Police Law

Tenth Edition

Jack English OBE QPM MA

Ex-Assistant Chief Constable, Northumbria Police
Ex-Director of the Central Planning, Instructor Training and
Police Promotion Examinations Unit
Ex-Chief Examiner to the Police Promotions Examinations Board

Richard Card LLB LLM FRSA

Emeritus Professor of Law
De Montfort University, Leicester

OXFORD
UNIVERSITY PRESS

OXFORD

UNIVERSITY PRESS

Great Clarendon Street, Oxford OX2 6DP

Oxford University Press is a department of the University of Oxford.
It furthers the University's objective of excellence in research, scholarship,
and education by publishing worldwide in

Oxford New York

Auckland Cape Town Dar es Salaam Hong Kong Karachi
Kuala Lumpur Madrid Melbourne Mexico City Nairobi
New Delhi Shanghai Taipei Toronto

With offices in

Argentina Austria Brazil Chile Czech Republic France Gre
Guatemala Hungary Italy Japan Poland Portugal Singapor
South Korea Switzerland Thailand Turkey Ukraine Vietnar

Oxford is a registered trademark of Oxford University Press
in the UK and in certain other countries

Published in the United States
by Oxford University Press Inc., New York

© Oxford University Press, 2007

The moral rights of the author have been asserted

Database right Oxford University Press (maker)

Crown copyright material is reproduced under Class Licence
Number C01P0000148 with the permission of HMSO
and the Queen's Printer for Scotland

Tenth edition published 2007

British Library Cataloguing in Publication Data

Data available

Library of Congress Cataloging in Publication Data

English, J. (Jack)
Police law/Jack English, Richard Card.—10th ed.
p. cm.
Includes index.
ISBN 978–0–19–921406–8 (pbk.: alk. paper) 1. Police—England.
2. Police—Wales. I. Card, Richard.
II. Title.
KD4839.E54 2007
344.4205'2—dc22

2006100978

Typeset by Laserwords Private Limited, Chennai, India
Printed in Great Britain on acid-free paper by
Ashford Colour Press Limited, Gosport, Hampshire

ISBN 978–0–19–921406–8

10 9 8 7 6 5 4 3 2 1

Preface

We originally wrote this book and titled it 'Butterworths Police Law' to fill the gap left by the demise of Moriarty's Police Law which for over fifty years had satisfied a particular need by explaining all aspects of the criminal law, together with those procedures which govern the processes of law enforcement, which are of particular concern to the police. Because of its concern with matters which also represented the day-to-day problems encountered by members of the public in coming to terms with the criminal law, it provided an explanation of the law in terms which were easily understood by those who had received no legal training. Butterworths have now transferred the publication of this, and other academic textbooks, to Oxford University Press.

As in previous editions, we have written Police Law with these points in mind. This book is not a reference book. It does not reproduce the law without explanation. Nor is the text broken up by constant references to footnotes which set out the effect of court decisions; instead, the effect of such decisions is incorporated in the explanations which are given of each aspect of the law as it is encountered by the reader.

We have prepared the material included in this book in a way which recognises the needs of police officers, of those who wish to study the criminal law, and of members of the public who wish to refer to a legal text which is written in terms which they can understand. However, it remains faithful throughout its pages to its title, Police Law, and sets out to cover comprehensively those areas of law and legal procedures with which all police officers are concerned. The syllabus of the qualifying examinations for promotion has been borne in mind throughout preparation of the text and it is our hope that the availability of this book will ensure the success of those who enter for either of the qualifying examinations for promotion. The book was extended when changes were made to the qualifying examinations with the introduction of 'OSPRE'. While it cannot be guaranteed that everything will be fully covered, little will be missed.

We have tried to summarise the law as it was on 1 September 2006, although we have been able to insert, in proof, some changes which have been made since that date. The previous edition has been extensively amended in consequence of two revisions of the codes of practice, the Gambling Act 2005, the Drugs Act 2005, Clean Neighbourhood and Environment Act 2005, the Prevention of Terrorism Act 2005, the Serious Organised Crime and Police Act 2005, the Identity Cards Act 2006, the Racial and Religious Hatred Act 2006 and the Terrorism Act 2006. We have indicated within the text those provisions which are not yet in force, but are expected to be brought into force at, or shortly after, publication. The provisions of the Road Safety Act 2006 have been written into the book although they are not in force at the time of writing. It is indicated within the text that the provisions are prospective. The Fraud Act 2006 was brought into force as the proofs of this edition were being finalised and it was possible to include the relevant provisions of the Act.

It is a trend with recent legislation, that it is placed on the statute book long before the provisions are brought into force and we have tried throughout to deal with this by providing a middle course which clearly indicates impending changes while retaining information which may be essential in the short term.

September 2006   Jack English
                                                                      Richard Card

Contents—Summary

CHAPTER 39 Burglary 1057

CHAPTER 40 Offences of fraud and corruption 1061

CHAPTER 41 Handling stolen goods and related offences 1075

CHAPTER 42 Forgery and counterfeiting 1087

CHAPTER 43 Preventive justice 1100

Index 1317
Notes 1235

Contents

CHAPTER 4
Police questioning and the rights of suspects   105

CHAPTER 8
The police   268

CHAPTER 10
Use of vehicles   399

CHAPTER 27
Pedlars, vagrancy and dealers 794

CHAPTER 28
Non-fatal offences against the person 803

CHAPTER 32
Public order offences related to sporting events and those connected with industrial disputes   910

CHAPTER 33
Terrorism generally   928

CHAPTER 37
Theft and related offences, robbery and blackmail   1015

For regular updates to chapters, please see the 'Police Law' companion website:
http://www.oup.co.uk/law/practitioner/cws

Table of Primary Legislation

Table of Secondary Legislation

List of abbreviations

AA	Automobile Association
ACPO	Association of Chief Police Officers
ACSA 2001	Anti-terrorism, Crime and Security Act 2001
ADBA	American Dog Breeders' Association
AHA 1981	Animal Health Act 1981
Arrest Code	PACE Code G: Code of Practice for the Statutory Power of Arrest by Police Officers
A-sBA 2003	Anti-social Behaviour Act 2003
ASCA 2001	Anti-terrorism, Crime and Security Act 2001
Audio Recording of Interviews Code	PACE Code E: Code of Practice in Audio Recording Interviews with Suspects
BGLA 1963	Betting, Gaming and Lotteries Act 1963
BNA 1981	British Nationality Act 1981
BRS	British Road Services
BTP	British Transport Police
CA 1992	Charities Act 1992
CA 2003	Communications Act 2003
CA(YP)A 1997	Confiscation of Alcohol (Young Persons) Act 1997
CAA 1981	Criminal Attempts Act 1981
CAA 1984	Child Abduction Act 1984
CDA 1971	Criminal Damage Act 1971
CDA 1998	Crime and Disorder Act 1998
ChA 1989	Children Act 1989
CJA 1967	Criminal Justice Act 1967
CJA 1988	Criminal Justice Act 1988
CJA 2003	Criminal Justice Act 2003
CJPA 2001	Criminal Justice and Police Act 2001
CJPOA 1994	Criminal Justice and Public Order Act 1994
CLA 1967	Criminal Law Act 1967
CLA 1977	Criminal Law Act 1977
CMA 1990	Computer Misuse Act 1990

CPIA 1996	Criminal Procedure and Investigations Act 1996
CYPA 1933	Children and Young Persons Act 1933
CYP(HP)A 1955	Children and Young Persons (Harmful Publications) Act 1955
D(FL)A 1996	Dogs (Fouling of Land) Act 1996
DA 1991	Deer Act 1991
DDA 1991	Dangerous Dogs Act 1991
Detention Code	PACE Code C: Code of Practice for the Detention, Treatment and Questioning of Persons by Police Officers
DPA 1998	Data Protection Act 1998
DPP	Director of Public Prosecutions
DVLA	Driver and Vehicle Licensing Agency
EA	Environment Agency
EC	European Community
ECE	European Community Equipment
ECHR	European Convention on Human Rights
EEA	European Economic Area
EPA 1990	Environmental Protection Act 1990
ESA 1883	Explosive Substances Act 1883
EU	European Union
FA 2006	Fraud Act 2006
FCA 1981	Forgery and Counterfeiting Act 1981
FiA 1968	Firearms Act 1968
FLA 1996	Family Law Act 1996
F(O)A 1991	Football (Offences) Act 1991
FSA 1989	Football Spectators Act 1989
GA 1968	Gaming Act 1968
GCHQ	Government Communications Headquarters
GM	genetically modified
GV(LO)A 1995	Goods Vehicles (Licensing of Operators) Act 1995
HA 1980	Highways Act 1980
HRA 1998	Human Rights Act 1998
IA 1971	Immigration Act 1971
IAA 1989	Immigration and Asylum Act 1999
Identification Code	PACE Code D: the Code of Practice for the Identification of Persons by Police Officers
IRA	Irish Republican Army
KA 1997	Knives Act 1997
LA 1964	Licensing Act 1964
LA 2003	Licensing Act 2003
LAA 1976	Lotteries and Amusements Act 1976
LGV	large goods vehicle
MCA 1988	Malicious Communications Act 1988
MDA 1861	Malicious Damage Act 1861
NCIS	National Criminal Intelligence Service
NCS	National Crime Squad
NHS	National Health Service
NRPSI	National Register of Public Service Interpreters

NSPCC	National Society for Prevention of Cruelty to Children
OAPA 1861	Offences against the Person Act 1861
OPA 1959	Obscene Publications Act 1959
PA 1871	Pedlars Act 1871
PA 1911	Perjury Act 1911
PA 1996	Police Act 1996
PAA 1911	Protection of Animals Act 1911
PACE	Police and Criminal Evidence Act 1984
PBA 1992	Protection of Badgers Act 1992
PCA 1953	Prevention of Crime Act 1953
PCA 1978	Protection of Children Act 1978
PCA 1999	Protection of Children Act 1999
PCA 2002	Proceeds of Crime Act 2002
PCV	passenger carrying vehicle
PEA 1977	Protection from Eviction Act 1977
PHA 1997	Protection from Harassment Act 1997
PII	public interest immunity
PNC	Police National Computer
POA 1936	Public Order Act 1936
POA 1986	Public Order Act 1986
PPVA 1981	Public Passenger Vehicles Act 1981
PRA 1976	Police Reform Act 2002
PRA 2002	Police Reform Act 2002
RAC	Royal Automobile Club
RD(A)A 1978	Refuse Disposal (Amenity) Act 1978
RIPA 2000	Regulation of Investigatory Powers Act 2000
RNLI	Royal National Lifeboat Institution
RSA	Road Safety Act 2006
RSPB	Royal Society for the Protection of Birds
RTA 1988	Road Traffic Act 1988
RTA 1991	Road Traffic Act 1991
RT(ND)A 1995	Road Traffic (New Drivers) Act 1995
RTOA 1988	Road Traffic Offenders Act 1988
RTRA 1984	Road Traffic Regulation Act 1984
RTSA 2003	Railway and Transport Safety Act 2003
SE(CA)A 1985	Sporting Events (Control of Alcohol etc) Act 1985
Searching of Premises Code	PACE Code B: Code of Practice for the Searching of Premises by Police Officers on Persons or Premises
SI	statutory instrument
SMDA 1964	Scrap Metal Dealers Act 1964
SOA 1956	Sexual Offences Act 1956
SOA 2003	Sexual Offences Act 2003
StOA 1959	Street Offences Act 1959
Stop and Search Code	PACE Code A: Code of Practice for the Exercise by Police Officers of Statutory Powers of Stop and Search
TA 1968	Theft Act 1968
TA 1978	Theft Act 1978
TA 1985	Transport Act 1985

TA 2000	Terrorism Act 2000
TMA 2004	Traffic Management Act 2004
TULR(C)A 1002	Trade Union and Labour Relations (Consolidation) Act 1992
UHF	ultra high frequency
V(C)A 2001	Vehicles (Crime) Act 2001
VA 1824	Vagrancy Act 1824
VAT	value added tax
VDU	visual display unit
VERA 1994	Vehicle Excise and Registration Act 1994
VHF	very high frequency
Visual Recording Code	PACE Code F: Code of Practice on Visual Recording with Sound of Interviews with Suspects
WCA 1981	Wildlife and Countryside Act 1981
WM(P)A 1996	Wild Mammals (Protection) Act 1996
YJCEA 1999	Youth Justice and Criminal Evidence Act 1999

CHAPTER I
General principles

We are concerned in this book with those branches of the law of England and Wales which are of particular relevance to police officers.

The word 'law' can be used in various senses, for example the laws of nature and the laws of cricket. We are concerned in this book with 'law' in the most commonly used sense of that term, namely a binding rule imposed on a person and governing his conduct, which is enforceable in the courts of the land by means of a penalty or sanction.

SOURCES OF ENGLISH LAW

There are two sources of English law: common law and legislation.

Common law

Common law is that part of English law which is not the result of legislation, ie it is the law which originated in the custom of the people and was justified and developed by the decisions and rulings of the judges.

In modern times legislation has played a preponderant part in the branches of the law dealt with in this book. As will be seen, very few offences are now governed and defined by the common law (ie the rulings of the judges). Moreover, the House of Lords, in its capacity as the senior appellate court in this country, has held that the judges do not now have the capacity to extend the criminal law, by creating new offences or widening existing ones. Examples of common law offences are murder, manslaughter and incitement.

Although most offences are now governed by legislation, most of the general principles of criminal liability are derived from the common law. For example, most of the general defences to crime and most of the rules concerning accomplices to crime are to be found in the rulings of the judges, and not in legislation.

The common law has been built up on the basis of the doctrine of precedent, under which the reported decisions of certain courts are more than just authoritative legal statements whose effect is persuasive, since they can be binding (ie must be applied) in subsequent cases. In the context of courts with criminal jurisdiction, it is the decisions of the House of Lords (from a day to be appointed, the Supreme Court), the Court of Appeal (Criminal Division), divisional court of the Queen's Bench Division of the High Court and a judge sitting in the Administrative Court of that Division (each of which has a criminal jurisdiction limited to appeals) which have binding effect. Whether or not such a decision is binding in a particular case depends on the relative standing of the court which made the decision and the court in which that decision is subsequently cited. The reason is that the doctrine of precedent depends on the principle that the courts form a hierarchy which, in the case of courts with criminal jurisdiction, is in the following descending order: House of Lords (Supreme Court); Court of Appeal (Criminal Division); divisional court; a judge in the Administrative Court; Crown Court and magistrates' courts. The basic rule is that a decision by one of the first four courts is binding on those courts below that in which it was given and, save in exceptional circumstances, will be followed by a court of equal status. A decision which is not binding under the above rules is nevertheless of persuasive authority, and may be cited to a court in a subsequent case.

Legislation

Statute

The majority of offences are defined and regulated by statutes, ie Acts of Parliament. Sometimes, statute has provided an offence where none previously existed: examples are the various offences relating to firearms. In other cases, statute has replaced common law offences with statutory offences: an example of this was the enactment of the offence of conspiracy in 1977.

The impact of statute has been limited in relation to the general principles of liability. As we have already said, most of these are still provided by the common law.

Subordinate legislation

A statute may give power to some body, such as the Queen in Council, a minister or a local authority or other public body, to make Orders in Council, regulations and byelaws (respectively) and prescribe for their breach. This method of creating criminal offences is of increasing importance in the present day, although it is not new. A good example is the power of the Secretary of State for Transport under the Road Traffic Act 1988 to make regulations concerning the construction and use of motor vehicles. Acting under this power, he has made a large number of detailed regulations on a variety of matters, such as the efficiency of brakes and the lighting of vehicles. Prosecutions for breach of these regulations are regularly instituted. Subordinate legislation made at central government level is normally required to be made by way of 'statutory instrument' (SI).

Legislation of the European Union

This has a limited impact on our criminal law, although that impact is growing. An example of a piece of European legislation which is of major importance to our law is Regulation 3820/85 (which is concerned with the driving hours of drivers of goods vehicles).

European Convention on Human Rights and the Human Rights Act 1998

The European Convention on Human Rights (ECHR), taken together with the Human Rights Act 1998 (HRA 1998), is of major importance. The provisions of the Act referred to below have great influence over the interpretation and development of the law by the judges and over new legislation.

Impact of HRA 1998 HRA 1998 'brings home' those Convention rights set out in HRA 1998, Sch 1. Essentially what this means is that remedies will be available in courts in England and Wales in respect of the Convention rights. This has not been achieved by the incorporation of the Convention rights into English law. Unlike the directly applicable legislation of the European Union (EU), the Convention does not automatically take priority over English law. Our courts have not been given a power to disapply an inconsistent Act of Parliament (primary legislation), but the effect of the main provisions in the Act comes close to permitting disapplication. On the other hand, subordinate legislation incompatible with a Convention right can be quashed unless (as is usually the case) primary legislation prevents removal of the incompatibility.

The Convention rights The Convention rights specified in HRA 1998, Sch 1 include:

(a) the right to life (ECHR, art 2);
(b) the right not to be deprived of liberty save in specified cases, for example after conviction or lawful arrest, and in accordance with a procedure prescribed by law (ECHR, art 5);
(c) the right to a fair trial (including the presumption of innocence) (ECHR, art 6);
(d) the right to respect for private and family life (ECHR, art 8);
(e) the freedom of expression (ECHR, art 10); and
(f) the freedom of assembly and association (ECHR, art 11).

The exercise of the last three rights or freedoms mentioned may be restricted by the law on specified grounds if this is necessary in a democratic society in (for example) the interests of national security, for the prevention of disorder or crime, for the protection of health or morals or for the protection of the rights and freedoms of others.

By ECHR, art 14 the enjoyment of the Convention rights must be secured without discrimination on any ground such as sex, race, opinion, national or social origin or other status.

We deal with the implications of HRA 1998 on the law of evidence on pp 262–263 and with its implications on public order offences on pp 906–907.

Statutory Interpretation Acts of Parliament and subordinate legislation must, *so far as possible*, be read and given effect to in a way which is compatible with the Convention rights, and this means even if there is contrary authority on the question. The courts, where necessary, will prefer a strained but possible interpretation which is consistent with Convention rights to one more consistent with the statutory words themselves. Where necessary to correct a defect in terms of ambiguity or omission the courts will be able to insert words into a statute to give effect to a Convention right. In the rare case where the mismatch between Convention rights and the statute is so great that a court cannot interpret the statute so as to be compatible, the court will have to make a declaration of incompatibility.

The Act clearly has a major impact on the doctrine of precedent. As a result of the present provision, the Crown Court may be obliged to ignore a decision of a superior court on the meaning of a statute in order to give effect to a Convention right.

Declaration of incompatibility   If a court is unable to interpret a statutory provision compatibly with a Convention right, it will have to proceed as normal. The issue of incompatibility can be raised on appeal. As far as criminal cases are concerned, a judge of the Administrative Court, a divisional court, the Court of Appeal or House of Lords (Supreme Court, from an appointed day), if satisfied that a provision of primary legislation is incompatible with a Convention right, may then (and presumably will feel obliged to do so) make a declaration of incompatibility. It may also make such a declaration in respect of a provision of subordinate legislation which is so incompatible if satisfied that (disregarding the possibility of revocation) the primary legislation prevents removal of that incompatibility.

If a declaration of incompatibility is made, the Government and Parliament are not required to take remedial action, although almost certainly they will. A fast-track route for doing so via a ministerial order is provided by HRA 1998, s 10.

By way of example, the Court of Appeal has upheld a declaration of incompatibility in respect of regulations which impose a liability upon the drivers and owners of lorries upon which illegal immigrants are discovered. The Court said that it was not possible to read and give effect to the legislation in a manner which was compatible with the Convention rights. The legislation has now been amended so as to be compatible.

Unlawful actions   It is unlawful for a public authority, such as a court, local authority or police officer to act in a way incompatible with a Convention right, unless:

(a) as the result of one or more provisions of primary legislation, the authority could not have acted differently; or
(b) in the case of one or more provisions of, or made under, primary legislation which cannot be read or given effect in a way which is compatible with the Convention rights, the authority was acting so as to give effect to or enforce those provisions.

This provides some protection for police officers who act in accordance with the law as it stands at the moment in question.

An individual may bring legal proceedings against any public authority in respect of any act which he considers to be unlawful in terms of the Convention rights. A court may grant such relief or remedy (including compensatory damages) or make an order as it considers appropriate within the terms of HRA 1998. The actions of police officers will therefore be subject to additional scrutiny, not only in relation to the direct exercise of powers or failure to fulfil their duties, but also in relation to orders which may be made by police officers in respect of processions, or directions to persons to quit land etc. In a recent case, for example, a chief constable was held vicariously liable for breaching a person's rights to life and to family life, when one of his officers failed to respond to the intimidation of a prosecution witness and to protect him, which led to that person's death. It is provided that damages in respect of a judicial act done in good faith may not be made otherwise than to compensate a person for arrest and detention in contravention of the terms of art 5.

GENERAL PRINCIPLES OF CRIMINAL LIABILITY

Criminal liability

Reference to a Latin maxim at this stage seems unavoidable. The maxim, which embodies the cardinal principle of criminal liability, is *actus non facit reus, nisi sit mens rea*—an act does not make a person legally guilty unless the mind is legally blameworthy. As is implied by this maxim there are two elements of criminal liability:

(a) the outward conduct which must always be proved against the accused (which is customarily known as the actus reus); and

(b) the state of mind which, apart from in exceptional offences, it must be proved that the accused had at the time of the relevant conduct (customarily known as the mens rea).

Of course, the definition of these two things varies from offence to offence, but if the relevant conduct and state of mind can be proved by the prosecution the accused is guilty unless he can rely successfully on a defence.

Actus reus

It would be wrong to think that proof of the relevant conduct required for an offence is limited to proof of an act on the accused's part. There are two reasons.

First, some offences can be committed (and, indeed, some can only be committed) by a failure to do a particular act on the part of a person who was under a legal duty to do that act; an example of such an offence is that of failing to provide a specimen of breath, without reasonable excuse, when required to do so under the Road Traffic Act 1988, s 6. It should also be noted that there are some offences whose definitions require neither an act nor an omission but simply the existence of a state of affairs on the part of the accused; an example is the offence of being found drunk in a public place, contrary to the Licensing Act 1872, s 12.

The second reason why more than an act on the accused's part must be proved is that rarely, if ever, is a mere act (or omission or state of affairs) sufficient for criminal liability for a substantive offence. The definitions of offences often specify surrounding circumstances, such as time and place, which are essential to render the act etc criminal. Sometimes the definition requires a consequence to result from the act or omission, such as the consequence of the unlawful death of another human being in murder. These specified circumstances and/or consequences are part of the actus reus of an offence.

Mens rea

Despite occasional judicial utterances to the contrary, it is clear from the application of mens rea in the courts that it has nothing necessarily to do with notions of an evil mind or knowledge of the wrongfulness of the act. The accused's ignorance of the criminal law is no defence, nor generally is the fact that the accused did not personally regard his conduct as immoral or know that it was so regarded by the bulk of society.

The expression mens rea refers to the state of mind expressly or impliedly required by the definition of the offence charged. This varies from offence to offence, but typical instances are intention, recklessness and knowledge.

Intention

A number of offences require the accused to have acted with a particular intent: in murder the accused must have acted with intent unlawfully to kill, or cause grievous bodily harm to, another person; in theft the accused must have dishonestly appropriated another's property with intent permanently to deprive him of it. Generally speaking, 'intention' refers to a state of mind in relation to a potential consequence of one's act. In some crimes, that consequence must actually result in order for there to be criminal liability; in others, such as theft, it is not necessary that the intended consequence should occur.

In law, a person 'intends' a consequence of his conduct if he has decided to bring it about, in so far as it lies within his power, no matter whether he desires that consequence or not. A person who has not decided to bring about a particular consequence may nevertheless be found by a jury or magistrates' court to have intended that consequence if it is proved that it was virtually certain to result from his conduct and he foresaw that it was virtually certain to result.

Recklessness

In some offences 'recklessness', either as to the consequence required for the actus reus or as to a requisite circumstance of it or as to some other risk, suffices for criminal liability as an alternative to some other mental state such as intention or knowledge.

A person acts recklessly with respect to:

(a) a circumstance when he is aware of a risk that it exists, or will exist;
(b) a consequence when he is aware of a risk that it will occur,

and it is, in the circumstances known to him, unreasonable to take the risk.

Knowledge

Many offences expressly or impliedly require 'knowledge' as to the circumstances by virtue of which an act, omission or state of affairs is criminal. Generally speaking, where 'knowledge' is required as to a circumstance it suffices that the accused actually knew of the existence of the circumstance or was wilfully blind as to it (ie he realised the risk that it might exist but deliberately refrained from making inquiries).

Proof of a state of mind

In proving whether the accused had a requisite intention, recklessness, knowledge or some similar state of mind, regard must be had:

(a) to the statements of the accused; and
(b) to the conduct and circumstances of the accused, and the presence of any motive, since these *may* give rise to the inference that he had the necessary state of mind.

Certain acts are known to be likely to produce certain consequences which are frequently spoken of as the 'natural and probable' consequences of those acts. The Criminal Justice Act 1967, s 8, provides:

A court or jury in determining whether a person has committed an offence—

(a) shall *not be bound* in law to infer that he intended or foresaw a result of his actions by reason only of its being a natural and probable consequence of those actions, but

(b) shall decide whether he did intend or foresee that result by reference to all the evidence, drawing such inferences from the evidence *as appears proper* in the circumstances.

Strict liability

In the case of some offences, the courts have held that a person can be convicted of a particular offence despite the fact that he was blamelessly inadvertent, that is, had no type of mens rea, as to a particular element of the actus reus (or sometimes even though he had no type of mens rea as to any element of the actus reus). These offences are known as offences of 'strict liability'. Most strict liability offences are minor in nature, but this is not always so; for example, a person can be convicted of the offence of raping a girl under thirteen despite the fact that he neither knew nor ought to have known that she was under thirteen.

The overwhelming majority of strict liability offences are statutory offences. Clearly, an offence is not one of strict liability if the statutory definition expressly uses a word such as 'intentionally', 'recklessly' or 'knowingly'. The fact that a statutory definition does not use any word importing the concept of mens rea does not necessarily mean that the offence is one of strict liability; it depends on whether or not the courts are prepared to imply a requirement of mens rea into the definition. The basic rule is that, where a statute is silent on the point, it is presumed that Parliament intended mens rea to be required to be proved (so that the offence is not one of strict liability), unless this is rebutted by clear evidence that Parliament intended the contrary. Such evidence includes the wording of the definition of the offence and of other offences in the statute, the subject matter of the offence, its aim, and the maximum punishment. Thus, if other offences in the statute contain a word like 'knowingly' and/or if the offence in question concerns something which is not 'truly criminal' and only punishable with a fine, the presumption that mens rea is required to be proved is liable to be rebutted. By way of example, many offences in the Road Traffic Acts have been interpreted as being of strict liability.

Where an offence is one of strict liability as to an element or elements of its actus reus, the prosecution must not seek to prove mens rea as to that element or those elements.

DEFENCES

Infancy

It is irrebuttably presumed that a child under ten years of age cannot be guilty of an offence.

Insanity

Everyone is presumed sane until the contrary is proved. The mere fact that a person is medically insane is no defence, but a person has a defence if he is proved to be legally insane. The test of insanity for the purposes of legal responsibility is provided by the *M'Naghten Rules*, which were laid down in 1843. These rules comprise three elements, which must be proved by the accused (unless it is the prosecution which alleges insanity). At the time of the conduct in question:

(a) *the accused must have been suffering from a 'disease of the mind'*, ie an impairment of the mental faculties of reason, memory and understanding due to a disease (whether organic or functional, and whether permanent or transient) as opposed to some external factor like a blow on the head;

(b) *the accused must have been suffering a 'defect of reason'* due to disease of the mind, ie a deprivation of reasoning power (as opposed to momentary confusion or absent-mindedness);

(c) *as a result, the accused must not have known the physical nature and quality of his act or, if he did know this, not have known he was doing 'a legal wrong'*. The mere fact that, because of a defect of reason due to a disease of the mind, the accused acted under an irresistible impulse is not enough.

It has been held by a divisional court that the defence of insanity is not available where the offence charged is an offence of strict liability as to every element of the actus reus, ie one where no mens rea is required.

Accused persons are rarely advised to plead insanity when tried in the Crown Court because, if their defence succeeds, they will be found not guilty by reason of insanity and are liable to be ordered to be detained in a secure mental hospital until the Secretary of State is satisfied that this is no longer necessary for the protection of the public.

Automatism

Generally, it is a defence that the accused was in a state of automatism at the time of the act in question. An act is done in a state of automatism if it is done by the muscles without any control of the mind (eg a reflex action, or a spasmodic or convulsive act) or if it is done during a state involving loss of consciousness (eg concussion, or a hypoglycaemic coma resulting from insulin taken by a diabetic).

It should be noted that, if the alleged cause of automatism in a case in the Crown Court is ruled by the trial judge to be a disease of the mind, he will direct the jury to consider only the defence of insanity, so that an acquittal on the ground of the defence of (non-insane) automatism will not be possible.

In the case of the defence of (non-insane) automatism, as opposed to insanity, the accused does not have to prove his defence. Instead he simply has the burden of adducing sufficient evidence to raise the issue; if he does this he must be acquitted unless the prosecution disproves his alleged automatism. In terms of his burden of adducing evidence, it is up to the accused to indicate the nature of his alleged incapacity and since, generally speaking, the mere statement 'I had a blackout' or 'I can't remember what happened' will be totally insufficient, the accused's evidence will very rarely be sufficient unless it is supported by medical evidence.

Sometimes, non-insane automatism is self-induced in that it results from something done or not done by the accused (as where a diabetic becomes an automaton as a result of taking insulin, or, having taken insulin, failing to eat sufficiently there-after). In such a case, the accused cannot be convicted of an 'offence of specific intent' (which is defined below). Nor can he be convicted of an offence which does not require a specific intent *unless* either his automatism was caused by his voluntary intoxication *or,* before he became an automaton, he was aware that something he did or failed to do was likely to make him aggressive, unpredictable or uncontrollable with the result that he might endanger others (as opposed simply to becoming unconscious), and he deliberately disregarded the risk.

Intoxication

The rules relating to the effect of intoxication in criminal liability are the same whether the intoxication was caused by drink or drugs. Intoxication is not in itself a defence. It is no excuse that, because of intoxication, the accused's power to judge between right and wrong, or to exercise self-control, was impaired.

In most cases a person's intoxication is regarded as 'voluntary'. Intoxication is voluntary if it results from knowingly taking alcohol or some other drug. There are two exceptions: intoxication is not voluntary where it is caused by something taken under and in accordance with medical advice, or where it is caused by a non-dangerous drug (ie a sedative or soporific drug) provided that the accused is not aware of the risk of becoming unpredictable or aggressive when he takes it. These cases of involuntary intoxication are dealt with below.

Where the accused was voluntarily intoxicated he may rely on his intoxication as evidence that he lacked mens rea if, but only if, the offence requires proof of a specific intent. Even if an offence is one of specific intent, an intoxicated, mistaken belief that he is acting in self-defence will not excuse the accused. Where an offence does not require a specific intent, an accused may be convicted of it if he was voluntarily intoxicated at the time of committing its actus reus, even though, because of his intoxication he did not have the mens rea normally required for that offence, and even though he was then in a state of automatism, provided that he would have been aware of the risk in question had he been sober.

The following have been held to be offences of specific intent in this context: murder; wounding or causing grievous bodily harm with intent contrary to the Offences Against the Person Act 1861, s 18; criminal damage contrary to the Criminal Damage Act 1971, s 1(1) or (2) (provided that it is only alleged that the accused intended to damage or destroy property, or intended to endanger the life of another by destroying or damaging property respectively); theft; robbery; burglary with intent to steal; the common law offences of kidnapping and false imprisonment; and attempt to commit an offence.

Conversely, the following have been held *not* to be offences of specific intent: manslaughter; maliciously wounding or inflicting grievous bodily harm (contrary to the Offences Against the Person Act 1861, s 20); assault occasioning actual bodily harm; assault on a constable in the execution of his duty; rape; taking a conveyance without lawful authority; and offences against the Criminal Damage Act 1971, s 1(1) or (2) (unless only an intention to damage or destroy property, or an intention to endanger life, respectively is alleged).

The situation is different where a person is involuntarily intoxicated. Intoxication is involuntary in the cases outlined above, and also where it is not self-induced (as where a person's glasses of lemonade have been laced with vodka or where he has been secretly drugged).

Where an accused is involuntarily intoxicated, he can use evidence of his intoxication as evidence that he lacked the mens rea for the offence in question (whether or not it is an offence of specific intent). However, if it can be proved that an accused had the necessary mens rea when the offence was committed, it is no defence that involuntary intoxication led him to commit an offence which he would not have committed when sober, and this is so even though, because of his intoxication, he acted under an irresistible impulse.

Duress

The defences of duress by threats and duress of circumstances are restricted to cases where an accused is impelled to act as he did because, on the facts as he reasonably believed them to be, he has good cause to believe that he or someone for whom he feels responsible is subject to a threat of imminent death or serious physical injury unless he acted as he did to avoid the threatened harm. The defence of duress by threats deals with the case where the threat comes from another person and, expressly or impliedly, is in the form of an order to do a particular nominated act or suffer the harm; the defence of duress of circumstances deals with the case where the threat of death or serious physical injury is of any other type (as where the threat comes from the surrounding circumstances). A threat of serious psychological injury or harm to property cannot give rise to either defence.

The threat must be such that an ordinary, sober person of reasonable firmness sharing the accused's characteristics would have responded as the accused did. Because this 'ordinary person' is someone of reasonable firmness he is not invested with a characteristic of the accused which did not make the accused less able to resist the threat than an ordinary person of reasonable firmness. In addition, the ordinary person of reasonable firmness is not invested with a characteristic of the accused, such as pliancy, vulnerability to pressure or timidity, since it would be a contradiction in terms to invest an ordinary person with these. On the other hand, if the accused is in a category of persons who might be less able to resist pressure than people outside that category, the characteristic which puts him in that category may be a relevant one. Obvious examples are age (a young person may not be as robust as a mature person); pregnancy (added fear for the unborn child); serious physical disability (may inhibit self-protection), and a recognised mental illness or psychiatric condition (may make the person more susceptible to pressure).

The defences of duress by threats and duress of circumstances are not applicable in respect of conduct committed after a threat has ceased to be operative or if the accused could have neutralised the threat by seeking police protection. Neither defence is available to a person who is charged with murder or attempted murder. Apart from this they are generally available in respect of other offences, including road traffic offences.

The defence of duress by threats is not available to a person if he foresaw or ought to have foreseen that his voluntary association with known criminals involved a risk of being subjected to any compulsion by acts of violence, not necessarily compulsion to commit crimes of the kind he was charged with. Thus, the defence is not available to an accused who joins a criminal gang, knowing that other members might bring pressure to bear on him to rob someone, and who is subsequently put under such pressure.

Coercion

This is an alternative defence to duress for married women in the circumstances which we now outline. It is a defence on a charge of any offence, other than murder or treason, for a wife to prove that she committed the alleged offence in the presence of, and under the coercion of, her husband. It will be noted that the accused wife has the burden of proving this defence. In contrast, an accused does not have to prove the defence of duress; he merely has to adduce evidence that he is covered by that defence, whereupon it is for the prosecution to prove that he is not (otherwise he must be acquitted). On the other hand, the defence of coercion can apply where the threat is of something less than death or serious bodily harm, although there must be some (as yet undetermined) limit on the type of threat that can suffice.

Autrefois acquit

Although not strictly a defence, the common law recognised that a person who was acquitted of an offence could not be tried for the same offence on another occasion. However, the Criminal Justice Act 2003 (CJA 2003), Part 10 makes provisions to allow retrial for serious offences (qualifying offences) in certain circumstances where a person has been acquitted of a qualifying offence on indictment or on appeal. The prosecutor may apply to the Court of Appeal, with the written consent of the Director of Public Prosecutions (DPP), for an order which quashes the acquittal and orders a retrial. Only one application may be made in respect of any acquittal and reporting restrictions apply to the contents of any submission.

Before such an application may be made there must be new and compelling evidence against the acquitted person. Evidence is new if it was not adduced at trial and is compelling if the court considers it to be reliable and substantial and that it appears to be highly probative. It is submitted that evidence would not be compelling if it related to a matter which was not in dispute at trial or was concerned with trivial matters. The Court of Appeal will consider whether, in total, it is in the interests of justice to order a retrial. An appeal lies to the House of Lords in respect of any point of law involved in making such an order.

Where issues are further investigated concerning such an application, no investigation may be carried out without the written consent of the DPP. The officer carrying out such an investigation may not, without the consent of the person acquitted (and then only with approval of the DPP), arrest or question him, search him or any premises or vehicle owned or occupied by him, or seize anything in his possession or take his fingerprints or any sample.

Provision is made for instances of urgency to prevent an investigation from becoming substantially and irrevocably prejudiced, which might be the case where there is a need to secure evidence without delay, perhaps during the course of some other investigation or the discovery of the location of relevant property. In such cases urgent action may be authorised by a superintendent (or above) provided that there has been no delay in seeking the approval of the DPP and there has been no previous refusal of consent. Any oral approval must be confirmed in writing as soon as possible.

Where there has been an acquittal in a trial on indictment or on an appeal against conviction the accused is also treated as being acquitted of any qualifying offence of which he could have been convicted in those proceedings (for example manslaughter as opposed to murder) except such offences of which he was convicted at the time, or found not guilty by reason of insanity.

Qualifying offences

The qualifying offences are set out in CJA 2003, Sch 5 and are murder, attempted murder, soliciting murder, manslaughter, kidnapping, rape, attempted rape, intercourse with a girl under thirteen (now repealed), incest by a man involving a girl under thirteen (now repealed), assault by penetration, causing a person to engage in sexual activity without consent, rape (or the attempt) of a child under thirteen, assault of a child under thirteen by penetration, causing a child under thirteen to engage in sexual activity, sexual activity with a person with a mental disorder impeding choice or causing such a person to so engage, unlawful importation or exportation of a Class A drug or fraudulent evasion in that respect, or the production of such a drug, arson endangering life, causing (or intending or inciting) an explosion likely to endanger life or property or war crimes, crimes against humanity, directing terrorism and hostage-taking and any conspiracy to commit such offences.

Arrest and charge in such cases

An arrest may be authorised by warrant (which may be issued by a justice who is satisfied that new evidence has been obtained) where the DPP's consent has not previously been obtained and urgent action is being taken. However, this does not affect a power to arrest for an offence other than a qualifying offence. A person arrested under the provision of CJA 2003 may be charged with the offence for which he was arrested in accordance with the provisions of the Police and Criminal Evidence Act 1984 (PACE) if an officer of the rank of superintendent (or above), who has not been involved with the investigation, considers that there is sufficient evidence for the case to be referred to a prosecutor with a view to making an application under these provisions. A custody officer must inform the superintendent of any evidence which became available during the investigation. Any decision as to bail or remaining in custody must be made by a Crown Court within twenty-four hours (excluding Sundays, bank holidays etc).

PARTIES TO A CRIME

There are a number of ways in which people may participate in an offence.

Perpetrators

A perpetrator is otherwise known as the principal. Normally, it is clear who is the perpetrator: he is the person who, with the relevant mens rea, fires the fatal shot in murder, or has intercourse in rape, and so on. Of course, there can be more than one perpetrator, as where a group of men enter a building as trespassers in order to steal therein; in such a case there are said to be joint perpetrators of the offence.

If a person makes use of an innocent agent in order to procure the commission of an offence, he is the perpetrator of the offence, even though he is not present at the scene of the offence and does nothing with his own hands. Thus, a person who kills another by posting a time bomb to him which is delivered by an innocent postman, or who employs a child under ten (the age of criminal responsibility) or a trained dog to remove goods from a shop, may be convicted of murder or theft, as the case may be, if he acts with the appropriate mens rea.

Accomplices

A person who aids, abets, counsels or procures the commission of an offence (an accomplice) is liable to be tried and punished for that offence as a principal offender.

The terms 'aiding' and 'abetting' are often used together, but they refer to different things: 'aid' describes the activity of a person who assists the perpetrator to commit the principal offence, and 'abet' describes the activity of a person who encourages the perpetrator to commit it, whether or not in either case he is present at the time of commission. 'Counsel', which means 'encourage', does not add anything strictly but is used to describe encouragement before the commission of the principal offence. A person 'procures' the commission of an offence where he sets out to see that it is committed and takes appropriate steps to produce its commission.

It can be seen from the above that basically there must be some assistance or encouragement by a person of the commission of an offence by another before he can be convicted as an accomplice to it. That assistance or encouragement must be given before, or at the time of, the commission of the offence. Someone who assists the perpetrator after the commission of an offence is not liable as a party to it, but one who assists the perpetrator to escape detection or arrest may be guilty of the statutory offence of assisting offenders, dealt with later in this chapter.

The assistance or encouragement of the perpetrator which must be proved against an alleged accomplice may take a variety of forms. Examples are: holding a woman down while she is raped; keeping watch; shouting words of encouragement; providing a jemmy to a burglar, and buying paper for use by a forger. A person is not an accomplice to an offence merely because he stands by when it is committed and does nothing to prevent its commission, but if he was deliberately present at the scene of the crime and it can be proved that his presence encouraged the perpetrator, as he intended it should, he can be convicted as an accomplice. Unless the deliberate bystander does something to signify his approval it will normally be difficult to prove these things, although his presence will be prima facie evidence of them.

The mens rea required of an accomplice is, first, an intent to assist or encourage the commission of the offence. This is proved by proving that the act of aiding, abetting etc was done intentionally, in the sense that he did it deliberately (and not accidentally), knowing that his conduct was capable of assisting or encouraging the commission of the principal offence, and with intent to assist or encourage the perpetrator. That intent can be found from evidence of the knowledge first referred to; an accused need not be proved to have acted with the aim or purpose that the principal offence be committed. Thus, for example, someone who deliberately sells someone a gun to be used for murdering a third party can be convicted as an accomplice to the subsequent murder, even if he was only interested in making money and was indifferent about whether or not the victim was killed. Second, it must be proved that the accused had knowledge of any circumstances required for the actus reus of the principal offence and contemplated as a real possibility that the perpetrator was acting or might act with the mens rea required for the offence (although, of course, the accused need not know that those facts constitute an offence, nor need he know any more details). These requirements apply even though the offence in question is one of strict liability.

Unforeseen consequences of a joint criminal enterprise

Sometimes an accomplice can be liable for the unforeseen consequences of the perpetrator's acts.

If, in the course of a joint criminal enterprise, a person accidentally commits the actus reus of an offence of a different type from that intended, neither he nor the accomplice will be guilty unless they have the necessary mens rea required for that offence. They may have that mens rea where the offence concerned is of a type which does not require foresight of the necessary consequence. Examples of such cases are manslaughter and unlawfully wounding or inflicting grievous bodily harm contrary to the Offences against the Person Act 1861, s 20, for example. A person is guilty of manslaughter if death results from the commission by him of an unlawful act likely to harm another, even though he did not foresee that death or grievous bodily harm was likely to result. If one person encourages another to assault a man with fists, and he unexpectedly dies in consequence of the blows received, they are each guilty of manslaughter.

It is different where, in carrying out a joint criminal enterprise with another, the perpetrator intentionally commits an offence which the other party has not assisted or encouraged him to commit. Where a person (X) encourages a second person (Y) to commit burglary and to use his jemmy to frighten off anyone who may come upon them and Y, disturbed by the householder in the course of the burglary, strikes him with the jemmy and kills him, both parties are guilty of burglary, X as accomplice and Y as perpetrator: but is X guilty of murder? The House of Lords has held that someone like X can be convicted of the further offence if it is proved that he contemplated as a real possibility that the perpetrator might commit it but still participated in the enterprise. In some cases the accomplice will have agreed to or authorised the commission of the further offence but this is not necessary. If it was proved that the accomplice in the circumstances set out above had contemplated as a real possibility that the jemmy might be used intentionally to kill or do grievous bodily harm to someone in such circumstances, the accomplice could be convicted as an accomplice to murder even without proof that he had agreed to its use for that purpose, and even though he had forbidden the use of violence.

In the case above, the accomplice contemplated as a real possibility the act carried out by the perpetrator. But what if he did not contemplate the act? The House of Lords has held that even if an accomplice intended or foresaw that the principal would or might act with the mens rea for the principal offence which was committed, he cannot be convicted as a party to that offence if the perpetrator's act is fundamentally different from the act intended or foreseen by the accomplice. On the other hand, if the perpetrator's act, though different, is as dangerous as that foreseen as a 'real possibility' by the accomplice, as where the actual act was stabbing with a knife and that foreseen as a real possibility was shooting to kill, an accomplice cannot escape liability for the offence.

A person who cannot in law perpetrate a particular offence may nevertheless be convicted as an accomplice to it. For example, a woman can be convicted of rape as an accomplice where she has encouraged or assisted a man to rape another woman.

Where an accused is alleged to be an accomplice to an offence, the charge may allege that he aided, abetted, counselled, or procured, it, and he will be convicted if he is proved to have participated in one or more of these four ways.

Vicarious liability

Vicarious liability means liability for the acts of another person which the accused has not authorised and of which he was ignorant.

Vicarious *criminal* liability is exceptional; it is imposed only on employers and, in some cases, certain other people with a similar status. It arises in three ways:

(1) Where a statute states that it is an offence for a person 'himself, or by his servant or agent', to do something, that person is vicariously liable if the prohibited act is done by his employee or agent in the course of his employment.
(2) Where a statutory strict liability offence uses a word like 'sell', 'expose for sale', or 'use', which connotes an activity which can be performed by an employee on behalf of his employer, an employer (or the like) can be vicariously liable for a prohibited 'selling' etc by his employee (or the like) in the course of his employment.
(3) Certain statutes impose duties on someone with a specified status and make it an offence for someone with that status knowingly to contravene them. If a person with the specified status completely delegates his statutory responsibilities to someone else such as an employee, and the delegate knowingly contravenes one of these duties, the conduct and the state of mind of the delegate are imputed to the person with the specified status, who is consequently vicariously liable for the offence in question. If this were not so, persons with the specified status could easily escape their statutory responsibilities by permanently absenting themselves from the premises, leaving someone else in charge.

Assisting offenders

The Criminal Law Act 1967 (CLA 1967), s 4 provides that, where a person has committed a relevant offence, any other person who, knowing or believing him to be guilty of the offence, or of some other relevant offence, does without lawful authority or reasonable excuse any act with intent to impede his apprehension or prosecution is guilty of an offence. A 'relevant offence' is (a) an offence for which the sentence is fixed by law (murder is the prime example); (b) an offence for which a person of eighteen years or over (not previously convicted) may be sentenced to a term of imprisonment for a term of five years (or might be so sentenced but for the restrictions imposed by the Magistrates' Courts Act 1980, s 33). Such a person is not guilty, as an accomplice, of the relevant offence which has been committed, because his conduct occurs after its commission; the offence under s 4 is a separate offence. By way of example, if A knows that his friend, B, has committed an offence of murder and, with intent to impede the arrest or prosecution of B, disposes of the gun used by B to commit the murder, A is guilty of the offence of assisting offenders contrary to CLA 1967, s 4.

Concealing offences

Like the last offence, this offence is not a form of participation in crime but is mentioned here for convenience. It is governed by CLA 1967, s 5, which provides that, where a person has committed a relevant offence (as defined above), any other person who, knowing or believing that the offence or some other relevant offence has been committed, and that he has information which might be of assistance in securing the prosecution or conviction of an offender for it, accepts or agrees to accept for not disclosing it any consideration other than the making good of loss or injury caused by the offence, or the making of reasonable compensation for it, is guilty of an offence.

Prosecutions for offences contrary to CLA 1967, s 4 or 5 may only be instituted by or with the consent of the DPP.

WASTEFUL EMPLOYMENT OF POLICE

The Criminal Law Act 1967, s 5(2) states that it is an offence for a person to cause any wasteful employment of the police by knowingly making to any person a false report tending to show that an offence has been committed or that the informant has any information material to any police inquiry, or giving rise to apprehension for the safety of any persons or property.

In the absence of the offence under CLA 1967, s 5(2), an informant would commit no offence by making a false report of events which could lead to extensive police activities and inquiries, as where a person falsely reports that he has seen a person drowning at sea and thereby causes expensive and time-consuming activities on the part of the police.

The Criminal Justice and Police Act 2001 (CJPA 2001) provides that this is a 'penalty offence' in respect of which a 'penalty notice' may be given: see pp 465 and 874.

CORPORATE LIABILITY

A company or other corporate body may be criminally liable:

(a) on the basis of vicarious liability (above); or
(b) for breach of a duty imposed on it as an 'occupier' of premises or as an employer etc,

in the same way as a natural person. The offences to which these principles apply are essentially ones of strict liability.

A company or other corporate body may also be liable for most offences requiring proof of mens rea where the actus reus of the offence is committed with the necessary mens rea by a 'controlling officer', ie, someone who represents the 'directing mind and will' of the corporation (such as a director). In such a case, the acts and state of mind of such an officer are regarded as the acts and state of mind of the corporation.

INCITEMENT, ATTEMPT AND CONSPIRACY

It is a common law offence to incite the commission of an offence, and a statutory offence to attempt to commit an indictable offence or to be a party to a conspiracy to commit an offence. These offences are committed on the making of the incitement, attempt or conspiracy and it is irrelevant that the substantive offence to which they relate is not committed or (except in the case of attempt) even attempted. If the substantive offence is committed, no question of attempt normally arises, and where there has been incitement the inciter becomes a party as an accomplice to the substantive offence and is not normally proceeded against for incitement. Conspiracy differs from the other two offences in that, even where the conspirators have committed the substantive offence, there are circumstances in which a charge of conspiracy is appropriate as best representing the overall gravity of what has occurred, although the appellate courts have discouraged the practice.

Quite apart from the statutory offence of conspiracy to commit an offence, there is also the common law offence of conspiracy to defraud.

We describe the elements of the offences of incitement, attempt and conspiracy in Chapter 43, below.

EXEMPTION FROM CRIMINAL LIABILITY

The Diplomatic Privileges Act 1964 provides that ambassadors and Commonwealth High Commissioners, and members of their families, and their administrative and technical staff, and their families, are immune from arrest and criminal proceedings whilst in the United Kingdom in that capacity. There is no immunity for a member of the family who is a national of the United Kingdom. Members of the service staff also have immunity but only in respect of acts in the course of their duties. The Home Office should be contacted in cases where a person who is dealt with for an offence claims diplomatic immunity. The Metropolitan Police maintain an index of persons who are entitled to diplomatic immunity.

In addition, the Consular Relations Act 1968 grants immunity from criminal proceedings to career consular officers and members of their administrative or technical staff in the exercise of consular functions. In addition, career consular officers may not be arrested or detained pending trial unless the offence is grave and the detention is authorised by a competent judicial authority. Honorary consular officers are not immune from the jurisdiction of our criminal courts nor from arrest or detention. Such persons are generally retained in a part-time capacity and will usually hold office on account of the status which it confers.

The provisions of the Road Traffic Act 1988, ss 6–11, which are concerned with drink/driving, apply to consular personnel (but not to Ambassadors etc). However, if a positive preliminary test is provided there can be no arrest of a career consular officer and the procedure must end there. Such a person would be liable to penalty if he failed to co-operate with a preliminary test.

CHAPTER 2
Elements of criminal procedure

INSTITUTION OF CRIMINAL PROCEEDINGS

Responsibility for prosecutions

Although the police may institute criminal proceedings, under what is known as the 'statutory scheme' it is now a matter for the Director of Public Prosecutions (DPP) to decide what charges should be laid against persons investigated by police in all but minor, routine cases. In cases where criminal proceedings are instituted on behalf of a police force (whether by a police officer or other person) the Director is obliged to take over their conduct (with the exception of various minor traffic offences, and even then only where the 'pleading guilty by post' procedure (described below) is adopted). This includes cases where the proceedings have been so instituted at the instigation of a private individual.

The DPP is the head of the Crown Prosecution Service (CPS). The Director is under the general supervision of the Attorney-General. The Director's functions are discharged on his behalf and under his direction by Crown Prosecutors working in the CPS.

There is generally nothing to prevent a private individual from instituting and conducting criminal proceedings, and such private prosecutions are occasionally instituted. In addition, criminal proceedings for various types of minor offences are instituted and conducted by officials of local authorities or other public bodies (in which case the Director is not obliged to take over even if the public officer has brought the accused to the police to be charged), and criminal proceedings for cases of serious or complex fraud may be instituted and conducted by the Director of the Serious Fraud Office. However, the DPP may intervene at any time and undertake the conduct of proceedings by a private individual or such an official, even if his purpose is to offer no evidence against the accused in the public interest and thereby to abort those proceedings.

An exception to the general rule that a police officer, private individual or public official may institute criminal proceedings is that there are numerous offences where the leave of the Attorney-General or of the DPP is required. For example, proceedings for an offence under the Official Secrets Acts 1911 and 1989 or for one of the offences relating to racial or religious hatred under the Public Order Act 1986 may only be instituted by or with the consent of the Attorney-General, and proceedings for over fifty offences may only be instituted by or with the consent of the Director. In the latter case, the Director's functions can, of course, be exercised by a Crown Prosecutor on his behalf. Where proceedings for an offence may only be instituted by or with the consent of the Attorney-General or of the Director, this is indicated at the appropriate point in this book.

Initiation of criminal proceedings

When the Criminal Justice Act 2003 (CJA 2003), ss 29 and 30, which are not in force at the time of writing, come into force, criminal proceedings will be initiated in one of three ways:

(a) a public prosecutor may institute criminal proceedings against a person by issuing a document (a written charge) which charges the person with an offence;

(b) a private person may institute criminal proceedings by laying an information and then securing the accused's presence before a magistrates' court by an arrest under a warrant or by a summons; or

(c) by an arrest without warrant, followed by a charge.

By a public prosecutor by means of a written charge

A 'public prosecutor' is (a) a police force; the Director of the Serious Fraud Squad; the DPP; the Attorney-General; the Secretary of State; the Commissioners of Customs and Excise; or in each case a person authorised by such a body or person to institute criminal proceedings; and (b) any person specified in an order made by the Secretary of State for this purpose or anyone authorised by such a person to institute criminal proceedings. CJA 2003, s 29 empowers such a prosecutor to institute criminal proceedings by issuing a written charge charging the person concerned with an offence. He must at the same time issue another document, a 'requisition', which requires a person to appear before a magistrates' court to answer the written charge. Both documents must be served on the person concerned and a copy must be served on the court named in the requisition. In view of these powers being available to him, a public prosecutor will no longer be empowered to lay an information for the purpose of obtaining a summons. These provisions, by removing the previous requirement for an information to be laid in respect of the issue of summonses for all criminal offences, remove the necessity to involve magistrates in the administrative process of bringing a person to court. In effect, for police purposes, the Crown Prosecution Service will take over the duties of the justices' clerk.

However, a public prosecutor may still apply for a warrant in respect of an indictable offence by means of laying an information, and nothing contained in ss 29 and 30 affects any power to charge a person with an offence while he is in custody. Where a written charge and requisition have previously been issued a warrant may be issued by a justice where a copy of the written charge is laid before him.

In consequence of the wide-ranging nature of this change, CJA 2003 provides that in any Act passed before its coming into force, there is a reference to an information or to a summons, that reference is to be read as including a reference to a written charge or a requisition respectively.

Private person laying an information

An information may be laid by a private person before a justice of the peace alleging that a person has, or is suspected of having, committed an offence. At the time of writing, this procedure could be used by a public prosecutor but, as noted above, it will be confined to private persons once the above provisions of CJA 2003 are brought into force.

Time limits

An information (or written charge) relating to an offence triable only summarily cannot generally be tried unless it has been laid within six months from the time when the offence was committed. An example of an exception to this general rule is provided by the Vehicle Excise and Registration Act 1994, which permits an information (or written charge) to be laid in respect of offences of using or keeping a vehicle without an excise licence up to three years after the commission of the offence. The general rule does not apply to an information (or written charge) relating to an offence which is triable on indictment. There is no set time limit in the case of such an offence, unless its parent statute expressly provides one.

Arrest without warrant, followed by charge

This is dealt with later in this chapter and in Chapter 4.

Summonses and requisitions

For an offence

A summons is a written order issued and signed by a justice of the peace or by a justices' clerk (or authorised assistant) on behalf of a justice. It is directed to the person named in the information and requires him to appear before a named magistrates' court at a specified time and date to answer the particular criminal charge(s) set out in it.

However, when the changes brought about by CJA 2003 are brought into force, summonses will only be issued to initiate criminal proceedings on the rare occasions upon which there is a private prosecution, and where a public prosecutor has issued a written charge it must at the same time issue a requisition requiring the person concerned to appear before a magistrates' court to answer the written charge.

For a breach of the peace

A summons may also be issued as a result of a complaint. A complaint is a written or verbal allegation made before a justice in respect of anything which is within the civil jurisdiction of a magistrates' court for the justices' petty sessions area to make an order. Of particular importance to a police officer is the fact that a complaint may be made to the effect that a person has committed a breach of the peace. Breach of the peace is *not in itself a criminal offence*. If the complaint is proved, that person may be bound over to keep the peace. A magistrates' court has jurisdiction to hear any complaint.

In respect of a witness

The Magistrates' Courts Act 1980, s 97(1) provides that, where a justice or justices' clerk (or authorised assistant) is satisfied that any person in England or Wales is likely to be able to give material evidence, or to produce any document or thing likely to be material evidence, at the summary trial of an information (or, when in force, written charge) or hearing of a complaint by a magistrates' court, and it is in the interests of justice to issue a summons to secure the attendance of that person to give evidence or produce the document or thing, the justice may issue a summons requiring that person to attend before the court to give evidence or produce the thing or document. Unlike other summonses, such a summons may not be served by post. A justice may refuse to issue a witness summons if he is not satisfied that the application was made as soon as reasonably practicable after the accused pleaded not guilty. Crown Courts are also empowered to issue witness summonses in prescribed circumstances.

Service of requisitions or summonses

The Criminal Procedure Rules 2005 deal with the various methods by which a requisition or summons may be served. It may be served by:

(a) delivering it to the person to whom it is directed; or
(b) by leaving it for him with some person at his last known or usual place of abode; or
(c) by sending it by post in a letter addressed to him at his last known or usual place of abode.

It is no longer necessary that, where a person fails to appear after service of a requisition or summons, either by leaving it for him with some person at his last or usual place of abode, or by sending it by post to him at his last known usual place of abode, it is proved that the summons or requisition came to his knowledge.

The Criminal Procedure Rules provide that, in any instance in which a requisition or summons may be sent by post to a person's last known or usual place of abode, the rule shall have effect as if it provided also for the document to be sent in the manner specified to an address given by that person for that purpose. Lawful service of such a document may therefore be effected and proved by sending the document for a summary offence, by post, to such a nominated address. The Interpretation Act 1978, s 7 provides that service is deemed to be effected when a pre-paid, properly addressed letter, which contains the document which is to be served, is posted. Unless the contrary is proved, service is deemed to be effected at the time at which the letter would be delivered in the ordinary course of post.

Service of a requisition or summons on a corporation may be effected by delivering it at, or sending it by post to:

(a) the registered office of the corporation, if that office is in the United Kingdom; or
(b) any place in the United Kingdom where the corporation trades or conducts its business, if there is no registered office in the United Kingdom.

Proof of service is usually by means of a certificate of service signed by the person who effected the service, or who posted the summons or requisition. Such a certificate contains details of the place, date and time of posting or of service by delivery.

Postal service of such a document issued in England and Wales is permitted throughout the United Kingdom. The Scots issue a 'citation' instead of a summons and this may be served by post in England and Wales. Northern Irish documents cannot be served by post in England and Wales.

The provisions concerning requisitions are not in force at the time of writing and this should be kept in mind in relation to matters which appear below.

Warrants of arrest

A justice of the peace (but not the justices' clerk or anyone else) may issue a signed warrant to arrest when information is laid before him to the effect that a person has, or is suspected of having, committed an offence. Such a warrant may be executed anywhere in England and Wales by any constable for the police area in which the warrant is issued. Alternatively, it may be executed by a constable for another police area within his police area. It may also be executed by a civilian enforcement officer or an approved enforcement agency.

An arrest warrant remains in force until it is executed or withdrawn. If the original is lost a justice may issue a replacement. However, an arrest warrant must not be issued in the first instance unless the offence to which it relates is either triable on indictment or punishable with imprisonment, or the accused's address is not sufficiently established for a requisition or summons to be served on him. An arrest warrant may be endorsed with a direction that the person to be arrested shall on arrest be released on bail, with or without sureties. This is known as 'backing for bail'.

Arrest warrants issued by judicial authorities in some EU countries may be executed in the United Kingdom.

Other warrants   For the sake of completeness, mention may be made of other warrants which may be issued by a justice or magistrates' court on an information being laid.

Warrants to arrest a witness   Such a warrant may be issued by a justice under the Magistrates' Courts Act 1980, s 97(2) where he is satisfied that a person who could give material evidence etc is unlikely voluntarily to attend court. Such a warrant will only be issued where a summons would be ineffective.

Warrant for distress or commitment   The Magistrates' Courts Act 1980, s 76 authorises a magistrates' court to issue a warrant of distress or of commitment where a person is in default of payment of a sum adjudged to be paid by a conviction or order of a magistrates' court.

The purpose of a warrant of distress is clear from its official title, 'a warrant of distress for the purpose of levying the sum which is unpaid'. Such a warrant is usually executed by a civilian enforcement officer or an approved enforcement agency but it may be executed by a constable in his police area. It requires that goods be seized; this is done initially by labelling the goods, after which they are in legal custody. Any electrical plant, line or meter belonging to a public electrical supplier cannot be seized, nor can wearing apparel or bedding, nor tools or implements of the person's trade. It is an offence for any person to remove the goods, or the marks placed on them to signify seizure.

A warrant of commitment orders the defaulter to be arrested and committed to prison. It may be issued *either* where it appears on the return to a warrant of distress that the defaulter's assets are insufficient to satisfy the sum adjudged *or* instead of a warrant of distress. If it considers it expedient, the magistrates' court may fix a term of imprisonment and suspend the issue of the warrant until such time and on such conditions as it thinks fit. A receipt must be obtained for the defaulter when he is handed over to a prison pursuant to a warrant of commitment.

Search warrants We discuss this type of warrant in Chapter 3, below.

This is not an exhaustive list of warrants which may be issued by a justice or magistrates' court, as will be seen below.

Execution of warrants

A warrant of arrest, or of commitment, or of distress, or a search warrant, may be executed anywhere in England and Wales by any constable for the police area in which the warrant is issued. Alternatively, it may be executed by a constable acting in his police area.

In addition, by the Criminal Justice and Public Order Act 1994, s 136 a warrant issued in England, Wales or Northern Ireland for the arrest or commitment (or a like warrant issued in Scotland) of a person may, without endorsement, be executed by a constable of a police force of the country of issue or of one of the 'home countries' or by a constable of the British Transport Police, as well as by any other persons within the directions of the warrant. As in the case of other arrest warrants, a constable who arrests the person named in the warrant is not liable for false imprisonment if that person is in fact innocent of the offence, unless there is malice on the part of the constable.

Certain warrants may be executed by a constable who does not have possession of the warrant at the time:

(a) warrants to arrest a person in connection with an offence;

(b) warrants under the Army Act 1955, Air Force Act 1955, Naval Discipline Act 1957 or Reserve Forces Act 1996 (desertion etc);

(c) warrants relating to the non-appearance of a defendant, warrants of distress, warrants of commitment, warrants issued in 'sending for trial' proceedings to arrest a potentially unwilling witness, and warrants to arrest someone for non-compliance with a requisition or summons issued in 'sending for trial' proceedings (under the Magistrates' Courts Act 1980, ss 55, 76, 93, 97 and 97A and the Crime and Disorder Act 1998 (CDA 1998), Sch 3); and

(d) warrants issued under the Youth Justice and Criminal Evidence Act 1999 Sch 1, para 3(2) (offender referred to court by youth offender panel).

However, in such cases the warrants must, on the demand of the person concerned, be shown to him as soon as practicable (Magistrates' Courts Act 1980, s 125D).

Except in the above cases, a warrant may not be executed by a constable who does not have it in his possession at the time. Thus, for example, a constable must be in possession of the warrant when executing a search warrant.

Entry to execute warrants   The Police and Criminal Evidence Act 1984 (PACE), s 17 permits a constable to enter and search premises, including any vehicle, vessel, aircraft or tent, for the purpose of executing a warrant of arrest issued in connection with or arising out of criminal proceedings, or a warrant of commitment issued under the Magistrates' Courts Act 1980, s 76. This power of entry and search is only exercisable where the constable has reasonable grounds for believing that the person whom he is seeking is on the premises. Where the premises consist of two or more separate dwellings, the entry and search is restricted to any common parts of the building and the dwelling in which the constable reasonably believes that the person may be.

This power of search under s 17 is only a power to search to the extent that is reasonably required for the purpose for which the power of entry is exercised.

CLASSIFICATION OF OFFENCES BY METHOD OF TRIAL

Offences can be classified as indictable offences, summary offences and offences triable either way, according to their mode of trial. The Interpretation Act 1978, Sch 1 defines these offences as follows:

(a) 'indictable offence' means an offence which, if committed by an adult, is triable on indictment, whether it is exclusively so triable (eg murder or robbery) or triable either way;

(b) 'summary offence' means an offence which, if committed by an adult, is triable only summarily (eg most driving offences); and

(c) 'offence triable either way' means an offence which, if committed by an adult, is triable either on indictment or summarily (eg theft or unlawful wounding).

COURTS OF CRIMINAL JURISDICTION

The guilt or innocence of persons charged with an offence against the criminal law is a matter to be decided in a court of justice. There are two methods of trying persons accused of criminal offences. One is by judge and jury in the Crown Court; the other is summarily by a magistrates' court without a jury. With a few exceptions, all criminal proceedings in the Crown Court begin in a magistrates' court since an accused tried in the Crown Court must normally have been sent for trial there by a magistrates' court.

Magistrates' courts

A magistrates' court is normally composed of two or three justices of the peace, unless a special exception applies. Some statutes permit particular offences to be tried by a single justice but such instances are rare. The normal sittings of a magistrates' court take place in a properly appointed court house on appointed days of the week. On other occasions, or in other places, a court may sit as an occasional court but with quite limited powers. A district judge (magistrates' courts), a legally qualified magistrate appointed on a salaried basis, may sit alone and has all the powers of two lay justices.

The court is advised by a justices' clerk. A justices' clerk has a five-year magistrates' court qualification; or is a barrister or solicitor who has served for not less than five years as an assistant to a justices' clerk; or has previously been a justices' clerk. Provision is made within the Courts Act 2003 for rules to provide that matters authorised to be done by, to or before a single justice, may be done before a justices' clerk or an assistant clerk.

A magistrates' court has jurisdiction to try any summary offence. Where a person is brought before a magistrates' court to be tried for an offence, the court may transfer the matter to another magistrates' court, and this may be done before or after beginning the trial, but all evidence must be heard by the court to which the matter is transferred.

In criminal matters a magistrates' court has jurisdiction in relation to the following matters.

Offences triable summarily only

The provisions set out under this heading are those which will exist when the amending provisions of the Courts Act 2003 are brought into force. A magistrates' court has jurisdiction to try any summary offence alleged to have been committed by a person who appears or is brought before the court.

Persons appearing before a magistrates' court do so either in answer to a requisition or summons or under arrest. At the commencement of a summary trial, the accused is asked to plead guilty or not guilty to a written charge which will have been read over to him by the clerk of the court.

Guilty plea   Persons who appear before the court will have the charge read over to them and will be asked if they plead guilty or not guilty. If an accused pleads guilty the court must be satisfied that it is a clear and unequivocal plea. On a plea of guilty being entered, the court may convict without hearing evidence. In practice, however, the facts of the case are outlined by the prosecution and the accused or his legal representative is at liberty to dispute those facts should he wish to do so and may also put before the court any mitigating facts which he feels that the court should consider before passing sentence. The court will also usually hear any evidence by the prosecutor of any previous recorded convictions of the accused and of his general character in order to enable it to decide the appropriate penalty. The accused may also ask the court to take into consideration, when passing sentence, other offences which he has committed.

Pleading guilty by post   In the case of many offences triable summarily only, the Magistrates' Courts Act 1980 permits pleas of guilty to be entered at a magistrates' court (or where the accused is sixteen or seventeen when the summons or requisition is issued, at a youth court) without the necessity for the accused person to attend the proceedings, or for any witnesses to be called. There are certain conditions which must be fulfilled:

(a) the proceedings must be by way of requisition or summons;
(b) it is not an offence specified by the Secretary of State;
(c) the designated officer for the court must have been notified by the prosecutor that the accused, when served with the requisition or summons for the offence, was also served with:
   (i)   a notice explaining the prescribed procedure;

   (ii)   *either* a concise statement of the facts of the case which will be put before the court in the event of him notifying the clerk of his plea of guilty *or* a copy of such written statement or statements complying with the Criminal Justice Act 1967, s 9(2)(a), (b) and (3) (proof by written statement, see pp 234–235) as will be so placed in those circumstances;

   (iii) if any information relating to the accused will or may, in the circumstances, be placed before the court by or on behalf of the prosecutor, a notice containing or describing the information; and

(d) the accused or his solicitor must have notified the clerk of the court that he wishes to plead guilty. On receipt of this notification, the clerk will inform the prosecutor.

Where the accused does not appear and proof of service of such documents is given, the court may hear and dispose of the case in the absence of the accused and the absence of the prosecutor. The documents are read to a court before a conviction is registered.

Should an accused appear, although the notification referred to in (d) has been received, the court may, with his consent, proceed as just described but the accused may make oral submissions with a view to mitigation of sentence, in place of a written submission which he may have sent to the clerk.

Not guilty plea   If an accused pleads not guilty the court must hear the evidence and, at the request of either party, the court will order all witnesses out of court so that evidence may be independently presented. The proceedings will be opened by the prosecutor outlining the facts of the case and calling his witnesses one by one to give evidence to the court. Each witness will either take the oath or affirm and will give his evidence during '*examination-in-chief* '. After the prosecutor has asked questions to introduce and identify his witness, he may not ask *leading questions* in relation to the facts in issue. Leading questions are those which may usually be answered 'yes' or 'no'. For example, a prosecutor may not ask, 'Did you see the defendant standing outside the premises at 2 East Street?' Instead he should ask, 'Where was the defendant when you saw him?'

When a witness has given evidence for the prosecution he may be *cross-examined* by the defence upon any aspect of the evidence which he has given. Leading questions may be asked. The object of a cross-examination is to test the truth or credibility of the evidence or to diminish its value.

At the conclusion of the cross-examination the prosecution has a right to *re-examine* the witness upon *any new facts* which have come to light, or to clear up ambiguities which may have arisen, during cross-examination. Leading questions may not be put, nor may new evidence be introduced.

The accused or his legal representative may then address the court, whether or not he calls witnesses. PACE, s 79, which also applies to trials in the Crown Court, requires that, if the defence intends to call two or more witnesses to the facts of the case and those witnesses include the accused, the accused must be called before the other witness or witnesses unless the court in its discretion otherwise directs. Such a direction is likely where, for instance, a witness is to speak of an occurrence before the matters about which the accused is to give evidence.

When a witness for the defence, including the accused, has given his evidence, he may be cross-examined by the prosecution and may then be re-examined by the defence on any new facts or ambiguities which have arisen during the cross-examination.

When the prosecution and defence have finished calling their evidence, each side has a right to address the court (except that the prosecution does not have the right if the accused has not called witnesses and is not legally represented), the prosecution's closing speech coming before that of the defence.

The court may adjourn to consider its verdict and may seek the advice of its clerk by specific request. If it decides to convict, its pronouncement of this verdict will usually be followed by evidence by the prosecutor of any previous recorded convictions of the accused and of his general character in order to enable the court to decide on the appropriate penalty. A plea in mitigation may be made by the accused or his legal representative. The accused may also take the opportunity to ask the court to take into consideration, when passing sentence, other offences which he has committed.

A magistrates' court may, before beginning to try an offence, or at any time during such proceedings, adjourn the proceedings to a time which it fixes. It may remand the defendant, either in custody or on bail. If the remand is in custody, the remand will be for a maximum of eight clear days; if the accused is allowed bail, the remand may be for longer with the consent of both parties. Remands may be for longer periods after conviction where the proceedings are adjourned for a medical report or for other inquiries to be undertaken.

Offences triable either way and offences triable only on indictment

Offences triable either way: where to be tried An offence which is triable either way may be tried either on indictment in the Crown Court or summarily in a magistrates' court. Where it is tried depends on the following rules.

At the time of writing, the procedure is as follows. Where an accused appears or is brought before a magistrates' court charged with an either-way offence, the court must cause the charge to be written down, if this has not already been done, and to be read to the accused. The court must explain to the accused that he may indicate whether (if the offence were to proceed to trial) he would plead guilty or not guilty; and explain that if he indicates that he would plead guilty:

(a) the court must proceed as if the proceedings constituted from the beginning the summary trial of the offence, and the court had asked whether he pleaded guilty or not guilty; and
(b) he may be committed for sentence to Crown Court if the court is of the opinion that certain grounds exist.

The court must then ask the accused whether (if the offence were to proceed to trial) he would plead guilty or not guilty. If he indicates that he would plead guilty the court must proceed as if the proceedings constituted from the beginning the summary trial of the offence and the accused had pleaded guilty. If the court is of the opinion that one of the specified grounds exists the court may commit the offender in custody or on bail to the Crown Court for sentence.

If the accused indicates that he would plead not guilty, or fails to indicate how he would plead, the court must decide whether the offence appears to be more suitable for summary trial or for trial on indictment. Before making that decision it must afford first the prosecutor and then the accused an opportunity to make representations as to which mode of trial would be more suitable. The court must consider the nature of the case; whether the circumstances make the offence one of a serious character; whether the punishment which a magistrates' court could inflict would be adequate, and any other relevant circumstances.

If, having considered these issues, the magistrates' court decides that trial on indictment is more suitable, it will commence to hold committal proceedings in respect of the offence to determine whether there is evidence on which a reasonable jury properly directed could convict of the offence. If there is, it will commit the accused to the Crown Court for trial. On the other hand, if the court decides that summary trial is more suitable, it must explain to the accused that the offence appears more suitable for the summary trial and that he can either consent to such trial or, if he wishes, be tried on indictment. He must also be warned that, if he is tried summarily and is convicted, he may be committed for sentence by the Crown Court if one of the grounds described above exists. If the accused consents to summary trial, the magistrates' court will proceed to it (in the same way as described above in relation to offences triable summarily only); if he does not so consent, committal proceedings will be held, just as it would if it had decided that trial on indictment was more suitable.

The Criminal Justice Act 2003 (the relevant provisions of which are not in force at the time of writing unless otherwise indicated) makes extensive amendments and additions to the above provisions in respect of the procedure to be followed by a magistrates' court in relation to an either-way offence. Many aspects of the new procedure are outside the objectives of this book and the following description is a brief summary of the provisions.

As previously, where an accused appears or is brought before a magistrates' court charged with an either-way offence, the court must cause the charge to be written down, if this has not already been done, and to be read to the accused. The court must explain to the accused that he may indicate whether (if the offence were to proceed to trial) he would plead guilty or not guilty; and explain that if he indicates that he would plead guilty:

(a) the court must proceed as if the proceedings constituted from the beginning the summary trial of the offence, and the court had asked whether he pleaded guilty or not guilty; and
(b) he may be committed for sentence to Crown Court if the court is of the opinion that certain grounds exist.

The court must then ask the accused whether (if the offence were to proceed to trial) he would plead guilty or not guilty. If he indicates that he would plead guilty the court must proceed as if the proceedings constituted from the beginning the summary trial of the offence and the accused had pleaded guilty. If the court is of the opinion that one of the specified grounds exists the court may commit the offender in custody or on bail to the Crown Court for sentence.

If the accused indicates that he would plead not guilty, or fails to indicate how he would plead, the court must decide whether the offence appears to be more suitable for summary trial or for trial on indictment.

The court must then decide in 'allocation of trial proceedings' whether the offence appears to be more suitable for summary trial or for trial on indictment. Before making a decision the court must give the prosecutor an opportunity to disclose any previous convictions, and both parties must be given an opportunity to make representations about the mode of trial. The court must consider whether the sentencing powers of a magistrates' court would be adequate for the offence(s), together with the representations made by both parties and any official guidelines issued.

Where a summary trial appears to be more suitable the court must explain to the accused that summary trial appears to be more suitable and that he can either consent to be so tried or, if he wishes, be tried on indictment and that, in the case of a specified offence (offence listed in CJA 2003, Sch 15, as sexual or violent offence), if he is tried summarily and convicted, he may be committed to a Crown Court for sentence. At this stage, the accused may request an indication of whether a custodial or a non-custodial sentence would be more likely to be imposed if he were to be tried summarily and plead guilty. The court may or may not give such an indication. If it does, it must ask the accused whether, on the basis of the indication, he wishes to change his plea. If the accused indicates that he would plead guilty the court must proceed to summary trial. Where the court does not give an indication as to sentence, or the accused does not indicate that he would plead guilty, the court must ask the accused whether he consents to summary trial or wishes to be tried on indictment. If he consents, the court must proceed to summary trial. In a case where a court has indicated whether or not a custodial sentence would be imposed no court may impose such a sentence unless that possibility was indicated. There is only one exception; it relates to the second type of committal for sentence described on p 31.

If the accused does not consent to summary trial, or the court decides that the offence appears to be more suitable for trial on indictment, or the prosecution request that the offence be tried on indictment, the court must proceed to send the accused to the Crown Court for trial.

In the case of a child or young person brought before a magistrates' court charged with an indictable offence (with certain exceptions), the procedure to be followed is similar. However, special provisions are made in the case of such a person who, by reason of his disorderly conduct before the court, makes it impracticable to proceed in that manner. In such a case, a court may proceed in the accused's absence but in the presence of his legal representative who may make the choices in relation to mode of trial.

Notice of transfer   Special provisions for notice of transfer apply in all respects where the case is one of serious or complex fraud and in certain cases involving children.

In serious or complex fraud cases a notice may be given under CDA 1998, s 51B by a designated authority (DPP, Director of the Serious Fraud Office, the Commissioners of the Inland Revenue or Customs and Excise, or the Secretary of State) in respect of an indictable offence where the authority is satisfied that there is sufficient evidence for the person charged to be put on trial and that a case of fraud of such seriousness or complexity is revealed making it appropriate that the management of the case should be, without delay, taken over by the Crown Court.

In the case of certain offences involving children, the DPP may give notice that he is of the opinion that the evidence is sufficient for the person to be put on trial for the offence; that a child would be called as a witness at the trial; and that for the purpose of avoiding prejudice to the welfare of the child, the case should be taken over and proceeded with without delay by the Crown Court. The offences are those which involve an assault on, or injury or a threat of injury to, a person; cruelty to a person under sixteen; a sexual offence under the Sexual Offences Act 2003 or the Protection of Children Act 1978; kidnapping, false imprisonment or abduction, or attempts, conspiracies to commit, aiding, abetting, counselling, procuring or inciting such offences. *For these purposes* a child is a person who is under the age of seventeen, or a person of whom a video recording was made when he was under the age of seventeen with a view to its admission as evidence-in-chief in the trial.

If a notice of transfer is served on a magistrates' court under either of these sets of provisions, the effect is that the magistrates must forthwith send the accused to the Crown Court for trial; they cannot allocate the case for summary trial if the offence is an either-way one.

Sending cases to Crown Court for trial   The information set out under this heading describes the procedure which will apply when the relevant provisions of the CJA 2003 are brought into force.

Where an *adult* (A) appears or is brought before a magistrates' court charged with an offence which is triable on indictment only, or where (under the above provisions) an offence triable either way is not to be tried by a magistrates' court, or where a notice of transfer has been given, the court must send him forthwith to the Crown Court for trial. It may at the same time send A for trial for any related either-way offence and for a related summary offence if it satisfies the 'requisite conditions', namely is punishable with imprisonment or involves obligatory or discretionary disqualification from driving. Other adult persons who are jointly charged with A with an either-way offence for which A is sent for trial must be sent for trial if they appear before the magistrates' court on the same occasion as A (and may be so sent if they appear later). If such another adult is so sent in respect of an either-way offence with which he is jointly charged with A, he must also be sent for trial in respect of any either-way offence, or any summary offences which fulfil the requisite conditions, related to that offence. In addition, where a court sends an adult for trial in this way, it may also send a child or young person for trial who is jointly charged with the adult with an indictable offence for which the adult is sent for trial, or an indictable offence related to that offence. If it does, it may also send the child or young person for trial for any related either-way offence or any related summary offence which fulfils the 'requisite conditions', if it considers it necessary to do so in the interests of justice.

Generally, *children and young persons* (ie persons under eighteen) have to be tried summarily in a youth court (or sometimes a magistrates' court other than a youth court); see below. However, in the following cases a person under eighteen may be sent to the Crown Court for trial. The first, mentioned above, is where such a person is jointly charged with an adult with an indictable offence for which the adult is sent for trial, or an indictable offence related to that offence. The second is where when a child or young person appears or is brought before a magistrates' court charged with an offence any of the following conditions is satisfied:

(a) that the offence is one of homicide, or one of a number of particular types of offence of possessing a prohibited weapon and the accused young person was aged sixteen or seventeen when he committed it;

(b) that the offence is one in respect of which a long period of detention may be ordered and the court considers that such a sentence ought to be possible;

(c) that a notice of transfer (see above) has been served in respect of the child or young person;

(d) that the offence is a 'specified offence', namely a range of violent or sexual offences, and it appears to the magistrates' court that if the accused child or young person is found guilty of the offence the criteria for the imposition of detention for public protection or an extended sentence would be met.

If one of the conditions (a) to (d) is satisfied, the magistrates' court must send the child or young person for trial. In such a case, it may also send the child for trial for any related indictable offence or any relevant summary offence which fulfils the 'requisite conditions'.

Where a court sends a child or young person for trial in such a case it may also send for trial an adult person who is jointly charged with an either-way offence or a related either-way offence or related summary offence which fulfils the 'requisite conditions'.

These provisions relating to a child and young person are in force except in relation to cases falling within conditions (a) to (c), as are the provisions relating to notices of transfer (referred to on pp 29–30) where a case is sent for trial under condition (d).

Until these provisions of CJA 2003 are brought into force magistrates' courts will continue to conduct committal proceedings, holding a preliminary inquiry into the circumstances of a case to decide whether there is evidence on which a reasonable jury properly directed could convict.

Notice and reporting   The court is required to give notice of the offence or offences for which a person is sent for trial and the place at which the trial is to take place. A copy of this notice must be served on the accused and given to the Crown Court.

CDA 1998, s 52A prohibits the publishing of written reports of any allocation or sending proceedings in England and Wales, or the inclusion of such an item in a broadcast, if it contains any information other than that permitted by the section. The permitted information is restricted to matters such as the identities of persons involved in the proceedings, the offence(s) charged, details of bail or an adjournment and the granting of legal aid.

Committal for sentence

In instances where a person over eighteen, charged with an either-way offence indicates his intention to plead guilty to it and the magistrates' court when dealing with sentencing considers that the offence, or the combination of the offence and one or more offences associated with it, was so serious that the Crown Court should have the power to deal with the offender in any way in which it could deal with him if he had been convicted on indictment, the court may commit him, in custody or on bail, to the Crown Court for sentence for that offence and any related either-way offences to which he has also pleaded guilty. Similar provisions are made in respect of children and young persons.

There are special provisions in respect of dangerous adult offenders who have been convicted on a summary trial of an offence triable either way. If it appears to the court that the criteria for the imposition of a sentence under CJA 2003, s 225(3) or 227(2) (imprisonment for public protection for serious offences and extended sentences for certain violent or sexual offences) would be met, the court must commit the offender in custody or on bail to the Crown Court for sentence. The Crown Court will not be bound by any indication given at the magistrates' court as to sentence and the same restrictions apply in relation to appeals. Similar provisions are made in respect of dangerous young offenders in relation to offences covered by CJA 2003, s 226(3) or 228(2).

In all cases, the Crown Court must inquire into the circumstances of the case and may deal with the offender in any way in which it could have dealt with him had he been tried and convicted before that court.

Youth courts

A youth court is a summary court (ie a magistrates' court) and is composed of justices who are specially appointed because of their qualifications. It sits for the purpose of hearing any charge against a child or young person or to exercise any other jurisdiction conferred on youth courts by the Courts Act 2003 or any other enactment.

The general public do not have a right of access to proceedings in a youth court.

A magistrates' court before which a person under eighteen (hereafter described as a 'juvenile') appears charged with an offence which, in the case of an adult, is triable only on indictment or triable either way must deal with it *summarily* unless (at the time of writing):

(a) the charge is one of homicide or
(b) the offence is so grave that under specific statutory powers he, if found guilty, may be sentenced to be detained for a long period; or
(c) he is charged jointly with an adult (ie a person who has attained eighteen) and the court considers it necessary in the interests of justice to commit the case for trial.

When the changes in CJA 2003 referred to above are in force, (a) to (c) will be abolished and replaced by the provisions referred to on pp 30–31.

With certain exceptions, no charge against a person under eighteen may be heard summarily by a magistrates' court other than a youth court. The exceptions, which allow trial by an 'adult' magistrates' court, are:

(a) where the juvenile is charged jointly with an adult;
(b) where an adult is charged with aiding, abetting, counselling, procuring, allowing or permitting an offence with which a juvenile is charged;
(c) where a juvenile is charged with aiding etc an offence committed by an adult;
(d) where the fact that the person is a juvenile is discovered in the course of proceedings in a magistrates' court;
(e) where the charge against a juvenile arises out of circumstances which are the same as, or are connected with, those which give rise to an offence by an adult (eg a theft by a youth and a handling by an adult).

The law recognises the specialist nature of youth courts by requiring a Crown Court or adult magistrates' court which finds a juvenile guilty of an offence other than homicide to send the case to a youth court for sentencing as if that juvenile had been found guilty by that court, unless satisfied that it would be undesirable to do so. In effect, subject to that exception, they must send the case to the youth court for sentence to be passed.

On occasions problems are caused in respect of the hearing of indictable offences where the person charged is a juvenile at the time of the commission of the offence but is an adult when it finally comes to trial. In such circumstances the appropriate date at which to determine whether an accused has turned eighteen for the purpose of the above procedures is the date of his appearance before the court when it determines which mode of trial is to be adopted, which is not necessarily his first appearance.

The 'pleading guilty by post' provisions described on pp 25–26 do not generally apply to proceedings in a youth court. The only exception is where the accused is aged sixteen or seventeen when the requisition is issued.

The sentencing powers of courts generally are limited in relation to children and young persons.

Crown Court

The Crown Court may sit in any part of England and Wales. For convenience the locations of the Crown Court are grouped in six circuits. The towns on the list of Crown Court locations are divided into three tiers. In the first, sittings of the High Court are held for civil cases as well as of the Crown Court for criminal cases (and such civil matters as are within its jurisdiction). On the other hand, in second and third tier locations only sittings of the Crown Court are held. The jurisdiction of a Crown Court is exercisable by any judge of the High Court, any circuit judge, any recorder, or a district judge (magistrates' courts), or, in the case of appeals from magistrates' courts, any High Court judge, circuit judge or recorder sitting with not more than four justices of the peace. It will be appreciated that, when a Crown Court is concerned with appeals, the presence of justices may be of benefit to the proceedings. However, the justices must defer to the judge or recorder on matters of law. High Court judges do not sit at third tier locations.

The Crown Court has jurisdiction over all offences which are triable only on indictment and also over offences triable either way in respect of which the accused has been committed, or sent, for trial on indictment. Trials on indictment are heard with a jury. There are exceptions under CJA 2003, Part 7 where there is a risk of jury tampering (in force), or where the prosecution has applied to the Crown Court to proceed in the absence of a jury for certain fraud cases (not in force at the time of writing); or there is a danger of jury tampering (in force). In addition, when the Domestic Violence, Crime and Victims Act 2004, s 17 is brought into force, the prosecution may apply to a judge of the Crown Court for a trial on indictment to take place on the basis that the trial of some, but not all, of the counts included on the indictment may be conducted without a jury as sample counts. Indictable offences are divided into four classes for the purposes of trial in the Crown Court; these classes depend on the seriousness of the offence. When committing, or sending, a person to a Crown Court, magistrates' courts will commit him to the appropriate tier of the Crown Court according to this classification.

A person who has been convicted by a magistrates' court may appeal to the Crown Court against sentence if he pleaded guilty, or against conviction or sentence if he pleaded not guilty. There is also a right of appeal against the making of certain orders, for example orders 'binding over' a person to be of good behaviour. The Crown Court also deals with people convicted in a magistrates' court who have been committed to it for sentence.

The Central Criminal Court in London is a Crown Court.

Court of Appeal (Criminal Division)

Appeals to this division are normally heard by a court consisting of three of the following: the Lord Chief Justice, the President of the Queen's Bench Division, Lords Justice of Appeal and judges of the Queen's Bench Division of the High Court. A circuit judge may take up one of these positions in certain specified circumstances.

If convicted of an offence on indictment before the Crown Court, a person may appeal to this court against *conviction* with the leave of the Court of Appeal or trial judge. On an appeal against conviction, the Court of Appeal can dismiss the appeal, allow it and quash the conviction, or substitute a conviction for another offence if it appears that the accused should have been convicted of that offence, rather than the one of which he was actually convicted. If fresh evidence has come to light, the court may order a new trial. It may also do so in any other case where the interests of justice so require.

A person convicted on indictment before the Crown Court may appeal against *sentence* with the leave of the Court of Appeal, and so may a person who has been sentenced by the Crown Court on committal for sentence. On *appeal* against sentence, the Court of Appeal may vary a sentence but cannot increase it. However, the Attorney-General may (in certain cases) refer a sentence to the Court of Appeal with its leave if it appears to him to be unduly lenient. On such a reference, the court may impose a more severe sentence.

CJA 2003, Part 9 permits a prosecutor to appeal to the Court of Appeal in relation to any ruling (decision, determination, direction, finding, notice, order, refusal, rejection or requirement), other than a ruling that a jury be discharged, made within a trial on indictment. Following notice proceedings may be adjourned and the judge's ruling has no effect within the period of adjournment. Such an appeal may only be made against one ruling but in the case of a submission of 'no case to answer' other rulings may be specified which are related to that submission. When certain provisions of CJA 2003, Part 9 are brought into force, the prosecution will be able to appeal one or more evidentiary rulings made by a judge at any time before the opening of the case for the defence.

Queen's Bench Division of the High Court

One function of the High Court is to hear appeals on points of law from magistrates' courts or from the Crown Court in respect of appeals from magistrates' courts to the Crown Court. Such appeal is known as appeal by case stated, since the magistrates' court or Crown Court is asked to 'state a case', that is set out its reasons for its finding on the basis of its interpretation of the law in relation to the facts found by it. The High Court is not concerned with any form of retrial.

Another function of the High Court relates to the issue of *habeas corpus*. This is a writ to secure the release of a person who is unlawfully or unjustifiably detained, whether in a prison or in some private place. It is available in any case in which it is alleged that a person has been deprived of his liberty without authority.

Cases of the above two types are dealt with by the Administrative Court, which is part of the Queen's Bench Division. They are heard by a divisional court or a single judge. A divisional court consists of two or more judges, normally two, one of whom is usually a Lord Justice of Appeal and the other a judge of the Queen's Bench Division.

Judges in the Administrative Court also deal with the *judicial review* of the decisions of an inferior court or other body. In such cases the court will examine whether there was authority or power by which the decision made could have been properly reached; whether the procedure followed the rules of natural justice; or whether the exercise of discretion on the part of the decision-making body was lawful. Thus the court is not examining the correctness of the decision but whether it was lawfully, reasonably and proportionately reached.

Following such a review, the court may issue certain orders.

Types of order

Mandatory order   This is an order of the court demanding that a person, inferior court or other body carries out a duty. It could be that a magistrates' court might refuse to hear a charge because the members of the court were in sympathy with the actions of the defendants. A mandatory order could be obtained in such a case to require that court to hear the case and decide it on its facts, disregarding any personal views which might be held.

Prohibiting order   This order requires an inferior court or tribunal not to do something improper.

Quashing order   This order is used to quash a decision made by an inferior court or tribunal. Such an order could be made where it is alleged that the justices had an interest or a bias in a particular case.

House of Lords

This Court is composed of Lords of Appeal in Ordinary and any other peers who hold or have held high judicial office. It is the highest court in the land and hears criminal appeals from the Court of Appeal or the Queen's Bench Division, but only where:

(a) the court has certified that a question of law of general public importance is involved; *and*
(b) the court or the House is satisfied that the point of law is one which ought to be considered by the House; *and*
(c) leave to appeal to the House has been given by the court or the House itself.

When the relevant provisions of the Constitutional Reform Act 2005 are in force the House of Lords' functions as an appellate court will be taken over by a new Supreme Court where members will be known as Judges of the Supreme Court.

JURISDICTION OF SERVICE AUTHORITIES TO DEAL WITH CRIMINAL OFFENCES

The Acts relating to service personnel make provisions for concurrent jurisdiction in respect of civil and service courts. The only offences with which a service court cannot deal are treason, murder (including aiding, abetting, counselling or procuring suicide), manslaughter and rape. It is for the chief officer of police to decide. He should, where practicable, consult the serviceman's commanding officer before making his decision. The chief officer may also consult the DPP before making a final decision. There are certain factors which should be considered:

(1) Where the person or property of civilians is affected, the offence should normally be dealt with by a civil court; where that is not the case, it should be dealt with by a service court where it has jurisdiction.
(2) It is desirable, where possible, to avoid preventing servicemen who are about to be sent overseas from travelling with their units, especially if there are reasons to believe that the offence was committed with a view to avoiding overseas service.

In most circumstances, therefore, unless the offence is serious or the service court does not have jurisdiction, proceedings should be instituted by a service court.

(3) Where the offence, whilst affecting the property of civilians, was committed on duty and amounted to a breach of that duty, or consisted of a minor assault on a civilian or minor offence against his property and was committed on service premises, it should be dealt with by the commanding officer.

(4) Difficulty and expense may be taken into account, as it would be unfair to ask witnesses to travel long distances to a service tribunal. The service court's jurisdiction does not extend beyond service personnel.

In circumstances where a serviceman and a civilian are jointly involved in the commission of an offence, the proceedings against both should take place in a civil court.

Persons who are arrested without warrant *and are charged with an offence* must be brought before a magistrates' court in accordance with PACE, s 46 (p 170) and this will equally apply to service personnel who have committed a criminal offence. Where it is considered that it will be desirable to have the case dealt with by a service tribunal, it may be best to apply for an adjournment. If any form of 'discharge' is granted by the civil court it may give grounds for a plea of autrefois acquit (ie be a bar to trial) before a court martial.

Where a serviceman commits a traffic offence whilst driving a service vehicle the appropriate service authority should be informed before the hearing.

CHAPTER 3
Police powers

Throughout this book, but particularly in this and the next five chapters, references are made to the Police and Criminal Evidence Act 1984; in the rest of this chapter we shall refer to it simply as PACE.

Conduct in breach or in excess of a relevant statutory or common law power may constitute a breach of a 'Convention right' under the Human Rights Act 1998 and may cause the police officer concerned to be liable in civil law or in criminal law. It may also render inadmissible evidence obtained as a result.

The term 'police officer' includes all branches of the British Transport Police, who are responsible for all offences relating to, or committed on, a railway or underground, the Docklands Light Railway, the Midland Metro Tram System and Croydon Tramlink.

CODES OF PRACTICE UNDER PACE

PACE, s 66 requires the Secretary of State to issue Codes of Practice, approved by both Houses of Parliament, to provide, within the terms of the Act, strengthened safeguards for the suspect and workable guidelines for the police. The Secretary of State has a limited power to provide by order that a code of practice then in force may be treated as having been modified. Such a modification does not require the approval of the Houses of Parliament, although it may be annulled by either House. It must be confined to one or more of the following:

(a) the modification of the effect of a Code in relation to such areas of England and Wales as may be specified in the order;
(b) the modification of the effect of a Code for a period, specified in the order, which must not exceed two years;
(c) the modification of the effect of a Code in relation to such offences or descriptions of offenders as may be specified in the order.

Seven codes of practice have been issued under PACE and apply throughout England and Wales. They are: Code A (stop and search); Code B (search and seizure); Code C (detention, treatment and questioning of persons); Code D (identification); Code E (audio recording of interviews); Code F (visual recording of interviews); Code G (arrest); and Code H (terrorism).

Code A: the Code of Practice for the Exercise by Police Officers of Statutory Powers of Stop and Search and Code B: the Code of Practice for Searches of Premises by Police Officers and the Seizure of Property Found by Police Officers on Persons or Premises deal, together with various provisions of PACE, with the search of persons or vehicles without first making an arrest and the search of premises and the seizure of property. In addition, Code A covers requirements on police officers and community support officers to record encounters not governed by statutory powers.

The notice of rights and entitlements which must be given to detainees provides that the rights and entitlements are guaranteed under the laws of England and Wales and comply with the European Convention on Human Rights (ECHR).

A police officer may be liable to disciplinary proceedings for a failure to comply with any provision in one of the Codes if that failure indicates that his conduct has not met the appropriate standards of behaviour, but such a failure does not of itself render him liable to civil or criminal proceedings (although it is admissible in such proceedings where a case is founded on some other ground). Evidence obtained in a way which involves a breach of a Code is not automatically inadmissible at the trial stage but the magistrates or judge may rule that it is inadmissible on the grounds (in the case of a confession) that it was obtained by oppression or is unreliable or (in the case of any evidence) that it poses a threat to the fairness of the proceedings. This is a matter to which we return on pp 238 and 254.

Wherever these codes of practice require the prior authority or agreement of an officer of at least inspector or superintendent rank, a sergeant is treated as holding the rank of inspector, and a chief inspector as holding the rank of superintendent, if he has been authorised by a superintendent to perform the functions of the higher rank under PACE, s 107.

Police powers are dealt with in the following order in this chapter:

(a) powers to stop and search;
(b) powers to conduct a road check;
(c) powers to arrest without warrant;
(d) powers of entry and search in relation to an arrest;
(e) powers to search under a search warrant;
(f)   general provisions on entry, search, seizure, access and retention;
(g) powers to arrest a person;
(h) powers as to surveillance and the conduct and use of 'covert human intelligence sources'.

POWERS TO STOP AND SEARCH

Before PACE, there was no general power (ie one possessed by all constables) to stop and search for stolen goods, articles for use in offences under the Theft Act 1968 and offensive weapons. However, Acts of local application did give (to varying extents) such stop and search powers to constables in the local police force in particular circumstances. These powers were repealed by PACE, s 1 of which gives *every* constable, subject to certain requirements, a power to stop and search for stolen goods, articles for use in offences under the Theft Act 1968 and offensive weapons. There is only one power to stop and search which is not possessed by every constable: it is provided by PACE 1984, s 6, which gives a special power to a constable employed by 'statutory undertakers' (ie bodies authorised by statute to carry out any railway, road transport, inland navigation or harbour undertaking). Such a constable may stop, detain and search any vehicle before it leaves a goods area included in the premises of the 'statutory undertakers'. A goods area is any area used wholly or mainly for the storage or handling of goods.

Before PACE, various statutes had given *every* constable the power to stop and search for particular articles, for example, controlled drugs, firearms, and game or poaching equipment. These general powers (which we deal with under the relevant offences) have not been affected by PACE. In addition, as we show at appropriate points, subsequent statutes have introduced general powers to stop and search for particular articles.

Code A: the Code of Practice for the Exercise by Police Officers of Statutory Powers of Stop and Search (hereafter referred to as the Stop and Search Code) applies to the following powers of stop and search:

(a) those requiring reasonable grounds for suspicion that articles unlawfully obtained or possessed are being carried (or under s 43 of the Terrorism Act 2000 (TA 2000) that a person is a terrorist);
(b) those authorised under the Criminal Justice and Public Order Act 1994 (CJPOA 1994), s 60 (p 42);
(c) those authorised under TA 2000, s 44(1) and (2) (p 44);
(d) those to search a person who has not been arrested in the exercise of a power to search premises.

On the other hand, it does not apply to the powers of stop and search under s 6, above, or under the Aviation Security Act 1982, s 27 (hijacking), or to searches carried out for the purposes of examination under TA 2000, Sch 7 and to which the relevant Code of Practice issued under that Act applies.

Power under PACE, s 1 to stop and search

PACE, s 1(2) states that a constable:

(a) may search any person or vehicle ('vehicle' includes vessels, aircraft and hovercraft), *and* anything which is in or on a vehicle, for stolen or prohibited articles or an article to which PACE, s 1(8A) applies or any firework to which subsection s 1(8B) applies; and
(b) may detain persons or vehicles for the purpose of such a search.

PACE, s 1(3) provides that a constable only has this power to search if he has *reasonable grounds for suspecting* that he will find stolen or prohibited articles or an article to which PACE, s 1(8A) applies or any firework to which PACE, s 1(8B) applies; he must of course have such grounds *before* carrying out a search. Reasonable force may be used in the exercise of these powers, but every effort should be made to persuade a person to co-operate and force should only be used as a last resort. A compulsory search may only be made if it is established that the person is unwilling to co-operate.

Where a police officer has reasonable grounds to suspect that a person is in innocent possession of a stolen or prohibited article, the power to stop and search exists notwithstanding that there would be no power of arrest. However, every effort should be made to secure the voluntary production of the article before the power is resorted to.

Stolen or prohibited articles

Section 1 merely empowers a constable to search a person or vehicle for stolen or prohibited articles or an article to which PACE, s 1(8A) applies if he has reasonable grounds for suspecting that he will find such articles. A 'prohibited article' is defined as:

(a) an offensive weapon (which, by PACE, s 1(9), means any article made or adapted for use for causing injury to persons, or intended by the person having it with him for such use by him or by some other person); or

(b) an article made or adapted for use in the course of or in connection with an offence of burglary, theft, taking a conveyance without authority, obtaining property by fraud contrary to the Fraud Act 2006, s 1 (when in force) or destroying or damaging property, or intended by the person having it with him for such use by him or by some other person. The word 'deception' replaces 'fraud' until the 2006 Act is brought into force.

An article to which PACE, s 1(8A) applies is any article in relation to which a person has committed, or is committing, or is going to commit, an offence under the Criminal Justice Act 1988 (CJA 1988), s 139, that is an article with a blade or point. An article to which s 1(8B) applies is any firework which a person possesses in contravention of a prohibition imposed by fireworks regulations. The term 'firework' has the same meaning as in the Fireworks Act 2003, s 1(1) and 'fireworks regulations' means the Firework Regulations 2004 referred to on pp 780–782. The term 'article' will also include any program or data held in an electronic form when the provisions of the Fraud Act 2006 are brought into force. Computer programs can generate credit card numbers; computer templates can be used for producing blank bills; and computer files may contain the credit card details of persons.

It is interesting at this stage to examine the existing police practice of searching persons on football coaches for offensive weapons before allowing them to proceed to football grounds. Many of the articles which such persons carry will no doubt fit the description of offensive weapons, but the likely possession of those weapons must be viewed objectively. The Code makes it clear that a reasonable suspicion cannot be founded upon a person's belonging to a particular group and, unless there are particular reasons for suspecting an individual of possession of such a weapon, a search would be unlawful and, in addition, the officer may be guilty of a disciplinary offence.

Places in which powers to search can be exercised

PACE, s 1(1) states that a constable may exercise any powers under s 1:

(a) in any place to which at the time when he proposes to exercise the power the public or any section of the public has access, on payment or otherwise, as of right or by virtue of express or implied permission; or

(b) in any other place to which people have ready access at the time when he proposes to exercise the power but which is not a dwelling.

Persons have a right to use streets and highways; they have express permission to enter cinemas, theatres or football grounds subject to paying an entry fee and they may remain there until that particular entertainment is over, when permission to be there ceases. There is an implied permission for persons to enter buildings to carry out business transactions with the owners, and even to use a footpath to a dwelling house for the purpose of paying a *lawful call* upon the householder. That implied permission remains until withdrawn by the householder or the owner of the business premises.

'Place to which people have ready access' in (b) is wide in meaning. It extends the power of search to any place (other than a dwelling) to which the public have access in fact, whether lawfully or not; for example, a private field or grounds into which people regularly gain access as trespassers.

PACE, s 1(4) states that, if a person is in a garden or yard occupied with, and used for, the purposes of a dwelling or on other land so occupied and used, a constable may not search him under s 1 unless the constable has reasonable grounds for believing that:

(a) he does not reside in the dwelling; and
(b) he is not in the place in question with the express or implied permission of a person who resides in the dwelling.

Similar restrictions apply to the search of a vehicle (or anything in or on it) in such a place. By PACE, s 1(5), a constable may not search it unless he has reasonable grounds for believing that:

(a) the person in charge of the vehicle does not reside in the dwelling; and
(b) the vehicle is not in the place in question with the express or implied permission of a person who resides in the dwelling.

In effect, the only places in which a constable cannot exercise these powers are dwelling houses, the curtilage of dwelling houses if the person or vehicle is there lawfully, or any other place which is secure and does not permit ready access.

Seizure of articles

PACE, s 1(6) provides that suspected stolen or prohibited articles, or an article suspected to be one to which s 1(8A) or (1(8B)) applies, found in a search may be seized.

Power under Sporting Events (Control of Alcohol etc) Act 1985 to stop and search

It is convenient at this stage to refer to related powers of search aimed at the prevention of football hooliganism which are provided by the Sporting Events (Control of Alcohol etc) Act 1985 (SE(CA)A 1985). By s 7(3) of the Act, a constable may stop a football coach or minibus containing football fans going to or from a match, and search it, if he has reasonable grounds to suspect that an offence under the Act of causing or permitting alcohol to be on the vehicle, or of possession of alcohol on it, or of drunkenness on it, is being or has been committed. A constable also has the same power under s 7(3) to search (but not to stop) a railway carriage.

The power to search under SE(CA)A 1985, s 7(3) is limited to searching the vehicle or carriage. However, under s 7(2), a constable has a general power to search a person whom he reasonably suspects is committing or has committed an offence under the Act. This power extends not only to the offences mentioned in the previous paragraph but also to offences under the 1985 Act of possessing alcohol, a firework (or other pyrotechnic device) or a bottle or can at a football match or while entering the ground.

The offences under SE(CA)A 1985 are explained in more detail in Chapter 32, below.

Power to stop and search in anticipation of violence

CJPOA 1994, s 60 provides further powers to stop and search. It provides that where a police officer of the rank of inspector or above reasonably believes that:

(a) incidents involving serious violence may take place in any locality in his police area, and that it is expedient to give an authorisation under the section to prevent their occurrence; or

(b) that persons are carrying dangerous instruments or offensive weapons in any locality in his police area without good reason,

he may give an authorisation that the powers conferred by the section are to be exercisable at any place within that locality for a specified period not exceeding twenty-four hours.

'Locality' is not defined and this was intentional, as the extent of a 'locality' will differ in relation to the nature of the incident. An anticipated serious disorder at a pub would be in a small 'locality' while one within a housing estate would be in an extensive 'locality'. Provided that thought has been given to defining the locality, and this can be proved, a court is unlikely to rule that the authorisation was invalid. The authorising officer should not set a geographical area which is wider than that he believes necessary for the purpose of preventing anticipated violence.

Whether or not it is expedient to give an authorisation may involve consideration of the effectiveness of other powers, and the resources available to deal with the type of incidents which may arise. Provided that such judgments are made in good faith, a court is unlikely to interfere.

The period during which these powers may be exercised must be the minimum considered necessary to deal with the risk of violence, the carrying of knives or offensive weapons, or terrorism.

The area within which these powers may be exercised must be carefully specified and officers must be aware of the geographical area enclosed. If the powers are to be used in response to a threat or incident which straddles police force areas, an officer from each of the forces affected must give an authorisation.

Where an inspector gives such an authorisation he must, as soon as it is reasonably practicable to do so, cause an officer of or above the rank of superintendent to be informed.

The authorisation may be extended once only for a further twenty-four hours on the authority of an officer of or above the rank of superintendent, where expedient, having regard to offences committed, or reasonably suspected to have been committed, in connection with an activity falling within the authorisation. Thereafter further use of the powers requires a new authorisation.

Police powers

Where an authorisation is in force under CJPOA 1994, s 60 a constable in uniform is empowered:

(a) to stop any pedestrian and search him and anything carried by him, for offensive weapons or dangerous instruments;
(b) to stop any vehicle and search the vehicle, its driver and any passenger for offensive weapons or dangerous instruments.

A driver of a vehicle which has been stopped is entitled to obtain a written statement to that effect, if he applies within twelve months. The same rights apply to pedestrians or a person in a vehicle.

These stops and searches may be carried out *whether or not the constable in question* has any grounds for suspecting that the person or vehicle is carrying weapons or articles of that kind. A constable may seize any dangerous instrument or article which he has reasonable grounds for suspecting to be an offensive weapon. A 'dangerous instrument' is one which has a blade or is sharply pointed; a vehicle includes a 'caravan'; and an 'offensive weapon' is as defined by PACE, s 1(9) (see p 40). A person carries a dangerous instrument or an offensive weapon if he has it in his possession.

In addition, where an authorisation under CJPOA 1994, s 60 is in force in relation to any locality, a constable in uniform is given by s 60AA(2) the power in that locality:

(a) to require any person to remove any item (eg a face mask) which the constable reasonably believes that person is wearing wholly or mainly for the purpose of concealing his identity;
(b) to seize any item which the constable reasonably believes any person intends to wear wholly or mainly for that purpose.

In addition, where an officer of or above the rank of inspector reasonably believes that activities may take place in any locality in his police area that are likely (if they take place) to involve the commission of offences, and that it is expedient, in order to prevent or control the activities to give the following authorisation, he may authorise under CJPOA 1994, s 60AA that the powers under s 60AA(2) shall be exercisable at any place within that locality for a specified period not exceeding twenty-four hours. Where it then appears to a superintendent that in view of offences which have been, or are reasonably suspected to have been, committed in connection with the activities to which the authorisation relates, he may direct that the authorisation continues in force for a further twenty-four hours. Where an inspector gives the initial authorisation he must, as soon as practicable, inform a superintendent (or above).

Further points

In the case of the British Transport Police references to a 'locality' or to ' a locality in his police area' are references to any locality in or in the vicinity of any policed premises, or to the whole or any part of such premises.

An authorisation under s 60 or s 60AA must be in writing and signed and must specify the grounds for it; the locality, and the period during which the powers are exercisable. If it is not practicable to do this at the time, it must be done as soon as possible. It is for the authorising officer to determine the period of time in which he proposes to exercise these powers. It should be the minimum period he considers necessary to deal with the risk of violence.

As indicated above, an officer exercising the power to require the removal of an item must reasonably believe that someone is wearing the face covering wholly or mainly for the purpose of concealing his identity. There is no power to stop and search for face coverings. However, it may be seized if it is discovered when searching for something else, or is seen to be carried, in circumstances in which an officer reasonably believes it is intended to be used for the purpose of concealing identity.

A person who fails to stop or (as the case may be) to stop his vehicle or to remove an item worn by him when required to do so by a constable exercising these powers commits an offence. Failure to remove an item when required is an arrestable offence.

Power to stop and search for the prevention of terrorism

TA 2000, ss 44, 45 and 46 provide police officers with powers in respect of vehicles and their occupants and pedestrians if an authorisation has been given under s 44(1) or (2).

The authorisation

By TA 2000, s 44(3) and (4), an authorisation may be given under s 44(1) or (2) only if the person giving it considers that it is expedient to do so in order to prevent acts of terrorism. For the meaning of 'terrorism' see pp 931–932. The House of Lords has confirmed that 'expedient' in these provisions has a meaning quite distinct from 'necessary', and that an order can be made even though the officer making the order does not have reasonable grounds for considering that it is necessary and suitable for the powers to stop and search to be exercised. It is enough if that officer considers it likely that the exercise of, and utility in seeking, the stop and search powers would be of significant practical value to prevent terrorism.

An authorisation under s 44(1) or (2) may be given by a police officer of or above the rank of assistant chief constable (or equivalent). The authorisation authorises the exercise of the powers under s 44(1) or (2) in an area or place (in the authorising officer's police area) specified in it. As a result of an amendment made by the Terrorism Act 2006, the power to give an authorisation specifying an area or place includes power to give such an authorisation specifying such an area or place together with the internal waters (ie waters not comprised in any police area) adjacent to that area or place, or such area of those internal waters as is specified in the authorisation. Although an assistant chief constable of the British Transport Police or the Ministry of Defence Police may give such an authorisation, it may only be given in respect of specified places or areas policed by that force.

The authorisation should be in writing which is signed, dated and timed; if it is given orally it should be confirmed in writing by the officer who gave it as soon as possible. The person who gives the authorisation must inform the Secretary of State as soon as is reasonably practicable. If the authorisation is not confirmed it will cease to have effect after forty-eight hours but this will not affect the lawfulness of things done before the end of that period. Where an authorisation is confirmed the Secretary of State may substitute an earlier date or time at which it must end. Such an authorisation may be renewed provided that the same procedure is followed once more. Authority may only be given to search for articles which may be connected with terrorism. The officer should set the minimum period he considers necessary in the circumstances, and a geographical area no wider than is necessary. The Court of Appeal has held that the power to make an authorisation under s 44 is an exceptional power because of threats to public safety, and that it must be used with appropriate circumspection.

An authorisation under s 44 cannot be extended. A new authorisation is required.

Where an authorisation is given under TA 2000, s 44, the Stop and Search Code requires that the officer giving that authorisation must cause the Secretary of State to be informed, as soon as reasonably practicable, that such an authorisation has been given. For this purpose, an authorisation may take effect before the Secretary of State has decided whether to confirm it, but it ceases to have effect if not confirmed by the Secretary of State within forty-eight hours of its having been given. The Secretary of State may confirm such an authorisation but for a shorter period; or confirm it as given. An officer authorising the use of powers under s 44 must take immediate steps to send a copy of the authorisation to the National Joint Unit, Metropolitan Police Special Branch, who will forward it to the Secretary of State. The Secretary of State should be informed of the reasons for the authorisation. The National Joint Unit will inform the force concerned, within forty-eight hours of the authorisation being made, whether the Secretary of State has confirmed, not confirmed, or altered the authorisation.

Vehicles and their occupants

An authorisation under s 44(1) authorises a constable in uniform to:

(a) stop any vehicle in an area or at a place specified in the authorisation; and
(b) search the vehicle, its driver, a passenger, or anything in or on the vehicle or carried by the driver or passenger for articles of a kind which could be used in connection with terrorism.

The exercise of these powers does not require the constable to have reasonable grounds for suspecting the presence of such articles.

In the exercise of these powers, the constable may seize and retain any article which he reasonably suspects is to be used in connection with terrorism. The person or vehicle may be detained for a reasonable time to enable the search to be carried out.

The driver of a vehicle which has been stopped is entitled to obtain a written statement to that effect if he applies within twelve months.

A constable may not require a person to remove any of his clothes in public other than any headgear, footwear, outer coat, jacket or gloves.

A person who fails to stop his vehicle when required to do so by a constable in the exercise of these powers, or who wilfully obstructs him in the exercise of these powers, commits an offence.

Pedestrians

An authorisation under s 44(2) may be combined with an authorisation to stop and search vehicles etc under s 44(1). An authorisation under s 44(2) authorises any constable in uniform to stop any pedestrian in an area or at a place specified in the authorisation and to search him, or anything carried by him, for articles of a kind which could be used in connection with terrorism. The constable does not need to have grounds for suspecting the presence of such articles before exercising his powers. He may seize and retain any articles which he reasonably suspects are intended to be used in connection with terrorism. The requirement to remove clothing in public must be limited to headgear, footwear, outer coat, jacket or gloves. An offence is committed by a person who fails to stop for a constable exercising these powers or who wilfully obstructs such a constable.

A person stopped by a constable under TA 2000, s 44(1) or (2) is entitled to obtain a written statement that he was stopped under these powers if he applies for such a statement within twelve months.

Exercise of these powers

The selection of persons stopped under TA 2000, s 44 should reflect an objective assessment of the threat posed by the various terrorist groups active in Great Britain. The powers should not be used to stop and search persons for reasons unconnected with terrorism. Particular care must be taken not to discriminate against members of ethnic minorities. There may be circumstances, however, where it is appropriate for officers to take account of a person's ethnic origin in selecting persons to be stopped in response to a specific terrorist threat (some international terrorist groups are associated with particular ethnic identities).

The period during which these powers may be exercised must be specified in the authorisation. It must be the minimum considered necessary to deal with the risk of terrorism. In any event it must not exceed twenty-eight days.

The area within which these powers may be exercised must be carefully specified and officers must be aware of the geographical area enclosed. If the powers are to be used in response to a threat or incident which straddles police force areas, an officer from each of the forces affected must give an authorisation. Exceptionally, at this time, Greater London has been designated as a stop and search area for articles connected with terrorism and designations have been granted on a 'rolling basis' since February 2001.

The extended powers of seizure under the Criminal Justice and Police Act 2001 (CJPA 2001), s 51 (p 74) apply to searches under TA 2000, s 44(1) or (2).

It is important for national monitoring purposes to specify in any record of a search under these provisions whether a stop and search was carried out under TA 2000, s 44(1) or (2).

The House of Lords has ruled that the powers to stop and search under TA 2000, s 44 are lawful and do not breach Art 5 (deprivation of liberty) of the ECHR.

Reasonable suspicion

The Stop and Search Code gives the following guidance on what may be 'reasonable suspicion' for the purposes of statutory powers of stop and search which require a reasonable suspicion.

Whether reasonable grounds for suspicion exist will depend on the circumstances in each case, but there must be some objective basis for it based on facts, information and/or intelligence which are relevant to the likelihood of finding an article of a certain kind, or in the case of searches under TA 2000, s 43 (p 935) to the likelihood that the person is a terrorist. Reasonable suspicion can never be supported on the basis of personal factors alone without reliable supporting intelligence or information or some specific behaviour by the person concerned. For example, a person's race, age, appearance, or the fact that the person is known to have a previous conviction, cannot be used alone or in combination with each other as the reason for searching that person. Reasonable suspicion cannot be based on generalisations or stereotypical images of certain groups or categories of people as more likely to be involved in criminal activity. A person's religion cannot be considered as reasonable grounds for suspicion and should never be considered as a reason to stop or stop and search an individual.

Reasonable suspicion can sometimes exist without specific information or intelligence and on the basis of some level of generalisation stemming from the behaviour of a person. For example, if an officer encounters someone on the street at night who is obviously trying to hide something, the officer may (depending on the other surrounding circumstances) base such suspicion on the fact that this kind of behaviour is often linked to stolen or prohibited articles being carried. Similarly, for the purposes of TA 2000, s 43, suspicion that a person is a terrorist may arise from the person's behaviour at or near a location which has been identified as a potential target for terrorists.

However, reasonable suspicion should normally be linked to accurate and current intelligence or information, such as information describing an article being carried, a suspected offender, or a person who has been seen carrying a type of article known to have been stolen recently from premises within the area. Searches based on accurate and current intelligence or information are more likely to be effective. Targeting searches in a particular area at specified crime problems increase their effectiveness and minimise inconvenience to law-abiding members of the public. It also helps in justifying the use of searches both to those who are searched and to the general public. This does not, however, prevent stop and search powers being exercised in other locations where such powers may be exercised and reasonable suspicion exists.

Where there is reliable information or intelligence that members of a group or gang habitually carry knives unlawfully or weapons or controlled drugs, and wear a distinctive item of clothing or other means of identification to indicate their membership of the group or gang, that distinctive item of clothing or other means of identification may provide reasonable grounds to stop and search a person. Other means of identification might include jewellery, insignias, tattoos or other features which are known to identify members of the particular gang or group.

A police officer may have reasonable grounds to suspect that a person is in innocent possession of a stolen or prohibited article or other item for which he or she is empowered to search. In that case the officer may stop and search the person even though there would be no power of arrest.

An officer who has reasonable grounds for suspicion may detain the person concerned for the purpose of carrying out a search. Before doing so he may ask questions about the person's behaviour or presence in circumstances which gave rise to suspicion. As a result of questioning the detained person, the reasonable grounds for suspicion necessary to detain that person may be confirmed or, because of a satisfactory explanation, be eliminated. Questioning may also reveal reasonable grounds to suspect the possession of a different kind of unlawful article from that originally suspected. Reasonable grounds for suspicion, however, cannot be provided retrospectively by such questioning during a person's detention or by refusal to answer any questions put.

If, as a result of questioning before a search, or other circumstances which come to the attention of the officer, there cease to be reasonable grounds for suspecting that an article which is being carried is of a kind for which there is a power to stop and search, no search may take place. In the absence of any other lawful power to detain, the person is free to leave at will and must be so informed.

There is no power to stop and detain in order to find grounds for a search. Police officers have many encounters with members of the public which do not involve detaining people against their will. If reasonable grounds for suspicion emerge during such an encounter, the officer may search the person, even though no grounds existed when the encounter began. If an officer is detaining someone for the purpose of a search, he should inform the person as soon as the detention begins.

The guidance in the Stop and Search Code on what might be 'reasonable suspicion' has been stated fully because of its importance to police officers. The issue of whether or not an officer had reasonable grounds for suspecting possession of stolen or prohibited articles will frequently arise, and, as we have indicated already, failure to observe the provisions of the Code may amount to a disciplinary offence, quite regardless of any other liability which might arise. The important factor is that the issue will be judged objectively in the light of the knowledge which was available to the police officer when he made his decision. This may be a description given to the officer when briefed for duty of a person suspected of offences. However, such a general description of a person would not allow a search by itself; the officer would have to apply his mind to the circumstances surrounding the particular person under observation. The fact that such person appeared to be seeking an opportunity to commit a similar type of crime might reinforce suspicion sufficiently to satisfy the objective test.

Again, although information received from a member of the public may constitute a basis for reasonable suspicion, whether it actually does so depends on the content and nature of the information as well as the credibility of the informant. If the manager of a filling station tells a police officer that a man, of whom he gives a description, stole two cartons of cigarettes from the kiosk before driving off in a green Golf which was damaged on the front offside wing, the issue is fairly clear. If the officer sees a Golf of that description, driven by a man of the description given by the station manager, he may accept that the information which he was given was clear and that it was given by a reliable witness. He may reasonably act upon that information since it provides him with the necessary reasonable suspicion.

The Stop and Search Code does not affect the ability of an officer to speak to or question a person in the ordinary course of his duties (and in the absence of reasonable suspicion) without detaining him or exercising any element of compulsion. It is not the purpose of the Code to prohibit such encounters between the police and the community with the co-operation of the person concerned and neither does it affect the principle that all citizens have a duty to help police officers to prevent crime and discover offenders.

Principles governing stop and search

There should be no unlawful discrimination. The Race Relations (Amendment) Act 2000 makes it unlawful for police officers to discriminate on the grounds of race, colour, ethnic origin, nationality or national origins when using their powers. The primary purpose is to allow officers to allay or confirm suspicions without the necessity for an arrest. It is important to explain such actions to the member of the public concerned.

An officer must not search a person, even with his consent, where no power to search is applicable. The Stop and Search Code specifies, as a sole exception, that an officer does not require a specific power when searching persons entering sports grounds or other premises carried out with their consent given as a condition of entry.

Factors to be considered before carrying out a search

PACE, s 2(1) provides that, if a constable detains a person or vehicle in the exercise of the power under s 1 or any similar power to stop and search, he need not subsequently carry out that search if it appears to him that no search is required or that a search is impracticable. These circumstances will frequently arise: a person will often be detained on valid grounds for the purpose of a search and then satisfy the constable of his bona fides by answering his questions, or because of other circumstances which come to the attention of the officer. In such a case it is unnecessary to search and the detention will not be unlawful merely because the search was not carried out.

The Stop and Search Code additionally points out that there is no power to detain a person against his will in order to find grounds for a search.

Procedure before carrying out a search

The following procedure is provided by PACE, s 2(2) to (5) and the Stop and Search Code. Before a search of a detained person or attended vehicle takes place the officer must take reasonable steps to give the person to be searched or in charge of the vehicle the following information:

(a) his name and the name of the police station to which he is attached;
(b) the object of the search; and
(c) his grounds or authorisation for making it.

If the inquiries are linked to the investigation of terrorism, the officer must give his warrant number or other identification number and not his name. If the officer is not in uniform he must show his warrant card. In doing so in the course of terrorism inquiries, he need not reveal his name.

A divisional court has held that the failure of a police officer to supply his name and station rendered the search of a person unlawful, even where multiple searches were being carried out. With respect to the court, their lordships' suggestion that officers in such situations could carry slips of paper containing such details, which could be handed out, fails to recognise the pressures existing in multiple search situations.

Unless it appears to the officer that it will not be practicable to make a record of the search (in a multiple situation perhaps), he must also state that a person who has been searched (or the owner or person in charge of a vehicle that has been searched, as the case may be) is entitled to a copy of the record of the search if he asks for it within one year. If a person wishes to have a copy and is not given one on the spot, he should be advised to apply to the officer's police station.

The Stop and Search Code requires that before any search of a detained person or attended vehicle takes place, the officer must take reasonable steps to state to the person to be searched or in charge of the vehicle that he is being detained for the purpose of a search; give his name (except where the inquiries are linked to terrorism investigation, or otherwise where the officer reasonably believes that giving his name might endanger him, in which case the officer's warrant or other identification number must be given), and the name of his police station; state the legal search power being exercised; and give a clear explanation of the purpose, the grounds for reasonable suspicion where the powers require such suspicion, or where they do not, the nature of the power and any authorisation and the fact that it has been given. Warrant cards must be shown by officers not in uniform. Before the search takes place the officer must inform the person (or the owner or person in charge of the vehicle to be searched) of his entitlement to a copy of the record of the search, and also inform him about police powers to stop and search and his rights in these circumstances.

If the person to be searched, or in charge of a vehicle to be searched, does not understand what is being said, or there is any doubt about his ability to understand English, the officer must take reasonable steps to bring to that person's attention his rights and any relevant provisions of the Stop and Search Code. If that person is deaf or cannot understand English and has someone with him, the officer must establish whether that person can interpret or otherwise help him to give the required information.

A constable asking a person to remove a mask pursuant to CJPOA 1994, s 60AA is not performing a search under PACE, s 2, so the requirements of that section do not apply.

Conduct of search

Every reasonable effort must be made to minimise the embarrassment that a person being searched may experience. By PACE, s 2(8) a person may be detained for a search for such time as is reasonably required to permit a search to be carried out either at the place where the person or vehicle was first detained or nearby.

The co-operation of the person to be searched must always be sought, even if he initially objects to being searched. A forcible search may be made only if it has been established that the person is unwilling to co-operate (eg by opening a bag) or resists. Reasonable force may be used as a last resort, but only if this is necessary to detain the person or to search him. The length of time for which a person or vehicle may be detained will depend on the circumstances, but it must be reasonable and not extend beyond the time taken for the search.

The Stop and Search Code advises that, where the exercise of the power requires reasonable suspicion, the extent of the search will be related to the nature of the article sought and the circumstances. If a person is seen to put an offensive weapon into a particular pocket, then, unless there are grounds for suspecting that it has been moved elsewhere, the search must be confined to that pocket; whereas, if the article sought may easily be concealed anywhere on the person, the search may have to be more thorough.

The term 'nearby' in PACE, s 2(8) is not defined but it is submitted that it should be interpreted quite narrowly. To move a vehicle from a congested spot into a side street, or a person from the public gaze into an alley, would be a reasonable action to take and would not prevent the search from being 'nearby'.

An officer who is not in uniform may not stop a vehicle for the purpose of a search.

Removal of clothing

The Stop and Search Code restricts searches in public to a 'superficial examination of outer clothing'. A constable is not authorised under s 1 of PACE, or under any other power of stop and search, to *require* a person to remove any of his clothing in public other than an outer coat, jacket or gloves (other than under TA 2000, s 44 of which grants a constable in addition the power to require a person to remove in public any headgear or footwear, or under CJPOA, s 60AA which grants a constable power to require the removal of any item worn to conceal identity). Where there may be religious sensitivities about asking someone to remove a face covering, as in the case of a Muslim woman, the police officer should permit the item to be removed out of public view (for example, in a police van or police station if there is one nearby). Where practicable, the item should be removed in the presence of an officer of the same sex and out of sight of anyone of the opposite sex. A search in public of clothing which has not been removed must be restricted to a superficial examination of outer garments. This does not prevent an officer placing his hands inside the pockets of outer clothing, or feeling around the inside of collars, socks and shoes if this is reasonably necessary. Subject to the restrictions upon removal of headgear, a person's hair may be searched in public.

If, on reasonable grounds, a more extensive search than a superficial examination of outer clothing is considered necessary (eg by requiring a person to take off a T-shirt or headgear) it must be done out of view of the public, for example in a police van or a police station if there is one nearby. Any search involving more than the removal of an outer coat, jacket or gloves, headgear or footwear, or any other item concealing identity, may only be made by an officer of the same sex as the person searched and may not be made in the presence of anyone of the opposite sex unless the person being searched specifically requests it.

Searches which involve exposure of intimate parts of the body must not be conducted as a routine extension of a less thorough search simply because nothing is found in the course of the initial search. Searches involving such exposure may be carried out only at a nearby police station or other nearby location which is out of the public view.

A search in a street itself should be regarded as being in public, even though the street is empty at the time the search begins. As a search of a person in public should be a superficial examination of outer clothing, such searches should be completed as soon as possible.

When a community support officer on duty and in uniform has been conferred with powers under TA 2000, s 44, by a chief officer, the exercise of these powers must comply with the requirements of the Stop and Search Code including the recording requirements set out below.

Record of search

The Stop and Search Code requires that a record of a search must be made at the time by an officer who has carried out the search, unless exceptional circumstances exist which would make it wholly impracticable (eg in public order situations or where a constable is urgently required elsewhere). If a record is not made at the time, it must be made as soon as practicable. There may be occasions where it is not practicable to obtain the information necessary to complete a record, but reasonable efforts should be made to do so. A copy must be given immediately to the person concerned. The officer must ask for the name, address and date of birth of the person searched, but there is no obligation for that information to be provided and no power to detain a person if he is unwilling to provide it. Where a stop and search is carried out by more than one officer, all should be identified on the record. There is nothing to prevent an officer who is present but not directly involved in the search from completing the record. In situations where it is not practicable to provide a written record of the stop or stop and search at that time, the officer should consider providing the person with details of the station at which a person may attend for a record. This may take the form of a simple business card, adding the date of the stop or stop and search.

Where an officer makes a record of the stop electronically and is unable to produce a copy of the form at the time, the officer must explain how the person can obtain a full record of the stop or stop and search and give the person a receipt which contains:

(a) a unique reference number and guidance on how to obtain a full copy of the stop or stop and search;
(b) the name of the officer who carried out the stop or stop and search (other than in a case involving terrorism); and
(c) the power used to stop and search him.

A note for guidance requires a record to be made of the self-defined ethnicity of every person stopped according to categories listed in Annex B to the Stop and Search Code. The person concerned should be asked to select a main category and a sub-category (eg White/British). The code number shown in Annex B should also be recorded. The purpose of obtaining such information should be explained. If an apparently incorrect response is given (a person who appears to be white states that he is black) the response given should still be recorded but the officer should give his own perception of the ethnic background of *every person stopped* by using the PNC/Phoenix classification system. If the 'not stated' category is used, the reason for doing so must be stated.

The following information should always be included in the record of a search even if the person does not wish to identify himself or give his date of birth:

(a) the name of the person searched, or (if he withholds it) a description of him;
(b) a note of the person's self-defined ethnic background;
(c) where a vehicle is searched, its registration number;
(d) the date, time and place the person or vehicle was first detained;
(e) the date, time and place the person or vehicle was searched (if different from (d));
(f) the purpose of the search;
(g) the grounds for making it, or in the case of those searches authorised under CJPOA 1994, s 60, or under TA 2000, s 44 (see above), the nature of the power and of any necessary authorisation and the fact that it has been given;
(h) its outcome (eg arrest or no further action);
(i) a note of any injury or damage to property resulting from it; and
(j) the identity of the officers making it (except in the case of inquiries linked to an investigation into terrorism, or otherwise where there is a reasonable belief that giving a name might endanger the officers, when the warrant or other identification number and duty station of the officer(s) should be recorded).

A record is required for each person and each vehicle searched. However, only one record is required where a person who is in a vehicle is searched in addition to the vehicle, and the object and grounds of the search are the same. Where only a vehicle is searched, the name of the driver and his or her self-defined ethnic background must be recorded, unless the vehicle is unattended. Records must include the reasons for searching the person concerned by reference to his behaviour and/or other circumstances. They must be made even though, following questioning, the detained person was not searched.

Unattended vehicles

If an unattended vehicle, or anything in or on it, is searched the constable is required by PACE, s 2(6) to leave a notice:

(a) stating that he has searched it;
(b) giving the name of the police station to which he is attached;
(c) stating where any application for compensation for any damage caused by the search should be directed; and
(d) stating where a copy of the search record may be obtained.

The notice must be left inside the vehicle if this can be done without damaging the vehicle. A vehicle which has been searched must, if practicable, be left secure.

Monitoring and supervising the use of stop and search powers

Supervising officers must monitor the use of stop and search powers and should consider whether there is evidence of such powers being exercised on the basis of stereotyped images or inappropriate generalisations and should satisfy themselves that officers are acting in accordance with the Stop and Search Code. They must also examine whether the records reveal any trends or patterns which give cause for concern, and, if they recognise such trends, take appropriate action. Senior officers with area or force-wide responsibilities must also monitor such matters on a broader basis. The Stop and Search Code requires the compilation of comprehensive statistical records of stops and searches at all levels. Disproportionate use by particular officers (or groups of them) or in relation to particular sections of the community should be investigated. Arrangements must be made, in consultation with police authorities, for records to be scrutinised by community representatives and for the use of these powers to be explained to them. However, such scrutiny of public records must take account of an individual's right to confidentiality. Anonymised forms and/or statistics generated from records should be the focus of the examination by members of the public.

Recording of encounters not governed by statutory powers

When an officer requests a person in a public place to account for himself, that is his actions, behaviour, presence in an area or possession of anything, a record of the encounter must be made at the time and a copy given to that person. The record must identify the officer. This does not apply to general conversations such as giving directions to a place or when seeking witnesses, nor does it include the seeking of general information or the questioning of people to establish background to incidents which have required intervention to maintain the peace or resolve a dispute. When stopping a person in a vehicle a separate form does not need to be given when a form HO/RT1, a Vehicle Defect Rectification Scheme Notice, or a fixed penalty notice is issued, nor does it apply when a preliminary specimen of breath is required under the Road Traffic Act 1988 (RTA 1988), s 6, or when stopping a person when a penalty notice is issued for an offence. The persons concerned must be informed of their entitlement to a copy of the record. In all such matters, the proviso relating to the identification of officers in cases of terrorism apply, as they apply to all subsequent references to identification.

The following information must be recorded:

(a) the date, time and place of the encounter;
(b) if the person is in a vehicle, the registration number;
(c) the reason why the officer questioned that person;
(d) a note of the person's self-defined ethnic background;
(e) the outcome of the encounter.

There is no power to require the provision of this information by the person. Where details of an ethnic background are refused the record must show a description of that background. If a person requests a record, such a record must be completed even if an officer considers that the nature of the encounter was such that a record is not required by the Stop and Search Code.

A record of an encounter must always be made when an officer requests a person to account for himself in a public place; but where this requirement is not met but the person requests a record, the officer should provide a copy of the form but record on it that the encounter did not satisfy the requirement. The requirement would not be used where an officer engages in conversation which is not pertinent to the actions or the whereabouts of the individual (eg because it does not relate to why the person is there, what they are doing or where they have been or are going). Situations designed to impede police activity may arise, for example, in public order situations where individuals engage in dialogue with the officer but the officer does not initiate or engage in contact about the individual's particular circumstances. The officer may refuse to issue a form if he reasonably believes that the purpose of the request is deliberately aimed at frustrating or delaying legitimate police activity.

These provisions apply equally to police staff designated as community support officers.

Search and seizure powers of community support officers

Community support officers are given powers, if their designation so provides, to search and seize by SOCPA 2005. These include powers to search for alcohol and tobacco; power to seize drugs and power to require names and addresses of persons found in possession of drugs.

The fact that it is necessary to attempt to spell out circumstances in which police staff may speak to members of the public without the necessity of making a record of the fact may be seen to sit uncomfortably with the concept of community policing.

POWERS TO CONDUCT A ROAD CHECK

Statutory power

PACE, s 4 governs the conduct of road checks by police officers for the purpose of ascertaining whether a vehicle is carrying:

(a) a person who has committed an offence other than a road traffic offence or a vehicle excise offence;

(b) a person who is a witness to such an offence;

(c) a person intending to commit such an offence; or

(d) a person unlawfully at large.

For the purposes of the section, a 'road check' consists of the exercise in a locality of the power conferred by RTA 1988, s 163 (power of a constable in uniform to stop a mechanically propelled vehicle or pedal cycle on a road) in such a way as to stop all vehicles or vehicles selected by any criterion.

PACE, s 4 is mainly concerned with setting up road checks to arrest actual or intending criminals or escaping prisoners. The purpose of the check will be to stop all vehicles or selected vehicles. It may be that the person the officers are seeking to arrest is known to be in a black Volkswagen Golf car and therefore only vehicles similar to that description will be stopped. Section 4 does not in any way affect an officer's powers to deal with road traffic matters and he may stop as many vehicles as he thinks necessary for that purpose. An officer who wishes to stop a single vehicle, which he reasonably suspects may be carrying a person who has committed or intends to commit an offence etc, may do so under the powers given by RTA 1988, s 163, which are unaffected in such circumstances.

Authorisation of road checks

A road check must be authorised in writing by an officer of the rank of superintendent or above. PACE, s 4 limits the instances in which authorisation may be given, as follows:

(a) if the commission of an offence, or the intention to commit an offence is involved, the officer must have reasonable grounds for believing that the offence is indictable and for suspecting that the person is, or is about to be, in the locality of the proposed check;

(b) if it is to trace a witness to an offence, the officer must have reasonable grounds for believing that the offence is an indictable offence; and

(c) if it is to arrest a person who is unlawfully at large, the officer must have reasonable grounds for suspecting that the person is, or is about to be, in that locality.

PACE, s 4 recognises that there will be emergencies in which it will not be practicable to obtain the authorisation of a superintendent in sufficient time for a road check to be effective. In such circumstances, authorisation may be given by an officer below the rank of superintendent, but the officer who authorises in such circumstances must, as soon as practicable:

(a) make a written record of the time of authorisation; and

(b) cause a superintendent (or above) to be informed.

The superintendent (or above) may then authorise, in writing, the road check to continue. If he decides it should not continue, he must record the fact that it took place, and its purpose (including the relevant indictable offence).

Time limits, records and searches

The maximum period for which a road check may be authorised is seven days, but written authorisation may be given for a further period not exceeding seven days if a superintendent (or above) believes that a road check ought to continue.

The authorisation may be for a road check to be carried out throughout the twenty-four hours of each day, or may be limited to specified times.

The record (ie written authorisation) which must be kept of a road check will show:

(a) the period during which the road check is authorised to continue;
(b) the name of the officer who authorised it;
(c) the purpose of the road check (including eany relevant indictable offence); and
(d) the locality in which vehicles are to be stopped.

The person in charge of a vehicle stopped in a road check is entitled to obtain a written statement of the purpose of the road check if he applies for such a statement within twelve months. It is only the purpose which needs to be stated in such a notice.

The Act does not give direct powers to a constable to search a vehicle stopped in a road check. However, he is empowered to do so:

(a) if he has reasonable grounds for suspecting that it contains stolen or prohibited articles (PACE, s 1); or
(b) for the purpose of arresting someone for an offence or certain other offences if he has reasonable grounds to suspect that the person is there (PACE, s 17); or
(c) under powers granted by any other statute, eg the Firearms Act 1968.

Common law powers

The power under PACE, s 4 does not affect or replace the existing common law power to set up road checks in relation to apprehended breaches of the peace. This common law power, which depends upon the immediacy of the threatened breach of the peace, was clarified in 1984 by a divisional court in a case concerning the stopping of vehicles carrying striking miners to picket lines. One of the judges expressed the relevant law in the following words:

If the police on reasonable grounds believe that a breach of the peace may be committed, the police officer is not only entitled but under a duty to take reasonable steps to prevent that breach occurring. Provided they honestly and reasonably form the opinion that there is *a real risk of a breach of the peace in the sense that it is in close proximity both in time and place*, then the conditions exist for reasonable preventive action. The possibility of a breach must be real to justify preventive action. The imminence or immediacy of the threat to the peace determines what action is reasonable.

Having stopped the vehicle under this power, the police may also search it thereunder. Anyone who insists on continuing his journey is liable to arrest under the common law power to arrest for an apprehended breach of the peace (see p 856).

Clearly, where the imminent breach of the peace would involve the commission of an indictable offence a road check can be operated either under PACE, s 4 or under the common law power. The procedural safeguards laid down for s 4 road checks do not, of course, apply to those under the common law power.

Prevention of terrorism: police cordons and prohibitions or restrictions of parking

TA 2000, ss 33 to 36 and 48 to 52 provide powers to impose a police cordon and to prohibit or restrict parking for the purposes of a 'terrorist investigation'. A 'terrorist investigation' means an investigation of:

(a) the commission, preparation or instigation of acts of terrorism (for the meaning of 'terrorism' see pp 931–932);
(b) an act which appears to have been done for the purposes of terrorism;
(c) the resources of a proscribed organisation (as to which see p 932);
(d) the possibility of making an order proscribing an organisation, or
(e) the commission, preparation or instigation of an offence under the Act or under TA 2006 other than an offence under s 1 or s 2 (encouragement of terrorism and dissemination of terrorist material).

TA 2000, s 34 permits an officer of at least the rank of superintendent, where he considers it expedient for the purpose of a terrorist investigation, to authorise a cordon to be imposed on an area specified by him in that authorisation. (An officer below that rank may do so where there is great urgency. He must, as soon as reasonably practicable, make a written record of the time of the designation of the area and ensure that an officer of at least the rank of superintendent is informed. Such an officer must confirm the designation or cancel it from a specified time, in which case his reason for doing so must be stated.) The area on which a cordon is imposed must, so far as is reasonably practicable, be indicated by means of police tape or in such other manner as appears to the police officer responsible for carrying out the arrangements for applying the cordon to be appropriate. The area concerned will be specified in the authorisation. The period of time initially specified must not exceed fourteen days, but may be extended by a superintendent (or above) by one or more written variations but the overall period must not exceed twenty-eight days. Persons must leave the area immediately when ordered to do so by a constable in uniform and persons must also leave premises which are wholly or partly in or adjacent to a cordoned area. Drivers or persons in charge of vehicles must move them out of the area (a constable has power to remove such vehicles). A constable in uniform may prohibit or restrict vehicular or pedestrian access to a cordoned area. Offences are committed by those who do not comply with the constable's requirements. A defence of 'reasonable excuse' exists in such cases.

TA 2000, s 48 permits a police officer of or above the rank of assistant chief constable (or commander), where it appears to him to be expedient in order to prevent acts of terrorism, to give an authorisation to any constable to prohibit or restrict the parking of vehicles on a specified road. This is to be done by the placing of traffic signs. A constable exercising his powers under the section may suspend a parking place and this will have the effect of permitting the removal of vehicles.

Such an authorisation may remain in force for a period not exceeding twenty-eight days, but this may be extended by further periods not exceeding twenty-eight days.

Persons who fail to move vehicles when ordered to do so by a constable commit offences, as do those who park in contravention of such a prohibition or restriction. The section provides defences for those who prove that they had reasonable excuse. Those with current disabled persons' badges are not exempt from these requirements and have no reasonable excuse for failure to comply on those grounds. The powers to impose these restrictions are additional to any other powers available to a constable.

POWERS TO ARREST WITHOUT WARRANT

An arrest may be authorised by a warrant issued by a justice of the peace. The law relating to the issue and execution of warrants has already been explained.

We are concerned here with the circumstances in which an arrest may lawfully be made without a warrant. SOPCA 2005, ss 110 and 111 made extensive changes to powers to arrest without a warrant and repealed all references in legislation to 'arrestable offences'.

PACE, ss 24 and 24A, as substituted by SOCPA 2005, deal with the powers of arrest available to constables and other persons respectively.

ARREST WITHOUT WARRANT: CONSTABLES (PACE, s 24)

(1) A constable may arrest without warrant:
   (a) anyone who is about to commit an offence;
   (b) anyone who is in the act of committing an offence;
   (c) anyone whom he has reasonable grounds for suspecting to be about to commit an offence;
   (d) anyone whom he has reasonable grounds for suspecting to be committing an offence.
(2) If a constable has reasonable grounds for suspecting that an offence has been committed he may arrest without warrant anyone whom he has reasonable grounds to suspect of being guilty of it.
(3) If an offence has been committed, a constable may arrest without warrant:
   (a) anyone who is guilty of the offence;
   (b) anyone whom he has reasonable grounds for suspecting to be guilty of it.
(4) The power of arrest conferred by (1), (2) or (3) is exercisable only if the constable has reasonable grounds for believing that for any of the reasons mentioned in (5) it is necessary to arrest the person in question.
(5) The reasons are:
   (a) to enable the name of the person in question to be ascertained (in the case where the constable does not know, and cannot readily ascertain, the person's name, or has reasonable grounds for doubting whether a name given by the person as his name is his real name);
   (b) correspondingly as regards the person's address;
   (c) to prevent the person in question:
      (i)   causing physical injury to himself or any other person;
      (ii)   suffering physical injury;
      (iii) causing loss of or damage to property;
      (iv)   committing an offence against public decency (but only where members of the public going about their normal business cannot reasonably be expected to avoid the person in question); or
      (v)   causing an unlawful obstruction on the highway;
   (d) to protect a child or other vulnerable person from the person in question;

(e) to allow the prompt and effective investigation of the offence or of the conduct of the person in question;

(f) to prevent any prosecution for the offence from being hindered by the disappearance of the person in question.

The effect of (4) and (5) is that the exercise of the arrest powers in (1) to (3) is subject to a test of reasonable belief in the necessity for an arrest on one of the specified grounds.

Code G, the Code of Practice for the Statutory Power of Arrest by Police Officers, gives guidance concerning arrest. Now that powers to arrest for specific offence are curtailed, the necessity for an arrest is likely to receive much attention within legal proceedings.

Reasonable suspicion

There must be some reasonable, objective grounds for the suspicion, based on known facts or information which are relevant to the likelihood that the offence has been committed and to the fact that the person to be questioned committed it.

Perhaps the most common arrest made by police officers is for the offence of being drunk and disorderly. There is no longer an unconditional power to arrest for the offence and a person who correctly identifies himself will no longer be liable to arrest. It will be interesting if he then continues with his disorderly conduct. Does an officer report him again or does he seek help from the common law power to arrest for a breach of the peace? If he does he must bear in mind the recent decision of a divisional court that there cannot be a breach of the peace on the part of a person unless there is an incident of violence on his part; verbal abuse is insufficient.

There may be grounds for arresting a suspect on the sole basis of the word of an informant but any police officer should treat that information with considerable reserve.

The term 'reasonable grounds for suspecting' means honest belief founded on grounds which would lead an ordinary cautious person to the conclusion that the person arrested was guilty. The information relied on need not be as compelling as that required to justify a conviction or the bringing of a charge. As in the case of most other police powers where phrases like 'reasonable grounds for suspecting' or 'reasonably suspects' are used, it is not enough that such reasonable grounds for suspicion exist; the constable must actually suspect the matter in question. The European Court of Human Rights has held that on the facts a police officer had reasonable grounds to suspect that the person arrested was guilty of a terrorist murder, even though the suspicion was formed as a result of a police briefing by a superior officer, because the information in that briefing specifically linked the person arrested to the murder. The Court of Appeal has held that when an arresting officer's suspicion is formed on the basis of a police national computer entry, that entry is likely to provide him with a reasonable suspicion.

The purpose of an arrest in these circumstances is to make a person answerable to a charge. Consequently, if a person who has been arrested on reasonable suspicion that he has committed an offence is able to prove that the arresting officer knew, at the time of the arrest, that there was no possibility of a charge being made, the arrest will be held unlawful because the arresting officer will have acted for an improper purpose. Thus, for example, arrests should not be made to teach a person a lesson where it is known that there is no possibility of a charge. On the other hand, there is no reason why an arrest should not be made for the purpose of interviewing a person reasonably suspected of committing an offence, in the hope of obtaining a confession, as in such a case the possibility of a charge still exists.

Points to be considered in relation to an arrest

Code G, the Arrest Code, deals with the essential elements surrounding arrest as follows, some of which simply repeats the terms of PACE, s 24.

The right to liberty is recognised by the ECHR. An arrest should not be effected if the necessary objectives can be achieved by other, less intrusive, means. Arrests must be exercised in a non-discriminatory and proportionate manner.

The Arrest Code states that a lawful arrest requires two elements:

(a) a person's involvement or suspected involvement or attempted involvement in the commission of a criminal offence; and
(b) reasonable grounds for believing that the person's arrest is necessary.

Arresting officers are required to inform the person arrested that he has been arrested, even if this fact is obvious, and of the relevant circumstances of the arrest in relation to both elements, and to inform the custody officer of these on arrival at the police station.

Involvement in the commission of an offence

A constable may arrest anyone:

- who is about to commit an offence or is in the act of committing an offence;
- whom the officer has reasonable grounds for suspecting is about to commit an offence or to be committing an offence;
- whom the officer has reasonable grounds to suspect of being guilty of an offence which he or she has reasonable grounds for suspecting has been committed;
- who is guilty of an offence which has been committed or anyone whom the officer has reasonable grounds for suspecting to be guilty of that offence.

The necessity criteria

The power of arrest is only exercisable if the constable has reasonable grounds for believing that it is necessary to arrest the person. The criteria for what may constitute necessity are set out below. It remains an operational decision at the discretion of the arresting officer as to:

- what action he or she may take at the point of contact with the individual;
- the necessity criterion or criteria (if any) which applies to the individual; and
- whether to arrest, report for summons, grant street bail, issue a fixed penalty notice or take any other action that is open to the officer.

In applying the criteria, the arresting officer has to be satisfied that at least one of the reasons supporting the need for arrest is satisfied.

Extending the power of arrest to all offences provides a constable with the ability to use that power to deal with any situation. However, applying the necessity criteria requires the constable to examine and justify the reason or reasons why a person needs to be taken to a police station for the custody officer to decide whether the person should be placed in police detention.

The criteria in PACE, s 24 are exhaustive. However, the circumstances that may satisfy those criteria remain a matter for the operational discretion of individual officers.

In considering the individual circumstances, the constable must take into account the situation of the victim, the nature of the offence, the circumstances of the suspect and the needs of the investigative process.

The criteria referred to above are that the arrest is necessary:

(a) to enable the name of the person in question to be ascertained (in the case where the constable does not know, and cannot readily ascertain, the person's name, or has reasonable grounds for doubting whether a name given by the person as his name is his real name);
(b) correspondingly as regards the person's address (an address is a satisfactory address for service of a summons if the person will be at it for a sufficiently long period for it to be possible to serve him or her with a summons; or that some other person at that address specified by the person will accept service of the summons on their behalf);
(c) to prevent the person in question:
    (i) causing physical injury to himself or any other person;
    (ii) suffering physical injury;
    (iii) causing loss or damage to property;
    (iv) committing an offence against public decency (but this only applies where members of the public going about their normal business cannot reasonably be expected to avoid the person in question); or
    (v) causing an unlawful obstruction of the highway;
(d) to protect a child or other vulnerable person from the person in question;
(e) to allow the prompt and effective investigation of the offence or of the conduct of the person in question;
(f) to prevent any prosecution for the offence from being hindered by the disappearance of the person in question.

This may include cases such as:

(a) where there are reasonable grounds to believe that the person concerned has:
    (i) made false statements;
    (ii) has made statements which cannot readily be verified;
    (iii) has presented false evidence;

    (iv) may steal or destroy evidence,

    (v) may make contact with co-suspects or conspirators; or

    (vi) may intimidate or threaten or make contact with witnesses; and

    (vii) where it is necessary to obtain evidence by questioning; or

(b) when considering arrest in connection with an indictable offence there is a need to:

    (i)   enter and search any premises occupied or controlled by a person;

    (ii)   search the person;

    (iii) prevent contact with others;

    (iv) take fingerprints, footwear impressions, samples or photographs of the suspect;

(c) to ensure compliance with statutory drug testing requirements;

(d) to prevent any prosecution for the offence from being hindered by the disappearance of the person in question, as where there are reasonable grounds for believing that if the person is not arrested he will not attend court, or that street bail after arrest would be insufficient to deter the suspect from trying to evade prosecution.

A police officer must consider carefully the necessity to arrest when deciding whether or not to do so. Not every refusal to provide a name and address at the officer's first request necessitates an arrest. Such a refusal should be followed by an explanation of the consequences of a continued refusal to provide an identity and an address which the officer believes to be true, and only if there is a continued refusal to provide such an identity and address should the arrest be made. However, a divisional court has accepted that where a person, whose name was unknown to a constable, was reasonably suspected by the constable of having committed an offence, these requirements are satisfied by the questions, 'What is your name?' and 'What is your address?' followed by a refusal to answer. In the event of refusal to answer, the offender should be told that he is being arrested in relation to the particular offence *and* for refusing to give his name and address. If an arrest is made, s 30 of the Act requires that a person arrested by a constable at a place other than a police station must be released if a constable is satisfied, before the person arrested reaches a police station, that there are no grounds for keeping him under arrest. It follows that, should an arrest be made on the grounds that a satisfactory name and address have not been provided but they are subsequently provided (or the person is identified in some other way), the arrested person must be instantly released. A record of such a release must be made as soon as practicable after the release.

Action to be taken in relation to an arrest

Cautions—when a caution must be given

Requirements relating to caution where there are grounds to suspect a person of having committed an offence are dealt with in Code C, the Detention Code (see p 111).

A caution need not be given or repeated when informing a person who is not under arrest that he may be prosecuted for an offence. However, a court will not be able to draw any inference under CJPOA 1994, s 34 if the person was not cautioned.

If it appears that a person does not understand the caution, the giver should explain it in his own words.

Records of arrest

The arresting officer must record in his pocket book or by any other method used for recording information:

(a) the nature and circumstances of the offence leading to arrest;
(b) the reason or reasons why arrest was necessary;
(c) the giving of the caution;
(d) anything said by the person at the time of arrest.

The record should be made at the time of the arrest unless impracticable to do so. If not made at the time, it must be completed as soon as possible thereafter.

The custody officer must open a custody record and the information given by the arresting officer on the circumstances and reason or reasons for arrest must be recorded. As an alternative, a copy of the entry made by the officer (as required above) may be attached to the custody record. The custody record stands as a record of the arrest.

Limits on powers resulting from arrest

The powers available to an officer as a result of an arrest—for example, entry and search of premises, holding a person incommunicado, setting up road blocks—are only available in respect of an indictable offence.

ARREST WITHOUT WARRANT: OTHER PERSONS (PACE, s 24A)

(1) A person other than a constable may arrest without warrant:
   (a) anyone who is in the act of committing an indictable offence (as defined on p 24);
   (b) anyone whom he has reasonable grounds for suspecting to be committing an indictable offence.
(2) Where an indictable offence has been committed, a person other than a constable may arrest without warrant:
   (a) anyone who is guilty of that offence;
   (b) anyone whom he has reasonable grounds for suspecting to be guilty of it.
(3) The power of arrest conferred by (1) and (2) is only exercisable if:
   (a) the person making the arrest has reasonable grounds for believing that for any of the reasons mentioned in (4) it is necessary to arrest the person in question; and
   (b) it appears to the person making the arrest that it is not reasonably practicable for a constable to make it instead.
(4) The reasons are to prevent the person in question:
   (a) causing physical injury to himself or any other person;
   (b) suffering physical injury;
   (c) causing loss of or damage to property; or
   (d) making off before a constable can assume responsibility for him.

The above provisions do not apply in relation to an offence under the Public Order Act 1986, Parts III or IIIA (racial and religious hatred offences).

Thus, the conditions under which an arrest can be made by some 'other person' are more limited than in the case of a constable. The reason in (4)(d) is included because of the power given to support officers to detain persons with a view to handing them over to a constable.

These provisions are difficult to recall until applied to practical circumstances. It is reasonable that all citizens should be allowed to arrest persons who are actually found committing, or are reasonably suspected to be in the act of committing, such an offence which is serious enough to be classed as an indictable offence. It would be quite ridiculous to require citizens to ignore such offences which were being committed. In the same way, if a person's house has been burgled and he finds someone hiding in the garden in suspicious circumstances with property concealed nearby, it would be unrealistic to deny him the power to arrest in such circumstances. He knows that an indictable offence has been committed and has clear grounds for suspecting the particular person to be guilty of it. The situation changes in circumstances in which a person is merely observed to be acting suspiciously when there is no knowledge that a particular indictable offence has been committed. In such a case, it is sensible to restrict to constables the power to arrest on reasonable suspicion that an indictable offence has been or is about to be committed, particularly since constables are trained to observe, question and apply their minds to circumstances which might amount to 'reasonable suspicion'.

OTHER POWERS OF ARREST WITHOUT WARRANT

Specific statutory power of arrest without warrant

PACE, s 26 repealed all previous statutory powers for a constable to arrest (including those provided by local Acts) with exceptions. These powers are listed in PACE, Sch 2, and were adjusted by the Serious Organised Crime Act 2005 (SOCPA 2005), leaving:

(a) the arrest of absentees and deserters from HM Forces and Visiting Forces;
(b) the arrest of persons under emergency powers or terrorism legislation;
(c) the arrest of persons who are absent from places of detention or who have broken bail;
(d) the arrest of persons under certain powers under the Immigration Act 1971;
(e) the arrest of persons under the provisions of the Mental Health Act 1983;
(f) the arrest at the direction of the presiding officer at a polling station of persons suspected of personation.

Power to arrest at common law

At common law a police officer or anyone else has power to arrest without warrant in certain circumstances, and this power is not affected by PACE. The common law power exists:

(a) where a breach of the peace is committed by the person arrested in the presence of the person making the arrest; or
(b) where no breach of the peace has occurred in the presence of the person making the arrest, but he reasonably believes that such a breach by the person arrested is

about to occur or is imminent; (he will not have such a belief if there is no real and present threat to the peace).

We define 'breach of the peace' on p 855.

These common law powers of arrest are important to police officers. They are in no way restricted by the nature of the place in which the breach of the peace occurs or is anticipated. The arrest within the above terms is a preventative measure and should be effected wherever it is necessary to preserve the peace; even on private premises and even if no member of the public is present. If two men are fighting, that is a breach of the peace regardless of all other considerations and an arrest by anyone who sees it occur is justified. It may be that the stage at which a fight actually occurs has not been reached but a constable reasonably believes that it will occur in the immediate future; in such a case he may arrest those in dispute. Likewise, where an actual fight may have been discontinued but a constable reasonably believes that the argument is not at an end and that the fight is likely to be resumed, and a breach of the peace occur, an arrest is justified.

Once a constable reasonably foresees a breach of the peace, he is entitled to remain on premises in which, until that time, he has been a trespasser.

Since a breach of the peace does not necessarily require anyone to be acting, or threatening to act, unlawfully, the power to arrest for breach of the peace is not limited to cases where unlawful conduct occurs, is suspected or anticipated. By way of a limit on the arrest of those who are not acting unlawfully, the Court of Appeal has set out four factors to be considered in such a case.

(1) There must be a real and present threat to the peace justifying depriving a citizen, not at the time acting unlawfully, of his liberty.
(2) The threat must come from the person arrested.
(3) The conduct must clearly interfere with the rights of others and its natural consequence must be 'not wholly unreasonable violence' from a third party.
(4) The conduct of the person to be arrested must be unreasonable.

Cross-border powers to arrest

The CJPOA 1994, s 137 provides that, where it appears to a constable that it would have been lawful for him to have exercised the power had the suspected person been in England or Wales, a constable of an English or Welsh police force, who has reasonable grounds for suspecting that an offence has been committed or attempted in England and Wales and that the suspected person is in Scotland or Northern Ireland, may arrest without warrant the suspected person wherever he is in Scotland or Northern Ireland. Scottish officers and those of the Northern Ireland Police Service have similar powers of arrest within England and Wales in respect of offences committed or attempted in Scotland or Northern Ireland respectively. This power may be exercised in England and Wales and Scotland (but not Northern Ireland) by a British Transport police officer. Thus, for example, such an officer can arrest someone in Scotland for an offence committed in England or Wales.

Where a person is arrested in Scotland or Northern Ireland under this power, he must be taken to the nearest convenient designated police station in England or Wales or to a designated police station in the police area where the offence is being investigated. This must be done as soon as reasonably practicable.

Arrest without warrant for fingerprinting

PACE, s 27 permits a constable to arrest without warrant a person who fails to comply with a requirement for fingerprinting made under that section. Section 27 provides that if a person:

(a) has been convicted of a 'recordable offence';
(b) has not at any time been in police detention for an offence; and
(c) has not had his fingerprints taken in the course of an investigation of the offence or since the conviction, any constable may at any time not later than one month after the date of the conviction require him to attend at a police station in order that his fingerprints may be taken. The requirement must give the person a period of at least seven days within which he must attend, and may direct him to attend at a specified time of day or between specified times of day.

A second set of fingerprints may be taken from a person convicted of a recordable offence who has already had his fingerprints taken in consequence of conviction of a recordable offence if they did not constitute a full set, or some were of insufficient quality to allow satisfactory analysis or matching.

The above provisions apply where a person has been cautioned for an admitted recordable offence, or where that person has been warned or reprimanded under the Crime and Disorder Act 1998, s 65, as they apply where a person has been convicted of an offence.

A constable may arrest without warrant a person who has failed to comply with a requirement under s 27.

The following offences are recordable:

(a)   any offence punishable with imprisonment (to be construed without regard to any prohibition or restriction imposed by or under any enactment on the punishment of young offenders);

(b)   loitering or soliciting for the purposes of prostitution (Street Offences Act 1959, s 1);

(c)   tampering with a motor vehicle (Road Traffic Act 1988, s 25);

(d)   touting for car hire services (CJPOA 1994, s 167);

(e)   giving intoxicating liquor to a child under five, exposing children under twelve to risk of burning, and failing to provide for safety of children at entertainments (Children and Young Persons Act 1933, ss 5, 11 and 12);

(f)   drunkenness in a public place (Criminal Justice Act 1967, s 91);

(g)   failing to deliver up authority to possess prohibited weapon or ammunition, possession of assembled shotgun by unsupervised person under fifteen, possession of air weapon or ammunition for air weapon by unsupervised person under fourteen and possession of air weapon in public place by unsupervised person under seventeen (Firearms Act 1968, ss 5(6), 22(3) and (4));

(h)   trespassing in daytime on land in search of game, refusal by such trespasser to give name and address, and five or more found armed in daytime in search of game and using violence or refusing to give name and address (Game Act 1831, ss 30, 31 and 32);

(i)   being drunk in highway or public place (Licensing Act 1872, s 12);

(j)   obstructing an authorised person exercising various powers under the Licensing Act 2003 (LA 2003), ss 59(5), 96(5), 108(3) and 179(4));

(k)   failing to notify licensing authority change of name or rules of club, or of convictions, or failing to notify court of the holding of a personal licence (LA 2003, ss 82(6), 123(2) and 128(6));

(l)   keeping alcohol on premises for unauthorised sale etc, allowing disorderly conduct on premises, selling alcohol to a drunken person, obtaining it for such a person, failing to leave licensed premises, keeping smuggled goods, and allowing unaccompanied children on certain premises (LA 2003, ss 138(1), 140(1), 141(1), 142(1), 143(1), 144(1) and 145(1));

(m) selling alcohol to children, allowing sale to, purchase by or on behalf of children, allowing consumption by or delivery to children, sending a child to obtain alcohol, and allowing unsupervised sale by children (LA 2003, ss 146(1), 147(1), 149(1), (3) and (4), 150(1) and (2), 152(1) and 153(1));

(n)   making false statements in applications for licences etc (LA 2003, s 158(1));

(o)   allowing premises to remain open following a closure order (LA 2003, s 160(4); SI 2005/3106);

(p)   making false statement in relation to an application for a sex establishment licence (Local Government (Miscellaneous Provisions) Act 1982);

(q)   falsely claiming a professional qualification (Nursing and Midwifery Order 2001, art 44);

(r)   taking or destroying game or rabbits by night (Night Poaching Act 1828, s 1);

(s)   wearing police uniform with intent to deceive and unlawful possession of police uniform (Police Act 1996, s 90);

(t)   conduct likely to cause harassment, alarm or distress, failing to give notice of public procession, failing to comply with condition imposed on public procession, taking part in prohibited public procession, failing to comply with a condition imposed on a public assembly, taking part in a trespassory assembly, and failing to comply with directions relating to such an assembly (Public Order Act 1986, ss 5, 11, 12(5), 13(8), 14(5), 14B(2) and 14C(3));

(u)   failing to provide a roadside specimen of breath (Road Traffic Act 1988, s 6);

(v)   kerb crawling, and persistently soliciting women (Sexual Offences Act 1985, ss 1 and 2);

(w) in connection with designated sporting events, allowing alcohol to be carried on public vehicles, being drunk on such a vehicle, allowing alcohol to be carried in some other vehicles, trying to enter designated sports ground while drunk, unauthorisedly drinking (or supplying) alcohol at a designated sports ground (Sporting Events (Control of Alcohol etc) Act 1985, ss 1(2), 1(4), 1A(2), 2(2), 5B(3), 5C(4), 5C(5), and 5D(3)) and throwing missiles, indecent or racialist chanting, and going on to the playing area (Football (Offences) Act 1991, ss 2, 3 and 4);

(x)   taking or riding a pedal cycle without the owner's consent (Theft Act 1968, s 12(5));

(y)   having article with blade or point in public place (CJA 1988, s 139(1));

(z)   purchasing or hiring a crossbow (or part) by person under seventeen, and unsupervised possession by person under seventeen (Crossbows Act 1987, ss 2 and 3);

(aa) begging (Vagrancy Act 1824, s 3);

(bb) persistent begging (Vagrancy Act 1824, s 4).

The provisions of PACE, s 27 require careful consideration. In the first instance it must be recognised that if a person has been in police detention for the offence, at any time, a requirement under s 27 for fingerprinting cannot be made. If a person is arrested for burglary, released on bail without his fingerprints having been taken, and is subsequently convicted of that offence, s 27 cannot apply at any future stage. Since the section is only concerned with those who have been convicted of a recordable offence, it has no application during the course of investigation at any stage prior to a person's conviction. In addition, if fingerprints have been taken during the course of the investigation, the section cannot apply even though those fingerprints may have been lost or spoiled.

In most instances involving the commission of recordable offences the person will have been in police detention at some stage; probably he will have been arrested at the time of commission and admitted to bail soon afterwards. Nevertheless, some offenders may be dealt with by way of requisition or summons for a recordable offence, there being no necessity to effect an arrest at or after the time of the offence. In such instances fingerprints may be taken after conviction within the provisions of s 27.

Arrest of service personnel—absentees without leave and deserters

The Army Act 1955 and the Air Force Act 1955 generally run in parallel. Section 186(1) of those Acts gives a constable power to arrest without warrant any person whom he has reasonable cause to suspect of being an officer, warrant officer, non-commissioned officer or soldier (or airman) of the regular forces who has deserted or is absent without leave. Warrants authorising such arrests may also be issued by justices of the peace. Persons so arrested must be brought before a magistrates' court as soon as practicable. The Naval Discipline Act 1957, s 105 makes similar provisions in respect of naval personnel. Whether or not such a person admits to being an absentee or deserter he *must* appear before a court. Where a court is satisfied that such a person is a deserter or absentee, it will remand him in custody to await a service escort unless he is also in custody for some other reason.

Immediately such an arrest has been effected, the appropriate service authority must be informed and provided with all particulars of the case, stating whether the identity of the person arrested is disputed and whether his behaviour is refractory. Details of escort arrangements should be noted. Where an escort arrives before the court rises the person concerned can be handed over immediately, thereby avoiding his committal to prison or to other civil custody. Where the escort is likely to arrive quite soon, the court will usually commit such a person to police custody. The court must provide a certificate giving details of the serviceman's arrest (or surrender, see below).

Absentees frequently surrender to the police, having simply overstayed their leave. Such persons need not be taken before a magistrates' court but they may be if this is desirable for any reason. In such a case the court will remand the person in custody to await a service escort, subject to the same rules as just set out. Where an absentee serviceman is not taken before a court, a certificate must be made out by the officer of police who causes the serviceman to be handed over to the escort. Care must be taken in completing this certificate. If it is incorrectly completed or is not signed by the officer in charge of the police station, it is inadmissible in evidence at a subsequent court-martial. In all such cases of arrest or surrender the appropriate authority to be informed is as follows:

(a) in the case of a naval rating or Royal Marine, the Commodore, HMS Nelson, Portsmouth PO1 3HH (Metropolitan Police report to Naval Provost Marshal, London);
(b) in the case of a soldier, the Central Criminal Record and Intelligence Office, Royal Military Police;
(c) in the case of an airman, the HQ RAF Provost and Security Services (United Kingdom).

On occasions the service authorities may issue a warrant to arrest a serviceman. In such a case, the serviceman should be arrested and handed to a service escort. He need not be placed before a court unless he is to be dealt with for some other reason. The appropriate certificate must be handed over to the escort.

OTHER POINTS ABOUT ARREST WITHOUT WARRANT

The nature of an arrest

An arrest involves a deprivation of liberty to go where one pleases. An arrest is normally effected by the seizing or the touching of a person's body with a view to restraint. Another example would be where a person is deprived of liberty where he is detained by the automatic activation of the door locks inside a car specially designed by the police as a trap. Where unreasonable force is used to effect an arrest the arrest is unlawful. It is possible to effect an arrest merely by words if they bring to the person's notice that he is under restraint and will be compelled to remain, and he submits to that compulsion.

The varied circumstances in which the arrests envisaged by PACE may occur dictate the likely processes of the arrest itself. If the arrest occurs outside, it is probable that some form of physical restraint will be applied as the constable will be anxious to ensure that his prisoner does not escape. However, if the person arrested is a quiet, elderly person who is not physically capable of such escape, physical restraint would be unnecessary and undesirable. In the same way, persons already in custody who are arrested for other offences do not require a show of restraint, nor would it serve any purpose.

Information to be given on arrest

PACE, s 28 provides that where a person is arrested, otherwise than by being informed that he is under arrest, the arrest is not lawful unless, as soon as practicable after his arrest, the person arrested is informed that he is under arrest. This is so whether or not the fact of his arrest by a constable is obvious. In addition, no arrest is lawful unless the person arrested is informed of the ground for arrest at the time of arrest, or as soon as practicable after. This is a separate requirement to that set out above. Hence, a person must be told two things: that he is under arrest; and the ground which exists for the arrest. An arrested person must be given sufficient information to enable him to understand that he has been deprived of his liberty and the reason for his arrest, for example when a person is arrested on suspicion of committing an offence, he must be informed of the suspected offence's nature and when and where it was committed. He must also be informed of the reason or reasons why arrest is considered necessary. When determining whether a person has been informed of the grounds for his arrest, the question is whether, in all the circumstances, he was told in simple, non-technical language that he could understand, the essential legal and factual grounds. Vague or technical language should be avoided. The adequacy of the information must be judged objectively having regard to the information reasonably available to the arresting officer.

While it is preferable that the person arrested is informed of the precise offence for which he is being arrested, for example: 'I am arresting you for an offence of burglary which I have seen you commit', this is not essential (although the ground given must be a valid one). It suffices if, by the use of commonplace language, he is informed of the type of offence for which he is being arrested, so that he has the opportunity to give information which would avoid the arrest. Thus, where a constable making an arrest reasonably suspected that the offence was theft, handling, or taking a conveyance (a car), her statement that she was arresting the suspect for unlawful possession of a car was held to be sufficient. The Court of Appeal has held that the requirements of s 28 are satisfied where a suspect is arrested by one officer, but informed by another of the reason for his arrest.

PACE, s 28 exempts an officer from the necessity to give either item of information if it was not reasonably practicable to do so by reason of the person's escape before the information could be given.

Code C: the Code of Practice for the Detention, Treatment and Questioning of Persons by Police Officers (hereafter referred to as the Detention Code) additionally requires that a person must be cautioned upon arrest for an offence unless:

(a) it is impracticable to do so by reason of his condition or behaviour at the time; or
(b) he has already been cautioned immediately prior to arrest and before questions, or further questions, were put to him as a person suspected of an offence.

The caution must be in the following terms:

'You do not have to say anything. But it may harm your defence if you do not mention when questioned something which you later rely on in court. Anything you do say may be given in evidence.'

The Detention Code states that a juvenile should not be arrested at school unless this is unavoidable. In the event of this happening, the head teacher or his nominee must be informed.

Arrest elsewhere than at a police station

PACE, s 30(1) requires that, where a person is arrested by a constable for an offence (or is taken into custody by a constable having been arrested for an offence by someone other than a constable) at any place other than a police station, he must be taken to a police station as soon as practicable. This is subject to the rules below concerning release on bail (s 30A) or without bail (s 30(7)). The inclusion of 'as soon as practicable' allows for the circumstances in which it would be unrealistic to take such a person directly to a police station. This is expressly stated by s 30(10) which provides that a constable may delay taking an arrested person to a police station (or releasing him on bail) if that person's presence elsewhere is necessary in order to carry out such investigations as it is reasonable to carry out immediately; in such a case any questions put to the arrested person should be confined to those investigations. It follows from all this that, where a person is arrested for a theft which he was seen to commit but the property was not in his possession when arrested after a chase, a constable carrying out one of the duties of his office, to protect property, could quite properly retrace the route of the chase with his prisoner in order to recover the stolen property as soon as possible. However, in circumstances where the property is not in imminent danger of being lost in consequence of any delay in effecting its recovery, the prisoner should be taken immediately to a police station unless it is essential that he indicates the precise place in which the property has been hidden or the place at which it was disposed of.

If there is any delay in taking an arrested person to a police station, the reason for it must be recorded on first arrival there or, as the case may be, when he is released on bail. With certain exceptions, the police station to which the person arrested must be taken under s 30 must be a 'designated police station'. This term is explained in Chapter 5, but in essence it refers to a police station approved for the purpose of detention of prisoners. In exceptional circumstances, a person arrested may be taken to any police station. These circumstances are where:

(a) the constable is working in a locality covered by a police station which is not a designated police station; or

(b) he is a constable belonging to a police force maintained by an authority other than a police authority (eg the British Transport Police).

The exception at (a) recognises the situation which exists within many police forces. A 'designated police station' may be many miles from the place at which an arrest is made. If a person is arrested for an offence in respect of which he is likely to be released on bail more or less immediately, it would be unrealistic to require him to be taken to a designated police station many miles from the scene of the arrest. Neither exception applies if it appears to the constable that it may be necessary to keep the arrested person in police detention for more than six hours, in which case the person arrested must be taken to a *designated* police station.

In addition, any constable may take an arrested person to *any* police station if:

(a) the constable has arrested him without the assistance of any other constable and no other constable is available to assist him; or

(b) the constable has taken him into custody from a person other than a constable without the assistance of any other constable and no other constable is available to assist him,

and (in either case) it appears to the constable that he will be unable to take the arrested person to a designated police station *without the arrested person injuring himself, the constable or some other person.*

This provision recognises the occasions upon which police officers, acting on their own, experience sufficient difficulty merely removing the prisoner to the nearest police station.

When the person is arrested and taken to a non-designated police station, and there is no officer present at that police station to act as a custody officer, the inspector at that designated police station to which that person would have been taken must be informed. If the first police station to which an arrested person is taken is not a designated police station, he must be taken to a designated police station within six hours unless he is previously released.

A separate custody record must be opened as soon as practicable for each person who is brought to a police station under arrest. We discuss custody records in the next chapter.

A person arrested by a constable at a place other than a police station may be released without bail if a constable is satisfied before that person reaches a police station that there are no grounds for keeping him under arrest (s 30(7)). The constable must record the fact of the release as soon as practicable.

Bail elsewhere than at a police station

PACE, s 30A provides that a constable may release on bail a person who has been arrested or taken into custody in the circumstances mentioned in s 30(1) above at any time before he arrives at a police station. Such a person must be required to attend at a police station. No requirement other than that of attendance may be imposed. A notice in writing must be given to such a person stating the offence for which he was arrested; the grounds on which he was arrested; the police station at which he is required to attend, and the time of attendance. (If the police station and time of attendance are not stated in the notice, a further written notice containing that information must be sent later. The provisions allow the sending of an amended notice requiring attendance at a different police station or at a different time.) The requirement to attend a police station may be cancelled by written notice. If a person is required to attend a non-designated police station he must be released or taken to a designated police station not more than six hours after his arrival. Nothing in the Bail Act 1976 applies to bail under s 30A, nor do the provisions of PACE prevent re-arrest without warrant of a person released on bail if new evidence justifying arrest has come to light since his release.

A constable may arrest without warrant a person who has been released on bail under s 30A but fails to attend the police station at the appointed time. A person so arrested must be taken to any police station as soon as practicable after the arrest. Such an arrest is treated as an arrest for an offence for the purposes of PACE, s 30 (above) and s 31 (below).

Arrest for a further offence

Where a person is under arrest at a police station for an offence and it appears that, if released, he would be liable to arrest for some other offence, PACE, s 31 requires that he be arrested for that other offence. The usual procedures to be followed after an arrest must be carried out; the person must be told that he is being arrested for that other offence and what the reasons are for that arrest, and he must be cautioned. This must be done whether or not it is intended to release him at that time.

POWERS OF SEARCH, ENTRY, AND ENTRY AND SEARCH, IN RELATION TO AN ARREST

Search and seizure on arrest for an offence

Search

PACE, s 32 provides that, where a person has been arrested elsewhere than at a police station, a constable may search him if the constable has reasonable grounds for believing that the arrested person may present a danger to himself or others. The constable may seize and retain anything which he has reasonable grounds for believing that the person searched might use to cause physical injury to himself or another.

PACE, s 32 goes further and also empowers a constable in such a case:

(a) to *search* the arrested person for anything which he might use to assist him to escape from lawful custody or which might be evidence relating to an offence; *and*
(b) if the offence for which he has been arrested is an indictable offence, to enter and search any premises in which he was when arrested or immediately before he was arrested for evidence relating to the offence.

The power to search only extends to a search which is reasonably required for the purpose of discovering any such thing or any such evidence. A constable may not search a person under (a) unless he has reasonable grounds for believing that the person may have concealed on him anything for which a search is permitted under (a). Similarly, a constable may not search premises under (b) unless he has reasonable grounds for believing that there is evidence for which a search is permitted under (b) on the premises.

Neither of the powers under PACE, s 32 authorises the removal of clothing in a public place other than an outer coat, jacket or gloves.

PACE, s 32 gives statutory authority to 'on the spot' searches at the time of an arrest. That search may be for weapons or dangerous articles, for things which may assist escape, or for things which may be evidence of an offence. Thus, if a man is arrested for burglary and pulls a knife on the constable at the time of arrest, the constable has reason to believe that he is a danger and may search him for other weapons; if the man has shown a will to escape the constable may search him for things which might assist him to do so; if the constable has reason to believe that he may find evidence of an offence, for example property stolen whilst committing the burglary for which the person was arrested and other burglaries which he may have committed prior to his arrest, he may search him for such evidence. The power to search for evidence is particularly important since, if such property is not recovered at the time of such arrest, it is likely to be disposed of by the arrested person if an opportunity presents itself.

Similar considerations will apply to arrests made upon premises. 'Premises' includes any place and, in particular, includes any vehicle, vessel, aircraft or hovercraft, any offshore installation, and any tent or movable structure. If a police officer is seen approaching the premises in which a thief is lodged, it is likely that the thief will conceal the property within those premises. If he leaves and is arrested outside, it is reasonable that the constable should be empowered to examine the premises which he has immediately vacated.

PACE, s 32 deals with the problem of communal occupation (including bedsit premises) by stating that where there are two or more separate dwellings, the search must be limited to the premises in which the arrest took place or in which the arrested person was immediately before his arrest *and* any part of the premises which the occupier of the dwelling uses in common with the other occupiers of other dwellings comprised in the premises. In the case of a bedsit, therefore, the constable would be able to search the room in which the arrested person was found and the common kitchen and lounge area used by all of the residents. It may be that a thief occupying one room may, on seeing the approach of a constable, enter the room of his neighbour and hand over property to him to conceal on his behalf. If the constable knows that the thief was in that room immediately before his arrest he is empowered to search it.

Seizure

A constable searching a person under PACE, s 32 may seize and retain anything, other than an item subject to legal privilege (see p 81), if he has reasonable grounds for believing that the person might use it to escape from lawful custody or that it is evidence of an offence or has been obtained in consequence of the commission of an offence. The Criminal Justice and Police Act 2001, s 51 provides additional powers of seizure from the person which apply to the power of seizure under PACE, s 32. CJPA 2001, s 51 deals with the case where a person carrying out a lawful search of any person finds something which he reasonably believes may be, or may contain, something for which he is authorised to search and to seize. It provides that if, in the circumstances, it is not reasonably practicable for it to be determined whether what he has found (or its contents) is (or are) something which he is entitled to seize, his powers of seizure include seizing so much of what he has found as is necessary to remove from the place of the search to enable that to be determined. The details of this power, and the circumstances in which it applies, are set out below in relation to the power of seizure of property on premises. The powers are the same, with the modifications necessary to recognise that CJPA 2001, s 51 applies to a search of a person.

Where a person exercises this power of seizure under CJPA 2001, s 51, he must give written notice to the person from whom such property is seized:

(a) specifying what has been seized;
(b) specifying the grounds under which the power was exercised;
(c) setting out the effect of CJPA 2001, ss 59 to 61 (remedies and safeguards);
(d) specifying the name and address of the person to whom any application for the return of the seized property must be made; and
(e) specifying the name and address of the person to whom an application may be made to be allowed to attend the initial examination of the seized property which must be held to determine how much of it is property for which the person seizing had a power to search.

Any person with a relevant interest in the seized property may apply to a judge for its return on the grounds that there was no power of seizure, or that the seized material contains matter subject to legal privilege or contains excluded or special procedure material.

CJPA 2001, s 51 also applies to a number of other powers of seizure from the person listed in CJPA 2001, Sch 1, Part 2, some of which are referred to later in this book.

Police officers must recognise that CJPA 2001, s 51 does not provide any general powers of search either of persons or premises when an arrest is made. The particular circumstances described in the section must exist. If a man is arrested for a sexual assault and is known to be of a non-violent disposition, there are no grounds for an 'on the spot' search; nor would there be, in most circumstances, reason to search premises unless articles had been used in the commission of the offence.

The powers of seizure under PACE, s 19 apply to a search of premises under PACE, s 32. In addition, CJPA 2001, s 50(1) deals with situations where a person who is lawfully on the premises finds objects there which he reasonably believes to contain something for which he is authorised to search and in respect of which there would be a power of seizure to which s 50 applies. CJPA 2001, s 50 provides that where it is not reasonably practicable to establish the nature of the contents on the premises, or the extent to which the contents comprise something which there is power to seize, the power of seizure includes power to seize so much of that which has been found as it is necessary to remove from the premises to enable its nature to be determined.

CJPA 2001, s 50(2) provides a power of seizure where a person lawfully on premises finds anything there ('the seizable property') which he would be entitled to seize but for its being comprised in something else that he has (apart from s 50(2)) no power to seize. CJPA 2001, s 50(2) provides that where:

(a) the power under which that person would have power to seize the seizable property is a power to which s 50 applies; and
(b) in all the circumstances it is not reasonably practicable for the seizable property to be separated in those premises from that in which it is comprised,

that person's power of seizure includes power to seize both the seizable property and that from which it is not reasonably practicable to separate it.

CJPA 2001, s 50 requires that factors to be taken into account in considering whether it is reasonably practicable should be confined to:

(a) how long it would take to carry out the determination or separation on those premises;
(b) the number of persons who would be required to carry out that determination or separation on those premises within a reasonable period;
(c) whether the determination or separation would (or would if carried out on those premises) involve damage to property;
(d) the apparatus or equipment that it would be necessary or appropriate to use for the carrying out of the determination or separation; and
(e) in the case of separation, whether the separation:
   (i) would be likely; or
   (ii) if carried out by the only means that are reasonably practicable on those premises, would be likely to prejudice the use of some or all of the separated seizable property for the purpose for which something seized under the power in question is capable of being used.

CJPA 2001, s 50 applies to powers, including that under PACE, s 18, set out in CJPA 2001, Sch 1, Part 1. More than one hundred powers are specified including all of the powers of seizure with which police forces are concerned in their day-to-day work. CJPA 2001 requires that at a subsequent examination, which must take place as soon as reasonably practicable, property must be separated into that in respect of which there was a power of seizure, that in respect of which there was no power of seizure, and any which appears to be subject to legal privilege or to be special procedure material (see p 82). Everything other than that in respect of which a power of seizure existed must be returned. Property which may be retained is that which there are reasonable grounds for believing to have been obtained in consequence of an offence, or is evidence in relation to any offence, which needs to be retained to prevent it from being concealed, lost, altered or destroyed.

Where such a power has been exercised, written notice must be given to the occupier of the premises, or some other person on the premises who is in charge. Where there is no person on the premises a notice must be attached, in a prominent place, to the premises. Perhaps the best example would be the finding of a safe which was reasonably believed to contain seizable material and there was no means of gaining entry to the safe on the premises.

Officers should be aware of the need for confidentiality in relation to the contents of any documents and property must be returned as soon as possible. Delay is only justified where there are clear and compelling reasons, for example that the person to whom the material is to be returned is unavailable or where it is necessary to make arrangements for the return of a large quantity of material.

Anything seized in accordance with the above provisions may be retained for as long as is necessary for:

(a) use as evidence at a trial for an offence;
(b) facilitating the use in an investigation or proceedings of anything to which it is inextricably linked (eg on a computer disk) without damaging evidential integrity;
(c) forensic examination or other investigation in connection with an offence;
(d) establishing its lawful owner when there are reasonable grounds for believing it has been stolen or obtained by commission of an offence.

The person who had custody or control of such property immediately before seizure must, on request, be provided with a list or description of the property within a reasonable time, and he or his representative must be allowed supervised access to examine the property or have it photographed or copied (or must be provided with a photograph or copy) within a reasonable time and at his own expense, unless the officer in charge of the investigation has reasonable grounds for believing that this would prejudice the investigation of the offence or criminal proceedings, or lead to the commission of an offence by providing access to unlawful material such as pornography. A record of such grounds must be made if access is denied.

Entry to premises to effect an arrest etc

PACE abolished all the common law rules which gave a constable power to enter premises without a warrant, except that the power still exists at common law to enter premises to deal with a breach of the peace or to prevent it.

PACE, s 17 provides that, without prejudice to any other enactment, a constable may enter and search any premises for the purpose:

(a) of executing a warrant of arrest issued in connection with or arising out of criminal proceedings, or a warrant of commitment issued under the Magistrates' Courts Act 1980, s 76;
(b) of arresting a person for an indictable offence;

(c) of arresting a person for an offence under the Public Order Act 1936, s 1 (prohibited uniforms), or an offence under the Public Order Act 1986, s 4 (fear or provocation of violence), or an offence against RTA 1988, s 4 (driving etc under the influence of drink or drugs), or an offence under RTA 1988, s 163 (failure to stop when required to do so by a police constable in uniform), or an offence against the Transport and Works Act 1992, s 27 (drink or drugs on public guided transport systems), or an offence under CJPOA 1994, s 76 (failure to comply with an interim possession order), or an offence to which the Animal Health Act 1981, s 61 applies (powers of entry and search as to rabies), or an offence contained in the Criminal Law Act 1977, ss 6 to 8, or 10 (offences of entering and remaining on property)—in this last case the arresting constable must be in uniform;

(d) of arresting, in pursuance of the Children and Young Persons Act 1969, s 32(1A), any child or young person who has been remanded or committed to local authority accommodation under s 23(1);

(e) of recapturing any person who is, or is deemed for any purpose to be, unlawfully at large while liable to be detained:

   (i)   in a prison, remand centre, young offender institution or secure training centre; or

   (ii) in pursuance of the Powers of Criminal Courts (Sentencing) Act 2000, s 92 (dealing with children and young persons guilty of grave crimes), in any other place;

(f) of recapturing any person who is unlawfully at large and whom he is pursuing (ie chasing); or

(g) of saving life or limb or preventing serious damage to property.

Except in the case of saving life or limb or preventing serious damage, the powers of entry and search under PACE, s 17 are only exercisable where a constable has reasonable grounds for believing that the person whom he is seeking is on the premises. With the same exceptions, they are limited in respect of premises consisting of two or more dwellings in the same way as with the powers to search described above. A search under s 17 may only be made to the extent that it is reasonably required for the purpose for which the power of entry is required. The Court of Appeal has ruled that a police officer, when exercising his right of entry by force under s 17, must give any occupant present the reason why he is seeking entry even if that reason is apparent in the circumstances. Otherwise the forcible entry will be unlawful, unless circumstances make it impossible, impracticable or undesirable. If the real reason is to arrest a person inside for an arrestable offence, for instance, it is insufficient to tell the occupants that the officer wishes to 'speak to' that person about the offence.

As in the case of search on arrest, the word 'premises' is given a wide meaning. It includes any place and, in particular, includes any vehicle, vessel, aircraft or hovercraft, any offshore installation, and any tent or movable structure.

Arguments will arise in respect of the power to enter and search for the purposes of arresting someone for an arrestable offence. They are likely to be concerned with whether this applies to an arrestable offence which is known to have been committed or whether reasonable suspicion that the person has committed the offence is sufficient. It is submitted that it would be unreasonable to interpret these powers to enter and search separately from the circumstances in which the Act allows an arrest without warrant for an arrestable offence; if so a reasonable suspicion will suffice.

It is a surprising gap in police powers that there is no power under s 17 or elsewhere to enter premises to find evidence of the next of kin of someone who is dead or seriously injured.

Entry, search and seizure after an arrest

Entry and search

PACE, s 18 empowers a constable to enter and search any premises occupied or controlled by a person who is under arrest for an indictable offence before the person is taken to a police station or released on bail under s 30A (above), if he has reasonable grounds for suspecting that there is on the premises evidence, other than items subject to legal privilege, which relates to that offence or to some other indictable offence which is connected with or similar to that offence. 'Premises' bears the same meaning as in the case of search on arrest, so that s 18 extends to the search of a vehicle, vessel or tent. A search of any person, who has not been arrested, which is carried out during a search of premises must be carried out in accordance with the Stop and Search Code. A search under s 18 is only permitted to the extent that it is reasonably required for the purpose of discovering such evidence. Premises in the occupation of a person arrested for burglary may therefore be searched for evidence of that offence, or for evidence of other similar offences (ie the proceeds of other burglaries or large-scale thefts). The arrest of that person would not authorise a search for drugs unless he was also arrested for an arrestable offence of that nature.

The Searching of Premises Code provides that a search under PACE, s 18 may not be made without the written authorisation of an officer of the rank of inspector or above, unless it is carried out before a person is taken to a police station in circumstances where the presence of that person at the place in question is necessary for the effective investigation of the offence. A mere record of an oral authorisation made in an inspector's notebook is normally insufficient to constitute a written authorisation; unless wholly impracticable the authorisation must be given on the Notice of Powers and Rights which should be given or left as explained on p 90. If a search is carried out without prior written authorisation in the situation described above, the constable must inform an officer of the rank of inspector or above that he has made the search as soon as practicable.

An officer who proposes to enter and search premises under a written authorisation under s 18 must explain to the occupier, in so far as it is practicable to do so, the reason why he intends so to act. Failure to do so will render his subsequent conduct unlawful. In one case a divisional court held that simply offering to show the warrant at a window to an occupier who refused to come to the window was insufficient; the reason must be stated.

The effect of PACE, s 18 is that if a man who is a television retailer is arrested in the living quarters above his shop premises on a charge of theft of television sets, the constable would be empowered to search not only his living quarters but also the shop premises after arrest as they are premises 'occupied or controlled' by that person. If the constable searches the shop premises before taking the man to a police station, he must inform an officer of the rank of inspector or above that he has done so as soon as practicable.

PACE, s 18 requires that an officer who authorises a search, or who is informed that a search has been made, must record in writing, in the custody record if there is one, otherwise in his notebook, or in the search record the grounds for the search and the nature of the evidence which was being sought. If the person in occupation or control of the premises is in police custody at the time that the search is carried out, the record must be made in his custody record.

Seizure

A constable may seize and retain anything on the premises for which he may search under the above power. (Although a vehicle, vessel or tent is 'premises' for the purpose of PACE, this does not prevent the seizure of the vehicle, vessel or tent itself.) The additional powers of seizure under CJPA 2001, s 50 (p 75) apply to this power of seizure.

POWERS TO SEARCH UNDER A SEARCH WARRANT

Power to issue warrants

There are many statutes which provide particular powers to enter and search premises under the authority of a warrant and PACE does not affect any of these provisions. However, PACE, s 8 does provide justices with a general power to issue warrants to enter and search premises. 'Premises' includes any place, including any vehicle, vessel, aircraft or hovercraft, any offshore installation, and any tent or movable structure. The Stop and Search Code provides that these powers to search premises also authorise the search of a person, who is not under arrest, who is found on the premises during a search, where the search is under CJA 1988, s 139B under which a constable may enter school premises to search for persons with a bladed or pointed article or other offensive weapon or under a warrant issued under the Misuse of Drugs Act 1971 to search premises for drugs or documents but only if the warrant specifically authorises the search of persons found on the premises. Before the powers under s 139B can be exercised there must be reasonable grounds to believe that an offence under s 139A (having a bladed or pointed article or offensive weapon on school premises) has been or is being committed. There is no requirement in relation to the 1988 or 1971 Act that there are specific grounds to suspect the particular person. A person authorised to accompany police officers or designated persons in the execution of a search warrant and the search and seizure of anything related to the warrant has the same powers as a police officer. (An officer of the rank of inspector or above may direct a designated investigating officer not to wear a uniform for the purpose of a specific operation.)

PACE, s 8(1) provides that if, on an application made by a constable, a justice is satisfied that there are reasonable grounds for believing:

(a) that an indictable offence (or a 'relevant offence' under the Immigration Act 1971) has been committed; and
(b) that there is material on premises mentioned in s 8(1A) (below) which is likely to be of substantial value (whether by itself or with other material) to the investigation of the offence; and
(c) that the material is likely to be relevant (ie admissible) evidence; and
(d) that it does not consist of or include items subject to legal privilege, excluded material or special procedure material (which are described in pp 81–82); and

(e) that *any* of the conditions specified in PACE, s 8(3) applies, in relation to each set of premises specified in the application;

he may issue a warrant authorising a constable to enter and search the premises. An indictable offence is an offence which, if committed by an adult, is triable on indictment, whether it is exclusively so triable (eg murder or robbery) or triable either way (eg unlawful wounding or theft): see p 24.

PACE, s 8(1A), inserted by SOCPA 2005, provides that the 'premises' mentioned in (b) above are:

(a) one or more sets of premises specified in the application (in which case the application is for a 'specific premises warrant'); or

(b) any premises occupied or controlled by a person specified in the application, including such sets of premises as are so specified in the application (in which case the application is for an 'all premises warrant').

PACE, s 8(1B), inserted by SOCPA 2005, provides that if the application is for an all premises warrant, the justice of the peace must also be satisfied:

(a) that because of the particulars of the indictable offence, there are reasonable grounds for believing that it is necessary to search the premises occupied or controlled by the person in question which are not specified in the application in order to find the material referred in (b) at the bottom of the previous page; and

(b) that it is not reasonably practicable to specify in the application all the premises which he occupies or controls and which might need to be searched.

These additional provisions will assist in the investigation of serious organised crime. Crime syndicates may occupy or control many sets of premises and the search of one may lead to the discovery of other premises upon which the material being sought is situated. Provided that the search continues within buildings which are within the syndicate's control, it will be authorised by an 'all premises warrant'.

PACE, s 8(1C), also inserted by SOCPA 2005, provides that a warrant may authorise entry to and search of premises on more than one occasion if, on the application, the justice of the peace is satisfied that it is necessary to authorise multiple entries in order to achieve the purpose for which he issues the warrant. PACE, s 8(ID), inserted by SOCPA 2005, requires that if multiple entries are authorised by a warrant, the number of entries authorised may be unlimited, or limited to a maximum.

PACE, s 8(2) authorises a constable to seize and retain anything for which a search has been authorised.

A constable should never apply for a search warrant under s 8 where the material in question may consist of or include items prima facie subject to legal privilege, excluded material or special procedure material. In such a case application should be made to a judge under the provisions of PACE, Sch 1 described in pp 82–84. However, the High Court has held that the retention of a small amount of legally privileged material inadvertently seized during a search does not render the execution of the search warrant unlawful.

It is vital to remember that the justice must be satisfied that all the points from (a) to (d) above are satisfied. If that is so, then it is necessary for him to be satisfied of the existence of any one of the conditions set out in PACE, s 8(3) referred to in (e) above, namely:

(a) that it is not practicable to communicate with any person entitled to grant entry to the premises;

(b) that it is practicable to communicate with a person entitled to grant entry to the premises but it is not practicable to communicate with any person entitled to grant access to the evidence;
(c) that entry to the premises will not be granted unless a warrant is produced; or
(d) that the purpose of the search may be frustrated or seriously prejudiced unless a constable arriving at the premises can secure immediate entry to them.

These conditions merely follow previously accepted practice, therefore: (a) would apply if there was no one occupying the premises at the time; (b) would apply if, for example, there was a caretaker to a block of flats who had master keys and who could therefore allow access but would have no right to grant access to the material; (c) would apply in the usual circumstances in which a warrant is sought; and (d) in circumstances in which the nature of the evidence is such that it could be easily disposed of if the occupier was aware of police interest. There are various terms included in PACE, s 8(1) which require explanation.

The Terrorism Act 2000, Sch 5 provides that a constable may apply to a justice of the peace for the issue of a warrant for the purposes of a terrorist investigation authorising a constable to: enter specified premises; search those premises and persons found there; and to seize and retain relevant material. The 'premises' may be one or more sets of premises specified in the application (in which case the application is for a specific premises warrant) or any premises occupied or controlled by a person specified in the application, including such sets of premises as are so specified (in which case the application is for an 'all premises' warrant).

Items subject to legal privilege

These are defined as communications between lawyer and client, the broad purpose of which is the giving and receiving of legal advice, and items enclosed with or referred to in such communications. A solicitor's record of appointments and attendances is, therefore, not subject to legal privilege. The exemption relating to items subject to legal privilege only applies if the material is in the possession of a person entitled to possess it. Items held with the intention of furthering a criminal purpose are specifically excluded from being items subject to legal privilege, even though that intention does not exist on the part of the holder (eg a solicitor) but does on the part of another (eg a solicitor's client).

Excluded material

This means:

(a) personal records (ie documents relating to the health of an individual or counselling given to him) acquired or created by a person in the course of a trade, business etc or for the purpose of any paid or unpaid office and held in confidence by him;
(b) human tissue or tissue fluid taken for diagnosis or medical treatment and held in confidence; or
(c) journalistic material (ie material acquired or created for the purpose of journalism and held by the person acquiring or creating it for that purpose) consisting of documents or other records and held in confidence.

Special procedure material

This is journalistic material, other than excluded material, and material, other than items subject to legal privilege and excluded material, held in confidence and acquired or created in the course of any trade, business etc (eg confidential business material, perhaps details of a motor company's intended new model).

Production orders etc

Although a justice may not issue a search warrant in respect of material of any of the three types set out above, PACE, s 9, as amended by SOCPA 2005, recognises that there may be occasions in which it is necessary to enter premises and search for excluded material or special procedure material by providing that a constable may obtain access to such material by making an application under PACE, Sch 1. PACE, s 9 does not provide for access to items subject to legal privilege. At the time of writing the power to make an order or issue a warrant under PACE, Sch 1 is exercisable only by a circuit judge but when amendments made by the Courts Act 2003 and SOCPA 2005 are brought into force the powers will also be exercisable by a judge of the High Court, recorder or a district judge (magistrates' court). For convenience, we shall use 'judge' hereafter to cover the existing and future positions.

Under Sch 1 such a judge may make a 'production order' or, in certain cases, issue a search warrant in respect of excluded material or special procedure material. Similar provision is made by TA 2000, Sch 5 for production orders and search warrants in respect of excluded or special procedure material for the purposes of a terrorist investigation.

These provisions are intended to protect the confidence of the maker or holder of the record etc, and not that of the suspect. Consequently, it is open to the maker or holder voluntarily to disclose the material. It is only where there is no consent on his part to do so that the special provisions of s 9 and Sch 1 come into play.

An application under PACE, Sch 1 must be made by a constable. The person who has custody of the material must be notified of the application for the order (and of the material sought) and allowed to attend the hearing of the application and make representations. Unless he is in custody of the material, there is no need to give notification to a suspected person. In exceptional circumstances, an application may be heard in the absence of notification of the application to the person with custody of the material.

The basic order which a judge may issue under PACE, Sch 1 is a 'production order'. This requires the person apparently in possession of the material in question *either* to produce it to the constable for him to take away *or* to give the constable access to it not later (*in either case*) than the end of a period of seven days from the date of the order or the end of such longer period as the order may specify. The making of such an order depends on one or other of two sets of 'access conditions' being fulfilled.

The first set of access conditions is fulfilled if:

(a) there are reasonable grounds for believing that:
    (i)   an indictable offence has been committed;
    (ii) there is material which consists of special procedure material or includes special procedure material and does not also include excluded material on

premises specified in the application, or on premises occupied or controlled by a person specified in the application (including all such premises on which there are reasonable grounds for believing that there is such material as it is reasonably practicable so to specify);

(iii) the material is likely to be of substantial value (whether by itself or together with other material) to the investigation in connection with which the application is made; and

(iv) the material is likely to be relevant evidence;

(b) other methods of obtaining the material:

(i)   have been tried without success; or

(ii) have not been tried because it appeared that they were bound to fail; and

(c) it is in the public interest having regard:

(i)   to the benefit likely to accrue to the investigation if the material is obtained; and

(ii) to the circumstances under which the person in possession of the material holds it, that the material should be produced or that access to it should be given.

The second set of access conditions is fulfilled if:

(a) there are reasonable grounds for believing that there is material which consists of or includes special procedure material or excluded material on premises specified in the application or on premises occupied or controlled by a person specified in the application (including all such premises on which there are reasonable grounds for believing that there is such material as it is reasonably practicable so to specify);

(b) prior to the enactment of PACE, s 9, a search of such premises for that material could have been authorised by the issue of a warrant to a constable under an enactment other than Sch 1; and

(c) the issue of such a warrant would have been appropriate.

It will be noted that the second set of access conditions is not limited to cases where it is reasonably believed that an indictable offence has been committed. A production order can be made even if it infringes or might infringe the privilege against self-incrimination of the person ordered to make production.

A divisional court has held that, before granting the application, the judge must be satisfied that it is substantially the last resort, ie that other practicable methods of obtaining the material have been exhausted without success.

The requirement of notice, together with the seven (or more) days' grace referred to above, gives a person plenty of time in which to dispose of incriminating material. Because of this, Sch 1 provides that a judge may issue a specific premises or all premises search warrant if satisfied that a set of 'access conditions' is not fulfilled. But he may only do so if he is also satisfied that:

(a) either set of access conditions is fulfilled; and

(b) any of the further conditions is also fulfilled in relation to each set of premises specified in the application:

(i)   that it is not practicable to communicate with any person entitled to grant entry to the premises;

(ii)   that it is practicable to communicate with a person entitled to grant entry to the premises but it is not practicable to communicate with any person entitled to grant access to the material;

(iii) that the material contains information which is subject to a statutory restriction or obligation and is likely to be disclosed in breach of it if a warrant is not issued;

(iv)   that service of notice of an application for a production order may seriously prejudice the investigation.

A judge may also issue a search warrant if satisfied that:

(a) the second set of access conditions is fulfilled; and
(b) a production order relating to the material has not been complied with.

The judge may not issue an all premises warrant unless he is satisfied:

(a) that there are reasonable grounds for believing that it is necessary to search premises occupied or controlled by the person in question which are not specified in the application, as well as those which are, in order to find the material in question; and
(b) that it is not reasonably practicable to specify all of the premises which he occupies or controls which might need to be searched.

A divisional court has emphasised that the issue of a search warrant under the present provisions is a major infringement on individual liberty and that, consequently, it is essential that the reason for authorising this procedure should be made clear.

Code B: the Code of Practice for the Searches of Premises by Police Officers and the Seizure of Property Found by Police Officers on Persons or Premises (hereafter referred to as the Searching of Premises Code) requires that an inspector or above be present and in charge of a search under a warrant issued under PACE, Sch 1 or TA 2000, Sch 5. The Code also contains further provisions concerning such a search.

Procedure before application is made for a search warrant or a production order

The relevant provisions are contained in the Searching of Premises Code. Where information is received which appears to justify an application for a search warrant or a production order, the officer concerned must take reasonable steps to check that the information is accurate, recent and has not been provided maliciously or irresponsibly. An application is not permitted on the basis of information from an anonymous source where corroboration has not been sought. The nature of the articles and their location must be established as specifically as possible.

The officer must also make reasonable inquiries to establish what, if anything, is known about the likely occupier of the premises and the nature of the premises themselves, and whether they have been previously searched (and, if so, how recently); he must also obtain any other information relevant to the application.

An application to a justice of the peace for a search warrant or to a judge for a search warrant or production order may not be made without the signed written authority of an officer of at least the rank of inspector, or, in a case of urgency where no officer of this rank is readily available, the senior officer on duty. Where the application is made to a judge under TA 2000 it must be supported by a signed written authority from a superintendent. In addition the Searching of Premises Code requires that other than in a case of urgency, the community relations officer must be consulted before a search takes place which might have an adverse effect on police/community relations. In urgent cases, the local police community liaison officer should be informed of the search as soon as possible after it has been made.

The making of an application

Between them, PACE, s 15 and the Searching of Premises Code provide the following rules for all search warrants. An application for a search warrant must be supported by information in writing, specifying:

(a) the enactment under which the application is made;
(b) (i) whether the warrant is to authorise entry and search of:
  • one set of premises, or
  • if the application is under PACE, s 8, or Sch 1, more than one set of specified premises or all premises occupied or controlled by a specified person;
  (ii) the premises to be searched;
(c) the object of the search;
(d) the grounds on which the application is made (including, when the purpose of the proposed search is to find evidence of an alleged offence, an indication of how the evidence relates to the investigation);
(e) where the application is under PACE, s 8 or Sch 1, for a single warrant to enter and search:
  (i) more than one set of specified premises, the officer must specify each set of premises which it is desired to enter and search;
  (ii) all premises occupied or controlled by a specified person, the officer must specify;
  • as many sets of premises which it is desired to enter and search as it is reasonably practicable to specify,
  • the person who is in occupation or control of those premises and any others which it is desired to search,
  • why it is necessary to search more premises than those which can be specified,
  • why it is not reasonably practicable to specify all the premises which it is desired to enter and search;
(f) whether an application under PACE, s 8 is for a warrant authorising entry and search on more than one occasion and, if so, the officer must state the grounds for this and whether the desired number of entries authorised is unlimited or a specified maximum;
(g) that there are no reasonable grounds for believing that material to be sought:
  (i) consists of or includes items subject to legal privilege (when applying to a justice of the peace or a judge); or
  (ii) consists of or includes excluded material or special procedure material (when applying to a justice of the peace);
  however, this does not affect the additional powers of seizure in the Criminal Justice and Police Act 2002, Part 2 (material to be sifted and examined elsewhere; see pp 74–76);

(h) if applicable, a request for the warrant to authorise a person or persons to accompany the officer who executes the warrant.

Although the identity of an informant need not be disclosed, the officer must be prepared to deal with questions about the accuracy of previous information provided by that source or other related matters. An application under PACE, Sch 1 must, where appropriate, indicate why it is believed that service of notice of an application for a production order may seriously prejudice the investigation. An application under TA 2000, Sch 5 must indicate why a production order would be inappropriate.

All applications must be supported by an information in writing and the constable must answer on oath any question asked by the justice. If an application is refused, no further application may be made for a warrant to search those premises unless supported by additional grounds.

There must be two copies of a warrant which specifies only one set of premises and does not authorise multiple entries. In the case of any other warrant, as many copies as are reasonably required may be made. Where a warrant authorises multiple entries it must specify whether the number of entries authorised is unlimited, or limited to a specified maximum.

Execution of a search warrant

An entry on or search of premises under a warrant is unlawful unless the provisions of PACE, s 15 just mentioned and those in PACE, s 16 are complied with. PACE, s 16 sets out the following provisions which apply to all search warrants.

A warrant may be executed by any constable. It may authorise other persons to accompany any constable executing it and a person so authorised has the same powers as a constable in relation to the execution of the warrant and the seizure of anything to which the warrant relates. Entry and search must be within three calendar months of issue and must be at a reasonable hour unless the purpose of the search may be frustrated by entry at such time. However, this does not apply to warrants issued under TA 2000, Sch 5 which are exercisable only within twenty-four hours of issue. PACE, s 16(3A), added by SOCPA 2005, covers the execution of all premises warrants. It provides that in the case of an all premises warrant, no premises which are not specified in the warrant may be entered or searched unless a police officer of at least the rank of inspector not involved in the investigation has in writing authorised them to be entered. Section 16(3B), also added by SOCPA 2005, together with the Searching of Premises Code, provides that no premises may be entered or searched for the second or any subsequent time under a warrant which authorises multiple entries unless a police officer of at least the rank of inspector not involved in the investigation has authorised that entry in writing.

Where the occupier of the premises is present, the constable must, before the search begins:

(a) identify himself (by warrant or other identification number in the case of terrorism inquiries) and, if not in uniform, show his warrant card (but in so doing in the case of terrorism inquiries, he need not reveal his name);
(b) produce the warrant to him; and
(c) supply him with a copy of it.

The constable must act likewise in relation to a person in charge of the premises in the absence of the owner.

A search under a warrant may only be a search to the extent required for the purpose for which the warrant was issued; the same applies where articles are seized for which the warrant has provided no authority.

Save in exceptional circumstances the media should not be invited to be present when a search warrant (or any other investigative procedure) is being executed, nor should they be invited to police briefings prior to the execution of a search warrant, because reports emanating from such involvement are liable to prejudice a fair trial.

GENERAL PROVISIONS ON ENTRY, SEARCH, SEIZURE, ACCESS AND RETENTION

In exercising the powers set out below, it must be remembered that the ECHR provides for the right to respect for family life (art 8). Any exercise of these powers which is not in accordance with the law will be in breach of art 8.

We have already described a number of specific rules in relation to this. In addition, the Searching of Premises Code lays down a number of rules which apply to searches of premises (whether those of the suspect or anyone else including the victim):

(a) undertaken for the purposes of an investigation into an alleged offence, with the occupier's consent, other than searches made in the following circumstances:
   (i) routine scenes of crime searches;
   (ii) calls to a fire or burglary made by or on behalf of an occupier or searches following the activation of fire or burglar alarms;
   (iii) searches where it is unnecessary to seek consent because in the circumstances this would cause disproportionate inconvenience to the person concerned;
   (iv) bomb threat calls;
(b) under powers conferred by PACE, ss 17 (entry to arrest/search), 18 (entry and search after arrest) and 32 (search on arrest); or
(c) undertaken in pursuance of a search warrant issued in accordance with PACE, s 15 (see p 85) or under PACE, Sch 1 (special procedure material and excluded material, see pp 81–82) or under TA 2000.

The exception for routine scenes of crime searches ceases to apply if the search develops into more than just a routine scenes of crime search. At that point, at the latest, the Searching of Premises Code applies.

On the other hand, the Searching of Premises Code does not apply to the exercise of a statutory power to enter premises or to inspect goods, equipment or procedures if the exercise of that power is not dependent on the existence of grounds for suspecting that an offence may have been committed and the person exercising the power has no reasonable grounds for such suspicion. This exception will exclude from the Code application inspections etc by local authority inspectors under health and safety provisions.

In what follows it must be borne in mind that 'premises' includes any vehicle, vessel or aircraft, and any tent or movable structure.

Entry other than with consent

The officer in charge must first attempt to communicate with the occupier or any other person entitled to grant access to the premises by explaining the authority under which he seeks entry to the premises and ask the occupier to allow him to do so, unless:

(a) the premises to be searched are unoccupied;
(b) the occupier and any other person entitled to grant access are absent; or
(c) there are reasonable grounds to believe that to alert the occupier or any other person entitled to grant access by attempting to communicate with him would frustrate the object of the search or endanger the officers concerned or other persons.

The circumstances at (c) might exist where there are known to be a number of persons on the premises all of whom are suspected of being involved in the offence, any of whom could dispose of the evidence whilst these procedures are being followed; or, in the case of entry to search for an armed criminal, where danger might arise if he was warned of imminent arrest. Although in the circumstances set out in (c), an officer need not comply with the requirements as to identification, production of his warrant card (if not in uniform) and search warrant (if any) before effecting entry, he must do so before conducting the search (except that it is enough if he gives a copy of the search warrant at the first reasonable opportunity if the search is under a search warrant).

Unless (c) above applies, where the premises are occupied, the officer in charge of the search must before the search begins:

(a) identify himself (by warrant or other identification number in a terrorist investigation) and, if not in uniform, show his warrant card (although he may do so without revealing his name in a terrorist investigation);
(b) state the purpose of the search and the grounds for undertaking it;
(c) identify and introduce any person accompanying the officer on the search (such persons should carry identification for production on request) and briefly describe that person's role in the process.

If a search warrant includes a schedule of documents to be searched for and the schedule has been detached when a copy of the warrant is given to the occupier of the premises, the search is unlawful and there is no right to retain anything seized. This is so even if an uncertified photocopy of the schedule is attached to the rest of the warrant.

Searches with consent

The Searching of Premises Code provides that, if it is proposed to search premises with the consent of a person entitled to grant entry, the consent must, if practicable, be in writing. Before seeking such consent the officer in charge must state the purpose of the proposed search and its extent. This information must be as specific as possible, particularly regarding the articles or persons being sought and the parts of the premises to be searched. The person concerned must be clearly informed that he is not obliged to consent and that anything seized may be produced in evidence. If, at the time, the person is not suspected of an offence the officer must tell him so when stating the purpose of the search. An officer cannot enter and search premises or continue to search premises if consent has been given under duress or is withdrawn before the search is completed.

In the case of a lodging house or other similar accommodation, a search should not be made on the basis solely of the landlord's consent unless the tenant is unavailable and the matter is urgent.

It is unnecessary to seek consent where in the circumstances this would cause disproportionate inconvenience to the person concerned; for example, where it is reasonable to assume that innocent occupiers would agree to, and expect that, police would take the proposed action. Examples are where a suspect has fled from the scene of the crime to evade arrest and it is necessary quickly to check surrounding gardens and readily accessible places to see whether he is hiding; or where police have arrested someone in the night after a pursuit and it is necessary to make a brief check of gardens along the route of the pursuit to see whether stolen or incriminating articles have been found.

Use of force

Where the police are acting under a warrant or under one of the above statutory powers, reasonable and proportionate force may be used if necessary in the following cases if the officer in charge is satisfied that the premises are those specified in the warrant:

(a) where the occupier or another person entitled to grant access has refused to allow entry;
(b) where it is impossible to communicate with such a person;
(c) where the premises are known to be unoccupied or the occupier etc is known to be absent; or
(d) where there are reasonable grounds to believe that to do so would frustrate the object of the search or endanger someone.

It is permissible to restrict the movement of occupants to one room while another room is being searched.

Designated officers

If a power conferred on a designated person (ie a person other than a police officer, designated under the Police Reform Act 2002, Part 4 who has specified powers and duties of police officers conferred or imposed on him):

(a) allows reasonable force to be used when exercised by a police officer, a designated person exercising that power has the same entitlement to use force;
(b) includes power to use force to enter any premises, that power is not exercisable by that designated person except:
    (i) in the company and under the supervision of a police officer; or
    (ii) for the purpose of:
        • saving life or limb; or
        • preventing serious damage to property.

Notice of powers and rights

An officer who conducts a search of premises under a search warrant issued under PACE or TA 2000 or under a power given by PACE (see below), or with the occupier's consent, must, unless it is impracticable to do so, provide the occupier with a copy of a notice in a standard format:

(a) specifying whether the search is made under warrant, or with consent, or in the exercise of powers under PACE, ss 17, 18 and 32;
(b) summarising the extent of the powers of search and seizure conferred in the Act;
(c) explaining the rights of the occupier and of the owner of property seized;
(d) explaining that compensation may be payable in appropriate cases for damage caused in entering and searching premises, and giving the address to which an application for compensation should be directed; and
(e) stating that a copy of the Searching of Premises Code is available to be consulted at any police station.

If the occupier is present, copies of the notice, and of the warrant (if the search is made under warrant), should if practicable be given to the occupier before the search begins, unless the officer in charge of the search reasonably believes that to do so would frustrate the object of the search or endanger the officers concerned or other persons. If the occupier is not present, copies of the notice, and of the warrant where appropriate, should be left in a prominent place on the premises or appropriate part of the premises and should be endorsed with the name of the officer in charge of the search, the name of the police station to which he is attached and the date and time of the search. The officer's warrant number, not his name, should be given in the case of a terrorism investigation. The warrant itself should be endorsed to show that this has been done.

Conduct of searches

Premises may be searched only to the extent required for the purposes for which the warrant was issued. This means that a search cannot be made in places where the articles specified in the warrant could not possibly be found or for longer than necessary to find those articles. This is emphasised by the Searching Code which states that premises may be searched only to the extent necessary to achieve the object of the search, having regard to the size and nature of what is sought. (A warrant to search for television sets would not authorise the examination of the contents of small drawers.) The constable executing the warrant must endorse it, stating:

(a) whether the articles or persons sought were found, and
(b) whether any articles were seized, other than articles which were sought,

and, unless the warrant is a warrant specifying one set of premises only, he must do so separately in respect of each set of premises entered and searched, which he must in each case state in the endorsement. Executed warrants and those not executed within the permitted time must be returned to the justices' clerk (or to the appropriate officer of the court if issued by a judge). A warrant which is so returned must be retained for a period of twelve months during which time it may be inspected by the occupier of the premises to which it relates.

A search under warrant may not continue under the authority of the warrant once all of the things specified in it have been found, or the officer in charge is satisfied that they are not on the premises.

The search itself must be conducted with due consideration for the property and privacy of the occupier of the premises searched, and with no more disturbance than necessary. Reasonable force may only be used to conduct the search where it is necessary because the co-operation of the occupier cannot be obtained or is insufficient for the purpose. An occupier must not be discouraged or prevented from securing the services of a friend, neighbour or other person to witness the search, unless the officer in charge has reasonable grounds to believe that this would seriously hinder the investigation or endanger the officers concerned or other people. A search need not be unreasonably delayed for this purpose. If the premises have been entered by force the officer in charge must satisfy himself, before leaving, that they are secured either by arranging for the occupier or his agent to be present or by any other appropriate means.

A person need not be cautioned before being asked questions which are solely concerned with the proper and effective conduct of a search; for example, to locate the key to a locked drawer or to otherwise seek co-operation during the search. If questioning goes beyond this point it may amount to an interview and would require the associated safeguards. No search may continue once the officer in charge is satisfied that what is being sought is not on the premises.

In determining when to make a search, the officer in charge must always give regard to the time of day at which the occupier is likely to be present, and should not search at a time when the occupier or any other person on the premises is likely to be asleep unless this is unavoidable. If the wrong premises are searched by mistake, everything possible should be done to allay any sense of grievance. In appropriate cases assistance should be given to obtain compensation.

The local police/community consultative group or its equivalent should be informed as soon as practicable after a search where there is reason to believe that it might have had an adverse effect on relations between the police and the community.

Records of searches

The Searching of Premises Code requires that, if premises have been searched, a record of the search must be made.

The record which is made of such a search must be made by or on behalf of the officer in charge of the search, and it must be made on his return to the police station. The record must include:

(a) the address of the premises;
(b) the date, time and duration of the search;
(c) the authority for the search (including a copy of the warrant and the written authority to apply for it, or the written consent where the search was made thereunder);
(d) the names of officer(s) in charge of and of the other officers conducting the search (except in the case of inquiries linked to the investigation of terrorism (or where it is reasonably believed that disclosing their names might endanger the officers), where the record must state the warrant or other identification number and duty station of each officer);

(e) the names of any persons on the premises (if known);
(f) any grounds for refusing the occupier's request to have someone present during the search;
(g) a list of articles seized (or a note of its location) and, if not covered by a warrant, the reason for seizure;
(h) whether force was used and, if so, the reason;
(i) a list of any damage caused, and the circumstances in which it was caused;
(j) if applicable, the reason it was not practicable to give the occupier a copy of the 'Notice of Powers and Rights'; and
(k) when the occupier was not present, the place where copies of the Notice of Powers and Rights and search warrant were left on the premises.

Search registers must be maintained at each sub-divisional or equivalent police station and the above record must be made, copied or referred to in the register.

On each occasion when premises are searched under a warrant, the warrant must be endorsed to show:

(a) whether any articles specified in the warrant were found and the address where found;
(b) whether any other articles were seized;
(c) the date and time at which it was executed and, if present, the name and address of the occupier, or if the occupier was not present, the name of the person in charge of the premises;
(d) the names of the officers who executed it and any authorised persons who accompanied them (except in the case of inquiries linked to the investigation of terrorism, in which case the warrant or other identification number and duty station of each officer concerned, and any identification number of police staff, should be given); and
(e) whether a copy, together with a copy of the Notice of Powers and Rights, was handed to the occupier; or whether it was endorsed with the name (warrant number in the case of a terrorism investigation) of the officer in charge, the name of his police station and the date and time of the search and left on the premises (and, if so, where).

A warrant must be returned to the appropriate person when it has been executed, or, in the case of a specific premises warrant which has not been executed, or an all premises warrant, or any warrant authorising multiple entries, on the expiry of three months from issue or sooner. The appropriate person is:

(a) if the warrant was issued by a justice of the peace, the designated officer for the local justice area in which the justice was acting when he issued the warrant;
(b) if it was issued by a judge, the appropriate officer of the court from which he issued it.

General powers of seizure

PACE, s 19 gives the police wide powers of seizure in addition to those otherwise provided by the Act or elsewhere. It provides that a constable lawfully on any premises (eg with the occupier's consent) may seize anything on the premises if he has reasonable grounds for believing that:

(a) it has been obtained in consequence of the commission of an offence; or

(b) it is evidence in relation to an offence which he is investigating or any other offence; *and* (in the case of (a) or (b))

(c) it is necessary to seize it in order to prevent it from being concealed, lost, altered or destroyed.

Although a 'vehicle', 'vessel' or 'tent' is premises for the purpose of PACE, the reference to anything 'on the premises' does not prevent the seizure of a vehicle, vessel or tent as a whole.

In the same circumstances (ie (a) to (c)), a constable may require any information stored in any electronic form contained in a computer and accessible from the premises to be produced in a legible form in which it can be taken away.

PACE, s 19 also provides that no relevant statutory power of seizure authorises the seizure of an item which the constable has reasonable grounds for believing to be subject to legal privilege as defined on p 81. Generally, a constable will have to examine an item to test a claim to legal privilege and, if no claim is made, the constable will not have reasonable grounds for believing it to be privileged until he has examined it. If the constable later obtains reasonable grounds, the item must be returned forthwith, but the seizure does not become unlawful.

Additional powers of seizure

The additional powers of seizure under CJPA 2001, s 50 and related provisions (pp 74–76) apply where there is a right of seizure under a search warrant or under PACE, s 19.

Record of seizure and access

PACE, s 21 provides that a constable who seizes anything *under any statutory power* must, on request, provide the occupier of premises or a person who had custody or control of the thing immediately before seizure with a record of what he seized. In such a case, the record must be provided within a reasonable time of the request.

The section also provides for access to a thing which has been seized, and for the photographing or copying of it, by a person who had custody or control of it immediately before seizure.

Retention

PACE, s 22 provides that anything seized or taken away under s 19 may be retained so long as is necessary in all the circumstances. In particular, anything seized under s 19 for the purposes of a criminal investigation may be retained (unless a photograph or copy would suffice) for use as evidence at a trial for an offence, or for forensic examination or investigation in connection with an offence. Moreover, anything may be retained to establish its owner, where there are reasonable grounds for believing that it has been obtained in consequence of the commission of an offence.

Nothing seized on the grounds that it may be used:

(a) to cause physical injury;

(b) to damage property;

(c) to interfere with evidence; or
(d) to assist in escape from police detention or lawful custody,

may be retained after the person from whom it was seized has been freed from detention or custody or has been bailed.

Any person who had custody or control of property prior to its seizure must, if it is retained, be provided within a reasonable time with a list or description of the property, if he asks for one. A person claiming property seized by the police may apply for its possession to a magistrates' court under the Police (Property) Act 1897 and should, where appropriate, be advised of this procedure.

REGULATION OF INVESTIGATORY POWERS

Telecommunications and public postal services

Part I of the Regulation of Investigatory Powers Act 2000 (RIPA 2000) deals with the interception of telecommunications and public postal services. Its provisions recognise the requirements of the ECHR. Article 8 of the Convention deals with the right to respect for private and family life and requires that:

1. Everyone has the right to respect for his private and family life, his home and his correspondence.
2. There shall be no interference by a public authority with the exercise of this right except such as in accordance with the law and is necessary in a democratic society in the interests of national security, public safety or the economic well-being of the country, for the prevention of disorder or crime, for the protection of health and morals, or for the protection of the rights and freedoms of others.

The provisions of RIPA 2000 also recognise art 5 of Council Directive 97/66/EC, the Telecommunications Data Protection Directive, which requires that the confidentiality of communications is safeguarded.

Most of the provisions of RIPA 2000 are aimed at protecting the confidentiality of public postal services and public telecommunications systems and some private systems which are attached to a public system. It is an offence intentionally and without lawful authority to intercept a communication in the course of its transmission by one of these means. The inclusion of some private systems means that someone who unlawfully intercepts a telephone conversation between a fellow employee and some other person, may incur a liability under RIPA 2000. However, in the case of a private system, an interceptor does not commit an offence if he has a right to control the operation or use of the system, which means the right to authorise or forbid the operation or use of the system, *or* if he has the express or implied consent of such a person to make the interception.

The recording by a covert listening device in a motor car of one person's voice speaking on a telephone is not an interception. Nor is the audio recording by an undercover police officer of a telephone conversation with a suspect, although it does amount to surveillance (dealt with below).

RIPA 2000 makes special provisions for the issue of *interception warrants* and provides for the lawful interception without an interception warrant where one or more of the parties has consented (for example, calls received from kidnappers). Such an interception will be authorised as surveillance, rather than by means of an interception warrant.

The Regulation of Investigatory Powers (Maintenance of Interception Capability) Order 2002 sets out the obligations which the Secretary of State considers to be reasonable to impose on the providers of public postal services or a public telecommunications service, for the purpose of securing that it is practicable for requirements to provide assistance in relation to interception warrants to be imposed and complied with. The Order enables the Secretary of State to ensure compliance with the obligations by providing that he may give a service provider a notice requiring it to take the steps described in the notice which specifies the period within which a person served with a notice may refer it to the Technical Advisory Board.

The Regulation of Investigatory Powers (Interception of Communications: Code of Practice) Order 2002 implemented a Code of Practice relating to the interception of communications, to which anyone exercising or performing a power or duty to which the Code applies must have regard.

Surveillance and the conduct and use of 'covert human intelligence sources'

Part II of the Regulation of Investigatory Powers Act 2000 also deals with these matters. It is these things which are of most direct concern to the police.

Surveillance

The forms of surveillance covered by the Act are:

(1) *Directed surveillance* which is covert, but not intrusive, surveillance and is undertaken for the purpose of a specific investigation or a specific operation in such a manner as is likely to result in the obtaining of *private information* about a person (whether or not one specifically identified for the purposes of the investigation or operation), and is otherwise than by way of an immediate response to events or circumstances the nature of which is such that it would not be reasonably practicable for an authorisation under this part to be sought for the carrying out of the surveillance. 'Private information' includes any information relating to a person's private or family life.

(2) *Intrusive surveillance* which is covert surveillance that is carried out in relation to anything taking place on any residential premises or in any private vehicle and involves the presence of an individual on the premises or in the vehicle or is carried out by means of a surveillance device.

These terms are defined by the Regulation of Investigatory Powers Act 2000, s 26. However, the Act provides that surveillance will not be intrusive if it involves no more than the placing of a vehicle location device, or it is surveillance involving the interception of a communication which is one sent by, or intended for, a person who has consented to the interception. In addition, it will not be intrusive if it is carried out by a device which is not present upon the premises or vehicle concerned. However, this does not apply if the device is such that it consistently provides information of the same quality and detail as might be expected to be obtained from a device which was actually present on the premises or in the vehicle. The Act also, of course, exempts devices designed to catch TV licence dodgers!

Surveillance is covert if it is carried out in a manner that is calculated to ensure that the persons who are subject to the surveillance are unaware that it is or may be taking place.

The conduct and use of a covert human intelligence source

The 'conduct of a covert human intelligence source' refers to any conduct of a person who:

(a) if he establishes or maintains a personal or other relationship with a person, for the covert purpose of facilitating the obtaining of information or the provision of access to information to another person;

(b) covertly uses such a relationship to obtain information or to provide such access; or

(c) covertly discloses information obtained by the use of such a relationship, or as a consequence of the existence of such a relationship.

The 'use of a covert human intelligence source' refers to inducing, asking or assisting a person to engage in the conduct of such a source, or to obtain information by means of such a source.

A purpose is covert in relation to the establishment or maintenance of a personal or other relationship only if the relationship is conducted in a manner that is calculated to ensure that one of the parties to the relationship is unaware of the purpose. A relationship is used covertly, and information obtained is disclosed covertly, only if it is used or disclosed in a manner that is calculated to ensure that one of the parties to the relationship is unaware of the use or disclosure in question.

The Regulation of Investigatory Powers (Covert Human Intelligence Sources: Codes of Practice) Order 2002 introduced a Code of Practice which must be observed by a person exercising or performing a power or duty to which that Code applies.

Lawful surveillance etc

RIPA 2000, s 27 provides that such conduct will be lawful if it is authorised and carried out in accordance with the authorisation. No civil liability will be incurred in respect of conduct 'incidental' to such lawful conduct and which is not in itself conduct in respect of which an authorisation or warrant is capable of being granted under a relevant enactment and might reasonably have been expected to be sought. A 'relevant enactment' means the RIPA 2000; the Intelligence Services Act 1994, s 5 (warrants for the intelligence services); or an enactment contained in Part III of the Police Act 1997 (powers of covert entry and interference with property by the police and customs officers).

Authorisation of directed surveillance and covert human intelligence sources

These matters are controlled by RIPA 2000, ss 28 and 29.

A 'designated person' may grant authorisations for the carrying out of directed surveillance. A designated person must believe that the authorisation is necessary:

(a) in the interests of national security;
(b) for the purpose of preventing or detecting crime or of preventing disorder;
(c) in the interests of the economic well-being of the United Kingdom;
(d) in the interests of public safety;
(e) for the purpose of protecting public health;
(f) for the purpose of assessing or collecting any tax, duty, levy or other imposition, contribution or charge payable to a government department; or
(g) for any other purpose which is specified for the purpose by order made by the Secretary of State,

and that the authorised surveillance is proportionate to what is sought to be achieved by carrying it out.

In the case of an authorisation of a covert human intelligence source, a designated officer must not only have the belief just referred to but must also believe that there are arrangements for the source's case that satisfy the following requirements:

(a) that there will be at all times a person holding an office, rank or position with the relevant investigating authority who will have day-to-day responsibility for dealing with the source on behalf of that authority, and for the source's security or welfare;
(b) that there will be at all times another person holding an office, rank or position with the relevant investigating authority who will have general oversight of the use made of the source;
(c) that there will be at all times a person holding an office, rank or position with the relevant investigating authority who will have responsibility for maintaining a record made of the use of the source;
(d) that the records relating to the source that are maintained by the relevant investigating authority will always contain particulars of all such matters (if any) as may be specified for the purposes of this paragraph in regulations; and
(e) that records maintained by the relevant investigating authority that disclose the identity of the source will not be available to persons except to the extent that there is a need for access to them to be made available to those persons; and
(f) that any other requirement imposed by order by the Secretary of State is satisfied.

The 'relevant investigating authority' in relation to the use of an informant is the public authority who handles him. If the informant's activities are to be for the benefit of more than one public authority, one of them must assume these duties.

An authorisation will specify the conduct which is authorised and require that it is carried out in accordance with the authorisation. In the case of informants the authorisation will be specific to the individual and the particular investigation.

Persons entitled to grant authorisations for directed surveillance and covert human intelligence sources

By RIPA 2000, s 30, the particular persons designated for the purposes of ss 28 and 29 are the individuals holding such offices, ranks and positions with the relevant public authorities as are prescribed by order. The Regulation of Investigatory Powers (Prescription of Offices, Ranks and Positions) Order 2000, as amended, specifies who is designated. So far as police forces are concerned, it specifies the rank of superintendent (inspector in urgent cases as provided by s 30). In the cases of an authorisation combining an authorisation under ss 28 or 29 and of an authorisation by the Secretary of State for carrying out intrusive surveillance (see below), the Secretary of State is the person designated for the purpose.

For the purposes of authorisations for directed surveillance, an authorisation may be granted by any public authority included in RIPA 2000, Sch 1, Part I or Part II. The Schedule, in addition to including any police force, the Serious Organised Crime Agency and the Serious Fraud Office, lists all government departments, local authorities, Customs and Excise, Ministry of Defence, post office and financial services and personal investment authorities as well as the Health and Safety Executive, NHS bodies in England and Wales, and the Royal Pharmaceutical Society for Great Britain. Orders of 2003 and 2006 extended the number of organisations quite extensively to embrace organisations other than government organisations, such as fire and rescue authorities, the Charity Commission, the Gaming Board and Postal Services Commission.

Authorisations of covert human intelligence sources may be granted by any public authority included in RIPA 2000, Sch 1, Part I (which includes all of the bodies listed in the paragraph above, except the Health and Safety Executive, NHS bodies in England and Wales, and the Royal Pharmaceutical Society for Great Britain).

Special provisions in relation to intrusive surveillance

In relation to *intrusive surveillance* authorisations, RIPA 2000, s 32 requires that authorisations may only be granted by the Secretary of State and senior authorising officers (chief constables and equivalents, plus assistant commissioners of the Metropolitan Police). Such authorisations will only be granted where it is believed that it is necessary:

(a) in the interests of national security;
(b) for the purpose of preventing or detecting serious crime; or
(c) in the interests of the economic well-being of the United Kingdom;

and that the authorised surveillance is proportionate to that which is sought to be achieved. In considering whether these requirements are satisfied, account must be taken of whether the information to be obtained could reasonably be obtained by other means. Any such authorisation must specify the conduct which is authorised.

Authorisations for intrusive surveillance may be granted under RIPA, s 34, by assistant chief constables or their equivalents (specified as a commander in the Metropolitan Police Force) in urgent cases where it is not reasonably practicable, in view of the urgency, for the senior authorising officer or his designated deputy to do so.

When an authorisation for intrusive surveillance is granted or cancelled, notice must be given to an ordinary Surveillance Commissioner. The Regulation of

Investigatory Powers (Notification of Authorisations etc) Order 2000 provides details of those matters which must be notified to an ordinary Surveillance Commissioner when such events occur.

RIPA 2000, ss 36 to 40 deal with the need for the approval of an ordinary Surveillance Commissioner before an authorisation for intrusive surveillance, other than one made by the Secretary of State, may take effect; the quashing of such an authorisation; appeals against a decision of an ordinary Surveillance Commissioner to the Chief Surveillance Commissioner (appointed under the Police Act 1997); and the information which is to be provided to Surveillance Commissioners.

The Regulation of Investigatory Powers (Covert Surveillance: Code of Practice) Order 2002 brought into force a Code of Practice relating to covert surveillance.

Retention of communications data held by communications providers

The Anti terrorism, Crime and Security Act 2001 (ACSA 2001), Part 11 empowers the Secretary of State to issue a code of practice relating to the retention by communications providers of communications data obtained by or held by them. The code, which was issued in 2003 is admissible in evidence in any legal proceedings in which the question arises whether or not the retention of any communication data is justified on the grounds that a failure to retain the data would be likely to prejudice national security, the prevention or detection of crime or the prosecution of offenders. A 'communications provider' is a person who provides a postal service or a telecommunications service. The code may contain such provisions as appear to the Secretary of State to be necessary for the purpose of safeguarding national security, or for the purpose of prevention or detection of crime, or the prosecution of offenders which may relate directly or indirectly to national security. A failure to comply with a provision of the code does not, by itself, render a provider liable to criminal or civil proceedings. However, the contents of the code will be admissible in evidence in any related legal proceedings.

ACSA 2001 provides that if, after reviewing the operation of the requirements included in the code, the Secretary of State considers it to be necessary, he may by order authorise the giving of directions concerning the retention of communications data to communications providers generally; to providers of a specified description; or to particular providers or a provider. The power to make such an order will lapse after the 'initial period' (which now extends until 14 December 2007) unless an order authorising the giving of such directions is made before the end of that time. In addition, the 'initial period' may be extended by statutory instrument.

The Independent Police Complaints Commission (Investigatory Powers) Order 2004 gives the Commission, its officers and employees powers equivalent to those exercised by the police. The Chairman of the Commission (or deputy or member of the Commission) may authorise interference and action in respect of wireless telegraphy on the application of a member of his investigative staff. The Deputy Chairman may appeal against a decision of the Chief Surveillance Commissioner to refuse or quash an authorisation.

The chairman is a senior authorising officer who may grant an authorisation for carrying out intrusive surveillance. Where, in an urgent case, it is not practicable for the chairman or deputy chairman to consider such an application, any other member of the Commission may do so. Grants or cancellations of authorities must be notified to an ordinary Surveillance Commissioner, whose approval is required to give effect to a grant of an authorisation by a member of the Commission. In addition, the chairman and deputy chairman of the Commission may cancel each other's authorisations and the chairman may cancel authorisations granted by any other member of the Commission.

The Independent Police Complaints Commissioners, its Regional Directors, its Director of Investigations and Deputy Director of Investigations are persons entitled to grant authorisations of directed surveillance and covert human intelligence sources. They may be granted only where it is believed that it is necessary for the purpose of preventing or detecting crime or preventing disorder. In urgent cases where none of these persons is available to authorise such activities, any senior investigating officer of the Commission may do so.

AUTHORISATION OF ACTION IN RESPECT OF PROPERTY

The Police Act 1997 (PA 1997), Part III introduced a system whereby authorisations may be given in respect of entry on or interference with property or with wireless telegraphy. No act carried out in accordance with an authorisation will be unlawful. Although authorisations may be given by 'authorising officers' (a chief constable, Commissioner or Assistant Commissioner of Police of the Metropolis, the Director General of the Serious Organised Crime Agency, or the officer of Revenue and Customs designated by the Commissioners of Revenue and Customs for the purpose) they are subject in some cases to approval by the Chief Commissioner or a Commissioner appointed by the Prime Minister for that purpose.

Authorisations by 'authorising officers'

Where an authorising officer believes:

(a) that it is necessary for the action specified to be taken on the ground that it is likely to be of substantial value in the prevention or detection of serious crime; and
(b) that what the action seeks to achieve cannot reasonably be achieved by other means,

he may authorise:

(a) the taking of such action, in respect of such property in the relevant area, as he may specify; or
(b) the taking of such action in the relevant area as he may specify, in respect of wireless telegraphy.

Conduct which constitutes one or more offences is regarded as serious crime if, and only if:

(a) it involves the use of violence, results in substantial financial gain or is conducted by a large number of persons in pursuit of a common purpose; or
(b) the offence or one of the offences is an offence for which a person who has attained the age of twenty-one and has no previous convictions could reasonably be expected to be sentenced to imprisonment for a term of three years or more;

and where the authorising officer is an officer of Revenue and Customs, it relates to an assigned matter within the meaning of the Customs and Excise Management Act 1979, s 1(1).

Provision is made for authorisations to be given by specified senior officers where it is not reasonably practicable for an authorising officer or his designated deputy to consider an application for an authorisation.

Authorisations must be in writing, although in urgent cases they may be given orally. Unless renewed, they will cease to have effect after seventy-two hours if given orally, or by a person other than the actual authorising officer or his designated deputy. In any other case an authorisation may last for three months. However, at any time before an authorisation would cease to have effect, it may be continued in effect for a further three months by the authorising officer. An authorisation may be cancelled at any time if such action is no longer required.

Notice of authorisations to be given to a Commissioner

The giving, renewal or cancellation of an authorisation must, as soon as is reasonably practicable, be notified to a Commissioner.

Authorisations requiring approval

Where an authorisation is given and, at the time at which it is given, the person who gives it believes that any of the property specified in the authorisation is used wholly or mainly as a dwelling or as a bedroom in a hotel, or constitutes office premises, or that the action authorised by it is likely to result in any person acquiring knowledge of matters subject to legal privilege, confidential personal information, or confidential journalistic material, the authorisation will not take effect until approved by a Commissioner and the person who gave the authorisation has been notified of the Commissioner's decision. However, this will not apply in a case of urgency.

Matters subject to legal privilege

The term covers communications between a professional legal adviser and his client, or any persons representing his client, which are made in connection with the giving of legal advice to the client. It also embraces communications made with or in contemplation of legal proceedings and for the purposes of such proceedings. Items enclosed with or referred to in communications of this kind are also included.

However, communications and items are not matters subject to legal privilege when in the possession of a person who is not entitled to possess them nor are communications and items held, or oral communications made, with the intention of furthering a criminal purpose.

Confidential personal information

This is (a) personal information which a person has acquired or created in the course of any trade, business, profession or other occupation, or for the purpose of any paid or unpaid office, and which he holds in confidence, and (b) communications as a result of which personal information is so acquired or created and is held in confidence. 'Personal information' is that concerning an individual (whether living or dead) who can be identified from it and relating to his physical or mental health, or to spiritual counselling or assistance given or to be given to him.

Information is held in confidence if it is held subject to an express or implied undertaking to hold it in confidence, or to a restriction on disclosure or an obligation of secrecy contained in any enactment.

Confidential journalistic material

This is (a) material acquired or created for the purpose of journalism which is in the possession of persons who acquired or created it for those purposes; is held subject to an undertaking, restriction or obligation (as above) and has been continuously held (by one or more persons) subject to such an undertaking, restriction or obligation since it was first acquired or created for the purposes of journalism; and (b) communications as a result of which information is acquired for the purposes of journalism and so held.

IDENTITY CARDS

The Identity Cards Act 2006 (ICA 2006) provides a framework for a National Identity Register and the issue of identity cards (ID cards) to those persons who are on the register. Existing documents may be designated as documents together with which an identity card may be issued (eg a passport) or documents which may themselves be classed as identity cards. Checks may be made against other databases to confirm the identity of persons,

Provisions are made which will allow public and private organisations to verify a person's identity, with the person's consent, before providing services; to define circumstances in which the police or other organisations prescribed within regulations could be provided, without consent, with information held in the Register.

ICA 2006, ss 25 to 29 create a number of offences relevant to the scheme of registration and the issue of ID cards, that is, various offences relating to false identity documents etc, an offence of unauthorised disclosure, an offence of providing false information, an offence of tampering with the National Identity Register, and new criminal offences relating to the misuse of identity cards and other identity issues in which fraud is involved.

Powers are provided to permit a future linking of access to specified public services to the production of an identity card or to an inspection of the Register.

The only substantive provisions of the ICA 2006 which are in force at the time of writing are those relating to false identity documents etc under ICA 2006, s 25.

Making or possession of false identity documents etc

It is an offence against ICA 2006, s 25(1) for a person with the requisite intention to have in his possession or under his control:

(a) an identity document which is false and that he knows or believes to be false;
(b) an identity document that was improperly obtained and that he knows or believes to have been unlawfully obtained; or
(c) an identity document that relates to someone else.

The requisite intention for the purposes of s 25(1) is:

(a) the intention of using the document for establishing registrable facts about himself; or
(b) the intention of allowing or inducing another to use it for establishing, ascertaining or verifying registrable acts about himself or about any other person (with the exception, in the case of an identity document that relates to someone else, of the individual to whom it relates).

ICA 2006, s 25(3) makes it an offence for a person to make or to have in his possession or under his control:

(a) any apparatus which, to his knowledge, is or has been specially designed or adapted to be used in the making of false identity documents; or
(b) any article or material which, to his knowledge, is or has been specially designed or adapted to be used in the making of false identity documents.

The requisite intention for the purposes of s 25(3) is the intention:

(a) that he or another will make a false identity document; and
(b) that the document will be used by somebody for establishing, ascertaining or verifying registrable facts about a person.

It is also an offence against s 25(5) for a person to have in his possession or under his control, without reasonable excuse:

(a) an identity document that is false;
(b) an identity document that was improperly obtained;
(c) an identity document that relates to someone else; or
(d) any apparatus, article or material which, to his knowledge, is or has been specially designed or adapted for the making of false identity documents or to be used in the making of such documents.

Meaning of terms

Identity document for the purpose of s 25

ICA 2006, s 26 provides that 'identity document' means any document that is, or purports to be:

(a) an ID card;
(b) a designated document;
(c) an immigration document;
(d) a United Kingdom passport (within the meaning of the Immigration Act 1971);
(e) a passport issued by or on behalf of the authorities of a country or territory outside the United Kingdom by or on behalf of an international organisation;
(f) a document that can be used (in some or all circumstances) instead of a passport;

(g) a UK driving licence; or

(h) a driving licence issued by or on behalf of the authorities of a country or territory outside the United Kingdom.

For the above purposes, immigration document means a document used for confirming the right of a person under the Community Treaties in respect of entry or residence in the United Kingdom, or a document which is given in exercise of immigration functions and records information about leave granted to a person to enter or to remain in the United Kingdom, or a registration card (within the meaning of IA 1971, s 26A).

For the purposes of ICA 2006, s 25, the Act defines the following terms as follows:

False identity document

An identity document is false only if it is false within the meaning of Part I of the Forgery and Counterfeiting Act 1981 (see p 1087). The primary factor is that it is not enough that the document tells a lie (ie contains a false statement); what is required is that it should tell a lie about itself (ie the document itself must pretend to be something which it is not). References to the making of a false identity document include references to the modification of an identity document so that it becomes false.

Identity document which was improperly obtained

An identity document is improperly obtained if false information was provided, in, or in connection with, the application for its issue or an application for its modification, to the person who issued it or (as the case may be) to a person entitled to modify it. References to the making of a false identity document include references to the modification of an identity document so that it becomes false.

CHAPTER 4

Police questioning and the rights of suspects

INTRODUCTION

In this and the following chapter, we shall make frequent reference to Code C, the 'Detention Code' (whose full title is the Code of Practice for the Detention, Treatment and Questioning of Persons by Police Officers). This Code applies to persons in custody at police stations, whether or not they have been arrested, and (except for its provisions as to reviews and extensions of detention) to those who have been removed to a police station as a place of safety under the Mental Health Act 1983, ss 135 and 136. However, persons who are voluntarily at police stations must be treated with no less consideration.

It cannot be pointed out too often that it is essential that police officers follow carefully the procedures set out below. Not only is evidence obtained in breach of them liable to be excluded in any subsequent court proceedings, but also a failure to comply with the Detention Code may lead to a disciplinary offence.

Nothing in the Detention Code prevents a custody officer from allowing civilian support staff who are not designated persons to carry out individual procedures or tasks at the police station if the law allows. However, the officer remains responsible for making sure that the procedures and tasks are carried out correctly in accordance with the Codes. Any such civilian must be a person employed by the police authority and under the direction and control of the Chief Officer, or employed by a person with whom the police authority has a contract for the provision of services relating to persons arrested or otherwise in custody. The term 'custody officer' includes any police officer, or designated staff custody officer acting in the exercise or performance of the powers and duties conferred or imposed on him by his designation, performing the functions of a custody officer. The designation of police staff custody officers applies only in police areas where an order commencing the provisions of the Police Reform Act 2002, s 38 and Sch 4 for designating police staff custody officers performing the functions of a custody officer is in effect, and these provisions are not yet in force. The Detention Code recognises that, whilst a custody officer is required to perform specified functions 'as soon as practicable', there may be unavoidable delays where a large number of suspects are brought to a police station simultaneously to be placed in custody, or interview rooms are all in use, or where there are difficulties in contacting an appropriate adult, solicitor or interpreter.

The Detention Code does not apply to the following persons in custody:

(a) persons arrested on warrants issued in Scotland by police officers under the Criminal Justice and Public Order Act 1994, s 136(2), or arrested or detained without warrant by officers from a police force in Scotland under s 137(2) of that Act. In these cases, police powers and duties and the person's rights and entitlements whilst at a police station in England and Wales are the same as those in Scotland;

(b) persons arrested for the purpose of fingerprinting under the Asylum and Immigration Act 1999, s 142(3);

(c) persons whose detention is authorised by an immigration officer under the Immigration Act 1971;

(d) persons who are convicted or remanded prisoners held in police cells on behalf of the prison service;

(e) persons detained for searches under stop and search powers except as required by the Stop and Search Code.

In addition, people detained under the Terrorism Act 2000 (TA 2000), Sch 8 and s 41 and other provisions of that Act are not subject to any part of Code C. Such persons are subject to the Code of Practice for the Detention, Treatment and Questioning of Persons detained by police officers under that Act.

Nothing in Code C requires the identity of officers or other police staff to be recorded or disclosed if the persons concerned reasonably believe that recording or disclosing their names might put them in danger. In such cases they shall use their warrant or other identification number and the name of their police station.

Where the Detention Code requires the prior authority or agreement of an officer of at least inspector or superintendent rank, that authority may be given by a sergeant or chief inspector authorised to perform the functions of the higher rank.

In the rest of this chapter, and the next three, there are frequent references to the Police and Criminal Evidence Act 1984, hereafter simply referred to as PACE.

VOLUNTARY ATTENDANCE AT POLICE STATION

PACE, s 29 deals with persons 'assisting the police with their inquiries' (or, as it describes them, those in voluntary attendance at a police station for the purpose of assisting with an investigation). It provides that, where, for the purpose of assisting with an investigation, a person attends voluntarily at a police station or at any other place where a constable is present, or accompanies a constable to a police station or any other place without having been arrested, he is entitled to leave at will unless he is placed under arrest. In addition he must be informed at once that he is under arrest if a decision is taken to prevent him leaving at will. The Detention Code goes further, requiring that at any stage at which a person voluntarily attending is cautioned, the officer must tell him that he is not under arrest and is free to leave and must remind him of his right to free legal advice. The police should assist a 'volunteer' who asks how he should go about obtaining such advice.

DOCUMENTATION

Custody records

When a person is brought to a police station under arrest, or is arrested at a police station having attended there voluntarily, or attends a police station in answer to bail, that person must be brought before the custody officer as soon as practicable after arrival, or following arrest at the police station. This equally applies to designated and non-designated police stations. Such a person is 'at a police station' if he is anywhere upon the premises or enclosed yards forming part of the premises.

As we stated in Chapter 3, above, a separate custody record must be opened as soon as practicable for each person who is brought to a police station under arrest or who is arrested at the police station, having attended there voluntarily.

Where the arresting officer is not physically present when a detainee is brought to the police station, the arresting officer's account must be made available to the custody officer remotely or by a third party on the arresting officer's behalf. All information which is required to be recorded under the Detention Code must be recorded as soon as practicable in the custody record unless otherwise specified. Any audio or visual recording made in the custody area is not part of the custody record. It is a matter for the custody officer to determine whether a record should be made of the property a detained person has with him or had taken from him on arrest. Any record made is not required to be kept as part of the custody record but the custody record should be noted as to where such a record exists. Whenever a record is made the detainee must be allowed to check and sign it as correct. Any refusal to sign must be recorded.

Where a person is answering street bail, the custody officer should link any documentation held in relation to the arrest with the custody record and any further action must be recorded in accordance with the Code.

In the case of any action requiring the authority of an officer of a specified rank, his name and rank must be recorded in the custody record, except where the person is detained under TA 2000, or where there are reasonable grounds to believe that naming him would endanger him (in which case the record must state the officer's warrant or other identification number and duty station).

All entries in the custody record must be timed and signed by the maker. In the case of a record held on a computer, this should be timed and contain the operator's identification. Warrant or other identification numbers and the name of the person's police station should be used rather than names in the case of detention under TA 2000 just mentioned or where it is reasonably believed that recording or disclosing his name would endanger that person.

The custody officer is responsible for the accuracy and completeness of the custody record and for ensuring that the record (or a copy) accompanies a detained person if he is transferred to another police station. The record must show the time of, and reason for, a transfer and the time a person is released from detention. As soon as practicable after his arrival at the police station, a solicitor or appropriate adult must be permitted to consult the custody record of a person detained. When a person leaves police detention or is taken before a court, he or his legal representative or his appropriate adult must be supplied on request with a copy of the custody record as soon as practicable. This entitlement lasts for twelve months after his release.

The fact and time of any refusal by a person to sign a custody record when asked to do so in accordance with the Detention Code must itself be recorded.

Interview records

An accurate record must be made of each interview with a person suspected of an offence, whether or not the interview takes place at a police station. The record must state the place of the interview, the time it begins and ends, the time the record is made (if different), any breaks in it, and the names of those present. The requirement to record names of those present does not apply to police officers interviewing a person detained under TA 2000 or where it is reasonably believed that the disclosure of names might endanger the officers; instead the record must state the warrant or other identification number and duty station of such officers. The Code provides similar protection for support staff involved in the investigation of serious organised crime where they fear harm. In cases of doubt as to the circumstances, an officer of inspector rank or above should be consulted.

An interview record:

(a) enables the prosecutor to make informed decisions;
(b) is capable of being exhibited to an officer's witness statement and used pursuant to the Criminal Justice Act 1967, s 9 (which is described on p 234);
(c) enables the prosecutor to comply with the rules of advance disclosure; and
(d) where the record is accepted by the defence, facilitates the conduct of the case by the prosecution, the defence and the court.

Such a record must, therefore, comprise a balanced account of the interview including points in mitigation and/or defence made by the suspect. Where an admission is made, the question as well as the answer containing the admission must be recorded verbatim in the record. Matters which might be considered to be prejudicial or inadmissible by a court should be brought to the attention of the prosecutor by means of a covering report.

An 'interview' is described in the Detention Code as 'the questioning of a person regarding his involvement or suspected involvement in a criminal offence or offences which, by virtue of the Code, is required to be carried out under caution'. For example, where, after arresting a man for possessing an offensive weapon, police officers asked him in the police car why he had the knife and he told them there had been some trouble and that he had it for his own protection, it was held that this amounted to an interview for the purposes of the Code, so that a record should have been made of it.

On the other hand, the statutory procedure for obtaining roadside specimens and specimens for analysis under the drink/drive legislation does not constitute an 'interview' for present purposes, so the requirements relating to such an interview do not apply to it. Nor does an informal conversation at or near the scene of a crime constitute an 'interview', but it will if it descends into detailed questioning.

In relation to interview records generally, when a suspect agrees to read records of interviews and of other comments and to sign them as correct, he should be asked to endorse the record with words such as 'I agree that this is a correct record of what was said' and add his signature. Where the suspect does not agree with the record, the officer should record the details of any disagreement and then ask the suspect to read these details and then sign them to the effect that they accurately reflect his disagreement. Any refusal to sign when asked to do so must be recorded.

Written interview records must be signed and timed by the maker.

With the exceptions mentioned below an interview at a police station must be audio recorded or visually recorded with sound in accordance with Code E: the Code of Practice on Audio Recording Interviews with Suspects (hereafter 'the Audio Recording Code') or Code F: the Code of Practice on Visual Recording with Sound of Interviews with Suspects (hereafter 'the Visual Recording Code'):

(a) with a person who has been cautioned in accordance with the Detention Code (on grounds of suspicion of his committing an offence) in respect of an indictable offence (including an offence triable either way);
(b) one which takes place as a result of a police officer exceptionally putting further questions to a suspect about an offence described in (a) after he has been charged with, or informed that he may be prosecuted for, that offence; or
(c) one in which a police officer wishes to bring to the notice of a person, after he has been charged with, or informed he may be prosecuted for, an indictable offence (including one triable either way), any written statement made by another person, or the content of an interview with another person, which may be done by playing an audio recording.

In addition, the Visual Recording Code suggests that it might be appropriate to visually record an interview when the interview is with, or in the presence of, a deaf, deaf/blind or speech impaired person who uses sign language to communicate, or where the presence of an appropriate adult is required, or where the suspect or his representative requests it.

However, audio recordings at police stations may be made of interviews with persons cautioned for other offences, at police discretion, provided that the Recording Codes are complied with. This also applies to responses after charge in such situations.

The TA 2000 makes separate provision for the audio or visual recording of interviews in relation to terrorism and the above requirements do not apply.

Any written record must be made during the interview, unless in the investigating officer's view this would not be practicable or would interfere with the conduct of the interview, and must constitute either a verbatim record or, failing this, an account of the interview which adequately and accurately summarises it. If the record is not made during the interview, it must be made as soon as practicable thereafter and the reason must be recorded in the officer's pocket book (or by other methods used for recording information) or the official book issued to a member of police staff.

The custody officer may authorise the interviewing officer not to audio record or visually record the interview in three cases:

(1) Where it is not reasonably practicable to do so, because of failure of the equipment or the non-availability of a suitable interview room or recorder, and the custody officer considers on reasonable grounds that the interview should not be delayed he may authorise the interviewing officer not to audio record the interview. Priority should be given to audio recording interviews with persons who are suspected of more serious offences.
(2) Where it is clear from the outset that no prosecution will ensue, the custody officer may authorise the interviewing officer not to audio record the interview.
(3) Where a person refuses to go into or remain in a suitable interview room and the custody officer considers, on reasonable grounds, that the interview should not be delayed, the interview may, at the custody officer's discretion, be conducted in a cell using portable recording equipment or, if none is available, recorded

in writing in accordance with the Detention Code and the reasons must be recorded.

The whole of an interview must be recorded, including the taking and reading back of any statement. If, during the course of any visually recorded interview, it becomes apparent that a terrorism offence may be involved, the equipment must be switched off and the interview should continue in accordance with TA 2000.

In these cases the interview must be recorded in writing and in accordance with the Detention Code. The custody officer must make a note, in specific terms, of the reason for not audio recording. Where a person refuses to enter or remain in an interview room and the custody officer considers that the interview should not be delayed, the interview may be conducted in a cell using portable recording equipment, or if such equipment is not available, it should be recorded in writing.

The recording of interviews must be carried out openly but unobtrusively, and it must be made clear to the suspect that there is no opportunity to interfere with the equipment or recording media. The 'master recording' will be sealed before it leaves the presence of the suspect. A master recording may be either one of two recording media used in a twin deck/drive machine or the only medium used in a single deck/drive machine. A second medium will be used as a working copy and it may be either the other medium in the case of a twin deck/drive machine, or a copy of the master used in a single deck/drive machine. Such a copy must be made in the presence of the suspect and without the master recording leaving his sight.

It must be borne in mind that the Criminal Justice and Public Order Act 1994, ss 34, 36 and 37 describe the conditions under which adverse inferences may be drawn from a person's failure or refusal to say anything about his involvement in the offence, when interviewed, after being charged or informed that he may be prosecuted. In effect, in the case of such a detainee at a police station who has asked for legal advice but has not yet been allowed an opportunity to consult a solicitor (including the duty solicitor), adverse inferences may not be drawn from his failure to say anything concerning his involvement in an offence. It would therefore be wrong to use the normal caution which includes the words 'But it may harm your defence if you do not mention when questioned something which you later rely on in court' as that simply would not be true. It has been held that no adverse inferences may be drawn where a person who has asked for legal advice has not received it. In such circumstances the words in inverted commas above are omitted from the caution. However, it must be remembered that when legal advice becomes available to the detainee, the full caution must then be given as any failure to respond may create circumstances which will permit adverse inferences to be drawn.

Checking the record

Unless it is impracticable, the person interviewed must be given the opportunity to read the interview record and to sign it as correct or to indicate the respects in which he considers it inaccurate. If the interview is audio recorded the arrangements set out in the Audio Recording Code apply.

If the person concerned cannot read or refuses to read the record or to sign it, the senior police officer present must read it over to him and ask him whether he would like to sign it as correct or to indicate the respects in which he considers it inaccurate. The police officer must then certify on the interview record itself what has occurred.

Records of comments outside interview

A written record should also be made of any comments made by a suspected person, indicating unsolicited comments, which are outside the context of an interview but which might be relevant to the offence. Any such record must be timed and signed by the maker. Where practicable the person must be given the opportunity to read that record and to sign it as correct or to indicate the respects in which he considers it inaccurate. Any refusal to sign must be recorded.

The present requirement does not extend to entries made in an officer's notebook and offered to the suspect for authentication. These do not have to be recorded in the custody record.

CAUTIONS

A person whom there are reasonable grounds (based on known facts or relevant information) to suspect of an offence must be cautioned before any questions about an offence, or further questions if the answers provide the grounds for suspicion, are put to him if either the suspect's answer or silence (ie failure or refusal to answer or answer satisfactorily) may be given in evidence to a court in a prosecution.

Statements made under caution may be used only for the purposes for which they are provided. To use them for an extraneous purpose, for example to leak to the press, whether or not for reward, is legally actionable as a breach of confidence.

Where no arrest has been made

Where a person has not been arrested but there are grounds to suspect him of an offence, he must be cautioned before any questions about it (or further questions, if it is his answers to previous questions that provide grounds for suspicion) are put regarding his involvement or suspected involvement in that offence if his answers or his silence (ie failure to answer a question or to answer satisfactorily) may be given in evidence to a court in a prosecution. The Court of Appeal has held that 'grounds to suspect' means 'reasonable grounds to suspect'.

A person need not be cautioned if questions are put to him for other purposes, for example solely:

(a) to establish his identity or his ownership of any vehicle; or
(b) to obtain information in accordance with any relevant statutory requirement or in furtherance of the proper and effective conduct of a search (for example, to determine the need to search in the exercise of powers to stop and search or to seek co-operation while carrying out a search); or
(c) to seek verification of a written record; or
(d) when examining persons in accordance with TA 2000, Sch 7 and the Code of Practice for Examining Officers issued under that Act, Sch 14, para 6.

Assistance is provided by a case where a suspect was being interviewed concerning burglaries and said he was wanted for 'something bad'. The police officer asked what it was, to which the suspect replied, 'I'm ashamed, I done a rape'. It was held that the officer, at the stage of asking his question, was merely trying to find out what was disturbing the suspect and that there had been no breach of the Detention Code by a failure to caution.

Wherever a person not under arrest is initially cautioned, or is reminded that he is still under caution after a break, he must at the same time be told that he is not under arrest; that he is not obliged to remain at the police station but that if he does he may obtain free and independent legal advice if he wishes. The officer must point out that the right to legal advice includes the right to speak with a solicitor over the telephone. The officer must ask the person whether he wishes to do so. A person who is arrested, or further arrested, must be informed that he is under arrest and given the grounds for that arrest.

Since the Detention Code obliges police officers to administer a caution if the answer to a question may be offered in evidence in criminal proceedings, it is necessary to caution motorists when pointing out to them that they have committed an offence as their reply is almost certainly going to be relevant to the proceedings. Indeed, although there is no direct requirement to caution when informing a person that he will be reported for an offence, the admissibility of his reply in evidence may depend upon whether or not he has been cautioned at some stage. Practice may still require that such a reply is included in an officer's report and, if this is so, the offender should be cautioned at some stage before he makes it. The use of a caution when dealing with offenders who commit minor offences is often misunderstood by members of the public who believe that the officer is being officious.

The caution prescribed by the Code is:

'You do not have to say anything. But it may harm your defence if you do not mention when questioned something which you later rely on in court. Anything you do say may be given in evidence.'

Minor deviations do not constitute a breach of this requirement provided that the sense of the caution is preserved.

Other forms of caution are prescribed by Annex C to the Detention Code for use where the restriction on drawing adverse inferences from silence applies (see below).

On arrest

A person must be cautioned on arrest for an offence unless:

(a) it is impracticable to do so by reason of his condition or behaviour at the time; or
(b) he has already been cautioned prior to arrest as described above.

After arrest

Following the arrest of a person, a police officer must caution him (or cause him to be cautioned or remind him that he remains under caution):

(a) before putting to him any questions or further questions for the purpose of obtaining evidence which may be given to a court in a prosecution (unless the questioning immediately follows the arrest);
(b) when arresting him for any further offence in accordance with the Police and Criminal Evidence Act 1984, s 31 (which we dealt with at p 72, above);

(c) when charging him with an offence (or informing him that he may be prosecuted for it); or
(d) when bringing to his notice a written statement or questioning him as permitted by the Detention Code.

Special cautions when the restriction on drawing inferences from silence applies

Annex C deals with these special cautions.

When a suspect who is interviewed at a police station or authorised place of detention after arrest fails or refuses to answer certain questions, or to answer them satisfactorily, after due warning, a court or jury may draw such inferences as appear proper under the Criminal Justice and Public Order Act 1994 (CJPOA 1994), ss 34, 36 and 37. This applies when:

(a) it was reasonable to expect the arrested person to have mentioned a fact on which he later relies;
(b) a suspect is arrested by a constable and there is found on his person, or in or on his clothing or footwear, or otherwise in his possession, or in the place where he is arrested, any objects, marks or substances, or marks on such objects, and the person fails or refuses to account for the objects, marks or substances found; or
(c) an arrested person was found by a constable at a place at or about the time the offence for which he was arrested is alleged to have been committed, and the person fails or refuses to account for his presence at that place.

These provisions are subject to an overriding restriction on the ability of a court or jury to draw inferences from a person's silence. This restriction applies:

(a) to any detainee at a police station who, before being interviewed, or being charged or informed that he may be prosecuted, has:
   (i) asked for legal advice;
   (ii) not been allowed an opportunity to consult a solicitor, including the duty solicitor, as in this Code; and
   (iii) not changed his mind about wanting legal advice.
   Note the condition in (ii) will apply when a detainee who has asked for legal advice is interviewed before speaking to a solicitor, but will not apply if the detained person declines to ask for the duty solicitor;
(b) to any person charged with, or informed that he may be prosecuted for, an offence who:
   (i) has had brought to his notice a written statement made by another person or the content of an interview with another person which relates to that offence;
   (ii) is interviewed about that offence; or
   (iii) makes a written statement about that offence.

Where a requirement to caution arises at a time when the restriction on drawing adverse inferences from silence applies, the caution must be:

'You do not have to say anything, but anything you do say may be given in evidence.'

Whenever the restriction begins or ceases to apply after a caution has been given, the person must be recautioned in the appropriate terms. The changed position in relation to inferences and the fact that the previous caution no longer applies must be explained to the detainee in ordinary language. The Code suggests, in a note for guidance, that where the restriction on drawing adverse inferences begins to apply it should be explained that the caution previously given no longer applies because after caution the detainee asked to speak to a solicitor but has not yet had an opportunity to do so (restriction (a)); or the detainee has been charged with or informed that he will be prosecuted for the offence (restriction (b)). He should be informed that this means that, from now on, adverse inferences cannot be drawn at court and his defence will not be harmed just because he chooses to say nothing. He should be asked to note that the new caution does not say anything about his defence being harmed.

Where any such restriction ceases to apply before or at the time the person is charged or informed that he may be prosecuted, the detainee should be told that the caution he was previously given no longer applies. This is because after that caution he has been allowed an opportunity to speak to a solicitor. He should be told to listen carefully as the caution now being given explains how his defence at court may be affected by his choosing to say nothing. The important factor is that where legal advice has been requested all bets are off in relation to silence until the detainee has had an opportunity to speak to a solicitor. This follows a ruling of the European Court of Human Rights.

General

Where there is a break in questioning under caution the officer in charge must ensure that the person being questioned is aware that he remains under caution; if there is any doubt the caution should be given again in full when the interview resumes. This is important because the officer may have to satisfy a court that the person understood that he was still under caution when the interview resumed.

If it appears that a person does not understand what the caution means, the officer who has given it should go on to explain it in his own words.

The Detention Code also requires that, if a person is not under arrest when an initial caution is given at a police station (or other premises), the officer must tell him that he is not under arrest and is not obliged to remain with the officer. The officer must also tell him that he is free to leave if he wishes *and remind him that he may obtain free legal advice* if he wishes and that the right to legal advice includes the right to speak to a solicitor on the telephone and ask him if he wishes to do so. This provision imports a significant requirement into the duties of police officers. Not only must an officer tell a person clearly that he is under arrest (and why he is under arrest) when that situation applies, but he must equally tell a person that he is not under arrest (if that is the case) whenever he cautions him if he is at a police station or before formally interviewing him at other premises.

Documentation

A record must be made when a caution is given, either in the officer's pocket notebook (or by other methods used for recording information) or in the interview record as appropriate.

Written statements under caution

All written statements made at police stations after caution must be written on the forms provided for the purpose and be taken in accordance with the rules in Annex D to the Detention Code. Before a person makes a written statement under caution at a police station he must be reminded about the right to legal advice. It is not normally necessary to ask for a written statement if the interview was recorded in writing, and the record signed, or audibly or visually recorded in accordance with the Audio Recording Code or Visual Recording Code.

Written by a person under caution

(1) A person must always be invited to write down himself what he wants to say.
(2) A person who has not been charged with, or informed that he may be prosecuted for, any offence to which the statement will relate, must, unless the statement is made at a time when the restrictions on drawing adverse inferences from silence applies, be asked to write out and sign the following before writing what he wants to say:

> 'I make this statement of my own free will. I understand that I need not say anything but that it may harm my defence if I do not mention when questioned something which I later rely on in court. This statement may be given in evidence.'

If the statement is made at a time when the restriction on drawing adverse inferences from silence applies, he must be asked to write out and sign the following before writing what he wants to say:

> 'I make this statement of my own free will. I understand that I do not have to say anything. This statement may be given in evidence.'

(3) When a person, on the occasion of being charged with, or informed that, he may be prosecuted for any offence, asks to make a statement which relates to any such offence and wants to write it he must, unless the restriction on drawing adverse inferences from silence applied when he was so charged or informed that he might be prosecuted, be asked to write out and sign the following before writing what he wants to say:

> 'I make this statement of my own free will. I understand that I do not have to say anything but that it may harm my defence if I do not mention when questioned something which I later rely on in court. This statement may be given in evidence.'

If the restriction on drawing adverse inferences from silence applied when the person was so charged or informed that he would be prosecuted, he must be asked to write out and sign the following before writing what he wants to say:

> 'I make this statement of my own free will. I understand that I do not have to say anything. This statement may be given in evidence.'

(4) Where a person, who has already been charged with or informed that he may be prosecuted for any offence, asks to make a statement which relates to any such

offence and wants to write it, he must be asked to write out and sign the following before writing what he wants to say:

> 'I make this statement of my own free will. I understand that I do not have to say anything. This statement may be given in evidence.'

(5) Any person writing his own statement must be allowed to do so without any prompting except that a police officer or civilian interviewer may indicate to him which matters are material or question any ambiguity in the statement.

Written by a police officer or other police staff

(6)   If a person says that he would like someone to write it for him, a police officer or other police staff must write the statement. If the person has not been charged with, or informed that he may be prosecuted for, any offence to which the statement he wants to make relates, he must, before starting, be asked to sign or make his mark, to the appropriate one of the following endorsements. Unless the statement is made at a time when the restriction on drawing adverse inferences from silence applies, the endorsement is:

> 'I, . . . , wish to make a statement. I want someone to write down what I say. I understand that I do not have to say anything but that it may harm my defence if I do not mention when questioned something which I later rely on in court. This statement may be given in evidence.'

If the statement is made at a time when the restriction on drawing adverse inferences from silence applies, the endorsement is:

> 'I, . . . , wish to make a statement. I want someone to write down what I say. I understand that I do not have to say anything. This statement may be given in evidence.'

(7)   If, on the occasion of being charged with or informed that he may be prosecuted for any offence, the person asks to make a statement which relates to any such offence, he must before starting be asked to sign, or make his mark to the following as appropriate. Unless the restriction on drawing adverse inferences from silence applied when he was so charged or informed that he may be prosecuted, the words are:

> 'I, . . . , wish to make a statement. I want someone to write down what I say. I understand that I do not have to say anything but that it may harm my defence if I do not mention when questioned something which I later rely on in court. This statement may be given in evidence.'

If the restriction on drawing adverse inferences from silence applied when he was so charged or informed that he may be prosecuted, the words are:

> 'I, . . . , wish to make a statement. I want someone to write down what I say. I understand that I do not have to say anything. This statement may be given in evidence.'

(8) If, having already been charged with or informed that he may be prosecuted for any offence, a person asks to make a statement which relates to such an offence, he must, before starting, be asked to sign or make his mark to:

'I, . . . , wish to make a statement. I want someone to write down what I say. I understand that I do not have to say anything. This statement may be given in evidence.'

(9) The person writing the statement must take down the exact words spoken by the person making it and he must not edit or paraphrase it. Any questions that are necessary (eg to make it more intelligible) and the answers given must be recorded contemporaneously on the statement form.

(10) When the writing of a statement is finished the person making it must be asked to read it and to make any corrections, alterations or additions he wishes. When he has finished reading it he must be asked to write and sign or make his mark on the following certificate at the end of the statement:

'I have read the above statement, and I have been able to correct, alter or add anything I wish. This statement is true. I have made it of my own free will.'

(11) If the person making the statement cannot read, or refuses to read it, or to write the above mentioned certificate at the end of it or to sign it, the person taking the statement must read it over to him and ask him whether he would like to correct, alter or add anything and put his signature or make his mark at the end. The person taking the statement must then certify on the statement itself what has occurred.

Summary

A statement must begin with a declaration to the effect that the person wishes to make a statement. The Code requires that, where police officers write the statement, they must record the exact words said by that person and that they must not edit or paraphrase those words. But for this latter provision, a shortened statement including only the words which a police officer considered to be important could still contain the exact words used, but perhaps not all of them. Provisions are made concerning alterations, corrections and signatures and that (in the event of an inability to read) *the senior officer present* shall read it over and deal with such matters. That officer must then certify on the statement what he has done.

Role of 'the appropriate adult'

The Detention Code also requires that, where the appropriate adult or another third party is present at an interview (see below) and is still in the police station at the time a written record is made, he must be asked to read it (or any written statement taken down by a police officer) and sign it as correct or to indicate the respects in which he considers it to be inaccurate. If he refuses to sign the record as accurate or to indicate the respects in which he considers it to be inaccurate, the senior officer present must record on the record itself, in the presence of the person concerned, what has happened. If the interview is audio recorded the arrangements set out in the Code of Practice for the Audio Recording of Police Interviews apply.

In the case of a *juvenile*, the 'appropriate adult' means:

(a) his parent or guardian (or, if he is in care, the care authority or organisation). The term 'in care' is used in the Code to cover all cases in which a juvenile is 'looked after' by a local authority under the terms of the Children Act 1989; or
(b) a social worker of a local authority; or
(c) failing either of the above, another responsible adult aged eighteen or over who is not a police officer or employed by the police.

A person, including a parent or guardian, should not be the appropriate adult if he is suspected of involvement in the offence in question, is the victim, is a witness, is involved in the investigation or has received admissions. In such circumstances it will be desirable for the appropriate adult to be someone else. If the parent or guardian of a juvenile is estranged from the juvenile, he should not be asked to be the appropriate adult if the juvenile expressly and specifically objects to his presence. The fact that a parent participates in questioning a juvenile during the interview does not disqualify the parent from being the appropriate adult. If a child in care admits an offence to a social worker, another social worker should be the appropriate adult.

Although the Code refers to 'the appropriate adult' in the singular, there may be cases where it is appropriate for more than one adult to be present as 'appropriate adults' during the interview of a juvenile, as where both parents are present or where a parent with language difficulties is present and a second adult is present to assist in questions of language.

In the case of a person *who is mentally disordered or mentally handicapped*, the 'appropriate adult' means:

(a) a relative, guardian or other person responsible for his care or custody; or
(b) someone who has experience of dealing with persons who are mentally disordered (as defined by the Mental Health Act 1983, s 1(2)) or mentally vulnerable (ie because of their mental state or capacity they may not understand the significance of what is said, of questions or of their replies) but who is not a police officer or employed by the police; or
(c) failing either of the above, some other responsible adult aged eighteen or over who is not a police officer or employed by the police.

In the case of people who are mentally disordered or vulnerable it may in some cases be more satisfactory if the appropriate adult is someone who has experience or training in their case rather than a relative lacking such qualifications. However, if the person himself prefers a relative to a better qualified stranger, his wishes should if practicable be respected.

A solicitor or independent custody visitor who is present at the police station in a professional capacity may not act as the appropriate adult.

A person should always be given an opportunity, when an appropriate adult is called to a police station, to consult privately with a solicitor in the absence of the appropriate adult if he wishes to do so. An appropriate adult is not subject to legal privilege.

INTERVIEWS

General provisions concerning interviews

As previously stated, the Detention Code defines an interview as 'the questioning of a person regarding his involvement or suspected involvement in a criminal offence or offences which, by virtue of the Code, is required to be carried out under caution'. Whenever a person is interviewed he must be informed of the nature of the offence, or further offence. Procedures undertaken under the Road Traffic Act 1988, s 7 or the Transport and Works Act 1992, s 31 (both dealt with in Chapter 17) do not constitute interviews for the purposes of the Code.

Thus, we are considering an 'interview' which takes place under caution, or which should have taken place under caution. Some decisions of the Court of Appeal continue to be helpful in establishing a divide.

In one case, police officers attended the house of a suspect to arrest him for handling stolen furniture and taking a lorry without consent. The officers put to him that they had seen him some days previously driving the stolen lorry. One of them said, 'What have you got to say about this?' He later said to him, 'But you are not doubting that we saw you last Thursday . . . in the lorry?' It was held by the Court of Appeal that these questions, asked without caution, were for purposes other than establishing identity as the officers already knew the name of the suspect. They were put for the purpose of obtaining evidence and therefore constituted an interview, and should not have been asked until arrival at the police station when the suspect had been informed of his right to legal advice.

In another case, an officer escorting a suspect to the custody office, saw the suspect drop a packet containing four ecstasy tablets. She said to him 'I have just seen you drop this. Things are looking a bit more serious now.' The suspect replied 'Yeah'. The officer asked 'Are these ecstasy tablets?' and the suspect replied 'Yes'. The Court of Appeal held that this was clearly an interview. Even one question regarding a suspect's involvement or suspected involvement in an offence can be sufficient in appropriate circumstances. On the other hand, the Court held, a conversation in which the suspect asks 'What will I get for this?', the officer replied 'What do you mean?', the suspect said 'At court for supplying drugs, what will I get?' and the officer replied 'That's not for me to say', did not amount to an interview. Clearly, the officer's question did not relate to the suspect's involvement in an offence. This conversation was simply an unsolicited comment which had to be recorded.

The Court of Appeal has given precise guidance in respect of any notes which might have been made in an interview.

(1) If such a note has, for whatever reason, not been shown to the suspect prior to the arrival of his solicitor, fairness both to the suspect and to the police themselves requires that it be shown in the presence of his solicitor.

(2) If such a note has been shown to the suspect before the arrival of the solicitor, fairness to both sides requires that the solicitor be informed of the facts when he arrives.

(3) Where the court concludes that the police have acted less than fairly the chances that the evidence of the conversation noted will be excluded will be considerably increased.

Before the start of an interview, other than one which is being recorded, it is required that each interviewing officer must identify himself and any other officers present to the prisoner by name and rank, except in the case of persons detained under TA 2000 when each officer must identify himself by his warrant or other identification number and rank rather than his name. In all interviews, mechanically recorded or not, there must be breaks at the recognised meal times and there must also be short breaks for refreshment at intervals of approximately two hours, subject to the interviewing officer's discretion to delay a break if there are reasonable grounds for believing that it would:

(a) involve a risk of harm to persons or serious loss of, or damage to, property; or
(b) delay unnecessarily the person's release from custody; or
(c) otherwise prejudice the investigation.

Meal breaks should normally last at least forty-five minutes and shorter breaks after two hours should last at least fifteen minutes. If a break is delayed as permitted by the Detention Code and prolongs the interview, a longer break should then be provided. If there is a short interview, and a subsequent short interview is contemplated, the length of the break may be reduced if there are reasonable grounds to believe that this is necessary to avoid any of the consequences set out at (a) to (c) above.

Interviews following arrest

Following a decision to arrest a suspect he must not be interviewed about the relevant offence except at a police station (or other authorised place of detention) unless the consequent delay would be likely:

(a) to lead to interference with or harm to evidence connected with an offence, or interference with or physical harm to other persons, or serious loss of, or damage to, property; or
(b) to lead to the alerting of other persons suspected of having committed an offence but not yet arrested for it; or
(c) to hinder the recovery of property obtained in consequence of the commission of an offence.

Interviewing in any of these circumstances should cease once the relevant risk has been averted or the necessary questions have been put in order to attempt to avert that risk.

Immediately prior to the commencement or recommencement of any interview at a police station or other authorised place of detention, the interviewing officer must remind the suspect of his entitlement to free legal advice and that the interview can be delayed for him to obtain legal advice (unless one of the exceptions to the right to legal advice applies, which are described on pp 132–133). At the beginning of an interview carried out in a police station, the interviewing officer, after cautioning the suspect, must put to him any significant statement or silence which occurred in the presence and hearing of a police officer or civilian interviewer before the start of the interview and which has not been put to the suspect in the course of a previous interview, and must ask him whether he confirms or denies that earlier statement or silence and whether he wishes to add anything. This does not prevent an interviewer from putting significant statements and silences to a suspect again at a later stage of a further interview.

A 'significant statement' is one which appears capable of being used in evidence against the suspect, in particular a direct admission of guilt. A 'significant silence' is a failure or refusal to answer a question or answer satisfactorily when under caution which might, allowing for the restriction on drawing adverse inferences from silence, give rise to an inference under CJPOA 1994. It is the responsibility of the interviewing officer to ensure that all such reminders are noted in the record of the interview.

No interviewer may try to obtain answers to questions or to elicit a statement by the use of oppression. Except as provided by the Detention Code, no police officer may indicate, except in answer to a direct question, what action will be taken on the part of the police if the person being interviewed answers questions, makes a statement or refuses to do either. If the person asks the officer directly what action will be taken in the event of his answering questions, making a statement or refusing to do either, the officer may inform the person what action the police propose to take in that event provided that the action is itself proper and warranted.

An interview concerning an offence with which the person has not been charged or for which they have not been informed that they may be prosecuted must cease when the officer in charge of the investigation:

(a) is satisfied that all relevant questions to obtain accurate and reliable information about the offence have been put to the suspect, including giving an opportunity for an innocent explanation to be put forward and asking any questions to test the accuracy or reliability of such explanation (eg to clear up ambiguities);
(b) has taken account of any other available evidence; and

the officer in charge of the investigation, or (in the case of a detained suspect) the custody officer, reasonably believes that there is sufficient evidence to provide a realistic prospect of conviction for that offence if the person was prosecuted.

This does not, however, prevent officers in revenue cases or acting under the confiscation provisions of the Criminal Justice Act 1988 or the Drug Trafficking Act 1994 from inviting suspects to complete a formal question and answer record after the interview is concluded.

In addition, according to the Court of Appeal, provided the officer has an open mind and is prepared not to charge (or not to refer to another officer responsible for charging) if the suspect produces a convincing account, the interviewer may proceed in order to see whether the suspect can produce an explanation.

Where a police officer proposes to question further a suspect, who has been arrested in respect of an offence, in respect of another more serious offence, he must first either charge him (or have him charged) with the more serious offence or at least ensure that he is aware of the true nature of the investigation. This is to enable the suspect to give proper weight to the nature of the investigation when deciding whether to exercise his right to legal advice and how to respond to the officer's questions. If an officer fails to take either of these steps, and the suspect (not knowing the true position) fails to seek legal advice and gives critical answers which might not otherwise have been given, the evidence will normally be excluded in any court proceedings.

Interviews while in detention

The Detention Code provides that if a police officer wishes to interview a detained person, or to conduct inquiries which require the presence of a detained person, it is the custody officer who must decide whether to deliver his prisoner into that officer's custody.

In any period of twenty-four hours a detained person must be allowed a continuous period of at least eight hours' rest, free from questioning, travel or any interruption by police officers in connection with the investigation concerned. This period should normally be at night or other appropriate time which takes account of when the detainee last slept or rested. If a detainee is arrested at a police station after going there voluntarily, the period of twenty-four hours runs from the time of arrival at the police station. The period of rest may not be interrupted or delayed except:

(a) when there are reasonable grounds for believing that not delaying or interrupting that period would:
   (i)   involve a risk of harm to people or serious loss of, or damage to, property;
   (ii)   delay unnecessarily the person's release from custody;
   (iii) otherwise prejudice the outcome of the investigation;
(b) at the request of the detainee, his appropriate adult or legal representative;
(c) when a delay or interruption is necessary in order to comply with the legal obligations and duties under s 15 of the Detention Code (reviews and extensions of detention) or to take the action required under s 9 (care and treatment of detained persons who are intoxicated or in need of clinical treatment and attention).

If such a period of rest is interrupted in accordance with (a), a fresh period must be allowed. Interruptions under (b) and (c) do not require that a fresh period be allowed.

As far as practicable, an interview must take place in a properly heated, lit and ventilated interview room. The detained person must not be required to stand.

A suspect whose detention without charge has been authorised under PACE, because his detention is necessary so that he may be interviewed with a view to obtaining evidence of the offence for which he was arrested, may choose not to answer questions. However, the police do not require a suspect's consent to interview him for this purpose. If a suspect takes steps to prevent an interview, such as refusing to leave his cell, or trying to leave the interview room, he must be cautioned and be told that refusal to co-operate could lead to the interview taking place in the cell and that such failure to co-operate may be given in evidence. A further invitation should then be given to co-operate by going to the interview room.

A record must be made of times during which a detainee was not in the custody of the custody officer, and why; of any reason for refusal to deliver the detainee out of that custody; of any reason why it was not practicable to use an interview room; and of any action taken in consequence of a refusal to be interviewed.

Audio recorded interviews

As stated above, these are governed by the Audio Recording Code. For the purposes of the Code, the term 'recording media' means any removable, physical audio recording medium (such as magnetic type, optical disc or solid state memory) which can be played or copied.

Recording and sealing master recordings

Recording of interviews must be carried out openly to instil confidence in its reliability as an impartial and accurate record of the interview. One recording, the master recording, will be sealed in the suspect's presence. A second recording will be used as a working copy. The master recording is either of the two recordings used in a twin deck/drive machine or the only recording in a single deck/drive machine. The working copy is either the second/third recording used in a twin/triple deck/drive machine or a copy of the master recording made by a single deck/drive machine.

The identity of officers or police staff conducting interviews need not be recorded or disclosed in the case of inquiries linked to the investigation of terrorism, or if the interviewer reasonably believes recording or disclosing their name might put them in danger. In these cases interviewers should use warrant or other identification numbers and the name of their police station.

Commencement of interview

When the suspect is brought into the interview room the interviewer must without delay, but in sight of the suspect, load the audio recorder with new recording media and set it to record. The recording media must be unwrapped or opened in the presence of the suspect. The interviewer must then:

(a) explain that the interview is being audibly recorded;
(b) give his name and rank and the name and rank of any other interviewer present, except in the case of inquiries linked to the investigation of terrorism, or where it is reasonably believed that this may endanger the individuals concerned, where warrant or other identification numbers must be stated rather than names;
(c) ask the suspect and any other person present (eg a solicitor) to identify themselves;
(d) state the date, time of commencement and place of the interview; and
(e) state that the suspect will be given a notice about what will happen to the copies of the recording.

The interviewer must then caution the suspect in the appropriate form (see p 112). He must remind the suspect of his right to free and independent legal advice and that he can speak to a solicitor on the telephone in accordance with the provisions of the Detention Code.

The interviewer must then put to the suspect any significant statement or silence (ie a failure or refusal to answer a question or to answer it satisfactorily) which occurred before the start of the audibly recorded interview, and must ask him whether he confirms or denies that earlier statement or silence or whether he wishes to add anything. A 'significant' statement or silence means one which appears capable of being used in evidence against the suspect, in particular a direct admission of guilt, or failure or refusal to answer a question or to answer it satisfactorily, which might give rise to an inference under CJPOA 1994, ss 34 (p 242), 36 or 37 (p 247).

The reader is reminded that a special warning must be given before inferences can be drawn under CJPOA 1994, ss 36 or 37 and of the fact that adverse inferences cannot be drawn where legal advice has been requested but has not yet been received.

Objections

If the suspect raises objections to the interview being audibly recorded either at the outset, or during the interview, or during a break in the interview, the interviewer must explain the fact that the interview is being audibly recorded and that the provisions of the Audio Recording Code require that the suspect's objections be recorded on the audio recording. The suspect's objections must be noted. When any objections have been recorded on the recording media or the suspect has refused to have his objections recorded, the interviewer may turn off the recorder. In this eventuality, he must say that he is turning off the recorder and give his reasons for doing so and then turn it off. The interviewer must then make a written record of the interview in accordance with the Detention Code. If, however, the interviewer reasonably considers that he may proceed to put questions to the suspect with the audio recorder still on, he may do so. He should bear in mind that a decision to continue recording against the wishes of the suspect may be the subject of comment in court.

If a suspect indicates that he wishes to tell an interviewer about matters not directly connected with the offence of which he is suspected and that he is unwilling for these matters to be recorded, he must be given the opportunity to tell the police officer about these matters after the conclusion of the formal interview.

Changing recording media

Where recording media are coming to an end, the interviewer must inform the suspect and round off that part of the interview. If the interviewer leaves the room for a second set of recording media, the suspect should not be left unattended. The interviewer will remove the recording media and insert new ones which must be unwrapped or otherwise opened in the suspect's presence. Recording media must be marked with an identification number immediately they are removed from the recorder.

Breaks in interview

When a break is taken, that fact must be recorded on the audio recording together with the reason for it and the time it was taken. If the interview room is vacated by the suspect, the recording media must be removed from the recorder and dealt with in the same manner as if the interview had been concluded (see below).

When a break is a short one and both the suspect and the interviewer remain in the interview room, the recording may be stopped. There is no need to remove the recording media. The time of recommencement of the interview must be recorded.

Whenever there has been a break in questioning under caution the interviewer must ensure that the person being questioned is aware that he remains under caution. If there is a doubt, the caution must be renewed. The interviewer must bear in mind that he may have to satisfy a court that the person realised that the caution still applied. He may also have to show that nothing occurred during a break in an interview or between interviews which influenced the suspect's recorded evidence. In view of this, he should consider, at recommencement or at a subsequent interview, summarising on recording media the reason for the break and confirming this with the suspect. See p 120 concerning lengths of breaks.

Equipment failure

In the event of an equipment failure which can be rectified quickly, for example by inserting new recording media, this must be done following the procedures laid down in relation to the changing of recording media. When the recording is resumed, the interviewer must record the reason and the time the interview recommences. Where the further use of the audio recorder is impossible and no alternative is readily available, the interview may continue without being audibly recorded but the authority of the custody officer must first be obtained.

Where the media or recording equipment fails during the interview the interviewer should stop the interview immediately. Where part of the interview is unaffected by the error and is still accessible on the media, that media must be copied and sealed in the suspect's presence and the interview recommenced using new equipment/media as required. Where the content of the interview has been lost in its entirety the media should be sealed in the suspect's presence and the interview begun again.

At the end of an interview

At the conclusion of the interview, the suspect must be offered the opportunity to clarify anything he has said and asked if there is anything he wishes to add. At the conclusion of the interview, including the taking and reading back of any written statement, the time must be recorded and the audio recorder stopped. The 'master' recording must then be sealed with a master recording label and treated as an exhibit. The interviewer must sign the label and ask the suspect and any third party to sign it also. If either, or both, refuse to sign the label, an officer of at least the rank of inspector, or if one is not available the custody officer, must be called in to the interview room and asked to sign it. The suspect must be handed a notice explaining the use which will be made of the audio recording and the arrangements for access to it and explaining that a copy of the audio recording will be supplied as soon as practicable if the person is charged or informed that he will be prosecuted.

After the interview

The interviewer must make a note in his pocket book of the fact that the interview has taken place, was audibly recorded, of its time, duration and date and of the identification number of the master recording. Where no proceedings follow in respect of the person whose interview was recorded the recording media must nevertheless be kept securely as required by the Audio Recording Code. Where proceedings follow, the interviewer must prepare a written record of the interview and sign it. Any record of an audibly recorded interview should be made in accordance with the national guidelines approved by the Secretary of State. Before preparing it the interviewer may refresh his memory by listening to the working copy of the recording media to check its accuracy. The interview record must be exhibited to any written statement prepared by the interviewer. If the interviewer's evidence of the interview is accepted by the defence, the evidence must refer to the fact that the interview was audio recorded and may be presented to the court in the form of the interview record. Where the interviewer's evidence is not accepted by the defence, the interviewer must refer to the fact that the interview was audio recorded and produce the master recording medium of the whole interview, as an exhibit, informing the court of any transcription which has been made of which he is aware.

Media security

The security of master recordings is the responsibility of the officer in charge of each police station. A police officer must not break the seal on a master recording required for criminal trial or appeal proceedings, except in the presence of a representative of the Crown Prosecution Service. In such a case, the defendant, or his legal adviser, must be informed and be given a reasonable opportunity to be present. If either is present, he must be invited to reseal and sign the master recording. If not present, or in the event of refusal, this will be done by the representative of the Crown Prosecution Service. If the recording has been delivered to the Crown Court following sending for trial, the Crown Prosecutor will apply to the Chief Clerk of the Crown Court for the release of the media for unsealing by the Crown Prosecutor.

Visual recording of interviews

The provisions of the Visual Recording Code applied experimentally in the first instance to police interviews conducted in specified areas within which they were compulsory. The Code is closely modelled on the Audio Recording Code. The orders requiring the mandatory visual recording of interviews in those areas have since been revoked. The situation now is that police officers may choose to visually record, with sound, interviews with suspects; if they do, they must have regard to the terms of the Visual Recording Code.

The rules governing the conduct of visually recorded interviews largely follow those applicable to audibly-recorded interviews. The recording must be carried out openly and the cameras should be placed in the interview room so as to ensure coverage of as much of the room as possible. The 'certified recording medium' (VHS or digital CD format) must be previously unused and the correct date and time in hours, minutes and seconds will be superimposed automatically and be recorded throughout the filming process. The master copy must be sealed before leaving the presence of the suspect. A second copy will be used as a working copy. The usual safeguards apply to identification of officers in terrorism cases or where it is reasonably believed that identification might endanger the officers. Such officers will be seated with their backs to the camera and must use their warrant number and the name of the police station to which they are attached.

The procedure concerning the explanation and identification of persons present is the same as that which applies to audio recording. Similar provisions also apply to objections.

Should the recording media run out before the interview is concluded further certified recording media will be used. As recording media near completion, a suspect should be warned and allowed to wind up that part of the interview. A suspect must not be left alone in the room while a further recording media are sought. Care must be taken when a number of recording media have been used to ensure that they are properly identified. If a break is due, provided that the persons concerned do not leave the room, it is sufficient that the fact is recorded and the equipment is switched off. If persons are to leave the room, the equipment must be switched off, the recording media removed and the interview should be properly concluded by sealing the master with a label and treating it as an exhibit. The label should be signed by the interviewer who should ask the suspect and any other person present to sign also. If no other such person will sign, an officer of at least inspector rank should be asked to do so and, if no such officer is available, the custody officer should sign the label. In addition, the suspect will be given a notice which explains the use to which the recording will be put and the arrangements for access to it. The notice will also advise the suspect that a copy of the recording will be supplied as soon as practicable if the person is charged or informed that he will be prosecuted.

The same procedures apply in relation to the security of the master copy and the breaking of the seal on a master copy which is required for criminal trial or appeal procedures, as apply in the case of audio recording media.

Complaints

If, at any stage, the detained person makes a complaint concerning a matter covered by the Detention Code, the Audio Recording Code or the Visual Recording Code, it must be recorded in the interview record and the interviewing officer must inform the custody officer who must deal with it in accordance with the Detention Code (see 'Complaints—treatment', p 143).

Where, during the course of an interview which is being recorded, a complaint is made about a matter not connected with the Detention Code, the Audio Recording Code or the Visual Recording Code, the decision to continue the interview or terminate it is at the discretion of the interviewing officer. If continued, the officer must inform the complainant that the complaint will be brought to the attention of the custody officer at the conclusion of the interview, which must be done as soon as practicable thereafter. Where the interview is being audio recorded, the recording media should be left running until the custody officer has entered the room and has spoken to the interviewee. Continuation or termination of the interview should be at the discretion of the interviewing officer pending action by an inspector.

Where a person raises objections to an interview being visually recorded the interviewer must explain that the objection must be recorded on the visual recording, When any objections have been visually recorded, or the person refuses to have his objections so recorded, the interviewer must say that he is turning off the recorder, giving his reasons for doing so. If a separate audio recording is being made, the interviewer must ask the person to record the reasons for refusal to agree to visual recording. If the person objects to audio recording, the provisions of the Audio Recording Code relating to objections by suspects will apply.

Other points

The custody record must show the times during which the prisoner was not in the custody of the custody officer and the reason why he was removed from his custody; if a request for the delivery of a prisoner out of that custody was refused, the reason for refusal must be recorded. Decisions to defer breaks must be recorded, with grounds, in the interview record. Assuming he is still at the police station when it is made, the person interviewed must be allowed to read the interview record and to sign it as being correct or to indicate what he considers to be inaccurate, but no person may be kept in custody for this sole purpose.

In conclusion, it should be noted that the Codes of Practice do not prevent a police officer from asking questions at the scene of a crime to elicit an explanation which could provide the arrested person with the opportunity to show that he was innocent. The reason is obvious: since the questions are not asked with a view to establishing admissions on which proceedings can be founded, there is technically no interview for the purposes of the Codes. If, in the course of asking such questions a suspect makes a confession, it is prima facie admissible (even if the suspect is a juvenile and no appropriate adult is present).

In addition, there is no universal rule that, whenever there is a breach of a Code of Practice in a police interview, all subsequent interviews must be tainted and evidence of them excluded. Such a rule would fetter a judge's discretion under PACE, s 78, which depends upon the facts of the particular case.

Persons at risk—juveniles and persons affected

If the detainee is a juvenile, is mentally handicapped, or otherwise mentally vulnerable, the custody officer must, as soon as practicable, inform the appropriate adult of the grounds for his detention and his whereabouts, and ask the adult to come to the police station to see the person. It is irrelevant that the person concerned is able to understand procedures and answer questions; this does not obviate the need for an appropriate adult to assist, guide and protect him.

If a juvenile is known to be subject to a court order under which a person or organisation is given any degree of statutory responsibility to supervise or otherwise monitor him, reasonable steps must also be taken to notify that person or organisation (the responsible officer). The responsible officer will normally be a member of a youth offending team, except for a curfew order which involves electronic monitoring when the contractor providing the monitoring will normally be the responsible officer.

A juvenile or someone who is mentally disordered or mentally vulnerable must not be interviewed regarding his involvement or suspected involvement in a criminal offence or offences, or be asked to provide or sign a written statement under caution or record of an interview, in the absence of an appropriate adult unless the special circumstances set out in the Detention Code apply. These provisions are concerned with urgent interviews which are authorised by a superintendent. If a juvenile or mentally disordered or vulnerable person is cautioned in the absence of the appropriate adult, the caution must be repeated in the appropriate adult's presence. Such a person may not be asked to give or sign a written statement. An interview is an indivisible process. A failure to involve an appropriate adult in some part of it is a breach of the Detention Code and may render the whole of the interview inadmissible.

If, having been informed of his right to legal advice, the appropriate adult thinks that legal advice should be taken, the provisions of the Code relating to the right to legal advice (p 131) must be followed.

If the appropriate adult is not at the police station when the provisions of the Code dealing with the juvenile's rights are explained, the provisions must be complied with again in the presence of the appropriate adult once that person arrives.

Juveniles may only be interviewed at their places of education in exceptional circumstances and then only when the principal or his nominee agrees and is present.

Every effort should be made to contact both the parents, or other person responsible for the juvenile's welfare, and the appropriate adult (if a different person). A reasonable time should be allowed to enable the appropriate adult to attend. Where this would cause undue delay, and unless the offence is against the educational establishment, the principal or his nominee can act as the appropriate adult for the purposes of the interview.

Juveniles should not be arrested at their place of education unless this is unavoidable. If this occurs, the principal or his nominee must be informed.

A juvenile or someone who is mentally disordered or otherwise mentally vulnerable may be particularly open to suggestion. Consequently, special care should always be exercised in questioning such a person, and it is important to obtain corroboration of any facts admitted wherever possible.

If the appropriate adult is present at an interview, he should be informed of the reason for his presence. He should be told that he is not expected to act simply as an observer. He should also be informed that the purposes of his presence are:

(a) to advise the person being interviewed and to observe whether or not the interview is conducted fairly and properly; and
(b) to facilitate communication with the person being interviewed.

The Detention Code directs that if a person appears to be blind or seriously visually impaired or unable to read, deaf, or unable to speak or has difficulty orally because of a speech impediment, he should be treated as such for the purpose of the Code in the absence of clear evidence to the contrary.

If a person is blind, seriously visually impaired or unable to read, the custody officer must ensure that his solicitor, relative, the appropriate adult or some other person likely to take an interest in him (and not involved in the investigation) is available to help in checking any documentation. Where the Detention Code requires consent or signing, then the person who is assisting may be asked to sign instead, if the detained person so wishes. However, there is no requirement that an appropriate adult be called solely to assist in checking and signing documentation in such circumstances.

Some vulnerable persons may not be interviewed unless an officer of superintendent rank or above considers delay will lead to the consequences set out at in the second list on p 120, and is satisfied that the interview would not significantly harm the person's physical or mental state. They are:

(a) a juvenile or person who is mentally disordered or otherwise mentally vulnerable if at the time of the interview the appropriate adult is not present;
(b) any other person who appears to be unable to appreciate the significance of questions and their answers, or to understand what is happening because of the effects of drink, drugs or any illness, ailment or condition;
(c) a person who has difficulty understanding English or has a hearing disability, if an interpreter is not present.

Such interviews must not continue once sufficient information has been obtained to avert the consequences referred to above.

A record must be made of the grounds for any decision to interview in these circumstances.

Interpreters

Foreign languages

The Detention Code provides as follows:

(1) If a person has difficulty in understanding English, the interviewer cannot himself speak the person's own language and the person wishes an interpreter to be present, he must not be interviewed in the absence of a person capable of acting as an interpreter, unless special circumstances apply (potential interference, harm, loss, etc and urgent interviews with vulnerable suspects, see pp 120 and 129).

(2) The interviewer must ensure that the interpreter makes a note of the interview at the time in the language of the person being interviewed for use in the event of his being called to give evidence and that he certifies its accuracy. The interviewer should allow sufficient time for the interpreter to note each question and answer after each is put, given and interpreted. However, in the case of a recorded interview there is no requirement on the interviewer to ensure that the interpreter makes a separate note of the interview. The person must be given an opportunity to read it or have it read to him and sign it as correct or to indicate the respects in which he considers it to be inaccurate. If the interview is audibly recorded or visually recorded, the arrangements in the Audio Recording Code or Visual Recording Code, respectively, apply.

(3) In the case of a person making a statement in a language other than English:
  (a) the interpreter must take down the statement in the language in which it is made;
  (b) the person making the statement must be invited to sign the statement; and
  (c) an official English translation must be made in due course.

These provisions merely follow the rules of common sense, recognising the need for persons who experience difficulty in fully understanding a language to be given every opportunity to compensate for that lack and ensuring that they are not required subsequently to sign a document which they do not understand.

Whenever possible, interpreters should be drawn from the National Register of Public Service Interpreters (NRPSI) or the Council for the Advancement of Communication with Deaf People (CADCP) Directory of British Sign Language/English interpreters.

The deaf and those with a hearing or speech difficulties

The Detention Code provides as follows:

(1) If a person appears to be deaf or there is a doubt about his hearing or speaking ability, he must not be interviewed in the absence of an interpreter unless he agrees in writing to be interviewed without one or the special circumstances exist (potential interference, harm, loss etc, see pp 120 and 129). Likewise, an interpreter should also be called if a juvenile is interviewed and the parent or guardian present as the appropriate adult appears to be deaf or there is a doubt about his hearing or speaking ability, unless he agrees in writing that the interview should proceed without one or those special circumstances exist.

(2) The interviewer must ensure that the interpreter is given the chance to read the record of the interview and to certify its accuracy in the event of being called to give evidence.
(3) Where an interview is being audibly recorded or visually recorded, the arrangements in the relevant Recording Code apply.

Chief officers are responsible for ensuring that arrangements are in place for the provision of interpreters for the deaf and those who cannot speak English.

General

Interpreters will be provided at public expense and all reasonable attempts should be made to make this fact clear to a detained person. The interpreter may not be a police officer or civilian support staff when interpretation is needed for the purpose of obtaining legal advice. In all other cases, a police officer or civilian support staff may only interpret if the detained person (and the appropriate adult if applicable) agrees in writing or if the interview is audibly recorded or visually recorded.

If a person who has difficulty in understanding English is charged with an offence, and the interviewer cannot himself speak the person's language, arrangements must be made for an interpreter to explain as soon as practicable the offence concerned and any other information given by the custody officer.

Where a person in detention cannot communicate with a solicitor, whether because of language, hearing or speech difficulties, an interpreter must be called.

Where a person charged with an offence appears to be deaf, or there is doubt about his hearing or speaking ability or ability to understand English, and the custody officer cannot establish effective communication, arrangements must be made for an interpreter to explain as soon as practicable the offence concerned and any other information given by the custody officer.

Documentation and guidance

The action taken to call an interpreter must be recorded, together with any waiver of the right not to be interviewed in the absence of an interpreter. As the interpreter may be needed as a witness at the person's trial, a second interpreter will be needed at that trial.

Legal advice

Access to solicitor

By s 58 of PACE, a person arrested and held in police custody is entitled, if he so requests, to consult a solicitor privately at any time. The Detention Code provides that the consultation may be in person, in writing or by telephone, and that independent legal advice is available free of charge from the duty solicitor. If a person asks for legal advice, he must be permitted to consult a specific solicitor or another solicitor from that solicitor's firm or the duty solicitor. If advice is not available by these means, or he does not wish to consult the duty solicitor, a person must be given an opportunity to select a solicitor from a list of those willing to provide legal advice. Where a choice is unavailable, two alternatives may be chosen and the custody officer has discretion to allow further attempts. A police officer must not advise the suspect about any particular firm of solicitors. No police officer may at any time do or say anything with the intention of dissuading a person in detention from obtaining legal advice.

In the case of a juvenile, an appropriate adult should consider whether legal advice from a solicitor is required. If a juvenile indicates that legal advice is not required the appropriate adult has the right to ask for a solicitor to attend if this would be in the best interests of the person. However, the detained juvenile cannot be forced to see the solicitor if he is adamant that he does not wish to do so.

A detainee who requests legal advice must be permitted to consult a solicitor as soon as practicable, except to the extent that delay is permitted under PACE, s 58 and Code C, Annex B. Whenever legal advice is requested (and unless delay is so permitted), the custody officer must act without delay to secure the provision of such advice. If, on being informed or reminded of the right to legal advice, the person declines to speak to a solicitor in person, the officer must point out that the right to legal advice includes the right to speak to a solicitor on the telephone and ask him if he wishes to do so. If the person continues to waive his right to legal advice the officer must ask him his reasons for doing so. Any reasons shall be recorded on the custody record or the interview record as appropriate. Once it is clear that a person neither wishes to speak to a solicitor in person, nor by telephone, he should cease to be asked his reasons, as he is not obliged to give such reasons.

When a detainee exercises his right to legal advice by consulting or communicating with a solicitor, he must be allowed to do so in private. This is a fundamental right. Except as allowed by TA 2000, Sch 8, para 9, if the requirement for privacy is compromised because what is said or written by the detainee or the solicitor for the purpose of the giving or receiving of legal advice is overheard, listened to, or read by others without the informed consent of the detainee, the right will effectively have been denied. Where a detainee speaks to a solicitor or on the telephone, he should be allowed to do so in private unless this is impractical because of the design and layout of the custody area or the location of the telephones. However, the normal expectation should be that facilities will be available, unless they are being used, at all police stations to enable such private communications to be made.

Delay

The right of access to legal advice may be delayed if the person is in police detention for an indictable offence (see p 24), has not yet been charged, and an officer of the rank of superintendent (or above) authorises the delay. If such authorisation is given orally it must be confirmed in writing as soon as practicable. Delay may only be authorised under this power in two types of case specified in Annex B to the Detention Code.

The first is where the superintendent (or above) has reasonable grounds for believing that access to a solicitor at a time when the detainee wishes to have access:

(a) will lead to interference with or harm to evidence connected with an indictable offence or interference with or physical injury to other persons; or
(b) will lead to the alerting of other persons suspected of having committed such an offence but not yet arrested for it; or

(c) will hinder the recovery of any property obtained as a result of such an offence.

Superintendents should authorise such delays only after careful consideration of these issues.

The Court of Appeal has ruled that a superintendent, attempting to justify such a decision, will be unable to do so 'save by reference to specific circumstances, including evidence as to the person detained or the *actual solicitor* sought to be consulted'. Thus, if it is felt that a particular solicitor may by any means bring about one of the consequences at (a) to (c) above, that suspicion would only be relevant to that particular solicitor and would not apply to others selected by the accused. The court stated that a solicitor who deliberately did something, knowing that it would result in consequence (a), (b) or (c), would commit a serious criminal offence. A superintendent must believe that, accident apart, a solicitor would do so.

The second type of case is that a superintendent may also authorise delay where the officer has reasonable grounds to believe that:

(a) the person detained for an indictable offence has benefited from his criminal conduct (decided in accordance with the Proceeds of Crime Act 2002, Part 2); and
(b) the recovery of the value of the property constituting that benefit will be hindered by the exercise of either right.

Access to a solicitor may not be delayed on the ground that he may advise the person not to answer any questions or that he was initially asked to attend by someone other than the detained person, provided the latter wishes to see him. In the latter case the detained person must be told that the solicitor has come to the police station at another person's request, and must be asked to sign the custody record to signify whether or not he wishes to see the solicitor.

If delay is authorised the detainee must be told the reason and the reason must be noted in his custody record. Once the reason for delay ceases, there may be no further delay in permitting access to a solicitor. *In any case* the detainee must be permitted to consult a solicitor within thirty-six hours from the 'relevant time' (a term defined later).

There are similar, but not identical, provisions about delaying access to legal advice when a person is detained under TA 2000, s 41 or Sch 7.

Where such a delay has been authorised and an interview takes place, a court or jury may not draw adverse inferences from a suspect's silence.

Arrival of solicitor etc at police station

Unless Annex B applies, when a solicitor arrives at a police station to see a particular person, that person must be informed of his arrival whether or not he is being interviewed, and asked if he wishes to see the solicitor. This applies even if the suspect has declined legal advice or having requested it, subsequently agreed to be interviewed without receiving advice. The attendance and the detained person's decision must be recorded. Where a consultation is permitted, a solicitor (or his representative etc) is entitled to be present whilst the detained person is interviewed if the detained person so wishes.

Non-accredited or probationary representatives

For the purposes of the Codes a 'solicitor' is a person who holds a current practising certificate, or an accredited or probationary representative included on the register of representatives maintained by the Legal Services Commission.

If a solicitor wishes to send a non-accredited or probationary representative to provide advice on his behalf, then that person must be admitted to the police station for this purpose unless an officer of the rank of inspector or above considers that such a visit will hinder the investigation of crime and directs otherwise. (Hindering the investigation of crime does not include giving proper legal advice to a detained person.)

In exercising his discretion as to admittance to such a person, an inspector must take into account in particular whether the identity or status of the non-accredited or probationary representative has been satisfactorily established; whether he is of suitable character to provide legal advice (a person with a criminal record is unlikely to be suitable unless the conviction was for a minor offence and is not of recent date); and any other matters in any written letters of authorisation provided. However, the Court of Appeal has held that a chief constable is not entitled to make a blanket order banning a particular probationary solicitor's representative from all police stations in his area. He may advise his officers that a particular representative is likely to hinder an investigation but the officer dealing with the case must decide whether, in the particular circumstances, the representative should be excluded.

If an inspector refuses access to a non-accredited or probationary representative or a decision is taken that such a person shall not be permitted to remain at an interview, he must forthwith notify the solicitor on whose behalf the non-accredited or probationary representative was to have acted, or was acting, and give him an opportunity of making other arrangements. The detained person must also be informed and the custody record noted. If an inspector (or above) considers that a particular firm of solicitors is persistently sending non-accredited or probationary representatives who are unsuited to provide legal advice, he should inform a superintendent (or above), who may wish to take the matter up with the Law Society.

A breach of the requirement that suspects should generally be allowed access to a solicitor does not necessarily justify exclusion of evidence obtained at the interview. Where a challenge is made, the court must establish whether a request was made and whether it had been refused. If this is so it must then consider whether a delay in compliance with such a request was permissible under PACE, s 58. If it was not, the court must then consider whether the evidence obtained at the interview should be excluded under PACE, s 78 or by any rule of common law.

Removal of solicitor

A solicitor (or his representative etc) may only be required to leave if his conduct is such that the investigating officer is unable properly to put questions to the suspect.

The solicitor's only role in the police station is to protect and advance the legal rights of his client. On occasions this may require the solicitor to give advice which has the effect of avoiding his client giving evidence which strengthens a prosecution case. The solicitor may intervene to seek clarification or to challenge an improper question to his client or the manner in which it is put, or to advise his client not to reply to particular questions, or if he wishes to give his client further legal advice. He may only be required to leave in accordance with the Detention Code if his approach or conduct prevents or unreasonably obstructs proper questions being put to the suspect or his response being recorded, as where a solicitor answers on his client's behalf or provides written replies for his client to quote.

If the investigating officer considers that a solicitor is acting in such away, he will stop the interview and consult an officer not below the rank of superintendent, if one is readily available, and otherwise an officer not below the rank of inspector who is not concerned with the investigation. After speaking to the solicitor the officer who has been consulted will decide whether or not the interview should continue in the presence of the solicitor. If he decides that it should not, the suspect will be given an opportunity to consult another solicitor before the interview continues and that solicitor will be given an opportunity to be present.

The Detention Code points out that the removal of a solicitor from an interview is a serious step and, if it occurs, the officer of superintendent rank, or above, who took the decision will consider whether the incident should be reported to the Law Society. If the decision was taken by an officer below the rank of superintendent, a superintendent must consider whether to make such a report. A note of guidance in the Code points out that where an officer takes the decision to exclude a solicitor, he must be in a position to satisfy the court that the decision was properly made. In order to do this, he may need to witness what is happening himself.

Other points

A detained person must be permitted to consult a solicitor etc for a reasonable time before any court hearing. The European Court of Human Rights has held that a detained person has a right (arising from its interpretation of art 6(3)(c) of the European Convention on Human Rights (p 137)) to communicate with his solicitor etc out of hearing of a third party unless there is good cause for restricting the right. If the detained person is not permitted to have private communication without good cause and this prejudices his defence and his chance to a fair hearing in court, there will be a breach of the Convention.

Any request for legal advice, and the action taken on it, must be recorded in the custody record. If a person has asked for legal advice and an interview has commenced in the absence of his solicitor etc (or the solicitor etc is required to leave) a record must be made in the interview record.

A detained person who asks for legal advice *may not be interviewed or continue to be interviewed* until he has received it unless:

(a) a delay has been authorised in accordance with the provisions in Annex B to the Detention Code (pp 132–133) set out above, in which case the restriction on drawing inferences from silence in Annex C (p 113) will apply because the detainee is not allowed an opportunity to consult a solicitor; or

(b) a superintendent (or above) has reasonable grounds to believe that:

    (i) the consequent delay might lead to interference with, or harm to, evidence connected with an offence; lead to interference with, or harm to, other people; lead to serious loss of, or damage to, property; lead to alerting other people suspected of having committed an offence but not yet arrested for it; or hinder the recovery of property obtained in consequence of the commission of the offence, or

(ii) where a solicitor, including a duty solicitor, has been contacted and has agreed to attend, awaiting his arrival would cause unreasonable delay to the process of investigation.

In these instances the restriction upon drawing adverse inferences from silence in Annex C would apply; or

(c) the solicitor nominated by the person, or selected by him from a list, cannot be contacted, has previously indicated that he does not wish to be contacted, or having been contacted has declined to attend, and the person has been advised of the Duty Solicitor Scheme but has declined to ask for the duty solicitor, or the duty solicitor is not available. In these cases the restriction upon drawing inferences from silence will not apply because the detainee has been allowed an opportunity to consult a solicitor; or

(d) the detainee who wanted legal advice changes his mind. In such a case there will be no restriction upon inferences being drawn.

Where (c) applies, the interview may be started or continued without further delay provided that an inspector (or above) has agreed to the interview continuing.

Where (d) applies the interview may be started or continued without further delay provided that the person has given an agreement in writing, or on recording media, to being interviewed without receiving legal advice and that an inspector (or above), having inquired into the person's reasons for his change of mind, has given authority for the interview to proceed. Confirmation of the person's agreement, his change of mind, his reasons where given, and the name of the authorising officer, except in terrorism cases or cases where it might endanger the officer to do so, must be recorded in writing or in the interview record made in accordance with the relevant Recording Code, at the beginning or recommencement of the interview. It is permissible for such authorisation to be given over the telephone, if the authorising officer is able to satisfy himself as to the reason for the suspect's change of mind and is satisfied that it is proper to continue the interview in those circumstances. The name of the authorising officer and the reason for the suspect's change of mind should be recorded and repeated on the recording media at the beginning or recommencement of the interview.

In considering whether awaiting the arrival of a solicitor would cause unreasonable delay (see (b) above), the superintendent should, where practicable, ask the solicitor for an estimate of the time he is likely to take in coming to the station, and relate this to the time for which detention is permitted, to whether a required period of rest is imminent, and to the requirements of other investigations in progress. If the solicitor says that he is on his way or that he will set off immediately, it will not normally be appropriate to begin an interview before he arrives. If it appears that it will be necessary to begin an interview before the solicitor's arrival he should be given an indication of how long the police could wait so that he has the opportunity to make arrangements for someone else to provide legal advice.

If an interview is begun before a person who has asked for legal advice receives it on the ground under (b) above that delay will involve an immediate risk of harm or serious loss or damage, questioning may not continue until the person has received legal advice once sufficient information to avert the risk has been obtained unless some other ground for delay applies.

Right to liberty and security and the right to a fair trial under articles 5 and 6 of the European Convention on Human Rights

Article 5 provides:

1. Everyone has the right to liberty and security of person. No one shall be deprived of his liberty save in the following cases and in accordance with the procedure prescribed by law:
   (a) the lawful detention of a person after conviction by a competent court;
   (b) the lawful arrest or detention of a person for non-compliance with the lawful order of a court or in order to secure the fulfilment of any obligation prescribed by law;
   (c) the lawful arrest or detention of a person effected for the purpose of bringing him before the competent legal authority on reasonable suspicion of having committed an offence or when it is reasonably considered necessary to prevent his committing an offence or fleeing after having done so;
   (d) the detention of a minor by lawful order for the purpose of educational supervision or his lawful detention for the purpose of bringing him before the competent legal authority;
   (e) the lawful detention of persons for the prevention of the spreading of infectious diseases, of persons of unsound mind, alcoholics or drug addicts or vagrants;
   (f) the lawful arrest or detention of a person to prevent his effecting an unauthorised entry into the country or of a person against whom action is being taken with a view to deportation or extradition.
2. Everyone who is arrested shall be informed promptly, in a language which he understands, of the reasons for his arrest and of any charge against him.
3. Everyone arrested and detained in accordance with the provisions of paragraph 1(c) above, shall be brought promptly before a judge or other officer authorised by law to exercise judicial power and shall be entitled to trial within a reasonable time or to release pending trial. Release may be conditioned by guarantees to appear for trial.
4. Everyone who is deprived of his liberty by arrest or detention shall be entitled to take proceedings by which the lawfulness of his detention shall be decided speedily by a court and his release ordered if the detention is not lawful.
5. Everyone who has been the victim of arrest or detention in contravention of the provisions of this Article shall have an enforceable right to compensation.

As part of the right to a fair trial, art 6(3) of the Convention provides that:

Everyone charged with a criminal offence has the following minimum rights:
(a) to be informed promptly, in a language which he understands and in detail, of the nature and cause of the accusation against him;
(b) to have adequate time and facilities for the preparation of his defence;
(c) to defend himself in person or through legal assistance of his own choosing or, if he has not sufficient means to pay for legal assistance, to be given it free when the interests of justice so require;
(d) to examine or have examined witnesses against him and to obtain the attendance and examination of witnesses on his behalf under the same conditions as witnesses against him;
(e) to have the free assistance of an interpreter if he cannot understand or speak the language used in court.

In effect, the provisions within our laws governing the arrest and detention of persons, and the conduct of police officers, will be measured against the provisions of arts 5 and 6; in addition other articles may also be relevant, for example art 8 (the right to private life). Where it is found that any provision is incompatible with the European Convention, the provisions set out at p 4 in Chapter 1 will apply, and a breach of the Convention by a police officer will be an unlawful action for which damages may be awarded (see p 4). A divisional court has, for example, said that a delay in providing access to legal advice to a vulnerable person who was being interviewed was a breach of art 6. By way of further example, the European Court of Human Rights has held that the covert recording of a suspect in a police cell contravened art 8.

The important factor for police officers is that there is strict compliance with the Convention. Challenges made within the provisions of the Human Rights Act 1998 can only be made by individuals and not by organisations set up with the object of ensuring the maintenance of human rights.

Other implications of the Human Rights Act are discussed on p 262 in relation to the law of evidence and Chapter 31 in relation to public order.

CHAPTER 5

Treatment, charging and bail of detainees

The comments made at the beginning of Chapter 4 concerning references to the Detention Code and the Police and Criminal Evidence Act 1984 (PACE) apply equally to the provisions of this chapter.

TREATMENT OF DETAINEES

A person detained at a police station as a place of safety under the Mental Health Act 1983 should not be questioned about any alleged offence or asked to make a statement. However, where such a person is, after such detention, reasonably suspected of having driven a motor vehicle with excess alcohol, it is permissible to commence the breath testing procedure where the attendance of those required to carry out a medical examination cannot be expeditiously arranged.

Whenever the Detention Code requires a person to be given certain information he does not have to be given it if he is incapable at the time of understanding what is said to him or if he is violent or in urgent need of medical attention, but he must be given it as soon as practicable.

Where video cameras are installed in the custody area, suspects and other people entering should be informed by prominently placed notices that cameras are in use. Any request by a suspect or other person to have video cameras switched off should be refused.

The Detention Code lays down a large number of rules concerning conditions of detention and medical treatment.

Conditions of detention

(1) So far as practicable, not more than one person shall be detained in each cell.
(2) Cells in use must be adequately heated, cleaned and ventilated. They must be adequately lit, subject to such dimming as is compatible with safety and security

to allow people detained overnight to sleep. No additional restraints should be used within a locked cell unless absolutely necessary, and then only approved restraint equipment which is reasonable and necessary in the circumstances having regard to the detainee's demeanour and with a view to ensuring his safety and the safety of others. If the detainee is deaf, mentally disordered or otherwise mentally vulnerable, particular care must be taken when deciding whether to use any form of approved restraints.

(3) Blankets, mattresses, pillows and other bedding supplied should be of a reasonable standard and in a clean and sanitary condition.

(4) Access to toilet and washing facilities must be provided.

(5) If it is necessary to remove a person's clothes for the purpose of investigation, for hygiene or health reasons or for cleaning, replacement clothing of a reasonable standard of comfort and cleanliness must be provided. A person must not be interviewed unless adequate clothing has been offered to him.

(6) At least two light meals and one main meal must be offered in any period of twenty-four hours. Drinks should be provided at meal times and on reasonable request between meal times. Meals should, so far as practicable, be offered at recognised meal times, or at other times that take account of when the detainee last had a meal. Whenever necessary, advice must be sought from the appropriate health care professional (clinically qualified person working within the scope of his practice) on medical or dietary matters. As far as practicable, meals provided must offer a varied diet and meet any special dietary needs or religious beliefs that a person may have. At the custody officer's discretion, the detainee may also have meals supplied by his family or friends at his or their own expense. However, especially in the case of a person detained under the Terrorism Act 2000 (TA 2000), immigration detainees and others likely to be detained for an extended period, a custody officer is entitled to take account of the risk of items being concealed in any food or package and of his (the officer's) duties and responsibilities under food handling arrangements.

(7) Brief outdoor exercise must be offered daily if practicable.

(8) A juvenile must not be placed in a police cell, unless no other secure accommodation is available and the custody officer considers that it is not practicable to supervise him if he is not placed in a cell or the custody officer considers that a cell provides more comfortable accommodation than other secure accommodation in the police station.

(9) A juvenile must not be placed in a cell with a detained adult.

(10) Detainees should be visited at least every hour. If no reasonably foreseeable risk was identified in a risk assessment, a sleeping detainee need not be awakened. A person suspected of being intoxicated through drink or drugs or having swallowed drugs, or whose level of consciousness causes concern, must, subject to any clinical directions given by the appropriate health care professional, be visited and roused at least every half hour, have his condition assessed and clinical treatment arranged if appropriate. His condition must be assessed by entering the cell, calling his name and shaking him gently, before asking his name and where he lives as well as where he thinks he is. (Some strange replies may be received.) He should be asked to open his eyes and to lift one arm and then the other. (These provisions apply to a person in police custody by order of a magistrates' court under the Criminal Justice Act 1988 (CJA 1988), s 152 (as amended by the Drugs Act 2005 (DA 2005), s 8) to facilitate the

recovery of evidence where that person has been charged with drug possession or drug trafficking and is suspected of having swallowed drugs. In the case of the health care needs of a person who has swallowed the drugs, the custody officer, subject to any clinical direction, should consider the necessity for rousing every half hour. This does not negate the need for regular visiting of the suspect in the cell.)

The visitor must be aware of the possibility of illness, injury, or the existence of a mental condition. A drowsy person who smells of drink may have diabetes, epilepsy, a head injury, or drug intoxication or overdose, or may have suffered a stroke.

It is important to remember that a person who appears to be drunk or behaving abnormally may be suffering from illness or the effects of drugs or may have sustained injury (particularly a head injury) which is not apparent, and that someone addicted to certain drugs may experience harmful effects within a short time of being deprived of their supply. Consequently, police officers should always err on the side of caution when in doubt about calling an appropriate health care professional, and act with all due speed. A detainee may be dependent upon certain drugs, including alcohol, and may experience harmful effects within a short time of being deprived of their supply. In these circumstances an appropriate health care professional should be consulted or an ambulance should be called. A record must be made of any intoxicating liquor supplied. Annex G to Code C limits the circumstances in which persons under the influence of drink or drugs or whose mental state is affected in some other way, may be interviewed. Those detained under the Mental Health Act 1983, s136 (p 105) should be taken to a hospital whenever it is practicable.

Visits or rousing of detainees made in accordance with the Code, or in accordance with medical advice, do not constitute an interruption to a rest period such that a fresh period must be allowed. Should the custody officer feel in any way concerned about the person's condition, for example because he fails to respond adequately when roused, then the officer must arrange for medical treatment. Nothing in the Code prevents the police from calling a police surgeon or, if appropriate, some other health care professional, to examine a detainee for the purpose of obtaining evidence relating to an offence in which he is suspected of being involved.

Documentation

A record must be kept of replacement clothing and meals offered. If a juvenile is placed in a cell, the reason must be recorded. The use of any restraints, the reason for such use and any arrangements for enhanced supervision must be recorded.

Clinical treatment and attention

(1) A custody officer must make sure that a detainee receives appropriate clinical attention as soon as reasonably practicable if that person appears to be suffering from physical illness, is injured, appears to be suffering from mental disorder or appears to need clinical attention. This applies even if no request for such attention has been received or if clinical attention has already been received elsewhere. If a detainee requests a clinical examination an appropriate health

care professional must be called. If an appropriate care plan cannot be produced, the advice of a police surgeon must be obtained. The custody officer must also consider the need for clinical attention in relation to those suffering from the effects of alcohol or drugs.

These rules about seeking medical attention are not intended to delay the transfer of a person to a place of safety under the Mental Health Act 1983, s 136, where that is applicable. Where an assessment under that Act takes place, the custody officer must consider whether an appropriate health care professional should be called to conduct an initial check on the detainee. This applies particularly where there is likely to be any significant delay in the arrival of a suitably qualified medical practitioner.

(2) If it appears to the custody officer, or he is told, that a person brought to the police station under arrest may be suffering from an infectious disease or condition, reasonable steps must be taken to safeguard the health of the detainee and others. Advice must be sought from an appropriate health care professional. The person and his property may be isolated pending clinical direction.

(3) If a detainee requests a clinical examination, an appropriate health care professional must be called as soon as practicable. If a safe and appropriate health care plan cannot be provided, the police surgeon's advice must be sought.

(4) If a detainee is required to take or apply any medication in compliance with clinical directions prescribed before his detention, the custody officer must consult the appropriate health care professional prior to the use of the medication; such consultation and its outcome must be noted in the custody record. The custody officer is responsible for the safekeeping of any medication and for ensuring that the detainee is given the opportunity to take or apply prescribed or approved medication. However, no police officer may administer medicines which are also controlled drugs subject to the Misuse of Drugs Regulations 2001, Sch 1, 2, or 3. A detainee may administer controlled drugs to himself only under the personal supervision of the registered medical practitioner authorising their use. Drugs listed in Sch 4 or 5 of the 2001 Regulations may be distributed by the custody officer for self-administration if the medical practitioner authorising their use has been consulted (which may be done by telephone) and both parties are satisfied that self-administration will not expose the detainee, police officers or anyone to the risk of harm or injury.

(5) Where appropriate health care professionals administer drugs or other medication, or supervise self-administration, it must be within the scope of their practice as defined by their professional body.

(6) If a detainee has in his possession, or claims to need, medication relating to a heart condition, diabetes, epilepsy or a condition of comparable potential seriousness then, even though (1), above, may not apply, the advice of the police surgeon must be obtained.

A record must be made in the custody record of any complaint made, together with a record of any clinical attention received, and of any request for a clinical examination under (3) and arrangements made in response. A note should also be made of any injury, ailment or condition causing such arrangements to be made, together with clinical directions and advice or clarifications given by a health care professional. Where applicable, a note should be made of responses made when attempting to rouse a detainee. Should a health care professional not record his clinical findings in the custody record, a note must be made in it of where the findings are recorded. Information necessary to ensure ongoing care and well being of a detainee must be recorded openly in the custody record. A custody record must include all medication in the possession of a detainee on his arrival, together with a note of medication which he claims to need.

Whenever an appropriate health care professional is consulted, the custody officer must ask for an opinion concerning risks or problems which need to be taken into account when making a decision about detention, when to carry out an interview if applicable and the need for safeguards. Any doubts concerning directions, particularly in relation to the frequency of visits, must be cleared up.

Complaints—treatment

If a complaint is made by or on behalf of a detainee about his treatment since his arrest, or it comes to the notice of any officer that he may have been treated improperly, a report must be made as soon as practicable to an officer of the rank of inspector (or above) who is not connected with the investigation. If the matter concerns a possible assault or the unnecessary or unreasonable use of force, the appropriate health care professional must also be called as soon as practicable; a record must be made of any arrangements made.

A record must be made of any complaint reported under the above provisions, together with any relevant remarks by the custody officer.

Independent custody visitors for places of detention

The Police Reform Act 2002, s 51 requires police authorities to make arrangements for detainees to be visited by persons appointed (independent custody visitors). They must be independent of both the police authority and the chief officer. The arrangements may provide rights of access to police stations; examination of records; meetings with detainees and the inspection of facilities. Access to a detainee may be denied if:

(a) it appears to an officer of or above the rank of inspector that there are grounds for doing so at the time that it is requested;
(b) those grounds are specified within the arrangements; and
(c) the procedural requirements imposed by the arrangements in relation to a denial of access are complied with.

The Secretary of State may issue a code of practice as to the carrying out by police authorities and independent custody visitors of their functions under the arrangements. The notice of rights and entitlements given to detainees explains that 'visitors' are members of the community who are allowed access to police stations unannounced to ensure that detainees have access to their rights. It explains that a detainee does not have a right to see an independent custody visitor and that he cannot request to see one; that such a visitor acts independently of the police to check that welfare rights are protected; and that the detainee does not have to speak to such a visitor if he does not wish to do so.

RECEPTION OF ARRESTED PERSONS AT POLICE STATIONS

PACE, s 35(1) requires that chief officers of police designate the police stations in their area which are to be used for the purpose of detaining arrested persons; their duty is to designate police stations which appear to them to provide sufficient accommodation for detaining arrested persons. By s 35(2A) the Chief Constable of the British Transport Police may designate police stations which (in addition to those designated under s 35(1)) may be used for the purpose of detaining arrested persons. Where a station is designated under s 35(1) or (2A), s 36 requires that one or more custody officers must be appointed by the relevant Chief Constable or his nominee. They must be of the rank of sergeant (or above) or (when the Serious Organised Crime and Police Act 2005, s 121 is in force) a staff custody officer, but the section allows another officer of any rank to perform the duties of a custody officer at a designated police station if such an officer is not readily available to perform those duties. Such an officer is only not 'readily available' if he is not actually at the police station and cannot, without much difficulty, be fetched there.

Where an arrested person is taken to a non-designated police station any individual not concerned in the investigation of the offence may, by PACE, s 36, assume the responsibilities of a custody officer or a staff custody officer. If no such officer or staff custody officer is available, it may be the arresting officer.

A custody officer's duties are laid down by PACE, ss 37 to 39 (dealt with on pp 146–147 and 171–172). Basically, and this is provided for by s 39, he is responsible for persons in detention and for ensuring that they and their property are treated in accordance with the Detention Code, and he is responsible for maintaining a chronological and contemporaneous record of every aspect of a person's treatment whilst in detention. These responsibilities cannot be overstated. The provisions in relation to detention are quite complex and the keeping of such a log means that omissions in the keeping of it cannot be corrected. If a duty is carried out but not recorded, the failure to record as required by the Codes is sufficient to raise the issue of disciplinary proceedings. Generally, custody officers must be independent of investigations in respect of detainees, but may be involved in identification processes or the obtaining of specimens of breath, blood or urine in accordance with the Road Traffic Act 1988, s 7.

Where PACE and its Codes require that certain things are done by a custody officer, the requirement also applies to a police officer other than a custody officer who is performing the functions of a custody officer.

Where a person has been arrested, a custody officer does not have to satisfy himself that the arrest is lawful before he can hold the arrested person in lawful custody.

A custody officer is required to perform the functions specified in the Detention Code as soon as is practicable. A custody officer is not in breach of the Code in the event of delay provided that the delay is justifiable and that every reasonable step is taken to prevent unnecessary delay. The custody record must indicate where a delay has occurred and the reason why.

Delays may occur in the processing of suspects because, for example, a large number of suspects are brought into the police station simultaneously to be placed in custody, or interview rooms are all being used, or where there are difficulties in contacting an appropriate adult, solicitor or interpreter.

Police detention

A person is stated by PACE, s 118 to be in police detention for the purposes of the Act if:

(a) he has been taken to a police station after being arrested for an offence, or after being arrested by a police officer under TA 2000, s 41 on reasonable suspicion of being a terrorist; or

(b) he is arrested at a police station after attending voluntarily at the station or accompanying a constable to it; and is detained there or is detained elsewhere in the charge of a constable.

In most circumstances, of course, a person's detention begins under (a) on arrival at a police station under arrest. If a person is subsequently removed from a police station, for example, to attend an identification parade or to visit the scene of a crime or on transfer to another station, he is in detention whilst he remains in the charge of a constable. This is important when periods of detention are to be considered by custody officers. By way of an exception, s 118 provides that a person who is at a court after being charged is not in police detention for the purposes of the Act.

As we have already stated, a separate custody record must be opened as soon as practicable for each person detained at a police station.

Limitations on police detention

PACE, s 34 provides that a person arrested for an offence (as opposed to a breach of the peace, which is not an offence) must not be kept in police detention, except in accordance with the provisions outlined below. However, no person in police detention may be released except on the authority of a custody officer.

Section 34 requires that if at any time a custody officer:

(a) becomes aware, in relation to any person in police detention at that station, that the grounds for the detention of that person have ceased to apply; and

(b) is not aware of any other grounds on which the continued detention of that person could be justified under the provisions of the Act,

the custody officer must order his immediate release from custody. However, persons who were unlawfully at large when arrested must not be released under these provisions. A person released in these circumstances must be released without bail, unless it appears to the custody officer that there is a need for further investigation of any matter in connection with which he was detained at any time during the period of his detention, or that in respect of any such matter proceedings may be taken against him or he may be reprimanded or warned under the Crime and Disorder Act 1998, s 65 (which is only possible where the offender is under eighteen), in which case he must be released on bail.

An investigating officer may bring facts to the notice of a custody officer but issues of further detention or release are to be decided by the custody officer. It will be appreciated that custody officers may find themselves in dispute with officers of senior rank in respect of detention issues. If this occurs the superintendent responsible for the police station must be consulted.

Duties of custody officer before charge

PACE, s 37 states that the decision as to whether or not there is sufficient evidence to charge a detainee arrested without warrant, or on a warrant which is not endorsed for bail, with the offence for which he was arrested is that of the custody officer. The person may be detained at a police station for such period as is necessary for him to make that decision. The custody officer must record on the custody record the offence(s) for which the detainee has been arrested (and the reasons). He should also note on the custody record any comment the person may make in relation to the arresting officer's account but should not invite comment. If the custody officer authorises a person's detention he must inform him of the grounds as soon as practicable and in any case before that person is then questioned about any offence. The custody officer must note on the custody record any comment the person may make in respect of the decision to detain him but may not invite comment, nor may he put specific questions to the person concerning his involvement in any offence, nor in respect of any comments he may make in response to the investigating officer's account or the decision to place him in detention. Such an exchange is likely to constitute an interview and would require the necessary safeguards. Section 37(2) provides that, if there is insufficient evidence of an offence, the custody officer must release that person either with or without bail, unless he has reasonable grounds for believing that detention is necessary to secure or preserve evidence of the offence or to obtain evidence by questioning him. If the person is detained without charge, the grounds must be recorded as soon as practicable by the custody officer.

Section 37(7) provides that, if the custody officer determines that he has sufficient evidence to charge the person arrested for the offence for which he was arrested, that person must:

(a) be released without charge and on bail for the purpose of enabling the Director of Public Prosecutions (DPP) to make a decision about charging or cautioning him;
(b) be released without charge and on bail but not for that purpose;
(c) be released without charge and without bail; or
(d) be charged.

By way of exception, if the person arrested is not in a fit state to be dealt with in this way (eg because he is under the influence of drink or drugs), he may be kept in police detention until he is in a fit state. If a person is released without charge and on bail under (a), the custody officer must inform him that he is being released to enable the DPP to make a decision about charging or cautioning him. In such a case, an officer involved in the investigation must send specified information to the DPP. The DPP must decide whether there is sufficient evidence to charge the person; must then decide whether he should be charged; and if so specify the offence and state whether the person might be given a caution (conditional caution, warning or reprimand). The DPP must notify the officer of his decision, at which stage the person must be charged, cautioned or told that he has been released from his bail. If a person is arrested for a breach of bail granted under these circumstances he may be charged or released without charge, either on bail or without bail. The custody officer may subsequently appoint a different time, or an additional time, at which the person must attend a police station. A person who surrenders to such bail may be kept in police detention to enable him to be dealt with.

If a person is released without charge under (b) or (c), and a decision has not yet been taken whether he should be prosecuted, the custody officer must inform him of this.

PACE, s 37A provides that the DPP may issue guidance in relation to decisions as to how persons should be dealt with under s 37(7) and also concerning the information to be sent to him so that he may make a decision. The Director must publish such guidance and any revisions which he may make.

Where the offence for which the person is arrested is one in relation to which a sample could be taken for a drug test under PACE, s 63B (see p 148) and the custody officer is required by s 37(2) to release that person and decides to release him on bail or decides in pursuance of s 37(7) to release that person without charge on bail, the detention of that person may be continued to enable such a sample to be taken, but this does not permit a person to be detained for more than twenty-four hours after the relevant time (as defined on pp 164–165).

Regulations made under PACE, s 45A may also provide for the functions relating to an arrested person taken to a non-designated police station, which, in the case of an arrested person taken to a designated police station, are a custody officer's functions under PACE, s 37, to be exercised by video-link facilities.

Conditional caution

The CJA 2003, Part 3 makes provision for 'conditional cautions'. An authorised person may give a conditional caution to a person aged eighteen or over if:

(a) he has evidence that the offender has committed the offence;
(b) a relevant prosecutor (the DPP and other official prosecution agencies, but not the police) has decided that there is sufficient evidence to charge him and that a conditional caution should be given;
(c) the offender admits the offence;
(d) the authorised person has explained the effect of the conditional caution to the offender and has warned him that failure to comply with any of the conditions may result in a prosecution for the offence; and
(e) the offender has signed a document which contains details of the offence; an admission of guilt; his consent to being given a conditional caution; and the conditions attached to the caution.

The conditions which may be attached to such a caution must have the object of facilitating the rehabilitation of the offender and ensuring that he makes reparation for his offence.

An 'authorised person' is a constable, an investigating officer, or a person authorised by a relevant prosecutor.

If an offender fails, without reasonable excuse, to comply with any of the conditions attached to the conditional caution, criminal proceedings may be instituted for the original offence and the documents referred to above are admissible in evidence. The caution ceases to have effect with the institution of proceedings.

The Secretary of State has issued a code of practice in relation to conditional cautions. Provision is made for the National Probation Service to provide assistance to authorised persons in deciding whether conditional cautions should be given, the conditions which might be attached and the supervision and rehabilitation of persons so cautioned.

Drug testing

PACE, s 63B permits the taking of urine or non-intimate samples from someone for the purpose of ascertaining whether he has any *specified* Class A drug in his body where:

(a) either the arrest condition or the charge condition is met;
(b) both the age condition and the request condition are met; and
(c) the notification condition is met in relation to the arrest condition, the charge condition or the age condition (as the case may be).

The arrest condition is that the person concerned has been arrested for an offence but has not been charged with that offence and either:

(a) that offence is a 'trigger offence' (theft, attempted theft, robbery, attempted robbery, burglary, attempted burglary, aggravated burglary, taking a motor vehicle or other conveyance without authority, aggravated vehicle-taking, obtaining property by means of fraud, attempted obtaining property by means of fraud, handling stolen goods or attempted handling, going equipped for stealing etc, and an offence under the Misuse of Drugs Act 1971 if committed in respect of a specified Class A drug (see below) associated with producing and supplying a controlled drug, possessing a controlled drug, or possessing a controlled drug with intent to supply, and begging or persistent begging contrary to the Vagrancy Act 1824, s 3 or s 4 respectively); or
(b) an inspector (or above), who has reasonable grounds for suspecting that the misuse by that person of any specified Class A drug caused or contributed to the offence, has authorised such a sample to be taken.

The charge condition is either:

(a) that the person concerned has been charged with a trigger offence; or
(b) that the person concerned has been charged with an offence and a police officer of at least the rank of inspector, who has reasonable grounds for suspecting that the misuse by that person of any specified Class A drug (ie cocaine and diamorphine (heroin), their salts and any preparation containing either drug or its salts) caused or contributed to the offence, has authorised the sample to be taken.

The age condition is:

(a) if the arrest condition is met, that the person concerned has attained the age of eighteen;
(b) if the charge condition is met, that he has attained the age of fourteen.

The request condition is that a police officer has requested the person concerned to give the sample (which in the case of a person under seventeen must be done in the presence of an appropriate adult).

The notification condition is that:

(a) the relevant chief officer has been notified by the Secretary of State that appropriate arrangements have been made for the police area as a whole, or for the particular police station, in which the person is in police detention, and
(b) the notice has not been withdrawn.

For the purposes of (a) appropriate arrangements are arrangements for taking samples under s 63B from whichever of the following is specified in the notification:

(a) persons in respect of whom the arrest condition is met;
(b) persons in respect of whom the charge conditions is met;
(c) persons who have not attained the age of eighteen.

Notification is treated as having been given for the purposes of the charge condition in relation to a police area if testing on charge was in force immediately before 1 December 2005; and for the purposes of the age condition, in relation to a police area or police station, if immediately before that day, notification that arrangements had been made for the taking of samples from persons under the age of eighteen (those aged fourteen to seventeen) had been given and had not been withdrawn.

Where a sample is taken from a person who satisfies the arrest condition, no other sample may be taken during the same continuous period of detention, but if the charge condition is met during that period, the sample already taken must be treated as one taken after charge. This must be recorded in the custody record.

In circumstances in which a person is arrested for a first offence which satisfies the arrest condition but not the charge condition and he would normally be liable to be released from custody before a sample is taken, but he remains in custody by reason of arrest for another offence not falling within the arrest condition, a sample may be taken before the end of a period of twenty-four hours following his *initial* arrest.

A sample must not be taken from a person in custody unless he is brought before the custody officer. It may only be taken by a person authorised by the Police and Criminal Evidence act 1984 (Drug Testing of Persons in Police Detention) Prescribed Persons Regulations 2001, viz a police officer or a person whose duties include taking samples for testing for the presence of specified Class A drugs. A sample may be taken from someone under seventeen only in the presence of an appropriate adult.

Information obtained from a sample taken under s 63B may be disclosed:

(a) for the purpose of informing any decision about granting bail in criminal proceedings (within the meaning of the Bail Act 1976 (BA 1976)) to the person concerned;
(b) for the purpose of informing any decision about the giving of a conditional caution under CJA 2003, Part 3 to the person concerned;
(c) where the person concerned is in police detention or is remanded in or committed to custody by an order of a court or has been granted such bail, for the purpose of informing any decision about his supervision;
(d) where the person concerned is convicted of an offence, for the purpose of informing any decision about the appropriate sentence to be passed by a court and any decision about his supervision or release;
(e) for the purpose of an initial or follow-up assessment which the person concerned is required to attend;
(f) for the purpose of proceedings against the person concerned for an offence of failing to attend such an assessment;
(g) for the purpose of ensuring that appropriate advice and treatment is made available to the person concerned.

A request for a sample must be preceded by an explanation of its purpose (to ascertain whether there is a specified Class A drug in his body); that failure without good cause to provide such a sample may make the person requested liable to prosecution; and, where authorised under (b) above, the grounds for giving the authorisation. In addition, the person requested must be reminded of his right to have someone informed of his arrest; of his right to consult privately with a solicitor; of the availability free of charge of independent legal advice, and of the right to consult the relevant code of practice. When warning a person who is asked to provide a urine or non-intimate sample, the following form of words may be used:

> 'You do not have to provide a sample, but I must warn you that if you fail or refuse without good cause to do so, you will commit an offence for which you may be imprisoned, or fined, or both.'

Custody officers may authorise continued detention for up to six hours from the time of charge to enable a sample to be taken. Where a sample is taken following authorisation by an inspector (or above), the authorisation and the grounds for suspicion must be recorded in the custody records. An authorisation given by an inspector may be given orally but must subsequently be confirmed in writing as soon as practicable. Details of authorisations and the giving of warnings must be recorded, together with the time of charge and the time at which a sample was given.

A person who fails without good cause to give any sample which may be taken from him is guilty of an offence.

Initial assessment

Where an analysis of a sample reveals the presence of a Class A drug a police officer may, at any time before the person's release, require a person of eighteen or over to attend an 'initial assessment' and to remain for its duration. A qualified 'initial assessor' will seek to establish dependency or a tendency to misuse any specified Class A drug and whether the person will benefit from further assessment or advice. If an initial assessor finds that a follow-up assessment is appropriate, he must inform the person of the time and place at which it is to take place, confirm this in writing and warn the person of he consequence of failing to attend.

Follow-up assessment

The police officer may, at the same time as he imposes a requirement to attend an initial assessment, require the person to attend a follow-up assessment and to remain for its duration. This requirement ceases to have effect if cancelled at the initial assessment. A follow-up interview will be concerned with a 'care plan'. If, at initial assessment, the assessor considers that a follow-up assessment is not appropriate, it may be cancelled. The provisions relating to follow-up assessments were not in force at the time of writing.

Attendance at assessments

A constable must inform the detainee (to be confirmed in writing) that failure to attend either or both forms of assessment without good cause, may result in prosecution. This must be done prior to release from custody and a record must be made in the custody record.

The DA 2005, s 12 provides that a person who is required to attend an initial assessment commits an offence if he fails, without good cause, to attend at the specified time and place, or attends but fails to remain for the duration of the assessment. Where such a failure occurs, any requirement imposed in relation to a follow-on assessment ceases to have effect. It is an offence against s 14 (not in force at the time of writing) to fail, without good cause, to attend a follow-on assessment. These offences are not committed if a subsequent analysis of a sample reveals that a specified Class A drug was not present in the person's body. This is because any requirement imposed ceases to have effect.

Information to be given to detainees

When the custody officer authorises the detention of a person who has not been charged, he is required by PACE, s 37 to make, as soon as practicable, a written record on the custody record of the grounds which exist for detention. This must be done in the person's presence and he must be informed at that time of those grounds. If he is asleep he must be woken and told. (However, if at that time a person is incapable of understanding what is said to him or is violent or is likely to be so, or is in urgent need of medical treatment, the information may be given as soon as practicable, and in any case before he is questioned for the offence.) At the same time the detainee must be informed clearly of the following rights: his right to have someone informed of his arrest, his right to consult privately with a solicitor and the fact that independent legal advice is available free of charge, and his right to consult the Codes of Practice (which must be available at all police stations). The detainee must also be told that he need not exercise those rights immediately; they may be exercised at any time whilst in detention.

The custody officer must also determine whether the detainee may be in need of medical treatment, requires an appropriate adult, requires assistance to check documentation or an interpreter and record his decisions in this respect. The custody officer must make a risk assessment in relation to himself or custody staff which should include a PNC. It may be necessary for him to consult others, eg the arresting officer or a health care professional. Chief officers are required to ensure a 'structured process' in this respect. The custody officer is responsible for implementing responses to such risks. The detainee must be given a written notice setting out those rights (audio versions must also be available) and informing him of his right to a copy of the custody record at the time of his release. The written notice must also set out the caution in the terms already described and explain the arrangements for obtaining legal advice. The custody officer must also give the detainee an additional notice setting out his entitlements while in custody, which have been described above. The custody officer should obtain the person's signature on the custody record acknowledging receipt of these notices; any refusal to sign must be recorded on the custody record. The person must be asked to signify on the custody record whether or not he wants legal advice at this stage. Where legal advice is requested (and unless delay has been validly authorised, see p 132), the custody officer must act without delay to secure the provision of such advice to the person concerned. A person attending a police station voluntarily who asks about his entitlement to legal advice should also be given such a notice.

The provisions concerning persons with language difficulties, those mentally ill etc, and juveniles, which have already been outlined in respect of persons being interviewed, apply equally to persons in custody. If the appropriate adult is already at the police station when information is given to the detainee under the above provisions, the information must be given to the detainee in his presence. If the appropriate adult is not then present, the information must be given to the detainee again in the presence of the appropriate adult once he arrives.

Communication by detainees with others

Notification of detention

A detainee has a right under PACE, s 56 to have someone informed at public expense and as soon as practicable of his detention. However, this extends only to one friend, relative or other person who is known to him or is likely to take an interest in his welfare. If the person cannot be contacted, the detainee may choose up to two alternatives. If they cannot be contacted the custody officer may allow further attempts. If a person is moved from one police station to another, the right to have someone informed of his whereabouts arises again.

PACE, s 56, together with Annex B to the Detention Code, provides that a delay in informing someone may be authorised by an inspector (or above) where the person is in police detention for an indictable offence and has not been charged with it. In such circumstances, the authorisation may only be given in two types of case. The first is where the inspector has reasonable grounds for believing that telling the person named of the arrest:

(a) will lead to interference with, or harm to, evidence connected with an indictable offence or interference with or physical harm to other persons; or

(b) will lead to the alerting of other persons suspected of having committed such an offence but not yet arrested for it; or

(c) will hinder the recovery of any property obtained as a result of such an offence.

The second type of case is that an inspector (or above) may also authorise delay where he has reasonable grounds for believing that the person detained for an indictable offence has benefited from his criminal activity (decided in accordance with Part 2 of the Proceeds of Crime Act 2002) and that the recovery of the value of the property constituting that benefit will be hindered by the exercise of either right.

There are similar, but not identical, grounds for delay where a person is detained under the TA 2000, s 41 or Sch 7. In such a case delay can only be authorised by a superintendent (or above) who has reasonable grounds to believe the necessary things.

If a delay is authorised, then, as soon as possible, the detainee must be informed of the reason for it and the reason must be noted on his custody record. If given orally, the authorisation must be confirmed in writing as soon as practicable. When the reasons for delay have been removed, for example by the arrest of other persons, the request to communicate must be granted. The right to communicate cannot be delayed for more than thirty-six hours.

Where an arrest is made under the TA 2000 communication to a friend etc may be delayed up to forty-eight hours.

Any delay authorised under the above provisions should be proportionate and last no longer than necessary.

Visits, letters and phone calls

A person in detention may receive visits at the discretion of the custody officer. Where inquiries by interested persons are received concerning his whereabouts, the information must be given if the detainee agrees and a superintendent (or above) has not authorised delay in the release of such information. The custody officer must exercise his discretion as to visits in the light of the availability of sufficient manpower to supervise a visit and any possible hindrance to the investigation.

The detainee must also be supplied on request with writing material. Letters and messages must be sent (at his expense) as soon as practicable, but all letters, other than those to his solicitor, may be read. The detainee may speak for a reasonable time to one person on the telephone. Whether or not the call can be made at police expense is a matter for the custody officer's discretion. Reasonable calls of a local character will probably be allowed at police expense. Unless the call is to a solicitor, a police officer may listen to the call and may terminate it if it is being abused. The detainee must be cautioned that what he says in a letter, call or message (other than to his solicitor) may be read or listened to and may be given in evidence. An interpreter may make a call on behalf of a detainee. Where an officer of the rank of inspector or above considers that the sending of a letter or the making of a telephone call may result in any of the consequences referred to in the list on p 152, and the person is detained in connection with an indictable offence or under TA 2000, s 41 or Sch 7, that officer can deny or delay the exercise of either or both these privileges.

Any delay or denial of these rights should be proportionate and should last no longer than necessary.

A record must be kept:

(a) of any request made in relation to matters of communication and of the action taken in consequence of that request;

(b) of letters or messages sent, calls made or visits received; and

(c) of any refusal by the prisoner to have information about himself or his whereabouts given to an outside inquirer.

The prisoner must be asked to countersign the record accordingly and any refusal to do so should be recorded.

Children and young persons

Where a child or young person is in police detention, the Children and Young Persons Act 1933 (CYPA 1933), s 34 requires that his parent or guardian must be informed as soon as practicable that he has been arrested; why he was arrested; and where he is being detained. If a court order is in force under which a person or organisation is given any degree of statutory responsibility to supervise or monitor the juvenile, reasonable steps must be taken to notify that person or organisation (the 'responsible officer' who will normally be a member of a youth offending team, except for a curfew order which involves electronic monitoring when the contractor providing the monitoring will normally be the responsible officer). If the juvenile is in care, the care authority or voluntary organisation must be informed in place of the parent or guardian. Such steps as are practicable must be taken to identify the person responsible for the juvenile's welfare.

For the purposes of CYPA 1933, s 34 a young person is a person who has attained the age of fourteen years and is under the age of seventeen years.

Aliens etc

The Detention Code provides that a citizen of an independent Commonwealth country or a foreign national may communicate at any time with his High Commission, Embassy or Consulate. Such a person must be informed as soon as practicable after being detained of his right to communicate with such agencies, and such agencies must be informed of an arrest. Consular officers may visit to advise such persons and those visits must take place out of the hearing of a police officer.

FURTHER RIGHTS OF PERSONS DETAINED

Access to legal advice

This matter has been dealt with in the previous chapter.

Searching and retention of property

PACE, s 54 charges the custody officer with a duty to ascertain the property which a person has with him when he is:

(a) brought to a police station after being arrested elsewhere or after being committed to custody by an order or a sentence of a court; or

(b) arrested at a police station or detained there when answering police bail or is arrested under PACE, s 46A (failure to answer police bail (see p 174)),

and the custody officer may record all or any of the items which he finds. In the case of an arrested person, this may be done in the custody record. To do this a person may be searched to the extent considered to be necessary by the custody officer, but an intimate search may not be carried out under s 54, and a strip search may only be carried out if the necessary requirements set out below are satisfied.

Articles other than those subject to legal privilege (eg letters from solicitors etc) may be seized and retained. However, clothes and personal effects (which do not include cash) may only be seized if the custody officer believes that they may be used by the person:

(a) to cause physical injury to himself or another;

(b) to damage property;

(c) to interfere with evidence;

(d) to assist him to escape,

or if the custody officer has *reasonable grounds* for believing that they may be evidence of an offence.

There will be some difficult decisions to be taken by custody officers who are required to allow a person in custody to retain property of a personal, non-dangerous character. Is a woman's vanity mirror likely to cause harm? It will not do so whilst it remains in its original condition but it will certainly do so if it is broken. This, perhaps, leads to a second question for the custody officer; is the woman in a mental state which might lead her to attempt to take her own life? Whatever decision the officer takes, he should apply his mind carefully to the particular situation which confronts him. If personal articles are retained by the custody officer he must explain why.

In addition, a person who is in custody at a police station or is in police detention otherwise than at a police station may at any time be searched by any constable in order to ascertain whether he has with him any articles which he could use for any of the purposes in (a) to (d) above. A constable may seize and detain anything found in such a search, except that clothes and personal effects may only be seized in the same circumstances as mentioned above. Designated community support officers may search detainees for dangerous items which could be used to assist escape.

An examination of the mouth is a non-intimate search which may be undertaken by a constable under PACE, s 54(8). A dentist has no power to conduct such examination without consent under these provisions.

Where articles are seized, the person must be told the reason unless he is violent or likely to be violent or is incapable of understanding. Items which are seized on the grounds that they may be used to cause injury, damage, interfere with evidence or assist escape must be returned when the person is released from police detention. The Detention Code states that the custody officer is responsible for the safekeeping of property taken from a person.

Search and examination to ascertain liability

A detainee at a police station may be searched or examined to establish:

(a) whether he has any marks, features or injuries that would tend to identify him as a person involved in the commission of an offence and to photograph any identifying marks; or
(b) his identity.

Where the appropriate consent has been withheld, or it is not practicable to obtain it, PACE, s 54A permits an officer of at least the rank of inspector to authorise the search and/or examination of a detainee to find marks under (a). If the person concerned has refused to identify himself or the officer has reasonable grounds for suspecting that the person is not who he claims to be, an inspector (or above) may under s 54A authorise a search to establish identity under (b). An authorisation under s 54A may be given orally but must be confirmed in writing as soon as is practicable.

Any identifying mark (including features and injuries) which is found may be photographed with consent, or if such consent is withheld or it is not practicable to obtain it, without consent. 'Photographed' covers the use of any means by which a visual image may be produced.

Such searches, examinations and taking of photographs may only be conducted or taken by constables of the same sex as the person concerned, who may use reasonable force. An intimate search may not be carried out under the authority of PACE, s 54A.

Photographs taken under PACE, s 54A may be used or disclosed for any purpose relating to the prevention or detection of crime, the investigation of an offence or the conduct of a prosecution. They may be retained after use or disclosure but may not be used or disclosed except for a related purpose.

The references to 'crime' in PACE, s 54A include conduct which is an offence (whether under United Kingdom law or the law of a country or territory outside the

United Kingdom) or which is or corresponds to conduct which would be an offence in the United Kingdom if it all took place in any part of the United Kingdom.

When a person is searched, examined or photographed under the above provisions, he must be informed:

(a) of the purpose of the search;
(b) of the grounds on which the relevant authority, if applicable, has been given; and
(c) of the purposes for which the photograph may be used, disclosed or retained.

This information must be given before the search or examination commences or the photograph is taken, except if the photograph is to be taken covertly.

A record must be made when a detainee is searched, examined, or a photograph of the person, or any identifying marks found on him, is taken. The record must include:

(a) the identity (subject to the usual exclusion) of the officer carrying out the search, examination or taking the photograph;
(b) the purpose of the search, examination or photograph and the outcome;
(c) the detainee's consent to the search, examination or photograph, or the reason the person was searched, examined or photographed without consent;
(d) the giving of any authority, the grounds for giving it and the authorising officer.

If force is used when searching, examining or taking a photograph in accordance with s 54A, a record must be made of the circumstances and those present.

SEARCHES

Strip searches

A strip search is any search involving the removal of more than outer clothing (including shoes and socks). The Detention Code states that, in order for such a search to take place, the custody officer must believe it to be necessary to remove an article which the detainee would not be allowed to keep and there is reasonable suspicion that the person might have concealed such an article. Strip searches should not be routinely carried out where there is no reason for suspicion that articles have been concealed.

Conduct

The following procedures must be observed when strip searches are conducted:

(1) A police officer carrying out a strip search must be the same sex as the person searched.
(2) The search must take place in an area where the suspect cannot be seen by anyone who does not need to be present, nor by a member of the opposite sex (except an appropriate adult who has specifically been requested by the person being searched).
(3) Except in cases of urgency, where there is a risk of serious harm to the person detained or to others, whenever a strip search involves exposure of intimate parts of the body, there must be at least two people present other than the person searched, and if the search is of a juvenile or mentally disordered or mentally vulnerable person, one of the people must be the appropriate adult. Except in

urgent cases as above, a search of a juvenile may take place in the absence of an appropriate adult only if the juvenile signifies in the presence of the appropriate adult that he prefers the search to be done in his absence and the appropriate adult agrees. A record must be made of the juvenile's decision and signed by the appropriate adult. The presence of more than two people, other than the appropriate adult, may be permitted only in the most exceptional circumstances.

(4) The search must be conducted with proper regard to the sensitivity and vulnerability of the detainee in these circumstances. Every reasonable effort must be made to secure co-operation and minimise embarrassment. Detainees who are searched should not normally be required to have all their clothes removed at the same time, for example, a person should be allowed to remove clothing above the waist and re-dress before removing further clothing.

(5) Where necessary to assist the search, the suspect may be required to hold his or her arms in the air or to stand with his or her legs apart and to bend forward so that a visual examination may be made of the genital and anal areas provided that no physical contact is made with any body orifice.

(6) If, during a search, articles are found, the person must be asked to hand them over. If articles are found within any body orifice other than the mouth, and the person refuses to hand them over, their removal would constitute an intimate search which must be carried out in accordance with the provisions of the Code set out below.

(7) A strip search should be conducted as quickly as possible, and the suspect allowed to dress as soon as the procedure is complete.

Documentation

A record should be made on the custody record of a strip search. It should record the parts of the body searched, who searched, the reason it was considered necessary to undertake it, those present and any result.

Intimate searches

An intimate search is a search which consists of the physical examination of a person's body orifices other than the mouth, ie the nose, ears, anus and vagina. The intrusive nature of such searches means the actual and potential risks associated with intimate searches must never be underestimated. Intimate searches are governed by PACE, s 55. Before an intimate search is authorised, every effort must be made to persuade a detainee to hand over the article. Whenever possible, a registered medical practitioner or registered nurse should be asked to make a risk assessment. The authorising officer must consider whether the grounds for believing that an article is concealed are reasonable. In cases of doubt, advice should be sought from a superintendent.

Authorisation

An intimate search must be authorised by an officer of at least the rank of inspector. To authorise such a search the officer must have reasonable grounds for believing that:

(a) an article which could cause physical injury to a detainee or others at the police station has been concealed; or
(b) the person has concealed a Class A drug which he intended to supply to another or to export; and
(c) in either case an intimate search is the only practicable means of removing it.

The authorisation of an intimate search may be given orally or in writing, but if orally it must be confirmed in writing as soon as practicable.

An intimate drug offence search may not be carried out without appropriate consent in writing. Before a detainee is asked to give such consent he must be warned that if he refuses without good cause his refusal may harm his case if it comes to trial. The following form of words may be used to give such a warning:

'You do not have to allow yourself to be searched but I must warn you that if you refuse without good cause, your refusal may harm your case if it comes to trial.'

The warning may be given by a police officer or member of police staff. If not legally represented, the detainee must be reminded of his entitlement to legal advice, and the reminder must be noted in the custody record. Where appropriate consent to a drug offence search is refused without good cause, a court or jury in any proceedings which follow may draw such inferences from that refusal as appear proper. Before the search begins, a constable, a designated detention officer or a designated staff custody officer must inform the person of the authorisation and the grounds for giving it and for believing that the item cannot be removed without an intimate search.

Execution

Intimate searches may take place only at:

(a) a police station (but not if it is a drug offence search);
(b) a hospital;
(c) a surgery; or
(d) other medical premises.

Before an intimate search takes place, the reasons why it is considered necessary must be explained to the person to be searched and he must be reminded of his entitlement to have legal advice and the reminder must be noted in the custody record.

An intimate search may only be carried out by a doctor or registered nurse, unless an inspector (or above) considers that it is not practicable and the search takes place because there are reasonable grounds for believing that an article which could cause physical injury to the detainee or others at the police station has been concealed, in which case it must be carried out by a constable of the same sex and the reason for the impracticability must be recorded. A proposal for a search to be carried out by someone other than a registered medical practitioner or a registered nurse must only be considered as a last resort where the risks involved in retention of the item outweigh those associated with its removal. Except in the case of a juvenile, no one of the opposite sex, other than a doctor or nurse, may be present, nor anyone whose presence is unnecessary, but a minimum of two people, other than the person searched, must be present during the search. A search should be conducted with proper regard to the sensitivity and vulnerability of the suspect in the circumstances.

An intimate search at a police station of a juvenile, or person who is mentally disordered or mentally vulnerable, must take place in the presence of the appropriate adult of the same sex (unless the person specifically requests the presence of a particular adult of the opposite sex who is readily available). In the case of a juvenile, the search may take place in the absence of the appropriate adult only if the juvenile signifies in the presence of the appropriate adult that he prefers it to be done in his absence and the appropriate adult agrees. A record should be made of the juvenile's decision and signed by the appropriate adult.

See p 204 concerning identification by way of intimate, non-intimate and other samples.

Documentation

After an intimate search has been carried out, a record must be made as soon as practicable on the custody record, stating the authorisation to carry out the search; the grounds for giving the authorisation; the grounds for believing that the article could not be removed without an intimate search; which parts of the detainee's body were searched; who carried out the search; who was present, and the result. Where the intimate search is a drug offence search, a record must also be made of the necessary warning and the fact that appropriate consent was given or (as the case may be) refused and, if refused, the reason given for the refusal.

The powers of seizure in respect of articles found are the same as those which apply to other searches. If an intimate search is carried out by a police officer, the reason why it was impracticable for a registered medical practitioner or a registered nurse to conduct it must be recorded.

X-rays and ultrasound scans

PACE, s 55A provides that where an officer of at least the rank of inspector has reasonable grounds for believing that a person arrested for an offence and in police detention may have swallowed a Class A drug, and was in possession of it with the appropriate criminal intent before his arrest, he may authorise an X-ray or an ultrasound scan (or both) to be taken. An X-ray or ultrasound scan must not take place without the appropriate consent in writing. Before an X-ray or scan is carried out, the detainee must be told by a police officer, designated detention officer or staff custody officer that the authority has been given and the grounds for the authorisation. Before being asked for his consent he must be warned that an unjustified refusal may harm his case if it comes to trial. This warning may be given by a police officer or member of police staff. A detainee who is not legally represented must be reminded of his entitlement to have free legal advice, and the reminder noted in the custody record. An X-ray or ultrasound scan may only be carried out by a suitably qualified person at a hospital, the surgery of a registered medical practitioner, or at some place used for medical purposes. The provisions on the previous page in relation to the inferences which may be drawn where consent to an intimate drug offence search is refused also apply to refusals to permit X-rays and ultrasound scans to be carried out.

If authority is given for an X-ray to be taken or an ultrasound scan to be carried out, or both, consideration should be given to asking a registered medical practitioner or registered nurse to explain to the detainee what is involved and to allay any concerns the detainee might have about the effect which such examinations may have upon him. If appropriate consent is not given, evidence of the explanation may, if the case comes to trial, be relevant to determining whether the detainee had good cause for refusing.

The following must be recorded as soon as practicable in the detainee's custody record:

(a) the authorisation to take the X-ray or carry out the ultrasound scan (or both);
(b) the grounds for giving the authorisation;
(c) the giving of the requisite warning;
(d) the fact that the appropriate consent was given or (as the case may be) refused, and if refused, the reason given for the refusal (if any); and
(e) if an X-ray is taken or an ultrasound scan carried out:
   (i)   where it was taken or carried out;
   (ii)   who took it or carried it out;
   (iii) who was present;
   (iv)   the result.

REVIEWS AND MAXIMUM PERIODS OF POLICE DETENTION

Reviews

PACE, s 40 requires periodic reviews of the detention of each person in police detention. The review will be carried out:

(a) in the case of a person who has been arrested *and charged*, by the custody officer; and
(b) in the case of a person who has been arrested *but not charged*, by an officer of at least the rank of inspector who has not been directly involved in the investigation.

The officer by whom the review is carried out is called the 'review officer'.

There will be some designated police stations at which the custody officer will be an officer of the rank of inspector. Where this is so he could carry out both of the above functions.

PACE, s 40 is precise in relation to when these reviews must be carried out:

(a) the first review must be not later than *six hours* after the detention was first authorised;
(b) the second review must be not later than *nine hours* after the first;
(c) subsequent reviews must be at intervals of *not more than nine hours*.

Failure to carry out a review in accordance with these rules renders the previously lawful detention unlawful and entitles the detainee to damages for false imprisonment.

The purpose of a review

The review officer is responsible under PACE, s 40 for determining whether or not a person's detention continues to be necessary. In the case of offences under the TA 2000, the powers and duties of a review officer are set out in Sch 8, Part II. Schedule 8,

Part III to that Act makes provision for a superintendent to apply to a judicial authority for a warrant of further detention.

The case of a person who has been arrested but not charged

Here the review officer must proceed as follows:

(1) Where the person was detained because he was not in a fit state to be charged or released without charge (with or without bail), eg because he was under the influence of drink or drugs, the review officer must consider whether he is now in a fit state to be charged or so released. If he is, one or other of these courses must be adopted. If he is not, further detention may be authorised, but consideration should be given to whether there is sufficient evidence to charge him with an offence.

(2) Where, although there is then insufficient evidence to charge him, the detention of the person has been authorised by the custody officer on the basis that there are reasonable grounds to believe that his detention without charge is necessary to secure or preserve evidence relating to an offence for which he is under arrest or to obtain such evidence, the review officer may authorise further detention if this is necessary on the same basis.

Before deciding whether to authorise continued detention the review officer must give an opportunity to make representations about the detention to the detainee, unless he is asleep; the detainee's solicitor, if available; and the appropriate adult.

PACE, s 40A permits the review of the detention of a person who has been arrested but not charged to be conducted by means of a discussion, conducted by telephone, with one or more persons at the police station where the arrested person is held. However, the Detention Code states that the telephone may be used to carry out a review of detention before charge when it is not reasonably practicable for the review officer to attend the police station holding the detainee, eg when severe weather conditions or an operational emergency prevent a review officer from attending a police station. In addition, a telephone review may not be conducted if the review is of a type authorised by regulations under PACE, s 45A to be carried out using video-conferencing facilities and it is reasonably practicable to carry out the review under those regulations. No such regulations have been made at the time of writing but experimental work is being evaluated. In the case of terrorism, telephone reviews may not be conducted. A telephone or video-conferencing review may only be carried out by an officer of at least the rank of inspector. Both telephone and video-conferencing reviews may be terminated by the review officer at any stage in favour of a review in person and a record should be made of such a decision.

The decision on whether the review takes place in person, by telephone or (when in use) by video-conferencing is a matter for the review officer. The review officer must always take account of the needs of the person in custody and the benefits of a personal review must always be considered with specific consideration being given to juveniles, the mentally vulnerable, persons with specific medical needs, and presentational or community issues surrounding the person's detention.

Where a review is conducted over the telephone or by video-conferencing facilities, the reviewing officer must require another officer at the station to fulfil the review officer's functions under PACE, s 40 and the Detention Code by making records connected with the review in the detainee's custody record in the presence of the detainee and giving the detainee information. The detainee or his solicitor must be given the opportunity to make representations either orally, or by using telephone or video-conferencing facilities (as the case may be), or in writing where facilities such as fax or email exist for the immediate transmission of written material.

The Regulations made under PACE, s 45A may also provide for the functions relating to an arrested person taken to a non-designated police station which, in the case of an arrested person taken to a designated police station, are a custody officer's functions under PACE, s 40, to be exercised by video-link facilities.

PACE, s 37 applies to the case of a person arrested but not charged in the same way as it does when a person is first detained at a police station, except that the obligations under s 40 are those of the review officer, and not of the custody officer, and that there will be no need to inform the detainee of a decision for his continued detention if he is asleep at the time.

The case of the person who has been charged

The person must be released, either on bail or without bail, unless:

(a) his name and address cannot be ascertained or there are reasonable grounds to doubt the name and address given; or

(b) there are reasonable grounds to believe that detention is necessary for his own protection or to prevent him causing physical injury to any person or loss of or damage to property; or

(c) there are reasonable grounds to believe that the person will fail to answer bail or that his detention is necessary to prevent him interfering with the administration of justice or with police investigations; or

(d) in the case of an arrested juvenile, detention is necessary in his own interests.

General

Before deciding whether to authorise continued detention the review officer must give an opportunity to make representations about the detention to:

(a) the detainee (unless in the case of a review, as opposed to an extension, the detainee is asleep);

(b) the detainee's solicitor if available at the time; and

(c) the appropriate adult if available at the time.

Other people having an interest in the detainee's welfare may also make representations at the authorising officer's discretion.

The representations may be made orally in person or by telephone or in writing. The authorising officer may, however, refuse to hear oral representations from the detainee if the officer considers him unfit to make representations because of his condition or behaviour.

After hearing any representations, the review officer must note any comment the person may make if the decision is to keep him in detention. No officer may put specific questions to the suspect regarding his involvement in any offence, nor in respect of any comments he may make in response to the decision to keep him in detention. Such an exchange is likely to constitute an 'interview' and would require the safeguard of the Code's provisions concerning interviews generally.

Before conducting a review the review officer must ensure that the detainee is reminded of his entitlement to free legal advice. This reminder must be noted in the custody record. PACE, s 40 requires that the person (unless he is asleep), or any solicitor who is representing him who is available at the time of the review, must be given an opportunity by the review officer to make representations to him concerning the detention.

If the detainee is likely to be asleep at the latest time when a review may take place, the review officer should bring it forward so that the detainee may make representations without being woken up.

If, in the light of the above considerations, the review officer authorises the detention of a person (whether charged or not) to continue, the review officer must make a written record of the grounds for the detention as soon as practicable. A detainee who is asleep at a review and whose continued detention is authorised must be informed about the decision and reason as soon as practicable after waking.

The grounds for, and the extent of, any delay in conducting a review must be recorded. Any written representations which are made must be retained. A record must be made as soon as practicable of the outcome of each review and of any application for a warrant of further detention (see p 167) or its extension.

Where a person is in police custody in circumstances which are not subject to statutory review, for example:

(a) someone arrested on warrant for failure to answer to bail or for breach of a condition of bail;
(b) someone in police custody under the Crime (Sentences) Act 1997 for a specific purpose and period;
(c) a convicted or remanded prisoner held on behalf of the Prison Service;
(d) someone detained to prevent him causing a breach of the peace;
(e) someone detained on behalf of the Immigration Service; or
(f) someone detained under CJA 1988, s 152 by order of a magistrates' court to facilitate the recovery of evidence where that person has been charged with drug possession or trafficking and is suspected of having swallowed drugs,

it is advised that reviews take place periodically to ensure that the power to detain still applies and that detention conditions are being complied with. Such reviews may be conducted by a sergeant.

Postponement of review

PACE, s 40 allows for the postponement of a review:

(a) if, having regard to all the circumstances prevailing at the latest time for the review in question, it is not practicable to carry out the review at that time;
(b) without prejudice to the generality of (a) above:
   (i) if at that time the person in detention is being questioned by a police officer and the review officer is satisfied that an interruption of the questioning for the purpose of carrying out the review would prejudice the investigation in connection with which he is being questioned; or

(ii) if at that time no review officer is readily available.

If a review is postponed it must be carried out as soon as practicable after the normal latest time for it. The reason for any postponement must be recorded in the custody record. In the event of a review being postponed, this does not affect the time at which any subsequent review must be carried out. This means that a second review must be carried out nine hours after the latest time at which the first review should have taken place, which time is six hours after the detention was first authorised.

Documentation

The grounds for, and the extent of, any delay in conducting a review must be recorded and reasons for there being a telephone review must also be recorded, together with the place where the review officer was, and the method by which representations were made. In addition, a record must be made of the outcome of each review. If the detainee was asleep at the time when a review was due and continued detention was authorised, a record must be made of when he was informed and by whom.

Limits on period of detention without charge

PACE, s 41 provides that a person must not be kept in police detention for more than twenty-four hours without being charged, except that detention beyond that period may be authorised in certain circumstances by an officer of the rank of superintendent (or above) (s 42) or by a magistrates' court (ss 43 and 44).

Calculation of period of detention

PACE, s 41 refers to the 'relevant time', which is the time from which the detention of a particular person is to be calculated. This may be:

(a) in the case where a person, whose arrest is sought in one police area in England and Wales, is arrested in another area, and is not questioned in the area in which he is arrested about the offence for which he has been arrested, *the time at which the person arrives at the first police station in the area in which his arrest is sought, or the time twenty-four hours after that person's arrest, whichever is the earlier;*

(b) in the case of a person arrested outside England and Wales, *the time at which that person arrives at the first police station to which he is taken in the police area in England and Wales in which the offence for which he is arrested is being investigated, or the time twenty-four hours after the time of that person's entry into England and Wales, whichever is the earlier;*

(c) in the case of a person who attends voluntarily at a police station, or who accompanies a constable to a police station without having been arrested, and is arrested at the police station, *the time of his arrest;*

(d) in the case of a person who attends a police station to answer bail under s 30A (released on bail without attending a police station), the time when he arrives at a police station;
(e) in any other case, it is the time at which the person arrested arrives at the first police station to which he is taken after arrest, *unless he is in detention in an area* in England and Wales and his arrest for an offence is being sought *in some other police area* in England and Wales and he is taken to that second area for the purpose of investigating that offence, without being questioned in the first area in order to obtain evidence in relation to it. In such a case the 'relevant time' will be twenty-four hours after he leaves the place where he is detained in the first area or the time at which he arrives at the first police station to which he is taken in the second area, whichever is the earlier.

These provisions appear to be extremely complicated at first sight but they may be summarised for ease of understanding. If we think of the 'relevant time' as the time at which we must start our detention alarm clock we find that the 'relevant time' is *normally the time of arrival at the relevant police station*. However, there are additions and variations which affect the time at which the clock must be started. *It must be started*:

(a) twenty-four hours after arrest (in the unlikely event of it taking longer than that to get the prisoner to a police station);
(b) if the person is arrested outside England and Wales, on arrival at the first police station in the area of the offence (or twenty-four hours after arrival in England and Wales if that is earlier);
(c) at the time of arrest at a police station (eg in interview room);
(d) at the time of arrival at the first police station in the area of the offence (when the prisoner is taken to other than a designated police station in the first instance); or
(e) if the person is in the detention of one force and his arrest is sought by another (and he is not questioned in the area of the first force), the detention clock of the second force will start on arrival at the first police station in the area where the offence was committed (subject to a maximum of twenty-four hours after leaving his place of detention in the area of arrest).

PACE, s 41 provides a safeguard in relation to a person in police detention who, whilst detained, is arrested for a second offence. The detention clock does not start again with his arrest for the second offence. It also provides for instances in which a person in police detention is removed to a hospital for medical treatment. Normally the period commencing with his journey to hospital and ending with his arrival back in police custody does not count towards his twenty-four hours in police custody; in effect, the clock may be stopped. However, any period, either during his journey or whilst in hospital, during which he is questioned by a police officer for the purpose of obtaining evidence in relation to an offence, is included in his period of police detention.

Release from detention after twenty-four hours

If a person has not been charged after twenty-four hours in police detention he *must* normally be released either on bail or without bail. A person so released must not be re-arrested without a warrant for the same offence unless new evidence justifying a further arrest has come to light since his release but this does not prevent his arrest for failure to surrender to police bail. It is submitted that evidence justifying further arrest would have to be substantial, probably sufficient in itself to justify arrest.

Release after twenty-four hours is not required if continued detention is authorised or a warrant of further detention is issued under the powers next discussed.

Continued detention

The relevant provisions are set out by PACE, s 42. Where an officer of the rank of superintendent (or above) who is responsible for a police station at which a person is detained has reasonable grounds for believing that:

(a) the detention of that person without charge is necessary to secure or preserve evidence relating to an offence for which he is under arrest or to obtain such evidence by questioning him;
(b) an offence for which he is under arrest is an 'indictable offence'; and
(c) the investigation is being conducted diligently and expeditiously,

he may authorise the keeping of that person in police detention for a period expiring at or before thirty-six hours after the relevant time.

This may not be done if the person has been in detention for more than twenty-four hours from the relevant time when the authorisation of continued detention is sought, nor may such an authorisation be given before the second review of that person's detention, that is the review at fifteen hours after detention was first authorised. If the first period of continued detention given does not take the detention time fully to thirty-six hours (a superintendent will not necessarily authorise an additional twelve hours), a further period may be authorised if the conditions in the previous paragraph are satisfied, up to the maximum of thirty-six hours. This further period may be authorised at any time during the first extension, and even though more than twenty-four hours has elapsed from the relevant time.

The detainee must be informed on all occasions of the grounds for his continued detention and the custody record must be endorsed with them. Before deciding whether to authorise continued detention the officer responsible must give an opportunity to make representations about the detention to the detainee, or his solicitor if available, and the appropriate adult if available. Any other person having an interest in the detainee's welfare may also make representations at the discretion of the officer authorising continued detention. Representations may be made orally or in writing. During consideration of authorisations of continued detention specific questions must not be put to a detainee regarding his involvement in an offence or in respect of any comments which he makes. Such an exchange could be considered to be an interview. If, when an extension of detention is authorised, the detainee has not yet exercised his right to have some person informed of his detention, or his right of access to legal advice, the custody officer must inform him of his rights, decide whether he shall be permitted to exercise them, and record his decision in the custody record. Detaining a juvenile or mentally vulnerable person for longer than twenty-four hours will be dependent upon the circumstances of the case and with regard to the person's special vulnerability, the legal obligation to provide an opportunity for legal representations to be made prior to a decision about extending detention, the need to consult and consider the views of an appropriate adult, and any alternatives to police custody.

A person who has been the subject of continued detention must be released, with or without bail, not later than thirty-six hours after the relevant time, unless he has been charged, or unless his continued detention is authorised or is otherwise permitted by a warrant of further detention. Such a person may not be re-arrested without warrant for the same offence unless new evidence justifying a further arrest has come to light since his release, but this does not apply to a person who fails to surrender to police bail.

Warrant of further detention

Such a warrant is governed by PACE, ss 43 and 44. A magistrates' court may issue a warrant of further detention following an application on oath by a constable which is supported by a written information. The court must be satisfied that there are reasonable grounds for believing that further detention is justified. A person's further detention is only justified for the purpose of ss 43 and 44 if:

(a) his detention without charge is necessary to secure or preserve evidence relating to the offence for which he is under arrest or to obtain such evidence by questioning him;

(b) an offence for which he is under arrest is an indictable offence; and

(c) the investigation is being conducted diligently and expeditiously.

The detainee must be given a copy of the information and he must be brought before the court. If he is not legally represented, but wishes such representation, the court must adjourn for this to be done and he may be kept in detention during the adjournment.

An application for a warrant of further detention may be made at any time before the expiry of thirty-six hours after the 'relevant time', or, if it is not practicable for the magistrates' court to sit at that time but it will sit during the six hours following that period, at any time before the expiry of those six hours. It is not sufficient for the police to have the application on the court lists for hearing within the sitting of the court. The application must be brought to the notice of the court before the end of the relevant period.

A warrant of further detention must state the time of issue and the period of detention which it authorises, which must not be longer than thirty-six hours. It may be extended for a further period, up to thirty-six hours, but must in no circumstances permit detention beyond ninety-six hours after the relevant time. A 'magistrates' court' in the present context is a court consisting of two or more justices, sitting otherwise than in open court for the purpose of these provisions.

Where a warrant of further detention is issued, the person must be released from police detention, with or without bail, on or before the expiry of the warrant unless he is charged. He may not be re-arrested for the same offence unless new evidence has come to light since his arrest, but this does not apply to a person who fails to surrender to police bail.

There are special provisions where a person has been arrested as a suspected terrorist pursuant to TA 2000, s 41 (p 934). By TA 2000, Sch 8, a judicial authority may extend (by stages) the duration of a warrant of detention for a period of up to twenty-eight days from the relevant time. Applications for a warrant of detention or further detention under Sch 8 may be made by a Crown Prosecutor, as well as by a superintendent (or above).

Documentation

A record must be made of the outcome of a determination whether to extend the maximum detention period without charge or an application for a warrant of further detention or its extension. Where an authorisation of continued detention has been given by a superintendent, the record must show the length of time by which detention was extended. The same applies where a warrant of further detention is granted.

CHARGING DETAINEES

Procedures

When the officer in charge of the investigation reasonably believes that there is sufficient evidence to provide a realistic prospect of a detainee's conviction, he must without delay inform the custody officer who will be responsible for considering whether or not the detainee should be charged. Where a person has been detained for more than one offence it is permissible to delay informing the custody officer until these conditions are satisfied in respect of all of the offences. If the detainee is a juvenile, or is mentally disordered or vulnerable, any resulting action must be done in the presence of the appropriate adult (if present at the time). Where guidance exists under PACE, s 37A a custody officer who determines in accordance with that guidance that there is sufficient evidence to charge the detainee, may detain that person for no longer than is reasonably necessary to decide how that person is to be dealt with under PACE, s 37(7) (see p 146), including, where appropriate, consultation with the duty prosecutor. The period is subject to the maximum period determined by PACE, ss 41 to 44 (above). Where a reference is made to the Crown Prosecution Service a custody officer is responsible for ensuring that all specified information is sent with that reference.

Where a person is arrested under the provisions of CJA 2003, which allow a person to be re-tried after being acquitted of a specified serious offence which is not precluded from further prosecution, an officer of the rank of superintendent or above, who has not been directly involved in the investigation, is responsible for determining whether the evidence is sufficient to charge. Where a Crown Prosecutor is unable to make a charging decision based upon the information available at the time, a detainee may be released without charge or on bail. A detainee should be informed of the circumstances of such a decision.

Unless the restriction on drawing adverse inferences from silence (see p 113) applies, a detainee who is charged or informed that he may be prosecuted for an offence must be cautioned in the terms set out at p 112. If the restriction does apply, the alternative terms of the caution set out on p 113 must be used. The detainee must also be given a written notice showing particulars of the offence charged, which must include the name of the officer (with the usual two exceptions) and the case reference number.

The charge must be stated in simple terms but must show the precise offence in law. The notice must begin with the following words:

'You are charged with the offence(s) shown below' [and be followed by the appropriate caution in the particular circumstances].

Where applicable the notice must be given to the appropriate adult.

The giving of a warning or the service of a notice of intended prosecution required by the Road Traffic Offenders Act 1988, s 1 does not amount to informing a detainee that he may be prosecuted for an offence and so does not preclude further questioning in relation to that offence.

If, after these procedures have been carried out, a police officer wishes to tell a detainee about any written statement or interview with another person relating to the offence, the detainee must either be handed a true copy of the written statement or have the content of the interview record brought to his attention. Nothing must be done to invite a reply or comment except to caution the detainee that he does not have to say anything, but that anything he does say may be given in evidence, and to remind him of his right to legal advice. If the detainee cannot read, the document may be read to him. In relevant cases, the appropriate adult must be given a copy of the document, or the interview record must be brought to his attention.

In addition, further questions relating to the offence may not generally be asked of a person after he has been charged with that offence, or informed that he may be prosecuted for it. Exceptions are: where they are necessary for the purpose of preventing or minimising harm or loss to some other person or to the public; or for clearing up ambiguity in a previous answer or statement; or where it is in the interests of justice that the person should have put to him (and have the opportunity to comment upon) new information concerning the offence; or where he volunteers to make a further statement. This could occur where a detainee mentions that property stolen was sold to a second party, or where a reference is made to a day of the week but no date is given, or where the name of a street is given without mention of the town. It could also occur where it would be advantageous to the accused and in the interests of justice for him to have another offence taken into consideration by the court, should he be prepared to admit responsibility. In such cases the detainee must be cautioned that he does not have to say anything, but that anything he does say may be given in evidence before further questions are put and the caution must be written at the head of any statement made. He must be reminded of his right to legal advice.

Where a juvenile is charged with an offence and the custody officer authorises his continued detention, the custody officer must try to make arrangements for the juvenile to be taken into the care of the local authority to be detained pending appearance in court. This requirement does not apply if the custody officer certifies that it is impracticable to do so, or, in the case of a juvenile of at least twelve years of age, no secure accommodation is available and there is a risk to the public of serious harm from that juvenile.

Neither a juvenile's behaviour nor the nature of the offence with which he is charged provide grounds for the custody officer to decide that it is impracticable to seek to arrange for his transfer to the care of the local authority. Similarly, the lack of secure local authority accommodation does not make it impracticable for the custody officer to transfer him. The availability of secure accommodation is only one factor in relation to a juvenile aged twelve or over when the local authority accommodation would not be adequate to protect the public from serious harm from the juvenile. The obligation to transfer a juvenile to local authority accommodation applies as much to a juvenile charged during the daytime as it does to a juvenile to be held overnight, subject to a requirement to bring the juvenile before a court under s 46 of PACE.

Documentation

A record must be made of anything a detainee says when he is charged. Questions put in an interview after a charge and answers given must be recorded in full during the interview on the forms provided and the record must be signed by the detainee or, if he refuses, by the interviewer and any third parties present. If the questions are audibly recorded or visually recorded the arrangements set out in the Audio Recording Code or Visual Recording Code apply.

If it is not practicable for a juvenile to be transferred to the custody of a local authority, the custody officer must record the reasons and make out a certificate to the effect that it is impracticable, which must be produced before the court together with the juvenile.

DETENTION AFTER CHARGE

PACE, s 46 requires that where a person:

(a) is charged with an offence; and
(b) after being charged, is kept in police detention or (in the case of a juvenile) is detained by a local authority,

he must be brought before a magistrates' court as soon as practicable, and in any event not later than the first sitting after he is charged (or, if he is to be brought before a magistrates' court in another area, not later than the first sitting of that court after his arrival in that area). If the person is to be brought before a magistrates' court in another area, he must be removed to that area as soon as practicable for the above purpose.

If no magistrates' court is due to sit on the day the person is charged (or on the day he arrives in the other area) or on the next day, the custody officer must inform the designated officer for a local justice area that there is a person in the area who has been detained after charge, and that person must arrange for a sitting of a magistrates' court not later than the day next following the day on which he is charged (or, if he has been transferred to another area, the day next following the day of his arrival in that area). Christmas Day, Good Friday and any Sunday do not count as 'days next following' for this purpose; thus, for example, the day next following Saturday is Monday.

None of the above provisions requires a person who is in hospital to be brought before a court if he is not well enough.

BAIL

When an investigating officer brings his prisoner before the custody officer, the custody officer may decide that there is insufficient evidence to justify a charge and that there is unlikely to be other evidence obtained; or that there is enough evidence to charge at that stage; or that there is not sufficient evidence available at that stage to charge the prisoner, but that there probably will be when further inquiries have been made. If the first of the decisions is reached the prisoner must be released at once without charge. If the second or third decision is reached, the following actions may be taken if it is decided that there are no further grounds for keeping the person in custody.

Police bail of person charged

Bail here means bail subject to a duty to appear before a magistrates' court.

Adults

PACE, s 38 requires that, when a person arrested otherwise than under a warrant endorsed for bail is charged with an offence, the custody officer must, subject to the Criminal Justice and Public Order Act 1994 (CJPOA 1994), s 25 (bail for accused charged or convicted for homicide or rape and related sexual offences (see p 175) after previous conviction for such an offence only if there are exceptional circumstances justifying it) order his release from police detention, either on bail or without bail, *unless:*

(a) his name and address cannot be ascertained or the custody officer has reasonable grounds for doubting the truth of a name or address provided by him; or

(b) the custody officer has reasonable grounds for believing that the person arrested will fail to appear in court to answer bail;

(c) in the case of a person arrested for an imprisonable offence, the custody officer has reasonable grounds for believing that the detention of the person is necessary to prevent him from committing an offence;

(d) in a case where a sample may be taken from the person under PACE, s 63B (see p 148), the custody officer has reasonable grounds for believing that the detention of the person is necessary to enable a sample to be taken from him;

(e) in the case of a person arrested for an offence which is not an imprisonable offence, the custody officer has reasonable grounds for believing that the detention of the person is necessary to prevent him from causing physical injury to any other person or from causing loss of or damage to property;

(f) the custody officer has reasonable grounds for believing that the detention of the person arrested is necessary to prevent him from interfering with the administration of justice or with the investigation of offences or of a particular offence; or

(g) the custody officer has reasonable grounds for believing that the detention of the person arrested is necessary for his own protection.

An 'imprisonable offence' is one punishable by imprisonment.

Juveniles

PACE, s 38 provides that if the person charged is a juvenile the custody officer must order his release from police detention, with or without bail, *unless* one of the above grounds applies or he has reasonable grounds for believing that the juvenile should be detained in the interests of his welfare. In the case of (d) this only applies if the juvenile has reached the minimum age specified by s 63B (at present fourteen).

Section 38 also requires that where a custody officer authorises an arrested juvenile to be kept in police detention, the custody officer must secure that the arrested juvenile is to be taken to local authority accommodation unless the custody officer certifies:

(a) that by reason of such circumstances as are specified in the certificate, it is impracticable to do so; or

(b) in the case of an arrested juvenile aged twelve or over that no secure accommodation is available and that keeping him in other local authority accommodation would not be adequate to protect the public from serious harm from him.

'*Secure accommodation*' is that provided for the purposes of restricting liberty. In the case of arrested juveniles who are charged with a violent or sexual offence (as defined by the Act; see below), the reference in (b) to protecting the public from serious harm is to protection from death or serious personal injury, whether physical or psychological, occasioned by further such offences. The term '*sexual offence*' in this context means an offence under one of the following Acts:

(a) the Protection of Children Act 1978 (indecent photographs of children);

(b) an offence under any provision of Part 1 of the Sexual Offences Act 2003 except s 52, 53 or 71 (causing or inciting or controlling prostitution for gain, and sexual activity in a public lavatory);

(c) conspiracy, incitement or attempt to commit any of these offences.

'*Violent offence*' means an offence which leads, or is intended or likely to lead, to a person's death or to physical injury to a person, and includes an offence which is required to be charged as arson (whether or not it would otherwise fall within this definition).

Except as provided above, neither a juvenile's behaviour nor the nature of the offence with which he is charged provides grounds for the custody officer to retain him in police custody rather than to seek to arrange for the transfer to the care of the local authority on the grounds of impracticability. Similarly, the lack of secure local authority accommodation does not make it impracticable for the custody officer to transfer him. The availability of secure accommodation is only one factor in relation to a juvenile aged twelve or over for whom other local authority accommodation would not be adequate to protect the public from serious harm from the juvenile.

Detention

If the release of a person arrested is not required by the above provisions of PACE, s 38, the custody officer may authorise him to be kept in police detention, but he may not authorise an adult to be kept in detention for a sample to be taken under PACE, s 63B after the period of six hours beginning when he was charged with the offence.

Use of video conferencing

Regulations made under PACE, s 45A may also provide for the functions relating to an arrested person taken to a non-designated police station which, in the case of an arrested person taken to a designated police station, are a custody officer's functions under PACE, s 38, to be exercised by video-link facilities.

Conditional bail

PACE, s 47 states that a release on bail under the detention provisions of the Act must be a release on bail granted in accordance with the BA 1976. However, this does not prevent the re-arrest without warrant of a person released on bail subject to a duty to attend at a police station if there is new evidence justifying a further arrest. A custody officer releasing a person on bail under s 37(7)(a) (release on bail and without charge pending a decision of the DPP) or s 38(1) (duties of custody officer after charge) or s 40(10) (which applies s 38(1) to review situations) has power to impose such conditions on bail as appear to him to be necessary:

(a) to secure that the person surrenders to custody;
(b) does not commit an offence whilst on bail; or
(c) does not interfere with witnesses or otherwise obstruct the course of justice whether in relation to himself or any other person.

Section 47(1B)–(1F) provides that no application by the prosecutor may be made under BA 1976, s 5B (reconsideration of decisions in granting bail) where a person is released under PACE, s 37(7)(a) (pending decision of the DPP) or s 37C(2)(b) (release on bail following breach of bail under s 37(7)(a)). Where a person is released on conditional bail in such circumstances, that person will not be entitled to apply to a magistrates' court for bail, but may seek variation of such conditions.

By BA 1976, s 3A(2), however, the custody officer does not have power to impose a requirement to reside in a bail hostel. This is obviously because a custody officer will not have sufficient time to make the necessary inquiries before such a condition might properly be imposed.

The combined effects of BA 1976, s 3(4), (5), (6) and (7) is to permit the following requirements to be made of a person before he is released on bail:

(a) he may be required to provide a surety or sureties to ensure his surrender to custody;
(b) he may be required to give security for his surrender;
(c) he may be required to comply with conditions which appear necessary to secure that he surrenders to custody, that he does not commit an offence whilst on bail, or that he does not interfere with witnesses or otherwise obstruct the course of justice;
(d) if a parent or guardian of a child or young person consents to be surety for it, the parent or guardian may be required to ensure that the child or young person complies with conditions imposed under (c) above, except that no such condition may be imposed where a young person will be seventeen before the time appointed for surrender, and that a parent or guardian may not be required to secure compliance with any requirement to which his consent does not extend and may not, in respect of those requirements to which his consent does extend, be bound in a sum greater than £50.

Where a custody officer has granted bail in criminal proceedings, he or another custody officer serving at the same police station may, at the request of the person to whom it was granted, vary the condition of bail, and in doing so he may impose conditions or more onerous conditions.

The BA 1976, ss 5 and 5A provide that, where a custody officer imposes conditions in granting bail or varies any conditions of bail, or imposes conditions in respect of bail, he must give reasons for doing so. This is to enable the person concerned to consider requesting the custody officer to vary those conditions. A note of the custody officer's reasons for imposing (or varying) conditions must be made in the custody record and a copy must be given to the person concerned.

A person who is bailed enters into a promise to appear as prescribed. That promise cannot be set against a recognisance from him that, if he fails to appear, a specific sum of money shall be forfeit. Instead the BA 1976 provides its own penalties for non-appearance. In serious cases it may be necessary for an accused to find one or more 'sureties', that is persons who *undertake to secure his attendance*. This is done by each surety entering a recognisance to forfeit a specified sum to the Crown in the event of the non-attendance of the accused.

Other points

When bail is granted by a constable a record must be made of the decision in the prescribed manner and the accused must be provided with a copy of that record if he so requests. In practice this copy is given on all occasions.

The Magistrates' Courts Act 1980, s 43 enables a magistrates' court to fix a later time for appearance before it and to enlarge recognisances.

Police bail of person not charged

If the custody officer decides, when the investigating officer brings the person detained before him, that there is insufficient evidence at that stage to charge him, but that there probably will be when further inquiries have been made, he may release the person detained on bail, such bail being conditional upon his appearance at a police station at a given time, as opposed to appearing at a court. The purpose is to re-assess the evidence then available to make a decision as to whether or not to charge the person detained. Such bail (ie the requirement to attend at a police station) may be cancelled at any time by notice in writing from the custody officer.

Arrest of person for failure to answer to police bail

PACE, s 46A provides that a constable may arrest without warrant any person who, having been released on bail subject to a duty to attend at a police station, fails to attend at that police station at the time appointed for him to do so. In addition, a person who has been released on bail for a decision to be made by the DPP, or who has been released on bail following an arrest for a breach of bail, may be arrested without warrant by a constable if he has reasonable grounds for suspecting that the person has broken any conditions of his bail.

Such a person must be taken to that police station as soon as practicable after his arrest.

General

By PACE, s 47(3A), where a custody officer grants bail to a person subject to a duty to appear before a magistrates' court, he must appoint for the appearance:

(a) a date which is not later than the first sitting of the court after the person is charged with the offence; or

(b) where he is informed by the designated officer for the relevant local justice area that the appearance cannot be accommodated until a later date, that later date.

PACE, s 47(6) provides that, where a person who has been granted police bail and either has attended at a police station or has been arrested under s 46A is detained at a police station, any previous time in custody must be included in any calculation of detention time. In practice, his old custody record will be continued.

PACE, s 47(2) provides that nothing in the BA 1976 prevents a re-arrest without warrant of a person released on bail subject to a condition to appear at a police station if new evidence justifying a further arrest has come to light since his release. If such a person is re-arrested the detention provisions in PACE apply as if he has been arrested for the first time but this does not apply to a person arrested for failure to surrender to police bail at a police station, or who has surrendered to that bail and has been arrested for that offence.

Where an offence of absconding whilst on 'police bail' is dealt with by laying an information, the limitation of six months in relation to the laying of an information (or, when the relevant provision is in force, issuing a written charge) applies from the time of the failure to surrender. Thus, it is suggested that an information is laid (or written charge is issued) when the failure to surrender occurs. Failure to surrender to police bail cannot be dealt with as a contempt, as there is no defiance of a court order.

Bail by a court

Section 4 of the BA 1976 states that when a person who is accused of an offence appears before a magistrates' court or a Crown Court in the course of, or in connection with, the proceedings for the offence, or when he applies to a court for bail or for a variation of the conditions of bail in connection with the proceedings, he must be granted bail if none of the exceptions specified in Sch 1 applies. However, this is subject to the provisions of CJPOA 1994, s 25 (bail for accused charged with or convicted of homicide, and offences under the Sexual Offences Act 2003, ss 1, 2, 4, 5, 6, 8, 30 and 31 involving rape, non-consensual penetration or sexual activity, the same activity with children under thirteen, and mentally disordered persons, after a previous conviction for such an offence only to be granted if there are exceptional circumstances justifying it). Section 25 also applies to a police officer considering the grant of bail in such circumstances. A court will also have regard, so far as it is relevant, to any misuse of a controlled drug by the accused.

Schedule 1 provides that bail need not be granted by the court where the offence (or one of them) is *punishable with imprisonment* if the court is satisfied that there are substantial grounds for believing that the accused, if released on bail (whether subject to conditions or not) would:

(a) fail to surrender to custody; or

(b) commit an offence whilst on bail; or

(c) interfere with witnesses or otherwise obstruct the course of justice, whether in relation to himself or any other person.

In addition, where the offence (or one of them) is punishable with imprisonment, and it appears to the court that the accused (who is eighteen or over) was on bail in criminal proceedings on the date of that offence, it need not grant bail unless it is satisfied that there is no significant risk of his committing an offence while on bail (whether subject to conditions or not). Where the accused is under the age of eighteen, in such circumstances, in deciding whether he is likely to commit a further offence while on bail, the court must give particular weight to the fact that the accused was on bail at the time of the offence. These provisions are not in force at the time of writing.

In deciding the above, the court must have regard to the nature and seriousness of the offence; the character, antecedents, associations and community ties of the accused; the record of the accused in respect of previous grants of bail; and the strength of the evidence available (except where the case is merely being adjourned for inquiries or a report).

Schedule 1 also provides that bail need not be granted by the court where the offence (or one of them) is *punishable with imprisonment*:

(d) if the court is satisfied that the accused should be kept in custody for his own protection or, if a child or young person, for his own welfare; or
(e) if he is in custody under a court order or in pursuance of any authority under the Services Acts; or
(f) if the court is satisfied that there has not been sufficient time to obtain information upon which a decision about bail may be made; or
(g) if, in certain circumstances, the accused has been arrested under BA 1976, s 7 for absconding or breaking conditions of bail.

Schedule 1 also provides that, where an accused charged with a non-imprisonable offence is arrested under s 7 (absconding or breaking condition of bail), bail may be refused only if the court is satisfied that there are substantial grounds for believing that if released on bail (whether subject to conditions or not) he would fail to surrender to custody, commit an offence while on bail, or interfere with witnesses or otherwise obstruct the course of justice.

CJA 2003, Part 2 makes provision for an appeal to a Crown Court against the imposition of conditions relating to residence, provision of surety or giving a security, curfew, electronic monitoring or contact. The prosecution may appeal to a Crown Court against a decision by magistrates to grant bail in the case of all imprisonable offences.

Special provisions in respect of drug users

An alleged drug offender aged eighteen or over who is charged with an imprisonable offence will not be granted bail (unless the court is satisfied that there is no significant risk of his committing an offence while on bail) where:

(a) a drug test indicates the presence of a Class A drug;
(b) the offence is a drugs offence involving a Class A drug or the court is satisfied that there are substantial grounds for believing that the misuse of a Class A drug caused or contributed to that offence or provided its motivation; and

(c) the person concerned does not agree to a dependency/propensity to misuse assessment test or, has undergone such assessment but does not agree to participate in any relevant follow-up offered.

However, these provisions only apply in areas where facilities are in place.

Arrest for breach of bail

BA 1976, s 7(3) provides a power to arrest without warrant. A person who has been released on bail in criminal proceedings and is under a duty to surrender into the custody of a court may be arrested without warrant by a constable if:

(a) the constable has reasonable grounds for believing that that person is not likely to surrender to custody, or
(b) the constable has reasonable grounds for believing that that person is likely to break any of the conditions of his bail, or has broken any of those conditions; or reasonable grounds for suspecting that that person has broken any of those conditions; or
(c) in a case where that person was released on bail with one or more sureties, if a surety notifies a constable in writing that that person is unlikely to surrender to custody, and that for that reason the surety wishes to be relieved of his obligations as a surety.

Unless he was arrested within twenty-four hours of the time appointed for surrender to custody, the arrested person must be brought before a justice as soon as practicable and in any event within twenty-four hours. Christmas Day, Good Friday and any Sunday are excluded from the calculation of twenty-four hours. A person arrested within twenty-four hours of the surrender time must be brought before the court at which he was to have surrendered to custody.

Remand to police custody

By the Magistrates' Courts Act 1980, s 128, a magistrates' court has power to remand a person for a period not exceeding three clear days (twenty-four hours if a juvenile) to 'detention at a police station' where there is a need to question him about other offences. Section 128 also requires that such a person must not be kept in detention at a police station unless there is a need for him to be detained for the purpose of inquiries into other offences. If he is kept in such detention he must be brought back to the magistrates' court which committed him as soon as the need for detention ceases. Such a person must be treated as a person in detention for the purposes of PACE (and this means that he must be treated in accordance with the Detention Code and his detention must be subject to reviews as prescribed by the Act).

Failure to surrender

By BA 1976, s 6 a person who has been bailed commits an offence if he fails without reasonable cause to surrender to custody as required. Moreover, if he had reasonable cause for failing to surrender at the appropriate time, he commits an offence if he fails to surrender to custody at the appointed place as soon after the appointed time as is reasonably practicable.

Where a person has been granted bail by a court and subsequently fails to surrender to custody, that person must be brought before the court at which proceedings in respect of which bail was granted are to be heard. No information should be laid (or, when the relevant provision is in force, written charge issued) to commence proceedings for such failure. The court in question should initiate proceedings for an offence of failing to surrender to bail on its own motion, following an express invitation by the prosecutor. On the other hand, where a person has been bailed from a police station to appear either at a magistrates' court or at a police station, proceedings for an offence of failure to surrender to bail should be initiated by way of charging the accused. The provisions of the Magistrates' Courts Act 1980, s 127 (which prevent summary proceedings from being instituted more than six months after the offence) do not apply in respect of offences against BA 1976, s 6.

General factors

PACE permits the enforcement of bail which is conditioned upon appearance at a police station in the same way as if conditioned for appearance at a magistrates' court.

The Act also allows a person arrested on a warrant endorsed for bail to be released on bail (ie admitted to bail 'on the spot') without being taken to a police station, provided that the endorsement for bail does not demand sureties. If sureties are required, the person must be taken to a police station.

CHAPTER 6
Identification methods

Identification may be made by witnesses who saw the crime committed who may make an identification in a video identification, identification parade, or similar procedure. There may be an identification by fingerprints, or by body samples such as blood or hair to generate a DNA profile. The Home Secretary is required by the Police and Criminal Evidence Act 1984 (PACE), s 66 to issue a Code of Practice in connection with the identification of persons. The relevant Code of Practice (Code D: the Code of Practice for the Identification of Persons by Police Officers, hereafter referred to as the Identification Code) is concerned with three methods used by police and police staff to identify people in connection with the investigation of offences: identification by witnesses, identification by fingerprints, identification by use of footwear impressions and identification by body samples, swabs and impressions. It is also concerned with the keeping of records and with the taking of photographs of arrested people. The provisions of the Code, together with PACE, are designed to ensure that approved procedures are followed in relation to all matters concerned with identification.

GENERAL PRINCIPLES

The Identification Code provides certain general principles which apply to all methods by which identification can be made. It provides that:

(1) Where a record is made of any action requiring the authority of an officer of a specified rank, the name (except in the case of terrorism inquiries, where the warrant or other identification number should be given) and rank of the officer must be included in the record. Where the Code requires the prior authority or agreement of an officer of at least the rank of inspector or superintendent, that authority may be given by a sergeant or chief inspector who has been authorised to perform the functions of the higher rank under PACE, s 107.

(2) All records must be timed and signed by the maker (or his warrant or other identification number given in the case of terrorism inquiries).

(3) In the case of a detained person records must be made in the custody record unless otherwise specified.

(4) Where the consent of the suspect to a procedure is required, the consent of a suspect who is mentally disordered or mentally vulnerable is only valid if given in the presence of the appropriate adult; and in the case of a juvenile his parent or guardian must consent in addition to the juvenile himself (unless he is under fourteen, in which case the consent of his parent or guardian suffices in its own right). These provisions follow the general rules of good practice. If there is a suspicion that a suspect is a child or young person or is mentally disordered or otherwise mentally vulnerable etc, the procedure should be followed as a matter of fairness to that individual.

(5) In the case of a person who is blind or seriously visually impaired or unable to read, the custody officer or identification officer must ensure that his solicitor, relative, the appropriate adult or some other person likely to take an interest in him (and not involved in the investigation) is available to help in checking any documentation. Where the Code requires written consent or signification, then the person who is assisting may be asked to sign if the detained person so wishes.

(6) If any information concerning the processes of an identification must be given to or sought from a suspect, it must be given or sought in the presence of the appropriate adult if the suspect is mentally disordered or otherwise mentally vulnerable, or a juvenile. If the appropriate adult is not present when the information is first given or sought, the procedure must be repeated in his presence when he arrives. If the suspect is deaf or there is doubt about his hearing ability or his ability to understand, the information must be given through an interpreter.

(7) Any procedure involving the participation of a witness who is or appears to be mentally disordered, otherwise mentally vulnerable or a juvenile must take place in the presence of the appropriate adult but the adult must not be allowed to prompt any identification of a suspect by a witness. The appropriate adult should not be (or be likely to be) a witness in the case.

The terms 'appropriate adult' and 'solicitor' where they appear above have the same meaning as in the Detention Code (see pp 118 and 134).

Persons other than police officers, including 'designated persons and other civilian support staff', must comply with the Identification Code. Such persons must be employees of a police authority under the control of the chief officer of police or employed by a person contracted to provide services relating to persons arrested or otherwise in custody.

IDENTIFICATION BY WITNESSES

Identification by witnesses arises, for example, if the offender is seen committing the crime and a witness is given an opportunity to identify the suspect in a video identification, identification parade, or similar procedure designed to test the ability of a witness to identify the person he saw on a previous occasion and to provide safeguards against mistaken identification.

A record must be made of the description of the suspect as first given by a potential witness. This must be made and kept in a form which enables details of that description to be accurately produced from it, in a visible and legible form, which can be given to the suspect or to the suspect's solicitor in accordance with the Code and, unless otherwise specified, be made before the witness takes part in any identification procedures. A copy must be provided to the suspect or his solicitor before any procedures under the Code are carried out.

Where the suspect is known and available

In a case involving disputed identification evidence, and where the identity of the suspect is known to the police and he is available, the methods of identification which may be used are:

(a) video identification (where the witness is shown video images of a known suspect, together with similar images of other people who resemble him). A general point relating to video identification is that moving images must be used unless the suspect is known but not available, or the suspect has unusual features and the identification officer does not consider that replication of a physical feature can be achieved or that it is possible to conceal the location of the feature on the image of the suspect. The identification officer may then decide to make use of video identification but using still images; Annex A to the Identification Code (p 186) governs video identification;

(b) identification parade (where the witness sees the suspect in a line of other people who resemble the suspect: Annex B to the Identification Code (p 189) governs this);

(c) group identification (where the witness sees the suspect in an informal group of people: Annex C to the Identification Code (p 192) governs this); and

(d) a confrontation by a witness (where the suspect is directly confronted by the witness: Annex D to the Identification Code (p 195) governs this).

A suspect is 'known' for present purposes if there is sufficient information known to the police to justify the arrest of a particular person (the 'suspect') for suspected involvement in the offence. A suspect is 'available' if immediately available to take part in the procedure or will become available in a reasonably short time and is willing to take an effective part in at least one of the identification procedures.

The arrangements for, and conduct of, these four types of identification are the responsibility of an officer *not below the rank of inspector* who must *not be involved in the investigation;* he is called the 'identification officer'.

No officer or any other person involved with the investigation may take any part in these procedures beyond the extent required by the procedures, or act as the identification officer. However, an identification officer may consult the officer in charge of an investigation to determine which procedure to use. Unless otherwise specified, the identification officer may allow another officer or member of civilian staff to make arrangements for, and to conduct any of, these identification procedures. The identification officer must supervise such persons effectively.

There will be a breach of this prohibition, not only if an officer investigating an offence participates in the actual identification process, but also if he takes the witness to the police station at which an identification is to be attempted. This is understandable since such contact permits the transfer of information concerning the identification.

Circumstances in which an identification procedure must be held

Whenever:

(a) a witness has identified a suspect or purported to have identified him prior to any identification procedure having been held; or

(b) there is a witness available, who expresses an ability to identify the suspect, or where there is a reasonable chance of the witness being able to do so, and he has not been given an opportunity to identify the suspect in any procedure and the suspect disputes being the person the witness claims to have seen,

an identification procedure must be held unless it is not practicable or it would serve no useful purpose in proving or disproving whether the suspect was involved in committing the offence. An example would be when it is not disputed that the suspect is already well known to the witness who claims to have seen him commit the crime.

An identification procedure may also be held if the officer in charge of an investigation considers that it would be useful.

Identification procedures must be held as soon as practicable.

Selecting an identification procedure

Where it is proposed to hold an identification procedure, the suspect must initially be offered either a video identification or an identification parade (the officer in charge of the case may choose freely between these two options) unless he considers that in the particular circumstances it is more satisfactory to hold a group identification and that it is practicable to arrange one. He should discuss with the identification officer which of the two options is the most suitable and practicable. An identification parade may not be practicable because of factors such as the number of witnesses, their state of health, availability and travelling requirements. A video identification would normally be more suitable if, in a particular case, it could be arranged and completed sooner than an identification parade.

Where a suspect refuses the offered identification procedure he must state his reason for doing so and may obtain advice from his solicitor and appropriate adult if present. All such persons must be allowed to make representations as to why another identification procedure should be used. A record must be made of these matters.

After consideration of such reasons and representations the identification officer must, if appropriate, arrange for the suspect to be offered an alternative which the officer considers to be suitable and practicable. If he decides that it is not suitable and practicable to offer an alternative, the reasons for that decision must be recorded.

If a suspect refuses or fails to take part in a video identification, or refuses to take part in the only practicable option from that list, the identification officer may make arrangements for a covert video identification or other arrangements to test the ability of a witness to identify the person. He may use suitable images of the suspect, whether moving or still, which are available or can be obtained.

Where none of these options are practicable the identification officer may arrange a confrontation.

Notice to suspect

Before a video identification, an identification parade or a group identification is arranged, the following must be explained to the suspect:

(a) the purpose of the video identification, identification parade or group identification;

(b) the suspect's entitlement to free legal advice;

(c) the procedures for holding it (including the suspect's right to have a solicitor or friend present);

(d) that he does not have to take part in a video identification, identification parade or group identification;

(e) whether, for the purpose of the video identification procedure, images of the suspect have previously been obtained and, if so, that he may co-operate in providing further suitable images which must be used in place of those previously taken;

(f) where appropriate, the special arrangements for juveniles;

(g) where appropriate, the special arrangements for mentally disordered or otherwise mentally vulnerable persons;

(h) that, if he does not consent to and take part in a video identification, identification parade or group identification his refusal may be given in evidence in any subsequent trial and police may proceed covertly without his consent, or make other arrangements to test whether a witness can identify him;

(i) that should he significantly alter his appearance between being offered an identification procedure and any attempt to hold it, this may be given in evidence and the identification officer may then consider other forms of identification;

(j) that a moving image or photograph may be taken of the suspect when he attends for any identification procedure;

(k) whether the witness has been shown photographs, a computerised or artist's composite likeness or similar likeness or picture by the police during the investigation before the identity of the suspect became known;

(l) that if the suspect changes his appearance before an identification parade it may not be practicable to arrange one on the day in question or subsequently and, because of his change of appearance, the identification officer may then consider alternative methods of identification; and

(m) that the suspect or his solicitor will be provided with details of the description of the suspect as first given by any witnesses who are to attend the video identification, identification parade, group identification, or confrontation.

The identification officer must also give to the suspect a written notice (the 'Notice to Suspect') containing this information and give him a reasonable opportunity to read it. The suspect must then be asked to sign a second copy of the notice to indicate whether or not he is willing to participate in the making of a video or take part in an identification parade or group identification. The signed copy must be retained by the identification officer.

The duties of an identification officer in respect of giving information and the giving of the Notice to Suspect may be performed by the custody officer or any other officer not involved in the investigation if:

(a) it is proposed to release the suspect, in order that an identification procedure can be arranged and carried out (as where the suspect is bailed to attend an identification parade), and an inspector is not available to act as identification officer before the suspect leaves the station; or

(b) it is proposed to keep the subject in police detention whilst the procedure is arranged or carried out, and waiting for an inspector to act as the identification officer would cause unreasonable delay.

Where it is suspected that the giving of a notice may lead the suspect to take steps to avoid identification

Where the identification officer and the officer in charge of the investigation have reasonable grounds to suspect that, if the suspect was given the information and notice as set out above, the suspect would thereafter take steps to avoid being seen by a witness in any identification procedure, the identification officer may arrange for images of the suspect for use in a video identification procedure to be obtained before giving the information and notice. If this is done, the suspect may then co-operate in providing suitable new images.

Where the suspect is known but not available

Where a suspect is known but is not available or has ceased to be available, the identification officer may make arrangements for a video identification (see p 186) in accordance with the Identification Code (eg by using images they already have of the suspect, or finding him and filming him). If necessary, the identification officer may follow the video identification procedures but using still images. Any suitable moving or still images may be used and these may be obtained covertly if necessary; covert activity must be limited to that which is necessary. Alternatively, the identification officer may make arrangements for a group identification. The identification officer may arrange a confrontation where no other option is available. The requirements for the giving of information to, and seeking it from, the suspect or for the suspect to have the opportunity to view the images prior to them being shown to a witness do not apply to a video identification where the suspect is not available. The record must indicate the reason for the suspect not being available.

These provisions would apply where a known suspect deliberately makes himself unavailable in order to delay or frustrate arrangements being made for obtaining evidence. It enables any suitable images of the suspect (moving or still) which are available or can be obtained to be used in a video identification. Examples include images from custody and other CCTV systems and from visually recorded interview records.

Where the identity of the suspect is not known

In such cases a witness may be taken to a neighbourhood or place to see whether he can identify the person whom he saw on the relevant occasion. Although it is appreciated that there can be no control over the general mix of people, their age, sex, race and general description or manner of dress, the principles governing formal identification procedures must be followed so far as practicable. For example:

(1) Before asking the witness to make an identification, a record must be made, where practicable, of any description of the suspect given by the witness.
(2) The witness's attention should not be directed towards any individual unless, having regard to the circumstances, this is unavoidable. This does not prevent a witness being told to look carefully at people who are around at the time, or to look towards a group or in a particular direction if this appears to be necessary to ensure that the witness does not overlook a possible suspect simply because the witness is looking in the opposite direction and also to enable a witness to make comparisons between any suspect and others who are in the area at the time.
(3) Where there is more than one witness, every effort should be made to keep them separate and, where practicable, witnesses should be taken to see whether they can identify a person independently.
(4) Once there is sufficient information to justify the arrest of a particular individual, for example after a witness makes a positive identification, formal identification procedures must be adopted for any other witnesses in relation to that individual.
(5) The officer or civilian support staff accompanying the witness must record in his pocket book the action taken as soon as practicable and in as much detail as possible. Such a record must include the date, time and place of the previous occasion upon which the witness claims to have seen the suspect; where any identification is made; how it was made and the conditions at the time (for example, the distance which the witness was from the suspect, the weather and light); if the witness's attention was drawn to the suspect; the reason for this; and anything said by the witness or the suspect about the identification or the conduct of the procedure.

A witness must not be shown photographs, computerised or artist's composite likenesses, or similar likenesses or pictures if the identity of the suspect is known to the police and the suspect is available to take part in a video identification, an identification parade or a group identification. If the identity of a suspect is not known, the showing of such pictures must be in accordance with Annex E to the Identification Code (see p 195).

Documentation

A record must be made of any identification procedure on the forms provided. Where an identification officer considers that it is not practicable to hold a video identification or identification parade, when either is requested by the suspect, a record must be made and the reasons explained to the suspect. Failure or refusal to co-operate in a video identification, identification parade or group identification must be recorded. If applicable, the grounds for obtaining images, where it was reasonably suspected that following notice a suspect would take steps to avoid being seen by a witness, must be recorded.

Showing films and photographs of incidents and information released to the media

Films or photographs may be shown to the public at large through the national or local media, or to police officers for the purposes of recognition and tracing suspects. However, when such material is shown to potential witnesses (including police officers) for the purpose of obtaining identification evidence, it must be shown on an individual basis so as to avoid the possibility of collusion, and the showing must, so far as possible, follow the principles for video identification if the suspect is known (see p 186) or identification by photographs if the suspect is not known (see p 195).

When a broadcast or publication is made, a copy of the material released by the police to the media for the purpose of recognising or tracing the suspect must be kept and the suspect or his solicitor must be allowed to see this material before any identification procedure is carried out, provided that it is practicable to do so and would not unreasonably delay the investigation. Each witness must be asked, after he has taken part in the identification procedure, whether he has seen any broadcast or published films or photographs relating to the offence or seen any description of the suspect. His reply must be recorded. This does not affect any separate requirement under the Criminal Procedure and Investigations Act 1996 to retain material in connection with an investigation.

Video film identification

The following rules are laid down by Annex A as to how video identification should be carried out.

General

The arrangements for obtaining and ensuring the availability of a suitable set of images to be used in a video identification must be the responsibility of an identification officer or investigation officers who have no direct involvement with the relevant case.

The set of images must include the suspect and at least eight other people who, so far as possible, resemble the suspect in age, general appearance and position in life. Only one suspect may appear on any set unless there are two suspects of roughly similar appearance in which case they may be shown together with at least twelve other persons.

If the suspect has an unusual physical feature, for example a facial scar, tattoo or distinctive hairstyle or hair colour which does not appear on the images of the other people that are available to be used, steps may be taken to:

(a) conceal the location of the feature on the images of the suspect and the other people; or
(b) replicate that feature on the images of the other people.

For these purposes, the feature may be concealed or replicated electronically or by any other method which it is practicable to use to ensure that the images of the suspect and other people resemble each other. The identification officer has discretion to choose whether to conceal or replicate the feature and the method to be used. If an unusual physical feature has been described by the witness, the identification officer should, if practicable, have that feature replicated. If it has not been described, concealment may be more appropriate.

If the identification officer decides that a feature should be concealed or replicated the reason for the decision and whether the feature was concealed or replicated in the image shown to any witness must be recorded. However, if the witness requests to view an image where an unusual physical feature has been concealed or replicated without that feature being concealed or replicated, the witness may be allowed to do so.

The images used to conduct a video identification must, so far as possible, show the suspect and other people in the same positions or carrying out the same sequence of movements. They must also show the suspect and other people under identical conditions unless the identification officer reasonably believes:

(a) that because of the suspect's failure or refusal to co-operate or other reasons, it is not practicable for the conditions to be identical; or

(b) that any difference in the conditions would not attract a witness's attention to any individual image.

The reason why identical conditions were not practicable must be recorded on the forms provided.

Provision must be made for each person filmed to be identified by number. If police officers are filmed, any numerals or other identifying badges must be concealed. If a prison inmate is filmed, either as a suspect or not, then either all or none of the persons filmed should be in prison clothing.

The suspect or his solicitor, friend or appropriate adult must be given a reasonable opportunity to see the complete set of images before it is shown to any witness. If the suspect has a reasonable objection to the set of images or any of its participants, he must be asked to state his reason. Steps must, if practicable, be taken to remove the grounds for objection. If this is not practicable, the suspect and/or his representative must be told why his objections cannot be met. The objection, the reason given for it and why it cannot be met must be recorded.

Before the images are shown the suspect or his solicitor must be provided with the details of the first description of the suspect by any witnesses who are to attend the video identification. The suspect or his solicitor must also be allowed to view any material released to the media by the police for the purpose of recognising or tracing the suspect, provided it is practicable to do so and to do so would not unreasonably delay the investigation.

Where practicable, the suspect's solicitor, or where one is not instructed the suspect himself, must be given reasonable notification of the time and place that it is intended to conduct the video identification in order that a legal representative may attend on behalf of the suspect. The suspect himself may not be present when the film is shown to a witness. In the absence of a person representing the suspect the viewing itself shall be recorded on video. No unauthorised person may be present.

Conduct of video identification

The identification officer is responsible for ensuring that, before they see the set of images, witnesses are not able to communicate with each other about the case, see any of the images which are to be shown, see, or be reminded of, any photograph or description of the suspect or be given any other indication as to the suspect's identity, or overhear a witness who has seen the material. There must be no discussion with the witness about the composition of the set of images and the witness must not be told whether a previous witness has made any identification.

Only one witness may see the set of images at a time. Immediately before the images are seen, the witness must be told that the person he saw may or may not appear in the images he is shown and that if he cannot make a positive identification he should say so. The witness must be advised that at any point he may ask to see a particular part of the set of images or to have a particular image frozen for him to study. Furthermore, it should be pointed out to the witness that there is no limit on how many times he can view the whole set of images or any part of them. However, he should be asked to refrain from making any decision until he has seen the entire set at least twice.

Once the witness has seen the whole set of images at least twice and has indicated that he does not want to view the images or any part of them again, the witness must be asked to say whether the individual he saw in person on an earlier occasion has been shown and, if so, to identify him by number. The witness will then be shown that image to confirm the identification.

Care must be taken not to direct the witness's attention to any one individual image, or to give any other indication of the suspect's identity. Where a witness has previously made an identification by photographs, or a computerised or artist's composite likeness or similar likeness, the witness must not be reminded of such a photograph or composite likeness once a suspect is available for identification by other means in accordance with the Identification Code. Neither must the witness be reminded of any description of the suspect.

As already indicated, where video films or photographs have been released to the media by the police, each witness must be asked after the procedure whether he has seen any broadcast or published films or photographs or any description of suspects relating to the offence and his reply must be recorded.

Image security and destruction

It is the responsibility of the identification officer to ensure that all relevant material containing sets of images used for a specific identification procedure is kept securely and its movement accounted for. In particular, no one involved in the investigation against the suspect may be permitted to view the material prior to its being shown to any witness.

Where a video film has been made all copies of it must be destroyed with the exceptions as apply to set out at pp 202–203. An opportunity of witnessing the destruction must be given to the suspect if he so requests within five days of being cleared or informed that he will not be prosecuted.

Records

A record must be made of all those participating in or seeing the set of images whose names are known to the police.

A record of the conduct of the video identification must be made on the forms provided. This must include anything said by the witness about the identification or the conduct of the procedure and any reasons why it was not practicable to comply with any provisions of the Identification Code governing the conduct of a video identification.

Identification parades

Identification parades must be carried out in accordance with Annex B to the Identification Code, which provides as follows.

A suspect must be given a reasonable opportunity to have a solicitor or friend present, and the identification officer must ask him to indicate his wishes in this respect on a second copy of the 'Notice to Suspect'. A parade may take place either in a normal room or in one equipped with a screen permitting witnesses to see members of the parade without being seen. The procedures for the composition and conduct of the parade are the same in both cases (except that a parade involving a screen may take place only when the suspect's solicitor, friend or appropriate adult is present or the parade is video recorded). This exception is an obvious safeguard, if the evidence of the identification is to have any value.

Before the parade takes place the suspect or his solicitor must be provided with the details of the first description of the suspect by any witnesses who are to attend the parade. The suspect or his solicitor should be allowed to view any material released to the media by the police for the purpose of recognising or tracing the suspect, provided it is practicable to do so and would not unreasonably delay the investigation.

Cases involving prison inmates

If a prison inmate is required for identification, and there are no security problems about his leaving the establishment, he may be asked to participate in an identification parade or video identification.

A parade may be conducted in a Prison Department establishment. If it is, it must be conducted as far as practicable under normal parade rules. Members of the public must make up the parade unless there are serious security or control objections to their admission to the establishment. In such cases, or if a video or group identification is arranged within the establishment, other inmates may participate.

If an inmate is the suspect, he should not be required to wear prison clothing for the parade unless the other persons taking part are other inmates in prison clothing or are members of the public who are prepared to wear prison clothing for the occasion.

The evidential value of a group identification in a prison could be high. Where prison clothing is worn by all, the similarity of dress of all participants will make identification difficult for witnesses who are not certain of the appearance of a suspect.

Conduct of an identification parade

Immediately before the parade, the suspect must be reminded of the procedure governing its conduct and given the appropriate caution. All unauthorised persons must be excluded from the place where the parade is held.

Once the parade has been formed, everything afterwards in respect of it must take place in the presence and hearing of the suspect and of any interpreter, solicitor, friend or appropriate adult who is present (unless the parade involves a screen, in which case everything said to or by any witness at the place where the parade is held must be said in the hearing and presence of the suspect's solicitor, friend or appropriate adult or be video recorded). No investigating officer should enter the room in which the parade is being held.

The parade must consist of at least eight persons (other than the suspect) who, so far as possible, resemble the suspect in age, height, general appearance and position in life. Where a suspect has an unusual physical feature, for example, a facial scar or tattoo or distinctive hairstyle or hair colour which cannot be replicated on other members of the identification parade steps may be taken to conceal the location of that feature on the suspect and other members of the parade if the suspect and his solicitor or appropriate adult agree. The use of a plaster or a hat may achieve such an objective. It is also permissible to take reasonable steps in good faith to make non-suspects resemble the suspect by the use of make-up, but this should not be done if there is an objection.

One suspect only may be included in a parade unless there are two suspects of roughly similar appearance, in which case they may be paraded together with at least twelve other persons. In no circumstances may more than two suspects be included in one parade, and where there are separate parades they must be made up of different persons.

Where all members of a similar group are possible suspects, separate identification parades must be held for each member of the group unless there are two suspects of similar appearance. Where police officers in uniform form an identification parade, numerals or other identifying badges must be concealed. It must be remembered that if a complaint concerns a police officer in uniform who was on duty at a particular time, all those on duty at the time who would have had an opportunity to be in the vicinity of any incident, whether in accordance with instructions or not, should be subjected to the identification procedure.

When the suspect is brought into the place where the parade is to be held, he must be asked whether he has any objection to the arrangements for the parade or to any of the other participants in it and to state reasons for any objections made. The suspect may obtain advice from his solicitor or friend, if present, before the parade proceeds. If the suspect has a reasonable objection to the arrangements or to any of the participants, steps must, where practicable, be taken to remove the grounds for objection. Where it is not practicable to do so, the officer must explain to the suspect why his objections cannot be met and a record must be made of the objection, the reason for it and why it cannot be met must be recorded on the forms provided.

The suspect may select his own position in the line. Where there is more than one witness, the identification officer must tell the suspect, after each witness has left the room, that he can if he wishes change position in the line. Each position in the line must be clearly numbered, whether by means of a numeral laid on the floor in front of each parade member or by other means.

Appropriate arrangements must be made to ensure, before they attend the parade, that witnesses are not able to:

(a) communicate with each other or overhear a witness who has already seen the parade;
(b) see any member of the parade;

(c) see, or be reminded of, any photograph or description of the suspect, nor are given any other indication of his identity; or

(d) see the suspect, either before or after the parade.

The person conducting a witness to the parade must not discuss with him the composition of the parade and, in particular, he must not disclose whether a previous witness has made any identification.

Witnesses must be brought in one at a time. Immediately before a witness inspects the parade, the identification officer or approved person must tell him that the person he saw may or may not be on the parade and that if he cannot make a positive identification he should say so. The witness must also be told that he should not make any decision before looking at each member of the parade at least twice. When the identification officer or civilian support staff member is satisfied that the witness has properly looked at each member of the parade, he must ask him whether the person he saw in person on an earlier relevant occasion is on the parade and, if so, to indicate the number of the person concerned. Where this takes place behind a screen it is desirable for the witness to be asked to make a note of the number of the person identified so that he may give direct evidence of that fact. However, if a witness is unable to recall that number at a subsequent trial, evidence from the person who conducted the parade as to the number called out by the witness is admissible as there is statutory authority for its admission. If the witness makes an identification after the parade has ended, the suspect and, if present, his solicitor, interpreter or friend must be informed. Where this occurs, consideration should be given to allowing the witness a second opportunity to identify the suspect.

If a witness wishes to hear any parade member speak, adopt any specified posture, or see him move, the witness must first be asked whether he can identify any persons on the parade on the basis of appearance only. When the request is to hear members of the parade speak, the witness must be reminded that the participants in the parade have been chosen on the basis of physical appearance only. Members of the parade may then be asked to comply with the witness's request to hear them speak, to see them move or to adopt any specified posture.

If the witness requests that the person indicated by him remove anything used to conceal the location of an unusual physical feature, that person may be asked to remove it.

Where video films or photographs have been released to the media by the police for the purpose of recognising or tracing the suspect, the investigating officer must ask each witness after the parade whether he has seen any broadcast or published films or photographs relating to the offence and must record his reply.

When the last witness has left, the suspect must be asked whether he wishes to make any comments on the conduct of the parade.

A video recording of the parade must be taken. Where this is impracticable a colour photograph must be taken. A copy must be supplied on request to the suspect or his solicitor within a reasonable time. The rules about the destruction and retention of such a video or photograph are the same as those described on pp 202–203.

If the identification officer or civilian support staff member asks any person to leave the parade because he is interfering with its conduct, the circumstances must be recorded. A record must be made of all those present at an identification parade whose names are known to the police and a record of the conduct of the parade must be made on the forms provided, including anything said by the witness or suspect about any identifications or the conduct of the procedure, and any reasons why it was not possible to comply with any provision of the Identification Code.

Group identification

Group identification must be carried out in accordance with Annex C to the Identification Code, which provides as follows.

General

The arrangements must as far as practicable satisfy the requirements of an identification parade.

A group identification may take place either with the suspect's consent and cooperation or covertly without his consent.

The location is a matter for the identification officer although he may take into account representations made by a suspect, appropriate adult, his solicitor or a friend. It should be a place in which other people are passing by, or waiting around informally, in groups so that the suspect is able to join them and is capable of being seen at the same time as others in the group.

A group identification could be held, for example, where people are leaving an escalator, walking through a shopping centre, passengers at railway or bus stations, waiting in queues or groups, or where people are standing or sitting in groups in other public places. Where identification is carried out covertly, it could take place on a route regularly travelled by the suspect, including buses, trains and public places.

While it is appreciated that the general description of people included in a group identification cannot be controlled, the identification officer must consider the general appearance and number of persons likely to be present. In particular, he must reasonably expect that persons broadly similar to the suspect will appear from time to time during the period of the witness's observation. A group identification need not take place where the identification officer believes that, because of the unusual appearance of the suspect, none of the locations which it would be practicable to use is likely to make the identification fair.

Immediately after a group identification (whether with or without the suspect's consent) a colour photograph or a video should be taken of the scene, where this is practicable, so as to give a general impression of the scene and the number of people present. Alternatively, if it is practicable, the group identification may be video recorded. If it is not practicable to take the photograph or video immediately after the group identification, such a record must be made later where practicable.

If at the time of the identification, the suspect is on his own, it remains a group identification.

Before the group identification takes place the suspect or his solicitor should be provided with details of the first description of the suspect by any witness attending it. In addition the suspect or his solicitor must be allowed to view any material released to the media for the purpose of recognising or tracing the suspect, provided that it is practicable to do so and it will not unreasonably delay the investigation. Where such releases have been made each witness must be asked after the procedure whether he has seen them and any reply must be recorded.

Identification with the consent of the suspect

A suspect must be given a reasonable opportunity to have a solicitor or friend present. He must be asked by the identification officer to indicate his wishes on a second copy of the Notice to Suspect. The witness, person carrying out the procedure, suspect's solicitor, appropriate adult, friend and any interpreter for the witness may be concealed from the sight of the persons in the group if this facilitates the identification. The person conducting a witness to the location must not discuss the forthcoming group identification nor disclose whether a previous witness has made an identification.

Anything said to or by a witness during the procedure regarding the identification must be said in the presence and hearing of those present at the procedure. Witnesses who have not yet attended the identification must not be able to communicate with each other about the case or overhear a witness who has already been given an opportunity to see the suspect in the group, nor see the suspect or see or be reminded of any photograph or description of the suspect or be given any other indication of his identity. Witnesses must be brought to the place singly and must be told that the person they saw may or may not be in the group and that if they cannot make a positive identification they should say so. The witness must then be asked to observe the group; the manner of doing so will depend upon whether the group is stationary or moving.

Moving group

The following provisions of Annex C apply when the group in which the suspect is to appear is moving, for example leaving an escalator.

If two or more suspects consent to a group identification, they should each be subject to different identification procedures, which maybe conducted consecutively. The person conducting the procedure must ask the witness to observe the group and ask him to point out any person he thinks he saw on an earlier relevant occasion. The suspect should then be allowed to take up what ever position in the group he prefers. When an identification is made, the witness must, where practicable, be asked to take a closer look to confirm identification. If this is not practicable, or the witness in unable to confirm the identification, the witness must be asked how sure he is that the person is the relevant person. The duration of the identification process must be such that the person conducting the procedure reasonably believes necessary for the witness to be able to make comparisons between the suspect and other individuals of broadly similar appearance.

Stationary group

When the group in which the suspect is to appear is stationary, for example people waiting in a queue, the following provisions of Annex C apply.

Where there are two or more suspects who consent to a group identification, there should generally be two separate procedures. However, if they are of broadly similar appearance, they may appear in the same group. Separate stationary group identifications must consist of different people.

The suspect may select his position. Where there is more than one witness, the suspect must be told, out of sight and hearing of any witness, that he may change his position between witnesses. The witness must be asked to pass along or amongst the group and to look at each person at least twice before making an identification. Once the witness has done so, he must be asked if the person he saw previously is in the group and to indicate that person by any means considered appropriate by the person conducting the identification. If this is not practicable, the witness will be asked to point out that person. He must, where practicable, be asked to take a closer look and confirm his identification. If this is not practicable, he must be asked how sure he is that the person is the one seen on a previous occasion.

Rules common to moving and stationary groups

An unreasonable delay by the suspect in joining the group, or (having joined the group) a deliberate concealment from the sight of the witness, may be considered as a refusal to co-operate in the identification.

Where a witness identifies someone other than the suspect, that person should be asked if he is prepared to give his name and address. He is not obliged to do so. There is no duty to record persons present in the group or at the place where the procedure is conducted.

At the end of the procedure the suspect must be asked to comment on the conduct of the procedure. If he has not previously been informed the suspect must be told of any identifications made by witnesses.

Group identifications without suspect's consent

These should, so far as possible, follow the rules set out above. As such an identification will take place without the suspect's knowledge, no solicitor etc will be present. Any number of suspects may be identified at the same time.

Group identifications in police stations

These must only take place for reasons of security, safety, or because it is impracticable to hold them elsewhere. The group identification may be in a room equipped with a one-way screen, or elsewhere in a police station. Safeguards applicable to identification parades must be followed where practicable.

Group identifications involving prison inmates

These may only take place in a prison or police station. They must follow the procedure which is applicable to group identifications in a police station. Where a group identification takes place in a prison, other inmates may participate. If the suspect is in prison clothing, all persons taking part must be so dressed.

Documentation

Where a photograph or video is taken a copy must be supplied on request to the suspect or his solicitor within a reasonable time. Such records must be destroyed or wiped clean in accordance with the rules described on pp 202–203. A record of the conduct of the identification must be made on the forms provided and must include anything said by the witness or suspect about any identification or the conduct of the procedure and any reason why it was not practicable to comply with any of the provisions of the Code governing the conduct of group identifications.

Confrontation by a witness

A confrontation may be used when it is not possible to arrange a video identification, identification parade, or a group identification. A confrontation does not require the suspect's consent, although he cannot be forcibly compelled to make his face visible to a witness.

As with the other identification procedures, the identification officer is responsible for the arrangements for, and conduct of, any confrontation of a suspect by a witness. The rules concerning confrontation, which are set out in Annex D to the Identification Code, are simple.

Before the confrontation takes place, the witness must be told that the person he saw may or may not be the person he is to confront and that if he cannot make a positive identification he should say so. In addition, before the confrontation, the suspect or his solicitor must be provided with the details of the first description of the suspect given by any witness who is to attend the confrontation. The note should be made available for examination at trial to act as a safeguard against the risk of auto-suggestion. Where a broadcast or publication has been made for the purpose of recognition and tracing of suspects, the suspect or his solicitor should also be allowed to view any material released by the police to the media, provided that it is practicable to do so and would not unreasonably delay the investigation. The suspect must be confronted independently by each witness, who must be asked 'Is this the person?' If the witness identifies the person but is unable to confirm the identification he must be asked how sure he is that the person is the person he saw on the earlier relevant occasion. Confrontation must take place in the presence of the suspect's solicitor, interpreter or friend, where he has one, unless this would cause unreasonable delay.

The confrontation should normally take place in the police station, either in a normal room or one equipped with a screen permitting a witness to see the suspect without being seen. In both cases the procedures are the same, except that a room equipped with a screen may be used only when the suspect's solicitor, friend or appropriate adult is present or the confrontation is recorded on video. After the confrontation each witness must be asked whether he has seen any broadcast or published films or photographs or any descriptions of suspects relating to the offence, and his reply must be recorded.

The showing of photographs

Annex E of the Identification Code sets out the procedures to be followed if photographs, or photofit, identikit or similar pictures are shown to a witness for identification purposes where the suspect's identity is not known. Where it is proposed to show photographs to a witness the officer in charge of the investigation must confirm to the officer responsible for supervising and directing the showing that the first description of the suspect given by the witness has been recorded. If it has not, the Annex E procedure must be postponed.

An officer of the rank of sergeant or above must be responsible for supervising and directing the showing of photographs, but the actual showing may be done by a constable or police staff. (This means that most of the responsibility remains with the sergeant etc. The accountability of a constable or approved person will be limited to non-observance of the directions given.) The supervising officer must confirm that the first description of the suspect given by the witness has been recorded before the witness is shown the photographs. If he is unable to confirm that the description has been recorded, he must postpone the showing.

Only one witness may be shown photographs at any one time. He must be given as much privacy as practicable and must not be allowed to communicate with any other witness in the case. The witness must be shown not less than twelve photographs at a time, which shall, as far as possible, all be of a similar type.

When the witness is shown photographs, he must be told that the photograph of the person whom he has said that he has previously seen may or may not be amongst them and that if he cannot make a positive identification he should say so. The witness must be told not to make a decision until he has viewed at least twelve photographs. He must not be prompted or guided in any way but must be left to make any selection without help. If a witness makes a positive identification from photographs then, unless the person identified is otherwise eliminated from the inquiries or is not available, other witnesses must not be shown photographs. However, both they and the witness who has made the identification must be asked to attend a video identification, an identification parade or group identification unless there is no dispute about the identification of the suspect. If the witness makes a selection but is unable to confirm the identification the person showing the photographs must ask the witness how sure he is that the photograph indicated is the person that he saw on a previous occasion.

Where the use of computerised or artist's composite likeness or similar likeness has led to there being a known suspect who can be asked to participate in video identification, appear on an identification parade or participate in a group identification, that likeness shall not be shown to other potential witnesses.

Where a witness attending a video identification, an identification parade or a group identification has previously been shown photographs or computerised or artist's composite likeness or similar likeness, the suspect and his solicitor must be informed of this fact before the video identification, identification parade or group identification takes place. The officer in charge of the investigation is responsible for informing the identification officer of this fact.

Any photograph used must be retained for production in court if necessary, whether or not an identification is made.

None of the photographs used shall be destroyed, whether or not an identification is made, since they may be required for production in court. The photographs should be numbered and a separate photograph taken of the frame or part of the album from which the witness made an identification as an aid to reconstituting it.

Documentation

Whether or not an identification is made, a record must be kept of the showing of photographs on forms provided for the purpose. The record must include any thing said by the witness about any identification or the conduct of the procedure, any reasons why it was not practicable to comply with any provisions of the Identification Code and the name and rank of the supervising officer, who must sign the record.

IDENTIFICATION BY FINGERPRINTS

PACE, ss 27, 61, 63A and 64 and the Identification Code deal with the taking of finger-prints and the circumstances in which fingerprints must be destroyed.

A person's fingerprints may be taken only with his consent (which must be in writing if given at a police station) or in accordance with the provisions of the following paragraph.

Powers to take fingerprints from a person over the age of ten years without consent are provided by PACE, ss 27 and 61. Those sections provide that fingerprints may be taken without consent:

(a) from a person detained at a police station, if an officer of at least the rank of inspector authorises them to be taken (which authority may only be given if the officer has reasonable grounds for suspecting the involvement of the person whose fingerprints are to be taken in a criminal offence and for believing that his fingerprints will tend to confirm or disprove his involvement *or will facilitate the ascertainment of his identity within the meaning of s 54A (authorisation of search and examination to ascertain identity) or both*; see below); or

(b) if the person is detained in consequence of his arrest for a recordable offence, or he has been charged with such an offence or informed that he will be prosecuted for it, and he has not had his fingerprints taken in the course of the investigation of the offence by the police. (Where such a person has had his fingerprints taken in the course of the investigation by the police, this does not prevent a second set of prints from being taken if the first did not constitute a full set or are of unsatisfactory quality for their purpose.); or

(c) if he has been convicted of a recordable offence or he has been cautioned for an admitted recordable offence, or he is a child or young person and has been warned or reprimanded under the Crime and Disorder Act 1998, s 65 for an admitted recordable offence; or

(d) a constable may take a person's fingerprints without the appropriate consent if the constable reasonably suspects that the person is committing or attempting to commit an offence, or has committed or attempted to commit an offence, and the name of the person is unknown to, and cannot readily be ascertained by the constable, or the constable has reasonable grounds for doubting whether a name furnished by the person as his name is his real name. This provision is not yet in force. The taking of fingerprints by virtue of this provision will not count for the purposes of PACE as taking them in the course of an investigation of an offence by the police.

The police may now use mobile digital fingerprint readers which are connected to the National Automated Fingerprint Identification System (NAFIS). This enables the taking of fingerprints (of two fingers) at a place other than a police station which may immediately be checked to assist an officer in deciding upon a course of action. Such fingerprints will also be subject to a speculative search against the database of fingerprints recovered from crime scenes.

Fingerprints taken prior to arrest will not be retained or added to NAFIS. These provisions are not in force at the time of writing.

'Recordable offence' is defined in p 66.

Paragraphs (a) and (b) do not apply to a person detained under the legislation relating to terrorism; special provision is made under the Terrorism Act 2000. An authorisation under PACE, s 54A may only be given where there has been a refusal by a person to identify himself, or the officer has reasonable grounds for suspecting that he is not who he claims to be. The section allows a detainee at a police station to be searched or examined or both, to establish (a) whether he has any marks, features or injuries that would tend to identify him as a person involved in the commission of an offence and to photograph any identifying marks, or (b) his identity. Such a search may only be carried out without the detainee's consent if authorised by an officer of at least inspector rank. Where it is done to establish identity, the authorising officer must be satisfied that the detainee has refused to identify himself or is reasonably suspected of giving a false identity.

In addition, the fingerprints of a person who has answered to bail at a court or police station may be taken without the appropriate consent if the court, or an officer of at least the rank of inspector, authorises them to be taken. This may be done where the court or officer reasonably believes that a person who has surrendered to bail is not the person admitted to bail and the person bailed has been previously fingerprinted, or the person who has answered to bail claims to be a different person from the person who had his fingerprints taken on a previous occasion.

In all cases an authorisation for fingerprinting may be given orally or in writing, but if given orally it must be confirmed in writing as soon as practicable. A person whose fingerprints are to be taken with or without consent must be told the reason before his fingerprints are taken. He must be told that his prints may be the subject of a speculative search against other fingerprints and a record must be made of this. This means that a check may be made against other fingerprints contained in records held by or on behalf of the police or held in connection with or as a result of an investigation into that offence.

PACE, s 64(1A) provides that where fingerprints or samples are taken from a person in connection with the investigation of an offence, and s 64(3) (below) does not require them to be destroyed, they may be retained after they have fulfilled the purpose for which they were taken but may not be used other than for purposes related to the prevention or detection of crime, the investigation of an offence, the conduct of a prosecution, or the identification of a deceased person or of the person from whom a body part came. However, by s 64(3), where fingerprints or samples are taken from someone who is not suspected of having committed the offence in question (elimination prints), they must be destroyed as soon as they have served their purpose, and neither the fingerprints or sample, or anything derived from the sample, may be used in evidence against the suspect, or for the investigation of any offence. Samples and fingerprints are not required to be destroyed under s 64(3):

(1) Where the non-suspected person consents in writing to the retention of the fingerprints or sample. Where this is done the use of the fingerprint or sample and the information gained from it is not restricted. Such consent cannot later be withdrawn.

(2) Where the fingerprint or sample was taken for the purpose of the same investigation of an offence for which a person from whom such a fingerprint or sample was taken has been convicted. This provision was introduced because there were found to be scientific reasons for processing some fingerprints or samples together and it is not technologically possible to separate them afterwards. This could occur where the fingerprints of a number of suspects were all found on a gun and were photographed together. However, the information derived from such a fingerprint or sample must not be used in evidence against that person, or for the purpose of any investigation of an offence. This restriction does not apply in cases where a written consent has been given under (1).

The House of Lords has held that PACE, s 64(1A) does not contravene the right to a private life under art 8 of the European Convention on Human Rights, nor the right not to be discriminated against under art 14. The reason was that the rule that fingerprints and samples could only be used for the purpose of 'the prevention or detection of crime, the investigation of an offence, or the conduct of a prosecution' meant that the interference with the right to privacy was not substantial and could be justified as necessary for that purpose. So far as discrimination is concerned, once such fingerprints or samples had been lawfully obtained, there was a clear and objective distinction between the individuals from whom these had been taken and those persons who had not been lawfully required to provide them.

Where fingerprints are destroyed, any copies must also be destroyed, and access to relevant computer data must be made impossible, as soon as it is practicable to do so. A person must be allowed to witness the destruction of his fingerprints if he so asks. In addition, if his fingerprints are destroyed or rendered in accessible he is entitled to a certificate, to be issued within three months of his application, certifying destruction or that access to the data has been made impossible.

PACE, s 63A(1), provides that, where a person has been arrested on suspicion of being involved in a recordable offence, or has been charged with a recordable offence, or has been informed that he will be reported for a recordable offence, fingerprints or samples or the information derived from samples taken under any power conferred by the Act from the person may be checked against (ie a speculative search may be conducted):

(a) other fingerprints or samples to which the person seeking to check has access and which are held by or on behalf of a police force, or are held in connection with or as a result of an investigation of an offence;

(b) information derived from other samples if the information is contained in records to which the person seeking to check has access and which are held as described in (a).

When the relevant provisions are in force, fingerprints taken by virtue of (d) on p 197 (reasonable suspicion that person whose name is not known is committing or has committed offence etc) may be checked against other fingerprints to which the person seeking to check has access and which are held by, or on behalf of, any one or more relevant enforcement authorities or which are held in connection with or as a result of an investigation of an offence.

The Identification Code deals with the taking of fingerprints for the purpose of Immigration Service inquiries in accordance with powers and procedures other than PACE and for which the Immigration Service (not the police) is responsible. Although the relevant legislation empowers police officers, as well as immigration officers, to take fingerprints, immigration officers will, almost without exception, be concerned. However, should it be necessary for a police officer to take such fingerprints, an officer is empowered to take fingerprints with or without consent, provided that the person is informed of the reason for which they are taken, and that they (and any copies) will be destroyed in accordance with the usual provisions concerning destruction which apply to fingerprints so taken.

Where public co-operation is being sought in relation to an investigation it is important to minimise the risk of confusion about the effect of giving consent to the provision of fingerprints. Fingerprints may be requested for the purpose of elimination or as a part of an intelligence-led screen and to be used only for that purpose. On other occasions they may be required to be retained for future use. Annex F to the Identification Code contains specimen endorsements in relation to the appropriate consent.

Documentation

A record must be made as soon as possible of the reason for taking a person's finger-prints without consent and of their destruction. If a person is detained at a police station when they are taken, the reason must be recorded on his custody record. If force is used a record must be made of the circumstances and those present.

A record must be made when a person has been informed that his fingerprints may be the subject of a speculative search.

Fingerprints taken from a person *suspected of committing a recordable offence but not arrested, charged or informed that he will be reported for it* may only be subjected to a speculative search if consent is given in writing. The Identification Code suggests a basic form of words for such written permission:

I consent to my fingerprints being retained and used only for the purposes related to the prevention and detection of crime, the investigation of an offence or the conduct of a prosecution either nationally or internationally.

I understand that my fingerprints or this sample may be checked against other fingerprint and DNA records held by or on behalf of relevant law enforcement authorities, either nationally or internationally.

I understand that once I have given my consent for the sample to be retained and used I cannot withdraw this consent.

IDENTIFICATION BY FOOTWEAR IMPRESSIONS

Taking of footwear impressions

PACE s 61A, added by SOCPA 2005, s 118, provides that, with the exceptions below, no impression of a person's footwear may be taken without the appropriate consent. Consent to the taking of an impression of a person's footwear must be in writing if it is given at a time when he is at a police station. Where a person is detained at a police station, an impression may be taken without appropriate consent from a person over the age of ten years if:

(a) he is detained in consequence of his arrest for a recordable offence, or has been charged with a recordable offence, or informed that he will be reported for a recordable offence; and

(b) he has not had an impression taken of his footwear in the course of the investigation of the offence by the police.

If a person mentioned in (a) has already had an impression of his footwear taken in the course of the investigation of the offence, that fact must be disregarded if the impression taken previously is incomplete, or is not of sufficient quality to allow satisfactory analysis, comparison or matching (whether in the case in question or generally). Reasonable force may be used, if necessary, to take a footwear impression from a detainee without consent.

In all cases, before an impression is taken, the officer must inform the person of the reason the impression is being taken and that the impression may be retained and may be the object of a speculative search, and this must be recorded as soon as practicable. If the person is at a police station, the fact must be recorded in the custody record. The person must also be informed that if destruction of the impression is required that he will be allowed to witness that destruction.

Before an impression of a person's footwear is taken (with or without consent) at a police station under the above provisions, the person must be told that the impressions may be retained and subjected to a speculative search, and the fact that he has been so informed must be recorded (in his custody record, if he is detained at a police station). He must also be told that if destruction of the impression is required he may witness it. Where an impression is taken without the appropriate consent, the reason must be given and must be recorded in the custody record. An impression taken without consent must be taken by a constable.

These provisions do not apply to cases of terrorism or to extradition.

The provisions of Annex F to the Identification Code concerning destruction and speculative search apply in relation to footwear impressions in the same way as they do to fingerprints and samples.

Where footwear impressions are voluntarily given for the purposes of elimination, or as part of an intelligence-led screening to be used only for the purposes of that investigation and destroyed afterwards, they should carry a written endorsement of consent. Annex F to the Identification Code contains specimen endorsements.

The Forensic Science Service maintains databases of footwear impressions recovered from crime scenes. Most manufacturers of footwear provide photographs and footwear impressions of new products. PACE, s 63A, referred to on p 199, as amended by SOCPA 2005, also applies to footwear impressions and permits footwear impressions to be retained and searched against the National Footwear Reference Collection and speculatively searched against the Mark Intelligence Index. The provisions of s 64 about the destruction of fingerprints and samples have been extended to footwear impressions by SOCPA 2005.

PHOTOGRAPHS

PACE, s 64A provides powers to take photographs of detainees with their consent, or without consent where it is withheld or it is not practicable to obtain consent.

In addition, as amended by SOCPA 2005, s 64A also authorises the taking of photographs elsewhere than at a police station with the person's appropriate consent, or without consent where it is withheld or it is not practicable to obtain it, if the person has been:

(a) arrested by a constable for an offence;
(b) taken into custody by a constable after a citizen's arrest;
(c) been required to wait by a community support officer;
(d) given a fixed penalty notice by an authorised enforcement officer.

For these purposes the term 'photograph' includes a moving image and corresponding expressions are construed accordingly. A photograph obtained without the suspect's consent may be obtained by making a copy of an image taken on a camera system installed anywhere in a police station. In the event of non-co-operation, where it is not possible to take the photograph covertly, reasonable force may be used to take the photograph. The use of reasonable force to take the photograph of a suspect elsewhere than at a police station must be carefully considered.

Only a police officer may take a photograph under s 64A. The officer may require the person to remove any item or substance worn on, or over, all, or any part, of the head or face. In the event of non-compliance, the officer may remove the item or substance. In order to obtain a suspect's consent and co-operation to remove an item of religious headwear to take a photograph, a constable should consider whether in the circumstances of the situation the removal of the headwear and the taking of the photograph should be by an officer of the same sex as the person. It would be appropriate for these actions to be conducted out of public view.

The suspect must be informed of the reason for taking the photograph and the purposes for which it may be used. This must be done beforehand, except if the photograph is taken covertly or by making a copy of an image (in which cases he must be informed as soon as practicable thereafter).

A photograph taken may be used or disclosed only for purposes related to the prevention or detection of crime, the investigation of an offence, the conduct of a prosecution, or the enforcement of a sentence. After being so used they may be retained thereafter but may only be used or disclosed for the same purposes. The term 'crime' includes conduct which constitutes one or more criminal offences, whether under United Kingdom law or that of a country or territory outside the United Kingdom, and is conduct, or corresponds to conduct, which, if it took place in the United Kingdom, would so constitute one or more criminal offences; and 'sentence' includes any order made by a court in England and Wales when dealing with an offender in respect of his offence.

When there are reasonable grounds for suspecting the involvement of a person in a criminal offence, but that person is at a police station voluntarily and not detained, the above provisions should apply, subject to the following modifications. Force may not be used to establish the identity of such a person or to take his photograph. The photograph of such a person which is not taken in accordance with the above provisions must be destroyed (together with any negatives and copies) unless such a person:

(a) is charged with, or informed that he may be prosecuted for, a recordable offence;
(b) is prosecuted for a recordable offence;
(c) is cautioned for a recordable offence or given a warning or reprimand in accordance with the Crime and Disorder Act 1998 for a recordable offence; or

(d) gives informed, written consent to the photograph being retained.

Such a person must be given an opportunity to witness the destruction or to have a certificate confirming destruction if he so requests within five days of notification that the destruction is required.

Whether or not he has consented to a photograph being taken, a suspect must be told that if he should significantly alter his appearance between the taking of the photograph and any attempt to hold an identification procedure this may be given in evidence if the case comes to trial.

He must also be informed that the photograph, negatives and all copies will be destroyed if he is cleared (unless he has a previous conviction for a recordable offence) or is not prosecuted (unless he admits the offence and is cautioned for it or he has a previous conviction for a recordable offence) and that he may witness its destruction or be provided with a certificate confirming its destruction if he asks to do so within five days of being cleared or informed that he will not be prosecuted.

Photographs must be kept in a secure manner to ensure that a potential witness in an identification procedure is unable to view them before any such procedure. The admissibility and value of identification evidence may be compromised if a potential witness in an identification procedure sees any photograph of the suspect otherwise than in accordance with the Identification Code.

SOCPA 2005, s 116 added s 64A(1A) and (1B). The combined effect is that, in certain circumstances, a person may be photographed elsewhere than at a police station with appropriate consent or, if that consent is withheld, or it is not practicable that it be so obtained, without it. The circumstances are, where a person has been:

(a) arrested by a constable for an offence;
(b) taken into custody by a constable after being arrested for an offence by a person other than a constable;
(c) made subject to a requirement to wait with a community support officer under the Police Reform Act 2002, Sch 4, para 2(3) or 3(B);
(d) given a penalty notice by a constable in uniform under the Criminal Justice and Police Act 2001, a penalty notice by a constable under the Education Act 1996, s 444A, or a fixed penalty notice by a constable in uniform under the Road Traffic Offenders Act 1988, s 54;
(e) given a notice in relation to a relevant fixed penalty offence (within the meaning of the Police Reform Act 2002, Sch 4, para 1) by a community support officer by virtue of a designation applying that paragraph to him; or
(f) given a notice in relation to such a relevant fixed penalty offence by an accredited person by virtue of accreditation specifying that the paragraph applies to him.

Documentation

A record must be made as soon as practicable of the reason for taking a person's photograph under the above provisions without consent and of the destruction of any photograph.

IDENTIFICATION BY BODY SAMPLES, SWABS AND IMPRESSIONS

PACE, ss 62 to 64 contains the basic provisions in this area, but (within the terms of these sections) it is the Identification Code which sets out the detailed procedures. The powers set out below are concerned with cases other than terrorism. The taking of such samples in cases covered by the Terrorism Act 2000 is specifically dealt with by that Act and is dealt with in Chapter 33.

Intimate samples

An intimate sample means a sample of *blood, semen or any other tissue fluid, urine, or pubic hair, a dental impression, or a swab taken from any part of a person's genitals or from a person's body orifices other than the mouth.* Intimate samples are governed by PACE s 62.

An intimate sample may be taken from a person in police detention only with his written consent. In the case of any procedure requiring a person's consent, the consent of a person who is mentally disordered or mentally handicapped is only valid if given in the presence of an appropriate adult; and in the case of a juvenile the consent of his parent or guardian is required as well as his own (unless he is under fourteen, in which case the consent of his parent or guardian is sufficient in its own right). An intimate sample may also be taken from a person not in police detention if, in the course of an investigation into an offence, two or more non-intimate samples have been taken which have proved unsuitable or insufficient for a particular form of analysis and such an officer as is mentioned below authorises it to be taken and the person concerned (or an appropriate adult) gives his written consent.

In these two cases an intimate sample may only be taken if an officer of at least the rank of inspector authorises it to be taken because he has reasonable grounds for suspecting the involvement of the person from whom the sample is to be taken is a recordable offence and for believing that the sample will tend to confirm or disprove his involvement.

A record must be made of the authorisation by virtue of which the sample was taken; the grounds for giving the authorisation; and the fact that the appropriate consent was given. This must be done as soon as is practicable after the sample is taken.

Before a person is asked to provide an intimate sample, he must be informed that it may be the subject of a speculative search (a check against other samples or against information derived from other samples) and the fact that this has been done must be recorded as soon as practicable after the sample has been taken. Where an intimate sample is taken from a person detained at a police station, the records referred to above must be made in the custody record.

Where a person refuses, without good cause, to consent to the taking of an intimate sample, in any proceedings for an offence, a court may draw such inferences from the refusal as appear proper.

An intimate sample, other than a sample of urine, may only be taken from a person by a registered medical practitioner or a registered nurse or registered paramedic. A dental impression may only be taken by a registered dentist.

Before a person is asked to provide one of these samples or swabs he must be warned that a refusal may be treated, in any proceedings against him, as corroborating relevant prosecution evidence. The Code suggests the use of the following words:

'You do not have to provide this sample/allow this swab or impression to be taken, but I must warn you that if you refuse without good cause, your refusal may harm your case if it comes to trial.'

The person must also be reminded of his entitlement to free legal advice and that the sample taken may be the subject of a speculative search against other samples. A record must be made of the giving of this warning and this reminder.

Non-intimate samples

There are separate provisions, contained in PACE, s 63, for the taking of a *non-intimate sample*. A non-intimate sample means hair, other than pubic hair, which includes hair plucked by the root; a sample taken from a nail or under a nail; a swab taken from any part of the body other than a part from which a swab taken would be an intimate sample; saliva; or a skin impression which means any record, other than a fingerprint, which is a record, in any form and produced by any method, of the skin pattern and any other physical characteristics or features of the whole, or any part of, a person's foot or any other part of the body. Where hair samples are taken for the purpose of DNA analysis (rather than for other purposes such as making a visual match) the suspect should be permitted a reasonable choice as to which part of the body he wishes the hairs to be taken from. When hairs are plucked they should be plucked individually unless the suspect prefers otherwise and no more should be plucked than the person taking them reasonably considers necessary for a sufficient sample.

Except in the following cases, a non-intimate sample may be taken from a suspect only with his written consent. The exceptional cases are:

(1) A non-intimate sample may be taken from a person without the appropriate consent if:
   (a) he is in detention as a result of an arrest for a recordable offence, and he has not had a non-intimate sample of the same type and from the same part of the body taken in the course of the investigation of the offence by the police, or he has had such a sample taken but it proved insufficient; or
   (b) he is being held in custody by the police on the authority of a court, and an officer of the rank of inspector (or above) has authorized it to be taken without his consent.

Such authorisation may only be given where the inspector (or above) has reasonable grounds to suspect that the offence in question is a recordable offence and that the sample will tend to confirm or disprove the suspect's involvement in it. An authorisation must not be given if the non-intimate sample concerned consists of a skin impression and such an impression has already been taken in the course of the investigation of the offence and that impression did not prove to be insufficient. Where such an impression is taken electronically it must be taken in the approved manner by an approved device.

Where an authorisation is given for the taking of a non-intimate sample, the suspect must be informed, before it is taken, of the grounds on which the authorisation has been given, including the nature of the suspected offence. He must also be told that any sample taken may be the subject of a speculative search.

(2) A non-intimate sample may be taken without the appropriate consent from any person (whether or not he is in police detention or held in custody by the police on the authority of a court) if:

(a) he has been charged with a recordable offence or informed that he will be reported for such an offence; and

(b) he has not had a non-intimate sample taken from him in the course of the investigation, or, if he has had a sample taken from him, it has proved unsuitable or insufficient for a particular form of analysis. An *unsuitable sample* is one which, by its nature, is not suitable for a particular form of analysis. An *insufficient sample* is one which is not sufficient either in quantity or quality for the purpose of enabling information to be provided for the purpose of a particular form of analysis such as DNA analysis.

(3) A non-intimate sample may be taken without the appropriate consent if the person has been *convicted* of a recordable offence. However, this does not apply to any person convicted before 10 April 1995 unless he is a person to whom the Criminal Evidence (Amendment) Act 1997 applies (persons imprisoned or detained by virtue of a pre-existing conviction for a sexual offence or an offence of violence or potential violence, listed in Sch 1 to the Act), and at the relevant time such person is serving a sentence of imprisonment in respect of that offence.

(4) A non-intimate sample may be taken without appropriate consent from a person detained following acquittal on the grounds of insanity or a finding of unfitness to plead.

Provision is made by PACE, s 63A, for a constable to require a person convicted of a recordable offence to attend a police station in order that non-intimate samples may be taken.

PACE, s 63A permits a constable within one month from the date of charge or conviction (as the case may be) or from the date of being informed that a sample is not suitable or is insufficient (as the case may be), to require a person who is neither in police detention, nor held in custody by the police on the authority of a court, to attend a police station in order to have a sample taken. While the section does not require this requirement to be in writing, as arrest may follow refusal, it is submitted that it would be wise to do so.

Reasonable force may be used to take a non-intimate sample without the suspect's consent under the above provisions.

General

Where public co-operation is being sought in relation to an investigation, it is important to minimise the risk of confusion about the effect of giving consent to the provision of a DNA sample. A DNA sample may be requested for the purpose of elimination or as a part of an intelligence-led screen and to be used only for that purpose. On other occasions it may be required to be retained on the National DNA database and used in the future. Annex F to the Identification Code contains specimen endorsements in relation to the appropriate consent.

A record must be made as soon as practicable of the reasons for taking a sample or impression and the warnings given. If force is used a record must be made of the circumstances and those present. If written consent is given to the taking of a sample or impression, the fact must be recorded in writing. A record must be made of the giving of a warning that a refusal without reasonable cause to provide an intimate sample may harm the suspect's case if it comes to trial. A record must also be made that the subject has been warned that a sample may be the subject of a speculative search.

Where clothing needs to be removed in circumstances likely to cause embarrassment to the person, no person of the opposite sex who is not a medical practitioner or nurse shall be present (unless, in the case of a juvenile or a mentally disordered or mentally handicapped person, that person specifically requests the presence of a particular adult of the opposite sex who is readily available), nor shall anyone else whose presence is unnecessary. However, in the case of a juvenile this is subject to the overriding proviso that such a removal of clothing may take place in the absence of the appropriate adult only if the juvenile signifies in the presence of the appropriate adult that he prefers the search to be done in his absence and the appropriate adult agrees.

A sample or impression must be destroyed as soon as practicable if the suspect is prosecuted and acquitted or not prosecuted (unless he admits the offence and is cautioned). However, although information derived from a sample which should have been destroyed must not be used in evidence against the suspect or for the purpose of any investigation of an offence, the House of Lords has held that evidence obtained by matching with that sample a sample taken from the suspect in another investigation is admissible at the trial judge's discretion.

Samples need not be destroyed if they were taken for the purpose of an investigation of an offence for which someone has been convicted, and from whom a sample was also taken.

VOICE IDENTIFICATION

The Court of Appeal has ruled that the Identification Code does not apply to identification by voice, and therefore there is no need for an identification parade (or, presumably, any other identification procedure) to be held. However, there is currently a difference of opinion between the judges about the relative values of 'auditory phonetic analysis' and 'quantitative acoustic analysis' as methods of identification. It would seem that the former is more valuable, because it tells one of the acoustic properties of the speech which depend on the individual's vocal tract, mouth and throat, whereas the latter tells one principally about the dialect or accent of the speaker.

INFORMAL IDENTIFICATION

While formal identification evidence is obtained in the course of procedures carried out under the Identification Code, informal evidence of identification may be admitted provided that the evidence was obtained in good faith and has no adverse effect on the fairness of the proceedings.

Where an accused and a witness are well known to each other, there is less need for any formal out-of-court identification procedure to be used. However, where the accused asks for a parade, the procedure is governed by the Identification Code and the failure to provide one may result in the exclusion of evidence whether the accused and the witness were previously known to one another or not. The House of Lords has made it clear that an identification parade should be provided, subject to the specified exceptions, when requested by an accused even though that person appears to have been positively identified by some other means.

SHOWING OF VIDEO RECORDINGS TAKEN BY SECURITY CAMERAS

Nothing in the Identification Code inhibits an investigating officer from showing a video film or photographs of an incident to the public at large through the national or local media for the purposes of recognition and tracing suspects. However, when such material is shown to potential witnesses (including police officers) for the purpose of obtaining identification evidence, it should be shown on an individual basis so as to avoid any possibility of collusion, and the showing should, as far as possible, follow the principles for video film identification or identification by photographs. A police officer who is a witness is subject to the same principles and procedures as a civilian witness.

Admissibility of evidence of person identifying suspect from video recording taken by a security camera

The Court of Appeal has held that in the following circumstances, subject to judicial discretion to exclude such evidence in particular circumstances, evidence that a person has committed an offence based upon photographic images from the scene of crime is admissible in the following cases:

(a) where the photographic image was sufficiently clear and the jury could compare it with the accused;
(b) where the witness knows the accused sufficiently well to recognise him as the person depicted;
(c) where a witness who did not know the accused had spent time viewing and analysing such photographic images thus acquiring a special knowledge that the jury did not have, such a witness could give evidence of identification based on a comparison of those images with a reasonably contemporary photograph of the accused, provided that both were available to the jury; and
(d) where a witness qualified in 'facial mapping' could give opinion evidence of identification based on a comparison of images from the scene (whether expertly enhanced or not) with a reasonably contemporary photograph, provided that both were available to the jury.

CHAPTER 7

The law of evidence

It is one of the functions of the courts to ensure that the rules of the law of evidence are observed.

It must be noted at the outset that the law of evidence determines two things:

(a) the means by which the facts in issue are proved in a court; and
(b) those facts which may (or may not) be proved in a court.

We shall be concerned with both senses of the term in the rest of this chapter.

In this chapter we are concerned only with the rules of evidence as they apply in criminal cases.

CLASSIFICATION OF EVIDENCE

It is important to explain briefly certain classifications of evidence because certain rules (whether common law or statutory) apply specifically to a particular class of evidence only. Evidence may be classified as follows.

Direct evidence and circumstantial evidence

Direct evidence is evidence which (if believed) directly establishes a particular fact in issue itself. For example, the existence of a firearm alleged to have been possessed by the accused may be proved by its production in court and the fact that he was in possession of it may be proved by a statement from a person who claims to have discovered him in possession.

Circumstantial evidence is evidence of a fact or facts from which a fact in issue may be inferred. Suppose that X is charged with murder. If an eyewitness gives evidence that he saw X fire a gun at the victim, this is direct evidence of a fact in issue. On the other hand, evidence that X was seen in possession of a gun near the scene of the crime shortly before it was committed is circumstantial evidence since it is evidence of a fact from which the fact in issue (that X fired the gun) may be inferred.

Oral evidence, documentary evidence and real evidence

Oral evidence

Most evidence given in a court is oral evidence. This consists of statements made in court by witnesses concerning matters of which they have knowledge, such as something which they have seen, or heard, or felt, or smelt, or touched.

Refreshing memory   Witness statements are usually recorded well in advance of trial. The Criminal Justice Act 2003 (CJA 2003), s 139 states that a witness in criminal proceedings may refresh his memory from a document made or verified by him at an earlier time provided that:

(a) he states in his oral evidence that the document records his recollections of the matter at that earlier time; and
(b) his recollection of the matter is likely to have been significantly better at that time than it is at the time of his oral evidence.

Recognising the difficulties associated with refreshing memory from an audio or video recording, provision is made for a witness to refresh his memory from a transcript. These provisions remove any suggestion that a witness should not have access to the statement which he made at an earlier time either before or during criminal proceedings and represents a significant step forward by eliminating from the giving of evidence a form of memory test of events.

Documents made at the time will almost invariably be recorded statements which can be shown to be:

(a) made or verified at the time, or shortly after the incident, while the circumstances were fresh in the mind of the witness;
(b) the document produced to the court; or
(c) where the witness has no recollection of the events, and is giving evidence as to the accuracy of the contents of the document, it is the original document which is used.

Where two witnesses have acted together (and this is common in the case of police officers) they may refresh their memories from notes which they made together. In relation to (a), a divisional court has held that a record made of a conversation which took place two hours after it occurred was made 'contemporaneously' where, throughout that period, the officer had been dealing with a person arrested for the offence which the person concerned was charged with aiding and abetting. The court considered that, as the officer had constantly been involved with the circumstances of the offence, the events which were then recorded must have been fresh in the officer's mind.

Hostile witness   If, during a trial in a Crown Court, a witness gives evidence which is hostile to the side calling him (it must be 'hostile' as opposed to unfavourable), that evidence may be contradicted by other evidence or, with the leave of the judge, it may be proved that the witness, on another occasion, made a statement which is inconsistent with his present testimony.

Special measures directions in case of vulnerable and intimidated witnesses

The relevant provisions are in the Youth Justice and Criminal Evidence Act 1999 (YJCEA 1999).

Witnesses who are eligible for special measures A witness may be eligible for special measures under YJCEA 1999, s 16 or 17 to help him in giving his evidence.

YJCEA 1999, s 16 provides that a witness (other than the accused) is *eligible* for special measures if:

(a) the witness is under seventeen at the time of the hearing (the time at which a court must decide whether he is eligible for such assistance); or
(b) if the court considers that the quality of the evidence given by the witness is likely to be diminished by reason of the witness:
    (i) suffering from mental disorder within the meaning of the Mental Health Act 1983; or
    (ii) otherwise having a significant impairment of intelligence and social functioning; or
    (iii) having a physical disability or suffering from physical disorder.

References to the quality of a witness's evidence are to its quality in the terms of completeness, coherence and accuracy. 'Coherence' refers to a witness's ability in giving evidence to give answers which address the questions put to him and can be understood both individually and collectively (ie in relation to a particular question as to his evidence generally).

YJCEA 1999, s 17 provides that a witness (other than the accused) is *eligible* for assistance where the court is satisfied that the quality of evidence given by him is likely to be diminished by reason of fear or distress on his part in connection with testifying in the proceedings. In determining whether it is so satisfied, the court must consider in particular:

(a) the nature and the alleged circumstances of the offence to which the proceedings relate;
(b) the age of the witness;
(c) such of the following matters which appear relevant:
    (i) the social and cultural background and ethnic origins of the witness;
    (ii) the domestic and employment circumstances of the witness;
    (iii) any religious beliefs or political opinions of the witness;
(d) any behaviour towards the witness on the part of:
    (i) the accused;
    (ii) members of the family or associates of the accused; or
    (iii) any other person who is likely to be an accused or a witness in the proceedings.

Where the complainant in a sexual offence (under the Sexual Offences Act 2003 (SOA 2003), Part 1 or the Protection of Children Act 1978) is a witness in proceedings relating to that offence (or other offence), there is a presumption that that person is *entitled* to 'assistance' unless the witness waives that entitlement.

Thus, YJCEA 1999, s 16 applies 'special measures' in relation to persons who are under seventeen at the time of the hearing, while s 17 is concerned with a witness of any age whose quality of evidence is likely to be affected by fear or distress. In either case, the court must consider any views expressed by the witness unless the witness is under seventeen.

YJCEA 1999, s 21 provides special protection for one type of person eligible for 'special measures' under s 16: 'a child witness' (ie someone under seventeen).

Where a court determines that a witness is a 'child witness', it must first have regard to the 'primary rule' that it must give in respect of that witness a special measures direction providing for a video recording of his evidence in chief to be admitted (unless this is contrary to the interests of justice) and providing for any evidence given by him which is not by means of video recording (whether in chief or otherwise) to be given by means of a live link. This primary rule does not apply to the extent that the court is satisfied that compliance with it would not be likely to maximise the quality of the witness's evidence so far as practicable (whether because the application to that evidence of one or more other special measures available in relation to the witness would have that result or for any other reason). However, this exception does not apply where the child witness is in need of 'special protection' which he will be if the offence (or one of them) in question is:

(a) a sexual offence, as defined at p 211 (s 17); or
(b) kidnapping, false imprisonment, an offence under the Child Abduction Act 1984, s 1 or 2, an offence under the Children and Young Persons Act 1933, s 1 (cruelty); or any other offence which involves an assault on, or injury, or a threat of injury to, any person.

Where a child is in need of special protection because the offence is a sexual offence, any special measures direction providing for video-recorded examination-in-chief must also provide for video-recorded cross-examination and re-examination otherwise than by the accused in person, unless the witness informs the court that he does not want that special measure to apply.

The essential point about YJCEA 1999, s 21 is that where a child witness is in need of *special protection*, a court will not have to consider (as it normally must) whether the special measures mentioned will improve the quality of his evidence. That requirement is treated as satisfied.

The House of Lords has held that YJCEA 1999, s 21 is not incompatible with the accused's right to a fair trial guaranteed by the European Convention on Human Rights (ECHR), art 6(2).

By YJCEA 1999, s 18, a range of special measures is made potentially available to witnesses who are eligible for special measures under s 16 or 17. The 'special measures' are set out in detail by YJCEA 1999, ss 23 to 30. Once a court has determined that a witness is eligible for special measures, it must then (except in the case of a child in need of special protection) determine whether any of those measures (or a combination of them) would be likely to improve the quality of the witness's evidence and, if so, determine which of those measures would be likely to maximise so far as practicable the quality of his evidence. Having made this second determination, it must give a 'special measures' direction in relation to the measure or measures so determined.

The special measures are:

(1) *Screening* Screens may be authorised to shield a witness from the accused (but the judge, jury, justices, a legal representative from each side, any interpreter, and any person appointed to assist the witness must be able to see the witness).

(2) *Evidence by live link* Usually this will be done by closed circuit television but the terms of the section are wide enough to permit any technology. Where a direction is given that evidence will be given in this way, evidence may not be given in any other way without the consent of the court. Where facilities are not available at a petty-sessional court house, the court may sit elsewhere where such facilities exist. A divisional court has held that evidence being given in this way does not breach an accused's human right to a fair trial.

(3) *Evidence given in private* The court may be cleared of non-essential personnel but this measure will only be available in relation to a sexual offence or when the court reason ably believes that someone has tried to intimidate, or will try to intimidate the witness. At least one member of the press must be allowed to remain in court.

(4) *Removal of wigs and gowns* This applies to the judiciary as well as legal representatives.

(5) *Video-recorded evidence-in-chief* Where this special measure is directed, it will provide for a video recording of an interview of the witness to be admitted in evidence-in-chief. However, the direction may not provide for a video recording, or part of it, to be admitted if its admission would not be in the interests of justice. If it is decided to permit only an edited version to be shown, the court must consider whether the exclusion of part of the recording is prejudicial. A court may later exclude a recording if its making is not properly proved, but may nevertheless admit it in such circumstances. The party tendering the evidence must call the witness, unless a special measures direction provides for cross-examination otherwise than in court or the parties have agreed to non-attendance. The witness may not give evidence-in-chief otherwise than by means of the recording as to any matter adequately dealt with in the recording or, without the court's permission, as to any other matter dealt with in the recording.

(6) *Video-recorded cross-examination or re-examination* The relevant provisions were not in force at the time of writing. For convenience they are described as if they were. Where a special measures direction provides for video recording of a witness's evidence-in-chief to be admitted, the special measures direction may also provide that the witness may be cross-examined before trial and that that cross-examination (and any re-examination) may be recorded for use at trial. This will not occur in the physical presence of the accused, although he will be able to see and hear it and to communicate with his legal adviser (live link). Nor need it take place in the physical presence of the judge or magistrates and the defence and prosecution legal representatives, although they must be able to see and hear the examination and to communicate with those present. However, a judge or magistrate must control the proceedings and it is intended that this person will normally be the trial judge or magistrate. Where a recording has been made of the examination of a witness under the above power, the witness may not be subsequently cross-examined or re-examined in respect of his evidence unless the court makes a further direction to this effect. Such a further direction may only be given: (a) where the proposed cross-examination is sought by a party to the proceedings as a result of having become aware since the original recording of a matter which he could not with reasonable diligence have ascertained by then, or (b) where it is in the interests of justice to do so.

The following additional measures are available only in the case of someone eligible for special measures under s 16 (ie persons under seventeen at the time of the hearing):

(1) *Examination of witness through intermediary* An intermediary is an interpreter or someone else whom the court approves to communicate to the witness the questions the court, the defence and the prosecution ask, and then to communicate the answers which the witness gives in reply. He may also explain such questions or answers, should that be necessary to facilitate understanding. It is foreseen that such an intermediary will normally be a specialist. An intermediary can act however and wherever the examination is conducted. The judge or magistrates, and at least one legal representative for each side, should be able to see and hear the witness and be able to communicate with the intermediary. The jury must be able to see and hear the witness unless the evidence is video recorded. An intermediary must declare that he will faithfully perform his function.

(2) *Aids to communication* A special measures direction may require a witness to be provided with an appropriate device to assist communication.

The status of evidence given under special measures   Evidence given using any of the special measures set out above must be treated in the same way as oral evidence. However, the judge may give such warning to the jury as he considers necessary to ensure fairness to the accused.

If the evidence of a witness who would normally be sworn gives unsworn evidence by means of a video recording, that evidence will be admissible at trial. However, where a person authorised to administer an oath is present, the evidence could be taken under oath in appropriate cases.

The *Consolidated Criminal Practice Direction* requires that the party who made the application to admit the video recording must edit the recording in accordance with the judge's directions and send a copy of the edited recording to the appropriate officer of the Crown Court and to every other party to the proceedings.

Where a video recording is to be adduced during proceedings before a Crown Court, it must be produced and proved by the interviewer, or any other person who was present at the interview with the child, at which the recording was made. The parties may agree to accept a written statement in lieu of the attendance of such a person. The party adducing the video recording must arrange for the operation of the video playing equipment.

Failure to so prepare, which leads to an adjournment for this to be done, may lead to an appropriate award for costs.

Live television links

Live television links at preliminary hearings   The Crime and Disorder Act 1998 (CDA 1998), s 57 provides for the use of live television links at preliminary hearings before a court, where an accused is being held in custody. The use of such a link (where it is possible) does not require the consent of the accused, or his legal adviser, but is a matter for the discretion of the court.

By CDA 1998, s 57(1), in any proceedings for an offence, a court may, after hearing representations from the parties, direct that the accused shall be treated as being present in the court for any particular hearing before the start of the trial, if, during that hearing:

(a) he is held in custody in a prison or other institution; and

(b) whether by means of a live television link or otherwise, he is able to see and hear the court and to be seen and heard by it.

The term 'particular hearing' used in CDA 1998, s 57(1) refers to any hearing before either a magistrates' court or Crown Court before the start of the trial.

Live television and other links in criminal proceedings generally   CJA 2003, Part 8 makes the following provisions in respect of such matters. These provisions are not in force at the time of writing.

A 'live link' is a live television link or other arrangement by which a witness, while at a place in the United Kingdom which is outside the building where the proceedings are being held, is able to see or hear a person at the place where the proceedings are being held, and to be seen and heard by the accused, judge, justices, jury, legal representatives and any interpreter.

CJA 2003, Part 8 provides that a witness (other than the accused) may, if the court so directs, give evidence through a live link in criminal proceedings whether on trial or during an appeal. The court may give such a direction on its own motion or on the application of a party to the proceedings. It cannot make a direction unless it has been notified by the Secretary of State that appropriate facilities are available in the area where the proceedings will take place. The court must be satisfied that it is in the interests of the efficient or effective administration of justice for this to take place. The court must consider all the circumstances, including the availability of the witness, the need to attend in person, the importance of the evidence and the views of the witness, the suitability of facilities and whether the absence of the witness may inhibit a party to the proceedings from effectively testing the witness's evidence. If the court refuses an application it must state in open court its reasons for doing so. When such evidence is given in a Crown Court the judge may direct the jury as he thinks fit to ensure that the same weight is given to the evidence as would be the case if oral evidence had been given in the place where the proceedings are held.

When such a direction has been given the witness may not give evidence by any other means but a court may rescind a direction (either on its own motion or the application of any party) if it appears to be in the interests of justice to do so.

Where a magistrates' court wishes to give such a direction and facilities are not available in the petty-sessional courthouse, the court may sit at any place appointed for the purpose of receiving such evidence and this may be outside the petty-sessional area.

Evidence by means of a video recording in other circumstances than 'special measures'

These provisions are not in force at the time of writing.

CJA 2003, s 137 permits a court to direct that a video recording of an interview with a witness (other than the accused), or a part of such a recording, be admitted as part of the evidence-in-chief in criminal proceedings for an offence triable only on indictment or for prescribed offences triable either way, where the witness claims to have witnessed an offence (or a part of it) or to have witnessed events closely connected with such events. The witness must have previously given an account of the events in question (whether in response to questions asked or otherwise) while the events were fresh in his memory.

In such circumstances the court may direct that the recording be admitted, provided that the witness's recollection of events is likely to be significantly better at the time he gave the recorded account than at the time of giving evidence, and it is in the interests of justice to admit the recording, having regard to the time which has passed since it was made; its quality; and any views of the witness as to whether the evidence-in-chief should be given orally or by means of the recording.

Any such evidence given by video recording must be treated as if it had been given orally provided that the witness asserts that it is true. Where such a recording is admitted the witness may not give evidence-in-chief otherwise than by means of the recording in respect of any matter which the court considers to have been dealt with adequately by the recording. Part of a video recording may be admitted, but a court must consider whether admitting only part of it would carry a risk of prejudice to the accused and, if this is likely, whether the interests of justice nevertheless require it to be admitted in view of the desirability of showing the whole, or substantially the whole, of the recorded interview.

Protection of witnesses from cross-examination by accused in person

Complainants in proceedings for sexual offences

YJCEA 1999, s 34 provides that no person charged with a sexual offence (ie an offence under SOA 2003, Part 1 (ss 1 to 79), discussed above or in the next chapter) may in any criminal proceedings cross-examine in person a witness who is a complainant, either in connection with the offence, or in connection with any other offence (of whatever nature) with which that person is charged in the proceedings.

Child complainants and other witnesses who are children

In relation to an offence to which it applies, YJCEA 1999, s 35 makes similar provisions concerning a 'protected witness'. A 'protected witness' is a witness who:

(a) either is a complainant or a witness to the offence; and
(b) either is a child or falls to be cross-examined after giving evidence-in-chief as a child (even if by the time of the cross-examination he or she is no longer a child).

YJCEA 1999, s 35 applies to any offence under the Protection of Children Act 1978 (indecent photographs etc of a child) and any offence under SOA 2003, Part I. It also includes kidnapping, false imprisonment, child abduction, cruelty to children or any offence involving an assault on, or injury (or a threat of injury) to, any person.

For the purposes of YJCEA 1999, s 35, where an offence is under one of the pieces of legislation just specified, a 'child' is someone under seventeen. For the purposes of the other specified offences, a 'child' is someone under fourteen.

Direction prohibiting cross-examination

YJCEA 1999, s 36, which is not limited to sexual offences or the other offences to which s 35 applies, permits a court to prohibit an unrepresented defendant from cross-examining witnesses in other cases, where the provisions of ss 34 and 35 do not apply.

This may be done where the court is satisfied that the quality of the evidence given by the witness on cross-examination is likely to be diminished if cross-examination is undertaken or continued by the accused in person, and would be likely to be improved if a direction was given, and that such a prohibition will not be contrary to the interests of justice. The court may discharge such a direction at any time.

A direction may be made on application by the prosecutor, or on the court's own motion.

The term 'witness' does not include any other person who is charged with an offence within the proceedings.

Representation of such persons for the purpose of cross-examination

Where a defendant is prohibited from cross-examining a witness under the provisions of YJCEA 1999, s 34, 35 or 36, the court must invite the accused to appoint a legal representative to cross-examine on his behalf. If no such appointment is made within the prescribed time limits, the court must consider whether it is necessary, in the interests of justice, for the witness to be cross-examined by a legal representative. If the court considers that it is necessary, it must appoint a legal representative. Such a court-appointed representative will not have been instructed by the accused and will not, therefore, be responsible to him. Material relating to the proceedings must be made available to an appointee.

In such a case, the judge must give the jury such warning as he considers necessary to ensure that the accused is not prejudiced:

(a) by any inferences which might be drawn from the fact that he has been prevented from carrying out a cross-examination in person;
(b) where the witness has been cross-examined by a legal representative appointed by the court, by the fact that such cross-examination was carried out by a representative other than a person acting as the accused's own legal representative.

Documentary evidence

Documentary evidence consists of information obtained by the production of a document (or of a copy of it, authenticated in a way approved by the court) as evidence of a matter contained in it. A 'document' includes, in addition to a document in writing, a map or drawing; a photograph; a disc, tape or the like; and any film or the like. Where a police officer offers in evidence the confession of an accused which is recorded in a written statement, it is the contents of the statement which are offered in evidence and the evidence is therefore documentary evidence.

Real evidence

Real evidence is the production of an object for the inspection of the court or jury. Where a document (or other object bearing writing) is produced as evidence of the matter contained in it, as opposed to proof of its physical existence, it is, as we have just seen, documentary evidence. The firearm which was produced by a witness in the example quoted above is real evidence. So, it has been held, is a computer printout recording attempts to enter a website, a paedophile website in the case in question. Police officers frequently give evidence of having recovered stolen property; this is oral evidence. When the property is produced for inspection in court, this is real evidence.

Original evidence and hearsay evidence

Original evidence is evidence of a fact by 'first-hand' evidence of it. Hearsay evidence is 'second-hand' evidence, since it consists of evidence of what someone else expressly or impliedly asserted orally, in writing or by conduct (eg a nod of the head) when the object of that evidence is to establish the truth of what was asserted. As an example, a policeman's notebook containing a statement about a stabbing is hearsay evidence of the stabbing. It must be emphasised that not all evidence of what someone else asserted is hearsay. If it is produced merely to prove the fact that it was asserted, as opposed to being produced with the object of establishing the truth of what was asserted, it is original evidence and not hearsay evidence. If the accused says that he acted under a threat to kill him made by Y, evidence of what he said is original evidence because it is produced as evidence that Y uttered a threat, but, if a witness says that X had told him that Y had broken the windows of a greenhouse, this is hearsay evidence since it is produced as evidence of the truth of what X stated, ie that Y had broken the windows.

The distinction between original evidence and hearsay evidence is important, because hearsay evidence is inadmissible in criminal cases unless its admission is permitted under a variety of rules.

PROOF

The general rule is that the prosecution must prove the existence of any fact on which it relies. There are, however, certain facts which do not need to be proved.

Facts which may be established by means other than proof

Judicial notice

The court may take 'judicial notice' of certain matters which are so notorious or well known that evidence of their existence need not be adduced. One does not have to prove that beer is intoxicating, for example, as this is a matter of general knowledge, whereas it may be necessary to prove that a less well-known drink is intoxicating. When screening devices for the purpose of breath testing were first introduced it was necessary to prove in each case the Secretary of State's approval of the type of device used. With the passage of time, the courts ruled that judicial notice could be taken of the existence of that approval.

Presumptions

Sometimes there is a presumption of law that if a particular fact is proved some other fact must be presumed to exist. There are two kinds of presumption of law: irrebuttable and rebuttable.

When the presumption is irrebuttable, no evidence can be received to contradict the presumed fact. An example of an irrebuttable presumption of law is provided by the rule that a child under ten is incapable of committing an offence.

Where there is a rebuttable presumption of law against the accused, the jury (or magistrates) must find that the presumed fact existed unless (depending on the presumption) the accused proves the contrary on the balance of probabilities, or there is evidence raising a doubt that the presumption is rebutted (in which case the prosecution will have to disprove that evidence beyond reasonable doubt).

Presumptions of law must be distinguished from presumptions of *fact*. When a jury (or magistrates' court) may find that a particular fact (the presumed fact) exists on proof of some other fact, the presumption is one of fact. Presumptions of fact play a very important part in the criminal law because they are often the only way by which the accused's state of mind can be proved. A judge may tell the jury that they *may* infer knowledge or intent from the fact that the prohibited act was done by the accused, and if the accused offers no explanation that will normally be drawn. This is a matter of common sense, because people generally are aware of the circumstances in which they act, and they generally do foresee that what does result from their conduct will result from it. Of course, the jury must consider the evidence as a whole, and, if they entertain any reasonable doubt, they must give the benefit of the doubt to the accused because of the general rule that the prosecution has the burden of proof. It must be emphasised that this presumption as to the accused's knowledge or intent is one which the jury (or a magistrates' court) *may* draw; they are never obliged to do so (as is confirmed in relation to intention by the Criminal Justice Act 1967(CJA 1967), s 8) and it is for this reason that the presumption is one of fact.

There are, of course, a wide range of other presumptions of fact, which arise because they are suggested by common sense. For example, if X is seen driving a car immediately after an accident, it may be inferred that he was driving at the time of the accident. As a moment's thought shows, presumptions of fact are merely particular and frequently occurring instances of the operation of circumstantial evidence since the nature of circumstantial evidence is that it consists of facts from which other facts may be presumed to exist.

Formal admissions

A confession is a statement wholly or partly adverse to the person who made it, whether made to a person in authority or not and whether made in words or otherwise.

A confession is a *means* of proving the fact admitted. On the other hand, a formal admission *dispenses with the need* for proving that fact since it is conclusive evidence of that fact as against the party admitting it. In criminal cases, provision is made for formal admissions, by or on behalf of either prosecution or defence, by CJA 1967, s 10. Such a formal admission may be made before or at the proceedings. Unless it is made in court, it must be made in writing. A written, formal admission must be signed by the person making it (or by an officer of the company if made by a company).

CJA 2003, s 118 preserves the common law rules under which in criminal proceedings an admission made by an agent of an accused (eg solicitor or counsel) is admissible as evidence against the accused of any matter stated, or a statement made by a person to whom an accused refers a person for information is admissible against the accused.

The burden of proof

The general rule is that the prosecution has the burden of proving the accused's guilt beyond reasonable doubt. In more detail, the position is as follows. The prosecution always has the burden of proving beyond reasonable doubt that the accused committed the actus reus of the offence charged with the requisite mens rea. In relation to defences, the accused normally has the burden of adducing sufficient evidence to raise a defence (an evidential burden); if he does so it is then for the prosecution to disprove the alleged defence beyond reasonable doubt.

Exceptionally, the accused has the burden of proving a defence on the balance of probabilities. This is called a 'persuasive burden'. The burden of proof is imposed on the accused in the following cases:

Defence of insanity   This was outlined in Chapter 1, above.

Express statutory provision   A statute sometimes provides that it is a defence if the accused proves certain facts. For example, under the Homicide Act 1957, s 2, the accused has the burden of proving the defence of diminished responsibility on a charge of murder.

Provisos and exemptions in statutory offences   Where a statute governing any offence provides any exception, exemption, proviso, excuse or qualification, as where it prohibits the doing of an act save in specified circumstances (or by persons of specified classes, or with specified qualifications, or with the licence or permission of specified authorities), the onus of proving such an exception, exemption etc is impliedly cast on the accused. This rule is provided in the case of summary proceedings by the Magistrates' Courts Act 1980, s 101, and applies in the case of trial of indictment by virtue of the common law.

Rebuttable presumption of law against the accused where the accused bears the burden of proving that the presumption is rebutted   We dealt with this on p 219 above.

Placing a persuasive burden on an accused may be incompatible with the presumption of innocence guaranteed by art 6 of the ECHR (see p 262), depending on the nature of the provision which imposes that burden. In each case it depends on whether imposing a persuasive burden serves a legitimate aim and is a justifiable and proportionate response to it; if not it will be incompatible. The Human Rights Act 1998 (HRA 1998), s 3 gives the courts a liberal power of statutory interpretation which enables them to read a statutory requirement for an accused to prove something as simply imposing an evidential burden on the accused if this makes the provision compatible with the Convention when it would not otherwise be so. To the extent that the courts have reached a conclusion about a particular provision which requires an accused to 'prove' something, we deal with the matter at the appropriate place in this book. The vast majority of such provisions have not yet been examined by the courts in terms of their compliance with the presumption of innocence; in respect of them what we have just said must be borne in mind.

Corroboration

'Corroboration' is evidence from a source (or sources) independent of the witness whose evidence is to be corroborated, which confirms or supports that evidence in some material particular. Corroboration is not generally required as a matter of law. This means that, generally, although corroboration may aid proof, it is possible for the prosecution to discharge its burden of proof by adducing only one item of evidence.

There are, however, exceptional circumstances in which corroboration is required, either by statute as a matter of law or as a matter of practice.

Corroboration required by statute

In cases under this heading a jury or magistrates' court cannot act, ie the relevant fact is not proved, on uncorroborated evidence given on behalf of the prosecution. These cases are:

(a) perjury (Perjury Act 1911); and
(b) speeding (Road Traffic Regulation Act 1984 (RTRA 1984)).

Corroboration and the Criminal Justice and Public Order Act 1994, s 32

Prior to the Criminal Justice and Public Order Act 1994 (CJPOA 1994) a judge was *required* to give a warning concerning the danger of convicting a person on the uncorroborated evidence of a complainant of a sexual offence or on the uncorroborated testimony of an accomplice. The need for such a warning in these cases has been abolished by s 32 of the 1994 Act. Subsequently, the Court of Appeal has stated that the judge has a *discretion* to give a warning to the jury in respect of a witness in one of these two types of case, just as he can in respect of any witness in any other type of case. It is up to the judge, where some warning is required, to determine what type of warning, if any, needs to be given. Much will depend upon the circumstances of the case, the issues raised and the content and quality of a witness's evidence. For it to be appropriate for a warning to be given, there must be an evidential basis for suggesting that a witness is unreliable; mere suggestions by counsel do not provide such a basis.

Proof of convictions and acquittals

The Police and Criminal Evidence Act 1984 (PACE), s 73 provides that, where the fact that a person has been convicted or acquitted of an offence otherwise than by a Service Court is admissible in evidence, it may be proved by producing a certificate of conviction or acquittal relating to that offence, and proving that the person named in the certificate is the person whose conviction or acquittal for the offence is to be proved. The certificate must be signed by a designated officer or by the clerk of the court, his deputy or any other person with custody of the court record (in the case of any other court) where the conviction or acquittal took place. A document purporting to be such a certificate is presumed to be such until the contrary is proved. Where such a certificate is relied on to prove a conviction against an accused it must be proved by the prosecution beyond reasonable doubt that the accused is the person named in that certificate (see, further, p 374, Ch 9—driving while disqualified). PACE, s 73 supplements other previous provisions. The Criminal Procedure Act 1865, s 6 allows convictions and acquittals to be proved by questioning, but if there is a refusal to answer the procedure under s 73 will have to be followed. CJPA 2001, s 82(2) provides that fingerprints which have lawfully been retained after they have fulfilled the purposes for which they were taken may be used for the purpose of the conduct of a prosecution and this provision should cover the proof of a previous conviction in relation to which the fingerprints were taken, where it is an essential element in an offence, such as driving while disqualified. The Road Traffic Offenders Act 1988, s 31 provides that where a person is convicted of an offence involving obligatory or discretionary disqualification, any previous conviction for a driving offence endorsed on a driving licence is prima facie evidence of that conviction.

In any proceedings where evidence is admissible of the fact that the accused has committed an offence, he is rebuttably presumed by PACE, s 74 to have committed it if he is proved to have been convicted (ie found guilty) of it by a United Kingdom court or a service court outside the United Kingdom.

PACE, s 74 also provides that the fact that a person other than the accused has been convicted of an offence by a United Kingdom court or a service court outside the United Kingdom is admissible in evidence for the purpose of proving that that person committed that offence, where evidence of his having done so is inadmissible. If that conviction is proved that person is rebuttably presumed to have committed it. However, where an accused is jointly charged with others who have pleaded guilty, proof of the convictions of those other persons jointly charged, in circumstances in which the jury is encouraged to rely on that evidence in determining the guilt of the accused, is liable to be held inadmissible by reason of its adverse effect upon the fairness of the proceedings in accordance with PACE, s 78. We explain the operation of s 78 on p 254.

Although it is possible to prove previous convictions by adducing Police National Computer (PNC) records admitted under the CJA 2003, s 117 (see p 230), s 117 cannot be relied on so as to make admissible details on the PNC about the offences (as opposed to the dates of convictions, the offences charged and the sentences), as explained on p 231.

COMPETENCE, COMPELLABILITY AND PRIVILEGE

Who can give evidence? Who is obliged to? When is a witness entitled to refuse to answer questions? The answers to these questions are to be found respectively in the law relating to competence to give evidence, to compellability to give evidence and to various types of privilege.

Competence and compellability

Competence

YJCEA 1999, ss 53 to 57 provide that anyone, of whatever age, is competent to give evidence unless he is unable to understand questions put to him as a witness, or unable to answer them in a way which can be understood. A witness may need the assistance of 'special measures' as set out at pp 211–214. However, an accused person is not competent to give evidence for the prosecution (whether or not he is the only accused, or is a co-accused in the proceedings). This does not preclude a person who is no longer liable to be convicted of the offence whether because of a guilty plea, or otherwise.

Questions of competence will be decided by the court and in the absence of the jury if there is one. The party calling the witness must satisfy the court that the witness, on the balance of probabilities, is competent to give evidence. Any questioning of the witness must be conducted by the court.

Compellability

PACE, s 80 deals with the 'compellability' of the spouse or civil partner of an accused to give evidence.

In any proceedings, the spouse or civil partner (X) of a person charged in the proceedings is compellable to give evidence on behalf of that person, unless he or she (ie X) is also charged in those proceedings. In addition, provided that he or she (ie X) is not also charged in those proceedings, the spouse or civil partner of a person charged in the proceedings is compellable to give evidence on behalf of any other person charged in those proceedings, but only in respect of any specified offence with which that other person is charged, or to give evidence for the prosecution but only in respect of any specified offence with which any person is charged in the proceedings. In relation to the spouse or civil partner of a person charged in any proceedings, an offence is a specified offence for these purposes if:

(a) it involves an assault on, or injury or a threat of injury to, the spouse or civil partner or a person who was at the material time under the age of sixteen;
(b) it is a sexual offence alleged to have been committed in respect of a person who was at the material time under that age; or
(c) it consists of attempting or conspiring to commit, or of aiding, abetting, counselling, procuring or inciting the commission of, an offence under para (a) or (b).

For the purposes of (b), a 'sexual offence' is an offence under:

(a) the Protection of Children Act 1978 (taking indecent photographs of children); or
(b) SOA 2003, Part 1.

The references above to a person charged in any proceedings do not include a person who is not, or is no longer, liable to be convicted of any offence in the proceedings (whether as a result of pleading guilty or for any other reason).

The failure of a spouse or civil partner of a person charged in any proceedings to give evidence in the proceedings must not be made the subject of any comment by the prosecution.

An ex-spouse or ex-civil partner is compellable to give evidence as if he or she had never been married to the accused.

Privilege

Self-incrimination

A person required to answer questions or produce documents may refuse to do so on the grounds that the evidence may incriminate him. Exceptions to this rule are created by a number of statutes concerned with 'trusts', the care and protection of children, and investigations carried out by the Serious Fraud Office. However, YJCEA 1999 provides restrictions in relation to the use of evidence obtained within such investigations.

Lawyer/client

Communications between a lawyer and his client which are concerned with the giving of legal advice or as to the presentation of material, and those between a lawyer, his client and a third party which are concerned with litigation and legal advice are privileged. Privilege is not afforded in respect of communications in the furtherance of crime or fraud. In addition, where such communications are disclosed from other sources (document coming into possession of police) or where privilege is waived by the lawyer's client, such evidence may be given.

Public policy and public interest immunity

Public interest immunity relates to the non-disclosure of material held by the prosecution on grounds of the public interest. The approach to be taken where such immunity is claimed is as follows:

(1) Does the material weaken the prosecution case or strengthen the defence case? If it does not, it should not be disclosed. If it does, the 'golden rule' is that disclosure should be made unless public interest immunity (PII) prevents it.
(2) In determining whether the golden rule can be derogated from, the court must consider whether there is a real risk of serious prejudice to an important public interest. If there is not, PII does not apply and the material must be disclosed.
(3) If the material does give rise to such a risk, the court must consider whether the accused's interests can be protected without disclosure or whether disclosure can be ordered in a way which would adequately protect the public interest and the interests of the defence. This requires the court to consider whether the prosecution should formally admit what the defence sought to establish or whether limited disclosure could be ordered.
(4) If the court is minded to order limited disclosure it must consider whether what it proposes in order to protect the defendant's interest and the public interest represents the minimum derogation to protect the public interest. If it does not, fuller disclosure should be ordered.
(5) If limited disclosure may render the trial process unfair to the accused, fuller disclosure should be ordered even if this leads to the discontinuance of the prosecution case. The court must keep the issue of unfairness under review as the trial proceeds.

Where a claim of public interest immunity is successful no adverse inference may be drawn against the witness's failure to give evidence. Notice should be given of an intention to claim such privilege. Approved special counsel may be appointed where it is necessary, in the interests of justice, to secure protection of the accused's right to a fair trial.

Public interest immunity may apply to many police matters: information relied upon for the issue of search warrants; reports to the DPP; the disclosure of the identity of informants or the siting of police observation posts. Public interest immunity may also apply to files relating to the investigation of complaints (although disclosure of working papers and reports prepared by investigating officers may be ordered where the public interest in disclosure outweighs that in preserving confidentiality) and disciplinary matters connected with the police.

On the other hand, any written complaint made about the conduct of a police officer is not privileged. Nor can privilege be claimed in respect of statements made within a police 'grievance' procedure alleging either racial or sexual discrimination.

Oral evidence: oath and affirmation

Normally, evidence must be given on oath (ie sworn). However, where it is not possible to administer the oath in the manner appropriate to the witness's religious beliefs, or where he objects to being sworn, the witness may make a solemn affirmation.

Determination of whether a witness should be sworn

The question whether a witness in criminal proceedings may be sworn, whether raised by a party to the proceedings or by the court of its own motion, is determined by the court as follows in accordance with YJCEA 1999, s 55.

A witness may not be sworn unless he has attained the age of fourteen and he has sufficient appreciation of the solemnity of the occasion and of the particular responsibility to tell the truth which is involved in taking an oath. If the witness is able to give intelligible testimony, he is presumed to have sufficient appreciation if no evidence is offered to the contrary. If such evidence is adduced, the issue of competence must be decided on the balance of probabilities.

Such issues must be dealt with in the absence of the jury.

Reception of unsworn evidence

YJCEA 1999, s 56 deals with unsworn evidence given by a person not permitted to be sworn by s 55. A deposition of unsworn evidence may be accepted as if it had been given on oath.

YJCEA 1999, s 57 provides that it is an offence for a person wilfully to give false evidence in such circumstances that, had the evidence been given on oath, he would have been guilty of perjury. The offence applies to all persons giving unsworn evidence, including those under fourteen.

Unsworn evidence may also be given by a person called simply to produce a document.

Documentary evidence

It is a general rule that the contents of a document may be proved only by production of the original. However, there are now so many exceptions to this general rule that it has lost much of its importance. When one of these exceptions applies, secondary evidence of the contents of the document may be given.

The principal exceptions whereby secondary evidence of the contents of a document may be given are as follows:

(1) Where the original is proved to have been lost or destroyed, secondary evidence of the contents may be given.
(2) The contents of public documents can always be proved by means of secondary evidence, although some statutes providing this exception for a particular type of public document limit the nature of this secondary evidence. A 'public document' is a document made for the purpose of the public making use of it and being able to refer to it. Examples are registers of births, deaths and marriages, the contents of which can be proved by a copy of an entry certified by a person who has lawful custody of the register.

   Judicial notice is taken of Acts of Parliament. A statutory instrument is proved by production of the Queen's Printer's copy.
(3) By the Bankers' Books Evidence Act 1879, ss 3 to 5, an examined copy of any entry in a banker's book kept in the ordinary course of business is admissible as prima facie evidence of such entry.

Under the heading of documentary evidence, mention may be made of certain statutory provisions which specially provide for evidence to be given by the production of a document. Examples of these appear later in this chapter, when we discuss exceptions to the rule against hearsay.

MEANS OF PROOF WHICH MAY BE INADMISSIBLE

Opinion

Opinion evidence is generally inadmissible because it is the function of the court or jury, and not of a witness, to draw conclusions from the facts proved. If a witness alleges that a particular driver was at fault and caused an accident, that evidence is inadmissible because that is the issue which the court or jury must decide. A fine line can sometimes exist between 'opinion' and 'fact', and for this reason evidence as to the identification of a person or thing (which must always be an opinion to some extent) is admissible. In addition, by way of exception to the general rule the following opinion evidence of experts is admissible:

(a) opinion evidence of experts on matters (outside the knowledge or experience of a jury) of a scientific, technical or artistic nature, such as doctors of medicine, forensic scientists, metallurgists or literary experts: a police officer can be an expert under this heading in appropriate circumstances; for example, the opinion evidence of a police officer that a quantity of drugs was too great for personal use was held admissible as expert evidence because the officer based his opinion on his seventeen years' experience and on published and unpublished material;

(b) opinion evidence from persons who are experts in handwriting comparison; and
(c) opinion evidence by a lawyer shown to have knowledge of a particular system of foreign law.

An expert witness should provide independent, objective assistance to the court in relation to matters within his expertise, and should never assume the role of advocate. An expert, whether instructed by the prosecution or the defence, is obliged to act in the cause of justice. His duties are owed to the court and override any obligation to those instructing or by whom he is paid. Consequently, for example, if an expert instructed by the prosecution carries out a test, or knows that a test has been carried out in his laboratory, which casts doubt on his opinion, he must disclose this to his instructing solicitor, who must disclose it to the defence. The Criminal Procedure Rules 2005, Part 24, prescribe procedures to be followed in relation to the mutual disclosure between parties of expert evidence which is to be offered in proceedings in the Crown Court. This enables experts, where possible, to agree points of agreement and disagreement.

Hearsay

As we have already said, hearsay evidence is 'second-hand' evidence since it consists of evidence of what someone else expressly or impliedly asserted orally, in writing or by conduct when the object of that evidence is to establish the truth of what was said or written. Hearsay evidence is inadmissible, unless its admission is permitted under a variety of rules, because the law of evidence generally requires a fact to be proved by direct evidence of it.

Of course, not all evidence of what someone other than a witness said or wrote is hearsay. If it is produced merely to prove the fact that it was said or written, as opposed to the truth of what was said or written, it is original evidence and not hearsay evidence, and therefore admissible if relevant to the facts in issue. This distinction can be illustrated as follows.

If a witness says that the deceased, while in hospital with injuries from which he unexpectedly died, told him, 'Fred did this to me', this is hearsay evidence since it is produced as evidence of the truth of what the deceased stated, that is, that Fred caused the injuries. For the same reason, it would be hearsay evidence for a witness to say (at a sexual assault trial), 'Hales told me that he saw Tate sexually assault Mrs Bird'.

By way of contrast, it is not necessarily hearsay evidence for evidence to be called to show that the accused said that he had acted under a threat of death made by Jones, or for a witness to say 'Mrs Bird complained to me that Tate had fondled her breasts'. This is original evidence of the fact that a threat had been made, or that an early complaint had been made (which is relevant in sexual offences, as we have seen). The latter statement is, however, hearsay if it is intended to show the fact that the sexual offence has been committed.

The rule against hearsay evidence has gradually been whittled away, culminating in CJA 2003, Part 11, Chapter 2 which abolished the common law rules about hearsay evidence and created a new set of rules about it.

The Criminal Procedure Rules 2005, Part 34 requires a party who wants to introduce hearsay evidence on one or more of the grounds set out in s 114, head(d) (see p 228), s 116 (see p 229), s 117 (see p 230) or s 121 (see p 233) to give notice to the court officer and all other parties. The prosecutor must give such notice, in a magistrates' court, at the same time as he complies or purports to comply with the initial duty of disclosure (see p 256), and, in the Crown Court, not more than fourteen days after the accused is admitted for trial, after service of a transfer notice, or, where he has been sent for trial, after the service of copies of the documents containing the evidence. An accused must give notice of hearsay evidence not more than fourteen days after the prosecutor has complied with or purported to comply with his initial duty of disclosure. A party who receives a notice of hearsay evidence may oppose it by giving notice within fourteen days to the court officer and all other parties. The court may vary these requirements.

The cases where a statement is admissible in criminal proceedings as evidence of the truth of its contents under an exception to the rule against hearsay are as follows.

Admissibility of hearsay evidence: the basic provisions

CJA 2003, Part 11, Chapter 2 commences in s 114 by stating that hearsay evidence is admissible in criminal proceedings as evidence of any matter stated if, but only if:

(a) a statutory provision makes it admissible (these are considered below);
(b) any rule of law makes it admissible (also considered below);
(c) all parties to the proceedings agree to it being admissible; or
(d) the court is satisfied that it is in the interests of justice for it to be admissible.

In deciding in (d) whether it is in the interests of justice, the court must have regard to the following factors (and any others it considers relevant):

(i)   how much probative value the statement has or how valuable it is for understanding other evidence;
(ii)   what other evidence has been, or can be, given on the matter or evidence mentioned in (i);
(iii)   how important the matter or evidence mentioned in (i) is in the context of the case as a whole;
(iv)   the circumstances in which the statement was made;
(v)   how reliable the maker of the statement appears to be;
(vi)   how reliable the evidence of the making of the statement appears to be;
(vii)   whether oral evidence of the matter stated can be given and, if not, why it cannot;
(viii)   the amount of difficulty involved in challenging the statement; and
(ix)   the extent to which the difficulty would be likely to prejudice the party facing it.

A court does not have to reach a conclusion about all nine of these factors in order to admit hearsay evidence under (d).

This does not affect the exclusion of evidence of a statement on grounds other than the fact that it is hearsay. For example, a confession (a type of admissible hearsay) might be excluded under the provisions of PACE.

For the purposes of CJA 2003, Part 11, Chapter 2, references to a 'statement' are to any representation of fact or opinion made by a person by whatever means, including a representation made in a sketch, photofit or other pictorial form. A 'matter stated' is one to which CJA 2003, Part 11, Chapter 2 applies only if the purpose (or one of the purposes) of the maker of the statement appears to have been to cause another person to believe the matter, or to cause another person to act or a machine to operate on the basis that the matter is as stated. As a result a statement which was not made with such a purpose, but from which a fact may be inferred (such as evidence of a request for drugs to be supplied made to the accused who is charged with supplying drugs), is not hearsay evidence and is admissible. This reverses the old law of hearsay, under which such a statement was hearsay.

We now turn to the exceptions to the hearsay rule to which (a) and (b) above relate.

Witness unavailable

CJA 2003, s 116 provides that in criminal proceedings a statement which is not made orally is admissible in evidence as evidence of any matter stated in it if:

(a) oral evidence given by the person making the statement would be admissible as evidence of that matter;

(b) the person who made the statement is identified to the satisfaction of the court; and

(c) that person is:
   (i) dead;
   (ii) unfit to be a witness because of his bodily or mental condition;
   (iii) is outside the United Kingdom and it is not reasonably practicable to secure his attendance;
   (iv) cannot be found although such steps as it is reasonably practicable to take to find him have been taken; or
   (v) through fear does not give (or continue to give) oral evidence in the proceedings, either at all, or in connection with the subject matter of the statement, and the court gives leave for the statement to be given in evidence.

'Fear' in (c)(v) is to be widely construed and (for example) includes fear of the death or serious injury of another person or of financial loss. Leave to admit may only be given where the court considers that the statement ought to be admitted in the interests of justice, having regard to its contents, to the risk of unfairness and, in appropriate cases, to the fact that a direction under YJCEA 1999 (special measures for the giving of evidence by fearful witnesses etc) could be made in relation to the person making the statement, and to any other relevant circumstances.

Any condition in (c)(i)–(v) which is in fact satisfied will be treated as not having been satisfied if any of the circumstances described in (c) are caused by the person in support of whose case it is sought to admit the statement, or by any person acting on his behalf, in order to prevent the person referred to in (c) from giving evidence in the proceedings.

A statement can be 'made in a document' by a person for the purposes of this section even though he himself did not write it, if his oral statement is contemporaneously recorded by the police officer to whom it was made. Normally the statement must be signed by its maker to be admissible, but if he is physically unable to sign the document it will also be admissible if he has clearly indicated that it is accurate after the document has been read back.

The words 'unfit to be a witness' apply not only to a person's physical inability to attend a court but also to his mental capacity when there to give evidence. The Court of Appeal has said that there is nothing to prevent the written evidence of a witness being admitted where he is too ill to give evidence at the time of the trial, even though his evidence is the only evidence against the accused. In the case concerned the landlord of a public house had seen three men burgling the pub and had them under observation in a well-lit room for five to ten seconds. He recognised two of them who were regular customers. Even though this was the only evidence upon which the prosecution relied, it was held that there was nothing which prevented such evidence from being given.

Where it is necessary to consider allowing a witness statement to be read on the grounds that it is not reasonably practicable to secure the witness's attendance, the judge should consider the matter as at the date of the application. It would be difficult to apply these provisions with any certainty if a judge had to consider future possibilities of securing attendance.

In relation to the aspect of 'fear' the issue may involve witnesses who have made statements concerning an offence and who later make a second statement saying that they are too afraid to give evidence. Where such events occur, the second statements concerning their state of mind are not excluded by the hearsay rule when they are put in evidence solely to prove the state of mind of the maker of the statement. Where a man committed an offence of aggravated burglary and made threats of violence towards two persons who later said that they were afraid to give evidence, the statements of those persons concerning the reasons for their fear were admitted as well as the statements which they had made immediately following the offence. Although it is sufficient that the witness is in fear as a consequence of the commission of the material offence or of something said or done (by the accused or anyone else) subsequently in relation to that offence and the possibility of that witness testifying as to it, the fear need not be in that form. It is enough that, for whatever reason, fear is established. A divisional court has ruled that the test of fear does not have to be based on reasonable grounds, so long as the court is sure that the witness is in fear. The fear need not have arisen as a result of something which has happened since the commission of the offence.

In order to satisfy the requirements of CJA 2003 there must, if possible, be direct evidence of fear from the witness. However, the evidence of fear may, for example, be given by a police officer. However, it is important to establish that the fear existed at the time of the trial. The Court of Appeal has said that it is not sufficient that the witness made a statement some months previously in which he said that he was afraid to give evidence because he feared repercussions against himself and his family. Before a court can properly be satisfied as to the requirements, it should be informed of what steps have been taken to persuade the witness to attend or to alleviate his fears.

Business etc documents and public information

CJA 2003, s 117 provides that in criminal proceedings a statement contained in a document is admissible evidence of any matter stated if:

(a) oral evidence given in the proceedings would be admissible as evidence of that matter;

(b) the following requirements are satisfied:

   (i)   the document or the part containing the statement was created or received by a person in the course of a trade, business, profession or other occupation, or as the holder of a paid or unpaid office;

   (ii) the person who supplied the information contained in the statement (the relevant person) had, or may reasonably be supposed to have had, personal knowledge of the matters dealt with; and

(iii) each person (if any) through whom the information was supplied from that relevant person to the person mentioned in (i) received the information in the course of a trade, business, profession or other occupation, or as the holder of a paid or unpaid office; and

(c) additional requirements are satisfied where the statement was prepared for the purpose of pending or contemplated criminal proceedings, or for a criminal investigation, but was not obtained pursuant to a request under the Crime (International Co-operation) Act 2003 or under the Criminal Justice Act 1988, Sch 13 (overseas evidence). The additional requirements referred to are any of the five conditions set out at (c) above under the heading 'witness unavailable', or that the relevant person cannot reasonably be expected to have any recollection of the matters dealt with in the statement (having regard to the length of time since he supplied the information and all other circumstances).

Where a court is satisfied that the statement's reliability as evidence is doubtful, either in its contents, the source of its information, the way or circumstances in which the information was supplied or received, or the way in which the document was created or received, it may make a declaration that the statement is not admissible.

The provisions of CJA 2003, s 117 are obviously sensible. It would be unnecessarily burdensome, and sometimes stultifying, if oral evidence was to be required in every case from a person who was either the creator or keeper of the document, or the supplier of the information contained in the document.

Where the supplier of the information and the creator of the document containing it are different people, the maker of the statement is the person who supplied the information. As a result, entries in a police officer's notebook (or a computerised crime record produced by a police officer) are admissible. Where a police officer has noted down a statement, the statement is made for the purposes of the present rules by the officer and not by the person who addressed it to him. In such a case, therefore, the question is whether the constable cannot reasonably be expected to recollect the matters in the statement, and not whether the person who addressed those matters to him can. Similarly, where a man presented a stolen Switchcard at a supermarket checkout and a supervisor saw him making off in a car, the registered number of which she noted, a record made by a second supervisor, at the dictation of the first, was held to be a document created or received in the course of a business, profession etc for these purposes; the fact that she could recall other matters which occurred at the time (such as the colour of the offender) did not mean that she could be expected to remember the registered number of the car. Section 117 admits a 'statement in a document' where a document was 'created or received' by a person in the course of a trade, business or profession.

It is important to note the limitations of s 117. It cannot be relied on, for example, to justify details about a previous offence of which a person has been convicted held on the PNC because those details (as opposed to the date, offence charged and sentence) will not be known personally to the person supplying the information as is required by condition (b)(ii) above. Likewise, where a shopper had left the offending vehicle's registration number on the damaged car's windscreen after it had been hit in a supermarket car park and that number had been reported in the police incident log after it had been given by the girlfriend of the owner of the damaged car, the Court of Appeal held that that information in the log should not have been admitted under s 117 because the girlfriend had not received it in the course of trade or business and therefore condition (b)(iii) was not satisfied. The Court of Appeal added that the police record would have been admissible under s 121(1)(c) (condition (c) referred to on p 233).

Evidence from computer records

The YJCEA 1999 repealed PACE, s 69, and Sch 3, which required that, if it was to be used in evidence, evidence by means of a document produced by a computer had to be accompanied by proof that the computer was operating correctly at the time and was being properly used.

The effect of the repeal is that it is presumed that a computer was operating correctly at the time in question in the absence of proof to the contrary. However, where there is a challenge to the reliability of the computer, the fact that it was working correctly has to be established. The ordinary law on evidence now applies to computer evidence. In the absence of evidence to the contrary, courts will presume that the computer system was working correctly. If there is evidence that it may not have been, the party seeking to introduce the evidence will need to prove that it was working.

Where the necessity for proof arises because the reliability of a computer is challenged, proof by the prosecution that the computer has been operating satisfactorily can be satisfied by the evidence of a person familiar with the operation of the computer, who need not be a computer expert. The House of Lords has held that evidence by a store detective that computerised cash tills were working satisfactorily was admissible where it was apparent from the nature of her evidence that she was thoroughly familiar with the operation of the tills and the central computer, even though she did not understand the technical operation of the computer. Lord Griffiths said that he suspected that it would rarely be necessary to call an expert and that in the vast majority of cases it would be possible to discharge the burden by calling a witness *who was familiar with the operation of the computer in the sense of knowing what the computer was required to do, and who could say that it was doing it properly.*

The CJA 2003 provides that where a statement is generated by a machine and is based on information implanted into the machine by a person, the statement will only be admissible where it is proved that the information was accurate. This is not directly related to proof of the reliability of the machine, but is associated, in that there is a requirement to show that accurate information was fed into the machine.

Inconsistent statements

CJA 2003, s 119 provides that, where a person gives oral evidence in criminal proceedings and he admits making a previous inconsistent statement, or a previous inconsistent statement made by him is proved to have been made, the statement is admissible as evidence of any matter in respect of which oral evidence would be admissible. Thus, the fact that he made a previous inconsistent statement does not merely affect the witness's credibility but it is also some evidence of the truth of the facts which he had previously stated. Evidence may be admitted to show that a witness has made a statement which is inconsistent with the evidence he has given. A witness may have denied in a previous statement having contact with an accused on a particular day, and then have stated in oral evidence that he did.

Other previous statements of a witness

Where it is suggested that a witness in criminal proceedings has fabricated oral evidence, a previous statement by the witness is admissible not only on the issue of credibility but also to prove the truth of the matters previously asserted. This is the effect of CJA 2003, s 120 which states that any previous statement which a witness has made is admissible in evidence as evidence of any matter which it contains in the same way as oral evidence would be admitted.

In addition, where a witness is refreshing his memory from a written document and is cross-examined on its contents and it is therefore received in evidence, that statement will become evidence of any matter stated in it.

A previous statement is also admissible as evidence of the facts contained in it if the witness states that he made the statement and believes it to be true and any one of the following conditions applies:

(a) that the statement describes or identifies a person, object or place;
(b) it was made by the witness when the matters stated were fresh in his memory and he cannot reasonably be expected to remember the matters stated well enough to give oral evidence of them;
(c) the witness claims to be a victim of an offence to which the proceedings relate and the statement consists of a complaint by the witness about conduct which (if proved) would constitute the offence (or part of it), and the complaint was made as soon as could reasonably be expected after the alleged conduct and not because of a threat or promise, provided the witness gives oral evidence in respect of the matter.

The provisions at (a) will apply to an object such as a motor vehicle and its registration number. In relation to (b), where a witness relies upon another person or a document to support his oral evidence the fact that he had to do so may affect the weight to be given to that evidence, but the fact that he had to be so assisted does not make the evidence inadmissible.

Additional requirements for admissibility of multiple hearsay

'Multiple hearsay' refers to the case where the witness has no personal knowledge of the matter stated to him, but repeats a hearsay statement made to him by another, as where X makes a statement to Y who repeats it to Z. Repetition of the statement by Z is multiple (or second-hand) hearsay, whereas if Y gave the statement in evidence it would be first-hand hearsay. CJA 2003, s 121(1) provides that a hearsay statement is not admissible to prove the fact that an earlier hearsay statement was made unless:

(a) either of the statements is admissible under CJA 2003, s 117 (business document), s 119 (inconsistent statement), or s 120 (other previous statements of witnesses); or
(b) all parties agree to its admissibility; or
(c) the court is satisfied that the value of the evidence in question, taking into account how reliable the statement appears to be, is so high that the interests of justice require the later statement to be admissible for that purpose.

CJA 2003, ss 116, 117, 119 and 120: general provisions concerning capability to make statements

A statement made under CJA 2003, s 116 (cases where a witness is unavailable), s 119 (an inconsistent statement), or s 120 (other previous statements by a witness) is not admissible in evidence if it was made by a person who did not have the 'required capability' at the time that he made the statement. In the case of a statement made under s 117 (business and other documents) such a statement is not admissible so far as the requirements of para (b) on pp 230–231 are concerned (created or received by the particular persons in the course of their business etc) if that person did not at the time have the required capability, or if that person cannot be identified but cannot reasonably be assumed to have had the required capability at that time.

A person has the 'required capability' if he is capable of understanding the questions put to him about the matter and of giving answers which can be understood. Where such capability is disputed, the fact must be determined in the absence of the jury (if there is one) and expert evidence may be received as well as that of any person to whom the statement was made. The burden of proof lies upon the party seeking to adduce the statement and the standard of proof is the balance of probabilities.

Evidence by certificate

The Criminal Justice Act 1948, s 41(1) permits a certificate signed by a constable, or qualified person, certifying that a plan or drawing exhibited in criminal proceedings is a plan or drawing made by him of the place or object specified in the certificate, and that the plan or drawing is correctly drawn to a scale so specified, to be accepted as evidence of the relative position of things shown on the plan or drawing. The plan etc is admissible to the same extent that oral evidence would be admissible. A 'qualified person' means a registered architect or a chartered engineer of one of certain types.

In order for the certificate to be admissible, a copy of such a plan etc must be served on the accused at least seven days before the hearing. Moreover, if the accused serves the appropriate notice that he requires the attendance of the person who signed the certificate, the certificate will not be admissible.

Evidence by written statements

CJA 1967, s 9 makes provision for the admissibility of written statements in proceedings. It provides that a written statement signed by the person who made it is admissible as evidence to the like extent as oral evidence given by that person. There are certain conditions which by s 9(2) must be satisfied:

(a) the statement must contain a declaration by that person to the effect that it is true to the best of his knowledge or belief and that he has made the statement knowing that, if it were tendered in evidence, he would be liable to prosecution if he wilfully stated in it anything which he knew to be false or did not believe to be true;

(b) before the hearing at which the statement is tendered in evidence, a copy of the statement must be served, by or on behalf of the party proposing to tender it, on each of the other parties to the proceedings; and

(c) none of the other parties or their solicitors must, within seven days from the service of the copy of the statement, have served a notice on the party so proposing objecting to the statement being tendered in evidence under the section.

In practice, statement forms carried by police officers incorporate the declaration at (a) so that the evidence of any witness can be offered in written form if it is accepted by the other side. Although the provisions at (b) and (c) seem to suggest that agreements are reached in advance of the hearing there is nothing to prevent agreement being reached at the trial itself.

A statement made by a person under eighteen tendered in evidence under CJA 1967, s 9 must, by s 9(3), state his age; if a statement is made by a person who cannot read, it must be read to him before he signs it and be accompanied by a declaration by the person who so read the statement to the effect that it was so read; and if the statement refers to any other document as an exhibit, the copy served on the other party must be accompanied by a copy of that document or by such information as may be necessary to enable that party to inspect that document or a copy of it. Copies of such written statements may be served in the same way as a summons or requisition.

Regardless of this procedure having been carried out, the party whose witness it is may nevertheless call that person to give evidence and the court may require, of its own motion or following an application from any party, that that person attends to give evidence.

Proof of convictions and acquittals

The provisions relating to how such proof may be made, which we discussed above, afford another exception to the rule against hearsay.

Statements received as part of the res gestae

An oral statement is part of the res gestae if it relates to a fact so connected with a fact in issue as to explain its nature or form in connection with one continuous transaction. At common law, under the 'res gestae rule', a statement which is part of the res gestae is admissible if the conditions set out below are satisfied.

The res gestae rule is specifically preserved by CJA 2003, s 118 which preserves any rule of law under which, in criminal proceedings, a statement is admissible as evidence of any matter stated if:

(a) the statement was made by a person so emotionally overpowered by an event that the possibility of concoction or distortion can be disregarded;
(b) the statement accompanied an act which can be properly evaluated as evidence only if considered in conjunction with the statement; or
(c) the statement relates to a physical sensation or mental state (such as intention or emotion).

An oral statement made by a person involved in an unusual, startling or exciting event is admissible as part of the res gestae as evidence of the facts stated, provided it was so clearly made spontaneously that, in the light of the circumstances, the possibility of concoction or distortion can be disregarded. If the issue is one of murder it is probable that a statement made by the victim, 'Don't shoot, Sidney', which was made as (or immediately before) the gun was fired would be admissible as part of the res gestae, although it is hearsay, and that likewise the victim's agitated shout immediately afterwards, 'Look what you've done. Get a doctor, quick', would be admissible. Where a man was stabbed and, whilst being given first aid treatment by a constable, named his attackers, this evidence was admitted as a part of the res gestae at the trial of the accused after the declarant had died.

While the length of time before or after the event about which the statement is made is relevant, admissibility is not restricted to circumstances in which statements are made at the time of the actus reus. In one case, an injured man crawled for an hour to reach a house at which he named his attacker. He subsequently named his attacker again when he identified him to a police officer whilst being transported to hospital by ambulance. It was submitted that too great a time had elapsed between the incident and the statements. It was held that the crucial question was whether there had been a real possibility of concoction or distortion. At the time that the deceased made the statements, were his thoughts so dominated by what had happened that they could be regarded as unaffected by ex post facto reasoning or fabrication?

Another example of the operation of the res gestae rule is provided by a case where two police officers saw a man being jostled by two others. The assailants went into a doorway where the victim's wallet was found. The victim lunged at the men and said 'they're the ones: these two mugged me of my wallet'. The victim, although summoned, did not attend the hearing and the issue surrounded whether these statements, which were clearly hearsay when repeated by the police officers, could be admitted as part of the res gestae. It was held that, looking at the nature of the incident as a whole, the statements were relevant and were properly admitted. Whilst the res gestae rule should not be used as a device to avoid calling a witness, there was no reason to believe that the Crown had done so in these circumstances.

Confessions

Although hearsay, a confession is generally admissible. A confession is an incriminating statement made by the accused. It may be a total confession of guilt by the accused, or a confession as to an act by him, or his state of mind, or some other fact relating to him. We deal with the law relating to confessions separately, below, but wish to point out here that this exception to the hearsay rule has been extended by the Court of Appeal to the case where, in the course of a routine inquiry, a police officer asks someone to identify himself and that person does so by saying 'I am Robin Hood of 15 High Street'. If, in later proceedings against Robin Hood of 15 High Street the officer cannot independently identify him as the person who spoke to him on the previous occasion, the officer may testify that that person had said 'I am Robin Hood of 15 High Street', despite the fact that this is hearsay, because it amounts to a confession. However, the jury must be directed to be sure that it was the accused who gave the identification on the previous occasion.

These rules were specifically preserved by CJA 2003.

Public information

CJA 2003, s 118 preserves the rule of law which permits, in criminal proceedings, the admissibility of facts of a public nature stated in published works dealing with matters of a public nature (eg histories, scientific works, dictionaries, maps), or in public documents (eg registers, returns under public authority with respect to matters of public interest), or in court records, treaties etc, or in birth certificates.

Expert reports

An expert report is admissible in evidence in criminal proceedings, whether or not the person making it attends to give oral evidence. However, if it is proposed that the maker of the report shall not give oral evidence, the report is only admissible with the leave of the court. In determining whether to give leave, the court must have regard to the contents of the report; the reasons why it is proposed that oral evidence shall not be given; the likely risk to fairness in relation to the accused; and any other relevant circumstance. An 'expert report' is one written by a person dealing wholly or mainly with matters on which he is (or would if living be) qualified to give expert evidence.

This common law rule was preserved by CJA 2003, s 118.

Reputation

CJA 2003, s 118 preserves the common law rules whereby, in criminal proceedings, hearsay evidence of a person's reputation is admissible for the purpose of proving his good or bad character, but only in so far as it allows the court to treat such evidence as proving his good or bad character. Some statutes make specific provisions in this respect and such provisions are not affected by the changes made by CJA 2003. Section 118 of the Act also preserves the admissibility of evidence of reputation or family tradition in relation to pedigree or the existence of a marriage, any public or general right or the identity of any person or thing but the use of such provisions will be rare.

Credibility of hearsay evidence

A challenge may be made to the credibility of the maker of a statement admitted as hearsay evidence if he does not give oral evidence in the proceedings. The person against whom the hearsay evidence has been admitted may produce, in certain circumstances, evidence to discredit the maker of the statement or to show that he has contradicted himself.

Stopping case where hearsay evidence unconvincing

A judge has the duty under CJA 2003, s 125 to stop a case and either direct acquittal, or discharge the jury, if a case is based wholly or partly on an out-of-court statement which is so unconvincing that, considering the importance of the case, a conviction would be unsafe. In a similar case in a magistrates' court the justices would be bound to dismiss the case or order a retrial where this was appropriate.

General discretion to exclude hearsay evidence

CJA 2003, s 126 gives a court a discretion to exclude a statement as evidence of a matter stated if the statement was made otherwise than in oral evidence in the proceedings, and the court is satisfied that the case for excluding the statement, taking account of the danger that to admit it would result in undue waste of time, substantially outweighs the case for admitting it, taking account of the value of the evidence. This is in addition to any discretion under PACE, s 78 or any other power of a court to exclude evidence.

CONFESSIONS

Confession by one accused: evidence against co-accused?

An out-of-court confession by *one accused is not evidence against another co-accused* unless the co-accused expressly or impliedly adopts the statements contained in it. There is one qualification to that statement because the House of Lords has held that, when in a joint trial of two or more accused for an offence alleged to have been committed jointly, proof of the guilt of one of the accused, A, was essential in proving the case against another accused, B, and the evidence against A consisted solely of his own out-of-court confession, then A's confession would also be admissible as evidence, not only against A but also against B in so far as the fact of A's guilt of itself established B's guilt.

Confession by accused as evidence against him

For the purposes of the rules which follow, a 'confession' is defined by PACE, s 82 as including 'any statement wholly or partly adverse to the person who made it, whether made to a person in authority or not and whether made in words or otherwise'. A wholly exculpatory statement is not a confession for these purposes. Because of the phrase 'in words or otherwise', an accused's confession may simply consist of a gesture of acceptance of a statement adverse to him made by another. Statements made which are intended to vindicate a suspect, for example, where he gives explanations intended to justify his possession of goods, and if taken to be true, would do so, do not amount to a confession, even if they are later shown to be false or inconsistent with the maker's evidence. In such a case, however, a record should be made as soon as possible; the reason for there being no contemporaneous notes should be recorded and the suspect should be given an opportunity to check the record.

A video re-enactment by the accused can constitute a confession. This was held in a case where a video recording made willingly by an accused (who had already made an oral confession and who had been reminded that he was under caution and that he was not obliged to participate) in which he re-enacted his actions when strangling a woman was held to be admissible evidence because the video recording had been made reasonably soon after the oral confession and the accused had been properly warned and made it voluntarily. In such a case the accused should be shown the recording and given an opportunity to make, and have recorded, any comment he wished to make concerning the recording.

PACE, s 76(1) allows a confession by an accused person to be given in evidence against him in so far as that confession is relevant to a matter in issue in the proceedings and has not been excluded by the court under s 76(2) on the basis explained below. Thus, if an accused makes a confession to an offence of burglary and mentions involvement in an offence of wounding on another occasion, his confession to burglary will be admissible at his trial for that offence since it is relevant to a matter in issue but, if he has not also been charged with wounding, his confession to wounding is not admissible since it is not relevant to a matter in issue in the proceedings.

Exclusion

PACE, s 76(2) provides that confessions by oppression must always be excluded. 'Oppression' includes torture, inhuman or degrading treatment, and the use of threats or violence. Apart from this, 'oppression' bears its ordinary dictionary meaning, namely, 'the exercise of power or authority in a burdensome, harsh, or wrongful manner; unjust or cruel treatment'. It will almost inevitably involve some impropriety on the part of the questioner. The fact that a confession has been obtained in circumstances involving a breach of a Code of Practice does not in itself constitute oppression. However, bullying questioning may exceptionally amount to oppression.

If a confession is induced by anything said or done which falls short of 'oppression' it will only be excluded if the thing said or done was likely, in the circumstances existing at the time, to render unreliable any confession which might be made by the accused in consequence thereof. An example of something which will be held to be likely to render a confession unreliable is the use of hostile and intimidating interview techniques. For such a likelihood of unreliability to be found there is no need for any hint of impropriety. Where a suspect was mentally handicapped and was interviewed without an adult person being present, it was held that once it had been established that there had been a breach of the code of practice, the onus was on the prosecution to satisfy the judge beyond reasonable doubt that the confession was not obtained in breach of PACE, s 76(2). 'The circumstances existing at the time' were all important in relation to reliability.

Where it is shown that there has been aggressive and hostile questioning it becomes a matter of degree as to whether the threshold is passed beyond which the behaviour of police officers has made the confession unreliable in all circumstances. However, all of the circumstances must be examined. In the course of an interview concerning drug offences an officer interjected, implying that if the suspect did not tell the truth he would be held in custody. Some sixteen minutes later he confessed to an offence. The trial judge refused to exclude his confession being satisfied that the accused was astute, had experience of being interviewed at a police station, and that his will had not been broken. He had continued to deny other offences. The Court of Appeal endorsed the trial judge's decision.

The question frequently arises whether or not, in relation to the issue of unreliability, the expert evidence of a psychiatrist or psychologist should be admitted as to a person's mental condition at the time when a confession was made. Such expert evidence may be admitted to show that a confession is unreliable because of psychological abnormalities if, but only if, it is to the effect that the accused was suffering from mental handicap, mental illness or a personality disorder so severe as to be categorised as mental disorder. It is not enough to allege that an accused is 'not exceptionally bright and is possibly of dull intelligence and very suggestible'.

It has not yet been decided whether interviewing a drug addict when he is withdrawing falls within the present provision. However, the Court of Appeal has held that, if it is, the question of 'likely to be rendered unreliable' depends on whether or not the addict was fit to be interviewed in the sense that his answers could be relied upon in the circumstances. This, the court held, is a matter for those present at the time. The court held that, where experienced police officers considered a person fit to be interviewed and a doctor who saw him after the interview was of the same opinion, there was no reason to believe that a confession was likely to be unreliable. (The court also refused to exclude the evidence obtained by the confession under its discretionary power to exclude unfair evidence provided by PACE, s 78, described on p 254.)

If it is alleged that a confession was, or may have been, obtained by oppression or in consequence of anything said or done which was likely to render the confession unreliable, the court must not allow the confession to be given in evidence against that person except in so far as the prosecution proves beyond reasonable doubt that the confession (notwithstanding that it may be true) was not obtained by these means.

PACE, s 76(4) provides that, even if a confession, or a part of it, is excluded under the above provisions, this does not affect the admissibility:

(a) of facts discovered as a result of the confession; or
(b) where the confession is relevant as showing that the accused speaks, writes or expresses himself in a particular way, of so much of the confession as is necessary to show that he does so.

The effect of (a) is as follows. If evidence of a fact is discovered as a result of a confession, or part of a confession, and that confession, or a relevant part of it, is excluded under PACE, s 76(2), that evidence may nevertheless be adduced by the prosecution. However, no reference should be made to the fact that the discovery was the result of a confession; only the accused, or someone acting on his behalf, may disclose this. Thus, if A is arrested for thefts of motor cars and makes a confession which includes details of the persons to whom he sold the vehicles, and that confession is excluded, the prosecution may give evidence of the recovery of the vehicles from those persons but it may not mention that they were discovered as a result of the excluded confession.

The effect of (b) is that, if there is something in a confession, or part, excluded under PACE, s 76, which shows that the accused writes, speaks or expresses himself in a particular manner, and this serves, for example, to identify him with whoever committed the offence, so much of the confession as is necessary to show the characteristic referred to is admissible.

Confessions given in evidence for co-accused

The discussion of confessions so far has concerned their use against an accused person. PACE, s 76A, inserted by CJA 2003, provides that a confession (as defined by s 82; see p 238) made by an accused person may be given in evidence by a co-accused in so far as it is relevant to a matter in issue unless excluded by the court on one of the two grounds under s 76. If it is alleged that one of them applies, the co-accused seeking to rely on the confession must prove on the balance of probabilities that the confession was not obtained by oppression etc. However, PACE, s 76A maintains the rule that the exclusion of a confession does not affect the admissibility of facts discovered in consequence of it.

Confessions by the mentally handicapped

PACE, s 77 is concerned with confessions (as defined by s 82) made by mentally handicapped persons. Where the case against such an accused depends wholly or substantially upon his confession and the court is satisfied that he is mentally handicapped and that the confession was not made in the presence of an independent person, the jury must be warned of, or the magistrates' court must heed, the need for special care before convicting the accused in reliance on the confession. A police officer or a person employed for, or engaged on, police purposes is not an independent person in this context. Generally speaking, to question a suspect in such circumstances amounts to a breach of the Detention Code (Code of Practice for the Detention, Treatment and Questioning of Persons by Police Officers).

In establishing whether an accused is mentally handicapped it is not appropriate to attempt to take figures provided by intelligence tests in one case and then to apply them slavishly to another in order to define some rigid line, the crossing of which would lead automatically to the exclusion of confession evidence. Each case must be looked at on its own facts.

Of course, if a mentally handicapped person's confession is obtained by oppression or by words or conduct likely to make it unreliable (as in a case where the accused confessed at a fifth interview after thirty-six hours' detention and without having received any legal advice), the confession will be inadmissible.

Procedure—audio recorded confessions at the Crown Court

The procedure to be followed in preparation for proceedings in the Crown Court in relation to audio recordings of police interviews with suspects is laid down in the *Consolidated Practice Direction*. Media must be produced and proved by the interviewing officer, or any other officer who was present at the interview; the prosecution must provide an audio machine operator; counsel must indicate the parts of a recording which it may be necessary to play, and the prosecution must be prepared in advance to do so.

ACCUSED'S RIGHT OF SILENCE

The CJPOA 1994 permits a court or jury to draw such inferences from an accused's failure to mention facts as appear proper. The circumstances, generally, in which such inferences may be drawn are:

(a) where an accused has failed, when questioned under caution or on being charged or officially informed that he may be prosecuted, to mention facts later relied upon as part of his defence, and which it is reasonable to expect him to have mentioned (CJPOA 1994, s 34);

(b) where an accused fails, without good cause, to give evidence or answer questions at trial (CJPOA 1994, s 35);
(c) where an arrested person fails or refuses to account for possession of objects, substances or marks when requested to do so (CJPOA 1994, s 36);
(d) where an arrested person fails or refuses to account for his presence at a particular place, when requested to do so (CJPOA 1994, s 37).

In the above cases, an inference may be drawn in relation to:

(a) the determination of applications for dismissal of charges made in relation to serious or complex fraud in respect of which notice of transfer has been given;
(b) the determination of the issue of whether a person accused of an offence (of whatever type) has a case to answer;
(c) the determination of whether a person is guilty of the offence charged.

However, an inference cannot be drawn under CJPOA 1994, ss 34 to 37 in respect of a failure to disclose facts in an interview or other questioning which is inadmissible in law or excluded by way of discretion.

An adverse inference drawn under CJPOA 1994, ss 34 to 37 cannot be the sole basis for a finding of a case to answer, for the issue of a notice to transfer, or for a finding of guilt. This is provided by s 38(3) and (4). For this reason, CJPOA 1999, ss 34 to 37 do not assist in overcoming the problems where one or both of the parents of an abused child must have injured it but both remain silent as to who did so. In such a case, the only evidence on the key issue of identity would be the inference, something which would be caught by the terms of s 38(3) and (4). As a result of s 38(3) and (4), the importance of ss 34 to 37 is that an adverse inference under them may enable the jury or magistrates to find that other evidence, when considered with the adverse inference, enables them to be sure beyond reasonable doubt of the truth and accuracy of that other evidence and in consequence of the accused's guilt.

When evidence is to be offered and admissibility

Subject to any directions given by the court, evidence which tends to establish the particular failure may be given before or after the evidence which tends to establish the fact which the accused is alleged to have failed to mention. Thus, where the interview is concerned with the accused's possession of a stolen watch, evidence of his failure to offer an explanation for his possession of it may be given before, or after, evidence of it being found in his possession. In most circumstances, the most appropriate time will be after evidence of his possession of the property has been given. These provisions do not prejudice the admissibility of evidence of his silence or other reaction which would be admissible apart from the section (eg reaction to things said in his presence and hearing which relate to his involvement in an offence).

Effect of accused's silence when questioned under caution or on being charged or officially informed that he may be prosecuted

By CJPOA 1994, s 34, where it was reasonable to expect the accused to have mentioned facts (as opposed to theory, possibility or speculation) on which he later relies in his defence, a court or a jury may draw such inferences as appear proper from a failure to mention any fact which a person could reasonably have been expected to mention when questioned under caution, charged or officially informed that he might be prosecuted. The Court of Appeal has held that s 34 does not permit an adverse inference to be drawn from an accused's failure to leave his police cell to be interviewed because this does not fall within the ambit of 'being questioned'. It has also been held that a person who gives the interviewing officer a prepared statement from which he does not depart when giving evidence at his subsequent trial has 'mentioned facts' and therefore falls outside s 34, notwithstanding that the prepared statement was not given in response to questioning and that he said 'no comment' to all subsequent police questions. The Court said that s 34 did not distinctly include police cross-examination of a suspect upon his account of events. Had that been intended, Parliament would have used different language.

Section 34 does not apply in a case where the accused was at an authorised place of detention (a police station or other prescribed place) at the time of the failure if he had not been allowed an opportunity to consult a solicitor prior to being questioned, charged or informed that he might be prosecuted.

It should be noted that there are significant areas of overlap between the rule under s 34 and that which applies under CJPOA 1994, ss 36 and 37 (referred to above and dealt with below). In addition, they share the similarity that drawing an adverse inference under them may infringe art 6 of the ECHR (right to a fair trial); see p 262. Whether or not it does must be determined in the light of all the circumstances of the case, including any explanation offered for the silence and the compulsion inherent in the situation. It would be contrary to art 6 to base a conviction solely on the accused's silence. Unlike ss 36 and 37, s 34 is not confined to the questioning of persons who are under arrest. In addition, ss 36 and 37 operate irrespective of whether a fact is relied upon as part of the defence, or irrespective of whether any defence is in fact made. By contrast, it is this reliance which is at the heart of s 34. Lastly, under s 36 or s 37, a constable is under a duty to explain the effect of the requirement in ordinary language, while the key pre-requisite in s 34 is the formal caution.

The Court of Appeal has held that there are six formal conditions to be met before an inference may be drawn by a jury from a failure to mention a fact later relied upon:

(a) there must be proceedings against a person for an offence;
(b) the alleged failure must occur before the person is charged (or—it is submitted—when charged or officially informed of the risk of prosecution);
(c) the alleged failure must occur during questioning under caution by a constable;
(d) the constable's questioning must be directed towards trying to discover whether or by whom the alleged offence had been committed;
(e) the alleged failure must be to mention any fact relied upon in his defence;
(f) the accused's failure to mention a fact which in the circumstances existing at the time the accused could reasonably have been expected to mention when so questioned. What is reasonable depends on all the circumstances of the case. 'Time' refers to the time of questioning and account must be taken of all the relevant circumstances existing at the time. 'In the circumstances' includes such matters as the time of day, the accused's age, experience, mental capacity, state of health, sobriety, tiredness, knowledge, personality and legal advice, which might all be relevant. These are matters for the jury.

For the purposes of (e), a fact can be relied on even though the accused does not give evidence at his trial, since an accused can rely on a fact by evidence through a witness on his behalf or through cross-examination of a prosecution witness.

The Court of Appeal has held that legal advice to remain silent cannot in itself prevent an adverse inference from being drawn under CJPOA 1994, s 34, otherwise s 34 would be rendered ineffective. In another case the Court of Appeal held that such advice is a very relevant circumstance to be taken into account in deciding whether it could reasonably have been expected to mention at that time the matter relied on. However, it said that the jury should not be concerned with the correctness of a solicitor's advice, nor with whether it complies with the Law Society guidelines. Another Court of Appeal has added that a jury may still draw an adverse inference if it is sure that the true reason for the accused's silence is that he had no, or no satisfactory, explanation consistent with evidence to give.

Subsequently, the European Court of Human Rights has held that the fact that an accused has been given legal advice to remain silent must be given appropriate weight by a domestic court because there may be good reason for such advice, and that a good reason for not drawing an inference was bona fide legal advice. The European Court has held that an accused's right to a fair trial under art 6 of the ECHR was violated where the judge's direction to the jury failed to strike the right balance between the right to silence and the circumstances in which an adverse inference may properly be drawn; in particular the jury should have been directed that if they were satisfied that the accused's silence at interview could not sensibly be attributed to his having no answers that would stand up to questioning or investigation, they should not draw an adverse inference. It added that particular caution was required before an adverse inference could be drawn from silence during questioning.

In its latest statement about silence in reliance on the advice of a solicitor, the Court of Appeal has summarised the law as follows. Where a solicitor's advice is relied upon by the accused, the ultimate question for the jury remains under s 34 whether the facts relied on at the trial were facts which the accused could reasonably have been expected to mention at interview. If they were not, that is the end of the matter. If the jury consider that the accused genuinely relied on the advice, that is not necessarily the end of the matter. It may still not have been reasonable for him to rely on the advice, or the advice may not have been the true explanation for his silence, the true reason being that he had no or no satisfactory explanation consistent with innocence to give.

Although under Code C: the Detention Code (Code of Practice for the Detention, Treatment and Questioning of Persons by Police Officers), a juvenile, or a vulnerable suspect, must not be interviewed in the absence of an appropriate adult, except in the case of an urgent interview, CJPOA 1994, s 34 is not confined to questioning that amounts to an 'interview'. However, Note 11C to that Code states that juveniles and vulnerable suspects may be particularly prone to provide information which is unreliable, misleading or self-incriminating. It goes on to state that 'special care should always be taken when questioning such a person'. This must be true with equal force in respect of any failure to state facts. There is also the distinct possibility that such a person will not understand the significance of the caution, or believe that an obligation to answer exists. For these reasons, a court would be slow to draw an inference from a failure of a vulnerable suspect to disclose facts subsequently relied upon, certainly in questioning which occurs in the absence of an appropriate adult.

An inference may be drawn from any failure to mention a fact later relied on as part of the accused's defence, and which occurs at or prior to (but not after) charge for the offence, or being officially informed etc. The fact that an accused was charged with one offence will therefore not prevent an inference being drawn in respect of another offence for which he is subsequently questioned. Where it was submitted that at the time of the interview the police were not attempting to discover who was responsible for the offence as they were already in possession of sufficient evidence upon which to charge the interviewee, the Court of Appeal said that the issue was not clear, as the police had come into possession of documents at the time of the arrest and the origin of these documents required investigation. It was desirable that police officers should have the opportunity to question suspects as explanations may be put forward which indicated that no offence had been committed, or that it had been committed by someone else. It is only where the officer is truly of the opinion that there is sufficient evidence upon which a successful prosecution may be based, that an interview should not take place or should be discontinued.

The rule that an inference may only be drawn from a failure to mention facts which the accused could have been reasonably expected to mention when questioned requires the court to assess the situation at the time of that questioning, not with the benefit of hindsight as at the date of trial. An inference cannot be drawn from a failure to mention a fact of which the accused was unaware when questioned.

The Court of Appeal has discouraged prosecutors from too readily seeking to activate CJPOA1994, s 34. Its mischief, it said, was primarily directed at the positive defence following a 'no comment' and/or 'ambush' defence. Where that was not the case, the Court warned against the further complicating of trials and summings-up by invoking s 34.

Effect of accused's silence at trial

CJPOA 1994, s 35(1) permits an inference to be drawn at the trial of a person who has attained the age of fourteen years unless:

(a) the accused's guilt is not in issue, or
(b) it appears to the court (from evidence, and not just from a submission by an advocate) that the physical or mental condition of the accused makes it undesirable (and not just difficult) for him to be called upon to give evidence.

However, this will not apply if, at the conclusion of the evidence for the prosecution, it is established that the accused will give evidence.

An accused's guilt will not be in issue if he has pleaded guilty and the hearing is merely concerned to resolve matters relevant to sentencing. Nor will it be in issue in preliminary hearings or in issues concerning the admissibility of evidence.

Where such an inference may be drawn, the court must, at the conclusion of the evidence for the prosecution, satisfy itself (in the presence of the jury where applicable) that the accused is aware that:

(a) the stage has been reached at which evidence can be given for the defence;
(b) he can, if he wishes, give evidence; and
(c) if he chooses not to give evidence, or, having been sworn, without good cause refuses to answer any question, it will be permissible for the court or jury to draw such inferences as appear proper from such failure or refusal.

It is mandatory to give such a warning. Where a court omits to do so but does not draw any adverse inference from a failure to give evidence, the omission does not render a conviction unsafe.

For the purposes of (c), a refusal will be taken to be without good cause where a person, having been sworn, refuses to answer any question unless:

(a) he is entitled to refuse to answer the question by virtue of any enactment, whenever passed or made, or on the ground of privilege; or
(b) the court in the exercise of its general discretion excuses him from answering it.

The privilege against self-incrimination and the common law doctrine of legal professional privilege will therefore apply. Outside such matters 'good cause' may be limited to relevance and propriety and perhaps where a question may be considered oppressive.

The Court of Appeal has rejected a submission that reasons or excuses for silence might exist which could properly be advanced by defence counsel without the need for evidence. An example had been given of an accused with previous convictions who had attacked the character of a prosecution witness and did not want to give evidence as he would then be liable to cross-examination concerning his criminal record. The Court of Appeal said that the acceptance of such a submission could lead to bizarre results. An accused with a record would be in a more privileged position than one with a clean record.

The Court of Appeal ruled that, apart from the exceptions included in CJPOA 1994, s 35(1), it is open to a court to decline to draw an inference from silence where the circumstances of the case justified such a course. However, there must be some evidential basis, or exceptional factors, making that a fair course to take. The inferences permitted by s 35 were only such as 'appear proper'.

The Court highlighted the need for a jury to be told that:

(a) the burden of proof remained on the prosecution;
(b) the accused was entitled to remain silent;
(c) an inference could not by itself prove guilt;
(d) the jury had to be satisfied that the prosecution had established a case to answer before drawing such an inference; and
(e) if despite any evidence relied upon to explain silence or in the absence of any such evidence, the jury concluded that silence could only sensibly be attributed to the accused's having no answer, or none that would stand up to cross-examination, they might draw an adverse inference.

In another case, a man who had been convicted of eight counts of theft and attempted theft claimed on appeal that, because the police had only interviewed him in respect of one of the offences, he had been deprived of his right to comment while matters were fresh in his mind and that the judge should not therefore have allowed the jury to draw inferences from his silence at trial. The Court of Appeal rejected this claim. It said that nothing had prevented him from making a statement to his legal advisers whilst matters were fresh in his mind.

Effect of accused's failure or refusal to account for objects, marks etc

CJPOA 1994, s 36 permits an inference to be drawn where:

(a) a person is arrested by a constable and there is:
 (i) on his person; or
 (ii) in or on his clothing or footwear; or
 (iii) otherwise in his possession; or
 (iv) in any place in which he is at the time of his arrest; any object, substance or mark, or there is any mark on any such object; and
(b) that or another constable investigating the case reasonably believes that the presence of the object, substance or mark may be attributable to the participation of the person arrested in the commission of an offence specified by the constable; and
(c) the constable informs the person so arrested that he so believes, and requests him to account for the presence of the object, substance or mark; and
(d) the person fails or refuses to do so,

then, if in any proceedings for the offence so specified, evidence of those matters is given, the court, judge or jury may draw such inferences from the failure or refusal as appear proper. These provisions apply to the condition of clothing or footwear as they apply to a substance or mark thereon. They do not preclude the drawing of inferences which could properly be drawn apart from the section.

   An inference may not be drawn under s 36 where the accused was at an authorised place of detention (a police station or other authorised place) at the time of the failure or refusal, if he had not been allowed an opportunity to consult a solicitor prior to the request being made.

Effect of accused's failure or refusal to account for presence at a particular place

CJPOA 1994, s 37 provides that in certain circumstances, a court may draw such inferences as appear proper from the failure or refusal to account for certain matters. Such inferences are permitted where:

(a) a person arrested by a constable was found by him at a place at or about the time the offence for which he was arrested is alleged to have been committed; and
(b) that or another constable investigating the offence reasonably believes that the presence of the person at that place and at that time may be attributable to his participation in the commission of the offence; and
(c) the constable informs the person that he so believes, and requests him to account for his presence; and
(d) the person fails or refuses to do so.

   Once again, the provisions of the section do not prevent the drawing of any other inference which could properly be drawn apart from the section.

   An inference may not be drawn under CJPOA 1994, s 37 where the accused was at an authorised place of detention (see above) if he had not been allowed an opportunity to consult a solicitor prior to the request being made.

EVIDENCE AS TO CHARACTER

By the accused of his good character

An accused person may always give evidence of his own good character.

If he does so, the judge must direct the jury that evidence of good character is relevant to the jury's assessment of the accused's credibility. It is also normally obligatory for the judge to direct the jury that the previous good character of the accused may be regarded by them as a relevant factor when they are considering whether he was the kind of person who was likely to have behaved in the way alleged by the prosecution. However, the judge is not required to give this latter direction if, although the accused is of good character (in that he had no previous convictions), he has been cautioned on one or more occasions.

Bad character

CJA 2003, s 98 provides that references in the relevant provisions to a person's 'bad character' are to evidence of, or of a disposition towards, misconduct on his part, *other than evidence which has to do with the alleged facts of the offence with which the accused is charged, or is evidence of misconduct in connection with the investigation or prosecution of that offence.* 'Misconduct' in this definition refers to the commission of an offence or other reprehensible behaviour. The Court of Appeal has held that evidence 'has to do with the alleged facts of the offence with which the accused is charged' if it is evidence relating to the very circumstances in which the offence occurred. It held that, on this basis, evidence of a conversation immediately before the robbery with which the accused had been convicted, in which (the accused said) the victim offered to supply him with drugs, was evidence relating to the alleged facts of the offence. It was evidence relating to the very circumstances in which the offence occurred; it was in effect contemporaneous to and closely associated with the alleged facts of the robbery. Where the evidence falls within either of the italicised exclusions it is admissible without more ado.

Evidence of non-accused's bad character

CJA 2003, s 100 provides that, in criminal proceedings, evidence of the bad character of any person other than the accused is admissible *only* if:

(a) it is important explanatory evidence;
(b) it has substantial probative value in relation to a matter which is in issue in the proceedings and is of substantial importance in the context of the case as a whole; or
(c) all parties in the proceedings agree to its admissibility.

The terms included in (a) to (c) are explained below. Section 100 applies to a witness, victim or any other person. So far as non-accuseds are concerned, evidence would be of probative value if it assisted in establishing an issue one way or another. This might arise where there was an issue of credibility as this would affect a court's finding in relation to an issue to be considered.

Except in the case of (c), evidence of the bad character of a non-accused may only be given with the leave of the court.

Under the Criminal Procedure Rules 2005, Part 35, a party who wants to introduce evidence of a non-accused's bad character or who wants to cross-examine a witness with a view to eliciting that evidence, must make an application which must be received by the court officer and all other parties to the proceedings (a) not more than fourteen days after the prosecutor has complied or purported to comply with his duty of initial disclosure, or disclosed the previous convictions of that accused, or (b) as soon as reasonably practicable, where the application concerns a non-accused who is to be invited to give (or has given) evidence for an accused. A party who receives a copy of such an application may oppose that application by giving notice in writing to the court officer and all other parties to the proceedings not more than fourteen days after receiving that application. The court may vary these requirements.

Evidence of accused's bad character

CJA 2003, s 101 deals with such matters. The previous rules which, in most instances, effectively prevented consideration of an accused's character, were abolished by the 2003 Act. The definition of 'bad character' given above embraces previous convictions (including convictions for offences committed after that being tried), evidence on other charges being tried concurrently, and evidence of offences for which a person has been charged where the charge is not prosecuted, or for which the person was subsequently acquitted. There is thus no barrier excluding evidence that a person has been involved in earlier offences even if he was acquitted of those charges, provided that the evidence is otherwise admissible.

Evidence of the accused's bad character is admissible in criminal proceedings only if:

(a) all parties agree to its being admissible;
(b) it is evidence adduced by the accused himself or is given in answer to a question asked by him during cross-examination and intended to elicit it;
(c) it is important explanatory evidence;
(d) it is relevant to an important matter in issue between the accused and the prosecution;
(e) it has substantial probative value in relation to an important matter in issue between the accused and a co-accused;
(f) it is evidence to correct a false impression given by the accused; or
(g) the accused has made an attack on another person's character.

Conditions (d), (f) and (g) are those most commonly relied on by the prosecution.

The court must not admit evidence under condition (d) or (g) if the accused has made an application to exclude it and the court considers that the admission of the evidence would have such an adverse effect on the fairness of the proceedings that it ought not to admit it. The test to be applied is that set out in PACE, s 78. The court must have regard, in particular, to the time which has passed between the matters to which the evidence relates and the matters forming the subject of the offence charged.

For the purpose of condition (c), evidence is important explanatory evidence if, in its absence, the court or jury would find it impossible or difficult properly to understand other evidence in the case, and its value for understanding the case as a whole is substantial. In an assault case, for example, evidence may be given that the accused (who claims that he acted in self-defence) has previously made unprovoked attacks on the victim. However, the evidence must be such that without it the court or jury would experience difficulty in understanding other evidence; the provisions are not intended to be a means of introducing support for trivial pieces of evidence. The probative value of evidence is that which assists the determination of the issue before the court.

Perhaps the most important factor is condition (d) above. The matters referred to include the issue of whether an accused has the propensity to commit the type of offence with which he is charged. An accused charged with assault could be shown to have a propensity to commit such an offence but this would only be relevant if the act of assault was in issue, but may not be so if that was admitted but other issues were taken. Propensity may be established by proof of previous convictions for similar offences. However, it is provided that where, due to the length of time since the previous conviction, or for any other reason, the court considers that it would be unjust, such evidence may be excluded.

CJA 2003, s 103(1) provides that, for the purposes of condition (d), matters in issue between an accused and the prosecutor include:

(a) the question of whether the accused has a 'propensity' to commit offences of the kind with which he is charged, except where his having that propensity makes it no more likely that he is guilty of the offence; and

(b) the question whether the accused has a propensity to be untruthful, except where it is not suggested that an accused's case is untruthful in any respect.

Section 103(2) provides that, where (a) applies, an accused's propensity to commit offences of the kind with which he is charged may (without prejudice to any other way of doing so) be established by evidence of a previous conviction for an offence of the same description as that with which he is charged, or an offence of the same category as that offence. For these purposes, two offences are of the same description as each other if the statement of the offence in a written charge or indictment would, in each case, be in the same terms, and two offences are of the same category if they are of the same *category of offences as prescribed by order*. The Criminal Justice Act 2003 (Categories of Offences) Order 2004 prescribes some categories of offences against the Theft Acts 1968 and 1978, and SOA 2003, as being of the same category. They are:

Theft Acts 1968 and 1978

(1)	Theft	1968 Act, s 1 (simple theft)
(2)	Robbery	1968 Act, s 8
(3)	Burglary if it was committed with intent to commit an offence of stealing anything in the building or part of a building in question	1968 Act, s 9(1)(a)
(4)	Burglary if the offender stole or attempted to steal anything in the building or that part of it	1968 Act, s 9(1)(b)
(5)	Aggravated burglary where that burglary was of the type described at (3) and (4) above	1968 Act, s 10
(6)	Taking a motor vehicle or other conveyance without authority	1968 Act, s 12
(7)	Aggravated vehicle-taking	1968 Act, s 12A
(8)	Handling stolen goods	1968 Act, s 22

(9)   Going equipped for stealing   1968 Act, s 25
(10) Making off without payment   1978 Act, s 3
(11) Aiding, abetting, counselling, procuring or inciting the
      commission of an offence of these descriptions, or
      attempting to commit such an offence

Sexual offences (persons under the age of 16)
The offences in the table below are those against the Sexual Offences Act 2003

(1)   Rape if it was committed in relation to a person   s 1
      under 16
(2)   Assault by penetration   s 2
(3)   Sexual assault if it was committed in relation to a   s 3
      person under 16
(4)   Causing a person to engage in sexual activity if   s 4
      committed in relation to a person under 16
(5)   Rape of a child under 13   s 5
(6)   Assault of a child under 13 by penetration   s 6
(7)   Sexual assault of a child under 13   s 7
(8)   Causing or inciting a child under 13 to engage in sexual s 8
      activity
(9)   Sexual activity with a child   s 9
(10) Causing or inciting a child to engage in sexual activity s 10
(11) Arranging or facilitating the commission of a child sex   s 14
      offence
(12) Abuse of position of trust: sexual activity with a child if s 16
      committed in relation to a child under 16
(13) Abuse of position of trust: causing or inciting a child to s 17
      engage in sexual activity if committed in relation to a
      person under 16
(14) Sexual activity with a child family member if   s 25
      committed in relation to a person under 16
(15) Inciting a child family member to engage in sexual   s 26
      activity if committed in relation to a person under 16
(16) Sexual activity with a person with a mental disorder   s 30
      impeding choice if it was committed in relation to a
      person under 16
(17) Causing or inciting a person with a mental disorder   s 31
      impeding choice to engage in sexual activity if it was
      committed in relation to a person under 16
(18) Inducement, threat or deception to procure activity   s 34
      with a person with a mental disorder if committed with
      a person under the age of 16
(19) Causing a person with a mental disorder to engage in   s 35
      or agree to engage in sexual activity by inducement,
      threat or deception if committed in relation to a person
      under 16
(20) Care workers: sexual activity with a person with a   s 38
      mental disorder if committed with a person under 16

(21) Care workers: causing or inciting sexual activity if   s 39
     committed in relation to a person under 16
(22) Aiding, abetting, counselling, procuring or inciting the
     commission of any of these offences or attempting to
     commit such a specified offence

So far as sexual offences are concerned, the related convictions for offences repealed by SOA 2003 are also prescribed. They are offences against the Sexual Offences Act 1956 (if committed against a person under sixteen unless otherwise stated in all cases against all previous Acts): s 1 (rape); s 5 (intercourse with girl under thirteen); s 6 (intercourse with girl under sixteen); s 7 (intercourse with a defective); s 10 (incest by a man); s 11 (incest by a woman); s 12 (buggery); s 13 (indecency between men); s 14 (indecent assault on a woman); and s 15 (indecent assault on a man). Also included are such offences against the Mental Health Act 1959, s 128 (sexual intercourse with patients); the Indecency with Children Act 1960 (indecent conduct towards young child); the Criminal Law Act 1977 (inciting a girl under sixteen to have incestuous sexual intercourse); and the Sexual Offences (Amendment) Act 2000 (abuse of a position of trust).

In referring to offences of the same description or category, CJA 2003, s 103(2) is not exhaustive of the types of conviction which may be relied on to show evidence of propensity to commit offences of the kind charged. Indeed, the provision is not limited to previous convictions; the fact that the accused has previously asked for offences to be taken into consideration can be admitted. There are no minimum number of convictions necessary to establish such a propensity, but the fewer the number, the weaker the evidence of propensity. Where the prosecution seeks to adduce evidence of an accused's bad character, in the form of previous convictions, in order to establish his propensity to commit offences of the kind with which he was charged, there are essentially three questions to be considered:

(1) Did the history of his convictions establish a propensity to commit offences of the kind charged?
(2) Did that propensity make it more likely that the accused had committed the offence charged?
(3) Was it unjust to rely on the convictions of the same description or category; and, in any event, would the proceedings be unfair if they were admitted?

An important point is that s 103 reverses the pre-existing general rule that evidence of bad character is inadmissible on the ground that its prejudicial effect is likely to outweigh its probative value.

By CJA 2003, s 103(3), s 103(2) does not apply if the court is satisfied, by reason of the length of time since the conviction or for any other reason, that it would be unjust for it to apply.

In the case of condition (e), a co-accused is restricted, in his introduction of evidence which shows no more than a propensity to lie on the part of the accused, to circumstances in which the co-accused's defence has been undermined by an accused, as in such a case credibility is at stake.

Condition (f) is concerned with evidence given by an accused which has created a wrong impression about himself. He may have claimed to be of good character where that is false, or have created an impression during evidence that his character is better than it really is. This covers assertions made by the accused, or by his representative, or a defence witness (if in response to a question by the accused which was likely to elicit it), or assertions made when questioned under caution or on being charged with the offence and out-of-court assertions made by any person if the matter is raised by the accused.

Condition (g) preserves the larger part of the old rule. An accused attacks the character of another person if he adduces evidence to the effect that that person has committed any offence or has behaved in a reprehensible way, or if he asks questions in cross-examination to elicit such evidence (or likely to do so), or if evidence is given of an imputation about the other person by the accused on being questioned under caution before charge or on being charged or informed that he might be prosecuted. Where evidence of an accused's bad character has been admitted as a result of his attack upon the character of another person, it can be used, if relevant, to establish a propensity on the part of the accused to commit offences of the type with which he is charged.

The provisions of the Children and Young Persons Act 1963, which required that a conviction for an offence by a person under fourteen must be disregarded in a trial for an offence alleged to have been committed by him over the age of twenty-one, are repealed by CJA 2003. Such convictions will now be treated in the same way as those outlined above, provided that both offences are triable only on indictment, and the court is satisfied that the interests of justice require that the evidence should be admitted.

CJA 2003, s 109 provides that any reference in its provisions about bad character to the relevance or probative value of evidence is a reference to its relevance or probative value on the assumption that it is true. However, in assessing the relevance or probative value of an item of evidence, a court need not assume that evidence is true if it appears, on the basis of material before it, that no court or jury could reasonably find it to be true.

Notice of introduction of evidence of accused's bad character

The Criminal Procedure Rules 2005, Part 35 provide as follows.

A prosecutor who wants to introduce evidence of an accused's bad character or who wants to cross-examine a witness with a view to eliciting that evidence must give notice to the court officer and all other parties to the proceedings. Such notice must be given:

(a) in a case to be tried in a magistrates' court, at the same time as the prosecutor complies or purports to comply with his duty of initial disclosure;
(b) in a case to be tried in the Crown Court, not more than fourteen days after:
    (i)   the committal for trial of the accused, or
    (ii) the service of a transfer notice, or
    (iii) where a person is sent for trial, the service of copies of the documents containing the evidence.

A co-accused who wants to introduce evidence of an accused's bad character or who wants to cross-examine a witness with a view to eliciting that evidence must give notice to the court officer and all other parties to the proceedings not more than fourteen days after the prosecutor has complied or purported to comply with his duty of initial disclosure.

A court may vary the above requirements.

Proof of a conviction

We explained on p 221 the provisions made by PACE, s 73 (in respect of the proof of conviction by the production of a certificate). Section 73 only relates to a conviction in England and Wales. In respect of a foreign conviction, there is a corresponding provision in the Evidence Act 1851, s 7. This refers to 'examined copies' or 'authenticated copies' of the foreign court's conviction records.

EXCLUSION OF UNFAIR EVIDENCE

The purpose of all the rules concerning the gathering of evidence and the manner of its presentation in court is to ensure absolute fairness to an accused person. PACE, s 78 provides that, in any proceedings, a court may refuse to allow evidence (including confessions) on which the prosecution proposes to rely to be given if it appears to the court that, having regard to all the circumstances, including the circumstances in which the evidence was obtained, the admission of the evidence would have *such an adverse effect on the fairness of the proceedings that the court ought not to admit it.* 'Fairness of the proceedings' is directed primarily to fairness of the actual conduct of the proceedings but it is not strictly limited to this. Although s 78 uses 'may' it does not in reality give the court a discretion to exclude evidence, the admission of which would have the requisite adverse effect on the fairness of the proceedings. The reason is that if the court decides that it would have that effect, it cannot logically exercise a discretion to admit it.

There is no general requirement for the police to have acted in bad faith before evidence is excluded under PACE, s 78. Bad faith on the part of police officers will usually lead to the exclusion of evidence, but evidence may be excluded even though the police acted in good faith. Likewise, a breach by the police of the ECHR does not necessarily render evidence inadmissible under s 78, but it is a matter which the judge must take into account when deciding whether to exclude evidence under s 78.

An example of the operation of PACE, s 78 is provided by a case where a person had been convicted on evidence based solely on a confession obtained after police had falsely pretended that his fingerprints had been found at the scene of the crime; the Court of Appeal ruled that such evidence should have been excluded under s 78 on the ground that it posed a threat to the fairness of proceedings. Another example is provided by various cases where evidence obtained after a significant and substantial breach of the provisions described in Chapter 4 relating to the right to legal advice or to the conduct of an interview has been excluded on the ground that in the circumstances of the case it would be unfair to admit it. A man was stabbed with a knife which had been handed to the assailant by the accused. The accused provided a written statement in which he said that he gave the assailant the knife and helped him to drive away. He was then cautioned and arrested for having an offensive weapon and impeding the arrest of the assailant. He was later interviewed in relation to these offences. The first statement which he made was excluded under s 78 on the grounds that it was not made within the limits of the code of practice, but the second interview, which related to his offences, was admitted. The Court of Appeal held that the second interview should have been excluded. The accused could have felt himself bound to the admission made in the first statement.

For such a second interview to be admitted the accused must have been given a *safe and confident* opportunity of withdrawing admissions. It is advisable in such cases that it be shown that the accused had the opportunity of taking legal advice between the first and second interview. Giving a caution is insufficient.

Section 78 does not affect the common law power of a court to exclude evidence on the basis that its prejudicial effect is likely to be greater than its probative value, and to exclude self-incriminatory evidence unfairly obtained from the defendant after the commission of the alleged offence, but there is no wider discretion at common law to exclude relevant admissible evidence on the ground that it was obtained by improper, unlawful or unfair means. Although s 78 goes much further than the common law power, particularly because it significantly widens the discretion to exclude evidence which has been unfairly or unlawfully obtained, there is one context in which the common law power is more extensive than s 78. This is where the evidence in question has already been adduced. Secion 78 does not apply in this context, but if the evidence ought not to have been admitted the court may, under the common law power, take any necessary steps to prevent an injustice, whether by directing the jurty to ignore the offending evidence or, if necessary, by discharging the jury.

Sometimes, in cases of unfairness to the accused, it is more appropriate for the court to stay proceedings on the grounds of an abuse of process on the basis that it would not be fair to try the accused, for example because the actions of the police threaten a basic human right. One such case recognised by the House of Lords is police entrapment, ie luring the accused into committing an offence and then seeking to prosecute him. Alleged entrapment does not prevent an accused also seeking to have the evidence obtained by entrapment excluded as inadmissible, but it must be borne in mind that the tests are different. In staying proceedings the test is whether it is unfair to try the accused; under s 78 it is whether admitting the evidence would have such an adverse effect upon the proceedings that the evidence ought not to be admitted.

ADVANCE DISCLOSURE OF EVIDENCE

The disclosure provisions

The Criminal Procedure and Investigations Act 1996 (CPIA 1996), Part 1 (ss 1 to 21) contains provisions relating to the advance disclosure of information which apply where:

(a) a person charged with a summary offence pleads not guilty;
(b) a person of eighteen or over charged with an either way offence, in respect of which a court proceeds to summary trial, pleads not guilty;
(c) a person under eighteen charged with an indictable offence, in respect of which a court proceeds to summary trial, pleads not guilty.

The provisions also apply where a person is charged with an indictable offence and is committed or sent for trial, or proceedings are transferred for trial, to the Crown Court.

Initial duty of prosecutor to disclose   The prosecutor must disclose to the accused previously undisclosed prosecution material which might reasonably be considered capable of undermining the prosecution case, or of assisting the case for the accused. At the same time, he must give the accused a document specifying any non-sensitive prosecution material which has not been disclosed to the accused.

Compulsory disclosure by the accused   Where cases are to be tried on indictment, and the prosecutor complies (or purports to comply) with his initial duty of disclosure, and provided that the accused has received documents containing the prosecution's case, the accused is required to provide the court and the prosecutor during the relevant period with a defence statement. Where there are other accused, and the court so orders, the accused will also have to give a defence statement to each other accused specified by the court when the relevant provision is in force. A defence statement may be supplied by the accused's solicitor. It must set out the nature of the accused's defence, including any particular defences which are to be relied upon; indicate the matters of fact which are disputed and why they are disputed; and indicate on any point of law (including any point as to the admissibility of evidence or an abuse of process) which the accused wishes to take and any authority upon which he intends to rely. Any defence statement which includes an alibi must give the name, address and date of birth of any witness the accused believes is able to give evidence in support of the alibi, or as many of those details as are known to the accused, and any other information in his possession which may assist in identifying or finding any such witness where details mentioned above are not known to the accused at that time. Evidence in support of an alibi is evidence tending to show that, by reason of the presence of the accused at a particular place or area at a particular time, he was not, or was unlikely to have been, at the place where the offence is alleged to have been committed at the time of its alleged commission. The Secretary of State has power to make regulations concerning the details of the matters to be included in defence statements.

Voluntary disclosure by the accused and notification of intent to call interesses   Where the case is to be tried summarily, and the prosecutor complies (or purports to comply) with his initial duty of disclosure, the accused or his solicitor may give a defence statement to the prosecutor during the relevant period. If he does so, he must also give the statement to the court.

Updated disclosure by the accused and notification of intent to call witnesses   The provisions described in this paragraph are not in force at the time of writing. Where the accused or his solicitor has given a defence statement, he must during the relevant period give to the prosecutor and the court (and any co-accused if the court so orders) an updated defence statement or a written statement that he has no changes to make to his defence statement. An accused or his solicitor must also give the court and the prosecutor notification of his intention to call witnesses (including experts) together with their identity or details which might lead to their identification. Changes must be notified.

Where it appears to a judge at a pre-trial hearing that an accused has failed to comply with these provisions and those relating to compulsory disclosure by the accused so that there is a possibility of comment being made, or inferences drawn, he must warn the accused.

Continuing duty of disclosure by prosecutor   After the prosecutor has complied (or purported to comply) with his initial duty of disclosure, the prosecutor remains under a continuing duty, up to the time of acquittal, conviction or a decision not to proceed with the case, to keep under review whether there is any undisclosed prosecution material which might reasonably be considered capable of undermining the case for the prosecution against the accused or of assisting the accused's case. If there is, the prosecution must disclose it as soon as reasonably practicable.

Where the accused gives a defence statement or an updated defence statement, as a result of which the prosecutor is required by the above provision to make any disclosure, or further disclosure, the prosecutor must do so within the relevant period. If he considers that he is not so required he must give the accused a written statement to that effect within that period.

Application by accused for further disclosure   Following compliance (or purported compliance) by the prosecutor with the provision just mentioned, or a failure by the prosecutor to comply with a duty (under that provision) to disclose, and provided that the accused has given a defence statement or an updated defence statement the accused may apply to the court for the disclosure of material which he reasonably believes is required to be disclosed to him but has not been. An order for further disclosure can only be made in respect of material in the possession of the prosecution in connection with the case against the accused; it cannot be made against a third party.

Protected material   such as photographs or pseudo-photographs of victims of sexual offences, or reports of medical examinations, are 'protected material' within the terms of the Sexual Offences (Protected Material) Act 1997 and may only be disclosed to an accused's legal representative who must give an undertaking that the material will not be retained by the accused and will not be shown to unauthorised persons except in connection with the proceedings or for the assessment or treatment of an accused (whether before or after conviction). Where an accused has no legal representative disclosure must be made to an authorised person such as a prison governor or his nominated representative or the officer-in-charge of a police station or any other person appearing to the prosecutor to be an appropriate person. These provisions are not yet in force and after the passage of nine years since the Act was passed it appears increasingly unlikely that they will be brought into force.

Inferences where there are faults in disclosure by accused   Where an accused:

(a) fails to give an initial defence statement; or
(b) gives one out of time; or
(c) is required to give an up-dated defence statement or a written statement indicating that there is no change but fails to do so; or
(d) gives such a statement out of time; or
(e) puts forward inconsistent defences in his defence statement; or
(f) puts forward at his trial a defence which differs from that set out in a defence statement, puts forward an undisclosed alibi, or calls a witness to support an alibi about whom he made no disclosure in his defence statement,

the court, or any other party, may make such comment as appears appropriate. In such circumstances, the court or jury may draw such inferences as appear proper in deciding whether the accused is guilty of the offence concerned.

Time limits   The Criminal Procedure and Investigations Act 1996 (Defence Disclosure Time Limits) Regulations 1997 require voluntary disclosure by the accused within fourteen days after disclosure by the prosecutor. That period may be extended by the court, on the application of the accused, if the court is satisfied that the accused could not reasonably have acted within that period. There is no limit upon such an extension, or further extensions.

Where such a period expires on a bank holiday or at a weekend, it is extended so as to expire on the next day which is not such a day.

The Regulations do not prescribe a particular period of time in relation to disclosure by the prosecution. However, CPIA 1996, s 13 requires such disclosure as soon as is reasonably practicable in the particular circumstances described in the section.

Non-disclosure where disclosure not in public interest   Information need not be disclosed by the prosecutor to the extent that the court, on an application by the prosecutor, concludes it is not in the public interest to disclose it and orders accordingly. Nor should it be disclosed if its disclosure is prohibited under the Regulation of Investigatory Powers Act 2000.

Police procedure

Police procedure is controlled by the revised 'Criminal Procedure and Investigations Act 1996: Code of Practice under Part II'. The Code was revised in consequence of revisions made to CIPA 1996 by CJA 2003. Most of these provisions are in force at the time of writing. In summary:

The officer in charge of an investigation

The officer in charge of an investigation is any police officer involved in the conduct of a criminal investigation. All investigators are responsible for the recording and retention of materials and this includes negative material resulting from the interview of persons who could give no positive evidence. The officer in charge of an investigation must make such material available to the disclosure officer. While the officer in charge of an investigation may delegate tasks to other investigators, he remains responsible for ensuring that the duties relating to disclosure are properly carried out. All reasonable inquiries, whether pointing towards or away from a suspect must be investigated. Where material is held on a computer, the investigating officer must decide which factors may reasonably be inquired into.

Where an investigating officer believes that other parties may be in possession of relevant material which has not been obtained he may invite those persons to retain the material in case a request for disclosure is received. The disclosure officer should inform the prosecutor that those persons have the material. There is no requirement to make speculative inquiries; there must be some reason to believe that the persons concerned have relevant material.

Material which may be relevant to a criminal investigation but is not recorded must be recorded in a durable or retrievable form. Information must be recorded at the time at which it is obtained or as soon as is practicable thereafter. There is no requirement to take a statement where it would not otherwise be taken. The investigator has a duty to retain material obtained in a criminal investigation which may be relevant to the investigation. Where material which previously has been examined but not retained becomes relevant, the officer in charge of an investigation must take steps to obtain it or ensure that it is retained. The duty to retain material includes:

(a) crime reports of all descriptions;
(b) custody records;
(c) records derived from tapes of telephone message containing descriptions of an alleged offence or offenders;
(d) final versions of witness statements (and draft versions if they differ) together with exhibits retained;
(e) interview records in any form with witnesses, potential witnesses or suspects;
(f) communications between police and experts (eg forensic scientists);
(g) records of first descriptions of suspects; and
(h) material casting doubt upon the reliability of a witness.

In addition, the duty to retain material which may be relevant to the investigation includes, in particular, the duty to retain material which may satisfy the test for prosecution disclosure, such as information provided by the accused which indicates an explanation for the offence with which he is charged, and material casting doubt on the reliability of a confession or a prosecution witness.

All such material which may be relevant to the investigation must be retained until a decision has been taken whether to institute proceedings against a person for an offence. If proceedings are instituted the material must be retained until the proceedings result in conviction or acquittal or a decision not to proceed has been taken. Where there is a conviction, material must be retained until the person is released from custody, or, in other circumstances, six months from the date of conviction. If a convicted person is released from custody within six months of conviction the material must be retained until the six months has elapsed. Where an appeal is lodged, material must be retained until the appeal is determined.

The disclosure officer

The disclosure officer is the person responsible for examining material retained by the police during an investigation; revealing material to the prosecutor during the investigation and any criminal proceedings resulting from it, and certifying that he has done this; and disclosing material to the accused at the request of the prosecutor. In any criminal investigation, one or more deputy disclosure officers may be appointed to assist the disclosure officer, and such a deputy may perform any of the above functions of the disclosure officer.

The functions of the disclosure officer may be carried out by the investigator or officer in charge of the investigation. Indeed, the functions of all three roles may be carried out by one person. Where this is not done there must be full consultation between both officers. The disclosure officer is the link between the investigators and the Crown Prosecution Service and is responsible for providing the material for 'primary disclosure' and performing any other tasks required by the prosecutor. He must ensure, by liaison with the officer in charge of the case where that is a different person, that all material is made available for examination.

The disclosure officer or officer in charge of an investigation, or an investigator, may seek advice from the prosecutor concerning which items are relevant to the investigation. Material which may be so relevant, which has been retained in accordance with the Code, and which the disclosure officer believes will not form a part of the prosecution case, must be listed on a schedule. There must also be a list on a schedule of material which the disclosure officer does not believe to be sensitive. Any material which is believed to be sensitive must be listed on a schedule of sensitive material or, in exceptional circumstances, it may be revealed to the prosecutor separately. If there is no sensitive material this must be recorded by the disclosure officer on a schedule of sensitive material. Sensitive material is material, the disclosure of which, the disclosure officer believes, would give rise to a real risk of serious prejudice to an important public interest. Examples of sensitive material include:

(a) material relating to national security;
(b) material received from the intelligence and security agencies;
(c) material relating to intelligence from foreign sources which reveals sensitive intelligence gathering methods;
(d) material given in confidence;
(e) material relating to the identity or activities of informants, or undercover police officers, or witnesses, or other persons supplying information to the police who may be in danger if their identities are revealed;
(f) material revealing the location of any premises or other place used for police surveillance, or the identity of any person allowing a police officer to use them for surveillance;
(g) material revealing, either directly or indirectly, techniques and methods relied upon by a police officer in the course of a criminal investigation, for example, covert surveillance techniques, or other methods of detecting crime;
(h) material, the disclosure of which might facilitate the commission of other offences or hinder the prevention and detection of crime;
(i) material upon the strength of which search warrants were obtained;
(j) material containing details of persons taking part in identification parades;
(k) material supplied to an investigator during a criminal investigation which has been generated by an official of a body concerned with the regulation or supervision of bodies corporate or of persons engaged in financial activities, or which has been generated by a person retained by such a body;
(l) material supplied to an investigator during a criminal investigation which relates to a child or young person and which has been generated by a local authority social services department, an Area Child Protection Committee or other party contacted by an investigator during an investigation; or
(m) material relating to the private life of a witness.

In exceptional circumstances, where an investigator considers that material is such that revelation by means of a schedule entry is inappropriate (and this will apply only where compromising the material would be likely to lead directly to the loss of life, or directly threaten national security), the existence of the material may be revealed to the prosecutor separately.

This lengthy list of exceptions illustrates the difficulties which arise following the provisions of a general duty to disclose material gained within an investigation.

In relation to all material, the appropriate schedule must be prepared where:

(a) the accused is charged with an offence which is triable only on indictment;
(b) the accused is charged with an offence triable either way, and it is considered either that the case is likely to be tried on indictment or that the accused is likely to plead not guilty at summary trial;
(c) the accused is charged with a summary offence, and it is considered that he is likely to plead not guilty.

In the case of either way or summary offences a schedule may not be necessary if the offence is admitted, or if it was witnessed by a police officer and the person concerned has not denied it. Where it is believed that an accused will plead guilty at a summary trial, a schedule need not be prepared in advance. However, if, contrary to this belief, there is a not guilty plea at a summary trial, or if the offence is to be tried on indictment, the disclosure officer must ensure that a schedule is prepared as soon as reasonably practicable thereafter.

All items must be listed separately (provided that it is practicable to do so) and numbered consecutively.

The disclosure officer must give the schedules to the prosecutor at the same time as he gives the file containing the material for the prosecution case (or as soon as possible after a decision concerning mode of trial or plea), drawing attention to retained material which may meet the criteria for prosecution disclosure. Where material is in a form other than in writing, it should be given to the prosecutor in a form agreed between the disclosure officer and the prosecutor.

Where at the time of the preparation of the schedule of non-sensitive material to the prosecutor, the disclosure officer does not know with certainty the material which will form a part of the prosecution case, but these matters are subsequently determined, the disclosure officer must, where necessary, provide an amended schedule listing additional material which may be relevant to the investigation but does not form part of the case against the accused, which is not already listed in the schedule and which is not believed to be sensitive.

The CIPA 1996, s 7A imposes a continuing duty upon the prosecutor, for the duration of criminal proceedings against the accused, to disclose material which might reasonably be considered to undermine the case for the prosecution, or which might assist the accused. After a defence statement has been given, the disclosure officer must look again at the material retained and must bring any material which might have this effect to the attention of the prosecutor.

The disclosure officer must certify that to the best of his knowledge and belief all relevant material which has been retained and made available to him has been revealed to the prosecutor. Further certification must follow subsequent developments.

If material has not already been copied to the prosecutor, and he requests its disclosure to the accused on the grounds that it satisfies the criteria for disclosure or a court has ordered its disclosure, the disclosure officer must disclose it to the accused. If material has been copied to the prosecutor, and it is so disclosed, it is a matter for agreement as to who should make the disclosure. Disclosure by the disclosure officer must be made by the provision of a copy or an opportunity to inspect it. Where a request is made for the provision of a copy of inspected material it must be given by the disclosure officer unless he considers that it is not practicable to do so (eg because the material consists of an object which cannot be copied, or because the volume of material is too great), or that it is not desirable (eg where the material is a statement by a child witness in relation to a sexual offence). Where information is recorded other than in writing, it is for the disclosure officer to decide whether it should be given in its original form or by means of a transcript certified as a true record.

If a court concludes that an item of sensitive material satisfies the prosecution disclosure test and that the interests of the defence outweigh the public interest in withholding disclosure, the material must be disclosed if the case is to proceed. The court, however, may in such circumstances direct that parts of the material be blanked out, or that the documents may be summarised, or that the prosecutor may make an admission concerning the substance of the material under CJA 1967, s 10.

THE RIGHT TO A FAIR TRIAL

Among the 'Convention rights' to which HRA 1998 applies is art 6 of the ECHR. Article 6 provides:

1. In the determination of his civil rights and obligations or of any criminal charge against him, everyone is entitled to a fair and public hearing within a reasonable time by an independent and impartial tribunal established by law. Judgement shall be pronounced publicly but the press and public may be excluded from all or part of the trial in the interests of morals, public order or national security in a democratic society, where the interests of juveniles or the protection of the private life of the parties so require, or to the extent strictly necessary in the opinion of the court in special circumstances where publicity would prejudice the interests of justice.
2. Everyone charged with a criminal offence shall be presumed innocent until proved guilty according to the law.
3. Everyone charged with a criminal offence has the following minimum rights:
   (a) to be informed promptly, in a language which he understands and in detail, of the nature and cause of the accusation against him;
   (b) to have adequate time and facilities for the preparation of his defence;
   (c) to defend himself in person or through legal assistance of his own choosing or, if he has not sufficient means to pay for legal assistance, to be given it free where the interests of justice so require;
   (d) to examine or have examined witnesses against him and to obtain the attendance and examination of witnesses on his behalf under the same conditions as witnesses against him;
   (e) to have the free assistance of an interpreter if he cannot understand or speak the language used in court.

There is little doubt that many of our laws relating to evidence and procedure will be put under the microscope in consequence of HRA 1998. It has been held, for example, that the Road Traffic Act 1988, s 172, which imposes a duty on the registered keeper of a motor vehicle to give such identity of the driver as may be required by the police, does not violate a person's right of silence and privilege against self-incrimination which are inherent in art 6 of the Convention. However, it is anticipated that this matter will receive further consideration because on a number of occasions the European Court of Human Rights, whose decision must be taken into account by our courts, has held that the imposition of criminal sanctions on a person who refused to supply information in other contexts in cases in other countries violated art 6.

In England, the Court of Appeal was asked to consider the human rights implications where a constable breached the Codes of Practice in relation to identification evidence, believing that he was entitled to do so by the terms of a Home Office circular giving guidelines on the use of equipment in police surveillance operations. The court held that the guidelines were not ultra vires, illegal or without effect and reference to the ECHR had simply not been appropriate. The court said that the Convention followed the Second World War and was intended to protect citizens from true abuses of human rights but it now appeared that lawyers were jumping on the bandwagon. It was possible not only that appeals of others might be unjustly delayed but that the Convention and the 1998 Act might themselves be brought into disrepute. However, our wager is still that the bandwagon will be crowded for some time to come!

See p 3 in relation to HRA 1998 generally and Ch 31 in relation to its possible effect upon public order law.

OFFENCES AGAINST ADMINISTRATION OF JUSTICE

Perjury

The Perjury Act 1911 (PA 1911), s 1(1) provides that it is an offence for any person, lawfully sworn as a witness or interpreter in a judicial proceeding, to wilfully make a statement material in that proceeding which he knows to be false or does not believe to be true.

A person is 'lawfully sworn' if the court or the person before whom the oath is taken is authorised to administer it, and no objection is made by the person taking it. A person, as an alternative to taking the oath, may affirm or declare that he will tell the truth if he has no religious belief, or his beliefs do not permit him to swear on oath, or it is not reasonably practicable, without inconvenience or delay, to administer an oath in the manner appropriate to his religious belief. A 'judicial proceeding' is a proceeding before any court, tribunal or person having by law power to hear, receive and examine evidence on oath. The presence of the word 'wilfully' means that it must be proved that the person concerned made that statement deliberately. A 'material statement' is one which may affect the decision of the court.

PA 1911, s 13 states that a person shall not be convicted of perjury solely on the evidence of one witness as to the falsity of any statement alleged to be false, so that there is a requirement of corroboration in this respect. PA, s 7 deals with aiding, abetting, counselling, procuring or suborning the commission of perjury. It provides that a person who commits such offences will be tried and punished as if he were a principal offender.

Perverting justice

The common law offence of perverting the course of justice may be committed by the destruction of evidence, the making of false statements, the intimidation of witnesses, attempting to influence members of a jury or other acts with a tendency to pervert the course of justice if, in each case, the accused intends to pervert the course of justice. Police officers may be prosecuted for these offences if they carry out such acts which are intended to defeat or pervert the due course of justice.

The Criminal Law Act 1967, s 5(2) described on p 16 provides an offence to deal with those who cause police time to be wasted, but the wasting of police time does not necessarily mean that any person was put in jeopardy. Where persons are put at risk of unnecessary arrest or wrongful conviction as a result of things done by another person, it may be more appropriate to charge such a person with perverting the course of justice.

INTIMIDATION OF WITNESSES, JURORS AND OTHERS

The offences generally

Jury nobbling and witness intimidation are significant problems. CJPOA 1994, s 51 is intended to deal with activities which prevent a prosecution being brought or being properly considered by a jury, and reprisals which are threatened or taken against certain persons after a criminal trial has been concluded.

Intimidation etc before or during a trial

CJPOA 1994, s 51(1) provides that a person commits an offence if:

(a) he does an act which intimidates, and is intended to intimidate, another person (the victim);
(b) he does the act knowing or believing that the victim is assisting in the investigation of an offence or is a witness or potential witness or a juror or potential juror in proceedings for an offence; and
(c) he does it thereby intending to cause the investigation or the course of justice to be obstructed, perverted or interfered with.

Thus, all that is required is the doing of an act which intentionally results in another person being intimidated. An act or threat made directly to a witness or juror will suffice but so will, for example, a threat to the wife of such a person to the effect that, unless her husband changes his evidence (or fails to vote for the acquittal of an accused), her face will be slashed. The person making such a threat clearly intends the husband to be intimidated, as well as the wife, and has thereby carried out an act to the husband through the medium of his wife. The husband will therefore be 'another person' for the purposes of the section. In addition, CJPOA 1994, s 51(3) makes it clear that it is immaterial that the act is or would be done, or that the threat is made otherwise than in the presence of the victim (or to a person other than the victim).

The Court of Appeal has held that 'intimidation' includes not only putting a person in fear by threat or violence, whether to persons or property, but also seeking to deter someone from some relevant action by an improper threat or violence which did not cause fear or deter that person from that cause of action. A threat need not necessarily be a threat of violence, but mere pressure is insufficient.

CJPOA 1994, s 51(1) does not require that the person who is intimidated be actually assisting in the investigation of an offence at the time, or is a witness or potential witness, or a juror or potential juror, in proceedings for an offence. By s 51(1)(b), it is sufficient that the accused believes that the person so intimidated is involved in that way. There must, however, be an investigation in progress; it is insufficient that a person believed that such an investigation was taking place. Evidence of that investigation must be before the court. An 'investigation into an offence' means an investigation by the police or other persons charged with the duty of investigating offences or charging offenders.

The accused must also intend, by the intimidating act done to the other person, to cause the investigation or the course of justice to be perverted, obstructed or interfered with. However, in this respect, CJPOA 1994, s 51(7) provides that if it is proved that such an act was done with the required knowledge or belief, it must be presumed, unless the contrary is proved, that the accused did the act with the required intention. Thus, the onus is upon the accused to show in such circumstances that he did not have such an intention.

Reprisals against witnesses, jurors and others

CJPOA 1994, s 51(2) provides that a person commits an offence if:

(a) he does an act which harms, and is intended to harm, another person or, intending to cause another person to fear harm, he threatens to do an act which would harm that other person;

(b) he does or threatens to do the act knowing or believing that the person harmed or threatened to be harmed (the victim), or some other person, has assisted in the investigation into an offence or has given evidence or particular evidence in proceedings for an offence, or has acted as a juror or concurred in a particular verdict in proceedings for an offence; and

(c) he does or threatens to do it because of that knowledge or belief.

It must be shown that the accused did (or threatened to do) something to another person, which results in harm (or would result in harm) to that other person. Moreover, by CJPOA 1994, s 51(3) it is immaterial that the act is or would be done, or that the threat is made, otherwise than in the presence of the victim (or to a person other than the victim). There is no requirement that the other person is actually intimidated thereby. As in the case of a s 51(1) offence, such an act may be carried out through the medium of a third party, with the intention of harming the second party. The remaining points which have to be proved are similar to those already discussed in relation to s 51(1). The act carried out or threatened must be intended to harm that person.

CJPOA 1994, s 51(4) provides that the harm which may be done or threatened may be financial as well as physical (whether to the person or a person's property), and similarly as respects an intimidatory act which consists of threats. The Court of Appeal has held that 'harm', other than financial harm or damage to property, bears the ordinary meaning of physical harm. As a result, it allowed the appeal against conviction under s 51(2) of a man who had spat in the face of a witness and verbally abused her. There had been no proof that the woman had been harmed.

Proof of knowledge or belief that the other person, or some other person, has assisted in an investigation or has given evidence etc is also required.

However, a third factor is involved which is not involved in the case of CJPOA 1994, s 51(1). It must be proved that the accused did, or threatened to do, the act because of what he knows or believes about the assisting in an investigation or the giving of evidence etc. In this respect, s 51(8) provides that if it is proved that within the 'relevant period':

(a) he did an act which harmed and was intended to harm, another person; or

(b) intending to cause another person fear of harm, he threatened to do an act which would harm that other person, and that he did the act, or (as the case may be) threatened to do the act, and with the knowledge or belief required by CJPOA 1994, s 51(2)(b) he is presumed, unless the contrary is proved, to have done the act, or (as the case may be) threatened to do the act, because of that knowledge or belief. Thus, it is clear that where there are threats within the relevant period to harm a witness or juror, there is no need for the prosecution to prove a connection between the threat and the trial.

For the purposes of this presumption, the 'relevant period' in relation to:

(a) a witness or juror begins with the institution of proceedings and ends with the first anniversary of the conclusion of the trial, or of any appeal;

(b) a person who has assisted in the investigation of an offence (or is believed by the accused to have done so) but who was not a witness in proceedings for an offence, is the period of one year beginning with the act (or believed act) which assisted the investigation; and

(c) a person at (b) above who was also a witness in proceedings for an offence, is the period beginning with the act (or believed act) which assisted in the investigation and ending with the first anniversary of the conclusion of the trial, or of any appeal.

However, it must be appreciated that the 'relevant period' is only of significance in relation to the presumption which leads to the burden of proof of motive being switched to the accused. It does not prevent a prosecution outside that time; if there is a prosecution outside such time, the presumption will no longer apply and it will be necessary to prove the requisite motive.

Common factors in relation to both offences

CJPOA 1994, s 51(5) provides that the intention/motive required (in either case) need not be the only or predominating intention/motive with which the act is done or threatened. This should exclude defences based upon the fact that the primary intention of the perpetrator was to avoid a miscarriage of justice.

Police powers

These offences are additional to existing common law offences. The common law offence of 'embracery' deals with interference with a juror with an intention to prejudice the administration of justice. Interference with witnesses or jurors is punishable at common law either as a criminal contempt of court or as perverting the course of justice. Reprisals against witnesses or jurors when a case has been disposed of may be punishable as a criminal contempt of court.

All of these offences, however, require positive proof of a specified intent on the part of the accused. It cannot be presumed in certain circumstances, as it can be in an offence under s 51.

Where the proceedings are other than those connected with an offence

CJPA 2001, ss 39 and 40 provide for the protection of witnesses in proceedings other than those in respect of an offence which take place before the Court of Appeal, the

High Court, the Crown Court, a county court or a magistrates' court. The offences provided by ss 39 and 40 shadow those set out above with the exception that they refer to 'relevant proceedings', a term which means proceedings which are not proceedings for an offence.

Intimidation

A person commits an offence against CJPA 2001, s 39 if he commits similar acts to those set out in CJPOA 1994, s 51(1), but those acts are related to actual or potential witnesses in proceedings other than for an offence. (Juries are extremely rare in civil cases.) In such a case, the act must be done knowing or believing that the victim is, or may be, a witness in such proceedings and with the intention to cause the course of justice to be obstructed, perverted, or interfered with.

Harming witnesses

A person commits an offence against CJPA 2001, s 40 if he commits similar acts to those set out in CJPOA 1994, s 51(2), but those acts are related to witnesses in proceedings other than for an offence. In such a case, the act must be done knowing or believing that some person (whether or not the person harmed or threatened or the person against whom harm is threatened) has been a witness in such proceedings and the accused must do or threaten to do the act because of that knowledge or belief. The acts must be committed within the 'relevant period' (beginning with the commencement of the proceedings and ending one year after they are finally concluded).

CHAPTER 8

The police

ORGANISATION, JURISDICTION AND LIABILITY

Organisation of police forces

The Police Act 1996 (PA 1996), ss 1, 2, 3 and 4 provide that England and Wales are divided into police areas. These police areas are those listed in Sch 1, together with the City of London police area and the Metropolitan Police District. A police force, with a police authority, must be maintained for every area listed in Sch 1, and for the Metropolitan Police District. Changes to police areas, including a reduction or increase in the number of them, are relatively simple matters, requiring no more than an order of the Secretary of State. He does not, however, have the power to alter the City of London police area nor to abolish the Metropolitan Police District. Police authorities must consist of seventeen members, but the Secretary of State may, by order, increase the size to a specified odd number greater than seventeen (subject to a maximum of twenty-three in the case of the Metropolitan Police). A police authority, other than the Metropolitan Police Authority, must consist of nine members of a relevant council (one wholly within the police area), five independent members appointed by the other members of the authority from a shortlist prepared by the Secretary of State, and three magistrates for the area concerned.

PA 1996, s 6 imposes the duty upon every police authority to secure the maintenance of an efficient and effective police force for its area. In discharging its functions, a police authority must have regard to:

(a) the Secretary of State's National Policing Plan;
(b) objectives determined by the Secretary of State and by itself;
(c) 'performance targets' set by itself at the direction of the Secretary of State (which direction may be general in character and applicable to all police authorities, or may be directed at one or more particular authorities);
(d) any local policing plan issued by the authority; and

(e) direction from the Secretary of State in consequence of a report from an inspector of constabulary to the effect that the force is not efficient or not effective, or that it will become so unless remedial action is taken.

PA 1996, s 6A requires every police authority for a police area to issue a three-year strategy plan before the beginning of every relevant three-year period specified by the Secretary of State. This plan sets out the authority's medium- and long-term strategies for the policing of the police are a during the period. Before a strategy plan is issued, a draft must have been prepared by the chief officer of police (after considering the views of the community on policing in the area) and considered by the authority. The authority must consult with the chief officer if it issues a strategy which contains a material difference from that submitted by the chief officer of police or if it later modifies it. The authority and the chief officer are obliged to take into account any guidance given by the Secretary of State as to the contents and form of a strategy plan. Before issuing or modifying a plan the authority must submit the plan or modifications to the Secretary of State. If he considers that there are grounds for considering that a strategy plan or modification issued by a police authority is inconsistent with any national policing plan applicable to a financial year in the three-year period he will inform the authority.

By PA 1996, s 7, a police authority must also set its local policing objectives before the beginning of each financial year after consulting the chief constable and considering the views of the community on policing in the area. Local policing objectives must be consistent with the Secretary of State's objectives. The police authority is required by PA 1996, s 8 also to produce a 'local policing plan' stating its priorities for the year and the resources available and setting out all of these objectives and targets. The draft of such a 'local policing plan' will be prepared by the chief constable for consideration by the police authority. The plan must give particulars of any objectives determined by the Secretary of State or in the authority's local policing objectives. It must be consistent with the three-year strategy plan. Changes must not be made to it without consultation with the chief constable. In discharging his duties, a chief constable must have regard to the local policing plan.

PA 1996, s 8A, added by the Serious Organised Crime and Police Act 2005 (SOC-PA 2005), places a duty on police authorities to produce a summary of information on local policing matters for members of the public as soon as possible after the end of each financial year. Section 3 empowers the Secretary of State to specify by order matters which must be included in such a summary. The Secretary of State has specified;

(a) a statement of the police authority's priorities for the year;
(b) an assessment of the extent to which the police force met the priorities set for the previous year; and
(c) an assessment as to the extent to which a police force has met the strategic policing priorities (if any) set by the Secretary of State.

The Metropolitan and City of London Police Forces are under the direction and control of their respective Commissioner.

Police forces for the areas listed in PA 1996, Sch 1 are under the direction and control of the chief constable appointed under PA 1996, s 11. PA 1996, ss 11, 11A and 12 permit a police authority to appoint chief constables, deputy chief constables and assistant chief constables subject to the approval of the Secretary of State and to call upon any of these officers to retire in the interests of efficiency or effectiveness. Appointments to the posts of chief constable and deputy chief constable have to be for a fixed term of a maximum of five years, which may be extended for a maximum of three years, and subsequently for a maximum of one year at a time, with the consent of the Secretary of State.

Under PA 1996, s 12A, a deputy chief constable may exercise any or all of the powers and duties of the chief constable during any absence, incapacity or suspension from duty of the chief constable, or during any vacancy in the office of chief constable, or at any other time with the chief constable's consent. A police authority may designate a particular assistant chief constable to exercise any or all of the chief constable's powers if both the chief constable and his deputy are absent, incapable or suspended or both their posts are vacant. That person may only act in that capacity for a period exceeding three months with the consent of the Secretary of State.

Each police authority must keep a 'police fund' into which all receipts will be paid and from which all expenditure will be met. The Secretary of State, for each financial year, makes a grant from central funds to police authorities and to the Receiver for the Metropolitan Police District. The remainder of the finance will be met from the council taxes of the local authorities within the police area. Civilian employees within a police force, although employed by a police authority, are under the direction and control of the chief constable.

Appointments and promotions to any rank below that of assistant chief constable are made by the chief constable. Those ranks are chief superintendent, superintendent, chief inspector, inspector, sergeant and constable.

The role of the Secretary of State

Although the courts have ruled that chief constables must carry out their duties independently, so that there may be no suggestion of direct government control in relation to law enforcement, PA 1996 empowered the Secretary of State to determine objectives for the policing of the areas of all police authorities. However, the determination of such objectives falls short of direct interference in matters relating to law enforcement, in that it does not place restrictions upon those persons who may be investigated or prosecuted. Part I of the Police Reform Act 2002 (PRA 2002) extended PA 1996 to introduce further elements of control, by authorising the Secretary of State to prepare annually a National Policing Plan setting out what ever the Secretary of State considers to be the strategic policing priorities for the year. However, provision is made for consultation with people representing police authorities and chief officers (ie the Association of Chief Police Officers (ACPO)).

The Secretary of State is also empowered to issue codes of practice relating to the discharge of their functions by chief officers of police.

The Crime and Disorder Act 1998 additionally makes provision for crime and disorder reduction partnerships in a police area involving councils, chief officers, police authorities, fire authorities and primary care trusts (and health authorities in Wales), giving the Secretary of State power to make an order merging two or more partnership areas. An order may require the reduction of crimes and forms of disorder described within it.

In addition, Part I of PRA 2002 extended PA 1996 so as to empower the Secretary of State to require inspectors of constabulary, in addition to carrying out their normal annual inspections of forces, to carry out a specific inspection of a police force or the Serious Organised Crime Agency. Where such an inspection leads to a conclusion that the force, or a part of it, is not efficient or effective, or will cease to be so unless remedial action is taken, the Secretary of State may direct the relevant authority to take such remedial measures as are specified in the direction. Alternatively, he may require the authority to submit an action plan setting out its proposed remedial measures for the Secretary of State's approval. Such action must be reported to Parliament. Reasons for his conclusion must be given to both the police authority and the chief officer. The PRA 2002 also extended the provisions of PA 1996 to permit the making of regulations requiring police forces in England and Wales to adopt particular procedures or practices. Before making such regulations, the Secretary of State must, after consultation, seek advice from the chief inspector of constabulary and the Central Police Training and Development Authority. Similar provisions are made in respect of the Serious Organised Crime Agency. The Act also extended the powers of the Secretary of State and police authorities to require the retirement of chief officers in the interests of efficiency and effectiveness so far as to allow for such an officer to be required to resign on such grounds. It also gives the Secretary of State power to call for the suspension of an officer above the rank of superintendent.

National police organisations

The SOCPA 2005 makes provision for the setting up of a Serious Organised Crime Agency (SOCA) which has its own Board whose duty is to maintain the service in question. In addition, the Criminal Justice and Police Act 2001 (CJPA 2001) provides for a body corporate designated as the Central Police Training and Development Authority which provides police training and promotes best practice in policing matters generally.

Serious Organised Crime Agency

SOCPA 2005 established SOCA which acts under a Director appointed by the Secretary of State for a period of five years. Its functions are to prevent and detect serious organised crime and to contribute to the reduction of such crime and to the mitigation of its consequences. It may also investigate revenue frauds and serious frauds, but only with the consent of the Commissioners for Revenue and Customs or the Serious Fraud Office as the case may be.

It is charged with gathering, storing, analysing and disseminating information relevant to the prevention, detection, investigation or prosecution of offences, or to the reduction of crime by other means or the mitigation of its consequences.

SOCA will provide information to police forces, special police forces and other law enforcement agencies as well as co-operating in other ways. While the Agency was set up to investigate serious crime, it may involve itself in lesser crime if that is the best means of securing a conviction and custodial sentence in respect of an organised criminal.

The activities of SOCA are supervised by its Board which consists of a chairman and members appointed by the Secretary of State, the Director General and other ex-officio members. SOCA is obliged to produce an annual plan and an annual report. The Secretary of State is empowered to establish strategic priorities and to issue codes of practice relating to the discharge of the Agency's functions. In addition, SOCA is subject to inspection by HM Inspectors of Constabulary. However, operational control remains with the Director General.

Voluntary arrangements may be made in relation to mutual assistance between SOCA and police forces. Where there is a failure to agree a voluntary scheme, the Secretary of State is empowered to direct that mutual assistance be arranged. SOCA will be liable for the actions of any police officer seconded to the Agency.

SOCA may disclose information in connection with the exercise of any of its functions if the disclosure is for any specified 'permitted purposes'. These are the prevention, detection, investigation or prosecution of criminal offences whether in the United Kingdom or elsewhere; the prevention, detection or investigation of conduct in respect of which penalties other than criminal penalties are provided by United Kingdom law or elsewhere; the exercise of any other function of SOCA; the exercise of intelligence functions under the Regulation of Investigatory Powers Act 2000 or the Football Spectators Act 1989; and the exercise of any other function of a public nature designated by order.

Any person may disclose information to SOCA in pursuit of its functions, although disclosure by revenue and customs must be authorised by the Commissioners or authorised persons.

Where a person becomes a member of staff of SOCA he loses any powers which he held in his previous office as a constable, revenue and customs or immigration officer. Powers may be designated by the Director General, or a designated officer (currently the Deputy Director), according to the needs of the organisation. SOCPA 2005, s 51 creates offences of assaulting, obstructing or impersonating designated members of SOCA staff.

The Director of the Serious Fraud Office and some other bodies are empowered to compel co-operation with investigations by the production of documents and answering questions. These powers are extended to police, SOCA and Revenue and Customs investigations into organised crime, terrorist or certain revenue offences. The powers may only be exercised by the Director of Public Prosecutions (DPP) or the Director of Revenue and Customs Prosecutions, or in Scotland, the Lord Advocate, or the delegate of such an office holder. Material obtained in consequence cannot be used in evidence, with extremely limited exceptions.

Central Police Training and Development Authority

This authority was established under CJPA 2001, s 87. Under CJPA 2001, s 88 its functions are to:

(a) provide police training and facilities for the provision of police training;
(b) promote the value of the provision of police training;
(c) give advice about the provision of police training to persons other than the authority who provides it or is proposing to do so;
(d) provide such persons with all such assistance in relation to the provision of police training as the Authority considers appropriate;
(e) provide persons serving or employed for policing purposes in England and Wales with advice and consultancy services with respect to police matters generally, and with respect to best police practice and the handling of incidents requiring police involvement.

In carrying out its functions, the Authority must have regard to any objectives set by the Secretary of State under CJPA 2001, s 89, after consultation with representative bodies. Performance targets may be set. The Authority must issue annual objectives and an annual 'Training and Development Plan' dealing with its priorities and the allocation of resources and specifying the objectives of the Secretary of State together with the Authority's own. Copies must be sent to the Secretary of State, and to every police authority and chief officer of police in England and Wales (CJPA 2001, ss 90 and 92).

Appointments to the Authority are made by the Secretary of State after consultation with police representative bodies. The Authority consists of not less than eleven members including a chairman, two members representing police authorities, two representing chief officers of police, and at least one civil servant.

The Secretary of State is authorised by CJPA2001, s 97 to make regulations concerning police training, and the qualification for deployment to perform particular tasks, of persons employed for policing purposes in England and Wales. If inspection reports indicate that a training need exists within a police force, or that there is a need for the provision of opportunities for professional development, the Secretary of State may direct the police authority to take appropriate measures.

Jurisdiction of constables

PA 1996, s 30 deals with this. It provides that every member of a police force has all the powers and privileges of a constable throughout England and Wales and the adjacent United Kingdom waters. A special constable has such powers within his police force area and, where the boundary of that area includes the coast, in the adjacent United Kingdom waters, and in areas contiguous with that area. 'United Kingdom waters' means the sea and other waters within the seaboard limits of the territorial sea. These powers are extended in the case of special constables for the City of London, whose powers extend not only to the Metropolitan Police area, but also to those areas contiguous to the Metropolitan Police area. Where special constables are sent to another police force area as part of a mutual aid scheme, they have all the powers of the special constables of that area.

The Criminal Justice and Public Order Act 1994 (CJPOA 1994), s 136 empowers constables of forces in England and Wales to execute arrest warrants issued in England and Wales in Scotland and Northern Ireland, and vice versa (see p 23).

The Anti-terrorism, Crime and Security Act 2001, ss 98 to 101 deal with the jurisdiction of officers of the Ministry of Defence Police and the British Transport Police in specified circumstances related to assistance provided to other police forces.

Exercise of police powers by civilians

PRA 2002, s 38 authorises chief officers of police to designate an employee of the police authority who is under his direction and control as:

(a) a community support officer;
(b) an investigating officer;
(c) a detention officer;

(d) an escort officer;

(e) staff custody officer (when SOCPA 2005, s 120 is in force)

A person designated under PRA 2002, s 38 has the powers and duties conferred or imposed on him by the designation. The complete range of powers and duties which may be conferred or imposed are set out in PRA 2002, Sch 4.

A community support officer

A designation may confer on a community support officer the power to issue prescribed fixed penalty notices for offences of disorder under CJPA 2001 (although the Secretary of State may by order restrict the powers granted under CJPA 2001 and the restriction has been applied in relation to offences against the Theft Act 1968, s 1 and the Environmental Protection Act 1990, s 87), and under other fixed penalty procedures for offences of failing to secure attendance of a pupil at school, of riding a cycle on a footpath, of allowing a dog to foul land under a dog control order, of writing graffiti, of fly-posting and of depositing litter. The above offences are all described as 'relevant fixed penalty offences'.

A designation may empower a community support officer to require a person to give him his name and address if he has reason to believe that that person has committed a 'relevant offence' (ie a relevant fixed penalty offence, or an offence which appears to have caused injury, alarm or distress to another or any damage to another's property, or certain other offences) or a relevant licensing offence. The designation may be limited to particular offences. It is an offence for a person to fail to comply with such a requirement. In addition, a designation may provide a power permitting a community support officer who is so designated and who has made a requirement for a name and address to require the other person to remain with him for a period, not exceeding thirty minutes, for the arrival of a constable, where the community support officer has reasonable grounds for suspecting that the person has given a false or inaccurate name or address. The alleged offender may elect to accompany the community support officer to a police station as an alternative to waiting. Such a person, on arrival at a police station, is under a duty to remain there until his custody is transferred to a constable. Failure to wait, or making off, is an offence. A designation may also empower search of a person asked to wait or the use of reasonable force to prevent an individual making off when subject to a requirement to give his name and address or while accompanying the officer to a police station.

A designation may also provide powers to require the name and address of someone reasonably believed to have been acting, or be acting, in an anti-social manner or to have ignored a traffic direction; to exercise a constable's powers in respect to alcohol consumption in designated public places, or confiscation of alcohol or tobacco; to enter to save life or limb or prevent serious damage to property; to disperse groups; to remove a child to its home in the event of a breach of a curfew order; to seize vehicles used to cause alarm etc; to exercise powers in respect of abandoned vehicles; to stop vehicles for testing; to control traffic for purpose of escorting heavy loads; to carry out road checks; to exercise a constable's powers in cordoned areas; and to stop and search vehicles etc in authorised areas.

An investigating officer

A designation may empower an investigating officer to exercise the powers under the Police and Criminal Evidence Act 1984 (PACE), s 8 to apply for a warrant to enter and search premises to be issued to him and to seize and retain articles found during a search. The safeguards etc provided by PACE in relation to searches apply equally to an officer so designated. A designation may permit a search warrant to be issued to, and executed under, the Theft Act 1968, s 26 or the Misuse of Drugs Act 1971, s 23 by an officer in respect of whom the designation applies these provisions. A designation may give the powers of a constable under PACE, s 9(1) (access to excluded and special procedure material) to an investigating officer. The various procedural matters prescribed by PACE in relation to such matters will apply to such an officer. Powers under PACE, ss 18, 19 and 21 to enter, search, seize and copy things seized may also be given by a designation, as may powers to arrest for a further offence at a police station for another offence. In addition, a designation may give powers under CJPOA 1994 to require arrested persons to account for certain matters. Amendments to PRA 2002 have empowered authorised persons with the same search and seize powers as possessed by an investigating officer whom they accompany.

A detention officer

A designation may authorise a detention officer to require a person to attend a police station for the taking of a sample, photograph or fingerprints (and to take those fingerprints without consent); to photograph a detained person; to carry out intimate or non-intimate searches; to carry out searches and examinations to establish identity (including the taking of a photograph of an identifying mark), and to take impressions of footwear.

A designation may empower a detention officer to use reasonable force to secure that persons in detention do not escape, or to assist others in securing this. A designated detention officer may carry out specified duties in relation to drug searches, X-rays and ultrasound scans carried out in respect of Class A drug searches.

An escort officer

An escort officer may be designated to take an arrested person to a police station or to escort a person in police detention. A designated escort officer taking an arrested person to a police station is required to keep him under control and may use reasonable force to do so. An escort officer designated to escort a person in police detention may also use reasonable force to keep the detainee under control. A designated escort officer remains in control until the detainee is handed over to the custody officer or other responsible person, and may use reasonable force to prevent that person escaping and to keep him under his control. A designated escort officer may carry out specified duties in relation to drug searches, X-rays and ultrasound scans carried out in respect of Class A drug searches.

A staff custody officer

SOCPA 2005, s 120 amended the provisions of PACE so that an employee of a police authority may be designated to act as a custody officer. Such a designated officer may perform all of the functions of a custody officer under PACE (other than under PACE, s 45A(4)—custody officer's duties in relation to video-conferencing facilities for decisions about detention) and under any other enactment which confers functions on such a custody officer. A designated person performing the duties of a custody officer at a police station designated under PACE, s 35 (see p 144) must first also be appointed a custody officer for that station under PACE, s 36(2). Except in PACE, ss 36 (particular police officers appointed at police stations; see p 144) and 45A(4), all references to a 'custody officer' within the meaning of PACE include references to such persons by virtue of such designation.

Community safety accreditation schemes

PRA 2002, s 41 authorises a chief officer to establish and maintain a 'community safety accreditation scheme' for the exercise in his area, by persons accredited by him, of powers related to community safety and security and (in co-operation with the local police) combating crime and disorder, public nuisance and other forms of anti-social behaviour. Any such scheme must contain provisions for arrangements to be made with employers who are carrying on a business in the police area for those employers to supervise the carrying out of such functions for the purposes of which accreditation powers are provided. The powers which may be conferred on accredited persons are set out in PRA 2002, Sch 5. Chief officers must also ensure that the employer has made satisfactory arrangements for the handling of complaints relating to the exercise of those powers.

Accredited persons may have conferred on them power to give fixed penalty notices for offences of cycling on a footpath, offences of disorder under CJPA 2001, the powers of an authorised officer under a dog control order, failing to secure attendance of a pupil at school, graffiti or fly-posting and of litter under the Environmental Protection Act 1990, s 88. They may also be given powers to deal with alcohol consumption in a designated public place, confiscation of liquor and tobacco and abandoned vehicles, to stop vehicles for testing, to stop cyclists committing offences of riding on a footpath, and the power to control traffic for the purpose of escorting a load of exceptional dimensions.

Accredited persons may be authorised to require names and addresses in relation to certain traffic offences, to control traffic, and to photograph persons given fixed penalty notices (see below under heading 'General').

General

A designated or accredited person must produce evidence of his designation or accreditation if requested to do so when exercising one of his powers. In addition, such persons may be restricted in the exercise of powers to times when wearing approved uniform or badge. However, a police officer of or above the rank of inspector may direct a particular investigating officer not to wear uniform for the purposes of a particular operation. PRA 2002, s 46 creates offences of assault upon designated persons, accredited persons, or other persons assisting such persons, in the execution of their duties; resisting or wilfully obstructing such persons; and, with intent to deceive, impersonating a designated or accredited person, making a statement or doing an act calculated falsely to suggest that a person is designated or accredited, or making any statement or doing any act calculated falsely to suggest that he has powers as a designated or accredited person which exceeds his actual powers. This last offence is, of course, committed by a designated or accredited person.

These auxiliary personnel must, in the discharge of their duties, have regard to the provisions of the Codes of Practice under PACE. A person lawfully in the custody of such a person must be treated as in police detention.

Where any power exercised by one of the above types of person includes power to use reasonable force to enter premises, that power may only be exercised in the company, and under the supervision of, a constable or to save life or limb or to prevent serious damage.

Traffic officers appointed under the Traffic Management Act 2004

The Secretary of State (in England) or the Assembly of Wales (in Wales), the 'national authority', may designate individuals as traffic officers and may authorise other persons to make such appointments. Appointments may be subject to limitations and conditions. The designation of individual officers will be in writing and will specify such limitations or conditions and its period of validity. Traffic officers must be employed by, or by persons providing services to, the authorised person. Because they are not designated by a chief officer of police, traffic officers are not police support officers. However, they are officers who will perform enforcement functions and are therefore dealt with within this chapter.

The Traffic Management Act 2004, Part 1 deals with the appointment of 'traffic officers' in England and Wales, their jurisdiction and powers. Traffic officers may be authorised by order made by, or authorisation given by, the Secretary of State or the Assembly to perform duties connected with the management of traffic on the network of 'relevant roads' in England or Wales, depending on which national authority appointed them. A 'relevant road' is a road for which the Secretary of State or the Assembly is responsible, as the case may be. They may also be authorised to perform any other function of the national authority (in its capacity as a traffic authority or highway authority). They have special powers:

(a) when engaged in the regulation of traffic in a road, power to direct persons driving or propelling a vehicle to stop the vehicle, or to make it proceed in, or keep to, a particular line of traffic (s 6(1)(a));
(b) in relation to a traffic survey being carried out on, or in the vicinity of, a road, power to direct a person driving or propelling a vehicle to stop the vehicle, or to make it proceed in, or keep to, a particular line of traffic, or to proceed to a particular point on or near the road on which the vehicle is being driven or propelled, subject to the restriction in the Road Traffic Act 1988 (RTA 1988), s 35(3) (person unwilling to take part in the survey not to be unreasonably delayed) (s 6(1)(b));
(c) the power of a constable to place temporary traffic signs under the Road Traffic Regulation Act 1984 (RTRA 1984), s 67(1) (placing of traffic signs in emergencies and where there are temporary obstructions).

A traffic officer may exercise these special powers on any road which is not a relevant road in England and Wales at the direction of the chief officer of police for the area in which the road is situated, or with the consent of the traffic authority for that area.

In consequence of these powers, RTA 1988, s 35 is amended to include a 'traffic officer' so that it becomes an offence for a driver or person propelling a vehicle to neglect or refuse to comply with a traffic direction given by such an officer in the execution of his duty in the regulation of traffic.

RTA 1988, s 37 is similarly amended to empower traffic officers engaged in the regulation of traffic to give directions to pedestrians, who commit an offence if they proceed across or along the carriageway in contravention of such a direction. In addition, RTA, s 163 is amended to give traffic officers the same power as that given to a constable to stop vehicles on a road in the performance of their duties. Traffic officers may deal with the removal of vehicles as authorised by regulations made under RTRA 1984, s 99 (removal of vehicles illegally, obstructively or dangerously parked, or abandoned or broken down). This includes the provisions of RTRA 1984, ss 100 to 102 (interim and ultimate disposal of vehicles and charges for removal, storage and disposal of vehicles). The appropriate national authority may provide further powers by way of statutory instrument where it considers this to be necessary.

A traffic officer has jurisdiction on any relevant road for which the national authority has responsibility, unless his designation is limited or subject to conditions which will be specified.

Traffic officers are required to comply with any directions given by a constable. Subject to that limitation, they must comply with any direction given by the appropriate national authority. However, such powers must only be exercised for the purpose of maintaining or improving the movement of traffic on a relevant road; preventing or reducing the effect of anything causing (or which has the potential to cause) congestion or other disruption to the movement of traffic; avoiding danger to persons or other traffic (or preventing it arising); preventing damage to the road, or to anything on or near a road; or for a purpose incidental to any of those purposes.

It is an offence to assault, or to resist or wilfully obstruct, a traffic officer in the execution of his duty, or with intent to deceive, to impersonate such an officer or to make a statement or perform an act calculated to suggest that that person is a traffic officer or (where the accused is a traffic officer) to suggest that he has powers which he does not have. It is also an offence for a person (having been given a direction which a traffic officer is empowered to give either by the traffic officer himself or by a traffic sign which he has lawfully placed on the road) to fail to give his name and address to that uniformed traffic officer on being required to do so.

Representation

The Association of Chief Police Officers, the Superintendents' Association and the Police Federation represent the interests of the various members of police forces. A member of a police force is not permitted to be a member of a trade union, or of any association having as one of its objects control or influence over pay, pensions or conditions of service of any police force. However, persons who were members of trade unions before joining the police force may retain that membership with the approval of their chief constable.

Liability

PA 1996, s 88 states that a chief officer of police is vicariously liable in civil law for any unlawful conduct of his constables (or an international joint investigation team which has been formed under the leadership of a constable who is a member of his force) in the performance or purported performance of their duties. This means that civil claims may be pursued against a chief officer, as well as against (or instead of against) the officer alleged to have committed a wrongful act. The chief officer can even be liable for the off-duty unlawful conduct of a constable if it was committed at a time when the constable was apparently acting in his capacity as a constable. However, it has been held in the High Court that a chief officer is not necessarily liable for conduct in the purported performance of a constable's duty if the conduct was clearly for a purpose unrelated to the constable's duty—as where he threatens not to report an illegal immigrant in return for sexual favours. Any damages or costs awarded against a chief officer must be paid out of police funds. Those awarded against the constable concerned may be paid or part paid from police funds at the discretion of the police authority, and it has been held that they should be so paid if the constable acted in good faith.

Special provision is made by PA 1996, s 97 in relation to officers seconded to central service or to an international organisation; it is the Secretary of State (and not their chief constable) who is vicariously liable for their torts.

Although the House of Lords has held that no action lies against a constable or his chief constable for injury caused to a person by a negligent failure to identify and arrest a criminal where that failure results in his committing further offences or for a negligent failure to give him reasonable protection, this does not necessarily mean that an action would never lie in respect of the negligent exercise of some other police function. The European Court of Human Rights has held that an absolute immunity would be a breach of the European Convention on Human Rights (ECHR), art 6 (right to a fair trial). The Court held that while the immunity may be permissible, it is open to an English court not to apply it if the public interest does not require the immunity.

An investigating officer conducting disciplinary proceedings (or his chief constable) cannot be liable under civil law to the officer under investigation if he negligently conducts the proceedings or acts in breach of his duty under the relevant regulations described on pp 293–304. Nor can a constable (or his chief constable) be liable to someone who suffers injuries in a foreseeable attempt to escape or to a road user for injuries caused by a constable's failure to give warnings of hazards of which the constable was aware but for which he was not responsible.

As a matter of public policy, chief constables are not generally liable to their subordinates who are injured by rioters in the course of controlling serious public disorder. In addition, chief constables are not liable for the negligent handling by a senior officer of a complaint made by one police officer against another, nor is the senior officer.

An individual police officer may be liable to pay damages under the Race Relations Act 1976 if he discriminates against someone, on the ground of his membership of a racial group, in performing his duties. In addition, a police officer's chief officer of police may be vicariously liable for such unlawful discrimination by that officer.

The 1976 Act makes provision for the payment out of police funds in respect of any compensation, costs or expenses awarded against a chief officer of police in any proceedings brought against him under the Race Relations Act 1976. Similar provisions are made in relation to actions brought against the Serious Organised Crime Agency.

It has been held that a chief constable is also vicariously liable for any unlawful sex discrimination on the part of a police officer.

Lastly, it must not be forgotten that a public authority, a term which includes a police officer, which acts incompatibly with a Convention right under the Human Rights Act 1998 can successfully be sued by a victim of that unlawful act and ordered to pay damages.

IMPERSONATING A POLICE OFFICER AND CAUSING DISAFFECTION AMONGST MEMBERS OF A POLICE FORCE

Impersonation

A person who, with intent to deceive, impersonates a member of a police force or a special constable, or makes any statement or does any act calculated falsely to suggest that he is such a member or constable, commits an offence against PA 1996, s 90. It is also an offence against that section for a person who, not being a constable, wears any article of police uniform in circumstances where it gives him an appearance so nearly resembling that of a member of a police force as to be calculated to deceive. The section also prohibits the possession of an article of police uniform, unless it was obtained lawfully and is possessed for a lawful purpose.

Causes disaffection

A person who causes, or attempts to cause, or does any act calculated to cause, disaffection amongst members of any police force, or induces, or attempts to induce, or does any act calculated to induce, any member of a police force to withhold his services commits an offence against PA 1996, s 91. The section applies to special constables appointed for a police force as it does to members of a police force.

POLICE COMPLAINTS AND DISCIPLINE

The foundations of the system

The PRA 2002, Part 2 and Sch 3, as amended by SOCPA 2005, Sch 11, deals with matters relating to complaints against the police. Police discipline, and the efficiency of officers, is dealt with by the Police (Conduct) Regulations 2004 and the Police (Efficiency) Regulations 1999. The Police (Complaints and Misconduct) Regulations 2004 apply the complaints procedures to detention officers and escort officers in respect of their appointed duties.

PRA 2002 established a body corporate known as 'the Independent Police Complaints Commission' which has wider powers than the Police Complaints Authority which it replaced. The investigation of many complaints continues to be carried out by police forces but those investigations may be carried out by a person serving with the police (of the force concerned or any other force), or SOCA. There is no requirement that the investigator must be a police officer. In addition, the Commission is empowered to carry out its own investigation of complaints and to supervise or manage other investigations.

The functions of the Commission include securing the maintenance by the Commission itself, and by police authorities and chief officers, of suitable arrangements for the handling of matters from which it appears that there may have been conduct by such persons which constitutes or involves a criminal offence or behaviour justifying disciplinary proceedings, the recording of matters from which it appears that a person has died or suffered serious injury during, or following, contact with a person serving with the police, and the manner in which such complaints or any such matters are investigated or otherwise handled and dealt with. The Commission is required to enter into arrangements with the chief inspector of constabulary for the purpose of securing co-operation between the Commission and the Inspectorate. However, PRA 2002 does not confer any function on the Commission in relation to any part of a complaint or conduct matter which relates to the direction and control of a police force by a chief officer of police.

The Commission is required to make an annual report to the Secretary of State, copies being sent to police authorities and service authorities (eg the Serious Organised Crime Agency).

Under PRA 2002, s 19, an order may be made by the Secretary of State authorising the use of directed or intrusive surveillance and the conduct and use of covert human intelligence sources to assist the Commission in carrying out its functions.

Complaints

The Independent Police Complaints Commission and complaints generally

PRA 2002, s 9 and Schs 2 and 3 deal with the constitution of a body corporate known as 'the Independent Police Complaints Commission' (hereafter 'the Commission') which consists of a chairman (who is appointed by the Queen) and not less than ten other members (who are appointed by the Secretary of State). The Secretary of State may appoint not more than two deputy chairmen from the membership. These appointments are for a maximum period of five years at a time. The Secretary of State may remove these members from office for various reasons. With the consent of the Secretary of State, the Commission may set up regional offices in any part of England and Wales.

The rules below apply whatever the rank of the officer against whom the complaint is made. As will be seen, various functions relating to complaints are carried out by the 'appropriate authority'. The 'appropriate authority' is the chief officer of police of the officer etc who is subject to the complaint. Where a complaint relates to the chief officer, his police authority is the appropriate authority.

Handling of complaints

PRA 2002, Sch 3, Part 1 requires that, where a complaint about the conduct of a person serving under his direction or control is submitted to a chief officer of police, or that chief officer becomes aware that such a complaint has been made to the Commission or to a police authority, he must take, as soon as reasonably practicable, any steps that appear to him to be desirable for the purpose of obtaining or preserving evidence relating to the conduct complained of. The term 'a person serving under his control and direction' includes members of a police force; police authority employees under the direction and control of a chief officer; and special constables.

PRA 2002, s 12 provides that a 'complaint' is any complaint about the conduct of a person serving with the police which is made (whether in writing or otherwise) by:

(a) a member of the public who claims to be the person in relation to whom the conduct took place;
(b) any other member of the public who claims to have been adversely affected by the conduct;
(c) a member of the public who claims to have witnessed the conduct;
(d) a person acting on behalf of a person in categories (a) to (c) above.

However, there is no 'complaint' where an allegation is made *by or on behalf* of a person who claims to have been adversely affected only as a result of having seen or heard the conduct or any of its alleged effects, unless it was only because that person was physically present, or sufficiently nearby, when the conduct took place or the effects occurred that he was able to see or hear the conduct or its effects, or unless the adverse effect is attributable to, or was aggravated by, the fact that the person in relation to whom the conduct took place was already known to the person claiming to have suffered the adverse effect. A person is taken to have witnessed conduct only if he acquired his knowledge in a manner which would make him a competent witness capable of giving admissible evidence, or if he has in his possession or under his control anything which would constitute admissible evidence.

In order to be authorised, for the purpose of (d), to act on behalf of another, a person must either be designated by the Commission as a person through whom a complaint may be made, or a person who has been authorised in writing by the person on behalf of whom he is acting.

Initial handling and recording of complaints

Where a complaint is made to the Commission, it must determine whether the complainant consents to the police authority or appropriate chief officer being notified; if he does it must give that notification. Where no consent is given, but the Commission believes that it is in the public interest for the subject matter of the complaint to be brought to the attention of the appropriate authority and recorded, the Commission may bring the matter to the attention of the appropriate authority as if it were a 'recordable conduct matter' (as to which term, see pp 286–287); where this is done the provisions of PRA 2002, Sch 3 have effect as if it were such a matter.

Where it receives a complaint about a police officer etc a police authority must notify the chief officer who is 'the appropriate authority' in relation to the officer etc against whom the complaint was made. If the chief officer who receives a complaint determines that he is not the appropriate authority, because the complaint relates to an officer in another force or to a senior officer, he must notify the 'appropriate authority'. Where notification of a complaint is given to an appropriate authority, the person who gave the notification or, as the case may be, the Commission, must notify the complainant.

PRA 2002, Sch 3 provides that if a chief officer determines that he is the appropriate authority in relation to a complaint, or if he is notified that he is, he must record the complaint. However, a complaint need not be recorded where the subject matter of the complaint has been, or is already being, dealt with by means of criminal or disciplinary proceedings or the complaint has been withdrawn.

Non-notification or recording of a complaint

Where a complaint has been received by, or notified to, an appropriate authority and the authority decides to take no action in relation to recording it, or notifying the appropriate authority, it must notify the complainant of the decision, the grounds for reaching it, and the complainant's right of appeal. The complainant has a right of appeal to the Commission against that decision. The Commission must decide whether action should have been taken and, if it thinks that it should, give directions to the appropriate authority which is bound to comply with such directions. All parties must be notified. Regulations may be made governing the procedures to be followed.

Reference of complaints to the Commission

A complaint must be referred to the Commission if:

(a) it alleges that the conduct complained of has resulted in death or serious injury;
(b) it is of a description specified in regulations; or
(c) the Commission notifies the appropriate authority that it requires the matter to be referred for consideration.

In cases other than those in which reference is mandatory, an appropriate authority may refer a complaint to the Commission if it considers that it would be appropriate to do so in view of the gravity of the subject matter or other exceptional circumstances. Such references may be made regardless of the fact that the complaint is already being considered by the Commission. Such action must be notified to the complainant and, except where any future investigation may be prejudiced, to the person complained against. In addition, where a death or serious injury matter (for definition see p 286) comes to the attention of a police authority, or a chief officer who is the appropriate authority, the matter must be recorded and if this has not been done the Commission may direct that it be done. Following the investigation of such matters a report will be submitted and the Commission may make recommendations or give advice. Where such an investigation reveals a conduct matter (a criminal or disciplinary offence) the matter will be treated as a conduct matter.

Where a complaint is referred to the Commission it must determine whether or not it is necessary for the complaint to be investigated. Where it considers that investigation is not necessary, it may, if it thinks fit, refer the complaint back to the appropriate authority for 'local resolution' and inform the complainant and (unless it considers that this may prejudice a possible future investigation of the complaint) the person complained against that it has done so.

The Police (Complaints and Misconduct) Regulations 2004 provide that a complaint of serious assault, a serious sexual offence, serious corruption, a criminal offence or behaviour which is liable to lead to a disciplinary sanction and which in either case was aggravated by discriminatory behaviour on the grounds of race, sex, religion, or other status identified in guidance issued by the Commission, or a 'relevant offence', are complaints for the purposes of (b) above. A 'relevant offence' is an offence for which the sentence is fixed by law, or an offence for which a person of eighteen years or over (not previously convicted) may be sentenced to imprisonment for a term of seven years (or might be so sentenced but for the restrictions imposed by s 33 of the Magistrates' Courts Act 1980).

Handling of complaints by the appropriate authority

Having recorded a complaint which does not need to be referred, the appropriate authority must then consider whether the complaint is suitable for local resolution. If it determines that it is suitable for local resolution, and the complainant consents (after having been informed of his right to appeal), it may make suitable arrangements. Any consent so given may not be withdrawn after the procedure has begun. If the complaint is not so suitable, the appropriate authority must take steps to investigate it formally.

A determination that a complaint is suitable for local resolution is dependent upon the appropriate authority being satisfied that the conduct complained of (even if it were proved) would not justify the bringing of any criminal or disciplinary proceedings or the Commission having approved such resolution. In order to approve a 'local resolution', the Commission must be satisfied that any disciplinary proceedings which might be justified would be unlikely to result in a dismissal, a requirement to resign or retire, a reduction in rank or other demotion or the imposition of a fine. Alternatively, the Commission must be satisfied that it would not be practicable for criminal proceedings which would be likely to result in a conviction, or disciplinary proceedings leading to one of those results, to be brought.

Dispensation by the Commission (other action or no action)

Where a complaint has been recorded, and not referred to the Commission, and the appropriate authority considers that it should be handled otherwise than in accordance with the procedures set out in PRA 2002, Sch 3, or that no action should be taken in relation to that complaint, and that the complaint falls within a description of complaints specified in regulations, it may apply to the Commission for permission to handle the complaint in an alternative manner. It must notify a complainant that this application has been made. The Commission must inform the authority and the complainant of its decision. Where the Commission gives permission for an appropriate authority to handle the complaint in whatever manner the authority considers to be fit, the authority needs do no more under Sch 3 than preserving the evidence, and take any action which it considers appropriate, or take no action at all.

Where the Commission does not grant permission the appropriate authority must consider whether the complaint is suitable for local resolution.

The Police (Complaints and Misconduct) Regulations 2004 prescribe the cases where dispensation may be granted. These are where the appropriate authority considers that:

(a) the incident is more than twelve months old and there is no good reason for the delay;
(b) the matter is already the subject of a complaint;
(c) the complaint does not disclose the name and address of the complainant or other interested party and such an address cannot reasonably be ascertained;
(d) the complaint is vexatious, oppressive or otherwise an abuse of the complaint procedures;
(e) the complaint is repetitious; or
(f) it is not reasonably practicable to investigate the complaint.

Local resolution of complaints

Where there is to be a local resolution of a complaint, the arrangements made by the appropriate authority for subjecting a complaint to local resolution may include the appointment of *a person who is serving with the police* and is under the direction and control of the chief officer of police of the relevant force, to secure the local resolution of the complaint. The requirement is not that it shall be *a police officer*. The Secretary of State has made the Police (Complaints and Misconduct) Regulations 2004 dealing with the procedural requirements. Any statement made for the purpose of such resolution is not admissible in any subsequent criminal, civil or disciplinary proceedings except to the extent that it consists of an admission relating to a matter which has not been subjected to local resolution.

If, after attempts to achieve local resolution, it appears to an appropriate authority that such resolution is impossible, or that the matter is unsuitable for such resolution, it must arrange for an investigation. In such a case, any attempt at local resolution must be discontinued. Such an attempt must also be discontinued if there is a requirement for the matter to be referred to the Commission or it is otherwise referred. Any person who has been involved in an attempt at local resolution is barred from participation in subsequently investigating the complaint.

Appeals relating to local resolution

A complainant has a right of appeal to the Commission against the conduct of the local resolution of a complaint. Where this is done, the only matter to be considered is whether there have been contraventions of procedural requirements relating to local resolution. The Commission must consider representations from both sides. Where the Commission rules in the complainant's favour, it must give binding directions to the appropriate authority as to the future handling of the complaint. This may take the form of requiring an investigation. Both parties must be informed.

The Police (Complaints and Misconduct) Regulations 2004 make provision for an appeal in relation to the conduct of the local resolution of a complaint (or the investigation of a complaint or a failure to record a complaint).

Withdrawn and discontinued complaints

The Police (Complaints and Misconduct) Regulations 2004 provide that where an appropriate authority receives from a complainant notification in writing, signed by him or by his solicitor or other authorised agent, to the effect that he withdraws his complaint or does not wish any further action to be taken, that withdrawal must be recorded and procedures discontinued. There may, however, be a decision to treat the matter as a recordable conduct matter. In addition, the Commission, or the appropriate authority, may suspend any investigation or other procedure which would, if it were to continue, prejudice any criminal proceedings. The Commission may direct such an investigation to continue if it is of the view that it is in the public interest to do so.

Where the investigation of a complaint has been suspended pending the outcome of criminal proceedings, the Commission or the appropriate authority must contact the complainant to establish whether or not he wishes the investigation to continue. If he does not wish to do so, or fails to reply within twenty-one days, the Commission or appropriate authority must decide whether or not it is in the public interest to treat the complaint as a recordable conduct matter.

Handling of conduct matters and death or serious injury matters

PRA 2002, Sch 3, Part 2 deals with these.

A 'conduct matter' is a matter which is not and has not been the subject of a complaint but in respect of which there is an indication that the person serving with the police may have committed a criminal offence or may have behaved in a manner which would justify disciplinary proceedings.

A 'death or serious injury matter' means circumstances (other than those which are or have been the subject of a complaint or which amount to a conduct matter) in or in consequence of which a person has died or has sustained serious injury and, in relation to which the requirements of subsections (2B) or (2C) of s 12 are satisfied. Those requirements are that: (a) at the time of the death or (b) serious injury the person had been arrested by a person serving with the police and had not been released from that arrest, or was otherwise detained in the custody of a person serving with the police, or that at or before the time of death or serious injury the person has contact (whether direct or indirect) with a person serving with the police who was acting in the execution of his duties, and there is an indication that the contact may have caused (directly or indirectly) or contributed to the death or serious injury.

Thus, such happenings are covered where a complaint or conduct matter has not yet been identified and may relate to matters concerning the direction and control of a police force.

Conduct matters arising in civil proceedings

Where a police authority or a chief constable has received notification that civil proceedings have been brought by a member of the public against him or are likely to be brought and it appears that these proceedings would involve a conduct matter, it or he should follow the same procedure in relation to recording that matter or notifying the appropriate authority about it. There is no requirement to record where the matter has already been dealt with by means of criminal or disciplinary proceedings.

Recording etc of conduct matters in other cases

Where a conduct matter comes to the attention of a police authority or chief officer of police in some other way from that just mentioned and it is conduct:

(a) which appears to have resulted in the death of any person;
(b) as a result of which a member of the public has been adversely affected by it; or
(c) it is of a description specified in regulations,

the matter must be recorded and the appropriate authority must consider whether it is a matter which must be referred to the Commission, or is one which it would be appropriate to refer. If it is not required to refer the matter and does not do so, it may deal with the matter in such other manner (if any) as it may determine. No such matter which has already been dealt with by means of criminal or disciplinary proceedings need be recorded.

The Commission may direct an appropriate authority to record a matter that has come to its attention and that it considers to be a 'recordable conduct matter' if it has not otherwise been recorded.

Duties to preserve evidence relating to conduct matters

The appropriate authority has a duty, as soon as practicable, to obtain and preserve evidence related to a recordable conduct matter.

Reference of conduct matters to the Commission

The same matters *must be referred* as in the case of complaints and there are similar arrangements in respect of voluntary references. Similar conditions apply in relation to notifications to interested parties.

Where reference has been made, it is the duty of the Commission to decide whether or not an investigation is necessary. Where it does not consider such an investigation to be necessary, it may refer the matter back to the appropriate authority to be dealt with in such manner (if any) as the authority determines.

The Police (Complaints and Misconduct) Regulations 2004 deal with the recording and reference of conduct matters. Those matters are similar to those applying in the case of a complaint, together with conduct the gravity of which, or other exceptional circumstances, make it appropriate to record such conduct.

Investigations and subsequent proceedings

Power of Commission to determine the form of an investigation

PRA 2002, Sch 3, Part 3 applies where a complaint or recordable conduct matter has been referred to the Commission and it decides that an investigation is necessary. The form of the investigation will depend upon the seriousness of the case and the public interest but must consist of:

(a) an investigation by the appropriate authority on its own behalf;
(b) an investigation by that authority under the supervision of the Commission;

(c) an investigation by that authority under the management of the Commission; or

(d) an investigation by the Commission.

The form of the investigation may be changed by the Commission at any time and the Commission may give directions to that effect.

Investigations by the appropriate authority on behalf of the Commission

The appropriate authority must appoint a person serving with the police (whether under the direction and control of the chief officer of police of the relevant force or of the chief officer of another force) to investigate the complaint or matter. The Police (Complaints and Misconduct) Regulations 2004 require that no person shall be appointed to carry out an investigation by the appropriate authority on its own behalf or, when the investigation is supervised or managed, unless that person has an appropriate level of knowledge, skills and experience to plan and conduct investigations and to manage the process and there must be no suggestion of bias. In the case of federated ranks, no member of a police force must be appointed, where the person to be investigated is also a member of a police force, unless that officer is of at least the rank of sergeant and is of at least the same rank as the person being investigated. Where the officer concerned is a chief superintendent or superintendent, the complaint must be investigated by an officer of at least the rank of assistant chief constable (commander in the case of the Metropolitan or City of London Police).

In the case of an investigation into the conduct of a chief officer, the investigating officer may not be a person under that chief officer's direction or control. In the case of the Commissioner of Police of the Metropolis or his Deputy, it must be a person nominated by the Secretary of State.

Investigations supervised by the Commission

The Commission may require that no appointment as an investigating officer may be made without its approval. If an appointment has already been made a further approved appointment must be made as soon as practicable.

The same conditions apply in relation to the investigation of chief officers. The person appointed to investigate the complaint or matter must comply with directions from the Commission which are authorised by regulations.

Investigations managed by the Commission

The same conditions apply as apply in the case of supervised investigations with the addition that the investigator must be under the direction and control of the Commission.

Investigations by the Commission itself

The Commission must designate a member of its own staff to take charge of the investigation on behalf of the Commission; it must also designate other members of its staff to assist that person. Any member of the Commission's staff so designated who does not already have all the powers and privileges of a constable throughout England and Wales and the adjacent United Kingdom waters has, for the purposes of carrying out the investigation and all purposes connected with it, all those powers and privileges of a constable. PRA 2002 authorises an order specifying that provisions of PACE may apply subject to specified modifications.

Restrictions on proceedings pending the conclusion of an investigation

No criminal or disciplinary proceedings may be brought in relation to any matter subject to an investigation (unless the investigation has been discontinued) until the appropriate authority has certified the case as a 'special case' or a report has been submitted to the Commission or appropriate authority. However, these provisions do not apply to proceedings by the DPP in exceptional cases where delay is undesirable.

SOCPA 2005, Sch 11 amended PRA 2002, Sch 3, to introduce an accelerated procedure in 'special cases'. These special conditions are met where there is good evidence that the police officer has committed a criminal offence which would justify dismissal and the appropriate authority considers that it is in the public interest for that police officer to cease to be a member of a police force. In such cases a report must be submitted before the completion of the investigation to enable disciplinary proceedings to be brought earlier than would otherwise have been possible. The DPP should be consulted in such cases and he may order the continuation of the investigation regardless of the disciplinary proceedings. It is difficult to see how any following trial for an alleged criminal offence will not be affected by the outcome of disciplinary proceedings in respect of which there are reduced standards of proof and majority verdicts.

Power of Commission to discontinue an investigation

The Commission may order the discontinuance of any investigation in relation to a complaint or matter specified in regulations made by the Secretary of State. Where an investigation is so discontinued, the Commission may give the appropriate authority directions, as authorised by regulations, or may act, as authorised by regulations, on its own behalf.

Final reports on investigations

Where the investigation is carried out on behalf of an appropriate authority, the investigating officer must submit his report to that authority. Where the investigation was supervised, or managed by the Commission, the investigating officer must send a report to the Commission and a copy to the appropriate authority. Where the Commission carries out the investigation itself, the investigating officer must report to the Commission. In all of these cases, the investigator is not prevented by any obligation of secrecy from including all such matters in his report as he thinks fit.

Action by the Commission in response to an investigation report

Where the Commission receives a report submitted to it in respect of an investigation which it has supervised, managed or carried out itself, it must send a copy to the appropriate authority and determine whether or not a criminal offence is disclosed. If it considers that such an offence is disclosed it must notify the DPP and send him a copy of the report, and it must notify the appropriate authority of this notification. The DPP must notify the Commission of his decision to take, or not to take, action in respect of the matter or matters investigated. If criminal proceedings are brought by the DPP, the Commission must inform, in the case of a complaint, the complainant and every person entitled to be kept informed in relation to the complaint as required by PRA 2002, s 21; in the case of a recordable conduct matter, every person entitled to be kept informed of that matter under s 21 must be informed. Where the Commission has determined that there is no indication of a criminal offence having been committed, or where it is notified that the DPP (having been sent the report) has decided to take no action, or where it is satisfied that any criminal proceedings have been concluded, the Commission must inform the appropriate authority requiring it to determine what action (if any) it will take in respect of matters dealt with in the report.

On being required to determine what action it will take, the appropriate authority must determine what action it will take and submit a memorandum to the Commission giving its decision and details of any proposed action. Where it decides that no disciplinary proceedings should follow, the reasons must be set out. The Commission must then consider whether the proposed action is appropriate and whether or not to make recommendations. It may make recommendations to the appropriate authority. The complainant and other entitled persons must be informed of those recommendations.

Action by appropriate authority in response to investigation report

The appropriate authority must decide whether the report submitted or sent to it indicates that a criminal offence may have been committed by the person whose conduct has been investigated. If it determines that it has, it must notify the DPP and send a copy of the report. If the DPP brings criminal proceedings, the appropriate authority must notify the complainant of this and every other person entitled to be kept informed under PRA 2002, s 21.

If the appropriate authority decides that the report does not indicate a criminal offence or (where a copy of the report has been sent to the DPP) it is notified that the DPP does not propose to bring criminal proceedings, the authority must decide upon what action (if any) it will take and make similar notifications in this respect. It must also do this once it is satisfied that any criminal proceedings in respect of matters in the report have been concluded (apart from any appeal). The notification must set out the report's findings; whether the appropriate authority has decided to take action; what action (if any) it has decided to take, and the complainant's right of appeal.

Except so far as it may be otherwise directed by regulations, an appropriate authority may (notwithstanding any obligation to secrecy imposed by any rule of law) give such a person notification of the findings by sending the person a copy of the report.

Complaints concerning officers who are no longer serving or whose identity cannot be ascertained

Where a complaint is recorded against an officer who is no longer serving, the preceding conditions will apply as if they did not include a requirement on the part of the appropriate authority to determine whether disciplinary proceedings should be brought.

The Regulations also make it clear that, where the person complained against has not been identified, all provisions concerning notices to be given to such a person and the determination of whether or not there may be criminal liability or liability to disciplinary proceedings do not apply.

Appeals to the Commission with respect to an investigation

A complainant has a right of appeal to the Commission:

(a) on the grounds that he has not been provided with adequate information about the findings of the investigation or any proposals in relation to the taking or not taking of action;
(b) against the findings of the investigation; and
(c) against any proposal of the appropriate authority to take, or not to take, action in respect of any of the matters dealt with in the report.

The Commission must notify all persons concerned that such an appeal has been lodged.

If such an appeal is brought, the Commission may require the appropriate authority to submit a memorandum specifying whether any action is proposed to be taken; and, if it is, specifying the nature of that action; and, where no disciplinary proceedings are proposed, specifying the reasons for so deciding. In addition, where the investigation was carried out by the appropriate authority on its own behalf, and the Commission so requires, it must be supplied with a copy of the report. If the Commission considers that the complainant has not been provided with sufficient information it must direct the appropriate authority to provide such information.

Where the Commission determines that the findings of the investigation need to be reconsidered it may review those findings without further investigation, or direct that the complaint be re-investigated.

Where the Commission considers that the appropriate authority is not proposing to take action which the Commission considers to be appropriate it must make such recommendations as it considers appropriate.

Any direction or recommendation made by the Commission as a result of determining an appeal must be notified to all persons concerned. An appropriate authority must comply with any directions.

The Police (Complaints and Misconduct) Regulations 2004, regs 8 to 10 deal with appeal procedures relating to a failure to determine who is the appropriate authority, or to record a complaint, local resolution, and investigations.

Review and re-investigations following an appeal

On a review of the findings of an investigation based upon the existing report, the Commission may:

(a) uphold the findings in whole or in part;
(b) give the appropriate authority such directions as to the review by the authority of the findings, as to the information to be provided to the complainant, and generally in respect of the handling of the matter in future, as it thinks fit; or
(c) direct that the complaint be re-investigated in a specified form.

All persons concerned must be informed by the Commission of any such determination or direction.

Duties with respect to disciplinary proceedings

Certain duties are imposed on the appropriate authority in the case of any investigation, where it has given, or is required to give, notification to entitled persons of the action which it is proposing to take, or it has submitted, or is required to submit, a memorandum setting out the action which it is proposing to take.

Subject to any recommendations or directions given by the Commission, the authority must take any action notified and, where that action consists of or includes disciplinary proceedings, it must secure that those proceedings are taken to a proper conclusion.

Where a memorandum has been submitted to the Commission, the Commission may make recommendations that disciplinary proceedings, or specified disciplinary proceedings, are brought against the person concerned, or that proposed disciplinary proceedings should be modified so as to include specified charges. The appropriate authority is then obliged to notify the Commission as to whether it accepts the recommendation and (if it does) to set out the steps which it is proposing to take. Where the appropriate authority does not take steps to carry out the recommendations of the Commission, the Commission may direct the authority to do so, setting out the steps to be taken, and the authority must comply. The Commission must supply a statement of its reasons for giving such a direction. The appropriate authority must keep the Commission informed of the action which it takes.

Information for complainant etc about disciplinary recommendations

The complainant, and all other persons entitled to be informed of such matters, must be notified by the Commission of any steps which it recommends to be taken by the appropriate authority, unless the authority has not notified its acceptance of the recommendation. If the appropriate authority notifies the Commission that it does not accept the recommendations, or fails to effect them, the Commission must determine what further steps, if any, should be taken. The Commission must also notify such persons of any determination not to take further steps or of the outcome of a determination to take further steps.

DISCIPLINE REGULATIONS

The police officer occupies a unique role within society and it is fitting that the highest possible standards are demanded of a constable, who, in addition to being answerable to the laws of the land in the same way as any other citizen, is also answerable to a disciplinary code. The code is set out in the Police (Conduct) Regulations 2004. There are some differences in the code as between the rules applicable to officers above the rank of chief superintendent and those applicable to chief superintendent and below. Set out below are the provisions of the Code as they apply to chief superintendents and below.

The Police (Conduct) Regulations 2004

Suspension from membership of a police force

The Police (Conduct) Regulations 2004, reg 4 provides that, where a report, complaint or allegation indicates that the conduct of a member of a police force does not meet the appropriate standard, the chief officer of the force concerned may suspend the member concerned from membership of the force and from his office of constable whether or not the matter has been investigated. These powers may be exercised at any time following receipt of the report, complaint or allegation until:

(a) the supervising officer decides not to refer the case to a hearing;
(b) the notification of a finding that the conduct of the member concerned did not fail to meet the appropriate standard;
(c) a sanction has been imposed after a hearing and the time limit for giving notice of intention to seek a review has expired, or any review has been completed.

Suspension will continue until such events occur, or until the chief officer decides to lift the suspension, which ever occurs first. Where a suspended member is subsequently required to resign, he will remain suspended during the period of notice.

This power to suspend may be delegated to a deputy chief constable or an assistant chief constable (or assistant commissioner or commander).

The *appropriate standard* referred to in reg 4 means the standard set out in the Code of Conduct which is included in Sch 1 to the Regulations (and is set out on pp 302–303). This Code of Conduct replaces the disciplinary offences which were included in the replaced disciplinary regulations. Although the Code is expressed in a way which suggests that it is concerned with the achievement of desirable objectives, this is not so. Failure to comply with any of the 'aims' of the Code amounts to an offence. A finding that an officer is guilty of any of the offences described in the code as *appropriate standards* means the officer may face any of the sanctions set out in reg 35:

(a) dismissal from the force;
(b) requirement to resign from the force as an alternative to dismissal taking effect either forthwith or on such date as may be specified in the decision;
(c) reduction in rank;
(d) fine;
(e) reprimand;
(f) caution.

However, PA, s 84(1) provides that the penalties of dismissal, requirement to resign, or reduction in rank cannot be imposed unless the member concerned has been given the opportunity to elect to be legally represented at the hearing. The provisions concerning legal representation may need to be looked at in consequence of a decision of the European Court of Human Rights which held that it was a breach of a prisoner's human rights for prison governors to deny them legal representation within disciplinary proceedings. It would be somewhat inconsistent to find that a police officer should be denied a protection afforded to prisoners.

In addition, reg 36 requires that those conducting the hearing must have regard to an officer's personal record and may receive evidence from witnesses. The member concerned, or his representative, must be given an opportunity to make oral or, if appropriate, written representations as respects the question or to adduce evidence relevant thereto.

Conduct of investigations

Where there are criminal proceedings outstanding against a member, proceedings under the Regulations (other than suspension) must not take place unless the chief officer believes that exceptional circumstances make it appropriate to do so.

Where a report, complaint or allegation received by the chief officer indicates that the conduct of the member did not meet the appropriate standard the chief officer may refer the case to an officer to supervise the investigation of the case. The officer is called the 'supervising officer'.

The supervising officer

The 'supervising officer' must be:

(a) at least one rank above that of the member concerned;
(b) of at least the rank of chief inspector;
(c) a member of the same force as the member concerned or a special constable appointed for the area; and
(d) not an interested party (ie not a witness or any person involved in the conduct which is the subject of the case nor anyone who has a direct interest in the case).

The investigating officer

The supervising officer may appoint an investigating officer, who must be:

(a) a member of the same police force as the member concerned or, if at the request of the supervising officer the chief officer of some other force agrees to provide an investigating officer, a member of that other force who is of at least of the rank of sergeant;
(b) if the member concerned is a superintendent or chief superintendent, of at least the rank of assistant chief constable or, if the investigating officer is a member of the City of London or Metropolitan Police Force, of at least the rank of commander;
(c) of at least the same rank as the member concerned; and
(d) not an interested party.

However, where the Independent Police Complaints Commission supervise the investigation they may require that no appointment is made without their approval.

The investigation

The investigating officer must, as soon as practicable (without prejudicing his or any other investigation) cause the member concerned to be given written notice:

(a) that there is to be an investigation into the case;
(b) of the nature of the report, complaint or allegation;
(c) informing him that he is not obliged to say anything concerning the matter, but that he may if he so desires, make a written or oral statement concerning the matter to the investigating officer or to the chief officer concerned;
(d) informing him that if he makes such a statement it may be used in any subsequent proceedings under these Regulations;
(e) informing him that he has the right to seek advice from his staff association; and
(f) informing him that he has the right to be accompanied by a member of a police force, who shall not be an interested party, to any meeting, interview or hearing.

The investigating officer must submit a written report on the case to the supervising officer and, if the Independent Police Complaints Commission are supervising the investigation, also to the Commission. If at any time during his investigation it appears to the investigating officer that it is likely that the case is a *special case* (as defined by Sch 2, Part I) namely:

(a) the conduct is of a serious nature and an imprisonable offence may have been committed;
(b) if referred to a hearing under reg 11 and proved, it may lead to dismissal from the force;
(c) the allegation is supported by written statements, documents or other material which is, in the opinion of the *appropriate officer*, sufficient without further evidence to establish on the balance of probabilities that the conduct of the member did not meet the appropriate standard; and
(d) the *appropriate officer* is of the opinion that it is in the public interest for the member concerned to cease to be a member of a police force without delay,

the investigating officer must, whether or not the investigation is at an end, submit to the supervising officer:

(a) a statement of his belief that the case may be one to which reg 45 and Sch 2 (which deal with special cases) applies and the grounds for that belief; and
(b) a written report on the case so far as it has then been investigated.

The *appropriate officer* is an assistant chief constable or an assistant commissioner.

When an investigation has been completed the supervising officer may refer the case to a hearing. Where the chief officer has a duty to proceed (memorandum has been sent to the Independent Police Complaints Commission stating that he intends to bring disciplinary proceedings), or the member has received two written warnings about his conduct within the previous twelve months and has admitted that his conduct failed to meet the required standard (see proceedings under Police (Efficiency) Regulations 1999 below), the supervising officer must refer the case to a hearing.

Where a supervising officer, on receipt of an investigating officer's report, is of the opinion that the case is a *special case* he must refer the case to the appropriate officer. If the appropriate officer does not consider it to be a *special case* he must return it to the supervising officer. If he considers it to be a *special case* he must certify it as such and refer it to a hearing, or if the circumstances make such certification inappropriate, return the case to the supervising officer.

Where a case is not referred to a hearing it must not be referred to in a member's personal record.

A supervising officer may direct withdrawal of a case at any time before a hearing unless the chief officer is under a duty to proceed.

The disciplinary hearing

Arrangements for hearing

Before any of the sanctions set out in reg 35 may be applied, there must be a disciplinary hearing. The supervising officer must inform the member concerned in writing of the decision to refer the case to a hearing as soon as practicable and must supply the member, not less than twenty-one days before the date of the hearing, with details of the time and place of the hearing and with any statement which he may have made to the investigating officer and any relevant statement (if an oral one an account of it), document or other material obtained during the course of the investigation. The conduct which allegedly amounts to a failure to meet the appropriate standard, together with the paragraph of the Code of Conduct in respect of which the appropriate standard is alleged not to have been met, must be specified.

A hearing may take place before the expiry of twenty-one days where a member is given written notice of a decision to refer a case to a hearing and he is at the time detained in prison in consequence of a sentence of a court, or has received a suspended sentence of imprisonment, and that member has not elected to be legally represented at the hearing.

Legal representation

Where a supervising officer is of the opinion that a hearing should have available the sanctions of dismissal, requirement to resign or reduction in rank, he must cause the member to be informed in writing at the time at which he receives notice of the hearing of his right to elect to be legally represented at the hearing and that this may be either by counsel or solicitor. He must also be informed that, alternatively, he may only be represented by a member of a police force.

When the European Court of Human Rights examined a case in which four prisoners were denied legal representation in prison disciplinary proceedings, the Court said that a person charged with a criminal offence who did not wish to defend himself in person must be able to have recourse to legal assistance of his own choosing. The denial of representation for breaches of the prison rules amounted to a breach of ECHR, art 6(3). It therefore appears that there is a case for legal representation at all police disciplinary proceedings.

Notice of hearing—procedure following receipt

A member must be invited to state in writing within fourteen days of receipt of the notice and documents:

(a) whether or not he accepts that his conduct did not meet the appropriate standard;
(b) where representation is allowed by these Regulations, whether he wishes to be legally represented at the hearing;
(c) whether he proposes to call any witnesses to relevant facts at the hearing and the names and addresses of any such witnesses whose attendance he wishes the supervising officer to arrange.

Police officers will be ordered to attend and other witnesses will be informed that their attendance is desired. The Regulations do not require that a hearing be adjourned where a witness is unable or unwilling to attend a hearing.

Where the allegation is accepted the member concerned will be supplied with a prepared summary of the facts of the case at least fourteen days before the hearing. If he does not agree with the facts he may respond within seven days. Where the allegation is not accepted, no summary of the facts shall be prepared.

The hearing itself

The case must be heard by three officers appointed by the chief officer. They must not be interested parties. The presiding officer must be an assistant chief constable or a commander. The other officers must be of at least the rank of superintendent each of whom shall be a member of a police force maintained under PA 1996, s 2. The officers hearing the case are immune from liability in the exercise of their functions.

If the member concerned is a superintendent or chief superintendent, the presiding officer must be assisted by assistant chief constables (or commanders) from a different force or forces than the member concerned.

The officers conducting the hearing will be supplied with a copy of the supervising officer's written notice to the member of his decision to refer the case to a hearing, and any summary of the facts, together with any response made by the member concerned. The case will be presented by a member of a police force appointed by the supervising officer (unless the member concerned has given written notice in an appropriate case that he is to be legally represented). The member concerned may conduct his own case either in person or by a member of a police force selected by him, or where, in an appropriate case, he has given notice of legal representation, by counsel or solicitor.

The officers conducting the hearing determine their own procedure. They must review the facts of the case and decide whether or not the conduct of the member concerned met the appropriate standard and, if it did not, whether in all the circumstances it would be reasonable to impose any, and if so which, sanction. Before there may be a finding that the conduct of a member concerned failed to meet the appropriate standard, the conduct must either be admitted or proved by the person presenting the case on the *balance of probabilities* to have failed to meet that standard. We return to the standard of proof later.

Police officers should give careful consideration to their actions when confronted by a number of suspects. The 'balance' of probability can be influenced by the number of persons who assert that a particular fact is true. Actions taken should be carefully recorded as soon as possible after the event and subsequent events should also be recorded and witnessed where possible.

The member concerned must be ordered to attend the hearing and if he fails to attend the case may proceed in his absence. Where his absence makes it impossible to comply with any of the procedures set out in the regulations, that procedure shall be dispensed with. The case may be adjourned where non-attendance is due to ill health or some other unavoidable reason.

Where the case for hearing is as a result of a complaint, the complainant must be allowed to attend the hearing while witnesses are being examined, or cross-examined, and may, at the discretion of the presiding officer, be accompanied by a friend or relative (spouse, partner, parent or adult child). However, if that complainant is to give evidence, he or his associate may not be present before he gives his evidence. If the member concerned gives evidence, following any cross-examination by the presenting officer, the presiding officer must put to the member any questions posed by the complainant which might have been properly put by the presenting officer. However, the presiding officer has the discretion to allow the complainant to put such questions directly to the member concerned.

The presiding officer is empowered by the Regulations to exclude such a complainant and any person accompanying him if they intervene in or interrupt the hearing, or behave in a disorderly or abusive manner, or otherwise misconduct themselves.

With the exceptions set out above, the hearing must be in private although the presiding officer has the discretion to allow a solicitor or any such other persons as he considers desirable to attend the whole or part of the hearing, subject to the consent of all parties to the hearing. Where the hearing is as a result of a complaint, any member of the Independent Police Complaints Commission is entitled to attend the hearing. This also applies where an investigation has been supervised by the Commission as required by PA 1996, s 72 (conduct resulting in death, serious injury etc). In addition, the member concerned may be accompanied at the hearing by a member of a police force and the presiding officer may allow witnesses to be accompanied by a friend or relative. However, where it appears that a witness may disclose information which it is not in the public interest to disclose, the presiding officer may require any member of the public, including the complainant and any person accompanying him, to withdraw while the evidence is given.

The presiding officer may determine issues of admissibility or the relevance of questions. With the consent of the member concerned, he may admit any document notwithstanding that a copy has not been supplied in advance as required by the Regulations.

The hearing may be adjourned if it appears to the officers conducting the hearing to be necessary or expedient to do so.

The decision of the officers conducting the hearing can be a majority decision. There will be no indication as to whether the decision was taken unanimously or by a majority.

The standard of proof

In 1991 the Police Complaints Authority, in its Triennial Review, voiced concern about the police complaints procedure. One of the concerns was the high standard of proof required to secure the conviction of a police officer for a disciplinary offence. The Authority called for the level of proof required in minor cases to shift from 'beyond reasonable doubt' to 'the balance of probabilities'.

In the event, the Police (Conduct) Regulations 2004, reg 27 provides for proof to be limited to the 'balance of probabilities' for all disciplinary offences including those in respect of which the punishments of dismissal from a police force and the office of constable, requirement to resign, and reduction in rank, may follow a finding of guilt. The 'balance' in favour of finding the charge proved need only exist in the minds of two of the three members of the disciplinary panel.

It is submitted that the validity of this legislation is open to challenge. The Police (Conduct) Regulations 2004 are made under powers conferred by a parent Act of Parliament, PA 1996, ss 50 and 84. The Regulations authorise severe penalties for failure to comply with the requirements. The Regulations create 'criminal' offences using the same procedure as is used in creating many other offences by way of statutory instrument. The seriousness of the offences created by the 2004 Regulations is reflected in the penalties provided. It is submitted that it is a basic human right to have a criminal offence proved beyond reasonable doubt. The European Court of Human Rights has said that in considering whether an offence is 'criminal' the issues to be considered were whether the proceedings are brought by a public authority under legislation which provides punishments, together with the severity of those punishments. In addition, the Court of Appeal has said that allegations of dishonest evasion of VAT which, if proved, would result in 'civil' penalties gave rise to criminal charges for the purposes of the ECHR, art 6. Consequently, a person made liable to a civil penalty under the Value Added Tax Act is entitled to the minimum rights provided for in art 6 of the Convention. The European Court has also ruled that 'fines' imposed by a tax authority for non-compliance with requests for the submission of documents amount to 'criminal proceedings'. The House of Lords has held that in proceedings for a civil anti-social behaviour order the standard of proof must be beyond reasonable doubt because that higher standard of proof should apply to allegations of quasi-criminal conduct which, if proved, would have serious consequences for the person against whom the allegations were made. The argument for the higher standard of proof is strengthened by the decision of the European Court of Human Rights that prison disciplinary procedures are 'criminal offences' for the purposes of art 6 because of the severity of the penalty (in one case an additional seven days of custody). It is submitted that that punishment scarcely compares with dismissal from the police service with its associated financial penalties.

Remission of cases for hearing

Where the presiding officer is an interested party, or it appears to him that the sanctions of dismissal, requirement to resign or reduction in rank, ought to be available and the member concerned has not been given the opportunity to elect to be legally represented and that it would be desirable for there to be another hearing at which the member could be so represented, he must remit the case for hearing by an officer of equivalent rank in the force concerned or to such an officer in another force. Where a case is so remitted notice in writing must be served on the member concerned inviting him to elect, within fourteen days of receipt, to be legally represented at that hearing. The officer to whom such a case is remitted must not be given any indication as to the presiding officer's assessment of the case or the sanction which might be imposed.

The presiding officer may remit any other case if, either before or during the hearing, he considers remission appropriate.

Record of hearing

There must be a verbatim record of the entire proceedings. A transcript of the record or a copy of it must be supplied to a member if he so requests within the time limit for any appeal and an appeal has been lodged.

Procedure following a hearing

The member must be informed orally of the finding and sanction imposed at the conclusion of the hearing and must receive written notification, together with a summary of reasons, within three days.

Review of a hearing

Where a sanction is imposed in consequence of a disciplinary hearing, a member may request in writing, stating the grounds on which the review is requested, within fourteen days of the receipt of the written summary of reasons (unless this period is extended by the reviewing officer), that the chief officer (or assistant commissioner) review the *finding* or *sanction* imposed or both the *finding and sanction*.

The reviewing officer should, if requested to do so, hold a meeting with the member, who may be accompanied by a member of a police force and, where appropriate, by counsel or solicitor. The member must be informed of the finding of the reviewing officer within three days. The reviewing officer may confirm the original decision, or impose a different sanction, but not one which is greater than that originally imposed. If the decision of the reviewing officer is such that the member is dismissed, required to resign or reduced in rank, he must be notified in writing of his right to appeal to a Police Appeals Tribunal.

The role of the reviewing officer may be undertaken by an assistant chief constable (or commander) designated to act on the chief officer's behalf where the chief officer is an interested party, or is suspended, or that post is vacant. Where the designated assistant chief constable is for any reason unavailable, the review will be conducted by the chief officer of another force. Where the Commissioner of the City of London Police is either absent or is an interested party, the review must be conducted by the chief officer of another force or an assistant commissioner of the Metropolitan Police Force.

Record of disciplinary proceedings

A book of record must be kept including details of every case brought against a member of a police force, including the finding and the record of the decision in any further proceedings.

Alternative procedures in special cases

The procedures are modified by reg 45 and Sch 2 to the Police (Conduct) Regulations 2004 where the case is *a special case*, that is one where the report, complaint or allegation indicates serious conduct of a criminal nature, and is supported by written evidence sufficient without further evidence to establish on the balance of probabilities that the officer's conduct did not meet the appropriate standard. In such a case the appropriate officer may direct that the case be returned to the supervising officer at any time before the beginning of the hearing.

The appropriate officer must ensure that, as soon as practicable, the member concerned is invited to an interview with the appropriate officer, at which he must be given written notice of the decision to refer the case to a hearing and be supplied with the relevant documentation. Where a member fails, or is unable, to attend the interview the notice and documentation may be delivered personally or left with some person at, or sent by recorded (signed for) delivery to, the address at which he is, with the approval of the chief constable, residing.

The date of any hearing must not be less than twenty-one nor more than twenty-eight days from the date of any notice. The appropriate officer must ensure that the member concerned is forthwith notified of the time, date and place of the hearing. The member must also be informed of his right to elect to be legally represented at the hearing and of the effect of PA 1996, s 84(1) to (3) (representation at disciplinary and other proceedings).

A special case must be heard by the chief officer concerned. However, where he is an interested party, it must be heard by the chief officer of another force. The officer conducting the hearing may adjourn the proceedings if it appears to him to be necessary or expedient to do so, but shall not do so more than once or for a period of more than one week or, on the application of the member concerned, four weeks.

The complainant must be allowed to attend the hearing and may at the discretion of the presiding officer be accompanied by a friend or relative. Such persons shall neither intervene in nor interrupt the hearing and if they behave in a disorderly or abusive manner, or otherwise misconduct themselves, the officer conducting the hearing may exclude them from the remainder of the hearing. However, the provisions which apply in cases other than special cases, which prohibit a complainant from being present before he gives evidence do not apply, nor do those which allow the presiding officer, in other cases, to put questions to the member on the complainant's behalf, or to allow the complainant to do so directly at the presiding officer's discretion. Regulation 31 (which, in other cases, allows the presiding officer to exclude members of the public if information may be disclosed by a witness which it is not in the public interest to disclose) does not apply to special cases.

In relation to the admission of statements in lieu of oral evidence, reg 32 is modified to recognise that witnesses will not be involved in the proceedings.

The regulation concerning the remission of cases is modified to recognise the different situation existing in a special case. The officer conducting the hearing may return the case to the supervising officer if, either before or during the hearing, the officer conducting the hearing considers it appropriate to do so.

In relation to the receipt of evidence of a member's personal record, the regulation is altered to permit the introduction of documentary evidence only.

The written notice of the finding must be provided within twenty-four hours where the case is a special one. So far as a request for a review is concerned, the regulation is adapted so that the request is for a review by the chief officer of another force. The member must be informed of the finding of any such review within twenty-four hours. In such a case, where the reviewing officer considers that the officer conducting the hearing should have returned the case to the supervising officer, he must so return the case.

The 'Code of Conduct'

Schedule 1 to the Police (Conduct) Regulations 2004 contains the Code of Conduct. The notes to the schedule draw attention to the extraordinary powers granted to the police and the high standards expected from police officers. They state that the Code does not seek to restrict an officer's discretion. It defines the parameters of conduct within which that discretion should be exercised. A breach of the principles in the Code may result in action being taken which, in serious cases, may involve dismissal. The Code applies while on duty, or while off duty if the conduct is serious enough to indicate that an officer is not fit to be a police officer. The notes indicate that the Code will be applied in a reasonable and objective manner.

However, it is important to remember that there is no basic difference between the old 'Discipline Code' and the new 'Code of Conduct'. Under the replaced Discipline Code offences were described as offences. Under the Code of Conduct the offences are set out in such a way that they have the appearance of performance objectives. They are not. They continue to be offences. Regulation 14(2) requires that a notice of hearing shall specify the conduct of the member concerned which, it is alleged, failed to meet the appropriate standard, and the paragraph of the Code of Conduct in respect of which the appropriate standard is alleged not to have been met. Thus, abuse of authority remains an offence but must now be described as failing to meet the appropriate standard by abuse of authority as required by para 4 of the Code of Conduct.

The paragraphs of the Code of Conduct are as follows:

Honesty and integrity

1.   It is of paramount importance that the public has faith in the honesty and integrity of police officers. Officers should therefore be open and truthful in their dealings; avoid being improperly beholden to any person or institution; and discharge their duties with integrity.

Fairness and impartiality

2.   Police officers have a particular responsibility to act with fairness and impartiality in all their dealings with the public and their colleagues.

Politeness and tolerance

3.   Officers should treat members of the public and colleagues with courtesy and respect, avoiding abusive or deriding attitudes or behaviour. In particular, officers must avoid: favouritism of an individual or group; all forms of harassment, victimisation or unreasonable discrimination; and overbearing conduct to a colleague, particularly to one junior in rank or service.

Use of force and abuse of authority

4.   Officers must never knowingly use more force than is reasonable, nor should they abuse their authority.

Performance of duties

5.   Officers should be conscientious and diligent in the performance of their duties. Officers should attend work promptly when rostered for duty. If absent through sickness or injury, they should avoid activities likely to retard their return to duty.

Lawful orders

6.   The police service is a disciplined body. Unless there is good and sufficient cause to do otherwise, officers must obey all lawful orders and abide by the provisions of legislation applicable

to the police. Officers should support their colleagues in the execution of their lawful duties, and oppose any improper behaviour, reporting it where appropriate.

Confidentiality

7. Information which comes into the possession of the police should be treated as confidential. It should not be used for personal benefit and nor should it be divulged to other parties except in the proper course of police duty. Similarly, officers should respect, as confidential, information about force policy and operations unless authorised to disclose it in the course of their duties.

Criminal offences

8. Officers must report any proceedings for a criminal offence taken against them. Conviction of a criminal offence or the administration of a caution may of itself result in further action being taken.

Property

9. Officers must exercise reasonable care to prevent loss or damage to property (excluding their own personal property but including police property).

Sobriety

10. Whilst on duty officers must be sober. Officers should not consume alcohol when on duty unless specifically authorised to do so or it becomes necessary for the proper discharge of police duty.

Appearance

11. Unless on duties which dictate otherwise, officers should always be well turned out, clean and tidy whilst on duty in uniform or plain clothes.

General conduct

12. Whether on or off duty, police officers should not behave in a way which is likely to bring discredit upon the police service.

Disciplinary appeals

PA 1996, s 85 provides that a member of a police force who is dismissed, required to resign or reduced in rank may appeal to a police appeals tribunal against such a decision. This appeal lies only after any other appeal has been exhausted, that is an application for a review by a chief officer. If the reviewing officer decides that the sanction imposed shall remain, this further appeal lies to a tribunal.

PA 1996, Sch 6 deals with appeals to police appeals tribunals.

A police appeals tribunal must consist of four members:

(a) a chairman chosen from a list of persons with a seven-year general qualification within the meaning of the Courts and Legal Services Act 1990 (currently only barristers and solicitors have such a general qualification) who have been nominated by the Lord Chancellor;
(b) a member from the police authority;
(c) a member from a list of persons maintained by the Secretary of State who are (or within the past five years have been) chief officers of police, other than those of the authority concerned; and
(d) a retired police officer of appropriate rank.

Where there is an equality of vote, the casting vote is that of the chairman.

An appeals tribunal may determine an appeal without a hearing but may not do so unless both the appellant and the respondent (chief officer of police concerned) have been afforded an opportunity to make written or, if either so requests, oral, representations and any such representations have been considered. At such a hearing the appellant has a right to be represented by a serving member of a police force or by counsel or solicitor. The respondent has similar rights and may also be represented by the clerk or other officer of the authority. The tribunal may have regard to all matters before it; it is not limited to simply deciding whether the decision appealed from was unreasonable.

Where a police appeals tribunal allows an appeal it may, if it considers it appropriate to do so, make an order dealing with the appellant in a way which appears to the tribunal to be less severe, and in which he could have been dealt with by the person making the original decision.

Any decision by a tribunal is final; there is no further appeal. The Secretary of State has made the Police Appeals Tribunal Rules 1999. Notice of appeal must be given within twenty-one days from the date on which the decision appealed against was notified to the appellant. The time limit is extended to twenty-eight days in certain circumstances if the case is a special case and criminal proceedings are involved. Rule 7 permits extension of the time limits where a police authority is satisfied that there are special circumstances and that it is just to do so.

Double jeopardy

The previous rule that, save where the disciplinary offence was that of being convicted of an offence, a member of a police force who had been convicted or acquitted of a criminal offence would not be liable to be charged with any offence against discipline which, in substance, was the same as the offence in respect of which he had been convicted or acquitted has now been removed. Disciplinary proceedings may now be taken, in any circumstances, following such conviction or acquittal.

THE POLICE (EFFICIENCY) REGULATIONS 1999

These Regulations, as amended, make provision with respect to the efficiency of members of a police force (whether police officers or civilian employees) and establish procedures by which members of a police force may be required to resign or may be reduced in rank. The provisions are additional to those contained in the Police (Conduct) Regulations 2004. They follow concern expressed by both the Government and chief officers that there existed no means by which chief officers could rid themselves of officers whom they considered to be lazy or incompetent. The Regulations were amended in 2003 to include unsatisfactory attendance by members of a police force.

The Regulations do not apply to a probationer constable who has not completed his period of probation.

First interview concerning performance

Circumstances and arrangement

Where the reporting officer (the member of the police force who has the immediate supervisory responsibility for the officer concerned) is a police officer and is of the opinion that the performance or attendance of a member is unsatisfactory he may require the member concerned to attend an interview (first interview) to discuss the member's performance or attendance (or both). Where the reporting officer is a civilian employee he may do likewise if of such opinion, but may only discuss the member's attendance. In addition, where the reporting officer is a civilian employee, any other member of the force who has supervisory responsibility for the member concerned may, if he is of the opinion that the performance of that member is unsatisfactory, require him to attend a first interview to discuss his performance. In such circumstances, references to a reporting officer will be taken to include references to that member with that supervisory responsibility. The reporting officer must send a notice in writing to the member concerned:

(a) requiring him to attend at a specified time and place, an interview with the report-ing officer or, if the member concerned so requests, the countersigning officer (a supervisor who is senior in rank to the reporting officer);
(b) stating the reasons why his performance is considered unsatisfactory;
(c) informing him that he may seek advice from a representative of his staff associa-tion and be accompanied at the interview by a member of a police force selected by him; and

the reporting officer must send a copy of the notice to the countersigning officer.

Not later than seven days after receipt (or such longer period as the reporting officer may permit) the member concerned may request by notice in writing that the inter-view be conducted by the countersigning officer. If he so requests, the interview will be so conducted.

Procedure at interview

The interviewing officer must explain the reasons why the reporting officer is of the opinion that performance or attendance is unsatisfactory and provide the member, or the officer who has accompanied him, or both, with an opportunity to make a response. If, after considering any representations, the interviewing officer is satisfied that performance has been unsatisfactory, he must:

(a) inform the member concerned in what respects his performance or attendance is considered unsatisfactory;
(b) warn the member of any specific action which he is required to take to achieve an improvement in his performance; and
(c) warn the member that, if a sufficient improvement is not made within such reasonable period as the interviewing officer shall specify, he maybe required to attend a second interview.

He may recommend that the member concerned seek assistance in relation to any matter affecting his health or welfare. The interviewing officer is also empowered to adjourn the interview to a specified later time or date if it appears necessary or expedient to do so.

Not later than seven days after the first interview, the reporting officer must:

(a) cause to be prepared a written record of the substance of the matters discussed at the interview; and

(b) send a copy to the member (two if he had been accompanied) together with a written notice informing him that he may submit written comments, or indicate that he has no comments to make, not later than seven days after the date of receipt.

Where the first interview is required in relation to attendance and the member has failed to attend that interview, the interviewing officer must, if he is satisfied that the attendance of the member has been unsatisfactory, not later than seven days after the date on which the first interview was to take place, send written notice (or two where the member representing the officer involved attended the interview) informing the member in what respects his attendance is considered unsatisfactory. The notice must also warn him of any specific action which he is required to take and warn him that, if sufficient improvement is not made within a specified period, he may be required to attend a second interview. A notice must also be sent informing the member concerned that he may submit written comments, or indicate that he has no comments to make, not later than seven days after the date upon which the notice is received by him. If made, such comments must be retained within the record of the interview. On application by the member, the interviewing officer may extend that period.

The interviewing officer must then send a copy of the record and any written comments to:

(a) the senior manager (the supervisory officer of the countersigning officer or, where the member concerned is a superintendent or chief superintendent, his supervising officer);

(b) the personnel officer (a person employed under PA 1996, s 15 which authorises civilian employees) or a member of a police force who, in either case, has responsibility for personnel matters relating to members of the police force concerned; and

(c) (i)   if the interview was conducted by the reporting officer, the countersigning officer; or

   (ii)   if the interview was conducted by the countersigning officer, the reporting officer.

Where a member has been required to attend a first interview in relation to his performance, attendance or both of those categories of behaviour, any second interview must only relate to the category or categories of behaviour that was or were the subject of the first interview.

Second interview concerning performance

Circumstances and arrangement

Where a reporting officer is of the opinion that a member who has been warned concerning his performance or attendance has failed to make sufficient improvement in his performance or attendance within the time specified, he may refer the case to the countersigning officer who may, after consultation with the personnel officer, require the member concerned to attend a second interview to discuss performance, or as the case may be, attendance. If the countersigning officer does require attendance at a second interview:

(a) he must send a notice to the member concerned:
  (i) requiring him to attend, at a specified time and place, an interview with the countersigning officer and the personnel officer;
  (ii) stating the reason why his performance or attendance is considered unsatisfactory and that further action will be considered in light of the interview; and
  (iii) informing him that he may seek advice from a representative of his staff association and be accompanied at the interview by a member of a police force selected by him; and
(b) he must send a copy of the notice to the reporting officer, the senior manager and the personnel officer.

Procedure at second interview

The second interview will be conducted by the countersigning officer and the personnel officer. The countersigning officer must explain the reasons why the reporting officer is of the opinion that the member concerned has failed to make a sufficient improvement in his performance or attendance or, as the case may be, that his performance or attendance is unsatisfactory. He must provide the member, or the member accompanying him, or both, with an opportunity to make representations. If after considering any such representations, he is satisfied that performance has been unsatisfactory during the period under review, he shall:

(a) inform the member concerned in what respects his performance or attendance is considered unsatisfactory;
(b) warn him that he is required to improve his performance or attendance in any such respect;
(c) inform him of any specific action which he is required to take to achieve such improvement; and
(d) warn the member concerned that, if a sufficient improvement is not made within such reasonable period as the countersigning officer shall specify, he may be required to attend an inefficiency hearing at which the officers conducting the hearing will have the power, if appropriate, to require the member to resign from the force or to order reduction in rank.

The countersigning officer may adjourn the interview if it appears necessary or expedient to do so.

Procedure following second interview

The countersigning officer must, not later than seven days after the interview, prepare, in consultation with the personnel officer, a written record of the matters discussed at interview and send a copy (or two copies where the member was accompanied) of that record to the member concerned, together with a notice confirming the terms of any warning given during the interview and informing the member that he may submit written comments, or indicate that he has no such comments, not later than seven days after receipt of the notice. However, this time limit may be extended by the countersigning officer. Any comments received must be retained in records.

Where a member fails to attend a second interview related to attendance, the countersigning officer must, if he is satisfied that the attendance of the member has been unsatisfactory during the specified period, not later than seven days after the date on which the interview was due to take place:

(a) prepare a written notice informing and warning the member of the unsatisfactory nature of his performance or attendance; of the improvement required and action necessary to achieve it; and stating that if sufficient improvement is not made within a specified period, he may be required to attend an inefficiency hearing at which the tribunal will have the power to require resignation or reduction in rank; and

(b) send a copy (two copies if member representing officer attended interview), together with a notice informing the member that he may submit written comments, or indicate that he has no comments to make, not later than seven days after the date on which the copy is received by him.

The countersigning officer must send a copy of the record and any comments by the member, to the reporting officer, the personnel officer and the senior manager.

Any subsequent efficiency hearing must be restricted to matters related to his second performance or attendance interview.

Not later than fourteen days after the end of the specified period for improvement, the countersigning officer and reporting officer must assess performance or attendance during that period and inform the member in writing whether they are of the opinion that there has been a sufficient improvement in performance or attendance. If the counter signing officer is of the opinion that there has been an insufficient improvement, the member must be informed in writing, within that period of fourteen days, that he may be required to attend an inefficiency hearing, to be notified separately, at which his performance will be considered. That hearing must not be sooner than twenty-one days and not later than fifty-six days after receipt of notice. The matter must then be referred to the senior manager who may, if he thinks it appropriate to do so, direct that such a hearing be arranged.

The inefficiency hearing

Arrangements

The personnel officer must send a notice, not less than twenty-one days before the hearing, giving the time and place of the hearing and stating the reasons why performance or attendance is considered to be unsatisfactory. It must also inform the member of his right to be represented at the hearing by counsel or solicitor, or a member of a police force selected by him. It must warn that if the officers conducting the hearing find that performance or attendance during the relevant period has been unsatisfactory they may:

(a) require the member concerned to resign from the force either one month after the date of his receipt of a copy of the decision, or such later date as may be specified;

(b) order reduction in his rank with immediate effect and issue a written warning that unless sufficient improvement in performance is made within a specified period, the member may, following consideration of his performance following the hearing (see below), be required to attend a first interview in respect of that performance; or

(c) issue such a written warning as is mentioned at (b).

Where there is a requirement to resign and the member does not do so, the effect of the decision shall be that the member is dismissed from the time specified.

The member concerned must give seven days' notice to the personnel officer if he wishes to call witnesses, giving their names and addresses.

The hearing

The chairman must be an assistant chief constable (or commander, or in the case of the City of London either an assistant commissioner or commander) and he will be assisted by two assessors. None of them must have been involved with the first or second interviews. Where the member concerned is a superintendent or chief superintendent, the other assessors must be assistant chief constables or commanders. Where the member is below the rank of superintendent, they will be superintendents. The personnel officer must send the chairman a copy of any document available to the interviewing officer at the first interview; any document which was available to the countersigning officer at the second interview; or which have been prepared within the procedure following the second interview. The member concerned must receive copies of all such documents.

The procedure shall be decided by the chairman and the hearing must be in private unless the chairman, with the consent of the member, decides otherwise. The member must be given an opportunity to make representations about any matter contained in the written notice sent to him with the arrangements for the hearing and to call any witnesses in respect of whom notice has been given. A verbatim record of the proceedings must be made and a transcript must be supplied to the member within the time limit for any appeal, notice of which has been lodged under PA 1996, s 85. In the event of non-attendance of the member, the hearing may take place in his absence if the chairman considers it proper to do so. In such a case, it may be assumed that any procedure involving the member has been complied with.

In the case of an inefficiency hearing, other than one in respect of which the member concerned has been sent a notice stating the reasons why his attendance is unsatisfactory, the chairman may postpone or adjourn the hearing if notified by the member that he is unable to attend, or where he is satisfied that there is a good reason for non-attendance. He may also adjourn the hearing if he considers, following representations made by the member, that it is appropriate to allow a further period of assessment of performance or attendance. A date must be fixed for resumption which allows further assessment by the reporting officer and the countersigning officer over a period not exceeding three months. Not later than fourteen days after the conclusion of the additional period of assessment, the reporting officer must prepare a report of the member's performance or attendance during that period and the countersigning officer must send it to the chairman and a copy of it to the member.

At the resumed hearing the chairman must allow the member to make representations and to call witnesses in respect of whom notice has been provided. Should the chairman be absent, incapacitated or suspended and the situation is likely to continue for more than twenty-eight days, the chief officer may arrange a suitable replacement.

The officers conducting the hearing must decide whether the performance or attendance of the member during the period considered following the second interview (or during any further period allowed within the period of adjournment together with the period following the second interview) has been satisfactory or not. It shall be a majority decision and no indication will be given of whether it was taken unanimously or by a majority. The decision may be deferred. Their decision must state the finding and the reasons why performance or attendance was considered to be unsatisfactory and the sanction imposed. A written copy of the decision must be sent to the member, senior manager and personnel officer within three days after the finding. The copy sent to the member must be accompanied by a notice explaining his right to have the decision reviewed.

Where there is a finding of unsatisfactory attendance the officers conducting the hearing may:

(a) require the member to resign;
(b) where it is established that insufficient support has been given during the relevant period in order to assist him to return to work, specify the measures which must be taken to give sufficient support in order to assist his return to work;
(c) issue a written warning that unless sufficient improvement in attendance is made within a specified period, he may be required to attend a second inefficiency hearing at which he may be required to resign;
(d) where it is established that the member's duties contribute directly to his unsatisfactory attendance record, order redeployment to alternative duties (which may involve a reduction in rank).

In the case of findings (b) or (d), a written warning must be issued that unless a sufficient improvement in attendance is made within a specified period, the member may be required to attend a first interview, a second interview, or an inefficiency hearing as specified by the officers conducting the hearing.

Assessment of performance following an inefficiency hearing

The Regulations, as explained above, permit the officers conducting an inefficiency hearing to issue a warning, where their decision has been to reduce the member in rank, or in any other circumstances other than a finding of requirement to resign, that unless sufficient improvement in performance is made within a specified period, he may be required to attend a first interview in respect of that performance. Performance, in such a case, must be assessed and reported upon not later than fourteen days after the conclusion of the appropriate period and a copy must be sent to the member. If performance has been satisfactory, no further action will be taken in respect of performance during that period. Where this is not so, the reporting officer must request the member to attend a first interview.

Where the inefficiency hearing has been considering the attendance of the member, and a written warning has been given that unless sufficient improvement in attendance is made within a specified period he may be required to attend a second inefficiency hearing at which he may be required to resign, not later than fourteen days after the specified period, the countersigning officer must assess attendance and prepare a report, a copy of which must be sent to the member concerned. Where it is concluded that attendance has been satisfactory no further action shall be taken in respect of attendance during that period. Where attendance has been unsatisfactory or insufficient improvement has been made, the countersigning officer may, where the member has already been given a written warning as set out at (c) above, require the member to attend an inefficiency hearing. Where steps under (b) or (d) have been taken, the member must be issued with a written warning that unless a sufficient improvement in attendance is made within a specified period, he may be required to attend a first interview, second interview or an inefficiency hearing as specified by the officers conducting the inefficiency hearing.

Review of a decision by an inefficiency hearing

The member has a right to request a review by the chief officer (or an assistant commissioner) of any finding or sanction (or both) imposed by such a hearing. A request for a review must be made within fourteen days of receipt (but this time may be extended by the reviewing officer) of a notice of the decision; state the grounds and indicate whether a meeting is required. The member may be accompanied at any meeting by a member of a police force and by counsel or a solicitor.

The member must be informed of the finding of the reviewing officer within three days. The reviewing officer may confirm the decision of the hearing or impose a different sanction but not one which is greater than that originally imposed. If the decision involves a requirement to resign, the member must be told in writing of his right of appeal to a Police Appeals Tribunal.

Where the chief officer is an interested party, or is absent, incapacitated or suspended, or during any vacancy in the rank of chief constable, the assistant chief constable designated to act as chief officer (or designated commander or an alternative assistant commissioner) shall act as reviewing officer. Where the Commissioner of the City of London police force is so absent, the review must be conducted by the chief officer of another force or by an assistant commissioner of the metropolitan police force.

If the designated assistant chief constable of a provincial force is also absent the review must be carried out by the chief officer of another force.

Maintenance of records of findings

Under the Police (Efficiency) Regulations 1999

Any sanction imposed under the Police (Efficiency) Regulations 1999, reg 17 is be expunged after two years free from any such sanction.

Under both the Police (Efficiency) Regulations 1999 and the Police (Conduct) Regulations 2004

Regulation 15(5) of the Police Regulations 2003 provides that if, following any review of a sanction imposed under either sets of Regulations, the reviewing officer substitutes a decision of the conduct hearing or inefficiency hearing, with a finding that the member concerned had not failed to meet the appropriate standard, or that the performance of the member concerned was not unsatisfactory, the sanction shall be expunged forthwith from the member's personal record.

RESTRICTIONS UPON PRIVATE LIVES OF MEMBERS OF POLICE FORCES

General

The Police Regulations 2003 impose a number of general restrictions upon the private lives of police officers. Schedule 1 to the Regulations lists the restrictions:

(1) A member of a police force must at all times abstain from any activity which is likely to interfere with the impartial discharge of his duties, or which is likely to give rise to the impression amongst members of the public that it may so interfere. However, the House of Lords has ruled that service as a school governor is not such an activity even though such service involved interviewing applicants for teaching posts, about whom a constable might have confidential information. The regulations specially provide that a member of a police force must not take any active part in politics, nor belong to any organisation specified or described in a determination of the Secretary of State.

(2) A member of a police force must not reside at premises which are not for the time being approved by the chief officer of police.

(3) A member of a police force must not, without the previous consent of the chief officer of police, receive a lodger in a house or quarters with which he is provided by the police authority or sublet any part of the house or quarters.

(4) A member of a police force must not, unless he has previously given notice to the chief officer of police, receive a lodger in a house in which he resides and in respect of which he receives a rent allowance or sublet any part of the house.

(5) A member of a police force must not wilfully refuse or neglect to discharge any lawful debt.

While not representing a 'restriction', the Police Regulations provide that every member of a police force must, on appointment, have a sample of hair or saliva taken. Such a specimen must be kept separate from specimens obtained under the provisions of PACE, s 63 and must be destroyed when the officer leaves the service. In addition, regulations provide the power to test for controlled drugs in respect of applicants to police forces, officers who give cause to suspect that they have used such drugs, probationers, officers whose work involves dealing with drugs and officers in specialist roles. In the case of officers in specialist roles, a power to test for alcohol is also provided. The Secretary of State is given power to set out in a determination the consequences of testing positive in any of these situations.

Incompatible business interest

The Police Regulations 2003 require that a member of a police force must inform the chief officer in writing of any business interests of himself or of a relative included in his family, unless that interest was disclosed on appointment. The chief officer must then decide if that business interest is compatible with the member's duties as a police officer. There is a right of appeal to the police authority against the decision of the chief officer. If an interest is found to be incompatible, the officer's services may be dispensed with after he has been given the opportunity to make representations.

A 'business interest' includes:

(a) any office or employment for hire or gain held by the member of the police force, or any business carried on by him;
(b) a shop kept in the area of the police force by a spouse (not being separated from the member) or a relative living with him; or
(c) a liquor or betting and gaming licence or permit (or certain similar types of licence) held by the member, his spouse (not separated) or a relative living with him, or a pecuniary interest in such a licence.

PROBATIONARY SERVICE

The Police Regulations 2003 provide that a member of a police force appointed in the rank of constable is always on probation for such period as the Secretary of State determines. This applies to all members of a police force appointed in the rank of constable other than a member who transfers to the force from another force, having completed the required period of probation therein. Where, in the opinion of the chief officer of police, the period of probation was seriously interrupted by a period of absence from duty, by reason of injury or illness, probation may be extended for a longer period, not exceeding twelve months, as determined in the particular circumstances. Such an extension may be made after the expiry of the initial probationary period if the probationer constable was on sick leave at the time of expiry. It may also be extended for other reasons. The power to extend a constable's period of probation may be delegated to an assistant chief constable, but a decision to dispense with the services of a probationer constable should only be taken by the chief officer himself.

An officer, who transfers from one force to another and has already successfully completed not less than one year of probationary service in that or any other police force, will thereafter be on probation for one year (unless extended as above). However, the chief officer of police may reduce this period, provided that the total probationary service is not less than two years.

This period of probationary service is used to establish whether or not a person is fitted mentally and physically to perform the duties of a constable. A probationer constable may be discharged at any time if his chief officer considers that he is not so fitted. The word 'mentally' is not used to indicate a level of academic acceptability. The demands of the job can be considerable and the pressures can be too much for those who are not equipped to handle certain situations. The chief officer may also dispense with the services of a probationer if he considers that he is not likely to become an efficient or well conducted police officer.

Where a chief officer is considering dispensing with the services of a probationary constable under these regulations, the probationer constable must be shown any report containing judgements and opinions on him. However, it has been held that where the grounds for dispensing with his services are that in the opinion of medical officers he is too overweight to carry out his duties satisfactorily, there would be no purpose in such action as any further observation could not alter the decision.

The term 'chief officer of police', for the purposes of the regulations relating to probationary service, includes an assistant commissioner of the Metropolitan Police.

DATA PROTECTION

The Data Protection Act 1998 (DPA 1998) is concerned with the regulation of processing of information relating to individuals, including the obtaining, holding, use or disclosure of such information.

Principles

Unless exempted by the provisions of the Act, a 'data controller' is obliged to comply with certain 'data protection principles' in relation to all 'personal data' in relation to which he is data controller. A 'data controller' is a person who (alone or jointly or in common with others) determines the purposes for which and the way in which any personal data are, or are to be, processed. It follows that each chief constable is a data controller.

The 'data protection principles' are:

(1) Personal data must be processed fairly and lawfully and, in particular, must not be processed unless:
   (a) the data subject has given his consent, or the processing is required by law, or is necessary in the interests of the administration of justice, or in certain other cases; and
   (b) in the case of 'sensitive personal data' (eg an individual's racial origin, his political or religious belief, his health or his commission (or alleged commission) of an offence), the data subject has given his explicit consent or the processing is necessary for the data controller to exercise or perform any right or duty imposed by law on the controller in connection with employment, or the processing is necessary in the interests of justice, or in certain other cases.

   This principle does not usually apply to the processing of personal data for the purpose of preventing or detecting crime.

(2) Personal data may be obtained only for one or more specified and lawful purposes, and may not be further processed in any manner incompatible with that purpose or those purposes.

(3) Personal data must be adequate, relevant and not excessive in relation to the purpose or purposes for which they are processed.

(4) Personal data must be accurate and, where necessary, kept up to date.

(5) Personal data processed for any purpose or purposes may not be kept longer than is necessary for that purpose or those purposes.

(6) Personal data must be processed in accordance with the rights of data subjects under DPA 1998.

(7) Appropriate technical and organisational measures must be taken against unauthorised or unlawful processing of personal data and against accidental loss or destruction of, or damage to, personal data.

(8) Personal data must not be transferred to a country or territory outside the European Economic Area unless that country or territory ensures an adequate level of protection for the rights and freedoms of data subjects in relation to the processing of personal data.

'Data' means information which:

(a) is being processed by means of equipment operating automatically in response to instructions given for that purpose;
(b) is recorded with the intention that it should be processed by means of such equipment;
(c) is recorded as part of a relevant filing system or with the intention that it should form part of a relevant filing system; or
(d) does not fall within paragraphs (a), (b) or (c) but forms part of an educational, health or public record of a prescribed type.

'Personal data' means data which relate to a living individual who can be identified:

(a) from those data, or
(b) from those data and other information which is in the possession of, or is likely to come into the possession of, the data controller,

and includes any expression of opinion about the individual and any indication of the intentions of the data controller or any other person in respect of the individual.

Registration

'Data controllers' must register with the Information Commissioner in order for personal data to be processed if the data falls within types (i) or (ii) above, but not (normally) in the case of the other types of data. Thus, the manual files retained within command and control systems do not require registration, but data stored on the Police National Computer do.

By DPA 1998, s 21(1), it is an offence to process personal data unless an entry in respect of that data controller has been registered.

Unlawful obtaining etc of personal data

DPA 1998, s 55(1) provides that a person must not knowingly or recklessly, without the consent of the data controller:

(a) obtain or disclose personal data or the information contained in personal data; or
(b) procure the disclosure to another person of the information contained in personal data.

Breach of s 55(1) is an offence.
DPA 1998, s 55(1) does not apply to a person who shows:

(a) that the obtaining, disclosing or procuring:
   (i) was necessary for the purpose of preventing or detecting crime (as where the data is passed from one police force to another for this purpose); or

(ii) was required or authorised by or under any enactment, by any rule of law or by the order of a court;

(b) that he acted in the reasonable belief that he had in law the right to obtain or disclose the data or information or, as the case may be, to procure the disclosure of the information to the other person;

(c) that he acted in the reasonable belief that he would have had the consent of the data controller if the data controller had known of the obtaining, disclosing or procuring and the circumstances of it; or

(d) that in the particular circumstances the obtaining, disclosing or procuring was justified as being in the public interest.

By DPA 1998, s 55(3), a person who sells personal data is guilty of an offence if he has obtained the data in contravention of s 55(1). Section 55(4) provides that a person who offers to sell personal data commits an offence if he has obtained it in contravention of s 55(1) or if he subsequently does so.

Prohibition of requirement as to production of certain records

DPA 1998, s 56(1) provides that a person must not, in connection with:

(a) the recruitment of another person as an employee;
(b) the continued employment of another person; or
(c) any contract for the provision of services to him by another person, require that other person or a third party to supply him with a relevant record or to produce a relevant record to him.

Likewise, DPA 1998, s 56(2) provides that a person concerned with the provision (for payment or not) of goods, facilities or services to the public or a section of the public must not, as a condition of providing or offering to provide any goods, facilities or services to another person, require that other person or a third party to supply him with a relevant record or to produce a relevant record to him.

Breach of either of these provisions is an offence. A 'relevant record' in these provisions includes any record of a conviction or caution obtained by a data subject from a data controller who is a chief officer of police or the Director General of the Serious Organised Crime Agency.

DPA 1998, s 56(1) and (2) do not apply to a person who shows that:

(a) the imposition of the requirement was required or authorised by or under any enactment, by any rule of law or by the order of a court; or

(b) in the particular circumstances the imposition of the requirement was justified as being in the public interest (which it will not be if the alleged justification is that it would assist in the prevention or detection of crime; in such a case a certificate of criminal record will be available from the Criminal Records Bureau).

DPA 1998, s 56 is the only section in DPA which is still to be brought into force. It is associated with the Police Act 1997, s 112 (not yet in force) (which provides for the issue by the Secretary of State of criminal conviction certificates), and with the Police Act 1997, ss 113A to 113F (inserted by SOCPA 2005) which deal with criminal record certificates, enhanced criminal record certificates relating to the suitability to work in a child care position or as a teacher, or to be a foster parent or special guardian, or a criminal records certificate or enhanced certificate relating to suitability to work in a care position in relation to adults. The Criminal Record Bureau may check passports and driving licences to establish identity and may access information held by the United Kingdom Passport Agency and the Driver and Vehicle Licensing Agency.

CHAPTER 9
Traffic: general provisions

TERMINOLOGY

Throughout the chapters which deal with traffic law, the terms 'mechanically propelled vehicle', 'motor vehicle' and 'road' will appear. These terms will have the meanings set out below, unless specifically defined in another manner within the particular context.

Mechanically propelled vehicle

This may be petrol driven, oil or steam driven or propelled by electricity. Whether or not a vehicle is mechanically propelled is a question of fact. Motor cars which are broken down on a road remain mechanically propelled vehicles. The fact that they may not be driven at that particular time is irrelevant. Before a vehicle can cease to be a mechanically propelled vehicle it must be in such a condition or in such circumstances that there is no reasonable prospect of it ever being driven again. The extent to which a vehicle has been immobilised will be the critical factor when considering whether or not it remains a mechanically propelled vehicle. A motor car in a scrap yard, which has been stripped of all of its mechanical means of propulsion without there being any reasonable prospect of the restoration of motive power, will obviously not be a mechanically propelled vehicle. However, a motor car which is similarly stripped down in a garage for the purpose of effecting repairs remains a mechanically propelled vehicle as there is a reasonable prospect of it being restored to its former mobility.

Motor vehicle

This is defined by the Road Traffic Act 1988 (RTA 1988), s 185 as being a mechanically propelled vehicle intended or adapted for use on a road. The words '*intended or adapted for use on a road*' are important. 'Adapted' does not mean 'altered'; it simply means 'fit and apt'. Some vehicles are quite obviously 'mechanically propelled' but they are not 'intended or adapted for use on a road'. Whether or not a mechanically propelled vehicle is intended or adapted for use on a road will depend upon the evidence as to its construction and appearance. The test is whether a reasonable person looking at the vehicle would say that one of the vehicle's uses is general use on a road. On this basis, for example, it has been held that a motorised scooter known as a 'Go-ped' was a motor vehicle within s 185. The Go-ped consisted of a small foot platform attached to a two-barred sub-frame on which the person using the Go-ped would stand. The vehicle was powered by a 22.5 cc engine which was attached to the rear. It was capable of a maximum speed of 20 mph. The braking system was such that it could not stop the vehicle if it was travelling at any great speed, or when the brakes were applied in an emergency situation. Severe braking caused the rear wheel to lift from the road surface. A divisional court said that the roadworthiness of a conveyance or its capability to be used safely on a road were not conclusive in relation to whether or not its use on a road was contemplated. There was no obvious place in which a Go-ped could be used, other than on a road. It could not travel on rough ground, soft or uneven surfaces. It was not designed for use in a place other than a road, such as was the case with a dumper truck, which was specifically constructed for use in connection with road construction. Regardless of the fact that the manufacturers said that it was not to be used on a road it would be and the reasonable person would recognise that to be so. The Scottish High Court of Justiciary has held that the 'mini-moto' (vehicle with a petrol engine, motor cycle tyres, exhaust system, normal handlebars and brakes similar to those found on a mountain bicycle) is a motor vehicle for the purposes of the RTA 1988. It found that the vehicle was mechanically propelled, a person had been riding it and it was capable of carrying an adult rider. The 'comfort' of the driver was not a factor for consideration.

The above test does not depend on the owner's or manufacturer's intention nor, unless there is evidence of regular use on a road, on the particular use to which it is put at the time. In one case, a dumper truck, which was used on a site for the transport of material around that site and was occasionally driven on adjoining roads for short distances, was held not to be a motor vehicle because there was no proof of general (as opposed to occasional) use on roads. On the other hand, in another case, a Euclid earth scraper, which was primarily used to dig up earth on a building site and carry that earth under its own power to other places, was held to be intended for use on a road when evidence of its general use on roads and of its capability of reaching a speed of 45 mph was given. Evidence was also offered to prove that the earth scraper was too large to be transportable and generally travelled from site to site by road.

RTA 1988, s 189 expressly provides that 'electrically assisted pedal cycles' are not motor vehicles nor are mechanically propelled invalid carriages of a prescribed type.

A mechanically propelled vehicle originally manufactured for use on a road may cease to be a 'motor vehicle' for the purposes of RTA 1988, s 185 if it is subsequently altered, but only if such alterations are very substantial.

Road

This is defined by RTA 1988, s 192 as meaning any highway and any other road to which the public has access and including bridges over which a road passes. The same definition is provided in relation to the Road Traffic Act 1960.

A highway allows members of the public a right of way on foot, riding, accompanied by a beast of burden or with vehicles and cattle. The term is therefore wide enough to embrace public footpaths, public bridleways and public carriageways, which we define below. It is reasonable to assume that the highway is the area of right of way as defined by its fences. Consequently, grass verges are generally a part of the highway, but this depends upon who erected the fences. If it was the highway authority, the fences will clearly mark the limits of the highway. If the fences were erected by an adjoining landowner, this will not necessarily be so.

Apart from a highway, 'road' in the road traffic legislation means any road to which the public has access. A road is a definable way for passage between two points and the essential factor is whether or not, as a question of fact, the public have access to it. A private road leading to a farmhouse, which was maintained by the farmer, has been held to be a 'road' on evidence being offered that there was no gate and that it was regularly used by persons who had no business at the farm. It is necessary to prove two things if it is alleged that a road is public for the purpose of the road traffic legislation. The first is to prove that it is a road (as described above) and the second that it is used by the public. It has been decided that any road may be regarded as a road to which the public have access, if members of the public are to be found on it who have not obtained access either by overcoming a physical obstruction or in defiance of a prohibition, express or implied. A pavement which is partly publicly owned and partly privately owned is a road if the public have access to the whole of it. It is essential to show that the public in general have access. Access which is restricted to certain classes of persons is not usually sufficient to make a road 'public'.

Save in exceptional circumstances, a car park is not a 'road', although it may be a 'public place' (a term used in other contexts in road traffic legislation), whose meaning is dealt with on p 590.

REGISTRATION

For a variety of reasons, all vehicles used or kept on roads in the United Kingdom must be registered with the Secretary of State. A 'vehicle' for this purpose is a mechanically propelled vehicle, or anything (whether or not a vehicle) that has been, but has ceased to be, a mechanically propelled vehicle (see p 334). All records relating to vehicles are retained by the Driver and Vehicle Licensing Agency (DVLA) at Swansea (or Coleraine, in the case of Northern Ireland). One of the purposes of central registration is to ensure the payment of vehicle excise duty; another is separately to identify all vehicles used or kept on roads by allocating to each a registration mark which is different from any mark assigned to any other vehicle. The Road Safety Act 2006 (RSA 2006), s 49 provides statutory authority for the Secretary of State to disclose information held by him under the Vehicle Excise and Registration Act 1994 (VERA 1994) (registration of vehicles) to the authorities of a country or territory outside the United Kingdom in respect of registration particulars.

The Road Vehicles (Registration and Licensing) Regulations 2002 provide a single set of Regulations for the whole of the United Kingdom.

VERA 1994, s 21 provides that it is the duty of the Secretary of State to register a vehicle on the first issue by him of a vehicle licence or a nil licence (ie a licence for a vehicle exempt from excise duty), or where particulars in respect of the vehicle are received by the Secretary of State from a motor dealer, before the first licence is issued.

The registration mark assigned to a vehicle must be fitted in the prescribed manner. Since it is the responsibility of the Secretary of State to register vehicles, the use of an unregistered vehicle on a road simply constitutes the offence of use without a vehicle excise licence. If it has been registered, but registration plates have not been fixed on it, an offence is committed by the driver or, if the vehicle is not being driven, by the person keeping the vehicle.

In addition to the assignment of a registration number on initial registration, the Secretary of State has power to assign new registration numbers to a vehicle in place of its existing ones. He also has power to assign to a vehicle (whether on first registration or not) registration numbers previously assigned to another vehicle. It is these powers which give effect to the practice of trading in personalised number plates. The Secretary of State may also grant to a person the right to retain a registration number by transferring it from one vehicle registered in that person's name to another such vehicle. This is of particular relevance where someone wishes to transfer a number to a new car from one which he is disposing of.

VERA 1994, s 22 authorises the Secretary of State to make regulations concerning the registration of vehicles. Regulation 10 of the Road Vehicles (Registration and Licensing) Regulations 2002 authorises the Secretary of State to register a vehicle in either the Great Britain or Northern Ireland records as he considers appropriate and to issue a registration document. He may require the keeper of a vehicle to produce it for inspection or to produce other evidence that the vehicle accords with the particulars furnished with the application. If he is not satisfied that the vehicle accords with the particulars, he may refuse to issue a registration document or replacement registration document. Regulation 11 provides that where a keeper of a vehicle requests that a particular registration mark is assigned to it, that mark having been previously assigned to another vehicle, that other vehicle shall be made available for inspection by the Secretary of State.

VEHICLES: REGISTRATION MARKS AND DOCUMENTS

Registration document

When the Secretary of State registers a vehicle he issues a registration document and, unless a registration mark has already been assigned by a motor dealer who has received a 'block' of numbers, assigns a registration mark to that vehicle. Even if a vehicle is exempt from the requirement to be licensed, it must still be registered. A registration document contains the registered particulars of the vehicle and the name and address of the person shown in the register as the owner or keeper of the vehicle. With effect from 31 January 2004 the Secretary of State must issue a registration document which complies with Community Directive 1999/37/EC in relation to dimensions, composition and the information to be contained in it. Registration documents which do not comply with the Directive will cease to have effect in the event of replacement and, in any case, on 1 July 2005. Registration documents issued by member states of the EU or Gibraltar must be recognised as such if they comply with the Directive. The Secretary of State must retain such former registration documents for not less than six months and notify the appropriate member state or Gibraltar in which the vehicle was previously registered. The Secretary of State is empowered to take action to satisfy himself as to the identity and address of an applicant for vehicle registration. The Secretary of State may issue a registration document in a microprocessor smart card format and he may issue that type of registration document without charging a fee where the old type of document is surrendered.

The registered owner of a vehicle is not necessarily its legal owner, and possession of a registration document is not in itself proof of ownership.

Regulation 13 of the Road Vehicles (Registration and Licensing) Regulations 2002 provides that where a registration document has been, or may have been, lost, stolen, destroyed, or damaged, or it contains any particulars that have become illegible, the registered keeper must apply for a replacement. In the case of damage or illegibility, the document must accompany the application. In any other case an oral application by telephone may be accepted. Provided that he is satisfied as to the circumstances, the Secretary of State must issue a replacement document. Before doing so, he may require the keeper of the vehicle to produce the vehicle, or evidence that it accords with its currently registered particulars.

Regulation 15(3) of, and Sch 3 to, the 2002 Regulations provide for the issue of a new registration document in certain circumstances where the vehicle concerned is one with regard to which an insurer has informed the Secretary of State that it has 'written off' the vehicle and destroyed the registration document, or the registration document has been surrendered under reg 20(5); the schedule requires the production and examination of the vehicle in order to ascertain that it is the vehicle concerned.

By reg 12, a police officer can require the *keeper* to produce a registration document and he must produce it for inspection if he is at any reasonable time required to do so. There are no provisions for later production as there are in the case of licences or insurance certificates.

VERA 1994, s 28A requires a person *using* a vehicle in respect of which a registration document has been issued to produce it for inspection by a constable or a person authorised by the Secretary of State (who must produce his authority). Failure to do so is an offence. However, no offence is committed if the document is produced personally at a police station specified by that person within seven days or as soon as is reasonably practicable. Nor is an offence committed if a vehicle is on lease or hire, and the vehicle is not registered (nor required to be registered) in the name of the lessee or hirer, and the person personally produces appropriate evidence of the lease or hire agreement in the same way as just described. That person, however, must reasonably believe (or it must be reasonable for him to expect) that the lessor etc is able to produce, or require production, of the registration document.

The Road Traffic (Vehicle Testing) Act 1999 provides a statutory basis for the establishment of a central computer database of motor vehicles and while this will be concerned with vehicle testing procedures at the outset, it is intended that the Act will provide, in due course, the option of a paperless form of vehicle relicensing.

Regulation 2 of the Motor Vehicles (Access to Driver Licensing Records) Regulations 2001 provides that the purposes for which constables may be given access to information made available to the Police Information Technology Organisation are:

(a) the prevention, investigation or prosecution of a contravention of any provision of the following enactments:
    (i)   the RTA 1988;
    (ii) the Road Traffic Offenders Act 1988;

   (iii) the Road Traffic (Northern Ireland) Orders 1981 and 1995;
   (iv) the Road Traffic Offenders (Northern Ireland) Order 1996;
(b) ascertaining whether a person has had an order made in relation to him under:
   (i)   the Child Support Act 1991, s 40B(1) or (5) (disqualifications from driving: further provisions);
   (ii)   the Criminal Procedure (Scotland) Act 1995, s 248A(1) (general power to disqualify offenders) or s 248B(2) (power to disqualify fine defaulters); or
   (iii) the Crime (Sentences) Act 1997, s 39(1) (offenders) or s 40(2) (fine defaulters).

In relation to further disclosure, reg 3 provides that information to which constables have been given access may be further disclosed to an employee of a police authority for any purpose ancillary to, or connected with, the use of the information by constables.

In addition, reg 27 of the Road Vehicles (Registration and Licensing) Regulations 2002 authorises the Secretary of State to make available particulars contained in the register to a local authority investigating a criminal offence or a decriminalised parking offence; a chief officer of police; or any person who can show satisfactory cause for requiring the information. Regulation 28 authorises the Secretary of State to sell such particulars to such persons as he considers fit, for a fee and within conditions which he considers appropriate, provided that the information does not identify any person or contain anything enabling such identification.

Notification of change of ownership

Regulation 22 of the Road Vehicles (Registration and Licensing) Regulations 2002 is concerned with changes of ownership affecting vehicles. Where there is a 'private' sale or transfer of a vehicle, that is to a person other than a motor vehicle trader, the registered keeper must give to the new keeper the part of the registration document which provides for particulars of a new keeper, and must forthwith send to the Secretary of State the remainder of the registration document giving:

(a) the name and address of the new keeper;
(b) the date of transfer;
(c) a signed declaration that this information is correct to the best of his knowledge; and
(d) a signed declaration made by the new keeper to the effect that this information is correct.

Where all parts of the registration document have been, or may have been, lost, stolen or destroyed, the new keeper must submit an application for a new registration document and send a fee of £19. If the new keeper can produce that part of the registration document which is to be given to the new keeper, no fee need be sent.

By reg 23, where the new keeper is a vehicle trader, the registered keeper must notify the Secretary of State, on the part of the registration document which relates to the transfer to a vehicle trader of the name and address of the vehicle trader and of the date on which the transfer took place, and he must send declarations from both himself and the vehicle trader to the effect that the transfer occurred on a specified date.

In addition, reg 24 deals with the duties of a vehicle trader. The trader must, on or before the 'appropriate date', notify the Secretary of State of the date of his acquisition of the vehicle. The 'appropriate date' is the earliest of the day of first use or keeping of the vehicle on a public road otherwise than under a trade licence, or the day following the expiration of a period of three months.

Where Regulation 13 provides that where the registration document has been, or may have been, lost, stolen or destroyed, notification must be by way of application for a new registration document and must be accompanied by a fee of £19. However, if the new keeper can produce the part of the document marked as the part which is given to the new keeper, no fee is payable.

If there is a transfer to another vehicle trader within the period of three months, the registration document must be transferred with the vehicle.

Where a vehicle trader transfers the vehicle to a person other than another vehicle trader or transfers the vehicle to another trader outside that period, he must, on the appropriate part of the registration document inform the Secretary of State of:

(a) the name and address of the new keeper;
(b) the date of transfer;
(c) a signed declaration to the effect that he transferred the vehicle to the new keeper on the date specified; and
(d) a signed declaration from the new keeper that the vehicle was transferred to him on the date specified.

Failure to notify the Secretary of State is not a continuing offence and therefore the time limitation upon proceedings runs from the day of the transfer of the vehicle. If, therefore, a period of six months has passed since the transfer of a vehicle no proceedings may be taken against either of the parties to the transaction if they have failed to comply with the requirement to notify the Secretary of State forthwith.

Notification of other changes

An owner of a registered vehicle who changes his name or address is required by reg 18 of the Road Vehicles (Registration and Licensing) Regulations 2002 forthwith to notify the Secretary of State and deliver the registration document to him. Where the registration document has been, or may have been, lost, stolen or destroyed, notification must be accompanied by a fee of £19.

In the event of a vehicle being sent permanently out of Great Britain or Northern Ireland, reg 17 requires notification of that fact and the surrender of the registration document. Regulation 17A requires that where an 'end-of-life' vehicle is transferred to an authorised treatment facility (facility operating under a waste disposal site licence) the facility must, in addition to issuing a 'certificate of destruction' to the last holder/owner of the vehicle, inform the Secretary of State of the issue of that certificate. No further records may then be made which are related to that vehicle.

Regulation 16 of the Road Vehicles (Registration and Licensing) Regulations 2002 is concerned with procedures which must be followed when there has been any alteration to a vehicle which renders the particulars in the registration document incorrect. Such alterations must be notified to the Secretary of State in writing by the owner and the registration document surrendered for amendment. Once again, if the registration document is not available, an application must be made for a new registration document and be accompanied by a fee of £19. This would apply, for example, if a motor car was resprayed or fitted with a new engine, since the details of colour and engine numbers are contained in the document. Should the alteration necessitate changes to the vehicle excise licence, it must also be surrendered by the owner for amendment.

Offences in respect of incorrectly registered vehicles

VERA 1994, s 43C, provides that it is an offence to use a vehicle on a public road or in a public place if excise duty is chargeable in respect of it, or it is an exempt vehicle which requires a 'Nil' licence, where the name and address of its keeper are not recorded in the register, or any particulars recorded in the register are incorrect. The offence is a fixed penalty offence.

It is a defence for the accused to show (as the case may be):

(a) that there was no reasonable opportunity, before the material time, to furnish the name and address of the keeper of the vehicle, or
(b) that there was no reasonable opportunity, before the material time, to furnish particulars correcting the incorrect particulars.

It is also a defence for the accused to show:

(a) that he had reasonable grounds for believing, or that it was reasonable for him to expect, that the name and address of the keeper or the other particulars of registration (as the case may be) were correctly recorded in the register, or
(b) that any exception prescribed in regulations is met. No such exception has been prescribed at the time of writing.

These details can be required of a vehicle keeper in addition to a purchaser or seller of a vehicle. The odometer reading of vehicles will be required.

The offence under s 43C was added to VERA 1994 by the Serious Organised Crime and Police Act, 2005 (SOCPA 2005) and has the effect of extending responsibility for ensuring that correct details are recorded in the register to those who use vehicles, subject to the defences provided.

Regulation of motor salvage operators

The Vehicles (Crime) Act 2001 (V(C)A 2001) was passed to tackle the problem caused where vehicles are stolen, and then either broken up for their parts or 'ringed' (ie the true identity of the car is swapped for a written-off car). Part I deals with motor salvage operators. It requires that all persons who carry on a business as 'motor salvage operators' must be registered with the local authority. The term 'motor salvage operator' covers those who carry on a business consisting:

(a) wholly *or partly* in the re-use or sale of salvageable parts from vehicles and the subsequent sale and other disposal for scrap of the remainder of the vehicle concerned (which definition covers scrap metal dealers);
(b) wholly *or mainly* in the purchase of written-off vehicles and their subsequent repair and resale;

(c) wholly *or mainly* in the sale or purchase of motor vehicles which are to be subject (whether immediately or on a subsequent re-sale) to any of the activities at (a) or (b); or

(d) wholly *or mainly* in activities falling within (b) and (c).

It will be noted that the Vehicles (Crime) Act 2001 refers to *motor vehicles* to which the Act gives a special definition. In the present context a 'motor vehicle' is one whose function is or was to be used on a road as a vehicle.

A local authority may refuse to register a person whom it considers to be unfit to carry on such a business. An appeal lies to a magistrates' court against such a decision. The V(C)A 2001 creates offences of failure to register, failure to keep appropriate records, and failure to notify the Secretary of State of the destruction of a motor vehicle. A person commits an offence if he makes a false statement in an application for registration, or if he fails to give notice of any change in the registered information. V(C)A 2001, s 12 makes it an offence for any person to give a false name or address to a motor salvage operator when selling a vehicle to him.

V(C)A 2001, s 9 provides a constable with a power of entry at any reasonable time into registered premises which are occupied as a 'motor salvage yard' by a person carrying on a business as a motor salvage operator or are occupied by him in relation to that business. At any reasonable time a constable may require the production of, and inspect, motor vehicles, salvageable parts, records, and may take copies or extracts of entries. Provision is also made for the issue of a warrant authorising entry and inspection. Force may not be used in respect of general entry, but it may be used in association with the execution of a warrant. When effecting entry without a warrant, a constable must, if required by or on behalf of the owner or occupier or person in charge of the premises, produce evidence of identity, and of his authority for entering, before doing so.

Regulations are to be made under V(C)A 2001, s 8 requiring registered motor salvage operators to notify the Secretary of State of the destruction of motor vehicles. These have not been made at the time of writing. The Motor Salvage Operators Regulations 2002 require motor salvage operators to keep records of such vehicles passing through their hands. The records must contain a range of specified information about a vehicle: registration number; vehicle identification number; make; model; colour; identity of supplier or receiver of the vehicle; details of proof of his identity and the condition of the vehicle; and the date on which the information was entered. It is an offence to fail to record any of this information, except information relating to proof of identity or the vehicle's condition.

Registration marks

Generally

The Vehicle Excise and Registration Act 1994, s 42 makes it an offence to drive a motor vehicle or (when it is not being driven) to be its keeper when a registration mark is not fixed to the vehicle as required by VERA 1994, s 23. An accused has a defence if he proves that he had no reasonable opportunity to register the vehicle and that it was being driven for the purpose of being registered.

The Road Vehicles (Display of Registration Marks) Regulations 2001 deal with the forms of registration marks and the manner in which they are fixed to vehicles.

Regulation 10 of, and Sch 2 to, the 2001 Regulations introduce a mandatory requirement for the use of registration plates made of retro-reflecting material conforming to British Standard specification BS AU 145a or an equivalent standard laid down by a European Economic Area (EEA) state on all vehicles first registered on or after 1 September 2001, and on all vehicles registered before that date but on or after 1 January 1973 if an existing plate is replaced. Regulation 10 and Sch 2 also set out the requirements for vehicles registered on or after 1 January 1973 and before 1 September 2001 in other circumstances (reflex-reflecting plates conforming to British Standard specification BS AU 145a or an equivalent standard laid down by an EEA state) but such vehicles *may* carry the forms of plates prescribed for vehicles first registered on or after 1 September 2001. In either case they must have black characters on a white background on a front plate; and black characters on a yellow background on a rear plate.

Schedule 2 also deals with vehicles registered before 1 January 1973. It provides optional specifications by requiring that where the plate is such that it may be illuminated from behind by virtue of the translucency of its characters they must be white translucent characters on a black background, and when illuminated the characters must appear white against a black background. Otherwise, plates must comply with BS AU 145 carrying black characters on a white background at the front and black characters on a yellow background at the rear; alternatively, they must be white, silver or light grey letters and numbers on a black surface which are indelibly inscribed on the plate and cannot readily be detached.

Permitted layouts

Regulation 13 of, and Sch 3 to, the 2001 Regulations govern this. Registration marks in any non-permitted format will be unlawful. The new marks may be, for example, a group consisting of two letters and two numbers followed by a group of three letters (eg DE51 ABC); a group consisting of a single letter and not more than three numbers followed by a group of three letters (eg A123 ABC); a group of three letters followed by a group consisting of not more than three numbers and a single letter (eg ABC 123A); a group of four numbers followed by a single letter or a group of two letters (eg 1234 A, 1234 AB); a group of not more than three numbers followed by a group of not more than three letters (eg 123 ABC, 123 AB, 12A); a group of not more than three letters followed by a group of not more than three numbers (eg ABC 123, AB 123, A12); a single letter or group of two letters followed by a group of four numbers (eg A 1234, AB 1234); and in Northern Ireland, a group of three letters followed by a group of four numbers (ABZ 1234) or a group of four numbers followed by a group of three letters (eg 1234 ABZ).

It is not necessary that these letters and numbers all follow one another. The plates may be square permitting the letters and characters to be placed in two or three rows as illustrated in the Schedule, except that plates containing three rows of characters are not permitted on vehicles first registered on or after 1 September 2001 or a replacement plate fixed to a vehicle first registered before then but on or after 1 January 1973. Plates containing all of the letters and numbers in a straight line are not permitted on motor cycles.

Character sizes and fonts

Regulation 14 of and Sch 3 to the 2001 Regulations makes provision in respect of character and size. They provide that the registration marks of vehicles first registered on or after 1 September 2001 or before 1 January 1973 must be 79 mm high. In respect of vehicles first registered on or after 1 January 1973 but before 1 September 2001 the registration marks may be 79 mm high instead of 89 mm, except where a plate is replaced after 1 September 2001. By way of exception to the above rules the required height is 64 mm in relation to a motor cycle, motor tricycle, quadricycle, agricultural machine, works truck or road roller. The width of characters, spacing and margins are all precisely prescribed by Table B in Sch 3.

Regulation 14A applies to a vehicle imported into the United Kingdom which does not have European Community Whole Vehicle Type Approval and is so constructed that the area available for the fixing of the registration plate precludes the display on the plate of a registration mark in conformity with the requirements of reg 14. In such a case the prescribed height of characters is 64 mm; the width (except for the letter 'I' or figure '1') must be 44 mm; the width of every part of a stroke and the spacing of characters within a group must be 10 mm, the vertical spacing between groups of characters and the width of a margin between the mark and the top and lateral sides of the registration plate must not be less than 5 mm; and the space between the bottom of the mark and the bottom of the registration plate must not be less than 13 mm.

Regulation 12(2) of the 2001 Regulations permits deviation from the prescribed height of characters provided that the deviation is not more than 1 mm either way. In the case of other dimensions, including spaces, the permitted deviation is 0.5 mm either way.

Regulation 15 and Sch 4 to the 2001 Regulations deal with the font of characters displayed on a registration plate fixed to a vehicle first registered on or after 1 September 2001, or on a new registration plate fixed to any other vehicle (except where the vehicle was first registered before 1 January 1973). They require that each of the characters must be in the prescribed font. In relation to other cases, characters must be in the prescribed font or in a style which is substantially similar to the prescribed font so that the character is easily distinguishable but, in the latter case, characters must not be formed in italic script (or other script which is not vertical), or in script in which the curvature or alignment of the lines of the strokes is substantially different from the prescribed font, or in script using multiple or a broken stroke or in such a way that a character, or characters, appear like a different character or characters. A character will not be treated as substantially different solely on the grounds that it has, or does not have, serifs (small lines at the extremity of a main stroke).

Fixing of rear registration plates: post-1938 vehicles

Regulation 5 of the 2001 Regulations (which applies to all vehicles first registered on or after 1 October 1938 other than works trucks, road rollers and agricultural machines) requires a rear registration plate to be fixed on the rear of the vehicle or (where it is towing a trailer) to the rear of the trailer or the rearmost trailer. However, where a vehicle or trailer has been constructed for rear plates to be fixed in accordance with relevant

EC type approval directives the plate may be fixed in the space provided in accordance with the directives. Regulation 9 requires a vehicle or trailer of the present type to be lit in accordance with the regulation when used on a road between sunset and sunrise.

Unless fitted in a space provided in accordance with an EC type approval directive, a rear registration plate must be fitted vertically (or, if that is not reasonably practicable, as close to vertical as is reasonably practicable) in such a position that the characters are easily distinguishable from a distance of 22 m (where the characters are of a width of 57 mm); 21.5 m (where the characters are of a width of 50 mm); and 18 m (where the characters are of a width of 44 mm). Regulation 9 provides that, except where a plate is fitted and lit in accordance with EC type approval requirements, the plate should be lit so that it is easily distinguishable from a distance of 18 m, but 15 m is substituted where the characters are of a width of only 44 mm.

Fixing of front registration plates: post-1938 vehicles

Regulation 6 of the 2001 Regulations deals with registration plates on a vehicle first registered on or after 1 October 1938, with the same exceptions as above in relation to rear plates. It requires that a front registration plate must be fixed vertically (or if that is not reasonably practicable, as close to vertical as is reasonably practicable) so that its characters are easily distinguishable from the rest of the plate in normal daylight. Regulation 6 requires that, in the case of motor cycles or motor tricycles which do not have a body of a type which is characteristic of the body of a four-wheeled vehicle, there must not be a front registration plate if the vehicle was first registered on or after 1 September 2001. A front registration plate need not be fitted if such a vehicle was registered before that date.

Pre-1938 vehicles, works trucks, road rollers and agricultural machines

Regulation 7 of the 2001 Regulations deals with registration plates fitted to the front of vehicles registered before 1 October 1938 and to their rear (and the rear of any trailer or rearmost trailer). It requires vertically fitted plates which are easily distinguishable.

There are similar provisions in respect of reasonable practicability and distinguishability of the characters on the front plate as under reg 6. Likewise, there is no need for a front plate to be fitted to a motor bicycle or motor tricycle. The lighting requirements of reg 9 apply to the rear plates of these vehicles.

Regulation 8 is concerned with works trucks, road rollers and agricultural machines. Registration plates must be fitted vertically on both sides of the vehicle, and on its rear. When the vehicle is towing a trailer and the plate is not fixed to the sides of the vehicle, a plate must be fixed on the trailer (or rearmost trailer) so that the characters of the mark are easily distinguishable from behind the trailer. In the case of a towing machine which is an agricultural machine (tractor, off-road tractor, light agricultural vehicle, agricultural engine or mowing machine) the plate displayed on the trailer may be that of any agricultural machine kept by the keeper of the towing vehicle. The lighting requirements of reg 9 do not apply to these vehicles.

Use of reflex-reflecting material and other impediments to true photographs

Regulation 11 of the 2001 Regulations prohibits the application of reflex-reflecting material to any part of the registration plate or the treatment of the plate in such a way as to cause the registration mark to become retroreflective. In addition, it requires that the surface of a registration plate must not comprise nor incorporate any design, pattern or texture, or be treated in any way which gives to any part of the plate the appearance of a design, pattern or texture. It also prohibits any treatment of a registration plate which has the effect of making it less distinguishable or would prevent or impair the making of a true photograph. The use of a screw or bolt or other fixing device in a manner which has the effect of changing the appearance or legibility of any characters of a registration mark, or would impair the making of a true photograph, is also prohibited.

GB plates and exemptions

Regulation 16 of the 2001 Regulations provides that no material other than a registration mark may be displayed on a registration plate, other than the display of the international distinguishing sign of the United Kingdom, adjacent to the registration mark in accordance with Council Regulation 2411/98.

Regulations 3 and 18 preserve the exemption of small purpose-built invalid carriages and pedestrian-controlled vehicles from the requirement to carry registration marks. The use of old style number plates on 'classic' vehicles is also preserved.

Breach of the Regulations: offences

The Vehicle Excise and Registration Act 1994, s 59 provides that a contravention of, or a failure to comply with, the above Regulations is an offence. An offence under s 59 is a fixed penalty offence if it relates to a failure to fix prescribed registration marks to a vehicle in accordance with the regulations relating to the size, shape and character of registration marks.

Registration plates

Regulation of suppliers of registration plates

Part 2 of the Vehicles (Crime) Act 2001 is concerned with the regulation of suppliers of registration plates.

By V(C)A 2001, s 17 a person commits an offence if he carries on business as a registration plate supplier without being registered with the Secretary of State. A person carries on a business as a registration plate supplier if his business consists wholly or partly in selling registration plates and he is not exempt (as provided by regulations) from the provisions of the Act. The Vehicles Crime (Registration of Registration Plate Suppliers) (England and Wales) Regulations 2002, reg 3 exempts a dealer in vehicles who has arranged a first registration in the United Kingdom on behalf of the intended purchaser or keeper, or where the registration plate was not fixed to the vehicle by the dealer or on his behalf.

Under V(C)A 2001, s 18, on payment of any prescribed fee, the Secretary of State must supply information from the register of registration plate suppliers on request by any person (subject to exceptions provided by regulations). Where a request is so made, and subject to any prescribed exception and fee, the Secretary of State must supply the information in the form of a certified copy of the register or of an extract from it. Any such certified copy is evidence of the matters mentioned in it. The Secretary of State may make all the information contained in the register, or prescribed parts of it, available to the Police Information Technology Organisation for use by constables or persons employed by a police authority under the Police Act 1996, s 15 (civilian employees) in the investigation of offences against Part 2. Regulations limit the further disclosure by constables of information to which they have been given access.

V(C)A 2001, s 19(3) provides that a person who, in making an application for registration, makes a statement which he knows to be false in a material particular, or recklessly makes a statement which is false in a material particular, commits an offence. On conviction for such an offence, a court may make an order under s 20 providing for the removal of the entry relating to him in the register, and/or prohibiting him from making an application for registration within a period not exceeding five years specified by the court.

Under V(C)A 2001, s 21, the Secretary of State may cancel a person's registration if he is satisfied that a person is not carrying on the business of a registration plate dealer and has not, while registered, been doing so for the past twenty-eight days, but may not do so without serving notice under s 22 and allowing time for representations. An appeal lies to a magistrates' court within twenty-one days.

The Vehicles Crime (Registration of Registration Plate Suppliers) (England and Wales) Regulations 2002 require registered persons who are in the course of selling registration plates to obtain prescribed information from the prospective purchasers before the completion of the sale. They also require registered persons to keep records of prescribed matters.

The information to be obtained by a registered supplier from a prospective purchaser is prescribed by reg 6. He is required to obtain:

(a) his name and usual address (or business address in the case of a firm);
(b) the name and address of any agent involved with the sale;
(c) the registration mark to be shown;
(d) where the request is from a vehicle body repairer on behalf of an insurance company, the name of that company and the number of the insurance policy (in such a case, if the record includes all of this information, no additional verification is needed);
(e) the connection of the purchaser with the registration mark or the vehicle on which it is to be affixed. (This does not apply where the registration plate is fixed to the vehicle to which there has been assigned the registration mark displayed on the registration plate and that vehicle is sold or transferred with the registration plate fixed to it.)

Identity must be verified by the registered person by production of a driving licence (whether or not issued in the United Kingdom), which contains a photograph. Alternatives are permitted but in each case there must be two documents:

(a) a valid passport whether or not issued in the United Kingdom;
(b) a valid national identity document issued by the government of a state or territory other than the United Kingdom;
(c) a valid debit card or credit card issued by a bank or building society;
(d) a valid police warrant card;
(e) a valid armed forces identity card;
(f) a bill or statement of account issued in respect of the supply of gas, electricity, water or telecommunications services to premises at a specified address;
(g) a council tax bill or statement of account; and
(h) a statement relating to an account held at a bank or building society.

The documents specified at (f) to (h) must be dated, or relate to a period ending, no later than six months before the time at which the plate is requested.

A driving licence containing a photograph amounts to an official document which proves both name and address. Other documents may only provide proof of a name and in such cases a further document will be required to establish an address.

In addition, the purchaser must establish his connection with the registration mark or the vehicle by:

(a) a registration document or registration certificate or that part of such document or certificate as is required to be furnished to a new keeper on the transfer of the vehicle;
(b) a certificate of entitlement to a registration mark;
(c) a retention document relating to the right of retention of a registration mark;
(d) a vehicle licensing reminder to registered keeper;
(e) a temporary registration certificate;
(f) an authorisation (issued by the Secretary of State) for the purchase of a number plate; or
(g) an authorisation for the purchase of the number plate (issued by a company owning more than one vehicle) stating that it holds the registration document or the registration certificate and giving the reference number of that document or certificate.

By V(C)A 2001, s 25(3), a person who contravenes any provision in reg 6 commits an offence, unless he shows that he took all reasonable steps and exercised all due diligence to avoid committing the offence.

Regulation 7 requires a registered person to keep records at his principal place of business or at any other premises at which he carries on the business of a registration plate supplier. Records must be retained for a period of three years from the date of registration. Such records must contain:

(a) the information required by reg 6;
(b) a statement of the document used to verify name and address and, if a driving licence, the number;
(c) a statement of such particulars or numbers (if any) appearing on the document referred to in (b) as purport to make the document or those particulars or numbers (or both) unique to the purchaser and which in the case of a driving licence must be the driver number;.
(d) the document used to verify connection with a registration mark or the vehicle; and

(e) where the document is a registration document, registration certificate or authorisation for purchase of the number plate issued by a company, the reference number of that document or certificate or the number referred to in that authorisation, as the case may be.

Failure to comply with these provisions as to records is an offence against V(C)A 2001, s 24(4), unless the accused shows that he took all reasonable steps and exercised all due diligence to avoid committing the offence.

V(C)A 2001, s 26 provides a power of entry and inspection to the registered premises of registered persons for a constable or authorised person (authorised by the Secretary of State or the local authority of the area in which the premises are situated) at any reasonable time. The constable or authorised person has power to require production of, and to inspect, any plates kept at the premises and any records which are required to be kept under Part 2, and to take copies or extracts of those. Provision is also made for the issue to a constable or authorised person of a warrant. While force may not be used to obtain entry in normal circumstances, it may be used in the exercise of the constable or authorised person's powers under the authority of a warrant. When effecting entry without a warrant, a constable must, if required by or on behalf of the owner or occupier or person in charge of the premises, produce evidence of identity, and of his authority for entering, before doing so. This also applies to an 'authorised person' when executing a warrant. The section also creates an offence of obstruction of an authorised person in the exercise of his powers under the section.

A person registered under Part 2 of V(C)A 2001 is required by s 27 to give notice of changes of circumstances. Section 27(4) creates the offence of failure to do so. The same defence as is set out above in relation to ss 24 and 25 is available to a person accused of this offence.

V(C)A 2001, s 28 is concerned with counterfeit registration plates and those which do not conform with regulations. It creates two offences: (a) of selling a plate or other device which is not a registration plate as a registration plate, knowing that it is not such a plate or being reckless as to whether it is a registration plate (hereafter 'unlawful activity'); and (b) of supplying such a plate, device or other object to a person who is carrying on a business which consists wholly or partly in such unlawful activity and he knows or reasonably suspects that the plate, device or other object will be used for the purposes of that other person's unlawful activity. RSA 2006, s 44 prospectively adds a s 28(1A) which makes it an offence to sell a plate or other device which is not a registration plate because the mark does not comply with regulations or is displayed otherwise than in accordance with regulations.

V(C)A 2001, s 29 creates the offence of supplying a plate, device or other object to an unregistered person (other than an exempt person to be defined by regulations) who is carrying on a business which consists wholly or partly in selling registration plates, knowing or reasonably suspecting that the plate, device or other object will be used for the purpose of that other person's business as a registration plate or as part of a registration plate.

Forgery, fraud or falsity

The Vehicle Excise and Registration Act 1994, s 44 makes it an offence to forge, alter, fraudulently use on a public road, fraudulently lend, or fraudulently allow another to use on a public road, a registration mark to be fixed to a vehicle. These offences also apply to trade plates (see below), licences and registration documents. Where a person is charged with forging a licence it is not essential to prove an intention to avoid paying duty, it is sufficient to prove an intention to induce a person exercising a public duty to accept it as genuine and, by reason of so accepting it, to act or refrain from acting in a way which he would otherwise not have done, to his own or another's prejudice. Thus, the alteration of a licence, to avoid attracting attention while an application for an excise licence was pending, is a forgery for the purpose of the section. By s 45, a person who is required by the Act to furnish particulars of the vehicle as its keeper (eg on a change of ownership) commits an offence if he furnishes particulars which to his knowledge are false or in any material particular misleading.

LICENSING

The Vehicle Excise and Registration Act 1994, s 1 provides that vehicle excise duty must be charged in respect of:

(a) every mechanically propelled vehicle registered under the Act or (if not so registered) used, or kept, on a public road. Whether or not a vehicle is 'mechanically propelled' has already been discussed. As we have seen, it is not necessary to prove that the vehicle was intended or adapted for use on roads. Any mechanically propelled vehicle, including a go-kart, which is actually used or kept on a public road requires a vehicle excise licence regardless of whether or not it was intended or adapted for use on a road;

(b) every *thing* (whether or not it is a vehicle) that has been, but has ceased to be, a mechanically propelled vehicle and is registered under the Act or (if not so registered) is used, or kept, on a public road.

In the rest of VERA 1994 'vehicle' means a mechanically propelled vehicle or any thing (whether or not it is a vehicle) that has been, but has ceased to be, a mechanically propelled vehicle. Vehicle excise duty charged in respect of a vehicle is paid on a vehicle licence.

VERA 1994, s 29 provides that if any person *uses or keeps* on a public road any vehicle for which no vehicle licence or trade licence (see p 342) is in force, not being a vehicle exempted from duty under the Act, he is guilty of an offence.

In addition, if a vehicle is unlicensed the registered keeper is guilty of an offence contrary to VERA 1994, s 31A, unless it is an exempt vehicle. However, s 31B provides a number of exceptions. The registered keeper does not commit an offence under s 31A if *at the relevant time:*

(a) he is not the person keeping the vehicle and, if previously he was the person keeping it, he has by the relevant time complied with *any requirements to furnish particulars or make declarations which apply on surrendering or not renewing a licence, or when keeping an unlicensed vehicle;*

(b) he is keeping the vehicle, it is neither kept nor used on a public road and he has complied with any requirement italicised in (a);

(c) the vehicle has been stolen and has not been recovered, and he has notified the prescribed person with prescribed details about the theft; or

(d) the period of 'grace days' has not expired since the expiry of the last licence and a licence is taken out within the 'grace days'.

The Road Vehicle (Registration and Licensing) Regulations 2002, reg 26A deals with the 'requirements to furnish particulars' etc referred to in (a). They are the requirements in relation to the surrender or destruction of a registration document; delivery of a registration document to the Secretary of State; notification of transfer to a vehicle trader; or where a vehicle trader notifies a sale or transfer of a vehicle.

These sections of VERA 1994 contain a number of terms which require definition.

Definitions

Uses

This term is described in Chapter 10, below. An employer is liable for use by his employee even though blamelessly unaware of what the employee is doing. It is not good practice to proceed against the employee in normal circumstances.

Keeps

VERA 1994, s 62(2) states that a person keeps a vehicle on a public road if he causes it to be on such a road for any period, no matter how short, when it is not in use there. If the description 'use' cannot be applied to the vehicle's presence on the road at any particular time, it is 'kept' on that road by any person who causes it to be there. It is a question of fact in each case who that person is. It may be a driver who has parked it there whilst the vehicle still remains under his control. It may be the owner who allows it to remain in a back street unlicensed, or it may be some person in temporary possession. If an unlicensed vehicle is repaired at a garage and placed outside on the road by the proprietor when the repairs have been effected, the garage proprietor is keeping the vehicle on a road without there being an excise licence in force.

Public road

A public road is one which is repairable at public expense. Whether or not a road is repairable at public expense can be established by the local authority who will be able to say whether it has been 'adopted' in the sense that a highway authority is responsible for its maintenance under the Highways Act 1980 (HA 1980) or under another enactment. In most instances, particular reference to authorities is unnecessary as the road concerned is commonly known to be a public road and justices are entitled to apply their knowledge to such matters. It is advisable that inquiries are made when use on roads within new housing estates is alleged, as it is possible that the roads are still the responsibility of the builder if development work is still continuing or has recently finished.

Licence is in force

The prosecutor invariably offers evidence of the lack of a vehicle excise licence but this does not strictly need to be proven. Once use or keeping of a vehicle on a public road has been established, the accused must prove that it was licensed. A 'licence' in this context includes a trade licence (discussed below). Where a licence is obtained by means of a cheque which is dishonoured the licence is void from the time of issue; consequently the use or keeping of a vehicle thereafter in such a case is a using or keeping of an unlicensed vehicle.

Not being exempted

Exemptions are listed in VERA 1994, Sch 2. The most significant exemptions from the necessity to be licensed under the Act are police vehicles, fire engines, ambulances and health service vehicles, veterinary ambulances, invalid carriages not exceeding 10 cwt, vehicles for export, vehicles imported by members of foreign armed forces, vehicles which are used only for purposes related to agriculture, horticulture or forestry and are on public roads only in passing between different areas of land occupied by the same person and the distance so travelled on public roads in doing so does not exceed 1.5 km, off-road tractors, agricultural engines, hedge- and verge-cutting tractors, mowing machines, electrically propelled vehicles, snow ploughs and gritters. An electrically assisted pedal cycle is also an exempt vehicle.

When used for particular purposes, a vehicle may also be exempt for that purpose only. One case is where the vehicle is used only for the purpose of submitting it by prior arrangement for examination or re-examination for a test certificate (or a vehicle weight test or identity check) or of taking it from such an examination or re-examination. This exemption also applies to a charge of 'keeping'. Thus, if a driver parks whilst on his way to the testing station simply for the purpose of buying something in a shop, such 'keeping' of the vehicle on a public road is exempt because it is still possible to say that the vehicle was on the road *solely* for the purpose of going to the testing station. Another case is where it is used in the course of that examination; another is where, having been refused a test certificate, a vehicle is taken by prior arrangement for repair etc.

Vehicles used by or for persons with particular disabilities may, in certain circumstances, be exempt.

Foreign vehicles are exempt if brought temporarily into the country for a period of one year. The term 'foreign' includes vehicles from the Isle of Man and the Channel Islands. Visitors from abroad may purchase a vehicle in this country with the intention of exporting it and then use it here without licensing it before taking it out of Great Britain. Northern Ireland licences are treated as licences issued here. The Road Vehicles (Registration and Licensing) Regulations 2002, Sch 5 exempts vehicles imported by members of visiting forces, members of a headquarters or other organisation, or a dependant of such a person. This exemption lasts for a period of twelve months only.

Documentary evidence of commission of offence of using or keeping

The Road Traffic Offenders Act 1988 (RTOA 1988), s 20 provides that evidence of a fact relevant to proceedings for an offence to which the section applies may be given by the production of a record produced by a prescribed device which is accompanied by a certificate as to the circumstances in which the record was produced, signed by a constable or a person authorised by or on behalf of a chief officer of police. An offence under VERA 1994, s 29 is prescribed as an offence to which RTOA 1988, s 20 applies and in respect of it a prescribed device is one designed or adapted to register:

(a) an image of a vehicle and its registration mark; and
(b) the time at which the image is registered,

and to record that information if, according to data stored by or otherwise accessible by the device, that vehicle is unlicensed. See p 448 for more about s 20.

Duration and issue of licence

Excise licences may be issued for a period of twelve months or for six months for vehicles in respect of which the annual rate of duty exceeds £50. In addition, where an application is made for a vehicle licence, the Secretary of State may issue a temporary licence for fourteen days or such other period as is prescribed by regulations. Other than temporary licences, licences are valid from the first day of the month on which they are taken out. An application may be made out by any person who must make a declaration and furnish particulars which are prescribed. The Vehicles (Crime) Act 2001 extended the provisions of VERA 1994 to permit the Secretary of State to require, in addition to the declaration and particulars originally required by VERA 1994, s 7, any other document or evidence prescribed. This is intended to counter the practice of 'ringing' stolen vehicles to assume the identity of legitimate vehicles.

The licence is issued to the vehicle, not the person who makes the application, and it does not authorise that person to use or keep any other vehicle. On the sale of a vehicle the licence must either be returned to DVLA with an application for a rebate of duty, or be transferred with the vehicle. It cannot be transferred to a new vehicle.

It has been the practice for many years to allow fourteen days' grace for the renewal of vehicle excise licences. The period of grace only applies where an application for a licence was made before the previous one expired and it is limited to a period of fourteen days which immediately follows the expiration of the previous licence. It would not therefore apply to a new vehicle or to one which had been laid up for the winter and then brought back into use. If a licence is not obtained within the period of fourteen days, then proceedings will probably be taken for unlicensed use whenever it occurred during that period, even though a licence was obtained in the currency of the rest of the month in question. Although the idea of this period of grace is to allow for postal delays in respect of licences which were applied for within the currency of the previous licence, proceedings are not usually taken in respect of use within the following period of fourteen days if a licence is applied for (and obtained) within that period. It cannot apply to the circumstances set out in the next paragraph.

Regulation 26 of, and Sch 4 to, the Road Vehicles (Registration and Licensing) Regulations 2002 require that, where a licence is surrendered or expires and a new licence is not taken out, the keeper must make a 'required declaration' (as approved by the Secretary of State in writing, orally or by electronic means) not later than the day upon which the licence ceases to be in force (or three months after such expiry in the case of motor traders). The declaration is to the effect that the vehicle will not be used or kept on a public road and that a licence will be taken out before any such use. It is an offence to fail to make such a declaration. If there is a transfer of such a vehicle during an unlicensed period and a licence is not taken out, a 'required declaration' must be made by the new owner.

A supplement of £80 is payable where a licence for a vehicle has expired and no vehicle licence is issued for the vehicle before the expiry of a period of one month from the date of expiry of the licence and no 'statutory off-road notification' has been made. That sum may be reduced to £40 if it is paid within twenty-eight days of the registered keeper being notified by the Secretary of State that a supplement may or has become payable. This supplement is payable by the person in whose name the vehicle is registered at the date of expiry of the licence by reason of whose late renewal the supplement became payable.

Rates of duty

Licences cost differing amounts depending upon the nature of the vehicle and its particular use. For example, motor cycles and tricycles attract lower rates of duty than private saloon cars. The Vehicle Excise and Registration Act 1994, Sch 1 sets out the rates of duty applicable to all vehicles. It sets the basic rate (which applies where no other rate is set by the schedule) and this is the rate which applies to private cars. Buses are charged according to their seating capacity and goods vehicles are charged according to their 'revenue weight'. This is, in most circumstances, the plated gross or plated train weight of the vehicle but where a vehicle does not have such a plated weight there will be a 'design weight certificate' in force in respect of the vehicle and the weight shown on that certificate is the revenue weight for the purposes of the VERA 1994. Provision is made by reg 5 of the Road Vehicles (Registration and Licensing) Regulations 2002 for reduced rates of vehicle excise duty to be applicable to certain buses, haulage vehicles and heavy goods vehicles which have been adapted to reduce pollution. Where this is so, a 'reduced pollution certificate' will be in force.

Some vehicles, which would otherwise have fallen within the goods vehicle rates of duty, are declared by Sch 1 to be 'special vehicles' or recovery vehicles.

Special vehicles

The basic rate of goods vehicle duty is payable in respect of *special vehicles* regardless of their revenue weight. Such vehicles have a revenue weight exceeding 3,500 kg and are digging machines, mobile cranes, works trucks or road rollers. 'Digging machines' are machines designed for use for trench digging, excavating or shovelling which are used on public roads for such a purpose or for getting to or from the place where they will so operate, and 'mobile cranes' are cranes designed for use on site which are used on public roads only in connection with work in the immediate vicinity of that road or in travelling to or from that place.

A 'works truck' is a goods vehicle (other than a straddle carrier) designed for use on private premises and used on public roads only for carrying goods between such premises and a vehicle on a road in the immediate vicinity, or in passing from one part of any such premises to another or to other private premises in the immediate vicinity, or in connection with roadworks while at or in the immediate vicinity of the site of such works. A drive of one and a half miles through congested roads is not from one set of premises to another which is in the immediate vicinity, nor is a journey of six-tenths of a mile. The test to be applied is concerned with the journey on a road, not with the distance the premises are apart. Whilst 'vicinity' connotes a degree of closeness, 'immediate vicinity' connotes a very considerable degree of closeness. Thus, the use of dumper trucks licensed at a special vehicle rate, for the purposes of local shopping on behalf of persons working at a 'roadworks' site or for a journey to the homes of employees, is not authorised.

Recovery vehicles

The rate of duty applicable to a recovery vehicle is the basic goods vehicle rate where the revenue weight exceeds 3,500 kg but does not exceed 25,000 kg, and 2.5 times that rate if the revenue weight exceeds 25,000 kg.

A 'recovery vehicle' is a vehicle which is constructed or permanently adapted primarily for the purpose of lifting, towing and transporting a disabled vehicle or for any one or more of those purposes. The approved purposes are set out in the Vehicle Excise and Registration Act 1994, Sch 1 and the Road Vehicles (Registration and Licensing) Regulations 2002, Sch 7. For a vehicle to be classified as a recovery vehicle for the purpose of attracting a lower rate of duty, it must be being used for:

(a) the recovery of a disabled vehicle;
(b) the removal of a disabled vehicle from the place where it became disabled to premises at which it is to be repaired or scrapped;
(c) the removal of a disabled vehicle from premises to which it was taken for repair, to other premises at which it is to be repaired or scrapped;
(d) carrying fuel and other liquids required for its propulsion and tools and other articles required for the operation of or in connection with integral or permanently mounted apparatus designed to lift, tow or transport a disabled vehicle;
(e) repairing a disabled vehicle at the place where it became disabled or to which it had been moved in the interests of safety after becoming disabled; or
(f) drawing or carrying one trailer if the trailer was, immediately before a vehicle became disabled, being drawn or carried by the disabled vehicle.

When recovering or removing a disabled vehicle from the place where it became disabled, a recovery vehicle may carry the driver, passenger and any load which was in or on the vehicle immediately before it became disabled and persons and their personal effects from the place where the vehicle is to be repaired to their destinations. Such a vehicle may also be used to remove vehicles at the request of a constable or local authority, and whilst proceeding to and from permitted assignments. If a recovery vehicle is used outside these purposes, it is no longer a recovery vehicle for the purposes of this Act. Nor is it a recovery vehicle if it is used to recover more than two vehicles at any time.

Exhibition of licences

An excise licence must be fixed to a vehicle in a holder sufficient to protect the licence from the effects of the weather to which it would otherwise be exposed. Consequently, an externally displayed licence must be completely enclosed in a waterproof container. Regulation 6 of the Road Vehicles (Registration and Licensing) Regulations 2002 set out the requirements. An excise licence must be exhibited on the vehicle so that the particulars are clearly visible in daylight from the nearside of the road, as follows:

(a) on an invalid carriage, tricycle or bicycle, on the nearside of the vehicle;

(b) on a bicycle with sidecar, on the nearside of the handlebars or the nearside of the sidecar;

(c) on a vehicle with a windscreen extending across the vehicle, on or adjacent to the nearside of the windscreen; or

(d) on any other vehicle, on the nearside window of the driver's cab (if it has one), or on the nearside of the vehicle in front of the driver's seat and not less than 760 mm and not more than 1.8 m above the surface of the road.

Immobilisation of unlicensed vehicles

The Vehicle Excise Duty (Immobilisation, Removal and Disposal of Vehicles) Regulations 1997 authorise the immobilisation and removal of stationary unlicensed vehicles on public roads in circumstances in which an 'authorised person' (a person, such as a police officer or local authority employee, authorised by the Secretary of State) has reason to believe that an offence is being committed under the Vehicle Excise and Registration Act 1994, s 29 (unlicensed vehicle used or kept on public road), where such a vehicle is stationary on a public road. The Regulations apply throughout England and Wales.

The vehicle may be wheelclamped where it stands, or moved to another place on the same or another public road and wheelclamped there. This may be done by the authorised person or a person acting under his direction. Where this has been done an immobilisation notice must be fixed to the vehicle indicating that the device has been fitted and warning that no attempt should be made to move the vehicle until it has been released from the device and providing other information, including the charge for release, removal and disposal. Before an authorised person can release such a vehicle a valid excise licence must be produced or a 'surety payment' must be made. A voucher will be issued to a person who makes such a payment. Where a licence cannot be obtained immediately the 'surety payment' permits the vehicle to be used unlicensed for a period of twenty-four hours. The payment will be returned upon production of a valid vehicle excise licence. The Regulations authorise the immediate removal of such a vehicle to the possession of an authorised 'custodian'. In addition, where a vehicle has been clamped for a period of twenty-four hours without release, it may be removed to the custody of such a person. Where this has been done, a removal fee will be charged additionally, together with charges for storage.

The 1997 Regulations create the following offences:

(a) unauthorised removal of or interference with an immobilisation notice: reg 7(1) and (2);

(b) removal, or attempted removal, of an immobilisation device: reg 7(3);

(c) false declaration to secure release of vehicle from an immobilisation device: reg 8(2);

(d) false declaration to secure possession of impounded vehicle: reg 13(1);

(e) false declaration in obtaining voucher or a refund relating to a surety payment: reg 16(1) and (3); and

(f) forgery, fraudulent alteration, fraudulent use, or the fraudulent lending of a voucher relating to surety payment: reg 16(2) and (3).

Offences related to licences

The most common offences committed contrary to the Vehicle Excise and Registration Act 1994 are as follows:

(a) using or keeping a vehicle on a public road without having in force an excise licence: VERA 1994, s 29 (described above);
(b) using or keeping a vehicle on a public road without the requisite licence being fixed to and exhibited on the vehicle in the way outlined: VERA 1994, s 33;
(c) forging, fraudulently altering, fraudulently using, fraudulently lending or allowing to be used by any other person, an excise licence: VERA 1994, s 44 (described above);
(d) making, in connection with an application for the issue of a licence, a declaration which to the accused's knowledge is false or in a material respect misleading: VERA 1994, s 45;
(e) supplying false information or producing false documents in relation to the design weight of a vehicle (for the purposes of establishing the revenue weight): VERA 1994, s 45(3A);
(f) forgery, alteration or use of a certificate (design weight certificate), or knowingly lending or allowing such a certificate to be used, or without reasonable excuse making or having in possession such a certificate: VERA 1994, s 45(3B);
(g) exhibiting anything which is intended to be, or could reasonably be, mistaken for a licence: VERA 1994, s 59 and the Road Vehicles (Registration and Licensing) Regulations 2002, reg 7.

Proceedings for offences and admissibility of evidence

VERA 1994, s 47 provides that proceedings for offences of using etc without a licence, of using a trade licence outside permitted uses (see later), and of using a licensed vehicle for a purpose which attracts a higher rate of duty than that paid, can only be instituted by the Secretary of State or a constable; such a person is known as the authorised prosecutor. Moreover, no prosecution may be instituted by a constable for these offences without the approval of the Secretary of State; proof that such approval has been given is required at the outset of proceedings in court.

Proceedings instituted by an authorised prosecutor for one of the above offences or for an offence under VERA 1994, s 44 or 45 (forgery or false statements etc) may be instituted within six months from the date on which sufficient evidence came to the prosecutor's knowledge to warrant proceedings, subject to a maximum limit of three years from the commission of the offence. This means that, if the Secretary of State institutes proceedings as the authorised prosecutor, the six-month time limit runs from the time when the required evidence came to his knowledge. The six-month limit replaces the normal rule requiring that proceedings for summary offences be taken within six months from the commission of the offence. VERA 1994, s 47 allows proof of the date upon which evidence came to the knowledge of the authorised prosecutor, or proof that the Secretary of State has approved the institution of a prosecution by a constable, to be given by means of a certificate signed by or on behalf of the authorised prosecutor or, as the case may be, the Secretary of State. Such a certificate is conclusive evidence of the facts stated, and is deemed to be properly signed unless the contrary is proved.

VERA 1994, s 52 allows certified extracts from DVLA records to be admissible to the same extent as oral evidence. Evidence may therefore be offered of the last date upon which a vehicle was licensed by means of such a certified extract.

VERA 1994, s 46 requires that, where one of the offences mentioned above (except forgery) is alleged to have been committed in relation to a particular vehicle, the person keeping the vehicle must give such information as he may be required by or on behalf of a chief officer of police or the Secretary of State to give as to the identity of the person or persons concerned in the offence. Failure to do so is an offence, unless the accused keeper satisfies the court that he did not know and could not with reasonable diligence have ascertained, the identity of the person or persons concerned. A divisional court has held that where there is evidence of using or keeping a vehicle on a road and a notice has been sent in accordance with this section to which the keeper does not respond, the justices should draw an adverse inference from the fact that there was a failure to respond and that this, coupled with the other evidence of using or keeping, is sufficient to support a conviction under s 46. The requirement is also extended to any other person (besides a 'keeper') who may have such knowledge, and (in cases of unlicensed use) to the person alleged to have been using the vehicle. Both types of person commit an offence if they fail to give such information as to identity as it is in their power to give. A request under s 46 is, in practice, made by serving on a person a form requiring the specified information. A reply to such a request must be made in writing.

TRADE LICENCES

Without modification, the requirement that all vehicles (as defined on p 334) used or kept on a road should be individually licensed under the Vehicle Excise and Registration Act 1994 would cause considerable problems for motor traders, through whose hands many vehicles pass, most of which are retained for a short period of time. The purpose of trade licences is to permit traders temporarily to use vehicles on public roads for restricted purposes without the necessity for licensing in the manner described above. Trade licences are inexpensive and in consequence their permitted uses are carefully defined.

Who may apply for a trade licence?

By VERA 1994, s 11, a motor trader may apply to the Secretary of State for a licence to cover all vehicles which are from time to time temporarily in his possession in the course of his business as a motor trader. Any motor trader who is a manufacturer may also be granted a licence for the purpose of allowing him to carry out research and development work in the course of his business as a manufacturer, and for all other vehicles which are from time to time submitted to him by other manufacturers for testing on roads in the course of that business.

The term 'motor trader' means a manufacturer or repairer of, or dealer in, vehicles. A person is treated as a dealer in vehicles if he carries on a business consisting wholly or mainly of collecting and delivering vehicles.

A person whose business is that of modifying vehicles (by fitting accessories or otherwise) or of 'valeting' vehicles (which means the thorough cleaning of a vehicle prior to first registration or in order to prepare it for sale, and includes removing wax and grease from the exterior, engine and interior) is also a 'motor trader'.

A vehicle tester may also apply for trade licences to cover his use of vehicles submitted to him for testing in the course of his business. A vehicle tester is a person, other than a motor trader, who regularly in the course of his business engages in the testing on roads of vehicles belonging to other persons.

Persons who satisfy the Secretary of State that they intend to commence business as motor traders or vehicle testers may also take out licences. Trade licences may be taken out for a period of twelve months. Shorter-term licences are also available but are seldom used. The holder of a trade licence is issued with two plates (which are generally referred to as 'trade plates') in respect of each licence held. These plates consist of red letters on a white background and show the registration mark assigned to the holder of the licence. One of the plates contains a means by which the licence may be fixed to the plate; it must be displayed at the front of the vehicle so as to be clearly visible at all times during daylight. The licence is therefore available for inspection by police officers and the registration mark itself is traceable to the motor trader who holds that licence. If the trader satisfies the Secretary of State that the vehicles which he will use in the course of his business will include motor bicycles as well as other vehicles, he may be issued with a second plate for the motor bicycles only. The licence duty is currently about half of that payable by the keeper of a private motor car. Trade licences for motor bicycles only are much cheaper. The plates remain the property of the Secretary of State and must be returned when the trader ceases to be the holder of the licence.

Non-permitted uses of trade licences

VERA 1994, s 12 provides that the holder of a trade licence is not entitled by virtue of *that licence:*

(a) to use more than one vehicle at any one time; or
(b) to use any vehicle for any purpose other than a permitted one (see below); or
(c) to keep any vehicle on a road if it is not being used thereon.

However, there is nothing to prevent a motor trader from holding more than one licence to permit use of more than one vehicle at any one time.

It is an offence, contrary to VERA 1994, s 34(1), for the holder of a trade licence to use on a public road a greater number of vehicles than permitted by his licence (or licences), or to use a vehicle for a non-permitted purpose. The subsection also punishes the keeping on a public road of a vehicle using a trade licence, if it is not being used at that time.

Restrictions on use of trade licences

Regulation 37 of and Sch 6 to the Road Vehicles (Registration and Licensing) Regulations 2002 provide that the holder of a licence must not permit any person to display a trade licence or trade plates on a vehicle other than one which that person is using for the purpose of the licence holder's business, or other than when the vehicle is being used for one or more of the prescribed permitted purposes. However, this does not prevent a person driving a vehicle on a road with the consent of the licence holder, when the vehicle is being used for the licence holder's business. Thus, an employee may drive vehicles in the course of his employer's (the licence holder's) business.

Permitted purposes

The use of vehicles by a motor trader under a trade licence is controlled by regs 38 to 42 of the Road Vehicles (Registration and Licensing) Regulations 2002.

Regulation 38 of and Sch 6 to the 2002 Regulations prescribe the purposes for which the holder of a trade licence may use a vehicle by virtue of a trade licence. Those purposes do not include the carrying of any person on the vehicle or any trailer drawn by it except a person carried in connection with such a purpose. The prescribed purposes are without prejudice to the provisions of VERA 1994, s 11(4) to (6) which specify classes of vehicle which a trade licence is for, in relation respectively to a motor trader who is a manufacturer of vehicles, any other motor trader and a vehicle tester.

Schedule 6, para 10 authorises the holder of a trade licence to use a vehicle on a public road for:

(a) business purposes, as specified by para 11;
(b) purposes specified by para 12; and
(c) purposes that do not include the conveyance of goods or burden of any description except specified loads (test load or built-in load which is returned to the place of loading without having been removed).

Business purposes, para 11

A vehicle is used for 'business purposes' if used for purposes connected with the motor trader's business:

(a) as a manufacturer or repairer of or dealer in vehicles;
(b) as a manufacturer or repairer or dealer in trailers carried on in conjunction with his business as a motor trader;
(c) of modifying vehicles (whether by the fitting of accessories or otherwise); or
(d) of valeting vehicles.

Permitted purposes, para 12

A vehicle is used for a para 12 purpose if it is used:

(a) for the test or trial of the vehicle, or its accessories or equipment, in the ordinary course of construction, modification or repair, or after completion;
(b) for proceeding to or from a public weighbridge to ascertain its unladen weight, or to or from any place for its registration or inspection by someone acting on the Secretary of State's behalf;
(c) for its test or trial for the benefit of a prospective purchaser, including going either to or from a place of such test or trial at the instance of the prospective purchaser;
(d) for its test or trial for the benefit of a person interested in promoting publicity in regard to the vehicle, including going either to or from a place of such test or trial at the instance of such a person;

(e) for delivering it to a purchaser;
(f) for demonstrating the operation of the vehicle or its accessories or equipment when handed over to a purchaser;
(g) for delivering it between parts of the motor trader's own premises or to the premises of another manufacturer, dealer or repairer, or bringing it back from there directly to his own premises;
(h) for proceeding to or from a workshop where a body, or a special type of equipment or accessories, is to be or has been fitted to it or where it is to be or has been painted, valeted or repaired;
(i) for proceeding from the premises of a manufacturer, repairer or dealer to a railway station, airfield or shipping dock for the purpose of transportation, or for proceeding to such premises from a railway station etc to which it has been transported;
(j) for proceeding to or from any garage, auction room or storage place where vehicles are usually stored or offered for sale and at which the vehicle is to be or has been stored or offered for sale as the case may be;
(k) for proceeding to or from a place of testing; or
(l) for proceeding to a place to be broken up or otherwise dismantled.

The use of a vehicle with a trailer is regarded as the use of a single vehicle under the licence.

Schedule 6, paras 14 and 15 to the 2002 Regulations deal respectively with manufacturers' research vehicles and use by vehicle testers. The first restricts use to manufacturers for research and development purposes and the second restricts testing to vehicles and trailers drawn thereby, or any accessory or equipment on the vehicle or trailer, in the course of a business as a vehicle tester.

The above purposes are the only purposes for which vehicles may be used under a trade licence, and even then only in the course of the business of the holder. If an employee used the trade plates and licence to remove his own private car to a paint shop for spraying, not in the course of his employer's business, the use would be unlawful. If the holder of the licence used under trade plates a vehicle which was in his possession in the course of his business to visit a cinema in the evening, that use of the motor vehicle would be unlawful as it would not be in the course of his business as a motor trader.

Carriage of goods or burden

Schedule 6, para 13 to the 2002 Regulations defines the 'specified loads' referred to in para 10 above. Regulations prohibit the use of a vehicle under trade plates for the conveyance of goods or burden of any description except:

(a) a load which is carried by a vehicle being used for the purpose of testing or demonstrating the vehicle, or its accessories or equipment, within the terms of (b), (d), (e) or (g), above, and is carried solely for that purpose, and which is returned to the place of loading without having been removed from the vehicle (except in the case of an accident or for demonstrating its operation to a purchaser when handed over to him, or when the load consists of water, fertiliser or refuse);

(b) in the case of a vehicle which is being delivered or collected and is being used for a relevant purpose (as described in (f) to (k) above), a load consisting of another vehicle used or to be used for travel to or from the place of delivery or collection;

(c) any load built in as a permanent part of the vehicle or permanently attached to it;

(d) in the case of a vehicle which is being used for a purpose falling within (h), (i) or (j) above, a load which consists of a trailer or of parts, accessories or equipment designed to be fitted to the vehicle and of tools for fitting them.

Although these provisions appear to be complex at first, their effect is simply to prohibit the carriage of goods on vehicles being used under a trade licence in all but the narrowest of circumstances. It may be that a 'test and trial' will necessarily involve the use of a vehicle with a load. If so, provisions limit the carriage of the load to the duration of that trial. In most circumstances in which a goods vehicle is observed being used under a trade licence whilst carrying a load, an offence will be committed. Some vehicles have what might be described as built-in loads, such as essential engineering equipment, and vehicles which are on their way to have accessories etc fitted may carry these accessories etc with them for that purpose. None of these loads is being carried for a commercial purpose connected with the use of the vehicle in the accepted sense of the word 'commercial'. The regulation makes similar restrictions in respect of use by vehicle researchers and vehicle testers.

Trade plate and trade licence offences

We have already dealt with the offence under VERA 1994, s 34(1) relating to non-permitted use of trade licences. Breach of the regulations relating to loads or passengers is also an offence.

Schedule 6, para 3 of the 2002 Regulations provides that the holder of a licence must not, or must not permit any person to, exhibit on any vehicle any trade licence or trade plate which has been altered, defaced, mutilated or added to; upon which the figures or particulars have become illegible; or upon which the colours has been altered by fading or otherwise. Breach of the Regulations is an offence.

VERA 1994, s 44 provides that the offences thereunder of forgery, fraudulent alteration or use, or fraudulent lending or allowing to be used by any other person, of excise licences and registration marks also apply to trade licences and trade plates.

DRIVING LICENCES, PENALTY POINTS AND DISQUALIFICATION

Driving licences

The licensing of drivers of motor vehicles is dealt with by Part III of the RTA 1988 and the Motor Vehicles (Driving Licences) Regulations 1999.

RTA 1988, s 87(1) states that it is an offence for any person to drive on a road a motor vehicle of any class otherwise than in accordance with a licence authorising him to drive a motor vehicle of that class. Once the prosecution has proved that the accused has driven a motor vehicle on a road, the onus is upon the accused to prove that he is licensed to drive as this is a fact peculiarly within his own knowledge. It is *desirable* that there should be, where possible, a statutory demand for production of the relevant licence, but there is no statutory obligation to do so.

The activities which may be described as 'driving' in relation to a motor vehicle are discussed in Chapter 16, below and it is sufficient to bear in mind that the essence of 'driving' is the use of the driver's controls (or, at least, one of them) in order to control the movements of the vehicle, however that movement is produced, provided that what occurs can in any sense be described as driving.

It is an offence, under RTA 1988, s 87(2), for a person to cause or permit another person to drive on a road a motor vehicle of any class otherwise than in accordance with a licence authorising that other person to drive a motor vehicle of that class. For the meaning of 'permit' and 'cause' see Chapter 10, below.

For driving licence purposes, motor vehicles are divided by the 1999 Regulations into various categories and it is essential that licences are checked, not only to establish the identity of the driver, but also to ascertain that he is authorised to drive the particular vehicle in which he is found. The classes are:

Category	Class of vehicle included	Additional categories covered
	Part 1	
A	Motor bicycles	B1, K and P
A1	A sub-category of category A comprising learner motor bicycles	P
B	Any motor vehicle, other than a vehicle included in category A, F, K or P, having a maximum authorised mass not exceeding 3.5 tonnes and having not more than 8 seats in addition to the driver's seat, including: (i) a combination of such a vehicle and a trailer where the trailer has a maximum authorised mass not exceeding 750 kg, and (ii) a combination of such a vehicle and a trailer where the maximum authorised mass of the combination does not exceed 3.5 tonnes and the maximum authorised mass of the trailer does not exceed the unladen weight of the tractor vehicle.	F, K and P
B1	A sub-category of category B comprising motor vehicles having three or four wheels and an unladen weight not exceeding 550 kg.	K and P
B + E	Combination of a motor vehicle and trailer where the tractor vehicle is in category B but the combination does not fall within that category.	
C	Any motor vehicle having an authorised mass exceeding 3.5 tonnes, other than a vehicle falling within category D, F, G or H, including such a vehicle drawing a trailer having a maximum authorised mass not exceeding 750 kg.	

Category	Class of vehicle included	Additional categories covered
C1	A sub-category of category C comprising motor vehicles having a maximum authorised mass exceeding 3.5 tonnes but not exceeding 7.5 tonnes including such a vehicle drawing a trailer having a maximum authorised mass not exceeding 750 kg.	
D	Motor vehicles constructed or adapted for the carriage of passengers having more than eight seats in addition to the driver's seat, including such a vehicle drawing a trailer having a maximum authorised mass not exceeding 750 kg.	
D1	A sub-category of category D comprising motor vehicles having more than 8 seats but not more than 16 seats in addition to the driver's seat and including such a vehicle drawing a trailer with a maximum authorised mass not exceeding 750 kg.	
C + E	Combination of a motor vehicle and trailer where the tractor vehicle is in category C but the combination does not fall within that category.	B + E
C1 + E	A sub-category of category C + E comprising any combination of a motor vehicle and trailer where: (a) the tractor is in sub-category C1, (b) the maximum authorised mass of the trailer exceeds 750 kg but not the unladen weight of the tractor vehicle, and (c) the maximum authorised mass of the combination does not exceed 12 tonnes.	B + E
D + E	Combination of a motor vehicle and trailer where the tractor vehicle is in category D but the combination does not fall into that category.	B + E
D1 + E	A sub-category of category D + E comprising any combination of a motor vehicle and trailer where: (a) the tractor vehicle is in sub-category D1, (b) the maximum authorised mass of the trailer exceeds 750 kg but not the unladen weight of the tractor vehicle, (c) the maximum authorised mass of the combination does not exceed 12 tonnes, and (d) the trailer is not used for the carriage of passengers.	B + E

Category	Class of vehicle included	Additional categories covered
F	Agricultural or forestry tractor, including any such vehicle drawing a trailer but excluding any motor vehicle included in category H.	K
G	Road roller.	
H	Track-laying vehicle steered by its tracks.	
K	Mowing machine or vehicle controlled by a pedestrian.	
P	Moped.	

Part 2

C1 + E (8.25 tonnes)	A sub-category of category C + E comprising any combination of a motor vehicle and trailer in sub-category C1 + E the maximum authorised mass of which does not exceed 8.25 tonnes.	
D1 (not hire or reward)	A sub-category of category D comprising motor vehicles in sub-category D1 driven otherwise than for hire or reward.	
D1 + E (not hire or reward)	A sub-category of D + E comprising motor vehicles in sub-category D1 + E driven otherwise than for hire or reward.	
L	Vehicle propelled by electrical power.	

Part 3

B1 (invalid carriage)	A sub-category of category B comprising motor vehicles which are invalid carriages.	None

So far as vehicles of category B1 (invalid carriages) are concerned, reg 5 of the 1999 Regulations provides that no licence may be issued for that sub-category to a person who did not hold one on 12 November 1999.

The term 'maximum authorised mass' has the same meaning:

(a) in relation to goods vehicles as 'permissible maximum weight' in RTA 1988, s 108(1); and

(b) in relation to any other vehicle or trailer as 'maximum gross weight' in the Road Vehicles (Construction and Use) Regulations 1986, reg 3(2) namely the weight which the vehicle is designed or adapted not to exceed when on a road.

Regulation 43 of the 1999 Regulations provides that where a person passes a test prescribed in respect of any category for a licence which authorises the driving of motor vehicles included in that category or in a sub-category of that category, the licensing authority must grant him a licence which will authorise him to drive vehicles of all classes included in that category or sub-category unless his licence is restricted to such vehicles fitted with automatic transmission, or vehicles specially adapted for the disabled, in which cases his entitlement will be restricted to similar vehicles within that class. Such holders are also authorised to drive those vehicles shown in column 3 above as additional categories or sub-categories with the same limitations as set out above, should the test have been taken on those types of vehicles. However, where the additional category is F, K or P the limitation in respect of 'automatics' will not apply.

Regulation 43 has since been amended in two ways. First in relation to a person passing the test of competence to drive a vehicle in category A after 1 February 2001, a licence to drive a vehicle in category B does not confer an entitlement to drive a vehicle in sub-category B1. Second, in relation to a person passing the test of competence to drive a vehicle in category B on or after 1 February 2001, a licence to drive a vehicle in category B does not confer entitlement to drive vehicles in category P unless that licence holder has successfully completed an approved training course for motor cyclists. In addition, reg 44A was inserted into the Regulations to provide for the grant of a licence restricted to three-wheeled vehicles in category P.

The 1999 Regulations parallel new categories of vehicles, introduced within the preceding 1996 Regulations, with the old categories which were described by the then replaced 1987 Regulations. They provide that licences (whether full or provisional) granted before 1 January 1997 are valid in respect of the new categories of vehicle, as set out in the table to the regulations.

Full driving licences issued to those who have passed the appropriate test are granted until the holder achieves the age of seventy years. After that age, the licence can be renewed for periods of three years. When the time for renewal arrives, it is the duty of the licence holder to make application for renewal: there is no requirement for reminders, nor are there any days of grace in respect of renewal. Those licences which authorise the holder to drive prescribed goods or passenger carrying vehicles will be renewable on the holder's forty-fifth birthday, or after five years, whichever is the *longer*, or where the licence is issued to a person between forty-five and sixty-five for the period ending on his sixty-sixth birthday or after five years, whichever is the *shorter*. A licence granted after the age of sixty-five will remain in force for one year only.

When there is a prosecution for an offence under RTA 1988, s 87, the issue is whether the accused was driving the vehicle otherwise than in accordance with the licence at the material time, and a licence taken out later in the day does not excuse unlicensed driving earlier in that day. However, RTA 1988, s 88 provides that it is lawful for a person to drive provided that an application for renewal of a licence under Part III of the Act has been received; or the driver holds a community licence, a Northern Ireland licence, a British external licence, a British Forces licence or an exchangeable licence. In the case of an application for a licence it must relate to a date which covers the driving in question; if the application is for a provisional licence, the conditions of such a licence must be complied with.

RTA 1988, s 97(1), requires the Secretary of State to issue a licence to a person who applies in the prescribed manner, pays the appropriate fee, and supplies necessary evidence to support his application. RTA 1988, s 97 will be amended by the RSA 2006, s 38 (when it is in force) so as to permit the grant of a licence subject to prescribed conditions:

(a) for a prescribed period; or
(b) until the happening of a prescribed event.

This will permit, for example, the imposition of conditions where a person disqualified for drink/driving had accepted a court order requiring participation in an alcohol ignition interlock programme, limiting driving to driving in accordance with that programme.

Section 98 requires the licence to be in the form of a photocard of a description specified by the Secretary of State, or in such other form as he may specify. Photocard licences were introduced in 1998, but pre-existing licences remain in force until they expire or the holder's details expire. Where a licence is issued in the form of a photocard an applicant must supply the licensing authority with a photograph which is a current likeness of him and with a specimen signature which can be electronically recorded and reproduced on the licence. If any other form of licence is granted, the holder must forthwith sign the licence in ink. Defaced or lost licences may be replaced by the licensing authority. If a lost licence is subsequently found it must be returned to the authority.

RTA 1988, ss 99ZA–99ZC provide for the making of regulations about compulsory driver training courses which may provide that persons who have not successfully completed a driver training course:

(a) may not take a test of competence to drive motor vehicles of a prescribed class (or a prescribed part of such a test),

(b) are not authorised to drive motor vehicles of a prescribed class (before having passed a test of competence to drive them) by a provisional licence (or by RTA 1988, s 98(2) or 99A(5)) (use of full licence as provisional);

(c) are not granted a licence authorising the driving of motor vehicles of a prescribed class by virtue of regulations under RTA 1988, s 89(6)(b) or (c) (authority to drive vehicles of other classes); or

(d) are not authorised to drive motor vehicles of a prescribed class in prescribed circumstances (despite having passed a test of competence to drive them).

Exemptions are made by s 99ZB in respect of (b), (c) and (d) where the person is undergoing training on a driver training course and is driving a motor vehicle as a part of that training. In addition, the regulations may provide exemptions in other circumstances. No regulations have been made at the time of writing.

Disqualification of persons under age

A person may also be disqualified from driving a particular class of vehicle by reason of age. A person is disqualified from holding or obtaining a licence to drive a motor vehicle of a particular class if he is under the age applicable to that class of vehicle. The minimum ages at which persons may drive particular classes of vehicles are listed by RTA 1988, s 101, which provides that a person below the minimum age to drive a particular class of vehicle is disqualified from holding a licence to drive that class of vehicle. The requirements of s 101 are amplified by the Motor Vehicles (Driving Licences) Regulations 1999, reg 9. The minimum ages are as follows:

(a) 16 years:
  (i) Invalid carriage.
  (ii) Moped. This means a motor vehicle which has fewer than four wheels and—
      (a) in the case of a vehicle the first use of which occurred before 1 August 1977, has a cylinder capacity not exceeding 50 cc and is equipped with pedals by means of which the vehicle is capable of being propelled, and
      (b) in any other case, has a maximum design speed not exceeding 50 kph and, if propelled by an internal combustion engine, has a cylinder capacity not exceeding 50 cc.

(iii) Agricultural or forestry tractor, provided it is a wheeled vehicle not exceeding 2.45 m in width and driven without a trailer (other than a two-wheeled or close coupled four-wheeled trailer not exceeding 2.45 m in width). The person must have passed a test for category F or be proceeding to or from such a test.

(iv) Disability living allowance. Sixteen-year-olds in receipt of a higher rate disability living allowance under the Social Security Contributions and Benefits Act 1992 may drive a small vehicle (see below) if it is driven without a trailer.

(b) 17 years:

(i) Motor cycle, other than a moped or a large motor bicycle.

(ii) Small vehicle. This means a motor vehicle (other than an invalid carriage, moped or motor bicycle) which—

(a) is not constructed or adapted to carry more than nine persons inclusive of the driver, and

(b) has a maximum gross weight not exceeding 3.5 tonnes, and includes a combination of such a vehicle and a trailer.

(iii) Incomplete large vehicle not exceeding 3.5 tonnes.

(iv) Road roller which is not steam-propelled, whose unladen weight does not exceed 11.69 tonnes, which has no pneumatic, soft or elastic tyres, which is not constructed or adapted to carry a load other than equipment of the vehicle.

(c) 18 years:

(i) Medium-sized goods vehicle. This means a motor vehicle constructed or adapted to carry or haul goods and not adapted to carry more than nine persons inclusive of the driver, with a permissible maximum weight exceeding 3.5 tonnes but not 7.5 tonnes and includes a combination of such a vehicle and a trailer where the relevant maximum weight of the trailer does not exceed 750 kg. However, the age of twenty-one applies if such a vehicle is drawing a trailer and the maximum authorised mass of the combination exceeds 7.25 tonnes.

(ii) Vehicle of a class included in sub-category D1 which is an ambulance and which is owned or operated by a health service body or a National Health Service Trust or a Primary Care Trust.

(iii) A motor vehicle and trailer combination of sub-category C1 + E the maximum authorised mass of which does not exceed 7.5 tonnes.

(iv) Other motor vehicles in special circumstances. A person of eighteen may drive a large goods vehicle of a category to which a training agreement applies, and which is owned by his employer or a registered heavy goods vehicle training establishment, provided that he is employed by a registered employer in accordance with the Training Scheme and that he is a registered employee. In addition, a person of eighteen may drive a large passenger vehicle where:

(a) the driver of the vehicle holds a provisional licence authorising the driving of the vehicle and is not engaged in the carriage of passengers, or

(b) the driver holds a full passenger-carrying vehicle driver's licence and—

(i) is engaged in the carriage of passengers on a regular service over a route which does not exceed 50 km, or

(ii) where he is not so engaged, is driving a vehicle of a class included in sub-category D1, and the vehicle is operated under a PSV operator's licence, a permit under the Transport Act 1985 (educational and other purposes), or a community bus permit.

(v) Incomplete large vehicle exceeding 3.5 tonnes but not exceeding 7.5 tonnes.

(d) 21 years:

(i) Large passenger vehicle, ie passenger vehicle with more than nine seats inclusive of the driver.

(ii) Large goods vehicle, ie exceeding 7.5 tonnes.

(iii) Large motor bicycles unless the person concerned passed a test on or after 1 January 1997 for a motor cycle in category A (other than sub-category A1) and the standard access period (two years before the date in question excluding any period of disqualification or during which the licence was not in force) has elapsed, or unless the vehicle is an armed forces vehicle or is being driven by someone subject to the orders of a member of such a force, or unless it is being driven by someone who (before 1 January 1997) passed a test authorising him to drive a large motor bicycle. A 'large motor bicycle' is, in the case of a motor bicycle without a sidecar, a bicycle the engine of which exceeds 25 kw or has a power to weight ratio exceeding 0.16 kw/kg, or in the case of a sidecar combination a bicycle whose engine has a power to weight ratio exceeding 0.16 kw/kg.

(iv) All other motor vehicles. This residual category covers generally those motor vehicles which do not normally carry passengers or carry or haul a load, eg a mobile crane.

The regulations permit members of the armed services, aged seventeen or over, to drive large motor cycles, and medium and large goods vehicles which are owned by the Secretary of State for Defence and are being used subject to his orders. Clearly this exemption is not a general one and the nature of the use of the vehicle at the time must be taken into account.

Although these provisions appear to be complex at first sight, the vehicles with which police officers are generally concerned are motor cycles, private saloon cars, goods vehicles and public service vehicles. Mopeds may be ridden at sixteen, motor cycles (unless they are large motor bicycles) and private cars at seventeen, those between 3.5 tonnes and 7.5 tonnes at eighteen and those in excess of 7.5 tonnes at twenty-one (eighteen when under an approved heavy goods vehicle training scheme) in most circumstances. Small passenger vehicles, which are generally private cars (as the seating of such a vehicle must not exceed nine) may be driven at seventeen. Passenger vehicles with more than nine seats may, with the exceptions outlined, only be driven by a person of twenty-one years; most vehicles of the 'Transit' type fall within this category.

Grant of licences

A person may apply for a driving licence at any time within two months of the date from which the licence will take effect. Where the application is for a large goods or passenger-carrying vehicle driver's licence, it must be made three months in advance of such date.

Full licences

Where the application is for a full licence, an applicant must satisfy the licensing authority that he has passed a test at the time of his application. In support of his application he must produce a certificate as prescribed by the Regulations certifying that he has passed the test of driving theory and hazard perception as the practical test cannot be taken without evidence being offered of success in the theory and hazard perception test. The hazard perception test is conducted by means of the exhibition of film clips which take the perspective of the driver of a motor vehicle and show, at some point during each film clip, one or more hazards to traffic occurring on or near the road and require the candidate (using electronic equipment capable of recording the exact moment of each response) to indicate during each film clip the moment he observed a hazard relating to traffic on a road.

The Motor Vehicles (Driving Licences) Regulations 1999, Part III deals with the constituent parts of driving tests, and the certificates to be issued to those who take tests. The regulations require that tests be conducted in two parts, a theory test and a practical or unitary test. Schedule 7 to the Regulations sets out the matters to be dealt with within a theory test and Sch 8 similarly deals with matters to be included in a practical or unitary test. The 1999 Regulations include a requirement that, where a person produces to an examiner an appropriate licence which does not include a photograph, he must satisfy the person conducting the test as to his identity by producing a document to establish his identity as prescribed by Sch 6 (all of which have a photograph) or a document of a like nature. However, if the person's identity is clearly apparent from the facts known to, or other evidence in the possession of, the person conducting the test, this will be satisfactory.

Provisional driving licences

Full licences may only be granted to those who have passed the relevant test of competence to drive that class of vehicle. Provisional licences are issued to those who wish to learn to drive motor vehicles and are issued subject to conditions set out in the Motor Vehicles (Driving Licences) Regulations 1999, reg 16. These conditions are concerned with the need for supervision, distinguishing marks, the drawing of trailers and the carriage of passengers. However, these conditions do not apply where a provisional licence holder has passed a test by virtue of which he is entitled to be granted a licence authorising him to drive a vehicle of the class then being driven.

Supervision   With the exceptions listed below, a provisional licence holder must not drive or ride a motor vehicle otherwise than under the supervision of a qualified driver who is present with him in or on the vehicle. A person is a qualified driver if he:

(1) is twenty-one years of age or over;
(2) holds a relevant licence (see below);
(3) has the relevant driving experience (see below); and
(4) in the case of a disabled driver, he is supervising a provisional licence holder who is driving a vehicle of a class included in categories B, C, D, C+E or D+E and would in an emergency be able to take control of the steering and braking functions of the vehicle in which he is a passenger.

Subject to provisions below relating to a disabled driver, a 'relevant licence' means a full licence authorising the driving of vehicles of the same class as the vehicles being driven by the provisional licence holder. However, subject to the provisions relating to a disabled driver, where a person holds a full licence authorising the driving of vehicles of the same class as that being driven by the provisional licence holder, which class is included in a category or sub-category specified in column 1 of the table below, and that person has held the licence for less than three years, 'relevant licence' has a special meaning. It means a full licence authorising:

(a) where that class of vehicle is included within any sub-category specified in column 1 of the table below, the driving of vehicles in the sub-category specified in column 2 which is opposite that sub-category, or

(b) where (a) above does not apply, the driving of vehicles in the category specified in column 2 of that table which is opposite the category specified in column 1 that includes the class of vehicle being driven by the provisional licence holder.

For the above purposes, the term 'full licence' includes a Northern Ireland licence and a Community licence.

In the case of a disabled driver who holds a licence authorising the driving of vehicles in category B, a relevant licence must authorise the driving of vehicles other than vehicles in category B1 or B1 (invalid carriages). A 'disabled driver' is a person who holds a relevant licence which is limited by virtue of a declaration made with his application for the licence or a notice under RTA 1988, s 92(5)(b) to vehicles of a particular class.

Where only (a) above applies, a person has relevant driving experience if he has held the relevant licence for a minimum period of three years. Where (b) above applies, a person has relevant driving experience if he has held the relevant licence authorising the driving of vehicles:

(a) of the same class as the vehicle being driven by the provisional licence holder for a minimum period of one year; and

(b) in the category or sub-category specified in column 2 of the table below for a minimum period of three years.

For the purpose of meeting these requirements the minimum period of time for holding a full licence may be met either by holding that licence continuously for that period or for periods amounting in aggregate to not less than that period.

The table referred to above is as follows:

Column (1)	*Column (2)*
Categories and sub-categories which include the vehicle being driven by the provisional licence holder	Categories and sub-categories authorised by the relevant licence
C	D
C1	D1
C + E	D + E
C + E	D1 + E
D	C
D1	C1
D + E	C + E
D1 + E	C1 + E

A number of attempts have been made to get this regulation right. An error in the Motor Vehicles (Driving Licences) (Amendment) (No 2) Regulations 2005 was corrected by the Motor Vehicles (Driving Licences) (Amendment) Regulations 2006 which re-instated the situation in respect of supervisors of learner-drivers of category B vehicles by requiring the holding of a category B licence for a minimum period of three years. In relation to supervisors of learner-drivers of large goods vehicles, coaches and buses, the Motor Vehicles (Driving Licences) (Amendment) Regulations 2006 replaced the table provided by the Motor Vehicles (Driving Licences) (Amendment) (No 2) Regulations 2005 so that, for example, a person who has held a full category C licence for a period of one year, which also authorises the driving of category D licences and has done so for a period of three years, may supervise the holder of a provisional category C licence. The reverse could apply where the supervision was of a provisional category D licence holder.

The conditions requiring that a qualified driver be over the age of twenty-one and that he has relevant driving experience do not apply to a member of the armed forces of the Crown acting in the course of his duties for naval, military or air force purposes. In addition, reg 8 provides that such a person may drive a dual purpose vehicle when it is being used to carry passengers for naval, military or air force purposes; where it does not exceed 3.5 tonnes, with a licence for a category B (not B1) licence; where it exceeds 3.5 tonnes but does not exceed 7.5 tonnes, a C1 licence; and in any other case, a C licence (other than C1).

The supervisor's duty is to make up for any deficiencies in the skill of the learner; as part of his duty he must participate in the driving to such extent as could reasonably be expected to prevent danger to other persons or property. Because he has a right of control over the learner driver, a supervisor can be convicted as an accomplice to a driving offence committed by the learner driver if he deliberately fails to prevent it when he could reasonably have done so. For example, if a learner drives with an excess alcohol level, his supervisor can be convicted as an accomplice, if he is aware that the learner has been drinking and may be 'over the limit', and deliberately refrains from stopping the learner driving.

A provisional licence holder is not required to be supervised while undergoing a test. Although an examiner will be with him, the examiner is there for the purpose of assessing his competence, not for the purpose of supervision (and therefore not for the purpose of interference when a lack of skill is evident). The examiner is not, therefore, similarly exposed to charges of aiding and abetting offences by the learner.

A provisional licence holder is not required to be supervised if he:

(a) is driving a motor vehicle of a class included in sub-category B1 or B1 (invalid carriages) or in category F, G, H or K which is constructed to carry only one person and not adapted to carry more than one person;

(b) is riding a moped or motor bicycle with or without a sidecar; or

(c) is driving a motor vehicle, other than a vehicle of a class in category C, C + E, D or D + E, on a road in an exempted island (a term which covers small islands like Lundy and the islands in the Isles of Scilly other than St Mary's).

Category B1 vehicles may have three or four wheels and an unladen weight not exceeding 550 kg. It follows, for example, that a small three- or four-wheeler with two seats requires a supervisor in order to be driven by a provisional licence holder, whereas if it is constructed with only one seat it does not (unless it has since been adapted to carry more than one person). The removal of a seat from a two-seater does not alter the position since it will have been constructed with two. It must be emphasised that there is a total exemption for two-wheeled motor bicycles, whether fitted with a sidecar or not.

Other licence conditions   Motor vehicles which are driven or ridden by persons holding a provisional driving licence must display on the front and on the back of the vehicle the letter 'L' (or 'D' in Wales) in such a manner that it is clearly visible from a reasonable distance to other persons using the road. It is an offence for the holder of a provisional licence to drive a vehicle which is not so marked.

The drawing of trailers by a motor vehicle driven by the holder of a provisional licence is prohibited, with the exception of the holder of a provisional licence authorising the driving of a vehicle of a class included in category B + E, C + E, D + E or F (combination vehicles where the tractor falls in category B, ie not exceeding 3.5 tonnes or nine seats or agricultural or forestry tractors), in relation to motor vehicles of that class.

Holders of provisional licences authorising the driving of mopeds or motor bicycles with or without a sidecar must not drive such a vehicle while carrying on it another person.

Regulation 16(7) deals with compulsory basic training on motor cycles. It requires that the holder of a provisional licence authorising the driving of a motor cycle other than a learner motor cycle must drive under the supervision of a 'direct access instructor' who is accompanying him on another motor bicycle; is able to communicate with him by radio other than a hand-held radio; who is supervising only that person or, at the most, one additional provisional licence holder; and who is carrying a valid certificate issued by the licensing authority. The requirement concerning communication by radio does not apply to a person who has impaired hearing provided that a suitable means of communication with the instructor is arranged in advance. Direct access instructors hold additional qualifications in respect of larger motor cycles.

It is a condition of a provisional licence to drive a moped or learner motor bicycle that, when undergoing 'relevant training' (receiving professional tuition from a paid instructor in driving on a road after compulsory basic training), the holder of the licence cannot be in a group of more than three other such learners. Such an instructor must be present with him and riding a moped, or learner motor bicycle, or any other motor bicycle.

Offences

We have already said that a person who drives a motor vehicle on a road otherwise than in accordance with a licence authorising him to drive the class of vehicle in question commits the offence of unlicensed driving, contrary to RTA 1988, s 87(1). Once it is proved that an accused drove a motor vehicle on a road it is for him to prove that he had a driving licence authorising the driving, as this is a fact peculiarly within his knowledge.

It should be noted that, when a police officer discovers an offence of driving without a driving licence in circumstances in which the offender's driving would not have been in accordance with any licence that could have been granted to him, the police officer should include in the report reference to whether or not the conditions applicable to that licence were being complied with. The reason is that this is important to the court in relation to the penalty points awarded for the offence.

Motor bicycles: some special rules

RTA 1988, s 97(3) provides that a provisional licence shall not authorise a person under the age of twenty-one years, before he has passed a test of competence to drive:

(a) a motor bicycle without a sidecar unless it is a 'learner motor cycle' or its first use occurred before 1 January 1982 and the cylinder capacity of the engine does not exceed 125 cc; or

(b) a motor bicycle with a sidecar unless its power to weight ratio is less than or equal to 0.16 kw/kg.

A 'learner motor bicycle' is one which is either propelled by electrical power or has the following characteristics:

(a) the cylinder capacity does not exceed 125 cc;

(b) the 'maximum net power output' of its engine does not exceed 11 kw.

The power to weight ratio is assessed on the basis of the relationship of the maximum power output to the actual weight of the machine with a full tank and normal equipment. 'Maximum net power output' means the maximum net power output measured under full engine load. Provisional licence holders who ride motor bicycles in excess of the power specified commit the offence of riding otherwise than in accordance with the conditions of their licences. The reason is that the provisional licence which they hold does not authorise the riding of that particular class of vehicle.

Motor cyclists and moped riders must undertake the two-part practical training which is applicable to them, within an approved training course for motor cyclists and moped riders. The first part is concerned with the basic handling and control of machines. The training for the first part of the test can be undertaken without the necessity to ride on a road. The second part of the test is the normal 'on the road' training to drive which takes place under the supervision of instructors.

A provisional licence does not authorise a person, before he has passed a test of competence to drive, to drive on a road a motor bicycle or moped, except where he has successfully completed an approved training course for motor cyclists or is undergoing training on such a course and is driving a motor cycle or moped on a road as part of the training. Certificates will be issued to those who have successfully completed such courses.

A certificate is not valid:

(a) if the person to whom it is issued is at the time of issue ineligible to undertake the training course; and

(b) after whichever is the earliest of the following dates, namely:

  (i) in a case where the person to whom the certificate was furnished is subsequently disqualified by order of a court under the Road Traffic Offenders Act 1988, s 36, the date on which the order is made;

  (ii) in a case where the licence of the person to whom the certificate was furnished is subsequently revoked by the Secretary of State under the Road Traffic (New Drivers) Act 1995 (RT(ND)A 1995), s 3(1), the date on which the revocation has effect in accordance with RT(ND)A 1995, s 3(2);

  (iii) in a case where the certificate was issued before 1 February 2001, the last day of the period of three years beginning with the date of the certificate; or

  (iv) in a case where the certificate was issued on or after 1 February 2001, the last day of the period of two years beginning with the date of the certificate.

Regulation 69 of the Motor Vehicles (Driving Licences) Regulations 1999 provides that the requirement that a person is not authorised to drive a motor bicycle on a road unless he has passed a test of competence to drive, without having successfully completed an approved training course, does not apply to a person who is a provisional entitlement holder by virtue of having passed a test in respect of category P (mopeds) on or after 1 December 1990, unless that person has subsequently been disqualified from driving until such time as he passes a test. Nor is such a person required to produce such a certificate on applying for a test of competence to drive a motor bicycle. Similar exemptions exist in favour of persons resident on exempted islands.

Regulation 69 has been amended by the addition of paras (2A), (2B) and (2C) to modify the exemptions from the requirements to complete such training courses. The general proposition is that no person shall be permitted to take a test of competence to drive a motor bicycle unless he produces the prescribed certificate of completion of an approved training course. The amended regulation provides that this will not apply to a person who is for the time being the holder of a full licence for a class of vehicle included in category A (motor bicycles) in respect of a test of competence to drive a vehicle of any other class included in that category. Such a holder shall also be exempt from the restrictions imposed by RTA 1988, s 97(3)(e) (which prevents the driving of a motor bicycle or moped on a road, by the holder of a provisional licence, before he has successfully completed an approved training course for motor cyclists) of his driving of a vehicle of another class included in that category. However, these exemptions do not apply in relation to the holder of a full licence authorising him only to drive a vehicle in category A having automatic transmission in respect of a test to drive vehicles with manual transmission or the driving of such a vehicle.

Regulation 44 of the 1999 Regulations provides that where a person passes a test for a licence authorising the driving of motor bicycles of any class other than a class included in sub-category A1, the licensing authority shall grant:

(a) where the test was passed on a motor bicycle without a sidecar, the engine of which has a maximum net power output of not less than 35 kw, a licence authorising the driving of all classes of motor bicycles included in category A;

(b) where the test was passed on any other motor bicycle without a sidecar, a licence authorising him to drive a standard motor bicycle (a motor bicycle which is not a large motor bicycle) but a licence granted under this provision will authorise the driving of all classes of motor bicycles in category A upon the expiration of the 'standard access period' (see below);

(c) where the test was passed on a motor bicycle and sidecar combination and the engine of the bicycle has a maximum net power output of not less than 35 kw, a licence authorising the driving of all classes of motor bicycle and sidecar combinations included in category A;

(d) where the test was passed on a motor bicycle and sidecar combination the power to weight ratio of which does not exceed 0.16 kw/kg but which does not fall within (c), a licence authorising the driving of standard motor bicycles and sidecar combinations, but such a licence will authorise the driving of all classes of motor bicycles and combinations after the expiration of the standard access period.

The 'standard access period' is the period of two years commencing on the date upon which a person passes a test for a licence authorising the driving of standard motor bicycles of any class other than a class included in sub-category A1 (which covers learner motor cycles except mopeds) but disregarding any period of disqualification or other period during which the licence has ceased to be in force.

At seventeen years or over, a person will be able to seek a licence to drive motor bicycles. If he is tested on a motor bicycle without a sidecar of 75 cc, but not more than 120 cc, success will bring a category A1 licence. Success in a test involving the use of a motor bicycle of 121 cc which is capable of a speed of 100 kph will bring a full standard licence (which, of course, includes A1 entitlement). Before being permitted to drive a 'large motor cycle' a candidate must be at least twenty-one and must pass a test on a motor bicycle with a maximum net engine power output of 35 kw. However, a person of less than twenty-one may take a test for a 'large motor cycle' entitlement if he has held a full standard category A licence for a period of two years. Someone over twenty-one is permitted, after holding a full standard category A licence for a period of two years, to drive large motor cycles without undergoing a further test.

Full licence as provisional licence

RTA 1988, ss 98(2) and 99A(5) provide that a full licence, other than one restricted to a specially adapted vehicle for a person with a physical disability, may act as a provisional licence for any other classes of vehicle, unless the holder is below the minimum age at which the other class of vehicle may be driven.

RTA 1988, ss 98(2) and 99A(5) do not apply to a licence in so far as it allows the holder to drive vehicles of a class included in category B + E, C + E, D + E, or K or in sub-category B1 (invalid carriages), C1 or D1 (not for hire or reward). Holders of full licences restricted to vehicles with automatic transmissions, may use those licences as provisional licences to drive manually-controlled vehicles of a category or subcategory as specified in the Table to reg 19. These provisions apply equally to holders of Community licences.

In the case of licences authorising the driving of motor bicycles of sub-category A1 (learner motor cycles) or of standard motor cycles (ie those which are not large motor bicycles), such licences do not authorise the driving of large motor cycles by a person under the age of twenty-one. A large motor cycle is one whose engine has maximum net power output exceeding 25 kw or has a power to weight ratio exceeding 0.16 kw/kg.

Physical fitness of drivers

RTA 1988, s 92 provides that an applicant for a driving licence must declare his physical fitness to drive, stating whether or not he is suffering, or has in the past suffered, from any relevant or prospective disability. The term 'disability' for the purposes of the section includes disease and the persistent use of drugs or alcohol, whether or not such misuse amounts to dependency, and:

(a) a relevant disability means any prescribed disability and any other disability likely to cause the driving of a vehicle by him to be a source of danger to the public; and
(b) prospective disability means any other disability which, by virtue of its intermittent or progressive nature, may become a disability of the type specified in (a) in course of time.

The disabilities prescribed for the purposes of (a) are:

(a) epilepsy;
(b) severe mental handicap;
(c) liability to sudden attacks of disabling giddiness or fainting;
(d) liability to sudden attacks of giddiness or fainting due to a heart condition for which a 'pacemaker' has been fitted;
(e) persistent misuse of drugs or alcohol, whether or not such misuse amounts to dependency; or
(f) inability to read in good daylight (with the aid of corrective lenses if worn) a vehicle registration mark containing letters and figures of the prescribed size; that is, where the characters are 79 mm high and 57 mm wide at a distance of 20.5 m (registration mark is one provided before 1 September 2001) or where the characters are 79 mm high and 50 mm wide at a distance of 20 m (registration mark is one provided on or after 1 September 2003). In the case of mowing machines and pedestrian controlled vehicles the distance is 12.3 m in the former case and 12 m in the latter.

The Secretary of State must refuse an applicant a licence if satisfied that the applicant is suffering from one of these disabilities. This does not apply to those who have had a previous licence and whose disability is one of absence of a limb, deformity or loss of use of a limb provided that the condition has not become more acute, nor does it apply if the application is for a provisional licence. Epileptics may be granted licences if free from attacks for one year, or if for the past three years attacks have been restricted to times while asleep, provided that the following conditions are satisfied: so far as practicable, the applicant must comply with medical directions including directions concerning regular check-ups given to him by a registered medical practitioner supervising his treatment; if required by the Secretary of State, the applicant must provide a signed declaration that he will observe such conditions; and the Secretary of State must be satisfied that the driving of a vehicle in accordance with the licence is not likely to be a danger to the public. Those fitted with 'pacemakers' may satisfy the Secretary of State that their driving will not be a source of danger. The Secretary of State may, by notice, require a person to be examined by one of his officers rather than a registered medical practitioner, if he suffers from visual defects, limb disabilities or impairment of cognitive function. Existing licences (including Community licences of persons normally resident in Great Britain) may be revoked totally if such a disability as described above actually arises, or may be revoked and replaced with shorter term licences if a prospective disability (as described above) arises. Licences may be issued which allow the driving of vehicles of a special construction; for example, a vehicle fitted with hand controls for a person who has lost both legs or they may allow driving subject to certain specified conditions. Persons holding driving licences who suffer an actual or prescribed disability must notify the Secretary of State forthwith. Failure without reasonable excuse to do so is an offence.

A person who holds a licence and drives a motor vehicle of the class authorised on a road commits an offence if he knowingly made a false declaration in relation to a relevant disability to obtain the licence. A similar offence is committed where he fails, without reasonable excuse, so to notify specified disabilities during the currency of the licence. A person who drives a motor vehicle on a road, otherwise than in accordance with a licence, commits an additional offence if a licence has earlier been refused on account of such a disability. These offences may also be committed by holders of Community licences normally resident in Great Britain.

RTA 1988, s 96(1) creates the offence of driving a motor vehicle on a road with uncorrected defective eyesight. The offence lies in driving while the eyesight is such that the requirement to read registration marks at the specified distances given above cannot be complied with. The defect in eyesight may be one which cannot be corrected or one which is not for the time being sufficiently corrected to enable the driver to satisfy the above requirement. Thus, a registered blind person necessarily commits the above offence if he drives on a road, whilst a person with impaired vision does not if his vision is sufficiently corrected by wearing spectacles (provided, of course, that he wears them).

A constable may require a person driving a motor vehicle to submit to an eyesight test; it is an offence to refuse to submit to such a test.

Foreigners and driving licences

Persons temporarily present (other than Community licence holders)

The Motor Vehicles (International Circulation) Order 1975, art 2 states that it is lawful for *a person resident outside the United Kingdom who is temporarily in Great Britain* to drive for a period of twelve months from the date of his last entry into the United Kingdom if he holds a Convention driving permit (see below) or a domestic driving permit of a country outside the United Kingdom authorising him to drive the vehicle in question, provided he is not disqualified (eg by age) from holding a British licence.

What has just been said is subject to qualification in respect of large passenger-carrying vehicles, privately operated passenger-carrying vehicles (vehicles not used for carrying passengers for hire or reward which are constructed or adapted to carry more than eight but not more than sixteen passengers), large goods vehicles and medium-sized goods vehicles (vehicles constructed or adapted to carry or haul a load which is not adapted to carry more than nine persons including the driver and exceeds 3.5 tonnes but does not exceed 7.5 tonnes). A holder of either type of permit may drive such a vehicle if he is resident in an EEA state, the Isle of Man, Jersey or Guernsey. Other holders of such a permit may only drive such a vehicle if it has been temporarily brought into Great Britain. In the cases set out in this paragraph no other licence is required.

Generally, any person may cause or permit holders of such Convention or domestic driving permits to drive vehicles which they are authorised by their permit to drive. In the phrase 'temporarily in Great Britain', 'temporarily' is an element other than simply a time element. It involves a presence for casual purposes, for example a holiday, as contrasted with regular habits. For example, an overseas student studying here is not 'temporarily' resident here.

A Convention driving permit is usually referred to as an 'international driving licence'. In Great Britain it is issued by the AA or RAC. The term 'domestic driving permit' refers to the licence issued by the driver's own country and it is therefore lawful for a visitor to Great Britain to drive for a period of one year on the authority of his own, local driving licence. Article 2, above, merely recognises that persons visiting from abroad would experience difficulty in undertaking a test in Great Britain while they are temporarily in this country. These permits are treated as driving licences in every respect and a constable's powers to demand production of a licence and to demand the holder's date of birth apply equally to them.

Resident foreigners (other than Community licence holders)

The Motor Vehicles (Driving Licences) Regulations 1999, reg 80 makes the same provision for a person from abroad who becomes resident in Great Britain, the twelve-month period in this case running from when he became a resident. Someone from abroad who is in this country but who falls outside the term 'temporarily in Great Britain', for example an overseas student, will be resident in Great Britain.

General

A person who becomes resident in Great Britain who is the holder of a relevant permit and is not disqualified for holding or obtaining a licence in Great Britain is, during the period of one year after he becomes so resident, treated as the holder of a licence authorising him to drive all classes of small vehicles (generally vehicles not constructed or adapted to carry more than nine persons inclusive of the driver and vehicles not exceeding 3.5 tonnes, including a combination of such a vehicle and a trailer), motor cycles or mopeds which he is authorised to drive by that permit. A 'relevant permit' is a 'domestic driving permit', or a 'Convention driving permit'. Where a question arises as to whether a person is normally resident in Great Britain or the United Kingdom, a person is deemed to be normally resident if he shows that he will have lived there for not less than 185 days preceding a test appointment.

Holders of driving licences issued by states within the EEA (community licences) who become resident in Great Britain are authorised to drive here without the need to exchange their licences for British licences within a year of becoming resident. Such persons do, however, have a right to exchange their licences. Where matters of validity, standards of health and fitness, and disqualification are concerned, the exchange of licences is mandatory. Resident Community licence holders are subject to the same medical requirements as holders of British licences. Community licence holders resident in Great Britain who wish to drive medium-sized or large goods vehicles and passenger-carrying vehicles of any class must, after a period of twelve months' residence, deliver their licences to the Secretary of State and provide details prescribed by RTA 1988, s 99B. They will be issued with counterparts. The right to the issue of British driving licences is restricted to persons normally resident in the United Kingdom. Community licence holders are also entitled to be licensed to drive a taxi or private hire vehicle or to drive small buses for charitable or similar purposes provided that their Community licence authorises them to drive cars.

Persons who become resident in Great Britain and who hold British external licences granted in the Isle of Man, Guernsey or Jersey authorising the driving of large goods vehicles or passenger-carrying vehicles, and who are not disqualified for holding or obtaining a licence in Great Britain, may drive such vehicles under the authority of those licences for a period of one year from the date upon which they became resident.

People permitted to drive in this country under a domestic driving permit etc who take out a provisional licence during the twelve-month period in order to take a driving test need not comply with the normal conditions applicable to a learner driver if they are still driving under the authority of their domestic permit etc at the time (ie within the twelve-month period).

RTA 1988, s 108(2) empowers the Secretary of State to designate a non-EEA country for the purpose of 'exchangeable licences' where he is satisfied that the driving test in that country is satisfactory. He may, however, restrict approval to the grant of exchange licences to particular circumstances, impose conditions to which they are subject, and limit the exchanged licence to particular classes of vehicles. An up-to-date list of the countries specified by order is contained in the Driving Licences (Exchangeable Licences) Order 2002.

Production of driving licences

By virtue of RTA 1988, s 164(1) a constable or vehicle examiner may demand the production of a driving licence and its counterpart by the following people:

(a) a person driving a motor vehicle on a road; or
(b) a person whom a constable or vehicle examiner has reasonable cause to believe has been the driver of a vehicle at the time when an accident occurred owing to its presence on a road; or
(c) a person whom a constable or vehicle examiner has reasonable cause to believe has committed an offence in relation to the use of a motor vehicle on a road; or
(d) a person who is supervising the holder of a provisional licence while the holder is driving a motor vehicle on a road; or
(e) a person whom a constable or vehicle examiner has reasonable cause to believe was supervising the holder of such a licence when an accident occurred owing to the presence of the vehicle on a road or when an offence is suspected of having been committed by the holder in relation to the use of a vehicle on a road.

When a licence is produced to a constable or vehicle examiner pursuant to a request under RTA 1988, s 164(1), he is entitled to ascertain the name and address of the holder of the licence, its date of issue and the authority by which it was issued. RTA 1988, s 164(2) also provides a power whereby a constable may require a person in circumstances prescribed by the Motor Vehicles (Driving Licence) Regulations 1999 to state his date of birth. These circumstances are:

(a) where that person fails to produce forthwith for examination his driving licence on being required to do so by a constable; or
(b) where, on being so required, that person produces a licence which the police constable has reason to suspect:
    (i)   was not granted to that person; or
    (ii) was granted to him in error; or
    (iii) contains an alteration in its particulars made with intent to deceive; or
(c) where, on being so required, that person produces a licence in which the driver number has been altered, erased or defaced; or
(d) where that person is a person supervising the holder of a provisional licence while the holder is driving a motor vehicle on a road, or is someone whom the constable reasonably suspects to have been supervising such a person when an accident occurred or an offence was committed, and the constable has reasonable cause to suspect that he is under twenty-one years of age.

It is an offence to fail to state a date of birth when so required.

RTA 1988, s 164(4A) provides that, where a constable to whom a provisional licence has been produced by a person driving a motor bicycle has reasonable cause to believe that the holder was not driving it as a part of the training being provided on a training course for motor cyclists, the constable may require him to produce the prescribed certificate of completion of such a course.

A traffic warden is empowered to demand the production of a driving licence where he has reasonable cause to believe that an offence has been committed in contravention of the pedestrian crossing regulations or by leaving a vehicle in a dangerous position.

The term 'licence' means a licence under RTA 1988, Part III or a Community licence.

Police officers have direct access to details of driving licences and their holders through the Police National Computer.

Failure to produce licence

RTA 1988, s 164(3) and (5) provides that:

(a) where a licence has been revoked by the Secretary of State but the holder has not surrendered it and its counterpart; or
(b) where the holder has failed to produce his licence and its counterpart to a court when lawfully required to do so; or
(c) where the Secretary of State has served notice on a Community licence holder in pursuance of s 99C (relevant disability) or s 115A (conduct of holder of LGV or PCV Community licence) requiring delivery of the licence to him,

a constable or vehicle examiner may require the holder to produce them and on production may seize them. RTA 1988, s 164(4) empowers a constable to require the holder of a licence to produce it and its counterpart where he has reasonable cause to believe that a false statement was knowingly made to obtain it.

A person who fails to produce his licence and its counterpart, or a certificate of completion of a training course for motorcyclists, when required to do so under any of the provisions of RTA 1988, s 164 commits an offence under RTA 1988, s 164(6). However, an offence of failing to produce a licence is not committed if the person produces a current receipt for the surrender of the licence issued under the fixed penalty procedure (p 465) and, if required, produces the licence in person immediately on its return at a police station specified at the time of the request, or if within seven days of the request he produces the receipt in person at that police station and, if requested, produces the licence there in person immediately on its return. In addition in proceedings against any person for an offence of failing to produce a licence it is a defence for him to show that:

(a) within seven days after the production of his licence and its counterpart was required he produced them *in person* at such police station as may have been specified by him at the time its production was required; or
(b) he produced them *in person* there as soon as was reasonably practicable; or
(c) it was not reasonably practicable for him to produce them there before the day on which proceedings commenced.

If a licence is not produced at the time its production was required, it is the usual practice of the police to make out a form HO/RT1 which will be produced at the police station nominated, together with the driving licence. This is merely a practice followed by the police and there is no statutory requirement that this be done

Disqualification by a court and penalty points

Prospective revision of system of recording penalty points

The provisions of RTA 1988, Part 3 and the fixed penalty provisions of the RTOA 1988 are prospectively amended. The previous provisions were such that a fixed penalty notice in respect of an endorsable offence could only be issued to a person holding a driving licence and a counterpart. Fixed penalty notices could not therefore be issued to unlicensed drivers. Nor could they be issued to non-GB residents unless they held a counterpart (to a Northern Ireland or EEA community driving licence) recording any penalty points previously awarded. Persons holding such licences may apply for counterparts but few do. The new system therefore makes provision for the issue of fixed penalty notices to drivers who do not have counterparts.

Provision, to be introduced in two stages, is made by the RSA 2006 for the Secretary of State to maintain a 'driving record' which will contain details of endorsements for driving offences.

(1) In the first stage, records will be made of offences by unlicensed and foreign drivers other than those holding counterparts to their driving licences. This will enable constables and vehicle examiners to give fixed penalty notices to such drivers who will not be liable to disqualification under the 'totting-up' procedure. The records kept by the Secretary of State may be instantly checked by enforcement officers. The Secretary of State may make the necessary endorsement in this record in relation to the offence for which the fixed penalty notice is then issued.

(2) The second stage will be introduced at a later stage and will involve all drivers within the new system and counterparts will become redundant. However, there will be two categories of drivers identifying those who hold GB licences and those who do not. Holders of GB licences will be required to produce their licences in order to be given a fixed penalty notice. Those community and Northern Ireland licence holders who previously held counterparts will no longer be treated in the same way as GB licence holders and will be dealt with in the same way as unlicensed and foreign drivers.

All references to 'counterparts' will be removed from existing legislation as these measures come into effect. However, it is likely to be some time before counterparts become obsolete so far as UK licence holders are concerned. A note will be made, where appropriate, in the following text to the effect that such records will replace counterparts when the prospective provisions of the RSA 2006 are brought into force.

Obligatory disqualification

RTOA 1988, s 34(1) deals with disqualification from driving following a conviction for an offence involving obligatory disqualification. On conviction for such an offence, a court must order disqualification for at least a specified minimum period, unless the court for special reasons thinks fit to order a shorter period of disqualification or not to order disqualification at all. These offences, which are all offences under the RTA 1988 unless otherwise indicated, are:

(a) manslaughter (common law offence, see RTOA 1988, Sch 2);
(b) causing death by dangerous driving (RTA 1988, s 1);
(c) dangerous driving (RTA 1988, s 2);
(d) causing death by careless driving when under the influence of drink or drugs (RTA 1988, s 3A);
(e) driving or attempting to drive whilst unfit through drink or drugs (RTA 1988, s 4(1));
(f) driving or attempting to drive with excess alcohol in breath, blood or urine (RTA 1988, s 5(1)(a));
(g) failure to provide specimen for analysis (where specimen required to assess ability or alcohol level at time offender was driving or attempting to drive) to see whether person guilty of an offence under RTOA 1988, s 3A, 4(1) or 5(1)(a)), RTA 1988, s 7(6) and s 7A(6);
(h) motor racing and speed trials on a public highway (RTA 1988, s 12); or
(i) aggravated vehicle-taking (Theft Act 1968, s 12A).

In the case of most of these offences, the specified minimum period of disqualification is twelve months. However, in the case of the offences of causing death by dangerous driving, manslaughter, or causing death by careless driving while under the influence of drink or drugs, it is two years. The same minimum period applies in relation to a person on whom more than one disqualification for a fixed period of fifty-six days or more has been imposed within the three years immediately preceding the commission of the offence. However, a disqualification imposed as a result of an offence committed by using vehicles in the course of crime or in respect of a conviction for stealing or attempting to steal a motor vehicle, joyriding or going equipped to steal etc a motor vehicle, or attempting to commit any such offence, is disregarded for this purpose, as is an interim disqualification on committal for sentence.

If the conviction is for any of the above offences which are connected with the drink-driving laws, that is an offence under RTA 1988, ss 3A, 4(1), 5(1)(a), 7(6) or s 7A(6) referred to above, and there has been a previous conviction for such an offence within the preceding ten years, a court *must* order disqualification for a period of not less than three years, unless there are special reasons for not doing so.

'*Special reasons*' are reasons special to the circumstances of the offence, as opposed to special to the offender. It is of no consequence that the loss of a driving licence will lose the offender his job, that he is a man of previous good character and/or that he has driven for many years without having been convicted of any motoring offence. The courts' approach is strict in this respect. They have refused to accept as special reasons the hardship to a country doctor and his patients or the problems caused for a disabled man. An example of a case where there would be reasons special to the offence is where a man, who thinks that he is drinking non-alcoholic drinks, has his drink 'laced' without his knowledge. In such a case, it is open to the court in its discretion to mitigate the period of disqualification, or not to disqualify at all, because of special reasons. Special reasons might have been found in the case of the country doctor if the country doctor had been called out to a man suffering a heart attack in circumstances in which no other doctor could reasonably have been summoned to attend.

Reduced period of disqualification for attendance on course

Where a person is convicted of an offence under RTA 1988, s 3A (causing death by careless driving when under the influence of drink or drugs etc); s 4 (driving or being in charge when under the influence of drink or drugs); s 5 (driving or being in charge with excess alcohol); or s 7(6) (failing to provide a specimen) and the court makes an order of disqualification for a period nor less than twelve months, an order may be made under RTOA 1988, s 34A that the period of disqualification shall be reduced if, by a date specified in the order, the offender satisfactorily completed an approved course. The reduced period must not be less than three months, nor more than on quarter of the period of disqualification. Section 34A is prospectively replaced by RSA 2006, s 35, the new s 34A referring to a 'relevant drink offence'. The term includes the offences above and also an offence against s 7(6A) (failure to allow a specimen to be subjected to a laboratory test). The new s 34A will also apply to a disqualification after a conviction for careless or inconsiderate driving, failing to comply with traffic signs, use of load contrary to scheme or regulations, or speeding.

Discretionary disqualification

RTOA 1988, s 34(2) deals with discretionary disqualification. Where a person is convicted of an offence which is shown in Sch 2 to the Act to be one which carries discretionary disqualification and either:

(a) the penalty points to be taken into account on that occasion number fewer than 12; or
(b) the offence is not one involving obligatory endorsement;

the court may disqualify for any period which it thinks fit. Disqualification may not be for an indefinite period, since the court must state the period of disqualification (although it may be for life). Particulars of any disqualification must be endorsed on the licence or its counterpart (or the driving record, when the RSA 2006 is in force). Offences which carry discretionary disqualification usually carry obligatory endorsement.

Endorsement and penalty points

RTOA 1988, s 44 provides that, unless there are special reasons not to do so, where a person is convicted of an offence involving obligatory endorsement the court must order particulars of the conviction to be endorsed on his licence (or the driving record, when the RSA 2006 is in force) and the endorsement must also include:

(a) if the court orders disqualification, particulars of the disqualification; or
(b) if the court does not order disqualification, particulars of the offence (including its date) and the number of penalty points to be attributed as shown in respect of the offence in RTOA 1988, Sch 2 (or, where a range of numbers is so shown, a number falling within the range).

It follows that, where an offender is convicted and the court imposes disqualification under RTOA 1988, s 34, no penalty points are to be attributed for that offence or any other offence in respect of which he is convicted on that occasion. This prevents the possibility of 'double disqualification'.

Where a person is convicted of two or more offences included in Sch 2, all of which are committed on the same occasion, the number of points awarded is generally the highest single figure applicable to one of those offences.

RTOA 1988, Sch 2 lists the offences which carry penalty points. Where a person is convicted for aiding and abetting offences involving obligatory disqualification the number of penalty points to be attributed to the offence is 10. The offences of dangerous driving, causing death by careless driving when under the influence of drink or drugs, driving or attempting to drive vehicles when under the influence of drink or drugs or with excess alcohol in breath, blood or urine, failing to provide a specimen for analysis, all carry obligatory endorsement of 3–11 penalty points, in addition to obligatory disqualification (unless there are special reasons). However, as indicated above, if disqualification is ordered the licence will not be endorsed with penalty points.

The offence of failing to stop after an accident carries 5–10 points, as does that of failing to report an accident. Insurance offences carry 6–8, careless driving 3–9 and failing to provide a specimen for a screening breath test 4. Any contravention of the construction and use regulations which constitutes an endorsable offence carries 3 points, as does a failure to comply with traffic directions, with the directions of school crossing patrols or with pedestrian crossing regulations. All offences of exceeding a speed limit carry 3–6 penalty points or 3 (fixed penalty). However, this is prospectively amended by RSA 2006, s 17 which extends the range of penalty points which may be given in respect of speeding to 2–6 or appropriate penalty points (fixed penalty). Offences concerned with driving licences carry 3–6 penalty points, except driving whilst disqualified by a court order which carries 6 points.

Unless there are special reasons for not doing so a court *must* endorse a person's licence if he is convicted of an offence shown in RTOA 1988, Sch 2 to be one in respect of which endorsement is obligatory.

Attendance on courses—effect upon penalty points

RTOA 1988, ss 30A, 30B, 30C and 30D (not in force at the time of writing) authorise courts to order a reduction in penalty points, to take effect on completion of a training course, where a person has been convicted of careless driving, inconsiderate driving, failing to comply with traffic signs, use of road contrary to scheme or regulations, or speeding, and is not disqualified but has his licence endorsed. There must be at least 7 but no more than 11 penalty points to be taken into account at the time of conviction. If such a person successfully completes a course within twelve months after the order, 3 points (or less if the court endorsed less) will cease to be taken into consideration under 'totting-up' considerations.

This option will not be available where a person who has committed one of these offences within the preceding three years and has successfully completed such a course, nor to a person who committed the offence during his probationary period under RT(ND)A 1995.

The Secretary of State is empowered to alter by regulations the three-year period and the minimum number of penalty points to be taken into account before such an order can be made.

Endorsement—holders of Community licences

RTOA 1988, s 91A provides that within those sections of the RTOA 1988 concerned with the production of a licence to a court in the event of conviction for an offence involving obligatory or discretionary disqualification, the term 'licence' includes references to a Community licence. RTOA 1988, s 91A(4) requires a court to notify the Secretary of State of any endorsement made to a counterpart of a Community licence and s 91A(5) requires a court to send a Community licence and its counterpart (if any) in the event of a convicted person being disqualified from driving. The Secretary of State will notify the EEA state concerned of the disqualification.

Duty to notify EU member state of driving disqualification of non-United Kingdom resident

The Crime (International Co-operation) Act 2003, Part 3, Chapter 1 (ss 54 to 75) deals with this as well as the matters described under the next heading. Part 3, Chapter 1 is not in force at the time of writing. C(IC)A 2003, s 55 provides that where an individual normally resident in another EU member state is disqualified by a United Kingdom court for holding or obtaining a driving licence, the appropriate Minister must generally notify the state in which the individual is normally resident of the details of the disqualification.

EU member states are similarly obliged to notify the United Kingdom about the disqualification by their courts of a United Kingdom resident.

Recognition of disqualification imposed in another EU state, Northern Ireland etc

By virtue of the Crime (International Co-operation) Act 2003, Part 3, Chapter 1, where an individual normally resident in the United Kingdom is convicted in another EU member state of an offence of reckless or dangerous driving, drink-driving, speeding, driving while disqualified or certain other offences, and is disqualified in that state for holding or obtaining a driving licence, and provided certain conditions are satisfied, the appropriate Minister in the United Kingdom must give a notice disqualifying that individual for holding or obtaining a licence for the unexpired period of the foreign disqualification beginning twenty-one days from the giving of the notice; where the unexpired period is less than one month the Minister is not required to give such a notice but may do so.

RTA 1988, s 102A also provides that a person disqualified for holding or obtaining a driving licence by a court in Northern Ireland, the Isle of Man, any of the Channel Islands, or Gibraltar, is disqualified for holding or obtaining a licence in Great Britain for the period of the disqualification.

Obligatory disqualification for repeated offences

RTOA 1988, s 35 applies to an offence involving discretionary disqualification and obligatory endorsement and to an offence involving obligatory disqualification in respect of which no order is made under s 34. Section 35 requires that where, on conviction for such an offence, the award of the penalty points for the offence, together with those already endorsed on the licence, brings the total to 12, the offender must be disqualified for a minimum period of six months if the points have been accumulated within three years of the commission of the offence for which penalty points are then awarded, unless the court is satisfied that there are grounds for mitigating the normal consequences of the conviction and thinks fit to order a shorter period of disqualification or not to order disqualification. If the total is in excess of 12 this may be recognised by disqualification for a longer period. Once the disqualification has been imposed the driving licence is in effect wiped clean. However, 'wiping clean' is restricted to disqualification under s 35 for repeated offences. Where a disqualification is imposed under s 34 for a specific offence, the penalty points previously accumulated remain effective at the end of the period of disqualification until the expiry of three years from the date of the offence for which they were imposed. It is important to note that disqualification as a result of this 'totting-up' procedure is in respect of convictions within the three years immediately preceding the commission of the offence in question (not a conviction for that offence).

It is also important to remember that, where the 'totting-up' rules are satisfied, a court must impose a disqualification for six months or more, unless it is satisfied, having regard to all the circumstances, that there are grounds for mitigating the normal consequences of the conviction and therefore thinks fit to disqualify for a lesser period or not at all. RTOA 1988, s 35(4) states that no account is to be taken, as a ground for mitigating the normal consequences, of any circumstances which are alleged to make the offence or any of the offences not a serious one; nor of any hardship other than exceptional hardship; nor of any circumstances which, within the preceding three years, have already been taken into account in ordering the offender to be disqualified for a shorter period or not to be ordered to be disqualified at all. Exceptional hardship which would be caused to a person other than the offender (for example a dependent, invalid wife) may be taken into account.

It follows from the above rules that, even if a court decides not to order disqualification when it is discretionary in relation to the offence in question, because of mitigating circumstances, it may be required to disqualify under RTOA 1988, s 35 as a result of the 'totting-up' of the penalty points attributed for the offence with previous penalty points.

A person who is already the holder of a driving licence authorising him to drive a vehicle of a particular class is disqualified by RTA 1988, s 102 from holding another licence for that class of vehicle. This is to prevent a person from holding more than one licence. If he was able to do so he could share out his penalty points by holding two licences indicating different addresses.

Use of vehicle in commission of crime: discretion to disqualify

The Powers of Criminal Courts (Sentencing) Act 2000, s 147 provides that if the Crown Court is satisfied that a motor vehicle was used (by the person convicted or anyone else) for the purpose of committing or facilitating the commission of an offence, it may disqualify the person convicted for such a period as it thinks fit from holding or obtaining a licence to drive. 'Facilitation' will include use after the offence for disposal of property or avoiding apprehension or detection. This power may only be exercised by the Crown Court on convicting an offender of an offence punishable on indictment with imprisonment for a term of two years or more, or when sentencing such a person after his conviction before a magistrates' court.

Disqualification: offenders in general

The Powers of Criminal Courts Crime (Sentencing) Act 2000, s 146 empowers a court on conviction of any offence to order the offender to be disqualified from holding or obtaining a driving licence. The Court of Appeal has held that this power is not limited to offences connected with the driving of a motor vehicle. However, there may be human rights implications where such disqualification is ordered for an offence, the commission of which was not aided, in any respect, by the use of a motor vehicle and which could not be prevented by the removal of the right to drive.

Legislation also empowers a magistrates' court to order disqualification in a case of default in paying a fine.

Effect of an order of disqualification

RTOA 1988, s 37 provides that, where a licence holder is disqualified by order of a court, the licence is to be treated as revoked with effect from the beginning of the period of disqualification. However, where the disqualification is for a fixed period shorter than fifty-six days in respect of an offence involving obligatory endorsement or the order is made under s 26 (interim disqualification), this will not prevent the licence from again having effect at the end of the period of disqualification.

Removal of disqualification

RTOA 1988, s 42 provides that a person who has been disqualified by a court may apply to have the disqualification removed as follows:

(a) if the disqualification is for less than four years, after two years;
(b) if it is for less than ten but more than four years, when half the disqualification has expired; or
(c) in any other case (life or ten or more years), when five years have passed.

Disqualification until passing of driving test

RTOA 1988, s 36 provides that, where a person is disqualified under s 34 (obligatory disqualification) on conviction for manslaughter by the driver of a motor vehicle, or for causing death by dangerous driving, or for dangerous driving, for causing death by careless driving while under the influence of drink or drugs, or is disqualified under ss 34 or 35 (repeated offences) in such circumstances or for such period as the Secretary of State may prescribe, or is convicted of an offence involving obligatory endorsement which may be prescribed by the Secretary of State, the court must order him to be disqualified until he has passed the appropriate driving test.

Where a person is disqualified under s 34 on conviction for any other offence carrying obligatory endorsement, the court may order him to be disqualified until he has passed the appropriate driving test.

An order of disqualification until the passing of a driving test ends when a certificate of competence is produced to the Secretary of State.

The term 'appropriate driving test' is prospectively amended by RSA 2006, s 37 so as to mean, in such circumstances as the Secretary of State prescribes, an extended driving test, and, otherwise, a test of competence to drive which is not an extended driving test. Currently, an extended driving test is required where a person is convicted of an offence involving obligatory disqualification or is disqualified under RTOA 1988, s 35, and the ordinary driving test is required in any other circumstances.

A person disqualified until he has passed a driving test under RTOA 1988, s 36 is permitted by s 37(3) to take out a provisional licence, once any fixed period of disqualification has expired, in which case he may drive under the conditions applicable to such a licence. A person who drives under a provisional licence granted by virtue of s 37(3), but who does not comply with the conditions attached to such a licence, commits an offence contrary to RTA 1988, s 103, of driving whilst disqualified. A person charged with driving while disqualified who relies on RTOA 1988, s 37(3) has the burden of proving that he is the holder of a provisional licence and that he was driving in accordance with the provisions of such a licence.

Revocation of licence of 'new driver'

Under the provisions of RT(ND)A 1995, where a qualified driver commits an offence involving obligatory endorsement during his 'probationary period' (two years from becoming a qualified driver) and the penalty points to be taken into account on that occasion number 6 or more, the court must send the Secretary of State a notice containing the particulars to be endorsed on the counterpart of the person's licence together with the licence (and counterpart). A similar requirement is made of a fixed penalty clerk, where a fixed penalty offence is involved. The Secretary of State must, by notice, revoke that licence. Such a licence may not be restored until the person concerned has passed a relevant driving test within the relevant period (not more than two years).

The prescribed probationary period will come to an end:

(a) where an order is made under RTOA 1988, s 36 (disqualified until a test is passed);
(b) after revocation of the licence by the Secretary of State (as described in the preceding paragraph) where the licence is restored, after passing a test; or
(c) where the driver has been driving on a provisional licence plus test certificate which have been revoked, where a full licence is granted after passing a test.

Obtaining licence, or driving, whilst disqualified

RTA 1988, s 103 creates two offences which can be committed by a person disqualified from holding or obtaining a licence: obtaining a licence while so disqualified, and driving a motor vehicle on a road whilst so disqualified. The section deals with those disqualified by a court (including those disqualified until they pass a test); these offences do not apply where the disqualification is by reason of age. We explain in Chapter 16 what constitutes 'driving' for the purposes of the commission of an offence under the RTA 1988. An order of disqualification remains valid unless it is suspended pending an appeal or is subsequently revoked. A subsequent revocation does not excuse driving whilst the order was in force. The prosecution must prove beyond reasonable doubt, not only the order of disqualification (by means of certificate of conviction or entry in a court register), but that the person before the court is the person so disqualified. There is no prescribed way that the identification of the accused as the person disqualified must be proved; it can be proved by any admissible means. Although a divisional court has stated that proof of identity may be given by:

(a) admission under the Criminal Justice Act 1967 (CJA 1967), s 10;
(b) fingerprints under the Criminal Justice Act 1948, s 39 (this method of proving previous convictions has since been abolished by the Criminal Justice and Police Act 2001 (CJPA 2001) but the Police and Criminal Evidence Act 1984 (PACE), s 64 (as amended by s 82(2) of the 2001 Act) provides that fingerprints may be used after the fulfilment of the purposes for which they were taken for the purpose of the conduct of a prosecution and this provision should cover the proof of a previous conviction, where it is an essential element in an offence (as in driving while disqualified), in relation to which the fingerprints were taken); or
(c) evidence of a person who was present in court when the disqualification was imposed;

this does not mean that an admission other than a formal one under s 10 is irrelevant. For example, a statement made under CJA 1967, s 9, which refers to a person whom the deponent knew and stating that the deponent knew him under a particular name, may entitle justices to find sufficient evidence of identification. It will normally be possible to establish a prima facie case on the basis of a match between the personal details of the accused and those recorded on the certificate of conviction. Indeed, although where the accused has a very common name and the date of birth on the certificate is not precisely the same as the accused's there may well not be a prima facie evidence of identity, where the accused has a highly unusual name it may not be necessary for the date of birth on the certificate to correspond with his. If an accused calls no evidence to contradict a prima facie case, it is open to the court to be satisfied that it has been proved that the accused was the person disqualified. In addition, if it is proper and fair to do so and warning has been given, a failure to give contradictory evidence can additionally give rise to an adverse inference under the Criminal Justice and Public Order Act 1994, s 35, which is dealt with on pp 245–246.

   In terms of proof of the order of disqualification, a divisional court has ruled that justices are not entitled to consult their own computerised records of convictions in order to establish whether a person charged with this offence is a person who has, on a previous occasion, been disqualified from driving. The justices had been advised that they were permitted to take notice of convictions which had occurred within their area of jurisdiction. The divisional court said that the prosecutor was obliged to prove that the person concerned was a disqualified driver. It was not for justices to satisfy themselves on such matters.

Offender escaping consequences of endorsable offence by deception

RTOA 1988, s 49 provides that where, in dealing with a person convicted of an endorsable offence (ie one involving obligatory or discretionary endorsement), a court was deceived regarding any circumstances that were or might have been taken into account in deciding whether, or for how long, to disqualify him and the deception constituted or was due to an offence committed by that person, then, if he is convicted of that offence (the one then before the court), the court has the same powers of disqualification as had the court which was deceived. However, the court must take account of the order made by the first court on his conviction for the endorsable offence.

If a person produces a licence which he has obtained free of endorsement by failing to provide particulars of those endorsements, he may escape disqualification on the 'totting-up' provisions of the penalty points system. This section allows a court, when convicting that person of an offence of obtaining such a licence without giving particulars of current endorsements, to disqualify him even though the offence then being dealt with is not one which carries penalty points.

Effect of disqualification upon holders of large goods vehicle or passenger-carrying vehicle drivers' licences

RTA 1988, s 115 requires that a large goods vehicle or passenger-carrying vehicle driver's licence must be revoked if, in relation to its holder, prescribed circumstances occur, or his conduct is such as to make him unfit to hold such a licence. RTA 1988, s 115A(1) makes similar provision in respect of the holder of a LGV Community licence or a PCV Community licence.

The 'prescribed circumstances' referred to in RTA 1988, s 115A are set out in respect of a large goods vehicle driver's licence or a LGV Community licence by reg 55 of the Motor Vehicles (Driving Licences) Regulations 1999. They are that, in the case of the holder of such a licence who is under the age of twenty-one, he has been convicted, or is by virtue of RTOA 1988, s 58 (*effect of endorsement without hearing* under fixed penalty points provisions) to be treated as if he had been convicted, of an offence as a result of which more than 3 penalty points are to be taken into account. Where such large goods vehicle licences are revoked, the cases in which such persons must be disqualified indefinitely or for a fixed period must be determined by the licensing authority. Where it determines that the disqualification shall be for a fixed period, such a person must be disqualified until he reaches the age of twenty-one or for such longer period as the licensing authority may determine. No corresponding provisions have been made in respect of large passenger-carrying vehicle licences.

Regulation 56 applies to circumstances in which large goods vehicle or passenger-carrying vehicle drivers' licences are treated as revoked by RTOA 1988, s 37 (effect of disqualification by order of court). RTA 1988, s 117 is modified by reg 56 to provide that, where the licence to be treated as revoked is a large goods vehicle driver's licence held by a person under the age of twenty-one, the licensing authority must order that person to be disqualified either indefinitely or for a fixed period, and where it determines that it shall be for a fixed period, he must be disqualified until he reaches the age of twenty-one or for such longer period as the licensing authority determines. Where the licence revoked is held by any other person, or is a large passenger-carrying vehicle driver's licence:

(a) the licensing authority may order that person to be disqualified either indefinitely or for a fixed period; or

(b) except where the licence is a provisional licence, if it appears to the licensing authority that, owing to that person's conduct, it is expedient to require him to comply with the prescribed conditions applicable to provisional licences until he passes a test, the licensing authority may order him to be disqualified from holding or obtaining a full licence until he passes the test.

Where a licensing authority orders disqualification until a test is passed, the test must be a test for a licence authorising the driving of any class of vehicle in Category C (other than C1), C + E, D or D + E which, prior to his disqualification by order of the court, the offender was authorised to drive by his revoked licence.

MOTOR VEHICLE INSURANCE

Using, causing or permitting use of, a motor vehicle on a road without insurance

RTA 1988, s 143(1) states that a person must not use, or cause or permit any other person to use, a motor vehicle on a road or other public place unless there is in force in relation to the use of that vehicle by that person or that other person, as the case may be, such a policy of insurance or such security in respect of third-party risks as complies with the requirements of Part VI of the RTA 1988. RTA 1988, s 143(4) states that Part VI of the Act does not apply to invalid carriages not exceeding 254 kg unladen weight. The few vehicles of this type which are still in use are covered by the Department of Health. Since electrically assisted pedal cycles are not motor vehicles (unless they fall outside the relevant regulations), the provisions dealing with insurance do not apply to them.

As in the case of driving without a driving licence, the onus is upon an accused who is proved to have used a motor vehicle on a road or other public place, to prove the existence of insurance as this is a fact peculiarly within his knowledge. However, a divisional court has said that it is *desirable* that there should be, where possible, a statutory demand for its production.

The terms 'use', 'cause' and 'permit' are discussed in Chapter 10, below. Basically, a person who drives a vehicle 'uses' it, but 'using' is not limited to driving. 'Use' means 'have the use of', with the result that, for example, if someone parks a motor vehicle on a road he can be said to be using it while it is parked, and it has been held that this is so even though the vehicle has been totally immobilised. Where an employee drives a motor vehicle owned by his employer in the course of his employment, his employer is regarded in law as also using it. A person 'causes' a vehicle to be used when, being in a position to do so, he expressly orders or authorises the vehicle to be used; and he 'permits' a vehicle to be used when he allows another person to use it. In each case, of course, the use must be on a road or other public place without there being in force in relation to the use of the person using the vehicle a requisite third-party policy of insurance or security.

The prohibition against using, or causing or permitting the use of, an uninsured vehicle is absolute in the sense that it is no defence that the accused reasonably believed that he, or the person allowed etc to drive, was covered by an insurance policy etc. There is one exception: under RTA 1988, s 143(3) it is a defence for a person charged with using an uninsured motor vehicle to prove that it did not belong to him and was not in his possession under a contract of hiring or loan, and that he was using it in the course of his employment and neither knew nor had reason to believe that it was not properly insured etc. This is reasonable: an employee will usually have no knowledge of the administrative affairs of his employer.

The Court of Appeal has said that there can be a 'user' of a motor vehicle by a person who is not the driver. The Court summarised factors established within appeal court hearings:

(1) A 'user' is by definition someone required to provide third-party cover and, if he fails to do so, is potentially liable both criminally and civilly.
(2) Not all passengers are users even when they know that the vehicle is being driven without insurance.
(3) There has to be present in the putative user some element of controlling, managing or operating the vehicle.
(4) That element can exist as a result of a joint venture to use the vehicle for a particular purpose or where the passenger procures the making of the journey.
(5) Not every joint venture or procurement, however, will involve the element of control or management necessary to constitute the passenger as a user.
(6) Whether in any given case there is sufficient element of control or management to constitute the passenger as a user is a question of fact and degree for the trial judge.

Can a person be said to permit his vehicle to be used on a road or other public place without insurance when he has lent it out on the express condition that it should only be used if its use is covered by insurance and its subsequent use is not so covered? The law provides a rather odd answer. If the condition is directly communicated to the person who uses the vehicle without insurance, the person imposing the condition does not permit his vehicle to be used without insurance. This seems sensible. How can you permit something which you have expressly forbidden? Thus, it is somewhat surprising that a divisional court has held that, if the condition as to use being covered by insurance has not been directly communicated to the user but has been communicated to someone else, for example to someone who borrows the vehicle, with a view to it being driven by the user, and it is used in breach of that condition, the person imposing the condition does in law permit uninsured use.

A person cannot permit another's use if he was not in a position to forbid it. Thus A, who supervises B, a learner driver, in B's own car cannot be convicted of permitting its uninsured use.

Keeping a vehicle which does not meet insurance requirements

RTA 1988, s 143 requires insurance in respect of the use of a motor vehicle on a road or public place. RSA 2006, s 22 prospectively inserts new ss 114A, 144B, 144C, 144D and 159A, and Sch 5 to that Act prospectively inserts a new Sch 2A, into the RTA 1988.

Section 144A creates an offence of keeping a motor vehicle which does not meet the insurance requirements. A vehicle will meet the insurance requirements if it is covered by a policy of insurance or a security complying with RTA 1988 and *either* the policy or security, or a related certificate, identifies the vehicle covered by its registration mark *or* the policy or security covers any vehicle, or any particular type of vehicle, owned by the person named in it or a related certificate. There are no penalty points to be imposed for this offence.

Section 144B specifies exceptions which are generally the same as those set out in s 144 (vehicles of local authorities, the police and National Health Service). Other exceptions may apply where the vehicle is no longer kept by the registered keeper, it is not kept for use on a road or other public place or has been stolen. However, these exceptions only apply if a prior statement (such as a SORN declaration) has been made in respect of the vehicle.

Section 144C authorises the Secretary of State to serve a fixed penalty notice on a person whom he believes to have committed an offence against s 144A. That penalty at present will be £100.

The Secretary of State is authorised by s 144D and Sch 2A to make regulations authorising the clamping of vehicles by an authorised person who has reason to believe that a s 144A offence has been committed, and their removal and disposal. Such regulations may exempt vehicles displaying a disabled person's badge and provide for the release of vehicles upon payment where the person shows that the vehicle can be driven away without committing an offence against the RTA 1988, s 143 and that he is not guilty of an offence against s 144A.

A new s 159A is prospectively inserted into the RTA 1988, which authorises the making of regulations requiring the Motor Insurers' Information Centre to provide information to prescribed persons for the purposes of their functions under the insurance provisions of RTA 1988.

Third-party insurance policies

Certificate of insurance

The requirement made by RTA 1988, s 143 is that there must be a policy of insurance (or a security: see later) in respect of third-party risks in accordance with Part VI (ie ss 143 to 162) of that Act in relation to the use of the vehicle by the person using it. By RTA 1988, s 147, no policy of insurance has effect unless the insurer has delivered to the person insured a certificate of insurance in the prescribed form. Therefore 'telephone insurance' is not valid; no certificate has been delivered at that time giving evidence of a contract between insurer and insured. Police officers frequently exercise discretion in circumstances in which a company has clearly accepted liability for third-party risks but some technicality has delayed delivery of a certificate. A cover note is a certificate.

What must be covered

RTA 1988, s 145 provides that, in order to comply with the requirements of Part VI of the Act, a policy must be issued by an 'authorised insurer' and must insure such person, persons or classes of persons as may be specified in it in respect of any liability which may be incurred by him or them in respect of the death of or bodily injury to any person (other than the driver) or damage to property up to a maximum value of £250,000 caused by, or arising out of, the use of the vehicle on a road or other public place in Great Britain.

The policy must also cover him or them:

(a) in respect of any liability for the emergency treatment of persons injured;
(b) in the case of a vehicle normally based in Great Britain, in respect of any liability which may be incurred as a result of its use within the territory of any member

of the EU, according to the law on compulsory insurance against civil liability in that state or, if it would give higher cover, the law which would be applicable if the vehicle was used in Great Britain; and

(c) in the case of a vehicle normally based in another EU state, in respect of any liability which may be incurred as a result of the use of the vehicle in Great Britain if, under the law of that other state, he or they would be required to be insured in respect of a liability which would arise under it had the event occurred in that state, and the cover required by that law is higher than that required as indicated in the previous paragraph.

Extent of cover

The nature of the policy held will be specified in the certificate. A policy covering use for social, domestic and pleasure purposes does not cover business use. However, to give a lift to a friend who is on business at the time is not a business use of the vehicle. To help move household goods for a friend without payment is not a business use, but it might be if payment was made. It is usual for non-business policies to exclude use for hire or reward, but RTA 1988, s 150 makes specific provisions for 'car-sharing' schemes. Provided that arrangements are made before the journey, that payment is in respect of running costs and depreciation only, and that the vehicle used is not adapted to carry more than eight passengers, the use is not for hire or reward.

Some policies allow persons to drive with the permission of the insured person if such a person 'holds or has held a driving licence' and is not disqualified. If that person has at any time held a licence, whether full or provisional, it is sufficient in law to satisfy such a requirement. The terms of the policy will have to be examined in circumstances in which the class of vehicle which the person is licensed to drive is different to the class of vehicle which is being driven. If the policy demands that such a person holds or has held a licence to cover the same class of vehicle as is covered by the policy, then use by a person who does not hold (and has not held) such a licence will amount to uninsured use, unless the licence which he holds may act as a provisional one to cover use of the vehicle in question. Similarly, where a person has borrowed a vehicle subject to an implied limitation, of which he was aware, concerning the purpose for which the vehicle was to be driven, he does not have the consent of the owner for a purpose outside that limitation. Where, therefore, insurance cover was dependent upon the driver having 'the consent of the owner thereof', use outside that limitation was uninsured use.

The use of trailers in Great Britain does not expressly need to be covered in respect of third-party risks, whereas this is essential in other EU countries. However, the use of trailers in Great Britain is generally covered in all policies of insurance and would seem to be within the use of the motor vehicle in any case. Injury caused to a person by a trailer is certainly caused due to the use of the motor vehicle on a road or other public place.

If the terms in which a policy is drawn up do not cover the particular use of the vehicle, an offence is committed regardless of the insurer's willingness to meet liabilities.

Validity

When a policy has been taken out it remains in force until it expires or is validly set aside. If a disqualified driver obtains insurance by failing to disclose his disqualification, then, although such insurance is obtained by means of a false declaration, it remains valid until the company takes steps to set aside the policy. If the company does set it aside, this only invalidates the policy for the future.

It is the practice of some insurance companies to insert restrictive clauses in their policies which can affect their validity in particular circumstances. However, RTA 1988, s 148 states that the third-party requirement of s 143 must be covered by companies regardless of restrictions which might be inserted covering the age, mental or physical condition of a driver; the condition of the vehicle; the number of persons carried; the load; the times or areas of use; the horse power cylinder capacity or value of the vehicle; the carrying of any special apparatus or the carrying on the vehicle of special identification marks. Where companies impose such restrictions, which might be, for example, to maintain the vehicle in good condition, not to exceed recommended loads, or to fit a crook lock or alarm system or 'identicar' markings, they are still liable for third-party risks because of s 148.

When a person is apprehended for taking motor vehicles without consent, it is good practice to check any certificate of insurance held by him in respect of motor vehicles. It is the terms of the policy which are important, not the moral implications. If his policy covers the use by him of another vehicle not owned by him or hired to him by a hire-purchase agreement, that policy will cover such use even though the vehicle has been taken illegally. It would be different if the use covered was similar but 'with the consent of the owner of such vehicle'.

Securities and other exemptions from insurance requirements

Securities

A security, rather than a policy of insurance, can satisfy the provisions of Part VI of the Act if it satisfies certain conditions set out in RTA 1988, s 146. The security must consist of an undertaking by the giver of the security (who must be an authorised insurer or some body of persons in the business of giving securities which has deposited with the Accountant General of the Supreme Court (the Accountant General of the Senior Courts, when the relevant provision in the Constitutional Reform Act 2005 comes into force) the sum of £500,000 in respect of that business). The undertaking must be to make good, subject to any conditions specified therein, any failure by the person covered by the security duly to discharge any third-party liability for which insurance would otherwise be required under Part VI of the Act. Use of securities is frequently made by large undertakings, such as bus companies, which would experience unnecessary difficulties in negotiating separate insurance in respect of a large fleet of vehicles. A security is of no effect for the purposes of Part VI unless there is a 'certificate of security' in force in relation to the vehicles.

Exemptions

The offences relating to use without third-party insurance or security, which are provided by RTA 1988, s 143, are subject to exemptions provided by RTA 1988, s 144. RTA 1988, s 144 also exempts from the requirement for third-party insurance or security:

(a) a vehicle owned by a local authority or a National Parks Authority, at a time when it is driven under the owner's control;

(b) a vehicle owned by a police authority or the Serious Organised Crime Agency, when driven under the owner's control;

(c) a vehicle being driven by a person for police purposes by or under the direction of a police constable, or by a person employed by a police authority; a police officer on duty using his own car for police purposes falls within this exemption;

(d) a vehicle being driven for salvage purposes pursuant to Part IX of the Merchant Shipping Act 1995;

(e) a vehicle being used for the purpose of its being furnished under a direction under the Army Act 1955 or the Air Force Act 1955;

(f) a vehicle owned by a health service body, at a time when the vehicle is being driven under the owner's control;

(g) an ambulance owned by an NHS Trust, at a time when it is being driven under the owner's control; or

(h) a vehicle made available by the Secretary of State to any person, body or local authority under the National Health Service Act 1977 when used within the prescribed terms.

The reasoning behind these exemptions is clear: the vehicles are either owned by or being used by undertakings which are in a position to meet liabilities which might be incurred. Crown vehicles appear to be similarly exempt, as RTA 1988, s 183, which deals with the application of the provisions of the Act to the Crown, does not mention RTA 1988, s 143.

Other requirements in respect of motor vehicle insurance

RTA 1988, s 147(4) requires that where a policy or security to which a certificate of insurance or security relates becomes cancelled, either by mutual consent or by virtue of the provisions of the policy or security, the certificate must be returned to the person who issued the policy within seven days. If a certificate has been lost or destroyed, a statutory declaration to that effect must be made within that period. An offence is committed by a person who fails to comply with these provisions.

RTA 1988, s 154 requires any person against whom a claim is made in respect of any such liability as is required to be insured against by s 145 (eg third-party risks involving death or bodily injury, damage to property or the cost of hospital treatment) to provide particulars of his insurance cover in respect of that liability. It is an offence to fail to comply with such a requirement without reasonable excuse, or wilfully to make a false statement in reply to such a demand. These provisions allow the administrative officers of hospitals etc to recover the cost of emergency treatment from vehicle insurers.

Details of existing insurance policies and securities to be made available to the Police Information Technology Organisation

The Vehicles (Crime) Act 2001, s 36 permits the Secretary of State to make regulations for relevant information which is required to be kept by reg 10 of the Motor Vehicles (Third Party Risks) Regulations 1972 (keeping of records by companies issuing a policy or security of names and addresses, specified motor vehicles, dates of validity and any conditions affecting indemnity) or by any subsequent regulations made under the RTA 1988 to be made available to the Police Information Technology Organisation. The term 'relevant information' means information relating to policies of insurance, securities or certificates issued with policies or securities, or information relating to motor vehicles to which RTA 1988, s 143 does not apply or to any certificates or other documents issued in connection with such vehicles.

SOCPA 2005, s 153 empowers the Secretary of State to make regulations requiring the Motor Insurers' Information Centre to make available 'relevant motor vehicle insurance information' to the Police Information Technology Organisation (PITO) for it to process with a view to making the processed information available for use by police officers. 'Relevant motor vehicle insurance information' means information relating to vehicles whose use was, but is no longer, insured. The Disclosure of Vehicle Insurance Information Regulations 2005 authorise the provision of such information at intervals specified by PITO. That organisation may process the information in a form which will be of assistance to a police officer in establishing whether or not an offence of uninsured use of a vehicle has been committed. Chief officers of police may further process that information to assist a police officer in deciding whether or not to demand production of evidence of insurance. All such information must not be disclosed other than for the purposes of proceedings.

Fraud, forgery etc

By RTA 1988, s 174(5) it is an offence to make a false statement, or to withhold any material information, for the purpose of obtaining the issue of a certificate of insurance or security, or any other document which may be produced in lieu of a certificate of insurance or security. Any person who issues such a document, which to his knowledge is false in any material particular, commits an offence against RTA 1988, s 175.

The alternative documents to which RTA 1988, s 174(5) refers are specified by reg 7 of the Motor Vehicles (Third-Party Risks) Regulations 1972 as follows:

(a) duplicates of certificates of security;
(b) certificates of deposit;
(c) a certificate signed by a police authority etc; or
(d) in the case of a vehicle normally based in another EU country, or Finland, Norway, or Switzerland, a document issued by the insurer in the prescribed form.

The making of false statements to obtain insurance is not uncommon. The disclosure of previous convictions for motoring offences, particularly those involving endorsement, can lead to high premiums which can be avoided by non-disclosure. In this context, the Rehabilitation of Offenders Act 1974 is important. The Act provides for convictions to become 'spent'. It also provides that where a question seeking information with respect to a person's previous convictions is put to him, otherwise than in proceedings before a judicial authority, the question must be treated as not relating to spent convictions and answers may be made accordingly. Most road traffic offences will have resulted in a fine and as a result will become spent after a period of five years.

The offence of making a false statement contrary to RTA 1988, s 174(5) is an absolute offence and it is not necessary to prove that the person who made the statement was aware of its falsity (or even of the risk that it might be false). It is submitted, however, that it would be essential to prove a deliberate act of 'withholding'.

RTA 1988, s 173 makes it an offence for a person, with intent to deceive, to forge, alter, use, lend for use, or allow to be used, a certificate of insurance or a document which may be used in lieu thereof. The section also provides an offence of making, or having in possession with intent to deceive, any document or other thing so closely resembling a document or other thing of the above types as to be calculated (ie likely) to deceive. Uncompleted insurance forms can be documents for this purpose. Thus, where a man was found to be in possession of bogus blank insurance certificates sequentially numbered, the Court of Appeal ruled that since the uncompleted forms were likely to deceive persons seeking insurance cover they could constitute documents so closely resembling genuine insurance certificates as to be calculated to deceive. An expired certificate, if used with intent to deceive, may be such a document.

Section 173 will also apply to documents evidencing the successful completion of a course of driver training when an amendment made by RSA 2006 is in force.

Persons temporarily in Great Britain

The Motor Vehicles (International Motor Insurance Card) Regulations 1971, reg 5 authorises a visitor to Great Britain to use his motor vehicle under the internationally recognised 'green card' insurance provision. 'Green cards' are referred to in the regulations as 'valid insurance cards'. A peculiarity of this provision is that a green card remains valid after the expiry date shown. This is to prevent the complications which would otherwise arise if holiday visitors decided to extend their stay. A constable's powers in respect of insurance certificates etc apply to 'green cards'.

Certificates of insurance or security issued in Northern Ireland are, of course, valid in Great Britain.

Police powers in relation to motor vehicle insurance

RTA 1988, s 165 states that:

(a) a person driving a motor vehicle, other than an invalid carriage, on a road;
(b) a person whom a constable or vehicle examiner reasonably believes to have been the driver of a motor vehicle on a road or other public place when an accident occurred etc; or
(c) a person whom a constable or vehicle examiner reasonably believes to have committed an offence in relation to the use of such a motor vehicle on a road,

shall, on being required by a constable or vehicle examiner, give his name and address and the name and address of the owner of the vehicle, and produce for examination the relevant certificate of insurance etc. Failure to do any of these things is an offence. The usual provisions concerning production of documents apply, allowing seven days for production; or production as soon as reasonably practicable; or proof that production was not reasonably practicable before the day on which proceedings were instituted. The documents (unlike a driving licence) need not be produced in person.

The provisions of RTA 1988, s 165 which require a person to give his name and address and the name and address of the owner of the vehicle also apply to a supervisor of a provisional licence holder in each of the three circumstances set out above.

Police powers of seizure of vehicles being driven without a driving licence or insurance

RTA 1988, s 165A, inserted by SOCPA 2005, s 152, provides that:

(a) where a constable in uniform requires, under RTA 1988, s 164 (see p 338), the production of a licence and counterpart, or under RTA 1988, s 165, the production of evidence of insurance; and

(b) in either case, there is a failure to produce the documents required and the constable has reasonable grounds for believing that the vehicle was being driven in contravention of RTA 1988, s 87(1) (requirement to have a driving licence) or s 143 (requirement to have insurance),

the constable may seize the vehicle and remove it.

RTA 1988, s 165A also provides that:

(a) where a constable in uniform has required, under RTA 1988, s 163, a person driving a motor vehicle to stop it; and

(b) there is a failure to do so, or a failure to do so for a sufficient time to allow the constable to make appropriate enquiries and the constable has reasonable grounds for believing that the vehicle is being driven in contravention of s 87(1) or 143,

he may seize and remove it.

Section 165A provides the constable with the power to enter any premises (other than a private dwelling house) on which he has reasonable grounds for believing the vehicle to be in order to seize it. The constable may use reasonable force to seize and remove the vehicle or to enter premises to seize and remove it.

Before seizing a vehicle under RTA 1988, s 165A, a constable must warn the person by whom it appears that the vehicle is, or was, being driven in contravention of either s 87(1) or 143 that he will seize the vehicle if the relevant documents are not produced, unless it is impracticable to do so in the circumstances. On seizing a vehicle under s 165A, a constable must give a seizure notice (see below) to the driver unless the circumstances make it impracticable to do so.

Where there has been a failure to stop, the power of seizure is valid for a period of twenty-four hours.

Retention and disposal of vehicles seized under powers provided by the Road Traffic Act 1988, s 165A

The Road Traffic Act 1988 (Retention and Disposal of Seized Motor Vehicles) Regulations 2005, make provision for the retention, safe keeping and disposal by an authorised person (ie a constable or other person authorised by the chief officer of police) of vehicles seized under s 165A of the RTA 1988.

Such as vehicle must be passed into, and remain in, the custody of an authorised person until the authorised person permits it to be removed from his custody by a person appearing to him to be the registered keeper or owner of the vehicle, or until it has been disposed of in accordance with the Regulations.

The authorised person must, as soon as is reasonably practicable after he has taken a vehicle into his custody, take such steps as are reasonably practicable to give a seizure notice to the person who is the registered keeper of the vehicle and to the owner, where that person appears to be someone different unless: (a) the authorised person is satisfied that a seizure notice has already been given, by a constable on seizing the vehicle, to the registered keeper and to the owner, where it appears that it is a different person; or (b) the vehicle has been released from his custody in accordance with the Regulations.

A seizure notice must contain information which can be or could have been ascertained from an inspection of the vehicle, or has been ascertained from another source, as to the registration mark and make of the vehicle. It must also include: a statement the place of seizure and the place where the vehicle is now being kept; a requirement that the keeper or owner claim the vehicle from the authorised person on or before a date specified in the notice (not less than seven working days from the date upon which the notice is given); a statement that unless the vehicle is claimed on or before that date, the authorised person intends to dispose of it; a notice that charges are payable and that the vehicle may be retained until they are paid; and a notice that the registered keeper or owner must either:

(a) produce at a specified police station a valid certificate of insurance covering his use of that vehicle and a valid licence authorising him to drive that vehicle; or
(b) nominate for this purpose a third person who produces at a specified police station such a valid certificate and such a valid licence.

The notice must also make clear that the vehicle may be retained until (a) or (b) is satisfied.

A seizure notice may be given:

(a) by delivering it to the person to whom it is directed;
(b) in the case of the registered keeper, by leaving it at the registered address or by sending it by registered post to that address;
(c) in the case of the owner, by leaving it at his usual or last known address, or by sending it by registered post to that address;
(d) in the case of a body corporate, by delivering it to the secretary or clerk of the body at its registered or principal office, or by sending it by registered post addressed to that secretary or clerk at that office.

Where, before a relevant motor vehicle is disposed of, a person satisfies the authorised person that he is the registered keeper or owner of that vehicle, pays the appropriate charge and produces at a police station specified in the notice a valid insurance certificate covering his use of the vehicle and a valid driving licence authorising him to drive the vehicle (or such documents are produced by a nominated person), the authorised person must permit him to remove the vehicle from custody. An authorised person may consider any documentary evidence produced to him in determining whether a person who claims to be the owner of a motor vehicle is in fact the owner.

A person, who would otherwise be liable to pay the appropriate charge, is not liable to pay it if he was not driving the vehicle at the time when it was seized under s 165A; did not know that the vehicle was being driven at that time; had not consented to it being driven, and could not, by taking reasonable steps, have prevented it from being driven.

An authorised person is empowered to dispose of a vehicle if:

(a) where the registered keeper and the owner appear to be the same person, that person fails to comply with any requirement in the seizure notice, or the authorised person was not able, after taking reasonably practicable steps, to give a seizure notice to that person;

(b) where the owner and registered keeper appear to be different:

   (i) where the seizure notice was given to both of those persons, neither the registered keeper nor the owner complies with all the requirements of the seizure notice;

   (ii) where, having taken such steps as were reasonably practicable, the authorised person was only able to give a seizure notice to one of them, that person fails to comply with any requirement in that seizure notice; or

   (iii) where, after taking reasonably practicable steps, the authorised person was not able to give a seizure notice to either the registered keeper or the owner.

An authorised person may not dispose of a vehicle:

(a) during the period of fourteen days starting with the date of seizure; or

(b) if that date has expired, until after a date specified in the seizure notice; or

(c) if not otherwise covered by (a) or (b), during the period of seven working days starting with the date on which the vehicle is claimed under the above provisions.

Where there is a disposal by way of sale, the net proceeds of that sale must be paid to any person who, within a period of one year, beginning with the date of sale, satisfies the authorised person that at the time of the sale, he was the owner of the vehicle. Where it appears that there may be more than one owner, the proceeds must be paid to such one of them as the authorised person thinks fit. The term 'net proceeds' refers to that part of the money remaining after the deduction of charges under the legislation.

INFORMATION AS TO IDENTITY OF DRIVER IN SPECIFIED CASES

The requirement to give information

RTA 1988, s 172(2) provides that where the driver of a vehicle is alleged to be guilty of an offence to which the section applies:

(a) the person keeping the vehicle must give such information as to the identity of the driver as he may be required to give by or on behalf of a chief officer of police; and

(b) any other person must if required as stated above give any information which is in his power to give and may lead to the identification of the driver.

The expression 'any other person' includes the driver himself. The section applies to:

(a) all offences against the provisions of the RTA 1988 except an offence under Part V (driving instruction), or s 13 (promoting motoring events on highway), s 16 (wearing of protective headgear), s 51(2) (certain test conditions—goods vehicles), s 61(4) (certain type approval requirements), s 67(9) (obstructing a vehicle examiner), s 68(4) (failing to proceed to place of vehicle inspection), s 96 (driving with uncorrected defective eyesight), or s 120 (offence against regulations dealing with licensing of drivers of large goods vehicles and passenger-carrying vehicles);

(b) an offence under the Road Traffic Offenders Act 1988, s 25 (information as to date of birth and sex after conviction), 26 (interim disqualification), or 27 (production of a licence on conviction);

(c) any offence relating to any other enactment relating to the use of vehicles on roads; and

(d) manslaughter by the driver of a motor vehicle.

A requirement may be made by way of written notice and served by post. Where it is so made it has effect as a requirement to give the information within the period of twenty-eight days beginning on the day on which the notice is served.

The offence

A person who fails to comply with such a requirement commits an offence. However, a person who keeps the vehicle is not guilty of the offence if he shows that he did not know, and could not with reasonable diligence have ascertained, who the driver of the vehicle was. Any other person must be proved to have had the information within his power to give. The fact that the accused does not know the identity of the driver does not excuse him if he simply fails to respond to a requirement for information (as opposed to responding and saying that he does not know). There must be evidence of the notice and that a requirement under s 172 has been made. This can be done by annexing a copy of the notice and requirement to a written statement under CJA 1967, s 9. The person on whom the notice is served is not guilty of the offence if he shows either that he gave the information as soon as reasonably practicable after the end of that period or that it had not been reasonably practicable for him to give it.

Procedure in respect of the notice

There is no requirement that the police specify the nature of the offence which it is alleged has been committed. A notice signed by an inspector with the authority of his superintendent, that superintendent having implied delegated authority from the chief officer of police to further delegate to his inspector, has been held to be a good and valid notice. In addition, it has been held that where a notice has been produced from an official source and has every appearance of authenticity, justices may draw an inference as to the validity of the notice. However, at the other end of the scale, it cannot be said that a police officer acting in the course of his duties is necessarily acting on behalf of his chief officer of police.

A divisional court has held that the obligation to respond is an obligation to respond in the manner specified in the notice. In that case the notice required (as is usual) that information be given in writing and signed. The driver had not done so but had provided the required information by telephone to an employee in the relevant fixed penalty office of the constabulary. The court held that the driver was guilty of failing to comply with the requirement for information.

The Road Traffic Offenders Act 1988, s 12(1) permits a court to accept a signed form as evidence that the person who signed the form was the driver of the vehicle at the time in question. A divisional court has held that where the name of the driver had been inserted in block capitals, but there was no signature, this could not be a statement in writing purporting to be signed by the accused for the purposes of the section in the circumstances existing within the cases concerned. However, the court observed that there may be circumstances in which it may be inferred, from the nature of the entries on a form, that driving was admitted. In a subsequent case, a divisional court accepted that an unsigned form did not indicate who had been the driver of the car as the information was not authenticated by a signature. Anyone could have written out the form. All such completed forms should be carefully examined when they are returned to ticket offices to avoid such difficulties arising.

Where a registered keeper endorsed the form sent by the police, 'please see covering letter enclosed', a divisional court allowed an appeal by the keeper against his conviction for failing to provide the required information. Within the letter the keeper had admitted that he was the keeper but explained that the vehicle concerned was one of a number of vehicles held by his medical practice and he could not ascertain who had been driving at the relevant time. The court said that while it had been decided that an oral reply to such a notice did not meet the statutory requirement, the letter had been written and signed. The justices' decision that the keeper had been acting unlawfully by responding in that way was erroneous. It was a proper and helpful way to respond to the request.

Human rights implications of such a statutory requirement

The Privy Council has concluded that the use of an admission by a driver obtained in pursuance of a requirement under RTA 1988, s 172(2)(a) is not incompatible with the accused's human rights under art 6(1) of the European Convention on Human Rights. The subsection merely provides for the putting of one simple question. The answer to that question cannot, by itself, incriminate the suspect. It does not permit prolonged questioning of a nature similar to that to which exception had been taken by the European Court of Human Rights. Although the origins of this case lie in Scotland, a divisional court has said that it would be exceptional, in a Convention matter, to depart from a considered decision of the Privy Council. A divisional court, having been asked to consider the position of 'any other person' required to provide information under s 172, concluded that the position was no different. Conclusive evidence should be admitted unless there is good reason for not doing so. The fact that, in this case, evidence could have been given by the driver's employer was not such a reason. It could not be unfair to admit the accused's own answer to a requirement made under the section. Parliament had sought to facilitate the giving of evidence as to the identity of drivers by means of written statements.

It is anticipated that this matter will receive further consideration because of the Privy Council's finding that special responsibilities follow the acquisition of a motor vehicle. While this is undoubtedly true, the question of the 'extent' of those responsibilities remains to be established as, it is submitted, they cannot go so far as to remove all of the safeguards set in place to protect other 'criminals'.

It is significant that RSA 2006, s 29 prospectively amends RTOA 1988, Sch 2, to permit a maximum of 6 penalty points to be awarded on conviction for the offence under RTA 1988, s 172. It may be suggested that this can be seen as a warning not to claim that the identity of the driver was unknown, even where that may be true. The difficulty of proving that this was so is likely to persuade most registered keepers to accept responsibility, together with a lesser number of penalty points. The measure might have sat more comfortably if the Act had made some provisions aimed at ensuring that camera evidence could be relied upon.

LAW RELATING TO HIGHWAYS

Highways

The meaning of the term 'highway' for the purposes of HA 1980 is given in HA 1980, s 328. The section states that the term includes the whole or part of a highway other than a ferry or waterway. Where a highway passes over a bridge or through a tunnel, the bridge or tunnel is, for the purposes of the Act, a part of the highway. HA 1980, s 328 does not define 'highway'; instead, that term is defined by common law. Basically, *a highway is a way over which all members of the public have the right to pass and repass* by foot, on horseback, or accompanied by a beast of burden or with vehicles or cattle. A highway bounded by a hedge or fence or buildings is presumed to extend up to that barrier. It follows that the term embraces carriageways, bridleways, and footpaths. In general terms these can be defined as follows.

A carriageway is a way constructed or comprised in a highway, being a way (other than a cycle track) over which the public has a right of way on foot, on horseback, or with vehicles and cattle.

A bridleway is a highway over which the public has a right of way while on foot, on horseback or leading a horse. By the Countryside Act 1968, s 30, the public also has a right to ride a pedal bicycle on a bridleway (provided that the cyclist gives way to pedestrians and persons on horseback). The right to ride a pedal cycle on a bridleway may be controlled by a local authority order. There may be a right on some bridleways to drive animals and such bridleways may be referred to locally as 'droves' or 'driftways'.

A footpath is a highway over which the public has a right of way on foot alone. The above definition of 'highway' can be contrasted with the definition of 'road' for the purposes of the Road Traffic Acts which is 'any highway *and any other road to which the public has access*' (see p 319 above).

Trunk road and motorway picnic areas

HA 1980, s 112 enables the Secretary of State to provide picnic areas on land adjoining or near to trunk roads and to manage them. Section 112 is prospectively extended to land adjoining or near to motorways by RSA 2006, s 55. The Secretary of State has the power to enforce waiting restrictions at such picnic areas by the removal of vehicles.

Obstruction of highway

The HA 1980, s 137 states that it is an offence for a person, without lawful authority or excuse, in any way wilfully to obstruct the free passage along the highway of whatever type.

Whether or not there was an *obstruction* is a question of degree for a court to decide; a complete blockage of the highway is not required. Whether or not a use of the highway amounts to an obstruction depends upon whether or not it was unreasonable having regard to all the circumstances of the case, including where it occurs, its duration, its nature, its extent and its purpose, and whether there is an actual, as opposed to a potential, obstruction. Where a supermarket left trolleys in a pedestrian precinct for the convenience of shoppers there was an obstruction even though no complaint had been made by a member of the public. In another case there was held to be an obstruction where for fifteen years a bridleway had been completely blocked by farm gates, tied by twine to hedges and held closed by a loop of twine, which could be opened easily. Simply to cause fear to users of a highway cannot amount to an obstruction. This was held by a divisional court in a case where the accused allowed his Rottweiler dogs to act in a menacing way behind a fence separating his land from a path constituting a highway. Pedestrians on the path were put in fear but, said the court, the highway was not obstructed.

The term '*wilfully*' in this context means that the particular obstruction was occasioned by some deliberate act which was freely carried out by the accused; consequently, a motorist who stops at a traffic light showing red does not wilfully obstruct the highway. In one case, a man who addressed a crowd, whose assembly interfered with traffic although traffic movement was not completely stopped, was held to have caused a wilful obstruction because, by the exercise of free will, he caused that obstruction to take place. On the other hand, if a queue forms outside a shop because many customers are attracted to it, it cannot be said that the shopkeeper has committed a deliberate and wilful act which caused the obstruction, as he is trading in a normal way. It would be different if the obstruction was caused because he was trading in an unusual way, for example through the window, as that unusual act would be wilful and would lead to an obstruction.

The question of whether or not a person has '*lawful authority or excuse*' will always be a question for the court to decide. PACE authorises police officers to set up road blocks in certain circumstances (see p 54). Clearly, a road block established in accordance with the provisions of the Act would be set up with lawful authority. Street traders or collectors for charity who are licensed for that purpose have lawful authority. 'Lawful excuse' embraces activities lawful in themselves which are a reasonable use of the highway or incidental to the right of passage. On the other hand, the right to protest does not give a right to obstruct the highway; consequently there is no lawful authority or excuse for such obstruction.

Dangerous parking

RTA 1988, s 22 makes it an offence for a person to cause or permit a vehicle or trailer drawn by a motor vehicle to remain at rest on a road in such a position, or in such condition or in such circumstances, as to involve danger of injury to other persons. The danger may be caused by the manner of the parking, the condition of the bodywork etc which may come into contact with persons, or other circumstances. It has been held that, where a vehicle has been parked without the brake being properly set and the vehicle moves and injures a pedestrian, the offence is committed. See below for other offences of causing danger on or near roads.

Causing danger to road users

RTA 1988, s 22A provides that a person is guilty of an offence if he intentionally and without lawful authority or reasonable cause:

(a) causes anything to be on or over a road; or
(b) interferes with a motor vehicle, trailer or cycle; or
(c) interferes (directly or indirectly) with traffic equipment, in such circumstances that it would be obvious to a reasonable person that to do so would be dangerous. If the danger would have been obvious to a *reasonable* person, it is irrelevant that the accused was unaware of it.

'*Danger*' refers to danger either of injury to any person while on or near a road, or of serious damage to property on or near a road. In determining what would be 'obvious' to a reasonable person in a particular case, regard must be had not only to the circumstances of which he could be expected to be aware but also to any circumstances shown to have been within the knowledge of the accused.

Where persons are seen on a bridge over a motorway in possession of large pieces of concrete, and then are seen to *balance* these objects on the parapet, they certainly cause those objects to be over a road and it is submitted that the circumstances are such that it would be obvious to a reasonable person that what they were doing was dangerous. The danger lies in the strong possibility that these pieces of concrete will fall. If pieces are dropped they are then caused to be 'on' a road and danger is caused, whether or not the road is being used by traffic at that particular time. While they remain there, they are a source of danger. Protesters who erect a barrier across a road will not normally be guilty of an offence under RTA 1988, s 22A if the barrier is solid and easily seen. Although their actions are otherwise unlawful, the essential element of 'danger' is normally missing in such circumstances. However, the stretching of a thin rope or wire across a road would cause the type of danger which the section seeks to outlaw.

A person who deflates a car tyre to a low pressure or interferes with its brakes or steering clearly interferes with it for the purposes of (b), above, in such circumstances that it would be obvious to a reasonable person that to do so would be dangerous.

For the purposes of (c) above, 'traffic equipment' means:

(a) anything lawfully placed on or near a road by a highway authority;
(b) a traffic sign lawfully placed on or near a road by a person other than a highway authority;

(c) any fence, barrier or light lawfully placed on or near a road, to protect street works or undertakings, or items placed by a constable or person acting on the instructions (whether general or specific) of a chief officer of police.

Any such thing placed on or near a road is, unless the contrary is proved, deemed to have been lawfully placed.

Thus, all official road signs, those indicating temporary works or obstructions, road accidents or diversions are covered by the section. The intentional interference with any such sign must be shown to have created the danger envisaged by the section. It is not sufficient merely to show that a sign has been interfered with. A person who removes a hazard warning sign will commit an offence provided that the hazard still exists. If the sign indicates the existence of a hazard associated with roadworks and those works have been completed (so that no danger then exists), there will be no offence under this section. Where a sign is removed which merely indicates the direction of a town, nuisance has certainly been caused but there is no danger associated with such removal in normal circumstances. If road surfacing operations are marked at night by a series of lamps, the removal of one lamp may or may not cause the type of danger which the section seeks to prevent. If lamps are set at intervals of inches, it may be that the removal of one lamp is insignificant. If there are few lamps and a gap is left completely unmarked, the situation changes.

Danger or annoyance on highway

HA 1980, s 161 prohibits any person, without lawful authority or excuse:

(a) from depositing anything on a highway in consequence of which a user is injured or endangered; or
(b) from lighting any fire on or over a highway which consists of or comprises a carriageway; or
(c) from discharging any firearm or firework within 50 feet of the centre of such a highway in consequence of which a user of the highway is injured, interrupted, or endangered.

HA 1980, s 161A(1) prohibits a person from lighting a fire on any land not forming part of a highway which consists of or comprises a carriageway, or from directing or permitting such a fire to be lit, when in consequence a user of any highway which consists of or comprises a carriageway is injured, interrupted or endangered by, or by smoke from, that fire or any other fire caused by that fire. However, s 161A(2) provides a defence to a charge under s 161A(1) if it can be proved that at the time the fire was lit the person was satisfied on reasonable grounds that it was unlikely that users of any such highway would be injured, interrupted or endangered by the fire or by smoke from it, or from others caused by it, and either that before or after the fire was lit he did all that he reasonably could to prevent the consequences or that he had reasonable excuse for not doing so. Section 161A is aimed at preventing smoke clouds, caused by straw burning in surrounding fields, blowing over motorways and main roads.

HA 1980, s 161 also punishes those who allow filth, lime or dirt, or other offensive matter or thing, to run on to a highway from any adjoining premises. It also prohibits the playing of football or any other game on a highway to the annoyance of a user of the highway. This offence creates many problems for police officers. Usually a complaint is received by telephone from a householder who wishes to complain that he is being annoyed by children playing football in the street. The offence is only committed when the game is 'to the annoyance of a user of the highway'; a person sitting in his house is not a 'user' in the sense intended by the section. Police officers frequently find themselves between the complainant and irate parents and it is helpful to appreciate the essentials of this factor when there is pressure to take action. A person who was not using the highway when annoyed cannot be subsequently annoyed by walking into the street unless the game continues to his annoyance when on the highway.

It is an offence contrary to HA 1980, s 162 to place, for any purpose, a rope, wire or other apparatus across a highway in such a manner as to be likely to cause danger to persons using the highway, unless the accused can prove that he had taken necessary means to give adequate warning. A washing line in a back street with white sheets suspended from it certainly involves the stretching of a rope across the highway, but in the circumstances it can easily be proved that adequate warning was given. However, if the washing is taken in and only the rope is left, there is an offence unless it can be proved that the necessary steps were taken to give adequate warning.

Builders' skips

HA 1980, s 139 provides that a builder's skip must not be deposited on the highway without the permission of the highway authority; otherwise an offence is committed.

Such permission must be in writing; it is granted to a named person and the highway where the skip is to be located is specified. Each skip must be authorised on each occasion; a general permission to place skips is not possible. The authority may impose conditions upon its permission. These may refer to the siting of the skip, its dimensions, the painting of the skip to make it visible, the care and disposal of its contents, the manner in which it is to be lighted or guarded and its removal at the end of the authorised period. Skips must be fitted with two oblong plates of diagonal red and yellow fluorescent or reflective material, similar to those fitted to heavy goods vehicles.

HA 1980, s 139 also provides that, whatever the conditions imposed, an owner must secure that the skip is properly lighted during the hours of darkness, that it is clearly and indelibly marked with the owner's name and with his telephone number or address, that it is removed as soon as possible after it has been filled, and that all conditions of the permission are complied with. Failure to do so is an offence on the part of the owner. The term 'owner' in relation to a skip which is hired for a month or more, or one which is the subject of a hire-purchase agreement, means the person in possession of the skip under the hiring agreement. 'Otherwise deposits in' is extremely wide and means no more than 'places or puts'. Where the commission by any person of an offence under s 139 is due to the act or default of some other person, that other person is also guilty and may be convicted whether or not proceedings are taken against the first-mentioned person.

It is a defence to a charge under HA 1980, s 139 for the accused to prove that the commission of the offence was due to the act or default of another and that the accused took all reasonable precautions and exercised all due diligence to avoid the commission of the offence by himself or any other person under his control.

HA 1980, s 140 provides that, regardless of whether or not permission has been obtained, the highway authority or a constable in uniform may require the owner of a skip to remove it, or reposition it, or cause it to be removed or repositioned. To fail to do so as soon as possible is an offence. A request by a constable must be made in person; a request by telephone, for example, is not sufficient.

Use of loudspeakers

The Control of Pollution Act 1974, s 62 bans the operation of loudspeakers in a street between 9 pm and 8 am the following morning for any purpose. It also bans their use at any other time for the purpose of advertising any entertainment, trade or business. The term 'street' means any highway and any other road, footway, square or court which is for the time being open to the public. The ban is therefore effective both in built-up areas and in the country, provided, in either case, the loudspeaker is operated in a 'street'.

The exemptions to these provisions are predictable. They are: use for police, fire and rescue or ambulance purposes, or by the Environment Agency or a water undertaking in the exercise of its functions or by a local authority; 'in vehicle' entertainments or announcements; telephones; use by showmen at a pleasure fair; and use in an emergency provided that the loudspeaker is operated so as not to give reasonable cause for annoyance to persons in the vicinity.

The most common exception to the general rule against the use of loudspeakers for advertising is in favour of those who have a loudspeaker fixed to a vehicle which is used for the conveyance of a perishable commodity for human consumption and is used solely for the purpose of informing the public, by means other than words, that the commodity is on sale from the vehicle. Such a loudspeaker must be operated so as not to give reasonable cause for annoyance to persons in the vicinity and it may only be used between noon and 7 pm of the same day. Thus 'ice-cream chimes' can be used between these times, but at no other.

NUISANCES

Generally

It is a common law offence to cause a public nuisance. To offend against the common law the act concerned must obstruct or cause inconvenience or damage to the public in the exercise of their rights. The essence of the offence is that the act is a nuisance to the public in general and not to an individual, or a restricted group of people. An act which is specifically authorised by law cannot be a public nuisance if carried out as prescribed. Despite its width, this common law offence is little used as most 'nuisances' are covered by statutes.

Nuisances related to noise

Because of difficulties experienced by local authorities and police officers in dealing with 'noise' nuisances, the Noise Act 1996 provides powers for local authorities to serve warning notices in respect of a dwelling ('the offending dwelling') or premises in respect of which a premises licence or a temporary event notice (see pp 665–671) has effect ('the offending premises') from which excessive noise is emanating, such noise being heard during the night. For the purposes of the Act, 'night' is the period between 11 pm and 7 am. Local authorities are equipped with approved measuring devices which establish noise levels. These powers were originally 'adoptive' but now apply generally to all local authorities in England and Wales. A local authority which receives a relevant complaint must secure that an officer of the authority takes reasonable steps to investigate the complaint.

Where a warning notice has been served in respect of an offending dwelling, it is an offence for any person who is responsible for the noise to emit from it, within a period specified in the notice, noise which exceeds the permitted level, as measured from within the complainant's dwelling or premises. This offence is subject to a defence of 'reasonable excuse', the onus of proving which is on the accused.

Where a warning notice has been served in respect of other premises and noise is emitted from them, within a period specified in the notice, which exceeds the permitted level, as measured from within the complainant's dwelling, the responsible person (see p 680) in respect of the offending premises commits an offence. No defence of reasonable excuse is provided.

The Act permits local authorities to introduce fixed penalty offences in relation to such nuisances. Local authority officers have a power of entry to a dwelling in respect of which a warning notice has been issued. It is a summary offence to obstruct such an officer and the Act provides powers of seizure and disposal of equipment causing such a noise nuisance.

If an authorised local authority officer has reason to believe that a person has committed or is committing the above offence, he may give that person a fixed penalty notice. Where this has been done, no proceedings shall be instituted for the offence before the expiration of fourteen days following the date of the notice. Such a person may not be convicted of that offence if he pays the fixed penalty within that period.

Depositing litter

There are several provisions dealing with forms of defacement which might generally be described as 'litter'. The Environmental Protection Act 1990 (EPA 1990), s 87, as amended by the Clean Neighbourhoods and Environment Act 2005 (CNAEA 2005), provides that a person commits an offence if he *throws down, drops or otherwise deposits*, any litter in any place in the area of a principal litter authority which is open to the air, *and leaves it*. However, s 87 does not apply to a place which is 'open to the air' on at least one side if the public does not have access to it, with or without payment. The offence of depositing litter is committed whether the litter is deposited on land or on water.

No offence is committed where the depositing of litter is authorised by law or is done with the consent of the owner or occupier or other person having control of the place where it is deposited. Consent may only be given to the depositing of litter in a lake, pond or watercourse by the owner, occupier or other person having control of all of the land adjoining that lake, pond or watercourse and all of the land into which water from those places directly or indirectly discharges, otherwise than by means of a public sewer.

The term 'litter' includes the discarded ends of cigarettes, cigars and like products and discarded chewing gum and the discarded remains of other products designed for chewing.

The major change to EPA 1990, s 87, brought about by CNAEA 2005 is that the revised EPA 1990, s 87 covers the dropping of litter on *any* private land.

The word 'leave' in EPA 1990, s 87 has been given a wide interpretation. In one case, a man and his family were living in a tent set up in a country lane. His lorry was parked nearby against which was a pile of scrap metal. The man was sorting through it when seen by police officers. He was convicted of depositing and leaving litter as it was judged that he intended to remove only that metal which was of value. A divisional court held that 'leave' for the purposes of the Act does not mean abandon. The metal had been deposited and permitted to remain beside the road for such a time and in circumstances that it could be said to have been left there. The court also held that an article deposited with no intention to remove it could be 'left' after only a short period of time. This is an important judgment. A man who throws down fish wrappers, and refuses to pick them up immediately, commits the offence of depositing and leaving litter. He has no intention of removing the wrappers and this is evidenced by his refusal.

The offence under EPA 1990, s 87 is a 'penalty offence' for the purposes of CJPA 2001, Part 1 and may be dealt with by a constable under a fixed penalty procedure under that Act: see p 874.

Where the offence under EPA 1990, s 87 is dealt with by a local authority 'litter warden' (who must be authorised in writing so to act on behalf of a litter authority), EPA 1990, s 88 (as amended by CNAEA 2005) permits the use of a fixed penalty procedure under that section. Where such an authorised officer finds a person who he has reason to believe has on that occasion committed an offence under s 87 in the area of that authority, he may give that person a fixed penalty notice. Where an authorised officer proposes to give a person a notice, he may require the person to give his name and address. Failure, or the giving of a false address, is an offence. Where this has been done, no proceedings may be instituted for the offence before the expiration of fourteen days following the date of the notice. Such a person may not be convicted of that offence if he pays the fixed penalty within that period. The amount of the fixed penalty under EPA 1990 procedure is that specified in the range of £50 to £80 by a principal litter authority in relation to its area or, where no amount is so specified, £75. Litter authorities may make provision for a lesser payment if made before the end of a period specified in the notice.

Refuse Disposal (Amenity) Act 1978

The Refuse Disposal (Amenity) Act 1978 (RD(A)A 1978), s 2(1(b)) provides the offence of abandoning, without lawful authority, on any land in the open air, or on any other land forming part of a highway, anything which has been brought to the land for the purpose of being abandoned there. The section is meant to deal with instances in which a motorist takes refuse quite deliberately into the countryside and abandons it there. Such a person may leave an old mattress at the side of the road or throw it over the fence into a field; in either event he commits an offence. There is no necessity to prove that the refuse was deposited from any particular place; it is sufficient that it is left there. Often such waste is identifiable as it includes marked articles traceable to the person who abandoned it.

Abandoned motor vehicles

RD(A)A 1978, s 2(1)(a) deals with the abandonment of motor vehicles in similar circumstances. The difference is that it is not necessary to prove that a motor vehicle was brought to the land for the purpose of abandonment. The offence is committed by a person who, without lawful authority, abandons on any land in the open air, or on any other land forming part of a highway, a motor vehicle or anything which formed part of a motor vehicle and was removed from it in the course of dismantling the vehicle on the land. The CNAEA 2005 added a s 2A to RD(A)A 1978 which makes provision for the offence under s 2(1)(a) to be dealt with as a fixed penalty offence by an authorised officer of the local authority. The fixed penalty is currently £200.

General

In terms of proof, RD(A)A 1978, s 2(2) contains a provision which is important in relation to both offences under s 2(1) mentioned in the last two paragraphs. RD(A)A 1978, s 2(2) deals with a person who leaves anything on land in such circumstances or for such a period that he may reasonably be assumed to have abandoned it or, as the case may be, to have brought it to the land for the purpose of abandoning it there. It provides that such a person is deemed to have abandoned it there or, as the case may be, to have brought it to the land for that purpose, unless the contrary is shown. The onus is therefore placed upon the accused to satisfy the court that the vehicle etc was not abandoned once it is proved to have been there in circumstances which suggest abandonment.

It follows from our description of the offences just mentioned that a person who abandons a motor vehicle at the roadside commits an offence against RD(A)A 1978, s 2(1). It can also be seen that the caravan traveller who dismantles vehicles either on the highway or adjoining land commits offences against EPA 1990 if he deposits and leaves pieces of metal, only some of which he intends to take away. When he moves on, abandoning stripped vehicle shells or pieces removed from vehicles, he commits an offence of abandonment under RD(A)A 1978.

Off-road driving

RTA 1988, s 34 prohibits a person from driving a mechanically propelled motor vehicle, without lawful authority, on to or upon any common land, moorland or land of any other description which is not a part of the road, or on any road which is a footpath, bridleway or restricted byway. However, the section permits the driving of a mechanically propelled vehicle within 15 yards of a road upon which a motor vehicle may be driven but only for the purpose of parking. RTA 1988, s 34 provides a further defence if the vehicle is so driven for saving life, or extinguishing fire, or for dealing with any other similar emergency.

The Police Reform Act 2002, s 59 provides powers for the seizure of vehicles in prescribed circumstances, see pp 576–577.

Nuisance on educational premises

Although not directly concerned with highways these offences are most conveniently examined here. They are provided by the Education Act 1996, s 547 (which deals with schools) and the Further and Higher Education Act 1992, s 85A (which deals with further education colleges). Both sections create an offence which may be committed by a person who is present on educational premises to which they apply, without lawful authority, who causes or permits nuisance or disturbance to the annoyance of persons who lawfully use those premises (whether or not any such persons are present at the time). The term 'premises' includes playing fields and other premises for outdoor recreation. A constable or an authorised local authority officer may remove such a person from the premises if he has reasonable cause to suspect that he is committing or has committed such an offence.

The offences are worded to embrace many possibilities from disturbances caused by irate parents, to nuisances caused by exercising dogs on playing fields. Many educational authorities do not appear to discourage the use of their facilities out of hours, even by those who are not students at those establishments. However, such use, in an orderly fashion, would not offend against the relevant section even where permission had not been directly given to a person to be on those premises.

CHAPTER 10

Use of vehicles

TERMINOLOGY

In various parts of this chapter we shall refer to 'motor cars', 'heavy motor cars', 'bus', 'large bus', 'coach', 'motor tractors' and 'locomotives'. These terms are defined by the Road Traffic Act 1988 (RTA 1988) or Road Vehicles (Construction and Use) Regulations 1986 (generally described in this chapter simply as the Construction and Use Regulations). All the terms are concerned, of course, with motor vehicles, and hereafter 'vehicle' must be understood in this sense. For the purposes of the present part of this chapter, the following definitions apply.

A 'motor car' is a vehicle constructed or adapted for use for the conveyance of any goods or passengers and whose unladen weight does not exceed 3,050 kg (3 tonnes), if it is constructed solely for the carriage of passengers and adapted to carry no more than seven of them as well as the driver, or if it is constructed for the conveyance of goods, or 2,540 kg (2.5 tonnes) in any other case. For the same purposes a 'heavy motor car' is a vehicle (not being a motor car) constructed to carry a load, whether goods or passengers, and whose unladen weight exceeds 2,540 kg (2.5 tonnes). Although this definition covers buses and coaches, there are some requirements of the regulations which are specific to them. For this reason 'bus', 'large bus' and 'coach' are separately defined. A 'bus' is a vehicle constructed or adapted to carry more than eight seated passengers in addition to the driver, and 'large bus' is a vehicle constructed or adapted to carry more than sixteen such passengers. A 'coach' is a large bus with a maximum gross weight of more than 7.5 tonnes and a maximum speed exceeding 60 mph. A 'dual-purpose vehicle' is a vehicle constructed or adapted for the carriage both of passengers and of goods or burden, being a vehicle whose unladen weight does not exceed 2040kg, and which either:

(a) is so constructed or adapted that the driving power of the engine is, or can be, transmitted to all the wheels of the vehicle; or
(b) is permanently fitted with a rigid roof; and
　　(i)　has at least one row of transverse, upholstered seats for two or more passengers permanently fitted;

(ii) has on each side and at the rear a window or windows having an overall area of not less than 1850 square cm on each side and not less than 770 square cm at the rear; and

(c) is such that the distance between the rearmost part of the steering wheel and the back-rests of the row of transverse seats in (b) (or, if there is more than one such row of seats, the distance between the rearmost part of the steering wheel and the back-rests of the rearmost such row), is not less than one-third of the distance between the rearmost part of the steering wheel and the rearmost part of the floor of the vehicle.

A 'motor tractor' is defined as a vehicle which is not constructed itself to carry a load (other than one concerned with its own propulsion or maintenance) and the unladen weight of which does not exceed 7,370 kg (7.25 tonnes). A 'locomotive' is a similar vehicle, the unladen weight of which exceeds 7,370 kg (7.25 tonnes).

ROAD VEHICLES (CONSTRUCTION AND USE) REGULATIONS 1986

The Road Vehicles (Construction and Use) Regulations 1986 are made under RTA 1988, s 41. They are divided into two main parts: one dealing with the construction, weight and equipment of motor vehicles and trailers; the other with the various uses of motor vehicles and trailers on roads. The 'construction' elements of the regulations are aimed at manufacturers in the main, as they amount to specifications for vehicle production. Many of these provisions are being replaced in relation to most modern vehicles by requirements of an international nature relating to 'type approved' vehicles, and arrangements for the transition to type approval are set out in reg 6 of the Regulations. The date of manufacture or first registration of vehicles will normally be the conclusive factor in deciding whether the 'construction' elements of these regulations apply, or those directed towards type approval. A vehicle which complies with the relevant type approval and has the relevant certificate of type approval or manufacturer's certificate of conformity to the type approval is exempt from certain parts of Part II of the Regulations concerned with the construction of motor vehicles. Police officers are much more frequently concerned with offences relating to the use of vehicles in contravention of the Regulations.

Certain special types of vehicles are authorised under the Road Vehicles (Authorisation of Special Types) General Order 2003 and do not have to comply with all of the requirements of the Road Vehicles (Construction and Use) Regulations. The clue to the nature of such vehicles lies within the term 'special'. The vehicles concerned are likely to be track-laying vehicles; those used for special engineering and maintenance purposes; military vehicles; and vehicles used for life-saving operations.

Type approval

As we have already stated, most modern vehicles, because they comply with certain international requirements, are exempt from those Construction and Use Regulations which are concerned with the *construction* of motor vehicles. These requirements are commonly referred to as 'Type Approval'.

Compulsory British type approval

Certain motor vehicles and their component parts, but *not trailers*, manufactured in Great Britain on or after 1 October 1977 must be wholly constructed to British Type Approval Standard. These vehicles are:

(a) passenger vehicles with four or more wheels adapted to carry not more than nine persons including the driver; and

(b) passenger vehicles with three wheels, not being a motor bicycle with sidecar attached.

There are various exemptions, examples of which are prototype vehicles, some vehicles which are manufactured for export, motor caravans and special ambulances.

Goods vehicles manufactured in Great Britain on or after 1 October 1982 and first used on or after 1 April 1983 are also subject to compulsory British type approval.

Again, there are various exemptions, for example prototype vehicles, fire engines, pedestrian-controlled vehicles and motor tractors.

The compulsory British type approval schemes are backed up by two offences:

(a) it is generally an offence to sell, supply, offer to sell or supply, or expose for sale a vehicle which does not have a Secretary of State's type approval certificate or a manufacturer's certificate of conformity to the type approval;

(b) using, or causing or permitting to be used, on a road, a vehicle subject in whole or part to compulsory British type approval is an offence, unless it appears from a certificate of the type referred to in (a) that the vehicle (or its parts) complies with the type approval.

Compulsory EU type approval

The optional system of EU type approval introduced by the Motor Vehicles (Type Approval) Regulations 1980 in respect of certain motor vehicles, trailers and their component parts now applies only to type approval of tachographs. With this exception, the 1980 Regulations have been superseded by the Motor Vehicles (EC Type Approval) Regulations 1998. The 1998 Regulations implement an EC Council Directive requiring member states to set up a system for granting EC type approval for '*light passenger vehicles*'. A light passenger vehicle is defined by the regulations as a motor vehicle which:

(a) has at least four wheels;

(b) has an internal combustion engine;

(c) is constructed or adapted for the carriage of passengers, and is not a goods vehicle;

(d) has no more than eight seats in addition to the driver's; and

(e) has a maximum design speed exceeding 25 kph.

To the extent that they overlap in their application, the EC system under the 1998 Regulations will prevail over the British type approval system.

The 1992 Regulations provide that, subject to specified exceptions, the Secretary of State must not as *from 1 January 1996* issue a first licence to or register a light passenger vehicle unless it either has an EC certificate of conformity or has a Minister's approval certificate issued under RTA 1988, s 58(1). An EC certificate of conformity is issued in respect of an individual vehicle covered by an EC type approval by the holder of that approval (normally the manufacturer). In a few cases, the operative date is 1 January 1998, or 1 January 2000, and not 1 January 1996.

Between 1993 and the relevant operative date, a vehicle with an EC certificate of conformity is deemed to comply with all type approval requirements, with the result that its use or sale will not constitute an offence under the British type approval regulations.

After the operative date, the use on a road of an unregistered light passenger vehicle which is not covered by an EC certificate of conformity or a Minister's approval certificate will be an offence, as will be the sale of a light passenger vehicle without one or other of these certificates.

CONSTRUCTION AND USE OFFENCES: GENERAL

RTA 1988, ss 40A, 41A, 41B and 42 provide various offences which may be committed in relation to the use of a vehicle in a dangerous condition and/or in contravention of the Regulations. RTA 1988, s 41 provides for regulations to be made covering the use of motor vehicles and trailers on a road, their construction and equipment and the conditions under which they may be so used. RTA 1988, s 41 (and s 66 which authorises regulations prohibiting the grant of an excise licence unless a vehicle complies with certain conditions) are prospectively amended by the Road Safety Act 2006 (RSA 2006), s 56 to allow regulations to be made requiring the examination by authorised persons of vehicles modified to run on liquefied petroleum gas and compressed natural gas which, because of their nature, carry a greater risk of explosion. Certificates will be awarded in respect of vehicles which comply with the regulations. Once these provisions are in place arrangements will be made for inspection to become a part of the 'MOT'.

RTA 1988, s 40A makes it an offence for a person to use, cause or permit another to use a motor vehicle or a trailer on a road when:

(a) the condition of the motor vehicle or trailer, or of its accessories or equipment; or
(b) the purpose for which it is used; or
(c) the number of passengers carried by it, or the manner in which they are carried; or
(d) the weight, position or distribution of its load, or the manner in which it is secured,

is such that the use of the motor vehicle or trailer involves danger of injury to any person. The question of whether there was a danger for the purposes of RTA 1988, s 40A is a matter which the justices must consider by reference to the matters set out above; the fact that an accident has occurred is irrelevant. On the other hand, they can take into account the nature of the locality and the classification of the road.

RSA 2005, s 25 prospectively provides that if this offence is committed within three years of a previous conviction for the same offence, disqualification is obligatory.

RTA 1988, s 41A makes it an offence for a person to:

(a) contravene or fail to comply with a construction and use requirement as to brakes, steering gear or tyres; or
(b) use on a road a motor vehicle or trailer which does not comply with such a requirement, or cause or permit a motor vehicle or trailer to be so used.

Offences against RTA 1988, ss 40A and 41A carry discretionary disqualification; the endorsement of 3 penalty points is obligatory.

RTA 1988, s 41B punishes offences in relation to 'weight'. A person who:

(a) contravenes or fails to comply with a construction and use requirement as to any description of weight applicable to:
   (i) a goods vehicle; or
   (ii) a motor vehicle or trailer adapted to carry more than eight passengers; or
(b) uses on a road a vehicle which does not comply with such a requirement, or causes or permits a vehicle to be so used,

commits an offence against the section. RTA 1988, s 41B(2) provides a defence where the alleged contravention relates to any description of weight applicable to a goods vehicle. It provides that in such a case it is a defence to prove either that the vehicle was going to or coming from a weighbridge, or, where the relevant weight limit is not exceeded by more than 5%, that that weight was not exceeded at the time of loading and that load had not been added to.

RTA 1988, s 42 is concerned with contraventions of a construction and use requirement other than those relating to brakes, steering gear or tyres, or those relating to weight, which are dealt with by ss 41A to 41B. It provides that a person who:

(a) contravenes or fails to comply with such a requirement; or
(b) uses on a road a motor vehicle or trailer which does not comply with such a requirement, or causes or permits a motor vehicle or trailer to be so used,

commits an offence.

Those who contravene RTA 1988, s 41B or 42 are not liable to disqualification or to obligatory endorsement under these sections.

An offence of using on a road a trailer which does not comply with regulations is an offence distinct from that of using a defective motor vehicle.

Since the relevant provisions are concerned with persons who use, cause or permit the use of motor vehicles or trailers in contravention of the Regulations, it is important that police officers understand the meaning of these terms.

Use

This term should be given its ordinary meaning. A person uses a vehicle if he controls, manages, operates or otherwise has the use of it as a vehicle.

In law, a person can 'use' a vehicle, even though he does not do so personally. This is because, if a driver of a vehicle is about his employer's business, the employer is also using the vehicle (and can therefore be held vicariously liable), and the words 'causing' or 'permitting' should not be considered. The offence of 'using' covers most eventualities where there is a employer/employee relationship.

RTA 1988, ss 40A, 41A and 42 impose a strict liability upon those who use motor vehicles in contravention of the Regulations; consequently, it is irrelevant that the accused did not know of the defect etc, nor ought to have known of it. In one case, a driver was convicted of using a vehicle on a road with a load which had not been properly secured, even though he had taken no part in the loading, and loading was not a part of his responsibility. In another, the driver of a motor lorry detected vibration on a wheel of the vehicle and pulled off at a service station, contacted his employer to arrange assistance, found that wheel nuts one wheel had loosened, and awaited assistance. At that stage a vehicle inspector who was carrying out routine checks at the service station, discovered the loose wheel nuts and a prosecution followed. A divisional court ruled that the justices had been wrong to decline to convict the driver of an offence of using the vehicle on a road in a dangerous condition. He had admitted driving on a road, the vibration would have been caused by the loose wheel nuts, and the offence being absolute that was all which needed to be proved. However, the divisional court declined to return the case to the justices on the grounds that, in view of the action taken by the driver, it did not merit punishment.

It is quite possible that the owner of a motor vehicle may be totally unaware that an offence of using in breach of the Regulations is being committed in relation to his vehicle which is being driven by an employee of his many miles away from his operating centre. Nevertheless, if the vehicle is on the road, upon his business, the employer is using it in addition to his employee driver, and both he and his employee can be convicted of the offence. In one case, where an owner had directed an employee driver to take the vehicle to a garage whenever it required maintenance, it was held that there had been a use with defective brakes by the employer as the vehicle was being used on his business; it was irrelevant that such a general direction as to maintenance had been given.

In general, where defects are 'discovered' which amount to contraventions of the Regulations, charges of 'using' should be considered in respect of the driver and of his employer if the vehicle is used upon his business. There must be clear evidence of an employee/employer relationship, and the employee must be acting in the course of his employment. Thus, where a driver used a stock car on a road he was properly convicted of using the vehicle with defective parts, but the owner, not being the employer of the driver in relation to the business of stock car racing, was held not to have been 'using' the vehicle. He was, however, held to have been permitting the offence because he had knowingly allowed the driver to drive the car in its defective condition (see below). Because it would not be in the course of his employment, a cleaner who made use of his employer's defective lorry would not render his employer guilty of using it.

In one case, a driver who was self-employed was paid on a daily basis. He paid his own tax and national insurance contributions, and did not work exclusively for the company. When he did work for the company, he wore its uniform, drove its vehicle and collected and delivered loads from and to specified locations. A divisional court held that the company was not 'using' the vehicle. It said that *a person is a user only if he is the driver or the owner of the vehicle, but an owner only uses his vehicle if the driver is employed by him under a contract of service and at the material time he is driving on his employer's business*, which the driver in the case was not. A divisional court has remarked upon the illogicality and artificiality caused by its insistence upon the need for a strict employer/employee relationship. The court on one occasion said that it found it difficult to accept that, if a man can 'use' his vehicle through the hands of his employee, he cannot be said to use it at the hands of someone else who, at his specific request, drives it on a journey at the express orders and with the full knowledge of the owner. Illogical or not, the court has persistently refused to extend the meaning of 'use' on the grounds that a line must be drawn somewhere. Where such a strict employer/employee relationship cannot be established, a charge of 'causing' or 'permitting' must be considered.

Where a vehicle is hired out with a driver for use by another firm, the driver will usually remain the employee of the owner of the vehicle, so that a 'using' by the driver will be a 'using' by the owner. Thus, where a haulier (BRS) hired a vehicle together with its driver to another haulier for a period of five years, and that other haulier operated the vehicle under its own livery, BRS was held to be using that vehicle when it was found to be overloaded. BRS had been in the business of hiring out vehicles with drivers who remained their employees and the vehicles were being used in the course of that business. Similarly, where the driver of a vehicle who was employed by A was ordered by telephone to pick up a return load on behalf of another company B, that company being responsible for loading the vehicle, its documentation and the selection of route, a divisional court held that company A was guilty of using the vehicle when it was found to be overloaded. The court said that, while it might be correct to argue that company B was using the vehicle, this did not mean that company A was not. It was their vehicle and their driver and that driver was employed under a contract of service. However, the owner will not be liable for using the vehicle when it is not being used on his business.

Where a company hires another company to transport its goods, the first company is not 'using' the vehicle at the time at which it sheds its load. This is so even where the first company supplies the means of securing the load. The first company is not 'operating' the vehicle at the time in question; it would be different if it had hired the vehicle and operated it itself.

A man who lends his private motor car to his friend is not liable for 'using' that vehicle if the Regulations are contravened by the friend. However, in certain circumstances, he could be guilty of permitting its use in contravention of the Regulations.

Where a trailer is towed by another vehicle and the offence concerned relates to the trailer, as, for example, where there is a defective part on the trailer, or it carries an insecure load, the information (or written charge, when the written charge system is in force) should specify that it was the trailer which was defective or improperly used. This is essential where the tractor unit and the trailer are owned by different persons or companies.

Cause the use

This term, together with 'permitting the use', covers circumstances in which charges of aiding and abetting would otherwise normally be appropriate. To be guilty of causing the use of a vehicle in contravention of the Regulations, an accused must actually have known of, or been wilfully blind as to, the contravention in question. The offence can only be committed by persons who are in a position to exercise some control over the driver who is using the vehicle. To 'cause' involves some express or positive command or direction from the person 'causing' to the person 'using'. If the foreman of a haulage depot, knowing that a vehicle has a defective tyre, orders an employee to drive the vehicle, the foreman 'causes' the driver to commit the offence. He is in a position to give orders to the employee in relation to the use of the vehicle and does so, and he has knowledge of the defect. In such a case the firm would also be guilty of using the vehicle as it was used on their business and knowledge is not an essential ingredient of that offence. Where a manager was responsible for five vehicle depots at each of which there was a vehicle superintendent, it was held that he could not be guilty of causing the vehicle to be used in a defective condition as he was not in a position to exercise control and could not have guilty knowledge in any case. In that case, for the superintendent to be guilty of causing the vehicle to be used, there would have to be evidence of a requirement to use it and knowledge of the circumstances.

A person who tows another vehicle is causing it to be used on a road.

Permit the use

Like 'causing the use' of a vehicle, 'permitting' a vehicle to be used in contravention of the Regulations requires proof that the accused actually knew of, or was wilfully blind as to, the contravention in question. However, the meaning of 'permitting' is much wider than the meaning of 'causing' because there does not need to be any express or positive mandate to use a motor vehicle by a person in a position to exercise control over the driver, and a general or particular permission to use a vehicle will be sufficient. However, for a person to be guilty of 'permitting' he must be in a position to forbid another person to use the vehicle.

Many employees of companies are given general permission to use a firm's vehicle in any way they choose. However, having been given such a general permission by an employer, it is unlikely that such an employer will be liable for contraventions of the Construction and Use Regulations in respect of that vehicle, but in some circumstances he may. There is a distinction between knowledge that the vehicle is being used and knowledge that it is being used unlawfully. A sales representative may be given total use of a motor car. As a driver he will be responsible for its use in contravention of these Regulations but his employers will not normally be liable for permitting, as they are unlikely to have knowledge of the particular unlawful use. However, if the vehicle is being used on company business, a charge of using may be appropriate. If such a person is using the vehicle privately at the time, the company will have no liability unless it can be shown that it knew of the defect but nevertheless gave permission for the vehicle's continued use. If such permission has been directly given, then a charge of permitting will lie.

In a case where a vehicle belonging to a company left its premises in good condition but, while out of the control of responsible officers of the company, employees coupled up a trailer in such a manner that the brakes were defective, it was held that the company officers could not be said to have permitted the offence as no formal permission to do the act was given. In such circumstances, however, the company 'used' the vehicle as it was on its business at the time. In the same way, where the accused was the owner of a lorry driven on a road by his employee while the brakes were defective, it was held that for a charge of permitting to succeed there must be proof of actual knowledge or wilful blindness on the part of the owner. It was pointed out, however, that the owner would have had no defence to a charge of 'using'.

A man who lends his car to his friend allows him to use it with his permission. That permission does not extend to unlawful use of a warning instrument as no permission has been given in that respect. If the tyres were defective, it would be a question of fact as to whether the owner of the vehicle knew of the defect when permission was given to use it.

PARTICULAR REGULATIONS UNDER THE ROAD VEHICLES (CONSTRUCTION AND USE) REGULATIONS 1986

Brakes

The differing braking systems with which differing types of vehicles must be fitted are dealt with in regs 15 and 16 and Sch 3. These provisions include exemptions from the provisions of the Construction and Use Regulations if type approval has been given. However, the fitting of various systems is not a matter of prime concern to police officers. On the other hand, the maintenance of brakes is. Regulation 18 deals with the maintenance of brakes and applies quite generally to braking systems (where fitted under these, or other, regulations).

The purpose of foot braking systems is to be able to stop the vehicle within a reasonable distance under the most adverse conditions. This is a fairly general description of the efficiency of a foot braking system but guidance is given in the Highway Code. The stopping distances given in the Code are related to good cars on dry roads with good brakes and alert drivers, and represent the shortest stopping distances. The Code sets out a table giving the overall stopping distances for vehicles travelling at 20, 30, 40, 50, 60 and 70 mph as 40, 75, 120, 175, 240 and 315 feet respectively. Although the provisions of the Code may be relied upon in a prosecution to show that the accused failed to comply with a standard contained in it and, therefore, as tending to establish negligence (eg in a criminal case, to establish dangerous or careless driving), the table is hearsay evidence as far as evidence of speeding is concerned.

Braking systems to which reg 15 applies

Regulation 15(1) of the Regulations requires that with certain exceptions (generally embracing specialist types of vehicles) all wheeled motor vehicles specified in the table set out within the regulation, which were first used on or after 1 April 1983, must comply with the construction, fitting and performance requirements of Community Directive 79/489/EEC. So must a trailer manufactured on or after 1 October 1982. The vehicles specified include most vehicles on our roads today. The table indicates the vehicle category set out in the Community Directive, specifying the construction, fitting and performance requirement of each type of vehicle. Other similar vehicles used or manufactured (as appropriate) before the relevant date may comply with these requirements as an alternative to reg 16.

Regulations 15(1A) and 15(1B) require that, with certain exceptions, the braking systems of most motor vehicles first used on or after 1 April 1989 (or trailers manufactured on or after 1 October 1988) must comply with the requirements of Community Directive 85/647/EEC. Motor cars, buses of a gross weight not exceeding 5,000 kg, and dual purpose vehicles, must comply if first used on or after 1 April 1990. By reg 15(1C), other motor vehicles (with certain exceptions) first used on or after

1 April 1992, and trailers manufactured on or after 1 October 1991, must comply with Community Directive 88/194/EEC. Regulation 15(1D) requires that all such vehicles as specified above first used on or after 1 April 1995 and trailers manufactured on or after that date must comply with Community Directive 91/422/EEC. Once again, other such vehicles may comply as an alternative to the other Directives specified above. Regulation 15(1E) requires the vehicles referred to below to comply with Community Directive 98/12/EC. It has the effect of extending the categories of vehicles which are required to be fitted with ABS braking systems at the point of manufacture to include all passenger-carrying vehicles with more than eight passenger seats in addition to the driver's seat, all goods vehicles over 3,500 kg (other than a street cleaning vehicle with a maximum design weight of 7,500 kg) and all trailers over 3,500 kg. Regulation 15(1E) applies to all motor vehicles of the relevant kinds first used on or after 1 May 2002 or, in the case of a trailer, manufactured on or after that date. Motor vehicles first used before 1 May 2002 or, in the case of a trailer, manufactured before 1 April 2002, may comply with these requirements as an alternative to reg 15(1), (1A), (1C) or (1D) or with reg 16.

For the purposes of reg 15, the date upon which a trailer was manufactured shall be taken to be the date on which its manufacture was completed except that, in the case of a trailer whose manufacture has been completed for more than eight years and which has been the subject of a notifiable alteration under reg 30 of the Goods Vehicles (Plating and Testing) Regulations 1988, it is the date on which the notifiable alteration was completed. Such a trailer must comply with all Community directives which applied to the trailer when the notifiable alteration was completed. This means, for example, that a rebuilt trailer manufactured more than eight years previously must be brought up to the latest braking standard applicable at the time of rebuilding.

Braking systems to which reg 15 does not apply

Most of the remainder of vehicles, that is those first used before 1 April 1983 and those specifically excluded from reg 15, are covered by the provisions of reg 16. However, all such vehicles *may* comply with the requirements of reg 15 as an alternative to the provisions of reg 16. Certain specialist vehicles are not covered by reg 16. It contains a table which specifies the requirements of Sch 3 to the Regulations which apply to particular vehicles.

Heavy motor cars and motor cars first used on or after 1 January 1968 to which reg 16 applies must be equipped with one efficient braking system having two means of operation; or one efficient split braking system having one means of operation; or two efficient braking systems each having a separate means of operation. No account is to be taken of a multi-pull means of operation unless, at first application, it operates a hydraulic, electric or pneumatic device which causes the application of the brakes with a total braking efficiency of not less than 25%. The braking system must be so designed that, in the event of failure of any part (other than a fixed member or brake shoe anchor pin) through or by means of which the force necessary to apply the brakes is transmitted, there is still available for application by the driver brakes sufficient under the most adverse conditions to bring the vehicle to rest within a reasonable distance. The brakes so available must be applied to at least one wheel if the vehicle is a three-wheeler and otherwise to at least half of the wheels. Braking systems must not affect or operate the pedals or hand lever of any other braking system, nor may they be rendered ineffective by the non-rotation of the engine. At least one means of operation must be capable of causing brakes to be applied directly, and not through the transmission, to at least half of the wheels of the vehicle. The parking brake must be so designed and constructed that it is independent and its braking force, when the vehicle is not being driven or is unattended, must be such that it can be maintained so as to hold the vehicle stationary on a gradient of at least 16% without the assistance of stored energy.

The provisions set out in the paragraph above also apply to heavy motor cars and motor cars first used *before* 1 January 1968 with the exception of those related to the parking brake. In the case of these vehicles the parking brake must be so designed and constructed that:

(a) its means of operation is independent of the means of operation of any split braking system;

(b) it is capable of being applied by direct mechanical action without the intervention of any hydraulic, electric or pneumatic device, or the brakes apply to all wheels; and

(c) it can at all times when the vehicle is not being driven, or is left unattended, be set so as to prevent the rotation of one wheel in the case of a three-wheeled vehicle, and of at least two wheels in the case of a vehicle with more than three wheels.

Two-wheeled motor cycles must be equipped with one efficient braking system having two means of operation; or two efficient braking systems each having a separate means of operation. The application of any means of operation of a braking system must not affect or operate the pedal or hand lever of any other means of operation.

Trailers, other than agricultural trailers, manufactured on or after 1 January 1968 and having a maximum gross weight exceeding 750 kg, must be equipped with an efficient braking system. The system must be such that in the event of failure etc the brakes available are applied to at least one wheel if the trailer has two wheels, and otherwise to at least two wheels. The braking power must be sufficient under the most adverse conditions to bring the vehicle to rest within a reasonable distance. Brakes may be of an overrun type. The brakes of these trailers must apply to all wheels. They must have a parking brake which can be applied and released by a person standing on the ground, by a means of operation fitted to the trailer.

Trailers manufactured before 1 January 1968 (and all agricultural trailers regardless of date of manufacture) require an efficient braking system if they have a maximum gross weight exceeding 750 kg. They may be of the overrun type. The brakes of the vehicle must apply to at least two wheels if the vehicle has no more than four wheels, and to at least half of the wheels if it has more than four wheels. The parking brake must be capable of being set so as effectively to prevent two at least of the wheels from revolving when the trailer is not being drawn.

Whilst the provisions of reg 16 do not apply to trailers which have a maximum total design axle weight not exceeding 750 kg, such trailers manufactured on or after 1 January 1997 are required:

(a) to have a braking device such that the trailer will stop automatically if the coupling separates while the trailer is in motion; or

(b) be provided with a secondary coupling (eg a chain or cable) which, in the event of separation of the main coupling, can stop the draw bar from touching the ground and provide some residual steering action in the trailer.

Such trailers manufactured on or after that date must carry a plate which carries their year of manufacture.

Maintenance and efficiency

Regulation 18(1) of the Construction and Use Regulations requires that every braking system and the means of operation thereof fitted to a vehicle must be maintained in good and efficient working order, and be properly adjusted. This applies to any vehicle to which a braking system is fitted, including a trailer which is not required to have a braking system fitted.

By reg 18(3) braking systems must be so maintained that service braking systems and secondary braking systems have prescribed braking efficiencies:

	Service	Secondary
(a) if the vehicle's construction etc complies with Community Directive 79/489, 85/647, 88/194 or 91/422:		
(i) not drawing a trailer	50%	25%
(ii) drawing a trailer	45%	25%
(b) vehicles first used on or after 1 January 1968 and complying with reg 16:		
(i) when not drawing a trailer or drawing trailer manufactured after 1 January 1968	50%	25%
(ii) drawing trailer manufactured before 1 January 1968	40%	15%
(c) goods vehicles and buses first used before 1 January 1968 having an unladen weight exceeding 1,525 kg being rigid vehicles with two axles (not artics):		
(i) when not drawing trailer	45%	20%
(ii) when drawing trailer	40%	15%
(d) vehicles not shown at (a) to (c) having at least one means of operation applying to at least four wheels (not a bus or artic):	50%	25%
(e) vehicles not shown at (a) to (c) having three wheels and at least one means of operation applying to all three wheels (not a motor cycle and sidecar) when not drawing a trailer, or when drawing a trailer if three-wheeler is classed as a motor cycle:	40%	25%
(f) other vehicles not shown at (a) to (c) when not drawing a trailer or, in the case of a motor cycle, when drawing a trailer	30%	25%

In certain circumstances where a defect arises in an ABS braking system during the course of a journey, it is permissible for the vehicle to complete its journey, or to be driven to a place where the ABS is to be repaired, without there being a breach of the requirement that every part of a braking system must be maintained in good and efficient working order. However, the affected braking system must still meet the braking efficiencies specified in reg 18(3).

The maintenance of brakes is further dealt with by reg 18(6) which is concerned with the efficiency of parking brakes. It requires that every vehicle or combination of vehicles specified in an item in column 2 of Table II of the regulation, shall be so maintained that the brakes are capable, without the assistance of stored energy, of holding it stationary on a gradient of at least the percentages specified in column 3 of that table. This means:

(i)	those vehicles specified at (a) above:	
	(A) when not drawing a trailer	16%
	(B) when drawing a trailer	12%
(ii)	those vehicles specified at (b) above	16%
(iii)	vehicles other than in (a) above drawing a trailer manufactured on or after 1 January 1968 and required by reg 15 or 16 to be fitted with brakes	16%

Anchorage points and seat belts

Regulations 46 and 47 of the Construction and Use Regulations deal with anchorage points and seat belts.

Anchorage points

Regulation 46 provides that, except in the case of an 'excepted vehicle', every bus first used on or after 1 April 1982; every wheeled motor car first used on or after 1 January 1965; every three-wheeled motor cycle the unladen weight of which exceeds 255 kg and which was first used on or after 1 September 1970; and every heavy motor car first used on or after 1 October 1988 must be fitted with anchorage points and seat belts as specified.

Excepted vehicles The following are excepted vehicles:

(a) a goods vehicle (other than a dual-purpose vehicle) which was first used:
   (i) before 1 April 1967; or
   (ii) on or after 1 April 1980 and before 1 October 1988 which has a maximum gross weight exceeding 3,500 kg; or
   (iii) before 1 April 1980 or, if the vehicle is a model manufactured before 1 October 1979, was first used before 1 April 1982 and, in either case, has an unladen weight exceeding 1,525 kg;
(b) an agricultural vehicle;
(c) a motor tractor;
(d) a works truck;
(e) an electrically-propelled goods vehicle first used before 1 October 1988;
(f) a pedestrian-controlled vehicle;
(g) an imported vehicle whilst travelling to be fitted etc;
(h) a vehicle having a maximum speed not exceeding 16 mph; and
(i) a locomotive.

Where points to be fitted   The rules are as follows:

(1)   A vehicle first used before 1 April 1982 must be equipped with anchorage points for seat belts in respect of the driver's seat and any specified passenger's seat. Where there is only one forward-facing seat alongside the driver's, that seat is the 'specified passenger's seat'. Where there is more than one forward-facing front seat, the term is applied to the one farthest from the driver's seat. A passenger or dual-purpose vehicle (other than a bus) first used on or after 1 April 1982 and not falling within (2) to (8) below must have anchorage points for every forward facing seat constructed or adapted to accommodate one adult.

(2)   A minibus, motor ambulance or motor caravan first used on or after 1 April 1982 but before 1 October 1988 must have anchorage points for the driver's and specified passenger's seats.

(3)   A minibus (not being within (7) or (8) below) with a gross weight not exceeding 3,500 kg, a motor ambulance or motor caravan first used on or after 1 October 1988 must have anchorage points for the driver's seat and each forward-facing front seat.

(4)   A goods vehicle first used on or after 1 October 1988 but before 1 October 2001 which has a maximum gross weight exceeding 3,500 kg must have anchorage points for the driver's seat and each forward-facing front seat.

(5)   A goods vehicle first used on or after 1 October 2001 which has a maximum gross weight exceeding 3,500 kg must have anchorage points for all forward-facing front seats.

(6)   A coach first used on or after 1 October 1988 but before 1 October 2001 must have anchorage points for all exposed forward-facing front seats (ie forward-facing seats at the front and any behind which are not immediately behind and level with a forward-facing high-backed seat).

(7)   A bus (other than an urban bus) with a gross vehicle weight of 3,500 kg and first used on or after 1 October 2001 must have an anchorage point for every forward-facing seat and every rearward-facing seat.

(8)   A bus (other than an urban bus) with a gross vehicle weight *not* exceeding 3,500 kg and first used on or after 1 October 2001 must have anchorage points for every forward-facing and every rearward-facing seat.

(9)   A passenger or dual purpose vehicle (other than a bus) first used on or after 1 April 1982 and not falling within (2) to (8) above must have an anchorage point for every forward-facing seat constructed or adapted to carry no more than one adult.

(10) In every other case a vehicle (other than a bus) first used on or after 1 April 1982 (and not within (2) to (8) above) must have anchorage points for every forward-facing front seat and every non-protected seat. A 'non-protected seat' is one which is not a front seat where the screen zones within the 'protected area' has a combined surface of less than 80 square cm.

Seat belts

Regulation 47, which deals with seat belts, applies to all vehicles covered by the requirements of reg 46 in relation to anchorage points. Such vehicles first used before 1 April 1981 must have seat belts for the driver's seat and the specified passenger's seat. They must be of an approved type and, in respect of these vehicles, 'diagonal belts' are approved. Those first used on or after 1 April 1981 must be provided with three-point seat belts for both the driver's seat and the specified passenger's seat.

Every passenger vehicle or dual-purpose vehicle (other than a bus) not falling within (b) to (h) of the text relating to anchorage points, and any other vehicle fitted with anchorage points and not falling within (2) to (8) in the last list, which is first used on or after 1 April 1987 must additionally be fitted with a three-point belt, lap or disabled person's belt for every forward-facing front seat which is not a specified passenger's seat. Thus, the 'Transit' type of vehicle will be required to have seat belts for all three front seats. Such vehicles must also be fitted with rear seat belts for passengers sitting in the rear of the vehicle who are using a forward-facing seat. Rear seat belts must be provided as follows:

(a) vehicles with not more than two forward-facing seats behind the driver's seat must have *either* an inertia reel belt for *at least one* of those seats, *or* a three-point, lap, disabled person's, or child restraint belt for each of those seats;
(b) vehicles having more than two forward-facing seats behind the driver's seat must have either:
  (i) an inertia reel belt for one of those seats being an outboard seat, and a three-point, lap, disabled person's, or child restraint belt, for *at least one other* of those seats; or
  (ii) a three-point belt for one of those seat sand either a child restraint or disabled person's belt for *at least one other* of those seats; or
  (iii) a three-point, lap, disabled person's, or child restraint belt for each of those seats.

The use of a coach or minibus for the purpose of carrying a group of three or more children in connection with an organised trip is prohibited by reg 48A unless the vehicle has at least as many forward-facing passenger seats as there are children, and each seat is fitted with seat belts. A disabled child in a wheelchair is disregarded for this purpose. For these purposes a child is a person who is three years or more but is under the age of sixteen. In the case of a coach or minibus first used on or after 1 October 2001 a rearward-facing seat is treated as a forward-facing seat if it has the appropriate anchorage point and belt.

Without prejudice to the generality of these requirements, a group of such children will be regarded as being on an organised trip if they are being carried to or from their school or from one part of their school premises to another.

A minibus not exceeding 3,500 kg gross weight, motor ambulance or motor caravan first used on or after 1 October 1988 must have three-point belts for the driver's and specified passenger's seats and a three-point or lap belt for any other forward-facing front seat. A coach first used on or after 1 October 1988 but before 1 October 2001 must have three-point, lap or disabled person's belts for all exposed forward-facing front seats. A goods vehicles first used on or after 1 October 2001 and having a maximum gross weight exceeding 3,500 kg must have a three-point belt or lap belt for the driver's seat and such a belt or a disabled person's belt for every forward-facing front seat. A bus falling within item (7) in the list relating to anchorage points must be fitted, as respects every forward- and rearward-facing seat, with an inertia reel belt, a retractable lap belt, a disabled person's belt or a child restraint. In the case of a bus falling within (8) the requirements are the same in respect of every forward- and rearward-facing seat except that a retractable lap belt may not be fitted in respect of a forward-facing seat.

Where lap belts are fitted to a forward-facing seat of a minibus, motor ambulance or motor caravan or to an exposed forward-facing seat of a coach (other than the driver's seat) either the requirements of Annex 4 to European Community Equipment (ECE), reg 21 must be met, or padding to a depth of not less than 50 mm must be provided on that part of the surface or edge of any bar or the top or edge of any screen or partition which would be likely to be struck by the head of a passenger wearing the lap belt in the event of an accident. Padding need not be provided on any surface more than one metre from the centre of the line of intersection of the seat cushion and the back rest, nor on the instrument panel of a minibus. The revised provisions concerning padding apply to vehicles registered from 7 September 1989. Such padding must extend for not less than 150 mm on either side of the central point of the seat. Thus, persons who may be thrown forward, and thereby come into contact with obstructions in front of them, are less likely to be seriously injured.

The requirements concerning the fitting of seat belts generally do not apply to vehicles being used under a trade licence or new vehicles in the course of delivery, nor do they apply (except in relation to the driver's seat or a front passenger seat) to vehicles constructed or adapted for the secure transport of prisoners.

Maintenance of seat belts

It is an offence to fail to maintain seat belts and their anchorage points. Buckles must be maintained so that they can be readily fastened and unfastened, and they must be kept free of any obstruction which would prevent them from becoming readily accessible to a person using the seat. Each end of a seat belt must be securely fastened to its anchorage point and the webbing must be free of cuts and other visible faults likely to affect its performance under stress. Within 30 cm of a seat belt anchorage point, the load bearing members or panelling of the vehicle structure must be maintained in sound condition.

Wearing of seat belts

The circumstances in which seat belts must be worn by passengers in motor vehicles are now prescribed in the Motor Vehicles (Wearing of Seat Belts) Regulations 1993 and the Motor Vehicles (Wearing of Seat Belts by Children in Front Seats) Regulations 1993 and not by the Road Vehicles (Construction and Use) Regulations. The 1993 Regulations implement the requirements of Council Directives 91/671/EEC and 2003/20/EC which apply to vehicles of less than 3.5 tonnes with four or more wheels and a design speed of more than 25 kph and to large and small buses and light goods vehicles. Directive 2006/20/EC requires additional measure in respect of the wearing of child restraining devices and places obligations upon bus operators to require the wearing of seat belts fitted to large and small buses. Both these Regulations and those of 1993, dealing with children in front sets which follow, were quite extensively amended by SIs 2006/1892 and 2006/2213.

The offences committed by breaches of the Seat Belt Regulations are punishable under RTA 1988, ss 14 and 15 and not by the RTA 1988, s 42 (unlike the other breaches in this part). The requirements created by the 1993 Regulations are not always confined to the description of vehicles set out in the Directive.

Front seat adult passengers

Regulation 5 of the Motor Vehicles (Wearing of Seat Belts) Regulations 1993 requires that every person driving a motor vehicle (other than a two-wheeled motor cycle with or without a sidecar) or riding in a rear seat of a motor vehicle (other than a two-wheeled motor cycle with or without a sidecar) must wear an adult belt. The regulation does not apply to a person under the age of fourteen years. Failure to comply with reg 5 is an offence under RTA 1988, s 14(3).

Regulation 6 provides the following exemptions from the requirement to wear a seat belt made by reg 5:

(a) a person holding a medical certificate to the effect that it is inadvisable for him to wear a seat belt;

(b) the driver of or a passenger in a motor vehicle constructed or adapted for carrying goods, while on a journey which does not exceed 50 metres and which is undertaken for the purpose of delivering or collecting anything;

(c) a person performing a manoeuvre which includes reversing;

(d) a qualified driver supervising a learner carrying out such a manoeuvre;

(e) a person by whom a test of competence to drive is being conducted where wearing a seat belt would endanger himself or another person;

(f) a person driving or riding in a vehicle being used for fire brigade or police purposes or for carrying a person in lawful custody (this includes the prisoner);

(g) the driver of a licensed taxi whilst being used to seek hire or answer a call, or when carrying a passenger for hire, or a private hire car whilst it is being used to carry a passenger for hire;

(h) a person in a vehicle being used under a trade licence for investigating or remedying a fault;

(i) a disabled person who is wearing a disabled person's belt; or

(j) a person riding in a vehicle whilst in a procession organised by or on behalf of the Crown.

There are two other exemptions. A person who is riding in a vehicle which is participating in a procession which is held to mark or commemorate an event is exempt from the requirement to wear a seat belt if the procession is one commonly or customarily held in a police area or areas, or if notice in respect of the procession has been given in accordance with the Public Order Act 1986, s 11 (see p 888). The second requirement in reg 5 relating to a person riding in a front or rear seat of a motor vehicle other than a two-wheeled motor cycle with or without a sidecar requiring him to wear a seat belt does not apply to a person riding in a small or large bus which is being used to provide a local service (within the meaning of the Transport Act 1985 (TA 1985)) in a built-up area (ie entirely on restricted roads or which is constructed or adapted for the carriage of standing passengers and on which the operator permits standing).

Rear seat adult passengers

Regulation 5 of the Motor Vehicles (Wearing of Seat Belts) Regulations 1993 also prohibits an adult person (ie someone aged fourteen or over) from riding in the rear seat of a motor car, or of a passenger car which is not a motor car, if he is not wearing an adult seat belt provided in the vehicle. Persons who fail to comply with the regulation offend against RTA 1988, s 14(3).

Front seat child passengers

It is an offence contrary to RTA 1988, s 15(1) and (2) for a person, without reasonable excuse, to drive a motor vehicle on a road in which a child under fourteen is in the front of that vehicle unless the child is wearing a seat belt in conformity with the Motor Vehicles (Wearing of Seat Belts by Children in Front Seats) Regulations 1993. Generally, it is irrelevant that a seat belt is not provided or available for the seat. The Regulations set out the rules with which a driver must conform. A 'front seat' is one which is wholly or partially in the front of the vehicle. The Regulations do not apply to two-wheeled motor cycles, with or without sidecars.

The description of the seat belts which satisfy the requirements of the Regulations relating to children is prescribed in reg 5 of the Motor Vehicles (Wearing of Seat Belts by Children in Front Seats) Regulations 1993, reg 5.

(a) in the case of a 'small child' travelling in a passenger car, light goods vehicle (not exceeding 3.5 tonnes), or a small bus (more than eight passenger seats but not exceeding 3.5 tonnes), the seat belt must be a child restraint with a marking required under the Road Vehicles (Construction and Use) Regulations 1986, reg 47(7) or a child restraint approved by another EU member state;

(b) in the case of a 'small child' in any other vehicle, the seat belt must be a child restraint approved under reg 47(7);

(c) in the case of a 'large child', the seat belt must be a child restraint approved under reg 47(7) of the 1986 Regulations or an adult belt.

For these purposes, a 'small child' is a child who is under twelve and under 135 cm in height, and a 'large child' is a child under fourteen who is not a 'small child'.

Regulation 7 exempts from these provisions:

(a) a 'small child' aged three or more who is riding in a bus and is wearing an adult belt if an appropriate seat belt is not available for him in the front or rear of the vehicle;

(b) a child for whom there is a medical certificate; or

(c) a disabled child who is wearing a disabled person's belt.

In addition, the prohibition created by RTA 1988, s 15(1) does not apply in relation to a child riding in a bus which is being used to provide a local service within the meaning of TA 1985 (see p 492), or which is constructed or adapted for the carriage of standing passengers and on which the operator (as defined on p 418) permits standing. The prohibition does not apply in relation to a 'large child' if no appropriate seat belt is available for him in the front of the vehicle.

RTA 1988, s 15(1A), added in 2006, requires that where:

(a) a child is in the front seat of a motor vehicle other than a bus;

(b) that child is in a rear-facing child restraining device; and
(c) the passenger seat where the child is placed is protected by a front air bag,

a person must not, without reasonable excuse, drive the vehicle on a road unless the air bag is deactivated' 'Deactivation includes the case where a bag is designed or adapted in such a way that it cannot inflate enough to pose a risk of injury to a child travelling in a rear-facing child restraining device in the seat in question. It is an offence contrary to s 15(2) for the person to drive a motor vehicle in contravention of s 15(1A). For the purposes of s 15, 'bus' means a motor vehicle with at least four wheels, constructed or adapted for the carriage of passengers, with more than eight seats in addition to the driver's seat and with a maximum design speed exceeding 25 kph.

Rear seat child passengers

RTA 1988, s 15(3), as substituted in 2006, and 15(4) makes it an offence for a person, without reasonable excuse, to drive a motor vehicle on a road where:

(a) a child under the age of three years is in the rear of that motor vehicle; or
(b) a child of or over that age but under the age of fourteen years is in the rear of the motor vehicle and any seat belt is fitted in the rear of that vehicle,

unless the child is wearing a seat belt in conformity with regulations. RTA 1988, s 15(3A) requires that a person must not, without reasonable excuse, drive a passenger car on a road where a child under the age of twelve and less than 135 cms in height, who is in the rear of a passenger car and no seat belt is fitted in the rear of the passenger car, but a seat in the front of the passenger car is provided with a seat belt and is not occupied by any person Exemption from these prohibitions is provided by reg 9 of the Motor Vehicles (Wearing of Seat Belts) Regulations 1993, as amended in 2006, which provides that they do not apply where the motor vehicle is a large bus, or where the vehicle is a licensed taxi or licensed hire car in which (in each case) the rear seats are separated from the driver by a fixed partition. Further exemptions are provided by reg 10, as amended, which provide that the prohibitions do not apply in relation to:

(a) a child for whom there is a medical certificate;
(b) a small child aged under three years who is riding in a licensed taxi, a licensed hire car or a small bus and wearing an adult belt if an appropriate seat belt is not available for him in the front or rear of the vehicle;
(c) a small child aged three years or more who is riding in a licensed taxi, a licensed hire car or a small bus and wearing an adult belt if an appropriate seat belt is not available for him in the front or rear of the vehicle;
(d) a small child aged three years or more who is wearing an adult belt and riding in a passenger car or light goods vehicle where the use of child restraints by the child occupants of two seats in the rear of the vehicle prevents the use of an appropriate seat belt for that child and no appropriate seat belt is available for him in the front of the vehicle;
(e) a small child who is riding in a vehicle being used for the purposes of the police, security or emergency services to enable the proper performance of their duty;
(f) a small child aged three years or more who is wearing an adult belt and who, because of an unexpected necessity, is travelling a short distance in a passenger car or light goods vehicle in which no appropriate seat belt is available for him; or

(g) a disabled child who is wearing a disabled person's belt or whose disability makes it impracticable to wear a seat belt where a disabled person's belt is unavailable to him.

The prohibition against the carriage of a child in the rear of a vehicle who is not wearing a seat belt does not apply in relation to a child under three years riding in a rear seat of a small bus. Nor does it apply to a small child aged three years or more riding in the rear of a small bus if neither an appropriate seat belt nor an adult seat belt is available for him in the front or rear of the vehicle In addition, it does not apply in relation to a 'large child' in any vehicle, if no appropriate seat belt is available for him in the rear of the vehicle. Lastly, the prohibition doe not apply to a child riding in a small bus which is being used to provide a local service (within the meaning of TA 1985) in a built-up-area (ie entirely on restricted roads) or which is constructed or adapted for the carriage of standing passengers and on which the operator permits standing.

For these purposes 'large buses' and 'small buses' are motor vehicles which have at least four wheels, adapted for the carriage of passengers, have more than eight seats in addition to the driver's seat, and have a maximum design speed exceeding 25 kph. The difference between them is that a large bus has a maximum laden weight exceeding 3.5 tonnes and a small bus has a maximum laden weight not exceeding 3.5 tonnes. A 'light goods vehicle' is a motor vehicle with at least four wheels, a maximum design speed of more than 25 kph, and a maximum laden weight not exceeding 3.5 tonnes. A 'small child' means a child under twelve years of age and under 135 cm in height, and a 'large child' is a child under fourteen who is not a small child. 'Operator' has the same meaning as in RTA 1988, s 15B below.

Wearing of seat belts in buses

The RTA 1988, s 15B(1), added in 2006, requires bus operators to notify passengers of the need to wear seat belts.

It provides that, subject to s 15B(6), the operator of a bus in which any of the passenger seats are equipped with seat belts must take all reasonable steps to ensure that every passenger is notified that he is required to wear a seat belt at all times when:

(a) he is in a seat equipped with a seat belt, and
(b) the bus is in motion.

'Operator' means the owner of the bus or, if the bus is in the possession of any other person under an agreement for hire, or hire-purchase, conditional sale, loan or otherwise, that person. 'Bus' has the same meaning as in RTA 1988, s 15 (see p 399).

Notification may be made by an official announcement, or an audio-visual presentation, made when the passenger joins the bus or within a reasonable time of his doing so, or a sign (a symbol of a seated figure wearing a belt) prominently displayed at each passenger seat equipped with a seat belt.

Section 15(6) provides that the offence against s 15B(1) does not apply in relation to a bus which is being used to provide a local service (within the meaning of TA 1985) in a built-up area (ie entirely on restricted roads) *or* which is constructed or adapted for the carriage of standing passengers and on which the operator permits standing.

The operator commits an offence against s 15B(4) if he fails to comply with the requirements of s 15(1). Where an offence committed by a body corporate is proved to have been committed with the consent or connivance of, or attributable to, any neglect on the part of a director, manager, secretary or other similar officer, or any person purporting to act in such a capacity, that person is equally liable.

A 'bus' for the purposes of s 15 is a vehicle with at least four wheels, constructed for the carriage of passengers, which has more than eight seats in addition to the driver's seat and has a maximum design speed in excess of 25 kph. For the purposes of the 1993 Regulations, reg 2 (general interpretation) defines the terms 'large bus', 'small bus' and 'light goods vehicle'. Both large and small buses have at least four wheels; are adapted for the carriage of passengers; have more than eight seats in addition to the driver's seat; and have a maximum design speed exceeding 25 kph. The large bus has a maximum laden weight exceeding 3.5 tonnes, the small bus must be 3.5 tonnes or less. A 'light goods vehicle' has more than four wheels; a maximum design speed of more than 25 kph; and a maximum laden weight not exceeding 3.5 tonnes.

The operator of either type of bus is the owner of that bus or, if the bus is in the possession of any other person under an agreement for hire. hire-purchase, conditional sale, loan or otherwise, that person.

'Availability' of seat belts

Schedule 2 to the 1993 Regulations describes the circumstances in which a seat belt will be regarded as not being available. They are where:

(a) another person is wearing the relevant belt;
(b) a child is occupying the relevant seat and wearing a child restraint which is an appropriate child restraint for that child and this renders use of the seat belt impracticable;
(c) a person holding a medical certificate is occupying the relevant seat;
(d) a disabled person (not being the person in question) is occupying the relevant seat and wearing a disabled person's belt and this renders use of the seat belt impracticable;
(e) by reason of his disability, it would not be practicable for the person in question to wear the relevant belt;
(f) [deleted];
(g) the person in question is prevented from occupying the relevant seat by the presence of a child restraint which could not readily be removed without the aid of tools; or
(h) the relevant seat is so designed that it can be adjusted to increase the space available for goods and effects and when it is so adjusted the seat cannot be used.

Speedometer

Regulation 35 of the Construction and Use Regulations provides that every motor vehicle must be fitted with a speedometer. It is unlikely that a revolution counter would be accepted by a court as a form of speedometer as it does not readily indicate speed since the needle reading needs to be converted into miles per hour, and the gear in which the vehicle is being driven affects that conversion. Regulation 35 also provides that speedometers fitted to vehicles first used after 1 April 1984 must indicate speed in both miles per hour and kilometres per hour; otherwise the indication given by a speedometer may be either in miles per hour or kilometres per hour. Instead of complying with reg 35, a vehicle may comply with the relevant Community directive or ECE regulations.

The provisions of reg 35 do not apply to a vehicle marked with a marking designated as a type approval mark. There are two types of approval marks in respect of speedometers, one for the traditional type of speedometer and one for speed recording equipment in tachographs. The importance of this is that failure to maintain a tachograph speedometer is an offence against the Transport Act 1968, s 97 if it is compulsorily fitted under the provisions of that Act. However, this will not usually be of concern to police officers since tachograph speedometers will be in addition to the ordinary instrument as they are unlikely readily to indicate speed to the driver.

Other vehicles exempt from the need to have speedometers fitted are:

(a) invalid carriages, motor cycles not exceeding 100 cc, and works trucks (provided in each case they were first used before 1 April 1984);
(b) agricultural vehicles which are not driven at more than 20 mph;
(c) vehicles which legally or physically cannot exceed 25 mph; and
(d) those which have an alternative type approved instrument.

Vehicles first used before 1 October 1937 are also exempt.

Regulation 36 requires that a speedometer must be kept free from any obstruction which might prevent its being easily read and must at all times be maintained in good working order. On a charge involving a breach of this requirement, it is a defence to prove that the defect occurred in the course of the journey being then undertaken or that steps had already been taken to have repairs or replacements effected as soon as possible. These defences cover so many possibilities, and if alleged are so hard to disprove, that enforcement is almost limited to admitted long standing defects in respect of which no repairs have been arranged or when the instrument registers incorrectly.

Speed limiters on motor vehicles

Regulations 36A, 36B and 70A of the Road Vehicles (Construction and Use) Regulations 1986 set out those vehicles which are required to be fitted with speed limiters and deal with the requirement to fix plates on such vehicles showing the speed at which the limiter has been set. Buses brought temporarily into Great Britain by a person resident abroad and registered in one or more member states of the EU must comply with the speed limiter requirements where the maximum gross weight exceeds 10 tonnes. Goods vehicles so registered must comply where the maximum gross weight exceeds 12 tonnes.

Regulation 36A (coaches, buses, etc)

Regulation 36A requires a speed limiter to be fixed to the following:

(1) Every coach first used on or after 1 April 1974 and before 1 January 1988, which would, without the fitting of a speed limiter, be capable of exceeding 112.65 kph,

must be fitted with a speed limiter calibrated to a set speed not exceeding 112.65 kph (reg 36A(1)).

(2) Every bus first used on or after 1 January 1988, which has a maximum gross weight exceeding 7.5 tonnes and which would, without the fitting of a speed limiter, be capable of exceeding 100 kph, must be fitted with a speed limiter calibrated to a set speed not exceeding 100 kph (reg 36A(2)). Speed limiters fitted to a vehicle as required by reg 36A(2), if the vehicle was first used before 1 January 2005 and has a maximum gross weight exceeding 10 tonnes, or was first used before 1 October 2001 and has a maximum gross weight exceeding 7.5 tonnes but not exceeding 10 tonnes, may be set at a maximum speed of 100 km/h.

(3) Regulation 36A(2A) extends the requirement to fit a speed limiter to every bus, not being a bus to which reg 36A(2) applies, first used on or after 1 January 2005, which has a maximum gross weight exceeding 5 tonnes but not exceeding 10 tonnes and would (without the fitting of a speed limiter) have a maximum speed exceeding 100 kph.

(4) Regulation 36A(2B) extends the requirement to fit a speed limiter to every bus, first used on or after 1 January 2005, which has a maximum gross weight not exceeding 5 tonnes and would (without the fitting of a speed limiter) have a maximum speed exceeding 100 kph. However reg 36A(2E) defers the requirements of (2B) until 1 January 2008 in the case of a vehicle used solely for national transport operations.

(5) Regulation 36A(2C) extends the requirement to fit a speed limiter to diesel-engined buses, not being buses to which reg 36A(2) applies, which comply with the limit values in respect of Euro III emission standards set out in the amended Directive 88/77/EEC, have a maximum gross weight not exceeding 10 tonnes, are first used between 1 October 2001 and 1 January 2005, and are capable of a maximum speed exceeding 100 kph. The requirement is deferred until 1 January 2006 in the case of a vehicle used for national and international transport operations, and until 1 January 2007 where the vehicle is used solely for national transport operations.

Speed limiters which are fitted to such vehicles must be sealed by an authorised sealer in such a manner as to protect the limiter against any improper interference or adjustment and against any interference of its power supply and must be maintained in good and efficient working order. In the case of limiters fitted before 1 August 1992 to vehicles first used before that date and those sealed outside the United Kingdom, the requirement that this must be done by an authorised sealer does not apply. Limiters fitted to coaches described at (1) above and fitted to buses described at (2) above before 1 October 1994 must comply with Part I of the British Standard or the Annexes to Community Directive 92/24/EEC. Those fitted after that date to such vehicles must comply with Community Directive 92/24/EEC as extended by Directive 2004/11/EC. However, these requirements do not apply to limiters fitted before 1 January 1988, nor where there is compliance with an equivalent standard.

The provisions of the regulation do not apply to vehicles being taken to a place where a speed limiter is to be installed, calibrated, replaced or repaired, or where the vehicle is completing a journey in the course of which the speed limiter has accidentally ceased to function.

Regulation 36B (goods vehicles)

Regulation 36B requires speed limiters to be fitted to:

(1) Goods vehicles of a maximum gross weight exceeding 7,500 kg but not exceeding 12,000 kg, and first used on or after 1 August 1992 and before 1 January 2005, which would (without the fitting of a speed limiter) be capable of exceeding a maximum speed of 60 mph. The speed limiter fitted must be calibrated to a set speed not exceeding 60 mph (reg 36B(1)).

(2) Goods vehicles of a maximum gross weight exceeding 12,000 kg, which are first used on or after 1 January 1988 and would (without the fitting of a speed limiter) be capable of a maximum speed exceeding 90 kph. The limiter must be set so that the stabilised speed of the vehicle cannot exceed 90 kph (reg 36B(2)).

(3) Goods vehicles of a maximum gross weight exceeding 3,500 kg but not exceeding 12,000 kg, which are first used on or after 1 January 2005, and which would, without the fitting of a speed limiter, have a relevant speed exceeding 90 kph (reg 36(1A)). However, the requirement is deferred until 1 January 2008 for such vehicles which do not exceed 7,500 kg when used solely for national transport operations (reg 36B(1A)).

(4) Goods-carrying diesel-engined vehicles which comply with the limit values in respect of Euro III emission standards set out in the amended Directive 88/77/EEC, have a maximum gross weight exceeding 3,500 kg but not exceeding 12,000 kg, are first used between 1 October 2001 and 1 January 2005, and would (without the fitting of a speed limiter) have a relevant speed exceeding 90 kph. However, this requirement is deferred until 1 January 2006 when the vehicle is used for national and international transport operations and to 1 January 2007 where it is used solely for national transport operations (reg 36B(1B)).

Exemptions

The provisions of reg 36A do not apply to a vehicle:

(a) being taken to a place where a speed limiter is to be installed, calibrated, replaced or repaired;

(b) where the vehicle is completing a journey in the course of which the speed limiter has accidentally ceased to function;

(c) which is owned by the Secretary of State for Defence and used for naval, military or air force purposes;

(d) which is used for naval, military or air force purposes while being driven by a person for the time being subject to the orders of a member of the armed forces of the Crown; or

(e) while it is being used for fire and rescue authority purposes or for or in connection with the exercise of any function of a relevant authority as defined in s 6 of the Fire (Scotland) Act 2005, for ambulance purposes or police purposes.

The provisions of reg 36B do not apply to a vehicle which:

(a) is being taken to a place where a speed limiter is to be installed, calibrated, repaired or replaced;

(b) is completing a journey in the course of which the speed limiter has accidentally ceased to function;

(c) is owned by the Secretary of State for Defence and used for such purposes or is so used by a person for the time being subject to the orders of a member of the armed forces of the Crown;

(d) is used for fire and rescue authority, ambulance or police purposes; or

when it is being used on a public road during any calendar week, is being used only in passing from land in a person's occupation to other land in his occupation, and it has not been used on a public road for distances exceeding an aggregate of six miles in that calendar week.

Regulation 70A (plates)

Regulation 70A provides the plating requirements in respect of all such vehicles. All vehicles to which reg 36A or reg 36B apply must be equipped with a plate which is in a conspicuous position in the driving compartment of the vehicle and is clearly and indelibly marked with the speed at which the speed limiter has been set.

Mirrors

Regulation 33 of the Construction and Use Regulations deals with these. With certain exceptions, every passenger vehicle, goods vehicle or dual-purpose vehicle first used on or after 1 June 1978 and before 26 January 2010, must be equipped with an interior rear view mirror and at least one exterior rear view mirror fitted to the offside of the vehicle. If for any reason the interior rear view mirror does not provide an adequate view to the rear, the vehicle must also have an exterior rear view mirror fitted to the nearside of the vehicle. In effect, this means that, when the internal mirror is obscured, the driver commits no offence if there are external mirrors on each side. Vehicles designed or constructed for the carriage of passengers and comprising no more than eight seats in addition to the driver's seat, must be fitted with an external rear-view mirror on both the driver's side and the passenger's side, if first used on or after 26 January 2010.

Two-wheeled motor cycles remain 'excepted vehicles' from the regulations relating to mirrors and therefore do not require any rear view mirrors. However, if mirrors are fitted to motor cycles first used on or after 1 October 1978, they must comply with the standards set out in the regulations. There are other types of 'excepted vehicles'. These include motor vehicles which are drawing trailers upon which there is some person who can communicate to the driver the intentions of other vehicles to the rear, works trucks with a clear view to the rear, pedestrian-controlled vehicles, and chassis being driven to a body plant.

Locomotives or motor tractors first used on or after 1 June 1978, agricultural motor vehicles not exceeding 7,370 kg unladen weight, agricultural motor vehicles first used after 1 June 1986 which are not driven at more than 20 mph, and some works trucks require only one mirror which must be fitted on the offside.

Vehicles first used before 1 June 1978 are subject to different requirements, as follows. Passenger vehicles adapted to carry more than eight seated passengers exclusive of the driver, goods vehicles and dual-purpose vehicles (except locomotives and motor tractors) must be fitted with at least two mirrors; one externally fitted on the offside, and the other internally or on the nearside externally. The remainder of vehicles (and this includes saloon cars) require only one mirror fitted either internally or externally in such a way that the driver can become aware of traffic to the rear.

The following rules apply where the goods vehicle concerned is first used on or after 26 January 2007:

(1) goods vehicles with a maximum weight exceeding 7.5 tonnes but not exceeding 12 tonnes which are first used on or after 26 January 2007 must be fitted with two wide-angle mirrors, a close-proximity mirror and a front mirror;

(2) goods vehicles with a maximum weight exceeding 3.5 tonnes but not exceeding 7.5 tonnes (but having cabins of a similar height to goods vehicles exceeding 7.5 tonnes) which are first used on or after 26 January 2007 must be fitted with two wide-angle mirrors and a close-proximity mirror;

(3) goods vehicles with a maximum weight exceeding 12 tonnes which are first used on or after 26 January 2007 must be fitted with an additional wide-angle mirror and a front mirror.

In all cases where a front mirror is specified, if it is not possible to fit a front mirror, a device for indirect vision (for example a camera and monitor device) may be used instead;

Passenger-carrying vehicles comprising no more than eight seats in addition to the driver's seat which are first used on or after 26 January 2010, must be fitted with an exterior rear-view mirror on both the driver's side and the passenger side of the vehicle. Previously such a vehicle was only required to have an exterior mirror on the driver's side.

In the case of vehicles first used on or after 1 June 1978, mirrors must be fitted in such a way that they remain steady under normal driving conditions; each exterior mirror must be visible to the driver from his driving position, either through a side window or through the area of the windscreen swept by a wiper blade. Interior mirrors and those fitted to the offside must be capable of adjustment by the driver from his driving position (except where the exterior mirror is a 'spring back' type). However, this does not prevent an exterior mirror being locked in position from the outside of the vehicle. In cases where the bottom edge of an exterior mirror is less than 2 m from the road surface when the vehicle is laden, the projection must not exceed 20 cm. If the vehicle is drawing a trailer which is wider than the towing vehicle, the projection of a mirror must not exceed the trailer width by more than 20 cm. However, where the lower edge of an exterior mirror, which complies with the requirements of Directive 2003/97/EC or ECE Regulation 46.02, is less than 2 m above the ground when the vehicle is loaded, the mirror must not project more than 25 cm beyond the overall width of the vehicle, where the vehicle is drawing a trailer and the trailer is wider than the towing vehicle, the mirror must not project more than 25 cm beyond the overall width of the trailer.

Instead of complying with the above requirements, a vehicle may comply with the relevant Community directive.

Windscreen wipers and washers

By reg 34(1) of the Construction and Use Regulations, all vehicles which are fitted with windscreens must be fitted with one or more efficient automatic windscreen wipers, unless the driver can obtain an adequate view to the front without looking through the windscreen, for example by opening the windscreen or looking over it (as is the case with 'wind open' screens and those which fold downwards, which are features of many cars produced before the 1950s).

The wipers fitted must be capable of clearing the windscreen so that the driver has an adequate view of the road in front of both sides of the vehicle and to the front of the vehicle.

Regulation 34(6), which deals with maintenance, demands that every windscreen wiper required by the Regulations to be fitted must, at all times while the vehicle is used on a road, be maintained in good and efficient working order and be properly adjusted. As we have stated, reg 34 demands one or more wipers. If the driver's wiper provides the view ahead and to both sides required by that regulation, any other wiper is not subject to the maintenance requirement.

By reg 34(2), a windscreen washer must be fitted to any vehicle which requires one or more automatic wipers, except an agricultural motor vehicle (other than one first used on or after 1 June 1986 and driven at more than 20 mph), a track-laying vehicle, a vehicle incapable of exceeding 20 mph, or vehicles being used to provide a local bus service. The washer must be such that, in conjunction with the wipers, it is capable of cleaning the area of the windscreen swept by the blades of mud or similar deposits.

In the alternative to the above requirement, a vehicle may comply with the relevant Community directive.

Audible warning instrument

The following provisions are made by reg 37 of the Construction and Use Regulations. All motor vehicles, which have a maximum speed of more than 20 mph, must be fitted with a horn but, in the case of an agricultural motor vehicle, only if it is being driven at more than 20 mph. In the case of motor vehicles first used on or after 1 August 1973 the sound emitted by any horn must be continuous and uniform and not strident. This is to ensure that the horns of such vehicles give a sound which is not offensive to the ear. With the exception of emergency vehicles, including vehicles of HM Revenue and Customs used in the investigation of serious crime, no motor vehicle may be fitted with a bell, gong, siren or two-tone horn, with the result that horns which play snatches of tunes, such as 'Colonel Bogey' are prohibited. However, vehicles may be fitted with an instrument or apparatus (not being a two-toned horn) to give a sound informing the public that goods are for sale from the vehicle; consequently, ice-cream chimes etc are not prohibited.

The rule against fitting gongs etc does not apply to an anti-theft device nor to an alarm to summon help to a public service vehicle. An anti-theft device must be fitted with a cut-out limiting its use to five minutes.

Where a horn can operate as an anti-theft device, a cut-out must be fitted if the motor vehicle was first used on or after 1 October 1982.

Regulation 37 permits the fitting of 'reversing alarms' to vehicles. These are devices to warn persons that the vehicle is reversing or about to reverse. Such a device is exempted from the requirement that the sound of a warning instrument shall be continuous and uniform but they must not be strident. Such alarms may be fitted to goods vehicles with a maximum gross weight not less than 2,000 kg, buses, engineering plant, refuse vehicles and works trucks. The sound emitted must be such that it is not likely to be confused with the sound emitted from a pedestrian crossing. A reversing alarm may only be used on a stationary vehicle if the vehicle's engine is running and it is about to move backwards or the vehicle is in danger from another moving vehicle.

Some public service vehicles are required to be fitted with a 'boarding aid alarm', which is an alarm for a power operated lift or ramp fitted to a bus to enable wheelchair users to board or alight which is designed to warn persons that the lift or ramp is in operation. Such an alarm is exempt from the provisions requiring a continuous and uniform sound but the sound must not be strident nor capable of being taken for the sound emitted from a pedestrian crossing. Horns and other audible warning instruments must be maintained in good and efficient working order at all times.

Instead of complying with the provisions mentioned above concerning the nature and maintenance of audible warning instruments, a vehicle may comply with the relevant Community directive or EC regulation.

Regulation 99 provides that no person shall sound, or cause or permit to be sounded, the horn or other audible warning device of a motor vehicle when it is stationary on a road at any time. The only exception is when there is danger due to another moving vehicle on or near the road. In addition, it provides that no person shall sound, or cause or permit to be sounded, in a vehicle in motion on a restricted road, a horn etc, between 11.30 pm and 7 am on the following day. This does not, of course, apply to anti-theft alarms, reversing devices, or boarding aid alarms. Instruments to advise the public of goods for sale from a vehicle must only be used for that purpose and must not be used between 7 pm and 12 am on the following day.

Silencer

Regulation 54 of the Construction and Use Regulations requires that every vehicle propelled by an internal combustion engine must be fitted with an exhaust system including a silencer, and that the exhaust gases from the engine must not escape into the atmosphere without first passing through its silencer. Specified noise levels are prescribed but they are directed at the manufacturers. Police officers detect faulty silencers by the nature of the sound emitted which indicates that the exhaust gases are escaping into the atmosphere without first passing through a silencer. This will occur where there is a break or large hole in the pipe. Instead of complying with the above provisions, a vehicle may comply with the relevant Community directive.

Alterations or replacements to exhaust systems are not permitted if they have the effect of increasing the noise.

Although not directly concerned with silencers, regs 97 and 98 also deal with noise. The first provision prohibits the use etc of a motor vehicle in a manner so as to cause excessive noise which could reasonably have been avoided by the driver. The second requires the driver of a stationary vehicle to stop the action of machinery attached to it, or forming part of the vehicle, so far as may be necessary for the prevention of noise or of exhaust emissions.

Wings

Regulation 63 of the Construction and Use Regulations requires that the following motor vehicles be fitted with wings or the like:

(a) invalid carriages;
(b) heavy motor cars, motor cars and motor cycles, not being agricultural motor vehicles or pedestrian-controlled vehicles;
(c) agricultural motor vehicles driven at more than 20 mph; and
(d) trailers.

Works trucks, unfinished vehicles, living vans, and some agricultural trailed appliances are exempt from the need to be fitted with wings as are the rear wheels of the motor vehicle part of an articulated vehicle whose trailer is used only in connection with the carriage of round timber. Otherwise motor vehicles must be equipped with wings or similar fittings to catch, as far as practicable, mud or water thrown up by the wheels. The provisions in relation to trailers are restricted to the rear wheels, if the trailer has more than two wheels. Instead of complying with these provisions, a vehicle may comply with the relevant Community directive.

Dangerous vehicles

Regulation 100(1) of the Construction and Use Regulations requires that a motor vehicle, every trailer and all parts and accessories of such vehicle or trailer must at all times be in such a condition that no danger is caused or is likely to be caused to any person in or on the vehicle or trailer or on a road. The provision is concerned with danger, and a distant possibility of such danger is not enough. For example, in a case where the radiator grille was missing, the court would not accept that sufficient danger existed of persons coming into contact with the revolving fan blades, because the engine was transverse. It might have been different had the fan blades been at the front of the engine. The provision applies to a vehicle which in its manufactured condition is inherently likely to cause danger to other road users, as well as to vehicles which have become dangerous through lack of maintenance. In relation to the requirement that all parts and accessories must be in such condition that no danger is caused, it is immaterial that parts may be in reasonable condition if they are dangerous because they are not in working order. In a case where a tow bar was in good condition, but the trailer was incorrectly coupled, the user of the vehicle was guilty of using it in a dangerous condition. Separate and distinct offences are involved in using a defective motor vehicle and a defective trailer on a road. This equally applies to articulated vehicles.

Regulation 100(1) also requires that the number of passengers carried, or the manner of their carriage, is such that no danger is caused or is likely to be caused to any person in or on the vehicle or trailer or on a road. Regulation 100(1) also requires that the weight, packing, distribution and adjustment of a load is such that no such danger is caused, or likely to be caused.

As can be seen, by reg 100(1), there are three quite separate and distinct prohibitions contained within the paragraph. The second prohibition is concerned with too many passengers. In one case, where a small four-seater car had been carrying eight passengers, it was found that this caused danger, in that it caused the vehicle to steer badly at all but low speeds. The third prohibition is really aimed at a badly loaded vehicle; insecure loads are dealt with by reg 100(2).

Regulation 100(2) requires that the load carried by a motor vehicle or trailer must at all times be so secured, if necessary by physical restraint other than its own weight, and be in such a position, that neither danger nor nuisance is likely to be caused to any person or property by reason of the load or any part of it falling or being blown from the vehicle or by reason of any other movement of the load or a part of it. In effect, this paragraph deals with insecure loads which for any reason cause danger or nuisance. It is necessary to specify which of these alternatives resulted from the insecurity of the load. Where a substantial part of a solid load falls onto a busy road there is little doubt that danger is caused. In circumstances where a goods vehicle, loaded with gravel, sheds part of its load steadily into the path of following traffic, there is no doubt that there is a breach of the requirement so to secure the load that no nuisance to persons or property is likely.

In considering whether a load has been adequately secured so that neither danger nor nuisance is likely to be caused one has to consider four things:

(a) the nature of the journey;
(b) the way in which the load was secured;
(c) the way in which the load was positioned; and
(d) the journey to be taken.

What might be secure for one journey in fine weather and on good roads might not be secure for another journey in poor weather and on less good roads. In applying the above test consideration must be given to the route taken. Thus, if the load is a high one, and too high to go under a bridge on the route, so that it is inevitable that the load will be knocked off, the load will not have been so secured that neither danger nor nuisance was likely.

Regulation 100(3) prohibits the use of a motor vehicle or trailer for any purpose for which it is so unsuitable as to cause danger or nuisance to any person on the vehicle, trailer, or on a road. The crucial question is whether the vehicle or trailer was unsuitable. If it is not properly loaded and it is the load which causes the danger or nuisance, this does not affect the suitability of the vehicle itself. In a case where an excavator which was loaded onto a trailer struck a bridge, it was held that the trailer did not become unsuitable when it was so loaded. It was the manner of the loading which was at fault.

Reference has already been made on p 402 to the offences under RTA 1988, s 40A of using, causing or permitting the use of a motor vehicle or trailer which is in a dangerous condition because of the condition of the vehicle's accessories or equipment, the purpose of its use, the number of passengers carried or the manner of their carriage and the weight, or the distribution and security of the load etc. It is submitted that most offences involving dangerous vehicles will now be charged under RTA 1988, s 40A and not under s 42, since a conviction of an offence under RTA 1988, s 40A involves the risk of discretionary disqualification and requires the obligatory endorsement of 3 penalty points. Where there is a conviction under RTA 1988, s 42 for a breach of reg 100 there can be no disqualification or endorsement of the offender's driving licence.

Some aspects of reg 100(2) and (3) have also been overtaken by the arrival of RTA 1988, s 40A as they also deal with elements related to danger being caused to persons in consequence of the user of the motor vehicle or trailer in the manner prohibited by s 40A. It may be, therefore, that reg 100(2) and (3) will be amended to restrict the prohibition created to those acts which result in nuisance only. This can be achieved by removing the word 'danger' from both of these paragraphs. At the time of writing, no such amendments have been made.

Maintenance of glass

All glass or other transparent material fitted to motor vehicles is required, by reg 30 of the Construction and Use Regulations, to be maintained in such condition that it does not obscure the vision of the driver while the vehicle is being driven on a road. This regulation is not limited to the windscreen but applies to all glass affecting the driver's vision, such as the rear window and side windows through which he needs to look.

Maintenance of fuel tank

By reg 39 of the Construction and Use Regulations a fuel tank on a motor vehicle first used on or after 1 July 1973 must be made of metal and reasonably secure from damage, and leakage from it must be adequately prevented (except that this does not prevent a tank being fitted with a pressure release valve). Those fitted before that date must be maintained so that leakage is adequately prevented.

Instead of complying with these requirements, a vehicle may comply with the corresponding requirements contained in EC directives and regulations.

Maintenance of tyres

Regulation 27 of the Construction and Use Regulations prohibits the use, on a road, of any motor vehicle or trailer, a wheel of which is fitted with a pneumatic tyre, if:

(a) the tyre is unsuitable for the use to which the vehicle or trailer is being put or to the type of tyres fitted to its other wheels;
(b) it is wrongly inflated for such use;
(c) it has a cut in excess of 25 mm or 10% of the section width of the tyre, whichever is the greater, measured in any direction on the outside of the tyre and deep enough to reach the ply or cords;
(d) it has a lump, bulge or tear caused by separation or partial failure of its structure;
(e) it has a portion of the ply or cord exposed;
(f) the tyre is not maintained in such condition as to be fit for the use to which the vehicle or trailer is being put or has a defect which might in any way cause damage to the surface of the road or damage to persons on or in the vehicle or to other persons using the road.

Also prohibited is the use on a road of:

(a) a passenger vehicle, other than a motor cycle, constructed or adapted to carry no more than eight seated passengers in addition to the driver;
(b) a goods vehicle with a maximum gross weight which does not exceed 3,500 kg; and
(c) a light trailer not falling within (b),

where a pneumatic tyre on a wheel does not have in grooves of the tread pattern a depth of at least *1.6 mm* throughout a continuous band comprising the central three-quarters of the breadth of the tyre and round the entire circumference of the tyre. There are special provisions for tyres on a vehicle first used before 3 January 1933.

In relation to large goods vehicles, motor cycles and other vehicles not included above, their use on a road is prohibited if a wheel is fitted with a pneumatic tyre and:

(a) the base of any groove which showed in the original tread pattern of the tyre is not clearly visible; or

(b) either it does not have a depth of 1 mm in the grooves of the tread pattern throughout a continuous band measuring at least three-quarters of the breadth of the tyre and round its entire circumference; or, if the grooves of the original tread pattern of the tyre did not extend beyond three-quarters of the breadth of the tread, any groove which showed in the original tread pattern does not have a depth of at least 1 mm.

As can be seen, all forms of damage to tyres which may result in danger are covered by this regulation. Potential danger is, of course, the reason for the requirement that the contact area of a tyre must have visible tread which must be at least 1.6 mm or (as the case may be) 1 mm deep for three-quarters of that contact area (subject to special provisions which apply to special tyres with narrow contact areas).

Regulation 27(2) makes special provision to allow for the use of tyres designed to be used safely when deflated. There are general exemptions in favour of agricultural trailed appliances, agricultural motor vehicles not driven at more than 20 mph and broken-down vehicles being towed at a speed not exceeding 20 mph. The tread pattern and minimum depth of tread provisions do not apply to three-wheelers not exceeding 102 kg with a maximum possible speed of 12 mph or less, nor to pedestrian-controlled works trucks. In addition, the minimum depth of tread provisions do not apply to motor cycles under 50 cc.

Regulation 27(5) prohibits a person using, or causing or permitting to be used, a motor vehicle on a road with a recut pneumatic tyre if its ply or cord has been cut or exposed in the process of recutting. Heavy duty tyres fitted to goods vehicles can usually be recut without causing danger, but tyres fitted to saloon cars do not usually have sufficient thickness of rubber to accept the process.

Special provision is made by reg 27(3) to allow passenger vehicles (not buses) to fit a temporary-use spare tyre, provided the vehicle does not exceed 50 mph.

Mixture of tyres

Regulation 26(1) of the Construction and Use Regulations provides that pneumatic tyres of different types of construction must not be fitted to the same axle of a vehicle. The regulation mentions three types of tyres:

(a) diagonal-ply tyres, which are commonly known as cross-ply tyres;

(b) bias-belted tyres, which are as above but have a reinforcing band around the outer circumference of the tyre under the tread, but on top of the cords; and

(c) radial-ply tyres.

Regulation 26(2) also provides that a motor vehicle having only two axles must not be fitted with the following combinations of tyres:

(a) cross-plys or bias-belted tyres on the rear axle and radials on the front; or
(b) cross-ply on the rear axle and bias-belted on the front.

This regulation is designed to prevent a gripping tyre from being fitted to the 'steering' wheels, whilst a tyre which is not so stable is fitted to the rear.

Not to emit smoke etc

Regulation 61 of the Construction and Use Regulations provides that no person shall use, or cause or permit to be used, on a road a motor vehicle from which is emitted any smoke, visible vapour, grit, sparks or oily substance which causes, or is likely to cause, damage to property or injury or danger to any person who is, or who may reasonably be expected to be, on the road. This could occur where oil spillage made the road unsafe or fumes badly affected visibility.

This regulation also provides that a vehicle must be maintained so as not to emit any avoidable smoke or avoidable visible vapour.

DUTIES OF DRIVERS AND OTHERS

Position to retain proper view and control

Regulation 104 of the Construction and Use Regulations provides that a driver must at all times be in such a position that he retains full control and has a full view of the road and traffic ahead. A man who drove with a sheepdog on his lap has been held to be in breach of this provision.

Reversing

By reg 106 of the Construction and Use Regulations, no person shall drive, or cause or permit to be driven, a motor vehicle backwards on a road further than may be requisite for the safety or reasonable convenience of the occupants of the vehicle or other traffic.

Unnecessary obstruction

Regulation 103 of the Construction and Use Regulations provides that a person in charge of a motor vehicle or trailer must not cause or permit it to stand on a road so as to cause any unnecessary obstruction. The various exemptions within local no-waiting orders in favour of goods vehicles which are loading or unloading has led to a belief by some van drivers that they may double park and even completely block roads for these purposes. This is not so. Any unreasonable use of the road which leads to the obstruction of other road users is an offence against this regulation. An obstruction can be caused by taking up so much of the road that normal two-way traffic is reduced to a one-way flow. In considering whether a particular use was reasonable or unreasonable, a court will apply its mind to the facts, including the duration of the obstruction, the nature of the place where it occurred, the purpose for which the vehicle was there and the *actual* (as opposed to potential) obstruction caused.

Parking facing the wrong way at night

Regulation 101 of the Construction and Use Regulations provides that, except with the permission of a uniformed police officer, a person must not cause or permit a motor vehicle to stand on a road between sunset and sunrise otherwise than with the left or nearside of the vehicle as close as may be to the edge of the carriageway.

The exemptions from this prohibition are predictable: vehicles being used for fire and rescue, police or ambulance purposes; taxi stands and bus stops; one-way streets; emergency operations etc. This regulation is not concerned in any respect with lighting requirements: it prohibits vehicles facing the wrong way at night because of the confusion which can be caused by the lights of other vehicles picking out reflective glass in circumstances which might cause the driver to fear that another vehicle is coming towards him on his side of the road. If lights are not displayed in a place where parking lights are required to be shown, then two offences are committed.

Stopping engine and setting parking brake

Regulation 107 of the Construction and Use Regulations provides that no person shall leave, or cause or permit to be left, on a road any motor vehicle which is not attended by a person duly licensed to drive it, unless the engine has been stopped and the parking brake effectively set. The exceptions include a vehicle being used for fire and rescue authority, police or ambulance purposes and special vehicles which use their engines for particular operations other than the driving of the vehicle. Although there is a requirement to do two things, that is stop the engine and set the handbrake, the failure to carry out either of these operations completes the offence under RTA 1988, s 42.

Opening of doors

Regulation 105 of the Construction and Use Regulations provides that no person shall open, or cause or permit to be opened, the door of a motor vehicle on a road so as to cause injury or danger to any person. Breach of this regulation can be committed by anyone—a driver, a passenger or any other person who opens the door of a vehicle. It is not necessary to prove negligence: if the action causes injury or danger that is sufficient.

Mobile telephones

Regulation 110(1) of the Construction and Use Regulations prohibits the driving of a motor vehicle on a road if the driver is using a hand-held mobile telephone, or a hand-held device of any kind, other than a two-way radio, which performs an interactive communication function by transmitting and receiving data. The term 'interactive communication function' includes:

(a) sending or receiving oral or written messages;
(b) sending or receiving facsimile documents;
(c) sending or receiving still or moving images; and
(d) providing access to the Internet.

The term 'two-way radio' refers to wireless telegraphy apparatus which is designed or adapted for the purpose of transmitting or receiving spoken messages and to operate on any frequency except a number of ranges. Such equipment is fitted to vehicles used by the emergency services and is therefore exempted from these provisions.

Regulation 110(2) prohibits causing or permitting any other person to drive a motor vehicle on a road while using a hand-held mobile telephone or hand-held device of the specified type. In addition, reg 110(3) forbids a person supervising a provisional licence holder to use a hand-held mobile telephone or such a hand-held device at a time when the provisional licence holder is driving a motor vehicle on a road. RSA 2006, s 26 prospectively provides 3 penalty points.

For the purposes of the regulation a mobile telephone or device is classified as 'handheld' if it is, or must be, held at some point during the course of making or receiving a call or performing any other interactive communication function.

Regulation 110(5) provides that there is no contravention where:

(a) the use is to call the police, fire, ambulance or other emergency service on 112 or 999;
(b) it is in response to a genuine emergency; and
(c) it is unsafe or impracticable to cease driving in order to make the call, or for the provisional licence holder to cease driving while the call is being made.

Trailers

Regulation 86 of the Construction and Use Regulations provides that, where a motor vehicle is drawing a trailer by means of a rope or chain, the length of the rope or chain must not exceed 4.5 m, and must not exceed 1.5 m unless the rope or chain is made clearly visible to other road users within a reasonable distance from either side.

Regulation 86A provides that trailers to which reg 15 (p 407 above) applies, which are not fitted with an automatic stopping device operative in the event of separation, must not be used on a road unless a secondary coupling is attached to the drawing vehicle and its trailer in such a way that, in the event of separation, the drawbar of the trailer would be prevented from touching the ground and there would be some residual steering of the trailer.

Trailers to which reg 15 applies which are fitted with a device which is designed to stop the trailer automatically in the event of separation must not be used on a road unless the secondary coupling is properly attached to the drawing vehicle and trailer.

Trailers which are living vans and have less than four wheels (or have two close-coupled wheels on each side) are prohibited by reg 90 from being used for the carriage of passengers. The only exception is in favour of testing, when a repairer etc may be carried in the van for that purpose.

Regulation 83 limits the number of trailers which may be drawn by a motor vehicle on a road. It limits locomotives to a maximum of three trailers, motor tractors to one laden trailer or two unladen trailers, and heavy motor cars and motor cars to one trailer. For the purposes of reg 83, a vehicle drawn by a steam powered vehicle and which is used solely to carry water for the purpose of the drawing vehicle is not a trailer. For the definition of 'locomotive', 'motor tractor', 'heavy motor car' and 'motor car', see pp 399–400.

Miscellaneous

Regulation 53 of the Construction and Use Regulations provides that mascots, emblems, or other ornamental objects fitted to vehicles first used on or after 1 October 1937 must not be in such a position that they are likely to strike persons with whom the vehicle may collide unless the nature of the mascot is such that injury is not liable to be caused.

Regulation 109 provides that no person shall drive, or cause or permit to be driven, a motor vehicle on a road if the driver is in such a position as to be able to see, whether directly or by reflection, a television receiving apparatus or other cinematographic apparatus used to display anything other than information concerning the vehicle or its journey.

CYCLES

Use of motor cycles

RTA 1988, s 23 restricts the carriage of passengers on a motor bicycle to one person who must be carried sitting astride the cycle on a proper seat securely fixed to the vehicle behind the driver's seat. Interestingly, a pillion passenger need not be carried facing the front. The driver commits an offence if a passenger is carried in contravention of this section. The Road Vehicle (Construction and Use) Regulations 1986, reg 102 prohibits the carriage of a passenger on a motor bicycle (whether it has a sidecar attached to it or not) on which there are not available suitable supports or rests for the feet for him.

The RTA 1988, s 16 empowers the Secretary of State to make regulations requiring persons driving or riding on a specified type of motor cycle (other than in a sidecar) which is on a road to wear protective headgear. The type of headgear is prescribed by the Motor Cycle (Protective Helmets) Regulations 1998. For the purpose of these Regulations, 'motor cycle' means a motor bicycle, including one with a sidecar, and motor tricycles where the paired wheels are less than 460 mm apart. The Regulations do not apply to mowing machines, motor cycles being propelled by a person on foot, or followers of the Sikh religion while wearing a turban. Helmets must comply with various British Standard or EEA (European Economic Area) specifications. Breach of the Regulations is an offence contrary to RTA 1988, s 17. However, there is no offence of aiding and abetting the failure to wear a crash helmet, unless the other party is under sixteen years of age. A divisional court has held that the BMW C1 motorcycle (which has a rigid rider cell in the form of a cab) is a motorcycle for the purposes of the Regulations and that a rider must wear a protective helmet although he is, in effect, inside a closed cab.

By virtue of the RTA 1988, s 18 it is an offence to drive or ride on a motor cycle on a road without wearing eye protectors of the type prescribed by the Motor Cycles (Eye Protectors) Regulations 1999. This is a fixed penalty offence. For the purposes of s 18, the Regulations define 'motor cycle' in the same way as in relation to protective helmets. The present requirement does not apply to a person driving or riding on a mowing machine nor does it apply to a person driving or riding on a motor cycle temporarily brought into Great Britain by a foreign resident, if it has been here for less than one year. In addition, the requirement does not apply to a member of the armed forces of the Crown who is driving or riding on a motor cycle on duty, if he is wearing an eye protector which is part of his service equipment. A person propelling a motor cycle on foot is not required to wear an eye protector.

Use of pedal cycles

By RTA 1988, s 24 the carriage of more than one person on a road on a bicycle not propelled by mechanical power is an offence by each of the persons carried, unless it is *constructed* or *adapted* for the carriage of more than one person. A tandem is a cycle *constructed* for the carriage of more than one person, and cycles which have a seat fitted to permit the carriage of a child have been *adapted* for the carriage of more than one person. Whether an attachment to a cycle amounts to an adaptation can be resolved by the question, 'If the vehicle had been originally produced in this form, would it have been produced for the carriage of two persons?'

The wilful riding of a pedal cycle on a footpath or causeway by the side of any road made or set apart for the use or accommodation of foot passengers remains an offence contrary to the Highway Act 1835, s 72. A person rides a cycle, even if he merely sits astride it and propels himself with his feet.

Races or speed trials

RTA 1988, s 31 provides that a person who promotes or takes part in a race or speed trial for pedal cycles on a highway commits an offence, unless that race or speed trial is authorised under, and conducted in accordance with, the Cycle Racing on Highways Regulations 1960. Time trials and bicycle races are dealt with separately by the Regulations.

For a time trial or bicycle race to be authorised, a promoter must in either case give twenty-eight days' written notice to the police, giving times, dates, routes, start, finish, maximum number taking part, arrangements for marshalling and supervision, and the rules of the competition.

Regulation 2 defines 'time trials' as a cycle race or trial of speed involving either single competitors or groups of not more than four competitors, starting at intervals of not less than one minute. In the case of groups they must not compete against one another. The result must depend upon the time taken by a competitor, or if a group any member of it, to reach a finishing point; or on the distance covered in a fixed time.

A 'bicycle race' is defined by reg 2 as a race or trial of speed which is not a time trial. In order for it to be authorised, the following additional requirements must be satisfied. The numbers taking part are restricted to, in not more than two races a year selected by the British Cycling Federation, a hundred competitors, and, in any other approved race, eighty. Races must not take place during the hours of darkness. If they follow a circuitous route, they must travel at least ten miles before passing the same point on a highway twice (in whichever direction). No continuous part of the race may be on more than one and a half miles of any road subject to a speed limit of 40 mph or less, and no further continuous part in a 40 mph restricted section may be within three miles of the previous one. A chief officer of police is empowered to make directions as to traffic movement and routes, including the closure of sections of roadway on such occasions.

The Road Traffic (Special Events) Act 1994 permits traffic authorities to make temporary orders restricting/prohibiting traffic in connection with special events or entertainments on a road.

Electrically assisted pedal cycles

An 'electrically assisted pedal cycle' is not a motor vehicle for the purpose of the Road Traffic Acts; such a cycle is a pedal cycle which has a kerbside weight not exceeding 40 kg, or if a tandem 60 kg, is fitted with pedals, has an electric motor of rated output not exceeding 0.2 kw (0.25 kw in the case of a tandem), and is incapable of propelling the vehicle when it is travelling at more than 15 mph. In other words, it is basically a pedal cycle with an auxiliary electric motor which cuts out when the vehicle is travelling in excess of 15 mph. A divisional court has held that the nature of the pedals fitted to such a cycle must be such that they are reasonably capable of propelling the vehicle in a safe manner in normal day-to-day use. It would not accept that pedals which were one inch wide and acted directly upon the front wheel of a tricycle without any form of chain or gearing were capable of propelling the vehicle safely.

The Pedal Cycles (Construction and Use) Regulations 1983, which have effect under the RTA 1988, s 81, require such pedal cycles to have a plate showing, inter alia, the continuous rated output of the motor. The battery must not leak so as to be a source of danger and the cycle must be fitted with a device, biased to the off position, which switches on the motor.

Electrically assisted pedal cycles may be driven by anyone aged fourteen or over. Unlike motor vehicles, their use does not require an excise licence or insurance. Nor do the requirements of testing, driving licences and protective headgear apply.

Brakes on cycles

The Pedal Cycles (Construction and Use) Regulations 1983 deal with the fitting and maintenance of brakes on pedal cycles and with matters affecting electrically assisted pedal cycles generally. The regulations also refer to fixed wheel and free wheel cycles, and these are defined as follows. Fixed wheel cycles are those so constructed that one or more of the wheels is incapable of rotating independently of the pedals. Free wheel cycles are those which are not so constructed.

Regulation 4 provides that no person shall ride, or cause or permit to be ridden, on a road an electrically assisted pedal cycle unless it is fitted with braking systems which comply with cl 6 of the 1981 British Standard. Regulation 5 prohibits a person from riding, or causing or permitting to be ridden, on a road such a cycle when the brakes have not been maintained in efficient working order.

The braking systems of pedal cycles which are not electrically assisted are also governed by these Regulations. Regulation 6 provides that no person shall ride, or cause or permit to be ridden, a pedal cycle which does not comply with the braking-system requirements in regs 7 or 8. Regulation 7 requires that at least one braking system be fitted to all pedal cycles with the exception of those on which the pedals act directly on the wheel rather than through a gearing system (eg a penny-farthing) and those temporarily in Great Britain when ridden by a visitor, such a cycle having a braking system or system complying with provisions of the International Convention on Road Traffic.

Pedal cycles manufactured on or after 1 August 1984 are subjected to additional braking requirements if the saddle height (fully raised and tyre fully inflated) is 635 mm (about 25 inches). Saddle height replaces wheel diameter as the yardstick in the case of cycles manufactured on or after 1 August 1984 because of the production of cycles with small wheels and high saddles which, because of their small wheels, were only required to have one braking system. The additional requirements are that fixed wheel cycles shall have a braking system acting on the front wheel or on at least two front wheels if there are more than one. Free-wheel cycles must have two independent systems, one acting upon the front wheel, or at least two front wheels if more than one is fitted, and the other acting upon the rear wheel, or at least two rear wheels if more than one is fitted. In the case of pedal cycles manufactured before 1 August 1984, these additional requirements apply to pedal cycles, any wheel of which exceeds 460 mm (approx 18 inches) in diameter including the fully inflated tyre, except that the braking system acting upon the rear need only act upon one rear wheel even if there is more than one rear wheel fitted. Non-goods tricycles may have two independent systems both acting upon the single wheel.

Regulation 10 prohibits riding, or causing or permitting to be ridden, on a road a pedal cycle the braking system of which, fitted in accordance with these Regulations, is not in efficient working order. This is the offence most frequently dealt with by police officers but it is not uncommon to find that one of two systems has been removed from a cycle.

Breach of regs 4, 5, 6 or 10 is an offence contrary to RTA 1988, s 91. A constable in uniform is empowered by reg 11 to test and inspect a pedal cycle for the purpose of ascertaining that the braking requirements are satisfied. This may be done on a road, or on any premises where the cycle is if the cycle has been involved in an accident (provided that the test and inspection are carried out within forty-eight hours of the accident with the consent of the owner of the premises).

TESTING AND INSPECTION

Powers to test and inspect vehicles are included in the RTA 1988 and in the Road Vehicles (Construction and Use) Regulations 1986. In effect, they permit authorised constables to test and inspect motor vehicles on roads, and all constables in uniform to test and inspect motor vehicles on premises, subject to certain conditions. It is helpful to consider both powers together.

Testing vehicles on roads: Road Traffic Act 1988, s 67

Authorised examiners may test a motor vehicle on a road for the purpose of ascertaining whether the requirements relating to its construction and use are being complied with, and also whether there is compliance with the requirement that the condition of the vehicle is not such that its use on a road would involve danger of injury to any person. There are two types of authorised examiners. First, certain police officers are specially authorised by their chief constables for this purpose. Second, vehicle examiners appointed under RTA 1988, s 66A by the Secretary of State are similarly authorised to carry out such tests. For the purpose of testing a vehicle an examiner may require the driver to comply with his reasonable instructions and may drive the vehicle. All authorised examiners must produce their authority if required to do so.

The provisions of the section do not mean that the requirement of the Act and the Construction and Use Regulations may only be enforced on a road by authorised constables. Particular offences may still be reported. In addition, a constable who is not an authorised examiner may test a vehicle with the owner's consent. This is borne out by a case where a constable who was not an authorised examiner tested the efficiency of a handbrake with the driver's consent; evidence of his findings was admitted even though he was not an authorised examiner. It is submitted that there is a difference between a power to make a general examination of a vehicle and the examination of a particular part of it because of the suspicion of an offence. If the wall of a tyre is badly split and the fabric exposed, this is observable by any police officer and the examination of the whole vehicle is unnecessary in order to deal with the particular infringement. It does not take a vehicle examiner to notice that the entire exhaust system of a motor vehicle is hanging off.

Where an examination of the vehicle under RTA 1988, s 67 is required by an authorised examiner, the driver may elect that the test shall be deferred to a time and place to be arranged. If the driver is the owner, he may choose a period of seven days, within the next thirty days, when the examination may be carried out on premises specified by him. If the driver is not the owner, he must give the owner's name and address and the examiner must make his arrangement with the owner. Once the period has been so specified, the police must give at least two days' notice of the day, within that seven-day period, when the test will be carried out. If no period is specified, seven days' notice must be given of the intention to test.

The right to defer does not apply when it appears to a constable that, following an accident on a road, the test must be taken forthwith. If this is so and the constable is not an authorised examiner, he may require that the vehicle is not taken away until the test has been carried out. The same powers are given when the vehicle appears to be so defective that it ought not to be allowed to proceed.

Traffic wardens may be authorised to stop motor vehicles for the purpose of tests under RTA 1988, s 67.

Testing vehicles off roads: Road Vehicles (Construction and Use) Regulations 1986

Regulation 74 empowers any police constable in uniform or vehicle examiner to test and inspect the brakes, silencers, steering gear and tyres, of any motor vehicle or trailer on any premises where that motor vehicle or trailer is, subject to the consent of the owner of the premises. This represents the basic difference between these powers and those set out above. The regulations are concerned with powers with respect to vehicles 'on premises', and RTA 1988, s 67 with powers with respect to vehicles 'on a road'.

The powers provided by the Regulations are always subject to the consent of the *owner of the premises*. This means that there is no power of entry onto premises for the purpose of inspection. In addition, the test and inspection cannot be carried out without the consent of the *owner of the vehicle*, unless notice of it has been served personally upon him at least forty-eight hours before the test, or seventy-two hours before it if service is effected by recorded delivery. The consent of the *owner of the vehicle* is not required if it has been involved in an accident, within the preceding forty-eight hours.

If an owner/driver is seen driving a motor vehicle in a defective condition but the police officer is not in a position to stop the vehicle, and the owner/driver garages his vehicle on return to his home, there is no means by which his vehicle can be examined without his consent as the owner of the premises. If, however, he took the vehicle to a garage proprietor, examination could take place on the garage proprietor's premises with his consent and the absence of consent of the owner of the vehicle could be overcome by notice.

Prohibition of unfit vehicles

RTA 1988, s 69 empowers an authorised constable to issue an immediate prohibition notice if, on an inspection under s 41, 45, 49, 61, 67, 68 or 77, it appears to him that, owing to any defects in the vehicle, driving it (or driving it for any particular purpose or purposes or for any except one or more particular purposes) would involve a danger of injury to any person. These sections referred to deal with powers in relation to construction and use; test certificates generally; inspections related to plated weights of goods vehicles, public service vehicles and vehicles adapted to carry more than eight passengers which are not public service vehicles; and the testing of the condition of used vehicles at sale rooms etc. A notice under s 69 may prohibit use absolutely, or for one or more specified purposes, or except for one or more specified purposes.

Vehicle examiners appointed under RTA 1988, s 66A have a similar power.

The Road Vehicles (Prohibition) Regulations 1992 make provision for a vehicle which is subject to a prohibition issued by an authorised constable, or vehicle examiner, to be driven on a road solely for the purpose of submitting it, by prior arrangement, for test with a view to removal of that prohibition, or for it to be driven in the course of any test for the purpose of the removal of the prohibition, or (within three miles from where it is being, or has been, repaired) to be driven solely for the purpose of its test or trial with a view to the removal of the prohibition.

Inspection of public passenger vehicles and goods vehicles

Special powers of inspection are provided by RTA 1988, s 68 in respect of goods vehicles, public service vehicles and vehicles adapted to carry more than eight passengers which are not public service vehicles. A vehicle examiner or any constable in uniform may require any person in charge of a stationary vehicle of such a type on a road to take the vehicle to any place within five miles, for the purpose of an inspection by a Ministry examiner, not by the police.

TEST CERTIFICATES

RTA 1988, ss 45 to 47 are concerned with tests of the satisfactory condition of motor vehicles, other than goods vehicles to which s 49 applies. The relevant provisions with regard to such goods vehicles are discussed in the chapter concerning goods vehicles. The Secretary of State is authorised by RTA 1988, s 45 to make regulations for the examination of all vehicles to which ss 45 to 47 apply and he has made the Motor Vehicles (Tests) Regulations 1981.

The Road Traffic (Vehicle Testing) Act 1999 amended the provisions of RTA 1988, ss 45 and 46 to provide a statutory basis for the central computer database of the MOT status of motor vehicles. This aids enforcement of the provisions of the Vehicle Excise and Registration Act 1994 and subordinate regulations. The revised sections permit the Secretary of State to supervise testing stations by nominating a supervisor for each testing station. A computer link with all testing stations enables the results of individual tests to be fed into the central database. The Secretary of State is empowered to release such information to prescribed persons on payment of a fee and to the police free of charge via the Police National Computer. Provision is also made for statements concerning the issue, and the date of issue of a test certificate to be admissible in evidence. The Motor Vehicles (Tests) Regulations 1981 have been amended to provide for the maintenance of electronic records in relation to vehicle tests. and for the authorisation of testers and examiners. The Motor Vehicles (Evidence of Test Certificates) Regulations 2004 provide for the production of evidence that a vehicle has passed the test to be provided in different forms in recognition of the existence of computer-based records.

By RTA 1988, s 47(1) a person commits an offence if he uses, or causes or permits to be used, at any time on a road a motor vehicle to which the section applies, and as respects which no test certificate has been issued within the appropriate period before the said time. In relation to 'use', 'cause' or 'permit', the reader is referred to pp 403–407. Once it is proved that the accused has used etc a vehicle on a road, the burden shifts to him to prove that there was in force a test certificate for the vehicle.

Which vehicles must be tested?

The answer to this question depends on two things, the type of vehicle and its age.

The following must be examined and receive a test certificate annually, after the period of three years defined in the next paragraph:

(a) passenger vehicles with not more than eight seats, excluding the driver's seat;
(b) rigid goods motor cars, the unladen weight of which does not exceed 1,525 kg;
(c) dual-purpose vehicles;
(d) motor cycles (including three-wheelers and mopeds); and
(e) motor caravans.

RTA 1988, s 47 applies to those motor vehicles of the types just specified which were first registered not less than three years before the time in question (ie the time of the alleged use without a test certificate). If, for any reason, a vehicle is used on a road in Great Britain or elsewhere before being registered, a test certificate must be obtained three years from the date of manufacture. Thus, a serviceman returning from duty abroad who brings into this country a vehicle which is more than three years old must have it tested immediately.

The RTA 1988 requires annual tests for the following motor vehicles after one year from first registration:

(a) motor vehicles used for the carriage of passengers and with more than eight seats, exclusive of the driver's (mainly public service vehicles);
(b) taxis licensed to ply for hire; and
(c) ambulances.

Exemptions

The Motor Vehicles (Tests) Regulations 1981 exempt:

(a) articulated vehicles other than articulated buses;
(b) invalid carriages not exceeding 306 kg unladen weight (or not exceeding 510 kg if supplied by the Department of Health);
(c) vehicles temporarily in Great Britain for a period of twelve months;
(d) police vehicles maintained in police workshops, or a vehicle provided for the purposes of the Serious Organised Crime Agency;
(e) electrically propelled goods vehicles not exceeding 1,525 kg;
(f) some licensed hackney carriages and private hire cars;
(g) a vehicle at a time when it is being used on a public road during any calendar week if it is being used only in passing from land in the occupation of its keeper to other land in his occupation, and it has not been used on public roads for more than an aggregate of six miles in that calendar week; and
(h) vehicles which have a Northern Ireland test certificate.

The Regulations also permit use without a test certificate when a vehicle is being taken to a testing station by previous arrangement for a test, or when it is being brought away from such a test, or while it is being so tested by an authorised person or under his direction. In circumstances in which a test certificate is refused, the vehicle may be moved without a test certificate for the purpose of work being done (once again, by previous arrangement), or for the purpose of delivering it, by towing, to a place where it is to be broken up. Imported vehicles which need to be tested may be driven on arrival in this country to the place of residence of the owner of the motor vehicle.

The test

The Motor Vehicles (Tests) Regulations 1981 require that certain parts of vehicles are tested. For the purposes of these tests motor vehicles are divided into Classes I to VII and specific testing requirements are set out for each class of vehicle in Sch 2 to the Regulations. The most commonly used vehicles are those falling within Class IV (motor cars and heavy motor cars not being vehicles which fall within other classes). The specified parts to be tested in relation to such vehicles include wheels and tyres, steering, audible warning instrument, front and rear position lamps, rear retro reflectors, stop lamps, direction indicators, rear registration plate lamps, rear fog lamps, hazard warning signal devices, braking, glass and field of vision, mirrors, windscreen cleaning, fuel tanks and pipes, seat belts and anchorages, exhaust (general condition), exhaust (emissions), vehicle identification number, structure and suspension (body, chassis, subframe, mounting or suspension which prejudices steering, braking or seat belt mountings or may otherwise cause danger), seats, doors and other openings to the extent that their condition may cause danger, and registration marks.

Due to the construction of the vehicles, the requirements in respect of vehicles in Classes I (light motor bicycles); II (motor bicycles); and III (light motor vehicles other than motor bicycles) are such that the parts to be tested differ on occasions.

The tests are even more extensive for vehicles which fall within Classes V and VI, and include speedometers, speed limiters and speed limiter plates, in addition to examination of many interior fittings. Class VII vehicles are inspected in a similar but extended fashion to those in Class IV, the test including such items as tyre loads and speed ratings.

The tests have been extended in relation to vehicles in Classes III to VII to include an annual check on the condition of any seat belts and anchorages which are fitted to such vehicles despite not being required to be fitted by the Construction and Use Regulations.

A vehicle may be tested in the one-month period (two months in the case of a public service vehicle) before the expiration of the current certificate, or the time when it must first be tested. This is to permit tests to be taken in sufficient time to have defects remedied prior to the expiry of an existing certificate. RTA 1988, s 48(2) permits test certificates which are renewed during the last month of the validity of the previous certificate to be issued to expire twelve months after the expiry of the last certificate, rather than twelve months from the date of the examination. Section 48(1A) makes similar provision in relation to a certificate issued in respect of a first test.

Refusal of test certificate

When a test certificate is refused, a notice of refusal must be issued and the grounds for refusal must be listed on a check list, except that in the case of a motor cycle the notice must state the grounds for refusal and a check list need not be given. All test certificates currently in use must be embossed by the stamp of the examiner or council on whose behalf it is issued. There is a right of appeal, against refusal, to the Secretary of State.

Contents of test certificate

The contents of a test certificate are not prescribed. A certificate must be in a form supplied by the Secretary of State. A certificate usually has a serial number, contains a statement to the effect that the vehicle complied with the requirements on the date of the examination, shows the registration mark of the vehicle, the vehicle testing station number, the date of issue of the certificate, the date of expiry and the signature of the person issuing the certificate. A signature may be a facsimile of the signature of the examiner or of a person so authorised by the Secretary of State. If the previous certificate had expired at the time of the examination, the serial number of the previous certificate may also be shown. Tests can only be conducted at testing stations authorised by the Secretary of State.

Requirement to produce test certificate

RTA 1988, s 165 empowers a constable or vehicle examiner to require a person driving, or reasonably believed by him to have been driving, when an accident occurred or when an offence was committed to give his name and address and the name and address of the owner of the vehicle and to produce certain documents, including a test certificate (if one is required for the vehicle). As with other types of document, there is a proviso which permits production within seven days at a specified police station; or production as soon as reasonably practicable; or proof that production was not reasonably practicable before the day on which proceedings were commenced. Production in person is not required.

CHAPTER 11
Control of vehicles

TRAFFIC SIGNS

These are governed by the Road Traffic Regulation Act 1984 (RTRA 1984) and regulations thereunder.

The term 'traffic sign' for the purposes of the RTRA 1984 is defined by RTRA 1984, s 64 as any object or device (whether fixed or portable) for conveying, to traffic on roads or any specified class of traffic, warnings, information, requirements, restrictions or prohibitions of any description:

(a) specified by regulations made by the relevant Ministers acting jointly; or
(b) authorised by the Secretary of State,

and any line or mark on a road for so conveying such warnings, information, requirements, restrictions or prohibitions.

The section authorises the making of regulations in respect of the size, colour and type of traffic signs. The current regulations are the Traffic Sign Regulations and General Directions 2002. Equipment which is used in connection with traffic signs must be of a type approved in accordance with the Directions.

RTRA 1984, s 65 empowers highway authorities to cause or permit traffic signs to be placed on or near any road in their area.

RTRA 1984, s 66 empowers a constable, or a person acting under the instructions (whether general or specific) of the chief officer of police, to place on a highway such authorised traffic signs indicating prohibitions, restrictions or requirements relating to vehicular traffic as may be required to prevent an obstruction on public occasions or near public buildings or at an authorised cycle race. This section permits police officers to place emergency signs on the road at special events such as air displays. A second power is given by s 67 to a police officer, traffic officer or a person under the instructions (general or specific) of the chief officer of police, to place on a highway authorised traffic signs indicating prohibitions, restrictions or requirements to prevent or mitigate congestion or obstruction of traffic, or danger to or from traffic in consequence of extraordinary circumstances. Among other things, this section empowers the police to place emergency signs on the road at the scene of an accident. Such signs may be maintained for a maximum period of seven days. The time starts when the signs are placed, so that a sign placed at 2 pm must be removed by 2 pm seven days after placement. The important feature of the section is that the authorisation is in respect of extraordinary circumstances and the section does not, therefore, authorise the regular placement of signs at locations selected by the police. If the need is a permanent one the matter must be dealt with by the highway authority.

Failure to comply with a sign placed under the provisions of RTRA 1984, ss 65, 66 and 67 is an offence contrary to the Road Traffic Act 1988 (RTA 1988), s 36.

Quite apart from the above, the Traffic Signs (Temporary Obstructions) Regulations 1997 authorise persons not otherwise authorised to do so to place specified traffic signs on roads in connection with temporary obstructions, other than roadworks. The indications given by the signs are specified in regs 4 to 7 of the 1997 Regulations and the form which the signs take is prescribed by regs 8 to 14.

Regulation 15 of the 1997 Regulations permits a 'keep right' sign to be placed by the crew of an emergency or breakdown vehicle which is causing a temporary obstruction. It is an offence against RTA 1988, s 36 to fail to comply with such a sign.

In addition, reg 15 authorises any person to place a 'road vehicle sign' on a vehicle, and to place on any road:

(a) a minimum of four 'flat traffic delineators', 'traffic cones', or 'traffic pyramids'; or
(b) a 'traffic triangle' (at least 45 metres from the obstruction) or 'warning lamp' (used in conjunction with one of any of these signs, including the 'road vehicle sign'),

for the purpose of warning traffic of a temporary obstruction, other than roadworks. It is not in itself an offence to fail to comply with any of these signs. A 'road vehicle sign' consists of a flexible sheet on which there is a triangle the outer edges of which are red, the inner part being either reflectorised white or fluorescent yellow. It is designed to be fixed to a stationary vehicle, facing approaching traffic. A 'traffic delineator', 'traffic cone' or 'traffic pyramid' is of the 'lane marker' type of device frequently used by emergency services and a 'traffic triangle' or 'warning lamp' (flashing amber signal) is the type of device frequently used by individual motorists.

The placing of traffic signs and road vehicle signs is, therefore, carefully controlled. The placing of signs otherwise than as prescribed is of no legal effect. Persons do not have a right to paint 'No Parking' on the roadway, or on a sign, outside their premises.

Failure to comply with a traffic sign

RTA 1988, s 35 deals with circumstances in which a constable or a traffic officer is for the time being engaged in the regulation of traffic in a road, and s 36 with that in which authorised traffic signs have been placed on or near a road.

Section 35 provides that, where a constable is for the time being engaged in the regulation of traffic in a road, a person driving or propelling a vehicle who neglects or refuses:

(a) to stop the vehicle; or
(b) to make it proceed in, or keep to, a particular line of traffic, when directed to do so by a constable in the execution of his duty,

is guilty of an offence. The word 'neglect' simply means 'fail'. The Functions of Traffic Wardens Order 1970 extends the offence of failure to comply so as to include failure to comply with directions given by a traffic warden employed in the control and regulation of traffic under the authority of that Order. Disqualification or endorsement cannot be ordered if the failure is to comply with the directions of a traffic warden. For an offence to be committed under s 35, the constable or warden must be acting in the execution of his duty which, in this context, means his duty to ensure public safety. It remains to be decided whether it is a defence that the driver did not see the signal.

RTA 1988, s 36 states that an offence is committed by a person driving or propelling a vehicle who fails to comply with the indication given by an authorised traffic sign. It is no defence for a driver to allege that he did not see a traffic sign. Photographic evidence of a car going through a red traffic light may be admitted as evidence in court proceedings. The cameras used must be approved by the Secretary of State.

Offences against s 36 are 'specified offences' for the purposes of the Road Traffic Offenders Act 1988 (RTOA 1988), ss 34A to 34C (reduced disqualification for attendance on courses) where an order of disqualification is made under the RTOA 1988, s 34 for a period of not less than twelve months. 'Specified offences' will be introduced by the Road Safety Act 2006 (RSA 2006) when in force.

Signs to which RTA 1988, s 36 applies

RTA 1988, s 36 applies to any traffic sign which indicates a statutory prohibition, restriction or requirement, *or* to any other traffic sign where it is expressly provided by or under the RTA 1988 or the RTRA 1984 that RTA 1988, s 36 shall apply to the sign; such express provision has been made by the Traffic Signs Regulations and General Directions 2002, reg 10. Examples of signs to which s 36 applies are described in the next three paragraphs, which deal in turn with signs indicating a prohibition, a restriction and a requirement.

Examples of signs which indicate a *prohibition* are 'No entry', 'No right turn', 'No U turn', 'Lorries prohibited', and 'No overtaking' signs. These signs frequently involve the use of symbols only. Except in the case of a 'No Entry' sign, these consist of a red circle with the enclosed symbol in black on a white background. Thus a sign prohibiting entry to lorries would carry the symbol of a lorry with a red circle around it.

Signs dealing with *restrictions* include those dealing with waiting restrictions. These signs have a red outer circle with a blue background and a red band cutting across the face from the top left to bottom right of the sign as seen by approaching drivers. Information concerning the nature of the restrictions in force is provided on a plate, usually attached to the post supporting the sign. A yellow plate with the words 'at any time' in black indicates a total ban on parking, while the words '8.00 am–6.00 pm' would indicate a restriction upon waiting between those hours. Where waiting is limited rather than prohibited, the sign will be of white lettering on a blue background. Restrictions on waiting may be additionally indicated by signs placed on the roadway but such a sign is only effective to create the prohibition or restriction if used in conjunction with a restriction sign or plate of the type referred to above. A single continuous yellow line running parallel with the kerb restricts waiting (other than for loading or unloading) for a period of at least eight hours between 7 am and 7 pm on a minimum of four days a week. A double continuous yellow line indicates that, additionally, the restrictions may extend on occasions beyond those hours. Broken yellow lines indicate other waiting restrictions, usually unilateral parking schemes, restricting waiting on particular sides of the road on particular days of the week.

Those signs which deal with *requirements* under the section are those which require a driver etc to do something. 'Stop', 'Give Way', 'Keep Right', 'Keep Left', 'Traffic Lights' are all signs which indicate a requirement. The driver must stop his vehicle, turn it in a particular direction or give way to other traffic. These signs vary in appearance. The modern 'Stop' sign is octagonal and coloured red with 'Stop' in white capitals on it, although variations still exist. Other statutory requirements relating to stopping are red traffic lights and manually operated 'stop' signs at road works. 'Give way' signs consist of a red inverted triangle on a white, circular background with the words 'give way' inside the triangle. White arrows on a blue background indicate the route which a driver must follow. Another example of a sign making a requirement is one requiring certain drivers to telephone for permission to cross automatic level crossings.

For the purposes of RTA 1988, s 36, traffic signs placed on or near a road are deemed to be of the prescribed size, colour and type, and to have been lawfully placed, unless the contrary is proved. Consequently, the prosecution do not normally have to offer evidence of the nature of the sign beyond that which satisfies the court of the nature of the restriction, prohibition or requirement in question. However, if the sign is proved not to be of the prescribed size etc, or not to have been lawfully placed, it will not be a valid sign and no offence can be committed in relation to it, unless the breach of the requirement is trivial. There is a presumption that automatic traffic lights are in working order, unless the contrary is proved.

Signs to which RTA 1988, s 36 does not apply

Where the provisions of s 36 do not apply to a sign but it is governed by regulations concerning traffic control made by the Secretary of State, RTOA 1988, s 91 states that contravention or failure to comply is an offence under that section.

Particular signs

Certain signs indicate particular requirements. A 'Stop' sign requires that:

(a) every vehicle must, before entering the major road, stop at the transverse lines at the junction, or, if the lines are not visible, at the major road; and

(b) no vehicle may proceed past the transverse line painted nearest to the major road, or, if the lines are not visible, may not enter the major road, in such a manner or at such a time as is likely to cause danger to the driver of any other vehicle on the major road, or such as to necessitate the driver of any such other vehicle to change its speed or course in order to avoid an accident.

The latter provision (ie (b)) also applies to 'Give Way' signs. Thus, it is not sufficient to stop, or give way, and then to proceed, if the results of so proceeding are as described. There should be no interference with traffic on the major road. To emerge in such circumstances also indicates an element of carelessness which may amount to careless driving.

Regulation 26 of the Traffic Signs Regulations and General Directions 2002 deals with double white lines, which consist of either two continuous white lines or one continuous white line together with a broken white line painted along the middle of the carriageway itself. Any white unbroken line must be immediately preceded by a white warning arrow painted on the road; otherwise the line is not valid as a sign. If there are two continuous white lines vehicles travelling in both directions are required to keep to the nearside of the nearest continuous white line. A broken line with a continuous line requires vehicles to keep to the nearside of the continuous white line when that line is the nearer of the two to the vehicle. Where there are two continuous white lines, therefore, vehicles travelling in both directions may not cross the nearest line to them. Where there is a broken line nearest, both lines may be crossed if it is seen by the driver that it is safe to do so. It is an offence to stop on either side of the road where there is a double white line marking of either description unless it is done:

(a) to pick up or set down passengers, to load or unload, or for building operations;
(b) in connection with road or public utility works;
(c) by a vehicle used for police, fire or ambulance purposes;
(d) by a pedal cycle without a sidecar (auto-assisted or not);
(e) to avoid an accident or because it is impossible to proceed;
(f) with the permission of a constable in uniform, or when directed by a traffic warden.

The reasons for these exemptions can easily be appreciated. For example, there may be a bus stop or a warehouse along the section of roadway covered by double white lines. Again vehicles may have to stop there because of a traffic jam, and in an emergency situation a driver must stop to prevent an accident.

Records produced as evidence

RTOA 1988, s 20 provides that evidence of a fact related to an offence involving a driver's failure to comply with a traffic sign, contrary to RTA 1988, s 36(1), may be given by the production of a record produced by a prescribed device. (Such a record is also admissible in respect of an offence relating to the abuse of a bus lane.) However, evidence may only be so given if (in the same or another document) there is a certificate as to the circumstances in which it was produced, signed by a constable, or by a person authorised by (or on behalf of) the chief police officer for the area. The effect of s 20 is that the record and certificate can be tendered in evidence without the need for a witness to be called to prove them. The device must be of a type approved by the Secretary of State and must be used in accordance with conditions subject to which the approval was given. The Secretary of State has approved a device designed or adapted for recording, by means of photographic or other image recording means, the position of vehicles in relation to light signals.

For a document of the type referred to above to be admissible under s 20, a copy of it must be served on the person charged with the offence not less than seven days before the hearing or trial. If the person charged, not less than three days before the hearing or trial, requires the attendance of the person who signed the document, the evidence of the circumstances in which the record was produced will not be admissible, although the record produced by the device will.

Where the prosecution does not serve the record and certificate on the accused within the seven days before the trial, a police officer may nevertheless attend as a witness to produce and prove those items as real evidence.

Traffic surveys

Before an offence can be committed under the provisions of RTA 1988, s 35 in relation to a neglect or refusal to comply with a constable or traffic officer's direction, he must beat the time engaged in the execution of his duty. At common law in the context of traffic control, that was limited to the duty to ensure public safety. As a result a constable who was stopping vehicles for the purpose of a traffic survey or census was not acting in the execution of his duty. However, RTA 1988, s 35(2) amends the common law position by providing that any directions given by a constable in this respect shall be treated as given in the execution of his duty. The constable's direction may be to stop or to proceed to a particular point, but no requirement to give information may be made and no unreasonable delay must be caused to a person who does not wish to provide information. RTA 1988, s 36(4) also provides that signs such as 'Stop at Census Point' and 'Census Point Stop if required' are traffic signs to which s 36 applies.

Other powers to stop drivers and pedestrians

Quite apart from the powers given to the police by RTA 1988, s 35 in relation to the regulation of vehicles, RTA 1988, s 163 requires that a person driving a mechanically propelled vehicle or riding a cycle on a road must stop his vehicle on being required to do so by a constable or traffic officer in uniform. Failure to do so is an offence.

In addition, by RTA 1988, s 37, a person on foot who fails to comply with the signals of a uniformed constable or traffic officer on traffic control commits an offence. Failure to give a name and address in such circumstances is a further offence.

Police officers should be aware that under the Fire and Rescue Services Act 2004, s 44 an authorised employee of a fire or rescue authority may close off streets, or stop or regulate traffic in any street, whenever he reasonably believes this is necessary for rescue or fire fighting purposes. It is an offence without reasonable excuse to obstruct or interfere with a fire and rescue authority employee taking action under s 44.

PEDESTRIAN CROSSINGS

RTRA 1984, ss 23 and 24 give powers to local authorities to provide pedestrian crossings on all roads other than trunk roads, and to the Secretary of State to do so in respect of trunk roads. Local authorities, before establishing, altering or removing a crossing, must consult the chief officer of police, give public notice, and inform the Secretary of State in writing. RTRA 1984, s 25 authorises the Secretary of State to make regulations in respect of the precedence of vehicles and pedestrians, and generally in respect of the movement of vehicles in the vicinity of crossings. Regulations have been made governing 'Zebra', 'Pelican' and 'Puffin' crossings. Zebra crossings are uncontrolled; Pelican and Puffin crossings are light-controlled. By RTRA 1984, s 25, a person who contravenes the regulations is guilty of an offence.

'Zebra' crossings

The 'Zebra', 'Pelican' and 'Puffin' Pedestrian Crossing Regulations and General Directions 1997 prescribe the nature of uncontrolled crossings and the rules governing them. The *limits* of the crossing itself (the walking area for the pedestrians) are indicated by lines of studs between which is an area marked by alternate black and white stripes. Flashing yellow globes indicate the presence of such a crossing to approaching drivers. The globes are mounted on poles which are also marked by black and white stripes. There must be a globe at either side of the crossing; if there is a central reservation or street refuge on the crossing, one or more globes may be placed there. The failure of the lamps does not prevent the crossing being a valid 'Zebra' crossing, so that the provisions of the regulations must still be complied with.

The approach to the crossing from each direction is marked out as a 'controlled area'. It is in effect a defensive area and drivers are made aware that they are entering such an area by white lines situated at each kerb and in the crown of the road on the approaching driver's side. This is known as the 'terminal line' and from it three zigzag lines stretch to a distance of one metre from the crossing itself where they join a broken white line which is the 'give way' line.

These regulations are concerned with 'Zebra' crossings at which traffic is not for the time being controlled by a police constable in uniform or a traffic warden. Immediately such an officer takes control of traffic movements at such a crossing, the crossing ceases to be an uncontrolled one and the provisions of the regulations cease to apply until that control ceases.

Precedence at a zebra crossing

Regulation 25 states that every pedestrian on the carriageway within the limits of an uncontrolled crossing shall have precedence within these limits over any vehicle. That precedence must be afforded by a driver before any part of his vehicle enters the pedestrian limits of the crossing itself. Where there is a central refuge each side of it is treated as a separate crossing. It must be emphasised that a pedestrian only has precedence when he or she is within the limits of the crossing before the vehicle enters the limits of the crossing. A pedestrian waiting at the kerbside is awaiting the courtesy of drivers who care to stop; such a person is not entitled to any precedence until he steps on to the crossing.

The driver of a vehicle must always approach an uncontrolled crossing in such a manner that he will be able to stop before reaching it unless he can see that there is no one in the vicinity. Evidence of negligence or a failure to take reasonable care is not necessary; there is a strict duty to accord precedence and the discharge of that duty requires an approach to such crossings that will allow precedence to be given in any circumstances. The only exceptions are in instances where there is a sudden defect in the vehicle or it is pushed on to the crossing by the vehicle behind; in such circumstances a driver is clearly unable through no fault of his to discharge his duty to accord precedence. It is important to recognise that the issue of precedence does not arise until there is the question of who goes first. Clear evidence should be offered that the passage of a pedestrian was interfered with by the passage of a motor vehicle over the limits of the crossing. Taken to extremes, where a crossing spans a very wide street, a vehicle might pass over the limits while a pedestrian was on the crossing without the progress of that pedestrian being in any way interfered with. Alternatively, where a vehicle is stopped at a crossing and the pedestrians have passed the point at which it is waiting, the driver is then at liberty to proceed as precedence has been afforded. If another pedestrian then steps on the crossing as the vehicle moves off, it is submitted that the driver commits no offence (provided no issue of 'who goes first' is raised).

'Pelican' and 'Puffin' crossings

A driver who ignores a red light at a pelican or puffin crossing commits an offence against reg 23 by 'proceeding beyond the stop line' or, if that line is not visible, the post on which the light signal is mounted. At a puffin crossing, a red with amber signal denotes an impending change to green, but it conveys the same prohibition as a red signal. At either type of crossing a steady amber signal when shown alone conveys the same prohibition as a red signal (with the usual proviso applicable to traffic lights), and there may be a green arrow showing, which signals that traffic may cross the stop line to proceed in a particular direction. It is an offence to fail to accord precedence when there is a flashing amber light at a pelican crossing. We explain below what is meant by 'according precedence'.

Both pelican and puffin crossings will have 'controlled areas' on each side of the crossing (or on one side in the case of one-way traffic), this controlled area being indicated by two or more zig-zag lines stretching from the terminal line to the stop line, a line which is met before the limits of the crossing itself are reached. The primary signals shown to both drivers and pedestrians are by synchronised light signals. Whilst a steady green light is shown to drivers, a steady red light is shown to pedestrians. The light signals to pedestrians are, in the case of pelican crossings, steady red, steady green and flashing green figures reinforced by the illumination of a sign which reads 'WAIT'. Those at puffin crossings are by means of red and green figures and the green figure must only be capable of showing when a red light is indicated to drivers.

Audible signals may be used at pelican crossings to indicate to pedestrians when it is safe to cross.

Precedence at a pelican or puffin crossing

The issue of precedence at these crossings is determined to a major extent by the light signals which are showing at the time. There are specific offences within the Regulations, dealing with failure to comply with such signals.

However, at pelican crossings a driver may encounter a flashing amber signal which indicates that pedestrians, who are on the carriageway or a central reservation within the limits of the crossing before any part of the vehicle has entered those limits, must be accorded precedence. It is an offence for a driver to fail to accord such precedence. The flashing amber signal is peculiar to pelican crossings alone and is not one of the signals shown at a puffin crossing.

Prohibition of waiting

Regulation 18 prohibits a driver from stopping his vehicle in the *limits* of any of the three types of crossing itself unless he is prevented from proceeding by circumstances beyond his control or it is necessary to avoid an accident. Moreover, reg 20 prohibits the driver of a vehicle from causing the vehicle or any part of it to stop in a '*controlled area*' (the zig-zag area). However, this regulation does not apply to pedal cycles without sidecars, whether mechanically assisted or not. Regulations 21 and 22 exempt from reg 20 vehicles:

(a) whose drivers have stopped to comply with requirements of the Regulations;
(b) whose drivers have been prevented from proceeding by circumstances beyond their control;
(c) whose drivers have stopped to avoid an accident;
(d) which have stopped for fire, ambulance, police or defence purposes; or
(e) which have stopped in connection with building works, road works or repairs to public utilities.

Vehicles may also halt to make right or left turns. Public service vehicles may stop to pick up or set down passengers but only on the far side of the crossing itself, not on its approach.

In conclusion, it should be noted that reg 19 prohibits a pedestrian remaining within the limits of a crossing longer than necessary for the purposes of crossing with reasonable despatch.

Prohibition on overtaking

Regulation 24 provides that a driver within a 'controlled area' of any of the three types of crossing must not overtake on the approach side to a crossing a moving motor vehicle or a stationary motor vehicle according precedence to a pedestrian on the crossing. Once the crossing has been passed it is not an offence to overtake within the controlled area on the other side. For the purpose of this regulation, a vehicle overtakes an other if any part of the vehicle passes ahead of the foremost part of another vehicle. The purpose of this regulation is to prevent pedestrians from being struck by overtaking vehicles. It is not surprising, therefore, that the regulation limits the prohibition on overtaking to cases where the vehicle overtaken is the only other vehicle in the controlled area, or is the foremost vehicle. If this was not so, where there were two lines of traffic approaching a crossing, it would not be possible for the traffic on the offside to close up. In relation to the prohibition on overtaking a vehicle which has stopped to accord precedence, such a vehicle includes one which has stopped for this purpose even though a pedestrian intending to cross has not yet stepped on to the crossing.

Because of the drafting of the provision, the ban on overtaking does not apply where the overtaking vehicle was actually on the crossing when it passed ahead of the foremost part of the overtaken vehicle.

School crossing patrols

RTRA 1984, s 26 authorises an 'appropriate authority' to make arrangements for the patrolling places where children cross roads on their way to or from school (or from one part of the school to another).

Arrangements may be made for patrolling such places at such times as the authority thinks fit. Persons may be appointed for this purpose by the 'appropriate authority' which (outside the Metropolis) is the county council.

The stopping of vehicles at school crossings is dealt with by RTRA 1984, s 28. There are various essential points to consider when dealing with an offence under this section. They are related to what a driver must do when required to stop by a school crossing patrol. When a vehicle is approaching a place in a road where a person is crossing or seeking to cross the road, a school crossing patrol wearing an approved uniform is empowered by exhibiting a prescribed sign, to require the person driving or propelling the vehicle to stop it. When such a person has been required to stop:

(a) he must cause the vehicle to stop before reaching the place where the person is crossing or seeking to cross and so as not to stop or impede his crossing; and

(b) the vehicle must not be put in motion again so as to reach the place in question so long as the sign continues to be exhibited.

It is an offence for a person to fail to comply with (a) or for him to cause a vehicle to be put in motion contrary to (b). These are separate offences.

The following should be noted about RTRA 1984, s 28. The duty to stop only exists if the patrol was wearing a uniform approved by the Secretary of State, and any uniform is deemed to be so approved unless the contrary is proved. Home Office Circular 119/1954 approves caps for men, or a beret for a woman, together with a white dust coat or mackintosh. Circular 108/1966 authorises fluorescent jerkins or sleeves to be worn over the approved uniform. The stopping of traffic may only be effected by exhibiting a sign prescribed by the School Crossing Patrol Sign (England and Wales) Regulations 2006. That sign will display the word 'Stop' in black letters with a black bar on a yellow fluorescent background surrounded by a red fluorescent border. RTRA 1984, s 28 states that where the sign is displayed by a school crossing patrol it will be presumed that it is a prescribed sign and, if displayed in circumstances in which it was required to be illuminated, that it was so illuminated.

As long as a prescribed sign has been properly exhibited, a driver must stop even if the persons have cleared the road and there are no others seeking to cross. In one case, where a party of children and adults were crossing while the sign was displayed and had cleared the crown of a road, a driver coming out of a side street drove past the exhibited sign, passing narrowly behind the last of the party. The justices dismissed a charge of failing to stop on the grounds that the driver had not impeded their crossing. A divisional court gave a direction to convict on the grounds that the words 'so as not to stop or impede their crossing' in (a), above, merely described the manner in which a driver should stop (ie he must not halt across the path which those children would take) and were not meant to indicate that drivers could ignore a properly displayed sign if, in doing so, they would not directly impede pedestrians. Drivers must, therefore, stop and remain stopped while the sign is properly displayed. The duty to stop is absolute. A properly exhibited sign is one on which an approaching driver can see the words on the sign but it need not be proved that it was full face to on coming traffic.

REMOVAL OF VEHICLES

The police have powers to require the removal of vehicles and to remove them themselves. Local authorities are legally obliged to remove abandoned vehicles.

Powers of police

Regulation 3 of the Removal and Disposal of Vehicles Regulations 1986 allows a constable to require the owner, driver or other person in charge or control of a vehicle which:

(a) has broken down, or been permitted to remain at rest, on a road in such a position, condition or circumstances as to cause obstruction to other persons using the road, or as to be likely to cause danger to such other persons; or

(b) has been permitted to remain at rest or has broken down and remained at rest on a road in contravention of a prohibition or restriction in or under any enactment mentioned in Sch 1 to the Regulations,

to move or cause it to be moved.

The statutory prohibitions or restrictions included in Sch 1, referred to in (b), are concerned with parking in 'no waiting' areas, in the controlled areas of pedestrian crossings or in contravention of traffic signs—including police 'no waiting' signs. The constable's requirement may include a requirement to move the vehicle to some other place which may not be on a road, or a requirement that it shall not be moved to a particular road or to a particular position.

It is an offence against the Road Traffic Offenders Act 1988, s 91 to fail to move or cause a vehicle to be moved as soon as practicable when required under the provisions of reg 3.

Regulation 4 of the 1986 Regulations allows a constable to remove or arrange for the removal of a vehicle which is on a road in the circumstances outlined in (a) or (b), above. He may also do so if the vehicle, having broken down on a road or on any land in the open air, *appears* to have been abandoned without lawful authority, or if the vehicle has been permitted to remain at rest on a road or any land in the open air in such a position or circumstances as to *appear* to have been abandoned without lawful authority.

In determining, for the purposes of (a), the question of 'obstruction', a different interpretation is given to that term from that accorded to it in the Highways Act 1980, s 137 and the Road Vehicles (Construction and Use) Regulations 1986, reg 103 (see pp 390 and 431, above). This has been stated by the Court of Appeal which held that 'obstruction' in (a) meant more than simply impeding the free access of members of the public to every part of the highway, since what was required was obstructing their passage by hindering or preventing them getting past. That 'obstruction', said the Court, need not be an actual one; it included obstructing people who might be expected to be using the highway. On the other hand, the mere fact that the use of a highway was unreasonable did not make it an obstruction.

The Court of Appeal has emphasised that reg 4 is not concerned with whether or not a vehicle has actually been abandoned, but whether it appears to a constable to have been abandoned. If a complaint is to be made concerning such removal it must be shown that in the particular circumstances the vehicle could not have appeared to the constable to have been abandoned. The burden of proof rests with the complainant.

The power to remove vehicles from land occupied by any person is subject to giving notice as prescribed by RTRA 1984, s 99 and the Removal and Disposal of Vehicles Regulations 1986, reg 8. The power under reg 4 is very useful when the driver, person in charge or owner of a vehicle cannot be found or that person refuses to move the vehicle.

Regulation 4A empowers a traffic warden, a community support officer, or a person accredited under a community safety accreditation scheme to remove a vehicle parked or broken down on a road in circumstances where it is causing an obstruction, where it is likely to cause danger to road users, or where an offence is being committed in relation to a statutory prohibition or restriction included in Sch 1 to the Regulations, referred to above.

Duties of local authorities

The Refuse Disposal (Amenity) Act 1978 (RD(A)A 1978), s 3(1) obliges local authorities to remove motor vehicles abandoned without lawful authority on any land in the open air or on any other land forming part of the highway within their area. Before removing vehicles from land other than a road the local authority must serve notice on the occupier of the land which is involved. It is an offence contrary to RD(A)A 1978, s 2 so to abandon a vehicle. We discuss this offence in Chapter 9, above, in relation to the law of litter.

DRIVING INSTRUCTION

RTA 1988, s 123 prohibits the giving of driving instruction of any prescribed description (ie prescribed by RSA 2006, Sch 6 when in force) for money or money's worth unless the person giving the instruction is a registered approved instructor or the holder of a licence authorising him to give such instruction. There must be fixed to, and exhibited on, the motor car the current licence or certificate of registration, in a similar position to that occupied by the vehicle excise licence. Free instruction given as a perk when buying a car from a motor trader is deemed to be given for payment. RTA 1988, s 123 only applies to motor cars, but RSA 2006, s 42 and Sch 6 prospectively substitute s 123 to apply these provisions to all motor vehicles. RTA 1988, s 123 does not apply to police instructors. Disabled drivers may become registered or licensed instructors.

The amendments effected by the RSA 2006 also enable the Secretary of State to make available information concerning persons offering driver training. Provision is made for regulations governing paid instruction in respect of lorries, buses and motor cycles.

A new s 123A creates offences in respect of the giving of paid driving instruction in contravention of s 123. Appropriate amendments are made to the provisions concerning registration.

A new s 162A is prospectively inserted into the RTA 1988 to provide for a statutory scheme regulating the use of persons who may be used as assistants to candidates who have difficulty in hearing, understanding or responding to instructions or questions.

Registered approved instructor

To be registered a person must satisfy the Registrar that he:

(a) has passed the official driving instructors' examination including a hazard perception test (except that a person who passed the written examination before 14 November 2002 is not required to undertake such a test);

(b) holds an appropriate full licence issued in Great Britain or Northern Ireland;

(c) has held that licence or a current foreign licence for at least four of the preceding six years;

(d) has not been disqualified from driving during any part of the previous period of four years;

(e) is a fit and proper person to have his name registered; and

(f) an application together with the fee has been received not later than one year after passing that examination.

Licensed instructor

To enable persons to gain experience with a view to undergoing the practical test of ability and fitness to instruct, which is part of the official driving instructor's examination, RTA 1988, s 129 allows the Registrar to grant a licence to give instruction in the driving of a motor car. If a previous licence has been granted, an application may be refused on that ground.

An applicant must have passed the written part of the official driving instructors' examination and the practical test of driving ability and fitness to drive, which is also part of the examination. Licence holders may only give instruction from premises named in the licence. If the premises are a driving school the licence holder may only give instruction if properly employed in accordance with rules that there can be no more than one licence holder to each registered instructor.

For the first three months of any licence (other than the second of two consecutive ones) the holder either must be under the direct personal supervision of a registered instructor for at least one-fifth of that time and keep a log to that effect, or must undertake a minimum of twenty hours' supplementary training. In the case of the latter alternative he must undertake five further hours of training in a second consecutive period.

Offences

A person giving the instruction in breach of RTA 1988, s 123 commits an offence, as does his employer if he is employed for that purpose. It is a defence for a defendant to prove that he did not know and had no reasonable cause to believe that his name, or that of his employee, was not in the register.

A person to whom a licence or a certificate of registration has been granted must produce it to a constable or authorised person on being required to do so. Failure to do so is an offence. However, it is a defence to prove in any proceedings for non-production:

(a) that the licence was produced within seven days at a police station specified by a constable or at a place specified by an authorised person (as the case may be); or

(b) that the document was produced at that police station or place (as the case may be) as soon as reasonably practicable; or

(c) that it was not reasonably practicable for it to be so produced at that police station or place before the day on which proceedings commenced.

RTA 1988, s 135(2) states that it is an offence for any unregistered person to wear or display a badge or certificate or to use any name, title or description which implies that he is registered. It also prohibits a person carrying on a driving instruction business from using any such title or description in respect of an unregistered employee, or from issuing any advertisement etc which is misleading in that respect. It is a defence for a person charged with this offence to prove that he did not know, and had no reasonable cause to believe, that his name, or that of his employee, was not in the register at the material time.

RTA 1988, s 125A permits the registration of disabled persons as driving instructors. Such persons may only be registered if they hold a current disabled person's limited driving licence and a current emergency control certificate. Such a certificate is only granted after assessment of the person's ability to take control of a motor car of a class covered by his disabled person's driving licence (with or without modifications). If an applicant for registration fails, without reasonable excuse, to disclose a relevant or prospective disability, he commits an offence. So does a registered disabled instructor or a disabled licensed instructor who gives paid instruction without holding an emergency control certificate or in an unauthorised motor car. A person who has employed the instructor to give that instruction will also be liable if one of these two offences is committed.

NOTICE OF INTENDED PROSECUTION

In the case of a number of moving traffic offences, the driver, if not stopped and interviewed by the police at the time, may experience considerable difficulty in recalling the circumstances some weeks after the event. For this reason, RTOA 1988, s 1 states that, in relation to certain named offences, a person shall not be convicted unless:

(a) he was warned at the time of the possibility of prosecution for the offence; or

(b) he was served with a summons (or, when the relevant provision is in force, a requisition) for the offence within fourteen days of its commission; or

(c) a notice of intended prosecution specifying the nature of the alleged offence and the time and place where it is alleged to have been committed was served within fourteen days on him or the person, if any, registered as the keeper of the vehicle at the time of the commission of the offence. (In the case of dangerous or careless cycling the notice must be served on the rider.)

The requirements of s 1 are deemed to have been complied with unless and until the contrary is proved.

The following offences require notice of intended prosecution in one of these forms:

(a) Road Traffic Act 1988

Section 2	Dangerous driving
Section 3	Careless, and inconsiderate driving
Section 22	Leaving a vehicle in a dangerous position
Section 28	Dangerous cycling
Section 29	Careless, and inconsiderate cycling
Section 35	Failing to conform with the indication given by a constable engaged in the regulation of traffic
Section 36	Failing to comply with the indication given by a traffic sign

(b) Road Traffic Regulation Act 1984

Section 16	Exceeding temporary speed restrictions imposed under s 14
Section 17(4)	Exceeding speed restriction on special road
Section 88(7)	Exceeding temporary speed limit imposed by order
Section 89(1)	Speeding offences generally

(c) Aiding and abetting any of the above offences.

However, such notice need not be given in relation to an offence in respect of which a full or provisional fixed penalty notice has been given or fixed under the provisions of the RTOA 1988.

Warning at the time of the offence

The words 'at the time of the offence' mean at the *time of the incident and not the moment of the offence*. In one case, a warning, given by a police officer at the scene of an incident thirty-five minutes after its occurrence and while it was still being dealt with, was held to have been given 'at the time'. In other circumstances, where the police immediately traced the driver but the process took two and a half hours, the notice was held to have been given 'at the time'. However, there is obviously a limit, and the matter should be judged in the context of the warning being given as a part of the continuous process of initial investigation. Whether or not warning was given at the time is a question of fact and degree and the best course of action, if there has been any delay at the scene, is to send a written notice.

The warning must be heard and understood by the person concerned, and it must be to the effect that the question of prosecuting him for one or other of the above offences will be taken into consideration. Police officers are advised to warn that the offender will be reported for consideration of the question of prosecuting him for whichever of the above offences is applicable. There is no prescribed form of words and any clear statement to the above effect will do. It is appreciated that it is not always possible to decide whether the prosecution may be for dangerous or merely careless driving but a warning that it may be for either will suffice as the evidence upon which the charge will be based will be similar.

Service of summons or notice of intended prosecution

In circumstances in which an oral notice is not given at the time, then either a summons (or requisition) or a written notice of intended prosecution must be served within fourteen days. In reckoning a period of fourteen days, the day on which the offence was committed is ignored. A notice sent by post must be despatched so that in the normal time of postal delivery it will arrive within fourteen days. If it is so posted, but is held up in the post and is delivered outside the fourteen-day period, it will be deemed to have been served in the fourteen-day period; consequently, the driver can still be convicted. It has been held that service of a notice on the wife of the defendant by a constable handing the notice to her was a valid service, since she was a person authorised to accept and deal with her husband's mail. It would be different if the notice was left with a hall porter, as he would not be so authorised. It is better to restrict service by hand to the offender. In the absence of personal service on the offender, it is advisable to serve a notice by sending it by registered post or recorded delivery since in such a case he is deemed to have been served if the notice was addressed to him at his last known address, notwithstanding that the notice is returned as undelivered or is for some other reason not received by him.

Where an accused alleges that he did not receive a notice of intended prosecution, the burden of proof is upon him to show on the balance of probability that notice was not given as required. It is insufficient that the prosecution did not produce proof of posting where no evidence of non-compliance is offered before the court.

Circumstances where non-compliance is no bar to conviction

RTOA 1988, s 2(3) states that a failure to comply with the above requirements is no bar to conviction if the court is satisfied that the name and address of the accused or of the vehicle's registered keeper could not with reasonable diligence have been ascertained in time for service of a summons or notice or that the accused by his own conduct contributed to the failure. These matters must always be resolved by the court but the difference can be appreciated between circumstances in which, on the one hand, the number of the vehicle was known to the police at the time and their inquiries were so slow that notice was served out of time, and, on the other, where the number was not known and extensive inquiries had to be undertaken to establish the identity of the driver.

RTOA 1988, s 2(1) waives the requirements of s 1 in relation to any offence if, at the time of the offence or immediately thereafter, an accident occurs owing to the presence on a road of the vehicle in respect of which the offence was committed. This exemption exists because, in such circumstances, the offender will normally be aware of the circumstances surrounding the offence. It does not apply, therefore, if the accident was so trivial that the driver was unaware that the accident had occurred. Here, the requirements of s 1 apply. On the other hand, the waiver of the requirements of s 1 does apply if the driver was unaware of the circumstances of an accident owing to the severity of his injuries, because subsequently the driver will be only too aware that the accident has occurred.

TRAFFIC WARDENS

Every police authority in England and Wales is authorised by RTRA 1984, s 95 to appoint traffic wardens to aid the police to discharge certain functions. By RTRA 1984, s 95(5), traffic wardens may only be used to discharge duties prescribed by the Secretary of State. Although appointed by the police authority, wardens act under the direction of the chief officer of police. Traffic wardens must wear the uniform prescribed by the Secretary of State; they must not act as traffic wardens when not in uniform.

RTRA 1984, s 95(4) authorises the use of wardens as school crossing patrols and as parking attendants at street parking places provided by the Secretary of State or a local authority. In addition, s 95(5) of the Act authorises the Secretary of State to make an order concerning the functions which traffic wardens may undertake. He has made the Functions of Traffic Wardens Order 1970, the Schedule to which provides that traffic wardens may be employed to enforce the law with respect to:

(a) offences of parking without obligatory lights or reflectors during the hours of darkness;
(b) offences of obstruction of a road by vehicles, or of vehicles waiting, or being left or parked, or being loaded or unloaded, on a road or other public place;
(c) offences against the Vehicles Excise and Registration Act 1994 (eg no vehicle excise licence);
(d) offences related to parking places on highways where charges are made (eg by meters or machines);
(e) offences committed by causing a vehicle, or any part of it, to stop in contravention of the pedestrian crossing regulations;
(f) to stop vehicles for the purpose of testing under RTA 1988, s 67; and
(g) to escort vehicles or trailers carrying loads of exceptional dimensions.

The Order also permits traffic wardens to be used in connection with obtaining information from the keeper of the vehicle or relevant person as to the identity of a driver alleged to be guilty of a road traffic offence. They are also permitted to perform duties connected with the interim disposal of vehicles removed in consequence of being illegally, obstructively or dangerously parked; the immobilisation of illegally parked vehicles; and the custody of vehicles removed under statutory powers. They are permitted to perform duties in the regulation and control of traffic and are permitted to stop vehicles generally under RTA 1988, s 163. Traffic wardens are not permitted to exercise any of their functions when in a moving vehicle.

To enable traffic wardens to carry out their various functions, art 3 of the Order provides that:

(a) drivers and pedestrians must comply with their traffic directions;
(b) traffic wardens have power to obtain the names and addresses of persons reasonably believed to have committed one of the following offences: parking without lights; obstruction; waiting or loading etc; failing to conform to a valid indication given for the regulation of traffic, or a traffic sign; a vehicle excise offence; or an offence in respect of charges for parking on the highway;
(c) traffic wardens also have power to obtain the names and addresses of pedestrians who fail to comply with traffic directions; and
(d) traffic wardens may require the production of driving licences where they have reasonable cause to believe that an offence has been committed by causing a vehicle, or any part of it, to stop in contravention of the pedestrian crossing regulations or by leaving the vehicle in a dangerous position, or where they are employed to perform functions in connection with the impounding of vehicles and have reasonable cause to believe that an offence of obstruction, waiting etc has been committed.

RTRA 1984, s 96 states that an order made under RTRA 1984, s 95(5) may provide that, for the purposes of any functions which traffic wardens are authorised by the order to discharge, references in a number of statutes to a constable shall include references to a traffic warden. However, this is subject to the limitations that any power of a constable for the purposes of RTA 1988, ss 163 (power to stop vehicles), 164(1), (2) and (6) (power to require production of driving licences etc), 165 (power to obtain names and addresses etc) (see pp 449, 364 and 383) is exercisable by a traffic warden only where he is assisting a constable, or (in the case of the power under s 163) where he is dealing with the control and regulation of traffic (including pedestrians), or where he reasonably believes that an offence has been committed of a type specified in the order.

PARKING GENERALLY

The Road Traffic Regulation Act 1984, ss 5 and 8 permit local authorities to make traffic regulation orders. Most of such orders will be 'no waiting' orders. There is no prescribed form which such orders must follow but they must be properly made in accordance with regulations.

Generally, such orders contain exemptions in favour of particular persons or particular types of vehicles. The offences which are committed when the provisions of such orders are contravened are contained in these sections of the RTRA 1984.

In addition, RTRA 1984, s 32 empowers a local authority to provide off-street parking places and to authorise the use as a parking place of any part of a road within their area not being a road within Greater London. RTRA 1984, s 35 permits local authorities to make parking place orders in respect of places so provided. RTRA 1984, ss 45 and 46 permit local authorities to designate parking places on highways within their areas and permit the imposition of charges in respect of such parking. It is an offence against s 47 to fail to comply with the requirements of any order so made.

RTRA 1984, ss 104 to 106 deal with the immobilisation of vehicles which are illegally parked in contravention of any statutory prohibition or restriction and such vehicles may be immobilised within areas specified by the Secretary of State, following an application by a local authority or the Traffic Director for London. Where a vehicle has been immobilised, a notice must be affixed warning against any attempt to release the vehicle and specifying the steps to be taken in order to secure its release. The vehicle will be released from the device upon payment of the appropriate sum. An offence is committed by any person who removes or interferes with any notice attached to such a vehicle, or who removes or attempts to remove an immobilisation device. A person who damages an immobilisation device in an attempt to release his vehicle is guilty of an offence of criminal damage and cannot claim that the act was carried out to protect his own property or release it from unlawful detention. This applies equally where a car is parked on private property and there is a notice clearly stating that vehicles which are unlawfully parked there will be clamped and a reasonable fee demanded for their release.

Permitted and special parking areas

The Road Traffic Act 1991 (RTA 1991), Part II (ss 50 to 82) makes provision for the decriminalisation of certain parking offences in London and the provinces. These offences lead to penalties being required to be paid by the appropriate authority without the offender appearing before a court. These penalties will be recovered in the same way as a civil debt, by 'certificated bailiffs'. There is a system of appeal to parking adjudicators. Once again, the particular orders will be made by local authorities which are empowered to employ parking attendants to enforce their provisions. The provisions of Part II apply within 'permitted' and 'special' parking areas which are designated as such by statutory instrument. Within a 'permitted' parking area, a parking offence under the RTRA 1984 is not committed in relation to contraventions of orders relating to the use of parking places and the offence is dealt with under the provisions of Part II in its decriminalised form. Within a 'special' parking area, existing no waiting orders (whether permanent or temporary), provisions relating to the parking of vehicles on verges or central reservations, the prohibition or restriction on waiting and loading, the prohibition on causing a motor vehicle to stop on a part of a road demarcated as a stopping place for a bus, the prohibition on driving or riding on cycle tracks similarly cease to apply (ie they are decriminalised and are dealt with under the provisions of Part II of the RTA 1991).

Where a parking attendant has reason to believe that a vehicle has been permitted to remain at rest in circumstances under which a penalty charge is payable, he, or another person acting under his direction, may fix an immobilisation device. A similar notice to that described above must be affixed to the vehicle and similar provisions apply concerning release.

At the time of writing, the provisions set out above in relation to permitted and special parking areas are those which are in force. However, the Traffic Management Act 2004 (TMA 2004), Part 6 (ss 72 to 93), when brought into force, will provide for civil enforcement in relation to penalty charges for 'road traffic contraventions' (ie parking contraventions, bus lane contraventions, London lorry ban contraventions and moving traffic contraventions) committed in a 'civil enforcement area', under regulations made by the 'appropriate national authorities'. These regulations must include provisions specifying the person or persons by whom a penalty charge must be paid (who may be the owner of the vehicle, its driver or any other appropriate person). In Greater London, 'civil enforcement area' means the whole of Greater London in relation to parking contraventions as specified in para (2) of Sch 7 (which are contraventions relating to parking places), bus lane contraventions and lorry ban contraventions, or such parts of Greater London as may be designated, in respect of parking contraventions not related to parking spaces and of moving traffic contraventions. Outside Greater London, the term means any area in respect of which an order has been made designating the whole or part of a local authority area as such a civil enforcement area for the purpose of parking contraventions, bus lane contraventions and/or moving traffic contraventions. The appropriate national authority is empowered to require a local authority to make an application for an order designating the whole or part of the local authority's area as a civil enforcement area for the purpose of parking contraventions. An area which, immediately before the coming into force of the above provisions under TMA 2004, Part 6, was designated as a special parking area or permitted parking area under RTA 1991 is a civil enforcement area for parking contraventions.

'Civil enforcement officers' may be appointed for dealing with such matters and will wear uniform when exercising specified functions. Parking attendants appointed under s 63A of RTRA 1984 by a local authority which is an enforcement authority will be civil enforcement officers in relation to parking contraventions, and may be given authority to deal with other road traffic contraventions.

In TMA 2004, ss 85 and 86, special provision is made in respect of 'special enforcement areas' designated for their purposes. An area which immediately before the commencement of TMA 2004, Part 6 was designated as a special parking area will thereafter be a special enforcement area. TMA 2004, s 85 prohibits double parking in special enforcement areas by providing that parking more than 50 cm from the edge of the carriageway is prohibited in places other than a designated parking place or where loading cannot be reasonably carried out (but not for more than twenty minutes). The usual exemptions apply in respect of essential works etc. Parking is prohibited by TMA 2004, s 86 in most instances in a special enforcement area where there is a 'dropped footway, cycle track or verge' (ie where the footway etc has been lowered at its join with the carriageway to assist pedestrians or cyclists or vehicles when entering or crossing the carriageway), or where the carriageway has been raised to meet the level of the footway etc for the same purpose.

Although not exclusively directed at parking offences, mention must be made of orders which restrict the use generally of motor vehicles within 'charging areas'. In London, the Road User Charging (Charges and Penalty Charges) (London) Regulations 2001 deal with the procedures relating to the imposition of charges and penalty charges (road user charging, commonly known as 'congestion charging') in Greater London. The Regulations include requirements concerning the imposition, setting and liability for charges and penalty charges; the examination of, and entry to, vehicles; powers of seizure and immobilisation; removal and disposal of vehicles; recovery of penalty charges in respect of removed vehicles; and the taking possession of vehicles and claims by owners of vehicles after their disposal.

Charges may also be imposed in respect of release from immobilisation; removal; storage and release; and the sale or destruction of vehicles.

An 'authorised person' (a local authority or its employee or an employee of Transport for London, a constable, or any other person authorized in writing by the charging authority) may examine a vehicle for the purpose of ascertaining whether any document required by a charging scheme is displayed; whether required equipment has been fitted, is in working order, or has been interfered with due to intent to avoid payment, and whether conditions of use are being complied with. Such a person may enter a vehicle on a road where he has reasonable grounds for suspecting that such equipment has been interfered with or that a false document is being used. He may seize anything (if necessary by detaching it from the vehicle) and retain it as evidence. These powers may not be exercised by an authorised person who is not a constable, except in the presence of a constable.

While the effect of these Regulations is limited to Greater London, the Transport Act 2000 makes provision for such schemes to be introduced elsewhere.

There are procedures for the enforcement and adjudication of road user charging schemes in Greater London. They deal particularly with notification, adjudication and enforcement, the determination of disputes, appeals against such determinations, the appointment of persons to hear appeals and the admissibility of evidence in such proceedings.

Provision is made for evidence of a fact to be given by production of a record produced by a prescribed device (a camera or other device designed to produce a record of the presence of a vehicle being used or kept on a road in a charging area together with the date and time at which this occurred, and the term includes any equipment used in conjunction with the camera or other device) which includes a certificate as to the circumstances in which it was produced, signed by a constable or person authorised for that purpose by the charging authority (this may be provided in a separate document). A record will be deemed to be such a record, or to be so signed, unless the contrary is proved.

Wheel-clamping on private property

Complaints are frequently made by persons who have had their vehicles 'wheel-clamped' on private property on the instructions of the occupier. Such wheel-clamping is not an offence, nor is it a civil wrong provided that the motorist was aware of the danger of wheelclamping (eg by a notice to that effect) and that the wheelclamping and charge for release amount to a reasonable means of the occupier protecting his property. In one case a divisional court held that immobilisation and a release fee of £25 was reasonable. In another case, the Court of Appeal considered that £40 was reasonable in the circumstances which it was considering (parking on private land in a town centre).

Wheelclampers employed by private companies must be licensed. It is an offence for a person to clamp a vehicle *on private land* when not so licensed. In all other respects, no offence is committed by an occupier who clamps, or causes to be clamped, vehicles which park on his land without authority if warning notices are displayed indicating that cars will be clamped. The issue is a civil matter between the occupier of the land and the trespasser.

Where a vehicle has been parked on private property, the owners of some private properties engage agents to send out notices of intention to take proceedings in relation to trespass and which offer an opportunity to pay a penalty in settlement. These are not fixed penalty notices. The particulars of the keeper of the vehicle will have been obtained from DVLA which is empowered to release such information to persons having cause to seek it.

A divisional court has held that a person who damaged a clamp in an attempt to recover his vehicle which had been clamped on private property, having seen signs warning that unlawfully parked (ie trespassory) vehicles would be clamped, was guilty of criminal damage. Its reason was that he had consented to the risk of his vehicle being clamped and had no lawful excuse for damaging the clamp. It would appear from another divisional court decision that it would have been different if the accused had not seen the warning sign. The Court of Appeal has held that a motorist who trespassed by parking on private property without permission, having seen a notice that those who did so would be wheel clamped and released on payment of a fee, is to be taken to have consented to the risk of his vehicle being clamped, provided that the release fee is reasonable, the vehicle would be released without delay on payment and there were means whereby an offer of payment might be made. No specific guidance has been given as to what constitutes a reasonable release fee. It should be noted that warning notices must be prominently displayed so that all who enter upon the land must see them. If they are not there cannot be a presumption that the driver consented to the risk of clamping having done so being aware of the consequences

Exposing vehicles for sale, or repairing vehicles, on a road

The Clean Neighbourhoods and Environment Act 2005 (CNAEA 2005), s 3 provides that a person is guilty of an offence if at any time, he leaves two or more motor vehicles parked within 500 metres of each other on a road or roads where they are exposed or advertised for sale, or causes two or more motor vehicles to be so left. However, a person will not be convicted of such an offence if he proves to the satisfaction of the court that he was not acting for the purpose of a business of selling motor vehicles.

CNAEA 2005, s 4 prohibits the carrying out of restricted works on a motor vehicle which is on a road. The term 'restricted works' means works for the repair, maintenance, servicing, improvement or dismantling of a motor vehicle or any part of or accessory to a motor vehicle or works for the installation, replacement or renewal of any such part or accessory. However, the offence is aimed at that which might be described as 'commercial works' and a person is not to be convicted if he proves to the satisfaction of the court that the works were not carried out in the course of, or for the purposes of, a business of carrying out restricted works, or for gain or reward. This defence does not apply where the carrying out of the works gave reasonable cause for annoyance to persons in the vicinity. A further defence exists where the works carried out were works of repair which arose from an accident or breakdown in circumstances where repairs on the spot or elsewhere on the road were necessary, and were carried out within seventy-two hours of the accident or breakdown or were, within that period, authorised to be carried out at a later time by the local authority for the area.

Where an offence against s 3 or s 4 is committed by a body corporate and it is proved that the act occurred with the consent or connivance of, or to have been attributable to, any neglect on the part of a director, manager or similar officer of that company, that officer is also guilty of the offence.

An authorised officer of the local authority may issue a fixed penalty notice in respect of such offences and, in such a case, no proceedings may be instituted within fourteen days. The penalty to be paid is currently £100. The officer may require an offender to provide his name and address. It is an offence to fail to do so or to provide a false or inaccurate name and address.

FIXED PENALTY OFFENCES

The application of the law on fixed penalties for road traffic offences requires police officers to be aware not only of the list of offences which can be dealt with by the fixed penalty procedure but also to be aware of those offences which carry obligatory endorsement of penalty points. RTOA 1988, Sch 3 lists the offences which are 'fixed penalty offences'. Schedule 2 indicates the offences which carry obligatory endorsement. To assist the memory of police officers in this respect, aides memoire have been prepared listing the various offences which are non-endorsable fixed penalty offences and those which are endorsable. The aide memoire in relation to endorsable fixed penalty offences also indicates the number of penalty points which apply, and gives a code number for each offence. That for non-endorsable fixed penalty offences includes advice concerning enforcement policies existing within a police force, particularly where a vehicle rectification scheme is in operation.

In general, the non-endorsable fixed penalty offences are concerned with those involving minor defects in the vehicle or its parts; vehicle registration and vehicle excise offences; failure to display goods vehicle plates; stopping on the verge or hard shoulder of a motorway; contravention of certain traffic directions (eg 'give way', 'no entry', 'no U turn', 'one-way' signs and temporary traffic signs); obstruction; waiting and parking offences; lighting and noise offences; offences relating to loads (other than dangerous loads); use of a vehicle without a test certificate; trailer offences; offences peculiar to motor cycles; offences of carrying more than one person on a pedal cycle and of cycling on a footway, and other miscellaneous motoring offences (eg failing to wear a seat belt).

The endorsable fixed penalty offences include those in the Road Vehicles (Construction and Use) Regulations 1986 which are concerned with danger (parts, loads, tyres etc); failure to comply with 'Stop' signs, double white lines, traffic lights, directions of a constable; illegal waiting at pedestrian crossings, overtaking a moving or stationary vehicle at such a crossing and failure to accord precedence, contrary to the 'Zebra', 'Pelican' and 'Puffin' regulations; speeding; stopping or reversing on the carriageway of a motorway; driving on a hard shoulder or central reservation; driving on a motorway by a provisional licence holder; use of offside lane of three-lane motorway by a large goods vehicle or passenger-carrying vehicle; breaches of conditions of provisional licences; use etc of a vehicle without insurance; failure to identify the driver; not exhibiting a licence; offences relating to motor cycle passengers; leaving a vehicle in a dangerous position; use of a vehicle in a designated play street; and driving or riding a motor cycle without wearing eye protectors of a prescribed type or using them in contravention of the relevant regulations.

The provisions discussed in this section dealing with fixed penalty offences are contained in the RTOA 1988, unless otherwise indicated.

The issue of a fixed penalty notice for a non-endorsable offence

RTOA 1988, s 54 states that a fixed penalty notice for a non-endorsable offence may be issued where a constable in uniform in England and Wales *finds a person* on any occasion and has reason to believe that on that occasion *he is committing or has committed* a fixed penalty offence. A fixed penalty notice for these offences must be issued at the time or immediately after an offence is committed. It cannot be issued where inquiries are necessary to trace the driver of a vehicle. For example, a driver seen to commit an offence by failing to give way at a junction controlled by a 'give way' sign may at the time or immediately afterwards be given a fixed penalty notice for that offence. If it is not possible to stop him at the time, and he is seen at home after a 'trace' through record systems, such a notice may not be issued to him under RTOA 1988, s 54 since he is not found on *that occasion* to be committing etc an offence. In such a case the conditional offer of a fixed penalty procedure (p 474) will have to be used or a prosecution will have to be instituted.

RTOA 1988, s 62(1) provides that where on any occasion a constable has reason to believe that a fixed penalty offence is being or has been committed in respect of a stationary vehicle, he may affix a fixed penalty notice in respect of the offence to that vehicle unless the offence appears to him to involve obligatory endorsement.

Only one fixed penalty notice may be issued on any one occasion. If more than one offence is committed on a particular occasion a constable should either issue a fixed penalty notice for one offence and administer a verbal warning in respect of all other offences, or report the offender in the normal way for all offences committed. However, this will not apply when offences are subsequently detected, as would occur when documents which were subsequently produced were found to be defective in some respect. These offences, subsequently detected, will be dealt with by the officer reporting the offender with a view to proceedings by way of a summons even though a fixed penalty notice has been issued for the original offence.

The issue of fixed penalty notices for non-endorsable offences by *traffic wardens* is restricted to those offences described in the Functions of Traffic Wardens Order 1970. The Schedule to the order provides that traffic wardens may be employed to enforce the law with respect to:

(a) offences of parking without obligatory lights or reflectors during the hours of darkness;
(b) offences of vehicles obstructing a road, or waiting or being left or parked, or being loaded or unloaded, on a road or public place;
(c) offences against the Vehicles Excise and Registration Act 1994 (eg no vehicle excise licence);
(d) offences relating to parking places on highways where charges are made (eg by meters or machines); or
(e) offences committed by causing a vehicle, or any part of it, to stop in contravention of the pedestrian crossing regulations.

RTOA 1988, s 86 permits the Secretary of State, by order, to permit the use of traffic wardens to deal with fixed penalty offences which involve obligatory endorsement where the vehicle concerned is stationary. At the time of writing, an order has been made adding the offences of vehicle obstruction and leaving a vehicle in a dangerous position.

Fixed penalty notices should not be given to juveniles as there are other recommended procedures for dealing with juveniles which recognise all the circumstances of each case.

The issue of a fixed penalty notice for an endorsable offence

RTOA 1988, s 54 states that, *subject to the provisions described below*, a fixed penalty notice for an endorsable offence may be issued where a constable in England and Wales finds a person on any occasion and has reason to believe that on that occasion *he is committing or has committed* a fixed penalty offence. As with a fixed penalty notice in respect of a non-endorsable offence, the notice under RTOA 1988, s 54 must be issued at the time of, or immediately after, the offence. If it is not so issued the conditional offer of a fixed penalty procedure (p 474) will have to be instituted.

Where it appears to a constable that the fixed penalty offence involves obligatory endorsement, he may only give the offender a fixed penalty notice in respect of the offence if:

(a) the offender produces his driving licence for inspection by the constable;
(b) the constable is satisfied on inspecting the licence that the offender would not be liable to be disqualified because the total number of penalty points would number 12 or more if he was convicted of the fixed penalty offence; and
(c) the offender surrenders his driving licence to the constable to be retained and dealt with in accordance with the Act.

In determining for such purposes whether a person convicted of an offence would be liable to disqualification it must be assumed, where the offence carries a range of penalty points, that the points to be attributed to the offence would be the lowest in the range.

The issue of a fixed penalty notice for an endorsable offence (or a non-endorsable offence) is a matter for the police officer's discretion so far as this is permitted by force policy. Within the limits of such policy, a constable may decide to give a verbal warning for the offence; issue a fixed penalty notice provided that existing penalty points permit such a course of action; or report the offender with a view to proceedings by way of summons (requisition when the relevant provision is in force).

When considering whether to deal with the offence by way of fixed penalty, and before he asks to see the offender's driving licence, the officer must ensure that the offender is aware of the implications of such a procedure and it is suggested that he uses a form of words which convey the following message:

'I am considering the issue to you of a fixed penalty notice for the offence of . . . It will be necessary for me to examine your driving licence and any penalty points which may be endorsed on it. If after examination I find that it is appropriate to issue you with a fixed penalty notice it will be necessary to surrender your licence to me.'

It is essential that, whatever form of words is used, the offender is not given the impression that he must permit the examination of penalty points endorsed on his licence or that he must surrender it. The Act does not extend the powers of a constable in relation to matters which may be examined in a driving licence, nor does it provide a power to seize a driving licence.

When licence produced at time

If the driver is able to produce his licence, and does so, and provided that the number of penalty points is not such that the driver will be liable to disqualification if points for the fixed penalty offence are added, the constable may issue a full fixed penalty notice. When the constable has examined the driving licence and is satisfied that he is able to issue a fixed penalty notice, because the addition of penalty points for the offence will not combine to a total of 12 or more, he should invite the driver to surrender his driving licence. Again, care must be taken in the choice of words. An officer might say:

'Your licence indicates that you may have this offence dealt with by fixed penalty notice. Are you willing to surrender your licence to me? You will be given a receipt.'

Part 3 of the fixed penalty notice gives advice on the procedure to be followed if the offender wishes to request a court hearing. If a driver contests the issue of a fixed penalty notice, his attention should be drawn to this part of the notice. Police officers completing fixed penalty notices should, wherever possible, obtain the full postcode as well as the address of the offender, as this assists the justices' clerk in relation to the registration of subsequent penalties with the offender's home court.

RTOA 1988, s 56 requires a constable or authorised person to give a receipt for a driving licence so surrendered. The receipt which is given by the officer is incorporated in the fixed penalty notice. Such a receipt is valid for two months from the date of issue (or such longer period as may be prescribed). However, a fixed penalty clerk may issue a new receipt on the application of the licence holder which will expire on such date as may be specified in the new receipt. In any event, a receipt ceases to have effect on the return of the licence to the holder. The section allows the receipt to be produced in place of a licence, subject to the same conditions concerning later production, on a request being made by a constable under RTA 1988, s 164, provided that, *if required to do so*, the licence holder subsequently produces his driving licence at the specified police station immediately it is returned.

When licence not produced at time

The procedure to be followed when an offender does not produce his driving licence at the time of the offence is dealt with by RTOA 1988, s 54(4). In any case where:

(a) the offence appears to the constable to be an offence involving obligatory endorsement; and
(b) the person concerned does not produce his licence for inspection by the constable,

the constable may give him a notice stating that if, within seven days after the notice is given, he produces the notice together with his driving licence in person to an authorised person at the police station specified in the notice (being a police station chosen by the person concerned) and the requirements of RTOA 1988, s 54(5) (set out below) are met he will then be given a fixed penalty notice in respect of the offence. An 'authorised person' is a person at a police station authorised for this purpose by a chief officer of police including the British Transport Police.

These provisions allow a constable to issue a 'provisional fixed penalty notice' in circumstances in which a driver does not produce his licence at the time of the offence. It would be unfair if there was not a procedure within which drivers who were not in possession of their driving licence at the time of the offence could not take advantage of an opportunity to pay a fixed penalty in preference to court proceedings.

RTOA 1988, s 54(5) allows a person to whom a provisional fixed penalty notice has been given to produce the notice together with his driving licence *in person* to an authorised person at the police station specified in the notice within seven days. If he does so and the authorised person is satisfied concerning the issue of accumulated penalty points and such person surrenders his driving licence to be retained and dealt with in accordance with the Act, the authorised person *must* give him a fixed penalty notice in respect of the offence.

It must be stressed that these provisions are concerned with extending the fixed penalty provisions to those drivers who are not in possession of their licence at the time of their offence. No offence is committed if the offender fails to produce his driving licence as a result of an offer made under RTOA 1988, s 54(4).

If the constable dealing with such an offender decides that he wishes to examine his driving licence for some reason other than substantiation of a provisional fixed penalty notice, or assessing penalty points on the spot, he must make a requirement under RTA 1988, s 164 and should make it clear that there is a quite separate demand for production to permit examination of those matters prescribed by RTA 1988, s 164(1), matters which are unconcerned with the issue of penalty points. If, in such a case, an offender fails to produce his licence under the provisions of the RTOA 1988, or on production it is found that his penalty points are such that the issue of disqualification arises, he will be prosecuted for the offence in the normal way and the provisional fixed penalty notice is of no further effect.

The form HO/RT 2 has been amended to deal with the production of driving licences consequent upon the issue of provisional fixed penalty notices and the production of driving licence receipts. When HO/RT 2 forms are made out specifically in connection with a provisional fixed penalty notice, the number of the notice should be included on the HO/RT 2.

Endorsements of licences without hearing

RTOA 1988, s 57 authorises the endorsement by the fixed penalty clerk (without any order of a court) of a driving licence surrendered by a person when he was given a fixed penalty notice under RTOA 1988, s 54. A licence may not be endorsed if a request for a hearing has been received before the end of the suspended enforcement period.

Licences so surrendered will be endorsed either at the time at which the fixed penalty is paid, if this occurs before the end of the suspended enforcement period, or, if it does not, when the fixed penalty plus one half of that penalty has been registered for enforcement as a fine. The number of penalty points to be endorsed on a licence for a fixed penalty offence may be particularly specified in the RTOA 1988, Sch 2 but where only a range of numbers is shown, it must be the lowest of those numbers. The Secretary of State may by order prescribe the number of penalty points to be awarded for offences. Such an order may provide different penalty points depending on the circumstances, including the nature of the contravention, its seriousness, where it occurred and whether the offender appears to have committed any offence or offences of a description specified in such order during a specified period.

RTOA, s 57A prospectively provides that where a fixed penalty notice is given to a person who is not the holder of a driving licence in respect of an offence involving obligatory endorsement, the Secretary of State may endorse the person's driving record accordingly.

RTOA 1988, s 83 deals with the case where a fixed penalty clerk is deceived into endorsing a licence in circumstances in which the licence holder should have been disqualified under the totting-up procedure and the deception constituted, or was due to, an offence committed by the licence holder. It provides that if the licence holder is convicted of that offence, the court before which he is convicted will have the same powers to disqualify as it would have had if it was convicting him of the endorsable offence.

Provisions related to fixed penalty offences generally

No proceedings may be brought for an offence to which a fixed penalty notice relates until twenty-one days following the day of the notice (or such longer period as may be specified in the notice). This period of time is referred to as the suspended enforcement period.

Where a fixed penalty notice has been given to an offender, no proceedings shall be brought unless that person has given notice requesting a hearing before the end of the suspended enforcement period. If no such notice has been received and the fixed penalty has not been paid before the end of the suspended enforcement period, a sum equal to the fixed penalty plus one half of that amount may be registered against that person as a fine.

In cases in which a fixed penalty notice is affixed to a vehicle and the fixed penalty has not been paid within the suspended enforcement period, *a notice to owner* may be served by or on behalf of the chief officer of police on *any person who appears to him* to be the owner of the vehicle (or a person authorised to act on such person's behalf). Such a notice must give particulars of the offence in question, of the fixed penalty concerned and of the period allowed for response to the notice. It must also indicate that, if the fixed penalty is not paid before the end of that period, the person on whom the notice is served must furnish, before the end of that period, a statutory statement of ownership. The period allowed for response to such a notice is defined by RTOA 1988, s 63(5) as twenty-one days from the service of the notice. However, a notice need not be served when a request for a hearing has been made with an admission by the person making the request that he was the driver of the vehicle on that occasion. If a person on whom a notice has been served by or on behalf of a chief officer of police was not the owner of the vehicle at the relevant time, and he furnishes in time a statutory statement to the effect that he was not the owner, he is not liable for the offence in question. Otherwise, where a notice is served within six months of the commission of that offence and the fixed penalty has not been paid within the period allowed, a sum equal to the fixed penalty, plus one half of that penalty, may be registered against the person on whom the notice to owner was served as a fine.

Where person receiving was not the driver

RTOA 1988 recognises that there will be occasions upon which the person who receives a notice to owner, in his capacity as such, will not have been the driver at the relevant time. RTOA 1988, s 63 therefore requires that the notice must indicate that the person on whom it is served may, before the end of the period permitted for response, either request a hearing or, if the person driving at the time wishes to give notice requesting a hearing, furnish, together with a statutory statement of ownership, a statutory statement of facts which has the effect of the actual driver requesting a hearing. (If such a driver is prepared to accept responsibility for the fixed penalty it is implied that he will do so by paying the penalty on behalf of the person to whom the notice is addressed.) Once a statutory statement of facts has been supplied, the person named in the notice to owner is relieved of further responsibility and any sums due by way of fixed penalty may not be registered for enforcement. Once a fixed penalty has been registered for enforcement as a fine against a person on whom a notice to owner has been served, however, no proceedings can be brought against any other person in respect of that offence.

Special provisions are applied to hire vehicles by RTOA 1988, s 66. For these purposes a hire vehicle is one which is hired for temporary use, as opposed to a vehicle on hire purchase. In such cases, provided a form of agreement has been drawn up between the hire firm and the hirer under the Road Traffic (Owner Liability) Regulations 2000 and provided the hire firm produces a copy of this to the police (together with a statement of hirer liability signed by the hirer under that hiring agreement), liability is removed from the hire firm; and the hirer of the vehicle becomes its owner for the purpose of the fixed penalty provisions.

Payment of penalties

Fixed penalties must be paid to a justices' clerk in a manner specified within the notice and the money must be dealt with as if it was a fine imposed on summary conviction. Payment may be made by way of a properly addressed, pre-paid letter. The payment is regarded as having been made at the time that the letter would be delivered in the course of normal post. In any proceedings a certificate from a fixed penalty clerk is admissible to prove that a fixed penalty was or was not received by a date specified in the certificate, or that a letter was marked as posted on a date so specified. If a fixed penalty is paid before the end of the suspended enforcement period, no further proceedings may be brought.

The fixed penalty to be paid in respect of an offence is such amount as the Secretary of State may by order prescribe, or one half of the maximum amount of the fine to which the person committing the offence would be liable on summary conviction, whichever is the less. RTOA 1988, s 53, as amended at the time of writing by the Domestic Violence, Crime and Victims Act 2004, s 16, permits the Secretary of State to prescribe graduated amounts in respect of penalties, taking into account the nature of an offence, its severity, the place at which it occurred and whether the offender appears to have committed any other prescribed offences within a prescribed period. The RSA 2006 provides that an order by the Secretary of State may provide for the fixed penalty for an offence to be different depending on the circumstances. The amounts prescribed by the Secretary of State are currently contained in the Fixed Penalty Order 2000. Under that Order the penalty for use etc of a motor vehicle without insurance is fixed at £200; for failure to identify a driver £120; and for offences involving obligatory endorsement £60. Where the offence is a non-endorsable offence the penalty is normally £30. However, where the non-endorsable offence consists of a fixed penalty parking offence committed in Greater London the penalty is £60 if it is committed on a red route, or £40 if it is committed otherwise than on a red route. The fixed penalty for use without a MOT certificate or for not exhibiting a licence is £60.

The term *fixed penalty parking offence* means:

(a) an offence under the Road Traffic Regulation Act 1984 which does not involve obligatory endorsement and is committed in respect of a stationary vehicle; and
(b) road obstruction offences under a variety of statutory provisions.

A 'red route' means a length of road on which there are traffic signs bearing the words 'red route' or red lines or marks.

Penalty registered against person who has no knowledge of the offence

Within such procedures it is obvious that there will be occasions when a penalty is registered against a person who, for some reason, has no knowledge of the offence. This may occur when fixed penalty notices are affixed to vehicles which have changed ownership without DVLA records being amended, or where a driver of someone else's vehicle does not inform the owner of the notice. RTOA 1988, s 72 therefore provides a procedure whereby registration may be declared void. If registration has followed non-receipt of a request for a hearing and the fixed penalty has not been paid, a statutory declaration may be made to the effect that the declarant was not the person to whom the fixed penalty notice was given or that he had requested a hearing before the end of the suspended enforcement period. Where the registration has followed service of 'notice to owner' on the owner of the vehicle in question, and the penalty has not been paid, the statutory declaration must state either that:

(a) the declarant did not know of the penalty, or fixed penalty notice, or notice to owner, until he received notice of the registration; or

(b) he was not the owner at the time of the offence alleged and that he has reasonable excuse for failing to comply with the notice to owner; or

(c) he requested a hearing as permitted by the notice to owner.

A declaration must be served on the proper officer of the relevant court, within twenty-one days of the receipt of the notification of registration. The effect of the declaration is that the relevant notice, registration or endorsement (as the case may be) is void.

Miscellaneous points

RTOA 1988, s 30 requires that, if a person is convicted of an offence involving endorsement and the court is satisfied that he is liable to have penalty points endorsed upon his licence within the fixed penalty procedure for an offence committed on the same occasion as those for which he is convicted, the court must reduce the number of penalty points endorsed on the licence by the number which will be attached in consequence of the fixed penalty offence.

It is an offence contrary to RTOA 1988, s 62(2) to remove or interfere with a notice affixed to a vehicle under s 62(1) unless it is done by or under the authority of the driver or person in charge of the vehicle or the person liable for the offence in question.

It is an offence by RTOA 1988, s 67 recklessly to furnish a statement which is false in a material particular, in response to a notice to owner issued under RTOA 1988, s 63, or to furnish such a statement knowing it to be false in that particular.

Financial penalty deposits

RSA 2006, s 11 inserts a new Part 3A into the RTOA 1988. It empowers a constable or vehicle examiner to require the payment of a financial penalty deposit from an offender who does not provide a satisfactory address in the United Kingdom. The offences in respect of which such deposits may be demanded will be prescribed. Thus, a means is provided to secure a deposit where an enforcement officer is not satisfied that a penalty or fine could be enforced in the United Kingdom. Where such a person is subsequently acquitted of the offence by a court, the deposit, with interest, will be returned to the alleged offender, otherwise it will be set against any penalty imposed. Police and vehicle examiners are empowered to prohibit the moving of the vehicle if the deposit is not paid immediately, although written permission may be given to remove it to a specified place. The prohibition will exist until the deposit is paid, or (where the offender has received a fixed penalty notice or conditional offer) the offender has paid the fixed penalty, or the offender is convicted of the offence or informed that he will not be prosecuted for it, or a specified period has elapsed. It is an offence to fail to comply with such a prohibition. These provisions are not yet in force.

Evidence in court proceedings in fixed penalty notice cases

RTOA 1988, s 79 permits the service of a constable's statement of evidence together with a fixed penalty notice or notice to owner. Such a statement will be deemed to have been served for the purposes of the Criminal Justice Act 1967, s 9 (which we referred to on p 234).

RTOA 1988 permits 'statutory statements of ownership or of facts' to be used in evidence. A statutory statement of ownership under the Act is one in which the declarant states whether or not he was the owner of the vehicle at the relevant time. If he was not it will state whether he was ever the owner and, if so, when. A statutory statement of facts is one in which the declarant states that he was not the driver of the vehicle at the relevant time and states the name and address of the person who was.

Conditional offer of fixed penalty

RTOA 1988, s 75 provides as follows. Where a constable has reason to believe that a fixed penalty offence has been committed and no fixed penalty notice has been given at the time or fixed to the vehicle concerned, a notice of 'conditional offer' may be sent to the alleged offender by, or on behalf of, the chief officer of police including the British Transport Police. A conditional offer must:

(a) give particulars of the circumstances and give reasonable information about the alleged offence;
(b) state the amount of the fixed penalty; and
(c) state that proceedings cannot be commenced for the offence until the end of twenty-eight days following the date of issue of the conditional offer (or such longer period as may be specified in it).

A conditional offer must indicate that if:

(a) within that period, the alleged offender pays the fixed penalty to the fixed penalty clerk, and, where the offence concerned involves obligatory endorsement, at the same time delivers his licence (and its counterpart) to the clerk; and
(b) where his licence and counterpart are delivered, the clerk is satisfied that, if the alleged offender was convicted, he would not be liable to disqualification under RTOA 1988, s 35 (disqualification for repeated offences),

liability to conviction will be discharged. In assessing liability to such disqualification, it is assumed (where penalty points awardable for the offence are within a range) that the number to be attributed for the offence would be the lowest in the range.

A person issuing a conditional offer must notify the fixed penalty clerk. If payment is made in accordance with the offer and the licence is delivered, no proceedings will be taken for the offence to which the conditional offer relates. The fixed penalty clerk must endorse the counterpart of the licence in appropriate cases and return it to the holder. Where the payment of a fixed penalty is made by means of a cheque which is subsequently dishonoured, the endorsement remains valid, even though the licence holder is then liable to prosecution for the offence. In such circumstances the fixed penalty clerk must, on the expiry of the period specified in the conditional offer, or (if that period has expired) forthwith, notify the person by whom the conditional offer was made that no payment has been made. Where proceedings are brought against a licence holder after he has been notified that a cheque tendered in payment has been dishonoured, the court must order the removal of the fixed penalty endorsement from the licence (or counterpart) and may make any competent order of endorsement or disqualification, in addition to sentence.

In consequence of the Secretary of State's power to order increased fixed penalty charges where an offender has, within a period of three years preceding the alleged offence, been disqualified from driving or had penalty points endorsed on any counterpart to any licence held by him, the Secretary of State has been authorised to provide by regulations for the payment of an increased charge in respect of a conditional offer, where it is subsequently revealed that either of those conditions exists.

The fixed penalty clerk must notify the Secretary of State of any endorsement made on the licence in accordance with these procedures.

Special provisions for dealing with offences by way of fixed penalty

The Road Traffic (Vehicle Emissions) (Fixed Penalty) (England) Regulations 2002 (2003 in Wales) make provision for specified local authorities to authorise persons to issue fixed penalty notices to users of vehicles within their areas who contravene, or fail to comply with, reg 61 (emission of oil, smoke, vapour, gases, oily substances etc) or reg 98 (stopping of engine when vehicle stationary) of the Road Vehicles (Construction and Use) Regulations 1986.

PARKING BY DISABLED DRIVERS

The Chronically Sick and Disabled Persons Act 1970 (CSDPA 1970), s 21 requires that a badge of the prescribed form be issued by authorities in England, Wales and Scotland for motor vehicles driven by, or used for the carriage of, disabled persons resident within their areas. TMA 2004, s 94 amended CSADPA 1971, s 21 to provide for the production of badges for inspection by enforcement officers (traffic wardens, civil enforcement officers and parking attendants).

A badge so issued may be displayed on a vehicle either inside or outside the area of the issuing authority, and exemptions afforded to such persons apply anywhere.

Badges may also be issued to institutions concerned with the care of the disabled.

Sections 21A to 21C of the CSDPA 1970 (added by the Disability Discrimination Act 2005 and not in force in Wales at the time of writing) sets out a system for the same recognition as that given to vehicles displaying a disabled person's badge to be given in England and Wales to badges issued under equivalent provisions in Northern Ireland or under corresponding provisions in those foreign jurisdictions set out in regulations. At the time of writing no such regulations have been made.

The Local Authorities' Traffic Orders (Exemptions for Disabled Persons) (England) Regulations 2000 and the Local Authorities' Traffic Orders (Exemptions for Disabled Persons) (Wales) Regulations 2000 contain a requirement that, except in respect of certain areas in central London, all no waiting orders etc made by local authorities must contain exemptions in favour of a vehicle displaying a disabled person's badge. The exemptions in favour of a disabled persons' vehicle are in respect of orders prohibiting vehicles waiting beyond a specified period of time, of orders prohibiting waiting for vehicles at all times of day or during specified periods of the day (whether in relation to some types or all vehicles), of orders prescribing charges and time limit restrictions at parking meters. The only restriction which may apply to disabled persons' vehicles is that, where there is a prohibition on waiting for a period of more than three hours, a vehicle displaying a disabled person's badge is exempt for a maximum of three hours (and must not return to the same road for an hour), and is only so exempt if a parking disc is displayed showing the time of arrival (disc parking scheme). However, the requirement to include an exemption does not apply to orders which prohibit the waiting of vehicles of all other classes.

Regulation 11 prescribes the forms of the badges to be issued and the Schedules to the regulations show the contents and various forms of badges. The background on the front and reverse sides of the badge is coloured light blue and includes a background of wheelchair symbols. The square box which contains the wheelchair symbol and the rectangular box containing the country identifier are coloured dark blue. All other boxes contained within the badge are coloured white. Those badges issued under the previous Disabled Persons (Badges for Motor Vehicles) Regulations 1982 will comply with the requirements of the 2000 Regulations and will contain similar information but will be coloured orange. These badges retain their validity until expiry.

Regulation 12 of the Disabled Persons (Badges for Motor Vehicles) (England) Regulations 2000 requires that a disabled person's badge be exhibited on the dashboard or facia of the vehicle, or where the vehicle is not fitted with a dashboard or facia, the badge is exhibited in a conspicuous position, in either case, so that the front of the badge is clearly legible from outside the vehicle. Similar provisions are made by the Local Authorities' Traffic Orders (Exemption for Disabled Persons) (England) Regulations 2000 for the display of parking discs, so that the quarter-hour period during which the period of waiting begins is legible from outside the vehicle.

Regulation 13 of the Disabled Persons (Badges for Motor Vehicles) (England) Regulations 2000 sets out the circumstances in which an individual's disabled person's badge may be displayed while the vehicle is being *driven*. These are:

(a) the holder is either driving or being carried in the vehicle; or
(b) if the vehicle is being used solely to collect the holder; or
(c) if the vehicle is leaving the place where the holder has got out.

For (b) and (c) to apply, it is necessary that a disabled person's concession (other than one relating to parking) would be available to a vehicle displaying such a badge; and it would not have been practicable for the vehicle to be lawfully driven to, or to stop at, or to have left the place where the holder is collected.

By reg 14 of the Disabled Persons (Badges for Motor Vehicles) (England) Regulations 2000 the circumstances in which an individual's disabled person's badge may be displayed while the vehicle is *parked* are:

(a) if it has been driven by the holder, or has been used to carry him, to the place where he is parked; or
(b) if it is to be driven by the holder, or is to be used to carry him, from that place.

A disabled person's vehicle must therefore be displaying a badge, and for that badge to be lawfully displayed, the relevant conditions set out above must apply. The Regulations provide that badges issued in Scotland and Wales are valid in England.

CSDPA 1970, s 21 makes it an offence for a person to drive a motor vehicle which is displaying badge purporting to be in a form prescribed under s 21 otherwise than in a manner or in circumstances prescribed by the Regulations.

The Traffic Management Act 2004 inserted new subsections (4BA), (4BB), (4BC) and (4BD) into s 21 of the 1970 Act which make provision for the inspection of badges. Section 21 provides where it appears to a constable or enforcement officer that there is displayed on any motor vehicle a badge purporting to be of a form prescribed under s 21 he may require any person who:

(a) is in the vehicle, or
(b) appears to have been in, or to be about to get into, the vehicle,

to produce the badge for inspection.

The term 'enforcement officer' is defined by s 21(4BB) as meaning:

(a) a traffic warden;
(b) a civil enforcement officer (within the meaning of s 74 of TMA 2004);
(c) a parking attendant (within the meaning of s 63A of RTRA 1984).

By s 21(4BC), the power conferred on an enforcement officer by s 21(4BA) is exercisable only for purposes connected with the discharge of his functions in relation to a stationary vehicle.

A person who, without reasonable excuse, fails to produce a badge when required to do so under subsection (4BA) is guilty of an offence against s 21(4BD).

The existing s 21(4C) which deals with penalties is extended to include the penalty for an offence against the new subsection (4BD).

The Order also amends RTRA 1984, s 117 (wrongful use of a disabled person's badge) so that in subsection (1)(a) after 'badge' the words 'purporting to be' are inserted.

TMA 2004 authorises a local authority to employ civil enforcement officers for the enforcement of road traffic contraventions for which it is the enforcement authority. Such an officer must be employed by the local authority or, where the authority has made arrangements with any person for the purposes of the section, an individual employed by that person to act as a civil enforcement officer. When exercising specified functions a civil enforcement officer must wear uniform. It also provides that a parking attendant appointed by a local authority, which is an enforcement authority under RTRA 1984, s 63A, is a civil enforcement officer in relation to parking contraventions for which the authority is the enforcement authority and such a person may also be appointed a civil enforcement officer in relation to other road traffic contraventions for which that authority is the enforcement authority. This provision is not yet in force.

The Disabled Persons (Badges for Motor Vehicles) (Wales) Regulations 2000 make similar provision in Wales and the offences which can be committed are identical.

The badge scheme does not permit parking:

(a) during the time a ban on loading or unloading is in force (indicated by one, two or three yellow marks on a kerb, at a time shown on a post-mounted plate);

(b) where there is a double white line in the centre of the road even if one of the lines is broken;

(c) in a bus or cycle lane when it is in use;

(d) on Zebra or Pelican crossings or on the zig-zag markings before or after these crossings;

(e) in parking places reserved for specific users, eg loading bays, residents, taxis or cycles; and

(f) in suspended meter bays or when the use of the meter is prohibited.

The Road Traffic Regulation Act 1984, s 117 deals with the wrongful use of a disabled person's badge. It provides that a person is guilty of an offence if, when he commits some other offence under the Act (eg contravention of an order relating to parking made under it), the following conditions are satisfied:

(a) there was displayed on the motor vehicle a badge of a prescribed form;

(b) he was using the vehicle in circumstances where a disabled person's concession would be available to a disabled person's vehicle,

but he is not guilty of an offence under s 117 if the badge was properly issued and displayed.

RESTRICTIONS ON THE USE OF MOTORWAYS

The Motorways Traffic (England and Wales) Regulations 1982 impose various restrictions upon the drivers of motor vehicles on motorways. Contravention of the Regulations is an offence. The Regulations limit the classes of vehicles which are permitted to use motorways.

Vehicles which may use motorways

Under the 1982 Regulations, Class I and Class II vehicles are, in normal circumstances, permitted to use motorways. Class I includes heavy and light locomotives, motor tractors, heavy motor cars, motor cars and motor cycles of not less than 50 cc and trailers drawn by such vehicles. (These terms are defined in Chapter 10.) Track laying vehicles are not within Class I. To be in Class I vehicles must be fitted with pneumatic tyres, must not be agricultural motor vehicles or machines and must not be pedestrian-controlled. All such vehicles must be capable of attaining a speed of 25 mph when unladen.

Class II vehicles are those specially made to transport abnormal, indivisible loads, and large vehicles (eg tank transporters) used by the armed services. In addition, earth movers and similar engineering plant are Class II vehicles if they are capable of attaining 25 mph when unladen.

Direction of driving

Regulation 6 of the Motorways Traffic (England and Wales) Regulations 1982 requires the observance of 'no entry' and 'no left or right turn' signs. It also requires that vehicles always have the central reservation on their right or offside, and that, if there is no central reservation, they continue to travel in the direction which was permitted on entry to the motorway and that they are not driven or moved so as to cause them to turn and proceed in, or face, the opposite direction.

Stopping

Regulation 7 of the Motorways Traffic (England and Wales) Regulations 1982 requires that no vehicle shall stop or remain at rest on a carriageway of a motorway. When a stop becomes necessary due to breakdown, mechanical defect, lack of fuel, accident, illness or other emergency, or to permit a person carried in the vehicle to recover or move an object which has fallen on to the motorway, or to permit a person to give help to another in any of those circumstances, the vehicle must, as soon and in so far as is reasonably practicable, be driven or moved off the carriageway on to a contiguous hard shoulder where it may stop and remain at rest. Such a vehicle must remain at rest in such a position that, as far as reasonably practicable, no part of it or its load obstructs or causes danger to vehicles using the carriageway. It must not remain for longer than necessary for such purpose.

The regulation makes the obvious exception in favour of drivers prevented from proceeding by 'traffic jams'. It also provides for stopping to pay motorway tolls.

Reversing

The driving or moving of a vehicle backwards is prohibited by reg 8 of the 1982 Regulations, unless it is necessary to do so to allow it to move forward or be connected to another vehicle.

General use

Regulations 9 and 10 of the Motorways Traffic (England and Wales) Regulations 1982 prohibit driving, stopping or remaining at rest on a hard shoulder (in circumstances other than those permitted) or on a central reservation. Regulation 11 prohibits the driving of motor vehicles on motorways by persons who are authorised to drive the vehicle which they are driving only by virtue of being the holder of a provisional licence. The regulation applies to:

(a) a motor vehicle in category A or B or sub-category C1 + E (8.25 tonnes), D1 (not for hire or reward), D1 + E (not for hire or reward), or P; and

(b) a motor vehicle in category B + E or sub-category C1 if the provisional licence authorising the driving of such a motor vehicle was in force at a time before 1 January 1997.

The Motor Vehicles (Driving Licences) Regulations 1999 provide for separate driving tests for motor cars with trailers (category B + E), trucks and vans of between 3.5 tonnes and 7.5 tonnes maximum authorised mass (sub-categories C1 and C1 + E) and for buses having more than eight but not more than sixteen passenger seats in addition to the driver's seat whether or not they carry passengers for hire or reward (sub-categories D1 and D1 + E). Provisional licences to drive such vehicles may only be issued to persons holding at least a full licence to drive motorcars (category B). Such holders of provisional licences are authorised to drive on motorways while holding provisional licences (as they are full licence holders in respect of category B).

It is an offence, contrary to the Road Traffic Regulation Act 1984, s 17(4), to walk on a motorway except when it is necessary to do so as a result of an accident or emergency, or as a result of a motor vehicle being at rest on a motorway in such circumstances or as a result of illness, or to assist in an emergency.

Regulation 14 provides that the person in charge of an animal shall, so far as is practicable, ensure that it is not removed from or permitted to leave the vehicle while on a motorway. If it escapes or it is necessary for it to be removed from or permitted to leave the vehicle, it must not go on or remain on any part of a motorway other than a hard shoulder, where it must be held on a lead or otherwise kept under proper control.

Use of right or offside lane

Regulation 12 of the Motorways Traffic (England and Wales) Regulations 1982 prohibits the following vehicles from using the offside lane of a three-lane motorway at any place where all three lanes are open to traffic:

(a) a goods vehicle which has a maximum laden weight exceeding 7.5 tonnes;

(b) a goods vehicle having a maximum laden weight exceeding 3.5 tonnes but not exceeding 7.5 tonnes to which reg 36B of the Road Vehicles (Construction and Use) Regulations 1986 applies (speed limiters) or would apply but for para (14)(a) or (b) of that regulation;

(c) a passenger vehicle which is constructed or adapted to carry more than eight seated passengers in addition to the driver, the maximum laden weight of which exceeds 7.5 tonnes;

(d) a passenger vehicle which is constructed or adapted to carry more than eight seated passengers in addition to the driver, the maximum laden weight of which does not exceed 7.5 tonnes to which reg 36A of the Road Vehicles (Construction and Use) Regulations 1986 applies (speed limiters) or would apply but for para 13(a) or (b) of that regulation;

(e) a motor vehicle drawing a trailer; and

(f) a motor vehicle which is a motor tractor or a locomotive.

The only occasion upon which such vehicles may enter the offside lane of a three-lane motorway, when all lanes are open, is when this is necessary to overtake a wide load.

However, where the number of lanes in a carriageway increases from two to three or more, for example, where motorways merge, a vehicle which is travelling in the outer lane may remain there until it is safe to move into the middle lane, or until such time as a change can be made without causing inconvenience to other traffic.

Exceptions and relaxations of effect of regulations

Regulation 15 of the Motorways Traffic (England and Wales) Regulations 1982 provides for vehicles other than those within Classes I and II to be permitted to use motorways in emergencies and certain other cases. There are occasions upon which vehicles which would normally be banned must be present to carry out maintenance work or repairs etc. This is permitted by reg 15. In addition, the Secretary of State may authorise limited use to allow excluded traffic access on occasions or in an emergency or to enable it to cross a motorway to gain access to premises abutting on or adjacent to a motorway. Lastly, a chief officer of police (or a superintendent acting on his behalf) may authorise usage by excluded traffic for a period of time during which the use of an alternative road is rendered impossible or unsuitable. The regulation also permits pedestrian use where this is authorised by a constable or appointed person to enable tolls to be paid.

Regulation 16 permits the use of a motorway otherwise than in accordance with the Regulations, upon the direction of a constable or traffic officer in uniform or as a member of the Serious Organised Crime Agency for the purposes of that Agency or in compliance with a traffic sign; with the permission of a constable or traffic officer for the purpose of the investigation of an accident; where necessary to prevent an accident or give help as a result of an accident or emergency; where the act is done in exercise of the duty of a constable, traffic officer, or member of a fire and rescue authority or of an ambulance service; or where necessary in connection with motorway maintenance or the removal of vehicles. These provisions have also been extended to permit permission to be given in relation to the payment of a toll.

Regulations 15 and 16 therefore provide the essential exceptions to the rules to permit maintenance, life saving and action by the emergency services.

CHAPTER 12
Public service vehicles

The Public Passenger Vehicles Act 1981 (PPVA 1981) consolidated the provisions of all previous Acts dealing with public service vehicles. Regulations have been made under the Act and regulations made under the previous legislation continue in force. It is essential that persons who offer bus or coach services to the general public maintain high standards and therefore provision for the licensing and control of the vehicles used is made by the Act and the regulations. Such vehicles must be correctly constructed, equipped and maintained to ensure the safety of the travelling public. Those who use the vehicles—drivers, conductors and passengers—must also comply with prescribed standards.

The Road Traffic Act 1988 (RTA 1988), s 193A makes special provisions in relation to tramcars which are not subject to the general provisions in respect of public service vehicles. Local regulations will be in force where tramcars are used within specific areas.

DEFINITION: PUBLIC SERVICE VEHICLE

PPVA 1981, s 1(1) defines a public service vehicle as a motor vehicle (other than a tramcar) which:

(a) if adapted to carry more than eight passengers, is used for carrying passengers for hire or reward; or
(b) if not so adapted, is used for carrying passengers for hire or reward at separate fares in the course of a business of carrying passengers.

There are, therefore, two types of public service vehicles (PSV). For the purposes of PPVA 1981, s 79A, referred to below, a vehicle within (a) is a 'large bus' and one within (b) is a 'small bus'. However, the definitions of both types contain a number of common elements, and we shall deal with these before giving separate consideration to the two types.

PPVA 1981, s 1(1) states that, to be a public service vehicle, a vehicle must be a *'motor vehicle (other than a tramcar)'*. The term 'motor vehicle' has already been fully discussed in Chapter 9, above, but the reader is reminded that it is defined as 'a mechanically propelled vehicle intended or adapted for use on roads'. Horse-drawn passenger carriages are therefore completely excluded from the legislation relating to public service vehicles.

The definitions of both types of public service vehicle require that the vehicle '*is used for carrying passengers for hire or reward*'. These words require further explanation.

Used

The meaning of this term has already been fully considered in Chapter 10, above, but PPVA 1981, s 1(2) adds that for the purpose of s 1(1) a vehicle is being used for a purpose mentioned in s 1(1)(a) or (b) if it is *being so used or if it has been so used and that use has not been permanently discontinued*. This extends 'use' to circumstances in which the motor vehicle is no longer being used at that moment as a public service vehicle, but it is the owner's intention to use it again. Consequently, a public service vehicle does not cease to be so classified merely because its journey is over; it remains such until permanently used for some other purpose. Persons who convey stock racing cars and dragsters to tracks frequently use modified buses or coaches for this purpose. These vehicles are no longer public service vehicles as their use for the carriage of passengers has been permanently discontinued. On the other hand, a bus or coach which, between service runs, is used by an employee to return to his home on an errand remains a public service vehicle as its use as such has not been permanently discontinued.

Hire or reward

Even though a vehicle may be able to carry fifty or more passengers it is not a public service vehicle unless it is used to carry passengers for hire or reward. Once it is so used, it will become a public service vehicle provided the requirements of one or other of the types of public service vehicle are satisfied. If a person owns a minibus and takes out his family, it is not a public service vehicle as it is not carrying passengers for hire or reward. If he owns a forty-seater coach which he only uses to take out his family and friends, then, provided that he never charges them a fare or the like, there is no carriage for hire or reward and therefore the coach is not a public service vehicle.

The term 'hire or reward' in a general sense means a monetary reward legally due under a contract. (However, as we show below, there are some cases of carriage for hire or reward, even though no contract exists.) Money paid or promised under a purely social arrangement (such as a car-sharing scheme) does not make the carriage for hire or reward. A contract to carry a passenger for hire or reward may be made before a passenger boards the vehicle (as in the case of a coach trip) or it may be made aboard the vehicle (as in the case of a bus journey).

The meaning of 'hire or reward' has been extended by PPVA 1981, s 1(5) as follows:

(a) a vehicle is to be treated as carrying passengers for hire or reward if payment is made for, or for matters which include, the carrying of passengers, irrespective of the person to whom the payment is made and, in the case of a transaction effected by or on behalf of a member of any association of persons (whether incorporated or not) on the one hand and the association or another member thereof on the other hand, notwithstanding any rule of law as to such transactions;

(b) a payment made for the carrying of a passenger is to be treated as a fare notwithstanding that it is made in consideration of other matters in addition to the journey and irrespective of the person by or to whom it is made;

(c) a payment is to be treated as made for the carrying of a passenger if made in consideration of a person being given a right to be carried, whether for one or more journeys and whether or not the right is exercised.

These provisions cover a number of possibilities. Paragraph (a) is concerned with circumstances which might arise in relation to a club or association. The club etc may own a coach and make it available to members for outings on payment by them. It could be argued that, as club members, they all own the coach and cannot, therefore, be using it for hire or reward. Because of (a), this argument will not succeed because (a) clearly states that the vehicle is to be treated as carrying passengers for hire or reward. Paragraph (b) will cover the circumstances of the 'all-in' holiday, where one payment is made to an agent for transport, accommodation, meals and courier service. This includes payment for carriage and such payment is deemed by (b) to be a fare, even though it is made in respect of other matters as well. Finally, (c) states that a payment is to be treated as made for the carriage of a person if it is made in consideration of a person being given a right to be carried, for example the purchase of a ticket, whether that ticket allows one or more journeys and even if the journey is never made.

These provisions are not an exclusive definition of the circumstances in which a vehicle is used for carrying passengers for hire or reward. For example, it has been held that, where there is a systematic carrying of passengers for hire or reward which goes beyond what might be described as 'social kindness', there is a carriage for hire or reward. There is no need to prove a legally binding contract. Thus, it has been held that, where school children are regularly carried to school in a private vehicle on the basis of 'petrol money' being paid, the vehicle is used for carriage for reward because there is a systematic carriage for hire or reward going beyond the bounds of social kindness and amounting to a business activity, whether or not direct demands have been made for payment. Likewise, it has been held that, where hotels regularly operate 'courtesy coaches' to be used free of charge by residents and visitors, there is a carriage for hire or reward as the service relates to the business activities of the hotel and the charges made for a room, or for a meal, can be taken to include such amenities.

The extended meaning of 'hire or reward' in s 1(5) is restricted in one special circumstance by s 1(6) which provides that, where a fare is paid in respect of a journey by air and, due to mechanical failure, bad weather or other circumstances outside the operator's control, part of the journey has to be made by road, no part of the fare is to be treated for the purposes of s 1(5) as paid in consideration of the carriage of passengers by road. Thus, the occasional use of coaches to facilitate air travel in emergencies can be made without those coaches becoming classified as public service vehicles.

We now turn to the separate requirements of the definition of the two types of public service vehicle.

Motor vehicle (other than a tramcar) adapted to carry more than eight passengers and used for carrying passengers for hire or reward

Such a vehicle may range from a minibus to a large luxury coach.

Whether or not a vehicle is 'adapted to carry more than eight passengers' is a question of fact to be decided in the particular circumstances. In the case where four of eleven seats in a minibus had been rendered unusable by being turned upside down and blocked off, a divisional court upheld a decision by magistrates that the vehicle in that state was not adapted to carry more than eight passengers. The term is not concerned with permanence, it is concerned with the situation existing at a particular moment. The words 'more than eight passengers' indicate that it must be adapted for at least nine. The issue of whether or not the driver is included in the nine is not clear. Previous legislation referred to passengers 'other than the driver' but PPVA 1981 makes no separate mention of the driver. Common sense suggests that a driver is not a passenger as he is not a traveller in the true sense. Additionally, the term 'driver' and 'passenger' are separately considered in the PPVA 1981 and in regulations made under its authority. It is noteworthy that parallel EU legislation refers to 'carrying not more than nine persons including the driver'. Until this issue is decided it is better to regard the definition as requiring adaptation to allow the carriage of a minimum of eight passengers plus a driver.

Motor vehicle (other than a tramcar) not adapted to carry more than eight passengers, which is used for carrying passengers for hire or reward at separate fares in the course of a business of carrying passengers

The obvious distinction between a public service vehicle of this type and one of the type just described is that the present type of motor vehicle is one which:

(a) is not adapted to carry '*more than eight passengers*' (a phrase discussed above); but
(b) is used to carry passengers *at separate fares in the course of a business of carrying passengers.*

Two examples of a vehicle not adapted to carry more than eight passengers, which automatically spring to mind, are a family saloon car and a London-type taxi. However, such vehicles will not be classed as public service vehicles unless they are used for carrying passengers for hire or reward at separate fares. Normally, of course, the family saloon car is not used to carry passengers at separate fares, and even if separate payments are made by passengers this will not normally make the car a public service vehicle. One reason is that, if the payments are made under a social arrangement (eg a car-sharing scheme), the passengers are not carried for hire or reward. The use of taxis in circumstances which would otherwise cause them to be classified as public service vehicles is specially provided for by the Transport Act 1985 (TA 1985) (see below).

The term 'separate fares' includes circumstances in which a man hires a vehicle and driver to take a party on a particular outing and then charges each person a separate fare for the journey. If an eight-seater vehicle is hired by one man, who then takes colleagues on the journey with him on payment of separate fares to him, that vehicle becomes a public service vehicle for the purpose of s 1 if the circumstances are outside those permitted by PPVA 1981, s 1(3), which is examined below.

In order for it to be a public service vehicle, the use of the vehicle must be not only to carry passengers for hire or reward at separate fares, but also be '*in the course of a business of carrying passengers.*' This phrase makes doubly certain that the *normal* type of 'car-sharing scheme' does not make the car in question a public service vehicle since such use of the car would not be in the course of a *business* of carrying passengers. This is made clear by PPVA 1981, s 1(4), which provides that a journey made by a vehicle in the course of which one or more passengers are carried at separate fares is not to be treated as made 'in the course of a business of carrying passengers' if:

(a) the fare or aggregate of the fares paid in respect of the journey *does not exceed the running costs* of the vehicle for the journey; and
(b) the arrangements for the payment of the fares by the passenger or passengers so carried were *made before* the journey began,

and for the purposes of (a) the running costs of the vehicle for a journey are taken to include an appropriate amount in respect of depreciation and wear and tear.

Therefore, the use of a vehicle for a car-sharing scheme does not make it a public service vehicle, provided the payments made cover no more than the sharing of the travel and the depreciation and wear and tear of the vehicle and that arrangements for payment of them were made before the journey began. If payments made within such a scheme were considered to go beyond these guidelines, it would be for a court to decide whether the elements of hire or reward and of business usage were present (see p 483).

Use of taxis at separate fares

The TA 1985, ss 10 to 16 make provision for the use of taxis for the carriage of passengers at separate fares in three types of case.

Under conditions prescribed in a scheme

TA 1985, s 10 provides that a licensed taxi may be hired for use for the carriage of passengers for hire or reward at separate fares without thereby becoming a public passenger vehicle if:

(a) the taxi is hired in an area where a scheme made under TA 1985, s 10 is in operation;
(b) the taxi is licensed by the licensing authority for that area; and
(c) the hiring falls within the terms of the scheme.

The licensing authority in London is the Secretary of State (or his nominee) and in other areas of England and Wales it is the authority responsible for licensing taxis. TA 1985 extends the provisions of the Town Police Clauses Act 1847, in respect of the licensing of taxis, to all areas.

The licensing authority is empowered to make a scheme for its area and must make such a scheme if the holders of at least 10% of the current taxi licences require the authority to do so. Such schemes *must* be concerned with the designation of places in the area from which taxis may be hired (authorised places), and should specify the requirements to be met in relation to the hiring at separate fares and other factors from time to time prescribed. They *may* deal with fares, display of documents, plates, marks or signs for indicating an 'authorised place', the manner in which arrangements are to be made for the carriage of passengers or the hiring, and the conditions to be applied to the hiring. For the purposes of s 10, the hiring of a taxi only falls within the terms of a scheme if it is hired from an authorised place and the hiring must meet the licensing authority's requirements. A taxi is hired from an authorised place if it is standing at that place when it is hired and the persons hiring it are all present there.

Shared taxis by arrangement

TA 1985, s 11 provides the second type of case. It states that a licensed taxi *or licensed hire car* may be used for the carriage of passengers for hire or reward at separate fares without these vehicles becoming a public service vehicle provided that the following conditions are satisfied. These are that all the passengers carried on the occasion in question booked their journey in advance and each of them consented, when booking his journey, to sharing the use of the vehicle on that occasion with others, on the basis that a separate fare would be payable by each passenger for his own journey on that occasion.

Taxi with restricted public service vehicle operator's licence

TA 1985, s 12 permits the holder of a taxi licence to apply for a restricted public service vehicle operator's licence. If the holder of the taxi licence states in his application that he proposes to use one or more licensed taxis to provide a local service, the traffic commissioner must grant the application. However, the commissioner *must* attach conditions to the effect that all vehicles used under the restricted licence must have taxi licences and that they shall not be used under the restricted licence otherwise than for providing a local service, although of course it may still be used as a taxi under its separate licence. The term 'local service' does not include an excursion or tour. Such vehicles are not treated as passenger service vehicles in every case. For example, they need not carry operator's discs and the drivers do not require public service vehicle drivers' licences. These restricted licences are referred to as 'special licences'. Vehicles operating under such licences must display a notice 'Bus' to the front plus the destination or route or nature of service, and must carry a fare table.

Circumstances affecting classification as public service vehicles

PPVA 1981, s 1(3) provides that a vehicle carrying passengers at separate fares in the course of a business of carrying passengers, but doing so in circumstances in which one of the following conditions is fulfilled, is to be treated as not being a public service vehicle *unless* it is adapted to carry *more* than eight passengers. The conditions are as follows:

(1) Where the making of the agreement for separate fares was not initiated by the driver or owner of the vehicle, or by any person who receives any remuneration in respect of the arrangements for the journey, *and* the journey is made without

previous, public advertisement of facilities for its being made by passengers to be carried at separate fares (except in the case of journeys, approved by a local authority, made to meet social and welfare needs).

(2) Where the arrangements for bringing together all the passengers were made otherwise than by or on behalf of the holder of the operator's licence under which the vehicle is to be used, or (if there is no such licence) the driver or owner of the vehicle, and otherwise than by any person who receives any remuneration in respect of the arrangements, and the journey is made without previous, public advertisement, and all the passengers are carried for the major part of the journey (allowing for different pick-up and set-down points), and the fares are the same regardless of the distance carried. Thus, a vehicle adapted to carry eight passengers or less is not a public service vehicle in these circumstances, which are exemplified by a group or club outing.

Small buses subject to regulation as private hire vehicles

In general, a 'small bus' (see p 482) cannot be used for private hire work by virtue of its operator having a public service vehicle operator's licence. Instead, it and its operator must be licensed by a local authority under the private hire vehicle licensing system. The only exception is where the small bus is provided in the course of a passenger- carrying business, all but a small part of which involves the operation of large buses (as defined on p 482).

PUBLIC SERVICE VEHICLE OPERATOR'S LICENCE

PPVA 1981, s 12(1) provides that a public service vehicle must not be used on a road for carrying passengers for hire or reward except under a public service vehicle operator's licence. Such a licence is granted by a traffic commissioner. It is granted to a person, rather than a vehicle. The country is divided into traffic areas, each with its own traffic commissioner, and if a person operating public service vehicles has an operating centre in more than one such area he must obtain separate operator's licences from the commissioner for each area. A public service vehicle licence authorises the holder to use vehicles anywhere in Great Britain. A person who uses a vehicle on a road as a public service vehicle without an applicable public service vehicle operator's licence is guilty of an offence, unless he proves that he took all reasonable care and exercised all due diligence to avoid the commission of that offence.

PPVA 1981, s 65 provides that it is an offence for a person with intent to deceive:

(a) to forge, alter or use or lend, or to allow to be used by any other person, such an operator's licence, or

(b) to make or to have in his possession a document or other thing so closely resembling such a document or other thing as to be calculated to deceive.

These offences also apply to licences, certificates of fitness or conformity, or certificates relating to the repute of an applicant, his financial standing or professional competence.

Operator's disc

Where a vehicle is used in circumstances requiring a public service vehicle operator's licence, an operator's disc must be fixed and exhibited on the vehicle adjacent to the vehicle excise licence so that it does not interfere unduly with the driver's view and can easily be read in daylight from outside the vehicle. The disc shows particulars of the operator and of his operator's licence under which the vehicle is being used. When a person is granted an operator's licence, the traffic commissioner will issue him with a number of such discs equal to the number of vehicles which he may use under the licence or a lesser number if the operator so requests. There are various detailed provisions as to the form, custody and production of operators' discs, and as to their replacement if they are lost, destroyed or defaced. If a vehicle is used without the requisite operator's disc in the prescribed form exhibited in the prescribed way, its operator is guilty of an offence unless he proves that he took all reasonable care and exercised all due diligence to avoid the commission of that offence.

Production of licence or disc

If he is required by a police officer or certain other officials to produce a public service vehicle operator's licence or disc for inspection, the holder must do so within fourteen days. It is enough, however, if he produces it at his operating centre, head office or principal place of business within the traffic area to which it relates.

Types of licence

A public service vehicle operator's licence may be either a standard licence or a restricted licence.

A standard licence authorises the use of any description of public service vehicle and may authorise use either:

(a) on both national and international operations; or
(b) on national operations only.

A restricted licence authorises the use (whether on national or international operations) of:

(a) public service vehicles *not adapted to carry more than eight passengers*; and
(b) public service vehicles *not adapted to carry more than sixteen passengers* (ie basically, minibuses) when used:
  (i) otherwise than in the course of a business of carrying passengers; or
  (ii) by a person whose main occupation is not the operation of public service vehicles adapted to carry more than eight passengers.

For the purposes of the above definitions, 'national operations' means transport operations wholly within this country. If an operator who requires a standard licence runs trips abroad as part of his operations, he will require a standard licence for both national and international operations.

If the holder of an operator's licence (eg a restricted one) uses a vehicle for a purpose not authorised by it (eg where a standard national licence would be required) he is guilty of an offence, unless he proves that he took all reasonable care and exercised all due diligence to avoid the commission of that offence.

Conditions attached to a PSV operator's licence

The TA 1985 provides that where it appears to a traffic commissioner, in relation to an operator to whom he has granted or is proposing to grant a public service vehicle operator's licence, that:

(a) the operator has failed to operate a local service registered under TA 1985, s 6 (see below); or
(b) the operator has operated a local service in contravention of that section; or
(c) the arrangements for maintaining the vehicles used under the licence in a fit and serviceable condition are not adequate for the use of those vehicles in providing the local service or services in question; or
(d) that the operator, or an employee or agent of his, has:
   (i)   intentionally interfered with the operation of a local service provided by another operator;
   (ii) operated a local service in a manner dangerous to the public; or
   (iii) been guilty of any other serious misconduct (whether or not constituting a criminal offence) in relation to the operation of a local service; or
(e) a condition attached under TA 1985, s 8 (traffic regulation condition) to the operator's licence has been contravened,

he may attach to the licence either a condition prohibiting the operator from using vehicles under it to provide any local service of a description specified in the condition or one prohibiting him from so using vehicles to provide local services of any description. In the circumstances set out at (a) and (b), above, the imposition of a condition is only possible if the operator did not have a reasonable excuse, or if the condition is appropriate in view of the danger involved to the public in the operator's conduct, or of the frequency of it.

Conditions may be imposed either when a licence is granted or thereafter.

If the traffic commissioner is required to do so by the holder of the operator's licence or the applicant for it, he must hold an inquiry before attaching a condition, except that he may attach a condition at once in an emergency. However, if he does attach a condition in any emergency before holding an inquiry, this must be followed by an inquiry as soon as reasonably practicable, if an inquiry is requested.

Revocation of PSV operator's licence

In circumstances in which a traffic commissioner revokes an operator's licence, he may order the holder to be disqualified indefinitely or for such period as he thinks fit. Such a disqualification may be limited to just one area.

Vehicle examiners' powers to issue fixed penalty notices

Under amendments made by RSA 2006, which are not yet in force vehicle examiners of the Vehicle and Operator Services Agency may issue fixed penalty notices in respect of offences which they are empowered to enforce in relation to passenger-carrying vehicles. Conditional offers under RTOA 1988, s 75 may also be issued.

This system will be operated independently of the police by the Secretary of State who is responsible for administering the system, collecting the penalties and the endorsement of the licences. The Vehicle Operator Service Agency will carry out this function on the Secretary of State's behalf.

When the relevant provisions of the Road Safety Act 2006 are in force, fixed penalty offences will be 'notifiable' in the same way as convictions in relation to the grant, variation, revocation of operator's licences.

Plying for hire by large PSVs

The TA 1985, s 30 prohibits operators from using on a road, in plying for hire, public service vehicles which are adapted to carry more than eight passengers. This provision therefore prevents the use of larger vehicles, by public service vehicle operators, in the manner of hire cars.

Community licences

Council Regulation 684/92/EEC, on common rules for the international carriage of passengers by coach or bus, prohibits the carriage of passengers in public service vehicles between member states without there being a Community licence in force. The Regulation has direct effect in Great Britain and reg 3 of the Public Service Vehicles (Community Licences) Regulations 1999 imposes a penalty for use of a vehicle in breach of the Council Regulation.

The Regulation requires each member state to issue a Community licence to any carrier established within that state who is entitled to carry out international transport operations. In Great Britain, this means operators holding a standard licence authorising both national and international operations, or holding a restricted licence. Such operators will be entitled to a Community licence.

The holder of a Community licence must keep the original, and a certified copy must be kept in each public service vehicle carrying out international transport operations. A Community licence must be produced to an authorised inspecting officer (a vehicle examiner appointed under RTA 1988, s 66A(1) (see p 438) and a police constable) on demand.

Regulation 7 of the PSV (Community Licences) Regulations 1999 makes it an offence to fail, without reasonable excuse, to comply with a condition of a Community licence.

In addition, the Road Transport (Passenger Vehicles Cabotage) Regulations 1999 have been made in consequence of Council Regulation 12/98/EC which lays down conditions under which road passenger transport carriers of member states may operate *cabotage transport operations*. A 'cabotage transport operation is one which involves the collection *and* delivery of passengers within a country other than that in which the operator is licensed'. The Regulations are therefore concerned with operating transport services for hire or reward *in* another member state within which the company has no base. The Regulation requires that cabotage services must be carried out under a Community licence or, if they take the form of 'occasional services' (ie vehicle hired for 'trip'), with a control document.

The Road Transport (Passenger Vehicles Cabotage) Regulations 1999 provide that a person who uses, or causes or permits the use of, a vehicle for the purpose of United

Kingdom cabotage operations must be a Community carrier with a Community licence authorising such use. Non-compliance with this requirement is an offence. In addition, a person commits an offence if he uses a vehicle, or causes or permits it to be used, for the purpose of United Kingdom cabotage operations taking the form of 'occasional services' without a control document.

The licence or control document must be carried on board and produced to a vehicle examiner appointed under RTA 1988, s 66A or constable in uniform. It is an offence to be without the necessary document or to fail, without reasonable excuse, to produce it when required.

OTHER PUBLIC SERVICE VEHICLE DOCUMENTS AND RESTRICTIONS

Registration of local services

The TA 1985 abolished the previous requirement for road service licences which were required in respect of services operated over prescribed routes. The provisions of the PPVA 1981 which dealt with road service licences are replaced by TA 1985, ss 6 to 9, which are concerned with the registration of local services.

By TA 1985, s 2, a 'local service' is a service, using one or more public service vehicles, for the carriage of passengers by road at separate fares other than:

(a) a journey organised privately by persons acting independently of the vehicle operators etc (see (2) on p 488); or

(b) a service within which every vehicle used is operated under a permit granted under TA 1985, s 19 (minibuses and buses operated by educational, religious, social, recreational and other beneficial bodies); or

(c) a service in relation to which (except in an emergency) *either* the place where each passenger is set down is fifteen miles or more, measured in a straight line, from the place where he was taken up *or* some point on the route between those places is fifteen miles or more from that place or both (limited stop vehicles).

The responsibility for the registration of local services is vested in the traffic commissioner for each traffic area.

By TA 1985, s 6, no local service shall be provided in any traffic area in which there is a stopping place for that service unless the prescribed particulars of the service have been registered with the traffic commissioner for that area by the operator of that service. These particulars are prescribed by the Public Service Vehicles (Registration of Local Services) Regulations 1986. Applications to operate a local service may only be accepted from the holders of unconditional public service vehicle operator's licences, or holders of permits under TA 1985, s 22 (operators of community bus services), or from persons who are using or proposing to use a school bus belonging to that person for fare paying passengers in accordance with the PPVA 1981, s 46(1). The term 'unconditional' in this respect, means that there is no condition attached to the licence prohibiting etc the provision of the particular service applied for. Applications for registration may be made in respect of two classes of service, standard and flexible. A flexible service is one which serves one or more local communities or neighbourhoods within a specific geographical area, which, while it may have fixed sections of route, is in the entirety of its operations so flexible that identification of its whole route is not practicable; it must be provided primarily for prebooked, fare paying individual passengers who collectively determine the route, and all seats must be available to the public. Applications are made to a traffic commissioner for the relevant area of operation. Where the area of operation covers more than one traffic area, application must be made, in the case of a standard service, to the traffic commissioner for the area in which the service will start. In the case of a flexible service, at the discretion of the operator, the application may be made either to the traffic commissioner for the area within which the greater part of the operation lies or to the commissioner for the area in which the greater number of fixed stopping places are situated.

The provisions of TA 1985 relating to the registration of local services do not apply to a London local service (ie a local stopping service with one or more stopping places in London). Local London services are governed by the Greater London Authority Act 1999, Part IV. Except in the case of a service provided under the London bus network determined by Transport for London, a local London service must be authorised by a London service permit granted by Transport for London.

Traffic regulation conditions

A traffic authority (county council) may ask the traffic commissioner for any area to determine traffic regulation conditions which must be met in the provision of services in the area to which the conditions are applied. If a trunk road is affected, the authority must have the consent of the Secretary of State to making the application. Before a traffic commissioner *determines* traffic regulation conditions, he must be satisfied that they are necessary to prevent danger to road users, or to reduce severe traffic congestion. In considering what conditions to apply he *must have regard* to the interests of those registered in respect of local services, users of those services and the elderly and disabled. He may then determine the routes of services, their stopping places, when vehicles may stop and for how long, and any other matters prescribed. Such conditions may affect different periods of the year, different days of the week, or different times during any period of twenty-four hours. In addition, he may impose conditions regulating the roads to be used and the manoeuvres to be performed when turning a vehicle, and limiting the number of vehicles which may be used (or the frequency at which vehicles may be operated) in the provision of a service along all or part of its route whether generally or during particular periods or at particular times.

Once made, these traffic regulation conditions apply generally to *all* services operated in the area or to such *class* of service as may be specified. There is one exception. Where the traffic commissioner is satisfied that the traffic regulation conditions which apply generally would be inappropriate in achieving the particular regulation of traffic which he considers necessary, he may determine conditions which apply only to a *particular* service or services.

Before determining any traffic regulation condition, a traffic commissioner must hold an inquiry if so requested by the traffic authority which has asked for such conditions or by a person who has registered a service. In an emergency he may make a condition without delay but this must be followed by an inquiry as soon as reasonably practicable if a request is received from any such party. The above provisions do not, of course, apply to a London local service, but if he grants a licence to such a service the traffic commissioner may insert into it conditions similar to those just mentioned.

Certificates of initial fitness

By PPVA 1981, s 6(1), a public service vehicle adapted to carry more than eight passengers must not be used on a road unless:

(a) an examiner appointed under the RTA 1988, s 66A has issued a certificate of initial fitness, stating that the prescribed conditions of fitness are fulfilled in relation to the vehicle; or

(b) a type vehicle or type approval certificate has been issued in respect of the vehicle.

Such public service vehicles must, therefore, have some form of certificate of initial fitness (or equivalent) for use as a public service vehicle. Such vehicles are subjected to stability tests and tests related to suspension, guard rails, brakes, steering gear, fuel tanks, exhausts, lighting, bodywork, windscreens and windows, and other pieces of miscellaneous equipment. The fitness requirements ('the prescribed conditions') may be met by a vehicle satisfying (1) the conditions prescribed in the Public Service Vehicle (Conditions of Fitness, Equipment, Use and Certification) Regulations 1981 or (2) the relevant requirements of the Annexes to Directive 2001/85/EC.

Applications for fitness certification in respect of single vehicles, or those adapted locally, are likely to be made to the traffic commissioner of the area, who will issue a certificate of initial fitness in respect of that particular vehicle.

It will be appreciated that this procedure would be somewhat tedious in relation to mass produced vehicles of a particular pattern. In such cases the Department of Transport will have caused the vehicle model to be subjected to inspection and will have approved that particular design by a certificate. Provided that there has been such a type approval and there is a certificate that the *particular* vehicle conforms with that type, PPVA 1981, s 6(1) is satisfied.

If a vehicle in used in contravention of PPVA 1981, s 6(1), the operator of the vehicle is guilty of an offence unless he proves that he took all reasonable precautions and exercised all due diligence to avoid the contravention.

Test certificates

Test certificates issued under RTA 1988, s 47(1) must be obtained in respect of public service vehicles one year after their original registration etc. There are provisions which allow the issue of a certificate of temporary exemption in certain circumstances, but the validity of such a certificate must not extend beyond three months. Provision is made for the testing of seat belts and anchorages fitted to public service vehicles, other than those which are required by law.

The provisions of RTA 1988, s 67, which deal with the testing of vehicles on roads for the purpose of ascertaining whether the requirements concerning a vehicle's construction and use and its general condition are satisfactory, apply equally to public service vehicles.

LICENCE TO DRIVE

The RTA 1988, Part IV is concerned with the licensing of drivers of large passenger-carrying vehicles. RTA 1988, s 110 states that licences to drive classes of vehicles which include large passenger-carrying vehicles, shall be granted by the Secretary of State in accordance with Part IV of the Act. Thus, licences to drive large passenger-carrying vehicles are subject to the provisions of both Parts III and IV of the RTA 1988.

RTA 1988, s 111 requires the traffic commissioner of an area to exercise the functions conferred by Part IV of the Act relating to the conduct of:

(a) applicants for and holders of large passenger-carrying vehicle drivers' licences; and

(b) holders of PCV Community licences.

The offence of driving a large passenger-carrying vehicle otherwise than in accordance with a licence arises under the RTA 1988, s 87 but the offence requires additional consideration within this chapter as there are variations, consequent upon the need to comply additionally with Part IV of the Act. In addition, there are requirements made by the Motor Vehicles (Driving Licences) Regulations 1999 ('the 1999 Regulations'), which apply only to large passenger-carrying vehicles.

A vehicle is a large passenger-carrying vehicle if it is constructed or adapted to carry more than sixteen passengers, whether or not they are being carried for hire or reward. Schedule 2 to the 1999 Regulations provides a multiplicity of categories and sub-categories of vehicles. The various forms of passenger-carrying vehicles are included in variations of category D types of vehicles.

Large passenger-carrying vehicle driving tests

The drivers of large passenger-carrying vehicles generally will be in possession of driving licences issued under Part III of the RTA 1988 for differing categories of vehicles. In order to obtain those licences, they will have been tested on different types of vehicles. The amended table set out below shows the various categories of passenger-carrying vehicles and gives details of the 'minimum test vehicle' which could be used within that test.

Category or sub-category		Specification
D1	8–16 seats in addition to driver's seat	Any vehicle in sub-category D1 having a maximum authorised mass of 4,000 kg, a length of at least 5 m, which is capable of an unassisted speed of 80 kph on the level
D1 + E	Combination vehicles not exceeding 12 tonnes	A combination of a minimum test vehicle for sub-category D1 and a trailer having a maximum authorised mass of 1,250 kg, which is capable of an unassisted speed of 80 kph on the level. The cargo compartment of the trailer must consist of a closed box body which is at least 2 m wide and at least 2 m high

Category or sub-category		Specification
D	more than 8 seats in addition to driver's seat	Any vehicle in category D having a length of at least 10 m, a width of at least 2.4 m, and capable of an unassisted speed of 80 kph on the level
D + E	D tractor but the combination falls outside that category	A combination of a minimum test vehicle for category D and a trailer of a width of at least 2.4 m, having a maximum authorised mass of 1,250 kg, the combination being capable of an unassisted speed of 80 kph on the level. The cargo compartment of the trailer must consist of a closed body which is at least 2 m wide and at least 2 m high

However, the provisions set out in the table above do not apply to a practical or unitary test conducted in a vehicle which was first used on a road, whether as a test vehicle or not, before 1 October 2003. In such cases the test vehicle requirement will be as required before the table was amended, namely D1 (D1 capable of 80 kph); D1 + E (D1 + trailer having maximum authorised mass of 1,250 kg and capable of 80 kph); D (D having length of 9 m and capable of 80 kph); and D + E (D + trailer of 1,250 kg and capable of 80 kph).

With effect from 1 July 2007 test vehicles in categories D or D + E must be fitted with anchorage points and seat belts for an examiner or authorised person present for the purpose of supervising it or otherwise.

OTHER PERSONS WHO MAY DRIVE LARGE PASSENGER-CARRYING VEHICLES

RTA 1988, Part III permits holders of Community licences authorising them to drive large passenger-carrying vehicles to drive those categories of vehicles in the United Kingdom. Those who become resident in the United Kingdom may exchange their licences for British ones, but are in any case, within a year of becoming resident, required to submit to the Secretary of State details of their driving entitlement and other information which is prescribed. Resident Community licence holders who hold licences entitling them to drive passenger-carrying vehicles are made subject to the code of conduct relating to such drivers. Such licences are referred to in the RTA 1988 as 'PCV Community licences'. Holders of Convention or domestic driving permits who are resident in the EEA (European Economic Area), the Isle of Man, Jersey or Guernsey may drive a large passenger-carrying vehicle which they are authorised to drive by that permit during a period of twelve months from the date of their last entry into the United Kingdom. Holders of such permits who are not residents of an EEA state, or the Isle of Man or Jersey, may only drive a large passenger-carrying vehicle brought temporarily into Great Britain.

Provisional licences

Persons who hold provisional licences to drive large passenger-carrying vehicles are subject to the general conditions under which persons, who are learner drivers, may drive particular classes of vehicles. These are the conditions prescribed by reg 16 of the Motor Vehicle (Driving Licences) Regulations 1999, the need for supervision, the display of learner plates, and the prohibition upon the drawing of a trailer. However, the supervisor of a learner driver of a large passenger-carrying vehicle must have held a full licence for the category of vehicle being driven by the learner driver for a continuous period of not less than three or for periods amounting in aggregate to not less than three years. Alternatively, where the vehicle is in category C, D, C + E or D + E he must have held the relevant licence (which includes a relevant provisional licence and a pass certificate) on 6 April 1998 and have held it continuously since that date; in addition, he must have held a full category B licence for not less than a total of three years.

However, the prohibition upon the drawing of a trailer does not apply to the holder of a provisional licence authorising the driving of a vehicle of a class included in category D + E (combination of passenger-carrying vehicle with more than eight seats in addition to the driver's seat where the tractor itself fits into category D but the combination does not) while driving such a vehicle.

Regulation 16(8) of the 1999 Regulations prohibits provisional licence holders from driving a passenger-carrying vehicle while carrying passengers. However, exceptions exist in favour of supervisors and holders of passenger-carrying vehicle drivers' licences who are receiving or giving instruction, have given or received it, or are to give or receive it.

Regulation 19 of the 1999 Regulations sets out details of certain full licences which do not carry provisional entitlement to drive all other categories of vehicles. Most significant to issues surrounding passenger-carrying vehicle drivers' licences is the provision that a category D1 licence only carries provisional entitlement to drive vehicles of category D1 + E and that a category D licence only carries provisional entitlement to drive vehicles of categories D1 + E and D + E.

Regulation 9(9) of the 1999 Regulations permit a person of eighteen to drive a passenger-carrying vehicle where:

(a) he holds a provisional licence authorising the driving of the vehicle and is not engaged in the carriage of passengers; or
(b) he holds a full passenger-carrying vehicle driver's licence and:
    (i) is engaged in the carriage of passengers on a regular service over a route which does not exceed 50 km, or
    (ii) where he is not so engaged, is driving a class of vehicle included in sub-category D1 (more than eight but less than sixteen seats in addition to the driver's seat),

and the vehicle is operated under a PSV operator's licence granted under PPVA 1981, s 12 or a permit granted under TA 1985, s 19 (vehicles used by educational and other bodies) or a community bus permit issued under TA 1985, s 22.

Regulation 7(6) of the 1999 Regulations provides that a category B licence holder (but not B1) who has held that licence for at least two years, is over twenty-one and receives no consideration other than out-of-pocket expenses may drive, on behalf of a non-commercial body, for social purposes but not for hire or reward, a vehicle of a class in sub-category D1 (more than eight but not more than sixteen seats in addition to the driver's seat) which is not drawing a trailer and has a maximum authorised mass not exceeding 3.5 tonnes excluding weight attributable to special equipment for carrying disabled passengers, and 4.25 tonnes otherwise. The usual proviso applies in relation to 'automatics'. Where such a driver is aged seventy or over, he must not be suffering from a relevant disability in respect of which the licensing authority would be bound to refuse him a Group 2 licence (within the meaning of reg 73—higher medical standards for large vehicles). Regulation 76 of the 1999 Regulations provides that a person who held a licence authorising, on 31 December 1996, the driving of vehicles in category D otherwise than for hire or reward, may drive the classes of vehicles included in category D which are driven under a permit granted under TA 1985, s 19. The amended Minibus and Other Section 19 Permit Buses Regulations 1987 provide that where such a licence was granted before 1 January 1997, such a person must be the holder of a full driver's licence for category B and sub-category D1 (not for hire or reward).

Validity of large passenger-carrying vehicle drivers' licences

A licence authorising its holder to drive large passenger-carrying vehicles remains in force, unless previously revoked, suspended or surrendered, but becomes renewable on the holder's forty-fifth birthday, or after five years, whichever is the *longer*, or where the licence is issued to a person between forty-five and sixty-five for the period ending on his sixty-sixth birthday or after five years, whichever is the *shorter*. A licence granted after the age of sixty-five will remain in force for one year only.

   RTA 1988, s 115 provides that a large passenger-carrying vehicle driver's licence must be revoked if there comes into existence in relation to the holder prescribed circumstances relating to his conduct, and must be revoked or suspended if his conduct is such as to make him unfit to hold such a licence.

Historic buses and those driven by a constable in an emergency

Regulation 50 of the 1999 Regulations provides that the provisions of RTA 1988, Part IV and the provisions of regs 54 to 57 of the Regulations shall not apply to:

(a) a passenger-carrying vehicle manufactured more than thirty years before the date upon which it is driven and not used for hire or reward or for the carriage of more than eight passengers;

(b) a passenger-carrying vehicle driven by a constable for the purpose of removing or avoiding obstruction to other road users or to other members of the public, for the purpose of protecting life or property (including the passenger-carrying vehicle and its passengers) or for other similar purposes.

Hours of driving

The number of hours during which a driver may be employed in the driving of a public service vehicle is strictly controlled. To avoid repetition, this matter is discussed in the next chapter.

BUSES OPERATED BY PARTICULAR ORGANISATIONS AND COMMUNITY BUSES

The TA 1985 contains provisions whereby, if certain conditions are observed, such vehicles are permitted to operate outside most, or all, of the general provisions of the Acts relating to public service vehicles. TA 1985, s 18 states that the provisions of PPVA 1981, s 12(1) (need to have a public service vehicle operator's licence) shall not apply to the use of a vehicle under a permit granted under TA 1985, s 19 or 22.

TA 1985, s 18 also provides that where a person is the holder of a licence under RTA 1988, Part III, which was first granted before 1 January 1977, he may drive a 'small bus' at a time when it is being used under such permits, notwithstanding that his licence does not authorise him to drive a small bus when it is being so used.

For these purposes, a 'small bus' is a vehicle which is adapted to carry more than eight but not more than sixteen passengers.

Where a Part III licence was granted on or after 1 January 1997, or a Community licence holder is authorised by RTA 1988, s 99A(1) to drive in Great Britain a motor vehicle of any class, the licence holder may drive a 'small bus' notwithstanding that he is not authorised by his licence to drive such a bus.

For these purposes a 'small bus' is one which when laden with the heaviest load which it is constructed to carry, weighs:

(a) not more than 3.5 tonnes, excluding any part of that weight which is attributable to specialised equipment intended for the carriage of disabled passengers; and

(b) not more than 4.25 tonnes otherwise.

Buses operated by particular organisations

TA 1985, ss 19, 20 and 21 authorise the use of buses of particular types under permits granted to a body which assists and co-ordinates the activities of bodies within an area which appear to be concerned with education, religion, social welfare, recreation or other activities of benefit to the community. Permits may be granted in respect of small buses (adapted to carry eight to sixteen passengers) or large buses (adapted to carry more than sixteen passengers). A permit for a small bus may be granted by a traffic commissioner or by a body designated by the Secretary of State, either to itself or to any other body to whom, in accordance with the order, it is entitled to grant a permit. A permit in respect of a large bus can only be granted by a traffic commissioner. It may be granted to any of the bodies mentioned above, with the exception of those concerned with recreational activity. Before granting a permit for a large bus, a traffic commissioner must be satisfied that there will be adequate facilities or arrangements for maintaining any bus used under the permit in a fit and serviceable condition. The Section 19 Minibus (Designated Bodies) Order 1987, as amended, lists those bodies approved by the Secretary of State for these purposes.

TA 1985, s 19(2) makes it clear that certain requirements must be met in relation to the use of a bus under a permit before the use of such a vehicle without a public service vehicle operator's licence will be exempt. The vehicle must be being used by the body to whom the permit has been granted; it must not be being used for carriage of members of the general public nor with a view to profit either directly or incidentally; it must be being used within the conditions of the permit and in compliance with any regulations made under TA 1985, s 21. If any of these factors are not being observed, the exemptions under s 18 do not apply, and the operator may be convicted of the offence of operating the vehicle without a public service vehicle operator's licence.

Discs carried by minibuses and other s 19 permit buses

Discs displayed on these vehicles will show the name of the body or person holding the permit, the number, the date upon which it was granted, the name of the issuing body and the words 'Transport Act 1985, section 19 permit vehicle'. The disc will also carry a code letter. The various code letters mean that the use is authorised for:

A — members of the body holding the permit
B — persons whom the body exists to benefit
C — mentally or physically handicapped persons or the seriously ill, and persons assisting them
D — pupils or students at any school, college, university or other educational establishment and staff or other helpers accompanying them
E — other class specified in the permit.

Community bus services

As stated above, TA 1985, s 18 states that the provisions in PPVA 1981 relating to the licensing of public service vehicle operators do not apply to the use of any vehicle under a permit granted under TA 1985, s 22 (a community bus permit). By TA 1985, s 22, a 'community bus service' is a local service provided by a body concerned for the social and welfare needs of one or more communities, without a view to profit, either on the part of that body or anyone else, and by means of a vehicle adapted to carry more than eight but not more than sixteen passengers. A 'community bus permit' may be granted by the relevant traffic commissioner for a public service vehicle which is providing a community bus service, or which is, in providing a community bus service, carrying passengers for hire or reward where the carriage of those passengers will directly assist the provision of the community bus service by providing financial support for it. If passengers are carried for hire or reward the vehicle must not be used in the course of a local service. The commissioner must be satisfied with the arrangements for the maintenance etc of the vehicle. A 'Community Bus' disc is issued with each permit.

The Community Bus Regulations 1986 permit a person who is not the holder of a passenger-carrying vehicle driver's licence to drive a vehicle in respect of which a community bus permit exists, provided that he complies with requirements relating to hand-held microphones, a driver's duty to ensure the safety of passengers, and giving his name, that of his employer, and particulars of his licence, to a constable or other person having reasonable cause. In addition, he must:

(a) hold a full licence authorising him to drive vehicles in category B other than vehicles in sub-category B1, and have held it for not less than two years in aggregate and be twenty-one or over; *or*
(b) where his full licence was granted under Part III of the RTA 1988 before 1 January 1997, hold a full licence authorising driving of vehicles in category B, other than

vehicles included in sub-category B1 and sub-category D1 (not for hire or reward), and be twenty-one or over; *and*

(c) if seventy or over, must not be suffering from a relevant disability in respect of which the licensing authority would be bound to refuse to grant him a licence to drive a category D1 vehicle (within the meaning of reg 65—higher medical standards for large vehicles).

A category D1 vehicle is one having more than eight but not more than sixteen seats in addition to the driver's seat.

The holder of a community bus permit commits an offence contrary to TA 1985, s 23(5) if a condition attached to a permit is contravened. The Community Bus Regulations 1986 set out the obligations of drivers and prescribe conditions of fitness.

These provisions recognise the difficulties in providing adequate bus services in rural areas. Where it is not economically sound to provide local services in some areas, community bus permits allow the use of 'Transit type vehicles'. These public service vehicles may be provided either free of charge, by a local authority or by some other body concerned for the social or welfare needs of communities, or for hire or reward where this will directly assist the provision of the community bus service by providing finance.

CONDUCT OF DRIVERS, CONDUCTORS AND PASSENGERS

The Public Service Vehicles (Conduct of Drivers, Inspectors, Conductors and Passengers) Regulations 1990 regulate behaviour on public service vehicles. Contravention of any of the following regulations is an offence. Each of the different forms of conduct specified gives rise to a separate offence.

A driver must not:

(a) while the vehicle is in motion, *hold* a microphone or any attachment there to unless it is necessary for him, either in an emergency or on the grounds of safety, to speak into that microphone;

(b) speak to any person either directly or by means of a microphone, whilst the vehicle is in motion, except that he may do so in an emergency or on the grounds of safety, or when speaking to a relevant person in relation to the operation of the vehicle; by way of exception the driver of a vehicle being used other than for an excursion tour, or sightseeing, may use a microphone to make short statements from time to time which are limited to indicating the location of the vehicle or operational matters, provided that he can do so without being distracted from his driving;

(c) fail to stop as close as is reasonably practicable to the left or nearside of the road when picking up or setting down passengers.

A driver or conductor must take all reasonable precautions to ensure the safety of passengers who are on, or who are entering or leaving, a public service vehicle.

A driver, inspector or conductor must:

(a) take all reasonable precautions to ensure that the provisions of the Regulations about the conduct of passengers are complied with;

(b) if requested by a constable or other person having reasonable cause, give his name and that of his employer; in addition a driver must give particulars of the licence by virtue of which he drives the vehicle;

(c) not smoke, except where the vehicle is not available for the carriage of passengers and it takes place in a 'smoking' area, or where the vehicle is hired as a whole and he has the permission of the operator and the hirer;

(d) not, subject to there being a space available, prevent a disabled person accompanied by an assistance dog (a dog trained by a charity to assist a physically disabled person), guide dog or hearing dog, from being allowed to board and travel in the vehicle with his dog.

A conductor must not, while the vehicle is in motion, distract the driver's attention or obstruct his vision without reasonable cause.

A Part IV was added to the Regulations in 2002 which applies to the conduct of drivers and conductors of regulated public service vehicles with respect to wheelchair users and other disabled persons. Part IV is primarily concerned with assistance and safety of disabled persons.

A passenger must not:

(a) put at risk or unreasonably impede or cause discomfort to any person travelling on or entering or leaving the vehicle, or to the driver, inspector, conductor, or employee of the operator, when doing his work on that vehicle;

(b) smoke or carry lighted tobacco or light a match or cigarette lighter in or on any part of the vehicle where passengers are by a notice informed that smoking is prohibited, unless the vehicle has been hired as a whole and both the operator and the hirer have given their permission to the contrary;

(c) speak to the driver whilst the vehicle is in motion except in an emergency or for reasons of safety, or to give directions as to the stopping of the vehicle;

(d) without reasonable cause, distract the driver's attention or obstruct his vision, or give a signal which might reasonably be interpreted by the driver as a signal to stop the vehicle in an emergency or as a signal to start the vehicle;

(e) remain on the vehicle when directed to leave by the driver, an inspector or conductor on the ground that his remaining on the vehicle would result in the number of passengers exceeding the maximum seating capacity marked on the vehicle in accordance with the Public Service Vehicles (Carrying Capacity) Regulations 1984, or that he has been causing a nuisance, or that his condition is such as would be likely to cause offence to a reasonable passenger, or that the condition of his clothing is such that his remaining on the vehicle would be reasonably expected to soil the fittings of the vehicle or the clothing of other passengers (however, such a direction may not be given solely on the grounds that a person is a disabled person);

(f) play or operate a musical instrument or sound reproducing equipment to the annoyance of any person on the vehicle, or in a manner which is likely to cause such annoyance;

(g) fail to place an article, substance or animal where directed by the driver, inspector or conductor, or fail to remove an article etc from the vehicle on such a direction being given. (This refers to bulky or cumbersome articles and those likely to cause annoyance, risk of injury or damage. There are certain exceptions in favour of assistance dogs, guide dogs and hearing dogs but a disabled person must comply with a direction to remove such a dog from the gangway.)

Certain other offences may be committed by passengers on a vehicle being used for the carriage of passengers at separate fares:

(a) using a ticket which has been altered or defaced or which has been issued to another person and is not transferable;
(b) failing to declare the journey to be taken when requested to do so;
(c) failing to pay the driver or insert the fare in a machine on one-man buses;
(d) failing to pay the appropriate fare to the conductor immediately upon his request;
(e) failing to accept or retain a ticket for the remainder of the journey;
(f) failing to produce a ticket to a driver, inspector or conductor during the currency of a journey; and
(g) failing to leave the vehicle or pay an excess fare at the end of the journey paid for.

Any passenger contravening these regulations may be removed from the vehicle by the driver or conductor. A passenger who is reasonably suspected by the driver or conductor of such contravention must give his name and address on demand.

Conduct which does not give rise to such an offence under the Regulations will sometimes constitute another offence. Staff or passengers who are rude or disorderly may be guilty of offences under the Public Order Act 1986 in serious cases. Passengers who spit upon, soil or deface any part of a public service vehicle may be guilty of an offence under the Criminal Damage Act 1971.

INSTITUTION OF PROCEEDINGS

Proceedings for any of the offences mentioned in this chapter (other than those committed by a passenger) may only be instituted by or on behalf of the Director of Public Prosecutions, or by a person authorised by a traffic commissioner, a chief officer of police or a local authority. For practical purposes, this means that a police officer can- not institute such proceedings unless authorised by his chief constable.

TOUTING FOR HIRE CAR SERVICES

The Criminal Justice and Public Order Act 1994, s 167 provides an offence which is committed by those who solicit persons, in a public place, to hire vehicles, whether licensed taxis or otherwise, to carry them as passengers in circumstances other than those described above in which a taxi would be operating lawfully. It is a defence for an accused to show that he was soliciting for passengers to be carried at separate fares by public service vehicles on behalf of the holder of a public service vehicle operator's licence.

The soliciting need not refer to any particular vehicle. The mere display of a sign is not soliciting.

CHAPTER 13

Goods Vehicles

DEFINITION

For the purposes of road traffic legislation, a 'goods vehicle' is a motor vehicle or trailer constructed or adapted for the carriage of goods; for this purpose the carriage of goods includes the haulage of goods. 'Adapted' means 'altered physically so as to make fit for the purpose'. If the seating is stripped from a public service vehicle and the vehicle is then fitted out as a mobile shop, it is thereby adapted to carry goods and becomes a goods vehicle. Of course, the opposite can apply. For example, where a goods van was adapted for the carriage of passengers and its only use for the carriage of goods was when it carried samples to the owner's place of business, it was held not to be a goods vehicle. When a vehicle is originally constructed as a goods vehicle, any alterations made to it must be *substantial and dramatic* if its initial classification is to be changed. The fitting of winches and support bars and ancillary equipment is insufficient to convert a goods vehicle into engineering plant for use in the drilling of wells. The test to be applied in cases in which a passenger vehicle has been converted to permit the carriage of goods is to examine its existing form and to ask whether, if it had been constructed in that form originally, it would have been classed as a passenger vehicle or as a goods vehicle. The mere removal of seats from an estate car to permit it to be used for the carriage of goods does not amount to an adaptation for these purposes. The seats can be replaced at any time.

In this chapter we shall be concerned with:

(a) the minimum age for driving a goods vehicle;
(b) large goods vehicles drivers' licences;
(c) plating and testing;
(d) operators' licences; and
(e) drivers' hours and records.

MINIMUM AGE FOR DRIVING A GOODS VEHICLE

This depends on whether the vehicle in question is a small, medium or large goods vehicle. The Road Traffic Act 1988 (RTA 1988), ss 101 and 108 provide as follows:

(1) A '*small vehicle*' is a motor vehicle (other than an invalid carriage, moped or motor bicycle) which:
   (i) is not constructed to carry more than nine persons inclusive of the driver; and
   (ii) has a maximum gross weight not exceeding 3.5 tonnes, and includes a combination of such a motor vehicle and trailer.
   Persons of seventeen or over (sixteen if in receipt of a mobility allowance) may drive small vehicles. The term 'permissible maximum weight' is explained below. It should be noted that unladen weights are of little significance in relation to the legislation concerning goods vehicles.
(2) A '*medium-sized goods vehicle*' is a motor vehicle which is constructed or adapted to carry or to haul goods, and which is not adapted to carry more than nine persons inclusive of the driver, and the permissible maximum weight of which exceeds 3.5 but does not exceed 7.5 tonnes and includes a combination of such a motor vehicle and a trailer where the relevant maximum weight of the trailer does not exceed 750 kg.
   Persons of eighteen or over may drive medium-sized goods vehicles.
(3) A '*large goods vehicle*' (although this term does not appear in the Road Traffic Act 1988, it is used in the Road Traffic (Driver Licensing and Information Systems) Act 1989) is for convenience used here to describe goods vehicles which exceed 7.5 tonnes permissible maximum weight or which have more than nine seats inclusive of the driver's.
   Persons of twenty-one or over may drive large goods vehicles.

The references to carriage of passengers occasionally cause confusion to those concerned with the problems related to goods vehicles. The limitation to nine persons in (1) and (2) means that a transit-type of vehicle will be classified as a goods vehicle if it is constructed or adapted to carry or haul a load, even though it retains some seating. This is important because, for example, transit-types of vehicles are frequently used by employers to carry goods (or to tow a trailer containing goods) in addition to carrying workers who are being transported to their place of work. If such a van seats nine or less it will be a small- or medium-sized goods vehicle, depending on its permissible maximum weight; if such a van seats more than nine it will be a large goods vehicle.

It should be noted that a person of a certain age may be permitted to drive a certain type of goods vehicle if it is used without a trailer because its permissible maximum weight is within the range which he would be allowed to drive, but that if a trailer is attached it is possible that the sum of the relevant maximum weights of the vehicle and the trailer will prohibit that person from driving it. For example, a person aged seventeen may drive a goods vehicle of 3 tonnes maximum relevant weight since, as its maximum relevant weight does not exceed 3.5 tonnes, it is a small goods vehicle. However, if a trailer is attached with a relevant maximum weight of 1 tonne, the sum of the weights is now 4 tonnes and the vehicle has become 'medium-sized' and may no longer be driven by him but only by someone aged eighteen or more. The situation is interesting when related to articulated vehicles. The tractive units of many articulated vehicles are quite small and will frequently have a relevant maximum weight under 3.5 tonnes. They may therefore be driven by seventeen-year-olds. However, when a semi-trailer is attached to the tractive unit the relevant maximum train weight is the deciding factor and this will almost invariably bring the vehicle into the 'medium' or 'large' category. If, for example, the tractive unit is of 3 tonnes and a semi-trailer is attached, and the maximum train weight is 6 tonnes, the vehicle becomes 'medium'. If it exceeds 7.5 tonnes, it would become 'large'.

Exceptions to normal minimum ages

There are certain exceptions to these general rules in relation to minimum permitted ages for the purpose of driving. Medium and large goods vehicles owned and used by naval, military or air force authorities may be driven by persons aged seventeen.

There is also an exception in relation to large goods vehicles where a person of eighteen or over is registered in the heavy goods vehicle training scheme. The Motor Vehicles (Driving Licences) Regulations 1999, reg 9, authorises persons of eighteen years to drive large goods vehicles of a category to which their training agreement applies, provided that they are employed by a registered employer and that they are registered employees of that employer. The vehicles which they are driving must be owned or operated by their employer or by a registered large goods vehicle driver training establishment. Regulation 54 of the Motor Vehicles (Driving Licences) Regulations 1999 prescribes additional conditions subject to which large goods vehicle drivers' licences are granted to persons under twenty-one, some of which are those set out above which relate to the employer/employee relationship.

PERMISSIBLE MAXIMUM WEIGHT

As can be seen from the above definitions, in relation to the ages of persons by whom they may be driven, goods vehicles are divided into three classes which are basically separated by their 'permissible maximum weights'. The permissible maximum weights of goods vehicles are prescribed by the RTA 1988, as follows.

An 'articulated goods vehicle' is a motor vehicle which is so constructed that a goods trailer may by partial superimposition be attached in such a manner as to cause a substantial part of the weight of the trailer to be borne by the motor vehicle. An 'articulated goods vehicle combination' is an articulated goods vehicle with the trailer (called a semi-trailer) attached. It is only in respect of such a combination that the phrase 'relevant maximum train weight' is relevant.

The 'relevant maximum weight' of a goods vehicle is the maximum gross weight which is shown on the relevant plate of the vehicle. The relevant plate is always the Ministry of Transport plate if the vehicle has then been fitted with one. If it has not, then the relevant maximum weight will be shown on the manufacturer's plate.

This means that in the case of vehicles which are fitted with both plates, the maximum weight shown on the Ministry plate is always the 'relevant' maximum weight. In the unlikely case of a vehicle having neither type of plate, the relevant maximum weight can be calculated by multiplying the unladen weight by a multiplier listed in the Goods Vehicles (Ascertainment of Maximum Gross Weight) Regulations 1976, Sch 2. This is unlikely to be of any operational significance to police officers.

The 'relevant maximum train weight' of an articulated goods vehicle combination is the gross weight of the unladen motor vehicle and its unladen trailer plus the maximum weight which the combination is permitted to carry. This is shown under the column marked 'gross train weight' on the plate attached to the vehicle.

The Road Vehicles (Authorised Weight) Regulations 1998 apply to all wheeled motor vehicles and trailers which fall within category M2, M3, N2, N3, O3 or O4 as defined in Annex II of Directive 70/156/EEC, as substituted by Directive 92/53/EC (in effect, buses, goods vehicles and trailers in excess of 3,500 kg). However, the Regulations do not apply in relation to vehicle combinations which for the time being fulfil the requirements of Parts II, III, or IIIA of Sch 11A to the Road Vehicles (Construction and Use) Regulations 1986 (exemptions relating to combined transport operations where the drawing vehicle and trailer are each carrying a relevant receptacle to or from a railhead as part of that combined transport operation).

Regulation 4 of the 1998 Regulations states that no vehicle to which the Regulations apply, which is of a description specified in a schedule to the Regulations, shall be used on a road if:

(a) the weight of the vehicle exceeds the maximum authorised weight for the vehicle determined in accordance with Sch 1;
(b) where the vehicle is used as part of a vehicle combination, the weight of the combination exceeds the maximum authorised weight for the combination determined in accordance with Sch 2; or
(c) the axle weight of the axle of any vehicle exceeds the maximum authorised axle weight for that axle determined in accordance with Sch 3.

Schedule 1 sets out weights which are not to be exceeded in relation to various types of rigid motor vehicles, tractor units, trailers which are not semi-trailers and articulated buses with from two to four axles. Schedule 2 is concerned with maximum authorised weights for vehicle combinations and Sch 3 deals with maximum authorised axle weights.

Regulation 4(2) of the 1998 Regulations provides that a vehicle to which any of the provisions of regs 75 to 79 of the Road Vehicles (Construction and Use) Regulations 1986 apply and which is being used in accordance with those provisions, shall be taken to comply with the 1998 Regulations.

Finally, reg 5 of the 1998 Regulations provides that nothing in the Regulations shall prejudice or affect reg 80 of the 1986 Regulations (which creates the offence of using, or causing or permitting the use of a vehicle on a road where the over-riding plated weight restrictions are exceeded). A person using or permitting a vehicle to be used in contravention of reg 80 commits an offence even if the weights authorised by the 1998 Regulations are not exceeded.

Where a Ministry plate contains particulars of 'maximum authorised weight' for the vehicle or combination, or for the axles of the vehicle, the vehicle or combination is being used in accordance with the 1998 Regulations.

LARGE GOODS VEHICLES DRIVERS' LICENCES

Large goods vehicles

For the purposes of the requirements relating to large goods vehicle drivers' licences, a large goods vehicle is a motor vehicle (not being a medium-sized goods vehicle within the meaning of Part III of the Road Traffic Act 1988) which is constructed or adapted to carry or to haul goods and the permissible maximum weight of which exceeds 7.5 tonnes.

The licensing requirement

General

The Road Traffic Act 1988, Part IV is concerned with the licensing of drivers of large goods vehicles. RTA 1988, s 110 states that driver licences under Part III of the Act shall be granted by the Secretary of State in accordance with Part IV of the Act. Such licences are, therefore, subject to both Parts III and IV of the Act. RTA 1988, s 111 requires the traffic commissioner for an area to exercise the functions conferred by Part IV of the Act relating to the conduct of:

(a) applicants for and holders of large goods vehicle drivers' licences; and
(b) LGV Community licence holders.

Section 112 provides that the Secretary of State shall not grant a large goods vehicle driver's licence unless he is satisfied, having regard to his conduct, that he is a fit person to hold the licence applied for.

The offence of driving a large goods vehicle otherwise than in accordance with a licence amounts to an offence under Part III (RTA 1988, s 87). The offences committed by learner drivers who breach conditions attached to their driving are, in most instances, the same as those committed by learner drivers of other vehicles. There are additional restrictions placed upon learner drivers of large goods vehicles who are under the age of twenty-one.

The provisions of RTA 1988 in relation to the licensing of drivers of large goods vehicles are extended by the Motor Vehicles (Driving Licences) Regulations 1999. Schedule 2 to the Regulations provides a multiplicity of categories and sub-categories of vehicles. The various forms of goods vehicles are included in variations of category C types of vehicles. However, reg 50(1) of the 1999 Regulations provides that Part IV of the Act shall not apply to vehicles of sub-category C1 + E (8.25 tonnes). Sub-category C1 + E is a sub-category of C + E. It comprises a combination of motor vehicle and trailer where the former is in sub-category C1, the maximum authorised mass of the trailer exceeds 750 kg but does not exceed the unladen weight of the tractor, and the maximum authorised mass of the combination does not exceed 12 tonnes.

For the purposes of the Regulations the term 'maximum authorised mass' has the same meaning, in relation to goods vehicles, as 'permissible maximum weight' as defined in RTA 1988, s 108(1). In relation to other vehicles or trailers, it has the same meaning as 'maximum gross weight' as defined by reg 3(2) of the Road Vehicles (Construction and Use) Regulations 1986.

The provisions of RTA 1988, Part IV which are concerned with driver licensing, and the provisions of regs 54 to 57 of the 1999 Regulations (large goods vehicle drivers' licences issued to persons under twenty-one; revocation of large goods vehicle drivers' licences and removal of disqualification) do not apply to large goods vehicles of a class included in categories F, G or H (some tractors, road rollers and track-laying vehicles) or to sub-category C1 + E (8.25 tonnes), or exempted vehicles. The list of other exempted vehicles is extensive, covering military vehicles, a variety of vehicles used in public works, industry, agriculture, articulated vehicles the unladen weight of which does not exceed 3.5 tonnes, forces vehicles and emergency vehicles.

The driving test

Goods vehicle drivers will be in possession of driving licences issued under Part III of the 1988 Act for differing categories of vehicles as described in Sch 2 to the 1999 Regulations. In order to obtain those licences they will have been tested on different types of vehicles. The table below sets out the various categories of goods vehicles and gives details of the 'minimum test vehicle' which would have been used in the relevant test.

Category or sub-category		Specification
C1	3.5 tonnes but not exceeding 7.5 tonnes + trailer not exceeding 750 kg	Any vehicle in sub-category C1 having a maximum authorised mass of 4,000 kg, a length of at least 5 m, and capable of an unassisted speed of 80 kph on the level. The cargo compartment of the vehicle shall consist of a closed box body which is at least as wide and as high as the corresponding dimensions of the cab.
C1 + E	C1 tractor, trailer exceeding 750 kg and mass not exceeding 12 tonnes	A combination of a minimum test vehicle for sub-category C1 and a trailer with a maximum authorised mass of 2,000 kg which combination is at least 8 m long and capable of an unassisted speed of 80 kph on the level. The combination must have an authorised maximum mass of 4,000 kg. The cargo compartment of the trailer shall consist of a closed box body which is at least as wide and as high as the corresponding dimensions of the tractor vehicle. The closed box body may be narrower than the tractor vehicle provided that

Category or sub-category		*Specification*
		the driver's view to the rear of the vehicle is only made possible by the use of the external rear-view mirrors of the tractor vehicle.
C	exceeding 3.5 tonnes + trailer not exceeding 750 kg	Any vehicle in category C, other than an articulated goods vehicle, having a maximum authorised mass of 12,000 kg, a length of at least 8 m and a width of at least 2.4 m, which is capable of an unassisted speed of 80 kph on the level. The cargo compartment of the vehicle shall consist of a closed box body which is at least as wide and as high as the corresponding dimensions of the cab.
C + E	tractor category C but combination does not fall within that category	Either: (a) an articulated goods vehicle combination having a maximum authorised mass of 20,000 kg, a length of at least 14 m and a width of at least 2.4 m, and which is capable of an unassisted speed of 80 kph on the level, or (b) a combination of a minimum test vehicle for category C and a trailer having a length of at least 7.5 m (each having a width of at least 2.4 m) a maximum authorised mass of 4,000 kg, and which has, in aggregate, a maximum authorised mass of 20,000 kg and an overall length of 14 m and which is capable of an unassisted speed of 80 kph on the level.

However, the vehicle specifications set out in the table do not apply in respect of a practical or unitary test conducted in a vehicle which was first used on a road, whether or not as a test vehicle, before 1 October 2003. Test vehicles may be as provided for by the revoked regulation 37, that is C1 (C1 vehicle of 4,000 kg and capable of 80 kph); C1 + E (C1 vehicle plus trailer of maximum authorised mass of 2,000 kg, 8 m in length and capable of 80 kph); C (C vehicle other than articulated vehicle, maximum authorised mass 10,000 kg, length 7 m and capable of 80 kph); C + E either an articulated combination of maximum authorised mass of 18,000 kg, length of 12 m and capable of 80 kph or C + trailer of 4 m, maximum authorised mass of

4 tonnes, in aggregate being of 18,000 kg, length of 12 m and capable of 80 kph.

Test vehicles in categories must be fitted with anchorage points and seat belts for examiners and authorised persons present for supervising it or otherwise. Test vehicles for categories C or C + E must provide a motor vehicle which is fitted with an exterior nearside and offside mirror providing adequate rearward vision from the seat occupied by the person conducting the test.

Provisional licences

These may be of two types. To permit those of eighteen years or more to be taught to drive within a training agreement, provisional trainee drivers' licences may be issued. Other learner drivers will be issued with a standard provisional driving licence.

Conditions applicable to provisional licences

Provisional licences of both types are subject to the general conditions prescribed by reg 16 relating to supervision, learner plates and the general restrictions placed upon vehicles being used to draw a trailer. However, a person supervising a learner driver of a large goods vehicle must have held a full licence for the category of vehicle being driven for a continuous period of not less than three years, or for periods amounting in aggregate to not less than three years, or, where the vehicle is of category C, D, C + E or D + E, have held the relevant licence on 6 April 1998 and have held it continuously since that date and have held a full licence authorising the driving of vehicles in category B for a continuous period of not less than three years, or for periods amounting in aggregate to not less than three years. In addition, reg 54(2) of the Motor Vehicle (Driving Licences) Regulations 1999 provides that where a person holds a LGV trainee driver's full licence, that person will still be subject to the condition that he must drive, as a registered employee of a registered employer, vehicles to which his training agreement applies, and which are owned or operated by that employer or by a registered LGV driver training establishment.

Full standard licences used as provisional licences

Regulation 19 sets out details of certain full licences which do not carry provisional entitlement to drive other categories of vehicles. The table included within this regulation sets out details of categories of full licences together with the provisional entitlement which is included within that licence. Most significant to issues surrounding large goods vehicles is the provision that a category C licence carries provisional entitlement to drive vehicles of categories C1 + E and C + E.

Regulation 54(4) provides that a LGV trainee driver's full licence authorising the driving of a vehicle of category C may not drive a vehicle in category C + E (other than vehicles included in sub-category C1 + E whose maximum authorised mass does not exceed 7.5 tonnes) as if he were authorised to do so by a provisional licence, before the expiration of six months commencing on the date on which he passed a test for category C. Thus, a trainee driver could pass a test for category C vehicles (exceeding 3.5 tonnes + trailer not exceeding 750 kg) but would be unable to use his full licence for category C vehicles as a provisional licence in respect of category C + E vehicles (combinations of motor vehicles and trailers which fall outside category C) until he has held that full licence for a period of six months.

Drivers from abroad

The Road Traffic Act 1988, Part III permits holders of Community licences authorising them to drive large goods vehicles to drive large goods vehicles in the United Kingdom. Those who become resident in the United Kingdom *may* exchange those licences for British ones, but are in any case required to submit to the Secretary of State details of driving entitlement and other information which is prescribed within a year of becoming resident. Such licences are referred to in RTA 1988 as LGV Community licences.

Holders of convention or domestic driving permits who are resident in the EEA, Isle of Man, Guernsey or Jersey may drive any large goods vehicle which they are authorised to drive by that permit during a period of twelve months from the date of their last entry into the United Kingdom. Holders of such permits who are not residents of an EEA state, or the Isle of Man or Jersey, may only drive a large goods vehicle brought temporarily into Great Britain.

PLATING AND TESTING

There is a system of 'Ministry plating and testing' of goods vehicles. Its purpose is to ensure that the provisions concerning their construction and use are complied with. Examinations for this purpose are carried out by, or under the direction of, vehicle examiners who may drive the vehicle for this purpose. The driver must remain with the vehicle throughout such an examination and must drive or operate the controls as required.

Before dealing with the system of Ministry plating and testing, we must say something about the rules relating to manufacturers' plates.

Manufacturer's plate

The Road Vehicles (Construction and Use) Regulations 1986 require the following vehicles to be fitted with a manufacturer's plate:

(a) every heavy motor car and motor car first used on or after 1 January 1968, which is not a passenger vehicle;
(b) every bus (whether or not it is an articulated bus) first used on or after 1 April 1982;
(c) every locomotive and motor tractor first used on or after 1 April 1973;

(d) every trailer manufactured on or after 1 January 1968 which exceeds 1,020 kg unladen weight (although living vans not exceeding 2,040 kg are exempted if fitted with pneumatic tyres); and

(e) every trailer which is a converter dolly manufactured on or after 1 January 1979.

The usual exceptions apply in respect of land, works, pedestrian-controlled and plant etc vehicles.

The various terms used in the above list are defined by the Road Traffic Act 1988 or by the Regulations themselves. For the purposes of the present part of this chapter, a 'motor car' is a mechanically propelled vehicle constructed or adapted for use for the conveyance of any goods or burden and whose unladen weight does not exceed 3,050 kg (3 tonnes) (or 3,500 kg (3.5 tonnes) if the vehicle carries a container or containers to permit its propulsion by gas). For the same purpose, a 'heavy motor car' is a mechanically propelled vehicle (not being a motor car) constructed to carry a load, and whose unladen weight exceeds 2,540 kg (2.5 tonnes). Although the full definition of these two types of 'car' also covers passenger vehicles, such vehicles are excluded from the present requirements, except that a 'bus' is separately specified. A 'bus' is a mechanically propelled vehicle constructed or adapted to carry more than eight seated passengers in addition to the driver.

A 'motor tractor' is defined as a mechanically propelled vehicle which is not constructed itself to carry a load (other than one concerned with its own propulsion or maintenance), and the unladen weight of which does not exceed 7,370 kg (7.25 tonnes). A 'light locomotive' is a similar vehicle, the unladen weight of which does not exceed 11,690 kg (11.5 tonnes) but does exceed 7,370 kg (7.25 tonnes). A 'heavy locomotive' is a similar vehicle, the unladen weight of which exceeds 11,690 kg (11.5 tonnes).

The Regulations extend the plating requirements to trailers of the 'converter dolly' type. These are trailers with two or more wheels enabling a semi-trailer to move without any part of its weight being directly superimposed on the drawing vehicle. A semi-trailer is the type hitched to an articulated tractive unit and it therefore has no wheels at the front as this part usually rests on the drawing vehicle. A converter dolly amounts to no more than a wheeled platform which provides the semi-trailer with front wheels.

The plate

The plate must be fitted to the vehicle in a conspicuous and readily accessible position. It must contain particulars set out in Sch 2 to the Regulations, including the maximum axle, gross and train weights for the vehicle.

In certain circumstances the only plate a goods vehicle will carry for the first year of its life is its manufacturer's plate, but those vehicles to which the Motor Vehicles (Type Approval for Goods Vehicles) (Great Britain) Regulations 1982 apply will be certified and fitted with a Ministry plate (see below) within fourteen days. So far as police officers are concerned, all such vehicles will be fitted with a plate which will give the necessary information concerning weights.

Plated weights are shown as 'gross weights', or where the vehicle is being used in accordance with the Road Vehicles (Authorised Weight) Regulations 1998, as 'maximum authorised weights'. The maximum gross weight is the unladen weight of a vehicle plus its maximum permitted load. It therefore represents the total weight of the vehicle as transmitted to the road surface. A vehicle of 5 tonnes unladen weight which is permitted to carry 4 tonnes of cargo would have a maximum gross weight of 9 tonnes. The term 'permissible maximum weight', which is used to establish whether goods vehicles are small, medium or large for the purpose of determining the minimum age for driving a goods vehicle, is the vehicle's 'relevant maximum weight'. In turn the relevant permissible maximum weight is the maximum gross weight shown on the plate. The weight shown on the plate is therefore the 'permissible maximum weight' for the above purpose.

The 'maximum authorised weight' in relation to a vehicle, vehicle combination or axle means the maximum authorised weight for the vehicle, vehicle combination or axle determined in accordance with the 1998 Regulations. See above at pp 506–507.

Ministry plate

The Goods Vehicles (Plating and Testing) Regulations 1988 make most heavy goods vehicles and trailers subject to provisions for annual testing. Goods vehicles which are not subject to type approval must have a first examination for the purpose of plating as well as testing. Other goods vehicles will be fitted with a Ministry plate within fourteen days and the requirement to have a first examination no longer applies to a motor vehicle where a certificate of conformity or a minister's approval certificate has been issued. The first examination includes assessment of the vehicle's axle and gross weights, or authorised weights, as well as a test of roadworthiness. These weights are recorded on a 'Ministry plate'.

Every motor vehicle which meets the following requirements, namely:

(a) a plating certificate is in force for the vehicle; and
(b) that plating certificate is a certificate of conformity or a minister's approval certificate that is treated as a plating certificate by virtue of RTA 1988, s 59(4),

must be submitted for a goods vehicle test on or before the appropriate day. Other motor vehicles, and every trailer, must be submitted for both a plating examination and a goods vehicle test on or before the appropriate day. The term 'appropriate day' means:

(a) in relation to a vehicle which is a motor vehicle, the last day of the calendar month in which falls the anniversary of the date on which it was registered; and
(b) in relation to a vehicle which is a trailer, the last day of the calendar month in which falls the anniversary of the date on which it was first sold or supplied by retail.

However, the prescription of such dates does not prevent the Secretary of State authorising the submission of a vehicle after the appropriate day.

A number of vehicles do not require a Ministry plate. For example, dual-purpose vehicles not constructed or adapted to form part of an articulated vehicle are exempt (although they are subject to the MOT test). So are breakdown, fire fighting or snow clearance vehicles, living vans whose gross design weight does not exceed 3,500 kg, police vehicles and vehicles temporarily in Great Britain (provided they do not remain for more than twelve months).

The requirements set out above under the heading 'Manufacturer's plate' are in respect of certain vehicles *at the time of manufacture*. On the other hand, the Ministry plating requirements are concerned with a subsequent examination, which on the first occasion includes a 'Ministry plating'. As a result there are differences in respect of the list of vehicles affected. Vehicles still exist which were not the subject of manufacturer's plating at the time of their manufacture, but will nevertheless be subject to Ministry plating and annual testing.

When the plated weight has been determined, a plating certificate is issued showing the date of issue, plated weights and tyre sizes. Those vehicles which were subject to the Motor Vehicles (Type Approval for Goods Vehicles) (Great Britain) Regulations 1982 will already have a certificate of conformity or approval and this, or a substitute issued by the Secretary of State for it, must be produced. The reason is that the certificate is treated as a plating certificate for the purposes of the Regulations and the examiner merely checks to see that no notifiable alterations have been made to the vehicle. If they have not, the certificate of conformity or type approval certificate is deemed to have been issued under the Plating and Testing Regulations.

The plate and plating certificate

The manufacturer's plate is a metal plate which is fixed to the vehicle. It is only significant until Ministry plating takes place, as the particulars on the Ministry plate are deemed to be correct after that examination is carried out. After a plating examination, a Ministry plate and a plating certificate will be issued in respect of the vehicle. They show the maximum gross weights or the maximum authorised weights for the vehicle; these may be the same as those shown on the manufacturer's plate but this will not necessarily be so as they may be lower if the Ministry does not accept the weights specified by the manufacturers. The Ministry will not set weights higher than those set by the manufacturer unless the vehicle has been altered to permit it to carry more weight. The Ministry plate is in fact a paper plate; it must be fixed in a conspicuous and readily accessible position in the cab of the vehicle, or (in the case of a trailer) in some such position.

Plates will be attached to both parts of an articulated vehicle, ie to the tractive unit and the semi-trailer. The 'plating certificate' is in most respects a copy of the plate attached to the vehicle but includes, additionally, details of the types of tyres fitted to the vehicle at the time of inspection. Plates issued since 24 March 1994 may contain a space for 'maximum train weight' where a vehicle is used for combined transport operations (the transport of loading units partly by rail in Great Britain and partly by road). Plates issued since 1 January 1998 may show maximum authorised weights.

Offences

It is an offence for any person to use, or to cause or permit to be used, on a road a goods vehicle of a class required by the 1988 Regulations to have been submitted for examination for plating if there is no plating certificate in force for the vehicle. The plating *certificate* will normally be held at the office of the company. The circumstances in which a constable may demand its production are the same as those applying to other vehicle documents. The same conditions apply, in relation to a defence being available to those who subsequently produce their certificate, as apply in the case of certificates of insurance (see p 384).

If a goods vehicle is to be permitted to draw a trailer, its plating certificate will specify its maximum laden weight together with its trailer, or its maximum authorised weight together with that trailer. If, after the relevant date for Ministry plating, it is used to draw a trailer when no such weight is specified, any person using or causing or permitting such use is guilty of an offence.

Any structural alterations made to vehicles after plating must be notified to the Ministry. It is an offence to fail to do so. However, alterations to plated particulars may be made without the necessity for a further examination where a plating certificate is in force for the vehicle and the alterations applied for would not affect the safety of the vehicle on a road.

Temporary exemption

The Ministry is empowered to issue certificates of temporary exemption if, due to exceptional circumstances, an examination cannot be carried out. An example of such a circumstance would be the destruction by fire of the testing station at which the examination was to be carried out.

Goods vehicle testing

Vehicles subject to goods vehicle testing must be submitted for testing on or before the appropriate day, as defined on p 514. Goods vehicles submitted for a first examination during the two months preceding the appropriate day may be issued with a certificate which expires on the next but one appropriate day. Provisions of the Road Safety Act 2006 (RSA 2006), s 48 will amend, when in force, RTA 1988, s 49 to require the Secretary of State to maintain records in respect of goods vehicle testing and these records may be checked against those maintained in accordance with the Vehicle Excise and Registration Act 1994 (VERA 1994).

Although vehicles which require plating are exempt from the normal MOT test applied to passenger motor cars, they are subject to a more stringent annual test by the Ministry at one of its testing stations. Computer-generated test certificates may be issued. The examiner is able to enter pass or fail marks into a hand-held computer which produces a certificate, or advisory note indicating the respects in which a vehicle has failed the test, or, where appropriate, a refusal form and if merited, a prohibition notice.

It is an offence to use on a road at any time after the relevant date any goods vehicle required to be tested by the Regulations, when there is no goods vehicle test certificate in force for it. It is also an offence to cause or permit this to be done. In the case of trailers, a disc is fitted to the trailer which gives the date on which its test certificate expires. The same exceptions to liability apply as in the case of MOT tests, for example where a vehicle is going by previous appointment to (and from) a test, or while it is undergoing a test, or where a vehicle refused a certificate is going to or from a place of repair, or where it is being towed to the breakers. In addition a certificate of temporary exemption may be issued on the same ground and in the same way as in the case of the Ministry plating requirement.

A goods vehicle test certificate must be produced to a constable in the same cases as a certificate of insurance. The usual time for production applies. It is an offence to fail so to produce it.

OPERATORS' LICENCES

Purpose of licensing

It is essential that strict control is kept over the operation of goods vehicles, partly to protect the environment, partly to promote safety on the roads, and partly to prevent damage to roads. The traffic commissioner for each area is the licensing authority for goods vehicles. He monitors the standard of maintenance of vehicles, checks that drivers do not exceed the maximum permitted periods of driving and working, and ensures that the recommended weight limits for vehicles are not exceeded.

Need for operators' licences

The Goods Vehicles (Licensing of Operators) Act 1995 (GV(LO)A 1995), s 2(1) states that, with the exceptions listed in s 2(2) (see p 523) no person shall use a goods vehicle on a road for the carriage of goods for hire or reward, or for or in connection with any trade or business carried on by him, except under the authority of an operators' licence. By s 2(5), a person who uses a vehicle in contravention of s 2(1) commits an offence.

If the vehicle belongs to the driver, or if it is in his possession under an agreement for hire, hire purchase or loan, he is deemed to be the user for licensing purposes. In any other case, the user will be the person whom the driver is serving or whose agent he is at the time. This is provided by GV(LO)A 1995, s 58(2). The offence of using a goods vehicle etc without the authority of an operators' licence is therefore one which is committed by the owner or hirer (or the like) of a vehicle if he is driving it, or by the employer of the driver where the owner or hirer is not personally driving the vehicle as is often the case. If Brown drives his own vehicle on a road for the carriage of goods for hire or reward without an operators' licence he commits this offence. If Green is driving Brown's vehicle in these circumstances, Brown, the employer, commits the offence, and Green does not. If a company leases vehicles with their drivers from a second company but the second company prescribes the drivers' duties; pays their wages; allocates their holidays; and is responsible for driver discipline and therefore remains the driver's employer, the second company is operating those vehicles and must hold the appropriate operators' licences. It is essential to prove that the goods vehicle was carrying goods at the time of the alleged offence. It must also be proved that the goods vehicle was being used *for hire or reward or for or in connection with any trade or business carried out by the user.*

Hire or reward

Generally speaking, a person uses a goods vehicle for hire or reward if he hires out the use of the vehicle, together with its driver, to another person. For example, a furniture remover who uses his employees and his vehicles to assist a customer to move his household effects, an agreed fee being paid by the customer, uses the vehicle for the carriage of goods for hire or reward. In one case, for instance, where a goods vehicle was hired out to empty a septic tank and dump effluent on to land some distance away, it was held that it had been used for the carriage of goods (the effluent) for hire or reward. In another case, a goods vehicle which was used to remove earth from a site for a fixed fee was held to be used for the carriage of goods for hire or reward.

For or in connection with any trade or business carried on by him

A large number of goods vehicles are used by firms solely for, or in connection with, their own trade or business, as opposed to hauling goods for hire or reward. Supermarket chains operate fleets of vehicles solely for the purpose of effecting deliveries to their retail outlets, with the result that the vehicles are used for or in connection with their own trade or business, and require operators' licences. Likewise, the builder who uses his goods vehicle to carry building materials to the sites where his building operations are being carried out uses the vehicle in connection with his own business and requires an operators' licence. On the other hand, it has been held that a person whose hobby was stock car racing and who transported the stock cars in a converted motor coach did not use that coach for or in connection with any trade or business, even though he competed for prize money and received sponsorship money.

GV(LO)A 1995, s 2(4) states that, for the purpose of operators' licensing, a local or public authority is deemed to be carrying on a business. Such an authority must therefore have operators' licences in respect of its vehicles.

Types of operators' licences

There are two types of operators' licences: standard operators' licences and restricted operators' licences.

Standard operators' licences

Standard operators' licences are all embracing in that they authorise the holder to carry goods for hire or reward or in connection with the holder's trade or business. On occasions a licence may be held by a company as opposed to an individual. Where a licence is held by a holding company, any business carried on by a subsidiary company is regarded as being carried on by the licence holder. This provision prevents the formation of subsidiary companies in an effort to avoid the responsibilities of the holder of a licence. However, a company which carries the goods of a second company which is its subsidiary or holding company may, in certain circumstances, hold a restricted licence instead of a standard licence.

Standard licences may authorise transport operations both nationally and internationally, or may be in respect of national operations only. A national transport operation is a transport operation involving the use of goods vehicles for the carriage of goods for hire or reward in the United Kingdom only. Therefore, if an operator wishes to transport goods to various centres in Europe for hire or reward he will require a standard licence which authorises international transport operations. If he does not hold such a licence he will only be able to deliver the goods to a port for despatch abroad, the goods to be picked up by another operator when unloaded at a European port.

Restricted operators' licences

A restricted operators' licence authorises the use of goods vehicles solely for, or in connection with, a trade or business carried on by the holder of the licence, other than that of carrying goods for hire or reward.

General

An operators' licence will normally authorise an operator to use several vehicles. It is issued to the operator and is generally kept at the offices of his company, usually his operating centre. The licence will specify the registration numbers of the vehicles which are authorised to be used. It will also specify, by type, the maximum number of trailers which may be used under the licence and also the maximum number of subsequently acquired motor vehicles which may be so used.

Identity discs

So that vehicles specified on an operators' licence may bear evidence of the fact that they are being used under the authority of a licence, an identity disc is issued in respect of each vehicle which is specified. The disc must be fixed to that vehicle in a waterproof container adjacent to the vehicle excise licence. The Transport Act 2000, s 263 substitutes GV(LO)A 1995, s 5(6) so as to provide that a motor vehicle which is not specified in an operators' licence is not authorised to be used under that licence unless the licence holder has notified the traffic commissioner by whom the licence was issued and has paid the prescribed fee. At the time of writing s 263 of the Transport Act 2000 has not been brought into force. The existing GV(LO)A 1995, s 5(6) permits a vehicle which is not specified in an operators' licence to be used by the operator for a period of one month after the vehicle first came into his possession, provided that the traffic commissioner is notified at some time within that period of one month, with a view to specifying that vehicle in the licence held by the operator.

The information which is given on an identity disc is sufficient to identify its authorised usage. It will show whether the licence is standard or restricted, and if standard whether it is valid in respect of international and national operations, or only of national ones.

The holder of the licence must cause the identity disc to be displayed at all times when the vehicle is specified in his licence, regardless of whether or not the vehicle is being used at the time for a purpose for which a licence is required. The person in control of the vehicle must keep the disc readily legible.

Production of licences etc for examination

The holder of an operators' licence must produce his licence if required to do so by a police constable, vehicle examiner, or by any person authorised by the licensing authority. He may elect whether to produce it at his operating centre, head office or principal place of business within the traffic area of the licensing authority by whom the licence was granted. It will be noted that there is no power to demand production of this document at a police station.

A requirement to produce must be complied with within fourteen days.

The GV(LO)A 1995, Sch 5 provides that no goods shall be carried on a large goods vehicle unless a consignment note is carried by the driver. The provisions do not apply if the goods could be carried without an operators' licence or if the vehicle is exempted by regulations. These powers may be exercised by a vehicle examiner, authorised person or a police constable. These provisions are not yet in force at the time of writing.

Vehicle examiners' powers to issue fixed penalty notices

Under amendments made by RSA 2006, which are not yet in force vehicle examiners of the Vehicle and Operator Services Agency may issue fixed penalty notices in respect of offences which they are empowered to enforce in relation to goods vehicles. Conditional offers under the Road Traffic Offenders Act 1988, s 75 may also be issued.

This system will be operated independently of the police by the Secretary of State who is responsible for administering the system, collecting the penalties and the endorsement of the licences. The Vehicle Operator Service Agency will carry out this function on the Secretary of State's behalf.

When provisions of RSA 2006 are in force, fixed penalty offences will be 'notifiable' in the same way as convictions in relation to the grant, variation, revocation of operators' licences.

Seizure of vehicle and load where vehicle is used without an operators' licence

The Goods Vehicles (Enforcement Powers) Regulations 2001 permit an 'authorised person' to detain a heavy goods vehicle and its contents in circumstances where the person using the vehicle does not have an operators' licence for that or any other vehicle. Schedule 1A defines the term 'authorised person' as an examiner appointed by the Secretary of State under RTA 1988, s 66A, or a person acting under his direction.

Regulation 3 provides that where an authorised person has reason to believe that a vehicle is being, or has been, used on a road in contravention of GV(LO)A 1995, s 2 (no operators' licence), he may detain the vehicle and its contents. However, no one other than a constable may stop such a vehicle on a road. By reg 4, a vehicle must be returned when it transpires that, at the time that the vehicle was being used, the person using it had an operators' licence (whether or not it authorised the use of the vehicle concerned), or when it transpires that, at the time of the detention of the vehicle, it was not, and had not been, used in contravention of GV(LO)A 1995, s 2.

Regulation 5 authorises the immobilisation of a detained vehicle. The device may be attached at the place of detention or at the place to which it has been moved. A notice must also be fixed to the vehicle stating that a device has been fitted to the vehicle; that release may only be effected by or under the direction of an authorised person; that the notice must not be removed or interfered with other than with the authority of an authorised person; and no attempt must be made to drive the vehicle. The removal of an immobilisation device or a notice, other than under the direction of an authorised person, is an offence. An immobilised vehicle may be released by an authorised person and must be released where it transpires that a licence was held (whether authorising the use of that vehicle or not) or it transpires that no offence was being committed against GV(LO)A 1995, s 2.

By reg 8, an authorised person may direct in writing that any property detained may be removed and delivered into the custody of a specified person. A detained vehicle may be driven, towed or removed by such means as are reasonable in the circumstances and necessary steps may be taken to facilitate removal. The contents may be separately removed to facilitate the removal of the vehicle; because there is good reason for storing the contents elsewhere; or their condition requires immediate disposal. A 'specified person' is one appointed by the authorised person, that specified person having made arrangements with the Secretary of State and agreed to take necessary steps for the safe custody of such property. However, where an authorised person has given a written direction concerning the detention of property, he may allow the driver to deliver its contents to their destination or some other suitable place before delivering the vehicle into the custody of a specified person.

An authorised person must publish a notice in the *London Gazette* giving details of the detention and the procedure for claiming the vehicle and its contents. In addition, not less than twenty-one days before the expiry of the period given in the notice (also twenty-one days), a copy must be served upon the owner, traffic commissioner and chief officer of police in whose areas the vehicle was detained, the Association of British Insurers, and the British Vehicle Rental and Leasing Association.

The Regulations also make provision for the owner of a vehicle so detained to apply in writing, within twenty-one days, to the traffic commissioner for the area in which the detention took place, for the return of his vehicle. An application may be made on the grounds that the person using the vehicle held a licence (whether or not authorising the use of the particular vehicle), that the vehicle was not being, and had not been, used in contravention of GV(LO)A 1995, s 2, or that the owner did not know that the vehicle was being used or had been so used. It must also state whether the applicant requires a hearing. Any determination of a traffic commissioner must be notified in writing. There is an appeal to a Transport Tribunal. Notice of such an appeal must be given before the expiry of twenty-eight days from that determination. Where the traffic commissioner or a Transport Tribunal finds that one of the grounds specified above is made out, he or it must order the authorised person to return the vehicle to the owner.

The Regulations provide for the disposal of vehicles where no application for return has been made, or where such an application has been made but the traffic commissioner or Transport Tribunal determines, on appeal, that none of the grounds set out in the paragraph above exist. An authorised person is empowered to sell or destroy the vehicle as he thinks fit. Notice of such disposal must be given to the persons and bodies to whom notice of detention is required to be sent, as set out above.

In relation to contents, an authorised person must return any contents detained under reg 3 (above) to a person who has given to an authorised person, within the permitted time, notice in writing of his claim and who produces satisfactory evidence of his entitlement to the contents and of his identity and address. Alternatively, where a person seeks to recover the contents as the agent of another person and produces satisfactory evidence of his status as agent and, of his principal's identity, address and entitlement to the contents, contents detained under reg 3 must be returned to him. Regulation 17 makes provision for the disposal of the contents of a vehicle.

It is an offence against reg 20 for a person intentionally to obstruct an authorised person in the exercise of his powers under reg 3 (detention of vehicle or contents) or reg 8 (removal). Regulation 21 creates the offence of making a declaration with a view to securing the return of a vehicle where that declaration is to the effect that the vehicle was not being, or had not been, used in contravention of GV(LO)A 1995, s 2 and that declaration is to the person's knowledge either false or in any material respect misleading.

Forgery etc of documents and powers of seizure

GV(LO)A 1995, s 38 provides that a person is guilty of an offence if, with intent to deceive, he forges, alters, uses, lends, or allows to be used, a document or other thing to which the section applies. Section 38 also provides that a person is guilty of an offence if, with intent to deceive, he makes or has in his possession a document or other thing so closely resembling a document or other thing to which the section applies as to be calculated to deceive. Section 38 applies to operators' licences and documents and other things (eg plates) ancillary to them.

GV(LO)A 1995, s 39 provides that a person is guilty of an offence if he knowingly makes a false statement in order to obtain the issue of an operators' licence or its variation, or in order to prevent its issue or variation, or in order to procure the imposition of a condition or limitation in relation to such a licence, or in order to obtain a certificate or diploma under the Act.

A vehicle examiner, a person authorised for these purposes by the traffic commissioner, or a police constable, may at any reasonable time enter any premises of an applicant for an operators' licence, or the holder of such a licence, and inspect the facilities for maintaining vehicles. It is an offence to obstruct such a person. Where such a person has reason to believe that a document or article carried on or by a driver, or a document produced to him under the Act, is a document or article in relation to which an offence under s 38 or s 39 has been committed, he may seize it.

When licences are not required

By way of exception to the general rule, that operators must hold licences in respect of all goods vehicles used by them for the carriage of goods for hire or reward, or for or in connection with their own trade or business, GV(LO)A 1995, s 2(2) states that this requirement does not apply to:

(a) the use of a small goods vehicle (as defined by Sch 1, see below);
(b) the use of a goods vehicle for international carriage by a haulier established in a member state of the EU (other than the United Kingdom) and not established in the United Kingdom;
(c) the use of a goods vehicle by a haulier established in Northern Ireland (and not in Great Britain) for international carriage; or
(d) to the use of any vehicle of any class specified in regulations (see below).

Small goods vehicle

A 'small goods vehicle' is a goods vehicle:

(a) which does not form part of a vehicle combination and has a relevant plated weight not exceeding 3.5 tonnes or (not having a relevant plated weight) has an unladen weight not exceeding 1,525 kg; or
(b) which forms part of a vehicle combination (not being an articulated combination) which is such that the total plated weight of the combination (except any small trailer) does not exceed 3.5 tonnes (or, if one or more of the vehicles in the combination, other than a small trailer, is not plated, if the total unladen weight of those vehicles, excluding such a trailer does not exceed 1,525 kg); or
(c) which forms part of an articulated combination which is such that the total of the unladen weight of the tractive unit and the plated weight of the trailer does not exceed 3.5 tonnes (or if the trailer does not have a plated weight, the total of their unladen weights does not exceed 1,525 kg).

The description of a 'small goods vehicle' appears to be quite complex until it is realised that the figures of 3.5 tonnes and 1,525 kg are all that it is essential to remember: 1,525 kg represents 30 cwt. Let us examine the type of vehicles which are small goods vehicles by virtue of Sch 1.

Rigid goods vehicles A single goods vehicle without a trailer, which is plated and whose relevant plated weight is 3.5 tonnes or less, is a small goods vehicle and does not need to be operated under a licence. The same is the case where the unladen weight of an unplated goods vehicle (and there are not many such vehicles) is 1,525 kg or less.

Rigid goods vehicles plus trailers The first point to note is that all draw-bar trailers with an unladen weight not exceeding 1,525 kg are classed as 'small trailers' and must be ignored in the following calculations. If both the goods vehicle and the trailer are plated, and the two relevant weights total 3.5 tonnes or less, the combination is a 'small' goods vehicle and does not need to be operated under a licence. If one or both parts of the combination are unplated, the relevant weight is 1,525 kg or less.

Articulated goods vehicle combinations   If the total of the unladen weight of the tractive unit and the plated weight of the semi-trailer is 3.5 tonnes or less, the combination is a 'small' goods vehicle and does not need to be operated under a licence; if the semi-trailer is unplated the relevant weight is 1,525 kg or less.

Vehicles exempt by regulations

Those vehicles which are exempted by regulations are set out in Sch 3 to the Goods Vehicles (Licensing of Operators) Regulations 1995. The list is extensive but, for ease of understanding, it is more practical to think in terms of categories of vehicles. Generally, the vehicles exempted are those used by public services. Thus, defence force, police, fire fighting, rescue and ambulance vehicles are exempt; so are vehicles used for purposes such as snow clearance, gritting and refuse disposal. Also exempted are vehicles used as agricultural tractors or machines, dual-purpose vehicles, showmen's goods vehicles, recovery vehicles, cement mixer lorries and vehicles used for funerals. Motor vehicles constructed or adapted primarily to carry passengers or their effects, together with any trailer, are exempt whilst being so used. Of course, the operation of public service vehicles must be licensed under other provisions described in the previous chapter.

Vehicles temporarily in Great Britain

The Goods Vehicles (Community Authorisations) Regulations 1992 established a Community-wide authorisation allowing goods vehicles access to the market in the carriage of goods by road between member states. The Goods Vehicles (Licensing of Operators) Act 1995 and the regulations bring into effect the provisions of Council Regulation No 881/92/EEC which requires that each member state must issue a Community authorisation to any haulier established in that state who is entitled to carry out international carriage of goods by road for hire or reward. Holders of such authorisations do not require operators' licences in other Community countries. The Council Regulation provides for the appointment of 'authorised inspecting officers' who are empowered to demand the production of a certified copy of the authorisation which must be carried on each vehicle operating under its authority. The 1992 Regulations appoint police constables and examiners appointed under the Road Traffic Acts as authorised inspecting officers. The Road Traffic (Foreign Vehicles) Act 1972 permits an examiner who is exercising the functions of an authorised inspecting officer to prohibit the driving of a foreign goods vehicle on a road where it appears to him that there may have been a contravention of the 1992 Regulations involving the vehicle's use without a Community authorisation or a failure to comply with the conditions governing the use of Community authorisations.

The Goods Vehicles (Licensing of Operators) (Temporary Use in Great Britain) Regulations 1996 exempt the users of foreign goods vehicles from the need to hold an operators' licence in specified circumstances. They define a 'foreign goods vehicle' as one:

(a) which is operated by a person who is not established in the United Kingdom and has been brought temporarily into Great Britain;
(b) which is not being used for international carriage by a haulier who is established in a member state other than the United Kingdom;
(c) which is engaged in carrying goods by road on a journey some part of which has taken place, or will take place, outside the United Kingdom; and
(d) which is not used at any time during the said journey for the carriage of goods loaded at one place in the United Kingdom and delivered at another place in the United Kingdom.

The 1996 Regulations, in addition, provide specific exemptions in favour of goods vehicles of named non-EU countries, in specified circumstances.

Evidence by certificate

The Goods Vehicles (Licensing of Operators) Act 1995, s 43 makes provisions for evidence to be given by certificate of the facts stated in it. The certificate must be signed by or on behalf of a traffic commissioner. It may certify that a person was the holder of an operators' licence on a particular date; the dates of validity of an operators' licence; the terms and conditions attached to such a licence; that a person is disqualified from holding or obtaining an operators' licence; or that a licence was suspended.

A certificate which purports to be signed by or on behalf of a traffic commissioner must be taken to be so signed unless the contrary is proved.

DRIVERS' HOURS AND RECORDS

The provisions set out below apply whether the driver is the driver of a goods vehicle or of a *passenger vehicle*.

There are two sets of provisions which apply: (a) the so called European rules; and (b) the rules provided by the Transport Act 1968, Part VI (which are of relatively limited application).

European rules

These rules, provided by the Community Drivers' Hours Regulation (and certain other Regulations) made by the Council of the EU, create common standards for the whole of the Community. Separate sets of regulations relate to drivers' hours and drivers' records. The rules apply to journeys on 'roads open to the public' by a goods or passenger vehicle (as specified below), whether it is laden or not, and whether it is registered in this country, in another EU member state, or in any other country. There is no distinction between journeys made for hire or reward and those made on an operator's own account.

It is to be noted that the rules are concerned with journeys on 'roads open to the public', a phrase otherwise unknown in our law. Where journeys are made entirely within an area which is privately owned, on roads which are privately maintained, the important question is not concerned with ownership of such roads, but with access to them and their use. The fact that they may only be used by persons with business in the privately owned area, eg an airport, is irrelevant. The question is whether the roads are open to the public.

The rules apply to carriage by:

(a) all goods vehicles which exceed 3.5 tonnes permissible maximum weight; and
(b) all passenger vehicles which in construction and equipment are suitable for carrying more than nine persons including the driver.

The meaning of 'permissible maximum weight' in (a) has already been given: essentially, it is the maximum gross weight shown on the relevant plate. Where a trailer is being drawn, the term refers to the aggregate of the maximum gross weight marked on the towing vehicle and the maximum gross weight marked on the trailer in actual use at the time; not to the total weight of the vehicle and the trailer which it might be capable of towing.

Exemptions

Quite apart from the vehicles to which the European rules do not apply because they are outside these general classifications, the European rules expressly do not apply to carriage by the following vehicles which would otherwise fall within them:

(a) vehicles used for the carriage of passengers on regular services where the route covered by the service in question does not exceed 50 km (approx 30 miles);
(b) vehicles with a maximum authorised speed not exceeding 30 kph (approx 20 mph);
(c) vehicles used by or under the control of the armed services, civil defence, fire services and forces responsible for maintaining public order;
(d) vehicles used in connection with sewerage, flood protection, gas, water or electricity services, highway maintenance and control, refuse collection and disposal, telegraph and telephone services, carriage of postal articles, radio and television broadcasting and the detection of radio or television transmitters or receivers;
(e) vehicles used in emergencies or rescue operations;
(f) specialised vehicles used for medical purposes;
(g) vehicles transporting circus or funfair equipment;
(h) specialised breakdown vehicles (regardless of the use to which they are being put at the time);
(i) vehicles undergoing road tests for technical development, repair or maintenance purposes, and new or rebuilt vehicles which have not yet been put into service;
(j) vehicles used for non-commercial carriage of goods for personal use;
(k) vehicles used for milk collection from farms and the return to farms of milk containers or milk products intended for animal feed.

In summary, these exemptions refer to vehicles used for the conveyance of passengers for short distances, vehicles of public services and public utilities, ambulances etc, many tractors, showmen's goods vehicles and some breakdown vehicles. As the purpose of keeping records is to exercise control over working hours, the reason for the exemptions can be appreciated. Such vehicles are not generally being used in the competitive business world in which there might be a temptation to use drivers for long periods of driving. In addition, most of the vehicles are controlled by public authorities or public utilities.

The exemptions are interpreted strictly. For example, in relation to exemption (a), buses used under contract by tour operators which are used for single journeys from airports to hotels, where the precise route to be taken is not predetermined, cannot be considered to be a 'regular service' within the terms of exemption granted in favour of regular services where the route covered does not exceed 50 kilometres. This is so whether or not there are occasional stops at tourist attractions. By way of further example, a vehicle used to transport gas appliances is not used 'in connection with gas services' under (d) above, since that phrase is limited to use in connection with the production, transport or distribution of gas, or the maintenance of installations for that purpose. Thus, a vehicle used to transport gas cookers and the like is subject to the European rules. Similarly, a vehicle used by a private company to collect builders' skips is not an exempted vehicle by reason of its use 'in connection with refuse disposal and collection' as that exemption has been held to be limited to a 'general service performed in the public interest', and not to extend to a commercial service to customers. A vehicle used to transport machinery to a highway maintenance site is not exempt; it has been held not to be a vehicle used in connection with highway maintenance and control. The reason given was that such a vehicle is being used for the carriage of goods and its connection with highway maintenance and control is too remote.

Further exemptions

Further modifications are provided by the Community Drivers' Hours and Recording Equipment (Exemptions and Supplementary Provisions) Regulations 1986. These regulations exempt from the provisions of the European rules the following vehicles:

(a) vehicles used for the carriage of passengers constructed or equipped to carry not more than seventeen persons including the driver;

(b) vehicles which on or after 1 January 1990 are being used by a public authority to provide public services otherwise than in competition with professional road hauliers (such as ambulances and medical vehicles, social services' vehicles for elderly and mentally and physically handicapped persons, those used by coast-guard, lighthouse, harbour, airports, railways and waterway authorities);

(c) vehicles used by agricultural, horticultural, forestry or fishery undertakings to carry goods within a 50 km radius of base (in the case of use by fishery undertakings only if used for the carriage of live fish or conveyance of a 'catch of fish');

(d) vehicles used for animal waste or carcasses not for human consumption;

(e) vehicles used for the carriage of live animals between farm and market or slaughterhouse;

(f) vehicles used as a shop, at a local market, for door to door selling, or for mobile banking etc;

(g) vehicles used for worship, library services or cultural events, which are specially fitted for such use;

(h) goods vehicles not exceeding 7.5 tonnes permissible maximum weight which are carrying equipment or material for the driver's use in the course of his work within a 50 km radius of his base provided that driving the vehicle is not his main activity;

(i)   vehicles which operate exclusively on offshore islands not linked to the rest of Great Britain;

(j)   gas or electrically propelled goods vehicles not exceeding 7.5 tonnes maximum permissible weight;

(k)   vehicles used for driving instruction with a view to gaining a licence provided there is no trailer used for goods purposes;

(l)   any tractor used on or after 1 January 1990 for agricultural or forestry work;

(m) any vehicle which is being used by the RNLI for the purpose of hauling lifeboats;

(n)   any vehicle manufactured before 1 January 1947; and

(o)   any vehicle which is propelled by steam.

Vehicles used for the collection of sea coal are exempt from the provisions of the European rules on drivers' records only.

Once again, these exemptions are interpreted strictly. In relation to (h) above, it has been held that the terms 'equipment or material' relate to goods which are in the possession of some person for the purpose of being worked on so as to produce some other article. It did not apply to greengrocery being taken from market to a retail outlet. The mere placing of such articles in bags does not make them 'material' for the driver's use in the course of his work, nor does the carriage of vehicle registration documentation upon a vehicle being taken to auction for disposal.

European rules on driving periods, rest breaks and rest periods

The rules are set out in the Community Drivers' Hours Regulation. For the purposes of the Regulation a 'driver' is any person who drives a vehicle, even for a short period, or who is in the vehicle in order to be available for driving if necessary; the term 'week' means the period between 00.00 hours on Monday and 24.00 hours on Sunday; and 'rest' means any uninterrupted period of at least one hour during which the driver may freely dispose of his time (which he will not be if he is engaged in doing some other type of work under the direction of his employer).

During breaks from driving a driver may not carry out any other work. The term 'other work' does not include waiting time spent on a moving vehicle by a driver who is not driving, or on a ferry or train. Where a driver accompanies a vehicle which is transported by ferry or train, the daily rest period may be interrupted (not more than once), provided that the period includes rest on land before or after the journey and the interruption is as short as possible and does not exceed one hour (including all embarkation, disembarkation and customs formalities etc) and during both portions of the rest period the driver must be able to have access to a bunk or couchette.

If a daily rest period is interrupted in this way, it must be increased by two hours. Thus, a driver may spend ten hours at rest in a bunk on land before embarkation on to a ferry for a journey. If at that stage his lorry has to be taken aboard the ferry by him, he may continue with a rest period, provided the break in his rest does not exceed one hour. If the journey takes four hours he will have had fourteen hours of rest. The normal daily rest period is eleven hours (extended by two in these circumstances), so the requirements are met. (If he had not already reduced three daily rest periods to nine hours in the course of the week, he would have complied with these requirements before he began the process of embarkation.) However, such interruptions to a daily rest period cannot occur at both sides of the Channel as the Regulation specifies that such interruptions can occur 'not more than once'.

Provided that road safety is not thereby jeopardised, the Regulation permits departure from the provisions to enable a driver to reach a suitable stopping place, but only to the extent necessary to ensure the safety of persons or of the vehicle or its load. In these circumstances the driver must indicate the nature of and the reason for his departure from these provisions on the record sheet of the recording equipment or in his daily roster. Such a deviation from the requirements of the Regulation may only be made by a driver at the time he is faced with an unexpected situation. It may not be pre-planned by an employer for reasons known before the journey commences.

Offences

A driver of a motor vehicle, who contravenes the above European rules concerning driving periods, rest breaks and rest periods whilst in Great Britain, commits an offence contrary to the Transport Act 1968, s 96(11A). An employer, or a person to whose orders the offender was subject, who causes or permits such a contravention, also commits an offence. However, it is a defence to prove that the contravention was due to unavoidable delay in the completion of a journey arising out of circumstances which the person charged could not reasonably have foreseen. In the case of an employer etc, he also has a defence if he proves that the contravention was due to the fact that the driver had for a particular period or periods driven otherwise than in his employment, and that he (the employer etc) could not reasonably have become aware of that fact.

'Cause' bears the same meaning as described on p 405. In the present context, 'permit' has been held by the House of Lords to mean failing to take reasonable steps to prevent a contravention. The House held that an employer's failure to check a driver's records amounts to prima facie evidence of permitting a contravention of the European rules and of being s reckless as to this.

European rules on drivers' records

The Community Drivers' Hours Regulation requires that a tachograph be installed and used in vehicles which are registered in a member state of the EU and are used for the carriage of goods or passengers by road. The Community Recording Equipment Regulation lays down rules as to the construction, installation, use and testing of tachographs.

The Community Recording Equipment Regulation requires that tachographs must be capable of detecting interruptions in the power supply, of recording driving time automatically, and of allowing the removal and refitting of seals by an approved centre to enable speed limiters to be fitted. It also requires the protection of cables connected to the transmitter by a steel sheath.

The Transport Act 1968, s 97 makes it an offence for any person to use, or cause or permit to be used, a vehicle to which the Community Drivers' Hours Regulation applies and in which a tachograph is required by the Community Recording Equipment Regulation, art 3 to be installed and used if that vehicle is not fitted with a tachograph, or it is not being used in compliance with the Community Recording Equipment Regulation. Where an approved tachograph was not in working order, it is a defence to prove that it had not been reasonably practicable to repair it and that alternative records were being kept. It is also an offence to use, cause or permit to be used, a vehicle in which there is recording equipment which has been repaired (whether before or after installation) otherwise than in accordance with the Community Recording Equipment Regulation.

The above offences are ones of strict liability, but it is a defence for an accused to prove that he neither knew nor ought to have known that the recording equipment had not been installed or repaired, as the case may be.

Tachographs may only be fitted and repaired by fitters or workshops approved by a member state. The tachograph is then sealed and marked. The employer and the driver are responsible for ensuring that the tachograph functions correctly and that the seals on it are unbroken. It is an offence contrary to Transport Act 1968, s 97AA to forge, alter or use any seal, with intent to deceive. A seal is 'forged' if it is made in order that it may be used as genuine.

Records must be made by the use of a 'digital tachograph' or an 'analogue tachograph'. The Passenger and Goods Vehicles (Recording Equipment) Regulations 2005 introduced the 'digital tachograph' as opposed to the 'analogue tachograph'. The digital tachograph created a need to recognise the different forms in which records were kept by digital, as opposed to analogue, tachographs. The analogue tachograph traces its records on a disk inserted into a machine; a digital tachograph 'stores' data in a similar way to that stored by a computer. However, it is useful to keep in mind that the provisions in these sections are, in character, the same in respect of both types of tachograph. The difference merely lies in the nature of the records kept, and because of their nature, the means which must be employed to inspect and copy records. Vehicles first put into public service on or after 1 May 2006 and which require a tachograph must be fitted with a digital tachograph.

The employer must issue sufficient tachograph record sheets or driver cards to each driver. Record sheets are circular discs upon which the tachograph records certain information. Driver cards store information in the same way as computer disks. Each driver is responsible for operating switches which separately cause records to be made of driving time, other work or attendance duties, breaks and rest periods. An employer must retain completed discs or downloaded data for a period of at least a year and produce them to an authorised inspector on request. The term 'authorised inspector' includes a constable who, if in uniform, is not required to produce a form of authority.

Each driver must enter on his tachograph record sheet or driver card:

(a) his full name;
(b) the date and place where the use of the sheet or driver card starts and ends;
(c) the registration number of the vehicle and of any other vehicle to which he changes during his duties;
(d) the odometer reading at the start of the first, and at the end of the last, journey recorded on the sheet and, if there is a change of vehicle, the same reading for the other vehicle or vehicles; and
(e) the time any change of vehicle takes place.

Drivers must not use dirty or damaged tachograph sheets or print-outs. Damaged sheets or print-outs must be attached to the sheet or print-out which replaces them so that an up-to-date record is always available. Drivers must ensure that tachographs are kept running continuously while they are responsible for the vehicle. Drivers must record on the tachograph record sheet or driver card:

(a) driving time;
(b) other periods of work;
(c) other periods of availability;
(d) breaks in work and daily rest periods.

'Other periods of work' includes time which a driver necessarily spends travelling to take over a vehicle subject to an obligation to use a tachograph and which was not at the driver's home or the employer's operational centre, and periods of driving by a driver performing a transport service outside the scope of the Regulations before taking over a vehicle to which they apply.

Where there is more than one driver, they must change the record sheets or driver cards to ensure that distance, speed and driving time are recorded in relation to each person's driving. Where there are two drivers the periods during which each is not driving are not rest periods if the driver remains in the vehicle and is available for driving if necessary. Article 8(7) of the Community Drivers' Hours Regulations provides that the daily rest period may be taken in a vehicle, as long as it is fitted with a bunk '*and is stationary*'.

It was pointed out in the case concerned that if the appeal was not allowed it would be lawful for owners to operate their fleet so that a substantial part of drivers' rest time would be spent in moving vehicles.

In respect of the requirement that the tachograph must be in operation, it must be in operation throughout the daily working period. If a lorry driver drives home having finished work for the day this driving comes within the daily working period. He will commit an offence if he has switched off the lorry's tachograph. It would be different, of course, if he drives home in his car, since that vehicle is not required to have a tachograph.

Tachographs must be designed so that an inspecting officer can read the recordings relating to the preceding nine hours without damaging the sheet or driver card, if necessary by opening the instrument. Drivers must be able on request at the roadside to produce record sheets/print-outs for the current week, and for the previous fifteen days (twenty-eight days after 1 January 2008). Tachographs must be capable of recording, automatically or semi-automatically, the distance travelled and speed of the vehicle, driving time, other periods of work, breaks from work and daily rest periods, and the opening of the part of the equipment which contains the record sheet or driver card. The tachograph fitted to vehicles with more than one driver must be capable of recording simultaneously, but distinctly and on separate sheets or driver cards, the activities of the two members. Employed drivers must return completed record sheets or print-outs to their employer within twenty-one days. It is an offence to fail to do so without reasonable cause, and it is also an offence for an employer to fail to secure that this is done. When considering charges alleging that a haulage company had permitted drivers to exceed maximum periods of driving, a divisional court drew attention to the fact that the law permits a driver to keep his records in his possession for a period of twenty-one days before handing them over to his employer. So far as the state of mind of the company is concerned, there must be a causal relationship between the driver's breach and the company's conduct. The divisional court considered that the justices had failed to consider that relationship and had not applied their minds to the company's knowledge, or means of knowledge, at the time of the breach. Neither had they expressly or impliedly found who it was in the company who represented the mind and brains of the company for the purpose of permitting such offences. The court has also said that mens rea, in practice, is likely to be established by showing that the employer's failure to take objectively reasonable steps to prevent contraventions was deliberate in the sense merely of not being due to 'honest mistake or accident'.

Any record made on a record sheet or print-out is evidence of the matters appearing in them, and entries made on record sheets or print-outs by drivers are evidence of the matters appearing therefrom. If a police officer requires a driver to remove the disc from his tachograph or print-out, he should indicate that this was done at his request. An authorised officer (eg a constable) may require a person to produce, and permit him to inspect and copy, any book or register which the person is required by regulations under the Transport Act 1968, s 98 to carry or have in his possession, or preserve, and any other relevant document kept by the owner of the vehicle. Records of drivers' hours must be kept for at least a year, in chronological order, and made easily available for inspecting officers.

Inspection

The Transport Act 1968, s 99ZA authorises an officer to require production, inspection, retention and the copying of owners' records, record sheets or hard copies of electronically stored data (or written records if these are being made as a substitute where a tachograph is inoperable).

The Transport Act 1968, s 99ZB gives a power of entry to an officer, to any vehicle to which s 97 applies (vehicles which must be fitted with a tachograph) to inspect the vehicle and its recording equipment including record sheets produced by an analogue tachograph or hard copy of data which is stored on digital recording equipment or on a driver card. Driver cards may be inspected and copied (using digital recording equipment in or on the vehicle or by temporarily removing the driver card for copying) and data on digital recording equipment may also be copied. Recording equipment may be removed and retained if it is suspected that it has been interfered with or that there is a device on the vehicle capable of interfering with the proper operation of the tachograph. The driver or the operator of a vehicle may be required to remove it to a specified address for this purpose. An officer may, at any reasonable time, enter premises upon which he has reason to believe that a vehicle is being kept; a relevant document is to be found; or a driver card or copy of data previously on a driver card, or digital recording equipment, is to be found. Upon those premises he may inspect vehicles, documents, data, driver cards or a copy of stored data; recording equipment; copy items; remove recording equipment and retain it as evidence if it is found that it has been interfered with, and search for, remove and retain any device capable of interfering with a tachograph.

The Transport Act 1968, s 99ZC authorises an officer to require that any hard copy of data be signed and endorsed to the effect that it is a true copy. Such copies (in whatever form) may only be retained for six months unless required as evidence in proceedings.

Offences

The Transport Act 1968, s 99ZD creates offences of failure, without reasonable excuse, to comply with the requirement of an officer made under the provisions relating to tachographs in ss 99ZA to 99ZC and of obstructing an officer exercising his powers under s 99ZB or 99ZF (see below). Section 99ZE deals with offences relating to false records and data: making a relevant record knowing it to be false; alteration of a record or entry with intent to deceive; destruction or suppression of a relevant record or entry made or kept under the Community Recording Equipment Regulation or as a substitute; failing without reasonable excuse to make a relevant record or entry; recording of data which the accused knows to be false on recording equipment or on a driver card; alteration or production of such false records with intent to deceive; destruction or suppression of data stored in accordance with the applicable Community rules on recording equipment or a driver card; and failing without reasonable excuse to record any data on recording equipment or a driver card.

An offence is committed by a person who produces, supplies or installs a device designed to interfere with the proper operation of recording equipment, or is designed to enable falsification, alteration, destruction or suppression of data which has been stored.

By s 99ZF, an officer may seize documents inspected under s 99ZA or ZB in respect of which he believes an offence has been committed under s 99ZE.

The Transport Act 1968, s 99A provides that:

(a) if a driver of a United Kingdom vehicle obstructs an authorised person (examiner or constable authorised by his chief officer) in the exercise of his powers under s 99 (see p 538) or 99ZB to enter a vehicle or premises to inspect a vehicle or its recording equipment or the records kept on premises, or fails to comply with a requirement from such a person to inspect or copy records made under s 99 or s 99ZA to 99ZC; or

(b) if it appears to such a person that there has been a contravention of ss 96 to 98 or the applicable Community rules (installation of recording equipment and keeping of records), or that such a contravention will occur if the vehicle proceeds; or

(c) if it appears that a false document has been made under s 99(5) or 99ZE,

the authorised person may prohibit the driving of the vehicle on a road either for a specified period or without limitation of time. He may also direct the removal of the vehicle to a specified place under specified conditions. Notice in writing of the prohibition must be given to the driver.

Company cards, control cards, drivers' cards and workshop cards for use with digital tachographs

The Passenger and Goods Vehicle (Recording Equipment) (Tachograph Card) Regulations 2006, came into force on 21 August 2006. They make provisions in relation to company cards, control cards, driver cards and workshop cards used with digital tachographs which are fitted to new vehicles first used on or after 1 May 2006.

While the Transport Act 1968, Part VI is concerned with the various offences which may be committed in relation to record keeping, be it by analogue means or digital means, the Passenger and Goods Vehicles (Recording Equipment) (Tachograph Card) Regulations 2006 are concerned with the misuse of the various types of 'cards' issued for use together with digital tachographs. The cards with which the 2006 Regulations are concerned are 'tachograph cards' which are smart cards intended for use with recording equipment and permit identification by the recording equipment of the identity (or identity group of the cardholder). They allow for data transfer and storage of information. The general term 'tachograph card' embraces cards of the following types:

(a) a driver card,
(b) control card,
(c) workshop card, and
(d) company card.

The driver card

This is a tachograph card which is issued by the authorities of a member state to a *particular* driver. The card identifies the driver and allows for the storage of the activities of that particular driver. The 'continuous driving time' is computed within the recording equipment in relation to the particular driver since the end of his last 'availability' or 'break/rest period' or 'unknown activity'. The computations take into account, as needed, past activities stored on the driver card. The amended Community Recording Equipment Regulation refers to 'over speeding' which occurs when the authorised speed of the vehicle is exceeded. It is defined as any period of more than sixty seconds during which the vehicle's measured speed exceeds the limit laid down for the setting of the speed limitation device as specified in Council Directive 92/6/EEC and such data will be stored on recording equipment.

The control card

This is a tachograph card issued by the authorities of a member state to a national competent control authority. The card identifies the control body and may identify a control officer. It permits access to the data stored in the data memory or on driver cards for the purpose of reading, printing and/or downloading. Thus, control cards will be used by enforcement officers for the purpose of accessing information stored on a digital tachograph.

The workshop card

This is a tachograph card issued by the authorities of a member state to a recording equipment manufacturer, a fitter, a vehicle manufacturer or workshop, approved by the member state. A workshop card identifies the cardholder and permits access for testing, calibration and/or downloading of information stored on the recording equipment. 'Calibration' means updating or confirming vehicle parameters to be held in the data memory and this information includes numbers identifying the vehicle and the registering member state.

Company card

This is a tachograph card issued by the authorities of a member state to the owner or holder of vehicles fitted with recording equipment. It identifies the company and permits display, downloading and printing of the data stored in the recording equipment which has been locked by the company.

Drivers' cards (offences)

Regulation 3(1) creates offences of

(a) using, attempting to use or being in possession of more than one driver card of which he is the identified holder;
(b) using or attempting to use a driver card of which he is not the identified holder;
(c) making with intent to deceive, a false statement, or forging or altering a document, for the purpose of obtaining a driver card;
(d) using or being in possession of a driver's card issued in consequence of an application, with intent to deceive, a false statement or forged or altered document;
(e) or using or possessing a driver's card which has been forged or altered.

The obvious exceptions are in respect of cards which will become time-expired within one month together with the card issued by way of renewal, or the holding of a time-expired card in combination with another card.

Workshop cards (offences)

Regulation 4(1) provides that a person commits an offence:

(a) if he uses, attempts to use or is in possession of more than one workshop card of which he is the identified holder, or more than one PIN (personal identification number for use in connection with a workshop card) in respect of the same place of work;
(b) if he uses or attempts to use a workshop card, or PIN, of which he is not the identified holder;
(c) if he uses or attempts to use a workshop card or PIN, in circumstances unconnected with his place of work for which that card, or PIN, was issued;
(d) if he makes a false statement or forges or alters a document, with intent to deceive, for the purpose of obtaining a workshop card or PIN;
(e) if he uses or is in possession of, a workshop card, or PIN, issued in consequence of an application which included, with intent to deceive, a false statement or forged or altered a document;

(f) if he uses or is in possession of, a workshop card, which has been forged or altered; or

(g) if he divulges to another person, or permits another person to use, the PIN used in connection with a workshop card of which he is identified as the holder.

Regulation 4(2) creates offences of causing or permitting any use, alteration or possession of a workshop card or PIN, or the making of any false statement or forgery or alteration of a document.

The same defences apply in respect of workshop card offences as is the case with offences against reg 3(1) in relation to drivers' cards.

Regulations 5 requires written notification to be given to the Secretary of State, of lost and stolen cards and the return to him of any damaged or malfunctioning cards. Regulation 6 requires a card holder to notify the Secretary of State of any changes to details included on the card and to return the card to him for alteration.

Regulation 7 requires a person in possession of a tachograph card (company, control, driver or workshop card), to surrender to the Secretary of State a card on which the person using it is not identified as the holder; or which has been falsified; or which has been issued in consequence of an application which included a false statement or forged or altered document.

Part VI of the Transport Act 1968

The legal requirements as to drivers' hours and records set out in Part VI of the Transport Act 1968, as amended, apply to the drivers of certain goods and passenger vehicles which are not subject to the European rules. The exclusion of those vehicles from those provisions does not necessarily mean that there are no rules about hours or records, since that exclusion only exempts them from the provisions of the European rules. Nevertheless, the provisions of Part VI are now limited to such a small range of vehicles that they are no longer particularly significant to police officers.

If a vehicle is one which is not subject to the European rules and:

(a) it is a passenger vehicle (ie a public service vehicle, or any other motor vehicle constructed or adapted to carry more than twelve passengers); or

(b) it is a goods vehicle which is a locomotive, motor tractor or articulated drawing unit; or

(c) it is constructed or adapted to carry goods other than the effects of passengers; or

(d) it does not fall within any of these classifications but is a vehicle within the meaning of art 1 of the Community Drivers' Hours Regulation other than those specified within art 4 of the Regulation (motor vehicles, tractors, trailers and semi-trailers, other than goods vehicles not exceeding 3.5 tonnes and passenger vehicles suitable for carrying no more than nine persons including the driver and various types of emergency and specialised vehicles),

it may be subject to these restrictions. However:

(a) light vans (not exceeding 3.5 tonnes plated weight or 30 cwt unplated);

(b) dual-purpose vehicles used for professional purposes by doctors, dentists, midwives, nurses or vets, or for services of maintenance, repair, installation or fitting, or by commercial travellers, or by the AA or RAC; or

(c) vehicles used for making motion pictures, radio or television broadcasting,

are exempted from all provisions except the requirement not to drive for more than ten hours a day. A day for these purposes is from midnight to midnight.

The plated weight referred to at (a) is the 'permissible maximum weight'. Where a trailer is towed, this term refers to the aggregate of the maximum gross weight on the motor vehicle and the maximum gross weight marked on the trailer in actual use at the time, not to the total weight of the vehicle and any trailer which it might be capable of drawing.

Part VI rules on driving periods, rest breaks and rest periods

For the purposes of the legislation, a driver may be either an employee-driver or an owner-driver. An employee-driver is on duty when he is on duty (whether for the purpose of driving or for other purposes) in the employment by virtue of which he is an employee-driver, or in any other employment of that employer. An owner-driver is on duty when driving the vehicle in connection with his trade or business or doing other work in connection with the vehicle or its load. A driver must not drive a Part VI vehicle for periods amounting in the aggregate to more than ten hours within a working day. A 'working day' is the aggregate of duty and breaks etc until an eleven-hour or, where permitted, a ninety-two-hour rest period is taken.

The Drivers' Hours (Goods Vehicles) (Modifications) Order 1986 restricts the application of the permitted hours provisions in Part VI in relation to goods vehicles, to requirements that the aggregate periods of driving on any working day must not exceed ten hours; the working day of a driver must not exceed eleven hours; and that no restrictions must apply where the vehicle is not driven for periods amounting in the aggregate to more than four hours, in each of the working days which make up a particular week. These regulations define 'working day' as any working period (duty period) which can be combined with any other working period which falls within a period of twenty-four hours.

In the case of passenger-carrying vehicles operating under Part VI of the Act, the provisions of s 96 apply in full and there are therefore additional requirements. Where, in a working day, a driver's hours on duty amount to five and a half hours without at least a thirty-minute break for rest or refreshment, the driver then must take such a break, unless that is the end of his work for the day. The working day may exceed eleven hours if, during the day, he has 'off-duty periods' at least equivalent to the amount of time by which that limit is exceeded, but not beyond twelve and a half hours. Moreover, if all the working day is spent driving limited stop or tour buses and he has a break of at least four hours for rest and refreshment, the working day may extend to fourteen hours. There must also be an eleven-hour rest period between two successive working days but this may be reduced to nine and a half hours once in a working week. A working week for these purposes begins at midnight between Sunday and Monday, unless altered by the licensing authority. A driver must not be on duty for more than sixty hours in a working week and during each working week a driver must be off duty for a period of at least twenty-four hours. That period of twenty-four hours may begin in one week and end in another, but may only be taken into account once.

Inspection

The Transport Act 1968, s 99 makes various provisions as to the inspection of records and other documents. An authorised officer (eg a constable) may require a person to produce, and permit him to inspect and copy, any record sheet. He may also require an owner to produce, and permit him to inspect and copy, any other document, book, register etc kept within the requirements of the European rules. The House of Lords has held that, although there is no direct power to do so under Transport Act 1968, s 99, an authorised officer may require tachograph records to be 'handed over' and he may take such records away for a detailed inspection. Where such a requirement is made, the company should be permitted to make copies. Failure to comply with such a requirement is an offence. An authorised person has power to detain, enter or inspect a vehicle and its equipment for the purpose of copying records etc and he may enter premises at reasonable times to copy records etc which are required by the rules to be kept. It is an offence to obstruct him in the exercise of the above powers. The existence of the various powers under s 99 does not preclude an officer making use instead of some other available procedure. This was held in a case where a police officer had previously used the powers under s 99 but not all of the relevant documents had been produced. Suspecting serious irregularities in the conduct of the company's business, including falsification of documents for financial gain, he obtained a search warrant under the Police and Criminal Evidence Act 1984, s 8 under which he seized some relevant documents. A divisional court held that the search warrant had been properly granted. The officer had had the choice between proceeding via s 99 or via a search warrant, since the suspected offence was one of forgery, an indictable offence, and it was irrelevant that a charge of forgery had not followed.

Offences

If a driver contravenes any of the above provisions, he commits an offence; so does his employer or a person under whose supervision he was if he caused or permitted the contravention. It is a defence to prove that the contravention was due to unavoidable delay in completing the journey because of circumstances which were not reasonably foreseeable. An employer or supervisor also has a defence if he proves that the contravention was due to the fact that the driver had for a particular period or periods driven otherwise than in the employment of that employer or, as the case may be, otherwise than in the employment to which the supervision relates, and that he (the employer etc) could not reasonably have become aware of this.

The Transport Act 1968, s 99(5) creates offences of making, or causing to be made, *entries in books, registers or other documents* which are known to be false, and of causing records to be altered with intent to deceive.

A record sheet may be seized if there is reason to believe that an offence under the Transport Act 1968, s 99(5) has been committed.

Part VI rules about drivers' records

The form of the records kept by drivers to whom Part VI applies are prescribed by the Drivers' Hours (Goods Vehicles) (Keeping of Records) Regulations 1987.

They consist of drivers' record books which include weekly record sheets divided up into boxes for entry of information relating to each day of the week. However, tachographs may be fitted and, if they are, they replace the need for record books.

Breach of any of the various requirements as to records is an offence.

CHAPTER 14
Lights and vehicles

The lighting requirements for vehicles are now set out in the Road Vehicles Lighting Regulations 1989, which were made by the Secretary of State under powers conferred by the Road Traffic Act 1988 (RTA 1988). Unless otherwise indicated, all references in this chapter to 'the Regulations' or to a regulation are to the 1989 Regulations, or a regulation in them.

The Regulations define certain terms which are used throughout:

Daytime hours   This means the time between half an hour before sunrise and half an hour after sunset.

Hours of darkness   This means the time between half an hour after sunset and half an hour before sunrise.

Obligatory   In relation to a lamp, reflector, rear marking or device, 'obligatory' means a lamp, reflector, rear marking or device with which a vehicle, its load or equipment, is required by the Regulations to be fitted.

Optional   In relation to a lamp, reflector, rear marking or device, 'optional' means a lamp, reflector, rear marking or device with which a vehicle, its load or equipment, is not required by the Regulations to be fitted.

OBLIGATORY LIGHTS

Required lighting equipment

Regulation 18 provides that a person must not use a vehicle on a road, or cause or permit it to be so used, unless it is equipped with obligatory lamps, reflectors, rear markings or devices as specified within the Regulations. Schedule 1 to the Regulations sets out the specific obligatory lighting requirements for different classes of vehicles. The tables included in Sch 1 deal with the obligatory lighting requirements of vehicles generally; in Part I with vehicles having three or more wheels; in Part II with solo motor bicycles and motor bicycle combinations; in Part III with pedal cycles; in Part IV with pedestrian-controlled, horse-drawn and track-laying vehicles; in Part V with vehicles drawn or propelled by hand; in Part VI with trailers drawn by motor vehicles, and in Part VII with trailers drawn by pedal cycles. Column 1 of Sch 1 lists the type of lamp, reflector, rear marking or device required; column 2 the installation and performance requirement (by reference to other Schedules), and column 3 any exceptions to the general rule.

In general, the Regulations specify the requirements for different classes of vehicles in relation to front position lamps, dim-dip devices or running lamps, dipped beam headlamps, main beam headlamps, direction indicators, hazard signal warning devices, side marker lamps, rear position lamps, rear fog lamps, stop lamps, end-outline marker lamps, rear registration plate light, side retro reflectors, rear retro reflectors and rear markings. These terms are defined by the Regulations as follows:

Front position lamp   This is a lamp used to indicate the presence and width of a vehicle when viewed from the front. (This type of lamp was previously referred to as a 'side lamp'.)

Dim-dip lighting device   This is a device which is capable of causing a dipped beam headlamp to operate at reduced intensity.

Running lamp   A lamp (not being a front position lamp, an end-outline marker lamp, headlamp or front fog lamp) used to make the presence of a moving motor vehicle readily visible from the front. (An alternative to a dim-dip device; in effect, a higher intensity front position lamp.)

Dipped beam headlamp   'Dipped beam' means a beam of light emitted by a lamp which illuminates the road ahead of a vehicle without causing undue dazzle or discomfort to oncoming drivers or other road users.

Main beam headlamp   'Main beam' means a beam of light emitted by a lamp which illuminates the road over a long distance ahead of the vehicle.

Direction indicator   This means a lamp on a vehicle used to indicate to other road users that the driver intends to change direction to the right or to the left.

Hazard warning signal device   This means a device which is capable of causing all the direction indicators with which a vehicle, or a combination of vehicles, is fitted to operate simultaneously.

Side marker lamp   A lamp fitted to the side of a vehicle or its load and used to render the vehicle more visible to other road users.

Rear position lamp   This means a lamp used to indicate the presence and width of a vehicle when viewed from the rear.

Rear fog lamp   This means a lamp used to render a vehicle more readily visible from the rear in conditions of seriously reduced visibility.

Stop lamp This means a lamp used to indicate to road users that the brakes of a vehicle or combination of vehicles are being applied.

End-outline marker lamp This means a lamp fitted near the edge of a vehicle in addition to the front and rear position lamps to indicate the presence of a wide vehicle.

Rear registration plate lamp This means a lamp used to illuminate the rear registration plate.

Side retro reflector This means a reflector fitted to the side of a vehicle or its load and used to render the vehicle more visible from the side.

Rear retro reflector This means a reflector used to indicate the presence and width of a vehicle when viewed from the rear.

Rear marking This means a marking as indicated in Sch 19, Part I, to the Regulations, ie a 'long vehicle' marking.

Each of these lamps, reflectors and devices is obligatory for motor vehicles (with exceptions mentioned later) and some of them are obligatory for trailers drawn by motor vehicles and for other vehicles. Such lamps etc must be fitted in the manner described by the Regulations.

As the requirements have increased over the years, the position of vehicles manufactured before new requirements were made has had to be safeguarded. The various regulations therefore specify the date of application by applying the requirements to vehicles first used on or after a given date. However, reg 4 provides that, even if a vehicle is first used on or after that date, it will be exempt from the requirements of the particular regulation if manufactured more than six months in advance of that date. In some instances this provision is expressly repeated in a particular regulation but generally it must be implied into a particular regulation from reg 4. For example, a vehicle first used on or after 1 April 1980 is required to have a rear fog lamp fitted, but (by virtue of reg 4) such a vehicle is exempt from the requirement if it was manufactured before 1 October 1979.

The Regulations require that obligatory lamps, reflectors, rear markings and devices are fitted and performing satisfactorily at all times. However, there are certain logical exceptions to this rule, such as incomplete vehicles proceeding to a works for completion, pedal cycles, pedestrian-controlled vehicles, horse-drawn vehicles, combat vehicles and vehicles being taken to, or removed from, a testing station by an authorised vehicle examiner in order to submit the vehicle for an examination there in order to ensure that the examination carried out at the station is carried out is in accordance with the required testing standards. To that list is added a vehicle which is not fitted with any front or rear position lamps, so that if a person is building a motor car from parts and has not yet installed such lights he will not commit an offence by using the vehicle on a road during daylight hours. In addition, the requirements of the Regulations relating to fitting do not apply to a vehicle based outside Great Britain which is on a journey in this country, provided that it has not been here for more than twelve months and that it complies with international requirements. Vehicles going to a port for export are similarly exempt. Hand-propelled vehicles, provided that their overall width does not exceed 800 mm, do not require lamps or reflectors if they are pushed close to the nearside of the carriageway.

For the purpose of the Regulations, a lamp is not treated as being a lamp if it is so painted over or masked that it is not capable of being immediately used or readily put to use, or if it is an electric lamp which is not provided with any system of wiring by means of which that lamp is (or can readily be) connected with a source of electricity.

If it is remembered that, apart from regulating the use of lamps on vehicles during the hours of darkness (and in some cases during daytime hours), the purpose of the Regulations is to ensure that lamps etc which are fitted are correctly fitted and comply with the Regulations, these exceptions are self-evident. A driver who finds that his wiring loom has burned out may lawfully drive that vehicle on a road during daylight hours, as the electric lights could not be connected without the provision of a new wiring system. An enthusiast who is building his own motor car may fit his headlamps and then be unable to secure professional assistance in setting the beams to comply with anti-dazzle requirements. Provided that he paints over or masks those lights, he may use the vehicle during daylight hours.

Front lights

Front position lamps

Vehicles with three or more wheels (other than invalid carriages and pedal tricycles) require two front position lamps. The maximum distance at which they may be placed from the side of the vehicle is 510 mm if the vehicle was first used before 1 April 1986 or was manufactured before 1 October 1985. Such lamps on motor vehicles first used or manufactured on or after those dates must be no more than 400 mm from the side of the vehicle (or 150 mm in the case of trailers manufactured on or after 1 October 1985).

Pedal cycles, solo motor bicycles, hand-propelled vehicles whose width (with load) does not exceed 1,250 mm, and invalid carriages require only one front position lamp, which must be fitted on the centre line or offside of the vehicle. Motor cycle combinations with a headlamp on the motor bicycle require a front position lamp on the centre line of the sidecar, or on the side of the sidecar furthest from the motor bicycle. A solo motor bicycle fitted with a headlamp need not be fitted with a front position lamp.

The maximum permitted height above the ground for vehicles first used before 1 April 1986 and trailers manufactured before 1 October 1985 is 2,300 mm. The maximum height restrictions do not apply to large passenger-carrying vehicles or road clearance vehicles. Vehicles and trailers used or manufactured after these dates must be fitted with front position lamps at a maximum height of 1,500 mm or, if the structure of the vehicle makes this impracticable, 2,100 mm. The height limit of 2,100 mm also applies to vehicles first used on or after 1 April 1986 with a maximum speed not exceeding 25 mph.

All front position lamps should be white in colour, unless they are incorporated in a yellow headlamp, in which case they may be yellow. They must be visible from a reasonable distance.

Dipped beam headlamps

Two dipped beam headlamps are required by motor vehicles with three or more wheels in most circumstances. The maximum permitted distance from the side of the vehicle is 400 mm (except in the cases of a vehicle first used before 1 January 1972, or of an agricultural vehicle, engineering plant or an industrial tractor, when there is no specific requirement). There is no minimum distance by which the two lamps must be separated. Solo motor bicycles or combinations, and three-wheelers first used before 1 January 1972 or with an unladen weight of not more than 400 kg and an overall width of not more than 1,300 mm, require only one headlamp on the centre line of the motor vehicle itself. A bus first used before 1 October 1969 need only have one dipped beam headlamp and there are no fitting requirements.

Dipped beam headlamps should generally be not more than 1,200 mm, and not less than 500 mm, from the ground. However, there are no minimum requirements in respect of vehicles first used before 1 January 1956, and no maximum for vehicles first used before 1 January 1952 or, regardless of the date of first use, for agricultural vehicles, road clearance vehicles, aerodrome fire tenders, aerodrome runway sweepers, industrial tractors, engineering plant or home forces vehicles.

The light emitted by a dipped beam headlamp must be white or yellow. The lamp itself must be so constructed that the direction of the beam of light can be adjusted whilst the vehicle is stationary. Where two dipped beam headlamps are required to be fitted, they must form a matched pair and be capable of being switched on and off simultaneously and not otherwise.

Main beam headlamps

The provisions concerning the number of obligatory headlamps to be fitted are the same as those relating to dipped beam headlamps with the exception that large passenger-carrying vehicles are required to have two main beam headlamps, even if first used before 1 October 1969. (This means that such vehicles must have two headlamps, although only one of them needs to be capable of being dipped.) The outer edges of the illuminated areas must not be outside those of the dipped beam headlamps and there is no maximum distance which should separate a pair of such lamps.

Main beam headlamps must emit a white or yellow light and must be constructed so that they can be deflected at the will of the driver to become a dipped beam, or so that they can be extinguished by the operation of a device which at the same time switches on a dipped beam or causes another lamp to emit a dipped beam. Thus headlamps of the 'long range' type are invariably wired so that as they are extinguished a dipped beam is emitted from the normal headlamps. Main beam headlamps must also be constructed so that the direction of the beam can be adjusted whilst the vehicle is stationary.

Dim-dip devices

The Regulations require that dim-dip devices must be provided on motor vehicles with three or more wheels first used on or after 1 April 1987. Vehicles having a maximum speed of 40 mph or less and home forces vehicles are exempt, as are vehicles which comply with Community Directive 76/756/EEC as last amended by

Directive 89/278/EEC or Directive 91/663/EEC. A running lamp may be fitted as an alternative.

Rear lights

Rear position lamps

Most vehicles with three or more wheels require two rear position lamps. The following vehicles, some of which have three or more wheels, require only one rear position lamp: buses first used before 1 April 1955; solo motor bicycles; pedal cycles with less than four wheels; trailers drawn by pedal cycles; trailers (the overall width of which does not exceed 800 mm) drawn by solo or motor cycle combinations; invalid carriages having a maximum speed not exceeding 4 mph; and vehicles propelled by hand. (See general exemption on p 542 for hand-propelled vehicles not exceeding 800 mm in width.) Some motor vehicles of maximum speed not exceeding 25 mph, and their trailers, require four rear position lamps; the details are set out in Sch 10 to the 1989 Regulations.

Where two rear position lamps are required to be fitted, motor vehicles first used before 1 April 1986 and any other vehicle manufactured before 1 October 1985 must have those lamps so fitted that they are not more than 800 mm from the side of the vehicle. Motor vehicles and other vehicles first used or manufactured on or after those dates must carry rear position lamps which are no more than 400 mm from the side of the vehicle.

There is no minimum distance by which the lamps need to be separated in the case of vehicles used before 1 April 1986 or manufactured before 1 October 1985. In the case of a vehicle first used or manufactured on or after the relevant date, the lamps must be at least 500 mm apart but this may be reduced to 400 mm if the overall width of the vehicle is less than 1,400 mm or to 300 mm if less than 800 mm.

In cases in which only one rear position lamp is required it must be fitted on the centre line of the vehicle or on its offside.

The rear position lamps should be at a maximum height of 2,100 mm, in the case of motor vehicles first used before 1 April 1986 other than buses, or trailers manufactured before 1 October 1985, or agricultural or horse-drawn vehicles, industrial tractors and engineering plant, but no maximum is specified for buses first used before 1 April 1986. There are no minimum height requirements in the case of these motor vehicles. In the case of a vehicle first used or manufactured on or after the relevant date, the maximum height will be 1,500 mm unless the structure of the vehicle makes this impracticable; in that case lights up to a height of 2,100 mm will be permitted. The rear position lamps of such vehicles are subject to a minimum height requirement of 350 mm.

All rear position lamps must be red.

Rear fog lamps

The Regulations require that, if it was manufactured on or after 1 October 1979 and first used on or after 1 April 1980, any motor vehicle having three or more wheels, and any trailer drawn by a motor vehicle, must, unless specifically dealt with elsewhere in the Regulations, have at least one rear fog lamp fitted, at or near the rear, on the centre line or offside of the vehicle. If two lamps are fitted there is no requirement concerning the distance these lights are placed from the sides of the vehicle. The minimum height which they may be above the ground is 250 mm. The maximum height is 1,000 mm except that agricultural vehicles, engineering plant and motor tractors may have lamps up to a maximum height of 2,100 mm. Rear fog lamps must be separated from stop lamps by a minimum distance of 100 mm. No more than two lamps may be fitted.

A rear fog lamp must show a red light. It must not be fitted so that it can be illuminated by the application of any braking system of the vehicle. A tell-tale must be fitted to show that the lights are in operation. If two lamps are fitted to a motor vehicle first used on or after 1 April 1986, or on a trailer manufactured on or after 1 October 1985, they must form a matched pair. If two rear fog lamps are fitted, the conditions set out above in relation to an obligatory fog lamp apply to both of them.

Vehicles first used before 1 April 1980 (and this therefore embraces vehicles which were manufactured before 1 October 1979 regardless of date of first use) do not need to be fitted with rear fog lamps. Nor do motor vehicles whose maximum speed is 25 mph or less, nor do motor vehicles or trailers which are no more than 1,300 mm in width, nor do agricultural vehicles or works trucks first used before 1 April 1986. If one of these exempt vehicles is fitted with such lamps there are no restrictions in relation to the number of lamps which may be fitted, but any which are fitted must be separated from stop lamps by a minimum distance of 100 mm and must not be capable of illumination by a braking system.

Stop lamps

Stop lamps must show a red light. Motor vehicles having three or more wheels, and trailers drawn by a motor vehicle, must, unless otherwise stated, be fitted with two stop lamps. Solo motor bicycles, combinations, invalid carriages and trailers drawn by motor cycles, together with motor vehicles or trailers first used before 1 January 1971, need only be fitted with one stop lamp. Motor bicycles of less than 50 cc first used before 1 April 1986 do not require any stop lamp, nor does any type of motor vehicle first used before 1 January 1936 or a motor vehicle whose maximum speed is 25 mph or less or an agricultural vehicle or works truck first used before 1 April 1986.

Schedule 12 to the 1989 Regulations lays down the following rules. If two stop lamps are fitted they should be on each side of the longitudinal axis of the vehicle. If only one is fitted it should be on the centre line or offside. The minimum separating distance of two stop lamps is 400 mm. The maximum permitted height from the ground is 1,500 mm or, if the structure of the vehicle makes this impracticable, 2,100 mm. The minimum permitted height is 350 mm. There are no maximum or minimum height specifications for motor vehicles first used before 1 January 1971 or for trailers manufactured before that date. There are detailed provisions about the angles of visibility.

The lamps must be operated by the application of the service braking system of the motor vehicle, and this also applies to the stop lamps of any trailer attached to that vehicle. In cases where two stop lamps are required to be fitted, they must form a pair.

It is common practice for enthusiasts to fit additional stop lamps and there is no restriction upon the number of lamps which may be fitted under the Regulations. If additional lamps are fitted, they must comply with the requirements of Sch 12 to the Regulations in all respects other than number, position and angles of visibility. Motor vehicles, other than motor bicycles, first used on or after 1 April 1991 are subject to control in relation to the intensity of such a light projected through the rear windows.

Rear registration plate lamp

All vehicles which are required to be fitted with a rear registration plate must have lighting which is capable of adequately illuminating the rear registration plate.

Other obligatory lights

Direction indicators

The requirements for direction indicators are as follows:

(1) Motor vehicles first used before 1 April 1936 and trailers manufactured before that date *may* have any arrangement of indicators so as to make the intention of the driver clear to other road users but they are not required to have any direction indicators at all.

(2) Motor vehicles first used on or after that date and before 1 April 1986, and trailers manufactured between 1 January 1936 and 1 October 1985, *must* be provided with any arrangement of indicators so as to satisfy the requirements for angles of visibility.

(3) Motor vehicles first used on or after 1 April 1986, and trailers manufactured on or after 1 October 1985, are subject to detailed restrictions, set out in Sch 7 to the Regulations. Motor vehicles with three or more wheels, other than motorcycle combinations, must have a single front indicator, one side repeater indicator and one rear indicator on each side. One additional optional rear indicator may be fitted and any number of side repeater indicators may be added. If fitted, they are subject to most of the restrictions imposed by Sch 7. Trailers manufactured after the specified date must have a rear indicator on each side. Additional optional indicators may be fitted as above. Motor bicycles and combinations must have a single front and a single rear indicator on each side of the vehicle. Paragraph 3 of the Schedule prescribes angles of visibility of direction indicators fitted to the vehicles within this category. Generally, the paragraph demands an outward angle of visibility of at least 80 degrees and this will control the placing of the indicator to allow such an outward angle to occur.

The colour of the light shown by direction indicators is amber in most instances. Motor vehicles first used before 1 September 1965, and the trailer of such a vehicle, may show white or amber to the front or red or amber to the rear. However, if such an indicator is visible from both the front and the back it must show an amber light regardless of the date of first use. All indicators on any side of a vehicle or its trailer must be operated by one switch. There must be a tell-tale to show that the indicators are in operation. Flashing indicators must flash constantly at a rate of not less than 60 and not more than 120 times per minute.

Vehicles whose maximum speed does not exceed 15 mph or invalid carriages having a maximum speed not exceeding 4 mph are not required to have direction indicators fitted, nor are vehicles first used before 1 August 1986 which are agricultural vehicles, industrial tractors or works vehicles.

Agricultural vehicles having an unladen weight not exceeding 255 kg do not require direction indicators.

End-outline marker lamps

These are required on motor vehicles first used on or after 1 April 1991, except those with a maximum speed not exceeding 25 mph; those having an overall width not exceeding 2,100 mm; and incomplete vehicles proceeding to works etc. Their purpose is to indicate the presence of a wide vehicle.

There must be two white lights fitted to the front and two red lights to the rear, not more than 400 mm from the side of the vehicle. Each set must be a matched pair. Any number may be fitted.

Hazard warning signals

These signals are obligatory on motor vehicles having three or more wheels and first used on or after 1 April 1986, with the exception of vehicles which are not required to be fitted with direction indicators. Hazard warning signals which are optionally fitted to other vehicles must comply with the same provisions. Each device must be operated by one switch which causes all direction indicators with which the vehicle or combination of vehicles is equipped to flash in phase. There must be a tell-tale, and the device must be capable of operation without the ignition being switched on.

Side marker lamps

Some motor vehicles, with three or more wheels, and trailers drawn by motor vehicles are required to have side marker lamps. Most are not, since motor vehicles first used before 1 April 1991 and trailers, the overall length of which does not exceed 6 m (or 9.15 m if manufactured before 1 October 1990), are not required to have side marker lamps, and nor are the following first used on or after that date:

(a) motor vehicles whose maximum speed does not exceed 25 mph;
(b) passenger vehicles;
(c) incomplete motor vehicles;
(d) those not exceeding 6 m in length;
(e) those first used before 1 April 1996 complying with Community Directive 76/756/EEC as amended by Directive 89/278/EEC and Directive 91/663/EEC (and trailers manufactured before 1 October 1985 which comply with these Directives);
(f) trailers, the overall length of which, excluding any drawbar and any fittings for its attachment, exceeds 6 m (9.15 m if manufactured before 1 October 1990);
(g) agricultural and works trailers;
(h) caravans and boat trailers; and
(i) trailers complying with the Community Directive.

A side marker lamp is a lamp which will show an amber light, if fitted to a vehicle first used on or after 1 October 1990, unless it is placed within 1 m of the rear of the vehicle, when it may be red. Trailers manufactured before that date may have lamps which show a white light to the front and a red light to the rear.

The obligatory requirements are to have, on each side, two and as many more as are sufficient to ensure that the maximum distance from the front of the vehicle (including any drawbar) to the first lamp is 4 m and the maximum distance from the rear in respect of the rearmost side marker lamp is 1 m. The maximum separation distance of adjacent obligatory lamps on the same side of the vehicle is 3 m or, if this is not practicable, 4 m.

A vehicle, or a combination of vehicles the overall length of which (including any load) exceeds 18.3 m must have additional side marker lamps, one lamp being no more than 9.5 m from the foremost part of the vehicle or vehicles and one lamp no more than 3.05 m from the rear (including loads in both circumstances). Other lamps must be placed to ensure that no more than 3.05 m separates the lamps. Where the length exceeds 12.2 m but not 18.3 m and the load is supported by any two vehicles, there shall be lamps placed behind the rearmost part of the drawing vehicle, but not more than 1,530 mm to the rear of that point. If the supported load extends more than 9.15 m to the rear of the drawing vehicle, the lamp shall not be forward of, or more than 1,530 mm to the rear of, the centre of the length of the load. These last provisions do not apply to articulated vehicles.

Side marker lamps must be fitted on each side of a vehicle or trailer as required. They must not be higher than 2,300 mm from the ground. There is no minimum height restriction.

Obligatory reflectors

Rear retro reflectors

The general requirement is for all vehicles to be equipped with two rear retro reflectors. By way of exception, the following vehicles only require one retro reflector: solo motor bicycles; pedal cycles with less than four wheels (with or without a sidecar); trailers drawn by pedal cycles; trailers not exceeding 800 mm drawn by solo motor cycles or combinations; invalid carriages having a maximum speed not exceeding 4 mph, and hand-propelled vehicles. Some restricted vehicles (maximum speed 25 mph) require four reflectors.

Reflectors must be fitted at or near the rear of the vehicle. Motor vehicles first used before 1 April 1986, and trailers manufactured before 1 October 1985, must have reflectors fitted no more than 610 mm from the side. In the case of vehicles first used or manufactured on or after those dates the distance is reduced to 400 mm. (There are certain exceptions to the general rules in respect of buses first used before 1 October 1954, some horse-drawn vehicles and vehicles for round timber; these are specified in Sch 18 to the Regulations.) Where there is only one reflector it must be on the centre line or offside of the vehicle.

Where reflectors are required to be fitted, the maximum permitted height above the ground is 1,525 mm if the vehicle is a motor vehicle first used before 1 April 1986 (or, if it is a trailer, manufactured before 1 October 1985). For a vehicle first used or manufactured on or after the relevant date, the maximum is 900 mm, unless the structure of the vehicle makes that height impracticable (in which case the maximum is raised to 1,200 mm). The colour of all rear reflectors must be red.

Side retro reflectors

The provision of side reflectors is obligatory on certain motor vehicles with three or more wheels and their trailers. The relevant requirements do not apply to a passenger vehicle (including private cars), nor to an incomplete vehicle travelling to a works for completion etc, mobile cranes, plant and certain earth removal vehicles, nor to a vehicle having a maximum speed not exceeding 25 mph. Nor do they apply to a goods vehicle:

(a) whose overall length does not exceed 6 m (if first used on or after 1 April 1986); or
(b) whose overall length does not exceed 8 m (if first used before that date).

The requirements therefore are restricted to long goods vehicles. In the case of such vehicles, first used before 1 April 1986, and trailers manufactured before 1 October 1985, there must be two side retro reflectors on each side of the vehicle. In the case of those first used or manufactured on or after the relevant date, there must be two on each side of the vehicle and as many more as are required by Sch 17 to the Regulations. Side retro reflectors must be amber or, within 1 m of the rear of the vehicle, they may be red. They must not be triangular in shape.

Rear markings

The provisions relating to rear markings relate to 'long vehicle' markings, and therefore most vehicles are exempted from them. In the case of those motor vehicles first used before 1 April 1996 which are not exempted, those which do not exceed 13 m in length need only carry the marker boards with diagonal lines, whereas those which exceed 13 m must carry marker boards with the words 'long vehicle' in black on a yellow background surrounded by a red border or, as an alternative, boards of yellow retro reflective material surrounded by a red fluorescent border. Those used on or after 1 April 1996, which are not exempted must carry boards of red and yellow diagonal stripes if they do not exceed 13 m in length; if they exceed 13 m, they must carry boards of yellow retro reflective material surrounded by a red fluorescent border. The same markings are required on certain trailers forming part of a combination of vehicles; if, in the case of a trailer manufactured before 1 October 1995, the overall length does not exceed 11 m, the marking must be of the diagonal line variety; if between 11 m and 13 m the marking may be of any approved variety; and if it exceeds 13 m it must be the 'long vehicle' type, or a board of yellow reflective material surrounded by a red fluorescent border. In the case of a trailer manufactured on or after 1 October 1995 which does not, in combination, exceed 11 m, it must carry a board of red and yellow diagonal stripes; if it exceeds 11 m but not 13 m it may carry boards of such red and yellow stripes or of yellow surrounded by red; and if it exceeds 13 m, the boards must be of yellow surrounded by red.

Pedal retro reflectors

These provisions do not apply to pedal cycles manufactured before 1 October 1985. Pedal cycles manufactured on or after that date must be provided with two amber reflectors on each pedal.

General

The legal requirements so far outlined are in respect of obligatory lights and equipment to be fitted to the various vehicles described. However, in most instances the Regulations do not prevent the fitting of additional lighting etc. The position is:

(1) Any number of optional front position lights may be fitted. If additional ones are fitted they must be white or, if incorporated in a yellow headlamp, yellow.

(2) Dim-dip devices in addition to running lamps and vice versa may be fitted optionally to vehicles.

(3) Any number of optional dipped beam headlamps may be fitted. If additional ones are fitted they must be white or yellow, comply with maximum and minimum height requirements, and be capable of adjustment while the vehicle is stationary.

(4) Any number of optional main beam headlamps may be fitted. They must be white or yellow, electrically connected so that they deflect or extinguish by the dip switch, and be capable of adjustment while the vehicle is stationary.

(5) Any number of rear position lamps may be fitted. They must be red. There are no other restrictions.

(6) The number of rear fog lamps is controlled in the case of vehicles first used on or after 1 April 1980 (or, in the case of trailers, manufactured on or after 1 October 1979). No more than two such lamps are permitted in such a case.

(7) Any number of stop lamps can be fitted. If additional lamps are fitted they must comply with the provisions set out above, except those relating to position and angles of visibility. Rear fog lamps and stop lamps must be red.

(8) Any number of side reflex reflectors may be fitted but all must be amber and none must be triangular in shape.

(9) Any number of rear reflex reflectors may be fitted. Additional ones must be red.

OPTIONAL LIGHTS

Regulation 20 of the Regulations provides that every optional lamp, reflector, rear marking or device fitted to a vehicle must comply with provisions set out in the respective Schedules to the Regulations. A table included in the Regulations describes the types of optional lamps etc and demands compliance with certain parts of the directions given in the relevant Schedule. These provisions have already been considered in a general sense, since those factors set out above from (1) to (9) are concerned with additional lamps etc which may be fitted (and are therefore optional lamps). However, reg 20 also deals with other optional lamps and devices which are not additional in that sense; there is no absolute requirement to have lamps of that type, but if they are fitted they must comply with certain provisions as follows:

Front fog lamps

These must be white or yellow lights. Where a pair of front fog lamps is used in conditions of seriously reduced visibility in place of the obligatory dipped beam headlamps, they must not be more than 400 mm from the side of the vehicle. There is no minimum height requirement but the maximum permitted height is 1,200 mm, except in the case of agricultural, road clearance and aerodrome vehicles, industrial tractors, plant vehicles and home forces vehicles.

Motor vehicles (other than motor bicycles) first used on or after 1 April 1991 may not have more than two front fog lamps.

Reversing lamps

Not more than two may be fitted; such a lamp must show a white light.

Warning beacons

Warning beacons on vehicles must be mounted so that the centre of the lamp is not less than 1,200 mm from the ground. The lights of such warning beacons must flash between 60 and 240 times per minute at constant intervals. They may be blue, amber, green or yellow as prescribed by reg 11:

(1) Blue—a blue and white chequered light is permitted from a chequered domed lamp fitted to a police control vehicle and intended for use at the scene of an emergency; a blue light is permitted from a warning beacon or rear special warning lamp on an emergency vehicle or a vehicle of HM Revenue and Customs used for the investigation of serious crime.

(2) Amber—permitted on road clearance, refuse or breakdown vehicles; those with an overall width exceeding 2.9 m; road service vehicles; special vehicles carrying abnormal loads; vehicles escorting an abnormal load; vehicles used for escort purposes other than escorting an abnormal load, while they are travelling at a speed not exceeding 25 mph, and vehicles of HM Customs and Excise (fuel testing vehicles). Regulation 17 requires motor vehicles with four or more wheels, other than those first used before 1 January 1947, which have a maximum speed which does not exceed 25 mph, or any trailer which they are drawing, to be fitted with, and display, at least one amber warning beacon when being driven on an unrestricted dual carriageway road. The Regulations do not apply to such vehicles when merely crossing such a road in the quickest possible manner.

(3) Green—permitted to be used by registered medical practitioners.

(4) Yellow—permitted to be used by airport vehicles.

Only permitted vehicles may be fitted with a warning beacon of the appropriate type. However, where a permitted vehicle which is fitted with a warning lamp is used for a purpose other than that to which the permission relates, as where an ambulance is used to take children to school, there is no requirement that the lamp should be covered or removed.

USE OF LAMPS, REFLECTORS ETC

The lamps, reflectors and devices which must, or may be, fitted to vehicles have been considered. We now turn to the various provisions relating to their use.

No red lights to the front

Regulation 11(1) provides that no vehicle may be fitted with a lamp which is capable of showing a red light or retro reflective material to the front. The important word is 'capable': the provision is not confined to the hours of darkness, nor is it necessary that the light is actually shown. The exceptions to the provision are obvious; they are (1) red and white chequered lamps (or red and white chequered beacons) fitted to a fire service vehicle for emergency purposes, (2) a red side marker lamp or a red side retro reflector, (3) red retro reflective material or a red side retro reflector fitted to any wheel or tyre of a pedal cycle (or its trailer or sidecar), a motor bicycle or motor bicycle combination or an invalid carriage, and (4) a traffic sign attached to a vehicle (such as a motorway maintenance vehicle).

Red lights to the rear

Regulation 11(2) provides that no vehicle may be fitted with a lamp which is capable of showing a light or retro reflective material to the rear other than a red light. The same comments apply to 'capable' as made above. The exceptions are plentiful and include direction indicators, reversing lamps, work lamps, interior illumination, rear number plates, taxi meters, public service vehicle route indicators, retro reflective material or side retro reflectors fitted to bicycles (or their sidecar or trailer), motor bicycles (or motor bicycle combinations) and invalid carriages, and the various emergency lights which have already been described. Pedal cycles may show an amber light to the rear from lamps fitted to their pedals. Pedal cycles, their trailers or sidecars may show a white or amber light to the rear from lamps fitted to their wheels or tyres if the lamp is designed to emit primarily to the side.

Maintenance of lamps, reflectors, rear markings and devices

Regulation 23(1) prohibits a person using, or causing or permitting to be used, on a road any vehicle unless every front position lamp, rear position lamp, headlamp, rear registration plate lamp, side marker lamp, end-outline marker lamp, rear fog lamp, retro reflector and rear marking with which it is required to be fitted is in good working order and, in the case of a lamp, clean.

Regulation 23, therefore, requires correct maintenance of all of the lamps, reflectors, markings and devices with which a vehicle is *required* to be fitted. Moreover, in the case of stop lamps and direction indicators reg 23 goes on to require that all stop lamps, running lamps, dim-dip devices, headlamp levelling device, hazard warning signalling devices, and direction indicators, even if they are in excess of those required by law, must be maintained at all times. However, the provisions of reg 23 do not apply to rear fog lamps on a vehicle which is a part of a combination of vehicles, if any part of the combination is not required to have a rear fog lamp. Nor do these provisions apply to a rear fog lamp on a vehicle drawing a trailer; nor to any defective lamp reflector, dim-dip device or headlamp levelling device where the defect arose in the course of the journey on a vehicle in use in the daytime (ie between sunrise and sunset), or if arrangements have been made to remedy the defect with all reasonable expedition; nor, during the daytime, to a lamp, reflector or rear marking fitted to a combat vehicle. (Combat vehicles are military vehicles used for the carriage of guns, tanks etc.)

Driving or parking without lights

Regulation 24 prohibits a person using, or causing or permitting to be used, a vehicle on a road between sunset and sunrise or (while the vehicle is in motion) during daytime hours in seriously reduced visibility unless every front position lamp, rear position lamp, rear registration plate lamp, side marker lamp and end-outline marker lamp required by the Regulations to be fitted is kept lit and unobscured. Subject to reg 24(5) to (9), it also prohibits allowing (or causing or permitting to be allowed) a vehicle to remain at rest (ie parked) in similar circumstances between sunset and sunrise. There are variations to these provisions in respect of motorcycles and trailers not required to be fitted with front position lamps, since the prohibitions are not breached if there are fitted to these vehicles 'ad hoc' front position lamps.

Regulation 24 is concerned with circumstances in which vehicles of certain classes may lawfully park between sunset and sunrise on roads subject to speed limits of 30 mph or less, without showing such lights. These classes of vehicles are goods vehicles not exceeding 1,525 kg, passenger vehicles other than buses, invalid carriages, and motorcycles or pedal cycles (in either case with or without a sidecar). The exemption will not apply to such a vehicle if it has a trailer attached or is carrying a load which requires lamps.

Regulation 24 only permits such a vehicle to park without lights in particular places. These are:

(a) designated parking places on roads; or
(b) a lay-by which is clearly shown to be such; or
(c) elsewhere, provided, if the vehicle is parked on a one-way road, it is facing in the correct direction on either side of the road as close as possible to the kerb, or, if it is parked on an ordinary road, it is properly parked and facing the correct way, and in either case no part of the vehicle is less than 10 m from a junction with the road upon which it is parked, whether the junction is on the same side of the road or not. For the purpose of measuring the distance from a junction, where a curving kerb exists there, the junction is regarded as beginning where the kerb begins to curve.

The specified vehicles may therefore park without lights on a restricted road provided they do so in a street car park, in a lay-by, or *elsewhere* on one-way streets or ordinary roads provided that they are not within 10 m of a junction on either side of the road.

The Regulations exempt solo motorcycles and pedal cycles, which are being pushed close to the nearside kerb, from the need to show front position lights. They also exempt altogether a pedal cycle which is halted and waiting to proceed (for example at traffic lights) if it is kept to the nearside, as well as a vehicle which is parked and properly outlined by lamps or traffic signs (eg a broken-down vehicle).

Use of headlamps

Regulation 25 provides that a person must not use, or cause or permit to be used, on a road a vehicle which is fitted with obligatory dipped beam headlamps unless every such lamp is kept lit:

(a) during the hours of darkness, except on a road which is a restricted one by virtue of a system of street lighting, when those lights are lit; and
(b) during daylight hours in seriously reduced visibility.

There are certain permitted variations; for example, motor vehicles with one obligatory dipped beam headlamp are exempt from the above requirement if a main beam or fog lamp is kept lit. Vehicles which are being towed, those which are parked, and those propelling snow ploughs are exempt from the above requirement. In addition, in the case of a motor vehicle other than a motor tricycle or motor bicycle combination, a pair of main beam lamps may be used as an alternative or, in seriously reduced visibility, a pair of front fog lamps may be used, provided that they are not more than 400 mm from the outer edges of the vehicle.

Regulation 25 appears to be clumsy at first sight but merely requires the use of obligatory dipped beam headlamps at night or during the day when visibility is seriously reduced. Roads in built-up areas with illuminated street lights set not more than 200 yards apart are the only ones in which a vehicle may be used without at least dipped beam headlamps during the hours of darkness. Any light from a headlamp operating a dim-dip device will not be sufficient to satisfy the requirement for minimum use of dipped-beam light in the circumstances described above.

Prohibition of particular use of lamps or devices

Regulation 27 provides that a person must not use, or cause or permit to be used, on a road any vehicle on which any lamp, hazard signal warning device or warning beacon of a specified type is used in the manner listed below.

Headlamps may not be used so as to cause undue dazzle or discomfort to other persons using the road and shall not be lit when a vehicle is parked. These prohibitions also apply to front fog lamps, with the addition of a prohibition upon use at any time other than in conditions of seriously reduced visibility.

The use of rear fog lamps is similarly restricted but the reference to undue dazzle or discomfort is predictably restricted to following drivers. They must also not be used when a vehicle, other than an emergency vehicle, is parked. Although their use generally is restricted to conditions of seriously reduced visibility, this appears not to be appreciated by some drivers, who switch them on as soon as they join a motorway.

Reversing lamps must not be used for any purpose other than that of reversing. Similarly the use of hazard warning signal devices is restricted to warning road users of a temporary obstruction (or the presence of a school bus which is stationary and loading or unloading school children under sixteen) when the vehicle is at rest, or, on a motorway or unrestricted dual carriageway, to warn of a temporary obstruction ahead, or, in the case of a bus, to summon assistance for the driver or conductor or an inspector who is on the vehicle.

Blue lamps and special warning lamps may only be used at the scene of an emergency, or to indicate the urgency of the journey or the presence of a hazard on the road. The use of amber lights is similarly restricted but they may also be used in connection with breakdowns or slow moving vehicles on dual carriageways. Green lights may only be used whilst the vehicle is occupied by a registered medical practitioner and used in an emergency. Yellow light beacons may not be lit on a road. Work lamps must not dazzle etc and must not be used other than for illuminating a working area, accident, breakdown or works in the vicinity of the vehicle. No other lamp which is fitted to a vehicle may ever be used so as to cause undue dazzle or discomfort to other persons using the road.

Movement of lamps or reflectors and nature of light

Regulation 12 provides that no person shall use, or cause or permit to be used, on a road a vehicle fitted with a lamp or reflector capable of being moved (by swivelling, deflecting or otherwise) while the vehicle is in motion. However, this does not prevent the fitting of rear lights, reflectors or indicators to a boot lid or other movable part of a vehicle. Nor does it refer to dipping headlights, lamps which may be adjusted to compensate for loads, those moved by the front wheels, retracting headlamps etc, direction indicators, work lamps, warning beacons, amber pedal reflectors, or retro reflective material or retro reflectors fitted to any wheel or tyre of pedal cycles (or their trailer or sidecar), motor bicycles (or motor bicycle combinations) or invalid carriages. In effect, reg 12 prohibits the movement of lamps statutorily fitted in a prescribed way, other than those lights which are exempted for predictable reasons.

Steady light

By regulation 13, the light shown by lamps covered by the Regulations must be a steady light, in that flashing lights are not permitted. There are exceptions for warning beacons prescribed for emergency vehicles etc. In addition, pedal cycles (or their trailer or sidecar) may be fitted with a front position lamp or a rear position lamp emitting a flashing light. As mentioned above, pedal cycles (or their trailer or sidecar) are permitted to have lights fitted to their pedals, wheels or tyres. They are also permitted to have flashing lights which may show red to the front or amber or white to the rear.

Overhanging or projecting loads

Regulation 21 prohibits a person using, or causing or permitting to be used, on a road:

(a) any trailer which projects laterally beyond the preceding vehicle in the combination; or
(b) any vehicle or combination of vehicles which carries a load or equipment, which (in either case) does not comply with the specifications set out in the regulation.

These specifications are as follows:

(a) a trailer, which (or whose load) projects laterally more than 400 mm from the outermost part of the obligatory front position light on that side of the vehicle in front of it, must have white lights to the front which are not more than 400 mm from the outermost projection of the trailer (or, as the case may be, of the load);
(b) a vehicle whose load projects laterally more than 400 mm must have lights at the front and rear not more than 400 mm from the outermost projection of the load;
(c) a vehicle whose load projects more than 1 m to the front or to the rear must have a front or rear lamp not more than 1 m from the foremost or rearmost projection of the load (except that that distance is 2 m in the case of an agricultural vehicle or a vehicle carrying a fire escape); or
(d) a vehicle carrying a load which obscures any obligatory lamps, reflector or rear markings must show a lamp etc in the prescribed position.

These requirements only apply when the vehicle/trailer is being used between sunset and sunrise or in circumstances of reduced visibility, except that in relation to stop lights and direction indicators in (d) the requirement applies in all circumstances.

TESTING AND INSPECTION OF LIGHTING EQUIPMENT ETC

Regulation 28 applies the provisions of reg 74 of the Road Vehicles (Construction and Use) Regulations 1986 to lighting equipment and reflectors with which a vehicle is *required* by the Regulations to be fitted. Regulation 74 empowers a constable in uniform to test and inspect lighting equipment on motor vehicles and trailers on any premises, subject to the consent of the owner of the premises.

OFFENCES

Contravention of any regulation contained in the Road Vehicles Lighting Regulations 1989 is an offence contrary to RTA 1988, s 42 except that a breach which relates to a pedal cycle is an offence contrary to the Road Traffic Offenders Act 1988, s 91.

It is also an offence under RTA 1988, s 42 for a person to use on a road a motor vehicle or trailer which does not comply with these Regulations or to cause or permit a vehicle to be so used.

CHAPTER 15

Traffic accidents

The legal obligations which arise in the event of a traffic accident are basically those of stopping and of providing certain information or subsequently reporting the accident to the police. In addition to these general obligations, there is also an obligation to produce proof of insurance at the time or subsequently at a police station if personal injury has been caused.

DUTY TO STOP ETC

The Road Traffic Act 1988 (RTA 1988), s 170(1) applies where, owing to the presence of a mechanically propelled vehicle on a road or other public place, an accident occurs by which personal injury is caused to a person other than the driver of that mechanically propelled vehicle or damage is caused to a vehicle other than that mechanically propelled vehicle or a trailer drawn by it, or to an animal other than an animal in or on that vehicle or a trailer drawn by it, or to any other property constructed on, fixed to, growing in or otherwise forming part of the land on which the road or other public place in question is situated or land adjacent to such land. By RTA 1988, s 170(2) in such a case the driver of the mechanically propelled vehicle shall stop and, if required to do so by any person having reasonable grounds for so requiring, give his name and address, and also the name and address of the owner and the identification marks of the vehicle.

Thus, if, owing to the presence of a mechanically propelled vehicle on a road or other public place, an accident occurs, and:

(a) a passenger in that vehicle or anyone else (whether or not in another vehicle) is injured;
(b) another vehicle is damaged; or
(c) an animal in another vehicle or running across the street is injured; or
(d) a bollard or street lamp (or some other thing fixed to or otherwise forming part of the land on which the road or other public place is situated or adjacent land) is damaged,

the driver of that mechanically propelled vehicle must stop etc.

Of course, an accident may occur owing to the presence of two or more vehicles on a road. If so, the driver of each vehicle must stop etc if the consequences set out above occur.

By way of contrast to the examples given in the last paragraph, the driver of a mechanically propelled vehicle, owing to the presence of which on a road or other public place an accident occurs, is not obliged by RTA 1988, s 170 (or any other legal provision) to stop etc if:

(a) no one (besides that driver) is injured; and
(b) no vehicle (besides that vehicle or its trailer) is damaged; and
(c) no animal (other than one in that vehicle or its trailer) is injured; and
(d) no property forming part etc of the road or land adjacent to it is damaged.

Having set out the basic framework of RTA 1988, s 170, we shall now proceed to examine the three component parts of the provision.

An accident must have occurred owing to the presence of a motor vehicle on a road or other public place

The term '*mechanically propelled vehicle*' has already been discussed in Chapter 9 above. Such vehicles may be petrol, oil or steam driven, or propelled by electricity. A vehicle is a 'mechanically propelled vehicle' whether or not it is intended or adapted for use on a road. RTA 1988, s 170 places duties only upon the drivers of mechanically propelled vehicles; the rider of a pedal cycle has no obligations under it.

We have also examined the word '*road*' previously and have seen that it means 'any highway and any other road to which the public has access, and includes bridges over which a road passes'.

The requirement that the *accident* must have occurred *owing to the presence* of a mechanically propelled vehicle on a road or other public place involves the following additional points. First, if the words 'owing to the presence' were to be given their widest possible meaning they would embrace circumstances in which a person, who had been allowed to cross a road by the courtesy of a driver who had stopped to allow him to do so, tripped over the kerb on turning to acknowledge this courtesy. This would clearly be ridiculous. The rule is, therefore, that there must be a direct causal connection between the presence of the mechanically propelled vehicle and the occurrence of the accident. If the driver of a vehicle brakes sharply on approaching a pedestrian who is crossing the road and the noise of that braking so startles the pedestrian that he falls and is injured, there is a direct causal connection between the vehicle and the accident. Likewise, if a cyclist collides with a motor car waiting at traffic lights, it is reasonable to accept that the accident occurred because the vehicle was on the road. There is a direct causal connection between the presence of the vehicle and the accident in that the cyclist was in contact with it. It would probably be different if, in moving to the crown of the road to avoid the motor car, the cyclist over-steered and fell off. The connection in such circumstances is not sufficiently direct. The cause of the accident was the cyclist's clumsy control, rather than the presence of the vehicle.

The second point is the meaning of the word 'accident'. A divisional court has held that that word bears its ordinary popular meaning (as opposed to any technical meaning) and that the question is whether an ordinary person would say that an accident has occurred. It also held that, subject to what has just been said, there can be an accident even though part of the chain of events leading to the injury or damage was a deliberate act on someone's part. For the obligations in RTA 1988, s 170 to apply to the driver of a mechanically propelled vehicle, it is not necessary that his vehicle is involved in an accident in the sense that it is in collision. For example, if X, the driver of a motor car, carelessly drives it across a junction with a major road, causing vehicles on the major road to take avoiding action which causes them to collide with each other, X certainly causes that accident although he is not involved in the collision. In such a case, the obligations in s 170 will have to be discharged by X, as well as by the drivers of the other motor vehicles.

The accident must have caused one of the specified consequences

As we have seen, these specified consequences are:

(1) Personal injury to a person other than the driver of the mechanically propelled vehicle owing to whose presence on a road or other public place the accident occurred. 'Injury' presumably bears its ordinary meaning and, as such, includes cases of shock. The corresponding provision in Northern Ireland has been interpreted to mean that the injury must be to a living person and not a corpse. It is irrelevant whether the person injured is a passenger in the driver's vehicle, the driver or a passenger in another vehicle, or someone else (such as a pedestrian).

(2) Damage to a vehicle other than the mechanically propelled vehicle, owing to whose presence on a road or other public place the accident occurred, or a trailer drawn by it.

   The term 'vehicle' is given a wide meaning and includes mechanically propelled vehicles, pedal cycles and horse-drawn vehicles. The dictionary meaning (ie carriage, cart or other conveyance) should be applied and this will include all types of wheeled vehicles, such as fairy cycles, prams or barrows, but not, it is submitted, skateboards, roller skates and similar toys, since they are not produced for some form of conveyance in a general sense.

   The essential factor is that the damage must be caused to a vehicle or trailer other than the driver's vehicle or trailer before the duties imposed by s 170 must be discharged. This is reasonable. A driver who damages his own vehicle or trailer is responsible for that damage. The argument is sometimes advanced that this also applies to injured passengers in a driver's vehicle but this is not so. The injured passenger may be a hitchhiker who is a complete stranger to the driver, and it is therefore reasonable that the law should make different demands in the case of personal injuries.

(3) Damage to any animal other than an animal in or on the motor vehicle, owing to whose presence on a road or other public place the accident occurred, or a trailer drawn by it.

   The term 'animal' means any horse, cattle, ass, mule, sheep, pig, goat or dog. Poultry are not included, nor are cats (no matter how valuable they may be). The section only applies if the injury is to an animal which is external to the vehicle at the time at which the accident occurs. The section assumes that animals of this description which are carried in the driver's motor vehicle will belong either to the driver or to someone who is known to him, and that therefore he need not stop and provide the specified information since his identity will be known to the owner of the animal.

(4) Damage to any other property constructed on, fixed to, growing in or otherwise forming part of the land on which the road or other public place in question is situated or land adjacent thereto.

Examples of such property are buildings, traffic signs, street lamps, fences, hedges and trees, provided they 'form part' of the land on which the road is situated or of land adjacent thereto. By way of example, if a motor car collides with a traffic bollard causing damage to it, it causes damage to property which is either constructed on or fixed to land on which the road or other public place is situated or land adjacent thereto. This is so whether the bollard is situated in the middle of the road or at the side of the road. It will be a question of fact to be determined by the justices whether or not property which is damaged forms part of, or is adjacent to, such land. If a car collides with the petrol pumps in a filling station adjacent to the road there is little doubt that a court would consider the petrol pumps to be on land adjacent to land on which a road or other public place is situated. Should damage be occasioned to a dwelling house which is immediately at the roadside, that house is undoubtedly constructed on land which is at least adjacent to land on which the road or other public place is situated. It is probable that, even if a garden exists at the front of the house, justices would consider that the house was constructed on land adjacent to the road. The same considerations would apply to damage to trees or plants which were growing in that garden. If, because of the presence on the road or other public place of a motor car, an accident occurs and the motor car leaves the road and is driven through a fence into a field of corn, the accident certainly causes damage to both the fence and the crops which are on land adjacent to the road. Of course, if the car had been driven, under control, through an open gate into a field of corn, the damage to the corn would not have been caused by an accident but a deliberate act of the driver. In such a case, the driver would be guilty of criminal damage to the corn, but would not be obliged by RTA 1988, s 170 to stop or provide any information.

The driver of the motor vehicle must stop and, if required by a person having reasonable grounds for so requiring, must give certain information

The term 'driver' has already been explained in a number of other chapters. However, it must be added that, for the purposes of RTA 1988, s 170, a person who takes out a vehicle on a road remains its 'driver' until that particular journey is over. Consequently, if a person who is driving to work sees a friend en route and stops his car (and switches off its engine) in order to talk to the friend, he remains the driver for the purpose of s 170 during that time, and, if the presence of the car on the road causes an accident, the obligations imposed by s 170 apply to him. Likewise, someone who parks his car, in order to post a letter or for some other purpose of his own, can be found to have remained its driver, because he is still en route on a journey, notwithstanding that an accident is caused by a passenger releasing the car's handbrake; the passenger lacks sufficient control to have replaced him as the driver. On the other hand, s 170 would not apply if the accident was caused by the car's presence on the road or other public place after he had parked it outside his place of work at the end of his journey.

The obligation to stop arises immediately the accident occurs. Thus, in one case, where a bus driver had injured a passenger by braking sharply and had driven on to a rendezvous with an ambulance which he had arranged by radio, a divisional court held that he had failed to stop as required by RTA 1988, s 170. Whether or not a driver has stopped 'immediately' may be controversial. Where a driver collided with a parked vehicle and drove on for a distance of about 80 yards before stopping and returning to the scene of the accident, justices convicted him of an offence of failing to stop. A divisional court said that it would not interfere with that finding, as it was one which was open to the justices on the facts of the case, but said that it was not sure that it would have reached the same conclusion. Because the duty to stop is an immediate one, a driver who leaves the scene and later returns to it does not 'stop' for the purpose of s 170. The term 'stop' means that the driver should stop and remain where he has stopped for such a period of time as in the prevailing circumstances will provide a sufficient period of time to enable persons who have reasonable grounds for so doing to require of him directly and personally the information which the driver may be required to supply. In determining what that period should be, particular regard should be paid to the character of the road or the place where the accident occurred. The duty is that of the driver and his responsibilities cannot be discharged by some other person whom he leaves at the scene. The driver must remain sufficiently near to the vehicle throughout this period of time to allow any person to make the requests permitted by the section. Common sense must be applied when considering the duty to stop. If a driver collides with a vehicle parked in a deserted country lane, it would be unreasonable to expect him to remain there indefinitely. The reasonable approach would be to consider whether his 'stop' was sufficient to allow any person who was nearby and aware of the accident to make such a request. In the case of a stationary vehicle, its driver cannot stop in the physical sense, but must 'stop at the scene' for sufficient time to permit persons to request information.

RTA 1988, s 170 also requires the driver to provide certain information if required so to do by 'any person having reasonable grounds for so requiring'. Such a person will usually be the driver of any other vehicle involved in the accident, a person injured, or the owner of property or of an animal. However, there are other persons who might quite reasonably demand information from the driver of a mechanically propelled vehicle; for example, a relative or friend of a person who has been injured, or a person who witnessed the accident and who is a friend of the owner of damaged property. It will be a matter for the courts to determine in cases of doubt. They may well look differently upon a demand made by a 'nosey parker' as opposed to one made by some person who quite genuinely had the other party's interests at heart.

RTA 1988, s 170(2), which requires a driver to stop and provide this information, is concerned with one offence which may be committed in two ways, either by failing to stop or if, having stopped, failing to provide the information which is required to be given by a person with reasonable grounds.

If the requirement is made by such a person having reasonable grounds, RTA 1988, s 170 obliges the driver to give:

(a) his name and address;
(b) the name and address of the owner of the vehicle; and
(c) the identification mark of the vehicle.

'Address' in (a) is not defined by RTA 1988, s 170. Section 170(2) can be satisfied by giving an address other than a home address, for example the address of the driver's solicitor or the driver's business address, provided it is an address at which the driver can be contacted via that address reasonably swiftly and easily.

This obligation is absolute in the sense that, if the requirement is made by a person having reasonable grounds to make it, the driver must supply this information. If he refuses or fails to do so he commits an offence which is not excused by any subsequent report which he might make to the police. However, if this information is supplied at the scene the obligations of the driver cease and there is no need to report the accident to the police. (If injury to some person is occasioned there is also a need to produce evidence of insurance; we deal with this below.)

In conclusion, it should be noted that the duty to stop does not cast on the driver the duty to go and seek persons to whom to give the above information.

DUTY TO REPORT TO THE POLICE

RTA 1988, s 170(3) deals with a driver's obligation to report an accident to the police and its wording is important:

If for any reason the driver of the mechanically propelled vehicle does not give his *name and address* to a person having reasonable grounds for so requiring, he must report the accident.

Two points must be made at the outset. First, the obligation to report an accident to the police arises whenever the driver has not given his name and address at the scene of the accident, whether or not he was required to do so by anyone there (and indeed, even though he was known personally to any person with reasonable grounds to require his name and address). Thus, a divisional court has held, the obligation to report arises even though the driver could not have given his name and address at the scene of the accident because he was unconscious throughout the time he was there. The obligation is not negated by the fact that police are in attendance at the scene of an accident from which an unconscious driver is taken to hospital. Second, the obligation to report is to do so at a police station or to a constable as soon as reasonably practicable and, in any case, within twenty-four hours of the occurrence of the accident and it can only be fulfilled officially and personally; telling a friend who is a police officer will not do, nor will a telephone message to a police station.

It must be remembered that RTA 1988, s 170(3) only specifies 'his name and address'. If, therefore, a driver gives his name and address to a person reasonably requiring information, but refuses to give the name and address of the owner or the identification mark of the vehicle, he will not be obliged to report the accident to the police, although he will commit an offence under s 170 in consequence of his refusal to give the other information. This one factor has caused more confusion for police officers carrying out their duties under s 170 than the remainder of the provisions of that section.

The obligation to report, of a driver who does not give his name and address at the scene of the accident, is subject to the following rules as to time. First he must report the accident at a police station or to a constable 'in any case within twenty-four hours'. This is the maximum period in which the report may be made, so that if the driver does not report until twenty-four hours or more have elapsed since the accident he is necessarily in breach of his obligation under RTA 1988, s 170. However, second, even if the report is made within twenty-four hours, the driver will nevertheless be in breach of his obligation if he has not made it 'as soon as reasonably practicable'.

What is 'reasonably practicable' is a matter for the court to decide upon in the particular circumstances of each case. If a driver who is not seeking urgent medical attention drives from the scene of an accident and past a police station, in order to go to his home, and only reports the accident twenty hours later, a court is unlikely to find that he reported the accident as soon as reasonably practicable. On the other hand, in a case where a motorist's car left the road and collided, causing damage, at 11 pm and the motorist left his address in his car at the scene and was interviewed by the police at 8.30 am the next day (at which point of time he reported the accident), the Divisional Court held that the justices were entitled to conclude that in the circumstances there had been no failure to report as soon as reasonably practicable.

OFFENCES

A person who fails to comply with any requirement of RTA 1988, s 170 commits an offence against s 170(4). In fact, if he fails to stop (or to give his name and address etc), contrary to s 170(2), and also fails to report the accident to the police, contrary to s 170(3), he commits two offences.

A person charged with such an offence has a defence if *he proves* that he did not know that an accident had occurred. However, in the case of an offence under RTA 1988, s 170(3), if, although unaware of the accident at the time of it, he subsequently becomes aware of it within the twenty-four-hour period and fails to report it to the police, he can be convicted of that offence since he will be obliged to report the accident and his failure at that time will be with knowledge of the accident.

INJURY ACCIDENTS: REQUIREMENT TO PRODUCE INSURANCE

Additional obligations are placed by the Road Traffic Act 1988, s 170(5) on drivers of motor vehicles concerned in accidents involving personal injury to another person.

RTA 1988, s 170(5) provides that if, in the case of a personal injury accident to which s 170 applies, the driver of the motor vehicle does not at the time of the accident produce such a certificate of insurance, or other evidence prescribed by regulations:

(a) to a constable; or
(b) to some person who, having reasonable grounds for so doing, has required him to produce it,

the driver must report the accident and produce such a certificate or other evidence.

As in the case of the duty to report an accident under RTA 1988, s 170(3), the driver must report the accident (and produce his insurance certificate etc) to a constable and must do so as soon as reasonably practicable, within twenty-four hours of the accident. It is an offence to fail to do so. However, the offence is subject to the proviso that a person is not to be convicted of this offence by reason only of a failure to produce a certificate etc if, within seven days after the accident, the certificate etc is produced at the police station specified by him when the accident was reported.

RTA 1988, s 170(5) imposes additional requirements upon a driver who is involved in an accident which involves personal injury to some person other than himself. In addition to providing to any person reasonably requiring such information his name and address, the name and address of the owner and the identification mark of the vehicle, he must also produce his certificate of insurance (or other evidence of insurance) to that person or to a constable. It is important to recognise that there are therefore no circumstances in which a driver must report an accident to the police if his duties are fully discharged at the scene. This is true even in circumstances in which a pedestrian is severely injured; if the driver is requested by the pedestrian, or someone acting reasonably on his behalf, to give the particulars required by s 170 and to produce a certificate of insurance, and he does so, that driver has carried out his legal obligations and need not report the accident to the police. It is, of course, not sufficient to wave a certificate of insurance in front of the eyes of a person requiring such information; it must be produced in the sense that the person is able to satisfy himself that an effective insurance is in force.

CHAPTER 16
Driving offences

INTRODUCTION

When we think of someone being put in fear, injured or killed, we tend to think about this being caused by a person who has embarked on activities which would generally be described as 'criminal'. The mugger, the man in the public house who breaks a bottle to provide himself with a weapon, and the sex attacker, all constitute some form of threat to other persons. However, it must not be forgotten that the driver of a mechanically propelled vehicle is in control of one of the most dangerous weapons of all and there is no limit to the harm which can be caused to persons or property by the irresponsible use of a mechanically propelled vehicle.

The common law offence of manslaughter has always been sufficient to deal with a driver who killed another person by driving which showed a culpable disregard for life. However, juries have been notoriously unwilling to convict a driver of manslaughter. It was for this reason that the offence of causing death by reckless driving was introduced in 1956; this offence was replaced by the offence of causing death by dangerous driving in 1992. Although the offence of 'motor manslaughter' may still be charged, it is now much more likely that proceedings will be taken for the offence of causing death by dangerous driving. In terms of maximum punishment, this is a lesser offence than manslaughter. In the relatively rare situation where 'motor manslaughter' is charged, the case will be governed by the rules set out on pp 847–848. The rules relating to causing death by dangerous driving are described later in the chapter.

In addition to the common law offence of manslaughter, statutory offences were created in the nineteenth century to deal with carriages and the like. Although these provisions were enacted before the days of mechanically propelled vehicles, they can be applied to such vehicles. This is important in relation to the third provision next mentioned. The Highway Act 1835 prohibits certain acts in relation to 'carriages', and the Town Police Clauses Act 1847, s 28 deals with the furious driving of any horse or carriage. The Offences Against the Person Act 1861, s 35 still punishes the causing of bodily harm by wanton or furious driving on a road or otherwise by a person having charge of a carriage or vehicle; this charge can be useful in circumstances in which the negligent driving of a mechanically propelled vehicle did not take place on a road or other public place. However, for all practical purposes, driving offences that are committed in relation to mechanically propelled vehicles are governed by the Road Traffic Act 1988 (RTA 1988). The most serious offences contained in that Act are the offences of dangerous driving and causing death by dangerous driving.

The offences described in this chapter contain a number of general terms, which it is appropriate to define at the outset.

'Driving'

The essence of 'driving' is the use of the driver's controls (or at least one of them) in order to control the movement of the vehicle, however that movement is produced, provided that what occurs can in any sense be regarded as 'driving'. Thus, a person who releases the handbrake and 'coasts' downhill in a car is 'driving' it (and this is so even though the steering is locked). So is a person in the driving seat of a car which is being towed if he has the ability to control its movements by means of the brakes or steering. This is so even if the vehicle is attached by means of a rigid tow bar which is attached to the towing vehicle by means of a ball hitch, and to the vehicle being drawn by means of a shackle. Such a combination leaves the person holding the steering wheel of the towed vehicle with a substantial potential for directional control because he is able (indeed he is required) to keep the towed vehicle in line with the towing vehicle by means of the steering wheel. In such a case it would be irrelevant that the towed vehicle does not have any brakes; directional control through steering is enough. On the other hand, a person in the driving seat of a vehicle on a fixed tow is not driving it, since he cannot control its movements by the use of any of the driver's controls. Nor is a person who is pushing a car and steering it with his hand through the window driving it because this cannot in any sense be so described. Two people may be driving a vehicle at the same time. For example, if A who is in the driving seat operates the clutch and brakes and gear shift but allows his passenger, B, to steer the vehicle, both A and B are driving.

RTA 1988, s 192 provides that, except for the purposes of the offence of causing death by dangerous driving, where a separate person acts as steersman of a motor vehicle he is driving the vehicle (as well as any other person engaged in driving it). This covers the case where one person is primarily concerned with the propulsion of the vehicle and another acts as its steersman. It is relevant only in the case of traction engines and the like.

A limited company cannot be convicted of an offence of driving physically committed by one of its employees; nor can any other employer.

It must be proved that the person alleged to have been driving was driving at the time of the alleged offence. Difficulties in this respect have arisen in cases in which a witness has reported an incident to a police officer and at the same time has provided, from memory, the registration mark of the vehicle. Even with the new rules about hearsay evidence introduced by the Criminal Justice Act 2003, there may be problems if the officer seeks to say in evidence that he was told that the number of the car involved in the incident was that given by the witness. In such cases, it would be good practice for the officer to record the number given to him in his notebook and to have the witness endorse the entry as being correct and sign it. Such a record then becomes 'joint' and may be referred to by either. The witness's statement should also include the fact that he gave that particular number to the officer and that it was the number of the vehicle seen on that occasion.

'Mechanically propelled vehicle'

This term has been discussed in Chapter 9 above. The offences under the Road Traffic Act 1988 involving dangerous or careless driving were extended to include the term 'mechanically propelled vehicle' in place of 'motor vehicle' by the Road Traffic Act 1991. The term 'mechanically propelled vehicle' includes all motor vehicles but also includes vehicles which would not be embraced by that term as they are not intended or adapted for use on a road.

'Motor vehicle'

This term has the normal meaning given to it under the Road Traffic Act 1988, s 185, namely a mechanically propelled vehicle intended or adapted for use on roads. We have discussed this term in Chapter 9 above.

'Road'

A 'road' is defined by RTA 1988, s 192 as any length of highway or any other road to which the public has access, including bridges over which a road passes. The question of whether or not a place is a road for the purposes of this offence will depend upon the question of usage. We dealt with these matters in more detail on pp 319–320.

'Public place'

For discussion as to what may or may not be a public place, in particular circumstances, see Chapter 17 below.

By RTA 1988, s 13A a person is not guilty of an offence involving dangerous or careless driving by virtue of driving a vehicle in a public place other than a road if he shows that he was driving in accordance with an authorisation for a motoring event given under the Motor Vehicles (Off Road Events) Regulations 1995 (see p 588 below). These Regulations empower prescribed bodies to issue authorisations.

DANGEROUS DRIVING, CAUSING DEATH BY DANGEROUS DRIVING, AND DANGEROUS CYCLING

Dangerous driving

RTA 1988, s 2 provides that it is an offence for a person to drive a mechanically propelled vehicle dangerously on a road or other public place. This offence replaced the offence of 'reckless driving'.

The ways in which driving may be dangerous are set out in RTA 1988, s 2A.

Dangerous manner

RTA 1988, s 2A(1) provides that a person is to be regarded as driving dangerously if:

(a) the way that he drives falls far below what would be expected of a competent and careful driver; and
(b) it would be obvious to a competent and careful driver that driving in that way would be dangerous.

RTA 1988, s 2A(3) states that 'dangerous' refers to danger either of injury to any person or of serious damage to property.

This test in RTA 1988, s 2A(1) is concerned with whether the manner of the accused's driving falls *far* below what would be expected of a careful and competent driver in circumstances where it would be obvious to a competent and careful driver that driving in that way would be dangerous. The presence of the word *'far'* will separate offences of dangerous driving from those which should more appropriately be charged as careless driving.

The standard of driving is defined objectively (ie in terms of a competent and careful driver) and it applies to all drivers regardless of the driving experience which they have gained. It would be no defence that the accused was doing his incompetent best or that he believed that he could drive as he did without causing danger to other road users because of his advanced driving skills, as recently held in a case involving a police advanced driver who was testing a new car at very high speeds. Nor would it be a defence that the accused did not intend to drive dangerously. This was held by the Court of Appeal in a case where a bus driver unintentionally pressed the accelerator when he meant to press the brake; as a result the bus travelled across a pedestrian island and pedestrians were killed. The court held that the driver's lack of an intention to drive dangerously was no defence. The objective standards to be applied will vary according to the prevailing conditions and to exceptional circumstances which might have existed. In fog, the competent and careful driver would drive in a manner quite different from that which he would adopt in dry, clear conditions. Whilst driving at a speed of 70 mph in an area restricted to 30 mph might be described as dangerous, it would not often be so on a dual carriageway. If it occurred in the middle of the night when the road was not being used by any other person or vehicle, such driving in a restricted area may not be 'dangerous', whilst driving at that speed on a dual carriageway which is restricted by road works may be.

The opinion of witnesses as to whether or not the accused drove dangerously is, of course, inadmissible.

Once it has been established that the actual driving fell far below standards of a competent and careful driver, it becomes necessary to consider whether or not it would be 'obvious' to a competent and careful driver that such driving would be dangerous.

In determining for these purposes what would be expected of, or obvious to, a competent and careful driver in a particular case, regard must be had not only to the circumstances of which he should be expected to be aware but also to any circumstances shown to have been within the accused's knowledge. Thus, some subjectivity is introduced at this stage as the court will have to determine the questions of what would be expected of a 'competent and careful driver', and of what would be obvious to him, by reference not only to the circumstances of which he could be expected to be aware but also to any circumstances within the defendant's *actual* knowledge. On the other hand, regard must not be had to any circumstance which the accused wrongly believed to exist. Consequently, it has been held that, where a police officer pursued a stolen car at speed through traffic lights at red, his mistaken belief that the junction was being controlled by other officers (so that he could cross safely) was irrelevant to the issue of dangerous driving.

The courts will therefore be concerned with that which 'falls far below' accepted driving standards and that 'which would be obvious' in relation to the danger caused.

A breach of the Highway Code does not necessarily mean that an offence has been committed, but the Code's provisions can be considered by a jury or magistrates, provided that it is clearly explained that they do not provide a 'standard'.

Dangerous state of the vehicle

The second way in which driving may be dangerous is provided by RTA 1988, s 2A(2) which provides that a person is also to be regarded as driving dangerously if it would be obvious to a competent and careful driver that driving the vehicle in its current state would be 'dangerous' (in the sense defined by s 2A(3), outlined above). In determining the state of the vehicle, regard may be had to anything carried on or in it, and the manner in which it is attached or carried.

Because the danger involved in driving the vehicle in its current state must be obvious, the offence will not be committed if the defect involved is a latent one. 'Current state' in s 2A(2) implies a state different from the original or manufactured state. Thus, where the alleged danger relates solely to something inherent in the original design of the vehicle (eg spikes forming part of a grab unit at the front of an agricultural vehicle) dangerous driving is not committed. It would be different if the original, unaltered state made the manner of the driving dangerous.

As with RTA 1988, s 2A(1), in determining what would be obvious to a competent and careful driver, regard must be had not only to the circumstances of which he could be expected to be aware but also to any circumstances shown to have been within the accused's knowledge. A danger is 'obvious' in this context only if it could be seen or realised at first glance by a competent and careful driver. It is not enough that such a driver would have taken steps to check out whether the vehicle was in a condition which was not dangerous, and by doing so would have discovered the defect, perhaps by examining the underside of the vehicle. Where a newly-purchased second-hand car swerved violently out of control and collided with another vehicle it was alleged that this was due to severe corrosion of the vehicle. A traffic examiner stated that it would be necessary to go beneath the vehicle to discover the corrosion. The Court of Appeal said that where a defect existed in a vehicle, it was necessary to show that it would be obvious to a competent and careful driver that driving the vehicle in that condition would be dangerous. However, as in this case, a defect might be such that even a competent and careful driver would not necessarily discover it. Such a defect was not 'obvious' and the issue of whether or not it would be obviously dangerous to drive the vehicle in that condition did not arise unless it could be shown that that knowledge existed.

Similarly, where a wheel detached itself from a vehicle and killed the driver of another vehicle and it was proved that visual checks upon the security of wheels were carried out daily and that a physical check was made once each week, the Court of Appeal said that 'obvious' meant something which could be seen or realised at first glance. In the case of an employee it is important to consider the nature of the instructions given to him and, generally, it would be wrong to expect him to do more that he had been instructed to do in the absence of evidence that those instructions were inadequate.

Another case concerned a goods vehicle which was fitted with a crane which in turn was fitted with outriggers for stabilisation when the crane was in use. The vehicle was fitted with devices for securing the crane and it was possible to see whether or not these securing devices were in position if they were examined (as they protruded slightly). The arm of the crane broke free and struck two pedestrians, killing one of them. The defence submitted that there was no case to answer on a charge of causing death by dangerous driving as there had been no evidence to show that it would have been obvious to a competent driver that the arm was not properly secured; it had not been used that day. The Court of Appeal said that the accused driver had been the only person to use the vehicle since he last secured the riggers. In the absence of any explanation, it was clearly open to a jury to conclude that it would have been obvious that they were not properly secured.

The Court of Appeal, when considering an appeal by a man convicted of aiding and abetting an offence of causing death by dangerous driving, examined the elements of dangerous driving involving a defective vehicle. It ruled that proof of guilt depended upon an objective test as to the standard of driving, namely, what would have been obvious to a competent and careful driver. The state of mind of the accused is relevant only if, and to the extent that, it attributes additional knowledge to the notional competent and careful driver. The threshold of proof is high. It must be shown that the defect would have been 'obvious' to the 'competent and careful driver'. It is not enough to show that a driver, had he examined the vehicle by going underneath it, would have seen the defect. Mens rea plays no part in the offence as it is concerned with defective vehicles.

Driving in a dangerously defective state through intoxication or consumption of drugs

Evidence of consumption of alcohol or drugs cannot by itself establish the fact that a driver has committed an offence of dangerous driving. The offence is concerned with the dangerous nature of the driving, not with the dangerous nature of the driver due to drink. While the consumption of a large amount of alcohol *is relevant* to an offence of dangerous driving it cannot be conclusive. Likewise the consumption of a drug, even if the amount is unquantified, has been held by the Court of Appeal to be relevant to an offence of dangerous driving, although it cannot be conclusive. In either case, there must be evidence that the vehicle was driven dangerously within the definition in RTA 1988, s 2A.

In relation to the consumption of drugs, the Court of Appeal has said that a jury is entitled to look at the consumption of cocaine per se as *relevant* to the issue of dangerous driving, in establishing whether a driver had been affected by drugs while driving. The Court said that the drug had a tendency or capacity to impair driving ability and was therefore relevant. Quantification of the amount taken is not essential.

Dangerous cycling

A person who rides a bicycle or tricycle dangerously on a road commits a separate and less serious offence. A person is to be regarded as riding dangerously if he rides in a *manner* which equates to the manner of driving described above.

Alternative verdicts

The Road Traffic Offenders Act 1988 (RTOA 1988), s 24 provides that, where a person is charged with an offence of dangerous driving or dangerous cycling and is found not guilty of such an offence and the allegations in the indictment or information amount to or include an allegation of an offence of careless driving or careless cycling, he may be convicted of that offence.

Causing death by dangerous driving

RTA 1988, s 1 provides that a person who causes the death of another person by driving a mechanically propelled vehicle on a road or other public place dangerously is guilty of an offence.

Proof of the offence requires proof that the accused drove a mechanically propelled vehicle on a road or other public place dangerously (in the sense just explained) and that the dangerous driving caused the death of another person (including someone else in the accused's vehicle). It is not necessary to show that the dangerous driving was the sole cause, since it is sufficient that it is more than a trifling cause. An example is a case where two drivers were engaged in a high speed chase and one of them was killed when she collided with an on-coming car, the other driver was convicted of this offence. His dangerous driving had been a cause of the death of the other driver and that 'cause' had been more than 'slight or trifling'. By way of a further example, if a driver deliberately accelerates towards people who are crossing at a pedestrian crossing and knocks down one of them, who later dies, he can be convicted of causing that death by dangerous driving. It will not assist him to allege that the victim was not seriously injured and would not have died if a heart condition from which he suffered had not been aggravated by the shock. His driving is a cause of that death and it is certainly not a trifling cause in such circumstances.

No mens rea need be proved as to the risk of death resulting from the dangerous driving; it follows that it is irrelevant that that risk was unforeseen or unforeseeable, as would be the case where the only obvious risk was of damage to property.

It is not necessary that the driver should have been driving the vehicle (ie it need not have been in motion) at the time that the fatal injury was caused. It is enough that there has been dangerous driving by the driver and that that driving is more than a trifling cause of death. This is shown by a case where a driver took his lorry on to a motorway after having been warned that his brake air pressure gauges were not working (which constituted dangerous driving), and the handbrake system was activated due to loss of air pressure. The trailer unit blocked the nearside lane of the motorway. Some twelve minutes later a lorry collided with it and the driver of that vehicle was killed. The Court of Appeal held that the consequences of dangerous driving are capable of outlasting the time the driver spends at the wheel. It held that the dangerous driving must have played a part, not simply in creating the occasion of the fatal accident, but in bringing it about. On the facts the consequences of the dangerous driving were not 'spent' and too remote from the accident, and were more than a trifling cause of the death. As a result the driver's conviction for causing death by dangerous driving was upheld.

Causing death by dangerous driving is a serious offence and it is important that the evidence offered to a court is well presented. Identification of the person fatally injured is of extreme importance. Medical evidence will be given at the Crown Court concerning the cause of death of the person injured in the accident. It is essential that a police officer, who was at the scene of the accident and saw the injured person, identifies that person to the pathologist who carries out the post mortem examination. In the absence of such evidence, there is nothing to connect the person upon whom the post mortem examination was carried out with the person injured in the accident. In addition, a careful note must be made of everything observed at the scene of the accident at the particular time at which it occurred. Whether driving can be described as dangerous will often depend upon the particular circumstances existing at the time, such as the state of street lighting and the nature and volume of traffic at that time of day. All fatal traffic accidents must be handled carefully and the possibility of the need for forensic evidence should be considered. There is little purpose in tracing a damaged vehicle suspected of having been involved in a fatal accident if samples of glass, paint and other vehicle debris were not collected at the scene at the time of the accident.

The ingredients of the offences of manslaughter and of causing death by dangerous driving are similar. However, it has been stated by the House of Lords that a person who caused death by reckless driving (the offence which previously existed) should normally be charged with that offence, and that a charge of manslaughter should only be brought in the most grave cases. It is assumed that the same view will be taken in relation to charges of dangerous driving. The House also held that counts of manslaughter and of causing death by reckless driving might not be joined in the same indictment; the prosecution must choose which offence to charge. The same will apply to offences of causing death by dangerous driving.

It is not the purpose of the offence of causing death by dangerous driving to punish the driver of a motor car who causes the death of one of his own family by the dangerous manner of his driving. Unless the circumstances are exceptional, it is probable that the punishment awarded by a court will be insignificant in relation to the punishment which such a driver will already have suffered. If particular circumstances exist which appear to make a prosecution desirable in such a case, the advice of the Director of Public Prosecutions should be obtained before such steps are taken.

Alternative verdicts

By the RTOA 1988, s 24 a person acquitted on a charge of causing death by dangerous driving can be convicted of dangerous driving, causing death by careless or inconsiderate driving (when the relevant provisions of the Road Safety Act 2006 (RSA 2006) are in force) or of careless driving, if the allegations in the indictment amount to or include an allegation of such an offence.

CARELESS AND INCONSIDERATE DRIVING, CAUSING DEATH BY CARELESS OR INCONSIDERATE DRIVING, CAUSING DEATH BY DRIVING WHEN UNLICENSED, DISQUALIFIED OR UNINSURED

Offences of careless driving

RTA 1988, s 3 creates two separate offences by providing that if a person drives a mechanically propelled vehicle on a road or other public place without due care and attention, or without reasonable consideration for other persons using the road or place, he is guilty of an offence. The level of 'bad' driving which must be proved in a charge of careless or inconsiderate driving is considerably less than that required in cases of dangerous driving.

Offences against s 3 are 'specified offences' for the purposes of RTOA 1988, ss 34A to 34C (reduced disqualification for attendance on courses) where an order of disqualification is made under RTA 1988, s 34 for a period of not less than twelve months. When provisions of the RSA 2006 are brought into force, offences against s 3 will be 'specified offences' for the purposes of RTOA 1988, ss 34A to 34C (reduced disqualification for attendance on courses) where an order of disqualification is made under RTA 1988, s 34 for a period of not less than twelve months.

Driving without due care and attention

RSA 2006, s 30 prospectively inserts a new s 3ZA into the RTA 1988 which defines the terms 'careless or inconsiderate driving'.

Section 3ZA provides that a person is to be regarded as driving 'without due care and attention' if (and only if) the way he drives falls below what would be expected of a competent and careful driver. In determining what would be expected of a competent and careful driver in a particular case, regard must be had not only to the circumstances of which he could be expected to be aware but also to any circumstances shown to have been within the knowledge of the accused. The definition of driving without due care and attention differs from that relating to dangerous driving in relation to the extent to which the accused's driving falls below the standard of a competent and careful driver. While dangerous driving requires a fall 'far' below what would be expected of a competent and careful driver, simply 'falling below' that standard, however marginally, suffices for careless driving.

Before careless driving was so defined it had been established that whether or not a person had committed an offence of careless driving was dependent upon whether he was exercising that degree of care and attention that a reasonable and prudent driver would exercise in those circumstances. It has been said that the standard is an objective standard, impersonal and universal, fixed in relation to the safety of the other users of the highway. It is in no way related to the degree of proficiency or degree of experience attained by the individual driver, and it is unaffected by the fact that the driver was driving to an emergency. The aim of s 3AZ seems to be very much in line with this.

Bearing in mind the objective approach to be applied, it is no defence that, as a learner, the driver was doing his best, if that best falls short of the standard which might be expected from a competent and careful driver. If a learner driver applies the accelerator instead of the footbrake and causes an accident he is guilty of driving without due care and attention. There is only one standard of competence and his actions fall short of it. In circumstances where a competent driver wears shoes with smooth leather soles and this causes his foot to slip from the brake pedal, the court will have to consider whether in the circumstances a competent and careful driver would have been aware of the possibility of this happening and would not have driven the car with such shoes. In the same way, it is essential to keep in mind that experienced drivers or specially trained drivers do not in consequence of that experience or training owe some higher standard of care. For example, the driver of a police vehicle owes the ordinary standard of care to other persons on the road.

There is no limit to the forms which this offence may take. If a driver gives false direction signals this amounts to driving without due care and attention since it falls below the standard of a competent and careful driver in the circumstances because such a driver, realising the possible risks of deluding other road users as to the intended movements of his vehicle, would ensure that he did not give false signals. There are numerous circumstances in which this offence is quite clearly committed. The Traffic Signs Regulations and General Directions authorise various road markings which demand a certain standard of care. Road markings at the junctions of roads frequently indicate that no vehicle shall pass the line markings in a side street in circumstances which will impede other traffic on the main road. If a collision occurs because a vehicle emerges from such a side street, having passed over the road markings, this provides clear proof that the driver was not paying sufficient attention.

Failure to observe a provision of the Highway Code does not of itself establish driving without due care and attention, but any such failure may be relied on as evidence of it.

In applying the appropriate test as to whether a defendant has driven without due care and attention, all of the circumstances of the case can be considered including evidence that the defendant had been affected by drink or that he had taken such an amount of drink as would be likely to affect a driver, since such evidence may indicate a lack of due care on the part of the driver in driving as he did.

Whether or not an accused driver has fallen below the objective standard of care is a question of fact in every case, and it must be decided upon the particular facts by the justices. These facts are very much within the knowledge of the local justices, and a divisional court will not interfere with one of their decisions unless it is one which no reasonable bench of justices could have reached in the circumstances. It will be appreciated that in most circumstances the local justices will be aware of the character of the road or junction at which the incident occurred, the volume and type of traffic which uses the roads and any particular hazards which exist. They are therefore in a much better position to assess whether or not a certain piece of driving was carried out without due care and attention than judges sitting in a divisional court who have no such local knowledge. In some cases, however, the facts are such that, unless the accused driver offers some explanation consistent with him having taken due care which is not disproved, the only proper inference is careless driving, in which case the justices must convict him (and if they do not a divisional court will order them to do so).

Driving without reasonable consideration

RTA 1988, s 3ZA, prospectively inserted by RSA 2006, s 30 provides that a person is to be regarded as driving without reasonable consideration for other persons only if those persons are inconvenienced by his driving. Those persons must be shown to have been inconvenienced. Thus a driver may deliberately drive at speed through a pool of water, but will only commit this offence if other persons were either dampened or forced to flee.

Once again, an objective test should be applied as to whether particular forms of driving are carried out without reasonable consideration for other persons using the road or place. Thus, the question is whether the accused drove without showing the consideration to other road users which would be shown by a considerate driver. The driver who occupies the fast lane of a motorway, or even the outside lane of a dual carriageway, in circumstances in which there is nothing to prevent him from regaining the nearside lane, because he is unreasonably interfering with the progress of other drivers. The irresponsible use of full beam headlamps may also amount to driving without reasonable consideration. A considerate driver certainly does not drive towards opposing traffic in this manner. A person may drive without reasonable consideration for other persons using the road even where his lack of consideration is to his own passenger.

Vehicle used in manner causing alarm, distress or annoyance

The Police Reform Act 2002 (PRA 2002), s 59(1) provides that, where a constable in uniform has reasonable grounds for believing that a mechanically propelled vehicle is being used on any occasion in a manner which contravenes RTA 1988, s 3 (careless and inconsiderate driving) and which is causing, or is likely to cause, alarm, distress or annoyance to members of the public, he has the power under PRA 2002, s 59(3):

(a) if the vehicle is moving, to order the person driving it to stop it;

(b) to seize and remove the vehicle;

(c) for the purposes of exercising a power falling within (a) or (b), to enter any premises (other than a dwelling home, but this term does not include any garage or other structure occupied with the dwelling house, or any land appurtenant to the dwelling house) on which he has reasonable grounds for believing the vehicle to be;

(d) to use reasonable force, if necessary, in the exercise of any power conferred by (a) to (c).

A constable additionally has the powers set out at (a) to (d) above where he has reasonable grounds for believing that a mechanically propelled vehicle has been used on any occasion in a manner falling within PRA 2002, s 59(1).

PRA 2002, s 59(4) provides that the power of seizure shall not be exercised unless:

(a) the constable has warned the person appearing to him to be the person whose use falls within PRA 2002, s 59(1) that he will seize the vehicle if that use continues or is repeated; and

(b) it appears to him that the use has continued or been repeated after the warning.

However, a warning need not be given if the constable would otherwise have the power to seize the vehicle under PRA 2002, s 59 if:

(a) the circumstances make it impracticable for him to give the warning;
(b) the constable has already on that occasion given a warning under PRA 2002, s 59(4) in respect of any use of that vehicle or of another mechanically propelled vehicle by that person or any other person;
(c) the constable has reasonable grounds for believing that such a warning has been given on that occasion otherwise than by him; or
(d) the constable has reasonable grounds for believing that the person whose use of that mechanically propelled vehicle on that occasion would justify the seizure is a person to whom a warning under PRA 2002, s 59(4) has been given (whether or not by that constable or in respect of the same vehicle or the same or a similar use) on a previous occasion in the previous twelve months.

It is an offence to fail to comply with an order under PRA 2002, s 59(3) to stop a motor vehicle.

The Police (Retention and Disposal of Motor Vehicles) Regulations 2002 provide for the safe keeping, retention, release and disposal of a vehicle seized under s 59. They provide that a person who would otherwise be liable to charges is not liable to pay if the use which caused the seizure was not a use by him and he did not know of the use of the vehicle in the manner which led to its seizure, had not consented to its use in that manner and could not, by the taking of reasonable steps, have prevented its use in that manner.

These powers also apply where a uniformed constable reasonably believes that an offence against RTA 1988, s 34 (prohibition of off-road driving; see p 397) has been committed, and that the manner in which the vehicle is being used is causing, or is likely to cause, alarm, distress or annoyance to members of the public.

General

Because RTA 1988, s 3 creates two offences, an information or (when in operation) written charge which alleges both alternatives is bad for duplicity. It is sufficient to allege that a person drove without due care and attention at a particular time or place, or that he drove without reasonable consideration at a time and place, since it is not necessary to specify the nature of his negligence in the information or written charge. If, following a fatal accident, it appears that there is sufficient evidence to support a charge of careless driving but not of dangerous driving, no such charge should be preferred until after the inquest has been held.

Causing death by careless or inconsiderate driving

RSA 2006, s 20 prospectively inserts a new s 2B into the RTA 1988 creating a new offence of causing death by careless, or inconsiderate, driving. Section 2B provides that a person who causes the death of another person by driving a mechanically propelled vehicle on a road or other public place without due care and attention, or without reasonable consideration for other persons using the road or place, is guilty of an offence.

Causing death by driving unlicensed, uninsured or disqualified

RSA 2006, s 21 prospectively adds a s 3ZB to the RTA 1988. It provides that a person is guilty of an offence if he causes the death of another person by driving a motor vehicle on a road and, at the time when he is driving, the circumstances are such that he is committing an offence under:

(a) RTA 1988, s 87(1) (driving otherwise than in accordance with a licence);
(b) RTA 1988, s 103(1)(b) (driving while disqualified); or
(c) RTA 1988, s 143 (using a motor vehicle while uninsured or unsecured against third party risks).

Causing death by careless driving when under the influence of drink or drugs

RTA 1988, s 3A(1), provides that it is an offence for a person to cause the death of another person by driving a mechanically propelled vehicle on a road or other public place without due care and attention, or without reasonable consideration for other persons using the road or place, and:

(a) he is, at the time when he is driving, unfit to drive through drink or drugs; or
(b) has consumed so much alcohol that the proportion of it in his breath, blood or urine at that time exceeds the prescribed limit;
(c) he is, within eighteen hours after that time, required under s 7 to provide a specimen, but without reasonable cause fails to provide it; or
(d) he is requested by a constable to give his permission for a laboratory test of a specimen of blood taken from him under s 7A of this Act, but without reasonable excuse, fails to do so.
(d) will apply when the relevant provisions of the RSA 2006 are brought into force.

It is also an indictable offence for the purposes of the provisions relating to search warrants.

The Police Reform Act 2002 inserted a s 7A into the RTA 1988 to deal with the taking of blood specimens from a person who has been involved in an accident and is, for some reason, incapable of giving a valid consent to the taking of a specimen of blood: see p 617. The provisions of RTA 1988, s 7A apply to offences against RTA 1988, s 3A.

In essence, to be guilty of an offence under RTA 1988, s 3A(1), the accused must be proved to have committed one or other of the offences of careless driving and thereby killed another and be proved to fall within one of the drink/drive elements in (a) to (c).

The term 'unfit to drive through drink or drugs' is explained in Chapter 17, as are other references to drink or drugs, prescribed limits etc. Other matters concerned with the evidential linking of the driver to the person who received fatal injuries, are discussed above.

Despite the wording of RTA 1988, s 3A(1), the offences at (b) and (c), which are based upon the consumption of alcohol in excess of the prescribed limit and upon failure to provide a specimen under s 7 within eighteen hours of driving, apply only to persons driving motor vehicles as opposed to mechanically propelled vehicles.

Alternative verdicts

RTOA 1988, s 24 provides that, where a person is charged with an offence under RTA 1988, s 3A and is found not guilty and the allegations in the indictment amount to or include an allegation of causing death by careless or inconsiderate driving (when the relevant provisions of the RSA 2006 are brought into force), careless driving or of a drink-driving offence or of failing to provide a specimen for analysis, he may be convicted of that offence.

Careless cycling

There are separate, and less serious, offences of riding a bicycle or tricycle on a road without due care and attention, or without reasonable consideration for other persons using the road.

DEFENCES TO DANGEROUS OR CARELESS DRIVING

Duress by threats and duress of circumstances

Where a person is compelled to drive dangerously or carelessly in order to avoid the threat of death or serious injury to himself or some other person, as where his car is being hotly pursued by an armed gang or where his car has been hijacked by an armed gang who order him to outdistance a pursuing police car, he may have the defence of duress of circumstances or of duress by threats. The requirements of these defences are set out on p 10.

Public emergencies

Unless the defence of duress of circumstances applies, police officers, firefighters and ambulance drivers may *not* use the emergency nature of their mission as a defence to a charge of dangerous or careless driving, as they owe the same duty of care to the public at all times.

Automatism

'Automatism' means the involuntary movement of a person's body or limbs, that is movements which are completely beyond his control. There are various medical conditions which may cause involuntary movements of part of the body or even unconsciousness. Some external factors may also cause such body movements. A driver may suffer an epileptic fit and thus lose control of a motor vehicle. A motor vehicle may be entered by a swarm of bees, with the result that the driver is prevented from exercising any directional control over the vehicle, any movements of his arms and legs being caused solely by the action of the bees. The question to be answered is how relevant these issues may be to dangerous and careless driving charges.

The answer is that *generally,* as in the case of other offences, it is a defence that the accused was an automaton. Consequently, a driver who suffers a totally unexpected epileptic fit, or who is overcome by a swarm of bees in the way just described, cannot be convicted of dangerous or careless driving. (We discussed automatism and the question of proof in Chapter 1, above, to which the reader is referred for further detail.)

However, by way of *exception*, it must be remembered that automatism does not excuse a person from liability for the crimes discussed in this chapter if his automatism resulted from his voluntary intoxication. Nor will automatism excuse such a person if, before he became an automaton, he appreciated the risk that something which he did or failed to do was likely to make him unpredictable or uncontrollable with the result that he might endanger others (as opposed to simply becoming an automaton) and he deliberately ran the risk or otherwise disregarded it.

Moreover, by way of further *exception*, an accused who, for example, falls asleep at the wheel or goes into a hypoglycaemic coma at the wheel can be convicted of careless driving under the ordinary principles of liability, not in relation to the time when he was an automaton but in relation to the time when he realised or should have realised that he was about to become unconscious and should have stopped driving. The reason is clear: to drive in such a case falls below the standard of a reasonable and prudent driver (since he would have stopped).

Mechanical defect

The fact that the driving complained of was due to the sudden mechanical failure of an essential part of a motor vehicle can provide a defence to charges of dangerous or careless driving, provided that the defect was not known by the accused to exist prior to the occurrence which forms the basis of the charge, and was not such that it should have been discovered by a reasonably prudent driver. Thus, where a driver knew that the brakes of his vehicle pulled to the offside but nevertheless drove it, the defence of mechanical defect was held not to be open to him.

Like the defence of automatism, the essence of this defence is that the dangerous situation was caused by a sudden loss of control which was in no way due to the fault of the driver.

SPEEDING

In considering offences of exceeding speed limits it is essential to separate them into those which are related to restricted roads, to roads subjected to a speed limit order, to speed limits on motorways, to speed limits introduced by temporary orders, and limits which affect particular vehicles in particular places.

With the exceptions noted below offences which are related to exceeding maximum speed limits are offences in respect of which there is discretionary disqualification; the endorsement of 3 to 6 or 3 (if fixed penalty) penalty points is obligatory. For offences of speeding which are contrary to the Road Traffic Regulation Act 1984 (RTRA 1984), ss 17(4) (speeding on special roads) and 89(1) (speeding elsewhere), the penalty points which a court may award will fall in the range of 2 to 6 or appropriate penalty points (fixed penalty). When provisions of the RSA 2006 are brought into force, speeding offences against these sections will be 'specified offences' for the purposes of RTOA 1988, s 34A to 34C (reduced disqualification for attendance on courses) where an order of disqualification is made for a period of not less than twelve months.

Restricted roads

By RTRA 1984, s 81 it is not lawful for a person to drive a motor vehicle on a restricted road at a speed exceeding 30 mph. It is an offence contrary to RTRA 1984, s 89 to do so.

In the present context, a 'restricted road' is basically defined as one upon which there is provided a system of street lighting furnished by means of lamps placed not more than 200 yards apart. A divisional court has held that an error of 12 yards between two lamps in a system of twenty-four does not prevent the road being restricted. In addition to this basic definition, RTRA 1984, s 82 provides that a direction may be given that a specified road with street lighting as described above shall cease to be a restricted road for the purpose of s 81 or that a road which is not provided with such lighting shall be a restricted road for the purpose of s 81. Such directions are made by the Secretary of State in the case of trunk roads and by the local authority in the case of other roads.

A road with street lighting which has been de-restricted by a direction must show the prescribed de-restriction signs (including repeater signs). Likewise, a road without such lighting which has been made a restricted road must be provided with the prescribed restriction signs (including repeater signs). If these are not in place, a driver cannot be convicted of exceeding the 30 mph speed limit. However, if they are, it is no defence to such a charge that the accused did not see the signs. The de-restriction or restriction signs which must be used are prescribed by the Traffic Signs (Speed Limits) Regulations and Directions 1969.

The requirement for restriction signs does not apply to a road which is restricted by virtue of having a system of street lighting with lamps not more than 200 yards apart. Consequently, it is no defence for a driver accused of exceeding 30 mph on such a road that no signs were provided.

Roads subject to speed limit orders

Quite apart from the 'restricted' (ie to 30 mph) roads just discussed, there are many other roads which are subject to speed limits. RTRA 1984, s 84 empowers a local authority to make an order prohibiting the driving of motor vehicles on a specified road at a speed exceeding that specified in the order (either at any time or during specified periods) or at a speed exceeding that indicated by traffic signs in accordance with the order. Where an order relates to a trunk road and certain other roads, the Secretary of State's consent is normally required. By s 89, a person who drives a motor vehicle at a speed in excess of that specified for the particular road is guilty of an offence. If a speed limit order is made under s 84, the specified road must bear the prescribed restriction signs (including repeater signs). If it does not, a person cannot be convicted of driving in excess of the specified limit.

Speed limits on motorways

The Motorways (Speed Limit) Regulations 1974 impose an overall speed limit of 70 mph on any motor vehicle using a motorway. If a section of motorway is subject to a lesser limit, this is expressly listed and that section must bear the prescribed signs indicating the lower limit (otherwise a driver cannot be convicted of exceeding that limit). Contravention of the Regulations is an offence contrary to RTRA 1984, s 17(4).

Temporary speed limits

RTRA 1984, s 88 permits temporary speed limit orders to be made by the Secretary of State when it is desirable to do so in the interests of safety or for the purpose of facilitating the movement of traffic. Such orders may impose temporary maximum speed limits.

The 70 mph, 60 mph and 50 mph (Temporary Speed Limit) Order 1977, which was made under the predecessor to s 88 and continues in force indefinitely, imposes a maximum limit of 60 mph on single carriageways and of 70 mph on dual carriageways. These are general limits which apply to all roads (other than motorways) unless some other speed limit operates by virtue of the provisions described in this chapter.

The 1977 Order also imposes a limit of 60 mph on certain specified lengths of dual carriageways and of 50 mph on certain specified lengths of single carriageways. Such lengths must be provided with the prescribed restriction signs (including repeaters).

By RTRA 1984, s 89, it is an offence for a person to drive a motor vehicle on a road in excess of an applicable temporary speed imposed under the Order.

Minimum speed limits

RTRA 1984, s 88 also permits orders to be made imposing minimum speed limits, subject to such exceptions as may be specified. Signs must be displayed if a minimum speed limit is in force in respect of any road. By s 88(7), breach of such an order is an offence. Neither disqualification nor endorsement can be ordered on a conviction for this offence. Such a minimum speed limit only applies, of course, to motor vehicles.

Temporary maximum limits by highway authorities

RTRA 1984, s 14 permits highway authorities to impose temporary speed limits because of roadworks or work which is being undertaken near a road, or because of the likelihood of danger to the public or of serious damage to the highway, or for the purpose of cleaning or clearing litter. Such an order cannot continue in force for more than eighteen months unless the Secretary of State consents to its further continuance or, in the case of roadworks, where the authority has stated in the order that the works will take longer, but in such a case the order must be revoked as soon as the works are completed.

A speed limit imposed under s 14 has been held not to be invalidated by being wrongly positioned, and consequently indicating that the length of the restriction was longer than that imposed by the order, if it gives adequate guidance on the speed limit on the part of the road properly subject to the order.

A person who contravenes a speed limit imposed under RTRA 1984, s 14 commits an offence contrary to RTRA 1984, s 16.

Speed limits on particular vehicles

Quite apart from the various speed limits which apply to roads, speed limits are also imposed on various types of vehicles. The result is that the driver of such a vehicle must not only observe the *speed limit applying to the road* in question but also the *speed limit applying to his vehicle on that road*. A person who drives a motor vehicle on a road at a speed in excess of a speed limit applicable to that vehicle is, by RTRA 1984, s 89, guilty of an offence.

RTRA 1984, Sch 6 sets out the speed limits applying to particular classes of vehicles as follows:

Class of vehicle	M/ways	Dual carr	Other roads
1 Invalid carriage	n/a	20	20
2 Passenger vehicle, motor caravan, car-derived van or dual-purpose vehicle drawing one trailer	60	60	50
3 Vehicle of the type mentioned in 2, drawing more than one trailer	40	20	20
4 Goods vehicle (except car-derived van) up to 7.5 tonnes mlw (maximum laden weight) not drawing a trailer	70	60	50
5 Articulated vehicle up to 7.5 tonnes mlw, and goods vehicles drawing one trailer where the combined mlw does not exceed 7.5 tonnes	60	60	50
6 Articulated vehicle over 7.5 tonnes mlw, goods vehicle over 7.5 tonnes mlw and goods vehicles drawing one trailer where the combined mlw exceeds 7.5 tonnes	60	50	40
7 Goods vehicle, other than a car-derived van, drawing more than one trailer	40	20	20
8 Motor tractor, light loco, heavy loco	20	20	20
9 Motor tractor, light loco, heavy loco with certain requirements as to springs and wings being met	40	30	30
10 Works truck	18	18	18
11 Passenger vehicle exceeding 3.05 tonnes u/w or adapted to carry more than 8 passengers:			
Not exceeding 12 m length	70	60	50
Exceeding 12 m length	60	60	50
12 Agricultural motor vehicle	40	40	40

The term 'car-derived van' means a goods vehicle which is constructed or adapted as a derivative of a passenger vehicle and which has a maximum laden weight not exceeding 2 tonnes. It is treated as if it was a passenger vehicle of the type from which it was derived.

A recovery vehicle equipped with a special boom for lifting vehicles is not a motor tractor. It is constructed to carry a load and is not, therefore, restricted to 40 mph on a motorway.

Exemptions from speed limits

RTRA 1984, s 87 exempts motor vehicles which are being used for fire and rescue, ambulance, or police purposes from the statutory provisions imposing speed limits on motor vehicles, if the observance of any such provision would be likely to hinder the use of the vehicle for the purpose for which it is being used on that occasion. Section 87 also applies in relation to vehicles being used for Serious Organised Crime Agency purposes, or for training drivers for use for Agency purposes, as it applies to a vehicle being driven for police purposes. However, other than in the case of training, s 87 does not apply in relation to a vehicle being driven for Agency purposes unless it is being driven by a person trained to drive vehicles at high speeds.

None of the above is a general exemption; the particular purpose of use on each occasion must be examined. The exemptions are clearly essential; otherwise, for example, police vehicles would not be permitted to pursue speeding vehicles and would not be permitted to respond as quickly as possible to emergency situations.

When the relevant provisions of the RSA 2006 are brought into force, the exemptions will expressly apply where the vehicle is being used for training purposes for any of the emergency services, but only if the driver has successfully completed a high speed driving training course, or is driving as part of such a course.

It has been held that the exemption extended to a police driver who was driving the Home Secretary to an engagement, in circumstances in which the driver had cause to fear that the Home Secretary might be in danger.

Procuring or inciting speeding: a special provision

RTRA 1984, s 89(4) provides that, if a person who employs others to drive motor vehicles on roads publishes or issues any timetable or schedule, or gives any directions, under which any journey or part of a journey is required to be completed within a specified time, and it is not practicable for that journey (or part) to be completed in the specified time without the commission of an offence under s 89, that publication or issue, or giving of directions, may be produced as evidence that the employer procured or (as the case may be) incited his employees to commit such an offence.

Proof

RTRA 1984, s 89(2) states that a person must not be convicted of an offence of speeding contrary to s 89 solely on the evidence of one witness to the effect that, in the opinion of the witness, the person prosecuted was driving the vehicle at a speed exceeding the specified limit. The subsection requires corroborative evidence; it does not require that there must necessarily be more than one witness. Although, technically, there is no reason why an offender should not be convicted on the evidence of two witnesses, where one corroborates the other by stating that in his opinion the vehicle was, for example, exceeding a limit of 30 mph, the courts would generally not be satisfied with two such opinions unless the speed was estimated to be far in excess of the limit imposed. Corroboration is therefore usually provided by some mechanical device, which is read by an operator (normally a police officer) who may then give evidence of its reading. These readings will provide corroboration of the operator's opinion of the speed of the vehicle in question. However, a divisional court in judicial review proceedings refused to interfere with a conviction where two experienced traffic officers saw a vehicle enter a built-up area at a speed which they both said was at least 45 mph. The court said that it was a matter for the court of trial to decide on the facts whether it accepted the evidence of the police officers or the explanation given by the accused. It was not its function, on an application for judicial review, to consider whether that court had reached the right conclusion; it could only interfere if the conclusion reached was such that no reasonable court, properly considering the evidence before it, could have reached. The court added that it would have reached the same conclusion.

Corroboration of speed may be obtained by the use of stop watches to assess speeds over a measured distance, but it is usually provided by a speedometer, radar speed meter, vascar or other approved device. Where a speedometer is used, it is important to establish that the police vehicle containing the speedometer maintained an even distance from the vehicle being checked as this is relevant to the issue of speed.

A police officer's opinion of a vehicle's speed may also be corroborated from scientific calculations made by him (or another) based, for example, on damage to the vehicle and skid marks where it has crashed.

In instances where two police officers are involved in detecting speeding offences, they may keep one record of the transaction provided that both check and acknowledge the accuracy of that record at the time. This frequently occurs where one officer is engaged in checking the speed of the vehicle, whilst another stops and deals with the offending driver.

Radar meters are extremely accurate devices, and the courts will accept evidence of speed which is based upon meter readings provided that the operator can satisfy the court that he is a trained operator and that there is clear evidence of the identity of the particular motor vehicle alleged to have exceeded the speed limit. The vehicle will have been stopped by another officer and clear proof will be required that the vehicle stopped by the second officer was the one which had exceeded a statutory speed limit. Hand-held radar guns have been criticised in the courts but, in the instances in which the readings obtained by such guns have been rejected, it is operator-error which has been the cause of the difficulties. Hand-held guns are accurate, provided the batteries are fully charged or, if they are operating from another source, provided they are properly connected. However, their accuracy is affected if they are operated within a quarter of a mile of powerful VHF or UHF transmissions or within 100 yards of high voltage cables. Care must also be taken to ensure that the beam is not bounced off metal objects and that it could not have picked up a reading from another moving object.

Vascar devices are also in common use within police forces. They record speeds averaged by a vehicle over a specified distance. Operators must be carefully trained as the device is operated by a series of switches. It is essential that the operator is able to satisfy a court that the switches were operated at the right time to ensure that correct distances are recorded, and that the vehicle was properly identified, together with the precise moment when it passes the object which marks the limit of the distance over which it is checked.

The above devices are approved by the Secretary of State.

Speed cameras

RTOA 1988, s 20 provides that records produced by prescribed devices are evidence of a fact related to any offence of speeding. The record must provide (in the same or another document) a certificate as to the circumstances in which the record was produced, signed by a constable or a person authorised by, or on behalf of, a chief police officer for the area in which the offence is alleged to have been committed. The device must be of a type proved to have been approved by the Secretary of State and must be used in accordance with conditions subject to which the approval was given. The Road Traffic Offenders (Prescribed Devices) Order 1992 gave approval to devices designed or adapted for measuring by radar the speed of motor vehicles. An identically named Order in 1993 approved devices designed or adapted for measuring speed by means of sensors, or cables on, or near the surface of a highway and those activated by means of a light beam or beams. Another identically named Order in 1999 gave approval to cameras designed or adapted to record speed by digitally recording the image of the motor vehicle as it passes two positions, digitally recording each image and the time it is photographed, and calculating the average speed between the two positions. The cameras do not require film but transmit computer images to a computer centre.

Evidence of the approval of the particular device used may be required and should be offered in the absence of judicial notice having been taken of its existence. This may be done by production of a valid copy of the instrument of approval. However, a divisional court has said that oral evidence may be given from a police officer who has knowledge of the approval, but approval may not be inferred merely from the fact that the device is in general use within police forces. Where a challenge had been made in relation to approval, the court approved of the officer in the case being recalled to give oral evidence and of the introduction of evidence of an entry in *Wilkinson's Road Traffic Offences* to the effect that the device had been approved by a particular Order and was in general usage within police forces. The court said that this entitled the justices to take judicial notice of the existence of approval.

A copy of evidence obtained by means of an approved device must be served on the person charged with the offence not less than seven days before the hearing or trial. If the person charged, not less than three days before the hearing or trial, requires the attendance of the person who signed the document, the evidence of the circumstances in which the record was produced will not be admissible, although the record produced by the device will; this limitation does not apply where the proceedings in question are committal proceedings.

Notices may be sent under the Road Traffic Act 1988, s 172, requiring the owner of the vehicle to identify the driver within twenty-eight days. A divisional court supported a finding by justices that an unsigned notice sent by a Central Ticket Office Manager 'For the Chief Constable' which was clearly identified as emanating from the Central Ticket Office of the Thames Valley Police had all the hallmarks of authenticity. The requirement that the notice be sent by or on behalf of the chief officer of police had been satisfied. The appeal courts have held that the requirement to respond to such a notice does not amount to a breach of the recipient's human rights.

Speed assessment equipment detection devices

RTA 1988, s 41 is prospectively amended by the RSA 2006 to permit the making of regulations to prohibit the fitting of a 'speed assessment equipment detection device' and to create an offence of using a vehicle fitted with such a device. The device is defined as 'a device, the purpose, or one of the purposes, of which is to detect, or interfere with the operation of equipment used to assess the speed of motor vehicles'. At present, it is not intended to prohibit devices which only contain information about fixed camera site locations.

The offence will be punishable in the same way as if the offender had been convicted of exceeding a prescribed speed limit when these provisions are brought into force.

Motor racing and rallies

It is an offence contrary to the Road Traffic Act 1988, s 12 to promote or take part in a race or trial of speed between motor vehicles on a highway. Thus, there is a complete ban on racing motor vehicles on a highway.

RTA 1988, s 13 creates the offence of promoting or taking part in a 'competition or trial' (other than a race or trial of speed) which involves the use of motor vehicles on a highway if that event is not authorised. Even if authorised, there is an offence if the event is not conducted in accordance with any conditions imposed. The Motor Vehicles (Competitions and Trials) Regulations 1969 deal with such events. Competitions or trials are authorised without the need for an application if:

(a) there are no more than twelve vehicles involved and the event does not take place within eight days of another similar event promoted by the same person or club;
(b) where no merit is attached to completing the event with the lowest mileage and there are no performance tests and no route, competitors are not timed or required to visit the same places, although they may be required to finish at the same place by a specified time;
(c) the highway factor is solely concerned with good road behaviour and compliance with the Highway Code; or
(d) all competitors are members of the armed forces of the Crown and the event is designed solely for the purpose of service training.

Regulation 6 permits the authorisation of other events by the Royal Automobile Club. Such authorisations may be varied or revoked by that organisation. Applications for such events must be made not less than two months before the event is due to be held. If it is to be held on more than one date (except in the case of a specified event, which is an event which is run not more than once a year, for example the 'Veteran Car Run' and is specified in the schedule to the Regulations), the application must not be made more than six months before the event.

RTA 1988, s 13A states that a person shall not be guilty of an offence under RTA 1988, ss 1, 2 or 3 by virtue of driving a vehicle in a public place other than a road if he shows that he was driving in accordance with an authorisation for a motoring event given under regulations. The Motor Vehicles (Off Road Events) Regulations 1995 authorise a number of bodies, including the RAC, to issue such authorisations.

RTA 1988, s 33(1) prohibits the promoting or taking part in a trial of any description between motor vehicles on a footpath or bridleway unless the holding of it has been authorised by the local authority.

CHAPTER 17

Drinking or drug-taking and driving

The Road Traffic Act 1988 (RTA 1988), ss 4 to 11 contain provisions concerning various offences relating to drinking and driving. The principal types of offence are driving or attempting to drive a motor vehicle with an alcohol concentration in excess of the prescribed limit (s 5), and driving or attempting to drive a mechanically propelled vehicle when unfit to drive through drink or drugs (s 4).

Apart from cases where the accused is unfit through drugs or he is below the prescribed limit or the mechanically propelled vehicle is not a motor vehicle, it is the almost invariable practice to prosecute for an offence under RTA 1988, s 5 rather than one under s 4. This is because s 5 lays down an objective test; whereas under s 4 it is necessary for the prosecution to prove that the accused's ability to drive properly was for the time being impaired by drink or drugs, which is a question of fact for the justices.

DRIVING ETC WITH EXCESS ALCOHOL

Under RTA 1988, s 5(1) it is an offence for a person:

(a) to drive or attempt to drive a motor vehicle on a road or other public place; or
(b) to be in charge of a motor vehicle on a road or other public place,

after consuming so much alcohol that the proportion of it in his breath, blood or urine exceeds the prescribed limit.

The charge must state whether the person was driving, attempting to drive, or in charge of the vehicle and the nature of the specimen in which the prescribed limit was exceeded. If it does not it is bad for duplicity.

The driving, attempted driving or being in charge referred to above must be on a 'road or other public place'. A 'road' is basically defined as any highway and any other road to which the public has access. A private road which leads to a farmhouse or the like is not a 'road' for present purposes because, although tradesmen are allowed to use it to get to the house, the access is limited to particular classes of people (as opposed to extending to the public at large). Where a road within a housing estate has not been adopted by the local authority, the determining factor is not whether the road is repairable at public expense but whether the public have access to it. If members of the public are seen there, and their presence is tolerated, it is a road. Care should be taken when alleging driving on a 'road' as opposed to a 'public place'. The House of Lords has ruled that a road was provided for the purpose of moving from one place to another as opposed to parking a car. It said that even though a part of a car park may be made up of routes giving access to parking bays this, by itself, was not enough if those routes merely gave access to parking bays and were not for the purpose of travelling from one place to another. In one case where a driver was charged with driving on a 'road' within a station car park on the grounds that station staff drove through it in order to reach their own private car park, a divisional court held that such use was insufficient to permit the car park to be described as a road. In another case, the 'road' concerned was within a caravan and camping site which contained privately owned residential caravans, but guests and campers were also permitted entry. A tarmac road encircled the site but driving could only be proved to have taken place on the grass area of the site. A divisional court rejected the magistrates' finding that this was a 'road' and observed that the justices appeared to have decided that a road was a place to which the public had access. The place concerned may have been a public place and the offence should have been so charged. It was not a road for the purposes of the RTA 1988.

The term 'other public place' means a place (other than a 'road') to which the public have access. The term therefore includes car parks which are open to the public at the time, and fields in which public events are taking place (such as galas, shows or race meetings). A distinction must be drawn between the car park of a public house and that of a members' club. The first is open to the public at large during licensing hours and is therefore a public place during those hours, but that of the members' club is restricted to members of that club and their guests and therefore it is never a 'public place'. A place can be a 'public place' even though access to it is only permitted after a person has been screened. If those who are admitted pass through a screening process because of a special characteristic or reason personal to themselves (eg because they are members of the caravan club to whose site they seek access, or because they are workers at a factory to whose car park they seek access), the place in question is not a public place. On the other hand, if anyone can pass through the screening process and gain access simply by paying an entry fee (eg a site fee at a caravan park), or by satisfying conditions imposed by the landowner (eg access only for private vehicles or the possession of a boarding pass), the place is a public place. For example, National Car Parks, traffic lanes leading to cross-channel ferries and the 'airside' of an airport have been held by a divisional court to be 'public places'.

On the other hand, the car park of a community centre, access to which is restricted to members who have been nominated and screened for membership is not a public place at a time when access is restricted to members. The absence of a physical obstruction or of a notice forbidding entry does not of itself mean that the public have access. It is irrelevant that the public could have had access; the question is whether they actually utilised access to the place.

Where a car park is a private one or its use has been allocated to a particular organisation it may nevertheless be a public place; the question is whether, as a matter of fact, the public have used it with regularity, so that it has become de facto a place where the public have access and therefore a public place.

Justices are entitled to rely upon their knowledge in determining whether a car park is a public place. When they do so they should indicate that fact to both the prosecution and the defence to give them an opportunity to comment.

'*Driving*' in the present context bears its normal meaning in road traffic offences. The essence of 'driving' is the use of the driver's controls (or, at least, one of them) in order to control the movement of the vehicle, however that movement is produced, provided that what occurs can in any sense be regarded as 'driving'. In most instances it is, of course, obvious whether or not a person is driving and this rather involved definition is particularly important in unusual circumstances which may confront a constable from time to time. A person who propels a motor cycle or moped by 'paddling' with the feet without the engine running is driving. In such circumstances the movement of the vehicle is being controlled by the driver's hands and he is 'on' the vehicle. Evidence of driving may be circumstantial. Police officers found a car which had collided with a lamp post and the windscreen had damage consistent with someone having hit the screen with his head. They visited the owner's home and found him hiding under the bed dressed only in trousers. A cut on his forehead was bleeding and he smelt strongly of alcohol. A divisional court said that the proximity of the time and place was important and, coupled with such other evidence, the justices were entitled to find that he had been driving. Where a man was found at 1.20 am in the driving seat of his car on a road, the keys were in the ignition and he replied 'Yes' when asked by a police officer if he had driven there, a divisional court said that a court could properly deduce that he had been driving. It did not have to depend upon his admission; the other circumstances supported that deduction. There is no reason why the oral admission of a driver to the effect that he was driving a car should not be admissible in evidence. A divisional court dismissed an appeal based on the grounds that the driver had been too drunk to give a reliable confession and that it was therefore prejudicial to admit it. Although the driver had been drinking heavily, he asked to see the custody officer and to make this admission to him. The custody officer had found him quite friendly, coherent and easy to deal with. In another case, a divisional court held that a man was 'driving' in circumstances in which there had been no movement of the vehicle. The car was on the grass verge outside his house and he was sitting in the driver's seat engaging in an activity which he described as 'wheel spinning'. This involved the use of the engine, accelerator, clutch and steering wheel with the vehicle in gear but the handbrake applied preventing any form of movement. The court held that the ordinary meaning of the word 'driving' included a situation where the person was ensuring that there was no movement but the wheels were spinning.

In relation to '*attempting to drive*', the reader is referred to the Criminal Attempts Act 1981 (CAA 1981), which we deal with in Chapter 43, below, and which regulates what is required for an attempt. It is clear from CAA 1981 that what is required is the doing of an act which is more than merely preparatory to the commission of the full offence, coupled with the intention to commit the full offence. It is therefore essential that some act must have been carried out which was more than a merely preparatory step towards the process of driving, and that the person doing the act had the intention of driving. For example, if a person gets no further than sitting in the driving seat of a motor car and searching his pockets for the ignition keys, it is almost certain that the justices would find that his acts were merely preparatory and that he was not attempting to drive (although he could be convicted of the offence of being in charge with excess alcohol). On the other hand, if he finds the keys and gets as far as placing them in the ignition switch it is almost certain that the justices would find that the act was more than merely preparatory, and that therefore he was attempting to drive.

CAA 1981 also provides that a person may be guilty of an attempt even though the facts are such that the commission of the full offence is not possible. Consequently, a person who is attempting to drive even though it was not possible for him actually to drive the vehicle in those circumstances is guilty of attempting to drive it.

In relation to the offence of '*being in charge*', as a general rule once a person takes a vehicle out on a road or other public place he remains in charge of it until he has taken it off the road or public place, unless he puts someone else in charge of it (as where he hands the ignition keys to another to prevent himself from being able to drive it) or loses effective control over the vehicle in some other way (as where it is stolen or where he has gone to bed). Persons other than the owner or a person in lawful possession or control of the vehicle may assume charge of it. In such cases consideration must be given to whether and where such a person was in the vehicle or how far from it, what he was doing, whether he was in possession of a suitable ignition key, evidence of intention to take control by driving or otherwise, and the position and circumstances of other persons who were also in the vehicle. Because more than one person can be in charge of a vehicle, someone sitting in a passenger seat supervising a learner driver is in charge of the vehicle.

RTA 1988, s 5(2) provides that it is a defence for a person charged with 'being in charge of a motor vehicle' etc to prove that, at the time he is alleged to have committed the offence, the circumstances were such that there was no likelihood of his driving the vehicle while the proportion of alcohol in his breath, blood or urine remained likely to exceed the prescribed limit; but in determining whether there was such a likelihood the court may disregard any injury to him and any damage to the vehicle. Where the accused's car had been wheel clamped and there was no evidence to show that the clamp could have been removed by any other means than paying for release, which the accused had refused to do, it was held that there was no likelihood of his driving. It was held that the fixing of a wheel clamp did not 'damage' the vehicle; there was no intrusion into the integrity of the vehicle. Normally, the accused will only succeed in proving this defence if there is expert evidence as to the rate of alcohol destruction by the body which indicates that his alcohol level would not have been above the limit at the time he intended to drive. The House of Lords has ruled that the accused bears a persuasive burden of proof of the s 5(2) defence (ie on the balance of probabilities), and not simply an evidential burden (see p 220), and that this is not incompatible with the presumption of innocence under art 6 of the European Convention on Human Rights.

'*Consuming*' is a wide enough term to include other methods of ingestion than through the mouth. Thus, for example, an alcohol level which may have, in part, resulted from the injection of a substance, comes about through 'consumption'.

The last element of the offence under RTA 1988, s 5(1) which needs to be explained concerns the *prescribed limits*. They are defined by RTA 1988, s 11 which states that the 'prescribed limit' means, as the case may require:

(a) 35 microgrammes of alcohol in 100 ml of breath;
(b) 80 mg of alcohol in 100 ml of blood; or
(c) 107 mg of alcohol in 100 ml of urine,

or such other proportion as may be prescribed by regulations made by the Secretary of State. So far, the Secretary of State has not prescribed any other proportion.

The 35 microgrammes is roughly equivalent to the 80 and 107 mg of the two other levels.

Having set out the requirements for an offence under RTA 1988, s 5, we must now describe the procedures which will normally precede a person being charged with that offence and which are regulated by the RTA 1988. These procedures will usually begin with a police officer on the beat requiring a 'screening' breath test; followed by an arrest (whether as a result of a positive test or of a failure to provide a breath specimen for it) and then be followed by a requirement for a specimen of breath (for an evidential breath test) or, in limited cases, a specimen of blood or urine (for analysis).

The details of the early part of this procedure are as follows.

PRELIMINARY TESTS

Under RTA 1988, s 6, as substituted by the Railways and Transport Safety Act 2003 (RTSA 2003), there are three types of preliminary tests whose purpose is to give an indication as to a driver's 'impairment' in consequence of consumption of alcohol and his impairment in consequence of taking drugs, by means of a breath test, an impairment test, or a drugs test.

Power to require preliminary tests

RTA 1988, s 6(1) provides that where sub-ss (2) to (5) apply, a constable may require a person to co-operate with one or more preliminary tests administered to that person by that constable or another constable. Section 6(2) provides that such a test may be required *if a constable reasonably suspects that the person*:

(a) *is* driving, *is* attempting to drive or *is* in charge of a motor vehicle on a road or other public place; and
(b) has alcohol or a drug in his body or is under the influence of a drug.

Section 6(3) similarly authorises a test where a constable reasonably suspects that a person *has been* driving, attempting to drive or in charge of a motor vehicle on a road or other public place while having alcohol or a drug in his body or *while unfit to drive because of a drug*, and that person still has alcohol or a drug in his body or is still under the influence of a drug.

Section 6(4) similarly authorises a test where a constable reasonably suspects that a person *is or has been* driving or attempting to drive or in charge of a motor vehicle on a road or other public place, and has committed a traffic offence while the vehicle was in motion. The type of traffic offence which the constable must reasonably suspect to have been committed is defined by RTA 1988, s 6(8), which provides that 'traffic offence' in this context means an offence under any provision of Part II of the Public Passenger Vehicles Act 1981, the Road Traffic Regulation Act 1984, the Road Traffic Offenders Act 1988 (RTOA 1988) except Part III, or any provision of the Road Traffic Act 1988 except Part V. This effectively covers the range of road traffic offences which could be described as 'moving traffic offences'. All offences which are set out in regulations made under those Acts are also included within this description; for example, offences contrary to the Road Vehicles (Construction and Use) Regulations 1986 or the Road Vehicles Lighting Regulations 1989. There are some exceptions to the definition of 'moving traffic offence' in the present context. Generally, they relate to the offence of giving driving instruction for payment without being registered or licensed under the Act, to offences related to fixed penalty procedures, and to some provisions concerning public service vehicles.

Section 6(5) applies so as to authorise a test if an accident occurs owing to the presence of a motor vehicle on a road or other public place, and a constable reasonably *believes* that the person was driving, attempting to drive or in charge of the vehicle at the time of the accident.

Thus, we are concerned with preliminary tests which may be required upon reasonable suspicion that a person:

(a) *is driving* etc and has alcohol or a drug in his body or is under the influence of a drug;

(b) *has been driving* etc while having alcohol or a drug in his body or while unfit to drive because of a drug and still has alcohol or a drug in his body or is still under the influence of a drug;

(c) *is or has been driving* etc and has committed a traffic offence while the vehicle was in motion.

In addition, we are concerned with preliminary tests where an accident occurs owing to the presence of a motor vehicle and a constable *reasonably believes* that the person *was driving* etc at the time of the accident.

The tests required (other than in the case of a test under s 6(5) (road traffic accidents)) may only be administered by a constable in uniform. Whether or not a constable was in uniform is a question of fact in each case. A constable wearing his uniform except for his helmet has been held to be in uniform so long as he is easily identifiable as a constable. A court is entitled to assume that a constable was in uniform unless this point is disproved.

The power to require a 'preliminary' test does not depend on the person actually having alcohol or a drug in his body or actually having committed a moving traffic offence. Instead, it arises simply because one of the four criteria is satisfied. In the case of the second criterion (s 6(3)), it is clear that the suspicion need not arise while the vehicle is in motion. Moreover, the same is true in the case of the first criterion (s 6(2)). Indeed, a uniformed constable may stop motorists, under his common law or statutory powers to do so, in order to see whether there is a reasonable suspicion that they have consumed alcohol, and if a reasonable suspicion then emerges of such consumption, go on to require a preliminary test. Thus, random stopping of motorists is not prohibited, although random preliminary tests are.

A constable does not have to administer a caution before requiring a preliminary test. It is only where the motorist has failed such a test (or failed to take it) that a caution needs to be administered.

Special circumstances which apply where an accident has occurred

As we have already said, there is a power, under RTA 1988, s 6(5), to require a 'preliminary' test if an accident occurs owing to the presence of a motor vehicle on a road or other public place. A constable may require any person whom he has *reasonable cause to believe* was driving or attempting to drive or in charge of the vehicle at the time of the accident to provide a preliminary test, subject to RTA 1988, s 9 (hospital procedure).

The fact that a constable's power to make a requirement of a person under RTA 1988, s 6(5) depends on an accident having occurred owing to the presence of a motor vehicle on a road or other public place raises the question of what is '*an accident*' for the purposes of s 6(5). The answer is that 'accident' bears its ordinary meaning, and it has been held that a crash which is deliberately caused falls within that meaning. The person's vehicle need not have been physically involved but there must have been a direct causal connection between his vehicle being on the road and the accident occurring. Where a sequence of events begins on a road and leads to a vehicle leaving the road and colliding with an object some distance from the road, there is an accident for the purposes of s 6(5).

Of course, the fact that an accident has occurred owing to the presence of a motor vehicle on a road or other public place does not entitle a constable to require a specimen of breath under RTA 1988, s 6(5) from anyone; that provision only empowers him to make such a requirement of any person whom he has *reasonable cause to believe was driving or attempting to drive or in charge of* the vehicle at the time of the accident.

The reader will remember that the power to require a breath specimen under the other provisions of RTA 1988, s 6 is framed in terms of a constable having *reasonable cause to suspect* that a person driving etc, has alcohol or a drug in his body or is under the influence of a drug, or has committed a moving traffic offence, or having *reasonable cause to suspect* that a person has been driving etc in those circumstances. However, s 6(5) uses the term '*has reasonable cause to believe*', which requires more than 'reasonable suspicion' since 'believe' requires more than mere suspicion and refers to having no substantial doubt about the facts. The fact that the constable uses the wrong term in expressing himself is not fatal. In one case, an officer stated in evidence that he had required the breath test because he 'suspected' that the defendant was the driver at the time of an accident. It was held that there was enough evidence to link the defendant with the accident and, whilst acknowledging that the words were different, it was recognised that the words used by the officer were no more than a careless use of language. Such decisions are not so important now that evidence of alcohol levels cannot be excluded merely because of a defect in procedure, but such an issue would still be relevant in cases of a failure to supply a preliminary breath test (as we explain below).

The nature of preliminary tests

Preliminary breath test

RTA 1988, s 6A provides that a preliminary breath test is a procedure whereby the person to whom the test is administered provides a specimen of breath to be used for the purpose of obtaining, by means of a device approved by the Secretary of State, an indication whether the proportion of alcohol in the person's breath or blood is likely to exceed the prescribed limit.

A preliminary breath test may be administered only at or near the place where the requirement to co-operate with the test is imposed; where it is administered following an accident it may be so administered or, if the constable who imposes the requirement thinks it expedient, at a police station specified by him.

Preliminary breath tests devices used by police officers must be approved by the Secretary of State before they may be used. Currently, the Secretary of State has approved two types of devices, one which might be described as the 'blow in the bag' type of device and the other 'electronic'. Approved devices of the 'blow in the bag' type are the Alcotest 80, the Alcotest R80A and the Alcolyser. The containers of such devices show the dates beyond which devices should not be used and it is important that these dates are checked. A number of electronic devices have been approved by the Secretary of State. They are various models of the Lion Alcolmeter, the Lion Alcolyser, the Alco-Sensor IV, the Draeger Alert, the Draeger Alcotest 7410, the Intoximeter Alco-Sensor FST and the Draeger Alcotest 6510. The Alcolmeter is a battery operated device of compact size into which a plastic tube is inserted. The suspect breathes into the tube until lights appear which register a result. The instrument incorporates a sensor which will respond to alcohol only and it is not affected by other breath contaminants. A person supplying a sample for a screening test must blow until the lights indicate that a sufficient sample has been received. Persons with breathing problems can, on occasions, find this difficult; constables should be aware of this and assist by giving precise directions and recognising on occasions that certain persons are unable to provide such a specimen. The Alert is a detector of the semi-conductor type, the conduction increasing in proportion to the concentration of alcohol in the breath. It is larger than the Alcolmeter but is extremely easy to operate, the lights clearly illustrating whether a sample is positive or negative. Its strength is its simplicity. The Alcotest 7410 is a one button device of high accuracy which gives both audible and visible indication of a positive test. If an alkaline battery is used, it will provide one thousand tests before charging becomes necessary. The Alcosensor IV contains a fuel cell and an electronically operated piston sampling pump. A signal is generated on the fuel cell as a result of the oxidation of any alcohol in the sample. The resulting electric current is translated into a breath alcohol concentration and the result is displayed.

The instructions which accompany all preliminary breath test devices warn that a breath test should not be given until at least twenty minutes have elapsed since the last intoxicating drink was taken. The reason for this is that it is the alcoholic content of deep-lung air, not mouth alcohol which is to be measured. If a drink has been taken within that period the constable should wait until twenty minutes has elapsed before carrying out the test. If a suspect driver is smoking he should be asked to stop and to take two or three deep breaths to clear the lungs of smoke. A divisional court has held that the innocent failure by a police officer to follow these instructions does not render the result of a subsequent analysis of a specimen by an Intoximeter device at a police station, and the arrest, unlawful.

Code C: The Code of Practice for the Detention, Treatment and Questioning of Persons by Police Officers (hereafter the Detention Code) referred to in Chapter 4, excludes the 'specimens for analysis' procedures under RTA 1988, s 7 (below) from the provisions of the Code which relate to 'interviews'; no similar exclusion is made in relation to s 6 procedures. It is therefore advisable that, where there is conversation between an officer and a suspect which relates to his condition, that conversation is recorded and read and signed by the suspect. A divisional court, however, refused to interfere with a decision of the justices not to exclude evidence subsequently obtained following an officer's inquiry as to whether a suspect had been drinking, to which the suspect replied, 'Yes, I've had a couple of pints'. It said that the justices, although recognising that there had been a breach of the Detention Code, were entitled to find that that breach had not been sufficiently 'significant and substantial' to merit exclusion of the evidence.

Nevertheless, care must be taken when engaging in conversation with drivers suspected of drink/drive offences. In one case police officers spoke to a man on three occasions, at his home prior to arrest and before caution; after his arrest and caution at his home; and in a police car in, the course of which he admitted that he had been to a funeral and had taken alcohol afterwards, that his last drink ('a couple of cans') had been taken at about 4 pm and that he had last driven his car at 5 pm and had not since taken a drink. It was held that these three conversations were 'interviews' for the purpose of the Detention Code. Additionally, it was stated that at the first interview at his home he had been entitled to legal advice which had not been offered. In this case the matter became unimportant as there was a subsequent 'untainted' interview at the police station but perhaps there is scope for some further guidance concerning the need for legal advice at such an exploratory stage as if this line of argument is extended, police officers will have to be accompanied by solicitors when on patrol.

The preliminary impairment test

RTA 1988, s 6B provides that a preliminary impairment test is a procedure whereby the constable administering the test observes the person to whom the test is administered in his performance of tests specified by the constable and makes such other observations of the person's physical state as the constable thinks expedient. Section 6B(6) requires that such tests may only be administered by a constable approved for the purpose by the chief officer of the police force to which he belongs. It may be administered at or near the place where the requirement to co-operate with the test is imposed or, if the constable who imposes the requirement thinks it expedient, at a police station specified by him.

Section 6B makes provision for the Secretary of State to issue (and from time to time revise) a code of practice about:

(a) the kind of task that may be specified for the purpose of a preliminary impairment test;
(b) the kind of observation of physical state that may be made in the course of a preliminary impairment test;
(c) the manner in which a preliminary impairment test should be administered; and
(d) the inference that may be drawn from observations made in the course of a preliminary impairment test.

The Secretary of State must ensure that a preliminary impairment test is designed to indicate:

(a) whether a person is unfit to drive; and
(b) if he is, whether or not his unfitness is likely to be due to drink or drugs.

A constable administering a preliminary impairment test must have regard to the Department of Transport Code of Practice for Preliminary Impairment Tests.

The Code of Practice provides as follows. Police officers may be trained and authorised to carry out Preliminary Impairment Tests. In each of the tests described below the officer must give a full explanation of what ie required, demonstrating actions which a subject is required to perform where this is essential to understanding and establishing whether or not a disability, injury or illness exists, whether physical or mental, which may affect performance during the test. Obesity and age may be factors. The tests are:

A pupillary examination   which involves the subject looking straight ahead with eyes wide open. The constable should establish whether or not he is wearing contact lenses. A gauge is held adjacent to the appropriate side of the subject's face to enable, by a process of comparison, estimation of the size of the pupils of the eyes. Conditions in which a subject's eyes are 'watering' or 'reddening' should also be noted.

The modified Romberg Balance Test   is concerned with a person's internal clock and ability to balance. He should be required to stand with heels and toes together and arms by his side and retain that position while tilting the head back slightly and closing the eyes and then to bring the head forward, open the eyes and say 'stop' when he thinks that thirty seconds has passed. A record will be made of ability to balance while being so instructed, whether he steps, sways or raises his arms and whether the eyes were opened, or the head straightened, during the test, together with the actual number of seconds which elapsed.

Walk and turn test   enables an assessment to be made of a person's ability to divide attention between walking, balancing and processing instructions. The constable should identify a line (other than a kerb or other place where a person may fall) and instruct the person to place his left foot on the line, his right foot on the line in front of the left foot touching heel to toe, put arms down by the side and keep them there throughout the test and to maintain that position while further instructions are given. On the instruction 'start', the subject should take nine heel to toe steps along the line; after these nine steps to leave the front foot on the line and to turn around using a series of small steps with the other foot (these manoeuvres can be demonstrated by the constable). After turning, the subject should take another nine heel to toe steps back along the line. The officer should count each step out loud.

A record must be made of whether a subject was able to stand still while being instructed, whether he started too soon, turned correctly, occasions when he stopped walking, missed heel to toe connection, stepped off the line, or raised his arms. A record must also be made of whether the steps were correctly counted; the point of any deviation from the straight line should be marked on a diagram on the appropriate form.

One leg stand   is to test balance and ability to count out loud. The subject should be instructed to stand with his heels and toes together and arms by sides; to maintain that position while receiving instructions and not to begin until told to do so. On the instruction 'start' he should raise his right foot 6 to 8 inches or 15 to 20 cm off the ground; keep the elevated leg straight with the toes pointing forward and the foot parallel with the ground; keep the arms by the side and to keep looking at the elevated foot throughout the test and while doing so to count out loud 'one thousand and one, one thousand and two, one thousand and three and so on progressively until told to stop. The test should be carried out using each foot in turn.

A record will be made over a timed period of thirty seconds, for each foot, any instances in which a subject sways, hops, puts a foot down or raises the arms, together with the point in the test where that occurred.

Finger to nose test   is designed to test depth of perception and balance. A subject must stand with both feet together and extend both arms in front, palms uppermost with the fists closed and the index finger of each hand extended (this must be carefully demonstrated) and he must maintain this position while waiting to be told to perform the remainder of the test. On being told to start he should tilt the head back slightly and *then* close the eyes and when told which hand to use, should attempt to touch the tip of his nose with the tip of the index finger and, having done so, to lower the hand, as the constable calls out the order in which hand should be used—Left, Right, Left, Right, Right, Left.

A record should be made where the subject steps, sways or raises an arm, and whether the correct hand was used, or touched a part of the face other than the tip of his nose and whereabouts.

Safety and site conditions

The safety of the subject must be considered. A hard, level, non-slippery surface should be chosen wherever possible in a well-lit unobstructed area out of the public view and in appropriate weather conditions. Where this is not possible, consideration must be given to the possibility of the test being conducted at another nearby location or at a police station. If not, appropriate allowance must be made in interpreting the tests. If the nature of footwear may be an impediment, the subject should be given the opportunity to remove it.

A constable should not close his eyes when demonstrating such a test. He should always stand away from the subject and remain still.

Disabilities, injuries or illness

Any such factors must be recorded, whether physical or mental, if they may affect the performance of the subject during a test. Obesity or age must be recorded if likely to affect the test.

Where these factors are evident or claimed, an officer may continue to require co-operation with the test. However, he must be particularly mindful of the possibility of the effect which this may have on performance when interpreting test results.

General

A constable may decide, in consequence of these tests, that there is sufficient evidence to justify an arrest under the RTA 1988, s 3A or 4. There is no pass/fail standard, nor a scoring system. A decision must be based upon overall observation during the tests and the records made of those performances. Prior to the tests being required, a suspicion will have arisen as to the subject's ability to drive properly, based upon his actual driving, the officer's assessment of his general condition, or any suspicion of the subject being under the influence of drugs.

The preliminary drugs test

This is dealt with by RTA 1988, s 6C. A preliminary drugs test is a procedure by which a specimen of sweat or saliva is obtained and used for the purpose of obtaining, by means of a device of a type approved by the Secretary of State, an indication whether the person to whom the test is administered has a drug in his body. It may be administered at or near the place where the requirement to co-operate with the test is imposed or, if the constable who imposes the requirement thinks it expedient, at a police station specified by him.

At the time of writing, no details of these tests have been published, nor has a device of this nature been approved by the Secretary of State.

Arrest

RTA 1988, s 6D provides:

(1) A constable may arrest a person without warrant if as a result of a preliminary breath test the constable reasonably suspects that the proportion of alcohol in the person's breath or blood exceeds the prescribed limit.
(2) A constable may arrest a person without warrant if
  (a) the person fails to co-operate with a preliminary test in pursuance of a requirement imposed under s 6, and
  (b) the constable reasonably suspects that the person has alcohol or a drug in his body or is under the influence of a drug.
(3) A person may not be arrested under this section while at a hospital as a patient.

The Serious Organised Crime and Police Act 2005 (SOCPA 2005), s 154, made significant changes to drink driving procedures. It adds two provisions to s 6D; they are s 6D(1A) and s 6D(2A).

Section 6D(1A) provides that the fact that specimens of breath have been provided under s 7(1) (see p 604) by the person concerned does not prevent s 6D(1) above having effect if the constable who imposed on him the requirement to provide the specimens has reasonable cause to believe that the device used to analyse the specimens has not produced a reliable indication of the proportion of alcohol in the breath of the person.

Section 6D(2A) provides that a person arrested under s 6D may, instead of being taken to a police station, be detained at or near the place where the preliminary test was, or would have been administered, with a view to imposing on him there a requirement under RTA 1988, s 7. Thus, a means is provided to carry out a second test at the roadside as an alternative to taking the person concerned to a police station.

These additions were made in consequence of modifications to s 7 (see below) which permit the taking of a specimen of breath for analysis at the roadside or at a hospital.

The power of arrest may therefore be exercised if, as a result of a preliminary breath test, a constable reasonably suspects that the proportion of alcohol in the person's breath or blood exceeds the prescribed limit. However, a driver must be requested to provide a breath specimen before he can be arrested under s 6D, even if his conduct makes this difficult. Where an officer is assaulted and thus prevented from making a proper request, the driver should be arrested under another appropriate provision.

The purpose of this power of arrest is to ensure that those suspected of having excessive alcohol in their bodies are taken to a police station to provide a specimen for analysis. It is therefore realistic to provide a power which allows a constable to arrest those who provide positive specimens.

Section 6D(2) is concerned with an arrest which may follow a failure to co-operate with a preliminary test in pursuance of a requirement imposed under s 6 and this refers to a requirement to provide any type of preliminary test.

It will be noted that it is not enough for the person required to co-operate with a preliminary test to fail so to co-operate; the constable must reasonably suspect that the person has alcohol or a drug in his body or that he is under the influence of a drug.

RTA 1988, s 11(2) provides that the word 'fails' includes 'refusal'. If a person is given an opportunity to do something and does not do it, there is a failure to comply with that request. Where a person refuses to reply to such a clear request, there has been a failure and it is no defence to allege that the refusal to reply was consequent upon a previous caution. It is essential that the constable makes it clear to the person concerned that he is required to co-operate in the test.

In a case where a driver refused to wait until a preliminary breath test device arrived at the scene, having been properly required to provide a specimen, it was held that he had failed to provide a specimen of breath. A demand that a test be deferred until the arrival of a solicitor amounts to a refusal. There can be no acceptance subject to conditions. The same considerations will apply to impairment tests and drug tests.

RTA 1988, s 11(3) provides:

A person does not co-operate with a preliminary test or provide a specimen of breath for analysis unless his co-operation, or the specimen, is sufficient to enable the test or analysis to be carried out, and is provided in such a way as to enable the objective of the test or analysis to be satisfactorily achieved.

This simplifies matters for police officers. The various preliminary breath test devices require breath to be supplied in various ways to allow a sufficient sample to be obtained. If sufficient breath has not been supplied there has been a failure. Where a preliminary breath test device requires the illumination of two lights before a satisfactory specimen has been obtained, there is a 'failure' where only one of those lights is illuminated and a police officer is not required to 'read' such a specimen. Similar considerations will apply to impairment tests and drug tests.

An important point to note about the power to arrest after a failure to co-operate is that the constable must have reasonable cause to suspect that the driver has alcohol in his body before effecting an arrest.

Clear words must be used in all cases to indicate the reason for arrest and that the person concerned is being compulsorily taken to a police station in consequence of such a failure.

Normally, a constable will exercise his power of arrest in the above two cases but this is not a pre-condition of further steps in the procedure being adopted and is unnecessary if the person concerned is quite happy to accompany the constable to a police station for the next steps in the procedure.

Power of entry

RTA 1988, s 6E provides a power of entry to premises in certain circumstances.

A constable may enter any place (using reasonable force if necessary) for the purpose of:

(a) imposing a requirement by virtue of s 6(5) following an accident in a case where the constable reasonably suspects that the accident involved injury of any person; or

(b) arresting a person under s 6D following an accident in a case where the constable reasonably suspects that the accident involved injury of any person.

This means that, with the one exception in (a), police officers do not have power to enter premises without the express or implied consent of the occupier for the purpose of requiring a preliminary breath, impairment or drug test. Thus, where officers pursued a driver whom they had cause to suspect of driving with excess alcohol and they followed him into the driveway of his house without permission, to carry out a breath test, the evidence of the subsequent analysis of a specimen was excluded under the provisions of the Police and Criminal Evidence Act 1984 (PACE), s 78 because the officers had acted quite deliberately outside their powers. Likewise, police officers, with the one exception in (b), do not have power to enter premises without the express or implied consent of the occupier for the purpose of making an arrest under RTA 1988, s 6D.

Clearly, the power to enter to require a breath test is limited to cases where the entry is for the purpose of requiring a person to provide a preliminary test under RTA 1988, s 6(5) *in a case where a constable has reasonable cause to suspect that the accident involved injury of any person.* A constable is therefore empowered by s 6E to enter premises to test a driver involved in an 'injury' accident or to arrest under s 6D where there has been an 'injury' accident, but he will not be empowered by s 6E to enter to arrest a person under s 6D who, having provided a positive test, or having failed to provide one, seeks sanctuary on private premises before arrest, in any case in which there has not been an 'injury' accident. This can hardly be supported as a logical or practical distinction. The amendments effected by the RTSA 2003 removed doubts which had previously existed concerning the meaning of the original legislation.

Offence of failure to co-operate with a preliminary test under s 6

RTA 1988, s 6(6) provides that a person commits an offence if without reasonable excuse he fails to co-operate with a preliminary test in pursuance of a requirement imposed under s 6.

This offence can be committed notwithstanding that the motorist has not been warned that refusal to co-operate will be an offence as there is no obligation to do so.

We have already explained what constitutes a 'failure to co-operate'. There cannot be a conviction for this offence unless the co-operation has been required under s 6, and it will not have been so required if the requirement made is invalid for some reason. For example, if the constable is a trespasser at the time of requiring a preliminary breath test he will be behaving unlawfully and his requirement will not be valid.

In addition, there cannot be a conviction for failing to provide a specimen if the requisite procedure is not validly administered, as will be the case if the device used is not an approved one, or if it is defective, or if the constable fails to comply with the manufacturer's instructions as to *assembly*. However, if the constable realises the defect or mistake he may validly require another breath test to be taken on another device. Provided the constable acts in good faith and not negligently, non-compliance by him with the manufacturer's instructions as to the use of the device does not invalidate the test unless the non-compliance is prejudicial to the accused.

A person cannot be convicted of failing to co-operate for a preliminary test unless his failure was without reasonable excuse. It is not a reasonable excuse that the accused did not think that he had consumed any alcohol, nor that he mistakenly believed that the requirement made was invalid, nor that he had consumed alcohol after driving.

It has been stated in a number of cases that no excuse can be adjudged reasonable unless the accused was physically or mentally unable to provide the specimen or its provision would entail a substantial risk to his health. This covers cases such as where the accused was unable to supply a sufficient specimen of breath because of a medical condition, such as bronchitis or shock, or where he was concussed and unable to appreciate the requirement made to him. However, it has also been held that a foreigner who is unable to understand the purpose of the requirement and the penal consequence of a failure to comply has a reasonable excuse. Not surprisingly, a person who has made himself so drunk as to be unable to understand these matters does not have a reasonable excuse, nor does someone who fails to provide a specimen because he is in a state of self-induced agitation. See also pp 625–627.

DRIVING ETC UNDER INFLUENCE OF DRINK OR DRUGS

RTA 1988, s 4 provides that:

(1) A person who, when driving or attempting to drive a mechanically propelled vehicle on a road or other public place, is unfit to drive through drink or drugs is guilty of an offence.

(2) Without prejudice to subsection (1) above, a person who, when in charge of a mechanically propelled vehicle which is on a road or other public place, is unfit to drive through drink or drugs is guilty of an offence.

The charge must state whether the person was driving, attempting to drive, or in charge.

Many of the elements of these offences have been dealt with already in relation to RTA 1988, s 5. It is worth noting that RTA 1988, s 4(3) provides a similar defence for persons charged with 'being in charge' to that provided by s 5(2) for those charged with the corresponding offence under s 5, namely, that it is a defence for the accused to prove that there was no likelihood of his driving the vehicle while he remained unfit through drink or drugs.

It remains to be added that 'drink' means alcoholic drink and 'drug' means any intoxicant other than alcohol, including medicines and glue.

Unfitness to drive

The element of these offences which does call for further explanation is that of unfitness to drive. RTA 1988, s 4(5) provides that a person is to be taken to be unfit to drive if his ability to drive properly is for the time being impaired. The evidence before the court on this point will normally include evidence of the accused's driving before his vehicle was stopped; any evidence of driving apparently outside the pattern of normal driving is relevant in that it may show some impairment of the ability to drive properly. In addition, the evidence of the speech of the accused after he was stopped, together with his general manner and demeanour and any apparent lack of co-ordination or control over bodily movements, may be important. The evidence before the court will also normally include the report of a medical examination by a police surgeon, which is extremely important since the surgeon will have required the accused to carry out a series of tests indicative of his ability (or lack of ability) to drive properly. Lastly, the evidence may include the result of the analysis of a specimen of breath, blood or urine required under RTA 1988, s 7. The procedure relating to such specimens, and the rules relating to the use of their analysis as evidence, are essentially the same as for the offences of driving etc with excess alcohol; we deal with these matters shortly. It must be remembered that the presence of a drug can be detected by a blood or urine test, but not by a breath test.

PROVISION OF SPECIMEN FOR ANALYSIS

RTA 1988, s 7(1) provides:

In the course of an investigation into whether a person has committed an offence under s 3A [causing death by careless driving while under the influence of drink or drugs etc], or s 4 or 5 of this Act a constable may, subject to the following provisions of this section and s 9 below (hospital procedures), require him:
(a) to provide two specimens of breath for analysis by means of a device of a type approved by the Secretary of State; or
(b) to provide a specimen of blood or urine for a laboratory test.

The offence under RTA 1988, s 3A is dealt with in Chapter 16.

The fact that a requirement under RTA 1988, s 7(1) can be made 'in the course of an investigation' into whether a person has committed an offence under RTA 1988, s 4 or s 5 indicates that it is not necessary that a preliminary test should have been required (although in a case under s 5 it will normally have been) and that, if there has been such a test, it is irrelevant that there has been some breach in the procedure relating to it or that the constable has acted unlawfully in some other way. Thus, where a constable, in good faith, had administered a preliminary test in a public house car park which, at the time, was not a public place, the subsequent specimen for analysis was held to have been properly required 'in the course of an investigation'. The procedure under s 7 does not constitute an 'interview' for the purposes of the Detention Code referred to in Chapter 4. However, a magistrates' court can exclude the evidence obtained from the analysis of a specimen if it appears to the court that, having regard to all the circumstances, including non-compliance with the preliminary test procedure under s 6, the admission of that evidence would have such an adverse effect on the fairness of the proceedings that the court ought not to admit it. This would be an application of PACE, s 78. PACE, s 78 was so applied in a case where a preliminary test was improperly required (because the officer did not have one of the requisite reasonable suspicions specified by s 6). A divisional court held that, since the defendant had been denied the protection afforded by s 6, the prosecutor had obtained evidence which he would not otherwise have obtained and, as a result, the defendant was significantly prejudiced in resisting the charge. The magistrates, it held, were therefore entitled to exclude the evidence, having directed themselves correctly in law.

In most circumstances, a person required to provide a specimen for analysis will have been arrested under RTA 1988, s 6(5). However, s 7 also permits the procedure to be followed if a person is at a police station other than under arrest, or if he has been arrested on suspicion of an offence other than one under s 5. Thus, if a driver reports an accident at a police station, and it is suspected that he has alcohol in his body, he may be required to provide specimens for analysis. Similarly, a person arrested for some other offence (eg burglary) may be so required if it is discovered that he has been driving a motor vehicle. No matter how a person came to be at a police station, if he is there in the course of an investigation into whether an offence under s 4 or 5 has been committed by him, a specimen may be required under s 7. In addition, a person who alleges that he was a passenger, not the driver of a car, at the time in question, may lawfully be required to provide a specimen as 'a person under an investigation for an offence under either s 4 or 5'. It is not necessary to show that he was driving or in charge. Although, of course, liability for an offence under s 4 or 5 will depend on proof that he was driving, attempting to drive or in charge at the material time, he can be convicted under s 7 of failing to provide a specimen even if he was not driving etc.

We now turn to the procedure to be adopted under s 7; it should be noted that where the person in question is a patient at a hospital a special procedure, governed by s 9, must be followed.

The specimen to be required

The important part of the procedure under s 7 is that, normally, it is two specimens of *breath* which must be required and that it is only in exceptional circumstances that alternative samples may be required.

SOCPA 2005, s 154 amends the RTA 1988, so that s 7(2) is substituted by a new s 7(2) to (2D) The new s 7(2) provides: that a requirement under s 7 to provide specimens of breath can only be made:

(a) at a police station;
(b) at a hospital; or
(c) at or near a place where a relevant breath test has been administered to the person concerned or would have been so administered but for his failure to co-operate with it.

For the purposes of s 7, s 7(2A) provides that 'a relevant breath test' is a procedure involving the provision by the person concerned of a specimen of breath to be used for the purpose of obtaining an indication whether the proportion of alcohol in his breath or blood is likely to exceed the prescribed limit.

Section 7(2B) states that a requirement under s 7 to provide specimens of breath may not be made at or near a place mentioned in (c) above unless the constable making it:

(a) is in uniform; or
(b) has imposed a requirement on the person concerned to co-operate with a relevant breath test in circumstances in which s 6(5) (see p 594) applies.

By s 7(2C) where a constable has imposed a requirement on the person concerned to co-operate with a relevant breath test at any place, he is entitled to remain at or near that place in order to impose on him there a requirement under s 7.

Section 7(2D) provides that if a requirement under s 7(1)(a) (specimen of breath for analysis) has been made at a place other than a police station, such a requirement may subsequently be made at a police station if (but only if):

(a) a device or a reliable device of the type mentioned in s 7(1)(a) was not available at that place or it was for any other reason not practicable to use such a device there; or
(b) the constable who made the previous requirement has reasonable cause to believe that the device used there has not produced a reliable indication of the proportion of alcohol in the breath of the person concerned.

The result of the analysis of a roadside evidential breath specimen is admissible in evidence to the same extent as the analysis of a specimen at a police station. The fact that a specimen for analysis may be taken at the roadside does not remove the availability of a preliminary test. In addition, the option of taking a person to a police station to obtain a specimen for analysis remains.

RTA 1988, s 7(3) provides that a requirement to provide a specimen of *blood* or *urine* can only be made at a *police station* or at a *hospital*; and that it cannot be made at a police station unless:

(a) the constable making the requirement has reasonable cause to believe that for medical reasons a specimen of breath cannot be provided (because of inability) or should not be required (for some other reason, such as the taking of a drug which affects blood/alcohol levels). Provided that a reasonable cause to believe that there are medical reasons exists, it is irrelevant that the constable himself does not believe that for medical reasons a breath specimen cannot be provided or should not be required. The present provision does not require the constable to seek medical advice; the question is whether on the facts before the constable he had reasonable cause to believe that medical reasons exist;

(b) specimens of breath have not been provided elsewhere, and at the time the requirement is made, an approved device or a reliable approved device is not available at the police station, or it is then for any other reason not practicable to use such a device there;

(bb) an approved device has been used at the police station or elsewhere but the constable who required the specimen of breath has reasonable cause to believe that the device has not produced a reliable indication of the proportion of alcohol in the breath of the person concerned;

(bc) as a result of the administration of a preliminary drug test, the constable making the requirement has reasonable cause to believe that the person required to provide a specimen of blood or urine has a drug in his body; or

(c)   the suspected offence is one under RTA 1988, s 4 and the constable making the requirement has been advised by a medical practitioner that the condition of the person required to provide the specimen might be due to some drug;

but may then be made notwithstanding that the person required to provide the specimen has already provided or been required to provide two specimens of breath.

The fact that, where the alleged offence is one under RTA 1988, s 4, the constable has been advised by a medical practitioner that the person's condition may be due to some drug, may be proved by oral evidence from the doctor or by the police officer saying what the doctor said to him. In addition, where unchallenged evidence has been given by the custody officer as to what the medical practitioner said and did and as to his completion of a procedural form recording the signed observations of the doctor, justices are entitled to find that this advice had been given. While the endorsement signed by the doctor is, in its contents, hearsay, the fact that the medical practitioner had signed the endorsement and said things which led the officer to complete the remainder of the form in a particular way, indicating that it was concerned with impairment through drugs after medical advice, has been held to be a matter to which the justices were entitled to have regard.

If a constable requires a specimen of blood or urine under RTA 1988, s 7(3), the decision as to whether it should be blood or urine is for the constable and he does not have to invite the motorist to express his own preference before making the decision. However, if the constable intends to require a specimen of blood, under the provisions of s 7(3), there are two mandatory requirements which must be fulfilled:

(a) he must, in accordance with RTA 1988, s 7(7), warn the person that a failure to provide a specimen may render him liable to prosecution (if this is not done the evidence of the analysis of the specimen is inadmissible);
(b) he must inform the person of the reason why specimens of breath could not be taken.

There are further factors which the constable should bring to the attention of the person concerned. While these factors have been held not to be mandatory by the House of Lords, the House has said that police officers, in order to seek to ensure that a driver is aware of the role of a doctor, should continue to use a formula recommended by Lord Bridge within a previous judgment given by the House. The additional factors included in the formula are:

(a) that the driver is informed that he is required to provide a specimen of blood or urine but that it is for the constable to decide which;
(b) that his only right to object to giving blood will be for medical reasons to be determined by a doctor;
(c) where a driver makes a representation in answer to a question about whether a specimen of blood should be taken, the constable must consider whether the statement proffered is capable of being a medical reason. It is a question of fact whether the statement raises a potential medical reason. A court is entitled to find on the facts that a police officer was not obliged to investigate the matter further;
(d) if the constable concludes that there is no medical reason, he may require a blood specimen, but if he has doubts about the matter, he should seek the opinion of a medical practitioner.

In relation to these non-mandatory requirements, the House of Lords said that what was necessary is that the driver should be aware, whether or not he was told by a police officer, of the doctor's role *so that he does not suffer prejudice*. If a driver appreciates that a blood specimen would be taken by a doctor and not by a police officer, a charge should not be dismissed merely because a police officer has failed to tell the driver that a specimen would be taken by a doctor. The House said that a court should follow a two-stage process:

(1) It should consider whether all of these matters had been brought to the attention of the driver. If the answer to that question was 'No' it should then consider (2).
(2) In relation to the non-mandatory requirements, the issue is whether the police officer's failure to give the full formula deprived the driver of the opportunity to exercise any option open to him, or caused him to exercise it in a way which he would not have done had everything been said.
    (a) If the answer is 'Yes' the driver should be acquitted.
    (b) If the answer is 'No' the police officer's failure to use the full formula should not be a reason for an acquittal.

The House of Lords said that it would only be in exceptional circumstances that a court would acquit on the grounds that a driver suffered prejudice without having heard evidence from the driver himself which raised the issue of prejudice. These issues are questions of fact. If the court, having heard the driver's evidence, is not satisfied beyond reasonable doubt that he was not prejudiced, he should be acquitted.

The House of Lords also ruled on this occasion that there is no statutory requirement, nor any considerations of fairness, which requires a police officer to ask a driver if any non-medical reason exists in consequence of which a specimen of blood should not be taken. Any such matter might support 'a reasonable excuse for failure to provide a specimen' but that is a matter for a court.

Where a constable said in evidence that she had completed the standard procedure form but could not recall the words which she used a divisional court expressed surprise that the justices had accepted a submission that there was no evidence of the giving of the warning, as the standard procedure was well known to them. If they were in doubt they should have asked for an explanation and the production of the forms.

A 'reliable device' referred to in RTA 1988, s 7(3)(b) is one which the police officer concerned reasonably believes to be reliable. The police officer must believe that the device *is unreliable, not* that *it might be*. Where a police officer thought that the device might be unreliable because the motorist did not appear to be as badly affected as the device indicated and required an alternative specimen, the conviction was quashed on the grounds that a belief that the device might be unreliable is insufficient. In another case where, during the morning and after a positive roadside breath test, a reading which was more than four times the legal limit was obtained and the driver gave no indication that she was so badly affected, a divisional court refused to interfere with the justices' conclusion that the intoximeter must have been unreliable even though she had not called expert evidence as to what the reading should have been following her admitted consumption of alcohol. The court said that the decision was very close to the line of perversity. For the officer to have required an alternative specimen he would have had to believe that the device had not produced a reliable reading.

It is 'not practicable to use a device' if there is no officer available at the station who has been trained to use the device.

Where a defendant has provided two specimens of breath on a machine which is then found to be defective, he may be lawfully required to provide two further specimens of breath for analysis by another device instead of being required to provide blood or urine. Where this involves a suspect being taken to another police station, a divisional court has said that it might be wise, *as a matter of an abundance of caution*, to repeat, at the second police station, the statutory warning that failure may render him liable to prosecution.

RTA 1988, s 7(3)(bb) was inserted by the Criminal Procedure and Investigations Act 1996. As interpreted by the appeal courts before 1996, RTA 1988, s 7(3)(b) requires evidence that the device was unreliable or that the officer had reasonable grounds for believing that the device was unreliable. While appellate decisions made in respect of s 7(3)(b) remain valid, the addition of s 7(3)(bb) makes, in some circumstances, the issue of the reliability of the machine itself irrelevant. An alternative specimen may be required where a breath testing device has been used and the constable who required the specimens has reasonable cause to believe that the device has not produced a *reliable indication* of the proportion of alcohol in the breath of the person concerned. Thus, if a device produces two readings which indicate significant differences in the levels of alcohol, it is open to the constable to require an alternative specimen if he reasonably believes that the device has not produced a reliable indication of alcohol in the breath. The latest evidential breath testing equipment incorporates new software which enables it to identify and flag up automatically where it is suspected an interfering substance may be present, or the alleged offender produces mouth alcohol, or the difference between the readings of two specimens is greater than 15%. In such situations a constable will be able to require blood or urine as an alternative.

Reliance on the guidance contained in procedural instructions about the use of breath testing equipment, which leads to the conclusion that an indication is unreliable, will mean that the constable has reasonable grounds to believe that the device has not produced a reliable reading.

It has been held by a judge in the Administrative Court that, where the constable has reasonable cause to suspect that the unreliable indication is due not to the unreliability of the device but to the way in which the individual provided the breath specimens, the officer may offer the individual the opportunity to provide further breath specimens (instead of requiring him to provide a blood or urine specimen).

Specimen of breath

RTA 1988, s 7 requires that the two specimens of breath which have been required under it be analysed by means of a device approved by the Secretary of State. A motorist who has provided one specimen of breath which exceeded the prescribed limit but has failed to provide a second specimen cannot, on the basis of that specimen, be convicted of driving with excess alcohol. He can, however, be convicted of failing to provide a specimen of breath.

Devices

Currently, the latest devices to be approved by the Secretary of State are as follows.

Camic Datamaster   The machine measures the amount of ethyl alcohol present in a person's breath. It looks only for ethyl alcohol and rejects any other substance which is present in a specimen of breath. The breath analyser is concerned with infrared absorption as a means of determining the presence of alcohol. The machine is combined with a microprocessor (computer) which calculates the validity of any sample provided. A 'run' button initiates the process of analysis and a 'print' button initiates a print-out of the last test. Accuracy checks are fully automatic. Print-outs from the Datamaster show the standard details from satisfactory specimens and record any circumstances in which a non-valid specimen has been detected. The machine detects and records the presence of 'interfering substances'. The clock can be reset by the operator to run in local time in the same way as setting a clock on the standard type of video recorder.

Lion Intoxilyzer 6000   This is a microprocessor controlled, multi-filtering infrared spectrometer. It works on the principle that the greater the concentration of alcohol in the breath, the greater the amount of infrared light which is absorbed. It will detect any interfering substance. The machine indicates its status. When ready for use it indicates 'standby'. It indicates that it is fully powered up and is ready for analysis, or has started to analyse a specimen, when it indicates 'analyse'. The print-outs include the standard details where there is a satisfactory specimen and otherwise indicate the defect which has been detected. So far as the clock is concerned, the computer software changes the reading between summer and winter time without intervention from the operator.

Intoximeter EC/IR   The machine incorporates two separately-controlled systems dealing with the analytical functions of the machine and the input/output control system which controls all aspects of the user interface and controls test sequences and protocols. The flow of electrons through the fuel cell is measured and this indicates the amount of alcohol consumed by the fuel cell. The infrared analysis system follows the general pattern of analysis and detects the presence of ethanol. Mouth alcohol and other 'interfering substances' are detected. The use of the 'enter' key initiates a test and the 'P' key produces a print-out of the latest test. The machine incorporates an internal clock and calendar.

For the purposes of the legislation relating to the provision of 'specimens of breath', 'breath' does not mean deep lung air but should be given its ordinary dictionary definition, ie 'air exhaled from anywhere'; therefore there is no need for the prosecution to prove that the reading from an approved device related solely to deep lung alcohol and was not related to mouth alcohol.

Analysis of breath by the machines

Instructors are trained by the Home Office to teach the use of the breath testing machines. The devices have been well designed to overcome the problems likely to arise from an evidential viewpoint. At the outset the devices are correctly calibrated but in actual use the devices check themselves for accuracy. They check their correct calibration both before and after each of the two breath samples and a record is made of those calibration checks on the eventual print-out slip. The slip therefore shows two separate readings of alcohol levels sandwiched between records of calibration checks to ensure that the devices are operating correctly. The accused is present throughout the procedure and has the opportunity to see the device at work. The officer carrying out the test is not obliged to explain to the motorist that the second specimen must be provided within three minutes of the first, or the test will abort.

The devices provide a timed and dated print-out which gives evidence of two separate readings of alcohol content in the breath of the accused. The normal procedure thereafter is that the constable who has operated the device certifies all copies of the print-out which shows, in addition to the readings, the particulars of the person from whom the sample is obtained, the signature of the officer, and the signature of the person (or a record that such a signature was refused). The constable's statement declares the lower of the two readings given by the device to be at the specified level and certifies that copies of the statement were signed by him and by the accused, or that the accused refused. Where a print-out is not produced in evidence and no oral evidence is given in relation to correct calibration, it is open to a court to find that calibration was correct where there is evidence that the machine was used by a trained operator.

The three devices are computers. Previously, PACE 1984, s 69 required that the constable certified that the computer had been properly used, was operating properly (and if not the defect was not such as would affect the production of the document) and that operating rules had been observed. However, PACE, s 69 was repealed by the Youth Justice and Criminal Evidence Act 1999 so there is now no requirement that the reliability of the computer be proved as a matter of course. Nevertheless, where reliability is challenged, such proof will be required. The ordinary law on evidence will now apply to computer evidence. In the absence of evidence to the contrary, courts will presume that the computer system was working correctly. If there is evidence that it may not have been, the party seeking to introduce the evidence will need to prove that it was working. It is therefore desirable that police officers continue to record on the appropriate procedural forms, the fact that the computer was operating correctly, together with any appropriate observations, as is done at present. Previous decisions concerning 'computers' will still be relevant to some instances in which reliability is challenged. Where a procedural form was offered in evidence and the certificate stating that the computer was operating correctly had not been fully completed in the spaces left for the insertion of particulars, a divisional court said that the justices were entitled to presume, from other evidence such as:

(a) the presence of a trained operator;
(b) the fact that calibration had been checked and found to be correct; and
(c) that the operator had not indicated, at the place where opportunity was provided, that the machine was not working,

that the computer was working. Similarly, where the sergeant had, when deleting a part of the procedural form which did not apply to the procedure which he was following, inadvertently struck out a part of the completed certificate, a divisional court said that the justices had been entitled to find that the certificate was valid. No objection had been made in respect of the forms which had been served on the accused and it was obvious, in view of the fact that proceedings had been taken, that the part of the certificate had been deleted in error. The fact that the clock on such a device is registering an incorrect time or date is not such a defect as would affect the production of such a document, where satisfactory evidence is offered to that effect. Nor is the fact that the printer omitted the second half of the first character and the second character in every line and printed some parts in smaller print. Provided that the part of the Intoximeter device which is a 'computer' was operating correctly at the time and that it was calibrated and correct, the malfunctioning of the printer does not affect in any way the manner in which the device processes, stores or retrieves the information which is used to generate the statement offered in evidence. A divisional court has also ruled that magistrates were not perverse in finding that a device was operating correctly in the case of a refusal, where the police officer had recorded that the machine aborted after only one minute, as opposed to the three minutes which it allegedly allowed. Expert evidence had been given by an experienced engineer to the effect that he had not encountered, in twenty years, an incident involving such a machine aborting after only one minute. The justices had been entitled to conclude that the officer had made an error in recording the time at which the machine aborted.

However, all such decisions will now have to be considered in the light of the fact that there is now no requirement and no regulated procedure by which proof of reliability may be measured.

The officer also certifies that he handed a copy of the statement to the accused who accepted, or declined to accept it. The mere fact that the copy handed to the accused is not signed by the officer does not affect the validity of the original. RTOA 1988, s 16(3) requires that a copy is either 'handed to' an accused at the time, or is served upon him not later than seven days before the hearing. Where an accused signed all three copies but refused to accept one, a divisional court held that s 16(3) had been complied with when the accused was offered a copy although there had been no physical transfer of possession of the document. Nevertheless, it will be good practice in such circumstances subsequently to serve a copy of the statement upon the accused in accordance with the section. However, the Act does not restrict evidence of the test to documentary evidence. Oral evidence may be given of the results of a test should the prosecutor, for some reason, choose not to use the simplified procedure. If this is done, oral evidence of calibration should also be given. It will be advisable, in such cases, to serve a copy of the evidence of the police operator on the defendant in accordance with the Criminal Justice Act 1967, s 9. A divisional court has said that, where an officer is giving oral evidence of the result of an analysis, there is no difference between those results having been seen on the screen, and those seen on a print-out.

Defence solicitors have no right to obtain documents kept in relation to breath testing devices, such as the log, repair reports and memory roll, with a view to searching for material which might support a submission that the device was defective. They must rely upon the prosecution to fulfil its duty to disclose material evidence which might be of assistance to the defence. The reliability of the approved device which has been used can be challenged either by direct evidence of some malfunctioning or by evidence from which the inference of unreliability can reasonably be drawn. On the other hand, the reliability of the device used cannot be challenged on grounds relating to all devices of the prescribed type because the type of device has been approved by the Secretary of State.

RTA 1988, s 8 provides that it is only the lower of the two readings given by the machine which may be used as evidence; the other must be disregarded. Where one of the two required readings is not obtained within the same operating cycle of the machine, a second cycle must be commenced. In such a case it is the lower of the first specimen taken and the first of the second cycle which should be offered in evidence.

However, where neither of the specimens in the first cycle is valid, a second cycle is undertaken and third and fourth specimens are, effectively, the first and second specimens recognised by the machine.

Where only one satisfactory specimen of breath has been obtained due to a failure of the breath-testing machine and an alternative blood or urine specimen has been, in consequence, obtained and a charge has been preferred alleging an excess of alcohol in that alternative specimen, evidence of the proportion of alcohol found in the one specimen of breath will be inadmissible, as it is not relevant to a charge of excess alcohol in another specimen. However, where the accuracy of the analysis of the alternative specimen is challenged, the prosecution is required to prove beyond reasonable doubt that the blood alcohol analysis was reliable and if the breath test result is broadly equivalent to the analysis of the alternative specimen then, notwithstanding the reason for requiring the alternative specimen, such evidence is at least capable of tending to support the reliability of the analysis of the alternative specimen. Provided that the significance of the relationship between the two analyses is explained by an expert, the evidence may be relevant.

RTA 1988, s 11(3) applies to specimens of breath for analysis. It provides that a person does not provide such a specimen unless it is sufficient to enable the test or the analysis to be carried out, and is provided in such a way as to enable the objective of the test or analysis to be satisfactorily achieved. This is an important provision, as it is necessary for the person providing the specimen to continue blowing until the indicator lights signify that sufficient breath has been obtained for analysis. If sufficient is not provided, there has been a 'failure' (see later).

Statutory option to replace specimen of breath with an alternative specimen

The prescribed limit in relation to alcohol in the breath is at present 35 microgrammes of alcohol in 100 ml of breath. In practice, machines are kind to persons suspected of these offences but, nevertheless, RTA 1988, s 8(2) provides that if the specimen with the lower proportion of alcohol contains no more than 50 microgrammes of alcohol in 100 ml of breath the person may claim that it should be replaced by a specimen of blood or urine. This is called the 'statutory option'. It applies even though the motorist admits driving with excess alcohol. The burden is upon the person from whom the specimen is required to exercise that option. However, he must be informed of his right to exercise it, unless he makes this impossible (as where he refuses to listen and walks away). Police officers must take care, when explaining this right, not to say anything which might have the effect of dissuading a person from exercising this right, or of depriving him of the opportunity to exercise the option, or of causing him to exercise it in a different way from that which he would have adopted if everything had been explained. If they do say something which might have one of these effects, any conviction resulting from the original analysis will be quashed. If the person who makes such a claim under s 8(2) was required to provide specimens of breath under s 7 at or near a place where a relevant breath test was administered (specimen for analysis taken at roadside), a constable may arrest him without warrant. This enables the constable to take the motorist to a police station for an alternative specimen to be provided.

The decision whether a 'replacement specimen' shall be of blood or urine is for the constable. In the light of this it is somewhat surprising that he must inform the motorist that he may claim blood or urine. On the other hand, it is not necessary to invite him to express a preference as to whether the specimen should be of blood or urine (since it suffices that he is told that, if he exercises the right to have a replacement specimen taken, it will be for the police officer to decide whether that specimen is to be of blood or urine). However, a divisional court held that, where a motorist had made it clear that his Rastafarian religious beliefs would not permit him to give blood before a constable had made a decision as to which specimen to require, the officer should at least have given consideration to the matter and that a decision to require blood, without any basis for doing so, would be an invalid requirement for blood. The House of Lords has ruled that where a police officer decides to require an alternative specimen of blood he must inform the person that the specimen of breath which he has given which contains the lower proportion of alcohol does not exceed 50 microgrammes in 100 millilitres of breath. See p 607–608 for non-mandatory procedural requirements in relation to the provision of a specimen of blood. In a RTA 1988, s 8(2) case, in addition to telling the driver that a specimen of blood 'will be taken by a doctor unless he considers that there are medical reasons for not taking blood', the constable should ask the driver if there are any medical reasons why a specimen of blood could or should not be taken by a doctor. Failure to do so will not lead to a dismissal of the charge unless the magistrates have a reasonable doubt as to whether or not the person was prejudiced by being deprived of the opportunity to exercise the option, or being caused to exercise it in a way which he would not have done if everything had been said. The motorist should be told of the role of the doctor at the outset of the procedure. Where a police officer has, at the outset, explained the whole procedure to a suspect who then exercises the option, it is not essential that the whole procedure be repeated when the suspect exercises the option. The reason is that the information will still be present and effective in the driver's mind. A divisional court has held that it is not *strictly* necessary for a police officer to inform the suspect that the breath specimen which that person has provided exceeds the statutory limit, since the fact that an alternative is being offered makes it obvious that the specimen provided shows an alcohol content in excess of the limit. Similarly, where an officer said that the replacement specimen would be used *for court purposes* a divisional court said that while those words served no useful purpose they were not misleading.

A suspect has no right to legal advice before deciding whether or not to exercise this option; the requirements of fairness inherent in the statutory option entitle the suspect to know of his option but do not entitle him to legal advice as to the result of exercising it. If a person, having been refused access to legal advice, declines to exercise his option, the original specimen is admissible. It would seem that if a suspect does not understand that the option exists, because, for example, of a breakdown in communication, the original specimen could be excluded by the court, although it will not be if the suspect's inability to understand is due wholly or partly to his consumption of alcohol. Where the option has been offered and refused, but the suspect then changes his mind, it is for the justices to decide, in accordance with the evidence, whether the procedure had come to an end at a time when the motorist changed his mind. It is likely that a more or less immediate change of mind will be acceptable as in other similar circumstances such words have been held to be 'relevant words and conduct to be taken into account'. However, once the procedure has moved on to the next stage, justices will have grounds to support a conclusion that the issue of acceptance or refusal had been finalised, in which case a claim to exercise the option would be ineffective. An example is provided by a case where, when asked if he wished to exercise his statutory option, a driver said 'No', at which the police officer recorded that reply into the computer which then began to print out the results of the analysis of the specimens of breath. Some two to three minutes later the driver claimed that he had a phobia concerning needles. A divisional court said that there had been an unequivocal refusal. What followed later was no more than an explanation for not wanting to give blood. Where an accused initially declined to exercise such option, but agreed to do so after legal advice one hour later, a court was held to be entitled to decide that enough time had passed to bring the statutory procedure to an end, and to admit evidence of the proportion of alcohol in his breath.

If the option to provide a blood or urine specimen is taken and a blood or urine specimen is provided, the results of the analysis of that specimen at the laboratory replace the lower of the readings of the breath specimen obtained by the machine for evidential purposes, regardless of whether the reading is higher or lower. Where a motorist gives a reason for not giving blood, which may amount to a medical reason (eg a medically recognised phobia against needles is such a reason), the police officer should ask him for an explanation of that reason (because this may establish that the alleged reason is unfounded) or, if necessary, call a doctor to establish whether there is a medical reason. If this is not done (for example where the motorist is a diabetic who is used to injections but nevertheless claims that he does not like other people putting needles into him), the prosecution cannot rely on the specimen of breath supplied. On the other hand, where a motorist says that he would prefer to provide urine as he does not like needles but accepts that there was no reason why a specimen of blood could not, or should not, be taken by a doctor, and then refuses to supply blood, the police officer is under no obligation to make further inquiries about the motorist's fear of needles. The motorist's two replies, taken together, did not create sufficient doubt as to a medical reason. Consequently, the prosecution will be entitled to rely upon evidence of the breath specimen.

It is a question of fact whether a driver's statement to the effect that he cannot provide blood raises a potential medical reason for not providing a blood specimen. A divisional court has held that, where a driver replied 'I do take tablets' when asked if there was a medical reason why he could not or should not give blood, this was capable in principle of being a valid reason and the police officer should not have gone on to arrange for a specimen of blood to be taken without making inquiries as to the nature of the medication and seeking medical advice if necessary.

Where a motorist has opted to replace the analysis of a specimen of breath with that of a specimen of blood which he opts to provide, it is not necessary for the prosecution to prove the calibration of the breath-testing device. The positive specimen of breath, in such circumstances, is no more than a pre-requisite for the supply of a specimen of blood; the analysis of the breath specimen ceases to have any probative value in proving the offence.

If a motorist given the statutory option is asked to provide a blood specimen, but the police officer is unable to contact a doctor, the police officer has power to ask the motorist to provide a urine specimen instead. If the motorist is unable to do so (eg because he has visited the lavatory in the meanwhile), the lower of the two breath specimens can be used in evidence since the statutory option procedure only prohibits either specimen of breath being used if a blood or urine specimen is provided under it.

Specimens of blood or urine

The option to provide blood or urine in the event of a reading being no more than 50 microgrammes on an evidential breath-testing machine has already been explained. Leaving aside this and the case (dealt with later) where the person concerned is a patient at a hospital, the only other exceptions to the rule that evidence must be obtained by means of such a machine are in the event of medical reasons, unavailability of a machine (or of a reliable machine), unreliability of indication, or where the person's condition might be due to a drug; see above.

As amended by the Police Reform Act 2002 (PRA 2002), RTA 1988, s 7(4) provides that, if the provision of a specimen other than a specimen of breath may be required in pursuance of the section, the question whether it is to be a specimen of blood or a specimen of urine and, in the case of a specimen of blood, the question who is to be asked to take it shall be decided (subject to s 7(4A), added by PRA 2002) by the constable making the requirement. The limitation in RTA 1988, s 7(4A) is that there must be no requirement to provide a blood specimen if:

(a) the medical practitioner who is asked to take the specimen is of the opinion that, for medical reasons, it cannot or should not be taken; or

(b) the registered health care professional who is asked to take it is of that opinion and there is no contrary opinion from a medical practitioner.

RTA 1988, s 7(4A) also provides that where by virtue of s 7(4A) there can be no requirement to provide a specimen of blood, the constable may require a specimen of urine instead.

The term 'registered health care professional' means a person (other than a medical practitioner) who is a registered nurse, or a registered member of a health care profession which is designated for the present purposes by an order made by the Secretary of State.

On requiring a person to provide a specimen of blood or urine, a constable must warn him that a failure to provide it may render him liable to prosecution, and state the reason why a breath specimen cannot be taken or used. Both requirements are mandatory; non-compliance with either of them results in a dismissal of the charge. In addition, in order to ensure that the person is aware of the role of the doctor, the constable should tell him that it is for the constable to decide whether the specimen is to be of blood or urine and, if (as is usually the case) the constable decides to require blood, ask the person if there are any medical reasons why a blood specimen cannot or should not be taken from him by a doctor. Failure to do so will not lead to a dismissal of the charge unless the magistrates have a reasonable doubt as to whether or not the person was prejudiced by not being told about the role of the doctor. Thus, for example, if he was aware that a doctor would take the blood specimen, the charge will not be dismissed.

RTA 1988, s 11(4) provides that:

A person supplies a specimen of blood if and only if:

(a) he consents to the taking of such a specimen from him; and
(b) the specimen is taken from him by a medical practitioner or, if it is taken in a police station, either by a medical practitioner or by a registered health care professional.

A constable requiring someone under RTA 1988, s 7 to provide a blood specimen is not required to ask the person whether there are any non-medical reasons why the specimen should not be taken. Nor need he give the person a chance to indicate his preference as to the alternatives of blood or urine.

Where a medical reason is given (for example that the motorist is taking tablets) there must be evidence that the police officer took this into account or had considered whether it could be a medical reason. Although medical possibilities might appear to be far-fetched, it is impossible to *know* that this is so. There must be evidence that the officer has asked questions. Where a 'medical reason' offered is capable of being valid the officer must refer the matter to a medical practitioner. If he does not, a requirement will not have been made pursuant to the Act and evidence of the resulting analysis will be inadmissible.

Whether or not there has been a valid requirement to provide a specimen of blood is a question of fact to be determined by a court, having regard to all of the circumstances. A divisional court has said that fairness can be achieved without the introduction of rigid judge-made formulae which can so easily mask the statutory language and needlessly complicate its construction. However, it is good practice to ensure that a direct requirement is made and to ensure that there has been a positive refusal.

Where a constable requires blood as an alternative and the person required to give blood refuses but offers urine as an alternative, there is a 'failure' unless such a medical reason exists.

Specimens of blood taken from a person incapable of consenting

RTA 1988, s 7A was inserted by PRA 2002 to deal with the taking of blood specimens from a person who has been involved in an accident and is, for some reason, incapable of giving a valid consent to the taking of a specimen of blood.

RTA 1988, s 7A(1) provides that a constable may request a medical practitioner to take a specimen of blood from a person ('the person concerned') irrespective of whether that person consents if:

(a) that person is a person from whom the constable would (in the absence of any incapacity of that person and of any objection under RTA 1988, s 9 referred to on p 620) be entitled under s 7 to require the provision of a specimen of blood for a laboratory test;
(b) it appears to that constable that that person has been involved in an accident that constitutes or is comprised in the matter that is under investigation or the circumstances of that matter;
(c) it appears to that constable that that person is or may be incapable (whether or not he has purported to do so) of giving a valid consent to the taking of a specimen of blood; and
(d) it appears to that constable that that person's incapacity is attributable to medical reasons.

RTA 1988, s 7A(2) provides that, under s 7A, the request:

(a) must not be made to a medical practitioner who for the time being has any responsibility (apart from the request) for the clinical care of the person concerned; and
(b) must not be made to a medical practitioner other than a police medical practitioner unless:
  (i) it is not reasonably practicable for the request to be made to a police medical practitioner; or
  (ii) it is not reasonably practicable for such a medical practitioner (assuming him to be willing to do so) to take the specimen.

A 'police medical practitioner' is a medical practitioner who is engaged under any agreement to provide medical services for purposes connected with the activities of a police force.

By RTA 1988, s 7A(3) it is lawful for a medical practitioner to whom a request is made:

(a) to take a specimen of blood from the person concerned irrespective of whether that person consents; and
(b) to provide the sample to a constable.

RTA 1988, s 7A(4) states that, if a specimen is taken pursuant to a request under s 7A, the specimen must not be subjected to a laboratory test unless the person from whom it was taken:

(a) has been informed that it was taken; and
(b) has been required by a constable to give his permission for a laboratory test of the specimen; and
(c) has given his permission.

On requiring a person to give his permission for the purposes of RTA 1988, s 7A for a laboratory test of a specimen, a constable is required by s 7A(5) to warn him that a failure to give the permission may render him liable to prosecution.

It is an offence under RTA 1988, s 7A(6) for a person, without reasonable excuse, to fail to give permission for a laboratory test of a specimen of blood taken from him under s 7A. It is a defence that a warning was not given under s 7A(5) or has not been understood by the person in question.

Other provisions about blood or urine specimens

If a specimen of blood is taken, RTOA 1988, s 15(4) provides that a specimen of blood shall be disregarded unless:

(a) it was taken from the accused with his consent and, if taken in a police station, was taken by a medical practitioner or a registered health care professional, or if taken elsewhere, was taken by a medical practitioner; or
(b) it was taken from the accused by a medical practitioner under RTA 1988, s 7A and the accused subsequently gives his permission for a laboratory test of the specimen.

Evidence that a specimen of blood was taken from the accused with his consent by a medical practitioner (or a registered health care professional) may be given by the production of a document purporting to certify that fact and to be signed by a medical practitioner (or registered health care professional). Blood specimen kits are provided by the forensic science laboratories and are kept at police stations.

A urine specimen must, by RTA 1988, s 7(5), be provided within one hour of the requirement and after the provision of a previous specimen. This means that a specimen must be taken and discarded, and another provided (for analysis) within one hour of the requirement. It is a question of fact for the justices to determine as to whether a period of one hour has passed since the requirement was made. Where justices had found that a requirement had been made at 2.10 am and no specimen had been provided by 3.10 am, a divisional court declined to become involved in consideration of the possibility of a few seconds' discrepancy. A police officer is not obliged to extend the time but, if he does accept a second specimen of urine outside the time limit, the result of the analysis of that specimen is nevertheless admissible. It has been held that a constable was entitled to require a specimen of urine where, the breath-analysis device being inoperable, he had required blood but a doctor was unable to obtain such a specimen when the motorist's vein collapsed. A divisional court said that the officer's right to change his mind continued up to the time at which *blood was actually taken*. This change of mind can take place either before or after a compliance with a requirement, or after a refusal to supply blood. The rule therefore is that an unproductive request for one specimen does not prevent a subsequent request for another specimen from being valid.

This proposition was supported where, after being asked whether there was any medical or other reason why blood should or could not be taken, the motorist said, 'Yes, there is a reason. Ask the doctor.' He then alleged that this had something to do with a condition from which he had suffered when in the army. The sergeant then asked if he would supply blood and he said 'No comment'. The motorist submitted that he could not be guilty of failing to supply urine as he had already refused to supply blood and at that stage he should have been charged with failure to supply blood and the procedure should have ended. A divisional court said that the sergeant, having been thwarted in his attempt to obtain a specimen of blood, was perfectly entitled to ask for a specimen of urine and the motorist's refusal to do so amounted to an offence.

RTOA 1988, s 15(5) provides that where, at the time a blood or urine specimen was required of the accused, he asked to be provided with such a specimen, evidence of the proportion of alcohol found in the specimen is not admissible on behalf of the prosecution unless the specimen is one of two parts into which the specimen was divided *at the time* it was provided and one part was given to the accused. 'At the time' does not mean 'then and there' nor 'in the presence of the accused'. It suffices that the division is closely linked in time and part of the same event as the taking of the sample. It is, however, desirable that the division takes place in the presence of the accused. There is no obligation to inform a motorist that he may request part of the specimen. Provided that at his request the specimen has been divided and one part has been given to the accused, but it is handed back to the police for some reason, it is irrelevant that he never collects it; the statutory requirement is satisfied, and evidence of the alcohol level in the part retained by the police is admissible.

RTOA 1988, s 15(5A) provides that where a specimen was taken under RTA 1988, s 7A from a person, evidence of the proportion of alcohol *or any drug* found in the specimen is not admissible on behalf of the prosecution unless:

(a) the specimen in which the alcohol or drug was found is one of two parts into which it was divided at the time it was taken; and

(b) any request to be supplied with the other part of the specimen taken from the accused, which was made by the accused when he gave his permission for a laboratory test of the specimen, was complied with.

When a specimen of blood or urine has been obtained from a person, the labels identifying the samples with that person must be carefully made out and attached securely to the samples. The sample is sent to the forensic science laboratory with completed forms FSL1. A divisional court has said that, where there is an allegation of mislabelling, each case must be considered on its own facts. Where the name and initial of the motorist was correct; the date and time of the taking of the specimen was correctly indicated; the name of the police force and the arresting officer were correct; the justices had been correct to be satisfied as to the admissibility of evidence of the analysis of the specimen. Errors in the name of the police station and the exhibit number were not sufficient to invalidate the specimen in these circumstances.

HOSPITAL PATIENTS

RTA 1988, s 9 lays down a special procedure which applies while a person is at a hospital as a patient. It is a question of fact, for the justices to decide, whether or not a person is a patient at a hospital at a particular time.

RTA 1988, s 9(1) states that, while a person is at a hospital as a patient, he must not be required to co-operate with a preliminary test or to provide a specimen under RTA 1988, s 7 unless the medical practitioner in immediate charge of his case has been notified of the proposal to make the requirement, and:

(a) if the requirement is made, it must be for co-operation within a test administered, or for the provision of a specimen, at the hospital; but

(b) if the medical practitioner objects on the ground specified in RTA 1988, s 9(2) (below), the requirement must not be made.

RTA 1988, s 9(1A) provides that, while a person is at a hospital as a patient, no specimen of blood may be taken from him under RTA 1988, s 7A (person incapable of consenting) and he must not be required to give his permission for a laboratory test of a specimen taken under that s 7A unless the medical practitioner in immediate charge of his case:

(a) has been notified of the proposal to take the specimen or to make the requirement; and

(b) has not objected on the ground specified in s 9(2).

By RTA 1988, s 9(2), the ground on which the medical practitioner may object is:

(a) in a case falling within RTA 1988, s 9(1), that the requirement or the provision of the specimen or (if one is required) the warning required by RTA 1988, s 7(7) would be prejudicial to the proper care and treatment of the patient; and

(b) in a case falling within s 9(1A), that the taking of the specimen, the requirement or the warning required by RTA 1988, s 7A(5) would be so prejudicial.

A divisional court has held that where a police officer has knowledge of a medical reason affecting the decision as to whether a blood sample should be taken he must pass on such knowledge to a hospital doctor dealing with the accused. This is also the case where a doctor is deciding under RTA 1988, s 7(4) whether for medical reasons the specimen should not be of blood.

If the medical practitioner objects on the ground that the requirement, or the provision of a specimen, or (in the case of a blood or urine specimen) the warning about the consequences of failing to provide it would be prejudicial to the proper care and treatment of the patient, the requirement in question must not be made.

If there is no such objection and the requirement is then made, it must be for the provision of a specimen at the hospital. Evidential breath tests cannot be conducted at a hospital, so that a blood or urine specimen must be required in lieu.

It should be noted that if a preliminary test undergone by a patient proves positive, or he fails to undergo it, he may not be arrested, but this does not prejudice the rest of the procedure being followed.

The procedure in relation to hospital patients is strictly controlled. The steps which a constable should take in a 'hospital case' in the normal case (ie where the patient does not appear incapable of consenting to the taking of a blood specimen) are as follows:

(a) seek out the medical practitioner in charge of the case;
(b) request his consent to the provision of a preliminary breath test explaining the method of operating the particular device to be used;
(c) obtain that consent before proceeding further: the doctor may not object if the process is not prejudicial to care or treatment;
(d) if the medical practitioner does not object, require a preliminary test;
(e) if the test is negative, explain that there will be no further action;
(f) if the test is positive or the patient fails to provide it, obtain the medical practitioner's consent to the taking of a specimen for laboratory analysis, after having explained the procedure: it must be of blood or urine in the case of hospital patients; and
(g) if the medical practitioner does not object, obtain a specimen of blood with the consent of the person, the sample being taken by a medical practitioner, or obtain a urine specimen followed within one hour by a second urine specimen (the evidential specimen).

The High Court of Justiciary in Scotland has held that where a police officer has received the consent of a medical officer in charge of such a patient at a hospital, he is not required to obtain the further consent of another doctor to whose charge the patient has been transferred. The legislation anticipates an interval between consent and the taking of a specimen.

Within the terms of RTA 1988, s 9 it is not strictly necessary to obtain a preliminary test before requiring a specimen for analysis but the explanatory circular states that it is assumed that this will be done. It is good practice to give a person the opportunity quickly to clear himself of suspicion.

Where a requirement to provide a specimen of blood has been made at a hospital but the patient is discharged before the specimen can be taken, that requirement is not varied or discharged by the mere fact that the person to whom the requirement was made is then taken to a police station. The specimen of blood may be taken there. The only exception is if a police officer abrogates the procedure started at the hospital by asking for breath specimens and thereby setting in train the procedure under s 7.

EVIDENCE IN PROSECUTIONS UNDER RTA 1988, s 4 or 5

The question of the admissibility and evidential value of documents made out in consequence of the various provisions of the Road Traffic Act 1988, s 4 or 5 is answered in RTOA 1988, ss 15 and 16. By RTOA 1988, s 15(2), evidence of the proportion of alcohol or any drug in a specimen of breath, blood or urine provided by or taken from an accused must, in all cases, be taken into account and it *must be assumed* that the proportion of alcohol in the accused's breath, blood or urine at the time of the alleged offence was at least that found in the sample. Evidence of a breath, blood or urine specimen is not the only admissible evidence. The result is that, if the analysis or test reveals a proportion below the prescribed limit, but the magistrates are sure from expert evidence that, given the lapse of time between the alleged offence and the provision of the specimen, the proportion of alcohol at the time of the alleged offence was over the prescribed limit, they may convict the accused of an offence under s 5. On the other hand, since the accused's alcohol level *must be assumed to be not less* than that found in the sample, he is not permitted to adduce evidence that, although above the limit when the specimen was taken, he was below it when actually driving.

The assumption made by RTOA 1988, s 15(2) does not apply if there is evidence that the evidential device was unreliable or that a blood or urine specimen is unreliable (eg because analysis of the part given to the accused is below the limit). Divisional courts have held that justices can assume that a device was reliable unless there is evidence that it was not and that if there is evidence that a device was unreliable the prosecution are obliged to prove its reliability. This differs from the previous understanding that it was for the accused to prove unreliability, and seems to reflect the impact of the Human Rights Act. Presumably, the same approach as taken in that case applies where the challenge is to the reliability of a blood or urine specimen. Evidence relating to unreliability may be direct evidence, but—depending on the disparity between the claimed consumption and the analysis—evidence of the unreliability may be provided by reference to the amount of alcohol allegedly consumed before the specimen was provided. Expert evidence of the reading which could be produced in the circumstances by the accused is not essential.

Although RTOA 1988, s 15 says that the proportion of alcohol or any drug in a specimen provided by the accused must in all cases be taken into account, there are exceptions. This is because RTOA 1988, s 15(4), (5) and (5A) expressly state that evidence derived from a specimen must be disregarded unless, in the case of a blood specimen, it was taken with the accused's consent in a police station by a medical practitioner *or a registered health care professional* or elsewhere by a medical practitioner; or it was taken from the accused by a medical practitioner under RTA 1988, s 7A (without consent) and the accused subsequently gave his permission for a laboratory test of the specimen. In the case of a blood or urine specimen, the evidence derived from it is inadmissible unless the accused's request for one of the parts into which it was divided was not properly complied with.

Breaches of the procedure laid down by RTA 1988, ss 7 to 9 will render the evidence obtained from the specimen inadmissible, because a specimen obtained in breach of that procedure cannot be said to have been obtained under the Act, as RTOA 1988, s 15(3) requires.

Hip-flask defence

RTOA 1988, s 15(3) allows the accused what is often described as the 'hip-flask' defence. It provides that, in all cases under RTA 1988, s 5 and in cases under s 4 involving drink, the assumption as to alcohol level must not be made if the accused proves that:

(a) he consumed alcohol before he provided the specimen or had it taken from him and,
  (i) in relation to an offence under RTA 1988, s 3A, after the time of the alleged offence, and
  (ii) otherwise, after he had ceased to drive, attempt to drive or be in charge of a vehicle on a road or other public place; and
(b) had he not done so the proportion of alcohol in his breath, blood or urine would not have exceeded the prescribed limit and, if the proceedings are for an offence under RTA 1988, s 4, would not have been such as to impair his ability to drive.

The burden of proof placed on the accused is a persuasive one, that is to prove the defence on the balance of probabilities. This has been held not to be incompatible with the presumption of innocence under art 6 of the European Convention on Human Rights.

This has been described as 'post-incident' drinking and this may occur where a driver, having been required to provide a preliminary test, locks the door of his car and drinks from a flask in the hope that he will then be in a position to allege that his alcohol level was so increased. It may also occur where a driver has driven home, following an accident, and has then taken a number of drinks in order to make it almost impossible to establish what the level might have been prior to his 'post-incident' drinking. While s 15(3) does not eliminate such possibilities, it places the burden on the accused of satisfying a court that, had he not done so, he would not have exceeded the prescribed limit in a specimen provided for analysis.

In such cases it will almost invariably be necessary for a defendant to call expert medical or scientific evidence in order to discharge this burden of proof, unless non-expert evidence which is called is such that it will enable the court reliably and confidently to reach a sensible conclusion without expert evidence. If justices have been given clear evidence from an expert as to the amount of alcohol necessary to cause a particular driver to exceed the legal limit and have been given plausible evidence as to the quantity of alcohol consumed after the driving etc in question, it is open to them, in spite of any unexplained discrepancies, to find that the defendant has discharged the burden necessary to establish a defence under RTOA 1988, s 15(3).

Accused who are able to prove the hip-flask defence may nevertheless be liable for the offence of wilfully obstructing a constable in the execution of his duty. This is because the deliberate consumption of alcohol after the alleged offence in order to frustrate the procedure for taking specimens has been held to amount to that offence. In any event, such deliberate consumption is liable to be self-defeating since the accused will often still be in charge of the vehicle at the time of the additional imbibing. It is therefore good practice, in instances in which a driver drinks from a bottle before submitting to testing procedures, to charge that person with an offence of 'being in charge etc' should tests prove to be positive.

Use of certificates

RTOA 1988, s 16(1) provides that evidence of the proportion of alcohol in a spec-imen of breath may be given by the production of the print-out produced by the breath-testing device together with the certificate signed by a constable (normally the operator) (which certification may be made on the print-out). As we have already explained, that certification is to the effect that the print-out relates to a specimen provided by the accused at the date and time shown in it. The print-out and certificate are only admissible in evidence on behalf of the prosecution if a copy of it (or both) has been handed to the accused when the print-out was produced, or has been served on him not later than seven days before the hearing. More-over, the certificate is not so admissible if the accused, not later than three days before the hearing or within such further time as the court may allow, has served notice on the prosecution requiring the attendance at the hearing of the constable who signed the certificate. While the Act makes specific provisions for print-outs to be offered in evidence, it does not require that this be done. Consequently, a police officer may give oral evidence of the readings obtained on the screen of the device, provided that he is able to testify that the device was working properly and was accurately self-calibrating.

RTOA 1988, s 16(1) also provides that evidence of the proportion of alcohol or a drug in a specimen of blood or urine may be given by the production of a certificate signed by an authorised analyst as to the proportion of alcohol or any drug found in the specimen identified in the certificate. However, such a certificate is only admissible in evidence on behalf of the prosecution if a copy of it has been served on the accused not later than seven days before the hearing. In addition, the certificate is not so admissible if, not later than three days before the hearing or within such further time as the court may allow, the accused has served notice on the prosecutor requiring the attendance at the hearing of the analyst who signed the certificate.

Where an accused indicates that he will not accept such documentary evidence because there are defects in those documents and new documents are subsequently served by the prosecutor, he must respond to the new documents. If he does not specify that he requires the attendance of the witnesses concerned (in consequence of the second documents) those documents may be admitted by the court.

For the purposes of RTOA 1988, s 16, the evidence of an analyst not authorised by the Secretary of State is admissible if it can be shown that he was fully qualified and experienced.

ALTERNATIVE VERDICTS

RTOA 1988, s 24 provides that, where a person is charged under the RTA 1988, s 4(1) with driving, or attempting to drive when unfit to drive through drink or drugs, and is found not guilty of that offence, but the allegations in the information (or, when in force, written charge) amount to, or include, an allegation of an offence of 'being in charge' in those circumstances, he may be convicted of that offence. The same applies where a person is charged with driving or attempting to drive with excess alcohol in his body under RTA 1988, s 5(1); he may be convicted of 'being in charge'.

OFFENCE OF FAILING TO PROVIDE A SPECIMEN REQUIRED UNDER s 7

RTA 1988, s 7(6) makes it an offence for a person, without reasonable excuse, to fail to provide a specimen when required to do so in pursuance of s 7. The subsection creates one offence; that is failing to provide a specimen for analysis. Whether that specimen is one of breath, blood or urine is immaterial, provided that there is a failure to provide a specimen. Where a person is charged with failure to provide a specimen of blood for laboratory analysis in circumstances in which an approved breath-testing device was not available, and the validity of the request for a sample of blood is challenged, the non-availability of the device must be proved in accordance with the laws of evidence. However, where a defendant contended that there was no direct evidence to prove that there was no approved device available at the police station as there could have been a second machine there, a divisional court ruled that evidence that the machine failed to operate together with evidence that the accused was told that it was not therefore possible to take specimens of breath was sufficient. As in the case of the offence under RTA 1988, s 6(4), there cannot be a conviction for this offence if the requirement made for it is invalid for some reason; the fact that the person was brought to the police station after a wrongful arrest or after a trespass by the police does not render the requirement invalid.

Fail

As we have already said 'fail' includes 'refuse'. However, where a motorist refused to supply a specimen of breath, but within five seconds said that he wanted to change his mind, there was no refusal. A divisional court said that the justices had ignored the motorist's words five seconds after his refusal. Regard must be had to all words and conduct in reaching a conclusion. It is submitted that, in the light of this and other rulings, the right to change one's mind will exist until the constable has moved on to the next stage of the procedure. Where a person declines to provide a specimen of breath, alleging a medical reason which is discounted by the police surgeon, there is a failure to provide a specimen without reasonable excuse. The police officer is not obliged to start the procedure all over again. If it were otherwise, recalcitrant motorists could play the system to gain some delay. Once required to provide a specimen an offence is committed if, without reasonable excuse, it is not provided.

In addition, where a motorist refuses to supply specimens of breath and it is subsequently found that, because of his limited lung capacity, he would have been unable to supply specimens, this cannot amount to a reasonable excuse. There must be a causative link between the refusal and the excuse and this cannot be so where the condition was not known to exist at the time of the refusal.

We have already referred to what is meant by a failure to provide a specimen of breath and what constitutes a 'reasonable excuse' for such a failure.

Reasonable excuse

We have seen that an excuse cannot be adjudged reasonable unless the accused was physically or mentally unable to provide the specimen, or its provision would entail a substantial risk to his health. We have also seen that a foreigner who is unable to understand the purpose of the requirement and the penal consequences of a failure to comply also has a reasonable excuse. In relation to the failure to provide a specimen of blood or urine, most reasonable excuses which a person may have in relation to a failure to provide a specimen of breath are equally applicable to whichever of the alternative specimens is selected by the constable. In addition, there would be a reasonable excuse for failing to provide a specimen of blood where the accused has an invincible repugnance, amounting to a medically recognised phobia, to blood being taken, or where he has refused to sign a form of consent (to providing a specimen of blood) until he has read it. While an invincible repugnance, amounting to a medically recognised phobia, to blood being taken is a reasonable excuse, the fear of the sight of blood is not; the accused can always close his eyes or look away. Where an accused claimed before a court that he had a 'phobia' in relation to needles but had made no mention of this to the police officer requiring the specimen, and had made no attempt to provide a specimen, making an outright refusal, a divisional court held that there could be no question of him having a reasonable excuse. The position was no different to that applying in the case of a requirement to give a specimen of breath.

An arrested person who has not been given time to read the Detention Code, or to refer to a law book, does not have a reasonable excuse for not providing a specimen in consequence of that lack of opportunity, nor does someone who has been advised by his solicitor not to provide a specimen. Nor does someone who refuses to supply a specimen unless he can first consult a solicitor, unless the consultation will not delay the taking of the specimen to any significant extent.

Stress caused by self-precipitated agitation cannot amount to a reasonable excuse for failure to provide breath, nor can mental anguish caused by conduct on the part of a police officer which the driver considered to be oppressive. There would have to be a causal connection between such anguish and the failure. Such a connection was found in one borderline case where the justices found that there had been a reasonable excuse where a lady driver was said by her doctor to be suffering from a condition in which any stress would cause her to suffer from extremes of agitation which would require chemical intervention. She had not taken medication which controlled her condition within the preceding week or so. The justices found that she had been suffering from a panic attack at the police station and this had prevented her from supplying specimens of breath. They noted the doctor's opinion that she would have understood the procedure and that there would be nothing of a physical or mental nature to prevent her from supplying breath, but considered that there was a causative link between her physical condition and her inability to supply breath. A divisional court refused to interfere with this finding.

The fact that a driver was so drunk that he could not understand the procedure which was being followed does not amount to a reasonable excuse because it does not relate to the defendant's *capacity* to supply a specimen. However, where a driver failed to provide two specimens of breath and two police officers gave evidence that he appeared to be too drunk to do so, a divisional court refused to overturn a decision of the justices that he had had a reasonable excuse for not providing a specimen due to stress resulting from adverse personal and family circumstances which had led to recent breathlessness, although no medical evidence was offered. The justices had reached their decision on unimpeachable findings of fact and a divisional court would not interfere.

While a fear of AIDS is not a reasonable excuse for not providing a specimen of blood, a medically recognised *phobia* in relation to contracting AIDS is, as stated above. A genuine fear of AIDS, short of a medically recognised phobia, *may*, however, provide grounds for 'special reasons' for not disqualifying the offender from driving. The wording of the relevant provisions is such that a person who fails to provide a specimen under RTA 1988, s 7 on the grounds that he has been unlawfully arrested also does not have a reasonable excuse.

A driver who does not attempt to provide a breath specimen at a police station cannot subsequently claim a reasonable excuse by reliance on having told a constable at the roadside about a medical condition, when he did not tell the constable at the police station who had no knowledge of the condition.

A driver who refuses to provide specimens of breath because he has a medical problem, and who is then made the subject of a medical examination by a medical practitioner at the instigation of the constable, with a view to seeing whether he should be charged with failing without reasonable excuse to provide a specimen, cannot claim a reasonable excuse on the ground that when the practitioner found no medical reason for not providing a specimen he (the driver) was not given another opportunity to provide a specimen of breath. The constable is not obliged to give him another chance.

The accused does not have the burden of proving reasonable excuse. There must, however, be evidence in support of facts which could constitute a reasonable excuse, otherwise the prosecution does not have to prove that there was no reasonable excuse. In almost every imaginable case of alleged physical or mental incapacity, that evidence must be medical evidence; in exceptional cases, however, other evidence—even that of the accused—can suffice. An example of such an exceptional case was where an accused had provided one specimen of breath but began to lose composure, sobbing continuously and experiencing difficulty in breathing. She was unable to provide a second specimen. A divisional court ruled that the justices were entitled to conclude that she was physically incapable of providing a specimen, whilst accepting that the case was close to the borderline. The need for medical evidence on such a point could not be accepted in absolute terms.

Other points

We have already indicated that, on requiring a person to provide a specimen in pursuance of RTA 1988, s 7, a constable must warn him that a failure to provide it may render him liable to prosecution. Although an omission to do so is no defence to a charge under RTA 1988, s 4 or 5, nor to a charge of failing to provide a screening breath test, contrary to s 6(4), it is a defence to a charge under s 7(6) that such a warning has not been given or has not been understood by the person from whom the specimen is required.

An offence under RTA 1988, s 7(6) is as serious as one under s 4 or 5, since it is punishable in the same way as the offence in respect of which the specimen was required for evidential purposes.

RTA 1988, s 7(6) does not create two separate offences of failing to provide a specimen for analysis, despite the fact that the maximum penalty is higher when the defendant is alleged to have been driving, or attempting to drive, the vehicle at the material time than it is when he is alleged to have been in charge of it. As a result, an information (or, when in force, written charge) framed in terms of s 7(6) alone, without reference to the circumstances in which the requirement was made, is not bad for duplicity. It would be *good practice* to inform an accused of the circumstances surrounding the charge as soon as they had been established. In most cases, the issue of whether a person was driving, attempting to drive, or was in charge of the vehicle will be known at the time of his arrest. It is therefore preferable that the charge should specify whether the investigation was being carried out under RTA 1988, s 4(1), (2), 5(1)(a) or (b).

DETENTION OF PERSONS AFFECTED BY ALCOHOL

RTA 1988, s 10(1) provides that a person who has been required under s 7 or 7A to provide a specimen of breath, blood or urine may be detained at a police station (or, if the specimen was provided otherwise than at a police station, arrested and taken to and detained at a police station) if a constable has reasonable grounds for believing that, if he was released and drove or attempted to drive, he would commit an offence against either s 4 or s 5 of the Act. In practice this may often involve detention until a negative screening test. On any question under s 10 whether a person's ability to drive properly is or might be impaired through drugs, a constable must consult a medical practitioner and must act on his advice.

Section 10(1) does not apply to a person if it ought reasonably to appear to the constable that there is no likelihood of his driving or attempting to drive while his ability to drive properly is impaired or while the proportion of alcohol in his breath, blood or urine exceeds the prescribed limit.

A hospital patient may not be arrested and taken to a police station if it would prejudice his proper care and treatment.

SPECIAL PROVISIONS—DRINK/DRIVE OFFENCES

High risk offenders

Such offenders are those who are disqualified for driving while two and a half times or more over the prescribed limit; disqualified from driving for failure, without reasonable excuse, to provide a specimen for analysis under RTA 1988, s 7; and those disqualified on two or more occasions within ten years for exceeding the legal limit for alcohol in a specimen, or being unfit to drive through drink or a drug. Currently, RTA 1988, s 88 deals with exceptions to the rule that someone may not drive a vehicle on a road without having an appropriate licence. One exception is where a person has previously held such a licence and the Secretary of State has received a qualifying application for a licence. The Road Safety Act 2006 (RSA 2006), s 13 (which will amend RTA 1988, s 88 when in force) provides that this exception will not apply where a high risk offender is awaiting the outcome of medical inquiries in relation to his application for the grant of a licence following a period of disqualification.

Endorsement—failure to allow a specimen to be tested

RTOA 1988, s 45(7) is prospectively amended by RSA 2006, s 14 (when in force) so as to provide that the period of effectiveness of an endorsement for an offence of failing to allow a specimen to be subjected to a laboratory test contrary to RTA 1988, s 7A(6) will remain effective for a period of eleven years. This corrects a consequential amendment missed from PRA 2002.

Alcohol ignition interlocks

New ss 34D, 34E, 34F, 34G and 41B are prospectively inserted into the RTOA 1988 by RSA 2006, s 15. Their effect is to empower courts to allow offenders to participate, at their own expense, in an 'alcohol ignition interlock programme'. Agreement permits the court to reduce a period of disqualification. The option applies to those convicted of a second 'relevant drink driving offence' within a period of ten years who would otherwise have to be disqualified for no less that two years. The programme must last for at least twelve months but must not exceed a half of the original unreduced period of disqualification. It cannot be offered to a person who in respect of whom a drink drive offenders' rehabilitation order is made.

The programme includes educational aspects and counselling but the main feature is that the offender is restricted to driving a vehicle which is fitted with an alcohol interlock device which is designed to prevent the vehicle from being driven until an acceptable specimen of breath has been provided (9 microgrammes of alcohol in 100 mm of breath). Such devices will be approved by the Secretary of State. Offences will be committed by those who interfere with such a device and a failure to comply with a condition will result in the restoration of the full period of disqualification. Any failure will result in the issue of a 'certificate of failing fully to participate' in a programme. A recipient may appeal to the supervising court.

These programmes are experimental at present and will continue until 2010 unless extended by order.

Reduced disqualification period for attendance on course for drink/drive and other specified offences

The RTOA 1988, ss 34A, 34B and 34C are substituted and a s 34BA is added by RSA 2006, s 35 (when in force).

The principle established in relation to the drink-drive rehabilitation scheme is extended to other offences. The scheme now relates to 'relevant offences' under RTA 1988 and 'specified offences' against RTA 1988 and RTRA 1984. Relevant offences are those against RTA 1988, s 3A(1)(a), (b) and (c) (where the offence relates to alcohol); s 4 (where the offence relates to alcohol); and ss 5(1), 7(6), and 7A(6). Specified offences are not relevant for the purposes of this chapter but are those against RTA 1988, s 3 (careless or inconsiderate driving) and s 36 (failing to comply with a traffic sign); RTRA 1984, s 17(4) (speeding on special road); and s 89(1) (speeding elsewhere). Courts are empowered to reduce a period of disqualification where an offender offers to undergo a training course at his own expense, upon the successful completion of the course, by an amount specified in the order. The reduced period must be not less than three months, nor more than a quanter of the disqualification period.

The option is only available where the offender has been disqualified for not less than twelve months. It is not available to those who have committed one of these offences within the preceding three years and successfully completed an approved course in consequence of such offences, nor to a person who is within his probationary period under the Road Traffic (New Drivers) Act 1995. Any appeals against a course provider's decision not to issue a certificate may be dealt with by the court making the order or by a relevant local court.

The specified offences, and the minimum period of disqualification to make a person eligible to take a course, may be varied by order.

OTHER OFFENCES

Cycling while unfit

By RTA 1988, s 30, it is an offence to ride a bicycle or tricycle on a road or other public place while unfit to ride through drink or drugs. Being in charge of a bicycle or tricycle in such circumstances is not an offence under the RTA 1988, but it is an offence under the Licensing Act 1872, s 12, which is described in the next paragraph.

Drunk in charge of a carriage, horse etc

By the Licensing Act 1872, s 12 it is an offence for a person to be drunk while in charge on any highway or other public place of any carriage, horse, cattle or steam engine. A motor vehicle, trailer, bicycle or tricycle is a 'carriage' for this purpose, but a person liable to be charged with an offence of driving or being in charge of a motor vehicle when unfit to drive through drink or drugs should not be charged with the present offence under the 1872 Act since its maximum punishment is far less severe than that for the appropriate offence under the RTA 1988. We deal with the offence under the 1872 Act in more detail in Chapter 19, below.

Drinking—guided public transport systems and airports

The Transport and Works Act 1992 (TWA 1992), s 27 applies to transport systems which are used, or are intended to be used, wholly or partly for the carriage of members of the public. Its provisions are restricted to railways, to tramways, and to other *guided transport systems* specified by the Secretary of State. The guided transport systems at Birmingham International Airport; Merry Hill Centre, West Midlands; and Gatwick and Stanstead Airports have been so specified. The first two systems are, however, no longer in use.

The Act creates two offences involving drink or drugs on such transport systems which can be committed by the following workers:

(a) drivers, guards, conductors, signalmen and others who control or affect the movement of vehicles operating under one of these systems;
(b) persons who couple or uncouple such vehicles or check that they are working properly;
(c) persons maintaining the permanent way (or other support or guidance structures), signalling systems and power supply used by such vehicles; and
(d) supervisors of, and look-outs for, persons engaged in the functions set out in categories (b) or (c) above.

An offence is committed where:

(a) a person in one of the categories in the above list carries out his duties when unfit to carry out that work through drink or drugs;
(b) a person in one of the categories in the above list carries out his duties after consuming so much alcohol that the proportion of it in the breath, blood or urine exceeds the prescribed limit (which is the same limit as prescribed by the RTA 1988).

A constable in uniform is empowered by TWA 1992, s 29 to require a preliminary breath test where he has reasonable cause to suspect that:

(a) a person working on a transport system has alcohol in his body; or
(b) a person has been working on a transport system with alcohol in his body and still has alcohol in his body.

This power is extended to circumstances in which there has been an *accident or dangerous incident* and a constable in uniform has reasonable cause to suspect that, at the time of that event, the person was working in one of the above capacities and that his act, or omission, while so working, may have been the cause of the accident or incident. A 'dangerous incident' means an incident which, in the constable's opinion, involved a danger of death or personal injury. Failure without reasonable excuse to comply with the request is an offence.

Similar powers to those under the RTA 1988 are provided by TWA 1992, ss 30 to 34 in relation to arrest and entry, the provision of specimens for analysis, the option to have a breath specimen replaced if the alcohol content in it does not exceed 50 microgrammes in 100 ml of breath, failure to comply with a request, hospital patients and the use of specimens in proceedings. There is, of course, no power of disqualification from driving. However, the consent of the Secretary of State or the Director of Public Prosecutions, is required before proceedings for such offences may be instituted.

The evidential provisions of the RTOA 1988 in relation to such offences are repeated in this Act, and so are the provisions about specimens without consent.

These provisions are important to all police officers. Following a train crash, it is the first police officer on the scene who will be expected to require a screening breath test if it applies.

Persons involved in shipping or aviation: alcohol and drugs

Although, like the provisions just discussed, these matters are not concerned with the subject 'drinking and driving' they are outlined here as a matter of convenience. Police officers on duty at ports and airports may be required to act under powers provided by the RTSA 2003 which are related to the consumption of alcohol or drugs by those involved in marine or aviation activities.

Persons involved in marine activities

RTSA 2003, s 78 provides that a professional master of a ship, a professional pilot of a ship, or a professional seaman while on duty on a ship, commits an offence if his ability to carry out his duties is impaired because of drink or drugs. He also commits an offence if the proportion of alcohol in his breath, blood or urine exceeds the prescribed limit. A master, pilot or seaman is 'professional' if (and only if) he is so acting as a master, pilot or seaman in the course of a business or employment.

By s 79, a professional seaman in a ship who is off duty but who in the event of an emergency would or might be required by the nature or terms of his engagement or employment to take action to protect the safety of passengers commits an offence if his ability to take such action is impaired because of drink or drugs, or the proportion of alcohol in his breath, blood or urine exceeds the prescribed limit.

By s 80, non-professionals on board a ship under way, who are exercising or purporting to exercise a navigational function, may commit the same offences.

The 'prescribed limit' in all of these cases is the same as that provided by the RTA 1988. The appropriate powers under the RTA 1988 to administer preliminary tests, to obtain specimens for analysis under s 7 and 7A, choice of specimen and protection for a hospital patient are applied with modifications to these circumstances, together with the provisions of the RTOA 1988 in relation to the use of specimens and documentary evidence.

A marine official is empowered to detain a ship if he reasonably suspects that a person on board is committing, or has committed, an offence under RTSA 2003, ss 78 to 80, provided that before doing so, or as soon as possible after doing so, he requests the presence of a constable.

Police powers   Unless the person concerned is a patient at a hospital, a constable may arrest a person without warrant if he reasonably suspects that the person is committing an offence under RTSA 2003, ss 78 to 80 or has committed such an offence and is still under the influence of drink or drugs.

A constable in uniform may board a ship, or enter any place, if he reasonably suspects that he may wish to exercise a power under s 83 (to obtain specimens) or s 85 (to arrest) in respect of a person who may be on that ship, or in that place. He may use reasonable force to board or enter and may be accompanied by one or more persons.

Persons involved in aviation activities

RTSA 2003, s 92 provides that a person commits an offence if he performs an aviation function at a time when his ability to perform the function is impaired because of drink or drugs, or if he carries out an activity which is ancillary to an aviation function at a time when his ability to perform the function is impaired because of drink or drugs. An 'aviation function' for the purposes of the RTSA 2003 is any of the following (and only any of the following):

(a) acting as a pilot, flight navigator, flight engineer, radio-telephony engineer of an aircraft during flight;

(b) acting as a member of the cabin crew of an aircraft during flight;

(c) attending the flight deck during flight to give or supervise training, to administer a test, to observe practice, or to monitor or record the gaining of experience;

(d) acting as a licensed air traffic controller (other than a licensed student); or

(e) acting as a licensed aircraft maintenance engineer.

An 'ancillary function' means an activity ancillary to an 'aviation function' which is undertaken by a person who has reported for a period of duty in respect of the function, and is carried out as a requirement of, for the purpose of or in connection with the performance of, the function during that period. A person who, in accordance with the terms of an employment or undertaking, holds himself ready to perform an aviation function if called upon to do so is to be regarded as carrying out an activity ancillary to the function.

By RTSA 2003, s 93, it is an offence for a person to perform an aviation function or a function which is ancillary to an aviation function at a time when the proportion of alcohol in his breath, blood or urine exceeds the prescribed limit. The prescribed limit in relation to 'aviation functions' is:

(a) in the case of breath, 9 microgrammes of alcohol in 100 ml;
(b) in the case of blood, 20 milligrammes of alcohol in 100 ml; and
(c) in the case of urine, 27 milligrammes of alcohol in 100 ml.

This limit does not, however, apply in respect of a licensed aircraft maintenance engineer. In that case the higher limits which apply to motor vehicle drivers, those involved in guided transport systems and those on ships apply.

The appropriate powers under RTA 1988 to administer preliminary tests, to obtain specimens for analysis under s 7 and 7A, choice of specimen and protection for a hospital patient are applied with modifications to these circumstances, together with the provisions of RTOA 1988 in relation to the use of specimens and documentary evidence.

Police powers Unless the person concerned is a patient at a hospital, a constable may arrest a person without warrant if he reasonably suspects that that person is committing such an offence or has committed such an offence and is still under the influence of drink or drugs.

A constable in uniform may board an aircraft, or enter any place, if he reasonably suspects that he may wish to exercise a power under s 96 (to obtain a specimen) or 97 (to arrest) on the aircraft, or in that place. For the purpose of boarding an aircraft or entering a place a constable may use reasonable force and may be accompanied by one or more persons.

CHAPTER 18
Children and young persons

The various statutes dealing with children and young persons are partly concerned with punishing adults, particularly those under a duty to care for a child or young person, whose conduct is physically or mentally harmful to him or otherwise harmful to his proper development. They are also concerned with the responsibilities of local authorities to receive a child or young person into their care, with the power of family proceedings courts to put a child or young person into care, when this is necessary on specified grounds for his welfare, and with the power of a court to make a child safety order or parenting order.

MEANING OF TERMS

Various terms are used in the relevant legislation with particular meanings. The most common of these terms are:

Child

For most legal purposes of relevance to a police officer, a child is a person under the age of fourteen years. However, there are occasions when the term is used in relation to persons who are fourteen or over. For example, the Education Act 1996 defines 'child' for the purposes of the legislation relating to child employment as meaning any person not over compulsory school age. In the legislation referred to below relating to street trading and performances abroad a 'child' means someone under the age of eighteen, and the same is the case in enactments dealing with the responsibilities of a local authority in relation to the welfare of children under the Children Act 1989 (ChA 1989).

For the purposes of law, a person attains an age on the relevant anniversary of his birth. The Children and Young Persons Act 1933 (CYPA 1933), s 99 states that when a person is brought before a court, other than as a witness, the issue of whether or not he is a child or young person must be decided upon inquiry by the court as to the age of the person. If it is later found that the age was different from that established by the court, any judgment or order will not be invalidated.

Young person

For the purpose of the Children and Young Persons Acts 1933 and 1969, in which the term is frequently used, a 'young person' is a person who has attained the age of fourteen years and is under the age of eighteen years.

Guardian

This term, for the purposes of the Children and Young Persons Acts, includes any person who, in the opinion of the court having cognisance of any case in relation to the child or young person or in which the child or young person is concerned, has for the time being the care of the child or young person.

The term is therefore wide in application, since it covers any person who, at the relevant time, appears to the court to be in charge or in control of a child or young person.

Generally, the Children and Young Persons Acts are concerned with 'guardians' in the wide sense just described rather than in the narrower sense of 'legal guardian'. A 'legal guardian' is a person appointed to have parental responsibility by a signed and witnessed document (including a will) or by order of a court.

RESPONSIBILITIES OF PARENT OR GUARDIAN

By CYPA 1933, s 34A where a child or young person is charged with an offence or is, for any other reason, brought before a court, the court may in any case, and must in the case of a child or young person who is under sixteen, require a person who is the parent or guardian to attend court during all stages of the proceedings, unless and to the extent that the court is satisfied that it would be unreasonable to require such attendance. 'Parent or guardian' in this context includes a local authority which has parental responsibility for a child or young person, and which has him in its care, or in accommodation which it provides under ChA 1989.

Where a child or young person under sixteen is convicted of an offence, the court is obliged by the Powers of Criminal Courts (Sentencing) Act 2000, s 137 to order that a fine, costs or compensation be paid by the parent or guardian (or where a child is in its care or accommodated by it, a local authority with parental responsibility), unless the court is satisfied that such parent or guardian cannot be found, or it would be unreasonable to make an order for payment, having regard to the circumstances of the case. In the case of a person of sixteen or more, the court may make such an order. These provisions also apply to circumstances in which such fines result from failure to comply with a community order.

The Powers of Criminal Courts (Sentencing) Act 2000, s 150 empowers a court, where a child or young person is convicted of an offence, to order a parent or guardian to enter into a recognisance to take proper care of him and to exercise proper control over him. A parent or guardian must consent to the making of such an order. If he refuses and the court considers his refusal unreasonable, it may order him to pay a fine not exceeding £1,000. Where the child or young person is under sixteen, it is the duty of the court to exercise these powers where it is satisfied, having regard to the circumstances of the case, that it is desirable in the interests of preventing him from committing further offences to do so. Where it does not exercise these powers, it must state in open court that it is not so satisfied and give its reasons for so finding.

Such a recognisance may be in a sum not exceeding £1,000 and be for a period not exceeding three years. The order must not extend beyond the date upon which the person becomes eighteen.

Such orders may not be made in respect of the binding over of a parent or guardian where a referral order is made under the Youth Justice and Criminal Evidence Act 1999.

Where a court has passed a community sentence it may include in such a recognisance a condition that the minor's parent or guardian ensures that the minor complies with the requirements of that sentence.

OFFENCES OF CRUELTY

There is much concern in society today about what has become labelled as 'child abuse'. Responsibilities are placed upon social agencies by various Acts of Parliament and this has had the effect of relieving the police of some of their burdens. The circumstances which are embraced by the abstract term 'child abuse' are dealt with by the offences of cruelty towards children and young persons which are governed by CYPA 1933, s 1. CYPA 1933, s 1 provides that a person who has attained the age of sixteen years and has the responsibility for any child or young person under that age commits an offence, if he wilfully assaults, ill-treats, neglects, abandons or exposes him, or causes or procures him to be assaulted, ill-treated, neglected, abandoned, or exposed, in a manner likely to cause him unnecessary suffering or injury to health.

There is much in CYPA 1933, s 1 which requires explanation and it is necessary to break it up for this purpose. In the first instance we will extract from the section the reference to 'or causes or procures etc' and bear in mind that each of the particular offences which we discuss below is equally committed by those who have the responsibility for a child or young person if they cause or procure the commission of these offences by someone else.

Responsibility for a child

For a person to be guilty of an offence contrary to CYPA 1933, s 1, he or she must have attained the age of sixteen years and have the responsibility for the child or young person under that age.

In this context a person is presumed to have responsibility for a child or young person if:

(a) he has parental responsibility for him under ChA 1989 (which the mother and father will both have if they were married to each other when the child or young person was born, or which only the mother will have if the mother and father were not so married, or which another person (including the father in the instance just given) or a local authority may acquire by operation of law); or

(b) he is otherwise liable to maintain him; or
(c) he has care of him.

The basic elements of the offence

CYPA 1933, s 1 specifies several ways in which an offence of cruelty can be committed by a person (of sixteen or over) with responsibility for a child or young person. It specifies the following, each of which must occur wilfully:

(a) assaulting;
(b) ill-treating;
(c) neglecting;
(d) abandoning; or
(e) exposing,

a child or young person under sixteen years in a manner likely to cause him unnecessary suffering or injury to health (including injury to or loss of sight, or hearing, or limbs or organs of the body, and any mental derangement).

CYPA 1933, s 1 does not prevent a parent, or other person with the right to do so, administering punishment to a child or young person. As we explain in Chapter 28, the right to administer corporal punishment is now very limited.

Wilfully

'Wilfully' makes it clear that any offence under CYPA 1933, s 1 requires mens rea on the part of the accused. For example, on a charge of wilfully neglecting there must be an element of mens rea as to the risk of unnecessary suffering or injury to health resulting from the neglect, and if (to continue the example) that charge involves failure to provide adequate medical aid, the requirement of wilfulness can only be satisfied where the accused was aware that the child's health might be at risk if he was not provided with medical aid or where his non-awareness of this risk was due to his not caring whether the child's health was at risk or not.

Assault

'Assault' for the purpose of CYPA 1933, s 1 requires more than a mere common assault or battery. An assault or battery may amount to no more than frightening a person or giving him a light slap, but this could hardly be done 'in a manner likely to cause unnecessary suffering or injury to health'. Although consent could be an issue in some minor assaults, it must be remembered that mere submission, particularly in the case of children, to a person in authority does not signify consent.

Ill-treat

The term signifies a continuous course of conduct leading to unnecessary suffering. A series of assaults each of which, if considered on its own, would not amount to an offence against the section, might together form ill-treatment over a period of time. Likewise, persistent frightening or bullying will suffice if it is likely to cause unnecessary suffering.

Neglect

The term signifies a want of adequate care. The likelihood of causing unnecessary suffering or injury to health can be caused by a deliberate omission to supply medical or surgical aid. Direct proof of such likelihood is not always strictly necessary as this may be inferred from the evidence of neglect and its actual effect. The section provides that a parent or other person legally liable to maintain a child or young person or his legal guardian is deemed to have neglected him in a manner likely to cause injury to health if he has failed to provide adequate food, clothing, medical aid or lodging for him or if, having been unable to provide such food, clothing, medical aid or lodging, he has failed to take steps to procure it to be provided under the enactments applicable in that behalf.

CYPA 1933, s 1 also declares that if the death of an infant under three years of age is caused by suffocation (other than by disease or a foreign body in the throat) while the infant was in bed with a person over sixteen who went to bed under the influence of drink, that person will be deemed to have neglected the infant in a manner likely to cause injury to health.

Abandon or expose

It is helpful to consider these terms together since an abandonment frequently leads to exposure. To abandon a child means leaving it to its fate. If a woman, who is living apart from her husband, takes her child to her husband's home and leaves the child at his door, she abandons that child. From the moment of abandonment the child is exposed and, if that exposure leads to suffering, the child has been abandoned and exposed in a manner likely to cause unnecessary suffering. It is also interesting to consider the position of the husband. If he is aware that the child has been left on his doorstep, then, as he cannot disclaim his custodial responsibilities, he also abandons and exposes the child by allowing it to remain there. This exposure does not cover exposure to risk. A father, who took his son and other boys on to a baulk of timber and floated the timber into deep water in London Docks, was not guilty of an offence under this section, because this was not the type of exposure to which the section refers.

Police action in cruelty cases

It is now standard procedure to refer reports of cruelty to children to officers of the National Society for the Prevention of Cruelty to Children (NSPCC). If the Society's investigations reveal evidence to suggest that criminal proceedings are desirable, the Society is empowered, as are the police, to initiate proceedings. However, the Society does attempt, through a process of encouragement, persuasion and warnings, to remedy the situation without recourse to the law whenever possible. The Society has set out the following advice to its branch secretaries:

(1) It is for the Society to decide whether to institute proceedings in any case in which its officers are involved, subject always to any action which the police may consider it necessary to take.
(2) If the Society is considering action, the issue of whether or not the case is one which should be prosecuted under the Offences Against the Person Act 1861 (Chapter 28 below) should be considered first. If the Society decides that this might be the case, it should be referred to the police.
(3) If the police then decide not to prosecute for an offence contrary to the Offences Against the Person Act 1861 they will return it to the Society for prosecution under CYPA 1933, s 1.
(4) The Society, when prosecuting under CYPA 1933, s 1, should bear in mind the advisability in serious cases of asking the magistrates' court to consider committing for trial in the Crown Court.

In all cases of non-accidental injury to children the police are likely to become involved at the outset when fulfilling their role as one of the emergency services. Local authorities, social services, the NSPCC and the police have the power to initiate any civil proceedings before a family proceedings court when a child appears to be in need of care. The police have power to detain children who appear to be in need of care and to take them to safe places. We deal with these matters later in this chapter. Police officers must never feel that the other social agencies have assumed responsibility for these matters. It is still the duty of the police to take some initial action to ensure the safety of any child in circumstances where a report of child abuse is received. Such cases may, in appropriate circumstances, later be referred to other agencies.

OTHER OFFENCES

There are a number of offences under CYPA 1933 which require little explanation. These offences are committed in relation to children of a specified age, which varies from offence to offence.

Brothels

By CYPA 1933, s 3, it is an offence for any person of sixteen years or more who has responsibility for a child or young person who has attained the age of four years, but is under sixteen, to allow that child or young person to reside in or frequent a brothel. What is and what is not a brothel is discussed in Chapter 35, below. It is important to remember that a woman who is a prostitute and receives men in her own room, but does not allow other women to use her room, is not keeping a brothel. This is the most likely situation to come to the notice of the police. Although an offence is not committed in these circumstances, care proceedings (see later) could perhaps be considered (as they should in the case of a brothel).

Begging

Causing or procuring a child or young person under sixteen to be in any street, premises or place for the purpose of begging or receiving alms, or of inducing the giving of alms (whether or not there is any pretence of singing, playing, performing, offering anything for sale or otherwise), is an offence contrary to CYPA 1933, s 4. There is a similar offence under the Vagrancy Act 1824, s 3.

It is also an offence under CYPA 1933, s 4 for the person having the responsibility for such a child or young person to allow him so to act. Such a person allows a child or young person to beg in the street if he fails to prevent it when he could and should have prevented it.

If it is proved that a child or young person was in a street etc for the purpose of begging etc and that a person with responsibility for him allowed him to be in the street etc, that person is presumed to have allowed him to be there for that purpose, until the contrary is proved.

Intoxicating liquor

It is an offence, contrary to CYPA 1933, s 5, to give, or cause to be given, intoxicating liquor to a child under the age of five years, otherwise than on the orders of a duly qualified medical practitioner or in a medical emergency. This is an offence for which a prosecution is improbable within modern society.

Tobacco

By CYPA 1933, s 7, it is an offence to sell tobacco or cigarette papers to any person under the age of sixteen, whether for his own use or not. 'Tobacco' includes cigarettes and any product containing tobacco intended for oral or nasal use, and smoking mixtures intended as a substitute for tobacco. Selling tobacco to a person under the age of sixteen is an offence of strict liability. The proprietor of a shop is guilty even when he has played no part in the transaction and knows nothing about it. However, s 7 provides that it is a defence for an accused to prove that he took all reasonable precautions and exercised all due diligence to avoid the commission of an offence. The fact that all possible precautions have not been taken does not rule out the application of this defence. This was held in a case where justices found that staff had been provided with written instructions setting out a procedure to be followed when in doubt about a customer's age, such procedures being regularly reviewed and supervised. A divisional court ruled that the justices were entitled to find that this defence had been made out, even though there were other things which the shop proprietor could have done to try to prevent the commission of the offence.

The general use of cigarette machines has led to a situation in which it is difficult to prevent cigarettes from falling into the hands of young people. If it is proved that a machine is being extensively used by persons under sixteen, a magistrates' court must order the owner to take precautions to prevent such use or, if necessary, to remove the machine. Failure to comply with such an order is an offence. CYPA 1933, s 7 places responsibilities upon constables and uniformed park keepers to seize tobacco or cigarette papers from a person apparently under sixteen whom they find smoking in any street or public place. These articles will then be disposed of by the appropriate authorities.

None of the above provisions about sale to a child applies to a child who is an employee of a tobacconist or a uniformed messenger employed by a messenger company.

The Children and Young Persons (Protection from Tobacco) Act 1991 prohibits the sale to anyone of unpacked (ie unpackaged) cigarettes by a person carrying on a retail business. It also requires notices to be placed on retail premises and machines concerning the illegality of tobacco sales to persons under sixteen.

Risk of burning

If a person of or over sixteen, having responsibility for a child under twelve, allows the child to be in a room containing an open fire grate or any heating appliance liable to cause injury to a person by contact with it and it is not sufficiently guarded against the risk of the child being burnt or scalded and in consequence the child is killed or seriously injured, he commits an offence contrary to CYPA 1933, s 11.

It will be noted that death or serious injury must result from the unguarded fire or appliance and it is almost certain that civil proceedings for a 'care order' (see later) would result from any incident likely to be charged as an offence under this section, which is punishable only by a fine.

The section does go on to say that any proceedings taken summarily under the section will not affect a person's liability to be proceeded against for any indictable offence. For example, if a child died as a result of his injuries it is probable that proceedings on indictment for manslaughter would follow.

Safety at entertainments

CYPA 1933, s 12 provides that, wherever an entertainment is provided in a building for an audience mainly of children, then, if there are more than a hundred children attending the entertainment, there must be a sufficient number of adult attendants, properly stationed and instructed in their duties, to prevent more people being admitted than can properly be accommodated and to control the movement of those entering and leaving and general safety. If these provisions are not complied with, the person providing the entertainment is guilty of an offence. A constable may enter any building in which he has reason to believe that such an entertainment is taking place, or is about to take place, to ensure that this is being done. The section does not apply to any entertainment in a dwelling house.

EMPLOYMENT

CYPA 1933, s 18 restricts the employment of children and young persons in many circumstances. It provides that no child or young person under compulsory school age shall be employed:

(a) under fourteen to do any work;
(b) to do any work other than light work;
(c) before the close of school hours on school days;
(d) before 7 am or after 7 pm on any day;
(e) for more than two hours on a school day or a Sunday;
(f) for more than twelve hours in any week in which he is required to attend school;

(g) for more than eight hours or, if he is under the age of fifteen years, for more than five hours in any day:
   (i) on which he is not required to attend school; and
   (ii) which is not a Sunday;
(h) for more than thirty-five hours or, if he is under the age of fifteen years, for more than twenty-five hours in any week in which he is not required to attend school;
(i) for more than four hours in any day without a rest break of one hour; or
(j) at any time in a year unless at that time he has had, or could still have, during a period in the year in which he is not required to attend school, at least two consecutive weeks without employment.

Breach of this provision renders the employer guilty of an offence, as well as any other person (other than the child or young person employed) to whose act or default the breach is attributable. However, if the employer is prosecuted, he has a defence if he proves that the contravention was due to the act or default of a third party (who has been brought before the court) and that he (the employer) has used all due diligence to comply with the above provisions. However, where the offence is against the provisions set out at (i) above the proviso does not apply, but it is a defence for him to prove that he used all due diligence to secure that the provisions were complied with.

Section 18 also empowers local authorities to make byelaws concerning the employment of children. In particular, such byelaws may authorise:

(a) the employment on an occasional basis of children aged thirteen by their parents or guardians in light agricultural or horticultural duties;
(b) the employment of children aged thirteen (notwithstanding what is said above) in categories of light work specified in the byelaw; or
(c) the employment of children or young persons for one hour before school on a day on which school is open (which is important in relation to the employment of children on newsrounds).

'Light work' in s 18 is defined as work which, on account of the inherent nature of the tasks which it involves and the particular conditions under which they are performed, is not likely to be harmful to the safety, health or development of children, and is not such as to be harmful to their attendance at school or to their participation in work experience, or their capacity to benefit from the instruction received or, as the case may be, the experience gained.

Street trading

CYPA 1933, s 20 provides that no child shall engage in, or be employed in, street trading. If there is a breach of this provision, the same rules apply as apply in the event of a breach of s 18 (see above). By way of exception, byelaws made by a local authority may permit children who have attained the age of fourteen to be employed by their parents in street trading; such parents must be authorised in writing. Byelaws must specify the days and hours during which, and the places at which, such children may engage or be employed in street trading.

Dangerous performances

By CYPA 1933, s 23, no person aged sixteen years or under may take part in any performance in which his life or limbs are endangered without a local authority licence. Anyone who causes or procures this to be done, or a parent or guardian who allows it, is guilty of an offence. A chief officer of police must authorise proceedings in such cases. The types of performance referred to are those in respect of which a charge is made, or which take place in licensed premises or registered clubs, or which are live or recorded broadcast performances or performances filmed for public exhibition.

Training for dangerous performances

By CYPA 1933, s 24, no person under twelve shall be trained to take part in any dangerous performance, and no one between twelve and eighteen shall be so trained except in accordance with the terms of a local authority licence. Every person who causes or procures a person, or being his parent or guardian allows him, to be so trained is guilty of an offence.

Performances abroad

CYPA 1933, s 25 provides that no person having the responsibility for any child under eighteen may allow him, nor may any person cause or procure such a child, to go abroad:

(a) for the purpose of singing, playing, performing or being exhibited for profit; or
(b) for the purpose of taking part in sport, or working as a model, where payment in respect of his doing so, other than defraying expenses, is made to him or to another person,

unless a licence has been granted. Such licences can only be granted by a justice of the peace and can only be granted in respect of children of fourteen or more. A person who contravenes these provisions commits an offence.

LOCAL AUTHORITY CARE

The ChA 1989 makes various provisions for children to be brought into the care of a local authority (ie the council of a county (including a unitary authority) or a metropolitan district or London borough council (in England) or a county or county borough council (in Wales)). For the purposes of these provisions, a 'child' is a person under eighteen, unless otherwise stated. The Act is extremely comprehensive and emphasises that the child's welfare is paramount in all matters particularly those concerned with his upbringing, and that delay in deciding such matters is likely to prejudice the child's welfare. The guiding principle of the Act is that the court should not make an order unless to do so is considered better for the child than making no order. Most of the Act's provisions relate to the functions of local authorities and the social service agencies. Those matters which most directly affect the police are considered below. ChA 1989, s 21 requires local authorities to make provisions for the reception and accommodation of children, including a child who is in police protection (see below). A child whom a custody officer has authorised to be kept in police detention after arrest must be received by a local authority where that officer so requests.

Care and supervision orders

ChA 1989, s 31 provides that, on the application of a local authority or authorised person (NSPCC or other body authorised by the Secretary of State), a family proceedings court (ie that part of a magistrates' court hearing proceedings under the 1989 Act) may make an order:

(a) placing the child with respect to whom the application is made in the care of a designated local authority; or
(b) putting him under the supervision of a designated local authority or of a probation officer.

A court may only make a care or supervision order if it is satisfied:

(a) that the child concerned is suffering, or is likely to suffer, significant harm; and
(b) that the harm, or likelihood of harm, is attributable to:
  (i) the care given to the child, or likely to be given to him if the order were not made, not being what it would be reasonable to expect a parent to give him; or
  (ii) the child being beyond parental control.

'Harm' means ill-treatment or the impairment of health or development, including, for example, impairment suffered from seeing or hearing the ill-treatment of another.

Such an order may not be made with respect to a child who has reached the age of seventeen (or sixteen in the case of a child who is married). A care order may not be made until the court has considered a care plan. On an application for a care order the court may make a supervision order, and vice versa.

As can be seen, where a child has been the victim of offences of cruelty or sexual abuse or neglect, an application may be made by a local authority or an authorised person for either of the above orders to be made. In addition, the provisions at (b)(ii), above, provide a means of obtaining a care order in circumstances in which a child who is below the age of criminal responsibility (ten) habitually commits a crime, or where a child receives adequate care from his parents but is so out of control that he is likely to harm himself.

Child assessment orders

ChA 1989, s 43 permits a local authority or authorised person to apply to the High Court, a county court, or a magistrates' court sitting as a family proceedings court for such an order where difficulties are being experienced in making an assessment of the needs of such a child. This may be due to lack of co-operation by those who have parental responsibility for the child. Such an order permits assessment to be made over a period not exceeding seven days and may require any person to produce the child to a person named in the order and to comply with specified instructions. However, a court should not make such an order if it is satisfied that there are grounds for making an emergency protection order and that it ought to do so rather than make a child assessment order.

Emergency protection order

There will be occasions upon which action must be taken immediately to protect a child. ChA 1989, s 44 empowers the High Court, a county court or a magistrates' court sitting as a family proceedings court, on the application of any person, to make an emergency order for the protection of a child. It may do so if it is satisfied that:

(a) there is reasonable cause to believe that the child is likely to suffer significant harm if:
  (i) he is not removed to accommodation provided by or on behalf of the applicant; or
  (ii) he does not remain in the place in which he is then being accommodated;
(b) in the case of an application made by a local authority:
  (i) inquiries are being made with respect to the child under the authority's duty to investigate where a child is suffering, or is likely to suffer, significant harm; and
  (ii) these inquiries are being frustrated by access to the child being unreasonably refused to a person authorised to seek access and that the applicant has reasonable cause to believe that access to the child is required as a matter of urgency; or
(c) in the case of an application made by an authorised person:
  (i) the applicant has reasonable cause to suspect that the child is suffering, or is likely to suffer, significant harm;
  (ii) the applicant is making inquiries with respect to the child's welfare; and
  (iii) those inquiries are being frustrated by access to the child being unreasonably refused to a person authorised to seek access and the applicant has reasonable cause to believe that access to the child is required as a matter of urgency.

An emergency protection order directs a person to produce a child and authorises the child's removal to accommodation provided by or on behalf of the applicant or the prevention of the removal of the child from a hospital or other place. It also gives the applicant parental responsibility for the child. An emergency protection order has effect for such period, not exceeding eight days, as is specified by the court, but the court has power (on one occasion only) to extend it for up to a further seven days. An emergency protection order can include an exclusion requirement in specified circumstances. Such a requirement enables the child to stay in its home by excluding someone else, such as a suspected child abuser, from it.

Where a police officer knows that an emergency protection order is in force in respect of a child, he should not exercise the power of removal under ChA 1989, s 46, unless there are compelling reasons to do so.

Removal and accommodation of children by police in emergencies

ChA 1989, s 46 empowers police officers to take a child into 'police protection' in prescribed circumstances. It also places responsibilities upon 'designated police officers', that is officers designated by chief officers of police to conduct inquiries into such cases.

Where a constable has reasonable cause to believe that a child would otherwise be likely to suffer significant harm, he may:

(a) remove the child to suitable accommodation and keep him there; or
(b) take such steps as are reasonable to ensure that the child's removal from any hospital, or other place, in which he is then being accommodated is prevented.

As soon as is reasonably practicable after taking a child into police protection, as above, the constable must:

(a) inform the local authority within whose area the child was found of the steps that have been, or are proposed to be, taken with respect to the child and the reasons for taking them;
(b) give details to the local authority within whose area the child is ordinarily resident ('the appropriate authority') of the place at which the child is being accommodated;
(c) inform the child (if he appears capable of understanding):
    (i) of the steps that have been taken with respect to him and of the reasons for taking them; and
    (ii) of the further steps which may be taken with respect to him under this section;
(d) take such steps as are reasonably practicable to discover the wishes and feelings of the child;
(e) secure that the case is inquired into by a designated officer; and
(f) where the child was taken into police protection by being removed to accommodation which is not provided:
    (i) by or on behalf of a local authority; or
    (ii) as a refuge (ie a voluntary home or registered children's home certified as a refuge);

secure that he is moved to accommodation which is so provided.

The constable must also, as soon as reasonably practicable, inform:

(a) the child's parents;
(b) every person who is not a parent of his but who has parental responsibility for him; and
(c) any other person with whom the child was living immediately before being taken into police protection,

of the steps that he has taken under s 46 with respect to the child, the reasons for taking them and the further steps that may be taken with respect to him under the section.

When the case has been inquired into by the designated officer, he must release the child from police protection unless he considers that there is still reasonable cause for believing that the child would be likely to suffer significant harm if released.

No child may be kept in police protection for more than seventy-two hours. However, at any time while the child is in police protection, the designated officer may apply *on behalf of the appropriate local authority* for an emergency protection order to be made with respect to the child. Such an application may be made whether or not the local authority knows of it or agrees to its being made.

Whilst a child is in police protection, the designated officer must do what is reasonable in all the circumstances of the case for the purpose of safeguarding or promoting the child's welfare (having regard in particular to the length of the period during which the child will be so protected).

The designated officer must allow:

(a) parents;
(b) any other person with parental responsibility;
(c) any person with whom the child was living immediately before he was taken into police protection;
(d) where there is a 'contact order' (an order permitting contact by named persons), any such named person; and
(e) any person acting on behalf of any of these persons,

to have such contact (if any) with the child as, in the opinion of the designated officer, is both reasonable and in the child's best interest. However, if a child who has been taken into police protection is in accommodation provided by, or on behalf of, the appropriate authority, these contact responsibilities are those of the authority rather than the designated officer.

Abduction of children in care etc

It is an offence against ChA 1989, s 49, for any person, knowingly and without lawful authority or reasonable excuse, to take a child to whom the section applies from the responsible person, or to keep such a child away from the responsible person, or to induce or assist or incite such a child to run away or stay away from the responsible person. The offences apply to a child who is in care, the subject of an emergency protection order, or in police protection. A 'responsible person' means any person who for the time being has care of him by virtue of a care order, emergency protection order, or the provisions of ChA 1989, s 46 (accommodation of children by police in emergencies).

Where such abduction has occurred, ChA 1989, s 50 permits a court to issue a 'recovery order'.

Police powers

An emergency protection order may include a requirement directed to a person to disclose the whereabouts of the child and may authorise an applicant to enter premises specified by the order and search for the child. Such a warrant may authorise a constable to assist an applicant where entry is being, or is likely to be, denied. It may also direct that a constable be accompanied by a registered medical practitioner, registered nurse or registered health visitor.

If a child or young person is absent without the consent of the responsible person:

(a) from a place of safety to which he has been taken under the Powers of Criminal Courts (Sentencing) Act 2000 (supervised person arrested on warrant and so placed);
(b) from local authority accommodation in which he was required to live as a condition of a supervision order; or

(c) from accommodation to which he had been remanded by a court either awaiting trial for an offence, or having been convicted of such an offence,

CYPA 1969, s 32 authorises a constable to arrest such a child or young person without a warrant. When so arrested he must be conducted to a place of safety, local authority accommodation, or such other place as the responsible person may direct.

Arrest of young offenders in breach of remand conditions

CYPA 1969, s 23A provides that a constable may arrest without warrant a young offender who has been remanded or committed to local authority accommodation in respect of any breach of a condition of that remand or committal if the constable has reasonable grounds for suspecting that the offender has broken any of those conditions.

The arrested person must be brought before a justice as soon as is practicable and in any event within twenty-four hours of his arrest (unless due to appear before a court within twenty-four hours of his arrest, for example, where he is on remand). In reckoning any period of twenty-four hours, no account shall be taken of Christmas Day, Good Friday or any Sunday.

Section 23B provides that where a court remands on bail a person aged ten or eleven who has been charged with or has been convicted of a serious offence (ie one punishable in the case of an adult with imprisonment for a term of two years or more), or who in the court's opinion is a persistent offender, the court may order the local authority to make an oral or written report specifying where the person is likely to be placed or maintained if he is further remanded to local authority accommodation. The order must specify the period (which must not be more than seven working days) within which the local authority must report; 'working days' do not include weekends and bank holidays, Christmas Day or Good Friday.

Parental compensation orders

The Serious Organised Crime and Police Act 2005, s 144 and Sch 10, which are only in force in specified areas at the time of writing, amend CDA 1998 by inserting s 13A which provides for a 'parental compensation order' to be made by a magistrates' court, on the application of a local authority, where the court is satisfied to the civil standard of proof (1) that a child under the age of ten has taken, or caused loss or damage to, property in the course of committing an act which would have been criminal if he had been ten or over or in the course of acting in a manner that caused or was likely to cause harassment, alarm or distress to someone of a different household, and (2) that the making of the order is desirable in the interests of preventing a repetition of the behaviour in question.

LOCAL CHILD CURFEW SCHEMES

The Crime and Disorder Act 1998 (CDA 1998), s 14 provides powers for local authorities and chief officers of police to set up local child curfew schemes for children under sixteen.

A local child curfew scheme is a scheme made by a local authority or a chief officer of police which enables the authority or chief officer to give a notice imposing, for a specified period, a ban on children of specified ages (under sixteen) being in a public place within a specified area:

(a) during specified hours (between 9 pm and 6 am);
(b) and otherwise than under the effective control of a parent (of whatever age) or of a responsible person aged eighteen or over.

The following local authorities may make a curfew scheme: the council of a district (or the equivalent, such as a unitary authority, or a London borough council) (in England) or a county or county borough council (in Wales). A 'public place' means 'any highway and any place to which at the material time the public or any section of the public has access, on payment or otherwise, as of right or by virtue of express or implied permission'. Streets, shops, the communal areas of blocks of flats, shopping centres, local authority parks and recreation grounds, and amusement arcades, all fall within this definition.

Before making a scheme, a local authority must consult:

(a) every chief officer of police any part of whose area lies within its area; and
(b) such other persons or bodies as it thinks appropriate, such as social services departments, voluntary agencies and the local community (eg residents groups).

Likewise, before making a scheme, a chief officer of police must consult:

(a) every local authority any part of whose area lies within the area to be specified; and
(b) such other persons or bodies as he considers appropriate.

A scheme does not have effect until confirmed by the Secretary of State.

Curfew notice

A local authority or chief officer of police may only give a notice imposing a curfew (a curfew notice):

(a) subject to and in accordance with the provisions of the local curfew scheme; and
(b) if, after such consultation as is required by the scheme, the authority considers it necessary for the purpose of maintaining order.

A curfew notice given under a curfew scheme may specify different hours in relation to children of different ages.

A curfew notice is required to be given:

(a) by posting it in some conspicuous place or places within the specified area; and
(b) in such other manner, if any, as appears to the local authority or chief officer of police (as the case may be) to be desirable for giving publicity to the notice.

The maximum duration of a curfew which may be specified by a curfew notice is ninety days. If the local authority wants an extension beyond the specified period it will have to consult again and go through the rest of the procedure set out above.

Contravention

CDA 1998, s 15 provides that, where a police officer has reasonable cause to believe that a child is in a public place, unaccompanied, in contravention of a ban imposed by a curfew notice, the officer may remove the child to the child's place of residence unless he has reasonable cause to believe that the child would, if removed there, be likely to suffer significant harm. The officer is not required to be in uniform.

It may be noted that there is no requirement to take the child home. The decision whether or not to do so is left to the police officer. In making that decision, the officer must also answer the question whether there is reasonable cause to believe that taking the child home would expose the child to the likelihood of suffering significant harm. This is the same question as has to be asked by a police officer before exercising the power under ChA 1989, s 46 (above) to remove a child to suitable accommodation.

The officer will normally have knowledge of the area; he may know the child's family and home circumstances. If, for example, he knows that there is a history of child abuse or neglect, he may well conclude that he should not take the child home because there are reasonable grounds to believe that otherwise the child would suffer significant harm and, the threshold criteria being the same, decide to remove the child to suitable accommodation under ChA 1989, s 46.

If the officer does decide to take the child home, he is not required to hand the child over to a responsible person. While it is a bar to the removal of the child in the first instance to its place of residence that there is reasonable cause to believe that the child's removal is likely to cause it significant harm, discovery of the absence there of a responsible person is not in itself a bar to the child being left there. However, it is likely that, if there is no responsible person there to look after the child, or that person is likely to abuse the child, the officer will use his power under ChA 1989, s 46 to remove the child to other suitable accommodation on the ground that otherwise the child would be likely to suffer significant harm.

The suitable accommodation to which a police officer will take a child in a breach-of-curfew situation will be a matter for discussion between the relevant agencies prior to the imposition of a curfew notice, so that appropriate arrangements will be in force during the curfew.

Where a police officer has reasonable cause to believe that a child is in a public place, unaccompanied, in contravention of a curfew notice made by a local authority, the officer must also, as soon as practicable, inform that local authority that the child has contravened the notice, however minor the contravention. The local authority will then send a social worker to the child's family to see why the child was in breach of the curfew and then to decide whether further action is necessary to prevent any repetition.

CHILD SAFETY ORDERS

These are governed by CDA 1998, ss 11 to 13.

A child safety order is an order which:

(a) places a child under ten, for a period specified in the order, under the supervision of the responsible officer; and

(b) requires the child to comply with such requirements as are so specified.

The permitted maximum period of supervision for the above purposes is three months.

The requirements that may be specified under (b) are those which the court considers desirable in the interests of:

(a) securing that the child receives appropriate care, protection and support and is subject to proper control; or
(b) preventing any repetition of the kind of behaviour which led to the child safety order being made.

The main responsibility of the responsible officer will be to the child and paramount to that will be the need to supervise the child and to ensure full compliance with the requirements of the order. However, the officer also has an important role to play in relation to the child's family circumstances.

The 'responsible officer' will be one of the following who is specified in the order:

(a) a social worker of a local authority social services department; and
(b) a member of a youth offending team.

The child safety order is directed to the child and requires or prohibits conduct specified in it. Where it is linked with a parenting order (below) that order could make associated requirements of the parent. For example, if the child safety order requires a child to be home by 7 pm, the associated parenting order could require the parent to ensure that the child is home by then.

Child safety orders are made by magistrates' courts sitting as family proceedings courts.

A child safety order cannot be made without an application by a local authority, that is a council of a county (including a unitary authority), a metropolitan district or London borough council or the Common Council of the City of London (in England) or a county or county borough council (in Wales).

A family proceedings court can make an order only if it is convinced that, with respect to a child under ten, one or more of the following conditions is satisfied:

(a) that the child has committed an act which, if he had been ten or over, would have constituted an offence;
(b) that a child safety order is necessary to prevent the child committing such an act;
(c) that the child has contravened a ban imposed by a curfew order; or
(d) that the child has acted in a manner that caused or was likely to cause harassment, alarm or distress to one or more persons not of the same household as himself.

Breach of a child safety order

Proceedings for breach of a child safety order must be brought by the responsible officer. Unlike an application for discharge or variation, an application in respect of a breach of a child safety order need not be heard by the same court as made the order; it can also be heard by another magistrates' court sitting as a family proceedings court for the same petty sessions area.

If on such an application it is proved that the child has failed to comply with any requirement in the order, a magistrates' court sitting as a family proceedings court may make an order varying the order in the same way as on a variation after an application for discharge.

Breach of a child safety order may also result in the making of a parenting order; it is one of the triggers of such an order.

PARENTING ORDERS AND PARENTAL CONTRACTS UNDER THE CRIME AND DISORDER ACT 1998, ss 8 to 10

Nature of a parenting order

What is a parenting order?

By CDA 1998, s 8, a parenting order is a court order requiring 'the parent' of a child (ie someone under fourteen) or (in some cases) a young person (ie someone of fourteen or over but under eighteen):

(a) to comply, for a period not exceeding twelve months, with such requirements as are specified in the order; and
(b) to attend, for a concurrent period not exceeding three months, such counselling and guidance programme as may be specified in directions given by the responsible officer.

A parenting order need not include a counselling and guidance-session requirement under (b) if the parent has previously been made subject to such an order under CDA 1998, s 8 or any other enactment, although it may do so. Apart from this, an order must contain such a requirement, although it need not contain any requirements under (a).

The reference in (b) to 'the responsible officer' who is to specify the counselling or guidance sessions to be attended is to one of the following, who is to be specified in the order:

(a) a probation officer;
(b) a social worker of a local authority social services department; and
(c) a member of a youth offending team.

The responsible officer's role is also to ensure that parents attend whatever sessions are specified in his directions and to ensure compliance with the order and any requirements under it.

The requirements which may be specified under (a) above are those which the court considers desirable in the interest of preventing any repetition of the kind of conduct which 'triggers' the making of a parenting order or (as the case may be) the commission of any further offence of the type which is a 'trigger'.

Examples of requirements which can be made under (a) are a requirement to ensure that the child is escorted to school every day by a responsible adult, a requirement to exercise control over him and a requirement to ensure that he is home by a certain time of night.

Against whom can it be made?

A parenting order may be made against various people depending on the context. First, it may be made against one or both 'parents', ie biological parents. It is not necessary that a parent should have parental responsibility. Thus an order can be made against the father of a child or young person, who was not married to the mother when the child was born and who has not acquired parental responsibility under ChA 1989.

A parenting order may also be made against a person who is a guardian of a child or young person. Guardians are defined here as any person who in the opinion of the court has for the time being the care of a child or young person. Hereafter, the term 'the parent' is used to cover these other people.

When can it be made?

Parenting orders may be made in any court proceedings where:

(a) a child safety order is made in respect of a child or the court determines that a child has failed to comply with such an order;

(b) an anti-social behaviour order or sex offender order is made in respect of a child or young person (ie someone aged under eighteen);

(c) a child or young person is convicted of an offence;

(d) a person is convicted of an offence under the Education Act 1996, s 443 (failure to comply with a school attendance order) or s 444 (failure to secure regular attendance at school of registered pupil); or

(e) a parental compensation order is made in relation to a child's behaviour.

By the nature of these terms, an order under (a) will be made by a magistrates' court, sitting as a family proceedings court; an order under (b), (d) or (e) by a magistrates' court; and an order under (c) by a youth court or (where the conviction is in the Crown Court) the Crown Court.

If the court is satisfied that 'the relevant condition' is fulfilled, it may (or must, see below) make a parenting order in respect of a person who is the parent or guardian of the child or young person.

The 'relevant condition' is that the parenting order would be desirable in the interests of preventing:

(a) in a case falling within (a), (b) or (e) above, any repetition of the kind of behaviour which led to the child safety order, anti-social behaviour, sex offender order or a parental compensation order being made;

(b) in a case falling within (c) above, the commission of any further offence by the child or young person;

(c) in a case falling within (d) above, the commission of any further offence under the Education Act 1996, s 443 or 444.

'Desirable in the interests of' is an unusual piece of legislative phraseology. It is not clear whether the requirement made by it can be satisfied where the object in question is desirable but it is clear that the parent will have no effect in relation to the child's behaviour.

CDA 1998 provides that a court is not normally obliged to make a parenting order if one of the relevant conditions is satisfied; it simply has the power to do so. There are two exceptions, both provided by CDA 1998 in relation to a child or young person under sixteen. If it is satisfied that one of the relevant conditions is satisfied, a court must make a parenting order (a) where such a person has been convicted of an offence; and (b) where a court makes an anti-social behaviour order against such a person. If such a person is convicted or subjected to an anti-social behaviour order, but the court is not so satisfied it must say so in open court and give its reasons why it is not so satisfied.

A parenting order cannot be made where an offender is referred to a youth offender panel.

Parenting contracts in cases of exclusion from school or truancy and in respect of criminal conduct and anti-social behaviour

The Anti-social Behaviour Act 2003 (A-sBA 2003), s 19, makes provision for 'parenting contracts' where a pupil has been excluded on disciplinary grounds from a school for a fixed period or permanently or where a pupil under sixteen has failed to attend his school regularly; such a contract is between the local authority or the school governing body and the parent of a pupil or child. A 'parenting contract' is a document which contains a statement by a parent agreeing to comply with requirements specified in the document for a period specified in it, together with a statement by the local education authority or governing body that it agrees to provide support to the parent for the purpose of complying with those requirements. The 'requirements' may include a requirement to attend a counselling or guidance programme. The purpose of the requirements is to improve behaviour or attendance, as the case may be. There is no requirement for education authorities to use parenting contracts, nor is there a requirement for a parent to sign such a contract. However, in the absence of such a signature, no parenting contract exists.

A-sBA 2003, s 25 also makes provision for 'parenting contracts' where a child or young person has been referred to a youth offending team. The team may enter into such a contract with a parent of a child or young person where a team member has reason to believe that the child or young person has engaged, or is likely to engage, in criminal conduct or anti-social behaviour. It similarly involves an agreement to comply with specified requirements and for support by the team for the purpose of achieving those requirements, which may include a requirement to attend a counselling or guidance programme.

Parenting orders in cases of exclusion from school and in respect of criminal conduct and anti-social behaviour

The provisions already existing in respect of parenting orders for parents convicted of a school attendance offence are complemented by the provisions of the A-sBA 2003, s 20. These enable applications for a parenting order to be made to a magistrates' court in relation to the parent of a pupil who has been excluded from school on disciplinary grounds, provided prescribed conditions are satisfied. A local education authority may apply for a parenting order as a first measure, or where a parent refuses to sign a 'parenting contract'.

The prescribed conditions referred to above are prescribed by the Education (Parenting Orders) (England) Regulations 2004. In the case of a pupil excluded for a fixed period the exclusion must be the second or subsequent exclusion of the pupil from any school within twelve months from the day on which the previous exclusion began. The application must be made within whichever of the following is applicable (if both are applicable whichever expires the later)—(a) the period of forty school days beginning with the next school day after the day on which the exclusion was considered by the governing body (or in the case of an exclusion from a pupil referral unit, the local education authority) or, if it was not so considered, the day on which it began; (b) the period of six months beginning with the day on which a parent of the pupil entered into a parenting contract. In the case of a pupil excluded permanently, the application must be made within whichever of the following is applicable (if both are applicable whichever expires the later)—(a) the period of forty school days beginning with the next school day after the day on which an appeal panel decided to uphold the exclusion, or, if there was no appeal, the last day on which an appeal could have been made; or (b) the period of six months beginning with the day on which a parent of the pupil entered into a parenting contract.

The court may make such an order in respect of a pupil's parent if the conditions are met and the court is satisfied that an order is desirable in the interests of improving the pupil's behaviour. The order will be for a period not exceeding twelve months. It will specify requirements and require attendance, for a period not exceeding three months during the order, at such counselling or guidance programme as may be specified (subject to the proviso that it need not contain such a requirement if a similar requirement has been made in a previous parenting order in respect of the parent).

Similar provision is made by A-sBA 2003, s 26 for a parenting order where a youth offending team applies to a magistrates' court for such an order in respect of a child or young person who has been referred to the team. If the court is satisfied that such a child or young person has engaged in criminal conduct or anti-social behaviour and that the making of the order is desirable in preventing further criminal conduct or further such anti-social behaviour, it may make such an order requiring a parent to comply with requirements specified in the order for a period not exceeding twelve months, and require attendance at a counselling or guidance programme not exceeding three months during the period (but this may not be necessary where there has been a parenting order in respect of the parent on a previous occasion).

In deciding whether to make a parenting order under A-sBA 2003, s 20 or s 26, a court must consider any refusal by a parent to enter into a parenting contract, or a failure by the parent to comply with any requirement of a contract. In the case of a person under sixteen, it must consider the pupil's family circumstances and the order's likely effect upon them.

The making of a parenting order requiring instruction in parenting techniques does not contravene art 8 of the European Convention on Human Rights.

General points about parenting orders

As long as a parenting order of any type is in force, it is an offence for a parent to fail without reasonable excuse to comply with any requirement included in a parenting order, or specified in directions given by the responsible officer.

Leaving aside the theoretical possibility of a private prosecution, the process of enforcement envisaged is that the responsible officer will report to the police an alleged breach of a parenting order. The police will investigate the allegation, taking statements etc and proceed from there. This can be contrasted with breach of a community order where it is the Probation Service which brings proceedings and conducts them.

REPRIMANDS AND WARNINGS

The circumstances in which they may be given

Where a constable has evidence that an offence, in respect of which there is a realistic prospect of conviction, has been committed by a child or young person who has not been previously convicted of an offence, the offence is admitted, and the constable is satisfied that it is not in the public interest to prosecute that child or young person, the provisions of CDA 1998, s 65 relating to reprimand and warning apply.

Reprimand

Where the circumstances are as set out above, the constable may reprimand the offender if he has not been previously reprimanded or warned (see below).

Warning

The constable may warn the offender, if he:

(a) has not been previously warned; or
(b) has been previously warned, the offence was committed more than two years after the date of the previous warning and the constable considers that the offence is not so serious as to merit prosecution. However, this special additional warning may only be given once.

Although a warning will not normally be given to an offender who has not previously been reprimanded, it may be given to such an offender if the constable considers the offence to be so serious as to require a warning.

The House of Lords has held that neither a warning given to a juvenile in respect of an admitted offence, nor the decision to warn him, following a decision not to prosecute him involves the determination of a criminal charge; consequently, the giving of such a warning is not incompatible with the juvenile's right under art 6 of the European Convention on Human Rights to have a charge against him determined by an impartial tribunal.

Procedure

A reprimand or warning under CDA 1998, s 65 must be given at a place approved by the Secretary of State. Where the offender is under seventeen, an appropriate adult must be present.

A constable giving a reprimand or warning must explain that it may be cited in criminal proceedings in the same circumstances as a conviction. In the case of a warning, the constable must refer the offender to a youth offending team as soon as practicable; the constable must explain this to the offender.

REMOVAL OF TRUANTS TO SCHOOLS OR DESIGNATED PREMISES

CDA 1998, s 16 provides that, where a direction has been given under the section, a police officer may remove a juvenile of compulsory school age whom he has reasonable cause to believe to be truanting to designated premises or to the juvenile's school.

In order for a direction to be given under s 16, a local authority, which in this context means the local education authority, must have designated premises to which children and young persons of compulsory school age may be removed under s 16, and notified the chief constable for the police area concerned (or the Metropolitan or City of London Police Commissioner, as the case may be) of the designation. The designated place could be a social services department; it could be a school where there are suitable facilities and staff able to deal with children who may have come from other schools.

Where premises have been designated in a police area under CDA 1998, s 16, a police officer of, or above, the rank of superintendent may direct that the powers set out below conferred on a police officer under s 16 are to be exercisable as respects any area falling within the police area, which is specified in the direction. The powers will only be exercisable during the period specified in the direction. A British Transport Police superintendent (or above) has power to make such a direction but in such a case the powers set out below are only exercisable in any area or in the vicinity of any premises policed by the British Transport Police or in the premises themselves.

A direction will probably be made only after discussions between a school and the police about a perceived truanting problem.

CDA 1998, s 16 provides that, where a police officer has reasonable cause to believe that a child or young person found by him in a public place in a specified area during a specified period:

(a) is of compulsory school age; and
(b) is absent from a school without lawful authority,

he may remove the child or young person to designated premises, or to the school from which he is so absent. Surprisingly, the constable does not have to be in uniform. The child must be 'found in a public place' by a police officer. There is no power to enter private premises (eg the child's home) nor to remove a truant found on private premises on which the police officer is already lawfully present. 'Public place' has the same meaning as in CDA 1998, s 14. Streets, shopping centres, local authority parks, recreation grounds and swimming pools, and amusement arcades, in many of which truanting children tend to congregate and make a nuisance of themselves are all 'public places' within this definition.

For the purpose of the requirement of a reasonable belief in the juvenile's absence from a school without lawful authority, a child's absence is deemed to be without lawful authority unless it is absent with leave, or because attendance at school is prevented by sickness or any unavoidable cause, or because the absence is on a day exclusively set aside for religious observance by the religious body to which his parent belongs.

If it transpired that the police officer did not have the necessary reasonable belief, or the child was not found in a public place, any force used by the officer would be unlawful and he would not be acting in the execution of his duty.

Penalty notice for an offence of failure to secure regular attendance at school

A-sBA 2003 amended the Education Act 1996 to make the offence of failure to secure regular attendance at a relevant school of a registered pupil one in respect of which a penalty notice may be given by an authorised officer. An 'authorised officer' for these purposes is a constable, community support officer, accredited person, an authorised local education authority officer, or an authorised staff member (head teacher or staff member authorised by the head teacher). A relevant school is a maintained school, a pupil referral unit, an Academy, a city technology college or a city college for the technology of the arts.

The Education (Penalty Notices) (England) Regulations 2004 prescribe the form of the notice and allow a period of forty-two days during which no proceedings will be taken. The Regulations require that a code of conduct be drawn up by each local education authority in consultation with other parties, to ensure consistency in the issuing of penalty notices. Records of the issue of notices must be kept by the education authority. The penalty to be paid is £50 where payment is made within twenty-eight days of receipt of the notice and £100 where paid within forty-two days of receipt of the notice (the prescribed period for the purpose of payment before proceedings may be taken).

RECORD OF PERSONS UNSUITABLE FOR EMPLOYMENT IN CHILD CARE POSITION

The Protection of Children Act 1999 (PCA 1999) set up a system within which the identity of persons who are unsuitable to work with children may be established. Child care organisations *must*, and other organisations *may*, refer an individual to the Secretary of State if he has been employed in a child care position and the organisation considers that he has been guilty of misconduct which harmed a child, or placed a child at risk of such harm.

The 'Consultancy Index List' which was maintained by the Department of Health (a list including the names of persons considered unsuitable for work with children) is given statutory recognition. The 'List 99' which was maintained by the Department of Education and Employment (a list of persons who are not considered fit and proper persons to be employed as teachers or in work involving regular contact with children) already enjoyed statutory recognition and the 1999 Act gives statutory authority for access, in prescribed circumstances, to the appropriate part of these records.

PCA 1999 amends the Police Act 1997 to permit the 'Criminal Records Bureau' established under that Act to include such information in addition to the criminal records of such persons. In this way, a check upon the suitability of a person applying for a job in child care can be carried out through one agency. The Police Act 1997 (Criminal Records) Regulations 2002 make provision for the issue of various forms of criminal record certificates in relation to convictions, or to cautions, reprimands or warnings given under CDA 1998. They also specify the information drawn from lists kept under specified pieces of legislation which will appear in criminal records certificates.

Child care organisations are required by PCA 1999, where they propose to employ someone in a child care position, to check that person against the records held by the Criminal Records Bureau. They must not employ persons identified on such records as being included on the 'Consultancy Index List' or the part of 'List 99' held by the Bureau under these provisions.

PCA 1999, s 1 requires that the Secretary of State establishes a list of those persons who are considered unsuitable to work with children. PCA 1999, s 2(1) requires that 'child care organisations' (providing accommodation, social services or health care services to children or the supervision of children etc) refer to the Secretary of State, for possible inclusion on the list, the names of persons who are or have been employed in child care positions and are eligible for such referral. Other organisations are permitted to do so.

Eligibility for referral under the provisions of PCA 1999 include circumstances where a person has been dismissed, transferred or suspended on the grounds of misconduct (whether or not in the course of their employment) that misconduct being such that it harmed a child, or placed a child at risk of harm. The provisions also embrace a person who would have been dismissed, or would have been considered for dismissal for such conduct had that person not resigned or retired. In addition, a referral should or may be made where an organisation has dismissed a person; that person has resigned or retired; or has been transferred by the organisation to a position within that organisation which is not a child care position. In circumstances where information which was not available to the organisation at the time of any such dismissal, resignation, retirement or transfer has since become available and the organisation is of the opinion that, if that information had been available at the time, and, in applicable circumstances that person had not resigned or retired, the organisation would have dismissed him or would have considered doing so, on the grounds of such misconduct, the provisions apply.

In the case of employment agencies, or agencies supplying nurses, the requirements are modified so that they refer to circumstances in which the organisation has refused to do business with the individual on the grounds of misconduct (whether or not in the course of employment) which harmed a child or placed a child at risk.

PCA 1999 requires that the Secretary of State, after considering observations from appellants and employers, must confirm the inclusion of an individual's name on the list. An appeal lies to a Tribunal established under PCA 1999, s 9. A person who is included on the list (otherwise than provisionally) may appeal against inclusion in the list or, with the leave of the Tribunal, against a decision not to remove his name from the list.

DISQUALIFICATION ORDER

The Criminal Justice and Court Services Act 2000, Part II provides for an order to be made by the Crown Court, the Court of Appeal, a court-martial or the Courts-Martial Appeal Court, where a person is convicted of specified offences committed against a child where a qualifying sentence is imposed (twelve months or more detention), disqualifying that person from working with children. The specified offences consist generally of those offences against a child which are of a sexual nature or involve cruelty, assault, abduction, prostitution, supplying drugs to children, or aiding, abetting etc such offences. 'Child' for the purposes of Part II means a person under the age of eighteen.

Where the person is convicted of an offence which was committed when he was eighteen or over the court must make an order unless, having regard to all the circumstances, it considers it unlikely that the individual will commit any further offences against a child. Reasons for not making an order must be stated and recorded. If the offence for which the individual is convicted was committed before he reached eighteen, the court must order disqualification if it is satisfied that, having regard to all of the circumstances, it is likely that the individual will commit a further offence against a child.

The court has a discretion to make an order if it is satisfied that it is likely that a further offence will be committed against a child, even though such a sentence has not been imposed. Where this is done the court must both state and record its reasons for doing so.

Wherever a court is under a duty to consider a disqualification order because of the sentence imposed and appears not to have done so, nor to have recorded reasons, the prosecutor may apply to a senior court for an order to be made.

CHAPTER 19

Licensed premises, licensed persons, clubs, places of entertainment and offences of drunkenness

INTRODUCTION

The Licensing Act 2003 (LA 2003) introduced a system of licensing operated by licensing authorities, essentially local authorities, who are empowered to issue various types of authorisations by means of personal licences, premises licences, club premises certificates and temporary events notices. The activities to which the provisions of the Act apply are not restricted to matters involving the sale or supply of alcohol; they extend to the control of various forms of entertainment and to the provision of late night refreshment.

The key to understanding the regime under LA 2003 is that premises where the above activities occur must always be authorised by a premises licence (or sometimes a club premises certificate or temporary event notice), and, in addition, a personal licence is required by a person selling alcohol by retail or supplying it by, or on behalf of, a club to, or to the order of, a member of the club on premises which have a premises licence.

On certain occasions it is an offence under LA 2003 intentionally to obstruct an officer of the licensing authority. These officers share powers with a constable in relation to the enforcement of many provisions of the Act. On each of these occasions it will also, of course, be an offence against the Police Act 1996 wilfully to obstruct a constable in the execution of his duties.

The key aims of LA 2003 are to reduce crime and disorder, to encourage tourism, to reduce alcohol misuse, and to encourage self-sufficient rural communities. The purpose in licensing the licensable activities with which the Act is concerned is to promote the 'licensing objectives' which are:

(a) the prevention of crime and disorder;
(b) public safety;
(c) the prevention of public nuisance; and
(d) the protection of children from harm.

TERMINOLOGY

Licensing authorities

A 'licensing authority' is defined by LA 2003, s 2 as meaning a council of a district in England, the council of a county in England in which there are no district councils, the council of a county or county borough in Wales, the council of a London borough, the Common Council of the City of London, the Sub-Treasurer of the Inner Temple, the Under-Treasurer of the Middle Temple, or the Council of the Isles of Scilly. Such councils must carry out their duties under the Act with a view to promoting the licensing objectives.

Licensable activities and qualifying club activities

These are the activities which are regulated by LA 2003 and require authorisation by the relevant licensing authority. They are defined by LA 2003, s 1.

Licensable activities

The following are licensable activities:

(a) the sale by retail of alcohol;
(b) the supply of alcohol by or on behalf of a club to, or to the order of, a member of the club, otherwise than a sale by retail;
(c) the provision of regulated entertainment; and
(d) the provision of late night refreshment.

The reference to 'sale by retail' in (a) means that 'business to business' wholesale sales are outside the provisions of the Act. The reference to 'otherwise than a sale by retail' in para (b) of this definition can be explained as follows. In the case of a members' club (as opposed to a proprietary one) the property of the club belongs to its members for the time being jointly in equal shares. Consequently if alcohol is supplied to a member at a price, this is not a sale by retail but a release by the other members of their interest in the drink supplied. This would not be covered by para (a), although a supply at a price to a guest of a member of a club would be.

LA 2003, s 173 excludes activities which would otherwise be licensable activities from being so if they are carried on in particular places, for example aboard an aircraft, hovercraft or train on a journey, at an approved wharf at a designated port or hover port, on board a vessel on an international journey, or the examination station of a designated international airport (area beyond security check-in). Premises permanently or temporarily used for the purpose of the armed forces are also exempted, together with royal palaces. Cabinet ministers or the Attorney-General may grant a certificate on the grounds of national security where inspection of the premises would involve a security risk; the effect is to prevent activities on the premises being licensable activities.

LA 2003, s 175 provides that the giving of a sealed container of alcohol as a prize in a lottery will not be a licensable activity if:

(a) the lottery is promoted as incidental to a bazaar, sale of work, fete, dinner, dance, sporting or athletic event or other entertainment of a similar character;

(b) after the deduction of all relevant expenses, none of the proceeds are used for private gain;

(c) none of the prizes are money prizes;

(d) the tickets or chances are sold or issued and the result of the draw is announced at the time of, and in the same place as, the entertainment;

(e) the lottery or draw is not the only or main inducement to attend the entertainment.

From a date to be appointed, s 175 is substituted by a provision whereby the promotion of a lottery will not constitute a licensable activity by reason only of one or more of the prizes in the lottery consisting of or including alcohol, provided that the alcohol is in a sealed container.

The expenses which are relevant are those incurred in arranging and holding the entertainment and those in connection with the lottery or draw including the printing of tickets and the purchase of prizes.

Regulated club activities

The following are qualifying club activities:

(a) the supply, otherwise than a sale by way of retail, of alcohol by or on behalf of a club to, or to the order of, a member of the club;

(b) the sale by retail of alcohol by or on behalf of a club to a guest of a member of the club for consumption on the premises where the sale takes place; and

(c) the provision of regulated entertainment where that provision is by or on behalf of a club for members of the club or members of the club and their guests.

A number of terms in the above definitions are defined as follows.

Alcohol

'Alcohol' in LA 2003 means spirits, beer, wine, cider or any other fermented, distilled or spirituous liqueur, except alcohol with a strength not exceeding 0.5% and obvious exceptions like perfume, medicinal products and liqueur confectionery.

Regulated entertainment

LA 2003, Sch 1 makes provision about what constitutes 'the provision of regulated entertainment' for the purposes of the Act. It provides that the term means the provision of one of the following types of entertainment:

(a) a performance of a play;

(b) an exhibition of a film;

(c) an indoor sporting event;

(d) a boxing or wrestling entertainment;

(e) a performance of live music;

(f) any playing of recorded music;

(g) a performance of dance;

(h) entertainment of a similar description to that falling within (e), (f) or (g),

where the entertainment takes place in the presence of an audience and is provided for the purpose, or for purposes which include the purpose, of entertaining that audience; or of the provision of entertainment facilities, ie facilities to enable persons to take part in entertainment in any of the following types for the purpose (solely or partly) of being entertained:

(a) making music;

(b) dancing;

(c) entertainment of a similar description to that falling within (a) or (b),

provided that the following two conditions are satisfied.

The first condition is that: the entertainment is, or entertainment facilities are, provided:

(a) to any extent for members of the public or a section of the public;

(b) exclusively for members of a club which is a qualifying club in relation to the provision of regulated entertainment, or for members of such a club and their guests; or

(c) in any case not falling within (a) or (b), for consideration and with a view to profit.

The second condition is that the premises on which the entertainment is, or entertainment facilities are, provided are made available for the purpose, or for purposes which include the purpose, of enabling the entertainment concerned.

As can be seen, the entertainments concerned include the performances of plays, films and shows. They also include all indoor sporting events (events which take place inside a building for spectators in that building). A venue with an opening/closing roof is not an indoor event, even if the roof is closed. 'Sport' includes any game in which physical skill is the predominant factor, and thus includes indoor bowls, indoor tennis and indoor athletics, but would not include a bridge competition or a 'sports quiz'. Outdoor boxing and wrestling matches are also included but no other form of outdoor sport. Live music, the playing of recorded music and the performance of dance where the entertainment takes place in the presence of an audience and is provided for its entertainment are activities included in the schedule.

LA 2003, Sch 1 provides that the following are not regulated entertainments:

(a) reception and playing of live TV and radio programmes within the meaning of the Broadcasting Act 1990;

(b) incidental music in a lift or a piano in a restaurant;

(c) films used for product demonstration, advertisement, information, education or instruction (such as in schools or shopping centres);

(d) entertainment incidental to a religious service or at a place of religious worship;

(e) entertainment at a garden fete;

(f) Morris dancing or dancing of similar type; and

(g) entertainment provided on vehicles in motion.

Premises licences (described below) which are issued to authorise the exhibition of films must include a condition requiring the admission of children to be restricted in accordance with recommendations given either by a body designated under the

Video Recordings Act 1984 or by the licensing authority. At the time of writing the only body so designated is the British Board of Film Classification.

No condition relating to the nature of the play or the manner of its performance may be attached to a club premises certificate (described below) authorising the performance of a play, unless such conditions are justified as a matter of public safety.

Late night refreshment

LA 2003, Sch 2 makes provision about what constitutes 'late night refreshment' for the purposes of the Act. It provides that the term means the supply of hot food or hot drink to the public for consumption on or off the premises, between 11 pm and 5 am. It also includes, when members of the public (or a section of it) are admitted to any premises, such supply on premises to anyone (or to a person of a particular type) on or off those premises. 'Hot' for the purposes of the Act means food or drink which is heated on the premises or elsewhere or that which, after it is supplied, may be heated on the premises.

There are exemptions:

(a) supply to guests of hotels or similar premises such as guest houses, lodging houses, caravan or camping sites or other premises supplying accommodation as their main purpose;
(b) supply to members of recognised clubs;
(c) supply to employees of particular employers (works canteens etc);
(d) premises already licensed under other Acts—'near beer' premises in London in which non-alcoholic beverages are sold;
(e) supply free of charge provided no charge has been made for admission to the premises or some other item;
(f) supply on a vehicle not permanently or temporarily parked.

The supply of food or drink free of charge by a registered charity is exempted, and so is provision by way of a vending machine where money is inserted by members of the public.

PREMISES LICENCES, CLUB PREMISES CERTIFICATES AND TEMPORARY EVENT NOTICES

Premises licence

These are governed by LA 2003, Part 3 (ss 11 to 59).

A premises licence is granted by the licensing authority for the area in which the premises are situated and authorises its holder to use the premises to which the licence relates for licensable activities (as defined on p 662).

A licence will set out the conditions subject to which it is issued, and remains in force unless revoked or suspended. However, an applicant may request a licence with a time limitation. Representations about the grant of a licence may be made to the licensing authority by local residents or businesses, the police, the fire authority and public environmental agencies. Following the grant of a licence, such persons may seek reconsideration of its conditions.

Where it is intended to build or extend premises a person may apply to the relevant licensing authority for a provisional statement. A schedule of works must be submitted. LA 2003 (Premises Licences and Club Premises Certificates) Regulations 2005 deal with procedural matters. Representations, as described above, may be made. Restrictions are imposed upon representations which may subsequently be made provided that the agreed work etc is carried out.

A constable or authorised person may enter the premises to which an application relates, before that application has been determined, in order to assess the likely effect on the promotion of the licensing objectives of the grant of the application, or as the case may be, the effect of the activities authorised by the licence which is applied for. Reasonable force may be used if necessary. It is an offence against LA 2003, s 59 intentionally to obstruct an authorised person exercising such a power.

Applications for a premises licence must be accompanied by an operating schedule, a plan of the premises and (if the application proposes that the licence will authorise the supply of alcohol) a form containing the consent of the individual whom it is proposed will be specified as the designated premises supervisor. The operating schedule must show the licensable activities to be carried out, the proposed hours of opening etc, the duration of the licence (if it has a fixed term), details about the individual who is to act as the designated premises supervisor, details of whether alcohol is to be supplied for on-sales, off-sales or both, and a statement of how the applicant intends to promote the licensing objectives (for instance the security arrangements). If the application is approved these factors will be incorporated into the licence.

Representations about the likely effect of the grant of the premises licence on the promotion of the licensing objectives may be made by residents, businesses, police, fire and enforcement authorities under health and safety provisions and the local council. However, objections concerning the proposed premises supervisor may only be made by a chief officer of police and on the grounds that he is satisfied that the designation of the person concerned as a premises supervisor would undermine the crime prevention objective.

If relevant representations are made, the authority must hold a hearing, unless the authority, the applicant and each person who has made representations agree that a hearing is unnecessary and, having regard to the representations, take such of the following steps as it considers necessary to promote the licensing objectives:

(a) grant the application subject to conditions, as in the case of an uncontested application but with conditions modified to promote the licensing objectives;
(b) exclude from the scope of the licence any of the licensable activities to which the application relates;
(c) refuse to specify a person in the licence as the premises supervisor;
(d) reject the application.

If no representations are made, a licensing authority is obliged to grant the application subject to conditions consistent with the operating schedule.

Where it is a condition that door supervision be provided anyone carrying out these duties must be licensed by the Security Industry Authority established under the Private Security Industry Act 2001.

Notice must be given to the applicant, objectors and the chief officer of police of the grant of the licence.

A premises licence authorising the supply of alcohol must include conditions prohibiting the supply of alcohol at a time when there is no designated premises supervisor in respect of the premises or such a supervisor does not hold a personal licence.

Variation and transfer of licences

The holder of a premises licence may apply to the relevant licensing authority to vary the licence. Such an application must be granted unless relevant representations are made. If relevant representations are made a hearing should be held unless, as above, all concerned agree that a hearing is unnecessary; having regard to the representations the authority may grant the application, or modify the conditions of the licence or reject the application. Notices, about the outcome of the application, must be sent to all interested parties. An application may be made merely to vary the name of the premises supervisor in the case of a licence concerned with the supply of alcohol. Representations may only be made by the chief officer of police in such a case on the grounds that granting the application would undermine the crime prevention objective. Notice of such an objection must be given to the licensing authority within fourteen days of notification of the application.

A 'designated premises supervisor' may give notice to the relevant licensing authority that he no longer wishes to be so designated. If that person is also the holder of the premises licence it must be submitted with his application. In any other case he must, within forty-eight hours, give a copy of his application to the premises licence holder with a request that the premises licence be sent to the licensing authority within fourteen days.

An application may be made for the transfer of an existing premises licence to the applicant and it must be accompanied by the premises licence. Notice of the application must be given to the chief officer of police who may, for the same reasons set out above, give notice of objection within fourteen days. The licence remains valid during the period between the application and its determination. The authority must transfer the licence where the holder has consented to the transfer or there is no need for such consent in the circumstances. The same conditions apply should the chief officer of police make representations in consequence of the crime prevention objective. Whether granted or rejected, the same notices are required.

Following the death, incapacity or insolvency of the holder of a premises licence, or where such a licence is surrendered, in the initial period of seven days after the lapse of the premises licence because of these circumstances, a person with a prescribed interest in the premises or connected to the licence holder (acting on his behalf) may submit an interim authority notice to the licensing authority. The effect will be to reinstate the lapsed licence and for the person who gave notice to become the premises licence holder for a period of two months, or until sooner terminated by such a person, or an alternative transfer takes place. However, the licence will lapse if the chief officer of police is not notified by the applicant within seven days. A chief officer may object within forty-eight hours of receipt of such a notice if he considers that a failure to cancel the notice would undermine the crime prevention objective. Alternatively, a person who may apply for the grant of a premises licence may so apply within seven days of the lapse for the transfer of the licence to him, where no interim authority notice has been submitted. In such a case, the licence will be re-instated with effect from receipt of the application. If the application is rejected or withdrawn, the licence lapses once more.

Register of authorisations

Section 8(1) requires each licensing authority to maintain a register containing the details of all authorisations which it issues; temporary event notices which it receives, any other notices and applications and any other prescribed information. The Secretary of State is empowered to make regulations. This register must be made available for inspection by the public during office hours free of charge. A charge may be made for a copy of such information. The Licensing Act 2003 (Licensing authority's register) (other information) Regulations 2005 make provisions in respect of the register.

Club premises certificates

These are dealt with by LA 2003, Part 4 (ss 60 to 98).

Club premises certificates will be granted by the licensing authority for the area in which the club is situated and will authorise the use of club premises for qualifying club activities specified in the certificate (see p 663). Representations may be made by the same persons as is the case in respect of a premises licence.

A club may wish to provide entertainment to members of the public on certain occasions and, in consequence, it may hold a club premises certificate in respect of its day-to-day activities and a premises licence authorising the provision of entertainment.

For a club to be a qualifying club in relation to a qualifying club activity:

(a) no one may be admitted as a member without an interval of at least two days after his nomination or application for membership;
(b) a person who is admitted as a member other than by prior nomination or application must wait at least two days before enjoying the privileges of membership;
(c) the club is established and conducted in good faith as a club;
(d) the club has at least twenty-five members;
(e) no alcohol is supplied, or intended to be supplied, on the club premises except by or on behalf of the club.

In relation to whether or not the club is established and conducted in good faith, account must be taken of the club's freedom to purchase alcohol; how money or property belonging to the club is used; giving members information about club finances; the club's accounts and the nature of its premises.

Where alcohol is to be supplied by a club the following additional conditions apply if it is to be a qualifying club for the supply of alcohol to members and guests: the purchase and supply must be managed by a committee; no commission or percentage deriving from the purchase of alcohol should be paid to any person at the expense of the club; and no one must receive a pecuniary benefit from the supply of alcohol by the club to its members.

If a club at any time ceases to meet the criteria its certificate will be withdrawn. A justice may issue a search warrant authorising a constable to enter club premises (if necessary by force) and to search them if he is satisfied that a club holding a club premises certificate ceases to meet the criteria necessary to be a qualifying club and evidence of that fact may be obtained at the club premises. The provisions of the

Criminal Justice and Police Act 2001 (CJPA 2001), s 50 (seizure of material which cannot be separated) apply to such a search.

An application for a club premises certificate must be advertised. It must be accompanied by similar information to that required in respect of a premises licence.

A club premises certificate may authorise the supply of alcohol to its *members* for consumption off the premises. Sale by retail to a guest is not authorised by the certificate. In general:

(a) a club premises certificate may not authorise the supply of alcohol for consumption off the premises unless it also authorises its supply to members for consumption on the premises;

(b) a club premises certificate authorising the supply of alcohol for consumption off the premises must include three conditions:

(i) the supply must be made at a time when the premises are open for the purposes of supplying alcohol, in accordance with the club premises certificate, to members of the club for consumption on the premises;

(ii) any alcohol supplied for consumption off the premises must be in a sealed container;

(iii) any supply of alcohol for consumption off the premises must be made to a member of the club in person.

No conditions attached to a club premises certificate may prevent the sale by retail of alcohol or the provision of regulated entertainment to associate members of a club or their guests if those are permitted activities.

A club premises certificate has effect until it is withdrawn or it is surrendered. The certificate must be produced at the request of the licensing authority. It is an offence against LA 2003, s 93 to fail, without reasonable excuse, to do so. A constable or authorised person may require production of a certificate (or certified copy). Failure to comply, without reasonable excuse, is an offence against s 94. Clubs must ensure that the certificate is held on relevant premises, and that a summary of the certificate and notice of the nominated individual responsible for it on the premises are prominently displayed.

A constable authorised by the chief officer of police or an authorised person may enter and inspect premises in respect of which an application has been made for the grant, variation or review of a certificate. Forty-eight hours' notice must have been given to the club. It is an offence to obstruct an authorised person exercising these powers.

By LA 2003, s 97 a constable may enter and search club premises where he has reasonable cause to believe that an offence in respect of controlled drugs has been, is being, or is about to be, committed or there is likely to be a breach of the peace. If necessary, reasonable force may be used.

Temporary event notices

Sometimes, a person wishes to carry out licensable activities at premises which are not licensed. He may wish, for example, to provide bar facilities at a wedding reception or to set up a disco in premises which, although licensed for the sale of alcohol, are not licensed for the provision of entertainment.

LA 2003, Part 5 (ss 98 to 110) deals with permitted temporary activities. Licensable activities can occur on premises which do not have a premises licence or club premises certificate on a temporary basis (a period not exceeding ninety-six hours) subject to conditions and limitations. A licensable activity (see p 662) is a 'permitted temporary activity' if it is one, carried on in accordance with a temporary events notice given to the relevant authority, which satisfies the following conditions:

(a) the temporary event notice has been duly acknowledged by the licensing authority and notified to the police;
(b) the temporary event notice has not been subsequently withdrawn by the individual giving the notice; and
(c) the licensing authority has not issued a counter-notice which would be issued, if necessary, following a hearing of any objections raised by the police to the effect that the crime prevention objective would be undermined by allowing the activity to go ahead or if the permitted limits attaching to the applicant or the premises would be exceeded.

Where it is proposed to use premises for one or more licensable events during a period not exceeding ninety-six hours, an individual may give the relevant licensing authority a notice of that proposal (a temporary event notice). That individual is called the 'premises user'. A premises user must be eighteen or over.

The form of the notice is prescribed by the Licensing Act 2003 (Permitted Temporary Activities) (Notices) Regulations 2005 which require details including:

(a) the licensable activities which are to be carried out;
(b) the total length of the event, which must not exceed ninety-six hours;
(c) the times during the event at which the licensable activities are to be carried out;
(d) the maximum number of people to be allowed on the premises at any one time, which must be less than 500;
(e) whether any alcohol sales are to be made for consumption on or off the premises (or both);
(f) any other information prescribed by regulations.

If the proposed licensable activities include the supply of alcohol, the notice must include the condition that all supplies will be made by, or under the authority of, the premises user. The temporary event notice must be given to the licensing authority and the chief officer of police at least ten working days before the event. The authority must acknowledge receipt no later than the day after receipt of the notice. A premises user can withdraw a temporary event notice up to twenty-four hours before the event is scheduled to take place. Once so withdrawn, the notice does not count towards the limitation upon numbers of notices which may be given, referred to below.

The police may object and if they do the authority must, if necessary, arrange a hearing to decide whether to issue a counter-notice.

Where the police consider that if the temporary event should proceed it would undermine the crime prevention objective, the premises user and the relevant licensing authority must be informed by an objection notice, setting out the reasons, not later than forty-eight hours after receiving the temporary event notice. If there is a police objection there must be a hearing unless all parties agree that it is unnecessary. Where the licensing authority accepts the objection it must issue to the premises user a counter-notice preventing the event from taking place and this must be done at least twenty-four hours before the proposed event. If the notice is not sent as required, the premises user may proceed with the event. However, at any time before a hearing the chief officer of police may, with the consent of the premises user, modify the terms of the temporary event notice.

In addition to the circumstances in which a police objection is accepted, a licensing authority must issue a counter-notice where the premises user holds a personal licence and has already given fifty such notices in the calendar year; where no personal licence is held and the premises user has already given five notices in that year; where twelve notices have been given in respect of the same premises in that year; or notices for events at the same premises have already covered fifteen days in a year.

There must be at least twenty-four hours between temporary events held on the same premises by a premises user, or by him and another person who is related to, associated with, or in business with that user.

The system of temporary events notices reverses the procedure which it replaces. Under legislation existing at the time of writing, application had to be made and formal approval given before the event took place. Notice must be given to the relevant licensing authority as prescribed by Part 5 of the Act, of an intention to hold an event and this may go ahead provided that no counter-notice is issued by the licensing authority.

LA 2003, s 108 provides that a constable or an officer of the licensing authority may, at any reasonable time, enter premises to assess the probable impact of the proposed event upon the crime prevention objective. The officer of the licensing authority must produce evidence of his authority, if requested. It is an offence to obstruct such an officer.

The premises user must ensure that the notice is displayed on the premises or is kept there under his control or that of a nominated person; where the notice is in the custody of a nominated person, the premises user must ensure that a notice to that effect is prominently displayed on the premises. It is an offence against LA 2003, s 109 for a premises user, without reasonable excuse, to fail to comply.

Where a temporary event notice is not displayed and there is no notice displayed as to its whereabouts, a constable or authorised officer may require the premises user to produce the temporary event notice. Where a notice relating to a 'nominated person' is displayed on the premises such a person may require the nominated person to produce the actual notice. It is an offence for a person to fail, without reasonable excuse, to produce a temporary event notice when requested to do so.

Opening hours of premises in respect of which there is a premises licence or club premises certificate

LA 2003 does not prescribe 'permitted hours' within which alcohol may be sold or supplied for consumption on or off the premises. In addition, there are no general restrictions placed upon any other licensable activity. An applicant for a premises licence or a club premises certificate may choose the hours within which it would like to be authorised to carry out the licensed activities. The licence will be granted on those terms unless, following representations, the authority considers it necessary to reject the application or alter its terms bearing in mind the 'licensing objectives' set out on p 661. Where a local authority had a 'cumulative impact policy' which required it to take into account relevant representations about the cumulative impact on the licensing objectives, in an area in which there were a significant number of licensed premises, a divisional court held that it was entitled to have such a policy in relation to applications for new licences and variations of existing licences.

PERSONAL LICENCES

A personal licence is required in the case of some persons involved in the sale or supply of alcohol on licensed premises. Personal licences are dealt with by LA 2003, Part 6 (ss 111 to 135). A personal licence is a licence granted by a licensing authority for the area in which the applicant is normally resident to an individual which authorises him to supply alcohol, or to authorise the supply of alcohol, in accordance with a premises licence. Supplying alcohol in this context means selling it by retail, or supplying it by or on behalf of a club to, or to the order of, a member of the club.

A personal licence is one which relates solely to the supply of alcohol. A personal licence is not required in respect of the other activities regulated by LA 2003 (ie regulated entertainment or late night refreshment).

The licensing authority must grant a personal licence if it appears to it that:

(a) the applicant is aged eighteen or over;
(b) he possesses a recognised qualification (awarded by an accredited body or a comparable qualification granted before the coming into force of LA 2003) or is a person of a prescribed description;
(c) no personal licence held by him has been forfeited in the period of five years ending with the date of application; and
(d) he has not been convicted of any 'relevant offence' or any 'foreign offence' (see below).

For the purposes of LA 2003, Part 6, 'relevant offences' are set out in Sch 4 to the Act and are, in general terms:

(a) offences under LA 2003 or similar offences under the previous legislation;
(b) offences in relation to the licensing of entertainments under previous legislation or the licensing of late night refreshment houses;
(c) most firearms offences;
(d) offence of false trade description where the goods in question are or include alcohol;
(e) offences under the Theft Acts 1968 and 1978;
(f) an offence under the Fraud Act 2006 (not in force at the time of writing);
(g) offences of production, supplying, possessing controlled drugs or permitting drug activities on premises;
(h) offences of fraudulent evasion of customs duty etc and of preparing to do so;
(i) most offences of forgery or counterfeiting;
(j) most copyright offences;
(k) offences against s 3A (causing death by careless driving while under the influence of drink), s 4 (driving etc a vehicle when under the influence of drink or drugs), or s 5 (driving etc a vehicle with alcohol concentration above prescribed limit);
(l) offences of selling food not of nature or quality demanded or falsely describing such products where the food is or includes alcohol;
(m) a sexual offence ie an offence (i) listed in the Criminal Justice Act 2003, Sch 15, Part 2 (which contains a very long list of sexual offences) other than

the repealed offence under the Sexual Offences Act 1967 of procuring other to commit homosexual offence; (ii) an offence under the repealed Sexual Offences Act 1956 (SOA 1956), s 8 (intercourse with a defective); (iii) an offence under the repealed SOA 1956, s 18 (fraudulent abduction of an heiress), or a violent offence, ie any offence which leads, or is intended or likely to lead, to a person's death or serious injury to a person, including an offence which is required to be charged as arson (whether or not it would otherwise fall within that definition);

(n) offence of engaging in certain activities relating to security without a licence, contrary to the Private Security Industry Act 2001, s 3; and

(o) offence under the Gambling Act 2005, s 46 (inviting, causing or permitting a child or young person to gamble) (not in force at the time of writing) if the child or young person was invited etc to gamble on premises in respect of which a premises licence had effect.

A foreign offence is an offence (other than a relevant offence) under the law of anywhere outside England and Wales.

Convictions for a relevant offence or a foreign offence must be disregarded if spent in terms of the Rehabilitation of Offenders Act 1974.

A licensing authority must reject an application if the applicant is under eighteen, or if he does not possess the required qualification, or if he has had a licence forfeited. If an applicant meets these three requirements but has a conviction for a relevant offence or a foreign offence, the authority must notify the chief officer of police for its area. If the chief officer is satisfied, by reference to any conviction for a relevant offence or any conviction for a foreign offence which he considers comparable to a relevant offence, that granting a personal licence to the applicant would undermine the crime prevention objective of the Act, he must within fourteen days of receiving the notification give the authority an objection notice. If he does not, the authority must grant the personal licence; if he does the authority must hold a hearing to consider the objection notice and decide whether or not to grant the personal licence.

A personal licence is valid for ten years and there is a presumption in favour of renewal if the licence holder has not been convicted of a relevant offence or a foreign offence. If an application for renewal has been made but it has not been determined before the expiry of the existing licence the licence continues to be effective until the matter has been determined. Where an application for renewal is received by the licensing authority it must notify the chief officer of police of any convictions for relevant or foreign offences.

A licence specifies the holder's name and address, the authority which granted it and convictions for relevant or foreign offences. The holder is under a duty to notify the authority of any change in address. It is an offence to fail, without reasonable excuse, to do so.

The system of personal licences permits licensed persons to move from one set of premises to another.

A personal licence authorises its holder to sell or supply alcohol from premises in respect of which there is a premises licence, and in accordance with that licence. On any such premises, the person nominated for the day-to-day running of the licensed premises must hold a personal licence and is known as the 'designated premises supervisor'. There may be more than one personal licence holder on licensed premises, but it is not necessary for all members of staff to have personal licences. However, all supplies of alcohol under a premises licence must be made by or under the authority of a personal licence holder.

The relevant licensing authority for the purpose of personal licences is the authority which granted it. It does not matter that the holder moves or works elsewhere.

Where, on an application for grant or renewal of a personal licence, an applicant is convicted of a relevant or foreign offence in the period between application and determination, but knowledge of the conviction came to notice after grant or renewal, the licence may be revoked by the licensing authority after consultation with the police. Provision is made for a record of convictions for relevant or foreign offences to be shown within a licence.

When charged with a relevant offence (see above), a personal licence holder must produce his licence to a court before the case against him is first heard in court. If for any reason it is not practicable for him to do so, he must explain why. If he is granted a personal licence *after being charged*, but before his conviction and sentencing, or acquittal, or before an appeal against such is dealt with, he must produce the licence to the court or explain why he is unable to do so. He must also notify the court if, after having first produced his licence, it is renewed, surrendered or revoked. LA 2003, s 128 makes it an offence to fail, without reasonable excuse, to comply with these requirements.

If a court convicts a personal licence holder of a relevant offence, it may forfeit the licence or suspend it for up to six months, but such a forfeiture or suspension may be suspended pending an appeal. The court by or before which a personal licence holder is convicted must notify the relevant licensing authority of his name and address, the nature and date of the conviction and the details of the sentence passed. Where a conviction is quashed or a sentence altered on appeal, the court must notify the relevant licensing authority. In circumstances in which a court was not aware of the existence of a personal licence at the time of the conviction for a relevant offence or a foreign offence, the holder must notify the licensing authority as soon as possible concerning the conviction and the outcome of any appeal. It is an offence against LA 2003, s 132 to fail, without reasonable excuse, to comply with these requirements.

Where the holder of a personal licence is on premises to sell or authorise the sale of alcohol by virtue of a premises licence or temporary event notice, he may be required by a constable or officer of the licensing authority to produce his licence. Failure to do so, without reasonable excuse, is an offence against LA 2003, s 135.

LICENSING OFFENCES

LA 2003, Part 7 deals with the various offences associated with licensing.

Unauthorised licensable activities

It is an offence against LA 2003, s 136 for a person to carry on, or attempt to carry on, a licensable activity on or from any premises without having the authorisation provided by a:

(a) premises licence;
(b) club premises certificate; or
(c) temporary event notice.

It is also an offence for such a person knowingly to allow such an activity to take place. In the case of regulated entertainment, a person does not commit an offence if his only involvement is as a performer or participant.

Exposing alcohol for unauthorised sale

It is an offence against LA 2003, s 137 to expose, on any premises, alcohol for sale by retail in circumstances where the actual sale by retail of that alcohol would be an unauthorised licensable activity because there is no applicable premises licence, club premises certificate or temporary event notice. It is not therefore essential that there has been a sale, or an attempted sale, provided that the alcohol is there to be sold and exposed to potential customers. A court which convicts a person of such an offence may order the confiscation of the alcohol for destruction or to be dealt with in some other way.

Keeping alcohol on premises for unauthorised sale

LA 2003, s 138 creates the offence of possessing, or having under control, alcohol, with the intention of selling it by retail, or supplying it, where that sale or supply would be an unauthorised licensable activity. A court has the same powers of confiscation as set out in the previous paragraph.

Defence of due diligence

LA 2003, s 139 provides a defence where a person is charged with carrying on an unauthorised licensable activity, exposing alcohol for unauthorised sale, or keeping alcohol on premises for unauthorised sale or supply if his act was due to a mistake, or to reliance on information given to him, or to an act or omission of another person, or to some cause beyond his control, and he took all reasonable steps and exercised all due diligence to avoid committing the offence.

DRUNKENNESS AND DISORDERLY CONDUCT

The offences described below are also dealt with by LA 2003, Part 7.

Allowing disorderly conduct on licensed premises etc

LA 2003, s 140 makes it an offence knowingly to allow disorderly conduct on licensed premises, premises in respect of which a club premises certificate is in force, or premises which may be used for a permitted temporary activity. The offence can be committed by any person who works on the premises in a capacity, paid or unpaid, which gives him the authority to prevent such conduct. On premises with a premises licence, the offence can also be committed by the premises licence holder or designated premises supervisor. In the case of a club, the offence can also be committed by an officer or member of the club who is present when the disorderly conduct takes place and who has the authority to prevent it. Members of a club committee would obviously be in such a position. In the case of a temporary event the offence can also be committed by the premises user.

Sale of alcohol to a person who is drunk or obtaining alcohol for such a person

It is an offence, contrary to LA 2003, s 141, knowingly to sell, or attempt to sell, alcohol to a person who is drunk, or to allow alcohol to be sold to such a person, on premises in respect of which there is a premises licence, or a club premises certificate, or premises which may be used for a permitted temporary activity. The offence also applies to the supply of alcohol by or on behalf of a club.

The offence may be committed by the same category of persons to which s 140 applies.

By LA 2003, s 142, it is an offence for a person knowingly to obtain, or attempt to obtain, alcohol for consumption on the above types of premises by a person who is drunk.

Failure to leave licensed premises etc

A person commits an offence against LA 2003, s 143 if he is drunk and disorderly and fails to leave premises in respect of which there is a premises licence, or a club premises certificate, or premises which may be used for a permitted temporary activity, without reasonable excuse, at the request of a police constable or:

(a) any person who works at the premises in a capacity, paid or unpaid, which gives him the authority to make that request;
(b) a premises licence holder or designated premises supervisor;
(c) an officer or member of a club who is present at the time and has authority to make that request; and
(d) a premises user who has given a temporary event notice in respect of the premises.

A person who is drunk and disorderly also commits an offence if, without reasonable excuse, he enters, or attempts to enter, such premises when requested not to do so by any such persons.

LA 2003, s 143 requires a constable to assist in the expulsion of persons who are drunk and disorderly from relevant premises, or to help prevent such a person from entering, if requested to do so by any of the persons described above.

KEEPING OF SMUGGLED GOODS

LA 2003, s 144 creates an offence committed by certain persons who knowingly keep, or allow to be kept, on relevant premises, any goods which have been imported without payment of duty or which have otherwise been unlawfully imported. The persons who may commit this offence are:

(a) any person who works at the premises in a capacity, paid or unpaid, which gives him the authority to prevent those goods from being on the premises;

(b) in the case of licensed premises, a premises licence holder or designated premises supervisor;
(c) in the case of premises with a club premises certificate, an officer or member of a club who is present at a time when the goods are kept on the premises and has authority to prevent them being so kept; and
(d) in the case of premises which may be used for a permitted temporary activity, the premises user (the person who gave the temporary event notice) in respect of the event in question.

This offence is aimed at those suppliers who obtain cheap supplies from those smugglers who arrange for large quantities of alcohol and tobacco to be imported into Great Britain. There is no legal limit on the amount of excisable goods which a person may bring into the United Kingdom for his personal use, as EU law prevents restrictions where duty has been paid within an EU state. HM Customs are obliged to prove that excisable goods bought within an EU state are not for personal use. Thus, any excisable goods bought within the EU which are then passed to some other person for sale within premises or supply within a club will be unlawfully imported goods upon which United Kingdom duty has not been paid.

OFFENCES IN RELATION TO PERSONS UNDER EIGHTEEN

Unaccompanied children prohibited from certain premises

It is an offence against LA 2003, s 145 to allow children under sixteen to be on certain categories of relevant premises if they are not accompanied by an adult (eighteen or over) and the premises are open for the supply of alcohol for consumption on the premises. The premises concerned are:

(a) those exclusively or primarily used for the supply of alcohol for consumption on the premises; or
(b) those open for the purpose of being used for the supply of alcohol for consumption on the premises by virtue of LA 2003, Part 5 (permitted temporary activities) and, at the time the temporary event notice in question has effect, they are exclusively or primarily used for such supplies.

It is also an offence against the section to allow an unaccompanied child under sixteen to be on such premises at a time between the hours of midnight and 5 am when the premises are open for the supply of alcohol for consumption there.

These offence may be committed by a person working on the premises in any capacity, paid or unpaid, with the authority to ask the child to leave, the premises licence holder or designated premises supervisor, an officer or member of a club with that authority, or the premises user who has given temporary notice in respect of the premises.

No offence is committed where the unaccompanied child is merely passing through the premises, where this is the convenient route.

A person charged with an offence under LA 2003, s 145 by reason of his own conduct has a defence if he believed the child to be sixteen or over, or that an individual accompanying him was eighteen or over, and had either taken all reasonable steps to establish the individual's age, or no one could reasonably have suspected from the individual's appearance that he was aged under sixteen or eighteen, as the case may be. A person will be treated as having taken all reasonable steps to establish an individual's age if he asked for evidence of it and the evidence would have convinced a reasonable person. Where a person is charged because of the default of some other person, it is a defence to show that he had exercised all due diligence to avoid committing the offence.

Sale of alcohol to persons under eighteen

LA 2003, s 146 prohibits the sale of alcohol to an individual aged under eighteen *anywhere*. It additionally provides that a club commits an offence if alcohol is supplied by or on its behalf to, or to the order of, a member under eighteen, or to a person under eighteen to the order of a member of a club. A person who supplies alcohol on behalf of a club in such circumstances also commits an offence.

LA 2003, s 146 provides a defence where the person charged believed that the purchaser was eighteen or over and either:

(a) took all reasonable steps to establish the purchaser's age; or
(b) no one could reasonably have suspected from the purchaser's appearance that he was under eighteen.

An accused will be deemed to have taken all reasonable steps if he asked the individual for evidence of his age and the evidence would have convinced a reasonable person. In the latter respect, the prosecution may show that the evidence of age produced was such that no reasonable person would have been convinced by it (it may be an obvious forgery or obviously belong to some other person).

Where a sale or supply was made by some other person than the person charged (as where a barman supplies a drink on behalf of a manager) it is a defence to show that the person charged exercised all due diligence to avoid committing the offence.

It is an offence against LA 2003, s 147 for a person knowingly to allow the sale of alcohol to a person under eighteen on licensed premises, premises with a club premises certificate or premises which may be used for a temporary permitted activity. The persons who can commit this offence are those workers, paid or unpaid, with authority to prevent sale or supply. An officer or member of a club, or the worker in it, with that authority commits an offence if he allows alcohol to be supplied to or to the order of a member under eighteen, or to someone under eighteen to the order of such a member.

Although liqueur confectionery is not alcohol for the purposes of LA 2003, by s 148 it is an offence to sell liqueur confectionery to a person under the age of sixteen, or for a club or person on behalf of a club to supply to, or to the order of, a member under sixteen or to a person under sixteen to the order of a member. It is good to know that in these dangerous times our children are protected from this evil! The same defences apply as in the case of unlawful sales under s 146.

PURCHASE OF ALCOHOL BY PERSONS UNDER EIGHTEEN OR ON THEIR BEHALF

LA 2003, s 149(1) makes it an offence for a person under eighteen to buy or attempt to buy alcohol (whether or not on licensed premises) or, if he is a member of a club, for him to have alcohol supplied to him by the club in circumstances in which he actively initiates the supply, or for him to attempt to do so. Test purchasing on behalf of a constable or trading standards officer is excepted from these provisions.

LA 2003, s 149(3) makes it an offence for a person to act as an agent for a child in purchasing, or attempting to purchase, alcohol. A person under eighteen may ask a stranger to purchase alcohol from an off-licence on his behalf and provide that person with the money in the same way as children request adults to take them into a cinema when a film is being shown which requires an accompanying adult.

LA 2003, s 149(4) provides an offence which is committed on licensed premises etc, by prohibiting a person from buying or attempting to buy alcohol for consumption by a person under eighteen on those premises. This would cover any relative or friend of a child who buys a drink for a child, or tries to do so, on licensed premises etc. However, the offence is not committed by an adult who buys beer, wine or cider for a person aged sixteen or seventeen to consume with a table meal (ie a meal eaten by a person seated at a table, counter or other structure used as a table by seated persons) taken on those premises in the company of an adult.

The offences under s 149(3) and (4) also apply in respect of the *supply* of alcohol in premises in respect of which there is in force a club premises certificate.

Consumption by or delivering to a child and sending a child to obtain alcohol

It is an offence against LA 2003, s 150(1) for an individual under eighteen knowingly to consume alcohol on relevant premises. Because of the presence of 'knowingly' the offence will not be committed where a child accidentally consumes alcohol, being unaware of the nature of his drink, or where something has been furtively added to it.

LA 2003, s 150(2) makes it an offence for a person knowingly to allow such consumption to take place on licensed premises etc. This offence can be committed, once again, by those responsible persons on licensed premises and officers and members of a club. The offence does not apply to persons of sixteen or seventeen who consume beer, wine or cider with a table meal (see above) on licensed etc premises and are accompanied by a person of eighteen or over.

LA 2003, s 151(1) is concerned with the *delivery* of alcohol to a person under eighteen. *Delivery* is a term which avoids 'sale or supply'. The offence lies in a person who works on licensed premises etc, knowingly delivering to a person under eighteen, alcohol which is sold on the premises or supplied by a club. It may be that his mother has bought and paid for a quantity of drink and has left it at the off-licence to be picked up. If a child goes to pick up the alcohol and it is handed over to that child, there has been a delivery.

It is an offence (by s 151(2)) for a person working on the premises with the necessary authority to prevent the delivery to allow it to take place.

A similar offence applies to clubs, where a person in authority allows such delivery. None of these offences is committed if alcohol is delivered to a home or work place, nor does it apply where the job of a minor involves the delivery of alcohol, nor where alcohol is sold or supplied for consumption on the licensed premises etc (as other offences are committed in this circumstance).

In view of the offences involving delivery to a person under eighteen, it is not surprising to find that 'sending' such a person to obtain alcohol sold, or to be sold, on licensed premises etc, or supplied or to be supplied by a club, is an offence against LA 2003, s 152. Thus where a parent orders by telephone from an off-licence and sends a child to seek the order, an offence against the section is committed. The section provides that the offence is committed whether the child is sent to the licensed premises etc or to some other delivery point. Thus, if the 'order' has been sent to a distribution centre and it is collected from those premises, the offence is still committed. No offence is committed where the minor works at the premises in a capacity involving the delivery of alcohol, nor if the child is assisting a constable or trading standards officer.

Unsupervised sales by persons under eighteen

It is an offence against LA 2003, s 153 for a responsible person knowingly to allow on licensed premises etc a person under the age of eighteen to sell or, in the case of a club, supply alcohol, unless each sale or supply has been specifically approved by a responsible person. A 'responsible person' means the holder of the premises licence, the designated premises supervisor or an adult (or club member) with authority to prevent the sale or supply or (at a temporary permitted activity) the premises user, as appropriate. Many of the checkout personnel in supermarkets which are authorised to sell for off-consumption are under eighteen, but provided that each sale is specifically approved (to prevent their young friends from conveniently going through their checkout) no offence is committed. Such youngsters are seen to gain the approval of more senior personnel. Section 153 exempts sales in a restaurant of alcohol to be taken with a table meal. Thus waiters and waitresses under eighteen may serve drinks in such a part of the premises.

CONFISCATION OF ALCOHOL—YOUNG PERSONS

The Confiscation of Alcohol (Young Persons) Act 1997 (CA(YP)A 1997), s 1 provides that, where a constable reasonably suspects that a person in any public place other than licensed premises, or any place (other than a public place) to which a person has unlawfully gained access, is in possession of alcohol and that either:

(a) he is under eighteen; or
(b) he intends that any of the alcohol should be consumed by a person under the age of eighteen in that or another similar place; or
(c) a person under the age of eighteen who is, or has recently been, with him, has recently consumed alcohol in that or another similar place,

the constable may require that person to surrender anything which he possesses which is, or the constable reasonably believes to be, alcohol, or a container for it, and to state his name and address. A person who, without reasonable excuse, fails to comply with such a requirement commits an offence. A constable who makes such a requirement must inform the person concerned of the suspicion and that failing without reasonable excuse to comply with the requirement is an offence. A constable may not require a person to surrender any sealed container unless the constable reasonably believes that the person is, or has been, consuming, or intends to consume, alcohol in any relevant place.

The Act provides a means by which the nuisance caused by young people assembling in public places and drinking from cans may be removed. The provisions of CA(YP)A 1997, s 1 effectively embrace all persons likely to be in such a group, including those who are over the age of eighteen if, as they are almost certain to be, they are associated with drinking by those who are under age. Where a person of eighteen or over is with a young person who is or has been drinking in such a place, (c) above requires the surrender of alcohol in the adult person's possession. The terms of CA(YP)A 1997 are such that everyone in a group containing some under-eighteen-year-olds with alcohol in their possession may be required to surrender it.

Police powers of disposal

A constable may dispose of anything surrendered to him under CA(YP)A 1997 in such a manner as he considers appropriate.

OTHER PROHIBITIONS UPON THE SALE OR CONSUMPTION OF ALCOHOL AND FALSE STATEMENTS

Prohibition of sale of alcohol on moving vehicles

LA 2003, s 156 creates the offence of selling alcohol by retail on or from a vehicle which is not permanently or temporarily parked. It is a defence where the sale was mistaken; was due to the seller relying on information given to him; was the fault of another person; or was due to some cause beyond his control and he took all reasonable precautions and exercised due diligence to avoid committing the offence. This could occur where it was believed that the refreshment served was non-alcoholic and there was some reason for a person to have held that belief.

While the section does not apply to trains, s 157 provides for the prohibition of sales of alcohol at specified stations or on trains travelling between specified stations for a particular period. A prohibition order may be made by magistrates on the application of a police officer of at least the rank of inspector, if the magistrates are satisfied than an order is necessary for the prevention of disorder. A copy of the order must be served by the police upon the operator or operators concerned. Thus provision is made for 'dry' soccer specials, at least so far as the operating companies are concerned.

Making of false statements in applications for licences and certificates and in notices

It is an offence against LA 2003, s 158 for a person knowingly or recklessly to make a false statement in or in connection with (1) an application for the grant, variation, transfer or review of a premises licence or club premises certificate, (2) an application for a local authority provisional statement in respect of a premises licence, (3) a temporary event notice or any other notice under the Act, or (4) an application for the grant or renewal of a personal licence. For the purposes of the section a person is treated as making a false statement if he produces, furnishes, signs or otherwise makes use of a document that contains a false statement. It is sufficient if he includes with his application any document which he knows to be false.

Alcohol consumption in designated public places

CJPA 2001, ss 12 to 16 address the issue of disorder and nuisance associated with such consumption.

CJPA 2001, s 12 gives a constable certain powers (set out below) where he reasonably believes that a person is, or has been, consuming alcohol in a designated public place, or intends to consume alcohol in such a place. The powers of a constable just referred to are to require the person concerned not to consume, in the designated place, anything which is, or which the constable reasonably believes to be, alcohol, and to surrender anything in his possession which is, or which the constable reasonably believes to be, alcohol or a container for alcohol. Anything so surrendered may be disposed of by the constable in a manner which he considers to be appropriate. Failure without reasonable excuse to comply with such a requirement is an offence. However, the constable making the requirement must inform the person concerned that failing without reasonable excuse to comply with the requirement is an offence.

As can be seen, it is not essential in order for a requirement to be made that an officer sees a person consuming alcohol. If a person has alcohol in a glass or an open container it raises the inference that he intends to drink it. Where alcohol is in a sealed container, notice will have to be taken of the surrounding circumstances. Possession of a 'four-pack' by a person who is walking home differs from possession by groups of persons assembled at that place for the purpose of drinking.

CJPA 2001, s 13 provides that a 'designated public place' is a public place within the area of a local authority which is identified in an order made by that authority. A local authority may make such an order where it is satisfied that:

(a) nuisance or annoyance to members of the public, or a section of the public; or
(b) disorder;

has been associated with the consumption of alcohol in that place. The making of orders is controlled by the Local Authorities (Alcohol Consumption in Designated Public Places) Regulations 2001.

By CJPA 2001, s 14, a place is not a designated place if it is:

(a) premises in respect of which a premises licence or club premises certificate has effect;
(b) a place within the curtilage of any such premises;
(c) premises which by virtue of LA 2003, Part 5 (permitted temporary activities) may for the time being be used for the supply of alcohol or could have been so used within the last twenty minutes; or
(d) a place where facilities or activities relating to the sale or consumption of alcohol are for the time being permitted by virtue of a permission granted under the Highways Act 1980, s 115E (council permission to set up objects and structures on a highway for the purpose of producing income).

CLOSURE OF LICENSED PREMISES DUE TO DISORDER OR DISTURBANCE

The making of a closure order

LA 2003, s 161 provides that a senior police officer (ie of or above the rank of inspector) may make a closure order in relation to any relevant premises (premises in respect of which there is a premises licence or a temporary events notice) if he reasonably believes that:

(a) there is, or is likely imminently to be, disorder on, or in the vicinity of and related to, the premises and their closure is necessary in the interests of public safety; or
(b) a public nuisance is being caused by noise coming from the premises and the closure of the premises is necessary to prevent that nuisance.

A closure order requires the premises to be closed for a period not exceeding twenty-four hours. An officer making a closure order must consider, in particular, any conduct of each appropriate person in relation to the disorder or nuisance. A closure order is effective as soon as notice of it has been given to the licensee or a manager of the premises.

A person who permits relevant premises to be open in contravention of a closure order, without reasonable excuse, commits an offence.

Extension of closure order

Where, before the end of the closure period the responsible senior police officer reasonably believes that:

(a) a magistrates' court will not have determined whether to exercise its powers under s 165(2) (see below) before the end of the closure period; and
(b) the conditions for an extension are satisfied;

he may extend the closure period for a further twenty-four hours. The conditions for an extension are:

(a) in the case of an order made on the grounds of public safety because of disorder, that those conditions still exist;
(b) in the case of an order made on the grounds of nuisance, that those conditions still exist.

To have effect, such a notice of extension must be given before the original period has expired.

Cancellation of a closure order

The responsible senior officer may cancel a closure order or any extension of it at any time between the making of the appropriate order but before determination by the magistrates. Such an officer must cancel an order if he does not believe that the original conditions which merited its making continue to exist. Notice of cancellation must be given.

Procedure following the making of an order

As soon as reasonably practicable after the making of the order, the responsible senior police officer (he who made the order or another senior officer designated for the purpose by the chief officer of police) must apply to a relevant magistrates' court for it to consider the order. The magistrates' court must as soon as reasonably practicable hold a hearing and may, under LA 2003, s 165(2):

(a) revoke the order and any extension of it;
(b) order that closure continues until the matter is considered by the relevant licensing authority;
(c) order the premises to remain closed until a time specified in an order subject to any stated exceptions; or
(d) order closure until a stated time unless prescribed conditions are satisfied.

An appeal lies to a Crown Court against any such decision by the magistrates.

The magistrates must notify the licensing authority of their decision in relation to any premises in respect of which a premises licence is in force. The licensing authority is required to review the premises licence within twenty-eight days of receiving notification from the justices. Regulations deal with notification to the holder of a premises licence. Where it has been ordered that premises remain closed an offence is committed by a person who, without reasonable excuse, allows the premises to remain open. Such premises are open if a person (other than a licence holder or person living there) enters the premises and is supplied with food or drink, or, while he is there, the premises are used for entertainment. Entries to premises which are not associated with licensable activities sit outside these provisions.

Police powers

A constable may use such force as may be necessary for the purpose of closing premises in compliance with a closure order. Neither a constable nor the chief officer of police will be liable for any damage which occurs in the course of such duties unless the act or omission is shown to have been in bad faith or to be unlawful because of the Human Rights Act 1998.

Closure of all premises in an identified area

LA 2003, s 160 deals with situations in which there is, or there is expected to be, disorder in a local justice area. In such cases, a magistrates' court acting for that area may make a closure order for a period not exceeding twenty-four hours, in relation to all premises situated at or near the place of the disorder or expected disorder and in respect of which a premises licence or a temporary event notice has effect. Application for such an order must be made by an officer of at least superintendent rank and the order must not be made unless the court is satisfied that it is necessary to prevent disorder.

It is an offence for a manager of premises, the holder of a premises licence, the designated premises supervisor or the premises user in the case of a temporary event to knowingly keep premises to which the order relates open, or to allow any such premises to be kept open, during the currency of that order.

A constable may use such force as may be necessary to close such premises.

Closure of unlicensed premises under provisions of the Criminal Justice and Police Act 2001

Where a constable or a local authority is satisfied that premises are being, or within the last twenty-four hours have been, used for unauthorised sale of alcohol for consumption on, or in the vicinity of, the premises, CJPA 2001, s 19 provides that he or it must serve a closure notice on a person having control of, or responsibility for, the activities carried on at the premises. A closure notice must also be served on any person occupying any other part of the building whose access would be impeded by the order. It may also be served on any other person with control of, or responsibility for, the activities on the premises, or any person with an interest in the premises. A closure notice must specify the nature of the alleged use of the premises, state the effect of s 20 (below) and set out the steps which may be taken to ensure that the alleged use of the premises ceases or (as the case may be) does not recur. Closure notices issued by a constable or a local authority may be cancelled at any time.

CJPA 2001, s 20 provides that when a closure notice has been served the constable or local authority may seek an order from the justices, not less than seven days, and not more than six months, after the service of the notice. An order should not be sought where the constable or local authority is satisfied that the offending use of the premises has ceased and that there is no reasonable likelihood of resumption. Where the justices on hearing the case are satisfied that a notice was properly served under s 19, and that the premises and/or the vicinity of those premises continue to be used for the offending purpose or that there is a reasonable likelihood that there will be such use, they may make a closure order under CJPA 2001, s 21, requiring in particular:

(a) immediate closure of the premises to the public until the constable or local authority (as the case may be) has certified that the need for the order has ceased (such an order may include conditions relating to admission and access to other parts of the building);

(b) any offending use to be discontinued immediately;

(c) any defendant to pay into court a sum of money which will not be released until the other requirements of the order have been complied with.

The constable or local authority (as the case may be) must fix a copy of the order to the premises.

An appeal against the making of such an order may be made to a Crown Court.

Affected persons may seek discharge of the order. If the justices are satisfied that the need for the order has ceased, they may discharge it.

A person who, without reasonable excuse, permits premises to be open in contravention of a closure order, or who otherwise fails to comply with it, commits an offence.

Police powers

Where a closure order has been made a constable or an authorised person, who identifies himself if so required, may enter the premises at any reasonable time, if need be by reasonable force, and do anything reasonably necessary to secure compliance with the order.

It is an offence for a person intentionally to obstruct a constable or an authorised person in the exercise of these powers.

Closure of noisy premises with premises licence or temporary event notice

The Anti-social Behaviour Act 2003, s 40 empowers the chief executive officer of a local authority to make a closure order in relation to premises in respect of which a premises licence or temporary event notice is in effect if he reasonably believes that a public nuisance is being caused by noise coming from the premises and the closure is necessary to prevent that nuisance. Such an order will require the specified premises to remain closed during a specified period which does not exceed twenty-four hours and begins when the manager of the premises receives written notice of the order. It is an offence, without reasonable excuse, to permit premises to be open in contravention of a closure order.

The chief executive officer must give notice of the order as soon as reasonably practicable to the licensing authority. A closure order may be cancelled by the chief executive officer by written notice. In addition, it must be cancelled as soon as reasonably practicable if the chief executive officer believes that it is no longer necessary in order to prevent a public nuisance being caused by noise from the premises.

The chief executive officer may authorise an environmental health officer to exercise the above powers on his behalf.

MISCELLANEOUS MATTERS

Exclusion of persons convicted of offences of violence from licensed premises

The Licensed Premises (Exclusion of Certain Persons) Act 1980 permits courts to make orders in respect of persons convicted of offences of violence or threats of violence on licensed premises (premises in respect of which a premises licence authorising the supply of alcohol for consumption on the premises is in force), prohibiting such a person from entering specified licensed premises without the express consent of the licensee, his employee or agent. A court will only interfere with an order if it is wrong in principle or manifestly excessive in extent. The Court of Appeal, for example, has refused to interfere with an order excluding a person from all licensed premises in the Borough of Crewe and Nantwich because that person's previous conduct suggested that this ban was appropriate. A person who enters in breach of an order commits an offence. The licensee, his employee or agent may expel a person who has entered, or whom he reasonably suspects of entering, in breach of an order. A constable must, on the demand of a licensee, his employee or agent, help to expel any person whom the constable reasonably suspects of being in breach of an exclusion order.

Opening hours generally

The Secretary of State is empowered by LA 2003, s 172 to make an order to provide for premises with a premises licence or a club premises certificate to open for specified, generally extended hours, on special occasions of international, national or local significance.

Prohibition of sales of alcohol at service areas, garages etc

LA 2003, s 176 provides that no premises licence, club premises certificate or temporary event notice has effect to authorise the sale by retail or supply of alcohol on or from excluded premises. These are premises on the land of a special road authority being used for the provision of facilities at motorway service stations or premises used primarily as a garage or which form part of such premises. The nature of prohibited premises may be altered by order. The Secretary of State may, for example, wish to exempt certain premises in rural areas where the business concerned with the provision of petrol etc is only a part of the business concerned.

Dancing and live music in certain small premises

LA 2003, s 177 is concerned with the situation where (1) a premises licence or a club premises certificate authorises the sale of alcohol for consumption on the premises and the provision of musical entertainment (ie live music or dancing), and (2) the relevant premises are used primarily for the sale of alcohol for consumption on the premises and have a capacity limit of up to 200. Section 177 provides that at any time when the premises are open for the supply of alcohol for consumption on the premises, and are being used for musical entertainment, and s 177(4) (below) does not apply, any conditions imposed in respect of musical entertainment by the licensing authority, other than those set out in the licence holder's operating schedule, will be suspended unless they were imposed for public safety or the prevention of crime and disorder.

LA 2003, s 177(4) provides that where a premises licence or a club premises certificate authorises the provision of musical entertainment and the premises have a capacity limit of less than 200 and, during the hours between 8 am and midnight, the premises are being used for live unamplified music but no other form of regulated entertainment, conditions imposed by the licensing authority, other than those set out in the operating schedule, will be suspended in relation to that entertainment.

Section 177 may be disapplied in relation to conditions in respect of particular premises following a review of the licence or certificate. There are exceptions where a licensing authority believes that a condition must continue to apply in the interests of the prevention of crime and disorder or the maintenance of public safety.

Police powers

LA 2003, s 179 provides for a police officer or other authorised person to enter premises where he has reason to believe that the premises are being, or are about to be, used for a licensable activity to ensure that the activities are being carried on under and in accordance with the appropriate authorisations. Reasonable force may be used if necessary. It is an offence to obstruct an authorised person.

LA 2003, s 180 provides that a police officer may enter and search premises where there is reason to believe an offence under the Act has been, is being or is about to be, committed, and may use reasonable force to gain entry.

OFFENCES OF DRUNKENNESS AND POLICE POWERS

Drunkenness is not in itself an offence but becomes so in certain circumstances, which are described below. Drunkenness in this context is limited to intoxication through drink and does not include intoxication through drugs or through glue-sniffing.

Simple drunkenness

The term 'simple drunkenness' is one of practice and not of law. Police officers have for many years used the term to separate the offence of being found drunk from various offences dealing with aggravated forms of drunkenness. This offence of simple drunkenness is often referred to, although not strictly accurately, as one of being drunk and incapable. The offence is governed by the Licensing Act 1872, s 12 which provides that a person is guilty of an offence if he is found drunk on any highway or other public place, whether a building or not, or on any licensed premises. The general arrest provisions of the Police and Criminal Evidence Act 1984, s 24, will apply to such circumstances. It is particularly worth remembering that that section permits an arrest if it is necessary to prevent the person from suffering serious physical harm. Such harm would be likely if he was left unconscious in the open.

This offence under LA 1872, s 12 is a 'penalty offence' for the purposes of Part I of CJPA 2001 and may be dealt with under a fixed penalty procedure: see p 874.

Drunk and disorderly

The Criminal Justice Act 1967, s 91 states that any person who in any public place is guilty, while drunk, of disorderly behaviour commits an offence. Where there is an intercom system and locks on the entrance to a block of flats, so that only those admitted by the occupiers are given access to the area, the landing area outside the flats is not a public place for the purposes of this offence. Nor would it be for the purposes of the offence of simple drunkenness.

An offence under Criminal Justice Act 1967, s 91 is a 'penalty offence' for the purposes of Part I of CJPA 2001 and may be dealt with under a fixed penalty procedure: see p 874.

Drunk in charge of particular things

LA 1872, s 12 also makes it an offence for a person to be drunk while in charge on any highway or other public place, of a carriage, horse, cattle, or steam engine, or to be drunk when in possession of a loaded firearm. 'Carriage' includes a motor vehicle, but if a person is drunk in charge of such a vehicle the appropriate offence is that under the Road Traffic Act 1988, s 4 (discussed in Chapter 17, above) and not the present one, since it is a more serious offence which reflects the gravity of the situation. Although a bicycle is a 'carriage', *riding* a cycle while unfit through drink is also an offence under the Road Traffic Act 1988, s 30, and if a person rides while unfit he should be dealt with under that section. However, a person *in charge*, eg pushing a pedal cycle, in such a condition commits an offence only against LA 1872, s 12. The Act does not define the term 'firearm' for the purposes of the section, but that term bears its everyday meaning and includes an airgun.

Drunk in charge of a child

The Licensing Act 1902, s 2 creates the offence of being found drunk on any highway or other public place, whether a building or not, or on any licensed premises, while having the charge of a child apparently under the age of seven years.

Being drunk at a designated sports ground

This offence is dealt with in Chapter 32.

CHAPTER 20

Betting, gaming and lotteries

INTRODUCTION

The Gambling Act 2005 (GA 2005) repealed all existing legislation covering the activities which would fall under these headings The Act provides a new regulatory system to govern the provision of gambling facilities in Great Britain, other than the National Lottery. The new system covers all the forms of betting, although some activities fall outside the terms of the Act in prescribed circumstances. GA 2005 responds to the fact that the nature of gambling activities has changed significantly since the enactment of previous legislation. Forms of communication (and thereby the forms of conducting betting transactions) have expanded. Television, the Internet and mobile telephones are just some examples of the means by which gambling transaction may be effected.

The provisions of GA 2005 which provide for the setting up of the Gambling Commission, or deal with transitory matters, are in force at the time of writing to enable the establishment of the system upon which the new law will be based. The parts of GA 2005 which deal with gambling establishments as encountered by the operational police officer will come into force in September 2007.

Some aspects of the new regulatory system of gambling will be dealt with by way of regulations, licence conditions, codes of practice and guidance.

This chapter deals with the situation as it will exist when all the provisions of GA 2005 are in force.

PRINCIPAL CONCEPTS

Licensing objectives

GA 2005 refers on a number of occasions to 'the licensing objectives'.
The licensing objectives are:

(a) preventing gambling from being a source of crime or disorder, being associated with crime or disorder or being used to support crime; and

(b) ensuring that gambling is conducted in a fair and open way; and
(c) protecting children and other vulnerable people from being harmed or exploited by gambling.

Gambling Commission and licensing authorities

In exercising its functions under GA 2005 the Gambling Commission must aim (a) to pursue, and wherever appropriate have regard to, the licensing objectives of GA 2005, and (b) to permit gambling, so far as it thinks that it is reasonably consistent with those objectives. Thus, the control of the issue of various forms of authorisation to permit people to provide gambling is in the hands of the Gambling Commission. The previous responsibilities for such matters, held by the Gaming Board and licensing justices, are removed by GA 2005. The members of the Gambling Commission are appointed by the Secretary of State.

The Gambling Commission is responsible for directly authorising the activities of *persons* who are involved in the provision of gambling facilities, including the person controlling and providing the facilities and specified members of staff. Licensing authorities (local authorities) are made responsible for the licensing of *premises* upon which gambling activities will take place, but these matters are supervised by the Gambling Commission.

The Gambling Commission, together with local authority inspectors, is closely involved with ensuring that the correct forms of authority are held by persons and in respect of premises involved in gambling activities. In consequence, the various forms of authorisation and the conditions which may be applied to them are dealt with below in a narrative form rather than by constant reference to Parts or sections of GA 2005. The Gambling Commission may carry out investigations and take proceedings for offences.

Both the Commission and the licensing authorities must maintain registers containing details of licences and permits issued.

Gambling

Gambling is defined by GA 2005, s 3 as meaning gaming, betting and participation in a lottery. These terms are defined on pp 692–695.

Remote gambling

GA 2005 is concerned with the various technological means by which gambling can take place. 'Remote gambling' is defined by GA 2005, s 4 as gambling in which persons participate by the use of 'remote communication', ie by using the Internet, telephone, television, radio or any other form of electronic or other technology for facilitating communication.

Facilities for gambling

The primary aim of the Act is to licence persons and organisations involved in gambling activities. There are many ways in which a person can provide gambling facilities or be involved in them. GA 2005, s 5 provides that a person provides facilities for gambling if he:

(a) invites others to gamble in accordance with arrangements made by him;
(b) provides, operates or administers arrangements for gambling by others, or
(c) participates in the operation or administration of gambling by others.

Thus, the term covers the provision of facilities (by individuals or companies) such as betting offices or casinos, or a website by means of which betting or gaming can take place. It also covers the administration of the arrangements for gambling by exercising some form of control, or being involved in the operation by participation, such as the part played by a croupier, or a person who assists others to complete betting transactions.

The suppliers of articles for gambling (other than gaming machines), eg packs of cards, are exempted, as are service providers of electronic communications. This is because they do no more than provide a commercial service, as opposed to a service which is directly aimed at gaming.

OTHER KEY CONCEPTS

Gaming

Gaming and game of chance

GA 2005, s 6 deals with these concepts. Gaming is the playing of a game of chance for a prize.

A game of chance includes (a) a game that involves both an element of chance and an element of skill; (b) a game that involves an element of chance that can be eliminated by superlative skill; and (c) a game that is presented as involving an element of chance. It does not include a sport. A person can play a game of chance whether or not there are other participants, and whether or not a computer takes the place of another participant. In this way, machine games or virtual games are brought within the scope of the Act.

Casino

By GA 2005, s 7, a 'casino' is an arrangement (whether conducted on premises or by remote communication) where people can participate in one or more casino games. 'Casino games' are games which are not equal chance games, as defined below. Thus, games which involve playing against a bank, or where chances are not equally favourable to all players, is a casino game. The Secretary of State is empowered to specify that an activity is or is not a casino game.

There are four categories of casino: regional, large, small or below the minimum size for a licensed casino. These terms will be further defined in regulations which may classify them by reference to:

(a) the number of gaming tables at which casino games (or classes of such games) are made available;

(b) the location and concentration of gaming tables; and
(c) the floor area used or designated for a specified purpose (a regional casino will have the largest floor area);
(d) any combination of (a) to (c), or
(e) any other matter.

The premises of a casino below the minimum size for a licensed casino will have been previously licensed under previous legislation. Transitional provisions permit this class to continue to operate.

Equal chance gaming

The distinction, recognised by previous legislation, between equal chance gaming and unequal chance gaming (including bankers' games) is retained. Gaming is equal chance gaming if (a) it does not involve playing or staking against a bank, and (b) the chances are equally favourable to all participants (GA 2005, s 8).

The right to conduct games of equal chance is more widely spread through clubs, private premises and non-commercial gaming. Unequal chance gaming is restricted, mostly to casinos.

Betting

In GA 2005, 'betting' means making or accepting a bet on:

(a) the outcome of a race, competition or other event or process;
(b) the likelihood of anything occurring or not occurring; or
(c) whether anything is or is not true (GA 2005, s 9).

In short, 'betting' involves the staking of money or other value on the outcome of a doubtful issue. The provisions of GA 2005 do not apply to 'spread betting' (a stock market activity).

GA 2005, s 11 provides that, despite the fact that no stake is deposited in the normal way of betting, prize competitions may amount to betting for the purposes of the Act if there is a requirement to pay to enter the competition generally. The term 'payment' includes a reference to paying money, transferring 'money's worth, and paying for goods and services at a price or rate which reflects the opportunity to participate in an arrangement under which a participant may win a prize. It is immaterial to whom the payment is made and who receives a benefit from it. An entry, or prize claim, by telephone where the call is charged at a standard rate, or by ordinary post, or by use of another comparable service at its standard price, does not amount to payment for entry. It does amount to payment to participate where an operator, or any third party, obtains income from the competition because the entrant must pay to find out whether he has won a prize (perhaps by use of a premium rate line). However, a competition will not be regarded as requiring payment for entry if there is a 'free entry route' (by letter or other means which is no more expensive or less convenient that the option for participating by paying). The free entry route must be displayed as prominently as that involving payment, and free entries must be no less likely to win all or any of the prizes than entries which are paid for.

Pool betting   GA 2005 refers to 'pool betting'. For these purposes betting is pool betting if made on terms that all or part of winnings:

(a) shall be determined by reference to the aggregate of stakes paid or agreed to be paid by the persons betting;
(b) shall be divided among the winners; or
(c) shall or may be something other than money (GA 2005, s 12(1)).

Pool betting is horse-race pool betting if it relates to horse-racing in Great Britain (GA 2005, s 12(2)).

Betting intermediary   In the days before licensed betting shops, there existed a well-known member of the local community who was known as a 'bookies' runner'. He journeyed from place to place throughout the day collecting bets on behalf of a bookmaker. GA 2005 provides the title 'betting intermediary', which is defined as follows by GA 2005, s 13. 'Betting intermediary' means a person who provides a service designed to facilitate the making or acceptance of bets between others. For the purposes of GA 2005 acting as a betting intermediary constitutes providing facilities for betting. As 'runners' have now mostly sought sanctuary in betting shops and become static, the new term is more appropriate.

Lotteries

For the purposes of GA 2005, there are two types of lottery: a simple lottery and a complex lottery. Both are defined by GA 2005, s 14.

An arrangement is a simple lottery if:

(a) persons are required to pay in order to participate in the arrangement;
(b) in the course of the arrangement one or more prizes are allocated to one or more members of a class; and
(c) the prizes are allocated by a process which relies wholly on chance.

An arrangement is a complex lottery if:

(a) persons are required to pay in order to participate in the arrangement;
(b) in the course of the arrangement one or more prizes are allocated to one or more members of a class;
(c) the prizes are allocated by a series of processes; and
(d) the first of those processes relies wholly on chance.

The definition of complex lottery recognises that a lottery may involve more than one process for determining prize winners. Where more than one person is involved, an arrangement is a lottery if the first process relies *entirely* upon chance. If this is so, it does not matter that any following process relies upon an element of skill or judgement. Where the first process does not rely wholly on chance, there will be no lottery, even if following procedures involve no more than chance.

'Payment' in the above definitions has the same meaning as it has in respect of 'betting'. The 'payment to enter' elements cannot be circumvented by offering two methods of entry, both of which involve premium rate communications, or where one involves payment and the other communication at a premium rate. Neither of these alternatives provides a mode of free entry.

Competitions which do not involve a minimum level of skill, judgement or knowledge are treated as relying solely on chance and are therefore lotteries. Moreover, a process which requires persons to exercise skill or judgement, or to display knowledge, is treated as relying wholly on chance if the requirement is unlikely to prevent a significant proportion of participants from receiving a prize, and is unlikely to prevent a significant proportion of persons who wish to participate from doing so. Where a competition is one for children, these levels of skill, judgement or knowledge must be examined accordingly; where it is provided within a publication produced for persons with a specialised skill or knowledge, 'challenge' will be looked at in recognition of the target population. The Secretary of State is empowered to specify within regulations types of arrangements which may be considered as lotteries.

Participating in the National Lottery is not gambling with the exception under GA 2005, s 42 referred to on p 698 (GA 2005, s 15).

Cross-category activities

With one exception, transactions which satisfy the definitions of betting and of gaming are treated by GA 2005, s 16 as gaming (and not as betting). This provision prevents games such as roulette being available on licensed betting premises. The exception is that a transaction satisfying both definitions which is pool betting is treated as betting (and not as gaming).

Transactions which satisfy the definitions of a game of chance and of a lottery are treated by GA 2005, s 17 as a game of chance (and not as a lottery) if a person who pays to join the class amongst whom members' prizes are allocated is required to participate in, or be more successful in, more than three processes before becoming entitled to a prize, and so is any other lottery besides a private society lottery, work lottery, residents' lottery, customer lottery, small society lottery, or non-incidental commercial lottery. These types of lottery (defined on pp 708–710) are treated as a lottery (and not as a game of chance).

Where a transaction satisfies the definition of participating in a lottery and also satisfies the definition of pool betting and of betting by virtue of the provisions relating to prize competitions, the transaction is treated by GA 2005, s 18 as participating in a lottery (and not as betting) if it is an incidental non-commercial lottery, private society lottery, work lottery, residents' lottery, customer lottery or small society lottery. Otherwise it is so treated as betting (and not as participating in a lottery).

Non-commercial society

The provisions of GA 2005 relating to operating licences and to lotteries refer to such a society. A society is non-commercial if established and conducted for charitable purposes, or for cultural or sporting purposes, or for any other non-commercial purpose other than that of private gain.

OFFENCES IN RELATION TO LICENCES

Provision of facilities for gambling

Generally

GA 2005, s 33 provides that the provision of facilities for gambling (as defined on p 691) is an offence unless that activity is authorised by an operating licence or is specifically exempted. Exempted activities are those which may take place without an operating licence, but may require a permit or some other authorisation, or do not require any form of authorisation, namely, equal chance gaming in certain circumstances in particular clubs or in miners' welfare institutes or in on-licensed alcohol premises, prize gaming, private gaming and betting, and non-commercial gaming. Those activities are dealt with on pp 710–713. In addition, the offence does not apply to the provision of facilities for a lottery or making a gaming machine available for use. Other offences may be committed in those circumstances.

It is immaterial whether facilities for gambling are provided in whole or in part by means of remote communication, or whether such facilities are provided inside or outside the United Kingdom or partly inside and partly outside.

However, where the gambling takes place by means of remote communication, the offence is committed only if one piece of remote gambling equipment is located in Great Britain. Where such equipment does not exist in Great Britain, no offence is committed even if people in Great Britain can participate. 'Remote gambling equipment' covers such equipment as a computer database or server which stores information about a person's gambling activities (virtual gambling); equipment used for determining the result or the effect of the result of a transaction (random number generators); and equipment to store information relating to the result. The term does not cover the equipment being used by the person participating (personal computer equipment) provided that it is not provided by the person providing the remote gambling facilities.

In instances in which the gambling concerned is other than by remote communication, the offence is committed only if any act of provision of unlicensed facilities takes place in Great Britain.

Provision of unlawful facilities abroad

A person commits an offence contrary to GA 2005, s 44 if he does anything in Great Britain, or uses remote gambling equipment situated in Great Britain, for the purpose of inviting or enabling a person in a prohibited territory to participate in remote gambling. 'Prohibited territory' means a country or place specified by the Secretary of State.

Relating to the use of premises

GA 2005, s 37 creates the offences of using premises, or causing or permitting the use of premises, for specified gambling activities, unless authorised by the appropriate premises licence or, in the case of bingo or betting in a casino, by a casino premises licence, or the activity is an exempted activity. An activity is exempted if it is:

(a) one in respect of which a temporary use notice exists;
(b) one in respect of which an occasional use notice exists;
(c) one on premises used for facilitating authorised football pools;
(d) one which relates to making available a gaming machine in specified circumstances;
(e) one which is covered by a prize gaming permit or involves prize gaming at an adult gaming centre, family entertainment centre (in specified circumstances) or travelling fair; or
(f) one to which an exception applies in relation to specific facilities such as the provisions of gaming machines on liquor licensed premises, at travelling fairs or at non-commercial events.

A temporary use notice, endorsed by the licensing authority (local authority), allows gambling temporarily on specified premises. By this means the holder of an operating licence may use other premises on a temporary basis. Regulations will provide for the extent of operations on temporary premises. These authorisations could cover some gambling activities at conference centres or entertainment venues. A temporary use notice must be submitted in writing by the holder of an operating licence and must relate to an activity covered by that operating licence. A set of premises cannot be subject to a temporary use notice for more than twenty-one days in any twelve-month period. Objections may be made by the Commission, the police and HM Revenue and Customs.

The term 'occasional use notice' is one which applies to tracks which are used only occasionally. Where they are not used for more than eight days in a year, such a notice may authorise the provision of betting facilities. A 'track' is a racecourse, dog track or any other premises used or intended for a race or other sporting event. Such a notice must be served by the occupier of a track, or a responsible officer, on the local authority and the police force of the area. However, persons providing betting facilities at the track will need to be authorised to act as betting operators.

Gaming is 'prize gaming' if neither the nature nor the size of the prize is determined by reference to the number of people playing, or the amount paid for or raised by the gaming. Where a permit is held in respect of prize gaming the charges and prizes must not exceed prescribed amounts and the gaming must take place on the relevant premises on one day only.

Other offences

Gambling software

GA 2005, s 41 provides that it is an offence to manufacture, supply, install or adapt, in the course of a business, computer software for remote gambling except in accordance with an operating licence held for that activity. Software which is used solely in connection with a gaming machine is excluded from the provisions of the section. Communication service providers do not supply or install gambling software simply by making facilities available to another which he uses to supply or install gambling software.

Cheating

GA 2005, s 42 creates offences of 'cheating' at gambling and of doing anything to enable or assist another so to cheat. 'Cheating' is not defined and should carry its normal meaning. There is no requirement that, as a result of his act, the offender should win, or that the act has the effect of improving the chances of success. The offences embrace actual or attempted deceptions, or interference with the process of gambling (for example, interfering with the operation of a roulette wheel). The event interfered with may be real or virtual.

An offence under s 42 extends to cheating etc in relation to the National Lottery.

Chain-gift schemes

GA 2005, s 43 deals with chain-gift schemes. A chain-gift scheme is an arrangement which requires a joining fee to be paid to one or more of the other participants, and where each participant is required or invited to invite others to take part and is encouraged to believe that he will receive more from joining fees from others than he paid. A joining fee may be money or money's worth, but not the provision of goods or services.

Section 43 makes it an offence to invite another to join, or knowingly to participate in the promotion, administration or management of a chain-gift scheme. No offence is committed by a participant in such a scheme. The offences are committed irrespective of whether the joining fees are paid directly between participants, or through a person responsible for managing or administering the scheme.

Offences involving children and young persons

For the purposes of GA 2005, a person aged less than sixteen is a child and a person aged sixteen or over, but under eighteen, is a young person.

Invitation to child or young person to gamble

By GA 2005, s 46, it is an offence to invite or cause or permit a person who is under eighteen to gamble.

The term 'invitation' includes intentionally sending the child or young person an advertisement of gambling or intentionally bringing to his attention information about gambling so as to encourage him to gamble. A person identified in such an advertisement as someone to whom payment may be made, or from whom information can be obtained, is deemed to have committed an offence under s 46, unless he proves that the document was sent without that person's consent or authority. If information about gambling is brought to the attention of a child or young person and identifies a person as to whom payment may be made or from whom information may be obtained, that person is deemed to have committed an offence under s 46, unless he proves that the information was brought to the child or young person's attention without his consent or authority or as an incident of the information being brought to the attention of adults and not with a view to encouraging the child or young person to gamble.

Inviting or permitting child or young person to enter a casino, betting shop or adult gaming centre

GA 2005, s 47 prohibits inviting or permitting a child or young person to enter licensed casino premises which are being used under that licence at the time. The offence does not apply to permitting a child or young person to enter the non-gambling area of a regional casino.

Section 47 also provides the following offences.

A person commits an offence if he invites or permits a child or young person to enter premises other than a track if a betting premises licence has effect in respect of the premises, and the premises are being used in reliance on that licence when the child or young person is invited or permitted to enter.

A person commits an offence if he invites or permits a child or young person to enter premises if an adult gaming centre premises licence has effect in respect of the premises, and the premises are being used in reliance on that licence when the child or young person is invited or permitted to enter.

A person commits an offence if he invites or permits a child or young person to enter an area at a track from which children and young persons are required by the premises licence to be excluded. These are areas where betting facilities are provided and gaming machines (other than Category D machines (see p 706)) are situated.

A person commits an offence if he invites or permits a child or young person to enter part of premises if:

(a) the premises are a licensed family entertainment centre;
(b) a person entering that part of the premises has access to a Category C gaming machine (see p 706); and
(c) at the time when the child or young person is permitted or invited to enter, a Category C gaming machine is being used or is available for use.

Offences by young persons

The following offences can be committed by a young person (but not by a child).

A young person commits an offence under GA 2005, s 48 if he gambles. But this does not apply in relation to participation in private gambling or non-commercial gaming or betting, or in a lottery or in football pools. Nor does it apply to the use of Category D gaming machines or participation in equal chance gaming in accordance with a prize gaming permit or at a licensed family entertainment centre, or in prize gaming at an unlicensed family entertainment centre or travelling fair.

By GA 2005, s 49, a young person also commits an offence if he enters premises of the type and in circumstances where it would be an offence under s 47 to invite or permit him to do so. An additional offence can be committed under GA 2005, s 50 by a young person who provides facilities for gambling other than private or non-commercial gaming and betting, lotteries, football pools and prize gaming at a travelling fair.

Employment of children or young persons to provide gambling facilities

By GA 2005, s 51, it is an offence to employ children or young persons for the purpose of providing gambling facilities other than facilities in connection with private or non-commercial gaming and betting, prize gaming at a travelling fair, a lottery or football pools. GA 2005, s 52 provides that a person commits an offence if he employs *a child* to provide facilities in relation to lotteries and football pool betting.

It is an offence against s 53 to employ *children* on premises where and at a time when facilities are provided for bingo or when gambling facilities are provided under a club gaming permit or club machine permit.

A person commits an offence under GA 2005, s 54 if he employs a child or young person to perform any function on premises where a Category A, B, C or D gaming machine (see p 706) is situated, and the child or young person is or may be required in the course of his employment to perform a function in connection with the gaming machine. Thus, a child may be employed at a family entertainment centre to carry out duties not connected with gaming, but he may not operate or handle the machines or pay customers prizes and he may not enter any area in which there are Category C machines.

A person commits an offence under GA 2005, s 55 if he employs a child or young person to perform any function on premises in respect of which any of the following have effect:

(a) a casino premises licence;
(b) a betting premises licence; and
(c) an adult gaming centre premises licence.

The offence does not apply to employment at a time when no activity is being carried on in reliance on the premises licence, or to employment on a part of premises which are being used for a regional casino at a time when that part is not being used for the provision of facilities for gambling.

A young person commits an offence if he is employed in contravention of s 54 or s 55.

The provisions which allow children and young persons to be employed in non-gambling areas are aimed at permitting them to carry out jobs which are not directly connected with gambling, such as an apprentice carrying out structural repairs to a building or its fittings.

Children and lotteries

It is an offence against GA 2005, s 56 to invite, or cause or permit a *child* to take part in a lottery other than a private lottery or an incidental exempt non-commercial one or the National Lottery. Thus, children may buy tickets at their school fete.

It is an offence under GA 2005, s 57 to invite, cause or permit a *child* to participate in football pools. The provisions of s 46 (p 698) relating to the meaning of 'inviting' and whereby a person may be deemed to have invited participation apply to the offence under s 57.

Defences

By GA 2005, s 63, it is a defence for a person charged with any of the offences under GA 2005, ss 46 to 57 where they relate to a child or (as the case may be) a young person to prove that he took all reasonable steps to establish a person's age and that he reasonably believed that the person was not a child or (as the case may be) young person.

Temporary or occasional use notices

By GA 2005, s 60, notices of these types authorising gambling at premises which do not have a premises licence are regarded as being premises licences for the purposes of the offences under GA 2005, ss 46 to 57.

OPERATING LICENCES

Operating licence are the principal authorisations issued under GA 2005. The Gambling Commission issues such licences and administers the licensing regime. There are ten types of operating licence:

(a) a casino operating licence;
(b) a bingo operating licence;
(c) a general betting operating licence;
(d) a pool betting operating licence;
(e) a betting intermediary operating licence;
(f) a gaming machine general operating licence;
(g) a gaming machine operating licence for a family entertainment centre;
(h) a gaming machine technical licence;
(i) a gambling software operating licence; and
(j) a lottery operating licence.

Both the Gambling Commission, by way of general and individual conditions attached to a licence, and the Secretary of State, by regulations containing specified conditions which must be attached to a licence, can make requirements in relation to operating licences.

Operating licences are of indefinite duration.

In the case of a bingo operating licence, the Secretary of State may make comprehensive regulations limiting stakes, participation charges and the payment of prizes. 'Multiple' and 'linked' bingo provisions are replaced by the necessity to obtain a remote operating licence for the operation of bingo by means of remote communication. No condition may be attached to such a licence prohibiting roll-over prizes.

A general betting operating licence is required by anyone wishing to accept or make bets by way of a business. Those providing facilities to accept another person's bets will require a betting intermediary operating licence. Employees of the holder of a general betting operating licence holder may accept or make bets on his behalf.

Conditions are also imposed on pool betting and horserace betting operating licences.

Lotteries, other than the National Lottery or exempt lotteries (as to which see p 708–9), must be licensed. A lottery operating licence may only be issued to:

(a) non-commercial societies;
(b) local authorities; and
(c) external lottery managers.

A non-commercial society (defined on p 695) requires an operating licence if the proceeds of a lottery (whether by way of entry, participation, sponsorship, commission or otherwise) are appropriated for the purposes of 'private gain'. If these thresholds are not exceeded the lottery is a 'small society lottery' and is exempt. However, such a lottery must be registered with the local authority.

An 'external lottery manager' may be authorised by licence to provide lottery management services on behalf of a local authority or non-commercial society. The Commission may impose upon a lottery operating licence requiring that all arrangements are to be made by an external lottery manager. An external lottery manager is someone who makes arrangements for a lottery on behalf of a society or authority of which he is not a member, officer or employee.

Delivery of lottery tickets by post may not be prohibited by regulations or by conditions. The Gambling Commission may impose conditions in respect of roll-overs. They include conditions that 20% of the proceeds of any lottery must go to good causes; the proceeds of a single lottery must be limited; the proceeds of all lotteries held in one year are restricted to an overall upper limit; and an upper limit may be imposed upon the size of a prize. Proceeds may not exceed £2,000,000 and the aggregate of the proceeds of lotteries in a calendar year must not exceed £10,000,000.

Non-remote operating licences and remote operating licences

An operating licence may authorise the provision of facilities on premises or by means of remote communication. It cannot authorise both. Where both activities are carried out, two licences must be in force. An operating licence must state whether it is a remote operating licence or not.

A non-remote operating licence authorises the operation of gambling facilities which are to be carried out on premises. However, the person to whom the licence is granted also requires a licence in respect of particular premises upon which such gambling will take place. This may be in the form of a premises licence, an occasional use notice or a temporary use notice. In addition, operating licences may be obtained to authorise the manufacture, supply, installation, adaptation, maintenance of gaming machines computer software.

A remote operating licence may carry conditions limiting the forms of remote gambling which are permitted. A form of communication may be specifically authorised.

One licence for more than one activity

Although it cannot authorise within one licence remote and non-remote activities, the Gambling Commission may issue a licence which covers more than one of the activities set out in the list at (a) to (j) on p 701.

A casino licence also authorises facilities for betting on the outcome of a virtual game, race, competition or other event or process, unless limited by a condition, and also authorises the provision of equal chance gaming other than bingo. A betting operating licence authorises facilities for betting on the outcome of such events (other than a game of chance) unless restricted by a condition. However, these provisions do not apply to virtual gaming by way of a machine.

Gaming machines—authorisations

Some forms of operating licence authorise making machines available for use. These are:

(a) a non-remote casino operating licence;
(b) a non-remote bingo operating licence;
(c) a non-remote general betting operating licence; and
(d) a non-remote pool betting operating licence.

PERSONAL LICENCES

Once a person has obtained an operating licence, there generally will be a need to have persons holding personal licences. A personal licence is a licence which authorises an individual to perform the functions of a specified management office, or to perform a specified operational function, in connection with the provision of facilities for gambling or in connection with a person who provides facilities for gambling. Thus, it authorises people to carry out certain duties on behalf of the licence holder. The Gambling Commission grants such licences. Every operating licence must specify at least one management office to be occupied by a personal licence holder (unless the operating licence holder is a 'small scale operator', in which case a personal licence requirement may not be attached to an operating licence). The term 'small scale operator' is to be defined by the Secretary of State in regulations. The regulations may, for example, refer to circumstances in which the betting operation is carried out by a very small staff under the direct supervision of the licence holder. This could occur at a race track where the operator takes an assistant to help to take bets and distribute winnings.

Additional management posts which must be occupied by a personal licence holder may be identified by the operating licence. As a result, personal licences may be required by persons directly involved in gambling activities such as croupiers and the operators of roulette wheels.

Personal licences are of indefinite duration.

PREMISES LICENCE

The licence

The Gambling Commission licences those operating gambling activities and makes requirements in respect of persons who must hold personal licences. It then becomes the duty of licensing authorities (local authorities) to licence specified premises through the grant of premises licences. Operators' licences cannot specify particular premises upon which gambling activities can take place, but may specify the maximum number of sets of premises upon which licensed activities may be conducted, or the number of people for whom facilities may be provided on any premises. A casino licence, for example, does not necessarily restrict activities to one set of premises. The provision of an operating licence by the Gambling Commission allows the specified person to provide specified gambling facilities, but, for these to be provided on particular premises, those premises must be licensed by the licensing authority.

Premises licences are required for:

(a) casino premises;
(b) bingo premises;
(c) betting premises (including tracks and premises used by a betting intermediary);
(d) adult gaming centres (for Category B, C and D gaming machines); and
(e) family entertainment centres (for Category C and D machines)

There are three types of casino premises licence: regional, large and small depending on which type of casino they relate to. There must be no more than one regional casino premises licence; eight large casino premises licences and eight small casino premises licences. The geographical distribution will be prescribed by order. The limitations on numbers may be varied.

An applicant for a premises licence must hold (or have applied for) a relevant operating licence. However, this requirement does not apply to an applicant for a premises licence which authorises a track to be used for accepting bets and for no other gambling purpose (except a maximum of four Category B, C or D gaming machines).

A licensing authority may issue a 'provisional statement' in advance of the construction or adaptation of premises to be used for providing gambling facilities, or where a person is intending to occupy premises.

Licensing authorities are required to maintain a register of premises licensed under GA 2005 which must be open to public inspection. The Gambling Commission, police and certain other public bodies have the right to make representations about applications for premises licences. Persons living close to the premises and those with business interests (or their representatives) may also make representations.

Unless the Secretary of State provides otherwise by regulations, premises licences are of indefinite duration.

Conditions

The Secretary of State and licensing authorities may include conditions within premises licences. They may be *mandatory* (to be set out in regulations) or *default* (also to be set out in regulations and to be applied unless the licensing authority excludes them in which case different conditions may be imposed concerning the same issues). However, a licensing authority may not impose a condition: (a) which would prevent compliance with a condition included in an operating licence; (b) which requires premises or a part of those premises to operate as a club or any other body which requires membership; or (c) which places a limit upon stakes, fees, winnings or prizes.

Other forms of premises authorisation

There are forms of authorisation of the use of premises for gambling other than premises licences. These are:

(a) occasional use notices (tracks) (see p 697);
(b) temporary use notices (for a specified activity) (see p 697);
(c) authorisation given in respect of football pools given by holder of pool betting operating licence;

(d) gaming machine permits for family entertainment centres (Category D machines only) issued by a licensing authority (local authority);
(e) authorisations or entitlements for alcohol licensed premises, clubs and miners' welfare institutes, and travelling fairs; and
(f) prize gaming permits.

People may provide facilities for private gaming and non-commercial gaming without the need for a premises licence if certain conditions are satisfied (see p 712).

REQUIREMENT TO PRODUCE A LICENCE

By GA 2005, s 108, a constable or an enforcement officer of the Gambling Commission may require the holder of an operating licence to produce it within a specified period. It is an offence for an operating licensee to fail, without reasonable excuse, to do so. In addition, by s 134, a constable or such an officer may require the individual who holds a personal licence to produce his licence. If the individual is carrying on a licensed activity or is on the licensed premises, the licence must be produced immediately. Failure by a personal licensee to comply with a requirement to produce a personal licence is an offence.

REQUIREMENT TO DISCLOSE A CONVICTION

Holders of operating licences, if convicted of an offence in Great Britain, or of a relevant offence outside Great Britain, must inform the Gambling Commission as soon as reasonably practicable.

Where a holder of an operating licence is convicted of a relevant offence in Great Britain, he must inform the court that he is the holder of such a licence. The court may then consider whether to exercise its power to order forfeiture as part of the sentence imposed. The court may also order the disqualification from holding a licence for a period of not more than ten years.

'Relevant offences' are defined in GA 2005, Sch 7 and are generally those related to 'gambling offences' whether committed under the Act or previous legislation, all forms of theft and associated offences involving dishonesty, sexual and violent offences as defined by the Powers of Criminal Courts (Sentencing) Act 2000, firearms offences, drug offences and those involving forgery or counterfeiting. Offences under the law of another country are relevant offences if of a similar nature.

GAMING MACHINES

Number and type of machines permitted in different circumstances

A gaming machine is defined by GA 2005, s 235 as a machine which is designed or adapted for use by individuals to gamble (whether or not it can also be used for other purposes). GA 2005 specifically excludes domestic or dual-use computers; a telephone or other communication device; a machine designed or adapted for betting only on future real events; a machine upon which someone enters a lottery; a machine for playing bingo or bingo prize gaming; or a machine used for playing real games of chance.

The definition of gaming machines is a wide definition within which all the various exceptions set out above may have been embraced.

Categories of gaming machines

The Secretary of State is required to define within regulations four classes of gaming machines to be identified as A, B, C and D. Category B may be subdivided into sub-categories. The categories will depend upon the maximum amounts paid to use the machine; the value or nature of the prize; the nature of the gambling for which the prize is available; or the type of premises upon which the machine is used. The lowest level of charges and prizes will apply to Category D machines, increasing in value up to Category A.

Entitlements to have gaming machines

GA 2005, s 172 sets out entitlements to gaming machines, which are framed in terms of different types of premises licences. Those entitlements are:

(a) licensed adult gaming centres: up to four Category B machines and any number of machines of Category C or D;

(b) licensed family entertainment centres: any number of machines of Category C or D;

(c) casinos:

(i) small casinos: 2 machines, which may be of Category B, C or D, per gaming table used in the casino, up to a maximum of 80 machines;

(ii) large casinos: 5 machines, which may be of Category B, C or D, per gaming table used in the casino, up to a maximum of 150 machines;

(iii) regional casinos: 25 machines, which may be of Category A, B, C or D, per gaming table used in the casino provided that there are at least 40 tables, up to a maximum of 1,250 machines. Where there are fewer than 40 tables, the entitlement is that of a large casino;

(d) bingo premises: up to four Category B gaming machines and any number of machines of Category C or D;

(e) betting premises: up to four gaming machines of Category B, C or D;

(f) tracks: where the licence permits the offer of pool betting, up to four machines of Category B, C or D.

Premises licences for different types of premises may not vary these statutory entitlements.

Offences in relation to gaming machines

GA 2005, s 242 provides that a person commits an offence by making a gaming machine available for use by another, unless he does so in accordance with an operating licence or a family entertainment centre gaming permit, club gaming permit which gives an automatic entitlement to operate the machine (see p 711), club machine permit (see p 711), or appropriate on-licensed premises gaming machine permit (see below), or unless he makes the machine available under the automatic permission relating to on-premises alcohol licensed premises (see below) or at a travelling fair (see below) or offers no or a limited prize.

Two gaming machines of Category C or D may be made available on on-licensed premises alcohol licensed premises in compliance with any relevant code of practice as to their location and operation but the alcohol related licence holder must have notified the licensing authority of his intention to install machines. An on-licensed premises gaming machine permit will authorise the provision of further machines of those categories as specified in the permit. Travelling fairs may provide unlimited Category D machines.

LOTTERIES

Promoting a lottery

For the purposes of GA 2005, a person promotes a lottery if he makes or participates in making arrangements for a lottery. In particular, a person promotes a lottery if he:

(a) makes arrangements for the printing of lottery tickets; or
(b) makes arrangements for the printing, distribution or publication of promotional material (ie a document that advertises, invites participation in, or contains information about how to participate in, a particular lottery, or lists winners in a lottery);
(c) possesses promotional material for distribution or publication;
(d) makes arrangements to advertise a lottery;
(e) invites a person to participate;
(f) offers or supplies, or possesses with intent to sell or supply, a lottery ticket;
(g) does or offers to do anything whereby someone becomes a member of a class among whom lottery prizes are to be distributed; or
(h) uses premises for purposes connected with the administration of the lottery.

Where there is an external lottery manager (see p 702) in relation to a lottery on behalf of a society or local authority, both he and the society or local authority promote the lottery.

It is an offence against GA 2005, s 258 for a person to promote a lottery unless:

(a) he holds an appropriate operating licence and is acting in accordance with it;
(b) he is acting (otherwise than as external lottery manager) on behalf of the holder of such a licence and in accordance with it; or
(c) the lottery is an exempt one.

As already noted, operating licences for lotteries may only be issued to local authorities, large non-commercial societies, or to an external lottery manager acting on their behalf. GA 2005, Sch 11 lists the following exempt lotteries:

(a) incidental non-commercial lotteries;
(b) private lotteries;
(c) customer lotteries; and
(d) small society lotteries (ie society lotteries which do not generate sufficient proceeds to require an operating licence and are registered with the local authority).

Exempt lotteries are dealt with further below.

A person charged with promoting a lottery contrary to s 258 has a defence if he shows that he reasonably believed that the lottery was exempt, or that a lottery operating licence was held and being complied with; that the arrangement in question was part of the National Lottery; or that it did not fall within the definition of a lottery under the Act.

Facilitating a lottery

It is an offence against GA 2005, s 259 to facilitate a lottery. For these purposes a person facilitates a lottery if (and only if) he advertises a particular lottery, or prints tickets or promotional material for it. The offence relates to 'a particular lottery' and therefore is not concerned with those who print lottery tickets to be used in lotteries generally. It does not apply to exempt lotteries or if what is done is done in accordance with the terms and conditions of an operating licence.

The same defences apply as in the case of the offence of promoting a lottery.

Misusing the profits of a lottery

It is an offence against GA 2005, s 260 where a promoter declares on a ticket or in an advertisement that the proceeds of a lottery are to be used for a specific purpose, and he uses, or permits to be used, any part of the profits for other than the stated purpose.

There is a separate offence in the case of exempt lotteries (which, in this context, means an incidental non-commercial lottery, a private society lottery and a small society lottery). Such lotteries are only exempt if they are run entirely for the purposes (ie for the benefit) of the charity or club. It is an offence against GA 2005, s 261 for a person to use, or permit the use, of any part of the profits of such a lottery for a purpose other than a permitted purpose.

Small society lottery: breach of condition

An offence against GA 2005, s 262 is committed by a non-commercial society if a lottery purporting to be an exempt lottery as a small society lottery is promoted on its behalf when it is not registered with the local authority, if the society fails to comply with a notification requirement or if it provides false or misleading information in relation to such a requirement.

Exempt lotteries

The following lotteries are exempt from the necessity to have an operating licence:

Incidental non-commercial lotteries

An exempt incidental non-commercial lottery is a lottery incidental to a non-commercial event, and in respect of which specified conditions are complied with.

An event is non-commercial if no money raised from the event is appropriated for the purposes of private gain. The specified conditions are:

(a) no deduction must be made from the proceeds of the lottery for prizes or for other costs in excess of the prescribed sum in respect of costs permitted by regulations;
(b) the lottery must be promoted for purposes other than private gain;
(c) the arrangements must not include a rollover; and
(d) tickets may only be sold at the event location during the event and the result must be declared during the event.

Private lotteries

These may be:

(a) a private society lottery (ie a lottery, promoted only by authorised members of a non-gambling society, where each person to whom a ticket is sold is a member or on the society's premises). A private society lottery may be promoted for any purpose of the society;
(b) a work lottery (ie a lottery where the promoters work on a single set of premises and each person to whom a ticket is sold or supplied also works there); and
(c) a residents' lottery which is similar to (b) but is restricted to persons who live in a single set of premises. A work lottery or residents' lottery must be organised so as to ensure that no profits are made.

Public advertisement of these lotteries is prohibited.

Customer lottery

A customer lottery is a lottery promoted by the occupier of business premises, ticket sales being restricted to customers who are on the premises. Certain conditions apply and must be satisfied in order to be exempt:

(a) the lottery must be so organised that no profits are made, ie the proceeds must be fully used in the reasonable expenses of the lottery and the provision of prizes;
(b) advertising must be restricted to the premises;
(c) no prize exceeding £50 in value may be received by a winner; and
(d) the arrangements must not include a rollover.

Small society lottery

A small society lottery is a lottery satisfying the following requirements. It must be: promoted on behalf of a non-commercial society (ie a society for cultural or sporting purposes); *the proceeds of the lottery* must fall below the thresholds prescribed (£20,000 per lottery and £250,000 for all lotteries in a year), and certain conditions must be satisfied. It may be promoted for any of the society's purposes. Such a lottery must be registered with the local authority. The conditions are:

(a) at least 20% of the proceeds must go to a purpose for which the society is conducted;

(b) no prize may exceed £25,000 per ticket;

(c) a rollover may be permitted only if each lottery liable to be affected by it is a small society lottery of the same society and the roll over does not permit any person to win more than £25,000 per ticket.

CLUBS, PUBS AND FAIRS

Gaming and the provision of gaming machines in members' clubs, commercial clubs, miners' welfare institutes, alcohol licensed premises and travelling fairs is dealt with by GA 2005. The provisions set out below do not apply to betting or lotteries which are dealt with separately.

Members' club, commercial club and miners' welfare institute

A members' club is a club with at least twenty-five members, established and conducted (a) wholly or mainly for purposes other than gaming (unless the gaming is of a prescribed type), and (b) (on a non-commercial basis) for the benefit of members. Such clubs must not be temporary. The Secretary of State may prescribe certain types of gaming which may take place.

A commercial club is a club with at least twenty-five members, established wholly or mainly for purposes other than gaming (unless the gaming is of a prescribed type). Such clubs may not be temporary. As in the case of members' clubs, the Secretary of State may prescribe forms of gaming which may take place.

A miners' welfare institute is an association established for social or recreational purposes, where the association is either managed by a group at least two-thirds of whom are miners' representatives or operates on premises regulated under a charitable trust which has, at some time, received funds from one of a number of mining organisations.

Exempt gaming

Certain facilities for club gaming may be provided by these clubs without the need for an operating licence or premises licence provided that certain conditions are observed:

(a) the gaming must be equal chance gaming;

(b) stakes and prizes must recognise limits prescribed by regulations;

(c) there must be no deduction by the club from the stakes or winnings;

(d) charges for participation must not exceed an amount prescribed by regulations;

(e) games played may only take place on one set of premises (no linking);

(f) each participant must be a member of the club or institute who has applied, or was nominated for membership, or became a member, at least forty-eight hours before playing, or is a genuine guest of such a person (but (f) does not apply in the case of commercial clubs).

Club gaming permit

Members' clubs (but not commercial clubs) and miners' welfare institutes may apply to a local authority for a club gaming permit authorising the provision of games of chance and gaming machines on club premises. A permit will allow gaming facilities, additional to those which are exempted, to be provided without an operating licence or premises licence.

A club gaming permit authorises a total of three gaming machines which may be in categories B, C or D, but no person under eighteen may be permitted to use a machine of Category B or C. Equal chance gaming may take place without the prescribed limits in (b) above applying to maximum stakes or prizes provided (c) to (f) are satisfied. Such other gaming as may be prescribed may also take place. The games which may be prescribed may involve a bank or unequal chances, such as pontoon or chemin-de-fer.

Club machine permit

Club machine permits are available to a miners' welfare institute or a commercial club. The provisions as to gaming machine permits are similar to those set out above in respect of club gaming permits. The permit obviates the need for a premises licence to be held in respect of such machines.

Alcohol licensed premises

Alcohol licensed premises are premises which contain a bar at which alcohol is served for consumption on the premises under an on-premises alcohol licence but only during such time as alcohol may be served under that licence. Thus, restaurants and similar premises which do not have a bar are not included within this category of premises.

The provision of equal chance gaming on such alcohol licensed premises is permitted subject to the following conditions: stakes and prizes must not exceed prescribed limits; no deductions are permitted from stakes or winnings; there must be no participation fee; games must be restricted to one set of premises (no linking); and children and young persons must be excluded from participation in the gaming.

Travelling fairs

A 'fair' means a fair consisting wholly or principally of the provision of amusements. Travelling fairs are those which travel from place to place, such a place not having been used for more than twenty-seven days in a calendar year for such a purpose.

A premises licence is not required if one or more Category D gaming machine is made available for use at a travelling fair and facilities for gambling amount to no more than an ancillary amusement at the fair.

Bingo in clubs, institutes and alcohol licensed premises

The authorisations set out above, applicable to clubs, miners' welfare institutes and alcohol licensed premises, do not cover 'high turnover bingo', ie bingo wherew the total stakes or prizes for bingo games played in any period of seven days exceed £2,000. If such bingo is to be played a bingo operating licence will be required.

PRIVATE AND NON-COMMERCIAL GAMING AND BETTING

Private gaming and private betting

To be private gaming, the gaming must take place in a private dwelling and on a domestic occasion, or in a hostel, hall of residence or similar establishment which is not administered in the course of a trade or business, provided that more than half of the participants are residents. In addition, there must be no charge, in any form, to participate and no public access, and the gaming must be equal chance gaming.

Despite the absence of an operating licence or a premises licence, people may offer facilities for private gaming or private betting without committing an offence, provided that certain conditions are met.

Private betting is betting which is domestic or workers' betting. It is domestic if made on premises in which each party to the transaction habitually resides. Workers' betting is betting restricted to persons employed under a contract of employment by the same employer.

Non-commercial gaming

Gaming is non-commercial if it takes place at a non-commercial event (whether as an incidental, principal or sole activity). A non-commercial event is one where no part of the proceeds is to be taken for private gain. Despite the absence of an operating licence or a premises licence, people may offer facilities for non-commercial prize gaming or non-commercial equal chance gaming without committing an offence under GA 2005, s 33 or s 37, provided that the following conditions are satisfied.

Players must be told that the purpose of the gaming is to raise money for a specified purpose other than that of private gain. The arrangements must be such that the profits will be applied for a purpose other than private gain. The gaming must not be remote. The non-commercial event must not take place on premises (other than a track) where a premises licence or temporary use notice has effect or on a track when activities are being carried on in reliance on a premises licence. In the case of equal chance gaming the arrangements must comply with regulations limiting stakes, participation fees and prizes.

It is an offence against GA 2005, s 301 to use the profit of such gaming other than for its specified purpose.

ENFORCEMENT

General provisions

Aspects of the administration and the enforcement of the various provisions of GA 2005 are placed in the hands of enforcement officers appointed by the Gambling Commission, authorised local authority officers and constables. In the course of their enforcement duties they may use children and young persons to test that the provisions of the Act in respect of such persons are being complied with.

Powers of entry

GA 2005, s 306 authorises a constable or enforcement officer of the Gambling Commission to enter premises if he reasonably suspects that an offence under GA 2005 has been, is being, or is about to be committed, on the premises.

Where a justice is satisfied that there are reasonable grounds for suspecting that an offence under GA 2005 has been committed, or that evidence of the commission of such an offence may be found on those premises, and that certain conditions are satisfied, he may grant a warrant authorising entry by a constable or enforcement officer. Those conditions are that entry has been refused, or is likely to be refused unless a warrant is produced, that the purpose of entry may be frustrated or seriously prejudiced unless immediate entry can be achieved, or that there is likely to be no-one on the premises to permit entry. Where there has been a refusal, or refusal is likely, a warrant can be issued only if the justice of the peace is satisfied that notice has been given to the occupier of an intention to apply for a warrant, or that the purpose may be frustrated or seriously prejudiced by the giving of such notice. Such a warrant is valid for twenty-eight days.

Inspection of gambling

For the purpose of inspection, a constable, enforcement officer of the Gambling Commission or authorised person of a local authority may enter premises if he reasonably suspects that facilities for gambling (other than private or non-commercial gaming or betting) may be provided on the premises. Such entry must be for the purpose (a) of establishing whether facilities for gambling other than private and non-commercial gaming or betting are being provided; of ascertaining whether an appropriate licence is in force; or of determining whether facilities are being, or will be or have been provided, in accordance with the terms or conditions of the licence.

Powers of entry to authorised establishments

Premises	Who may enter	Purpose
Of holder of operating licence where offence suspected (s 308)	A constable or enforcement officer of the Gambling Commission.	To enter premises upon which, although gambling may not be taking place, are used in connection with gambling activities eg head office of a casino operator.
Family entertainment centre (s 309)	A constable, enforcement officer or authorised local authority officer.	To determine whether licensed activities are being carried on in accordance with terms and conditions of operating licence.
Premises licensed for alcohol (s 310)	Enforcement officer or authorised local authority officer. PLUS, additionally, a constable.	Any purpose connected with the application for Category C or D machines. PLUS, additionally, for purposes of ensuring that gaming satisfies the conditions for exempt gaming; that conditions applying to any operating licence for bingo are being complied with; whether 'high turnover bingo' is being played; and to check the number and category of machines.
Prize gaming permit (s 311)	A constable, enforcement officer or authorised local authority officer	Any purpose connected with an application for a permit and to ascertain whether the gaming complies with the requirements of the Act and regulations.
Clubs (s 312)	Authorised local authority officer. PLUS, a constable or enforcement officer.	Any purpose connected with an application for a club gaming permit or a club machine permit. PLUS, where premises are reasonably believed to be used by a members' club, commercial club or miners' welfare institute, to determine whether gaming is taking, or is about to take place, or whether any gaming is in accordance with the provisions in respect of exempt gaming, a club gaming permit or a club machine permit.

Premises	Who may enter	Purpose
Licensed premises (s 313)	A constable, enforcement officer or an authorised local authority officer.	Any purpose connected with an application for a premises licence or a review of that licence.
Lotteries: registered societies (s 314)	Enforcement officer and authorised local authority officer.	Any purpose connected with a lottery promoted on behalf of the society.
Temporary use notice (s 315)	A constable, enforcement officer or an authorised local authority officer.	To determine whether the activities carried on are in accordance with the notice, or to assess likely effects of activity in reliance on notice.

Persons exercising powers of entry may inspect any part of the premises or any machine or other thing on the premises, access written or electronic records and require copies. Material may be seized and retained where it is reasonably believed to contain or constitute evidence of an offence or a breach of licence conditions. Regulations will make rules governing the procedure. Where material is seized other than under a warrant, it must relate entirely to matters to which the power of entry relates. Where records are 'mixed' they may only be seized under a warrant.

GA 2005, s 323 authorises a constable to use reasonable force to enter premises when exercising powers under the Act. An enforcement officer may do so if he reasonably suspects that an offence under GA 2005 has been, is being, or is about to be committed on the premises, and he or an authorised person may do so where he reasonably suspect that gambling (other than private or non-commercial gambling) is taking place.

The exercise of all such powers must be at a reasonable time and that which is reasonable will vary according to circumstances.

GA 2005, s 326 makes it an offence without reasonable excuse to obstruct or fail to co-operate with a constable, enforcement officer or an authorised local authority officer exercising any of the powers set out above.

Production of authorisations

GA 2005, s 316 provides that a constable or enforcement officer of the Gambling Commission may require the holder of an operating licence who has given a written authorisation, or the person to whom the authorisation was given, to produce a copy of it. Failure to comply, without reasonable excuse, is an offence. The types of authorisations concerned are:

(a) an authorisation relating to pool betting, where the licence holder has authorised a person to accept bets at a track, or in relation to football pools, where the holder has authorised a person to receive payments on his behalf, or has authorised a person to provide facilities for horse race pool betting;

(b) an authorisation relating to a casino premises licence, where the licence holder has authorised a person to use those premises for providing betting, bingo or both.

ADVERTISING

For the purposes of GA 2005 'advertising' embraces anything which is done to encourage one or more persons to take advantage of facilities for gambling, or is done with a view to increasing the use of gambling facilities. Persons who knowingly participate in or facilitate such an activity are also advertising for the purposes of the Act. 'Advertising' also includes entering into arrangements such as sponsorship or brand-sharing agreements under which a name is displayed in connection with an event or product and either (a) the provision of gambling facilities is the sole or main activity under that name, or (b) the way the name is displayed is designed to draw attention to the fact that gambling facilities are provided under that name.

Regulations are to be made to control the form, content, timing and location of advertising for gambling. It is an offence against GA 2005, s 328 to contravene a requirement of such regulations, and this is a continuing offence. By s 330, the advertising of unlawful gambling is also an offence, but this does not apply to lotteries. The offence will cover circumstances in which advertising takes place in advance of obtaining an operating licence.

The advertising of foreign gambling, other than lotteries, is prohibited by s 331. 'Foreign gambling' means (a) non-remote gambling in a non-EEA state, and (b) remote gambling none of the arrangements for which are subject to the gambling law of an EEA state.

CHAPTER 21
Aliens

ILLEGAL ENTRY AND SIMILAR OFFENCES

The Immigration Act 1971 (IA 1971), s 24 states that a person who is not a British citizen is guilty of an offence:

(a) if, contrary to the Act, he knowingly enters the United Kingdom in breach of a deportation order or without leave;

(b) if, having only a limited leave to enter or remain in the United Kingdom, he knowingly either:
  (i) remains beyond the time limited by the leave; or
  (ii) fails to observe a condition of the leave;

(c) if, having lawfully entered the United Kingdom without leave by virtue of IA 1971, s 8 (crew member of ship or aircraft), he remains without leave beyond the time allowed by that section;

(d) if, without reasonable excuse, he fails to comply with any requirement imposed upon him under IA 1971, Sch 2 to report to a medical officer of health, or to attend or submit to a test or examination, as required by such an officer;

(e) if, without reasonable excuse, he fails to observe any restriction imposed on him under IA 1971, Sch 2 or 3 as to residence, as to his employment or occupation or as to reporting to the police or to an immigration officer;

(f) if he disembarks in the United Kingdom from a ship or aircraft after being placed on board under IA 1971, Sch 2 or 3 with a view to his removal from the United Kingdom;

(g) if he embarks in contravention of a restriction imposed by or under an Order in Council under IA 1971, s 3 (provisions aimed at preventing persons from going to specified places on the grounds of safety).

IA 1971, s 24 provides that a person who commits an offence under (b) above by remaining beyond the time limited by the leave commits that offence on the day when he first knows that the time limited by his leave has expired and continues to commit it throughout any period during which he is in the United Kingdom thereafter. However, a person may not be prosecuted under (b) more than once in respect of the same limited leave.

It is an offence contrary to IA 1971, s 24A for a person who is not a British citizen, by deception, to obtain or seek to obtain leave to enter or remain in the United Kingdom, or to secure or to seek to secure the avoidance, postponement or revocation of enforcement action against him. 'Enforcement action' means direction for removal from the United Kingdom under the Immigration and Asylum Act 1999, or deportation orders against those seeking asylum, or a person's removal from the United Kingdom under such a direction or deportation order. The offence embraces claims made by those who seek to remain on the basis of unfounded asylum claims involving the use of deceit. It is a defence for a refugee in certain circumstances to prove that he had come from a country where his life or freedom was threatened.

IA 1971, s 26 includes offences which can be committed:

(a) in relation to statements or representations made to an immigration officer during examination which are known to be false, or are not believed to be true; and

(b) in relation to alterations to documents and the possession of documents known, or reasonably believed, to be false.

Assisting breach of immigration law etc

IA 1971, s 25(1) provides that a person commits an offence if he:

(a) does an act which facilitates the commission of a breach of immigration law by an individual who is not a EU citizen;

(b) knows or has reasonable cause for believing that the act facilitates the commission of a breach of immigration law by the individual; and

(c) knows or has reasonable cause for believing that the individual is not a EU citizen.

By the Immigration Act 1971, s 25A(1), a person commits an offence if:

(a) he knowingly and for gain facilitates the arrival in the United Kingdom of an individual; and

(b) he knows or has reasonable cause to believe that the individual is an asylum seeker.

The offence set out in IA 1971, s 25A(1) does not apply in relation to anything done by a person acting on behalf of an organisation which aims to assist asylum seekers, and does not charge for its services. An 'asylum seeker' is a person who intends to make a claim that it would be contrary to the United Kingdom's obligations under the Refugee Convention or the European Human Rights Convention for him to be removed from, or required to leave, the United Kingdom.

Prosecutions

IA 1971, s 28 provides that an extended time limit will apply to the prosecution of offences under s 24, 24A, 25 or 26. An information relating to an offence may, in England and Wales, be tried by a magistrates' court if it is laid within six months of the commission of the offence, or if it is laid within three years of the commission of the offence and not more than two months after the date certified by a police officer above the rank of chief superintendent to be the date on which evidence sufficient to justify proceedings came to the notice of an officer of the police force to which he belongs. A person charged with such an offence may be tried where the offence was committed or at any place in which he may be.

In proceedings for an offence under IA 1971, s 24 of entering the United Kingdom without leave:

(a) any stamp purporting to have been imprinted on a passport or other travel document by an immigration officer on a particular date for the purpose of giving leave is presumed to have been duly so imprinted, unless the contrary is proved;

(b) proof that a person had leave to enter the United Kingdom lies on the defence if, but only if, he is shown to have entered within six months before the date when the proceedings were commenced.

PERSONS WHO HAVE THE RIGHT OF ABODE IN THE UNITED KINGDOM

IA 1971, s 2(1) provides that a person is entitled to have the right of abode in the United Kingdom if:

(a) he is a British citizen; or
(b) he is a Commonwealth citizen who:
    (i) immediately before the commencement of the British Nationality Act 1981 was a Commonwealth citizen having the right of abode in the United Kingdom by virtue of IA 1971, s 2(1)(d) or (2) as then in force; and
    (ii) has not ceased to be a Commonwealth citizen in the meanwhile.

IA 1971, s 2(2) provides that, in relation to Commonwealth citizens who have the right of abode in the United Kingdom by virtue of (b) above, the Act applies as if they were British citizens.

The British Nationality Act 1981 (BNA 1981) is the principal Act now dealing with citizenship. It deals with three categories of citizen:

(a) those who have British citizenship because of a right which is associated with descent, birth, adoption, naturalisation etc;
(b) persons who are citizens of British Overseas Territories which are set out in BNA 1981, Sch 6; and
(c) persons who are British Overseas citizens and became such, having been a citizen of the United Kingdom and Colonies, whilst not becoming a British citizen or a citizen of the British Overseas Territories, at the commencement of BNA 1981.

Any person who immediately before 21 May 2002 was a British Overseas Territories citizen automatically became a British citizen on that day, except someone who became a British Overseas Territories citizen solely through a connection with the Sovereign-Base Areas in Cyprus. Those within (b) and (c) are categorised as Commonwealth citizens.

There are no restrictions upon the movements of persons who are classed as British citizens who may enter, remain and work in the United Kingdom at any time. Such persons are not liable to deportation.

LEAVE TO ENTER UNITED KINGDOM—PERSONS OTHER THAN BRITISH CITIZENS

In consequence of IA 1971, s 3 a person who is not a British citizen:

(a) must not enter the United Kingdom unless given leave to do so in accordance with the Act or regulations thereunder;

(b) may be given leave to enter the United Kingdom (or, when already there, leave to remain in the United Kingdom) either for a limited or indefinite period.

If a person who is not a British citizen is given a limited leave to enter or remain in the United Kingdom, the leave may be given subject to conditions restricting his employment or occupation in the United Kingdom, or requiring him to register with the police, or both.

Leave may be varied in relation to its duration or conditions. If the limit on duration is removed, conditions are automatically revoked. A person's leave to enter or remain lapses on his going to an area outside the common travel area (which is defined as the United Kingdom, Channel Islands, Isle of Man, and the Republic of Ireland), whether or not he lands there, unless within the period of his original leave he returns to the United Kingdom in circumstances in which he is not required to obtain leave to enter. If he does so return, his previous leave and any conditions attached to it will continue to apply.

The Immigration, Asylum and Nationality Act 2006, s 30 provides that a person seeking to enter the United Kingdom and claiming to have a right of abode must prove that right by the production of a United Kingdom passport describing him as a British citizen or a British subject with a right of abode; an Identity Card which so describes him; or a certificate of entitlement.

IA 1971, s 3A authorises the Secretary of State to make further provisions, by order, in respect of the giving, refusing or varying of leave to enter the United Kingdom. The nature of the authorisation will permit the Secretary of State to make provisions allowing individuals to be granted or refused leave to enter by British Embassies or High Commissions overseas, before their arrival in the United Kingdom.

DEPORTATION

By IA 1971, s 3(5) a person who is not a British citizen is liable to deportation from the United Kingdom if:

(a) the Secretary of State deems his deportation to be conducive to the public good; or

(b) another person to whose family he belongs is or has been ordered to be deported.

In addition, IA 1971, s 3(6) provides for the deportation of a non-British citizen, who has attained the age of seventeen years, if he is convicted of an offence punishable by imprisonment and deportation is recommended by a competent court.

The Immigration, Asylum and Nationality Act 2006, s 47 provides that where leave to enter or remain in the United Kingdom has been extended pending an appeal, the Secretary of State may decide that the person should be removed from the United Kingdom in accordance with directions given by an immigration officer. This section is not yet in force at the time of writing.

IMMIGRATION GENERALLY

As has been seen above, IA 1971 provides an element of control in respect of non-British citizens. Leave to enter the country must be obtained from an immigration officer and leave may be limited and may be subject to restrictions. Registration with the police may be one of the conditions which is imposed. On the other hand, unlimited leave to enter may be granted and such leave cannot be subject to conditions. The Immigration (Leave to Enter and Remain) Order 2000 introduced a system which allows entry to a person who produces an 'entry clearance' which specifies the purpose for which that person is entering the United Kingdom and the permitted duration of his stay. The Order provides quick entry to persons where there has been an opportunity to examine their reasons for coming to the United Kingdom in advance of arrival. However, the important factor is that leave and conditions will be endorsed on the passport or travel document of the person concerned. EU nationals are admitted on proof of European citizenship. Endorsements which are made on such documents are authenticated by a date stamp which shows the immigration officer's identity number and the port of entry. Where entry is refused, the date stamp is applied to the document by means of a cross.

Police officers are often asked to assist immigration officers with their inquiries (it makes a change from others assisting police officers with their inquiries). Such inquiries are frequently urgent and merit a speedy reply by telephone. Confirmation may be required.

No immigration controls are imposed upon persons entering the United Kingdom from the Republic of Ireland but the Secretary of State may exclude or deport persons in certain circumstances. Conditions which are imposed where a person enters at another place within the 'common travel area' apply elsewhere within it. The Immigration (Control of Entry through the Republic of Ireland) Order 1972 applies special provisions in relation to leave to enter, and, in respect of certain foreign nationals and police registration, in the case of entry via the Republic of Ireland.

IA 1971, Sch 2, para 16 provides that a person who may be required to submit to examination under para 2 of the Schedule (a person who has arrived in the United Kingdom by ship or aircraft) may be detained under the authority of an immigration officer pending examination and a decision in relation to entry. A person liable to be so detained may be arrested without warrant by a constable or immigration officer. This power is useful where the police have been notified that persons intending to seek entry to the United Kingdom have been discovered on a ship and are to be brought into a port. Such persons may be detained under these provisions for interview by an immigration officer.

The Immigration, Asylum and Nationality Act 2006, s 32 empowers a superintendent to require the owner or agent of a ship or aircraft to provide passenger or service information. Passengers and crew members must provide information to the owner of agent where such a requirement has been made. These powers also apply to 'freight information'. A person commits an offence if he fails, without reasonable excuse, to comply with any such requirement. This section is not yet in force at the time of writing.

Asylum seekers

The Immigration and Asylum Act 1999 (IAA 1999) represents a far-reaching attempt to regularise immigration procedures by streamlining the process for those who have a genuine reason for wishing to enter the United Kingdom, and by providing measures to combat illegal entry and 'overstaying'. Formal arrangements are made for the welfare of genuine asylum seekers and the procedure is tightened in respect of bogus asylum seekers. Most of the changes which are important to police officers have been achieved by the amendment of provisions of IA 1971. So far as police officers are concerned, those persons who have entered the United Kingdom without leave may be arrested under the amended provisions of IA 1971 and detained for examination by an immigration officer. The various offences which can be committed under the provisions of IA 1971 or IAA 1999 are likely to be prosecuted by the Immigration Service.

However, it is important to appreciate the additional heavy penalties introduced by IAA 1999 (as amended) for those involved in smuggling immigrants or asylum seekers into the United Kingdom. By IAA 1999, s 32, a person is classed for the purposes of the Act as a clandestine entrant if:

(a) he arrives in the United Kingdom concealed in a vehicle, ship, aircraft or rail freight wagon;

(b) he passes, or attempts to pass, through immigration control concealed in a vehicle; or

(c) he arrives in the United Kingdom on a ship or aircraft, having embarked:
  (i) concealed in a vehicle; and
  (ii) at a time when the ship or aircraft was outside the United Kingdom,

and claims, or indicates that he intends to seek asylum in the United Kingdom, or evades, or attempts to evade, immigration control. Where this occurs, s 32 empowers the Secretary of State to require a person who is responsible for a clandestine entrant to pay a penalty in respect of the clandestine entrant and of anyone concealed with him in the same transporter. The following are 'a person responsible': where the transporter is a ship or aircraft, the owner and captain; where it is a vehicle (but not a detached trailer), the owner, hirer and driver; where it is a detached trailer, the owner, hirer and operator of the trailer; where it is a rail freight wagon, the train operator who certified at the train's last scheduled stop outside the United Kingdom that it was fit to travel to the United Kingdom (except where it is a freight shuttle wagon, in which case the shuttle train operator is the responsible person). IAA 1999, s 34 provides that a person is not liable to a penalty if he has a defence under that section. By s 34(2) and (3), it is a defence for him to show that he was acting under duress; or that he did not know, and had no reasonable grounds for suspecting, that a clandestine entrant was, or might be concealed in the transporter, that an effective system was in operation for preventing such carriage, and that, on the occasion in question, the person or persons responsible for carrying out the system had done so correctly. By s 34(3A), it is also a defence for a person to show that:

(a) he knew or suspected that a clandestine entrant was or might be concealed in a rail freight wagon, having boarded after the wagon began its journey to the United Kingdom;

(b) he could not stop the train or shuttle-train of which the wagon formed part without endangering safety;

(c) an effective system for preventing the carriage of clandestine entrants was in operation in relation to the train or shuttle-train; and

(d) on the occasion in question the person or persons responsible for operating the system did so properly.

Penalties are imposed by notice and provision is made for a 'notice of objection'. A notice of objection may be either to the imposition of a penalty or its amount. If the notice of objection is unsuccessful, there is a right of appeal to a county court.

Power is given to a senior officer of the Immigration Service to detain any relevant vehicle, small ship (500 tonnes), small aircraft (5,700 kilogrammes) or rail freight wagon where such notice has been given, until all penalties and expenses reasonably incurred by the Secretary of State have been paid. This power to detain will only be exercised where there is a significant risk of non-payment.

It is important, therefore, when such persons are found by a police officer, either wandering around the countryside after having been set down by a vehicle, or aboard such a vehicle, that the necessary details are obtained so that these penalties may be applied. These penalties are in addition to penalties provided by IAA 1999, ss 40 to 42 (as amended) which are concerned with persons arriving by such means who do not have proper documents. In such circumstances the Secretary of State may charge the owner of the ship or aircraft, in respect of that person, the sum of £ 2,000 or any other sum prescribed. The section provides a number of defences.

REGISTRATION WITH POLICE

The Immigration (Registration with Police) Regulations 1972 deal with the registration of aliens. An 'alien' is a person who is neither a Commonwealth citizen, nor a British protected person, nor a citizen of the Irish Republic. Such persons may be required to register with the chief officer of police for the area in which they reside. They will have been granted limited leave to enter which will be subject to a condition of registration and their passports will have been endorsed accordingly. If, in any circumstances, EU nationals are required to register, the Home Office will notify the appropriate police force. Where this occurs, the residence permit will be endorsed in the space provided and this endorsement fulfils the purpose of a police registration certificate.

In respect of other persons who must register with the police, a police registration certificate will be issued which carries the photograph of the person concerned. Police forces maintain records of aliens living within their areas who are subject to registration requirements. Changes of residence must be reported within seven days and changes in other registered particulars, within eight days. This may be done by post but personal attendance may be required.

An immigration officer or constable may require an alien to whom the Regulations apply either to produce a certificate of registration, or to give to the officer or constable a satisfactory reason for failure to produce it, forthwith. Where alterations are being made in registered particulars, a registration officer may require the alien concerned to produce his certificate of registration so that necessary amendments can be made. Where there is a failure to produce at the time, the officer or constable may require that person to produce a certificate of registration at a police station specified by the officer or constable within the following forty-eight hours.

A person who fails to register as required or to comply with any registration requirement offends against the Immigration Act 1971, s 26(1).

FINGERPRINTING

The persons who may be fingerprinted

IAA 1999, s 141 applies to:

(a) any person who, on arrival in the United Kingdom, fails to produce a valid passport with a photograph or some other document satisfactorily establishing identity and nationality;

(b) any person who has been refused leave to enter but has been temporarily admitted pending removal if an immigration officer reasonably suspects that the individual will not comply with a reporting or residence requirement;

(c) an illegal entrant subject to a direction under IA 1971, Sch 2 or subject to a deportation order where a direction has been given for his removal;

(d) a person about whom a decision to give leave to enter has not yet been made, who has been arrested or detained;

(e) an asylum seeker; and

(f) a dependent of anyone in (a) to (e).

The taking of fingerprints and powers to enforce

Fingerprints may be taken by an 'authorised person' and this term includes a constable, an immigration officer, a prison officer, an officer appointed for the purpose, or a person employed under a contract at a detention centre.

IAA 1999, s 142 makes provision for requiring the attendance of a person to whom s 141 applies at a specified place, within a time specified in a notice, for the purpose of fingerprinting. The section gives a constable or immigration officer a power of arrest without warrant where a person fails to comply with such a requirement.

CHAPTER 22

Animals, birds and plants

DISEASES OF ANIMALS

The Animal Health Act 1981 (AHA 1981) sets out the duties of various persons in relation to notification of certain animal diseases and the action which must be taken. The administrative responsibilities lie with the Secretary of State for Environment, Food and Rural Affairs (in Wales, the National Assembly for Wales) but local authorities must appoint their own inspectors. Constables are frequently appointed as inspectors under the Act and when this occurs they have additional duties and responsibilities to those which all constables have under the Act.

Animals for the purposes of AHA 1981 are cattle, sheep, goats, and all other ruminating animals, swine (ie pigs), horses, asses, mules and jennets (ie small Spanish horses). The Secretary of State (in Wales, the National Assembly for Wales) has power, by order, to add to this list and, for the purposes of the special provisions relating to rabies mentioned on the next page, dogs and cats have been added to the definition of 'animal'.

The Act and orders thereunder specify the diseases with which it is concerned, the most important of which are foot-and-mouth disease, swine fever and rabies. Persons having animals affected by a specified disease must so far as possible separate them from unaffected animals and speedily inform a constable. A constable on receipt of such information must forthwith inform a local authority inspector and the Department's divisional veterinary inspector.

The action which follows is very much related to the particular disease, but action is always directed towards the prevention of the spread of disease. Foot-and-mouth disease can spread rapidly and the action taken in such cases provides a good example of the general nature of action to be taken. On receiving notification of the suspicion of the disease, the local authority inspector serves a Form 'A' on the stockholder. This makes his premises an infected place and prohibits movement in or out by unauthorised persons or materials. The divisional veterinary inspector, if he serves Form 'C', creates an infected area of five miles radius and this can be extended further if necessary. Where foot-and-mouth disease is suspected to exist susceptible animals must be slaughtered (although the Secretary of State (in Wales, the National

Assembly for Wales) may decide not to slaughter zoo animals; animals kept in a wildlife park or other premises for display and education of the public; animals in an enclosed area principally used for shooting; or in an approved conservation area or premises, for display, education or scientific purposes). In addition, the Secretary of State (in Wales, the National Assembly for Wales) may authorise vaccination under licence. He may make declarations in respect of 'vaccination zones' and 'vaccination surveillance zones'. Movement of vaccinated animals, which will be identified by eartags, is controlled and 'cattle passports' may be required. Local authorities are required to erect signs indicating such zones. Authorised measures will enable the creation of 'buffer zones' in any outbreak of foot-and-mouth disease.

Any person who does anything prohibited by AHA 1981, or by an order of the Secretary of State (in Wales, the National Assembly for Wales) or a regulation of a local authority, or who omits to do something required of him by the Act or an order or regulation, commits an offence if he does not have lawful authority or excuse. It is also an offence for any person, without lawful authority or excuse, to refuse entry to an inspector or other officer, or to obstruct or impede him in entering, or to obstruct or impede an inspector, constable or other officer in the execution of his duty, or to assist another to do so. In the case of each offence, the accused has the onus of proving lawful authority or excuse.

Duties and powers of a constable

AHA 1981, s 62(2), provides that a constable may, for the purpose of exercising any power to seize an animal or cause an animal to be seized, where an order is in force under the Act or a power is given for the purpose of preventing the introduction of rabies into Great Britain, enter (if need be by force) and search any vessel, boat, aircraft or vehicle in which there is, or in which he with reasonable cause suspects that there is an animal to which that power applies. The offences to which this power applies are the landing or attempted landing of any animal (including a dog or cat) in contravention of a Rabies Order, or the failure by a person in charge of a vessel or boat to discharge any obligation under such an order, or the unlawful movement of any such animal into, within or out of a rabies infected area. However, there will be no contravention if the provisions of the Pet Travel Scheme have been complied with.

PROTECTION OF ANIMALS

The Protection of Animals Act 1911 deals with the various ways in which a person can be cruel to animals. The Act defines the term 'animal' as meaning any 'domestic' or 'captive' animal, and goes on to provide further definitions of 'domestic' and 'captive' animals. Cruelty to an animal not covered by these definitions is not an offence under this Act but may be an offence under the Wild Mammals (Protection) Act 1996, the provisions of which are examined below.

Domestic animal

A 'domestic animal' is defined as a horse, ass, mule, bull, sheep, pig, dog, cat, or fowl, or any other animal of whatsoever kind or species, and whether a quadruped or not, which is tame or which has been or is being sufficiently tamed to serve some purpose for the use of man.

This definition embraces most farmyard animals and the two major household pets. Most of the decisions of the courts in relation to whether or not an animal is a domestic animal are unimportant as the animals concerned would certainly have been held to be captive animals. A fighting cock has been held to be a domestic animal, as have wild birds kept in confinement and trained as decoy birds for bird-catching. The first falls within the description 'fowl', and the second within the term 'tame or being sufficiently tamed to serve some purpose for the use of man'.

Captive animal

A 'captive animal' is defined as any animal (not being a domestic animal) of whatsoever kind or species, and whether a quadruped or not, including any bird, fish, or reptile, which is in captivity or confinement, or which is maimed, pinioned, or subjected to any appliance or contrivance for the purpose of hindering or preventing its escape from captivity or confinement.

The definition of 'captive animal' covers most animals which have become, in some way, captive or confined or hindered or prevented from escaping. The definition clearly includes all zoo animals, including captive fish, birds and reptiles, but it is certainly not limited to them. However, the definition does not cover invertebrates; consequently it is not an offence to be cruel to spiders and similar insects, whether captive or not.

The usual question to resolve in relation to wild animals is whether or not they are captive. Temporarily to trap a wild animal does not make it captive nor does restraint incidental to capture; there must be some control exercised over a period of time. A wild squirrel which is temporarily trapped in a tree does not thereby become a captive animal. The cruel maiming of a hedgehog, by repeatedly beating it with a stick, does not make that animal a 'captive animal' within the meaning of the Act.

Cruelty to animals

The Protection of Animals Act 1911 (PAA 1911), s 1(1) provides the offence of cruelty to animals. It defines such cruelty in wide terms. First, it makes it an offence cruelly to beat, kick, ill-treat, over-ride, over-drive, overload, torture, infuriate or terrify an animal. It is not necessary to prove that ill-treatment was deliberate or wilful. The section then goes on to declare that those who cause or procure, or being an owner permit, such conduct are also guilty of cruelty to animals. A wanton or unreasonable omission to look after an animal which results in causing unnecessary suffering also constitutes cruelty, as does a wanton or unreasonable positive act which has that result. Reasonableness must be judged in the light of all the circumstances. A High Court judge has held that a licence to trap a wild animal cannot justify unnecessary suffering to it, nor can it make the suffering necessary. Section 1 also provides that the following constitute the offence of cruelty to animals: conveyance in a cruel manner, fighting or baiting animals (those who permit premises to be used for this purpose are also guilty), wilful poisoning without reasonable cause, and subjecting animals to operations conducted without due care and humanity. The tethering of a horse, ass or mule under conditions or in such manner as to cause unnecessary suffering also amounts to cruelty to animals under s 1.

Although PAA 1911, s 1 specifies so many ways in which the offence can be committed, the offence is essentially concerned with any unnecessary abuse of a domestic or captive animal which causes pain or suffering.

PAA 1911, s 1(3)(a) excepts things done in the slaughtering, or preparation for slaughtering, of animals for food, unless done in such a way as to cause unnecessary suffering. Section 1(3)(b) excepts coursing or hunting of captive animals, unless the animals are liberated in an injured or exhausted condition, or unless they are hunted in a confined area from which there is no escape. However, the reference to coursing or hunting in the exception in s 1(3)(b) does not include a reference to participation in a hare coursing event or the coursing or hunting of a wild mammal with a dog.

Animal fights

A person who, without reasonable excuse, is present when animals are placed together for the purpose of their fighting each other commits an offence under PAA 1911, s 5A. Someone who publishes or causes to be published an advertisement, knowing its nature, of such a fight commits an offence under s 5B. These offences are particularly relevant to dog fights.

Abandoning animals

It is an offence for an owner or a person in charge or control of any animal to abandon it without reasonable cause or excuse, whether permanently or not, in circumstances likely to cause it unnecessary suffering. The offence extends to those who cause or procure or, being the owner, permit such abandonment. The offence is set out in the Abandonment of Animals Act 1960, s 1 which declares that such acts render a person guilty of the offence of cruelty to animals under PAA 1911, s 1 and subject to the provisions of that Act which apply to cruelty.

'Abandonment' in the present context does not require permanent abandonment, although it means something more than merely leaving unattended. For abandonment, it must be proved that the accused had intentionally relinquished, wholly disregarded or given up his duty to care for the animal. Where a person has made or attempted to make arrangements for the animal's welfare during a period where he cannot look after it himself, there is no abandonment. Proof of abandonment is not enough; the abandonment must be in circumstances where unnecessary suffering is likely to be caused by it.

Destruction of injured animals

Where the owner of an animal is convicted of cruelty under the above provisions, and the court is satisfied that it would be cruel to keep the animal alive, the court may order the destruction of the animal. Where such an order is not made, but there is evidence that the animal is likely to be exposed to further cruelty, the court may deprive its owner of his ownership and dispose of the animal as it thinks fit.

Police officers frequently find that animals have been injured in accidents. PAA 1911, s 11 allows a constable to summon a registered veterinary surgeon to any animal, which he finds so diseased, or so injured, or in such a physical condition, that in his (the constable's) opinion it could not be moved without cruelty. It is the opinion of the constable which is important; if the owner is present and refuses to call a veterinary surgeon the constable may nevertheless do so. If the veterinary surgeon finds that it is cruel to keep the animal alive, and issues a certificate to that effect, the constable may have the animal humanely slaughtered. The expenses incurred are recoverable from the owner as a civil debt.

Dogs and cats are excluded from the definition of 'animal' for the purposes of this section. Nevertheless, it is the duty of the police to take action to prevent such suffering and similar action should be taken, although in such circumstances the Act does not authorise the recovery of the money by civil process. If the owner of the dog or cat is present then it is unlikely that difficulties will arise, but the police officer should direct his mind towards the condition of the animal. If a veterinary surgeon is called to an injured cat or dog, his advice should be followed. It must be remembered that the police do not have a specific power to sanction the destruction of an injured cat or dog, but if a constable has such an animal destroyed on the ground that it would be cruel to keep it alive, there can be no doubt that he would have a defence to a criminal charge.

Pets—sale and boarding

The Pet Animals Act 1951 requires that the keepers of pet shops must be licensed with the local authority. Under other legislation, dog-breeding kennels and boarding kennels for dogs or cats must be similarly licensed.

For the purposes of Pet Animals Act 1951, the keeping of a pet shop refers to the carrying on at premises (including a private dwelling) of a business of selling animals or pets, including the keeping of animals on those premises for the purposes of such a business. However, a person who only keeps or sells pedigree animals bred by him does not keep a pet shop.

It is also an offence to sell a pet to a child under twelve years, or to sell pets in a street or public place (except at a stall or barrow in a market).

Dog kennels for breeding purposes include any premises, even a private house, where more than two bitches are kept for breeding purposes.

The local authority ensures that licensees comply with the conditions of their respective licences by authorising its officers or a veterinary surgeon to inspect pet shops and kennels. The Breeding of Dogs Act 1973 empowers local authorities to grant a licence for the keeping of a breeding establishment for dogs and to impose conditions. Records must be kept as prescribed by the Breeding of Dogs (Licensing Records) Regulations 1999. It is an offence for such a breeder to sell a dog which is not wearing an identifying tag or badge containing information concerning the breeding establishment at which it was born, including any identification number allocated to the dog, and its date of birth.

BADGERS AND OTHER WILD ANIMALS

Badgers

Badgers are not domestic animals and are therefore not protected by PAA 1911. However, the Protection of Badgers Act 1992 (PBA 1992), s 1 gives special protection to badgers by creating offences of wilfully killing, injuring or taking any badger, or attempting to do one of these things in contravention of the Act. Section 1(2) provides that if, in any proceedings for attempting to kill, take, or injure a badger, there is evidence from which it could be reasonably concluded that at the material time the accused was doing so, he shall be presumed to have been doing so, unless the contrary is shown. If a person is found in possession of a dead badger, or any part of it, he is guilty of an offence under PBA 1992, s 1(3), unless he can show that the badger had not been killed in contravention of the provisions of the Act, or that the badger, or part, had been sold (whether to him or another) and, at the time of the purchase, the purchaser had no reason to believe that the badger had been killed in contravention of the Act.

Licences may be granted by the Department for the Environment, Food and Rural Affairs to permit killing or taking to prevent serious damage to crops. Licences may also be granted by the Department to permit killing or taking to prevent the spread of disease, and by the appropriate conservation body to allow taking for scientific purposes, zoological needs or for ringing or marking. Acts authorised by such a licence are of course exempted from being an offence.

Offences of cruelly ill-treating, using badger tongs, or digging for badgers are dealt with by PBA 1992, s 2(1). PBA 1992, s 2(2) provides, in relation to the offence of digging for a badger, that if there is clear evidence from which it could reasonably be concluded that the accused was digging for a badger, he must be presumed to have been doing so, unless the contrary is shown. Digging for badgers is quite common in some parts of Great Britain. When the badger is unearthed, dogs are released to fight it. In addition, s 2(1) provides that the use, for the purpose of killing or taking a badger, of a firearm, other than a smooth bore weapon of not less than 20 bore or a rifle using ammunition having a muzzle energy not less than 160 footpounds and a bullet weighing less than 38 grains, is an offence.

PBA 1992, s 3 creates offences of interfering with a badger sett by intentionally or recklessly damaging it, destroying it, obstructing access to it, causing a dog to enter it or disturbing a badger when it is occupying it. A 'badger sett' for the purposes of s 3 means the tunnel and chambers created by badgers and the immediate areas outside the entrance holes to those tunnels and chambers. The term may also apply in other circumstances, as where badgers have occupied coverts or disused sheds as their shelter or refuge.

Under s 4 it is an offence to sell, offer for sale or have live badgers in one's possession or control.

There are also exceptions from liability for an offence under the Act for those who find an injured badger and either take it to tend it or kill it as an act of mercy, and for those who unavoidably kill or injure a badger as an incidental result of lawful action. Farmers and others who consider that the action in question is necessary to prevent serious damage to land, crops, poultry or other property are also exempted from an offence of killing, taking or injuring etc. This exemption is subject to a major qualification; if it was apparent before the time that the action was taken that it would prove necessary to prevent such damage (ie there is not a situation of urgency), a person is not exempted if he had not applied for a licence for this purpose as soon as reasonably practicable after the fact became apparent or if an application for such a licence had been under consideration.

Where a constable has reasonable grounds for suspecting that a person is committing an offence under this Act, or has committed such an offence, and that evidence is to be found on that person, or in any vehicle or article he has with him, the constable may without warrant stop and search that person, vehicle or article. He may seize and detain anything which may be evidence of the commission of such an offence. These powers are wide; persons reasonably suspected of badgering may be stopped and searched. If they have dogs, tongs and spades with them, these may be seized.

Where a dog is used in commission of offences of taking etc, cruelty and interference with setts, a court may order its destruction, or may disqualify the offender from keeping or having the custody of a dog for such period as it thinks fit.

Dangerous wild animals

It is an offence to keep a dangerous wild animal without having a local authority licence. The term 'dangerous wild animal' is defined in the Dangerous Wild Animals Act 1976. The animals described could generally be described as zoo animals.

Cruelty to wild mammals

The Wild Mammals (Protection) Act 1996 (WM(P)A 1996), s 1 makes it an offence for any person to mutilate, kick, beat, nail or otherwise impale, stab, burn, stone, crush, drown, drag or asphyxiate any wild mammal with intent to inflict unnecessary suffering upon it.

WM(P)A 1996, s 2 exempts from the provisions of s 1:

(a) the attempted mercy killing of a wild mammal which has been so seriously disabled (by an act which is not the act of the person concerned) that there is no chance of recovery;
(b) the reasonably swift and humane killing of a wild mammal injured or taken in the course of either lawful shooting, hunting, coursing or pest control;
(c) acts authorised under any enactment;
(d) any act made unlawful by s 1 if it was by means of a snare, trap, dog, or bird lawfully used for the purpose of killing or taking any wild mammal; or
(e) the lawful use of a poison or noxious substance.

For the purposes of WM(P)A 1996, s 2 hunting a wild mammal with a dog is treated as lawful if, and only if, it is exempt hunting within the meaning of the Hunting Act 2004 (as to which see p 732).

A 'wild mammal' is any mammal which is not a domestic or captive animal within the meaning of the Protection of Animals Act 1911.

Thus, all mammals which are outside the protection of pre-existing legislation are afforded protection by WM(P)A 1996. Mercy killings and attempted mercy killings are generally exempted from the provisions of the Act, as are authorised acts under existing legislation, and established methods of pest control such as the snaring of rabbits.

It is submitted that some of the exemptions included in WM(P)A 1996, s 2 are unnecessary as s 1 carefully defines the ways in which the offence might be committed. Those who are carrying out a 'mercy' killing are unlikely to adopt any of the methods described in s 1, nor are those who follow what is described as 'country pursuits'. It is also submitted that, in any case, such acts as mercy killings and those authorised by law could not be described as being carried out 'with intent to inflict unnecessary suffering'.

WM(P)A 1996, s 4 provides that where a constable has reasonable grounds for suspecting that a person has committed an offence under the provisions of the Act and that evidence of the commission of the offence may be found on that person or in or on any vehicle which he may have with him, the constable may:

(a) without warrant, stop and search that person and any vehicle or article he may have with him; and

(b) seize and detain for the purposes of proceedings under any of those provisions anything which may be evidence of the commission of the offence or may be liable to be confiscated under WM(P)A 1996, s 6 (a convicting court may order confiscation of any vehicle or equipment used in commission of the offence).

It is essential that police officers dealing with offences under the Act specify the number of animals which were subjected to such cruelty. WM(P)A 1996, s 5 provides that the maximum fine which may be imposed shall be determined as if the person had been convicted of a separate offence in respect of each such wild animal.

Hunting

The Hunting Act 2004 (HA 2004), s 1 makes it an offence for a person to hunt a wild mammal with a dog, unless such hunting is exempt. Exemptions ('exempt hunting') are specified in Sch 1.

Under Sch 1 stalking and flushing out a wild mammal is exempt if carried out in accordance with prescribed conditions. The first condition is that the stalking or flushing out must be undertaken for the purpose :

(a) of preventing or reducing serious damage which such a mammal would otherwise cause to livestock, game birds, food for livestock, crops, growing timber, fisheries or other property, or the biological diversity of an area;

(b) obtaining meat for human or animal consumption; or

(c) participation in a field trial (ie a competition in which dogs flush animals out of cover or retrieve shot animals so as to assess the dog's usefulness in connection with shooting).

The second condition is that the stalking or flushing out must take place on land which belongs to the person carrying out the activity, or in respect of which permission has been granted for that purpose by the occupier or land owner. The third condition is that not more than two dogs may be used for the purpose of stalking or flushing out. The fourth condition is that the stalking or flushing out must not involve the use of a dog below ground otherwise than in accordance with Sch 1, para 2 below. The fifth condition is that reasonable steps must have been taken to ensure that the animal concerned is shot dead by a competent person and the dogs are kept under control. The use of a dog below ground in the course of stalking or flushing out is in accordance with Sch 1, para 2 if the stalking or flushing out is undertaken for the purpose of protecting game birds or wild birds which a person is keeping or preserving for the purpose of shooting; only one dog is used below ground at any one time; and participants carry written evidence of ownership of the land or of consent to so act which is provided by the occupier or owner of the land. Reasonable steps must be taken to ensure that as soon as possible after being found the wild animal is flushed out from below ground and to prevent injury to the dog used for below ground.

As the term 'wild mammal' embraces vermin, exemptions are provided in respect of the hunting of rats and rabbits. There are also exemptions in respect of the flushing of a wild mammal for the purposes of falconry, in respect of the hunting of a wild mammal in order to recapture it or rescue it, and in respect of the observation or study of a wild mammal.

It is a defence for a person charged with an offence of hunting contrary to s 1 to show that he reasonably believed that the hunting was exempt. HA 2004, s 3, provides that a person commits an offence if he knowingly permits land which belongs to him to be entered or used in the course of the commission of an offence against s 1. It also provides that a person commits an offence if he knowingly permits a dog which belongs to him to be used in the course of the commission of such an offence. For the purposes of the Act, a dog belongs to a person if he owns it, is in charge of it, or has control of it.

A person commits an offence against HA 2004, s 5 if he participates in a hare coursing event, or attends, or knowingly facilitates such an event, or permits land which belongs to him to be used for such an event. Offences are committed by those who enter dogs, permit dogs to be entered, or who control or handle a dog within such an event.

By s 8, a constable who reasonably suspects that a person is committing or has committed any of the offences set out above has the following powers. If he reasonably believes that evidence of the offence is likely to be found on the suspect, he may search that person, and if he reasonably believes that evidence of the offence is likely to be found on or in a vehicle, animal or other thing of which the suspect appears to be in possession or control, he may search the vehicle. He may seize and detain such a vehicle, animal or other thing if he reasonably believes that it may be used in evidence or may be made subject to a forfeiture order. A constable may without a warrant enter land, premises (other than a dwelling) or a vehicle for the purpose of exercising these powers.

DOGS AND THE LAW

Dogs worrying livestock

The Dogs (Protection of Livestock) Act 1953 declares that the owner of a dog, and, if it is in the charge of a person other than the owner, that person also, shall be guilty of an offence if the dog worries livestock on any agricultural land. Not surprisingly, exceptions are made in relation to certain dogs at large in a field of sheep; dogs of the occupier of the field or the owner of the sheep are not included, nor are police dogs, guide dogs, trained sheep dogs, working gun dogs or, perhaps unexpectedly, a pack of hounds.

The term 'worry livestock' covers *attacking* livestock, or *chasing* livestock in such a way as may reasonably be expected to cause injury or suffering to it, or, in the case of females, abortion, or loss of or diminution in their produce. It also covers a dog *being at large* (meaning not on a lead or under close control) in a field or enclosure in which there are *sheep*.

'Livestock' means cattle, sheep, goats, swine, horses or poultry. For the purposes of this definition, 'cattle' includes bulls, cows, oxen, heifers or calves; 'horses' includes asses and mules and 'poultry' means domestic fowls, turkeys, geese or ducks. Thus 'livestock' can generally be described as farm animals. 'Agricultural land' means land used as arable, meadow or grazing land or for the purposes of poultry farming, pig farming, market gardens, allotments, nursery grounds or orchards. Generally, the land described is agricultural in the general sense of the word but the inclusion of 'allotments' gives a wider meaning to the term. There are many allotment gardeners who keep poultry on their land in towns. Offences of worrying livestock are most frequently encountered on agricultural land near to towns. The town-dweller is more likely to leave his dog free to roam. The country-dweller is usually careful in this respect.

There are two defences which can be offered in cases of livestock-worrying. The first is that the owner of the dog may prove that at the time in question the dog was in the charge of some other person, whom he reasonably believed to be a fit and proper person to be in charge. This would apply where an owner had left his dog with a reliable friend while absent on holiday, or even where some reliable person had taken the dog for a walk. The other defence is related to circumstances in which livestock trespass upon someone else's land. If the dog which attacks the livestock is owned by, or in the charge of, the occupier of that land or a person authorised by him, a defence is open to that person provided that he did not cause the dog to attack the livestock.

A constable is empowered to seize a dog, found anywhere, which he reasonably believes to have been worrying livestock on agricultural land and to retain it until the owner is found and has paid the expenses of its detention. This power is unaffected by the repeal of police powers in respect of stray dogs effected by the Clean Neighbourhood and Environment Act 2005. This power cannot be exercised if there is a person present who admits to being the owner of the dog or in charge of it. If, on an application by a constable, a justice is satisfied that there are grounds for believing that:

(a) an offence under the Act has been committed; and
(b) the dog in question is on premises specified in the application,

he may issue a warrant authorising a constable to enter and search the premises in order to identify the dog.

The Animals Act 1971 allows the owner of livestock worried by a dog to claim compensation by way of civil process. This Act also provides that a person who is sued in the civil courts for killing or injuring a dog has a defence if he acted in protection of his livestock and gave notice to the police of what he had done within forty-eight hours.

Stray dogs

The Environmental Protection Act 1990 (EPA 1990), s 149 requires every local authority to appoint an officer to deal with stray dogs found in its area. Where the officer has reason to believe that any dog found in a public place or on any other land or premises is a stray dog, he must, where possible, seize it and detain it. Where the place concerned is not a public place, he may only seize and detain the dog with the consent of the owner or occupier of the place. Where the dog wears a collar on which appears a person's name and address, or its owner is known, a notice must be served on that person, stating that the dog will be liable to be disposed of if it is not claimed within seven clear days and the expenses of its detention met. After the dog has been detained for seven clear days (or, where a notice has been served, if it has not been claimed and the expenses paid within seven clear days after service of the notice) the dog may be disposed of by way of sale or destruction. Where a dog is sold under the provisions of this section to a person acting in good faith, the ownership of the dog is vested in the buyer.

The officer must keep a register giving particulars of all dogs so seized and disposed of. The register must be available, at all reasonable times, for inspection by the public without charge. The officer must ensure that all such dogs are properly fed and looked after while they are detained.

EPA 1990, s 150 requires the finder of a stray dog to:

(a) return it to its owner; or
(b) take the dog to the appointed officer of the local authority for the area;

and to inform the officer of the local authority. Failure to comply with these requirements is an offence. Where a dog has been taken to an appointed officer, the finder may keep the dog, if he wishes, on informing the officer of this and his name and address. In such a case the finder must keep the dog for at least a month; he commits an offence if he fails to do so.

The Dogs Act 1906 (DA 1906), s 3 makes similar provisions in relation to the seizure, detention and disposal of stray dogs by the police but, in consequence of EPA 1990, such dogs will be detained by the local authority officer. DA 1906, s 4 makes similar provision to that in EPA 1990, s 150 concerning the situation where the finder takes a stray dog to a police station and wishes to keep it. It provides that, on informing the police officer of this and of his name and address, he must be given a certificate which includes a description of the dog and gives details of its finding. The finder is, in consequence, obliged to keep the dog for a period of one month. If he does not he commits an offence. This must be explained to him before he agrees to keep the dog. If the finder does not wish to keep the dog it must be dealt with by the police by sale or destruction in the same way as described above in relation to an appointed local authority officer.

DA 1906, s 3 and s 4 are prospectively repealed by the Clean Neighbourhoods and Environment Act 2005 (CNEA 2005) and this will relieve police officers of any responsibility for stray dogs. The provisions of these sections are not yet in force.

Further offences which may be relevant to 'straying' dogs are discussed below under the heading 'Specific offences in relation to dangerous dogs' (pp 739–740).

Control of dogs

Collars

The Control of Dogs Order 1992 requires that every dog while on a highway or in a place of public resort must wear a collar with the owner's name and address inscribed upon it, or on a plate or badge attached to it. There are certain exceptions which refer to working dogs used in the countryside in conditions which might make the wearing of a collar dangerous, or to other similar circumstances in other working environments. The exceptions apply to:

(a) any pack of hounds;
(b) any dog while being used for sporting purposes;
(c) any dog while being used for the capture or destruction of vermin;
(d) any dog while being used for the driving or tending of cattle or sheep;
(e) any dog while being used on official duties by a member of HM Armed Forces or HM Customs and Excise or by the police force for any area;
(f) any dog while being used in emergency rescue work; or
(g) any dog registered with the Guide Dogs for the Blind Association.

Where a dog is found in a highway or place of public resort without the requisite collar, the owner or the person in charge of the dog who, without lawful authority or excuse, the proof whereof is on him, causes or permits the dog to be there without that collar is guilty of an offence.

Leads and muzzles

The Road Traffic Act 1988, s 27 empowers local authorities to make orders designating certain roads within their areas as roads upon which dogs must at all times be kept on a lead. The chief officer of police must be consulted before such an order is made and the local authority is required to publish it and to place signs on the road affected. When such an order is in force, it is an offence to cause or permit a dog to be on such a road if it is not held on a lead. The section permits exceptions to be made by the order, and it expressly provides that the offence just mentioned does not apply to dogs tending cattle or sheep in the course of a business nor to those being used for sporting purposes.

The Dangerous Dogs Act 1991 (DDA 1991), s 1(2) makes it an offence for the owner, or person for the time being in charge, of a dog which is bred for fighting and to which the section applies (any dog of the type known as pit bull terrier, Japanese tosa and any other type of dog designated by order of the Secretary of State, currently the *dogo argentino* and the *fila braziliero*) to allow such a dog to be in a public place without being muzzled and kept on a lead. We deal with what constitutes a 'public place' on p 741. It will be noted that a 'public place' includes the inside of a car which is in the public place. The prohibition in s 1 is a strict one. If a dog of the requisite type is in a public place, it must not be allowed to be unmuzzled and must be kept on a lead. Thus, where an owner removed the muzzle from a pit bull terrier because it developed kennel cough and it was therefore cruel to muzzle it, it was held that neither the Act nor the common law allowed a person in control of such a dog to make a value judgement between the safety of the public or the well-being of the dog, and that there were no circumstances in which the necessity of the situation could overtake the prohibition. The word 'type' is not synonymous with 'breed'. 'Type' has a wider meaning than 'breed'. Determining the limits of a type is a question of fact for determination by the magistrates or Crown Court. They are entitled to look at the American Dog Breeders' Association (ADBA) breed standard as a guide. The fact that a dog does not meet that standard in every respect is not conclusive that it is not one of the specified types. Thus, for example, it has been held that the fact that a dog is near to, or has a substantial number of, characteristics of a pit bull terrier as set out in the ADBA standard is sufficient for the dog to be found to be of the pit bull terrier type. It is relevant to consider whether the dog exhibited the behavioural characteristics of a pit bull terrier but that evidence would not be conclusive.

By DDA 1991, s 5 a constable (or authorised local authority officer) may seize any dog which appears to him to be a dog to which s 1 applies and which is in a public place when it is not muzzled or kept on a lead. The additional powers of seizure provided by the Criminal Justice and Police Act 2001, s 50 apply to this power of seizure.

Dogs fouling land

The Dogs (Fouling of Land) Act 1996 was repealed by the CNEA 2005 which makes provision for dog control orders to be made by local authorities which may include requirements in relation to these, and other matters concerned with dogs.

General controls related to dogs

Dog control orders

CNEA 2005, Part 6 provides local authorities with powers to make dog control orders providing for offences in relation to the control of dogs in respect of any land in its area. For these purposes an offence relates to the control of dogs if it relates to one of the following matters:

(a) fouling of land by dogs and the removal of dog faeces;
(b) the keeping of dogs on leads;
(c) the exclusion of dogs from land;
(d) the number of dogs which a person may take on to any land.

Dog control orders made may apply to any land in the open air to which the public are entitled or permitted to have access, with or without payment. Land which is open to the air on one side is land open to the air.

Land may be designated by statutory instrument as land to which these provisions do not apply. The Control on Dogs (Non-application to Designated Land) Order 2006 designates the following as such: land which is placed at the disposal of the Forestry Commission (for the purpose of making a dog control order) and land over which a road passes (for the purpose of making a dog control order which provides for an offence relating to the exclusion of dogs from land).

The offences which are provided for in a dog control order must be prescribed by regulations. Such regulations may specify the wording to be used in an order, limit times during which an offence may be committed, and deal with failures to comply with directions of specified persons. The Dogs Control Orders (Prescribed Offences and Penalties, etc) Regulations 2006 prescribe the offences of:

(a) failing to remove faeces deposited by a dog on land in respect of which a Fouling of Land by Dogs Order applies;
(b) failing to keep a dog on a lead on land in respect of which a Dogs on Leads Order applies;
(c) failing to put, and to keep, a dog on a lead when directed to do so by an authorised officer, on land in respect of which a Dogs on Leads by Direction Order applies;
(d) permitting a dog to enter land in respect of which a Dogs Exclusion Order applies;
(e) taking more than the maximum number of dogs onto land in respect of which a Dogs (Specified Maximum) Order applies.

These offences must be committed without reasonable excuse or without the consent of the owner, occupier or other person or authority who has control of the land. Persons who are registered blind or who have some other disability which make them dog-dependent do not commit the offences at (a) and (d).

CNAEA 2005, s 59 makes provision for offences to be dealt with by an authorised officer of the local authority way of a fixed penalty. The amount of the fixed penalty may be specified in the order. If it is not it is currently £75. An authorised officer is empowered to require a person to whom he intends to give a notice, to give his name and address. Failure to do so, or the giving of a false or inaccurate name and address, is an offence.

The CNAEA 2005 provides that community support officers and accredited persons may deal with these matters by way of a fixed penalty.

Dangerous dogs

Order to keep under control

Complaints are frequently received by police officers to the effect that a particular dog is dangerous. The Dogs Act 1871 lays down the following powers for a magistrates' court in relation to a dangerous dog.

If it appears to a magistrates' court that a dog is dangerous and not kept under proper control, it may order the owner to keep it under control or may order that it be destroyed. Depending on the circumstances, the court can be satisfied that a dog is dangerous on the basis of a single act; in other cases further evidence will be required. The proceedings must be by way of complaint and if initiated by information they are invalid. Complaints may be preferred by a police officer.

Such an order may be made whether or not the dog is shown to have injured any person. It may specify the measures to be taken for keeping the dog under control, whether by muzzling, keeping on a lead or by excluding it from specified places or otherwise. Such an order may also require the neutering of a male dog.

A divisional court held that it is not necessary that the dog is dangerous to mankind; it is enough that it is dangerous to other animals of whatever kind. However, in one case, a dog which killed two pet rabbits was held by a divisional court not to be dangerous as it was within the natural instincts of a dog to chase, wound or kill other small animals. This is a surprising view. If followed generally it would undermine the Dogs Act 1871. In contrast in a more recent case, where a Japanese Akita dog slipped its lead and attacked a Jack Russell terrier which died as a result of its injuries, a divisional court held that a dog could be dangerous and not under proper control even if the only danger it presented was to another dog. It held that 'dangerous' was to be given its ordinary everyday meaning and was not limited to danger to mankind or particular species of animals or birds.

As indicated above, the saying that every dog may have two bites is not necessarily true. This saying has arisen because the court will often order the owner to keep the dog under control on the first occasion that a complaint is made. However, the court has the power to order destruction from the outset. There is an appeal to the Crown Court against an order of destruction, but not against an order to keep the dog under control.

The Dangerous Dogs Act 1989 empowers a magistrates' court, when it makes an order under the 1871 Act directing a dog to be destroyed, to appoint a person to do it and to require the custodian to deliver it up. It may also disqualify the owner from having custody for a specified period. There is an appeal to the Crown Court.

The Dangerous Dogs Act 1989 also creates offences of failing to keep a dog under proper control as ordered under the 1871 Act, and failing to deliver up a dog for destruction as ordered. The offences are punishable by fine and disqualification from having custody of a dog for a specified period.

Specific offences in relation to dangerous dogs

DDA 1991, ss 1 and 3 make further provisions in relation to dangerous dogs.

The most important provision is DDA 1991, s 1(3) which makes it an offence for a person to have in his possession or control a dog to which s 1 applies (see p 736 above). However, by the Dangerous Dogs Compensation and Exemption Schemes Order 1991, this offence does not apply to a dog born before 30 November 1991 if the following set of conditions is satisfied:

(a) the person wishing to keep the dog must have notified the police of its address, name, age and gender;
(b) the dog must have been neutered;
(c) there must be third-party insurance in respect of bodily harm caused by it;
(d) a certificate of exemption must have been issued; and
(e) the terms of the certificate must be complied with.

DDA 1991, s 1(2) prohibits breeding, selling, exchanging, giving or offering to give, advertising or exposing for sale, exchange or gift, a dog specified above in relation to leads etc. It also makes it an offence for the owner to abandon such a dog, or for the owner or person in charge of it to allow it to stray.

DDA 1991, s 3 creates two offences which apply to all dogs.

First, where a dog is dangerously out of control in a public place, the owner or the person for the time being in charge of it is guilty of an offence under DDA 1991, s 3(1). The offence is aggravated if the dog, whilst so out of control, injures any person. Strict liability is imposed by s 3(1) on the owners or handlers of such dogs. The test is objective and the state of mind of the owner is irrelevant. However, an owner has a defence under s 3(2) if he can prove that at the time of the offence the dog was in the charge of a person whom he reasonably believed to be a fit and proper person to be in charge of it. A divisional court has held that the defence only applies if there is plain evidence that 'charge' has been transferred to an identified person. The fact that a dog was let out of the house by a person other than the owner was not evidence from which it can be inferred that charge of the dog had been transferred to that other person.

Second, the owner or person in charge of a dog commits an offence against DDA 1991, s 3(3) if he allows it to enter a place which is not a public place but where it is not permitted to be and, while it is there, it injures any person, or there are grounds for reasonable apprehension that it will do so. There would be such grounds, for example, if a dog attacks someone without prior warning. The offence can be committed by omission if it results in the dog entering the place in question. Consequently, for example, a person who fails to take adequate precautions to prevent a dog escaping into another place 'allows' it to enter that place. Where a dog was secured by a chain which proved to be inadequate and it escaped from a garden, entered a place where it was not permitted to be, and bit the face of a young child, the owner was held to have 'allowed' the dog to enter that place, even though he thought that the chain was adequate. Like the offence under s 3(1), the present offence is one of strict liability.

An aggravated offence under DDA 1991, s 3(1) or (3) is committed if the dog does injure any person in these circumstances.

Destruction and disqualification orders

These are dealt with by DDA 1991, s 4 or s 4A. Section 4(1) provides that, where a person is convicted of an offence against s 1 or 3, the court may order destruction of the dog concerned. Indeed, it *must* do in the case of an offence under s 1 or an aggravated offence contrary to s 3, unless it is satisfied that the dog would not constitute a danger to public safety and, where the dog was born before 30 November 1991 and is subject to a prohibition on its possession under s 1(3), that there is good reason why the dog has not been exempted from that prohibition.

A court may also order a person convicted of any of these offences to be disqualified from keeping a dog for such a period as it thinks fit. Dogs may not be destroyed during the period allowed for notice of, and determination of, any appeal.

Similar provisions are made in DDA 1991, to those set out above in the Dangerous Dogs Act 1989, in relation to the appointment of a person to undertake the destruction of a dog and requiring it to be delivered up for that purpose.

Offences are committed against DDA 1991, s 4(8) where a person has custody of a dog while disqualified, or where he fails to deliver up a dog for destruction as ordered.

DDA 1991, s 4A provides that where:

(a) a person is convicted of an offence under DDA 1991, s 1 or an aggravated offence under DDA 1991, s 3(1) or (3);
(b) the court does not order destruction of the dog under DDA 1991, s 4; and
(c) in the case of an offence under DDA 1991, s 1, the dog is subject to the prohibition under DDA 1991, s 1(3),

the court must order that, unless the dog is exempted from that prohibition within the requisite period, the dog shall be destroyed. The requisite period, currently two months, may be extended by the court.

DDA 1991, s 4A also provides that, where a person is convicted of a simple offence under DDA 1991, s 3(1) or (3), the court may order that, unless its owner keeps it under proper control, the dog must be destroyed. Such an order may specify the measures to be taken to keep the dog under control whether by muzzling, keeping on a lead, excluding it from specified places or otherwise, and, if it appears to the court that the dog is a male and would be less dangerous if neutered, may require that the dog be neutered.

Public place

DDA 1991 defines a 'public place' as any street, road or other place (whether or not enclosed) to which the public have or are permitted to have access. A private garden is not a public place in this context and neither is any other type of place which people enter by express or implied invitation. On the other hand, a dog in a private car on a public highway is in a public place.

Police powers

As already mentioned, by DDA 1991, s 5(9), a constable (or authorised local authority officer) may seize any dog which appears to him to be a dog to which s 1 applies and which is in a public place when its possession or custody is unlawful by virtue of s 1. Such a person may also seize any dog in a public place which appears to him to be dangerously out of control.

If a justice of the peace is satisfied by information on oath that there are reasonable grounds to believe that one of the above offences has been committed, or that evidence of such an offence is to be found on any premises, he may issue a warrant authorising a constable to enter and search them and to seize any dog or other thing which is evidence of such an offence. This power is given by DDA 1991, s 5(2).

DDA 1991, s 4B makes provision for an order of destruction which may be made by a justice of the peace in respect of a dog which has been seized under DDA 1991, s 5(1) or (2) of the Act where there is no prosecution, or where the dog cannot be released without contravention of DDA 1991, s 1(3). A justice is not required to make such an order if he is satisfied concerning the factors mentioned in relation to DDA 1991, s 4(1) above.

Dogs owned by young persons

DDA 1991, s 6 provides that, where a dog is owned by a person who is less than sixteen years old, the term 'owner' in the above provisions includes a reference to the head of the household, if any, of which that person is a member.

Guard dogs

The Guard Dogs Act 1975 sets out to control the use of guard dogs on premises. It is an offence for any person to use or permit the use of a guard dog on any premises unless:

(a) a person ('the handler') who is capable of controlling the dog is present on the premises and the dog is under the direct control of the handler; or
(b) the dog is so secured as to prevent it from being at liberty to go freely about the premises.

However, the Act is concerned with what might be described as the commercial use of guard dogs, rather than the family watchdog. It therefore excludes from the term 'premises' agricultural land and land in the curtilage of a dwelling house, thus exempting farm dogs and those confined within a dwelling house or its yard or garden.

When guard dogs are kept upon 'premises' warning notices must be clearly displayed at all entrances to the premises; failure to display such notices is an offence.

A 'guard dog' is one which is used either to protect the premises or property on them, or to protect a person guarding the premises or property. The handler must keep the dog under his personal control at all times unless he has handed over responsibility to another handler, or he has secured the dog so that it is not at liberty to go freely about the premises; otherwise he commits an offence. If the dog is properly secured it is not necessary for the handler to be on the premises all the time. If secured on a long chain, it is a question of fact, for the justices to determine, whether the dog was at liberty to go freely about the premises.

STRAYING ANIMALS

The Highways Act 1980, s 155 states that if horses, cattle, sheep, goats, or swine are found straying or lying on or at the side of a highway their keeper is guilty of an offence. A person in whose possession animals are is their keeper, whether or not he derives any personal benefit from them. Highways which pass over common or unenclosed land are exempted from these provisions.

Police officers frequently receive reports of straying animals, usually during the night. They are empowered to return them to the keeper's land or to any other place provided for the safe custody of animals. Such places, or common pounds as they were known, are extremely rare today. It is, therefore, usually left to police officers temporarily to secure such animals. It is inadvisable to place animals in a field in which other animals are already grazing, unless it is known that they escaped from that field. The consequences of mixing non-attested cattle with those which have been attested can be expensive.

WILD BIRDS, ANIMALS AND PLANTS

Wild birds

Killing, destroying, damaging or possessing

The relevant statute is the Wildlife and Countryside Act 1981 (WCA 1981). WCA 1981, s 1 creates the offences of intentionally killing, injuring or taking any *wild bird*, of intentionally taking, damaging or destroying the *nest of such a bird*, and of intentionally taking or destroying an *egg of such a bird*. It is equally an offence to possess a wild bird, whether alive or dead (including one which has been stuffed and mounted), or any part of it, or an egg (or part of it) of such a bird. 'Knowledge' that the bird is wild is not required. Consequently, an accused's belief that a wild bird was bred in captivity and was therefore not a 'wild bird' does not afford an excuse.

The purpose of the legislation is to provide complete protection to wild birds against the activities such as those of the falconer at one extreme and those of the youthful 'birds'-nester' at the other. The term 'wild bird' is widely defined to include all wild birds which are resident in, or are visitors to, Great Britain, with the exception of poultry (birds which could not readily be described as wild even if free ranging) or game birds (which are protected by separate legislation discussed in the next chapter). In addition, as already implied, 'wild bird' does not include a wild bird which has been bred in captivity. For a bird to be bred in captivity the parent birds must have been in captivity when the egg was laid. This restriction is to prevent the 'nest robbers' from legally rearing falcons and other rare birds in captivity. Captive birds must be ringed and registered.

It is an offence against WCA 1981, s 1(5) intentionally or recklessly to disturb any wild bird mentioned in Sch 1 to the Act whilst it is building a nest, or is in, on or near such a nest containing eggs or young birds, or to disturb dependent young of such a bird. Schedule 1 contains all but the commonest of birds. It includes all birds of prey resident in the United Kingdom with the exception of the kestrel and sparrow hawk. Nest robbers target the nests of peregrine falcons, goshawks and eagles. The peregrine, particularly, is highly valued by falconers. Frequent use is made of the provisions relating to 'disturbance' to combat such nest robbers. Where chicks are found in the possession of persons licensed to keep birds of prey, and the circumstances are suspicious, the parenthood of such chicks can be established by DNA fingerprinting. The RSPB will assist in this respect.

Exceptions

For the purpose of day to day enforcement, it is almost certain that persons found in the act of killing wild birds, or in possession of their eggs, will be guilty of an offence against this Act. However, there are some limitations on the offence of killing, taking or injuring a wild bird. Some birds may be killed or taken outside their close season (generally their nesting season); these include the commoner species of duck and goose, plover, snipe and woodcock, which are listed in WCA 1981, Sch 2, Part I. There are a number of other exceptions, relating to wild birds in general, where the action taken is done by an authorised person (ie a landowner or the occupier, or someone authorised by him or by an official body of a specified type) or officially required or done in relation to a disabled bird and in certain other cases.

Sale etc

It is an offence under AHA 1981, s 6 to sell, or to expose or offer for sale, or to possess for sale, live wild birds or their eggs, or to publish, or cause to be published, advertisements to that effect.

Wild animals

WCA 1981 contains similar offences to protect wild animals. These provisions are not so easy for police officers to enforce as those relating to wild birds. The reason is that the protection afforded to wild animals by WCA 1981 is restricted to animals described in Sch 5 to the Act. This leads to problems of identification, concerning which specialist help will be needed.

By WCA 1981, s 9 it is an offence intentionally to kill, injure or take any wild animal listed in WCA 1981, Sch 5, or for a person to possess such animal alive or dead (in whole or part), without proper authority. The same provisions as in the case of wild birds apply in relation to sale, exposing or offering for sale, possessing for sale, or advertising for sale, a wild animal listed in WCA 1981, Sch 5.

The animals listed in Sch 5 include most of the less common butterflies, moths, frogs, lizards and newts, porpoises, dolphins, red (but not grey) squirrels and the common otter.

Wild plants

That part of WCA 1981 which concerns wild plants is more direct as it begins (in s 13) by providing that it shall be an offence for any person intentionally to pick, uproot or destroy any wild plant included in WCA 1981, Sch 8. Schedule 8 contains quite an extensive list of wild plants; all but the most common of our wild plants are listed.

It is also an offence under s 13 for someone who is not an authorised person intentionally to uproot any wild plant not included in Sch 8. An 'authorised person' has the same meaning as defined in relation to the killing of wild birds.

The *uprooting* of wild plants is perhaps not so common as the picking of flowers. As can be seen, the intentional picking or destruction of wild plants, other than by uprooting, is only an offence if the plant concerned is one listed in Sch 8 to the Act.

As in the case of wild animals, it is an offence under WCA 1981, s 13 to sell, offer or expose for sale, possess for sale or advertise for sale etc any live or dead wild plant included in WCA 1981, Sch 8.

Licences

The above offences relating to wild birds, animals and plants are not committed by a person acting within the terms of a licence granted by the appropriate authority.

Additional police powers

By WCA 1981, s 19(1) if a constable suspects with reasonable cause that any person is committing or has committed any of these offences, he may without warrant stop and search that person and search or examine anything which that person may then be using or have in his possession. In each case, if he with reasonable cause suspects that evidence of the offence is to be found, he may seize and detain for the purpose of proceedings under the Act anything which may be evidence of the commission of the offence or may be liable to be forfeited.

For the purpose of exercising his powers as set out above, or for the purpose of arresting a person under the Police and Criminal Evidence Act 1984, s 24 for any of the offences under WCA 1981, a constable is empowered by WCA 1981, s 19(2) to enter onto any land other than a dwelling house. A justice may issue a search warrant under s 19(3) subject to the usual conditions in respect of the offence disclosed.

OFFENCES RELATED TO DEER

The Deer Act 1991 (DA 1991) deals with the protection of deer by provisions relating to close seasons, the times of day when deer may be taken and the methods by which this may be done. It also deals with deer poaching.

Taking or killing of deer: in close season or at night

DA 1991, Sch 1 provides close seasons for red, fallow, roe and sika deer. These vary considerably because of the breeding seasons of the different species. It is an offence to take or intentionally kill a deer during its close season. Deer farmers are permitted to take or kill deer out of season, but their deer must be conspicuously marked. Authorised persons (occupiers of land, persons with shooting rights, and persons authorised by them) may *shoot* deer out of season in protection of crops etc. The DA 1991 also prohibits the taking or intentional killing of *any* deer by night (ie between one hour after sunset and one hour before sunrise). This offence relates to *any part* of the year. Neither offence is committed if the taking or killing is done to prevent suffering by an injured or diseased deer.

Other offences

The DA 1991 also prohibits the setting of traps, snares, poisoned baits etc (unless this is done to prevent suffering to an injured or diseased deer) and the use of smooth-bore guns and guns having a calibre of less than .240, air pistols, air rifles and bullets other than those which are soft- or hollow-nosed. It also prohibits the discharge at deer of firearms from mechanically propelled vehicles or the use of such vehicles for the purpose of driving deer, and the use of arrows, spears or similar missiles, or of drugged missiles containing a poisoned or stupefying drug.

Deer poaching

The DA 1991 prohibits entry onto land without the consent of the owner or occupier or other lawful authority in search or pursuit of any deer with the intention of taking, killing or injuring it.

Offences are also committed by persons who:

(a) intentionally take, kill or injure any deer (or attempt to do so);
(b) search for or pursue any deer with the intention of taking, killing or injuring it; or
(c) remove the carcass of any deer.

A person is not guilty of any of these offences if his act is done in the belief that:

(a) he would have had the consent of the owner or occupier of the land if such person knew of his doing it and the circumstances of it; or
(b) he has other lawful authority to do it.

Police powers

The DA 1991 provides a constable, who suspects with reasonable cause that any person is committing or has committed any offence under the Act, with a power, without warrant, to search or examine persons, vehicles, animals, weapons or other things on whom or on which he reasonably suspects evidence of the offence is to be found, and to seize and detain anything which is evidence of an offence and any deer, vehicle, animal, weapon or other thing liable to be forfeited by a court under the Act. For the purpose of exercising the above powers, or of exercising his power of arrest, a constable may enter any land other than a dwelling house.

CHAPTER 23
Game laws

The term 'game laws' refers to the law relating to poaching, trespassing in pursuit of game of all varieties, close seasons and the need for licences.

The various game laws are designed to protect the rights of the owners or occupiers of land to kill and take game on their land. In the first instance the right to take game rests with the landowner. However, if he leases the land, the right to take game on it automatically passes to the tenant, unless the landowner expressly reserves that right. Frequently the person with the right to take game may let the 'shooting rights' to another person or to a syndicate of persons.

POACHING BY DAY AND BY NIGHT

Powers in public place

It is best to begin by considering the most likely exercise of a constable's powers in the course of his routine duties. If a constable in any highway, street or public place has good cause to suspect a person of coming from land where he has been unlawfully in search or pursuit of game, and of having in his possession any game unlawfully obtained, or any gun, ammunition, nets, snares, traps or other devices of a kind used for the killing and taking of game, he may search that person or an accomplice of his. He may also stop and search conveyances. The constable may seize and detain any game, articles or other things connected with poaching which he finds. Dogs and ferrets may not be seized.

The above powers are provided by the Poaching Prevention Act 1862, s 2 which goes on to provide that when the person summoned appears before the justices he will be convicted of an offence if it is proved that:

(a) he has obtained the game by unlawfully going on any land in search or pursuit of game;
(b) he has used any article or thing for unlawfully killing or taking game; or
(c) he has been an accomplice to conduct of the type mentioned in (a) or (b).

For the purpose of the above provisions, 'game' includes hares and rabbits and pheasants, partridges, woodcocks, snipes, grouse, black or moor game and *the eggs of each of these birds.*

Day poaching

The Game Act 1831, s 30 provides an offence of poaching by day. It provides that anyone who trespasses by entering or being upon land in the daytime in search or pursuit of game, woodcocks, snipes or rabbits commits an offence. For the purposes of the Game Act 1831 'game' includes hares and pheasants, partridges, grouse, heath or moor game, and black game.

'Daytime' begins one hour before sunrise and ends one hour after sunset.

'Trespass' indicates an entry on to land (or presence there) without authority. If a person enters upon another's land without authority, the occupier of that land may order that person to leave at once and is entitled to use reasonable force to eject him should he refuse to go. It is not a criminal offence, at the moment, merely to trespass but a trespasser is criminally liable for any damage which he may cause whilst trespassing. The present offence is committed when a trespass is aggravated by a search for or pursuit of game.

Parliament considered that it was essential to provide protection for gamekeepers as it was quite common for bands of poachers to become violent. It therefore increased the penalties under the Game Act 1831, s 31 in cases where five or more persons trespass together during the daytime for such purposes. This recognises the threat offered by large numbers. The Game Act 1831, s 32 seeks to deal with the individual threatening actions of any of these persons. If any one of the five is armed with a gun and he uses violence, intimidation or menaces to prevent any person from exercising his powers under the Act, he and those with him commit a further offence.

The Game Laws (Amendment) Act 1960, s 4A(1) provides that where a person is convicted of an offence under the Game Act 1831, s 30 as one of five or more persons liable under the section and the court is satisfied that any vehicle belonging to him or in his possession or under his control at the relevant time has been used for the purpose of committing or facilitating the commission of the offence, the court may make an order of forfeiture in respect of that vehicle.

'Facilitation' includes the taking of any steps after the commission of the offence to avoid apprehension or detection, or removing from the land any person or property connected with the offence. Thus, the use of the vehicle 'after the event' is also included. The court is not required, when exercising its powers under this section, to have regard to the value of the property and to the likely financial and other effects upon the offender of such an order.

Powers

A constable has power to require any trespasser in search or pursuit of game to quit and give his name and address. If a constable has reasonable cause for suspecting that a person is committing the offence of trespassing in pursuit of game in the daytime he may enter land for the purpose of exercising this power.

Night poaching

The Night Poaching Act 1828 is concerned with offences of poaching by night. Night commences one hour after sunset and continues until one hour before sunrise. The Night Poaching Act 1828, s 1 creates two general offences:

(a) by night, unlawfully taking or destroying by night any game or *rabbits* on land, open or enclosed (including a public road, highway or path); and
(b) by night, unlawfully entering or being on any land, open or enclosed, with any gun, net, engine or other instrument for the purpose of taking or destroying game.

For the purposes of these offences, 'game' means hares, pheasants, partridges, grouse, heath or moor game, black game or bustards; it does not include rabbits. The two offences can be contrasted as follows. First, the man who has taken or destroyed *game or rabbits* by night has committed an offence wherever that killing or taking has occurred, be it in a field, in a street or public place. Second, the man who has not killed or taken game, must have unlawfully entered upon land with an instrument for the taking of *game*; for this purpose, the land may be open or enclosed but a public road, highway or path is not within the offence.

Like the Game Act 1831, the Night Poaching Act 1828 provides increased penalties for more aggravated offences. By s 2 of the 1828 Act, anyone committing an offence under s 1 who assaults or offers violence with a gun or other offensive weapon towards any person authorised to apprehend him is liable to an increased penalty. Section 9 provides that if three or more people together enter or are on land by night to take or destroy game or rabbits, and one of them is armed with a gun or other offensive weapon, all are guilty of an aggravated offence.

Powers

A constable who has reasonable grounds for suspecting that one of these offences is being committed may enter land to deal with the offence.

GAME

Rights to take game

We have mentioned the rights of landowners, their tenants and authorised persons to take game on their land. At the opposite extreme, we have looked at those who trespass to take or destroy game or who actually take or destroy it. There is only one further Act which should be considered in order to complete an understanding of the rights of persons to take game. This is the Ground Game Act 1880 which provides that an occupier of land will always have the right to kill and take ground game (ie hares and rabbits) on the land which he occupies, whether or not the landowner has contracted to some other person game rights generally. The occupier may also give written authorisation to other people to kill and take ground game, but he may only authorise (again in writing) one person, in addition to himself, to kill ground game with firearms. Authorisations of these types may only be given by the occupier to his own resident household, people in his ordinary employment on the land and one other person bona fide employed by him in the taking and destruction of ground game.

Game licences

Quite regardless of the issue of whether or not a person is authorised to kill or take game on land, all persons must have a game licence to kill, pursue or take game, or to use dogs or devices for such purpose. The Game Licences Act 1860 requires that a licence be taken out for game, woodcocks, snipes, rabbits or deer. There are exceptions to the rule which are generally related to the authorised killing of deer and the killing of rabbits by landowners. The occupiers of land, and persons authorised, do not need game licences in their taking of hares. The Game Act 1831 requires that a licence be held if a person searches for game, but 'game' for the purpose of that Act does not include rabbits.

Close season for game

The Game Act 1831 prohibits taking or killing game on Sundays or Christmas Days. In addition, it prohibits the taking or killing of particular types of game birds during their close seasons, which are as follows:

(a) partridges   —   1 February to the following 1 September;
(b) pheasants   —   1 February to the following 1 October;
(c) black game   —   10 December to the following 20 August;
(d) grouse   —   10 December to the following 12 August.

OFFENCES IN RELATION TO FISH

As fishing increases in popularity as a sport and more fisheries are created (either by the Environment Agency for the general public or by clubs for their members), the likelihood of police involvement at some stage in the enforcement of the freshwater fishery laws increases. There are certain provisions of the Salmon and Freshwater Fisheries Act 1975 which are quite general in nature and can directly concern the police. The provisions of the Theft Act 1968, Sch 1 are also important.

Salmon and Freshwater Fisheries Act 1975

Licensing

The Act requires the Environment Agency (EA) to regulate fishing for salmon, trout, freshwater fish and eels by means of a system of licensing. The fishing licence granted by a water authority authorises the person to whom it is granted to use the instrument specified (commonly a rod and line) to fish for fish named in specified waters between certain dates. A salmon licence will include trout, and any licence which allows fishing for trout also permits fishing for lesser freshwater fish and eels.

The EA licence is usually referred to as a 'rod licence', and it is important to realise that all a person is authorised to do by that licence is to use a rod in the EA area.

It is an offence to fish for, or take, fish of a description other than that authorised by the licence, or by means other than that authorised by the licence. It is also an offence to possess, with intent to use it for fishing, any instrument other than that authorised by the licence.

A water bailiff appointed by the EA, or any constable, may require any person who is fishing, or whom he reasonably suspects of being about to fish (or to have, within the last half-hour, fished), in the area of the EA to produce his licence or other authority to fish and to give his name and address. (This power is also available to the holder of a licence if he produces his own licence at the time of his demand.) The 'other authority' referred to must be some alternative form of authority issued by the EA; it does not refer to a riparian owner's consent to fish. Clearly, a person could reasonably be suspected of being about to fish if he was seen approaching water with a rod and tackle, and he could reasonably be suspected of having fished in the preceding half-hour if he was seen leaving the water with such equipment on the approach of a constable.

Failure without reasonable excuse to comply with such a request is an offence, except that, if within seven days after the requirement the person requested produces his licence or other authority at the office of the EA, he cannot be convicted of failing to produce it.

Illegal methods

Quite regardless of the licensing situation, there are certain methods of fishing which are prohibited by the Salmon and Freshwater Fisheries Act 1975 (SFFA 1975). The use of any firearm, as defined by the Firearms Act 1968, is prohibited, as is the use of otter-boards, snares, crosslines, setlines, spears, gaffs, stroke-hauls, snatches or other like instruments, or any light. These are typical poaching devices. The otterboard is a floating board to which are attached a number of lines. A crossline is one which is stretched across a river with a number of lines etc attached. A setline is any line which is left unattended. Stroke-hauls and snatches are used for the purpose of dragging for fish which are foul hooked. Gaffs may, at certain times, be lawfully used for landing fish which have been caught by rod and line, but not for catching fish. The use of fish roe is also prohibited. This is important because some poachers prepare fish roe into a sticky substance, often referred to as 'taffy', which is attached to the line to attract fish to the bait. The use of explosives, poison or electrical devices with intent to take fish is always an offence unless carried out with consent of the EA.

Powers

A water bailiff appointed by the EA may examine rods, instruments or baits if he has good cause to suspect that they are illegal. He may also stop and search a boat or vessel used in fishing in a water authority area or any vessel or vehicle which he reasonably suspects to contain fish caught in contravention of the provisions of the SFFA 1975, and he may seize fish, instruments, vessels or vehicles or other things liable to be forfeited under the Act. It is an offence to refuse to allow, or to resist, the execution of the above powers by a water bailiff. However, the bailiff must produce his appointment before searching. It is important that police officers are aware of the powers of a water bailiff as they are frequently called to their assistance.

Water bailiffs and other officers of the EA have power to impose a fixed penalty notice on those whom they find, and reasonably believe to be committing or to have committed an offence under the SFFA 1975, in lieu of court proceedings and conviction. This fixed penalty system has similarities with that operating in relation to road traffic offences.

The point to remember in resolving disputes arising between officials and anglers is that these powers are only given to a water bailiff appointed by the EA. Superintendents of club fisheries are frequently referred to as bailiffs but unless they have been authorised by the EA they are not water bailiffs for the purpose of fishery legislation.

At night (as defined by the Night Poaching Act 1828 described above), a water bailiff may arrest without warrant any person illegally taking or killing salmon, trout, freshwater fish or eels, or whom he finds near water with that intent, or who has in his possession any prohibited instruments. The bailiff must place such persons in police custody as soon as possible. Such arrested persons may therefore be placed in the care of a custody officer.

Close seasons for game fishing

SFFA 1975, Sch 1 deals with the annual close seasons for taking game fish. There is no purpose in setting out the details as the Schedule places the responsibility upon the EA to make byelaws fixing for their area, or the respective parts of it, the annual close season for fishing for salmon and trout other than rainbow trout. In doing so, the EA is required to observe minimum closure periods. The Schedule gives guidelines in respect of fishing by rod and line for salmon and trout which are subject to variation by local bylaws:

(a) salmon   —   31 October and the following 1 February;
(b) trout   —   30 September and the following 1 March; and
(c) rainbow trout —   close season may be dispensed with altogether.

Theft Act 1968

Fish can be the subject of theft but only if:

(a) they are ordinarily kept in captivity, as where someone has bought a dozen live trout and placed them in his private pond, or as in the case of fish at fish farms; or
(b) they have been reduced into possession by or on behalf of someone other than the accused, or that other person is in the course of reducing them into possession, as where an angler (the other person) has put fish in a keep net or has hooked it and is reeling it in.

The Theft Act 1968, Sch 1 deals with the situation where fish do not fall within the above provisions, so that the taking or destroying of them is not theft (nor criminal damage). It provides that it is an offence for a person unlawfully to take or destroy, or attempt to take or destroy, any fish:

(a) in water which is private property (such as reservoirs and privately owned lakes); or

(b) in water in which there is any private right of fishery.

'Private right of fishery' can be explained as follows. The water in *non-tidal* rivers or parts of rivers is not owned by the landowners through, or between, whose land the river flows. However, these landowners (or, to give them their technical description, riparian owners) have a private right to fish in the waters bounded by their banks (or up to mid-stream if the banks are in separate ownership). The public cannot acquire a right to fish in non-tidal rivers by common usage. The right always remains with the landowner unless he lets the land to a tenant, at which time it passes to the tenant unless expressly reserved by the landowner. Of course the owner of a right to fish can, if he wishes, give general permission to the public to use his fishery. By way of contrast, a private right of fishery cannot exist in tidal waters, including the tidal part of a river, with the result that there is generally a public right to fish in them, although it must be noted that salmon is almost universally reserved by fishery boards, and that local Acts may affect other fisheries.

If an offence contrary to Sch 1 is committed by night it is more severely punishable than if committed by day. 'Night' and 'day' bear the same meaning as they do under the legislation mentioned earlier in this chapter.

CHAPTER 24

Firearms

There is no general right to possess firearms in Great Britain. The Firearms Act 1968 (FiA 1968) controls the sale and acquisition of all types of firearms and the possession or carrying of those weapons on particular occasions. Other Acts punish the possession of firearms on particular occasions.

DEFINITIONS

FiA 1968, s 57 defines the term 'firearm' for the purposes of that Act as a *lethal barrelled weapon* of any description *from which any shot, bullet or other missile can be discharged*. It also provides that the term includes any *prohibited weapon*, whether it is such a lethal weapon as aforesaid or not, and any *component part* of such a lethal or prohibited weapon, and any *accessory* to any such weapon designed or adapted *to diminish the noise or flash caused by firing the weapon*.

Nothing in FiA 1968 relating to firearms applies to an antique firearm which is sold, transferred, purchased, acquired or possessed as a curiosity or ornament.

Firearms

Lethal weapon

It is clear from judicial decisions that a lethal weapon means a weapon which is capable of causing injury from which death might result. It need not be designed or manufactured for the purpose of causing such injury; if it is not, it is enough that it is capable of causing such injury if misused.

Consequently, even though the purpose of its designer and manufacturer was to produce a toy, a spring pistol which can fire pellets through a barrel will be a lethal weapon (and therefore a firearm) if, even though only through misuse, it is capable of causing an injury from which death might result.

By way of further example, a signalling pistol which fired an explosive magnesium and phosphorus flare, and which was capable of killing at short range, has been held to be lethal; the fact that the manufacturer did not produce it for the purpose of killing or injuring being held to be immaterial. Many of the air guns which are manufactured would normally only cause a trivial injury but they may be classed as lethal since they could cause death by a pellet striking an extremely vulnerable part of the body, for example, an eye.

Whether or not a weapon is lethal must be assessed in relation to the particular weapon in question, and not to weapons of its type. If the particular weapon is not in working order and is therefore incapable of causing injury from which death might result it is not a lethal weapon, even though a weapon of its type is so capable when in working order.

Under the *basic* definition of a 'firearm', the 'lethal weapon' must be *barrelled* and capable of *discharging* any shot, bullet or other *missile*. To these matters we now turn.

Barrelled

A barrel, in relation to a gun, is a tube through which a bullet or shot is discharged. Traditionally, that tube has been made of metal. However, in the modern world of newly discovered substances which might act as substitutes for metal, it is unlikely that the nature of the substance would be restricted to metal.

Shot, bullet or other missile

The terms 'shot' and 'bullet' are self-explanatory, and the term 'other missile' should be taken to relate to some similar solid object which can be discharged from some form of 'barrelled weapon'. It is unlikely that much difficulty will be experienced in relation to this term as the only 'guns' which are excluded thereby are those weapons designed or adapted to discharge some form of gas, and these are almost certain to be 'prohibited weapons' (see below), and therefore a firearm, in any case. However, a weapon which simply discharged compressed air would not be a prohibited weapon for the purposes of FiA 1968.

Apart from its basic definition, 'firearm' also includes 'prohibited weapons', component parts of a lethal barrelled weapon from which any missile can be discharged or of a prohibited weapon, and certain accessories to any such weapon.

In addition, under the Firearms Act 1982, s 1 the provisions of FiA 1968 are made to apply (with limited exceptions) to an imitation firearm which has the appearance of being a firearm to which FiA 1968, s 1 (firearms requiring a firearm certificate) applies and which is so constructed or adapted as to be readily convertible into such a firearm.

Prohibited weapons

There are two provisions creating offences relating to prohibited weapons: FiA 1968, s 5(1) and (1A). These impose controls over and above the need to have a firearm certificate.

For the purposes of the offence under FiA 1968, s 5(1), a prohibited weapon is:

(a) any firearm which is so designed or adapted that two or more missiles can be successively discharged without repeated pressure on the trigger;
(b) any self-loading or pump-action rifled gun other than one chambered for .22 inch rim-fire cartridges;
(c) any firearm which either has a barrel less than 30 cm in length or is less than 60 cm in length overall, other than an air weapon, a muzzle-loading gun or a firearm designed as a signalling apparatus;
(d) any self-loading or pump-action smooth-bore gun which is not an air weapon (as defined on p 760) or chambered for .22 inch rim-fire cartridges and either has a barrel of less than 24 inches in length or is less than 40 inches in length overall;
(e) any smooth-bore revolver gun other than one which is chambered for 9 mm rim-fire cartridges or a muzzle-loading gun;
(f) any rocket launcher, or any mortar designed for line-throwing or pyrotechnic purposes or as a signalling apparatus;
(g) any air rifle, air gun or air pistol which uses, or is designed or adapted for use with, a self-contained gas cartridge system;
(h) any weapon of whatever description designed or adapted for the discharge of any noxious liquid, gas or other thing.

This covers a wide variety of weaponry from a flame thrower, or a high voltage electric stunning device, to the small gas pistols frequently used by women for self-protection in America. The fact that a stun-gun designed for an electrical charge is not working due to some unknown fault does not change its character as a prohibited weapon. The words 'designed or adapted' mean that any other type of weapon which is converted in any way for these purposes is a prohibited weapon as it has been 'adapted'. These weapons do not need to be either lethal or barrelled *provided* they are capable of discharging noxious liquid, gas or other thing. If the weapon is capable of discharging such a substance, and was either designed or adapted for that purpose, it is prohibited. A water pistol used to discharge gas would not be a prohibited weapon if it was used in an unaltered state, since it would not have been designed to discharge one of the prohibited substances, nor adapted in any way to allow it to do so. The same applies to a washing-up liquid bottle filled with hydrochloric acid. The container was neither designed nor adapted for the discharge of a noxious liquid. Although the issue has not been tested to date, there appears to be little doubt that the word 'noxious' before 'liquid, gas or other thing' applies to all three things. A substance is noxious if it is harmful, hurtful or injurious. All forms of gas projectors are therefore prohibited, from the tear gas gun to the small gas pistol.

In relation to (a), the Court of Appeal has held that the words 'so designed or adapted that two or more missiles can be successively discharged without repeated pressure on the trigger' relates to what is objectively possible and not to the intention of the designer of the weapon. Thus, if that effect could be brought about, even if only in expert hands, the weapon is designed as a prohibited weapon.

The prohibition set out at (c) above was that introduced by the Firearms (Amendment) Act 1997 to restrict the use of handguns. For the purposes of (c) and (d) above, any detachable, folding, retractable or other movable butt-stock are disregarded in measuring the length of any firearm.

References to muzzle-loading guns are references to guns which are designed to be loaded at the muzzle end of the barrel or chamber with a loose charge and a separate ball (or other missile).

The air weapons referred to at (g) were added by the Anti-social Behaviour Act 2003 which provided that such weapons possessed at the time of the Act coming into force may be retained subject to the need to obtain a firearms certificate. It also provided that a chief officer shall not refuse an application for a firearm certificate in such circumstances, nor an application for renewal on the ground that the person does not have a good reason for having the weapon.

Slaughtering instruments, humane killers, shot pistols used for killing vermin, starting pistols, trophies of war, firearms of historic interest and weapons used for treating animals are exempted from the prohibitions imposed upon weapons falling within (c) above (or, in the case of weapons used for treating animals, within (c) or (g)) subject to conditions set out in the Firearms (Amendment) Act 1997, ss 2 to 8.

For the purposes of FiA 1968, s 5(1A), the following are prohibited weapons:

(a) any firearm which is disguised as another object;
(b) any launcher or other projecting apparatus which is not a prohibited weapon under s 5(1) which is designed to be used with any rocket or ammunition which is designed to explode on or immediately before impact and is prohibited ammunition under s 5(1) or (1A).

In relation to FiA 1968, s 5(1A) only, there are a number of exemptions in terms of weapons and of ammunition. They relate principally to collectors and to possession, purchase or acquisition for use for certain authorised purposes, namely slaughtering animals, sporting purposes, shooting vermin, estate management purposes, and competition and target shooting purposes.

Changes in type

A weapon which at any time has been classified as a prohibited weapon (or as a FiA 1968, s 1 firearm or as a shotgun) remains so classified notwithstanding anything done to convert it into a weapon of another type (eg prohibited weapon into a s 1 firearm) or to render it incapable of discharging a missile.

Component parts and accessories

The fact that any component part of a lethal barrelled or prohibited weapon (as defined above) is stated by FiA 1968, s 57 to be a firearm in itself is important. In cases of doubt concerning whether or not a weapon is 'lethal barrelled' in the general sense, it is helpful to remember that if it consists of component parts, which are essentially parts of a 'firearm', then those parts are included within the term 'firearm' and their possession etc is equally controlled. For example, it has been held that an article such as a starting pistol, incapable of discharging a missile because the barrel is solid, but capable of being adapted to do so by boring the barrel, was a firearm because the other parts of the weapon were component parts of a revolver. Likewise, if replicas of firearms are produced for the public but with soft metalled firing pins which render the weapons unusable, they are still firearms if the other components are those of a firearm.

The only accessories which are included within the term 'firearm' by FiA 1968, s 57, and are therefore controlled by FiA 1968, are those designed or adapted to diminish noise or flash, ie silencers and flash eliminators. Any other accessory to a firearm is not included. A telescopic sight is an accessory but it is not one covered by the term 'accessory' for the purposes of FiA 1968.

What is ammunition?

For the purposes of FiA 1968, 'ammunition' is defined by FiA 1968, s 57 as meaning ammunition for any firearm; a blank cartridge is ammunition. Section 57 provides that the term also includes grenades, bombs and other missiles, whether capable of use with a firearm or not, and also includes prohibited ammunition. A 'bomb' is any explosive substance in a case, or a case containing poison gas, smoke, or inflammable material which might be dropped from an aircraft, fired from a gun or thrown or placed by hand.

Prohibited ammunition for the purposes of FiA 1968, s 5(1) is:

(a) any cartridge with a bullet designed to explode on or immediately before impact (eg a 'dum-dum bullet'),

(b) any ammunition which contains, or is designed or adapted to contain, any noxious liquid, gas or other thing; and

(c) if capable of being used with a firearm of any description, any grenade, bomb (or other like missile), or a rocket or shell designed to explode on or immediately before impact,

other than ammunition used for treating animals.

Therefore containers designed or adapted to contain any noxious gas etc for use as a missile or bomb are prohibited ammunition, whether filled or not. The other types of prohibited ammunition are explosive bullets and (if capable of being used with a firearm) grenades, bombs, rockets and shells.

Prohibited ammunition for the purposes of FiA 1968, s 5(1A) is:

(a) any rocket or ammunition which is not prohibited ammunition for the purposes of FiA 1968, s 5(1) which consists in or incorporates a missile designed to explode on or immediately before impact and is for military use;

(b) any ammunition for military use which consists in or incorporates a missile designed so that a substance contained in the missile will ignite on or immediately before impact;

(c) any ammunition for military use which consists in or incorporates a missile designed, on account of its having a jacket and hard-core, to penetrate armour plating, armour screening or body armour;

(d) any ammunition which incorporates a missile designed or adapted to expand on impact;

(e) anything which is designed to be projected as a missile from any weapon and is designed to be, or has been incorporated in:
   (i) any ammunition falling within any of the preceding paragraphs; or
   (ii) any ammunition which would fall within any of those paragraphs but for its being specified in FiA 1968, s 5(1).

What is an antique firearm?

As we have said, antique firearms are exempt from the provisions of FiA 1968 relating to firearms, provided they are sold, transferred, purchased, acquired or possessed as a curiosity or ornament. The term 'antique' is not defined. Basically, it is a question of fact and degree for the court to decide; it is unlikely that a court will consider that anything made in this or the last century is an antique.

POSSESSION, PURCHASE OR ACQUISITION OF FIREARMS OR AMMUNITION

Section I firearms and ammunition

FiA 1968, s 1(1) states that, subject to any exemption under FiA 1968, it is an offence for a person:

(a) to have in his possession, or to purchase or acquire, a firearm to which the section applies without holding a firearm certificate in force at the time, or otherwise than as authorised by the certificate; or

(b) to have in his possession, or to purchase or acquire, any ammunition to which the section applies without holding a firearm certificate, or otherwise than as authorised by such a certificate, or in quantities in excess of those so authorised.

The section applies to every firearm except:

(a) a shotgun, that is to say a smooth-bore gun (not being an air gun) which:
   (i)   has a barrel not less than 24 inches in length and does not have any barrel with a bore exceeding 2 inches in diameter;
   (ii) either has no magazine or has a non-detachable magazine incapable of holding more than two cartridges; and
   (iii) is not a revolver gun; and

(b) an air weapon (that is to say an air rifle, air gun or air pistol not of a type declared by rules made by the Secretary of State under FiA 1968 to be specially dangerous).

FiA 1968, s 1(1) applies to ammunition for a firearm except:

(a) cartridges containing five or more shot, none of which exceeds .36 inch in diameter;

(b) ammunition for any air gun, air rifle or air pistol; and

(c) blank cartridges not more than 1 inch in diameter.

A person can be in possession of a firearm or ammunition even though he does not have physical custody of it nor keeps it in his home; it is enough that he has control of it (as where he keeps a firearm at the home of a relative for safe-keeping). Indeed, someone can be in possession of a firearm even though he is not aware that he has a firearm under his control. For example, if a man has custody of a firearm in a hold-all for only a matter of minutes without giving thought to the nature of its contents, he is in possession of those contents and if a firearm is proved to be a part of them, then possession of it has been established. The fact that possession was brief, or that he did not know or could not reasonably have been expected to know that it contained a firearm, affords no defence. The nature of the legislation was intended, by Parliament, to be draconian. It does not have to be proved that the accused knew that the article possessed was a firearm or ammunition within the relevant meaning of those terms. As already indicated, the offence is one of strict liability as to the nature of the article possessed; consequently, for example, an honest and reasonable mistaken belief that the article was an antique firearm (and therefore exempt from FiA 1968) is no defence. There is one exception; where the alleged offence involves an imitation firearm which is readily convertible into a firearm to which s 1 applies, it is a defence for the accused to prove that he did not know and had no reason to suspect that it was readily convertible.

An offence contrary to FiA 1968, s 1(1) is an offence. It is also an offence for a person to sell or transfer a firearm or ammunition to which s 1 applies to a person other than a registered firearms dealer or person who has a certificate authorising its purchase or acquisition.

Shotguns

For the purposes of FiA 1968, a 'shotgun' is a smooth-bore gun (not being an airgun) which:

(a) has a barrel not less than 24 inches in length and does not have any barrel with a bore exceeding 2 inches in diameter;
(b) either has no magazine or has a non-detachable magazine incapable of holding more than two cartridges; and
(c) is not a revolver gun.

If the barrel of a shotgun is shortened to less than 24 inches it is no longer a shotgun, but becomes a firearm to which FiA 1968, s 1 applies.

Shotguns are excepted from the provisions of FiA 1968, s 1 but FiA 1968, s 2 states that, subject to any exemption under FiA 1968, it is an offence for a person to have in his possession, or to purchase or acquire, a shotgun without holding a certificate under FiA 1968 authorising him to possess shotguns. The reason for these special provisions in relation to shotguns is that the conditions for obtaining a shotgun certificate are different from those which apply in the case of FiA 1968, s 1 firearms.

What we said about possession and an accused's state of mind in relation to FiA 1968, s 1 is equally applicable here.

Air weapons

Air weapons essentially operate by the release of compressed air and therefore contain no explosive charge. An 'air weapon' (ie an air rifle, air gun or air pistol) which is not a prohibited weapon and which has not been declared by the Secretary of State to be specially dangerous does not require a firearm certificate for its possession, acquisition or purchase. The Secretary of State has declared that an air weapon will be specially dangerous (and therefore a firearm to which FiA 1968, s 1 applies) if:

(a) on discharge from the muzzle there is a kinetic energy in excess of 6 ft/lb in the case of an air pistol, or 12 ft/lb in the case of a weapon other than a pistol; or
(b) it is disguised as another object.

This has had the effect of compelling manufacturers to keep within these limits. If weapons are sold as air weapons, it is reasonable to assume that they have been tested to confirm that they are inside these limits.

The Firearms (Amendment) Act 1997, s 48 provides that any reference in the Firearms Acts of 1968 to 1997 to an air rifle, air pistol or air gun includes a reference to a rifle, pistol or gun powered by compressed carbon dioxide. On the other hand, a gas-fired rifle, gun or pistol is not an air weapon and therefore requires a firearm certificate for its possession etc.

Ammunition for shotguns and air weapons, and blank cartridges

Ammunition for a shotgun is excepted from the definition of ammunition for the purposes of FiA 1968, s 1 provided the cartridge contains five or more shot (none of which exceeds .36 inch diameter). Consequently, if a cartridge contains only four shot, or one of five shot exceeds 0.36 inch in diameter, it is not exempt from the provisions of FiA 1968, s 1 and a firearm certificate is required for its possession, purchase or acquisition.

The Firearms (Amendment) Act 1988, s 5 makes special provisions in relation to ammunition to which FiA 1968, s 1 does not apply and which is capable of being used in a shotgun or in a smooth-bore gun to which s 1 applies. It makes it an offence to sell such ammunition to any person who is neither a registered firearms dealer nor a person who sells ammunition by way of trade or business, unless such person produces a shotgun certificate; or shows entitlement to possess without a certificate; or produces a certificate authorising another person to possess such a gun, together with that person's written authority to purchase ammunition on his behalf.

Ammunition for an air weapon is also excepted from the definition of ammunition for the purposes of FiA 1968, s 1. This exception even applies to ammunition for a weapon which may have been declared to be specially dangerous.

Blank cartridges not more than one inch in diameter are also excepted from the definition of ammunition for the purposes of FiA 1968, s 1.

Firearm certificates and shotgun certificates

Firearm certificates

A person wishing to possess, purchase or acquire a firearm or ammunition covered by FiA 1968, s 1 must have a firearm certificate, which is a certificate granted by a chief officer of police under FiA 1968 in respect of any firearm or ammunition to which the section applies. The term includes certificates granted in Northern Ireland.

To obtain a certificate an applicant must apply to the chief officer of police of the area in which he resides and must state such particulars as may be required by the form. Information concerning previous names, residence and convictions, other than those for minor traffic offences, must be given. The applicant must sign a statement to the effect that the statements are true, rather than believed to be true. It is an offence knowingly or recklessly to make a statement false in a material particular. An applicant must provide up to four photographs and the names and addresses of two persons who have agreed to act as referees. Before considering the application, the chief officer will verify the particulars included in the application and the likeness to the applicant of the photographs provided. The information which the applicant is required to give on the application form must be verified by each of two referees by a signed statement that the information is, to the best of his knowledge and belief, correct. In addition, each referee must provide a reference to the effect that he knows of no reason why the applicant should not possess a firearm.

FiA 1968, s 27 states that a firearm certificate must be granted by the chief officer of police if he is satisfied that:

(a) the applicant is fit to be entrusted with a firearm to which FiA 1968, s 1 applies and that he is not a prohibited person;

(b) he has good reason for having in his possession, or for purchasing or acquiring, the firearm or ammunition in respect of which the application is made;

(c) in all the circumstances the applicant can be permitted to have the firearm or ammunition in his possession without danger to the public safety or peace.

A chief officer is empowered to impose conditions subject to which the firearm certificate is held. These conditions may refer to the nature of the storage of the weapons or their use. Conditions can be varied at any time by notice in writing to the holder, who may be required to return his certificate for variation.

A person under eighteen who applies for such a certificate is capable of having a good reason for possessing it *only* if he has no intention of using if for a purpose other than an authorised purpose under the European weapons directive. An authorised purpose is a sporting purpose, the shooting of vermin, a purpose related to estate management activities, competition shooting or target shooting.

Police officers are required to carry out inquiries on behalf of the chief officer and, with these provisions in mind, they are required to check upon the intended usage of the weapon. If the applicant wishes to have a .22 rifle to shoot vermin in his garden, which is quite small and is surrounded by other dwellings, it is apparent that he could not use it for the purpose declared without danger to the public. However, if he wishes to keep the firearm at home but to use it at an approved rifle club, that would be a different matter. The officer conducting the inquiry should always check the secure place in which the weapon will be stored.

If a firearm certificate is granted, the holder must on receipt sign it in ink. He must at all times keep the firearm and ammunition in a safe place and must inform the chief officer of the theft or loss of the firearm or a change of address.

Shotgun certificates

The conditions relating to applications for shotgun certificates are not quite so strict. An application must be made in the prescribed form to the chief officer of police and there are similar requirements in respect of the submission of photographs, verification and a reference by one referee, signature of the certificate, and notification of the loss or theft of the certificate or of a change of address.

Such a certificate must be granted by the chief officer of police if he is satisfied that the applicant can be permitted to possess a shotgun without danger to the public safety or to the peace, unless he has reason to believe that the applicant is prohibited by FiA 1968 from possessing a shotgun (see below), or is satisfied that the applicant does not have a good reason for possessing, purchasing or acquiring one. It has been held that a refusal to grant a certificate to the wife of a man with two previous convictions for drug offences was justified, where they both continued to associate with drug users.

A sporting or competitive purpose is declared by FiA 1968 to be a good reason. A person under eighteen who applies for such a certificate is capable of having a good reason for possessing it *only* if he has no intention of using it for a purpose other than an authorised purpose. An 'authorised purpose' has the same meaning as under FiA 1968, s 5(1A), see p 757.

A shotgun certificate must specify the description of the shotguns to which it relates including, if known, the identification numbers of the guns.

Transfer of firearms etc between authorised persons

The Firearms (Amendment) Act 1997, s 32 requires that where:

(a) a s 1 firearm is sold, let on hire, lent or given; or
(b) a shotgun is sold, let on hire, given or lent for a period of more than seventy-two hours, by any person,

to a person who is not a firearms dealer nor exempt from holding a certificate, the following requirements must be complied with:

(a) the transferee must produce to the transferor an appropriate certificate;
(b) the transferor must comply with any instructions contained in the certificate; and
(c) the transferor must hand the firearm to the transferee personally.

It is an offence to fail to comply with these requirements. The provisions of the Firearms (Amendment) Act 1997, s 32 apply to transfers of s 1 ammunition.

Each party to the transfer (as described above) of a s 1 firearm or of a shotgun who is the holder of a firearm or shotgun certificate must give notice of the transfer within seven days to the chief officer of police. It is an offence against FiA 1968, s 33 to fail to do so.

De-activation, destruction or loss of firearms or shotguns

The Firearms (Amendment) Act 1997, s 34 requires that where a firearm to which a firearm certificate or shotgun certificate relates is de-activated, destroyed or lost, the certificate holder must give notice to the chief officer of police within seven days. It is an offence to fail to do so without reasonable excuse.

Grant, refusal, revocation, etc

Persons aggrieved by the refusal of a chief officer of police to grant or renew a firearm or shotgun certificate may appeal to the Crown Court. There is a corresponding right of appeal against a chief officer of police's refusal to vary a firearm certificate or the refusal to vary such a condition.

A firearm certificate may be revoked if the chief officer of police has reason to believe that:

(a) the holder is of intemperate habits or unsound mind or is otherwise unfitted to be entrusted with a firearm; or
(b) the holder can no longer be permitted to have the firearm or ammunition to which the certificate relates without danger to the public safety or peace;
(c) the holder is prohibited from possessing a s 1 firearm;
(d) the holder no longer has a good reason for having, purchasing, or acquiring the firearm or ammunition, which the certificate authorises him to have etc.

A firearm certificate may also be revoked if the holder has failed to comply with a notice requiring him to deliver up his certificate.

In addition, a chief officer may partially revoke a certificate in relation to any particular firearm or ammunition held under its authority.

A shotgun certificate may be revoked only if the holder becomes a 'prohibited person', or cannot be permitted to possess a shotgun without danger to the public safety or to the peace.

It has been held that a chief officer, in deciding whether to revoke a shotgun licence, is entitled to take into account irresponsible conduct by the licence holder which does not involve the use of a shotgun. It is a matter for the chief officer's discretion to what extent he should investigate a particular offence.

Where a certificate is revoked the holder must be notified in writing and required to surrender his certificate. It is an offence to fail to comply with such a notice within twenty-one days of the date of the notice.

An appeal against the revocation of a certificate lies to the Crown Court.

Persons prohibited from possessing a firearm

Certain restrictions are placed on the possession of any firearm or ammunition by a person who has been convicted of a crime and been sentenced to:

(a) custody for life, or to preventative detention, or imprisonment, or corrective training, or youth custody or detention in a young offender institution for three years or more; such a person is banned for life; or
(b) imprisonment or youth custody or detention in a young offender institution from three months to three years, or has been subject to a secure training order; such a person is banned for five years.

Suspended sentences do not count unless they are actually served at a later date. Air weapons are included in this prohibition.

Lawful possession without a certificate

Persons who hold a permit from the chief officer of police of the area in which they reside may possess a firearm (including a shotgun and ammunition) in accordance with the terms of the permit. Such permits are frequently issued where the holder of a firearm certificate dies and a relative requires some form of authority to possess the firearm pending its sale or disposal. It is unusual for such permits to be valid for more than one month. Firearms dealers (if registered—see below) and their employees may possess such a thing without a certificate.

FiA 1968, ss 9 to 15 and 54 are concerned with persons who may lawfully possess firearms and ammunition without holding a certificate. These exemptions are generally concerned with those who possess firearms in the course of their duties, that possession in many cases being of a transitory nature. The principal exemptions provided by FiA 1968, ss 9 to 15 and the Firearms (Amendment) Act 1988, s 15 are as follows:

(a) an auctioneer, carrier, warehouseman, or the employee of such a person is frequently required to handle other people's firearms and ammunition in the course of his duties. Sensibly this is permitted, but it is necessary for such persons to take reasonable precautions for safe custody and to report loss or theft forthwith to the police;

(b) a slaughtering instrument and its ammunition may be possessed by a licensed slaughter man;

(c) a person carrying a firearm or ammunition belonging to another person who is the holder of a certificate may possess that firearm or ammunition under instructions from, and for the use of, that other person for sporting purposes only. The person carrying the firearm etc can best be described as a 'gun bearer';

(d) a starter at an athletic meeting may possess a firearm for the purpose of starting races only. The Act does not allow him to possess ammunition, so that he is restricted to blanks not exceeding one inch in diameter (which do not, of course, require a certificate);

(e) a member of an approved cadet corps may possess a firearm and ammunition when engaged as such a member in connection with drill or target shooting;

(f) subject to any exclusion of the club or restriction to specified types of rifle by the Secretary of State, a member of an approved rifle club (including a miniature rifle club) or of an approved muzzle-loading pistol club may possess a firearm and ammunition when engaged as such a member in connection with target shooting; an approval of a club may be limited to specified weapons;

(g) possession at a miniature rifle range (usually a side show at a fair) provided that no weapons are used exceeding .23 inch calibre. It should be noted that the owner of the range, unless only air weapons are used, will have a certificate listing the weapons in use. The exception is in favour of the public briefly using those weapons;

(h) a person who does not hold a shotgun certificate may borrow a shotgun from the occupier of private premises and use it on those premises, provided the occupier is present;

(i) a person may use a shotgun at a time and place approved by the chief officer of police for shooting at artificial targets. This exemption is designed to cover a person who is interested in shooting or wishes to receive instruction, but has not got a shotgun certificate. Commonly approved places at which the exemption permits him to shoot include agricultural shows and permanent shooting grounds run by firearms dealers;

(j) a person taking part in a theatrical performance, rehearsal or film may possess a firearm during the performance. This exception does not extend to ammunition, so that any ammunition used would have to be blanks not more than one inch in diameter;

(k)　signalling apparatus may be possessed on board an aircraft or at an aerodrome as a part of its equipment. It may also be transferred at an aerodrome from one aeroplane to another, or from or to an aeroplane at an aerodrome to or from an appointed place of storage there;

(l)　firearms and ammunition may be possessed on board a ship as a part of its equipment. However, if it is to be removed from the ship a permit to do so must be obtained from a constable. A similar permit is required if the signalling apparatus described at (k) is to be transferred from one aerodrome to another;

(m)a Northern Ireland shotgun certificate authorises possession of a shotgun in Great Britain; and

(n)　any Crown servant or member of a police force who is in possession of a firearm or ammunition in his capacity as such does not require a certificate.

In addition, the Firearms (Amendment) Act 1988 permits a person of seventeen or over, without holding a firearm certificate, to borrow a rifle from the occupier of private premises and use it on the premises in the presence of the occupier or an employee of the occupier, if the person so accompanying him holds a firearm certificate in respect of that rifle and its possession and use complies with any conditions in the certificate.

The Firearms (Amendment) Act 1988 also makes provision for 'visitor' permits in relation to both s 1 firearms and shotguns. A firearm permit permits a person to possess a firearm and ammunition and to acquire ammunition for it, and a shotgun permit permits a person to possess or acquire a shotgun (although there are exceptions in the case of a shotgun with a magazine). 'Group' applications may be made for not more than twenty permits. These will cover persons visiting Great Britain to take part in competitions. In addition, the Firearms Acts (Amendment) Regulations 1992 extended the Firearms Acts to permit the use of a European Firearms Pass. Persons holding such passes are entitled to acquire in another EU member state firearms to which the pass relates. Such 'passes' are issued in Great Britain by the chief officer of police to holders of an appropriate firearm certificate. Lastly, the Firearms (Amendment) Act 1988, ss 16A and 16B authorise, respectively, persons under the supervision of a member of the armed forces to possess a firearm and ammunition on service premises, and persons being trained or assessed under the supervision of a member of the Ministry of Defence Police to do so on premises used for any purpose of the Ministry of Defence Police, without holding a firearm certificate. They also authorise such persons in such circumstances to possess a prohibited weapon or prohibited ammunition without obtaining the Secretary of State's authority.

A European Firearms Pass must be produced on demand by a constable.

Lists of exceptions to any rule are always difficult to remember if one attempts to memorise them without bearing in mind some overall rule to which each exception relates. Each of these exceptions is concerned with occasions when persons will possess firearms in Great Britain temporarily. Most of them are concerned with a very brief moment in time. Imagine the difficulties if each person using a rifle range at a fair had to obtain a firearm certificate before shooting; if each pilot or ship's captain had to apply for a certificate before setting out on a journey; if each starter at an athletic meeting had to obtain a certificate before he started a race. This approach to the recall of these exceptions makes the task much easier.

Prohibited weapons and ammunition

We have already defined these terms. Because weapons and ammunition of this type can only properly be regarded as suitable for military use, FiA 1968, s 5(1) and (1A) provide that a person commits an offence if he has in his possession, or purchases or acquires, any prohibited weapon or ammunition to which s 5(1) or (1A) respectively apply without the written authority of the Secretary of State. An offence under FiA 1968, s 5(1) or (1A) is one of strict liability as to the fact that the weapon or ammunition is prohibited, so that it is no defence that the possessor is reasonably unaware of the characteristic which makes the weapon or ammunition prohibited.

Museum licences

By virtue of the Firearms (Amendment) Act 1988, s 19 and Sch 1 specified museums do not need to have a firearm certificate, shotgun certificate or s 5 authority, as the case may be, in relation to exhibits displayed or stored at the museum if they have a museum firearm licence granted under those provisions. Specified museums are those registered with the Museums and Galleries Commission for the purpose of making them eligible for a museum firearm certificate.

POSSESSION BY YOUNG PERSONS

FiA 1968, ss 22 to 24 deal with the possession of all types of firearms by juveniles. The provisions are difficult to remember because of the differing ages which are associated with various weapons in particular circumstances. However, there are certain general rules which assist the memory.

No one under fourteen years may have a *firearm* certificate in any circumstances. Those between fourteen and seventeen years may have a firearm certificate but they may not buy or hire the firearm which they are authorised to possess. Those over seventeen years may have a firearm certificate and may buy or hire the firearm which they possess.

A person of any age may have a *shotgun* certificate but if he is less than seventeen years he must have acquired the weapon by way of a gift. The detailed provisions of these sections are set out below. In the case of each type of weapon, we shall start our explanation at the age of seventeen years.

Section 1 firearms and ammunition

If a person under seventeen wishes to have a s 1 firearm, or ammunition for it, he cannot buy or hire it himself; if he does so he commits an offence (and so does the seller or person letting it on hire). However, provided that he is fourteen years or over he may receive it, together with ammunition, by way of a gift or loan. Where an adult wishes to buy a firearm as a gift for such a youth, he must obtain a firearm certificate and so must the youth. The seller may then sell to the adult, who may then transfer the weapon to the youth, both notifying the chief officer of police of the transaction by registered post within forty-eight hours. Certificates granted to persons under seventeen are endorsed to the effect that firearms or ammunition cannot be sold or hired to them until the specified date, which is the date of their seventeenth birthday.

A holder of a firearm certificate who is under the age of eighteen may only use that firearm for purposes authorised by the European weapons directive. Such purposes are likely to be specified in the certificate. It is an offence to use the weapon for a purpose other than those so specified. An authorised purpose is a sporting purpose, the shooting of vermin, a purpose related to estate management activities, competition shooting or target shooting.

It is an offence to give or lend a s 1 firearm or ammunition to a person under fourteen years of age. It is also an offence for such a person to possess such a thing, with certain exceptions. In recalling these exceptions it is helpful to consider those persons who are permitted to possess s 1 firearms without a certificate and to identify the exceptions which might apply to persons under fourteen years. The exceptions are:

(a) when he is carrying the firearm or ammunition for another for sporting purposes, and that other person is the holder of a firearm certificate; or
(b) when, as a member of an approved cadet corps, he is engaged in connection with target shooting or drill; or
(c) when he is using the firearm or ammunition at a miniature rifle range or shooting gallery where the only weapons used do not exceed .23 inch calibre; or
(d) when, as a member of an approved rifle club, he is engaged in connection with target shooting.

Shotguns

It is an offence for a person under seventeen to purchase or hire any shotgun. Likewise, someone who sells or lets on hire a shotgun to such a person commits an offence. It is also an offence to make a gift of a shotgun to a person under fifteen. (These rules also apply to ammunition for a shotgun.) It is, of course, possible for a person of fifteen or sixteen lawfully to acquire a shotgun by the same process as that outlined in relation to s 1 firearms.

All young persons in possession of shotguns must have a shotgun certificate. Although FiA 1968 does not prescribe a minimum age at which a shotgun certificate may be granted, control is exercised by the chief officer of police who must consider the grant of such a certificate in the context of public safety.

Even if he has a shotgun certificate, it is an offence for a person under fifteen to 'have with him' an assembled shotgun, except:

(a) while under the supervision of a person of twenty-one years or more; or
(b) while it is so securely fastened with a gun cover that it cannot be fired.

In addition, a holder of a shotgun certificate who is under eighteen may not use the weapon for a purpose which is not authorised by the European weapons directive.

Air weapons

The same general rule applies. It is an offence for a person under seventeen years to purchase or hire an air weapon or ammunition. The seller or person who lets on hire in such a case also commits an offence. However, as there is no need to obtain any form of certificate, a person under seventeen needs only to enlist the aid of an adult to effect the purchase. There are, however, restrictions in relation to possession and they are predictable. A person under seventeen commits an offence if he has with him in a public place an air weapon except when:

(a) as a member of an approved club, he is engaged in connection with target shooting; or
(b) he is using the weapon or ammunition at a shooting gallery or miniature range where the only firearms used are either air weapons or miniature rifles not exceeding .23 inch calibre.

These exceptions parallel those in relation to s 1 firearms and it would be surprising if this was not so.

There are additional restrictions in relation to a person under seventeen. It is an offence for such a person to have with him an air weapon or ammunition *in any place* (except at a shooting gallery or in a rifle club), *unless* under the supervision of a person of twenty-one years or over. However, if the person under seventeen fires any missile beyond the premises (including land) on which he is being supervised he commits an offence despite being supervised, and so does the supervisor if he allows him to use the weapon in this way. In the case of a person under the age of fourteen it is not an offence for him to have an air weapon or ammunition on private premises with the consent of the occupier but, where such a person has that weapon with him in circumstances where such possession would be otherwise prohibited, it is an offence for him to use it for firing missiles beyond the premises.

It is an offence for any person to make a gift of an air weapon or ammunition to a person under seventeen. It is also an offence to part with the possession of an air weapon or ammunition to a person under seventeen except where that person is not prohibited from having it with him under the circumstances (member of approved club etc) outlined above.

In summary, no one under the age of seventeen may have an air weapon in his possession at any time unless supervised by someone of at least twenty-one years or as part of target shooting at a club or shooting gallery.

OTHER FIREARMS OFFENCES

Conversion of firearms

It is an offence under FiA 1968, s 4 to shorten the barrel of a shotgun within the meaning of FiA 1968 (ie a smooth-bore gun other than one which has a bore exceeding 2 inches in diameter) to a length of less than 24 inches. It is not an offence for a registered firearms dealer to shorten a barrel for the sole purpose of replacing a defective part so as to produce a barrel not less than 24 inches in length. It is also an offence for anyone other than a registered firearms dealer to convert into a firearm anything which, though having the appearance of a firearm, cannot discharge a missile through its barrel.

Possession with intent to endanger life

The offence is that contrary to FiA 1968, s 16 of possessing a firearm or ammunition with intent by means thereof to endanger life, or to enable another person by means thereof to endanger life, whether an injury has been caused or not.

The section is intended to dissuade criminals from using firearms. If criminals set out to rob a bank and possess loaded firearms there is some evidence to suggest that they intended to endanger life. If they use the firearms to stage a hold-up that inference is reinforced because this strongly suggests that they are prepared to use the firearms against all who might oppose them.

There are two factors to prove: that the accused was in possession of a firearm; and that at the time of that possession he had an intention by means thereof to endanger life. A person who carries a loaded gun merely to give it to a colleague to use, should he be challenged, is equally guilty because he intends to enable another by means thereof to endanger life. The same would be true of an accomplice who carries ammunition for a gunman for use, if necessary, in a bank raid. However, possession with intent that another person should, by means of the firearm or ammunition, endanger life, means more than merely making those objects available to known criminals who could or might endanger life. Such possession is too remote from any subsequent act on the part of the criminal which might show an intention to endanger life. An intention to endanger the life of a person abroad is sufficient for this section; consequently, it covers possession by terrorist groups who may intend their mischief elsewhere. Possession with intent to commit suicide is not covered by this section; an intent to endanger life must relate to the life of another. The present offence is not committed by a person who intended to endanger life for a lawful purpose, as where a person whose house is besieged by an armed gang threatened them with his firearm in self-defence.

Possession with intent to cause fear of violence

It is an offence by FiA 1968, s 16A for a person to have in his possession any firearm or imitation firearm with intent:

(a) by means thereof to cause; or
(b) to enable any other person by means thereof to cause,

any person to believe that unlawful violence will be used against him or another.

FiA 1968, s 16A was added to the Act to cover the use of firearms by bank robbers who use such weapons to terrorise bank staff and customers.

In this offence, 'imitation firearm' is defined by FiA 1968, s 57 (and not by the Firearms Act 1982, s 1), as meaning anything which at the material time has the appearance of being a firearm (other than a weapon for the discharge of a noxious liquid, gas or other thing) whether or not it is capable of discharging any shot, bullet or other missile. An automatic pistol with the firing pin removed has been held to be such an imitation firearm; clearly, it fell within the definition. So may things which have the appearance of being firearms in particular circumstances on specific occasions, but not in others. A piece of roughly fashioned wood held in the hand in a darkened room may certainly have the appearance of being a firearm. It would be a matter for the jury to decide whether something actually did have the appearance of being a firearm in the circumstances in question. The House of Lords has held that fingers positioned in a jacket so as to appear to be a gun are not in law capable of constituting a firearm.

Use of firearms to resist arrest

It is an offence by FiA 1968, s 17(1) for a person to make, or attempt to make, any use whatsoever of a firearm or imitation firearm with intent to resist or prevent the lawful arrest or detention of himself or another person.

If a firearm or imitation firearm is used in resisting lawful arrest or detention, whether of the person using the firearm, or some other person, the offence is complete. The important words are 'to make, or attempt to make use of' the firearm and the issue of whose possession the firearm was in before that moment does not arise. A man who grabbed a gun from the person arresting him and made use of it in this way would be guilty. It must be proved that the firearm was used intentionally for such a purpose. The offence would not be made out, for example, if the firearm was used with the intention of preventing a search of premises and an arrest was not intended at that time.

FiA 1968, s 17(2) creates a second offence of possessing a firearm or imitation firearm at the time of committing or being arrested for an offence specified in FiA 1968, Sch 1, unless that person can show that he possessed it for a lawful object. The offences in Sch 1 include theft, robbery, burglary, blackmail, taking a conveyance, assaulting a constable in the execution of his duty, assaulting a prison custody officer acting in pursuance of prison escort arrangements or performing custodial duties at a contracted-out prison, assaulting a secure training centre custody officer in the execution of his duty, rape, assault by penetration, causing a person to engage in sexual activity without consent where the activity caused involved penetration, rape of child under thirteen, assault of a child under thirteen by penetration, causing or inciting a child under thirteen to engage in a sexual activity where any activity involving penetration was caused, sexual activity with a person with a mental disorder impeding choice where the touching involved penetration, causing or inciting a person with a mental disorder impeding choice to engage in sexual activity where penetration was caused, criminal damage, malicious wounding, assault occasioning actual bodily harm and assault with intent to resist arrest. The second offence is concerned with possession at the time of commission of certain offences, or at the time of arrest for their commission. For example, a person who takes a motor car whilst in possession of an air pistol, or even an imitation firearm, commits this offence. Even if he had not possessed the firearm at the time of taking the conveyance, he would be equally liable if he was in possession of it at the time of his arrest. Where the case is one of possession *at the time of arrest*, there is no requirement that the prosecution prove that the defendant actually committed the specified offence. It is only necessary to prove that the defendant was in possession of the firearm when lawfully arrested for a specified offence. The physical possession of the firearm is not essential. The Court of Appeal has said that FiA 1968 distinguishes between the concept of 'having a firearm with him' and 'having a firearm in his possession', and that 'possession' in s 17(2) simply refers to 'custody and control'. Consequently, for example, a person remains in possession of a firearm for the purposes of s 17(2) if he has left it in a nearby van at the time of committing a specified offence elsewhere.

For the purposes of both subsections of FiA 1968, s 17, a 'firearm' does not include a component part or accessory.

'Imitation firearm' in s 17(1) and (2) has the same meaning as in FiA 1968, s 16A (see p 770).

Carrying firearm with criminal intent

FiA 1968, s 18 deals with the offence committed by a person who has with him a firearm or imitation firearm with intent to commit an indictable offence, or to resist arrest or prevent the arrest of another, in either case while he has the firearm or imitation firearm with him.

This is another offence which refers to 'having with him' rather than 'possessing', and we would remind the reader of the narrower meaning of the former term, which we set out above. 'Imitation firearm' has the same meaning as in FiA 1968 s 16A and s 17 (see p 770).

The intent required by this section is a particular one. It is not sufficient that the accused intended to commit an indictable offence or to resist etc the arrest. He must also intend to have a firearm or imitation firearm with him at the time of that commission or resistance. On the other hand, he does not have to intend to use or carry the gun in furtherance of the indictable offence. Section 18(2) provides that, for the purposes of the section, proof that the accused had a firearm or imitation firearm with him and intended to commit an offence, or to resist or prevent arrest, is evidence that he intended to have it with him while doing so.

Having a firearm in a public place

A person commits an offence contrary to FiA 1968, s 19 if, without lawful authority or reasonable excuse (the proof whereof lies on him), he has with him in a public place a loaded shotgun or any air weapon (whether loaded or not), or any other firearm (whether loaded or not) together with ammunition suitable for use in that firearm, or an imitation firearm. 'Imitation firearm' has the same meaning as in FiA 1968, ss 16A, 17 and 18 (see p 770).

This section is intended to deter people having with them firearms in a state of readiness for use. Where the firearm is a shotgun it must actually be loaded in order for the offence to be committed; on the other hand, in the case of any other firearm this is not necessary (although the accused must have with him suitable ammunition for the firearm in question other than when it is an air gun when the possession of ammunition is unnecessary). A shotgun which has a loaded magazine is loaded, even though there is no round in the breach.

FiA 1968, s 19 does not use the term 'possession' but 'having with him'. The latter term is a narrower one. As we have seen, a person can be in possession of a firearm if he has control of it, even though it is not in his physical custody and is not immediately available to him. In contrast, although a person can have a firearm with him, even though he is not carrying it, he must have a close physical link with it and it must have been readily accessible to him. A man who has a gun in his pocket clearly has it with him, and the same is true if it is in a bag which he is carrying or in the glove compartment of the car which he is driving. Provided that the firearm is readily accessible to him, a person may even have with him at the time a firearm which has left in his car which he has parked down the street. Of course, to be guilty of the present offence he must be in a public place at the material time.

The offence is one of strict liability as to the nature of the item in question. Where a woman was arrested and threw away a handbag which was found to contain a loaded pistol which was wrapped in paper, she claimed that she knew that she had the parcel with her, but did not know that it contained a loaded pistol. The Court of Appeal supported the judge's ruling that her knowledge, or lack of knowledge, that the parcel contained a gun was irrelevant as a matter of law. Similarly, where a man took possession of a loaded shotgun from a co-accused, who was in the course of a robbery at the time, it was held to be sufficient to prove that he knew he was in possession of the shotgun; it was not necessary to prove that he knew that it was loaded. The fact that it turned out to be loaded made him automatically guilty of the offence.

It is difficult to imagine circumstances in which a man could, with lawful authority or reasonable excuse, have with him a loaded shotgun in a public place. The possession of a shotgun certificate certainly does not authorise this. Depending on the circumstances, a gamekeeper, crossing a public highway in the course of his duties, might be considered to have a reasonable excuse for having a loaded shotgun with him. A man who is going to his rifle club with a .22 rifle in his hand and ammunition in his pocket would doubtless be able to prove a reasonable excuse for having the rifle and ammunition with him, provided that he possessed a firearm certificate. It would be otherwise if he was not going to his rifle club.

Trespassing with a firearm

An offence is committed against FiA 1968, s 20(1) if a person, while he has any firearm or imitation firearm with him, enters or is in any building or part of a building as a trespasser and without reasonable excuse (the proof whereof lies on him). A less serious offence is committed under FiA 1968, s 20(2) where the trespass is on land; the other ingredients of this offence are identical to those in s 20(1). 'Imitation firearm' bears the same meaning as in FiA 1968, ss 16A to 19 (see p 770).

We have just said something about 'has with him'. The term 'enters' requires the bodily presence of the defendant to some degree. For the purposes of FiA 1968, s 20(1), 'building' refers to a structure which has a roof and is of a reasonably permanent nature; the term 'part of a building' is included to cover instances in which a person may have a right to be in a building, for example a hotel, but is a trespasser in someone else's room, which would be a part of that building. For the purposes of FiA 1968, s 20(2), the expression 'land' includes land covered with water, so that a person with a firearm trespassing in a boat on a lake is guilty of this offence.

General

The offences under FiA 1968, s 16, 17 or 18 are indictable offences to which the law relating to search warrants applies.

If a robber leaves home with a loaded shotgun, intending to use the gun to threaten those who might oppose him or attempt to arrest him, but having no intent to shoot at anyone in any circumstances, he commits an offence against s 19 as soon as he leaves his house, since he has a loaded shotgun with him in a public place without reasonable excuse. His conduct also contravenes s 18, as he intends to commit an indictable offence (robbery) and to resist arrest if necessary. He is also guilty under s 16A, as he intends to cause fear of violence. At this stage, he cannot be guilty of offences against ss 16 and 17 as he does not intend to endanger life etc, has not made use, or attempted to make use, of the firearm for the prohibited purposes, has not committed a Sch 1 offence whilst in possession of the firearm, and has not been arrested while in possession.

POLICE POWERS

Stop and search in certain cases

FiA 1968, s 47 authorises a constable to require any person whom he has reasonable cause to suspect:

(a) of having a firearm, with or without ammunition, with him in a public place; or
(b) to be committing or about to commit, elsewhere than in a public place, an offence of 'having with him' a firearm or imitation firearm with intent to commit an indictable offence or to resist arrest (contrary to s 18, above) or an offence of trespassing with a firearm (contrary to s 20, above),

to hand over the firearm or ammunition for examination. It is an offence for a person so required to fail to do so.

FiA 1968, s 47 also provides that a constable who has reasonable cause to suspect the existence of one of the above circumstances (ie (a) or (b)) may search that person and may detain him for the purpose of doing so. This power extends to the search of vehicles and the constable may require a driver to stop for that purpose. A constable may enter any place to exercise his powers under this section.

Production of certificates

FiA 1968, s 48(1) states that a constable may demand, from any person whom he believes to be in possession of a firearm or ammunition to which s 1 applies, or of any shotgun, the production of his firearm certificate or his shotgun certificate. If such a person fails to produce the certificate or to permit the constable to read it, or to show that he is exempt from the requirement to have a certificate, the constable may seize and detain the firearm, ammunition or shotgun and may require the person immediately to declare his name and address. It is an offence to refuse to give a true name and address.

FiA 1968, s 48(1A) provides that, where a constable has made a demand under s 48(1) and the person to whom it is made fails:

(a) to produce a firearm certificate or (as the case may be) a shotgun certificate; or
(b) to show that he is a person who is not entitled to be issued with a document identifying that firearm under any provisions which in the other member states of the EU correspond to the provisions for the issue of European Firearms Passes; or

(c) to show that he is in possession of the firearm only in his capacity as a recognised firearms collector of another member state,

the constable can demand from that person the production of the certificate issued to that person in another member state relating to the firearm in question. It is an offence for such a person to fail to comply with such a demand. The powers of seizure etc under FiA 1968, s 48 then apply.

Search warrant

By FiA 1968, s 46, a justice, who is satisfied by information on oath that there is reasonable ground for suspecting that:

(a) an offence relevant for the purposes of the section has been, is being, or is about to be committed; or
(b) in connection with a firearm or ammunition, there is a danger to the public safety or to the peace,

may grant a search warrant. The warrant will authorise a constable or civilian officer:

(a) to enter at any time any premises or place specified, if necessary by force, and to search them or any person found there;
(b) to seize and detain anything which he may find on the premises or place, or on any such person, in respect of which or in connection with which he has reasonable grounds for suspecting that:
   (i) a relevant offence has been, is being or is about to be committed; or
   (ii) in connection with a firearm, imitation firearm or ammunition there is a danger to the public safety or to the peace.

In relation to the power of seizure and detention, this includes power to require information which is stored in any electronic form and is accessible from the premises or place to be produced in a form in which it is visible and legible (or from which it can readily be produced in such form) and can be taken away. The additional powers of seizure provided by the Criminal Justice and Police Act 2001, s 50 apply where a search warrant is executed under FiA 1968, s 46. A 'relevant offence' is any offence under FiA 1968 except that under s 22(3) (person under fifteen having assembled shotgun otherwise than under supervision) or an offence related specifically to air weapons.

It is an offence to intentionally obstruct a constable or civilian officer in the exercise of these powers.

Entry into rifle clubs

A constable duly authorised in writing by a chief officer of police, on producing (if required) his authority, may enter any premises occupied or used by an approved rifle club, miniature rifle club, or pistol club and inspect those premises and anything on them, for the purpose of ascertaining whether the requirements relating to its use and any limitations in the approval are being complied with. This power is provided by the Firearms (Amendment) Act 1988, s 15(7).

FIREARMS OFFENCES UNDER OTHER ACTS

Drunk in charge

It is an offence contrary to the Licensing Act 1872, s 12 to be drunk when in charge on any highway or other public place of any loaded firearm (including a loaded air rifle).

Discharge near the highway

The Highways Act 1980, s 161 provides that a person is guilty of an offence if, without lawful authority or excuse, he discharges any firearm within 50 feet from the centre of any highway which consists of or comprises a carriageway, *and in consequence thereof* a user of the highway is injured, interrupted or endangered. It is important to remember that the discharge is not prohibited in itself. It must also be proved that there was an injury to someone, or that someone's passage was interrupted or interfered with (for example, by being forced to make a detour) or that someone was endangered, ie put in danger of injury. 'Highway' for the purposes of this section is restricted to a public right of way for the passage of vehicles, consequently it does not include footpaths, cycle tracks, bridleways or cattle tracks.

The offence is not committed if the person discharging the firearm has a lawful authority or excuse for doing so, as where the discharge occurred during a clay pigeon shoot which involved shooting down the field and away from the highway.

Wanton discharge in a street

By the Town Police Clauses Act 1847, s 28 it is an offence wantonly to discharge a firearm in any street to the obstruction, annoyance or danger of residents or passengers.

BUSINESS TRANSACTIONS

A 'firearms dealer' is defined by FiA 1968, s 57 as a person who, by way of trade or business, manufactures, sells, transfers, repairs, tests or proves firearms or ammunition to which FiA 1968, s 1 applies or shotguns. It is an offence for a person to do any of these things without being registered under FiA 1968 as a firearms dealer. By way of exception, it is not an offence for an auctioneer to sell by auction a firearm or ammunition without being registered as a firearms dealer, provided he holds a police permit for that purpose.

The chief officer of police must keep a register of firearms dealers. An applicant must provide details of every place of business (including storage places) in the area, at which he proposes to carry on business as a firearms dealer, and details of the precise nature of the business which he intends to conduct. A registered firearms dealer or his employee is permitted to keep, purchase or acquire firearms and ammunition in the ordinary course of his business without holding firearms certificates in respect of them, and this is so even though the place where the firearm or ammunition is possessed, purchased or acquired by the dealer or employee is not the dealer's place of business or has not been registered as his place of business.

Except on certain specified grounds, the chief officer of police must enter the applicant's name and place(s) of business in the register and grant him a certificate of registration. The chief officer of police may, however, impose conditions upon registration. These conditions are generally concerned with ensuring the safekeeping of firearms. They usually include the following conditions; that:

(a) the dealer shall, on being given reasonable notice, allow a police officer authorised in writing by the chief officer to enter and inspect his premises;
(b) hand-guns must be kept in a locked safe;
(c) other weapons must be chained together by the trigger guards and locked in a rack;
(d) ammunition is to be stored separately and locked up;
(e) rifle bolts must be removed and kept separately;
(f) the windows of cabinets for storage must be illuminated at night; and
(g) glass door panels and windows must be barred.

In addition, conditions are usually imposed concerning notification of dealings in various types of weapons.

The Act does not permit registration for particular purposes. A person is either a firearms dealer or he is not; there is no right to restrict dealings to shotguns. There is, of course, no need to be registered to deal in air weapons. All certificates of registration are renewable every three years. A new place of business must be notified to the chief officer and must be registered by him, unless the use of those premises for firearms dealing would endanger the public safety or the peace. A registered dealer may be removed from the register if he ceases to deal in firearms, or to have a business place within the area, or if he cannot be permitted to continue in business without danger to the public safety or the peace. Failure to comply with conditions also provides reason for removal from the register. Particular premises may be removed from the register on safety grounds.

Dealer to keep records

A dealer must keep a register of transactions. He must immediately enter in his register the particulars of persons to whom firearms and ammunition are sold or transferred. In the case of a sale or transfer of a firearm to which FiA 1968, s 1 applies (but not of ammunition) he must generally send a notification of this, by registered post or recorded delivery, to the chief officer of police with whom he is registered within forty-eight hours. Dealers may only sell and transfer such things to a person who holds the necessary certificate, or to a person who is legally entitled to purchase or acquire the firearm or ammunition without a certificate.

Registered dealers must allow police officers, authorised in writing by the chief officer of police, to enter and inspect all stock in hand and must produce their registers for inspection. It is an offence to fail to do so, or knowingly or recklessly to make any false entry in a register. A police officer who is authorised in writing by his chief officer of police to carry out these duties must produce that written authority if required to do so.

CROSSBOWS

Crossbows are not firearms. The Crossbows Act 1987 creates specific offences in respect of crossbows with a draw weight of at least 1.4 kg.

It is an offence for any person to sell or let on hire a crossbow or part of a crossbow to a person under the age of seventeen. No offence is committed if the seller or hirer believes the person so acquiring to be seventeen years of age or older, provided he has reasonable ground for that belief. Similarly it is an offence for a person under seventeen:

(a) to purchase or hire such a crossbow or part of a crossbow; or
(b) for him to have with him a crossbow capable of discharging a missile, or parts which together (and without any other parts) can be assembled to form a complete crossbow,

unless in either case he is under the supervision of a person who is twenty-one years of age or older.

Where a constable suspects with reasonable cause that a person is committing or has committed an offence of having with him a crossbow or parts, he may:

(a) search that person for a crossbow or part of a crossbow; or
(b) search any vehicle, or anything in or on a vehicle, in or on which the constable reasonably suspects there is a crossbow or part of a crossbow connected with the offence.

A person or vehicle may be detained by the constable for the purpose of such searches and evidence may be seized. The constable may enter any land other than a dwelling house to exercise these powers.

CHAPTER 25
Explosives

The law controlling explosive substances is concerned with various aspects of their use. From day to day we are concerned with fireworks and their use in public places. The manufacture and general control of explosives need to be regulated; their storage needs to be made safe, and the unlawful use of such substances must be punished.

FIREWORKS

For practical purposes, the significance of the Explosives Act 1875 is contained in its provisions relating to the storage and use of fireworks. Shopkeepers who wish to store fireworks must be registered with the local authority. Once premises are registered they are subject to inspection by inspectors appointed under the Health and Safety at Work etc Act 1974. Generally, small shops and businesses can store up to 500 lb of small fireworks which are not likely to explode violently. Up to 100 lb can be kept in the part of the premises to which the public have access and the remaining 400 lb must be kept elsewhere in closed metal containers, each container having no more than 100 lb of fireworks inside it. The 100 lb kept in the public part of the shop must be secure, for example in a glass showcase. The idea is that no one should be able to throw a lighted match into a box of fireworks in the shop.

The Fireworks (Safety) Regulations 1997 prohibit the supply of fireworks of erratic flight and mini-rockets, aerial shells, shells-in-mortar, aerial maroons and maroons-in-mortar. These Regulations also prohibit the supply of bangers, including banger/combination fireworks but not wheels with bangers, and prohibit persons under eighteen from purchasing fireworks other than caps, crackers, snaps, novelty matches, party poppers, serpents and throw-downs. There are exceptions in relation to supply to 'professional' organisations providing firework displays.

Retailers must not sell fireworks removed from a primary pack or selection pack.

By the Explosives Act 1875 (EA 1875), s 30, it is an offence to hawk, sell or expose for sale any gunpowder (including fireworks containing gunpowder) in any street or public place and this prevents the sale of fireworks in markets. The sale of fireworks containing gunpowder to a child apparently under the age of sixteen years continues to be an offence under the EA 1875, s 31. These provisions will be repealed when the Fireworks Act 2003 is fully in force.

Throwing fireworks

It is an offence to throw, cast or fire any fireworks in or onto any highway, street, thoroughfare or public place. This offence, provided by EA 1875, s 80, is extremely useful. Although there are other offences in relation to the use of fireworks in streets and public places, for example under the Highways Act 1980 and the Town Police Clauses Act 1847, this offence is the most easily proved. Cases covered by it include throwing in a street a firework which fails to explode, or the firing of a firework in any street or public place. There are no exceptions to the offence; even the celebration of 'Guy Fawkes' must be restricted to the use of fireworks otherwise than in streets or public places.

The offence under EA 1875, s 80 is a 'penalty offence' for the purposes of the Criminal Justice and Police Act 2001, Part I and may be dealt with under a fixed penalty procedure: see p 874. EA 1875, s 80 will be repealed when the Fireworks Act 2003 is fully in force.

Offences under the Fireworks Act 2003

The Fireworks Regulations 2004 made under the Fireworks Act 2003 contain a number of prohibitions.

The Fireworks Act 2003, s 11 provides that any person who contravenes a prohibition imposed by fireworks regulations, or who fails to comply with a requirement imposed by or under such regulations, is guilty of an offence. The defence of 'due diligence' provided by the Consumer Protection Act 1987, s 39 applies to these offences. The offence is a 'penalty offence' for the purposes of the Criminal Justice and Police Act 2001, s 1. In addition, s 11 provides that where there is a requirement to give information under fireworks regulations, a person is guilty of an offence if he gives a statement which he knows to be false in a material particular, or recklessly makes a statement which is false in a material particular.

Prohibition of supply of adult fireworks without licence

By reg 9, no person may supply or expose for supply any adult firework (defined below) except in accordance with a licence granted by the local licensing authority. However, this does not prevent the supply of such fireworks without a licence:

(a) on the first day of the Chinese New Year and the three days immediately preceding it;
(b) on the day of Diwali and the three days immediately preceding it;
(c) during the period beginning on 15 October and ending on 10 November; or
(d) during the period beginning on 26 December and ending on 31 December.

Prohibition on possession

Regulation 4 of the Fireworks Regulations 2004 provides that no person under the age of eighteen years may possess an 'adult firework' in a public place. The term 'public place' bears its usual meaning. An adult firework is one which does not comply with Part 2 of the BS 7114 or any firework (except for a cap, cracker, snap, novelty match, party popper, serpent, sparkler or throw down) which does comply with those requirements. Each of these types of fireworks are defined by reg 3 and are the least dangerous fireworks which are available.

Regulation 5 prohibits anyone from possessing a 'category 4 firework'. This is a firework classified as category 4 under Part I of BS 7114.

However, reg 6 provides that nothing in regs 4 and 5 prohibits the possession of any firework by:

(a) any person who is employed by, or in business as, a professional organiser or operator of firework displays and who possesses the firework in question for such purposes;

(b) any person who is employed in, or whose trade or business (wholly or partly) is, the manufacture of fireworks or assemblies containing fireworks and who possesses the firework in question for the purposes of his trade, employment or business;

(c) any person who is employed in, or whose trade or business (wholly or partly) is, the supply of fireworks or such assemblies, for the purposes of supplying them in accordance with the Fireworks (Safety) Regulations 1997;

(d) any person who is employed by a local authority, or the Government of the United Kingdom, who possesses the firework in question for the purpose of a display or in connection with a national public celebration, or in the course of carrying out enforcement powers in relation to fireworks (or, in the case of Government employees, use for research or investigation);

(e) any person for use, in the course of a trade, business or employment, for special effects purposes in the theatre, on film or on television;

(f) any person who is in business as or is employed by a supplier of goods designed and intended for use in conjunction with fireworks or assemblies containing fireworks who possesses the firework in question for testing those goods in connection with safety;

(g) any person who is employed by a naval, military or air force establishment who possesses the firework in question for the purpose of a display or at a public celebration or a national commemorative event.

Prohibition of use at night

The Fireworks Regulations 2004, reg 7 prohibits the use of an adult firework during 'night hours' (11 pm to 7 am) otherwise than on a permitted fireworks night or by a local authority employee in the course of a local authority display or at a national public celebration or commemorative event. Permitted fireworks nights are Chinese New Year (11 pm to 1 am); 5 November (11 pm to midnight); the day of Diwali (11 pm to 1 am); or 31 December (11 pm to 1 am).

Enforcement by police

The Fireworks Regulations 2004, reg 12 requires chief officers of police to enforce the provisions of the Regulations in relation to offences of possession or use. It would seem that possession of a copy of BS 7114 will be essential for the purposes of enforcement! The enforcement of the parts of the Fireworks Regulations relating to licensing and certain other matters is a matter for the local weights and measures authority, except that in a metropolitan county licensing enforcement is a matter for that county's fire and rescue authority.

EXPLOSIVE SUBSTANCES ACT 1883

The Explosive Substances Act 1883 (ESA 1883) deals with many offences which can be committed in relation to 'explosive substances'. It is therefore necessary to establish the meaning of that term.

Explosive substance

The term is defined by ESA 1883, s 9. This Act declares that an explosive substance is deemed to include:

(a) any material for making any explosive substance;
(b) any apparatus, machine, implement, or materials used, or intended to be used, or adapted for causing, or aiding in causing, any explosion in or with any explosive substance;
(c) any part of any such apparatus, machine or implement.

This is a wide definition. It covers, for example, an ingredient which would go into the making of an explosive substance, an empty bomb case, and a detonator for a bomb.

The ESA 1883 does not define the essential term 'explosive' but the Court of Appeal has held that the term should be interpreted in the light of the definition of 'explosive' in the Explosives Act 1875, s 3, which states that the term means:

(a) gunpowder, nitro-glycerine, dynamite, gun-cotton, blasting powder, fulminate of mercury or of other metals, coloured fires and every other substance, whether similar to those already mentioned or not, used or manufactured with a view to producing a practical effect by explosion or a pyrotechnic effect; and
(b) includes fog-signals, fireworks, fuses, rockets, percussion caps, detonators, cartridges, ammunition of all descriptions, and every adaptation or preparation of an explosive as above defined.

Reference to this definition confirms the view that 'explosive substance' is, indeed, a wide term. A petrol bomb has been held to be an explosive substance within the above definition.

Causing an explosion likely to endanger life

ESA 1883, s 2 makes it an offence for any person unlawfully and maliciously to cause by an explosive substance any explosion of a nature likely to endanger life, or to cause serious injury to property, whether such injury or damage is caused or not. This offence is also punishable in United Kingdom courts if such an act is carried out by a British citizen in the Republic of Ireland or if committed in relation to hijacking offences in aircraft. An offence under s 2 is an offence. It is also an indictable offence for the purpose of the law relating to search warrants.

'Unlawfully' means without lawful justification, ie otherwise than in self-defence, prevention of crime or the like, which will rarely be the case. 'Maliciously' simply requires the accused to have intended to cause some harm to another or to property, or to have been reckless as to the risk of this resulting from the explosion. It does not mean or require spite or ill-will.

Therefore, if someone, without lawful justification or excuse, intending to cause bodily harm or damage to property, causes an explosion of such a nature that its probable result will be to endanger life or cause serious damage to property, the fact that the explosion has occurred is all that is necessary for the offence to have been completed. If a man explodes a bomb in a crowded cinema it is probable that life will be endangered. It is equally likely that there will be serious damage to property. The fact that the bomb does not kill, or cause such serious damage as might have been expected, is unimportant. The important point to remember in relation to this offence is that the explosion has occurred.

Attempt to cause explosion; making or keeping explosives with intent

ESA 1883, s 3 creates two types of offence. Both offences apply even where the relevant conduct occurs outside the United Kingdom or a dependency, provided in such a case that the accused is a British citizen. The first offence is being concerned with acts done with the specified intent to cause an explosion, and the second with making or possessing an explosive substance with the specified intent. The offences relate to consequences intended to result in the United Kingdom or elsewhere.

In examining circumstances which might lead to the identification of offences contrary to this section we should think in terms of those who have not yet caused an explosion but are doing some act with that intention in mind. The section extends, by its terminology, the normal concept of an 'attempt' by making punishable acts which would normally be considered to be preparatory acts. The offences are unlawfully and maliciously:

(a) to do any act with intent to cause by an explosive substance an explosion of a nature likely to endanger life or cause serious injury to property, or to conspire so to cause; or

(b) to make or have in one's possession or under one's control an explosive substance with intent by means thereof to endanger life or cause serious injury to property, or to enable any other person to do so.

'Unlawfully' has the same meaning as in ESA 1883, s 2. 'Maliciously' is redundant in this offence because of the specific nature of the required intent.

If we consider the legal position of our offender who caused the explosion in the cinema in our earlier example, before he caused the explosion, the situation is as follows. Whilst preparing the bomb upon his premises he is making an explosive substance with the necessary intent. From the moment he has completed the making of the bomb, he is in possession of it with intent to cause the explosion in the cinema. When he begins to plant the bomb in the cinema he certainly does an act with the necessary criminal intent. It is unnecessary for any explosion to take place. If it did, an offence under ESA 1883, s 2 would be committed. Unless the prosecution is in a position to prove that some positive act was done, it is probably better to charge possession.

Making or possessing an explosive under suspicious circumstances

It will be appreciated that there will often be practical difficulties associated with proving that explosive substances were made or possessed for the purpose of causing explosions likely to endanger life etc. On occasions, the circumstances of the finding, any admissions, and the nature of the explosive device itself may tend to support a charge under ESA 1883, s 3, but on other occasions there may be difficulties in proving a particular intention.

ESA 1883, s 4, as interpreted by the Court of Appeal, provides that any person who knowingly makes or knowingly has in his possession or under his control any explosive substance, under such circumstances as to give rise to a reasonable suspicion that he is not making it or does not have it in his possession or under his control for a lawful object (whether an object to take place in the United Kingdom or abroad), commits an offence. If the accused claims that he made, possessed or controlled it for a lawful object, he must prove that this was so, in which case the offence is not committed.

ESA 1883, s 4 does not define what constitutes a 'lawful object' but it has been held that self-defence or the like against an imminent attack would be a lawful object if the accused intended to use the explosive in a way which was no more than reasonably necessary to meet the imminent attack.

The serious view which is taken of explosive offences is evident from the heavy term of imprisonment which may follow conviction for making, possessing or controlling explosive substances even when no specific intention to use them can be proved. The discovery of a 'bomb factory' today would at the very least lead to charges under ESA 1883, s 4 for all persons concerned.

The two offences under ESA 1883, s 4 (making and possession) cover many modes of involvement. If several persons are concerned in the making, they are equally guilty of the offence; so are those who 'control' the explosive substances as well as those who actually possess them. Each person in a group, if such group has a common design, is responsible for the conduct of a member of that group within the common design: if that amounts to 'possession', all will be guilty.

Prosecutions

A prosecution for an offence under ESA 1883 may not be instituted without the consent of the Attorney-General.

POLICE POWERS AND DUTIES

By EA 1875, s 73 a constable may enter at any time, by force if necessary, any place (including a building, vehicle or vessel) upon reasonable cause for believing that any offence has been or is being committed in that place with respect to an explosive if he is in possession of:

(a) a justices' warrant granted following information on oath; or

(b) a written order from a superintendent or other officer of police of equal or superior rank, which may be issued if the case is one of emergency and delay in obtaining a warrant would be likely to endanger life,

and to search for explosives, and take samples of any explosives and ingredients of an explosive. It is suggested that if information is received that explosives are stored upon any premises in a locality in which people normally reside, the case will be one in which delay would be likely to endanger life.

There are certain duties which must be carried out by the police when thefts of explosives are reported. The Hazardous Substances Division of the Health and Safety Executive should be informed of the exact nature and quantity of explosives stolen, the circumstances of the theft, whether the explosives have been stolen from a store or conveyance, and the use to which the explosives are normally put. The Division also require the identity of the caller and details of place, time and date of the theft, together with details of any explosives left behind by the thieves. Where explosives are found, similar notification should be given to the Division.

HM Explosives Inspectorate require details of all cases of illegal manufacture of explosives, even in the case of trivial experimentation by children. The usual details of the person, time, date etc, of offence are required together with details of police action, court action and details of any forensic report on the substance. HM Inspectorate also like to know where the persons concerned obtained their knowledge of the manufacture of explosives.

OTHER OFFENCES IN RELATION TO EXPLOSIVES

ESA 1883 deals with the likely activities of a bomber quite extensively but police officers should always remember, when considering charges which can be preferred in relation to the activities of terrorist bombers, that the Offences Against the Person Act 1861 and the Criminal Damage Act 1971 also deal with similar offences to those set out in ESA 1883. (These offences are described in Chapters 28 and 38, below.)

BOMB HOAXES

The offences which generally attract the description of bomb hoaxes are those dealt with by the Criminal Law Act 1977 (CLA 1977), s 51.

Placing or despatching an article

CLA 1977, s 51(1) creates two offences. The first is committed by any person who places an article in any place whatsoever with the intention of inducing some other person to believe that it is likely to explode or ignite and thereby cause personal injury or damage to property. The subsection declares that the term 'article' includes any substance. The offence would be committed by the man who produced a parcel in a tube train, or in an arena or elsewhere, to which wires were attached together with something which resembled a timing device. If he then, in view of other passengers, pushed the parcel under the seat or elsewhere and left the train, arena etc, he would quite clearly intend to induce others to believe that it was an explosive device.

The second offence is to despatch any article by post, rail or any other means whatever of sending things from one place to another with the intention to induce in some other person a belief that it is likely to explode or ignite and thereby cause personal injury or damage to property. The offence therefore embraces any form of despatch, provided the article in question is intended to have the specified effect upon people. A man may send through a post office sorting office a number of such false devices with the intention of causing fear of an explosion to be aroused in the staff of that office. Although the article is incapable of exploding or igniting, the offence is complete.

It is not necessary for either offence for the accused to have any particular person in mind as the person in whom he intends to induce the relevant belief.

False messages

CLA 1977, s 51(2) is concerned with false messages to the effect that an explosive device has been planted. It states that it is an offence for a person to communicate any information, which he knows or believes to be false, to another person, with the intention of inducing in him or any other person a false belief that a bomb or other thing liable to explode or ignite is present at any place or location whatever. The use of the words 'there is a bomb' by a hoaxer is sufficient to give rise to the offence. It is not a necessary ingredient that the person communicating the false information should identify a location.

This offence is aimed partly at the hoax telephone caller. It must be proved that the accused knew or believed that the information which he passed was false, and the circumstances will normally make this issue quite clear. However, it would be different if a man asked a boy to ring the manager of a cinema to warn him of the presence of a bomb on the premises and the boy, believing the story to be true, made the call. The boy would commit no offence as he did not believe that the story was false. On the other hand, the man would commit the offence because he knowingly communicated false information to the boy, with the intention of inducing him to believe that a bomb was liable to explode at the cinema.

When police officers receive such a call, it is essential to gain as much information as possible from the caller, or from the person who is passing on a message received from such a caller. The details should include sex, estimated age, urgency in voice, emotion and accent, together with details of the time, date, duration of call, whether from a private telephone or a call box, and any background voices. All information given by the caller must be established; where, when and why the bomb is likely to explode, description of the type of bomb and its appearance and as many of the actual words used as can be recalled.

Although the offence is most commonly committed by means of a telephone call, it can equally be committed by word of mouth, a letter, or a form of general advertisement. It is not necessary that the accused had any particular person in mind in whom he intends to induce the relevant belief.

CHAPTER 26

Railways

There are a number of offences which are specifically concerned with railways. Some of them are provided by two Acts of Parliament, the Offences against the Person Act 1861 (OAPA 1861) and the Malicious Damage Act 1861 (MDA 1861), which were not generally limited to 'railway matters', while others are provided by 'railway legislation'. The enforcement of much of this legislation frequently falls to police officers other than those of the British Transport Police because they happen to be the first to arrive on the scene.

Basically, the two Acts of Parliament named above are concerned with the throwing of articles at railway trains and interference with the railway system itself. In resolving problems concerned with which offences are committed in particular circumstances, it is helpful to remember that the provisions of MDA 1861 are concerned with damage to property while OAPA 1861 deals with injuries to persons. Of course, in many circumstances where obstructions are placed on a railway line there may be evidence of offences contrary to both Acts of Parliament.

ENDANGERING THE SAFETY OF PASSENGERS

Interfering with the railway system with intent

OAPA 1861, s 32 is concerned with persons who unlawfully and maliciously carry out certain acts with intent to endanger the safety of any person travelling or being on a railway. Basically, these acts involve *interference* with the railway system itself. The placing of obstructions on a railway, the displacing of parts of it, the moving of points and similar fittings, the showing of a false signal, the concealment of a real one, or the doing or causing to be done of anything else, are all offences contrary to s 32 provided (in each case) that there is an intent to endanger the safety of any person travelling or being upon such railway.

Throwing things with intent

OAPA 1861, s 33 deals with the *throwing* of missiles. It provides that it is an offence for any person unlawfully and maliciously to throw, or cause to fall or strike, any wood, stone or other matter or thing, at, against, into or upon any engine, tender, carriage or truck used upon any railway with intent to injure or endanger the safety of any person on the train. In considering the appropriate charge it must be remembered that s 33, as well as s 32, requires the accused's acts to be unlawful and malicious and in particular to be carried out with the specified intent (which, in the case of s 33, is an intent to injure or endanger the safety of any person on the train). Neither section requires the specified intent to be directed at a particular person. Consequently, if a man throws a brick at a train intending to injure or endanger people in general who are on it, he commits an offence under s 33.

The British Transport Commission Act 1949, s 56 creates an offence of throwing stones and other objects on railways. This is a 'penalty offence' for the purposes of Part I of the Criminal Justice and Police Act 2001 and may be dealt with under a fixed penalty procedure: see p 874.

General

In the light of the intent to endanger required for OAPA 1861, s 32 and of the intent to injure or endanger required for OAPA 1861, s 33, it is clear that both offences are of a serious nature.

Endangering passengers

There are, of course, occasions where it may not be possible to prove that the act was carried out with an intention to injure anyone or to endanger anyone's safety. Although mischievous and completely irresponsible, many of the acts which are reported to the police are carried out in circumstances which do not give rise to any clear inference of such an intention. To cover such eventualities, OAPA 1861, s 34 creates a lesser offence which can be committed by any person who, by any unlawful act, or by any wilful omission or neglect, endangers or causes to be endangered the safety of any person conveyed or being in or upon a railway, or who aids or assists therein.

The general nature of OAPA 1861, s 34 requires examination. If young persons throw stones at railway trains but cannot be shown to have done so with the intention to injure or endanger, as specified in OAPA 1861, s 33, they may nevertheless be convicted of an offence under s 34 since, by their unlawful acts, they have endangered the safety of railway passengers. The same would be so where someone who placed an obstruction on a railway line cannot be proved to have had the intent to endanger a person on the train, which is required by OAPA 1861, s 32, provided that the obstruction is of such a nature as (in the view of experts) to endanger passengers. In respect of such conduct, and any other conduct covered by s 34, it is irrelevant whether or not the accused ever considered the consequences of his conduct. Section 34 also punishes wilful omissions or neglect. These offences are likely to be committed by railwaymen. A driver who neglected to keep a lookout for signals would certainly be guilty of this offence.

The selection of appropriate charges in instances of dangerous conduct relating to railways is often difficult. Selection may be aided by reference to the consequences of the act but in some cases the crucial point will not be the actual consequences of an act but the potential danger attached to it. For example, where a man cut three spans of copper wire linking together signal boxes, thereby disrupting the signalling system, it was held that he was properly convicted of an offence under OAPA 1861, s 32 even though the operation of a hand signalling device by an alert signalman averted danger.

It has been held that an acquittal for an offence against OAPA 1861, s 32 is not a bar to a subsequent indictment for an offence contrary to s 34.

OBSTRUCTION ETC OF ENGINES AND THE LIKE

In considering the offences committed in circumstances involving obstruction etc by objects being unlawfully placed upon a railway line it is helpful to consider from the outset the parallel offences under OAPA 1861 and MDA 1861. While there is, understandably, no parallel offence to that of throwing missiles with intent, the Malicious Damage Act almost repeats the substance of the other two offences already discussed.

Interfering with the railway system with intent

MDA 1861, s 35 is almost identical to OAPA 1861, s 32. The only difference is in relation to intent. The intention required by MDA 1861 must be to obstruct, upset, overthrow, injure or destroy an engine, tender, carriage or truck using such railway.

Obstruction

MDA 1861, s 36 parallels the offence previously described in OAPA 1861, s 34. There must have been an unlawful act, or a wilful omission or neglect, which led to the obstruction of an engine or carriage using a railway (as opposed to endangering the safety of passengers as required by the Offences against the Person Act). If, therefore, persons unlawfully obstruct a line, they commit an offence of the same gravity, whether they do so in such a way that the safety of passengers is threatened, or merely in such a way that an engine etc was obstructed. A person who causes a train to stop or to slacken speed by altering signals or by making unauthorised signals with the arms is guilty of obstructing a train contrary to MDA 1861, s 36. The offence is also committed by those who cause an obstruction to take place, or who aid or assist this.

An acquittal for the major offence under MDA 1861, s 35 is no bar to a prosecution under s 36.

RAILWAY TRESPASS

The question of trespass upon a railway needs to be carefully considered as there are many occasions upon which persons, particularly intending users, are permitted to be upon railway property. A trespasser is one who goes upon the land of another without a right by law to do so or any express or implied permission of the occupier (or his authorised agent). Consequently, any unauthorised entry upon the land of another is a trespass. There may also be occasions where the original entry onto the premises was authorised, but for a particular purpose; a person who uses the property outside the terms upon which entry was permitted becomes a trespasser. For example, a person who is permitted to enter a railway station to meet a passenger is not thereby permitted to trespass upon the railway lines. A person who is validly requested to leave a railway station becomes a trespasser after the expiry of a reasonable time for him to leave has elapsed from the withdrawal of his permission to remain.

Trespass offence

Trespass on railways is an offence under the British Transport Commission Act 1949, s 5. This offence is committed when any person trespasses upon any of the lines of railway or sidings, or in any tunnel, or upon any railway embankment, cutting or similar work belonging, leased to or worked by a successor to the British Railways Board, *or* trespasses upon *any other lands* of a successor to the British Railways Board in dangerous proximity to any such lines of railway or other works or to any electrical apparatus used for, or in connection with, the working of the railway. However, a person must not be convicted of this offence unless it is proved to the satisfaction of the court that public warning has been given to persons not to trespass upon the railway by a notice clearly exhibited at the station on the railway nearest to the place where the offence is alleged to have been committed. The notice must be renewed as often as it is obliterated or destroyed; if it is not, a person cannot be convicted of the offence. The significance of such a notice at railway stations is difficult to assess as the station is likely to be miles distant from the scene of trespass.

It should be noted that the offence only applies to trespassing on the track, land etc of Network Rail. It does not apply where a person who is not trespassing on such land jumps onto (and thereby trespasses on) a passing train, nor does it apply where the trespass is on the track, land etc of one of the various companies running restored steam trains. It is useful to police officers to be aware of the provisions of the British Transport Commission Act 1949, but it is preferable to leave enforcement to the British Transport Police and to officers of a successor to the British Railways Board. However, in the interests of the safety of such trespassers it may be necessary for any police officer to take action in such cases. A refusal by a trespasser to leave railway property on such an occasion will amount to an obstruction of a police officer in the execution of his duty, that is the enforcement of the law and the removal of criminal trespassers, within the meaning of the Police Act 1996, s 89(2).

The offence under the British Transport Commission Act 1949, s 5 is a 'penalty offence' for the purposes of Part I of the Criminal Justice and Police Act 2001 and may be dealt with under a fixed penalty procedure, see p 874.

Offence of refusal to quit

The Railway Regulation Act 1840, s 16 states that it is an offence for any person wilfully to trespass upon the railway or any station or premises connected therewith and to refuse to quit upon request by any officer or agent of the railway company. This offence of trespass is not restricted to the operational areas of a railway system nor to the property of the railway company, as is the case under the British Transport Commission Act 1949. It can occur anywhere on railway property but the offence is not complete until there is a refusal to quit at the request of any officer or agent of the railway company. Police officers, other than officers of the British Transport Police, are not 'officers of the company'. There is no need to prove that notices are displayed in such a case.

TICKET OFFENCES

Generally, all offences related to tickets will be dealt with by a railway employee or by British Transport Police officers, but there may be occasions upon which a police officer from a local force may be called to a dispute centred upon whether or not a person has committed a ticket offence. It is therefore helpful to have some understanding of the legal position of those who may be involved in such a dispute.

Travelling without a ticket

In the first instance, the Regulation of Railways Act 1889, s 5(1) provides that every passenger on a railway, on request by an officer or agent or servant of the railway company, must *either* produce, and if requested deliver up, a ticket showing that his fare is paid, *or* pay his fare from the place where his journey started, *or* give his name and address. In default of doing so, the passenger commits an offence. Put in everyday language, a railway passenger must at the request of a railway employee or British Transport Police officer, show, and if required surrender, his ticket. If he does not for any reason, he must pay the fare for his journey; if he is unable to do this he must give his true name and address so that the fare may be recovered from him by civil process, if necessary.

Travelling with intent to avoid paying fare

On occasions a constable may be called to a dispute centred upon an allegation that some person is travelling, or attempting to travel, without having previously paid his fare and with intent to avoid payment. One of two offences may be involved here. Both are provided by the Regulation of Railways Act 1889, s 5(3).

Section 5(3) of the 1889 Act provides, first, that if any person travels, or attempts to travel, on a railway without having previously paid his fare, and with intent to avoid payment thereof, he commits an offence. The intention to avoid payment may be proved by showing that the passenger has ignored opportunities to pay his fare or has taken measures to avoid a ticket inspector. A person who leaves a train without paying his fare when there has been an opportunity to do so indicates such an intention. In addition, a person who travels on a ticket issued to another person, which is not transferable, clearly indicates an intention to avoid payment. It is not essential to prove knowledge on the part of the accused that the ticket was not transferable. A person, therefore, who produces a concessionary ticket issued to a young person or a senior citizen to which he is not entitled, clearly shows an intention to avoid payment of his true fare. In this respect the term 'fare' means the correct fare for the particular journey and the class of carriage by which the person travels. A person who travels in a first-class carriage with a standard-class ticket may be convicted of travelling without having previously paid his fare, if an intention to avoid payment of the correct fare is indicated by his refusal to pay the excess. It is usual in such circumstances for a ticket collector, if one is carried, to ask such a person to move if he alleges that he has made a mistake, but if the journey has almost been completed it is probable that the ticket collector will demand the excess fare and a refusal to pay indicates an intention to avoid payment.

Second, it is also an offence under the Regulation of Railways Act 1889, s 5(3) knowingly and wilfully to proceed by train beyond the distance for which a fare has been paid. Opportunities exist on all trains to obtain an additional ticket for the excess journey and if opportunities to do so are ignored on the journey, this *may* be taken to indicate a knowing and wilful act. It would be different if the passenger fell asleep and was accidentally taken beyond the destination for which he has paid as he could not be said to have proceeded knowingly and wilfully beyond that point.

Penalty fares

The Railways (Penalty Fares) Regulations 1994 made under the Railways Act 1993, make provision for the charging of penalty fares for failure to produce, when required to do so, a ticket or other authority authorising a person to travel by train or to be present in a compulsory ticket area at a station. The Regulations apply to all train operators.

By reg 3, subject to the provisions of the regulations, and to any rules made under them:

(a) any person travelling by, present on or leaving a train must, if required by or on behalf of the train operator, produce a ticket or other authority authorising his travelling by or his being present on that train, as the case may be; and

(b) any person present in or leaving a compulsory ticket area must, if so required, produce a ticket or other authority authorising him to be present in or leave that area.

Failure to produce a ticket or other authority when so required renders the person liable to be charged a penalty fare by the train operator or someone acting on its behalf. A person is not liable to pay a penalty fare in a case covered by (a) if, when he boarded the train (or a preceding train on his journey, which was operated by the same operator):

(a) there were no ticket etc facilities available for the journey in question;

(b) there was no notice in a prescribed form indicating the penalty fare scheme;

(c) at the station where and when he commenced his journey, a notice was displayed indicating that it was permissible to travel without having such ticket or authority; or

(d) a person in authority (or apparently in authority) at the originating station gave permission to travel without a ticket etc.

These exemptions do not exempt a person who had the opportunity to obtain a fare ticket while on the train (or one of them used on the journey).

There are similar exemptions from liability to pay a fixed penalty fare in respect of a person in a compulsory ticket area.

A person who fails to pay a penalty fare at once must provide his name and address on being required to do so by an authorised person.

In an action to recover a penalty fare, which is a civil action, a defendant may provide the claimant with a 'relevant statement' explaining his failure to produce a ticket etc and including particulars of his journey, which must be submitted within twenty-one days. Where this has been done it will be for the claimant to show that the facts of the case do not fall within the exemptions provided by the Act. In any other case it is for the defendant to show that the facts of the case fall within those exemptions.

If a person has been charged a penalty fare in respect of his failure to produce a ticket or other authority when required and he is then prosecuted under the Regulation of Railways Act 1889, s 5(3) (see above) or for breach of a railway byelaw in respect of the lack of a ticket etc, he ceases to be liable to pay the penalty fare. If he has already paid it, it must be refunded.

CHAPTER 27

Pedlars, vagrancy and dealers

PEDLARS

The Pedlars Act 1871 (PA 1871) still exists to provide some element of control over those who engage in some forms of door-to-door trading. Not the least of the reasons for this control is that peddling provides for those who commit crime a convenient cover or excuse to visit houses, where they may take advantage of opportunities to steal.

The definition of 'pedlar'

The term 'pedlar' is defined by PA 1871 as meaning a hawker, pedlar, petty chapman (another name for a pedlar), tinker, caster of metals, mender of chairs, or other person who, without any horse or other beast bearing or drawing burden, travels and trades on foot, and goes from town to town or to other men's houses, carrying to sell, or exposing for sale, any goods, wares or merchandise, or procuring orders for goods etc immediately to be delivered, or selling or offering for sale his skill in handicraft.

An important part of this definition is 'travels and trades on foot', which has been held to require that, to be a pedlar, a person must *go round* selling things; he must *trade as he travels on foot*, although he may stop to conduct a particular sale, rather than simply selling from a stall or pitch. Thus, a door-to-door salesman is a pedlar, but someone who stands in one place with a pitch, soliciting custom, is not. Nor is a person who moves a barrow from place to place, waiting at each place for customers to come to him. Provided the words of the definition are satisfied, it is irrelevant that the trade is carried out on a part-time basis or on the basis that the proceeds of sale will go (in whole or in part) to a charity.

Pedlars' certificates

Under PA 1871, a person who acts as a pedlar without a pedlar's certificate commits an offence, subject to certain exceptions. A pedlar's certificate is obtained from the chief officer of police of the district in which the applicant has resided during the month preceding his application. Before granting a certificate the chief officer must be satisfied that the applicant is over seventeen, is of good character and in good faith intends to carry on the trade of a pedlar. It is an offence to make a false representation with a view to obtaining a pedlar's certificate.

The certificate is renewable annually and authorises the holder to carry on the trade of a pedlar in any part of the United Kingdom. It also permits the pedlar to sell vegetables and fruits within the limits of a market, but only in the district in which it was granted. A chief officer of police may not deprive a pedlar of his certificate during its currency. The only way in which a pedlar may be deprived of a certificate is by order of a court in circumstances set out in PA 1871, s 16.

Chief officers of police must maintain a register of certificates. The Act permits a chief officer to delegate his functions under PA 1871 and, in practice, certificates are usually issued within police divisions and signed by the divisional commander on behalf of the chief officer.

An applicant may appeal to the justices against a refusal to issue a pedlar's certificate; the applicant must give to the chief officer, within one week of the refusal, written notice of his wish to appeal.

Justices may summon a pedlar to appear before them at any time and if he fails to appear or, having done so, fails to satisfy them that he is carrying on the business of a pedlar in good faith, the justices may deprive him of his certificate.

Exemption from need for a certificate

PA 1871 states that it is not necessary for certain persons to obtain pedlar's certificates, and these are:

(a) commercial travellers or other persons selling or seeking orders for goods, wares or merchandise, to or from dealers therein, and who buy to sell again;
(b) those who sell or seek orders for books as agents authorised in writing by the publishers of such books;
(c) sellers of vegetables, fish, fruit or victuals; and
(d) persons selling or exposing for sale goods etc in any public market or fair which is legally established.

These exemptions are easily understood when one recalls that the purpose of PA 1871 is to give some form of supervision to door-to-door trading activities which would otherwise be uncontrolled and require control. The commercial traveller who, on foot, visited business premises which were also 'houses', in that the businessmen lived on the premises, would have become a pedlar if he was delivering goods to them; but for the exemption he would have required a certificate in such a case. Parliament did not think that this situation required control and the same is true of the other exceptions. The encyclopaedia salesman is already authorised by the publishers to sell their product and his purpose in calling at houses is only to sell books. The sellers of vegetables, fruit etc from door to door are local businessmen who are already well-known to both the public and the police. It is, however, interesting to note that a High Court judge has held that lavender is a vegetable and that those who sell lavender from door to door are exempt from the necessity to obtain a pedlar's certificate. The exemption in relation to markets appears to be unnecessary as market traders do not go to other men's houses in any case.

Offences

It is an offence for a pedlar to refuse on demand to show his pedlar's certificate to a justice or constable or to a person to whom he offers his goods for sale (or upon whose private grounds or premises he is found), or to refuse to allow it to be read.

STREET AND HOUSE-TO-HOUSE COLLECTIONS

Street collections

The Police, Factories etc (Miscellaneous Provisions) Act 1916 permits local authorities to make regulations with respect to the places where and the conditions under which persons may be permitted, in any street or public place within their area, to collect money or sell articles for the benefit of charitable or other purposes. It also provides that a contravention of any regulations so made is an offence.

House-to-house collections

The House to House Collections Act 1939 prohibits house-to-house collections for charitable purposes unless the collection is authorised. Such a collection may be authorised by a *licence* (issued by a district council, Commissioner of the Metropolitan Police, or the Common Council of the City of London), or an *order* of exemption (granted by the Secretary of State where the charitable purpose is to be pursued throughout the whole of England or a substantial part of it), or a *certificate* of exemption (granted by a chief officer of police in respect of a collection which is local in character and likely to be completed within a short period of time).

The House to House Collections Regulations 1947 deal with such matters as badges, certificates of authority, collecting boxes and receipt books and duties of collectors and promoters. They prescribe a minimum age of sixteen years in respect of collectors. The 1947 Regulations do not apply to a collection under a certificate of exemption. Breach of the regulations is an offence. The House to House Collections Act 1939, s 5 punishes the unauthorised use of prescribed badges or certificates of authority, or a thing so closely resembling those articles as to be calculated to deceive.

A constable may require any person whom he believes to be acting as a collector for the purposes of a collection for charitable purposes to declare to him his name and address and to sign his name. Failure to comply with such a requirement is an offence.

The Charities Act 1992

The Charities Act 1992 (CA 1992) deals, among other things, with public charitable collections, ie charitable appeals made in any public place or by house-to-house visits.

CA 1992, s 66 prohibits any public collection from being conducted except in accordance with a permit issued by the district council or with an order of the

Charity Commissioners. Breach of this prohibition is an offence on the part of the promoter (ie any organiser or controller) of the charity appeal. CA 1992, s 73 permits regulations to be made along the lines of the 1947 Regulations. CA 1992, s 74 replicates the offence under the House to House Collections Act 1939, s 5.

These provisions are not in force at the time of writing. When they are, CA 1992 will repeal the Police, Factories etc (Miscellaneous Provisions) Act 1916 and the House to House Collections Act 1939.

VAGRANCY OFFENCES

Begging

The Vagrancy Act 1824 (VA 1824), s 3 punishes persons who wander abroad, or place themselves in any public place, street, highway, court or passage, to beg or gather alms, or who cause, procure or encourage any child to do so. The divisional court has decided that workmen on strike who seek assistance by asking for contributions towards their cause are *not* begging for the purposes of this section. It should be remembered that the purpose of the section is to prevent persons from frequenting the streets for the purpose of begging to the annoyance of the general public. It is not really concerned with trivial and occasional incidents. It must be shown that the person concerned had, in a sense, taken up the profession of a beggar in preference to work.

VA 1824, s 4 deals with the aggravated forms of begging by the exposure of wounds or deformities in public or by seeking charitable contributions of any kind by false pretences.

Begging is a recordable offence.

Sleeping out etc

It is an offence contrary to VA 1824, s 4 for any person, wandering abroad and lodging in any barn or outhouse, or in any deserted or unoccupied building, or in the open air, or under a tent, or in any cart or waggon, not to give a good account of himself.

It must be emphasised that the offence is only committed by a person who fails to give a good account of himself. People holidaying at a static caravan site and genuine hikers who, being tired and hungry, rest in a barn or outhouse are not guilty of this offence because they can easily give a good account of themselves by explaining their presence. In contrast, a tramp found sleeping in a barn would find it much more difficult to give a good account of himself, particularly if he has made a temporary home in that building.

Two important limits were imposed on the offence by the Vagrancy Act 1935. First, the Act amended VA 1824, s 4 by providing that the reference to a person lodging under a tent or in a cart or waggon does not include a person lodging under a tent, cart or waggon with or in which he travels. It was thereby made quite clear that the present offence was not concerned with gypsies travelling in their own waggons, nor with persons sleeping out in their own tents.

The Vagrancy Act 1935 also requires that before a person can be guilty of the present offence, it must be proved either that:

(a) on the occasion in question, he had been directed to a reasonably accessible place of free shelter and that he failed to apply for, or refused, accommodation there; or

(b) he is a person who persistently wanders abroad and, notwithstanding that a place of free shelter is reasonably accessible, lodges or attempts to lodge in a way described above; or

(c) by, or in the course of, lodging in a way described above he caused damage to property, infection with vermin, or other offensive consequence, or he so lodged in such circumstances as to appear to be likely to do so.

As a result, the present offence is of little practical significance to police officers. The reason is that there are few places of free shelter to which people may be directed, or which are reasonably accessible to the person who persistently sleeps out. The provision of greatest practical significance is that at (c), which can apply to the roadster who destroys hay or feed in a barn by his presence, or who causes the barn or outbuilding to become verminous by his presence.

SCRAP METAL DEALERS AND MOTOR SALVAGE OPERATORS

Registration of dealers

The Scrap Metal Dealers Act 1964 (SMDA 1964) requires every district council (hereafter 'the local authority') to maintain a register of persons carrying on business in their area as scrap metal dealers.

It is an offence for a person to carry on a business as a scrap metal dealer in the area of a local authority unless he is registered with that authority. The essential elements to prove for this offence are that a business is being carried on in the area of a particular local authority, that the business is one of being a scrap metal dealer, and that the person carrying on the business is not registered with the local authority.

Carrying on a business

For the purposes of SMDA 1964, a person carrying on business as a scrap metal dealer is treated as carrying on that business in the area of a local authority if, but only if:

(a) a place in that area is occupied by him as a scrap metal store; or

(b) no place is occupied by him as a scrap metal store, whether in that area or elsewhere, but he has his usual place of residence in that area; or

(c) no place is occupied by him as a scrap metal store, whether in that area or elsewhere, but a place in that area is occupied by him wholly or partly for the purposes of that business.

(For the purpose of these provisions, 'place' includes land, whether enclosed or not, and a 'scrap metal store' means a place where scrap metal is received or kept in the course of the business of a scrap metal dealer.)

Therefore, a person who has a scrap metal store in the area of a local authority is clearly carrying on a business in the area of that authority and must be registered with it. Also, a person who does not have a scrap metal store in the area of the X local authority but nevertheless lives in the area of that authority must register with it, as must a person with a business address in the area of the X local authority if that business is one of being a scrap metal dealer.

Business as a scrap metal dealer

A person carries on business as a scrap metal dealer if he carries on a business which consists wholly or partly of buying and selling scrap metal, whether the scrap metal sold is in the form in which it was bought or otherwise, other than a business in the course of which scrap metal is not bought except as materials for the manufacture of other articles or as part of the carrying on of a business as a 'motor salvage operator' and is not sold except as a by-product of such manufacture or of such a business or as surplus materials bought but not required for such manufacture or of such a business. A 'motor salvage operator' is someone who carries on a business which consists:

(a) wholly or partly in the recovery for re-use or sale of salvageable parts from motor vehicles and the subsequent sale or other disposal for scrap of the remainder of the vehicle concerned;
(b) wholly or mainly in the purchase of written-off vehicles and their subsequent repair and resale;
(c) wholly or mainly in the sale or purchase of motor vehicles which are to be the subject (whether immediately or on a subsequent resale) of any of the activities set out at (a) or (b) above; or
(d) wholly or mainly in activities falling within (b) and (c).

The above definition of carrying on business as a scrap metal dealer is quite complex and difficult to follow unless it is broken up into pieces. In the first instance, the person must carry on a business which consists wholly or partly of buying and selling scrap metal. Therefore persons who merely buy scrap metal are not scrap metal dealers, nor are those who merely sell it. If this was not so, a farmer who quite regularly sells scrap metal which gathers about the farm might be considered to be carrying on business as a scrap metal dealer if it could be said that his business was partly that of selling scrap metal. If a person both buys and sells it does not matter that the metal is sold in a different form. Consequently, a person who buys scrap washing machines and crushes them into cubes of metal, which he then sells to some other person, is quite clearly a scrap metal dealer. In terms of the exclusion of motor salvage operators from the definition of 'carrying on business as a scrap metal dealer', it must be remembered that such operators are subject to the special regulatory regime under the Vehicles (Crime) Act 2001, which we described in Chapter 9. If a motor salvage operator also deals in scrap in ways falling outside the above list, he must comply with the Scrap Metal Dealers Act 1964.

The Vehicles (Crime) Act 2001, s 2 requires local authorities to establish and maintain a register of persons carrying on business as motor salvage operators. Registration with the local authority may be cancelled if the authority is satisfied that the person (or a director of or partner in a company) concerned is not a fit and proper person to conduct such a business.

The Motor Salvage Operators Regulations 2002 will provide for the keeping of records by registered motor salvage operators. SMDA 1964, s 4A inserted by the Vehicles (Crime) Act 2001 empowers the Secretary of State to make regulations providing for the notification by persons registered as scrap metal dealers of the destruction of motor vehicles and for the keeping of appropriate records. SMDA 1964, s 4A(3) creates an offence of failure to comply with such regulations.

Scrap metal

The SMDA 1964 describes scrap metal as including any old metal, and any broken, worn out, defaced or partly manufactured articles made wholly or partly of metal, and any metallic wastes, and also as including old, broken, worn out or defaced tooltips or dies made of any of the materials commonly known as hard metals or of cemented or sintered metallic carbides. References to metals, other than 'hard metals' or 'metallic carbides', are references to aluminium, copper, iron, lead, magnesium, nickel, tin and zinc, or, subject to the next sentence, to brass, bronze, gun metal, steel, white metal or any other alloy of these metals. However, if any alloy has 2% or more of gold, silver, platinum etc, it is not treated as such an alloy. It follows that a person who deals only in precious metals is not a scrap metal dealer.

Alteration in registered particulars

Dealers must notify the local authority within twenty-eight days of any change in their registered particulars, or if they cease to carry on business as a scrap metal dealer. This requirement is the same as that imposed on motor salvage operators.

Records to be kept by scrap metal dealers

A scrap metal dealer must keep a bound record book at each place occupied by him as a scrap metal store. He must make entries concerning:

(a) all scrap metal received at that place; and
(b) all scrap metal either processed at, or despatched from, that place.

He may, if he wishes, keep two separate bound books recording matters at (a) and (b) separately but otherwise may not extend the book-keeping by keeping any other books recording dealing in that store.

Records of metals received

The records must show:

(a)   the description and weight of the scrap metal;
(b)   the date and time of receipt of the scrap metal;
(c)   if the scrap metal is received from another person, his full name and address;
(d)   the price, if any, payable, if ascertained at the time of the entry;

(e) if the price has not been ascertained, the dealer's estimate; and
(f) if the scrap metal has been delivered by mechanically propelled vehicle, the registration mark of the vehicle (even if it is the dealer's).

Records—metals processed or despatched

The records must show:

(a) the description and weight of the scrap metal;
(b) the date of processing and the process applied, or, as the case may be, the date of despatch;
(c) if despatched on sale or exchange, the full name and address of the person to whom the scrap is sold or with whom it is exchanged, and the consideration for which it is sold or exchanged; and
(d) if processed or despatched otherwise than on sale or exchange, the value of the scrap before its processing or despatch as estimated by the dealer.

These provisions can be easily remembered if it is kept in mind that the provisions are concerned with the prevention of dealings in stolen metals. With this in mind it is logical that dealers will have to be registered and that meticulous records will have to be kept of metals. The idea is that, from the moment that scrap metal is received by the dealer, the records will provide a continuing history of its origin, including the person from whom it is obtained and his mechanically propelled vehicle, through its processing to its ultimate disposal.

Itinerant collectors

Where a person, who is registered by a local authority as a scrap metal dealer satisfies the authority that he carries on, or proposes to carry on, the business of a scrap metal dealer as part of the business of an 'itinerant collector', and not otherwise, the authority may make an order exempting him from keeping the records set out above, but making him subject to the following requirements:

(a) that, when he sells scrap metal, he obtains a receipt from the purchaser showing its weight and aggregate price; and
(b) that he keeps such receipts for two years in such a way that he can produce them on demand to any authorised person.

Before making an order of the above type, the local authority must consult the chief officer of police for their area. This order, limiting the need to keep records, may be revoked by the local authority at any time. Failure to comply with the requirement to keep records as an itinerant collector is an offence.

An 'itinerant collector' is a person regularly engaged in collecting waste materials, and old, broken, worn out or defaced articles, by means of visits from house to house. Most 'tinker' collectors will fit this description as they are regularly engaged in such activities.

Police powers of entry

SMDA 1964, s 6 empowers a constable at all reasonable times:

(a) to enter and inspect any place registered as a scrap metal store, or as a place occupied by a scrap metal dealer wholly or partly for the purposes of his business; and

(b) to require production of, and to inspect, any scrap metal kept at that place and any book, or record which the dealer is required to keep at that place, or, as the case may be, any receipt (itinerant dealers), and to take copies of or extracts from any such book, record or receipt.

The term 'reasonable times' is not defined, and must therefore be given a normal, commonsense meaning. Any time during working hours would be reasonable unless particular circumstances (such as some internal operation within the yard which demanded the dealer's uninterrupted attention) indicated the contrary.

Entry under this power can only be effected by force on the authority of a justice's warrant. Such a warrant may be issued under SMDA 1964, s 6 if a justice is satisfied by information on oath that admission is reasonably required in order to secure compliance with the provisions of the Act, or to ascertain whether those provisions are being complied with. The warrant authorises those having a right of entry to enter within one month, if need be by force.

It is an offence for any person to obstruct the exercise of a right of entry or inspection under SMDA 1964, s 6, or to fail to produce books, records or other documents which a person has a right to inspect thereunder.

Power of courts to impose additional requirements

Where a person is convicted of carrying on business as a scrap metal dealer without being registered, or being registered, he is convicted of failing to keep records or of any offence involving dishonesty, the court *may* make an order subjecting him to certain additional requirements in respect of his scrap metal store, namely that:

(a) no scrap metal shall be received between 6 pm and 8 am;

(b) all scrap metal received at such place shall be kept in the form in which it is received for a period of not less than seventy-two hours.

The duration of the order specified by the court must not exceed two years. A dealer commits a further offence if he does not comply with the requirements of an order. If he is convicted of such an offence, a further order may be made against him.

Miscellaneous offences

It is an offence, contrary to SMDA 1964, s 5(1), for a scrap metal dealer to acquire scrap metal from a person apparently under the age of sixteen, whether that metal is offered on his own behalf or on behalf of someone else. The accused dealer has a defence if he proves that the person from whom he acquired the scrap metal was in fact of or over the age of sixteen.

By SMDA 1964, s 5(2), a person who gives a false name or false address to a scrap metal dealer, on selling him scrap metal, commits an offence.

CHAPTER 28

Non-fatal offences against the person

This chapter is concerned with various non-fatal offences against the person, which are distinguishable in a number of ways, such as the degree of harm caused, the way in which it is inflicted and the status of the victim.

The first two offences to be discussed are the separate offences of assault and battery, contrary to the Criminal Justice Act 1988 (CJA 1988), s 39. Rather confusingly, the word 'assault' is used in some statutes to refer to assault or battery. Even more confusingly, the word 'assault' has sometimes been used in decided cases as meaning only a 'battery', which is not altogether surprising since this is the meaning normally given to 'assault' in common parlance. Obviously, an officer must take care to ascertain the relevant meaning of 'assault' when he comes across that term in a particular context.

COMMON ASSAULT AND BATTERY

Assault

A person is guilty of the separate offence of assault if he intentionally or recklessly causes another person to apprehend the immediate application to himself of unlawful force.

The actus reus which must be proved is some act by the accused which causes the victim to fear the immediate application of unlawful force against him.

Any act, even mere words, can suffice if it has the requisite result. An example would be where, during an argument in a pub, someone holding a beer glass loses his temper and shouts out to his antagonist, 'I'll glass you for that.' Although words alone can constitute an assault, threatening words are more likely to be prosecuted as an offence under the Public Order Act 1986 (POA 1986), ss 4, 4A or 5.

The requirement that the immediate application of unlawful force must be apprehended means that it is an assault to aim a blow at someone, whether or not that blow hits him, unless he is blind or the blow is aimed from behind him or there is some other circumstance which means that he does not apprehend force.

The requirement of 'immediacy' has been given a liberal interpretation by the courts. It has been held to be satisfied where a woman has been put in fear by a 'peeping tom' whom she saw through a window, or by a malicious telephone caller who had repeatedly 'hung up', because the woman would not know what the person was going to do next. In another case, where a woman had been caused psychiatric harm after repeated telephone calls and letters from a stalker, the last two of which contained threats, the Court of Appeal held that the jury were entitled to find that the last letter had caused the woman fear of immediate force. It emphasised that the accused, who was known to the woman, lived near her and she thought that something could happen at any time. In a curious statement, the Court of Appeal, albeit accepting the requirement of the apprehension of immediate force, said that it was enough for the prosecution to prove fear of force 'at some time not excluding the immediate future'. In the light of these decisions, the requirement seems to mean little. Cases involving repeated conduct such as the last two cases just described are now better dealt with by bringing a prosecution for an offence under the Protection from Harassment Act 1997, described on pp 878–880.

If a person is put in fear of immediate force, it is irrelevant that the accused could not in fact carry out his threat; for example, pointing an unloaded gun or an imitation gun at someone who is unaware of its harmlessness can be an assault.

The mens rea required for an assault is an intention to cause the victim to apprehend the immediate application of unlawful force or recklessness as to whether the victim might so apprehend. Recklessness requires that the accused realised the possibility that his act might cause the victim to apprehend immediate unlawful force but nevertheless persisted in doing that act without any justification.

If a person, indulging in a piece of horseplay and mistakenly believing that the other is doing so as well, playfully throws a punch at the other, meaning to miss, he is not guilty of an assault—even though the other does fear immediate force—because he does not intend the other to fear immediate unlawful force and is not reckless in this respect. On the other hand, rowdies who throw bottles at passers-by on the opposite pavement clearly indicate an intention to cause them to fear being hit (ie immediate force) if they take deliberate aim; if they lob the bottles in the general direction of the passers-by, this may indicate recklessness as to whether any of the passers-by may be put in fear of immediate force.

Battery

A person is guilty of battery if he intentionally or recklessly applies unlawful force to another person. Most batteries are preceded by an assault, but this is not always so. If a person is clubbed down from behind there is certainly a battery, but, if he was unaware that the blow was coming, there cannot be an assault, because there would have been no apprehension by him of the immediate application of unlawful force.

The actus reus of the offence of battery is some conduct on the part of the accused which results in unlawful force being applied to another. Technically, the slightest degree of force, even a mere touching, suffices, but a prosecution is most unlikely unless some harm has been caused. The force can be applied directly, as where a person hits another with his fist or an instrument, or indirectly, as where someone puts a tripwire across an alley over which another person trips or puts acid in a hand drier which is blown onto the hands of the next user. The fact that a battery requires an application of force, whether by a fist, an implement, a projectile or a liquid, means that those who cause harm in some other way than by applying force, for example by poisoning, do not commit a battery. Causing someone psychiatric harm by a threat does not involve a battery because it does not involve the application of force. However, a divisional court held that there was a battery of a child where the assailant punched the mother causing her to drop the child to the floor. This represents a recognition of the doctrine of 'transferred malice' where an unlawful and dangerous act leads to the injury of a third person to whom the violence was not directly offered.

Normally, the force must be applied as a result of an act by the accused. However, liability can also be based on an omission (with the appropriate mens rea) to take such steps as are in the accused's power to counteract a dangerous situation created by him, even if inadvertently. In one case which states this, P, a police officer, approached D and told him that she intended to carry out a full body search. She asked him to turn out his pockets. He did so and produced some syringes without needles. P asked D if he had any needles on him and he replied 'No'. When P searched one of D's pockets her finger was pierced by a hypodermic needle, at which D smirked. A divisional court held that, by giving P a dishonest assurance about the contents of his pockets, D thereby exposed her to a reasonably foreseeable risk of the injury which materialised. Clearly, D had failed to counteract a danger, which his assurance had created, by not warning P not to put her hand in the pocket. As a result force (the needle) had been applied to P's finger and there could be a conviction for battery since D had the mens rea for that offence.

The mens rea required for a battery is an intention to apply unlawful force to the other or recklessness as to whether unlawful force might be so applied. It follows that, if the horseplay referred to above results in a blow landing on the other, there is no battery if the blow is a light one and the person throwing it believed that the other was engaging in the horseplay and therefore consenting to such a blow (because, as we shall see, he will not have intended, nor been reckless as to, the application of *unlawful* force).

Clearly, it is not a battery to hit or shoot someone accidentally (since there is no intention to apply force to another), unless the accused can be proved to have realised the risk that his act, eg of swinging his arm or pulling the trigger, might possibly result in unlawful force being applied to another and unjustifiably decided to do the act regardless (in which case he would be proved to have been reckless as to the risk).

Assault and battery: unlawful force

It is an integral part of both offences that the force apprehended by the victim, or applied to him, must be unlawful force. In this context, the essential point is that if the victim has given a valid consent to it, or if the force is threatened or applied in self-defence, prevention of crime or the like, it is lawful force. This point is also important in relation to the other non-fatal offences discussed later in this chapter.

Consent

When no actual bodily harm is caused, the consent of the victim is valid (except in the cases referred to at the top of p 807). However, generally, a person cannot give a valid consent to 'actual bodily harm' which was intended or likely. 'Actual bodily harm' means any injury which is not so trivial as to be wholly insignificant. See further pp 809–810. The result of all this is that if a person intentionally causes another actual bodily harm or the actual bodily harm caused was likely, it is generally irrelevant whether or not the latter has consented, since, generally, he cannot give a valid consent in such a case. Thus, assuming the other elements of the offence are proved, there can generally be a conviction for an assault or battery or some other non-fatal offence against the person in such a case, despite the victim's apparent consent. For example, men who agree to fight each other to 'settle a score' commit an assault and a battery (or a more serious non-fatal offence) when they fight each other, since actual bodily harm is clearly intended and/or caused. For the same reason, willing and enthusiastic participants in sado-masochistic acts of violence for the sexual pleasure engendered in the giving and receiving of pain can be convicted of an assault, or of a battery (or of a more serious non-fatal offence).

There are, however, exceptions, based on grounds of public policy, to the general rule just stated. A person can give a valid consent to 'any actual bodily harm' caused by reasonable surgical operations or procedures; if he could not the surgeon would commit a battery or an assault occasioning actual bodily harm (below) or some more serious offence against the person.

Likewise, it has been held that a valid consent can be given to ear-piercing, to being tattooed or, even, to being branded with one's spouse's initials, since the causing of bodily harm of these types is not contrary to public policy.

Similarly, those who agree to take part in a lawful sport consent to the rules of that sport and, if those rules allow forms of physical contact, they validly consent to the risk of actual bodily harm which is likely to result from physical contact which is within the rules or is a minor infringement of them. For example, a blow struck in a boxing match under the Queensberry Rules (in which boxers wear approved gloves) is not a battery or any other offence, regardless of the injury caused, unless the blow is struck in circumstances far outside the rules (eg hitting an opponent when he is lying unconscious on the floor, or hitting an opponent with a glove in which is concealed a heavy object). Likewise, in soccer and rugby, the participants consent to the risk of actual bodily harm resulting from something within the rules of the game or not too far removed from them, but not to the risk of such harm resulting from something which is far outside the rules, such as a head-butt or deliberately kicking a player who is on the ground. The fact that the play is within the rules of the game gives a firm indication that what has happened is not criminal. In judging whether conduct is criminal or not, it must be remembered that, in highly competitive sports, conduct outside the rules can be expected to occur in the heat of the moment, and even if the conduct justifies a sending off, it still may not reach the threshold level required for it to be criminal. That level is an objective one and does not depend upon the views of individual players. The type of the sport, the level at which it is played, the nature of the act, the degree of force used, the extent of the risk of injury, the state of mind of the defendant are all likely to be relevant in determining whether the defendant's actions go beyond the threshold.

Not all sports are lawful. For example, a prize-fight, where gloves are not worn and the fight continues until one of the participants can no longer continue, is an unlawful sport. Thus, the participants cannot give a valid consent to the actual bodily harm intended and/or caused, with the result that the force which they apply to each other is always unlawful.

Other points on consent Sometimes when a person has consented to the application of force, his consent is invalid, even though actual bodily harm is not caused by the force. This occurs where he is so young or mentally impaired as not to be able to comprehend the nature of the act committed, or where his apparent consent has been procured by duress or has been given under a mistake as to the identity of the other party or as to the nature of the act. The Court of Appeal has held that a mistake as to the quality of the act, as opposed to its essential nature, will also invalidate consent, but this proposition is questionable. In that case it was held that women who consented to their breasts being touched by a man who had fooled them into thinking that he was medically trained did not give a valid consent to touching. They knew they were being touched but made a mistake as to the quality of that act; they were consenting to being touched for medical purposes not to indecent behaviour.

When considering a claim of consent one must consider what it is that is supposed to have been consented to. A person does not consent to something if he does not give an 'informed consent' to it. Suppose that someone consents to have intercourse with an AIDS sufferer in ignorance of that person's disease. While he will have consented to the intercourse (bodily contact) involved, this does not mean that he will have consented to run the risk of becoming diseased with AIDS (grievous bodily harm). In such a case, the consent to contact means that there will not be a battery but there can be liability for a more serious offence (see later) based on the infliction or causing of grievous bodily harm.

Assuming it is valid, a consent need not be express; it can be implied from the circumstances. Everyday living demands a certain amount of physical contact. People are often touched in order to attract their attention, and there are constant collisions in shopping precincts, and the consent of people to such things can normally be implied. It is, of course, different if the person touched has indicated that he does not want to be touched. If A tells B, who has been pestering him, to go away, A clearly does not impliedly consent to B touching him soon after in order to attract his attention. Of course, there is a limit to what a person impliedly consents to. There is certainly no consent to a violent blow, allegedly to attract attention, perhaps as a person walked away after an argument. Similarly, one does not impliedly consent to collisions in a shopping precinct caused by hooligans charging about.

Another way of expressing cases based on implied consent is that they fall within a general exception embracing all physical contact which is generally acceptable in the ordinary conduct of daily life.

Normally, the consent of sports players referred to above is implied from their participation in the game, rather than being expressly given.

Other factors which render force lawful

Disciplinary use of force and corporal punishment Subject to the limitations below, parents and other people in loco parentis are entitled as a disciplinary measure to apply a reasonable degree of force to their children or charges old enough to understand its purpose. In relation to the following offences:

(a) wounding or causing grievous bodily harm with intent, or unlawful wounding or infliction of grievous bodily harm;

(b) assault occasioning actual bodily harm; or

(c) cruelty to a person under sixteen,

battery of a child cannot be justified on the ground that it constituted reasonable punishment.

Teachers are no longer entitled by virtue of their position as such to apply reasonable corporal punishment as a disciplinary measure.

Prevention of crime or effecting arrest   The Criminal Law Act 1967, s 3 provides that it is lawful to use such force as is reasonable in the circumstances in the prevention of crime (ie a crime under the law of England and Wales) or in effecting (or assisting in) the lawful arrest of offenders, suspected offenders or persons unlawfully at large. Where the accused acts under a mistake as to the circumstances, this provision is applied to the circumstances as he believed them to be. The effecting of an arrest will almost always involve some form of restraint, even if it is only symbolic, and this would be a battery but for the present defence. It must be emphasised that, if the force used to prevent a crime or to make an arrest is unreasonable in the circumstances, it will be unlawful and the person using it will not have a defence to a charge of battery or of another offence against the person. A person has no defence, even though he uses reasonable force, if he is acting in furtherance of an unlawful arrest.

Self-defence and defence of property or of another   Self-defence and the defence of property or of another are common law defences. However, a person who acts in defence of himself or another or of property is almost invariably acting in the prevention of crime, in which case he also has the defence under the Criminal Law Act 1967, s 3. For practical purposes, the terms of both the common law and the statutory defences are identical in their requirements.

The issue of self-defence as an excuse for a non-fatal offence against the person has been summarised extremely well by the Court of Appeal. The Court said that it was both good law and good sense that a person who is attacked may defend himself but that in doing so, he may only do what is reasonably necessary. The test of whether or not the force is reasonable is an objective one, but it is assessed on the facts as the person concerned believed them to be.

The law on defence of property or of another is essentially the same as in self-defence, the essential question being 'was the force used reasonable in the circumstances' as the accused believed them to be. An occupier of land who uses force against persons who trespass upon his land without offering force would be most unlikely to be found to have used reasonable force if he has not first asked the trespassers to leave. If he has, and they refuse, any force used thereafter to remove them from the land must be reasonable in the circumstances as he believes them to be. Of course, if a trespasser offers force, then it may be met with whatever force is reasonable self-defence to overcome it and remove him.

For the avoidance of doubt, it must be stated that the mere fact that a person who has used force against another was provoked to lose self-control (as opposed to acting in self-defence etc) is no excuse. Of course, if a person who has used provocative words or conduct then makes some immediately threatening move towards the person to whom his words or conduct are directed, he has carried out an assault and reasonable resistance to it would amount to self-defence. If no more than provocation is involved, this is only relevant in relation to the penalty which the court may award.

Assault and battery: procedural matters

Assault and battery are separate statutory offences of common assault and common battery and should be so charged, under CJA 1988, s 39. Where the person has been merely 'put in fear' the person must be charged that he 'did assault' that person. If force has been applied, the charge should allege 'did assault by beating'. Proceedings are frequently instituted by private persons. A common example of the institution of a private prosecution for a common assault or battery is where an argument with a spouse or an acquaintance has got out of hand and led to a threat of harm or to fairly minor harm being done. It quite often happens in such a case that proceedings are discontinued by the private prosecutor after a period of reflection.

Witnesses

When common assaults or batteries are committed against children or young persons the wife or husband of the person charged may be called as a witness without the consent of the person charged. Justices may accept the depositions of children whose attendance they consider likely seriously to endanger their life or health. The evidence of a child of tender years is admissible unless it appears that he is incapable of giving intelligible testimony, although such evidence is not sworn.

Certificate of dismissal

If, on a charge of common assault or battery brought by or on behalf of the victim, the justices find that the charge is not proved, or that the assault was justified or so trifling as not to merit punishment, they must make out a certificate of dismissal which (like a conviction for common assault or battery) has the effect of releasing the person concerned from all further proceedings in relation to that offence, whether criminal or civil (ie for damages). Clearly it is important that the victim realises this before an information is laid by him (or on his behalf).

AGGRAVATED ASSAULTS

There are a number of offences of aggravated assault. Among them are assault with intent to rob, and racially- or religiously-aggravated assault, which are discussed elsewhere. Like the aggravated assaults discussed below, they require an assault or battery which is accompanied either by a particular intention or by a special circumstance or consequence.

Assault occasioning actual bodily harm

It is an offence, contrary to the Offences Against the Person Act 1861 (OAPA 1861), s 47 to assault any person, thereby occasioning him actual bodily harm. What is required is an assault or battery which has occasioned actual bodily harm. Actual bodily harm means any injury which is not so trivial as to be wholly insignificant. It must be more than transient but it need not be permanent. 'Bodily' refers to injury to any part of the body (including a person's hair) or psychiatric injury (but not mere emotions such as fear, distress or panic which are not themselves evidence of an identifiable clinical condition). Consequently, to cause someone psychiatric injury by a threat of 'immediate' force can amount to an offence under s 47. Where a victim claims to have suffered psychiatric illness or injury as a result of a non-physical assault, there must be psychiatric evidence as to whether the symptoms alleged by the victim amount to a psychiatric illness or injury. A judge in the Administrative Court has held that loss of consciousness falls within the meaning of 'harm', because it involves an injurious impairment to the victim's sensory functions. He added that, even though the loss of consciousness was momentary, the bodily harm was 'actual'.

There must be a direct connection between the 'assault' and the bodily harm occasioned and in most circumstances this will be apparent. If the assailant punches his victim in the face and causes actual bodily harm, for example cuts or bruises, there has been a battery and the harm has been occasioned thereby. It may be, however, that an assailant chases his victim who, fearful of the consequences of being caught, attempts to jump over a fence and thereby injures himself. In such circumstances there has been an assault, ie the putting of another in fear of immediate force, and that assault has led to the harm done. It is a question of sufficient connection between the two elements. To attempt to escape in that way is reasonable and there is therefore sufficient connection. Only if the action taken by the person assaulted, which led to the bodily harm, was unreasonable in the circumstances would there be an insufficient connection.

The mens rea required for this offence is the mens rea required for an assault or battery (as the case may be). It is not necessary to establish that the defendant intended to cause some bodily harm or was reckless as to the risk of doing so.

Assault with intent to resist arrest

Although assaults upon police officers are dealt with in detail by the Police Act 1996 (PA 1996), s 89, it remains an offence under OAPA 1861, s 38 for a person to assault (ie by an assault or by a battery) any person with intent to resist or prevent the lawful apprehension or detainer of himself, or any other person, for any offence. The provisions of this section are still extremely useful as it deals with assaults on any person effecting an arrest, and therefore includes members of the public who are making 'citizens' arrests'.

The offence is proved if it is proved that the arrest was lawful; that the accused intended to resist it; and that he knew that the person whom he assaulted was seeking to arrest him. The issue of whether or not an offence which merited arrest had been committed is irrelevant as is an alleged belief on the accused's part that he had not committed the offence. The Court of Appeal said that this must be so, as many lawful arrests were effected following a reasonable suspicion on the part of the person arresting.

Assault on a constable in the execution of his duty

The Police Act 1996, s 89(1) makes it an offence for a person to assault (by an assault or by a battery) a constable in the execution of his duty. While, of course, the accused must have the necessary mens rea for the assault or battery which he commits, it is irrelevant that he does not know that the victim was a constable acting in the execution of his duty. However, if the accused, ignorant that the victim is a constable, applies force to the constable who is exercising one of his powers, and that force would have been reasonable on the ground of self-defence if the victim had not been a constable, the accused does not commit an offence. He will not have intentionally or recklessly applied unlawful force (the mens rea for a battery) because of his ignorance of his victim's status.

The key point about this offence is that the constable must be acting in the execution of his duty. At first sight the offence seems to be quite straightforward as there is a tendency to assume that police officers are in the execution of their duty at all times while they are carrying out duties in the course of their routine work. This is not so, and it is important to remember that on every occasion upon which it is alleged that this offence has been committed the particular duty which was being executed at the time will be examined by the courts.

To be acting in the execution of his duty, a constable must be acting within the general scope of a duty imposed on him by law (such as his duties to protect life and property, to keep the peace, to prevent and investigate crimes and to prevent obstruction of the highway) and he must not be acting unlawfully at the time. Thus, even if a constable is acting within the general scope of one of his duties, he is not acting in the execution of his duty if he has no power to do the thing in question (and is, therefore, committing a trespass against a person or his property). In one case, a man kicked a constable, used foul language and started to walk away. The constable laid a hand on the man's shoulder, not with the intention of arresting him but to detain him for further conversation. This was held to be an unlawful detention against the man's will and therefore the constable was held not to be acting in the execution of his duty in so acting. It would have been different if he had been exercising his power of arrest, as he was entitled to do. Similarly, where a police officer laid a hand on a man during a domestic incident but was not intending to arrest him at that stage and the man believed that he was being arrested and struggled, resulting in the officer falling through a window, the Court of Appeal held that, as there was no arrest, the defendant's mistaken belief that he had been arrested did not affect his right to resist unlawful restraint. Where police officers arrest a man and it is not practicable to give the reason for that arrest at the time, the arrest will be lawful and an assault upon the police officers will, at that time, be committed while they are in the execution of their duty. This is so even if the arrest is subsequently made unlawful by a failure to give the reason for arrest as soon as it is practicable to do so. In another case, a constable stopped a motor vehicle pursuant to the Road Traffic Act 1988, s 163 and detained it, suspecting it to be stolen. He was acting in the execution of his duty, where his suspicion was justified.

The test of whether a police officer is acting in the execution of his duty is judged objectively. Thus, for example, an officer who makes an unlawful arrest is not acting in the execution of his duty even though he believes that he has the necessary reasonable grounds for making an arrest.

Police officers are frequently asked to assist with the expulsion of persons from premises, where the owner of the premises considers them to be intruders or for some other reason they are unwelcome. An officer may lawfully assist the owner of property in these circumstances, but he is not bound to do so. Unless there are particular circumstances which demand such expulsion, for example, the removal of violent, quarrelsome, disorderly persons from various premises as required by law, or where a breach of the peace is taking place or apprehended, it is unlikely that he will be considered to have been acting in the execution of his duty. Similarly, a constable who arrested a man who was wanted on a warrant for non-payment of a fine, without having the warrant in his possession, was held not to be acting in the execution of his duty as what he did was unlawful. Police officers who arrest without warrant are not acting in the execution of their duty if a power does not exist in the circumstances. Since the revision of the powers of arrest under PACE by the Serious Organised Crime and Police Act 2005, it is now always essential for police officers to show that the arrest was necessary and this factor will have to be taken into account when considering whether an officer was acting in the execution of his duty.

However, a constable does not act outside the execution of his duty if what he does involves no more than a trivial touching; indeed there is probably not an assault or battery in any event. In one case, for example, a constable, who touched a man on the shoulder to attract his attention because he wished to speak to him in relation to an offence, was held to have been acting in the execution of his duty. It would not have been so if he had tried to detain him where there was no power to arrest.

Assaults upon constables frequently occur in police stations and, once again, the nature of the duties being undertaken at the time must be examined before this charge is preferred. A person who has not been arrested is entitled to leave a police station at any time unless he is detained under particular provisions which allow detention. An officer who attempts to prevent him from leaving a police station is not acting in the execution of his duty. In one case, two policewomen, in searching a prisoner in accordance with their interpretation of the chief constable's instructions, removed her brassiere and were assaulted by the prisoner. It was held that, regardless of those instructions, they were not acting in the execution of their duty if they had not personally considered whether such a search was necessary for a lawful purpose, or whether the removal of that garment was necessary for that particular person's protection. This is an interesting decision which clearly places responsibility for lawful search upon the officer conducting it.

Most assaults upon police officers still occur when they are dealing with disorderly persons in the street. The onerous nature of these duties is very much appreciated, as is the immediate pressure placed upon the officer and the suddenness with which assaults occur. However, the actions of the officer will always be considered in the calm of the courtroom! In one case, a group of noisy youths were told to move on by a constable. They were not sufficiently disorderly to merit arrest (under a power then existing for the offence of being drunk and disorderly). All moved with the exception of one who was lying on a seat. He eventually stood up and the officer took hold of his arm whilst he spoke to him, and refused to release it. It was considered that the constable was not acting in the execution of his duty as he did not apprehend a breach of the peace. However, on another occasion youths were shouting, swearing and causing a disturbance in the early hours of the morning. Constables told them to be quiet and go home. One refused and continued with his conduct and assaulted a constable who warned him that he would be arrested. The officer was held to have been acting in the execution of his duty as he had the power to arrest in this instance for a breach of the peace committed in his presence. In another case, where a constable witnessed an argument between a man and his girlfriend which resulted in the girl running away, it was held that he was entitled, after giving the girl directions to her home, to detain the man to speak to him to ensure that he would not follow the girl as he was acting in the execution of his duty to preserve the peace.

On occasions constables are given the authority to enter premises, and if they enter under such an authority they are acting in the execution of their duty. For example, the common law authorises a constable to enter premises to deal with a breach or apprehended breach of the peace (and it also authorises him to remain for this purpose if he is already on the premises); such a constable is acting in the execution of his duty. Response to a burglar alarm gives police an implied authority to enter premises for a reasonable time for the purpose of a search, but there is no legal right to enter premises found insecure at night. Where a constable is invited to enter premises by a member of the family and is later told to leave by the occupier, and he is assaulted by the occupier while he is immediately complying with that request, it is an assault upon him in the execution of his duty. On the other hand, he would no longer be in the execution of his duty if he did not comply with the request within a reasonable time because he would become a trespasser; if he was assaulted after the expiry of such a time an offence under PA 1996, s 89(1) would not be committed. Of course, it would be an offence under s 89(1) if the constable had remained to deal with a breach of the peace, because he would then be acting in the execution of his duty.

Under PA 1996, s 89(1) it is also an offence to assault a person assisting a constable in the execution of his duty. The reference to 'a person assisting a constable in the execution of his duty' includes reference to any person who is neither a constable nor in the company of a constable but who is a member of a joint investigation team (ie an investigation team established under an international framework) led by a member of a police force.

By PA 1996, s 89(3) the offence under s 89(1) may also be committed against constables of Scottish forces or the Police Service of Northern Ireland who are executing warrants or acting in England and Wales by virtue of any enactment. Similar amendments have been made to the laws of those countries to apply equivalent offences to acts against police officers of England and Wales so acting in those countries. Section 89(1) also applies to a constable of the British Transport Police Force in the same way as it applies to other constables in England and Wales (Railways and Transport Safety Act 2003, s 68(1)). A person carrying out surveillance in England and Wales under the Regulation of Investigatory Powers Act 2000, s 76A is treated as if he were acting as a constable in the execution of his duty (Crime (International Cooperation) Act 2003, s 84(1)).

The Police Reform Act 2002, s 46 creates similar offences in relation to assaults on, or the obstruction of, a designated or accredited person acting in the execution of his duty, or someone assisting such a person: see pp 276–277.

Obstructing or resisting a constable in the execution of his duty

It is an offence under PA 1996, s 89(2) for a person to resist or wilfully obstruct a constable in the execution of his duty, or a person assisting him. The provisions in PA 1996, s 89(3), the Railways and Transport Safety Act 2003, s 68(1) and the Crime (International Co-operation) Act 2003, s 84(1), mentioned above also apply to an offence under s 89(2).

To obstruct is to do any conduct which prevents or makes it more difficult for a constable to carry out his duty, and in this sense those who give warning of police speed checks obstruct the constables in the execution of their duty. A man who deliberately drinks alcohol after an accident to negative the breath testing procedure is also guilty of this offence. It has been held that a person who warns motorists of a police speed check is only guilty of obstructing a constable in the execution of his duty if the prosecution proves that the motorists warned were in fact speeding or were likely to be speeding at that location.

The obstruction must be 'wilful', which in this context means that:

(1) The accused's conduct which has resulted in the obstruction must have been deliberate and intended by him to bring about a state of affairs which, in fact, prevented or made it more difficult for the constable to carry out his duty, whether or not the accused realised that that state of affairs would have that effect.

(2) Also, the accused must have had no lawful excuse. Police officers often experience difficulty in obtaining names and addresses from offenders but a refusal to give such information will not amount to a wilful obstruction unless that person has a duty to give that information, because otherwise he will have a lawful excuse for his refusal. Nor, for the same reason, is it a wilful obstruction to advise someone not to answer police questions which he is not obliged to answer, even if the advice is given in an abusive way. Where a man told his brother repeatedly and in colourful language to say nothing to police officers who were seeking to question him in the street, it was held that, although he might have committed other offences, he did not thereby obstruct a police officer in the execution of his duty. It was not unlawful to so advise a person. Much of the traffic legislation imposes a duty to give particular types of information, but there is no such requirement in relation to most offences. Just as in the case of a failure to provide information, so in the case of other failures to assist the police (eg by failing to accord entry to a constable), there is only a wilful obstruction if the constable has the right to require the assistance in question, so that the accused is under a legal duty to provide it. An example would be where a constable has a statutory right of entry. A refusal to admit the constable in breach of the duty to admit him would be a wilful obstruction.

It has been held that an accused who believed that the person obstructed was not a constable could not be convicted of the present offence.

Like obstruction, resistance does not require an assault or battery. Probably, any resistance is also an obstruction, but resistance is a more appropriate word in certain cases (such as where a person arrested by a constable tears himself away).

What we said above about 'acting in the execution of his duty' is equally applicable to the offences of obstruction and resistance. Thus, for example, where a person seeks to prevent an arrest which, in the circumstances, is not a lawful arrest, he is not guilty of a wilful obstruction of a police officer acting in the execution of his duty since the officer will not be acting *in the execution of his duty*.

OFFENCES INVOLVING WOUNDING OR GRIEVOUS BODILY HARM

Malicious wounding or infliction of grievous bodily harm

OAPA 1861, s 20 provides two offences: malicious wounding, and malicious infliction of grievous bodily harm. Section 20 provides:

Whosoever shall unlawfully and maliciously wound or inflict any grievous bodily harm upon any other person, either with or without any weapon or instrument, shall be guilty of an offence.

Both offences have two elements in common: 'unlawfully' and 'maliciously'. The difference between them relates to their actus reus: 'wounding' and 'infliction of grievous bodily harm', and these terms will be discussed first.

Wounding or infliction of grievous bodily harm

The term 'wound' indicates a breaking of the continuity of the skin and means both layers of the skin. It is not possible, therefore, to allege that a wound has been inflicted if there is no breaking of the skin. Consequently, all injuries involving broken bones are excluded unless the bone pierces the skin. However, such injuries will amount to grievous bodily harm.

'Grievous bodily harm' means really serious harm; 'bodily harm' can include psychiatric injury or loss of consciousness but, of course, such injury must be serious in order to be grievous. It is not necessary that the nature of the harm should be either permanent or dangerous.

A wound can be caused or grievous bodily harm can be 'inflicted' even though it does not result from a battery; it is enough, instead, that it directly results from something done by the accused, as where someone infects another with AIDS or some other serious disease (which he conceals from the other) by having intercourse with him. A further example would be where the accused bangs on the locked door of a third-floor flat, threatening to kick it down and injure its occupant, and the terrified occupant jumps out of a window and breaks a leg when he hits the ground. Another example would be where a stalker behaves in such a way as to cause the woman serious psychiatric injury. In all these situations convictions for unlawfully and maliciously inflicting grievous bodily harm have been upheld on appeal. However, there may be difficulty in proving that a 'stalker' or anyone else who causes serious harm by a threat acted with the necessary mens rea, ie with intent or recklessness as to his conduct causing harm. Consequently, it will normally be more appropriate to charge an offence under the Protection from Harassment Act 1997, s 4 in such a case. We deal with this on p 880.

Unlawfully

This means 'without lawful justification' and is merely intended to except from the offence, in certain circumstances, acts done with a justification rendering the harm lawful, for example harm lawfully caused in self-defence.

Maliciously

The mens rea of an offence under OAPA 1861, s 20 is that the accused should have wounded or inflicted grievous bodily harm 'maliciously'. This does not mean that he must have acted out of spite or ill-will. Instead, what is required is that the accused must have intended his act to cause some unlawful harm to another, or been reckless as to whether some unlawful harm might result from his act (and this means that he must have realised the risk that some harm might result but unreasonably persisted in taking that risk). It must be emphasised that it is not necessary that the accused should have intended or foreseen harm of the gravity described in the section, ie a wound or really serious harm; foresight that some harm, albeit of a minor character, might result, is enough.

The fact that recklessness as to the risk of causing some unlawful bodily harm to another suffices for s 20 means that if the accused (D), knowing that he has the HIV virus or some other serious sexually transmitted disease, and therefore aware of the risk of infecting her, has intercourse with a woman (P) who consents to the intercourse in ignorance of D's disease, as D knows, D will be guilty of the present offence if P becomes infected with the disease and suffers grievous bodily harm in consequence.

Wounding or causing grievous bodily harm with intent to do grievous bodily harm or to resist or prevent arrest

OAPA 1861, s 18 provides:

Whosoever shall unlawfully and maliciously by any means whatsoever wound or cause grievous bodily harm to any person with intent to do grievous bodily harm to any person, or with intent to resist or prevent the lawful apprehension or detainer of any person, shall be guilty of an offence.

Clearly, an offence under s 18 is a very serious one; the nature of the maximum punishment (life imprisonment) is a factor to bear in mind when deciding which of the various nonfatal offences against the person to charge.

OAPA 1861, s 18 provides two offences: wounding with intent to do grievous bodily harm or with intent to resist the lawful apprehension or detainer of any person, and causing grievous bodily harm with one of these intents.

Actus reus

What was said in relation to OAPA 1861, s 20 in relation to the words 'unlawfully', 'wound' and 'grievous bodily harm' is equally applicable to OAPA 1861, s 18. However, s 18 specifies that grievous bodily harm must be 'caused' (as opposed to 'inflicted'). This difference in terminology between s 18 and s 20 raises the question of whether there is a difference of substance. Grievous bodily harm can be 'caused' by a deliberate and culpable omission to act; but opinions differ as to whether such harm can be 'inflicted' by a deliberate and culpable omission to act.

Mens rea

If the accused is charged with wounding with intent to do grievous bodily harm, or with causing grievous bodily harm with such intent, the word 'maliciously', the meaning of which was explained above, is redundant. An accused may wound or cause grievous bodily harm to any person with intent to cause grievous bodily harm to any person. It is not essential that the harm is caused to the particular person intended. An accused may be convicted of wounding Smith with intent, even though the accused thought that Smith was someone else or fired at Jones and hit Smith by accident. If a person fires a gun into a group of people without taking particular aim, but intending to harm someone, he may be charged with a s 18 offence against the person whom he hits.

The basic distinction between wounding or causing grievous bodily harm with intent to do grievous bodily harm and attempted murder is that, in the former offences, only an intent unlawfully to do grievous bodily harm is required, while the latter requires an intent unlawfully to kill.

Where the accused is charged with wounding with intent to resist or prevent the lawful apprehension or detainer of any person (whether himself or another), or with causing grievous bodily harm with such intent, 'maliciously' is relevant. It must be proved that the accused intended his conduct to cause *some* unlawful harm to another (or was reckless as to this occurring), ie that he was 'malicious', *and* that he intended to resist or prevent the lawful apprehension or detainer of himself or another.

Clearly, there is some overlap between the two specified intents. Thus, if an accused strikes a police officer, who is attempting lawfully to arrest him, with an iron bar which causes a serious wound it would be possible to charge him in one of two ways. If it is alleged that the wound was inflicted with the intention of causing grievous bodily harm, then the evidence offered should be to support that intention. It will serve no purpose to offer evidence of intention to resist arrest. However, out of the same circumstances the accused could be charged with wounding the officer with intent to resist his own arrest, and in such a case it would be necessary only to offer evidence of the nature of the wound, that he realised his act of striking the officer might cause some harm and that he struck the officer in order to resist arrest. In the circumstances described, where an iron bar was used to cause the wound, there would probably be little difficulty in proving either charge. If a less formidable weapon was used which nevertheless caused a serious wound, it might be difficult to prove an intention to cause grievous bodily harm. It would be much better to prefer a charge alleging an intention to resist arrest.

Differences between OAPA 1861, ss 18 and 20

It is interesting to consider the essential differences between offences described in OAPA 1861, ss 18 and 20. If, during an argument, an accused strikes a person with a stick, causing a cut to his head which requires stitches, there has certainly been a wound which was unlawful, in that it could not legally be excused. Malice was apparent, as the act indicated a decision on the part of the assailant to do some unlawful bodily harm. All the essential points required under s 20 to be proved are therefore capable of proof. If we are to consider whether an offence contrary to s 18 is disclosed, we must ask ourselves if it can be proved that the assailant intended to cause grievous bodily harm when the blow was struck. The surrounding circumstances will help; any words said by the accused at the time, the ferocity of the attack and the nature of the weapon used. If the stick used was light in weight and one blow was struck, this would not support the allegation that the accused intended to cause grievous bodily harm. If the stick was heavy and metal tipped, the blow struck was severe, and it could be shown that the accused shouted an intention to do serious harm to the person injured, then an intention to cause such harm could be more easily established.

Finally, an important fact to remember is that 'maliciously' for the purpose of OAPA 1861, s 20 suggests an awareness, at least, that the act may cause some physical harm to some other person. It is not necessary that an accused should have foreseen physical harm of the gravity described in the section, that is, a wound or serious bodily harm. It is enough that it is foreseen that some harm might result. This would not suffice for s 18; an intention to cause grievous bodily harm must be proved, or an intention to resist etc arrest.

RACIALLY- OR RELIGIOUSLY-AGGRAVATED NON-FATAL OFFENCES AGAINST THE PERSON

The Crime and Disorder Act 1998 (CDA 1998), s 29 has introduced the following new offences.

CDA 1998, s 29(1) provides that:

A person is guilty of an offence under this section if he commits:
(a) an offence under section 20 of the Offences against the Person Act 1861;
(b) an offence under section 47 of that Act;
(c) common assault [or battery];
which is racially or religiously aggravated for the purposes of this section.

CDA 1998, s 29(1) does not create one offence which can be committed in various ways but a number of separate ones.

On a charge of an offence under CDA 1998, s 29, the prosecution must prove that the accused has committed one of the relevant specified basic offences and that it (the basic offence) was racially- or religiously-aggravated.

By CDA 1998, s 28(1), any of the specified basic offences is racially- or religiously-aggravated if:

(a) at the time of committing the offence, or immediately before or after doing so, the offender demonstrates towards the victim of the offence hostility based on the victim's membership (or presumed membership) of a racial or religious group; or
(b) the offence is motivated (wholly or partly) by hostility towards members of a racial or religious group based on their membership of that group.

In (a), 'membership', in relation to a racial or religious group, includes association with members of that group; 'presumed' means presumed by the offender (CDA 1998, s 28(2)). 'Racial group' means a group of persons defined by reference to race, colour, nationality (including citizenship) or ethnic or national origins (CDA 1998, s 28(4)). These words are given a broad, non-technical interpretation. A group will be a racial group defined by reference to race if, in ordinary speech, those people would be regarded as belonging to a named race. On this basis 'African' denotes a racial group. It has been held that, just as all who are black or all who are white, form a racial group within the definition, so do all who are foreign. A 'religious group' is a group of persons defined by reference to religious belief or lack of religious belief, eg Muslims or Rastafarians.

Because (a) does not require the accused's conduct to be motivated by racial or religious hatred, but simply requires the demonstration of such hatred (as defined), it is possible for a person to fall within (a) even though he is of the same colour etc as the victim of his conduct. This was held by a divisional court in a case where it upheld the conviction of an accused whose conduct had demonstrated hostility based on the victim's membership of a racial group which was the same as the accused's.

For the test under (a) to be satisfied, the accused must have formed the view that the victim was a member of a racial group (or religious group, as the case may be) and the accused must have done or said something which demonstrated hostility towards the victim based on that membership. Words used need not expressly identify the racial or religious group to which the victim belongs. This was held by the Court of Appeal in a case where the victim was Indian and brown skinned. He was called an 'immigrant doctor' by the accused immediately before the accused assaulted him. The Court of Appeal held that it was open to the jury to conclude that the accused had identified her victim as falling within the racial groups of Indian and brown-skinned and that the use of 'immigrant' demonstrated hostility based on the victim's membership of such groups.

(a) does not require the hostility demonstrated to be based only on the victim's membership of a racial or religious group, or even principally on it. Thus, in one reported divisional court case, the fact that the hostility demonstrated was based more on a dispute over food at a kebab shop than a racial hostility did not prevent racial aggravation being proved under (a). However, the more incidental the words or other conduct with a racial or religious content, the more difficult it will be to prove that the accused has demonstrated racial or religious hostility. In this context it must be emphasised that it is not enough simply to refer, for example, to the victim's race or religion; the accused must be proved to have demonstrated 'hostility' based on the victim's membership, or presumed membership of a racial or religious group. Where a man of Asian origin attacked an Asian caretaker at a community centre and called him a 'white man's arse licker' and a 'brown Englishman' it was held that what he said was not in any material sense based upon the caretaker's membership of the Asian race but upon hostility to the caretaker's conduct on that night. The phrases used did not, therefore, make the assault into a racially aggravated one. The Court of Appeal said that an offence of racially-aggravated common assault might be made out if a white man was to assault another white man and make such a remark as 'nigger lover' when noting that man's association with a group of black persons.

The word 'immediately' in (a) qualifies 'after' as well as 'before'; (a) strikes at words uttered or acts done in the immediate context of the basic substantive offence. Thus, a divisional court held that a racially aggravated offence was not made out where the accused demonstrated racial hostility to the victim only twenty minutes after committing the basic offence, while being questioned by the police.

Although (a) requires proof of what the accused did at the time of committing the offence, (b) can be established by evidence relating to what the accused may have said or done on other occasions (since such evidence may be relevant to the accused's motivation at the time of the offence).

OTHER OFFENCES INVOLVING BODILY INJURY

The OAPA 1861 includes other offences which are associated with the causing, or attempted causing, of forms of bodily harm. These offences and the other offences set out in the rest of this chapter should be considered when circumstances are presented involving actual or attempted harm to a person. They are concerned with particular ways of inflicting harm.

Attempting to choke etc

This offence, which is provided by OAPA 1861, s 21, consists of an attempt by the accused, by any means whatsoever, to choke, suffocate or strangle any other person, or an attempt by the accused, by any means calculated to choke, suffocate, or strangle, to render any other person insensible, unconscious or incapable of resistance, with intent in any such case thereby to enable himself or any other person to commit any indictable offence, or with intent to assist another to do so.

The offence differs from those against OAPA 1861, ss 18 and 20. There needs to be only an attempt to render a person unconscious, or incapable of resistance, with intent to commit any indictable offence. A wound etc is not necessary.

Using chloroform etc to commit an indictable offence

This offence is provided by OAPA 1861, s 22. There must be an unlawful application or administration to, or causing to be taken by, a person a stupefying or overpowering drug, matter or thing, with intent thereby to enable the accused or another person to commit an indictable offence.

Administering poison etc so as thereby to endanger life etc or with intent to injure etc

OAPA 1861, s 23 provides that a person is guilty of an offence if he unlawfully and maliciously administers to, or causes to be administered to or taken by, any other person any poison, or other destructive or noxious thing, *so as thereby to endanger the life of such person, or so as thereby to inflict upon such person any grievous bodily harm.*

OAPA 1861, s 24 provides that a person is guilty of an offence if he unlawfully and maliciously administers to, or causes to be administered to or taken by, any other person any poison, or other destructive or noxious thing, *with intent to injure, aggrieve, or annoy such person.*

A 'poison' means a recognised poison, in whatever quantity it may be administered etc; a 'noxious thing' is any other drug or thing which is harmful in the dosage in which it was administered etc. 'Administer' does not necessarily involve the application of direct physical force and covers, for example, the spraying of tear gas from a distance. Where a person acts in concert with another who self-injects a drug (for example by holding a tourniquet around that person's arm while he self-injects or by preparing and giving that person the drug for immediate self-injection), both persons can be regarded as administering the drug because their actions are interlinked (though separate) parts of the overall process of administering the drug. A poison, or other destructive or noxious thing, is caused to be taken if it is left for a person who then drinks it. To leave it for the purpose of it being taken would be to attempt to cause it to be taken.

The consent of the person to whom the poison is given is no defence to charges under OAPA 1861, s 23 or 24. For example, heroin can be a noxious substance for the purposes of these offences. If a shot of heroin is administered to another with his consent, this will amount to an administration for the purposes of this section.

The distinction between the offences under OAPA 1861, ss 23 and 24 lies partly in the fact that the offence under OAPA 1861, s 23 requires the additional element that the administration must be such as thereby to endanger life or to inflict grievous bodily harm, and partly in the fact that the requirement of mens rea is not the same for each offence. The differences between the two offences are shown by the words italicised in the definitions given above.

The mens rea required is as follows. The offence under OAPA 1861, s 23 requires proof of intention or recklessness in relation to the administration etc of a poison or other destructive or noxious thing and as to the causing of some bodily harm, but not in relation to the second element of the actus reus, the endangering of life or causing grievous bodily harm. In the case of an offence under s 24 not only must an intentional or reckless administration etc of a poison or other destructive or noxious thing be proved but also an intention to injure, aggrieve or annoy. The intention or recklessness referred to above is what is meant by 'maliciously' in the definitions of the two offences.

Torture

The offence of torture is governed by CJA 1988, s 134. A public official or person acting in an official capacity, whatever his nationality, commits the offence of torture if in the United Kingdom or elsewhere he intentionally inflicts severe pain or suffering on another in the performance or purported performance of his official duties. A person not acting in such an official capacity commits the offence of torture if he commits such an act at the instigation, or with the consent or acquiescence, of a public official or person acting in that capacity, and the official or other person is performing or purporting to perform his official duties when he instigates the commission of the offence or consents to or acquiesces in it.

It is immaterial whether the pain or suffering is physical or mental and whether it is caused by an act or omission. It is a defence for a person to prove that he had lawful authority, justification or excuse for that conduct.

The consent of the Attorney-General is required for a prosecution in England and Wales for the offence of torture. Police officers will certainly find themselves in situations which expose them to allegations of offences under this section, particularly in view of the inclusion of 'mental' suffering. It is submitted that this offence is not applicable to those situations which might arise in the course of interviews in normal circumstances.

CHILD ABDUCTION

Two offences of child abduction are provided by the Child Abduction Act 1984 (CAA 1984). These offences contain a number of common features; these will be dealt with after the separate offences have been outlined.

Abduction from the United Kingdom by parent etc

By CAA 1984, s 1, a person connected with a child under sixteen commits an offence if he takes or sends the child *out of the United Kingdom* without the appropriate consent. A person is regarded as 'sending' a child if he causes the child to be sent. A prosecution for this offence may only be instituted by or with the consent of the Director of Public Prosecutions.

For the purposes of the offence, a person is 'connected with' a child if:

(a) he is the child's parent, guardian or special guardian; or
(b) he has custody of the child (ie has sole or joint custody, legal custody or care and control of the child by a United Kingdom court order); or
(c) in the case of a child, whose parents were not married to each other at the time of his birth, there are reasonable grounds for believing that he is its father; or
(d) he is a guardian or special guardian of the child; or
(e) he is the person in whose favour a residence order is in force in respect of the child.

Only persons falling within these categories can commit the present offence.

The reference to the 'appropriate consent', in relation to the removal or sending of the child out of the United Kingdom, means:

(a) the consent of *each* of the following:
    (i)   the child's mother;
    (ii) the child's father, if he has parental responsibility for him;
    (iii) any guardian or special guardian of the child;
    (iv) any person in whose favour a residence order is in force with respect to the child;
    (v) any person who has custody of the child; or
(b) the leave of the court granted under or by virtue of Part II of the Children Act 1989; or
(c) if any person has custody of the child, the leave of the court which granted custody to him.

A person does not commit the present offence by taking or sending a child out of the United Kingdom without the appropriate consent:

(a) if he is the person in whose favour there is a residence order in respect of the child, and he takes or sends the child out of the United Kingdom for a period of less than one month; or
(b) if he is a special guardian of the child and takes or sends it out of the United Kingdom for a period of less than three months,

unless he is in breach of an order under Part II of the Children Act 1989.

A person does not commit the present offence by doing anything without the consent of another person whose consent is required if:

(a) he does it in the belief that the other person has consented or would consent if he was aware of all the relevant circumstances; or
(b) he has taken all reasonable steps to communicate with the other person but has been unable to communicate with him; or
(c) the other person has unreasonably refused to consent.

However, the last alternative (ie (c)) does not apply where the person who refused consent is a person in whose favour there is a residence order, or who is a special guardian of the child, or who has custody of the child; or where the taking or sending is in breach of any court direction under certain statutory provisions.

There are special provisions where the child is in the care of a local authority or a voluntary organisation, or is the subject of custodianship proceedings or of proceedings (or an order) for adoption, or is in a place of safety.

Abduction of child by other persons

This offence is governed by CAA 1984, s 2. It can be committed by anyone other than:

(a) the father or mother (if they were married when the child was born) or the mother (if they were not); or
(b) the child's guardian; or
(c) a person with a residence order, or custody, in respect of the child.

Another important difference from the offence under CAA 1984, s 1 is that the child need not be abducted from the United Kingdom.

CAA 1984, s 2 provides that anyone, other than a person mentioned above, commits an offence if, without lawful authority or reasonable excuse, he takes or detains a child under sixteen so as either to remove him from the lawful control of anyone having lawful control of him or to keep him out of the lawful control of any person entitled to it. Removal from control does not require any removal in a geographical sense; it suffices to deflect the child from what he would be otherwise doing with the consent of those having lawful control of him into some activity induced by the accused, as where the accused finds a child in a park pursuing a particular activity (eg playing football) and induces it to go elsewhere in the park for another activity (eg to look for an alleged lost bicycle).

There can be a 'taking' for the purposes of CAA 1984, s 2 despite the fact that a child consents provided that the acts of the accused were a cause of the child accompanying him and such acts are more than just peripheral or inconsequential. If the acts of the accused are an effective cause of the child accompanying him, that is sufficient.

A person is regarded as detaining a child if he causes him to be detained or induces the child to remain with him or another.

It must be proved that the accused intended, when taking the child, to keep him out of the control of someone known to be entitled to such control.

It is a defence for the accused to prove that, at the time of the alleged offence, he believed the child was sixteen or over. Alternatively, in the case where the father and mother of 'the child in question' (ie the child taken or detained) were not married to each other at the time of birth, it is a defence for the accused to prove that he is the father of the child taken or detained or that he had reasonable grounds to believe he was that child's father. Lastly, a person is not guilty of an offence under CAA 1984, s 2 if he mistakenly believed, reasonably or not, in facts which—if they had been as he believed—would have given him a lawful authority or reasonable excuse. On this basis, a man who takes a child, thinking that it is his child whereas in truth it is another child, will not be guilty if, on the facts as he believes them to be, he would have a lawful authority or reasonable excuse for taking the child.

General

For the purposes of both offences, a person is regarded as taking a child if he causes or induces the child to accompany him or any other person, or causes the child to be taken.

It is irrelevant that the child consents to what occurs.

KIDNAPPING

The offences which have just been discussed are concerned with the abduction of particular persons, specially protected because of their age. The common law offence of kidnapping knows no such boundaries and can be committed whenever there is an unlawful taking or carrying away of any person by force or by fraud.

In 1984 the House of Lords held that the offence involves four requirements:

(a) The taking or carrying away of one person by another

It is irrelevant whether the taking or carrying away is to some other place within the jurisdiction or to some place outside it. Although the person taken or carried away is often secreted thereafter, this is not a requirement of the offence. The offence can be committed even though the defendant only took the victim where the victim wanted to go, if the taking is by fraud.

(b) The taking or carrying away must be by force or by fraud

'Force' is not limited to physical force or the threat of it. It encompasses any conduct which, coupled with the taking or carrying away (ingredient (a)), overrides the true consent of the person taken or carried away (ingredient (c)). Thus, the exercise of mental or moral power or influence to compel another to do something against his will can suffice if it overcomes his will. Any fraud which induces the victim to consent to being taken or carried away will suffice, and will invalidate the victim's apparent consent.

(c) The taking or carrying away must be without the consent of the person taken or carried away

This requirement must be satisfied whatever the age of that person. However, there can be a kidnapping, even though the person carried away consents at first, if he changes his mind and ceases to consent while still being carried away. In the case of a very young child, it does not have the understanding or intelligence to give consent so that the absence of consent will be a necessary inference from its age. In the case of an older child, it is a question of fact for the jury whether the child had sufficient understanding or intelligence to give consent and, if so, whether absence of consent has been proved. Unlike child abduction, the presence or absence of consent on the part of the person having custody or care and control of a child victim is immaterial (except that such consent may support a defence of lawful excuse). Likewise the presence or absence of consent on the part of other people, such as the spouse of a person who is taken, is immaterial.

The Court of Appeal has stated that, because taking or carrying away by fraud is part of the definition of kidnapping, issues of consent will rarely arise, if ever, because a victim who has been deceived will not have consented to being taken or carried away by fraud where fraud is involved.

It must be proved that a person charged with kidnapping knew or was reckless that he did not have the victim's consent.

(d) The taking or carrying away must be without lawful excuse

Clearly, for example, a parent (or other person) with custody of a child will often have a lawful excuse for taking or carrying away the child. An exception would be where this contravenes a court order in relation to the child.

Procedural points

Kidnapping is a relevant indictable offence for the purposes of the law relating to search warrants.

The House of Lords has held that the conduct of a parent who snatches his own child in defiance of a court order relating to its custody or care and control (such as one making the child a ward of court) should normally be dealt with as a contempt of court rather than as the subject matter of a prosecution for kidnapping, unless the parent's conduct was particularly bad.

The Child Abduction Act 1984, s 5 provides that the consent of the Director of Public Prosecutions to the institution of a prosecution for kidnapping is required wherever the victim is under sixteen or where the prosecution is against a parent or guardian etc.

HOSTAGE TAKING

The Taking of Hostages Act 1982, s 1 makes it an offence for a person of any nationality to detain in the United Kingdom or elsewhere any other person (a hostage) and, in order to compel any state, international governmental organisation, or person, to do or abstain from doing any act, to threaten to kill, injure or continue to detain the hostage. The consent of the Attorney-General is required before a prosecution may be brought for this offence.

CONTAMINATION OF GOODS ETC WITH INTENT

POA 1986, s 38(1) provides that it is an offence for a person to contaminate or interfere with goods, or make it appear that goods have been contaminated or interfered with, or to place goods which have been contaminated or interfered with, or which have that appearance, in a place where goods of that description are consumed, used, sold or otherwise supplied, with the intention:

(a) of causing public alarm or anxiety;
(b) of causing injury to members of the public consuming or using the goods;
(c) of causing economic loss to any person by reason of the goods being shunned by members of the public; or
(d) of causing economic loss to any person by reason of steps taken to avoid any such alarm or anxiety, injury or loss.

POA 1986, s 38(2) makes it an offence for a person to threaten that he or another will do, or claim that he or another has done, any of these acts with such intention as is mentioned in (a), (c) or (d) above. Possession of contaminated goods, apparently contaminated goods, materials with which to contaminate goods or to make it appear that goods have been contaminated, is also an offence.

Thus, the activities of groups, including animal rights groups, calculated to hit at businesses with which they are not in sympathy are made punishable under this section. However, it must be remembered that such activities may also amount to attempts to commit offences (for example, attempted murder, if poisons are placed in foodstuffs with an intention of killing, since the placing of the contaminated goods is more than merely a preparatory act which can amount to an attempt). In addition, if someone actually consumes a contaminated product and suffers harm, there will be liability for the relevant 'full' offence against the person, depending on the degree of harm.

A defence is available to a person who, in good faith, reports or warns that such acts have been, or appear to have been, committed. Thus, the broadcast of a warning received, if carried out in good faith, is excused.

GUNPOWDER ETC OFFENCES

The OAPA 1861 creates a number of offences related to the use of explosives.

OAPA 1861, s 28 provides that anyone, who unlawfully and maliciously, by the explosion of gunpowder or other explosive substance, *burns, maims, disfigures, disables or does any grievous bodily harm to any person*, is guilty of an offence.

OAPA 1861, s 29 provides that anyone, who unlawfully and maliciously causes an explosion, or sends or delivers an explosive substance (or any other dangerous or noxious thing), or places or throws at someone any corrosive fluid or any destructive or explosive substance, *with intent to burn, maim, disfigure, or disable any person, or to do some grievous bodily harm to any person*, is guilty of an offence, whether or not any bodily injury is effected.

OAPA 1861, s 30 provides that it is an offence unlawfully and maliciously to place or throw in, into, upon, against or near any building or vessel an explosive substance *with intent to do any bodily injury to any person, whether or not any explosion occurs and whether or not anyone is injured.*

It has been held that a petrol bomb is an explosive substance under s 29, since where a person puts petrol and air into a bottle together with a wick, lights that wick and throws the bottle, an explosion must be caused. This decision is equally applicable to the meaning of 'explosive substance' in ss 28 and 30.

Clearly, there is a good deal of overlap between the three offences, especially those under OAPA 1861, ss 28 and 29. The major distinguishing features of each offence is indicated by the words italicised. The basic distinction is that s 28 is concerned with where really serious bodily harm is actually caused by an explosion, while it suffices for s 29 that the accused caused an explosion with intent to cause such harm, whether or not it occurred; in fact, s 29 does not require an explosion to occur since it is also concerned with sending or delivering, or placing or throwing, explosives and certain other substances with such intent. Section 30 does not require anyone to be harmed but it does require the accused to act with the specified intent to do bodily injury (which need not be serious injury).

OAPA 1861, s 64 makes it an offence to make, manufacture or knowingly possess explosive substances or machines, engines, or instruments with intent to commit any offence under OAPA 1861, or with intent to enable others to do so.

When circumstances are being considered involving the use of explosives, it must be remembered that offences under the Criminal Damage Act 1971 and the Explosive Substances Act 1883 must also be considered. However, if the bomber etc has the requisite specified intent to cause really serious bodily harm (OAPA 1861, s 29) or bodily injury (OAPA 1861, s 30), or actually causes really serious bodily harm (OAPA 1861, s 28), an offence will always be committed under OAPA 1861.

CHAPTER 29
Disputes

Quite a large part of a police officer's time is spent in advising members of the public of action which they may take in relation to disputes involving them and their spouses, cohabitees, other members of their families, landlords and the like. On occasions it is appropriate to have recourse to the criminal law, but on most occasions the most useful approach may be to put them in touch with one of the various agencies which are equipped to deal with such situations. In many cases civil remedies are available and particularly appropriate. It is important for police officers constantly to be aware that they are what might be described as a front line agency. Because the police service offers an immediate response throughout twenty-four hours of the day, police officers will most often be involved in such disputes, or incidents, when they occur or very soon afterwards.

DOMESTIC VIOLENCE

For convenience, we shall refer to the victim of domestic violence as a woman but it must not be forgotten that sometimes the victim in such a case is a man. Domestic violence accounts for a quarter of reported violent crime. Quite rightly the Crown Prosecution Service does not regard violence in the domestic context as a mitigating factor but as an aggravating one. The subject of non-fatal offences and homicide offences is considered elsewhere. A woman who has been injured by her husband, civil partner or cohabitee is competent and compellable to give evidence against that person in a criminal court in relation to the offence in question, and may wish to do so. Likewise, a family member who has been subject to domestic violence is competent and compellable. However, it will be appreciated that this is frequently an extremely difficult decision for a wife, partner or family member to make. Many women, for example, feel trapped and helpless and, being unable to face up to life on their own, prefer to remain with a husband who treats them badly. In such circumstances they will not wish to give evidence against their husbands because of their fear that this will lead to a final breakdown of the marriage. The social services are experienced in the handling of these situations and will help if the wife will accept such aid.

Where a woman (or member of a family who is a child) has been subjected to domestic violence, the courts can assist without the necessity for the woman to give evidence in a criminal court. She can seek assistance by applying for one of the orders under the Family Law Act 1996 (FLA 1996), described below, which are not limited to proceedings between spouses (or ex-spouses), civil partners (or ex-civil partners) or cohabitees (or ex-cohabitees).

Non-molestation orders

A non-molestation order is an order containing either or both of the following provisions:

(a) provision prohibiting a person (the respondent) from molesting another person who is associated with the defendant;
(b) provision prohibiting the respondent from molesting a relevant child.

A person 'associated with' the respondent may apply for a non-molestation order under FLA 1996, s 42. A person is 'associated with' the respondent if she is the spouse (or ex-spouse), civil partner (or ex-civil partner) or cohabitant (or ex-cohabitant) of the respondent, or a member (or ex-member) of the same household, or a relative, or a fiancée (or ex-fiancée) or (when the Domestic Violence, Crime and Victims Act 2004, s 4 is in force) has had an intimate personal relationship with the respondent which is or was of significant duration. 'Cohabitant' means someone who, although not married to the respondent, is living together with him as wife and husband (or (if of the same sex) in an equivalent relationship). In addition, where the proceedings brought by the applicant relate to a child, the respondent is associated with the child if he is the parent or has had parental responsibility for it.

A 'relevant child' in relation to such proceedings is any child who is living with or might reasonably be expected to live with either party to the proceedings, or any child in relation to whom an order under the Adoption Act 1976 or the Children Act 1989 is in question in the proceedings, or any other child whose interests the court considers relevant.

Such an order may be made:

(a) on the application (whether in other family proceedings or without any other family proceedings being instituted) of a person who is associated with the respondent; or
(b) during family proceedings to which the respondent is a party, if the court considers that such an order will benefit any other party or a relevant child even though no application has been made.

In deciding whether to make a non-molestation order, the court must consider all the circumstances, including the need to secure the health, safety and well-being of the applicant or any relevant child.

A non-molestation order may refer to molestation in general, to particular acts of molestation, or both. It may be made for a specified period, or until a further order is made. An order which is made in other family proceedings ceases to have effect if those proceedings are withdrawn or dismissed.

Complaint without notice to the other party

Where it appears to be just and convenient to do so a court may, under FLA 1996, s 45, make a non-molestation order even though the party against whom the complaint is made has not been given notice of the proceedings. In such cases, the court must consider:

(a) the risk of significant harm if the order is not made immediately;
(b) whether if such an order is not made the applicant will be deterred or prevented from pursuing the application; and
(c) whether there is reason to believe that the party complained against is aware of the proceedings but is deliberately evading service of the notice and the other applicant, or a relevant child, will be seriously prejudiced by the delay involved in effecting service (or substituted service) of the proceedings.

Where an order is made on a complaint without notice to the other party, it must afford the person against whom it is made an opportunity to make representations as soon as just and convenient, at a full hearing.

Offence of breaching non-molestation order

Under FLA 1996, s 42A, a person who without reasonable excuse does anything that he is prohibited from doing by a non-molestation order is guilty of an offence. In the case of an order made without notice to the other party, a person can be guilty of the offence only in respect of conduct engaged in when he was aware of the existence of the order.

Undertakings

Where a non-molestation order could be made, a court may accept an undertaking from any party to the proceedings. Where such an undertaking is given breach of it is not an offence. However, the undertaking is enforceable in civil law in the same way as a court order, except that no power of arrest attaches to its breach. Where a power to arrest appears to be appropriate, an undertaking should not be accepted by a court.

Rights associated with the matrimonial home

Where domestic disputes occur, regardless of whether or not a non-molestation order has been sought, the issue of occupational rights in relation to the home still remains. The FLA 1996 seeks to ensure that all sides to a dispute are protected from eviction.

Where one spouse has no estate, etc

FLA 1996, s 30 provides that, where one spouse or civil partner (A) is legally entitled to occupy a dwelling house and the other spouse or civil partner (B) has no such legal entitlement, B has 'home rights' which means that:

(a) if B is in occupation, B has a right not to be evicted or excluded from the dwelling house or any part of it by A without the leave of the court under FLA 1996, s 33;
(b) if B is not in occupation, B has a right with the leave of the court under FLA 1996, s 33 'to enter and occupy the dwelling-house'.

There is, therefore, no lawful way by which one party to a marriage or civil partnership can be removed from the matrimonial home without the circumstances being examined by a court (ie the High Court, a county court or a magistrates' court sitting as a family proceedings court). However, FLA 1996, s 59 provides that a magistrates' court will not be competent to entertain any application, or make any order, where there is a dispute as to a party's entitlement to occupy property by virtue of beneficial estate, interest or contract or by virtue of any enactment giving him the right to remain in occupation, unless it is unnecessary to determine the question in order to deal with the application or make the order. In any case, a magistrates' court may decline jurisdiction if it considers that the application can more conveniently be dealt with by another court. In addition, a magistrates' court has no power to suspend or rescind orders made under FLA 1996.

Occupation orders

FLA 1996, s 33 provides for the making of an occupation order where the applicant has an estate or interest etc entitling him to occupy a dwelling house or has home rights in it and the dwelling house is or has been the home of the applicant and of someone else with whom he is associated (or was intended by both such people to be their home). If an occupation order is made it may:

(a) enforce the applicant's occupation rights as against the other person (the respondent);
(b) require the respondent to permit the applicant to enter and remain in that dwelling house or part of it;
(c) regulate the occupation by both parties;
(d) if the respondent is legally entitled to occupy, prohibit, restrict or suspend the exercise by him of his occupation rights;
(e) if the respondent has home rights and the applicant is the other spouse, restrict or terminate those rights;
(f) require the respondent to leave the dwelling house or part of it; or
(g) exclude the respondent from a defined area in which the dwelling house is included.

In deciding whether to make an occupation order and (if so) in what manner, the court must have regard to all of the circumstances including the housing needs and housing resources of both parties and any child, the financial resources of both parties, the likely effect of any order (or of a failure to make an order) on the health, safety or well-being of each party and child, and the conduct of the parties in relation to each other and otherwise.

Former spouse, civil partner, cohabitee and situations in which neither spouse has an entitlement to occupy

FLA 1996 makes similar provisions in relation to former spouses, civil partners and cohabitees where one of them is legally entitled to occupy a dwelling house. It also makes provision for circumstances in which neither spouse or civil partner (or ex-spouse or ex-civil partner) has a legal entitlement to occupy a dwelling house which is (or was) the matrimonial home. These provisions are set out in FLA 1996, ss 35 to 38.

Breaches of occupation order and other points

There is a power to arrest without warrant for breach of an occupation order where such a power has been attached to the order; otherwise an application must be made for an arrest warrant. 'Undertakings' and orders without notice to the other party may be made in respect of these orders in the same way as in the case of non-molestation orders.

Police action

Arrest for other offences

Serious or minor offences may have been committed, or be reasonably suspected within such incidents. If so, a constable will have the normal power of arrest if the requirements of PACE, s 24 are satisfied. However, note must be taken of the changes to a constable's powers to arrest under s 24 effected by the Serious Organised Crime and Police Act 2005.

The powers which exist at common law in relation to breaches of the peace may also be relevant in the circumstances.

Police action—when contact is first made

When a first contact is made with the police, it should be determined whether immediate response is required or whether there is no immediate danger. Such complaints must be recorded bearing in mind that where a crime is alleged, it should be so recorded. Existing records should be checked to establish whether there is any previous record of incidents involving the complainant. Generally, if the victim claims to have been violently assaulted, reconciliation should not be attempted. Where the victim is a woman, a woman police officer should attend such incidents where possible as a woman who has been assaulted may prefer to be dealt with by another woman. A woman police officer should also attend where the victim is a girl or young boy. Any interview at the time should not take place in the presence of the alleged assailant. However, if a complainant wishes to repeat any allegation in the presence of the alleged assailant, she may do so and any reply made by the assailant should be noted.

If hospital treatment is not required, a victim may be taken to a victim examination suite if one is available. A medical examination by a police surgeon or some other doctor with forensic science training is preferable to examination by her own general practitioner. It is important to ensure that children are adequately cared for throughout this procedure. Other members of the family, or neighbours, may prove to be good witnesses in such cases, particularly where the victim is reluctant to become involved.

In domestic violence cases it is essential that the Crown Prosecution Service is fully informed of the circumstances surrounding the family relationships involved, the domestic circumstances and the likely course of future events including whether there is any likelihood of any lasting reconciliation.

It is important to ensure that victims continue to receive help and guidance in such cases from bodies such as Women's Aid Federation, Refuge, and Childline. It may also be necessary to remove the victim to a place of shelter (or, in the case of children, a place of safety) before making long-term arrangements with some other social agency. Some police forces have domestic violence units which specialise in such matters. Where it is necessary for the victim to live elsewhere, the police should assist in taking her to a place of refuge. If she subsequently wishes to visit the home for any reason she should be accompanied by a police officer.

Recent changes in the law permit the setting up of a system within which female victims of domestic violence will be spared court appearances which bring them into contact with their attackers.

Where complainant subsequently withdraws complaint

Where a victim subsequently decides to withdraw her complaint and states that she will be unwilling to give evidence in court she should be asked to make a statement to that effect. This will be taken into account by the Crown Prosecutor who may, nevertheless, take steps to compel the complainant to give evidence against her husband.

The Crown Prosecutor will also wish to take into account the views of the officer who recorded that statement concerning the validity of the complainant's reasons and her likely reaction to being compelled to give evidence. Where a victim refuses to give evidence it may be possible to continue the case by offering her statement in evidence in accordance with the rules set out on pp 229–230.

EVICTION AND HARASSMENT

It is essential for the law to protect tenants of property. If it were otherwise they would be subject to the risk of instant eviction from the premises at the whim of a landlord, or to the risk of extreme measures to ensure that they left the property, such as shutting off the essential services to the dwelling house.

Police officers frequently become involved in disputes concerning landlords and tenants and, although they are usually called to prevent a breach of the peace, it is essential that the correct advice is given to both parties. Personal sympathies must be set aside and a clear explanation of the legal position must be provided together with advice concerning the agencies which may be approached to assist in resolving the dispute.

The Protection from Eviction Act 1977 (PEA 1977), s 1 provides two offences whose aim is to protect tenants: the offences of eviction and of harassment. The Act specifically authorises district councils to institute proceedings for these offences. Both offences use the term 'residential occupier' and this must first be explained.

A 'residential occupier', in relation to any premises, means a person occupying the premises as a residence, whether under a contract or by virtue of any enactment or rule of law giving him the right to remain in occupation or restricting the right of any other person to recover possession of the premises. Therefore, a tenant, or even a lodger who is living in a furnished room under an agreement with the owner, is a residential occupier. However, a person who hires a room for a short period of time is not a residential occupier. This is fortunate, because otherwise landladies who offered holiday accommodation would be unable to repossess rooms to meet their obligations towards successive visitors. The issue is best resolved by common sense; could the accommodation in question be properly described as the person's residence?

Eviction

PEA 1977, s 1(2) provides:

If any person unlawfully deprives the residential occupier of any premises of his occupation of the premises or any part thereof, or attempts to do so, he is guilty of an offence unless he proves that he believed, and had reasonable cause to believe, that the residential occupier had ceased to reside in the premises.

The manner in which the residential occupier is unlawfully deprived of his occupation is unimportant as any unlawful method will constitute an offence. It is not necessary that any form of violence or intimidation is used; it would be sufficient if the residential occupier was tricked into leaving so that the owner could regain occupation, or that the owner entered by stealth during the residential occupier's absence. The offence requires something in the nature of an eviction. The deprivation of occupation need not be permanent. Consequently, a person who unlawfully excludes a residential occupier from his premises, intending the exclusion to be permanent, can he convicted under PEA 1977, s 1(2) even though he repents almost immediately and lets the occupier back in.

An offence is committed by any person who unlawfully deprives, or attempts to deprive, a residential occupier of his premises. The commission of the offence is not restricted to the owner or any person having an interest in the property; it can be committed by anyone and this is meant to prevent the use of other persons to apply pressure in an attempt to dispossess. The only defence, which must be proved by the accused, is one of reasonable belief that the residential occupier has ceased to reside in the premises. The House of Lords has held that putting the onus of proving this defence on the accused is not incompatible with the presumption of innocence under the European Convention on Human Rights, art 6(2).

Harassment

PEA 1977, s 1(3) deals with harassment and provides:

If any person with intent to cause the residential occupier of any premises—

(a) to give up the occupation of the premises or any part thereof; or
(b) to refrain from exercising any right or pursuing any remedy in respect of the premises or
part thereof;

does any act calculated to interfere with the peace or comfort of the residential occupier or members of his household, or persistently withdraws or withholds services reasonably required for the occupation of the premises as a residence, he shall be guilty of an offence.

Section 1(3) is therefore concerned with persons who, with the requisite intent, either do some act likely to interfere with the peace or comfort of the residential occupier etc or persistently withdraw services. The actus reus may, therefore, consist of any act, such as intimidation, threats, or even interference with the building, perhaps by removing window frames or doors on the pretence that they are to be replaced. Alternatively it can consist of a lack of action which results in services reasonably required for the occupation of the premises being persistently withdrawn or withheld. This would be so if the landlord failed to pay for essential services to the building or part of the building occupied by the tenant. The use of the word 'persistently' which is used as an adverb to both 'withdraws' and 'withholds' indicates that this must be done for some period of time before those services could be reasonably described as having been persistently withdrawn or withheld.

The intention must be to cause a *residential occupier* to give up permanently occupation of the premises or to refrain from exercising any right or pursuing any remedy in respect of the premises or part of them. This offence therefore cannot be committed in relation to squatters who are in occupation of premises without agreement or any form of residential status.

Where an act likely to interfere with the peace or comfort of the residential occupier or members of his household is carried out with intent to cause the residential occupier *to give up occupation*, it is irrelevant that the act in question is not wrongful in civil law. This was stated by the House of Lords in a case where it held that a landlord who had disconnected a tenant's doorbell could be convicted of an offence under PEA 1977, s 1(3), even though the tenant was not entitled under his tenancy agreement to a front door bell (so that the disconnection was not a civil wrong).

The fact that the offence under PEA 1977, s 1(3) requires proof of the requisite intention means that proof of the offence may not always be easy. Consequently, s 1(3A) provides that the landlord of a residential occupier or an agent of the landlord commits an offence if he does acts likely to interfere with the peace or comfort of the residential occupier or members of his family, or if he persistently withdraws or withholds services reasonably required for the occupation of the premises, and (in either case) *he knows or has reasonable cause to believe that that conduct is likely to cause* the residential occupier to give up occupation of the whole or part of the premises or to refrain from exercising any right or pursuing any remedy in respect of the whole or any part of the premises. By s 1(3B), a person is not guilty under s 1(3A) if he proves that he had reasonable grounds for doing the acts or withdrawing or withholding the services in question.

Disputes involving anti-social behaviour

The Anti-social Behaviour Act 2003, Part 2 made changes to the Housing Act 1996 by giving local authorities, housing action trusts, and social landlords registered with the Housing Corporation, new powers to deal with anti-social behaviour in social housing. In particular, they may apply in the civil courts for an anti-social behaviour injunction. Where there are persistent reports of anti-social behaviour on housing estates in which the properties are owned or administered by such persons or organisations, the attention of the appropriate person or authority should be drawn to any conduct alleged to be that of tenants or their families.

Caravans: eviction and harassment

The Caravan Sites Act 1968, s 3 makes similar provisions to those under PEA 1977 in relation to residential caravans on 'protected sites'.

It is an offence for any person unlawfully to deprive the occupier of his occupation on a protected site of any caravan which the occupier is entitled by the contract to station and occupy, or to occupy, as his residence on that site, if this deprivation occurs during the subsistence of a residential contract.

Moreover, even after a residential contract has expired or been ended, it is an offence for a person to enforce, otherwise than by court proceedings, a right to exclude the occupier from the protected site or from any such caravan, or to remove or exclude the caravan from the site.

There is a defence available to a person if he proves that he believed and had reasonable cause to believe that the occupier of the caravan had ceased to reside on the site. This could occur when an occupier left for an extended period without informing the owner and without paying his rent. It would be reasonable for an owner after a period of time to form the belief that such a person had left without paying and without the intention of returning.

The offence of harassment also applies to caravans on protected sites. The acts forbidden in relation to other tenancies are forbidden in relation to caravans both during or after a residential contract, if they are done with intent to cause *the occupier to abandon occupation of the caravan or to remove it from the site or to refrain from exercising rights or remedies.*

In addition, the owner of a protected site or his agent is guilty of an offence if, whether during the subsistence or after the expiration or determination of a residential contract:

(a) he does acts likely to interfere with the peace or comfort of the occupier or persons residing with him, or
(b) he persistently withdraws or withholds services or facilities reasonably required for the occupation of the caravan as a residence on the site,

and (in either case) he knows, or has reasonable cause to believe, that that conduct is likely to cause the occupier to do any of the things italicised above. It is a defence to prove that the accused had reasonable grounds for doing the acts or withdrawing or withholding the services or facilities in question.

A 'protected site' is:

(a) any land in respect of which a site licence is required under the Caravan Sites and Control of Development Act 1960, Part I; or
(b) gypsy or other local authority sites exempt from the necessity of becoming so licensed.

The term 'protected site' does not extend to those which are for holiday use only or are part-time sites.

The term 'the occupier' for the purposes of the Act includes a person who was the occupier within the terms of a residential contract which has expired or been terminated. In the event of the death of the occupier, the widow, widower or surviving civil partner of that person (provided they were then residing together) or, in default, any member of the occupier's family (if then residing with the occupier) is 'the occupier'.

Police action

The primary duty of police officers will always be the prevention of a breach of the peace. When allegations are made concerning a dispute affecting a landlord and tenant a police officer should make all inquiries which are possible at that time at the scene of the dispute. If it appears that there may have been an offence in relation to the provisions outlined above in respect of dwellings or caravans, the officer should explain the provisions to the landlord and should warn him of the possibility of prosecution. However, whether or not such a warning is issued at the time, a comprehensive report of the circumstances should be sent to the local housing authority immediately. In appropriate cases, the police should inform the complainant in writing that the complaint has been referred to the housing authority.

Homelessness

The Housing Act 1996, Part VII requires every local housing authority to secure that advice and information about homelessness, and the prevention of homelessness, is available free of charge.

In addition, if someone applies to the authority for accommodation, or assistance in obtaining it, and the authority have reason to believe that he is or may be homeless or threatened with homelessness, the authority is required by Part VII to inquire into his eligibility for assistance (persons from abroad who are not eligible for housing assistance are not eligible for assistance under Part VII, nor are asylum seekers or their dependants in any event) and the circumstances.

In cases of apparent priority need, the authority must provide temporary accommodation while they make their inquiries.

If the authority are satisfied as a result of their inquiries that the applicant is intentionally homeless but has a priority need, they are required to ensure that accommodation is available for such period thereafter as will give him reasonable opportunity to find accommodation, and to give him advice and assistance in finding it; if a person found intentionally homeless does not have a priority need, he is only entitled thereafter to advice and assistance.

If the authority are satisfied that the applicant is homeless, but not intentionally so, and are satisfied that he does not have a priority need, their obligation thereafter is simply to provide advice and assistance in finding accommodation; they have power, however, to secure that accommodation is made available to him. On the other hand, if they are aware that an applicant who is not homeless intentionally has a priority need, the authority must secure that accommodation is made available to him; this duty comes to an end in certain circumstances specified by the Act.

Persons who are apparently homeless and seek advice from police officers should be referred to the local housing authority, whether or not the persons concerned have been previously resident in that area. The authority are permitted to make inquiries with the housing authority of an area in which such persons have previously resided, should they wish to do so.

CHAPTER 30

Homicide and abortion

The term 'homicide' means the killing of a human being by a human being and when expressed in this all embracing way does not attempt to differentiate between those which are unlawful and those which are not. Offences of homicide are categorised as follows: murder, manslaughter, infanticide, causing death by careless driving while under the influence of drink or drugs, causing death by dangerous driving, and, when certain provisions of the Road Safety Act 2006 are brought into force, the offences of causing death by careless or inconsiderate driving and of causing death by driving when the driver was unlicensed, disqualified or uninsured, will be added to this definition. Some acts which are carried out in emergencies to prevent violence, either in the commission of crime or against the person, may be sufficiently excusable to escape the criminal law.

MURDER

Murder continues to be a common law offence. It is defined as follows:

The crime of murder is committed where a person of sound mind and discretion unlawfully kills any reasonable creature in being, and under the Queen's peace, with intent unlawfully to kill or cause grievous bodily harm.

In three types of exceptional case a person is not guilty of murder, even though the definition of that offence is satisfied. Those exceptions are where the accused has the defence of provocation, where the accused suffered from diminished responsibility, or where the person was acting in pursuance of a suicide pact. If any of these defences is successful, the accused is guilty of voluntary manslaughter rather than murder.

The definition of murder is made up of a number of words or phrases, each of which requires explanation. With the exception of the reference to the accused's intent, the terms of the definition of murder also apply to involuntary manslaughter, which is discussed later in this chapter.

Person of sound mind and discretion

This phrase is really redundant. It simply refers to the general rule that a person is not legally liable if he is excused from liability under the rules relating to the liability of those who are insane or who are under ten (the age of criminal responsibility).

We discussed the defence of insanity in Chapter 1.

Unlawfully

A killing is unlawful unless it falls within one of the following categories:

Prevention of crime or effecting arrest

The Criminal Law Act 1967, s 3 provides that it is lawful to use such force as is *reasonable* in the circumstances in the prevention of a crime under the law of England and Wales or in effecting (or assisting in) the lawful arrest of offenders, suspected offenders, or persons lawfully at large. It follows that a police officer who accidentally causes the death of someone whom he is lawfully arresting is not guilty of manslaughter, let alone murder, provided that the force used by him was reasonable in the circumstances as he believed them to be (including the degree of resistance offered by the deceased).

Self-defence and defence of another or of property

Self-defence and defence of another or of property are common law defences, and they render a killing lawful. However, a person who acts in defence of himself, or of another or of property, is invariably acting in the prevention of crime, in which case he also has the defence under the Criminal Law Act 1967, s 3. For practical purposes, the terms of both the common law and the statutory defences are identical in their requirements since the crucial question in the common law defence is also whether the force used was *reasonable* in the circumstances as the accused believed them to be. We have explained this in more detail in Chapter 28, above. A police officer who shoots an armed terrorist who is shooting at him (or someone else) would clearly be using reasonable force, assuming that there is no other way of preventing the terrorist continuing to fire, and he can successfully plead the statutory defence of prevention of crime or the common law defence of self-defence (or defence of another). The use of fatal force to protect property is unlikely to be found to be reasonable by a jury.

Misadventure

Death is caused by misadventure where the killing is not murder, manslaughter, infanticide, causing death by dangerous driving or causing death by careless driving when under the influence of drink or drugs. As an example, if a patient dies as a result of a lawful operation carried out by a surgeon with proper care, the killing is by misadventure, and so not unlawful, and therefore the surgeon is not guilty of any offence of homicide.

Kills

Generally, some form of action is required which proves to be a substantial cause of death. However, 'substantial' in this context simply means 'more than minimal'. Although generally some 'act' is required, if the accused is under a legally recognised duty to act (as where a parent or similar person has the care of a child or helpless person), and fails to act, that failure being a substantial cause of death, he may be convicted of an offence of homicide. Normally the contribution to the death of an act will be easily proved, for example shooting, stabbing, pushing over a cliff, or violently assaulting, a person with fatal consequences, but the act does not need to be so violent nor so obviously connected with the death. Thieves who lock bank staff in a sealed, airtight vault to secure their escape without an alarm being raised kill their victims as surely as they would by any direct act. A person who steals the food and water left to sustain an injured man who is lost on the fells, while his companion seeks assistance, kills that man if he dies from the lack of sustenance, even though the man is not touched in any direct way. If someone deliberately tells a shocking lie to a person suffering from a serious heart condition, his act may kill that person although there is no hostile touching.

If the original act of the accused was a substantial cause of death it does not matter that some other intervening event finally caused the death, provided that that intervening event (as opposed to its details) was reasonably foreseeable in the ordinary course of things. If A knocks B unconscious on the beach and B is killed by the incoming tide, A's act is regarded in law as the cause of B's death because the incoming tide was clearly reasonably foreseeable. On the other hand, if two men (A and B) fight in a park and A leaves B unconscious but not seriously hurt and B is later killed by a tree which falls upon him when it is blown down by a gale, the fact that the fall of the tree was not reasonably foreseeable means that A's act is not regarded in law as a cause of B's death. A similar rule applies where the accused threatens someone who takes evasive action and is killed in doing so, as where a woman jumps out of a first floor window to avoid rape. Provided that the evasive action is likely, the threatened act will be a cause of death if it was a substantial cause (as almost inevitably it will be).

If the injuries inflicted by the accused are an operating cause of death it is irrelevant that an intervening act by a third party also contributed to the death, provided that the accused's act was a substantial contribution. Suppose that an assailant causes such serious injuries to his victim that the victim can only be kept alive by a life support machine. If, subsequently, because there is no hope of recovery, doctors switch off that machine, the assailant has still killed that person as his act was a substantial and operating cause of death. Suppose, on the other hand, that the accused's act is not an operating cause of death but merely provides the setting in which an intervening act by a third party is the immediate cause of death. The accused's act will not be a legal cause of death unless the third party's act is not free or not deliberate or not informed. In one case a man in attempting to evade arrest snatched a girl in front of him as he fired at police officers. The officers fired back instinctively, killing the girl. Although the officers' act resulted in the girl's death, it was held that the man's act was in law a cause of the girl's death; the officers' reaction was instinctive (and therefore not deliberate) and was done in self-defence (and therefore not free).

In a number of modern cases, the Court of Appeal has developed a special rule in respect of cases where the accused has helped the deceased to inject a controlled drug by applying a tourniquet, or by handing over a drug for *immediate* self-injection, and death has resulted from the injection. The Court of Appeal has held that the accused's conduct constitutes jointly engaging with the deceased in administering (injecting) the drug, and that therefore the accused's conduct is in law a cause of death.

Even where negligence in the treatment of a victim was the immediate cause of death, this does not exclude the responsibility of the accused, unless the negligent treatment was so independent of his acts and itself so potent in causing death that the accused's contribution was insignificant.

If an act is committed which leads to death, it is legally immaterial that the person injured refused medical treatment. Where a girl was stabbed by an assailant and refused a blood transfusion and died, the act of her attacker was held to be a cause of the killing. A person who commits violent acts likely to lead to the death of his victim must take his victim as he finds him. If the victim's beliefs prevent him from taking actions which might save his life the accused cannot claim successfully that he was not responsible for the death which results.

Sometimes a victim contributes to his death by doing something (other than taking evasive action, dealt with above) after the accused's act. The normal rule here is that if the victim's intervening act is not free, or is not deliberate, or is not informed, the accused's act will be a legal cause of death, whereas if the victim's act was free, deliberate and informed the accused's act will not be a legal cause of death. In one type of case, however, a different rule has been applied by the Court of Appeal. This is the case where the accused, in order to assist the victim, a drug addict, gives the victim a controlled drug which the victim knowingly administers to himself with fatal results. Under the rule just mentioned the accused's act would not be a legal cause of death, the victim's act of self-infliction being free, deliberate and informed. The Court of Appeal, however, did not apply this rule. Distinguishing between an ordinary occurrence (which the self-injection was on the facts) and an extraordinary one, it held that an ordinary occurrence would not prevent the accused's act of giving the victim a drug being a legal cause of the victim's death.

Reasonable creature in being

Any human being, however deformed or subnormal, is a 'reasonable creature in being' and therefore protected by the law of homicide, provided that it is 'in being' at the material time.

This raises the question of the point of time at which a foetus becomes a human being and therefore a 'reasonable creature in being'. To be a reasonable creature in being a child must have completely emerged into the world and have a separate existence from its mother. To have had that separate existence it is not essential that the cord has been severed or even that the afterbirth has been expelled, but it must have breathed.

The wilful destruction of a child capable of being born alive before it is born alive may amount to the offence of child destruction, while the intentional procuring of a miscarriage may constitute the offence of abortion; we discuss these offences later in this chapter. If someone injures a pregnant woman, and as a result of the attack she goes into premature labour and her child, although born alive, subsequently dies owing to its prematurity, the assailant is guilty of manslaughter but cannot be convicted of murder despite the fact that he intended to kill the woman or seriously harm her. It would make no difference that he intended also to destroy the foetus in the womb because such an intent does not suffice for murder.

Under the Queen's peace

For the purposes of murder, all persons are under the Queen's peace whether they are Her Majesty's subjects or not. The only persons who are not under the Queen's peace are alien enemies (and possibly rebel subjects) in the actual heat and exercise of war. However, while it is not murder to kill an alien enemy in battle, it is murder intentionally to kill an alien enemy in other circumstances (as when he is a prisoner of war).

When did death occur in relation to the act which caused it?

An offence of homicide may be committed by a person who carries out an appropriate act with the necessary mens rea regardless of the time which has passed since the injury etc was inflicted. However, where the injury alleged to have caused the death was sustained more than three years before the death occurred, or where the person whom it is intended to prosecute for an offence of homicide has already been convicted of an offence in circumstances alleged to be connected with the death, no prosecution for an offence of homicide may be brought without the consent of the Attorney-General. These provisions also apply to the offences of aiding, abetting, counselling or procuring suicide and of causing or allowing the death of a child or vulnerable adult.

With intent unlawfully to kill or cause grievous bodily harm

The mens rea required for murder is an intent unlawfully to kill another human being or unlawfully to cause grievous bodily harm to another human being. This is described as 'malice aforethought'. To apply the term 'malice' strictly to the offence of murder can be misleading. The killing itself need not be such that it would normally attract the description 'malicious'; it may even be compassionate, as when a person kills a close relative, who is suffering considerably in the final stages of an incurable illness, by means of a drug overdose. In addition, the word 'aforethought' is also misleading because it suggests that the killing must have been premeditated, which is certainly not a legal requirement. Provided that the accused's fatal act was done with intent unlawfully to kill or cause grievous bodily harm, it is irrelevant that he acted on the spur of the moment, the intention only being formed a brief second before the killing. A person who intends to kill or cause grievous bodily harm will not intend to do so unlawfully if on the facts, as he believes them, his use of force is reasonable to prevent crime, effect an arrest or in self-defence.

Provided that the accused intended unlawfully to kill or cause grievous bodily harm to another human being he is guilty of murder, even though the person whom he killed was not the intended victim. Thus if A fires at B, intending to kill him, but misses and kills C, A is guilty of murder.

MANSLAUGHTER

Manslaughter is a term which covers a variety of unlawful homicides which do not amount to murder. For ease of understanding of the offences of manslaughter, it is better to divide the offence into two varieties, voluntary and involuntary manslaughter.

Voluntary manslaughter

Voluntary manslaughters embody all the characteristics of murder including the necessary malice aforethought. It is the presence of particular circumstances acting upon the mind of the person carrying out the fatal act, which has the effect of reducing the nature of the crime. At common law extreme provocation, acting upon the person at the time, lessened his blameworthiness. Hot blooded killings were less offensive to society than cold blooded killings. The Homicide Act 1957 added two further circumstances in which blame might be lessened; first, where the person was suffering from 'diminished responsibility' at the time of his fatal act or omission, and, second, where a killing occurred in consequence of a suicide pact. Where their terms are satisfied, the rules relating to provocation, diminished responsibility and suicide pacts operate as a defence to a charge of murder, and reduce liability to manslaughter. A person cannot, for example, be charged with manslaughter under provocation.

Provocation

Provocation is not a defence to any charge other than murder, not even to attempted murder. It is quite distinct from the defence of self-defence, and is based on a sudden loss of self-control in circumstances where the accused may not entertain any belief that he is in danger.

The common law defence of provocation was extensively amended by the Homicide Act 1957, s 3. The present law can be stated as follows: Provocation can be by acts or words, or a combination of acts or words, and the defence can apply even though the provocative conduct came from someone other than the person killed. Thus, a person who is provoked by grossly insulting words uttered by A and, having lost self-control, attacks A and his companion, B, killing B but not A, may have the defence of provocation. A person may have the defence of provocation even though the provocative conduct was directed at somebody other than himself. Lastly, a person may have the defence of provocation even though the provocative conduct is a reaction to something which he has done, as where the accused's conduct in blackmailing X leads X to provoke him by taunts about his sexual inclinations.

The test of whether the defence of provocation is entitled to succeed is a dual one. The first test is that the alleged provocative conduct must have actually caused in the accused a sudden and temporary loss of self-control as the result of which he killed the deceased; the loss of self-control must have been to such a degree that the accused was for the moment not master of his mind. This is known as the subjective test. It must be emphasised that such a loss of self-control must be sudden (although it need not follow immediately after the provocative conduct); the defence of provocation is not open where a killing contains an element of deliberation or premeditation. Because the loss of self-control need not be immediate, the defence of provocation may be available to a 'battered wife' who undergoes a 'slow-burn' (rather than immediate) reaction to the final incident in a protracted series of violence and kills her husband while deprived of the power of reflection.

The second test is known as the objective test. To use the words of the Homicide Act 1957, s 3, the question is whether the alleged provocative conduct was enough to make a reasonable man do as the accused did, that is, enough to cause a reasonable man (ie an ordinary person) suddenly and temporarily to lose his self-control and to do as the accused did. In applying this test, the reasonable man is a person with the power of self-control of an ordinary person of the same age and sex as the accused, and with such other characteristics (other than intoxication) and factors as would affect the gravity of the provocation to the accused, but not with characteristics of the accused which would affect his power of self-control. Thus, if a person of Chinese origin who is highly sensitive about being a dwarf, is suffering from a depressive illness affecting his self-control and who is also drunk is provoked by a grossly insulting remark about his lack of height, the reasonable man test is applied on the basis of whether a reasonable man of the accused's age who was a dwarf and who was sensitive about this, these characteristics being ones which would affect the gravity of the provocation to the accused, would have been provoked. The reasonable man would not be invested with the characteristic of Chinese origin (since this would not affect the gravity of the provocation on the facts of the case) nor with the accused's drunkenness or his depressive illness. It is not enough simply that a reasonable man would have been provoked, since the test also requires that the reasonable man (as defined) would have been provoked to do as the accused did.

The accused does not have to prove to the jury's satisfaction that both tests are satisfied. The Homicide Act 1957, s 3 provides that if, but only if, there is *evidence* on which the jury can find that the accused was provoked to lose his self-control, the judge must leave the defence to the jury. If the defence is left to the jury, the accused must be acquitted of murder and convicted of manslaughter unless the prosecution proves to the jury that one or other or both of the two tests is not satisfied.

For operational purposes, the question of provocation does not affect the action taken by the police officers as it can only be settled at the trial for murder.

Diminished responsibility

The Homicide Act 1957, s 2 provides that where a person kills, or is party to the killing of, another, he shall not be convicted of murder if he was suffering from such abnormality of mind (whether arising from a condition of arrested or retarded development of mind or any inherent causes or induced by disease or injury) as substantially impaired his mental responsibility for his acts and omissions in doing or being party to the killing. These are matters for the defence to prove. If proved they will have the effect of reducing murder to manslaughter on the part of the person so affected, but will not affect the liability of other parties to the crime.

'Abnormality of mind' indicates a state of mind so different from that of the ordinary human being that the ordinary man would describe it as abnormal. For this purpose, a person's 'mind' includes his mental ability to control his physical acts in accordance with his judgements, as well as his ability to make rational judgements. The questions of both judgement and will-power therefore arise. It may be that an accused knew that his acts were wrong but some abnormality of mind prevented him from repressing his urge to kill.

For the defence to succeed, the abnormality of mind must have resulted from one of the specified causes, that is, it must result from a condition of arrested or retarded development of mind or any inherent causes or be induced by disease or injury. Thus, abnormality of mind due to hate, jealousy or intoxication is outside the defence. However, an abnormality of mind would be due to a specified cause (disease or injury), if due to alcoholism of such a degree that *either* the brain had been injured so that there was gross impairment of judgement and emotional response *or*, where the brain had not been damaged to that extent, the drinking was involuntary in that the accused was unable to resist the impulse to take the first drink.

The last requirement for the defence to succeed is that the abnormality of mind must have substantially impaired the accused's mental responsibility for his conduct. This requirement is concerned with the extent to which the accused's mind was answerable for his conduct. Whether there was a substantial impairment in this sense is a question of degree; the impairment need not be total but it must be more than trivial or minimal.

Suicide pacts

The Homicide Act 1957, s 4 declares that it is manslaughter, and not murder, for a person to kill another or be party to someone else killing another, if he was acting in pursuance of a suicide pact between himself and the person killed. This is a matter for the defence to prove.

A 'suicide pact' is a common agreement between two or more persons, having for its object the death of them all, whether or not each is to take his own life. Nothing done by a person entering into a suicide pact may be treated as in pursuance of such a pact unless it is done while he has the settled intention of dying in pursuance of the pact.

A related offence is that of aiding and abetting another's suicide contrary to the Suicide Act 1961, s 2, which provides that a person who aids, abets, counsels or procures the suicide of another, or an attempt by another to commit suicide, commits an offence. A prosecution for this offence requires the consent of the Director of Public Prosecutions.

Although there is little difference between the offence of manslaughter and that of aiding and abetting suicide, it must be remembered that one essential difference is that in the case of manslaughter we are considering the survivor of a suicide pact. There is no mention of this in relation to the offence under the Suicide Act 1961, s 2. The person aiding, abetting, counselling or procuring an offence does not need to be a partner in a pact. The offence is aiding etc another to commit suicide (or to attempt to commit suicide). The fact that this offence can be committed even though the suicide attempt fails marks another distinction between the offences.

In some cases the distinction between the two offences is clear. If X and Y make a suicide pact under which X is to shoot Y and then himself and, having shot Y, X is prevented from shooting himself, his liability is for manslaughter under the Homicide Act 1957, s 4; there is no question of aiding and abetting suicide. Conversely, if M gives N a lethal poison which N then takes, there being no suicide pact, M's liability is clearly only for the offence of aiding and abetting suicide. The difficulty arises in a case where two or more people have agreed to die, and one, at least, of them survives, and it is not clear exactly who did what. A good example is the case of a couple who try to asphyxiate themselves with fumes in a car. They are both found in the back seat, one is alive and the other dead. The survivor will be guilty of manslaughter under the Homicide Act 1957, s 4 if he took the necessary steps (in whole or part) to kill the deceased but only of aiding and abetting suicide if those steps were taken wholly by the deceased. Proving who did what can be difficult.

Involuntary manslaughter

This category covers cases where the accused, who has unlawfully killed another (ie has committed the actus reus of murder), is not guilty of murder because he lacked malice aforethought (ie an intent unlawfully to kill or cause grievous bodily harm) but acted with some lesser degree of mens rea.

There are three types of involuntary manslaughter, between which there is a degree of overlap:

(a) killing by gross negligence;
(b) killing with recklessness as to death or serious bodily harm;
(c) killing by an unlawful and dangerous act.

Killing by gross negligence

This type of manslaughter may be committed by an act or by a failure to act (if the accused has failed in breach of a legal obligation to do an act); it is irrelevant whether or not the accused's act or omission would have constituted an offence if death had not resulted.

The requirements of manslaughter by gross negligence are:

(a) the existence of a duty of care, ie not to act in a way which puts another in peril (unless there is a legally acceptable excuse for doing so) or, as the case may be, not to fail to do an act which one is under a legally recognised duty to do;
(b) a gross breach of duty. Normally, proof of negligence simply involves proof that, whether or not he realised the risk (of which he should have been aware) the person subject to the duty did something, or failed to do something, in a way which fell below the standard of conduct expected of a reasonable person in all the circumstances (including the defendant's expertise and training, if they are relevant in the context). This is not enough in the case of gross negligence. For there to be gross negligence, the accused's conduct must have involved a risk of death to another and in respect of that risk his conduct must have fallen so far below the standard to be expected of a reasonable person, ie be so bad that it should be judged criminal;
(c) the breach must cause death. This simply repeats the requirement of causation which applies to offences of homicide generally.

Killing with recklessness as to death or serious bodily harm

In this context, a person is reckless as to a risk of death or serious bodily harm if he himself foresees that risk as a highly probable consequence of the fatal act or omission and he takes that risk, and in all circumstances it is unreasonable for him to do so.

The present type of involuntary manslaughter will often overlap with constructive manslaughter (referred to below) and manslaughter by gross negligence, but it will not do so where the fatal act is not otherwise unlawful and there is no risk of death.

Killing by an unlawful and dangerous act

This mode of committing manslaughter is commonly known as 'constructive manslaughter'. It cannot be committed by an omission to act; an unlawful act by the accused is required. Three elements must be proved by the prosecution:

(a) *that the accused has committed the actus reus of an offence (other than homicide) with the mens rea required for that offence*; proof of this is proof of the 'unlawful act'. In most cases the offence will be a battery, but constructive manslaughter is certainly not limited to that offence, for example it is not unusual for a constructive manslaughter conviction to be based on the offence of administering a noxious thing (see p 820, where it was noted that 'administration' is a wide term), although dangerous driving or careless driving which results in death can never constitute constructive manslaughter;

(b) *that the unlawful act was a cause of death*; and

(c) *that the unlawful act was dangerous*, in the sense that all sober and reasonable people would inevitably recognise that the unlawful act must subject another person to the risk of some harm, albeit not serious harm.

This test is applied on the basis of the facts known to the accused at the time of his unlawful act or, if the act continues over a period of time, which became known during that period. Suppose that a burglar, being confronted by the householder and becoming aware that the householder is old and physically frail, continues his burglarious trespass. If the householder suffers a heart attack and dies in consequence of that trespass and, on the facts which became known to the accused, all sober and reasonable people would inevitably recognise that his burglarious trespass must subject the householder to the risk of some harm, the burglar is guilty of manslaughter.

INFANTICIDE

The offence of infanticide arose out of a desire to separate certain acts committed by a disturbed mother, who had recently given birth to a child, from the general rules associated with the common law offence of murder. The Infanticide Act 1938, s 1 states that where a woman by any wilful act or omission causes the death of her child, being a child under the age of twelve months, but at the time of that act or omission the balance of her mind was disturbed by reason of not having fully recovered from the effect of giving birth to the child, or by reason of the effect of lactation consequent on the birth of her child, then the offence, regardless of other circumstances, is infanticide rather than murder. If the Infanticide Act 1938 had not dealt with these special circumstances the vast majority of the cases within the Act would constitute manslaughter by reason of diminished responsibility in any case. The basis of the law on infanticide is that depression after childbirth, or the effect of breast feeding a child, are factors which can cause a mother to act out of character by committing some wilful act, or omitting to do something which a caring mother would do, that act or omission leading to the death of a child. The Infanticide Act 1938 only refers to children under the age of twelve months and this is not surprising, as Parliament had in mind a nursing mother who, in a fit of depression, killed the child which she was nursing. However, it leads to problems when such a mother kills more than one of her children, the other being over the age of twelve months. A charge of infanticide will lie in respect of the child who is under the age of twelve months and one of murder in respect of the child who is over the age of twelve months. However, the defence of diminished responsibility would normally be available to the mother in respect of the killing of the older child.

While infanticide may be charged as an offence in the first instance, it may alternatively be raised as a defence to a charge of murder.

CAUSING OR ALLOWING DEATH OF A CHILD OR VULNERABLE ADULT

In cases of child abuse or abuse of a vulnerable adult where the victim has died as a result of the act or default of someone in the same household, it is sometimes difficult to prove who perpetrated the crime, or to prove that A aided and abetted B to do so or B aided and abetted A to do so (so that both can be convicted of an offence of homicide described above).

This problem has been resolved by the Domestic Violence, Crime and Victims Act 2004, s 5, which provides that a person ('D') is guilty of an offence if:

(a) a child under sixteen or vulnerable adult ('V') dies as a result of the unlawful act of a person who:
   (i) was a member of the same household as V; and
   (ii) had frequent contact with him;
(b) D was such a person at the time of that act;
(c) at that time there was a significant risk of serious physical harm (ie grievous bodily harm) being caused to V by the unlawful act of such a person; and
(d) either D was the person whose act caused V's death or:
   (i) D was, or ought to have been, aware of the risk mentioned in para (c);
   (ii) D failed to take such steps as he could reasonably have been expected to take to protect V from the risk; and
   (iii) the act occurred in circumstances of the kind that D foresaw or ought to have foreseen.

The prosecution does not have to prove whether it is the first alternative in (d) or the second ((i) to (iii)) that applies.

If D was not the mother or father of V:

(a) D may not be charged with an offence under s 5 if he was under sixteen at the time of the act that caused V's death;
(b) for the purposes of (d)(ii), D could not have been expected to take any such step as is referred to there before attaining that age.

For the purposes of s 5, (a) 'act' includes a course of conduct and also includes omission; (b) an 'unlawful' act is one that constitutes an offence, or would constitute an offence but for being the act of a person under ten or of a person (other than D) who has the defence of insanity; (c) 'vulnerable adult' means a person aged sixteen or over whose ability to protect himself from violence, abuse or neglect is significantly impaired through physical or mental disability or illness, through old age or otherwise; (d) a person is to be regarded as a 'member' of a particular household, even if he does not live in that household, if he visits it so often and for such periods of time that it is reasonable to regard him as a member of it.

THREATS TO KILL

By the Offences Against the Person Act 1861 (OAPA 1861), s 16 it is an offence for any person, without lawful excuse, to make to another person a threat to kill that other or a third person, intending that that other person would fear that it would be carried out. The substance of this offence is therefore quite straightforward. An unborn child is not 'another person' for the purposes of this section.

It is not necessary that the person making the threat intends to kill. If a man writes or telephones to another and says that he is a member of a terrorist group and that the group intends to kill that person or someone else, the offence is complete if the person making the threat intends that the person receiving the message should fear that the threat will be carried out. Whether or not the accused is a member of that organisation is immaterial. However, if a similar telephone call was made by a man to his friend as an intended joke, and he admitted at the end of the call that it was a joke, this would be clear evidence that the accused had not intended that it be taken seriously.

Self-defence can amount to lawful excuse for a threat provided that the threatened force is reasonable in the circumstances as the maker of the threat believes them to be. A householder who, hearing a burglar in his house, arms himself with a gun and threatens to kill the burglar with it when the burglar threatens him with a crowbar, might well be found by a jury to have threatened reasonable force in self-defence

SOLICITING ANOTHER TO COMMIT MURDER

It is an offence contrary to OAPA 1861, s 4 for a person to solicit, encourage, persuade or endeavour to persuade or propose to any person, to murder any other person. There must be some form of communication and this may be in any form. It is not essential that the person solicited etc was affected by the communication.

CHILD DESTRUCTION

The common law offence of murder requires the killing of a 'reasonable creature in being' and this left a gap in the law where a child was yet unborn. It was therefore necessary to protect unborn children, and this is now done by the statutory offences of child destruction and abortion. The offence of child destruction is associated with those unborn children who are capable of being born alive.

The Infant Life (Preservation) Act 1929 is concerned with persons who, with intent to destroy the life of a child capable of being born alive, by any wilful act, cause a child to die before it has an existence independent of its mother. There is a proviso to the offence, namely that a person is not guilty of it unless it is proved by the prosecution that the accused did not act in good faith for the purpose only of preserving the life of the mother. This proviso has been construed by the judges as including acting to preserve the mother's physical or mental health. In addition, the Abortion Act 1967, s 5(1) provides that no offence under the Infant Life (Preservation) Act 1929 is committed by a registered medical practitioner who terminates a pregnancy in accordance with the provisions of the Act of 1967, which we explain on p 852.

The offence is concerned with 'wilful acts' and there must be some positive action on the part of the person charged, such as strangling a baby as it emerges from its mother. The wilful act must be done with the intention of destroying the life of a child 'capable of being born alive'. 'Capable of being born alive' means capable of being alive at the time when the act was done. A child is capable of being born alive when it has reached a state of development in the womb in which it is capable, if born then, of living and breathing through its own lungs without any connection with its mother. The Act provides a presumption that a child is capable of being born alive at any time after the twenty-eighth week of pregnancy. However, the offence can be committed in relation to a younger child if it is proved that it was capable of being born alive. Provided that the child was capable of being born alive, it is irrelevant that it is not capable of sustained survival.

Perhaps this offence is best understood by examining extreme circumstances. If a man deliberately shoots his pregnant girlfriend in the stomach, her child having developed beyond seven lunar months and the child is born dead, the man will be guilty of child destruction. The act was wilful, he intended to destroy the life of a child capable of being born alive and the child died without having had a separate existence. However, if the child had been born alive and had died after having an existence independent of its mother, the man would be guilty of manslaughter.

ABORTION

The offence commonly known as abortion is somewhat misleadingly described in this way, because the relevant offence does not require the abortion (miscarriage) of a foetus but merely that one of a number of specified acts should be done with intent to procure a miscarriage (whether or not it occurs). However, for convenience, we shall describe the offence as abortion hereafter. Because there must be an intent to procure a miscarriage, someone who does something to *prevent* the implantation of a fertilised ovum in the uterus (as where the 'morning-after' pill is used) does not commit an offence of the present type because a pregnancy only begins, and a miscarriage can only occur, after implantation.

It may be the pregnant woman who acts to end her pregnancy and the law deals with this situation. The actual acts carried out with the intention to procure a miscarriage may be carried out by someone else and that is a separate issue. There is also the question of the criminal liability of any person who knowingly supplies the means to bring about an abortion.

The woman herself

OAPA 1861, s 58 states that it is an offence for a woman, being with child and with intent to procure her own miscarriage, unlawfully to administer to herself any poison or other noxious thing, or unlawfully to use any instrument or other means whatsoever.

There are several points to be proved within this offence. In the first instance, the section provides that the woman must be pregnant if she is charged with abortion upon herself; it is not sufficient for her to imagine that she is pregnant. There are a number of means by which the offence can be committed. She may take (or unlawfully administer to herself, as the section describes it) any poison or other noxious thing. 'Poison' has been defined as a recognised poison. If such a thing is taken etc, it is irrelevant that the quantity is too small to cause harm. The term 'noxious thing' means any substance, other than a recognised poison, which is harmful in the dosage in which it was administered even though it might be harmless in smaller quantities. Clearly 'noxious thing' is a wide term; even certain forms of oil used in cooking and some forms of soap can be harmful in a given dosage. If a dosage is insufficient to render a substance a noxious thing, although the accused believes it is, there can be a conviction for an attempt to commit an offence under OAPA 1861, s 58. The term 'instrument' would cover the range of surgical instruments usually associated with medical operations and also the instruments used by the back street abortionist, such as knitting needles. The term 'other means whatsoever' embraces any other way in which a person may seek to bring about an abortion, such as manual manipulation with the fingers. These comments concerning the nature of substances and instruments are equally valid in relation to this offence when carried out by some other person.

If X urges a woman to take something to procure a miscarriage, X can be convicted of incitement, and this is so even though that thing (unknown to X) was harmless and incapable of causing a miscarriage.

The intent to procure a miscarriage requires an intent to cause the expulsion of an ovum implanted in the uterus.

Any other person

OAPA 1861, s 58 goes on to provide that anyone (other than the woman herself) who, with intent to procure the miscarriage of any woman, unlawfully administers to her, or causes to be taken by her, any poison or other noxious thing, or who, with the same intent, unlawfully uses any instrument or other means whatsoever commits an offence, *whether or not the woman is pregnant*. The words italicised indicate an important distinction between the offence committed by the woman herself and the offence committed by other persons.

This offence is concerned with the abortionist in the generally accepted sense of the word.

Unlawfully: the effect of the Abortion Act 1967

By the Abortion Act 1967, s 5(2) anything done with intent to procure a woman's miscarriage (or, in the case of a woman carrying more than one foetus, her miscarriage of any foetus) is unlawfully done unless authorised by s 1 of the Act.

The Abortion Act 1967 legalises abortions (including abortion operations which are unsuccessful or not completed) carried out by a registered medical practitioner in prescribed circumstances. In order for an abortion to be lawful under the Act two registered medical practitioners must in good faith be of the opinion that:

(a) the pregnancy has not exceeded its twenty-fourth week and that the continuance of the pregnancy would involve risk, greater than if the pregnancy was terminated, of injury to the physical or mental health of the pregnant woman or any existing children of her family (a question in the determination of which account may be taken of the mother's actual or reasonably foreseeable environment); or

(b) the termination is necessary to prevent *grave* permanent injury to the physical or mental health of the pregnant woman (a question in the determination of which account may be taken of the woman's actual or reasonably foreseeable environment); or

(c) the continuance of the pregnancy would involve risk to the life of the pregnant woman, greater than if the pregnancy was terminated; or

(d) there is a substantial risk that if the child were born it would suffer from such physical or mental abnormalities as to be seriously handicapped.

In order to be lawful, such an abortion must be carried out in a NHS hospital, NHS Trust hospital or other approved place.

In an emergency an abortion may be carried out by a registered medical practitioner without complying with the above requirements if it is necessary to do so immediately to save the life of a pregnant woman, or to prevent grave permanent injury to her physical or mental health. This might occur during an operation upon the woman or at the scene of, or immediately following, a serious road accident.

The person supplying the means

OAPA 1861, s 59 punishes those who unlawfully supply or procure any poison or other noxious thing, or any instrument or thing whatsoever, knowing that it is intended to be unlawfully used or employed with intent to procure the miscarriage of any woman, whether she be or be not with child. 'Supply' should be given its ordinary meaning of transferring physical control from one person to another. 'Procure' means to obtain possession of something for some other person. To procure, therefore, indicates going out deliberately to seek something for a particular purpose, while something may be supplied to a woman which was already in the possession of the accused. As to 'intent to procure miscarriage', see p 851.

CONCEALMENT OF BIRTH

OAPA 1861, s 60 provides that if any woman is delivered of a child, every person who, by any secret disposition of the dead body of that child, endeavours to conceal its birth is guilty of an offence. It is irrelevant whether the child died before, at or after its birth. However, in the case of a stillborn child, it must have reached a sufficient state of maturity that, but for some accidental circumstance, it might have been born alive.

The secret disposition may be done by anyone or by a number of persons, but typically it is done by the mother following an unattended birth. In such a case, the offence is of importance where it cannot be proved how and/or when a child died, so that the mother cannot be convicted of an offence of homicide or of child destruction.

It is not enough to prove that a woman, who denied giving birth, had in fact given birth and abandoned the child's body. There must be evidence of a secret disposition of the child's body in an endeavour to conceal its birth. By 'concealment' is meant concealment from the world at large, but this is not prevented by the fact that some of the woman's friends or confidantes know. Clearly, a secret disposition in an endeavour to conceal the birth from a particular person, for example the woman's father, does not constitute the offence. Apart from what has just been said, it is difficult to be precise. Placing the body in a secluded spot, without covering it, may be sufficient if the particular circumstances permit this to be described as a secret disposition in an endeavour to conceal.

CHAPTER 31

Public order offences other than those related to sporting events or industrial disputes

THE QUEEN'S PEACE

One of the fundamental duties of a police officer is the preservation of 'the Queen's peace'. This term is used in a different sense here from that which applies in the case of murder (see p 843). It has been described in many ways but is generally descriptive of that public peace and good order which is expected to be preserved to allow Her Majesty's subjects to live their lives without due interference from other citizens. It has been described as 'that normal state of the peace and tranquillity' which should always exist in an ordered society and as a 'normal and ordered' state of society.

At the outset, it is essential to give the legal definition of that well known term, 'breach of the peace'.

BREACH OF THE PEACE

To be a breach of the peace, the conduct in question does not have to be disorderly. However, there cannot be a breach of the peace on the part of a person unless there is an incidence of violence on his part; verbal abuse is insufficient.

There is a breach of the peace whenever and wherever (even on private premises):

(a) harm is *actually done*, or is *likely* to be done, to a person, whether by the conduct of the person against whom a breach of the peace is alleged or by someone whom it provokes; or

(b) harm is *actually* done, or is *likely* to be done, to a person's property in his presence; or

(c) a person is genuinely in fear of harm to himself or to his property in his presence as a result of an assault, affray, riot, or other disturbance.

It is for the justices to decide whether or not there has been a breach of the peace in particular circumstances.

A breach of the peace is not a criminal offence, but it (or the risk of it) can result in an arrest being lawfully made or in a binding over order being made. In addition, the courts have held that a police officer in whose presence a breach of the peace is being, or reasonably appears to be about to be, committed has the right to take reasonable steps to make the person breaking or threatening to break the peace refrain from doing so.

A police officer has power to arrest without a warrant where:

(a) a breach of the peace is committed in his presence;
(b) he reasonably believes that such a breach will be committed in the near future by the person arrested although he has not yet committed any breach; or
(c) a breach has been committed and it is reasonably believed that a renewal of it is threatened.

Although the power of arrest will normally be exercised against a person who commits a breach of the peace or reasonably appears to be about to do so, it can also be exercised against someone whose lawful conduct is reasonably believed to be liable to provoke a breach of the peace by others if it is unreasonable conduct in the circumstances. The Court of Appeal has held that mere agitation or excitement does not amount to a breach of the peace where there is no question of injury or threat of injury.

BINDING OVER

'Binding over' is a precautionary measure; it is not a conviction or punishment. It should not be ordered for some act that is past and not likely to be repeated.

The powers of a magistrates' court to bind over a person to keep the peace or to be of good behaviour, or both, may be exercised either as a complaint (under the Magistrates' Courts Act 1980, s 115) or on the court's own motion under the Justices of the Peace Act 1361 and common law powers. Other courts can also bind over on their own motion, but we shall limit ourselves to the powers of a magistrates' court.

The importance of the fact that a magistrates' court can bind over of its own motion is that a person can be bound over whether or not he has been convicted of an offence; if he has been so convicted, the binding over may be in addition to any punishment imposed.

Where the magistrates act on complaint under the Magistrates' Courts Act 1980 they can only bind a person over if the facts complained of have been proved beyond reasonable doubt. If they act of their own motion, it must be proved beyond reasonable doubt that there is a risk of a breach of the peace or of an offence in the future.

On occasions where there is a breach of the peace, or the risk of one, the person concerned may be engaged upon a lawful activity, for example a demonstration. On such occasions it must be shown that in all the circumstances it was the defendant who was acting unreasonably rather than the other person.

The process of binding over is effected by requiring the individual to enter into a recognisance, with or without sureties, to keep the peace or, alternatively, to be of good behaviour.

A person enters into a recognisance if he undertakes to pay a sum of money fixed by the court if he fails within the time specified by the court to comply with the terms of the recognisance, and a person becomes a surety if he agrees to pay a sum so specified if that other person so fails to comply.

The power to bind over independently of any conviction is exercisable either after an arrest without warrant for an actual or apprehended breach of the peace or upon complaint. Before a person is bound over, he will be told by the court of its intention to do so, and he, the complainant and their witnesses will be heard by the court. The court cannot impose a binding over if the person does not consent but, in the event of a refusal to be so bound, or to find sureties, the person concerned may be committed to prison for a fixed term not exceeding six months or until he sooner complies with the requirements of the court.

RIOT

The Public Order Act 1986 (POA 1986), s 1(1) provides that, where twelve or more persons who are present together use or threaten unlawful violence for a common purpose and the conduct of them (taken together) is such as would cause a person of reasonable firmness present at the scene to fear for his personal safety, each of the persons using unlawful violence for the common purpose is guilty of riot. Riot is the most serious offence against public order.

Basically, what is required is that an accused uses violence in the following circumstances that:

(a) twelve or more persons (including the accused) who are present together use or threaten unlawful violence for a common purpose; and

(b) the conduct of them (taken together) is such as would cause a person of reasonable firmness present at the scene to fear for his personal safety; and

(c) the accused's use of unlawful violence was for the common purpose.

Riot may be committed in private as well as in public places. Thus, a riot can take place at factory premises, in a club, in a college, at a tickets-only dance at a dance hall or—even—in someone's home.

Use of unlawful violence

A person does not perpetrate the offence of riot merely by threatening unlawful violence; he must actually use violence in the prescribed circumstances. If twelve or more people simply threaten violence for a common purpose in a frightening way, but none of them uses violence, riot is *not* committed.

On the other hand, provided one of twelve or more people actually uses violence for the common purpose, the offence of riot is perpetrated by him (or by all those who so use violence if more than one does). Those who merely threaten violence for the common purpose can, however, be convicted as accomplices to riot if, with the appropriate mens rea, they aid, abet, counsel or procure the use of violence by another (like anyone else who does so).

'Violence' is defined by POA 1986, s 8 as 'violent conduct'. It is not limited to violent conduct towards a person or persons since it includes violent conduct towards property (for example, smashing shop windows or overturning cars). Nor is it limited to conduct causing or intended to cause personal injury or damage to property, since it 'includes any other violent conduct (for example, throwing at or towards a person a missile of a kind capable of causing injury which does not hit or falls short)'. Swinging a knife at someone or firing a gun in his direction is violence under the definition in s 8, even though he is not hit.

The requirement that the violence be unlawful excludes from riot the use of violence which is justified by law (for example, under the common law rules relating to the use of reasonable force in self-defence and the defence of another or of property, or under the statutory provisions relating to the use of such force in the prevention of crime or the effecting of an arrest).

Use or threat of unlawful violence for a common purpose by twelve or more present together

The phrase 'present together' does not mean that the twelve or more people should form a cohesive group. Nor need they be present pursuant to an agreement to come together; consequently, they may be 'present together' by accident.

The same comments apply to 'use' and 'violence' as have been made above. If, during public disorder, the residents of a street use or threaten reasonable violence for the common purpose of defending themselves or their property from attack, their use or threat of violence does not constitute a riot because their violence is not unlawful.

In relation to threats, they may be by gestures alone (eg the brandishing of a weapon) or be by words alone, or be by a combination of both (eg waving a car-jack accompanied by words such as 'I'll get you with this'). Although, in the case of words, they will normally be spoken, there seems no reason why it will not do if the threat is communicated by words on placards or banners if the other conditions for riot are satisfied. Indeed, it has been held by the House of Lords that the overt possession of offensive weapons can amount to a threat of violence, for example, by the pointed display of a weapon or the visible possession of a petrol bomb.

POA 1986, s 1(2) provides that it is immaterial whether or not the twelve or more use or threaten violence simultaneously. Equally, it is immaterial whether or not *any* of the others used or threatened violence at the time of the use of violence by the accused. Provided that twelve or more persons who use or threaten violence are present *together* throughout, and that the violence is used or threatened by twelve or more for a common purpose, the offence of riot can be committed. Thus, it covers the situation where violence is used or threatened in one part of a crowd, then dies away, only to break out in another part at a later time.

It must be proved that the use or threat of violence by the twelve or more present together was for a purpose common to them (or at least to twelve of them). The question is not whether the twelve or more were present for a common purpose but whether they threatened or used violence for a common purpose. The common purpose need not be violence and it need not be an unlawful purpose (although, no doubt, it will normally be so). The common purpose may be inferred from the conduct of those involved; if a large group advance towards police officers, shouting 'kill the pigs', it may be inferred that they are threatening violence for a common purpose.

Conduct such as would cause fear

The question is not whether the conduct of an individual accused would cause fear but whether the conduct of the 'twelve or more present together . . . ' is such as would, *taken together,* cause fear (ie alarm or apprehension). The conduct of the twelve or more must be such as *would* cause a person (ie a third-party bystander) of reasonable firm-ness present at the scene to fear for his *personal safety*; it does not matter whether it actually caused fear to a person present at the scene or even *might* have.

No person of reasonable firmness need actually be, or be likely to be, present at the scene; in fact, no one else (besides the twelve or more) need be present or likely to be present at the scene. No doubt the case where there are no bystanders will be exceptional; where it occurs proof of the riot may be particularly difficult.

Mens rea

By POA 1986, s 6(1), a person is guilty of riot only if he intends to use violence or is aware that his conduct may be violent. POA 1986, s 6(5) provides that, for the purposes of the offence of riot, a person whose awareness is impaired by intoxication shall be taken to be aware of that of which he would be aware if not intoxicated, unless he shows either that his intoxication was not self-induced (as where his drink has been 'laced') or that it was caused solely by the taking or administration of a substance in the course of medical treatment. 'Intoxication' here means any intoxication, whether caused by drink, drugs or other means (eg glue), or by a combination of means.

VIOLENT DISORDER

POA 1986, s 2(1) provides that, where three or more people who are present together use or threaten unlawful violence and their conduct (taken together) is such as would cause a person of reasonable firmness present at the scene to fear for his personal safety, each of the persons using or threatening unlawful violence is guilty of violent disorder.

To perpetrate the offence, an individual accused must use or threaten unlawful violence in the following circumstances that:

(a) three or more people (including the accused) together use or threaten unlawful violence (whether towards persons or towards property);
(b) the conduct of them (taken together) is such as would cause a person (ie a third-party bystander) of reasonable firmness present at the scene to fear for his personal safety. No person of reasonable firmness need actually be, or be likely to be, present at the scene.

As in the case of riot, violent disorder may be committed in private as well as in public places.

The prohibited conduct for this offence is substantially the same as that of riot (and the comments made when discussing the identical elements in riot are equally applicable here) with the exceptions that:

(a) an individual accused is guilty if he uses or *threatens* unlawful violence;
(b) only three persons (including the accused) who are present together are required to use or threaten unlawful violence;
(c) neither the accused nor the other participants are required to use or threaten unlawful violence for a common purpose.

The operation of the above can be illustrated as follows. If a racist march or static demonstration takes place in the centre of an immigrant community, accompanied by threats of immediate violence which would make a person of reasonable firmness fear for his personal safety, the offence is committed; but not if the taunts are merely (if that word may be used) of a racist nature highly offensive to local inhabitants, although they may give rise to an offence under POA 1986, ss 4A, 5 or 18 or the Crime and Disorder Act 1998 (CDA 1998), s 31.

By POA 1986, s 6(2) a person is guilty of violent disorder only if he intends to use or threaten violence or is aware that his conduct may be violent or threaten violence.

As in the case of riot, a person whose awareness is impaired by intoxication is to be taken to be aware of that of which he would be aware if not intoxicated, unless he shows either that his intoxication was not self-induced or that it was caused solely by the taking or administration of a substance in the course of medical treatment.

Violent disorder is a useful offence to charge since it is not restricted to incidents which might be described as serious public disorder. If three or more gather outside a dance hall using or threatening violence against others, they can be convicted of violent disorder if they are acting collectively and their conduct (taken together) is sufficiently frightening to be liable to affect a person of reasonable firmness.

Where evidence of the involvement of three or more persons is affected by the dismissal of the charges against all but one or two, the one or two may nevertheless be convicted of violent disorder if it is proved that others not charged were also involved; if it is not so proved, the one or two may be convicted of an offence of affray. However, if there is only evidence of violence towards property, a conviction for an offence of affray will not be possible.

AFFRAY

POA 1986, s 3(1) provides that a person is guilty of affray if he uses or threatens unlawful violence towards another and his conduct is such as would cause a person of reasonable firmness present at the scene to fear for his personal safety.

The prohibited conduct is that:

(a) the accused must use or threaten violence *towards* another; and
(b) his conduct must be such as would cause a person of reasonable firmness present at the scene to fear for his personal safety.

Like riot and violent disorder, affray may be committed in private as well as in public places. One result is that, if a fight breaks out at a party in someone's home or at a private function at a discotheque, those who participate in it can be guilty of affray if the terms of the offence are satisfied. In fact any assault—even a domestic one—wherever committed, accompanied by the use or threat of violence, is an affray if it would cause a person of reasonable firmness present at the scene to fear for his personal safety. *Most* of the elements of the actus reus are common to riot and violent disorder.

Use or threat of unlawful violence towards another

Unlike the position in riot and violent disorder, 'violence' here does not include violent conduct towards property.

Another important difference between affray and riot and violent disorder is that a threat of violence cannot be made by the use of words alone, whether the words are uttered orally or displayed or distributed in writing, and however aggressively they are expressed. Of course, an affray can be committed where a threat of violence is made by a combination of words and gestures (such as shouting out, 'I'll get you for that', while brandishing a weapon or even shaking a fist) as well as by gestures alone. As in the case of riot and violent disorder, the overt possession of weapons which are not waved or brandished can amount to a threat of violence. A threat of violence must be directed towards a person or persons actually present at the scene.

It has even been held that inciting an excited dog off the lead to attack someone can constitute a threat of violence. It would be different, of course, if a person merely said 'seize him' to a quiet dog lying at his feet, since the threat would be by words alone.

An affray, like riot and violent disorder, can only be committed if the violence is 'unlawful' as defined on p 858. Thus, a person who fights another in self-defence cannot be guilty of an affray, although his assailant can be if his use of violence would make a person of reasonable firmness fear for his personal safety.

Conduct such as would cause a person of reasonable firmness present at the scene to fear for his personal safety

This requirement provides an important limit on the offence, and excludes many fights from it. For example, it is most unlikely that a fight between two people, arising out of a personal quarrel but without any danger of the involvement of others, would constitute an affray. On the other hand, a violent street fight outside a pub at closing time undoubtedly constitutes an affray. If three or more are involved it will also constitute the more serious offence of violent disorder.

The reference to the hypothetical person 'present at the scene' is to an 'innocent member of the public within sight or earshot' of the violence.

Where two or more people use or threaten the unlawful violence, it is the conduct of them taken together that must be considered for the purpose of ascertaining whether the conduct would have the required effect.

As in the case of riot and violent disorder no one besides the participants (ie no bystander) need be present, or be likely to be present, at the scene, and it is expressly provided by POA 1986, s 3(4) that no person of reasonable firmness need actually be, or be likely to be, present at the scene. The offence of affray is, in reality, concerned with *three* persons: a person using or threatening unlawful violence, a person towards whom the violence or threat is directed, and a notional person of reasonable firmness. It is not enough that the victim of the violence or threat is put in fear for his personal safety. The question is whether, if the *notional* person of reasonable firmness had been so present, he would have been caused to fear for his personal safety.

Mens rea

By POA 1986, s 6(2), a person is guilty of affray only if he *intends* to use or threaten violence or is *aware* that his conduct may be violent or threaten violence. As in the case of riot, a person whose awareness is impaired by intoxication—whether by drink, drugs or other means (or a combination of these)—must be taken to be aware of what he would have been aware of if not intoxicated, unless he shows that his intoxication was not self-induced or that it was caused solely by the taking or administration of a substance in the course of medical treatment.

FEAR OR PROVOCATION OF VIOLENCE

POA 1986, s 4(1) provides that a person is guilty of an offence if he:

(a) uses towards another person threatening, abusive or insulting words or behaviour; or

(b) distributes or displays to *another person* any writing, sign or other visible representation which is threatening, abusive or insulting,

with intent to cause that person to believe that immediate unlawful violence will be used against him or another by any person, or to provoke the immediate use of unlawful violence by that person or another, or whereby that person is likely to believe that such violence will be used or it is likely that such violence will be provoked.

Threatening, abusive or insulting

The words 'threatening, abusive or insulting' do not bear an unusual legal meaning. Instead, the magistrates will decide as a question of fact whether the accused's conduct was threatening, abusive or insulting in the ordinary meaning of those terms, and this is to be judged according to the impact which the conduct would have on a reasonable member of the public. Masturbation in a public convenience in the view of a stranger is capable of being insulting behaviour because he might be a heterosexual who would be insulted at being taken for a homosexual. Behaviour is not threatening, abusive or insulting merely because it gives rise to a risk that immediate violence will be feared or provoked, nor simply because it gives rise to anger, disgust or distress. This is shown by a case where the accused's activities in disrupting a tennis match at Wimbledon (by running onto No 2 court and distributing leaflets) caused anger among spectators, some of whom tried to hit him as he was removed. The House of Lords did not disturb the magistrates' finding that, albeit annoying and irritating, the accused's behaviour was not threatening, abusive or insulting.

If conduct is threatening, abusive or insulting, it does not matter whether or not anyone who witnessed it felt himself to be threatened, abused or insulted.

The distribution or display of any writing, sign or other visible representation which is threatening, abusive or insulting covers handing out leaflets (distribution) or holding up a banner or placard (display).

POA 1986, s 4 requires that threatening, abusive or insulting words or behaviour must be used *towards another person* or that threatening etc written material be distributed or displayed to *another*. In relation to the use of threatening, abusive or insulting words or behaviour, 'towards another' imports a requirement that the words or behaviour in question must be directed towards (ie deliberately aimed at) another particular person or persons; if they are not, one must rely on the offence under POA 1986, s 4A or the lesser offence under POA 1986, s 5. Conduct is not used towards another if he is not present, in the sense that he can perceive with his own senses the threatening words or behaviour etc. Thus, a person who makes a threat against a person who is out of earshot and only learns of it through a third party who is not under the control or direction of the maker of the threat cannot be convicted of an offence under this section. However, whilst the person towards whom the behaviour was aimed must have been present to perceive it, this does not mean that the only means of proving that the victim perceived the behaviour is by hearing evidence from that person. Justices may rely solely on evidence from a bystander and may draw the inference that the victim did perceive what was said and done by an accused.

The insertion of 'to another' after 'distributes or displays' requires that the written material be directed towards another particular person or persons (or brought to his notice), rather than simply being distributed (eg by leaflets being left lying around in a shopping centre) or displayed (eg by pinning a poster to a wall in the middle of the night).

Public or private place

With one exception, an offence under POA 1986, s 4 can be committed in private places, such as factory premises, clubs or college premises, as well as in public places, such as football grounds, dance halls, public car parks and shopping precincts. Thus, an offence can be committed by pickets who threaten working colleagues, whether the pickets are inside or outside factory premises, or by protesters who invade a military base.

The exception is that, in order to exclude domestic disputes, POA 1986, s 4 has the effect of providing that the use of words or behaviour inside a dwelling is only an offence if the addressee (ie another person towards whom the words or behaviour are used or the writing etc is displayed) is not inside that dwelling or any other dwelling. Thus, to use threatening, abusive or insulting words towards someone else in the same house cannot be an offence under s 4, and the same is true if such words are shouted to someone in the house next door or displayed so as to be visible only to him. On the other hand, if such words are shouted in a house at a next-door neighbour who is in his back garden, an offence under s 4 will be committed, provided that the other elements of the offence are satisfied.

For the above purpose, 'dwelling' means any structure or part of a structure occupied as a person's home or as other living accommodation (whether the occupation is separate or shared with others) but does not include any part not so occupied, such as a garage, a shop with accommodation over or the communal parts of a block of flats. Thus, if threatening words are shouted from a flat to a shop below, an offence under POA 1986, s 4 may be committed, and so may it if the words are shouted from the shop to the flat upstairs. 'Structure' here includes a tent, caravan, vehicle, vessel or other temporary or movable structure.

Mens rea

The accused must either intend the words, behaviour or writing etc to be threatening, abusive or insulting or be aware that they or it may be. The result of this requirement is that a person, who uses words which are seemingly innocuous but which are addressed to, or heard by, persons to whom (unknown to him) they are highly insulting, is not guilty of the present offence.

A person whose awareness is impaired by intoxication must be taken to be aware of that of which he would be aware if not intoxicated, unless he shows either that his intoxication was not self-induced or that it was caused solely by the taking or administration of a substance in the course of medical treatment.

POA 1986, s 4 also requires that the accused's use of the words or behaviour towards another (hereafter described as 'an addressee'), or the accused's distribution or display to another ('an addressee') of the writing etc, must be intended by the accused or be likely (whether or not the accused realises this) either:

(a) to provoke the immediate use of unlawful violence *by an addressee or another*; or
(b) to cause *an addressee* to believe that immediate unlawful violence will be used against him or another.

It will be noted, under para (a), that it is not necessarily an addressee who must be intended or likely to be provoked to immediate violence. It is sufficient that someone else present, towards whom the threatening etc behaviour etc was not directed, was intended or likely to be provoked. Thus, if X shouts at a coloured person whom he knows cannot speak English, 'Paki bastard, go home', intending that this should provoke immediate violence on the part of a group of skinheads who are in the near vicinity, the present offence is committed. On the other hand, for the purposes of para (b), fear of immediate violence, intended or likely, the fear must be on the part of an addressee (although it need not be fear of violence against himself, nor of violence by the accused).

It is important to note that the offence under POA 1986, s 4, unlike those under ss 1 to 3, is not concerned with the reactions of a hypothetical person of reasonable firmness. It has been held that, since constables are under a common law duty to preserve the peace, they are unlikely to respond to threatening, abusive or insulting conduct by using violence. Nevertheless, such conduct directed towards a constable will constitute an offence under s 4 if it is intended or likely to put him in fear of immediate unlawful violence or is intended to provoke him to such violence. If the conduct is so serious as to amount to a breach of the peace and make it likely that a constable to whom it is addressed will have to use violence in the exercise of his common law power to arrest for a breach of the peace, an offence under s 4 will not be committed because the violence likely to be provoked will not be unlawful.

The fact that the unlawful violence which is intended or likely to cause a person to believe will be used or provoked must be *immediate* must be emphasised. However, that term has been given a liberal interpretation by a divisional court. 'Immediate' does not mean 'instantaneous'. Instead violence will be 'immediate' if it is likely to result in a relatively short period of time and without any intervening occurrence.

As with the term 'unlawful violence' in other offences in POA 1986, the immediate violence which is intended, or is likely, to be feared to be used, or to be provoked, will not be unlawful if it is reasonable force in self-defence, or in prevention of crime, or is otherwise legally justified.

A speaker must take his audience as he finds it. If he uses insulting words at a meeting, he is guilty of the present offence if they are likely to provoke the immediate use of violence by the particular audience he is addressing, even though he does not intend to provoke this and even though his words would not be likely to cause a reasonable person so to react, provided that he intends his words to be insulting or is aware that they might be.

In the reference to an intention to cause, or the likelihood of causing, the apprehension of immediate unlawful violence or the provocation of it, 'violence' means any violent conduct. It includes fear or provocation of violent conduct towards property as well as violent conduct towards persons, and it is not restricted to conduct causing or intended to cause injury or damage but includes any other violent conduct (such as throwing at or towards a person a missile of a kind capable of causing injury which does not hit or falls short).

HARASSMENT, ALARM OR DISTRESS

POA 1986, s 4 does not deal with many minor acts of hooliganism or other anti-social behaviour which are prevalent, particularly in inner city areas. Such conduct is a particular cause for concern when it is directed at members of especially vulnerable groups, such as the elderly and members of religious groups, who may feel unable to act themselves to remove the nuisance or who may be deterred from participating in everyday activities or even from leaving their homes. It is at problems such as these, in particular, that the offences under POA 1986, ss 4A and 5 are aimed.

POA 1986, s 4A provides that a person is guilty of an offence if, with intent to cause a person harassment, alarm or distress, he:

(a) uses threatening, abusive or insulting words or behaviour, or disorderly behaviour; or
(b) displays any writing, sign or other visible representation which is threatening, abusive or insulting,

thereby causing that or another person, harassment, alarm or distress.

POA 1986, s 5 provides that a person is guilty of an offence if he:

(a) uses threatening, abusive or insulting words or behaviour or disorderly behaviour; or
(b) displays any writing, sign or other visible representation which is threatening, abusive or insulting,

within the hearing or sight of a person likely to be caused harassment, alarm or distress thereby.

As these two definitions indicate, there is much common ground between these two offences. We shall deal with this first and then consider the elements which distinguish the two offences.

The common elements are that a person must use threatening, abusive, insulting or disorderly words or behaviour, or display any writing, sign or other visible representation which is threatening, abusive or insulting. The words 'threatening, abusive or insulting' have already been discussed and what is said there is equally applicable here. A similar approach applies to 'disorderly', a term with which magistrates are already familiar via the offence of being drunk and disorderly. Thus, it is a question of fact for the magistrates whether the accused's conduct was disorderly in the ordinary meaning of the term. A divisional court, in confirming this, has held that an element of 'violence' is not essential for there to be disorderly behaviour, and that neither is an abusive, threatening or insulting character to the behaviour required nor any feeling of insecurity, in an apprehensive sense, on the part of a member of the public.

'Behaviour' is not limited to overt behaviour. It would be open to a court to find that the conduct of a 'Peeping Tom' constitutes insulting behaviour. Indeed, in one case, where a trader installed a video camera in an area used by ladies to try on swim wear, a divisional court held that he had been properly convicted of an offence against POA 1986, s 5. The guilty act was the setting up of the camera and letting it run, which amounted to insulting behaviour. This decision is of importance in relation to an offence under s 5, although a more appropriate offence to charge would now be one of the offences under the Sexual Offences Act 2003, s 67 (see p 971).

In relation to any threatening, abusive or insulting writing, sign or other visible representation, the offence is limited to displaying and cannot (unlike an offence under POA 1986, s 4) also be committed by distribution. One result is that handing out threatening, abusive or insulting leaflets is not caught by s 4A or s 5, unless the leaflets are so printed, and so held, that their contents can be said to be displayed in the sight of another. An important application of s 5 will be the display of graffiti or slogans likely to cause racial harassment.

Another distinction between the offences under the POA 1986, s 4A and s 5 and that under POA 1986, s 4 is that the words or behaviour need not be used *towards* another person (nor need writing etc be displayed to another). It follows that words or behaviour need not be directed towards another, nor need written material be deliberately brought to the attention of another.

An offence under POA 1986, s 4A or s 5 may be committed in a public or a private place, except that no offence is committed where the words or behaviour are used, or the writing, sign or other visible representation is displayed, by a person inside a dwelling and the other person who is harassed, alarmed or distressed thereby (s 4A), or, within whose sight or hearing it occurs and who is likely to be harassed, alarmed or distressed thereby (s 5), is also inside that or another dwelling. Consequently, displaying an abusive poster in the front window of a house adjacent to the street is capable of being an offence under s 4A or s 5, whereas if the poster was displayed in a place where it could only be seen by a person in the house or by a person in the first floor flat of the house next door a s 4A or s 5 offence would not be committed. It will be remembered that there is a corresponding provision in relation to an offence under s 4.

The separate elements: POA 1986, s 4A

While the accused's conduct need not be directed towards another (and written material need not be displayed by him to another), there must be a victim in the sense that someone else is actually caused harassment, alarm or distress. 'Harassment, alarm or distress' are not defined by POA 1986. They are somewhat vague terms. It has been held that 'harassment' does not require any apprehension about one's personal safety, nor (probably) does 'distress'.

The fact that there has to be an identifiable victim means that some (possibly many) cases falling within POA 1986, s 4A will not be prosecuted under that section because victims of harassment may well be reluctant to go to court and give evidence for fear of reprisals, and without such evidence it will normally be impossible to prove that a particular person was caused harassment, alarm or distress. The offence is intended to protect the vulnerable, and the vulnerable are most likely to be influenced by the fear of reprisals.

The offence is inadequate to deal with harassment (racial or otherwise) for another reason. In some cases, such as racist graffiti on walls or racist chanting, there is no identifiable individual victim who is harassed, alarmed or distressed but, rather, an offence to a section of the public at large.

The offence can be committed by an isolated piece of conduct; persistence is not required.

The accused must either intend his words or behaviour, or the writing etc, to be threatening, abusive or insulting or be aware that they or it may be threatening, abusive or insulting, or (as the case may be) intend his conduct to be or be aware that it may be disorderly.

The accused must also intend his threatening etc words or behaviour or his display of a threatening etc visible representation to cause a person, harassment, alarm or distress; it is irrelevant that the person who was actually caused the harassment etc was not the intended victim. The need for an intent to harass to be proved by the prosecution is a significant limiting factor on the offence, particularly because its proof may be difficult in practice. However, given that the prohibited conduct can be satisfied if an unduly sensitive person is inadvertently caused distress by disorderly conduct, some sort of subjective state of mind does seem to be essential if the offence is not to be too wide. It would have been better if awareness (recklessness) as to the risk of causing harassment etc had been specified as an alternative to intention.

POA 1986, s 4A(3) provides two defences which also apply on a charge under s 5. POA 1986, s 4A(3)(a) provides a defence for an accused who alleges that he was inside a dwelling at the material time. It states that it is a defence for him to prove that he was inside a dwelling and had no reason to believe that the words or behaviour used, or the writing, sign or other visible representation displayed, would be heard or seen by a person outside that or any other dwelling.

POA 1986, s 4A(3)(b) provides that it is a defence for an accused to prove that his conduct was reasonable, reasonableness being judged objectively. It would be reasonable, for example, to shout a threat at a pickpocket across the street to deter him. This is an exceptionally vague defence and proving it may often be difficult.

The separate elements: POA 1986, s 5

While the accused's conduct need not be directed towards another (and written material need not be displayed by him to another), there must be a victim in the sense that what the accused does must be within the hearing or sight of a person likely to be caused harassment, alarm or distress thereby, although no likelihood of violence being provoked or feared is required. Whilst there must be evidence that someone was able to see or hear the words or conduct complained of, the prosecution does not have to call evidence that the words or conduct were actually heard or seen. We have already commented upon the vagueness of 'harassment, alarm or distress'.

A police officer is a person capable of being subject to 'harassment, alarm or distress' for the purposes of this offence (and for the purposes of the POA 1986, s 4A offence). It is not necessary that a person who is likely to be alarmed should be alarmed for his own safety; it suffices that he is likely to be alarmed about the safety of someone unconnected with him.

The accused must either intend his words or behaviour, or the writing etc, to be threatening, abusive or insulting or be aware that it may be threatening, abusive or insulting, or (as the case may be) intend his conduct to be or be aware that it may be disorderly. Consequently, a person who gives no thought to the nature of his conduct, or who honestly believes that there is no risk of it being threatening etc, does not commit this offence. The provisions concerning intoxication, discussed above, apply equally to an offence under POA 1986, s 5.

Although the accused's conduct must be in the hearing or sight of a person likely to be caused harassment, alarm or distress thereby, the accused is not required to intend this or to be aware that it might occur. On the other hand, POA 1986, s 5(3)(a) provides that it is a defence for the accused to prove that he had no reason to believe that there was any person within hearing or sight who was likely to be caused harassment, alarm or distress. There are two other defences, which correspond with those in s 4A. Section 5(3)(b) provides a related defence to that in s 5(3)(a) for an accused who alleges that he was inside a dwelling at the material time. It states that it is a defence for him to prove that he was inside a dwelling and had no reason to believe that the words or behaviour used, or the writing, sign or other visible representation displayed, would be heard or seen by a person outside that or any other dwelling.

POA 1986, s 5(3)(c) provides that it is a defence for an accused to prove that his conduct was reasonable. As with the defence in s 4A, 'reasonableness' is judged objectively. A divisional court has held that if the prosecution proves, as it must, that the defendant's behaviour was threatening, abusive or insulting, and that he intended it to be, or was aware that it might be, it would in most cases follow that his conduct was objectively unreasonable. The court also stated that, in considering whether conduct was reasonable, the court must have regard to all the circumstances, and to the European Convention on Human Rights, art 10(2), which sets out the grounds on which the freedom of expression may be interfered with. This latter point had already been made by another divisional court, which stated that a court must presume that conduct is protected by art 10 unless and until it is established that a restriction on that freedom is strictly necessary in a democratic society for the protection of the rights of others and proportionate to the need to protect such rights. In this case, a protester had defaced the American flag in the sight of American servicemen. A district judge had considered that the protester's right to freedom of expression under art 10 was necessarily restricted by s 5 for the protection of the rights of others and convicted her of the offence. Allowing the protester's appeal against conviction, the divisional court held that the district judge had given insufficient weight to the presumption in favour of the protester under art 10. It said that the fact that the protester could have made her point in another way was only one factor to consider when determining the overall reasonableness and proportionality of her behaviour and the state's response to it. In another case, a divisional court supported a conviction by magistrates where an evangelical Christian preacher displayed a sign reading 'Stop immorality, Stop homosexuality, Stop lesbianism' holding that the justices had found as a fact that the words had been 'threatening, abusive or insulting' and that the preacher was aware that this was so. They were entitled to reach such a conclusion. The restriction placed upon his freedom of expression had the legitimate aim of preventing disorder.

Offences against POA 1986, s 5 are 'penalty offences' for the purpose of the Criminal Justice and Police Act 2001 (CJPA 2001), s 1, which is explained on p 874.

RACIALLY- OR RELIGIOUSLY-AGGRAVATED PUBLIC ORDER OFFENCES

A person commits an offence under CDA 1998, s 31 if he commits an offence under POA 1986, ss 4, 4A or 5, which is racially or religiously aggravated. There are three separate offences under s 31, each based on one of the three basic offences under POA 1986.

By CDA 1998, s 28(1), an offence is racially- or religiously-aggravated for the purposes of CDA 1998, s 31 if:

(a) at the time of committing it, or immediately before or after doing so, the offender demonstrates towards the victim of the offence (or, in the case of a basic offence under POA 1986, s 5, the person likely to be caused harassment, alarm or distress) hostility based on that person's membership (actual or presumed) of a racial or religious group; or

(b) the offence is motivated (wholly or partly) by hostility towards members of a racial or religious group based on their membership of that group.

For this purpose, in (a) 'membership of a racial or religious group' includes association with members of that group, and 'presumed' means presumed by the offender. A 'racial group' means a group of persons defined by reference to race, colour, nationality (including citizenship) or ethnic or national origins. A 'religious group' is a group of persons defined by reference to religious belief or lack of religious belief. (a) does not require the hostility demonstrated to be based only on the victim's membership of a racial or religious group, or even principally on it. 'Immediately' in (a) qualifies 'after' as well as 'before'. This was held in a case where a conviction for a racially aggravated offence was quashed on the basis that the demonstration of racial hostility twenty minutes after the basic offence was not 'immediately after' that offence.

An offence under CDA 1998, s 31 can be committed by someone of the same racial group as that at which his offence is 'aimed'. This is demonstrated by a case where a man of the same racial group addressed a bus conductress from Sierra Leone as a 'stupid African bitch'; the Court of Appeal held that the term 'African' did describe a racial group and that it was possible for a person to show hostility to another who was of the same racial group.

For the test under head (a) to be satisfied, the defendant must have formed the view that the victim was a member of a racial group and the defendant must have done or said something which demonstrated hostility towards the victim based on that membership. Where victims of the words 'bloody foreigners' were Spanish; it was held that these words were capable of satisfying (a); all who were black formed a racial group within s 28(4), as did all who were white; and it was no great extension of the concept to embrace within a single racial group all who were foreign). Words used may or may not expressly identify the racial group to which the victim belongs; this was held in a case where the victim, Indian and brown skinned, was called an 'immigrant doctor' by a defendant immediately before the defendant assaulted him. The Court of Appeal held that it was open to the jury to conclude that the defendant had identified her victim as falling within the racial groups of Indian and brown-skinned and that the use of 'immigrant' demonstrated hostility based on the victim's membership of such groups.

Although (a) requires proof of what the accused did at the time of committing the offence, (b) can be established by evidence relating to what the accused may have said or done on other occasions (since such evidence may be relevant to the accused's motivation at the time of the offence).

PROTECTION OF ACTIVITIES OF ANIMAL RESEARCH ORGANISATIONS

Interference with contractual relationships so as to harm animal research organisation

The Serious Organised Crime and Police Act 2005 (SOCPA 2005), s 145 provides that a person commits an offence if, with the intention of harming an animal research organisation, he:

(a) does a relevant act; or
(b) threatens that he or someone else will do a relevant act,

in circumstances in which that act or threat is intended or likely to cause a second person (B) :

(a) not to perform any contractual obligation owed by B to a third person (C) (whether or not such non-performance amounts to a breach of contract);
(b) to terminate any contract B has with C;
(c) not to enter into a contract with C.

A 'relevant act' is an act amounting to a criminal offence, or to a tortious act (ie an act giving rise to liability for damages) causing B to suffer loss or damage of any description (other than an act which is actionable on the grounds only that it induces another person to break a contract with B). For these purposes, 'contract' includes any other arrangement, and to 'harm' an animal research organisation means to cause the organisation to suffer loss or damage of any description, or to prevent or hinder the carrying out by the organisation of any of its activities.

Section 145 does not apply to any act done wholly or mainly in contemplation or furtherance of a trade dispute within the meaning of the Trade Union and Labour Relations (Consolidation) Act 1992. The Trade Union and Labour Relations (Consolidation) Act 1992 deals with similar acts committed in contemplation or furtherance of trade disputes.

Section 145 may do much to limit the activities of animal rights groups which have, for many years, targeted animal research organisations in an effort to compel them to cease activities authorised by law. Other legislation dealing with forms of harassment and disorder left many gaps which could be exploited by those who engaged in activities aimed at 'persuading' such organisations to abandon all forms of research which involved the use of animals. Targeting was not restricted to the actual animal research establishments, since it was also aimed at other organisations which were alleged to have any form of business dealings with such animals research establishments, or with other organisations which had such dealings.

Activities aimed directly at business premises frequently involved, in addition to criminal damage, activities which interrupted the smooth workings of the businesses concerned, such as the use of loud hailers and flooding of the switchboards with constant calls with no relevance to business activities. The nature of these activities created problems for the police in gathering evidence of offences connected with public disorder, while recognising the rights of the protesters to protest.

The effect of SOCPA 2005, s 145 is to prohibit such activities, being 'relevant acts', either criminal, or tortious in that they are intended to cause the company concerned to suffer loss or damage *of any description*. As s 145(3) provides that a tortious act does not include an act which is actionable on the ground only that it induces another person to break a contract with such organisations, it can be anticipated that animal protest groups will, at some stage, claim that any acts which they commit which are not in themselves criminal offences because they are solely directed at inducing another person to break a contract. It is submitted that the presence of the word 'only' will be the significant factor. Most of the acts carried out in the past could not be described as actionable 'only' on such grounds.

Intimidation of persons connected with animal research organisation

Animal rights groups are extremely well organised and encounter few difficulties in acquiring the names and addresses of directors and employees of organisations alleged to have connections with animal research establishments. Many research establishments, and the business premises of organisations with a connection with such establishments, are able to take effective measures to protect their property, to a large extent, but the residences of employees present an easier target to protesters, leading to houses being damaged and cars covered with paint stripper.

SOCPA 2005, s 146 therefore provides that a person (A) commits an offence if, with the intention of causing a second person (B) to abstain from doing something which B is entitled to do (or do something which B is entitled to abstain from doing):

(a) A threatens B that A or somebody else will do a relevant act; and
(b) A does so wholly or mainly because B is:
    (i)   an employee or officer of an animal research organisation;
    (ii)   a student at an educational establishment that is an animal research organisation;
    (iii)   a lessor or licensor of premises occupied by an animal research organisation;
    (iv)   a person who has a financial interest in, or who provides financial assistance to, such an organisation;
    (v)   a customer or supplier of such an organisation; or
    (vi)   a person contemplating becoming someone within (iii), (iv) or (v);
    (vii)   a person who is, or is contemplating becoming, a customer or supplier of someone within (iii), (iv), (v) or (vi);
    (viii) an employee or officer of someone within (iii), (iv), (v), (vi), or (vii);
    (ix)   a person with a financial interest in, or who provides financial assistance to, someone within (iii), (iv), (v), (vi) or (vii);
    (x)   a spouse, civil partner, friend or relative of, or a person known personally to, someone within (i)–(ix); or
    (xi)   a person who is, or is contemplating becoming, a customer or supplier of someone within (i), (ii), (viii), (ix) or (x);
    (xii)   an employer of someone within (x).

The provisions in s 146 do not apply to trade disputes.

For the purposes of s 146 'relevant act' has the same meaning as in s 145, except that the limitation whereby a tortious act does not include an act actionable only because it induces a breach of contract with B does not apply.

General

Proceedings for an offence under SOCPA 2005, s 145 or 146 may not be taken without the consent of the Director of Public Prosecutions.

'Animal research organisations' means any person or organisation (a) who or which is the owner, lessee or licensee of premises licensed or designated by the Animals (Scientific Procedures) Act 1986, or (b) who or which is the employer of, or engages under a contract of service, a person who is the holder of a licence under that Act or who is specified by it. The Secretary of State is empowered to amend this provision.

ANTI-SOCIAL BEHAVIOUR ORDERS

CDA 1998, s 1 empowers:

(a) a council for a local government area;
(b) a county council (in England);
(c) a chief officer of police (including the British Transport Police (BTP));
(d) any person registered under the Housing Act 1996, s 1 as a social landlord who provides or manages any houses or hostel in a local government area;
(e) a housing action trust established under the Housing Act 1988, s 62;
(f) the Environment Agency; or
(g) Transport for London,

to apply by way of complaint to a magistrates' court for an anti-social behaviour order to be made in respect of any person aged ten or over. Before applying for an order, a council must consult the local chief officer of police (and vice versa) before making an application. A registered social landlord or housing trust must consult the council and the chief officer of police before making an application. A chief officer of police can delegate the consultation process and the application for an order to officers in his force.

By CDA 1998, s 1B, a relevant authority additionally may apply for an order within county court proceedings. A relevant authority may apply to have a person who is not a party to the principal proceedings in a county court, but whose behaviour is material, to be joined in those proceedings so that an order can be applied for.

Applications for orders by housing action trusts are limited to applications which would protect their tenants.

The circumstances in which a complaint may be made are that:

(a) the person has acted in an anti-social manner, that is to say, in a manner that caused or was likely to cause harassment, alarm or distress to one or more persons not of the same household as himself; and
(b) such an order is necessary to protect relevant persons from further anti-social acts by him.

Such acts need not have occurred within the previous six months of the making of the complaint as there is no corresponding six-month limit which applies to the laying of an information. Evidence of events which took place more than six months before the application was made are admissible in respect of either limb of CDA 1998, s 1(1).

In the case of a complaint by a council or a chief officer of police (other than BTP), 'relevant persons' are those within the council or county council area, or police area, respectively. In the case of a complaint by the chief officer of BTP 'relevant persons' are those who are within (or are likely to be within) areas which may briefly be described as railway land within the jurisdiction of the BTP. In the case of a complaint by a registered social landlord or a housing action trust, 'relevant persons' are people who are in (or are likely to be in) the premises subject to their control or the vicinity of those premises.

In considering whether to make such an order, the court must disregard any acts which are shown to have been reasonable. The House of Lords has held that, although the proceedings described above to obtain anti-social behaviour orders are civil (and not criminal) in nature, and therefore the laws of evidence which apply in civil cases will apply to such proceedings, the standard of proof is the criminal one: proof beyond reasonable doubt. Its reason was the seriousness of the matter involved.

An anti-social behaviour order can also be made on conviction in criminal proceedings, if a court considers that the conditions set out in CDA 1998 have been fulfilled, and this may be done whether or not an application has been made. The order must be additional to a sentence for the offence or an order of conditional discharge.

The prohibitions which may be included in an order are those necessary for the purpose of protecting persons (whether relevant persons or persons elsewhere in England and Wales) from further anti-social acts by the defendant.

CDA 1998, s 1AA, which requires that where a court makes an anti-social behaviour order in respect of a defendant who is a child or young person (ten to seventeen), it must consider whether individual support conditions are fulfilled. These conditions are:

(a) that it would be desirable in the interests of preventing any repetition of the behaviour which led to the order;
(b) the defendant is not already subject to an individual support order; and
(c) the court has been notified that arrangements are in place for implementing such orders.

If all of those conditions are fulfilled then the court must make an individual support order for a period not exceeding six months. Such an order requires the defendant to comply with its requirements and to comply with directions given by a 'responsible officer' (social worker, education officer or member of a youth offending team) to participate in specified activities, to report and to comply with educational arrangements but attendance at an appointed place may not be required on more than two days each week. Before the court makes such an order it must obtain information from the local authority or a member of a youth offending team. An individual support order will cease if the anti-social behaviour order to which it is linked ceases.

Variation of an order may be applied for by way of complaint but no order can be discharged before the end of the period of two years other than with the consent of both parties.

Breach of a prohibition in an anti-social behaviour order without reasonable excuse is an offence. A local authority may prosecute for this offence where it obtained the order or where the person subject to the order appears to reside in its area, but the Crown Prosecution Service may do so if it wishes. In proceedings for the offence, a copy of the order certified by a proper officer of the court, is evidence of the making of the order and its contents to the same extent that oral evidence would have been admissible. Reporting restrictions do not apply to such proceedings but may be restricted provided that the court states its reasons.

The Police Reform Act 2002 (PRA 2002), s 50 provides that if a constable in uniform has reasonable grounds to believe that a person has been acting in an anti-social manner within the meaning of CDA 1998, s 1, he may require that person to give his name and address. Failure to do so, or the provision of a false or inaccurate name and address, is an offence.

SOCPA 2005, s 142 amended CDA 1998 to permit local authorities to 'contract out' Anti-Social Behaviour Order (ASBO) functions. The Secretary of State may by order specify a person to whom local authorities may contract out these functions. Such an order may specify conditions and may empower a local authority to make its own conditions.

Section 143 makes provision for special measures under the Youth Justice and Criminal Evidence Act 1999 (see p 211) to apply to vulnerable and intimidated witnesses in the context of ASBO proceedings.

The Drugs Act 2005, s 20 inserted a s 1G into CDA 1998 which permits a relevant authority which is applying for an anti-social behaviour order in respect of a person of eighteen or over, to also apply for an 'intervention order' where it has received a report relating to the effect of the use of controlled drugs upon a person's behaviour. In such circumstances a court may, additionally, make such an order in the interests of preventing further such behaviour. Such an order may be valid for no more than six months and will require the person to comply with requirements specified in the order. In the event of failure to comply, the appointed supervisor must inform the relevant authority. Failure, without reasonable excuse, to comply with a requirement of the order is an offence.

PENALTY NOTICES FOR DISORDERLY BEHAVIOUR

CJPA 2001, s 2 provides that a constable in uniform who has reason to believe that someone aged ten or over has committed a 'penalty offence' *may* issue a 'penalty notice'.

If a child under sixteen is given a penalty notice, the chief officer of police must within twenty-eight days notify in writing such parent or guardian of the child as he thinks fit, either by first class post or by delivery to the parent or guardian personally, of the giving of the penalty notice. The chief officer is given power to cancel the original notification within twenty-one days of its service if it is discovered that the person on whom the notification was served was not the parent or guardian of the child, or if it is desired that the notification should have been served on another parent or guardian of the child (in which case the parent or guardian served with the original notification must be informed in writing of the cancellation). If the chief officer cancels the original notification, he must notify such other person who is a parent or guardian of the child of the giving of the penalty notice.

The term 'penalty offence' means:

(a)	Being drunk in a highway, other public place or licensed premises	Licensing Act 1872, s 12
(b)	Throwing fireworks in a thoroughfare	Explosives Act 1875, s 80 (prospectively repealed)
(c)	Knowingly giving false alarm of fire	Fire and Rescue Services Act 2004, s 49
(d)	Trespassing on a railway	British Transport Commission Act 1949, s 55
(e)	Throwing stones etc at trains or other things on railways	British Transport Commission Act 1949, s 56
(f)	Sale of alcohol to person who is drunk	Licensing Act 2003, s 141
(g)	Sale of alcohol to children	Licensing Act 2003, s 146(1) and (3)
(h)	Purchase of alcohol by or on behalf of children	Licencing Act 2003, s 149(1)
(i)	Buying or attempting to buy alcohol for consumption on licensed premises, etc by a child	Licencing Act 2003, s 149(4)
(j)	Consumption of alcohol by children or allowing such consumption	Licensing Act 2003, s 150
(k)	Delivering alcohol to children or allowing such delivery	Licensing Act 2003, s 151
(l)	Drunk and disorderly in a public place	Criminal Justice Act 1967, s 91
(m)	Wasting police time or giving false report	Criminal Law Act 1967, s 5(2)
(n)	Theft	Theft Act 1968, s 1
(o)	Destroying or damaging property	Criminal Damage Act 1971, s 1(1)
(p)	Using a public electronic communications network in order to cause annoyance, inconvenience or needless anxiety	Communications Act 2003, s 127
(q)	Contravention of a prohibition or a failure to comply with a requirement imposed by or under fireworks regulations or making false statements	Fireworks Act 2003, s 11
(r)	Behaviour likely to cause harassment, alarm or distress	Public Order Act 1986, s 5
(s)	Depositing and leaving litter	Environmental Protection Act 1990, s 87
(t)	Consuming alcohol in designated public place	Criminal Justice and Police Act 2001, s 12

By way of exception to the 'in uniform' requirement, where a penalty notice is given at a police station by a constable authorised by the chief officer of police that officer need not be in uniform.

A penalty notice offers the opportunity to discharge liability for such specified offences by the payment of a penalty. The amount of such penalty will be prescribed by order but must not be more than a quarter of the maximum penalty on conviction summarily. CJPA 2001, s 3, which deals with the amount of penalties, is prospectively amended by the Domestic Violence, Crimes and Victims Act 2004 (DVCVA 2004), s 15, to give the Secretary of State power to add to prescribed penalties 'a half of the relevant surcharge'. The 'relevant surcharge' in relation to a person of a given age is the amount payable by way of surcharge under CJA 2003, s 161A by a person of that age who is fined the maximum amount for the offence.

The Penalties for Disorderly Behaviour (Amount of Penalty) Order 2002 as amended prescribes penalties of £80 for offences of knowingly giving a false alarm to a fire brigade; sale of alcohol to a person who is drunk; sale of alcohol to someone under eighteen; buying alcohol on behalf of such a person; delivering alcohol to such a person; wasting police time or giving false report; using a public electronic communications network in order to cause annoyance, inconvenience or needless anxiety; behaviour likely to cause harassment, alarm or distress; throwing fireworks in a thoroughfare; theft; criminal damage; and breach of fireworks regulations (and false statements), and penalties of £50 for the remainder. Where the penalty notice is given to a child under sixteen the penalties are £40 and £30 respectively.

The provisions in respect of penalty notices; their effect; their restriction upon proceedings; the payment of penalties; registration of penalties and sums payable in default; and enforcement are the same as those provided in relation to fixed penalties for road traffic offences.

It is not intended that a penalty notice should always be issued in respect of the specified cases; the constable has discretion. Penalty notices are designed for minor and straightforward cases. More serious cases should be dealt with by using the traditional criminal process.

Community support officers and accredited persons may issue penalty notices under CJPA 2001, except they may not issue a notice in respect of theft or of depositing and leaving litter, and in addition an accredited person may not issue a notice in respect of criminal damage.

POWER TO DISPERSE GROUPS IN AREAS WHERE PERSISTENT ANTI-SOCIAL BEHAVIOUR HAS OCCURRED

A-sBA 2003 provides the police with powers to designate areas where they can disperse groups causing intimidation, direct that groups disperse, and after 9 pm return those under sixteen to their homes.

The principal provision is A-sBA 2003, s 30. It applies where an officer of above the rank of superintendent has reasonable grounds for believing:

(a) that any members of the public have been intimidated, harassed, alarmed or distressed as a result of the presence or behaviour of groups of two or more persons in public places in any locality in his police area (the 'relevant locality'); and

(b) that anti-social behaviour is a significant and persistent problem in the relevant locality.

A-sBA 2003, s 30 provides that that officer may give an authorisation that the powers conferred on a constable in uniform by s 30(3) to (6) are to be exercisable for a period specified in the authorisation, which must not exceed six months.

By A-sBA 2003, s 30(3) and (4), a constable in uniform who has reasonable grounds for believing that the presence or behaviour of a group of two or more persons in any public place in the relevant locality has resulted, or is likely to result, in any members of the public being intimidated, harassed, alarmed or distressed may give one or more of the following directions. These are:

(a) a direction requiring the persons in the group to disperse (either immediately or by such time as he may specify and in such way as he may specify);
(b) a direction requiring any of those persons whose place of residence is not within the relevant locality to leave the relevant locality or any part of the relevant locality (either immediately or by such time as he may specify and in such way as he may specify); and
(c) a direction prohibiting any of those persons whose place of residence is not within the relevant locality from returning to the relevant locality or any part of the relevant locality for such period (not exceeding twenty-four hours) from the giving of the direction as he may specify.

The Court of Appeal has held that, provided a uniformed constable has the necessary grounds for belief, he may give a direction even though the group is of a different type, and their behaviour of a different kind, from that contemplated when the authorisation was given.

In two cases, a constable may not give such a direction: where a group is engaged in conduct which is lawful under the Trade Union and Labour Relations (Consolidation) Act 1992, s 220 (see p 925); or where it is participating in a public procession to which POA 1986, s 11 (see p 888) applies and the requisite advance notice has been given or is not required (A-sBA 2003, s 30(5)).

A-sBA 2003, s 30(6) provides that, if, between 9 pm and 6 am, a constable in uniform finds a person in any public place in the relevant locality who he has reasonable grounds for believing:

(a) is under sixteen; and
(b) is not under the effective control of a parent or a responsible person aged eighteen or over,

he may remove the person to the person's place of residence unless he has reasonable grounds for believing that the person would, if removed to that place, be likely to suffer significant harm.

The Court of Appeal has ruled that the power of removal given to a constable is coercive, so that the reasonable force may be used, if necessary, to remove a person under s 30(6).

Protests are not excluded from the application of s 30.

A-sBA 2003, s 31 requires that an authorisation under s 30 must be in writing, and signed, and must specify the relevant locality, the grounds for the authorisation and its duration. It must not be given without the consent of the district council(s) (or equivalent) for the relevant locality. The public must be made aware of the making and terms of an authorisation, by publication in a local newspaper or posting notices in the locality.

Police powers and duties

By A-sBA 2003, s 32 the directions which may be given by a constable may be given orally and to a person individually or to two or more persons together and may be withdrawn or varied. A person who knowingly contravenes a direction commits an offence.

Where the persons concerned are under the age of sixteen and the action described above has been taken, the local authority must be notified.

A-sBA 2003, s 33 amended PRA 2002 to allow community support officers to be given these powers to disperse groups and to remove persons under sixteen to their place of residence.

HARASSMENT BY STALKERS ETC

Prohibition of harassment

The Protection from Harassment Act 1997 (PHA 1997) sets out two prohibitions of harassment. The first, contained in s 1, prohibits a person from pursuing a course of conduct:

(a) which amounts to harassment of another person; and
(b) which he knows or ought to know amounts to harassment of the other person.

SOCPA 2005, s 125 added the second prohibition of harassment, contained in s 1(1A) to PHA 1997, which prohibits a person from pursuing a course of conduct:

(a) which involves harassment of two or more persons, and
(b) which he knows or ought to know involves harassment of those persons, and
(c) by which he intends to persuade any person (whether or not one of those mentioned above),
    (i)   not to do something that he is entitled or required to do, or
    (ii) to do something that he is not under any obligation to do.

Section 1(1A) was added to protect company employees from harassment by animal rights groups. Section 1(1) does not protect such employees who may only be harassed on one occasion. Section 1(1A) refers to a course of conduct and prohibits harassment of two or more persons on different occasions with knowledge that the conduct amounts to harassment and it is done for the purpose of compelling someone not to do something he is entitled to do, or to do something which he is not obliged to do.

The definition of 'a course of conduct' is amended to provide that it must involve, in the case of conduct relating to single person (see s 1(1)), conduct on at least two occasions in relation to that person or, in the case of conduct in relation to two or more persons (see s 1(1A)), conduct on at least one occasion in relation to each of those persons. 'Conduct' includes 'speech'. Publishing a series of articles in a newspaper can constitute a course of conduct.

Although there can be a course of conduct comprising only two incidents, the fewer the incidents and the wider apart they are spread, the less likely it is that a finding of harassment can be made. Nevertheless, incidents as far apart as one year can constitute a course of conduct if connected in type and context, eg a threat made once a year on someone's birthday.

By PHA 1997, s 7(3A), a person's (X's) conduct on any occasion which is aided, abetted, counselled or procured by another (Y) is taken:

(a) also to be on that occasion the conduct of Y; and

(b) to be conduct in relation to which Y's knowledge and purpose (and what Y ought to have known) are the same as they were in relation to what was contemplated or reasonably foreseeable at the time of the aiding, abetting etc.

This means in relation to the wording in s 1(1) that there can be a breach of the prohibition on harassment by Y if, for example, on one occasion the harassing conduct is by X aided and abetted by Y and on the second occasion it is by Y himself provided that the two pieces of conduct can be regarded as a 'course' and that part (b) of s 7(3A) is satisfied. The same principle will apply to conduct aimed at different company employees so far as s 1(1A) is concerned.

It is provided that the person whose course of conduct is in question ought to know that his conduct amounts to harassment of another if a reasonable person in possession of the same information would think the course of conduct amounted to harassment of the other. The reasonable person in this context is not imbued with any mental illness or other characteristic which the accused has.

Although it seems that a company cannot be harassed within the terms of this Act, individual employees of such companies which are subjected to harassment (eg by animal rights protesters) may be harassed within the terms of the Act.

'Harassment' includes alarming another person or causing that person distress.

While the Act was fashioned with 'stalkers' in mind, it is worth noting that its terms are wide enough to embrace situations in which harassment is caused to neighbours or to persons living in a particular area in which unruly juveniles tend to congregate. It can also cover the activities of political protesters and members of the 'paparazzi'. The courts, however, have shown an inclination to construe the Act as narrowly as they can. In one case, it was held that acts done in the conduct of oppressive litigation fell outside the terms of the Act.

The prohibitions of harassment in PHA 1997, s 1(1) and (1A) do not apply to a course of conduct for the purpose of preventing or detecting crime; nor to a course of conduct pursued under any enactment or rule of law or to comply with a condition or requirement lawfully imposed; nor to a case where, in the particular circumstances, the pursuit of the course of conduct was reasonable. This last limitation is an important curb on the potential width of s 1. It has been stated in the High Court that PHA 1997 was clearly not intended by Parliament to be used to clamp down on the discussion of matters of public interest or upon the rights of political protest and public demonstration. The Court said that it would resist any wide interpretation of the Act. It would have been better if Parliament's intentions had been more clearly set out in the first instance. Perhaps the reasonable man would view certain of the activities of protest groups as harassment. It has been stated in a divisional court that whether conduct was reasonable involves balancing the interests of the victim against the purpose and nature of the course of conduct pursued, including the right to peaceful protest. However, the court agreed in that case that, if the course of conduct involved breach of an injunction, it could not be reasonable conduct, at least unless the circumstances were very special.

PHA 1997, s 2 makes it an offence to break the prohibition of harassment.

Civil remedy

PHA 1997, s 3 makes provision for an actual or apprehended breach of the prohibition of harassment under s 1(1) to be the subject of a civil claim by the victim. Damages may be awarded for (among other things) any anxiety caused by the harassment and any financial loss resulting from the harassment. An employer can be liable in damages for a breach of the prohibition of harassment by an employee. The High Court or a county court may grant an injunction for the purpose of restraining a defendant from pursuing any course of conduct which amounts to harassment. Breach of such an injunction, without reasonable excuse, is an offence.

SOCPA 2005 added a s 3A to the PHA 1997 to permit an injunction to be sought where there is an actual or apprehended breach of s 1(1A). It permits a person who is or may be the victim of the course of conduct in question, or any who is or may be a person falling within s 1(1A)(c), to apply to the High Court or a county court for an injunction to forbid such conduct.

Victims should be made aware of these possibilities.

Putting people in fear of violence

PHA 1997, s 4 creates the offence of putting people in fear of violence. It is committed where a person whose course of conduct causes another to fear, on at least two occasions, that violence will be used against him, where the perpetrator knows or ought to know that his course of conduct will cause that other person to fear that consequence on each of the occasions in question. For the purposes of s 4, the course of conduct must cause another person to fear on at least two occasions, that violence will be used against him. 'Conduct' includes 'speech'. Direct evidence from the victim that he was caused to fear such violence is not essential, because a court may infer such fear if there is other evidence entitling them to do so, but without direct evidence from the victim proof may be difficult.

The section provides similar defences with the substitution of 'circumstances in which the pursuit of his course of conduct was reasonable for the protection of himself or another or for the protection of his or another's property', for 'the pursuit of the course of conduct being reasonable in the circumstances'.

Where a person is charged before a jury with an offence against PHA 1997, s 4 and the jury find him not guilty, they may find him guilty of an offence contrary to PHA 1997, s 2.

Breach of restraining order

PHA 1997, s 5 makes provision for the sentencing court in the case of a conviction under s 2 or s 4, in addition to any other sentence imposed, to make an order protecting the victim of the offence (who must be named), or any other person mentioned in the order, from further conduct which amounts to harassment or will cause a fear of violence. If, without reasonable excuse, a person does anything which is prohibited by the order, he commits an offence. When an amendment to s 5 is in force a restraining order will be capable of being made under s 5 where a defendant is convicted of any offence.

PHA, s 5A (which is not in force at the time of writing) permits a court before which a defendant is acquitted of an offence, if it considers that it is necessary to do so to protect a person from harassment by the defendant, to make an order prohibiting the defendant from doing anything specified in the order.

Police directions stopping the harassment etc of a person at his home

CJPA 2001, s 42 provides that a constable who is at the scene may give a direction to a person if:

(a) that person is present outside, or in the vicinity of, premises used by someone (the resident) as a dwelling;
(b) that constable believes, on reasonable grounds, that that person is there for the purpose (by his presence or otherwise) of representing to the resident or another individual, or of persuading the resident or other individual that:
    (i) he should not do something which he is entitled or required to do; or
    (ii) he should do something which he is not under any obligation to do; and
(c) the constable also believes on reasonable grounds that the presence of that person (either alone or together with others who are likely to be present):
    (i) amounts to, or is likely to result in, the harassment of the resident;
    (ii) or is likely to cause alarm or distress to the resident.

A direction under CJPA 2001, s 42 is one which requires its addressee to do things which the constable considers to be necessary to prevent the harassment of the resident or the causing of alarm or distress to the resident. It may be given orally, either to an individual or a group. A direction may require a person or persons to leave the vicinity of the premises (either immediately or after a period of time). It may include exceptions and may make exceptions subject to conditions, including conditions as to the distance from the premises in question at which, or the location where, those who do not leave must remain, and conditions as to the numbers, or identity, of the persons who are authorised by the exception to remain in the vicinity. SOCPA 2005, s 127, amended s 42 of CJPA 2001 so that it provides that requirements that may be made under s 42 include:

(a) a requirement to leave that vicinity of the premises in question, and
(b) a requirement not to return to it within such period as the constable may specify, may be for a period not being longer than three months.

When there is more than one officer at the scene, only the senior officer present may give the direction. The power to give a direction under CJPA 2001, s 42 does not include the power to direct a person to refrain from activity which is lawful under the Trade Union and Labour Relations (Consolidation) Act 1992, s 220 (p 925). Any direction given may be varied or withdrawn.

A person who knowingly contravenes such a direction commits an offence.

SOCPA 2005, s 126 added a s 42A to CJPA 2001 which provides that a person commits an offence if:

(a) he is present outside or in the vicinity of any premises that are used by any individual (the resident) as a dwelling, and
(b) he is there to represent to the resident or another individual, or to persuade the resident or other person, that he should not do something which he is entitled or required to do, or should do something he is not obliged to do, and
(c) he intends his presence to amount to harassment, alarm or distress to the resident, or knows or ought to know that his presence is likely to do so, and
(d) his presence amounts, or is likely to result in, harassment of the resident, a person in the resident's building or a person in another dwelling in the vicinity of the resident's dwelling.

RACIALLY- OR RELIGIOUSLY-AGGRAVATED HARASSMENT OFFENCES

A person commits an offence under CDA 1998, s 32 if he commits an offence under the Protection from Harassment Act 1997 which is racially or religiously aggravated. There are two separate offences under CDA 1998, s 32, each based on an offence under PHA 1997, s 2 or s 4 respectively.

By CDA 1998, s 28(1), an offence is racially or religiously aggravated for the purposes of s 32 if:

(a) at the time of committing it, or immediately before or after doing so, the offender demonstrates towards the victim hostility based on that person's membership (actual or presumed) of a racial or religious group; or
(b) the offence is motivated (wholly or partly) by hostility towards members of a racial or religious group based on their membership of that group.

In (a) 'membership of a racial or religious group' includes association with members of that group, and 'presumed' means presumed by the offender. A 'racial group' means a group of persons defined by reference to race, colour, nationality (including citizenship) or ethnic or national origins. A 'religious group' is a group of persons defined by reference to religious belief or lack of religious belief. We discussed s 28(1) on p 869; what was said there is equally applicable here.

RACIAL OR RELIGIOUS HATRED

POA 1986, Part III (ss 17 to 29) provides offences relating to racial hatred. The Racial and Religious Hatred Act 2006 inserted a Part IIIA (ss 29A to 29N) into the POA 1986, which added offences relating to religious hatred. To a large extent, the offences of religious hatred mirror those under ss 17 to 29, which forbid threatening, abusive or insulting words, behaviour or material intended or likely to cause racial hatred, but they are limited to words, behaviour or material which is 'threatening' and the accused must intend thereby to stir up religious hatred. It is convenient to deal with these matters together within the parallel offences.

POA 1986, s 17 provides that racial hatred means hatred against a group of persons defined by reference to colour, race, nationality (including citizenship) or ethnic or national origins. Hereafter, such a group is described for convenience as a 'racial group'. As can be seen, a group of persons defined by reference to religion is not a racial group and therefore falls outside the protection of POA 1986, Part III. Where the accused intends to stir up religious hatred, POA 1986, Part IIIA is the relevant part. POA 1986, s 29A provides that 'religious hatred' means hatred against a group of persons defined by reference to religious belief or lack of religious belief.

All offences under Part III of the 1986 Act require that the material, words or behaviour in question are 'threatening, abusive or insulting'. These words do not bear an unusual legal meaning. Instead, as with offences under ss 4, 4A and 5, the magistrates or jury must decide as a question of fact whether the material etc was threatening, abusive or insulting in the ordinary meaning of those terms, and this is judged according to the impact which it would have on a reasonable member of the public.

References to 'abusive' or 'insulting' were excluded from Part IIIA during Parliamentary debate upon the original proposals following members' concerns in relation to freedom of expression. In addition, POA 1986, s 29J provides that nothing in Part IIIA of the Act should be read or given effect in a way which prohibits or restricts discussion, criticism or expressions of antipathy, dislike, ridicule, insult or abuse of particular religions or the beliefs or practices of their adherents, or of any other belief system, or the beliefs or practices of its adherents, or proselytising or urging adherents of a different religion or belief system to cease practising their religion or belief system. In view of the savings in respect of 'freedom of expression', to offend against Part IIIA the form of 'threat' will have to be very direct such as carrying a banner urging the killing of non-believers in circumstances which make it clear that a particular religion is the only true religion, or the making of a similar threat in some other way.

Use of words or behaviour or display of written material

POA 1986, s 18(1) provides that a person who uses threatening, abusive or insulting words or behaviour, or displays any written material which is threatening, abusive or insulting, is guilty of an offence if:

(a) he intends thereby to stir up racial hatred; or
(b) having regard to all the circumstances, racial hatred is likely to be stirred up thereby.

The parallel offence created by s 29B requires the use of *threatening* words or behaviour, or the display of written material which is *threatening*, and an *intention* thereby to stir up religious hatred.

'Written material' includes any sign or other visible representation. POA 1986, s 18 does not apply to words or behaviour used, or written material displayed, solely for the purpose of being included in a television or sound broadcasting or cable service. In such a case, however, an offence may be committed under s 22 (or s 29F) when the programme is transmitted.

As in the case of an offence under POA 1986, s 4, 4A or 5A, these offences may be committed in a public place (for example, a football ground) or a private place. There is one limit in relation to private places. As in the case of an offence under s 4, 4A or 5, an offence is not committed by the use of words or behaviour, or the display of written material, by a person inside a dwelling which is not heard or seen except by other persons in that or another dwelling. Thus, racist taunts (or religious threats) shouted from a house to people in the street or displayed on a poster on a window visible in the street are caught, but not racist abuse (or religious threats) shouted inside a house or flat (and only audible within it or another house or flat) or a racist (or threatening religious poster) displayed in an inner room of a house.

It is a defence for the accused to prove that he was inside a dwelling and had no reason to believe that his words, threat or behaviour, or the written material displayed, would be heard or seen by a person outside that or any other dwelling.

As already seen, the prosecution must prove in the case of s 18 offences, that the accused intended to stir up racial hatred by his words, behaviour or display or that such hatred was likely to be stirred up thereby. Where an offence against s 29B is alleged, there must be proof that the accused intended by his threatening words, behaviour or display to stir up religious hatred.

POA 1986, s 18(5) provides that a person who is not shown to have intended to stir up racial hatred is not guilty of an offence under s 18 if he did not intend his words or behaviour or the written material to be, and was not aware that it might be, threatening, abusive or insulting. Unlike comparable provisions in other offences in POA 1986, Part III, the accused does not have the burden of proving this lack of intent or awareness. There is no parallel provision to s 18(5) under s 29B as that section is limited to cases where the accused intended to stir up religious hatred.

Racial or religious abuse or harassment unaccompanied by the mental element just described may, nevertheless, result in liability for an offence under CDA 1998, s 31 or 32.

Publishing or distributing

POA 1986, s 19 provides that a person who publishes or distributes written material which is threatening, abusive or insulting is guilty of an offence if:

(a) he intends thereby to stir up racial hatred; or
(b) having regard to all the circumstances, racial hatred is likely to be stirred up thereby.

There must be a publication or distribution to the public or to a section of the public. 'The public' and 'section of the public' are not defined by the Act. In the only reported case which has referred to the point, the Court of Appeal held that a distribution of racialist pamphlets to members of a family living together in one house was not a distribution to 'the public at large'. There is no minimum number of persons to whom publication or distribution must be made in order for it to be to 'the public'. Ultimately, the question must be solved by common sense, the question being whether the publication or distribution has been on a scale and on a basis such as to be describable as being to 'the public'.

A publication or distribution only to members of a club or association is not a distribution to 'the public' but to a 'section of the public', as will be seen. In the case referred to above, the Court of Appeal held that the family was not a 'section of the public'. This decision was sensible; a family group would not normally be described as a section of the public (and doubtless the same is true of other small, domestic groups). In the case the Lord Chief Justice said that 'section of the public' refers to some identifiable group, 'in other words members of a club or association'. However, it is arguable that the term also covers any identifiable group of people whose connection is *not* a private relationship (ie a familial or domestic one) provided that that group is identifiable by some common interest or characteristic. If this is so, the employees of X Ltd are a section of the public, as are the inhabitants of houses in Y Street, Members of Parliament, teachers, a football crowd and persons of West Indian descent.

Although the prosecution must prove that the accused intended to stir up racial hatred by the publication or distribution or that such hatred was likely to be stirred up thereby, it does not have to prove any knowledge on the part of the accused in relation to the content of the written matter which he has published, or distributed, although he will almost inevitably have had such mens rea if he is proved to have intended to stir up racial hatred. However, under POA 1986, s 19, it is a defence for an accused who is not proved to have intended to stir up racial hatred to prove that he was not aware of the content of the matter and neither suspected nor had reason to suspect it of being threatening, abusive or insulting. The defence under s 19 is of obvious importance to innocent publishers or distributors, like newsagents.

POA 1986, s 29C provides that a person who publishes or distributes written material which is threatening is guilty of an offence if he intends thereby to stir up religious hatred. It also provides that references within Part IIIA to the publication or distribution of written material are to its publication or distribution to the public or a section of the public.

Possession of racially inflammatory material

POA 1986, s 23 provides that a person who has in his possession written material which is threatening, abusive or insulting, with a view to its being displayed, published, distributed, or included in a programme service (whether or not by himself) is guilty of an offence if:

(a) he intends racial hatred to be stirred up thereby; or
(b) having regard to all the circumstances racial hatred is likely to be stirred up thereby.

POA 1986, s 23 makes similar provision in relation to a person who has in his possession a film or sound or video tape.

For the above purposes, regard must be had to such display, publication, distribution, showing, playing, or inclusion in a programme service as the accused has, or it may reasonably be inferred that he has, in view.

The Act does not define what is required for 'possession' in this context but reference to other areas of the law suggests that actual custody is not necessary provided that there is control over the written matter. The intended publication or distribution need not be by the person in possession. The result of all this is that, if racially inflammatory pamphlets printed by X are deposited with Y for safekeeping in his warehouse until X wishes to collect and distribute them, the present offence can be committed by X and by Y (as long as the pamphlets are in the warehouse) because, since Y (as well as X) is in control of the pamphlets, Y and X are in possession of them.

As with POA 1986, s 19, the prosecution does not have to prove any mens rea on the part of a person charged with possession contrary to s 23 in relation to the content of the written matter possessed by him. Likewise, it need not necessarily be proved that the accused intended racial hatred to be stirred up by the publication or distribution, since it is enough that, if the matter were published or distributed, racial hatred would be likely (having regard to all the circumstances) to be stirred up as a result of the publication or distribution. However, under POA 1986, s 23(3), it is a defence for an accused who is not proved to have intended to stir up racial hatred to prove that he was not aware of the content of the written material or recording, and neither suspected nor had reason to suspect it of being threatening, abusive or insulting. This is of obvious importance to 'innocent' possessors of racialist material, such as warehousemen.

The person in possession of the written material must have been in possession with a view to its publication or distribution. If there is a dispute about this, the magistrates or jury will have to draw such inferences as seem reasonable from the quantity and nature of the material possessed.

POA 1986, s 29G parallels this offence in relation to religious hatred. In this case, however, the material must be 'threatening' and intended to stir up religious hatred.

A justice of the peace, if satisfied by information on oath laid by a constable that there are reasonable grounds to suspect that a person has possession of written material or a recording in contravention of POA 1986, s 23 or s 29G, may issue a warrant authorising the entry and search of premises where it is suspected the material or recording is situated. A constable executing such a warrant may use reasonable force if necessary.

Other offences

POA 1986, ss 20, 21 and 22 respectively provide offences relating to threatening, abusive or insulting words, behaviour or material in public plays, visual or sound recordings, and programmes in broadcasts or cable services, which are intended or likely to stir up racial hatred. A detailed explanation of these offences is outside the scope of this book.

POA 1986, ss 29D, 29E and 29F respectively provide offences corresponding to those under ss 20, 21 and 22 in relation to threatening words, behaviour or material in public plays, visual or sound recordings and programmes in broadcasts or cable services. In all cases the play, recording, programme, broadcast must be intended to stir up religious hatred.

General

Under POA 1986, ss 28 (racial hatred) and 29M (religious hatred), the directors, secretaries and similar officers of bodies corporate are liable for offences under Part III or IIIA of the Act which have been committed by the body corporate with their consent or connivance.

None of the above offences applies to a *fair and accurate* report of:

(a) proceedings in Parliament, the Scottish Parliament or National Assembly of Wales; or
(b) proceedings publicly heard before a court or tribunal exercising judicial authority.

However, in the case of a report of the proceedings of a court or tribunal, the exemption *only* applies if the report is published *contemporaneously* with those proceedings or, if it is not reasonably practicable or would be unlawful to publish a report of them contemporaneously (because of the law of contempt of court), is published *as soon as publication is reasonably practicable and lawful.*

No prosecution for an offence under Part III or Part IIIA of the POA 1986 may be instituted except by or with the consent of the Attorney-General.

INDECENT OR GROSSLY OFFENSIVE COMMUNICATIONS

Two statutes are relevant under this heading.

The Malicious Communications Act 1988 (MCA 1988), s 1 makes it an offence for any person to send to another person:

(a) a letter, electronic communication or article of any description which conveys:
    (i) a message which is indecent or grossly offensive;
    (ii) a threat; or
    (iii) information which is false and known or believed to be false by the sender; or
(b) any other article or electronic communication which is wholly or partly of an indecent or grossly offensive nature,

if his purpose or one of his purposes in sending it is that the message, threat or information should cause distress or anxiety to the recipient or to any other person to whom he intends that it, or its content or nature, should be communicated.

In relation to the sending of a threat, a defence exists if the accused shows that the threat is to reinforce a demand made by him on reasonable grounds and that he believed and had reasonable grounds for believing that it was a proper means of reinforcing the demand.

For the purposes of MCA 1988 the term 'electronic communication' includes any oral or other communication by means of an electronic communication system, and any communication (however sent) that is in electronic form.

The Communications Act 2003 (CA 2003), s 127(1) provides that a person commits an offence who:

(a) sends by means of a *public* electronic communications network, a message or other matter which is grossly offensive or of an indecent, obscene or menacing character; or
(b) causes any such message or matter to be so sent.

In addition, it is an offence against CA 2003, s 127(2) to send, for the purpose of causing annoyance, inconvenience or needless anxiety to another, by means of a public electronic communications network, a message which is known to be false, or to cause such a message to be sent, or persistently to make use of such a network for such a purpose.

These offences under CA 2003, s 127 are restricted to the use of 'public' networks.

The House of Lords has ruled that whether a message or other matter is grossly offensive for the purposes of the Communications Act 2003, s 127(1) must be judged by the standards of an open and just multi-racial society; the words must be judged taking account of their context and all other relevant circumstances. To be guilty of an offence under (a) the sender of the message must intend his words to be grossly offensive to those to whom they related, or be aware that they might be taken to be so. If the sender has such a state of mind he can be convicted under (a) even if a recipient of the message was not offended.

An offence under CA 2003, s 127(2) is a 'penalty offence' for the purposes of CJPA 2001, Part I and may be dealt with under a fixed penalty procedure: see p 874.

PUBLIC PROCESSIONS

Advance notice

POA 1986, s 11 requires that, where it applies, written notice specifying the date a procession is intended to be held, the time when it is intended to start, its proposed route, and the name and address of the person (or one of the persons) proposing to organise it, must be given to a police station in the police area in which it is proposed the procession will start. Section 11 applies if the procession is public and it is intended:

(a) to demonstrate support for or opposition to the views or actions of any person or body of persons;
(b) to publicise a cause or campaign; or
(c) to mark or commemorate an event.

If such a procession starts in Scotland, it is the first police area in England along the proposed route which must be given notice. The notice may be given by hand not less than six clear days before the date upon which the procession is intended to be held, or if that is not reasonably practicable, as soon as delivery is reasonably practicable. It will be appreciated that it may be impossible to give six clear days' notice of processions which occur quite spontaneously, following some incident concerning which a group feels inclined to demonstrate.

The section permits delivery of the notice by recorded delivery service, if the notice is delivered not less than six clear days in advance. The provisions of the Interpretation Act 1978 under which a document sent by post is deemed to have been served when posted and to have been delivered in the ordinary course of post do not apply to the service of such notices.

The provisions of the section do not apply to processions commonly or customarily held (for example, a procession connected with an annual gala, a Remembrance Day procession or a monthly campaigning mass cycle ride), or to funeral processions organised by funeral directors (as opposed to processions which suddenly appear in protest at a death).

Each of the persons organising a public procession is guilty of a offence if notice has not been so given, or if the details given in the notice differ from the actuality of the procession. It is a defence for a person to prove that he did not know of, or suspect the failure to give such notice, or that differences in the time, date or route occurred due to circumstances beyond his control, or with the agreement of a police officer, or by his direction.

Conditions

By POA 1986, s 12, the senior police officer (the chief officer of the area or senior officer present at the procession) may impose conditions in relation to any public procession, having regard to its time, place or circumstances, including its route, if he reasonably believes that:

(a) it may result in serious public disorder, serious damage to property or serious disruption to the life of the community; or

(b) the purpose of the persons organising it is the intimidation of others with a view to compelling them not to do an act they have a right to do, or to do an act they have a right not to do.

These conditions may include any measures which appear necessary to prevent such disorder, damage or disruption or intimidation, including conditions as to the route of the procession or prohibiting it from entering any specified public place.

Offences are committed by organisers and participants who knowingly fail to comply with a condition. It is a defence for an accused to prove that the failure arose from circumstances beyond his control. A person who incites another to participate in a procession and to fail to comply with a condition also commits an offence.

Prohibition

A chief officer of police may apply under POA 1986, s 13 to the council of the district for an order prohibiting for a period, not exceeding three months, the holding of all public processions (or any class of procession specified) within that district. The chief officer must reasonably believe that, because of particular circumstances existing, his power to impose conditions will not be sufficient to prevent serious public disorder. Such an order may be made by the council with the consent of the Secretary of State. The Commissioners of the Metropolitan and City of London Police Forces may themselves make such an order in respect of their police areas with the consent of the Secretary of State.

Persons who organise, or take part in a public procession commit an offence if they know that it has been prohibited. Those who incite others to participate in a prohibited procession are also guilty of an offence.

ENTERING AND REMAINING ON PROPERTY

In an effort to protect premises from unlawful occupation, the Criminal Law Act 1977 (CLA 1977) provides certain offences relating to entering and remaining on premises. Although these offences are often associated with 'squatters', the relevant provisions extend to situations beyond those involving squatting.

The definitions of the various offences refer to 'premises'. CLA 1977, s 12 defines 'premises' as any building, any part of a building under separate occupation, any land ancillary to a building, and the site comprising any building or buildings together with any land ancillary thereto. The definition would therefore cover a block of flats, a single flat or even the grounds in which the block has been erected. The section goes on to say that the term 'building' includes any immovable structure, and any movable structure, vehicle or vessel designed or adapted for use for residential purposes. In this way protection is extended to residential caravans, houseboats etc.

Violence for securing entry

By CLA 1977, s 6, it is an offence for any person, without lawful authority, to use or threaten violence for the purpose of securing entry into any premises either for himself or for any other person, provided that:

(a) there is someone present on those premises at the time who is opposed to the entry which the violence is intended to secure; and

(b) the person using or threatening the violence knows that that is the case.

Use or threat of violence

The essence of this offence is the use or threat of violence for the purpose of securing entry into premises on which a person opposed to the entry is present: actual entry is not required. It is immaterial whether the entry which the violence is intended to secure is for the purpose of acquiring possession of the premises or for some other purpose. People who use or threaten violence in order to secure entry to a dance are guilty of the present offence if they know that someone inside is opposed to their entry; so are squatters who, with such knowledge, seek to enter a house by such means, and so are protesters who likewise seek to enter a public building or a factory.

The violence used or threatened may be against a person or property (whether he or it is on or off the premises). It is important to recognise that the offence is to use 'violence', not 'force'. Although the difference may seem to be small, it is considerable in certain circumstances. It would no doubt amount to violence against the property to set fire to it to drive out those inside and thereby gain entry, but the degree of force necessary to insert a key and to secure entry does not amount to violence. It would be different if the lock was burst open by using violence against the door.

Someone on the premises opposed to the entry

Someone must be physically present on the premises who is opposed to the entry to them which the violence is intended to secure. One person will suffice and he might equally be the owner of the premises or a trespasser who is opposed to the owner's re-entry. The section does not demand that this person physically opposes entry; it merely requires that the intended entry is against his will. Clearly, the present offence is not committed where someone breaks into an empty house.

Mens rea

In terms of the mens rea required for the offence, the accused must:

(a) intend to use or threaten violence;

(b) intend that violence or threat to secure him entry to the premises for himself or another; and

(c) know that there is someone on the premises at the time who is opposed to the entry in question.

Without lawful authority

An offence is not committed under CLA 1977, s 6 if the person using or threatening violence has lawful authority for acting in the prescribed way. This exemption is essential to protect the violent entries which may have to be made by police officers or bailiffs in executing warrants or orders of courts. However, the only entries so protected will be those where the form of violence used to secure entry is authorised by law.

It might be assumed that the owner of the property would always have lawful authority for re-occupying his property which had been unlawfully occupied by those who would exclude him, but this is not so. CLA 1977, s 6(2) states that the fact that a person has any interest or right to possession or occupation of any premises does not give him lawful authority to use or threaten the use of violence for the purpose of securing his entry into those premises.

This situation is interesting. If the tenant of office accommodation went to enter his premises in the morning and found that the office had been taken over by homeless persons, he would commit the offence under CLA 1977, s 6 if he attempted to secure immediate entry by the use or threat of violence, knowing that there was someone on the premises at the time who was opposed to such entry, because he would have no lawful authority for his action. Likewise, if a restaurateur, who has been thrown out of his restaurant by rowdies, uses force to re-enter the premises and evict them he will have no lawful authority for his use of violence and can be convicted under s 6.

This means that landlords and other non-residential occupiers must seek to recover possession of their premises by an action in the civil courts, unless it is possible for them to effect a peaceful re-entry.

Of course, if an occupier does succeed in re-entering his premises, he does not commit any offence by proceeding to eject any trespasser, whatever liability he may incur by virtue of his entry.

Displaced residential occupiers and protected intending occupiers

Special provision is made for people falling within the definition of a 'displaced residential occupier' or 'protected intending occupier' of premises or any access to them.

The term 'displaced residential occupier' is defined by CLA 1977, s 12:
any person who was occupying any premises as a residence immediately before being excluded from occupation by anyone who entered those premises, or any access to those premises, as a trespasser is a displaced residential occupier of the premises as long as he continues to be excluded from occupation of the premises by the original trespasser or by any subsequent trespasser.

A person who is regarded as a displaced residential occupier of premises by virtue of this provision is regarded as such an occupier also of any access to those premises.

CLA 1977, s 12 also provides that a person who was himself occupying the premises as a trespasser before being excluded is not a displaced residential occupier.

The obvious example of a displaced residential occupier is the householder who discovers squatters in his house when he returns from work or from holiday.

An involved definition of 'protected intending occupier' is provided by CLA 1977, s 12A.

The first type is an individual who, at the time of the request to leave:

(a) has in the premises in question a freehold interest or leasehold interest with not less than two years still to run;
(b) requires the premises for his own occupation as a residence;
(c) is excluded from occupation of them by a person who entered them, or any access to them, as a trespasser; and

(d) holds, or a person acting on his behalf holds, a written statement, signed by him
and witnessed by a magistrate or commissioner for oaths, which:
   (i)   specifies his interest in the premises; and
   (ii) states that he requires the premises for occupation as a residence for himself.

The purpose of the statement is to enable the police to identify the protected
intending occupier and thereby prevent abuse of the protection given by the Act.

The second type of protected intending occupier is an individual who, at the time
of the request to leave:

(a) has a tenancy of the premises (other than a tenancy falling within the other two
definitions) or a licence to occupy them granted by a person with a freehold
interest or a leasehold interest with not less than two years still to run in the
premises;
(b) requires the premises for his own occupation as a residence;
(c) is excluded from occupation of the premises by a person who entered them, or
access to them, as a trespasser; and
(d) holds, or a person acting on his behalf holds, a written statement:
   (i)   which specifies that he has been granted a tenancy of those premises or a
         licence to occupy them;
   (ii) which specifies the interest in the premises of the person who granted that
         tenancy or licence to occupy (the landlord);
   (iii) which states that he requires the premises for occupation as a residence for
         himself; and
   (iv) in respect of which there is a statement signed by the landlord and by the
         tenant or licensee and witnessed by a magistrate or commissioner for oaths.

The third type of protected intending occupier is an individual who, at the time of
the request to leave:

(a) has a tenancy of the premises in question (other than a tenancy falling within the
other two definitions) or a licence to occupy them granted by a local authority,
the Housing Corporation, or a registered housing association or certain other
bodies;
(b) requires the premises for his own occupation as a residence;
(c) is excluded from occupation of them by a person who entered them, or any
access to them, as a trespasser; and
(d) has been issued by or on behalf of the authority, corporation or association with
a certificate stating that the authority etc is one to which these provisions apply
and that he has been granted a licence or tenancy to occupy the premises as
a residence.

Even a displaced residential occupier or protected intending occupier does not have
lawful authority to use or threaten violence to secure entry to his home. However,
CLA 1977, s 6(1A) provides that the offence under s 6(1) does not apply to a person
who is a displaced residential occupier or a protected intending occupier of the
premises in question or who is acting on behalf of such an occupier. This exemption
does not have to be proved by the accused. Instead, if he adduces sufficient evidence
(ie evidence which raises a reasonable doubt) that he was, or was acting on behalf of,
such an occupier he is presumed to be, or to be acting on behalf of, such an occupier
unless the contrary is proved by the prosecution. This exemption applies only to a

charge under s 6. However, if such an occupier is charged with assault or some other offence he may have the general defence of using reasonable force in the prevention of crime (if he has unsuccessfully asked the trespasser to leave, since the latter's failure to do so will be an offence under s 7 (below)) or in defence of property.

Adverse occupation of residential premises

CLA 1977, s 7 creates an offence of 'adverse occupation'. It provides that any person who is on any premises (including any access to them whether or not any such access constitutes premises within the meaning of CLA 1977) as a trespasser, after having entered as such, is guilty of an offence if he fails to leave those premises on being required to do so by or on behalf of a displaced residential occupier, or a person who is a protected intending occupier of the premises.

CLA 1977, s 7 is of great importance because it gives a displaced residential occupier or a protected intending residential occupier of premises who has been excluded from them by trespassers, for example squatters, a swifter remedy for recovering possession of them than the available civil remedy. He may require the trespassers to leave and they commit an offence if they fail to do so.

The term 'protected intending occupier' is explained above. The effect of CLA 1977, s 7 is to protect not only the owners or tenants of houses, but also buyers of houses, private tenants and council tenants who have not taken up residential occupation of the premises before being excluded by trespassers. Protection does not, however, extend to persons who occupy premises for business purposes.

There is no time set upon departure and it is submitted that this indicates that the requirement is immediate.

Three defences are provided by CLA 1977, the burden of proof in each case being on the accused:

(1) It is a defence that the accused believed that the person requiring him to leave was not a displaced residential occupier or a protected intending occupier of the premises, or someone acting on his behalf. This plea will rarely succeed, particularly in the light of the requirement in the case of a protected intending occupier of a written statement or certificate to this effect.

(2) Where he was requested to leave by a person claiming to be (or to act on behalf of) a protected intending occupier, it is a defence for the accused to prove that, although asked to do so by the accused at the time that he was requested to leave, the person requesting him to leave failed at that time to produce a written statement, or certificate, complying with CLA 1977.

(3) It is a defence that the premises in question are or form part of premises used wholly or mainly for non-residential purposes. This means, for instance, that people involved in a factory sit-in do not commit the present offence if they fail to leave when required by a resident caretaker, so long as they are not in his flat or in part of the premises used wholly or mainly for access to, or in connection with, the flat.

Trespassing with weapon of offence

CLA 1977, s 8 provides an offence of trespassing with a weapon of offence, which can be committed whether or not the trespassory entry was secured by the use or threat of violence. Where an armed trespasser commits an offence under s 6 or s 7, discussed above, the effect of the present offence is to impose further liability on him because of the element of aggravation of his being armed.

CLA 1977, s 8 states:

A person who is on any premises as a trespasser, after having entered as such, is guilty of an offence if, without lawful authority or reasonable excuse, he has with him on the premises any weapon of offence.

The term 'weapon of offence' means any article made or adapted for use for causing injury to or incapacitating a person, or intended by the person having it with him for such use. We discuss an identical definition on p 1059.

INTERIM POSSESSION ORDERS IN RELATION TO PREMISES

Obtaining a final possession order in respect of premises can take rather longer than desirable. As a result an interim possession order, which can be obtained more speedily, has been introduced by rules of court. Breach of such an order was made an offence by the Criminal Justice and Public Order Act 1994 (CJPOA 1994). CJPOA 1994, s 76(2) makes it an offence for a person to be present on premises as a trespasser at any time during the currency of such an order. However, the subsection provides that no offence will be committed if such a person leaves within twenty-four hours of the time of service of the order and does not return, or if a copy of the order was not affixed to the premises in accordance with the rules of court. A person in occupation at the time of service, who leaves the premises, commits an offence if he re-enters the premises as a trespasser or attempts to do so after the expiry of the order but within a period of one year from service of the order.

CJPOA 1994, s 75 provides that a person commits an offence if, for the purpose of obtaining an interim possession order, he makes a statement which he knows to be false or is misleading in a material particular, or recklessly makes such a statement. Likewise, a person commits an offence if he knowingly or recklessly makes such a statement to resist the making of an interim possession order.

POWER TO REMOVE TRESPASSERS

Direction to leave

CJPOA 1994, s 61 provides that if the senior police officer (the most senior in rank of police officers present at the scene) reasonably believes that two or more persons are trespassing on land, that they are present with the common purpose of residing there for any period, that reasonable steps have been taken by or on behalf of the occupier to ask them to leave and that:

(a) any of those persons has caused damage to property on the land or used threatening, abusive or insulting words or behaviour towards the occupier, a member of his family or an employee or agent of his; or

(b) those persons have between them brought six or more vehicles onto the land, he may direct those persons, or any of them, to leave the land and to remove any vehicles or other property they have with them on the land. The direction must be to leave immediately or as soon as reasonably practicable, rather than at a future time.

Where the persons in question are reasonably believed by the senior officer present to be persons who were not originally trespassers but have become trespassers on the land, he must reasonably believe that the above conditions are satisfied after those persons became trespassers before he can exercise these powers.

There are a number of factors to consider. The senior officer must reasonably believe that two or more persons are present on the land as trespassers with the common purpose of residence, no matter how brief that intended period of residence may be. A person may have a purpose of residing in a place notwithstanding that he has a home elsewhere. While these provisions are adequate to deal with mass trespass by New Age Travellers, they are similarly adequate to deal with trespass by gypsies. The term 'land' does not include buildings other than agricultural buildings, nor does it include scheduled monuments or land forming part of a highway unless it is a footpath, bridleway or byway open to all traffic, restricted byway or cycle track. The term includes 'common land', whether public or privately owned common land. The senior officer must also reasonably believe that reasonable steps have been taken by or on behalf of the occupier (the person entitled to possession of the land by virtue of an estate or interest held by him) to require the trespassers to leave. The senior police officer present, reasonably believing these facts, may require such persons to leave without further reason if he reasonably believes they have brought six or more vehicles onto the land. If they have not, he must reasonably believe that any of those persons has caused damage to the land or to property on the land, or has used threatening, abusive or insulting words or behaviour towards the persons specified (the occupier of the land, a member of his family or an employee or agent of his). Thus overnight campers are outside these provisions, provided that they have caused no damage to property on the land, or used such words or behaviour.

Where the land in question is common land, the references in s 61 to trespassing and trespassers include acts and persons doing acts which constitute a trespass as against the occupier or an infringement of the commoners' rights, and references to 'the occupier' include the commoners or any of them or, where the public has access to the common, the local authority as well as any commoner.

The requirement concerning damage is in relation to the land or to property on the land. Damage to growing crops, trees or hedgerows would clearly be within the provisions of the section and by CJPOA 1994, s 61, 'damage' includes the deposit of any substance capable of polluting the land.

For the purposes of this section, the term 'vehicle' includes any vehicle, whether or not it is in a fit state for use on roads, and includes any chassis or body, with or without wheels, appearing to have formed part of such a vehicle, and any load carried by, and anything attached to, such a vehicle, and a caravan.

Offences

If a trespasser directed to leave complies with that direction, he commits no offence. On the other hand, he commits an offence under CJPOA 1994, s 61 if, knowing that a direction has been given which applies to him:

(a) he fails to leave the land (with any vehicle or other property he is required to remove), as soon as reasonably practicable; or
(b) having left, he again enters the land as a trespasser within a three-month period beginning on the day on which the direction is given.

Paragraphs (a) and (b) are separate offences. It is a defence for the accused to prove that:

(a) he was not trespassing on the land; or
(b) he had a reasonable excuse for failing to leave the land as soon as reasonably practicable or, as the case may be, for again entering the land as a trespasser.

The defence of 'not trespassing' refers to not trespassing at the time that the senior police officer forms his reasonable belief, and not the time of the prohibited conduct.

Police powers

The purpose of CJPOA 1994, s 61 is to give the occupier of the land a swifter remedy for recovering possession of it than the available (and possibly costly) civil remedy.

By CJPOA 1994, s 62, where a direction under s 61 has been given, a constable may seize and remove a vehicle if he reasonably suspects that a person to whom it applies has, without reasonable excuse, failed to remove a vehicle which appears to belong to him or be in his possession or control. The same powers apply where such a person has re-entered the land within a period of three months from the date of the direction.

POWER TO REMOVE TRESPASSERS WHERE AN ALTERNATIVE SITE IS AVAILABLE

The Anti-social Behaviour Act 2003 added ss 62A, 62B, 62C and 62D to CJPOA 1994. CJPOA 1994, s 62A provides that, where the senior police officer present at the scene reasonably believes that certain conditions are satisfied in relation to a person and land, he may direct the person to leave the land and to remove any vehicle and other property which he has with him on the land. The conditions are:

(a) that the person and one or more others ('the trespassers') are trespassing on land;
(b) that the trespassers have between them at least one vehicle on the land;
(c) that the trespassers are there for the common purpose of residing there for any period;
(d) if it appears to the officer that the person has one or more caravans in his possession or control on the land, that there is a suitable pitch on a relevant caravan site (ie a site in the same local authority area managed by that authority or a registered social landlord) for the caravan(s); and
(e) that the occupier of the land or someone acting on his behalf has asked the police to remove the trespassers.

Such a direction may be communicated to the person to whom it applies by any constable at the scene. The term 'land' does not include buildings other than agricultural buildings or scheduled monuments. A person may be regarded as having a purpose of residing in a place even if he has a home elsewhere, as would be the case where there is a 'sited' residential caravan. 'Occupier', 'trespassing', 'trespassers' and 'vehicle' have the same meaning as in CJPOA 1994, s 61. By CJPOA 1994, s 62D the same provisions apply in respect of s 62A as apply to s 61.

Where a police officer proposes to give such a direction he must consult every local authority within whose area the land is situated as to whether there is a suitable pitch for the caravan or each of the caravans on a relevant caravan site situated in their area.

By CJPOA 1994, s 62B, a person commits an offence if he knows that such a direction has been given which applies to him and (a) he fails to leave the land as soon as reasonably practicable, or (b) he enters any land within the area of the relevant local authority as a trespasser within a period of three months. The section provides defences where an accused can show:

(a) that he was not trespassing on land in respect of which he is alleged to have committed the offence; or
(b) that he had a reasonable excuse for failing to leave as soon as reasonably practicable, or for entering land in the area of the relevant local authority as a trespasser with the intention of residing there; or
(c) that at the time the direction was given he was under the age of eighteen and was residing with his parent or guardian.

CJPOA 1994, s 62C provides that, where a constable reasonably suspects that a person subject to such a direction has, without reasonable excuse, failed to remove any vehicle which appears to belong to him or to be under his possession or control, or that such a person has entered any land in the area of the relevant local authority as a trespasser with a vehicle within the period of three months from the day of the direction, he may seize and remove the vehicle.

UNAUTHORISED CAMPING WITH A VEHICLE

CJPOA 1994, s 77 empowers a county council, district council or London borough council to direct unauthorised vehicular campers to leave:

(a) any land forming part of a highway;
(b) any other unoccupied land in the open air; or
(c) any occupied land in the open air where they are camping without the consent of the occupier of the land.

Such a direction may be addressed to a particular person or persons or to all of the occupants of vehicles on the land. It is not necessary for the local authority to show that there has been any form of nuisance caused by their presence.

Where such notice of a direction has been served, any person who knows that the direction has been given, and that it applies to him, commits an offence:

(a) if he fails, as soon as practicable, to leave the land or remove from the land any vehicle, or any other property which is subject of the direction; or
(b) if, having removed any such vehicle or property, he again enters the land with a vehicle within a period of three months from the day upon which the direction was given.

The section provides a defence where such failure to leave or remove a vehicle or other property as soon as practicable, or the re-entry with a vehicle, was due to illness, mechanical breakdown or other immediate emergency. The onus is upon the accused to prove such a defence.

If a direction under CJPOA 1994, s 77 is not complied with, the local authority can make an application to a magistrates' court under s 78 for an order for the removal by local authority officers and employees of persons and vehicles on the land in contravention of the direction. Wilful obstruction of someone acting under such an order is an offence. Although police officers do not actually execute an order under s 78, they will often be in attendance in view of the risk to public order.

AGGRAVATED TRESPASS

Offence of aggravated trespass

CJPOA 1994, s 68 states that a person commits the offence of aggravated trespass if he trespasses on land and, in relation to any lawful activity which persons are engaged in, or are about to engage in, on that land or adjoining land, does there anything which is intended by him to have the effect:

(a) of intimidating those persons or any of them so as to deter them or any of them from engaging in that activity;
(b) of obstructing that activity; or
(c) of disrupting that activity.

For this purpose, an activity on the part of a person or persons on land is 'lawful' if he or they may engage in the activity on the land on that occasion without committing an offence against English law or trespassing on the land. Even if the activities on land did constitute a crime under international law this would not render the activity unlawful for the purpose of s 68, if those undertaking the activity were not committing an offence under English law and were not trespassing. This was held by the House of Lords in a case where those accused of aggravated trespass at military bases unsuccessfully alleged before the House that the activity carried on there was not a lawful activity because the bases were being used to further the war in Iraq and that the attack on Iraq constituted the crime of aggression under international law.

The persons engaged, or about to engage, in the relevant lawful activity must physically be present on the land in question at the time of the alleged trespass. The provisions were originally aimed particularly at the activities of hunt saboteurs who often went beyond peaceful protest. However, they would equally apply to the disruption of shooting, angling or even the obstruction of new motorway workings.

Some act is required in addition to trespass. It must be specified in the charge and must be shown to be intended to have one of the effects set out at (a) to (c). Thus a trespasser who gives drugged meat to gundogs commits such an act, as does someone who immobilises a bulldozer on a construction site. Indeed, a divisional court has held that a trespasser commits an offence under CJPOA 1994, s 68 if he does an act with intent to commit a further act, which is not committed, and thereby to intimidate, obstruct or disrupt a lawful activity, if the act done is sufficiently closely connected with the intended intimidation etc as to be more than merely preparatory to it. On this basis, the Court upheld the conviction under s 68 of a person who had trespassed on land and run after a hunt with the intention of getting close enough to do something to disrupt it. The act must be committed on land. 'Land' does not include land forming part of a highway unless it is a footpath, bridleway etc. A failure to do something is not enough. Trespassers who were already at a particular spot, who refused on an impulse to move to allow other persons to pass, would not commit an offence under s 68; whereas it would be an offence if they deliberately placed themselves there with the intention of disrupting the activity.

The offence is one requiring 'intent' to create one of these specified effects. The trespassing rambler who walks through grouse moors will not commit this offence even though he disrupts a shoot, if that was not his intention. Those who protest at the building of a new road will commit the offence if they deliberately sit down on private land in front of the machines because they intend to obstruct or disrupt the lawful activity of the developers.

Unless they are acting to prevent an unlawful act, protesters cannot rely on the common law defence of defence of property as a defence to a charge of aggravated trespass. This was held in a case where a group of protesters trespassed on land and attached themselves to tractors being used to plant genetically modified crops a district judge ruled that they had the common law defence of property as they held a genuine belief concerning the dangers of GM crops and feared for the well-being of surrounding property. A divisional court allowed the prosecutor's appeal. The common law defence was one related to the commission of an unlawful act. The act concerned had not been unlawful.

Direction to leave

By CJPOA 1994, s 69, where the senior police officer present at the scene reasonably believes that:

(a) a person is committing, has committed or intends to commit the offence of aggravated trespass on land; or

(b) two or more persons are trespassing on land and are present there with the common purpose of intimidating persons so as to deter them from engaging in a lawful activity or of obstructing or disrupting a lawful activity,

he may direct that person, or those persons (or any of them), to leave the land. It is not necessary for an offence of aggravated trespass to have been committed before a direction can be given under CJPOA 1994, s 69.

A person who, knowing that such a direction has been given which applies to him, fails to leave the land as soon as practicable or, having left, again enters the land as a trespasser within the period of three months beginning with the day on which the direction was given, commits an offence.

It is a defence to a charge of either of the above offences for the accused to prove that he was not trespassing on the land, or that he had a reasonable excuse for failing to leave the land as soon as practicable or, as the case may be, for again entering the land as a trespasser.

PUBLIC ASSEMBLIES

Generally

The POA 1986, s 14 authorises the senior police officer, on the basis of the same grounds of reasonable belief as in the case of conditions on public processions (see p 888), to impose such conditions in relation to the place at which any public assembly (an assembly of two or more persons in a public place which is wholly or partly open to the air) may be (or continue to be) held, its maximum duration, or the maximum number of persons who may constitute it, as appear to him to be necessary to prevent serious public disorder, serious damage to property, serious disruption to the life of the community or intimidation. A divisional court has held that conditions may be imposed under this provision requiring those assembled to disperse by a specified route and to stay in a specified place as long as necessary to enable dispersal to take place safely and without disorder.

In the case of an assembly which is actually being held, the senior police officer is the police officer most senior in rank present at the scene; it is not necessary for reasons to be given in such a case. In the case of an assembly which is intended to be held, the senior police officer is the chief officer of police; in such a case the chief officer must identify the particular ground (or a combination of grounds) on which he is relying. Although extensive detail is not required, the chief officer must provide sufficient detail of the reasons for his belief in the ground (or grounds) for a demonstrator to understand why a direction is being given.

Offences under s 14 are committed by the same classes of persons as in relation to a breach of a public procession condition.

Section 14 does not apply to a public assembly which is also a demonstration in a public place in a designated area in the vicinity of Parliament. Such a demonstration is dealt with by the provisions set out on pp 902–903.

Trespassory assemblies

These are dealt with by POA 1986, ss 14A, 14B and 14C.

POA 1986, s 14A is concerned with the prohibition of a trespassory assembly before it has taken place. Where a trespassory assembly has already commenced, police involvement is limited to the prohibition of its continuance if an officer believes that this is necessary to prevent a breach of the peace. Section 14A is, inter alia, aimed at assemblies of New Age Travellers at such places as Stonehenge at summer solstice time. However, its provisions are more extensive and will cover an assembly which might cause serious disorder, obstruction of the highway, or noise.

POA 1986, s 14A provides that where a chief officer of police reasonably believes that an assembly of twenty or more people is intended to be held in any district at a place on land in the open air to which the public has no right of access or only a limited right of access and that the assembly:

(a) is likely to be held without the permission of the occupier of the land or to conduct itself in such a way as to exceed the limits of any permission of his or the limits of the public's right of access; and

(b) may result:
   (i) in serious disruption to the life of the community; or
   (ii) where the land, or a building or monument on it, is of historical, architectural or scientific importance, in significant damage to the land, building or monument,

he may apply to the council of the district (or Secretary of State in the case of the Metropolitan and City of London Police Forces) for an order prohibiting for a specified period the holding of all trespassory assemblies in the district, or a part of it as specified. An order may only be made with the Secretary of State's consent. Where such an order is made, it will operate to prohibit the holding of an assembly on land in the open air to which the public has no right of access or only a limited right of access and takes place without the permission of the occupier, or in excess of his permission or the public's right of access. Such an order may not prohibit such an assembly for a period exceeding four days or in an area exceeding a circle with a radius of five miles from a specified centre.

It is irrelevant that the anticipated assembly is open to the public or is a private ceremony, but it must be held on land in the open air. This can be contrasted with the power to impose conditions on a public assembly under POA 1986, s 14; there the assembly may be held wholly or partly in the open air. 'Land' in s 14A includes land forming part of the highway. It follows, for example, that an intended obstructive assembly of twenty or more on the highway (which is by definition trespassing, since the public only have a right to pass and repass on it and make other reasonable use of it) can be the trigger for an order under s 14A.

It is important to understand that these powers are restricted to assemblies which are reasonably believed to be trespassory in nature. Assemblies *with permission* are not covered by the legislation unless there is a reasonable belief that they will be conducted in such a way as to exceed that permission.

Offences

A person who organises an assembly which he knows to be prohibited under POA 1986, s 14A commits an offence against s 14B. So does a person who takes part, or who incites another to do so.

Central to these offences is that the assembly must be prohibited under POA 1986, s 14A, and an assembly is prohibited only if, within the area and duration of the prohibition order, it:

(a) is held on land in the open air to which the public has no right of access or only a limited right of access; and
(b) takes place in the prohibited circumstances, ie without the permission of the occupier of the land or so as to exceed the limits of any permission of his or the limits of the public's right of access.

In the case of assemblies on the highway, the public's right of access to the highway has been held by the House of Lords to include the right to hold a public assembly which is peaceful and non-obstructive of the rights of passage of other users of the highway if the assembly is a reasonable use of the highway.

Police powers

By POA 1986, s 14C, if a constable in uniform reasonably believes that a person is on his way to an assembly within the area to which such an order applies, which the constable reasonably believes is likely to be an assembly which is prohibited by that order, he may, within the area specified in the order:

(a) stop that person; and
(b) direct him not to proceed in the direction of the assembly.

A person who fails to comply with such a direction which he knows has been given to him commits an offence.

Trespass on protected site: demonstrating on a protected site

SOCPA 2005, s 128 provides that a person commits an offence if he enters, or is on, any protected site in England or Wales as a trespasser. A 'protected site' is either a nuclear site (ie the outer perimeter (fences etc) of premises in respect of which a nuclear site licence exists and other premises within that perimeter) or a 'designated site'. A 'designated site' is one specified or described by order by the Secretary of State. A site may only be designated if:

(a) it is comprised in Crown land;
(b) it is comprised in land belonging to Her Majesty in Her private capacity or to the immediate heir to the Throne in his private capacity, or
(c) it is considered appropriate in the interests of national security.

It is a defence for a person charged with an offence under s 128 to prove that he did not know, and had no reasonable cause to suspect, that the site was protected. No proceedings for such an offence may be instituted without the consent of the Attorney-General.

The Serious Organised Crime and Police Act 2005 (Designated Sites) Order 2005 designates Her Majesty's Naval Base, Clyde; Northwood Headquarters; RAF Brize Norton; RAF Croughton; RAF Fairford; RAF Feltwell; RAF Fylingdales; RAF Lakenheath; RAF Menwith Hill; RAF Mildenhall; RAF Welford; Royal Navy Armaments Depot Coulport, and Sea Mounting Centre Marchwood as designated sites.

Demonstrations in the vicinity of Parliament

SOCPA 2005, s 133 requires written notice to the Commissioner of Police of the Metropolis of any such proposed demonstration in a designated area in the vicinity of Parliament. Such notice must be given, if reasonably practicable, not less than six clear days before the proposed demonstration, or if that is not reasonably practicable, not less than 24 hours before the demonstration. By s 134, the Commissioner must issue an authorisation but may impose conditions with a view to preventing specified acts and guaranteeing public safety.

The 'designated area' has been defined by order. The order specifies places none of which are more than one kilometre from Parliament Square.

A person who organises a demonstration in a public place in the designated area, or takes part in such a demonstration, or carries on such a demonstration by himself, commits an offence against SOCPA 2005, s 132 if, when the demonstration starts, authorisation for it has not been given. It is a defence for such a person to show that he reasonably believed that authorisation had been given. No offence is committed where the demonstration is in the form of a procession which has been authorised. In addition, the section does not apply to conduct which is lawful under the Trade Union and Labour Relations (Consolidation) Act 1992, s 220 (referred to on p 925).

The conditions which the Commissioner may specify in an authorisation are conditions which in his reasonable opinion are necessary for the purpose of preventing—

(a) hindrance to any person wishing to enter or to leave the Palace of Westminster;
(b) hindrance to the proper operation of Parliament;
(c) serious public disorder;
(d) serious damage to property;
(e) disruption to the life of the community;
(f) a security risk in any part of the designated area;
(g) risk to the safety of members of the public (including any person taking part in the demonstration.

The conditions may, in particular, impose requirements as to the place where the demonstration may, or may not, be carried on; the times at, and the period during which, it may be carried on; the number of persons who may take part; the number and size of the banners or placards used; and the maximum permitted noise levels. Each person who takes part in or organises a demonstration in the designated area is guilty of an offence if he knowingly fails to comply with a condition imposed, or he knows or should have known that the demonstration was carried on otherwise than in accordance with the particulars set out in the authorisation. It is a defence for the accused to show that the offence arose because of circumstances outside his control, or that the act was done with the agreement, or by the direction, of a police officer.

Police powers at the scene of such a demonstration

SOCPA 2005, s 135 authorises the senior police officer present, if he reasonably believes that it is necessary to do so to prevent any of the things mentioned at (a) to (g) above, to impose additional conditions or to vary existing conditions. It is an offence for an organiser of, or participant in, the demonstration knowingly to fail to comply with such additional conditions, or varied conditions. It is a defence for him to show that the failure arose from circumstances beyond his control.

Loud speakers in designated area

Section 137 provides that the operation of a loudspeaker in a street within the designated area is prohibited, subject to specified exceptions (emergency, public utility, local authority vehicles and loudspeakers fixed to vehicles used within that vehicle for directions or entertainment). Those who operate loudspeakers in a designated area, or who permit them to be used, in contravention of this prohibition commit an offence.

Raves

The Criminal Justice and Public Order Act 1994, ss 63 to 65 provide the police with certain powers to deal with 'raves'. Section 63 is the main provision. By s 63(1), s 63 applies to a gathering on land in the open air of twenty or more persons (whether or not trespassers) at which amplified music is played during the night (with or without intermissions) and is such as, by reason of its loudness and the duration and the time at which it is played, is likely to cause serious distress to the inhabitants of the locality; and for this purpose:

(a) such a gathering continues during intermissions in the music and, where the gathering extends over several days, throughout the period during which amplified music is played at night (with or without intermissions); and
(b) 'music' includes sounds wholly or predominantly characterised by the emission of a succession of repetitive beats.

For the purposes of s 63(1), 'raves' do not need to be trespassory, nor do they need to be totally in the open air. 'Land in the open air' includes a place partly open to the air. Thus, both an aircraft hangar without doors, or a Dutch barn, would be such a place.

The Act does not define the term 'during the night'. The Minister said during debate in the Commons that it was not intended to mean lighting-up time and that he was content to leave the provisions vague. This is all very well, but it can be argued that 'night' is quite limited during the summer. More importantly, the law should properly define those acts which are prohibited.

By CJPOA 1994, s 63(1A), added by the Anti-social Behaviour Act 2003, CJPOA 1994 s 63 also applies to a gathering if:

(a) it is a gathering on land of twenty or more persons who are trespassing on the land; and
(b) the gathering would be of a kind described above if it took place on land in the open air.

Thus, the provisions of s 63(1A) now also cover gatherings in a building where the persons attending the rave are trespassing.

In the first instance, it must be recognised that CJPOA 1994, s 63 does not apply to a gathering which is licensed by a local authority entertainments licence.

Where a police officer of at least the rank of superintendent reasonably believes, in respect of any land, that:

(a) two or more persons are making preparations for the holding there of a gathering to which this section applies;
(b) ten or more persons are waiting for such a gathering to begin there; or
(c) ten or more persons are attending such a gathering which is then in progress,

he may give a direction that those persons and any other persons who come to prepare or wait for or to attend the gathering are to leave the land and remove any vehicles or other property which they have with them on the land. The direction may be conveyed to the gathering by any constable. If reasonable steps have been taken to convey the direction, it shall be deemed to have been given.

Persons occupying or working on the land and their families are exempt from a direction under s 63.

A person who knows that such a direction has been given which applies to him who:

(a) fails to leave the land as soon as reasonably practicable; or
(b) having left, again enters the land within a period of seven days beginning with the day on which the direction is given,

commits an offence. It is a defence for the accused to show that he had a reasonable excuse for failing to leave the land as soon as reasonably practicable or, as the case may be, for again entering the land.

A person also commits an offence if:

(a) he knows that such a s 63 direction has been given which applies to him, and
(b) he makes preparations for or attends a gathering to which s 63 applies within the period of twenty-four hours starting when the direction was given.

This means that those who have been given a direction to leave a rave cannot simply move to another site (and carry on raving) with impunity.

Police powers

CJPOA 1994, s 64 provides that, where a superintendent reasonably believes that circumstances exist which would justify giving such a direction, he may authorise a constable to enter the land without warrant to ascertain that these circumstances exist and to exercise powers conferred upon him. Where such a direction has been given, and a constable reasonably suspects that any person to whom the direction applies has, without reasonable excuse:

(a) failed to remove any vehicle or sound equipment on the land which appears to the constable to belong to him or to be in his possession or under his control; or
(b) entered the land as a trespasser with a vehicle or sound equipment within the period of seven days beginning with the day on which the direction was given,

the constable may seize and remove that vehicle or sound equipment.

CJPOA 1994, s 66 permits a court to order the forfeiture of sound equipment but also allows the owner of the equipment (if he is not the person from whom it was seized) to claim it by applying to the court within six months. The Police (Disposal of Sound Equipment) Regulations 1995 provide for the disposal of the equipment where the court has made no such order.

Where a constable in uniform reasonably believes that a person is on his way to such a gathering in respect of which a direction has been given, he may stop that person and direct him not to go in the direction of the gathering. This power is provided by CJPOA 1994, s 65. It may only be exercised at a place within five miles of the boundary of the site of the gathering. This does not apply to occupiers of the land etc. A person who, knowing that such a direction has been given, fails to comply with such a direction commits an offence.

PUBLIC MEETINGS

It is an offence, contrary to the Public Meeting Act 1908, s 1 for any person at a lawful public meeting to act in a disorderly manner for the purpose of preventing the transaction of the business for which the meeting was called together. It is also an offence to incite others to do so.

The term 'public meeting' is used in the sense that the meeting is open to the public and not restricted to members of a particular organisation or club. Meetings which are open to the public but held on private premises are therefore public meetings. In such a case, a police officer who reasonably suspects a breach of the peace may enter the private premises. The fact that a meeting is held on a highway does not render it unlawful merely because it is so held. However, the circumstances in which the meeting is held may make the participants liable for other offences, such as obstructing the highway.

The Public Meeting Act 1908, s 1 gives constables the power to require a person at a public meeting immediately to give his name and address. However, a constable may only execute this power if requested to do so by the chairman of the meeting. Even when so requested, he must reasonably suspect the person concerned of being guilty of the offence described above before acting. The constable must therefore decide whether or not the person to whom his attention is directed is merely asking questions and making points which the chairman and platform party do not like, or is acting in a disorderly manner for the purpose of preventing the transaction of the business. Refusal or failure to give a name or address, or the giving of a false name and address, is an offence.

PUBLIC ORDER OFFENCES AND HUMAN RIGHTS

We dealt on pp 3–4 with the effect of the Human Rights Act 1998 in general terms.

Public order law can interfere with the exercise of the Convention rights, particularly those under Articles 10 and 11 referred to below.

Article 10 is concerned with freedom of expression. It declares that:

1. Everyone has the right to freedom of expression. This right shall include freedom to hold opinions and to receive and impart information and ideas without interference by public authority and regardless of frontiers. This Article shall not prevent States from requiring the licensing of broadcasting, television or cinema enterprises.
2. The exercise of these freedoms, since it carries with it duties and responsibilities, may be subject to such formalities, conditions, restrictions or penalties as are prescribed by law and are necessary in a democratic society, in the interests of national security, territorial integrity or public safety, for the prevention of disorder or crime, for the protection of health or morals, for the protection of the reputation or rights of others, for preventing the disclosure of information received in confidence, or for maintaining the authority or impartiality of the judiciary.

The following provisions of Article 11, which are concerned with the freedom of assembly and association, are likely to lead to further challenges. It provides:

1. Everyone has the right to freedom of peaceful assembly and to freedom of association with others, including the right to form and join trade unions for the protection of his interests.
2. No restriction shall be placed on the exercise of these rights other than such as are prescribed by law and are necessary in a democratic society in the interests of national security or public safety, for the prevention of disorder or crime, for the protection of health or morals or for the protection of the rights and freedoms of others. This Article shall not prevent the

imposition of lawful restrictions upon the exercise of these rights by members of the armed forces, of the police or the administration of the State.

As can be seen, Articles 10 and 11 begin with a wide declaration concerning an individual's rights in relation to freedom of expression and to freedom of assembly and association and continue with a list of matters which can justify limiting those rights. Where someone is able to show that there has been interference with a specific right, it may be shown that the interference was justified, being prescribed by law; having a legitimate aim; being necessary in a democratic society in the interests of a legitimate aim; and that interference must not be discriminatory. For a restriction to be 'prescribed by law', a citizen must have access to the information and the law must be formulated with sufficient degree of precision to enable a citizen to regulate his conduct. It will not be sufficient that an interference is reasonable or desirable, there must be a pressing social need. An interference within a law must be proportionate to the legitimate aim pursued. While such assessment will be made by the state concerned initially, the 'reasonableness' of that assessment will be subject to scrutiny by the European Court of Human Rights if the individual concerned ultimately takes his case there.

Some of the matters listed as legitimate aims can be described as 'essential', eg matters affecting national security or public safety, where the limitation is necessary in a democratic society for such a purpose. Some of the other limitations, such as the prevention of disorder or the protection of the rights of others, are particularly likely to arise in public order situations. The question will be whether any interference with freedom of expression or of assembly or association is prescribed by law and necessary in a democratic society for such a purpose. It is inevitable that freedoms will come into conflict with other competing rights or interests and it is the duty of Parliament and of the courts to balance the rights of the individual against the needs of society. Inevitably, it is frequently the rights of individuals who seek to act in defiance of the agreed norms of society which appear to be supported, and the needs of society in general which appear to be ignored. One thing is certain, there will be continue to challenges to public order law, and its application, in consequence of the Act.

The challenges to our public order laws will occur in three principal ways:

(a) by way of an appeal against a criminal conviction in which case the court may hold that a statutory provision is incompatible with a Convention right;
(b) on an application for a declaration in any judicial proceedings that a statutory provision is incompatible with a Convention right.

Contravention of a Convention right may lead to a court holding that the exercise of the police power in question was invalid and therefore unlawful.

PUBLIC ORDER ACT 1936

The Public Order Act 1936 (POA 1936) governs the wearing of political uniforms and participation in quasi-military organisations. It was passed at a time at which the activities of the British Fascist Movement were attracting much attention.

Political uniforms

It is an offence under POA 1936, s 1 for any person to wear uniform, in any public place or at any public meeting, which signifies his association with any political organisation or with the promotion of any political object. By way of exception, a chief officer of police, with the consent of the Secretary of State, may by order permit the wearing of such uniforms at a ceremonial, anniversary or other special occasion. The consent of the Attorney-General is required for the continuation of the prosecution of a person charged with this offence.

A 'public meeting' is a meeting held for the purpose of discussing matters of public interest, and may be in a public place or in a private place if the public are permitted to attend (whether on payment or otherwise). There are many organisations (whose objectives are quite harmless) whose members wear some form of identifying clothing within their organisation. This would be within the scope of the section, but for the fact that it only deals with cases where the uniform signifies association with a political organisation or the promotion of a political object *and* it is worn in a public place or a public meeting. It must be emphasised that even members of a political organisation may wear uniforms in private, even in meetings if these are restricted to their own membership.

The term 'uniform' includes any particular article of clothing which is worn by each member of a group and which is intended to indicate his association with such an organisation or object. The article does not have to cover any major part of the body and it is sufficient to prove that the article has been commonly used by members of a political organisation. The berets, dark glasses and dark pullovers used by the IRA identify its members, in the eyes of the public, with a political organisation. In the same way, the wearing of a swastika arm band will still symbolise, in the eyes of the public, association with the Nazi Party.

Quasi-military organisations

POA 1936, s 2 is concerned with the preparation of private quasi-military forces of any description. Persons who take part in the control or management of any association, or in its training, commit offences if its members or adherents are:

(a) organised, trained or equipped for the purpose of enabling them to usurp the functions of the police or armed forces; or

(b) organised and trained or organised and equipped either to promote a political object by the use or display of physical force, or to arouse reasonable apprehension of that purpose.

In relation to the last word in (b), it has been held that the fact that there was no evidence of actual attacks on opponents, or of plans to attack them, did not necessarily remove grounds for 'reasonable apprehension of that purpose'.

Where a person is charged with taking part in the control or management of such an association, as opposed to training, he has a defence if he proves that he neither consented to nor connived at the organisation, training or equipment in contravention of the section. It will be appreciated that in any political organisation in which such military preparations have taken place there may be officials who were unaware of the activities of some of its members, and this defence is intended to cover such officials.

The provision of a reasonable number of stewards to assist in the preservation of order at a public meeting held on private premises is permitted, as is the provision of badges and insignia for them. The instruction of such persons in their lawful duties is also permitted.

CHAPTER 32

Public order offences related to sporting events and those connected with industrial disputes

Because of the high incidence of unruly behaviour before, during and after soccer matches, a number of Acts deal specifically with offences committed by persons attending such sporting events and give police officers particular powers to deal with such persons.

Recognising the high level of emotional feeling surrounding industrial disputes, the Trade Union and Labour Relations (Consolidation) Act 1992 seeks to ensure that disruption is kept to a minimum, while at the same time recognising the rights of individuals to protest concerning their working conditions.

PUBLIC ORDER AND SPORTING EVENTS

Alcohol on coaches, trains, etc

The Sporting Events (Control of Alcohol etc) Act 1985 (SE(CA)A 1985), ss 1 and 1A provide a number of offences whose aim is to prevent drunken behaviour by football fans en route to or from matches, and to prevent them arriving at grounds drunk. These offences are offences of:

(a) causing or permitting the carriage of alcohol on a specified vehicle;
(b) being in possession of alcohol on such a vehicle; and
(c) being drunk on a specified vehicle.

Vehicles specified

SE(CA)A 1985, s 1 provides these offences in relation to public service vehicles (ie coaches, buses and the like) and passenger trains. It does not apply to all such vehicles but only to those which are being used for the principal purpose of carrying passengers for the whole or part of a journey to or from a 'designated sporting event'. Thus, it does not apply to a bus or train on a normal scheduled service because it is not being used for the principal purpose of carrying passengers to or from a designated sporting event, even if the majority of the passengers are travelling to or from a match, since the words 'used' and 'principal purpose' must refer to use by, and the principal purpose of, the bus or rail company. However, it does apply to a 'football special' or to a coach or train chartered by the supporters' club, provided that it is travelling to or from a designated sporting event.

SE(CA)A 1985, s 1A provides substantially identical offences to those in s 1 in relation to a motor vehicle which:

(a) is not a public service vehicle but is adapted to carry more than eight passengers; and

(b) is being used for the principal purpose of carrying *two or more* passengers for the whole or part of a journey to or from a designated sporting event.

It will be noted that the definition is not limited to minibuses. It therefore includes the few types of private car which are adapted to carry more than eight passengers.

Designated sporting event

'Designated sporting event' is defined by SE(CA)A 1985, s 9(3). It means 'a sporting event or proposed sporting event for the time being designated, or of a class designated, by order made by the Secretary of State'. It also 'includes a designated sporting event within the meaning of the Criminal Justice (Scotland) Act 1980, Part V'. A designation order made by the Secretary of State may apply to events or proposed events outside Great Britain as well as those in England and Wales.

For the purposes of SE(CA)A 1985, the Sports Grounds and Sporting Events (Designation) Order 2005 designates as sporting events to which the Act applies:

(a) association football matches, at any sports ground in England or Wales, in which one or both of the participating teams represents a club which is for the time being a member (whether a full or associate member) of the Football League, the Football Association Premier League, the Football Conference National Division, the Scottish Football League or Welsh Premier League, or represents a country or territory;

(b) association football matches, at any sports ground in England and Wales, in competition for the Football Association Cup (other than in a preliminary or qualifying round);

(c) association football matches at a sports ground outside England and Wales in which one or both of the participating teams represents a club which is for the time being a member (whether a full or associate member) of the Football League, the Football Association Premier League, the Football Conference National Division, the Scottish Football League or Welsh Premier League, or represents the Football Association or the Football Association of Wales.

The Act does not apply to any sporting event or proposed sporting event where all competitors are to take part otherwise than for reward, and to which all spectators are to be admitted free of charge.

All matches in the Scottish Football League, all matches in the Highland Football League, all Scottish Football League and Association cup matches, all football matches in the three European cups, and soccer internationals, provided in each case that they take place at a designated ground, have been designated by the Sports Grounds and Sporting Events (Designation) (Scotland) Order 1980. The grounds designated by the Order are Hampden Park and the grounds of members of the Scottish Football League or of the Highland League. In addition, the Order designates rugby internationals at Murrayfield as designated sporting events.

Causing or permitting carriage of alcohol on a vehicle

SE(CA)A 1985, s 1(2) provides that a person who knowingly causes or permits alcohol to be carried on a vehicle to which s 1 applies is guilty of an offence:

(a) if the vehicle is a public service vehicle and he is the operator of the vehicle or the employee or agent of the operator; or

(b) if the vehicle is a hired vehicle (eg a chartered train or a football special) and he is the person to whom it is hired or the employee or agent of that person. Thus, an organiser of the supporters' club (or his agent) can be convicted if he permits alcohol to be carried on a chartered train, but a train guard who fails to prevent this cannot because, although he permits it, he is not a person to whom the train is hired (nor the employee or agent of such a person).

SE(CA)A 1985, s 1A(2) provides that a person who knowingly causes or permits alcohol to be carried on a motor vehicle to which s 1A applies is guilty of an offence:

(a) if he is its driver; or

(b) if he is not its driver but its keeper, the servant or agent of its keeper, a person to whom it is made available (by hire, loan or otherwise) by its keeper or the keeper's servant or agent, or the servant or agent of a person to whom it is so made available.

The causing or permitting of the carrying of alcohol on the vehicle must be done 'knowingly', which means that the accused must actually know or be wilfully blind that he is causing or permitting the carrying of alcohol on the vehicle.

Possession of alcohol on vehicle

SE(CA)A 1985, s 1(3) makes it an offence for a person to have alcohol in his possession while on a vehicle to which s 1 applies. There is a corresponding offence under SE(CA)A 1985, s 1A(3) in relation to motor vehicles to which s 1A applies.

Being drunk on a vehicle

SE(CA)A 1985, s 1(4) provides that a person who is drunk on a vehicle to which s 1 applies is guilty of an offence. There is a corresponding offence under SE(CA)A 1985, s 1A(4) in relation to motor vehicles to which s 1A applies.

Police powers

By SE(CA)A 1985, s 7(3), a constable may stop a public service vehicle to which SE(CA)A 1985, s 1 applies or a motor vehicle to which SE(CA)A 1985, s 1A applies (but not, for obvious reasons, a railway passenger vehicle) and may search such a vehicle or a railway passenger vehicle if he has reasonable grounds to suspect that an offence under s 1 or s 1A is being or has been committed in respect of that vehicle. The provisions of the Police and Criminal Evidence Act 1984 (PACE), s 2 and Code A, the Stop and Search Code, apply to such a search.

It will be noted that the power to search under SE(CA)A 1985, s 7(3) is to search the vehicle, and not a person on board it. There is, however, a general power under s 7(2) for a constable to search a person, whom he reasonably suspects is committing or has committed an offence under the Act. This is discussed later.

Alcohol, containers, fireworks, etc at designated sports grounds

SE(CA)A 1985, s 2 provides two offences relating to alcohol, containers, fireworks and the like, at a designated sports ground. It is aimed at preventing drunkenness at matches and at preventing the use of bottles and cans as missiles.

Designated sports ground

A 'designated sports ground' is defined by SE(CA)A 1985, s 9(2) as any place:

(a) used (wholly or partly) for sporting events where accommodation is provided for spectators; and
(b) for the time being designated, or of a class designated, by order made by the Secretary of State.

The provisions of the 2005 Order are set out above.

Period of a designated sporting event

Offences under SE(CA)A 1985, s 2 can only be committed during 'the period of a designated sporting event'. 'Designated sporting event' is defined on p 911. Normally, the period of such an event is the period beginning two hours before the start of the event or (if earlier, as where the start is delayed) two hours before the time at which it is advertised to start and ending one hour after the end of the event. Where a match is postponed or cancelled, the period ends one hour after the advertised start time. In respect of a room in a designated sports ground from which the designated sporting event may be directly viewed to which the public are not admitted (eg the directors' box), there is a different period in relation only to an offence of possession of alcohol etc. This is a 'restricted period' beginning fifteen minutes before the start of the event (or advertised start) and ending fifteen minutes after the end of the event or fifteen minutes after the advertised start (if the event is postponed or cancelled).

Possession of alcohol etc at designated ground

SE(CA)A 1985, s 2(1) provides that a person who has alcohol or an article to which s 2 applies in his possession:

(a) at any time during the period of a designated sporting event when he is in any area of a designated sports ground from which the event may be directly viewed; or

(b) while entering or trying to enter a designated sports ground at any time during the period of a designated sporting event at that ground,

is guilty of an offence.

The reference to an article to which SE(CA)A 1985, s 2 applies is to various types of drinks containers, for example bottles or a crushed-up can, which can be used as missiles or weapons. Because these are not offensive weapons per se (except in the case of a deliberately broken bottle or the like), a conviction for possessing an offensive weapon is most unlikely if a container is not actually used to cause injury because the necessary intent to use it to cause injury would be impossible to prove. Consequently, it was not normally possible for the police to take preventive action before a container was used offensively. The present provision is aimed at plugging this gap.

To turn to detail, SE(CA)A 1985, s 2(3) states that an article to which s 2 applies is any article capable of causing injury to a person struck by it, being:

(a) a bottle, can or other portable container (including such an article when crushed or broken) which is for holding any drink and is of a kind which, when empty, is normally discarded or returned to, or left to be recovered by, the supplier; or

(b) part of an article falling within (a).

However, the definition expressly does not apply to anything that is for holding any medicinal product.

The container need not be made specifically to hold alcohol, and it is irrelevant that it has never contained alcohol or that it is broken. An empty lemonade bottle is caught, as is a coke tin. On the other hand, a re-usable plastic drinks container, a mug, a thermos flask, a decanter or hip flask is not (although the latter two are likely to excite suspicion of possession of alcohol), since it is not the kind of container which is normally discarded or returned to, or left to be recovered by, the supplier.

Possession of fireworks etc

SE(CA)A 1985, s 2A(1), which is essentially aimed at reducing the risk of fire, makes identical provision in relation to the possession of a firework or of distress flares, fog signals, canisters of smoke or visible gas and similar articles. Matches and cigarette lighters are expressly excluded.

It is a defence for a person charged with an offence under s 2A(1) to prove that he had possession with lawful authority.

Being drunk at a designated sports ground

SE(CA)A 1985, s 2(2) provides that a person who is drunk in a designated sports ground (as defined above) at any time during the period of a designated sporting event (see above) at that ground, or who is drunk while entering or trying to enter such a ground at any time during the period of a designated sporting event at that ground, is guilty of an offence.

Misbehaviour at a designated football match

The Football (Offences) Act 1991 (F(O)A 1991) creates a number of offences. They can only be committed at a 'regulated football match'. Such matches are designated by the Football (Offences) (Designation of Football Matches) Order 2004. They are association football matches in which one or both of the participating teams represents a club which is for the time being a member (whether a full or associate member) of the Football League, the Football Association Premier League, or the Football Conference or the League of Wales, or represents a country or territory.

References in the Act to things done at a designated football match include anything done there in the period beginning two hours before the start of the match or (if earlier) two hours before the advertised start time and ending one hour after the end of the match. If the match does not take place, the period is two hours before the advertised start time until one hour after that time.

Throwing objects

F(O)A 1991, s 2 creates offences of throwing anything at or towards:

(a) the playing area or any area adjacent to the playing area to which spectators are not generally admitted; or
(b) any area in which spectators or other persons are or may be present,

without lawful authority or excuse (which it is for the accused to prove).

Thus, those who throw objects onto the pitch, into the players' tunnel etc, or into spectator areas will commit offences. Those who may prove 'lawful authority or excuse' would include vendors who throw packets of crisps etc into the crowd, or spectators who throw money to such persons.

Chanting

The F(O)A 1991, s 3 makes it an offence to engage or take part in chanting of an indecent or racist nature at a designated football match. 'Chanting' means the repeated uttering of words or sounds whether alone or in concert with one or more others, and 'racist nature' means consisting of or including matter which is threatening, abusive or insulting to a person by reason of his colour, race, nationality (including citizenship) or ethnic or national origin. Where visiting football supporters chanted 'You're just a town full of Pakis' a district judge ruled that this was merely doggerel amounting to no more than a statement that 'our town is better than your town'. Moreover, the district judge held, 'Paki' was nothing more than an abbreviation of 'Pakistani' and thus no more insulting or racialist than the use of the words 'Pom', 'Brit', 'Yank', 'Aussie' or 'Kiwi'. A divisional court allowed the prosecutor's appeal, holding that 'Paki' was commonly understood to be racially offensive and certainly was in the context in which it was used in the case. That was plain from the presence of 'just' in the chant.

Pitch invasion

By F(O)A 1991, s 4, it is an offence for a person to go on to the playing area, or any area adjacent to the playing area to which spectators are not generally admitted, without lawful authority or lawful excuse (which it is for the accused to prove).

It is not easy to obtain a conviction where spectators surge forward on to the pitch. Most will contend that they were carried forward unwillingly by the momentum of the crowd. If this is not disproved, a conviction for an offence under F(O)A 1991, s 4 will not be possible, since a person cannot generally be convicted if his conduct was beyond his control. Those who would have lawful excuse for going on to the pitch include trainers and official first aiders.

Sporting events: general police powers

Under the Sporting Events (Control of Alcohol etc) Act 1985

A constable may, at any time during the period of a designated sporting event at any designated sports ground, enter any part of the ground for the purpose of enforcing SE(CA)A 1985. It will be noted that the constable's power of entry is not limited to the 'public' parts of the ground; if necessary for the purposes of enforcing SE(CA)A 1985, he can enter the directors' suite or the manager's office.

In addition, a constable may search a person he has reasonable grounds to suspect is committing or has committed an offence under SE(CA)A 1985.

The power to search is extensive but it must be remembered that 'reasonable grounds to suspect' is a term which is now carefully defined in Code A, the Stop and Search Code. There must be a sound basis of fact upon which a police officer forms his reasonable suspicion that such an offence is being committed. Searches of supporters entering grounds cannot be carried out under a general belief that such persons are likely to commit these offences and this is specifically stated in the Code. If a person is seen to be carrying a supermarket bag with the distinctive bulge of a 'four-pack', or the outline of bottles etc can be seen inside coat pockets, then a reasonable suspicion exists. The suspicion is directed towards an individual and there is reason to suspect him.

The Code provides that its requirement that a person must not be searched except under a specific power of search does not affect the routine searching of persons entering sports grounds or other premises, *with their consent or as a condition of entry*. The searches which take place outside soccer grounds do not generally take place with consent (they may be accepted under the belief that the police have a right to do so) and a search as a condition of entry to a sports ground is not a search which should be conducted by a police officer, even if he is paid by the proprietor of the ground to do duty there. If a proprietor makes such a condition, it should be enforced by his own stewards as it is no part of a police officer's duty to enforce the rights of such proprietors.

BANNING ORDERS

The Football Spectators Act 1989, Part II deals with these.

Regulated football match

A 'regulated football match' is an association football match (whether in England or Wales or elsewhere) which is a prescribed match or a match of a prescribed description. The Football Spectators (Prescription) Order 2004 prescribes 'regulated football matches in England and Wales' and 'regulated football matches outside England and Wales'.

Regulated football matches in England and Wales

This is an association football match in which one or both of the participating teams represents:

(a) a club which is for the time being a member (whether a full or associate member) of the Football League, the Football Association Premier League, the Football Conference or the League of Wales;

(b) a club whose home ground is for the time being situated outside England and Wales, or

(c) represents a country or territory.

It is no longer a requirement that, to be a regulated match, the match must be played at a specified type of ground.

Regulated football matches outside England and Wales

This is an association football match involving:

(a) a national team appointed by the Football Association to represent England or the Football Association of Wales to represent Wales;

(b) a team representing a club which is for the time being a member (whether a full or associate member) of the Football League, the Football Association Premier League, the Football Conference or the League of Wales;

(c) a team representing any country or territory whose football association is for the time being a member of FIFA where the match is part of a competition or tournament organised by or under the authority of FIFA or UEFA and it is one in which a national team referred to in (a) is eligible to participate, or has participated; or

(d) a team representing a club which is for the time being a member (whether a full or associate member) of, or affiliated to, a national football association which is a member of FIFA, where the match is part of a competition or tournament organised by, or under the authority of, FIFA or UEFA and the competition is such that a club from the Football League, the Football Premier League, the Football Conference or the League of Wales is eligible to participate, or has participated.

When can a banning order be made?

A banning order may be made under the Football Spectators Act 1989 (FSA 1989), s 14A, s 14B or s 22.

Banning orders following a conviction for a relevant offence

FSA 1989, s 14A is concerned with a situation in which an offender is convicted of a 'relevant offence'. The relevant offences are set out in FSA 1989, Sch 1. They are:

(a) any offence contrary to the Football Spectators Act 1989, ss 2(1), 14J(1) or 21C(2) (unauthorised attendance at a regulated match (not yet in force), failure to comply with banning order requirement, or non-compliance with a notice under s 21B, respectively);

(b) any offence contrary to the Sporting Events (Control of Alcohol etc) Act 1985, s 1, s 2 or s 2A (possession of alcohol, containers or fireworks) committed at a regulated football match or while entering or trying to enter the ground;

(c) any offence involving harassment, alarm or distress contrary to the Public Order Act 1986 (POA 1986), s 5, or racial hatred contrary to POA 1986, Part III:
  (i)   committed during a period relevant to a regulated football match while at, entering or leaving the ground (or trying to do so), or
  (ii) if the court makes a declaration of relevance (ie declares that the offence related to regulated football matches), while on a journey to or from a regulated football match;

(d) any offence involving the use of violence or threat of violence towards another person or property:
  (i)   committed during a period relevant to a regulated football match, while at, entering or leaving the ground (or trying to do so), or
  (ii) if the court makes a 'declaration of relevance', committed while on a journey to or from a regulated football match;

(e) any offence involving harassment, alarm or distress (POA 1986, s 5) or racial hatred (POA 1986, Part III) which does not fall within (c), or any offence involving the use or threat of violence towards another person or property which does not fall within (d), which was committed during a period relevant to a regulated football match (normally the period from twenty-four hours before the start of the match to twenty-four hours after its end) and as respects which the court declares that the offence related to that match or that match and other regulated football matches during that period;

(f) any offence of drunkenness (ie being found drunk, or being drunk and disorderly, in a public place), committed while on such a journey, as to which offence the court makes a declaration of relevance);

(g) any offence contrary to the Sporting Events (Control of Alcohol etc) Act 1985, s 1 (alcohol on coaches or trains) committed on a journey to or from a regulated match, as to which offence the court makes a declaration of relevance;

(h) any offence contrary to the Road Traffic Act 1988, s 4 or 5 (drink and driving etc) committed while the accused was on a journey to or from a regulated football match, as to which offence the court makes a declaration of relevance;

(i) any offence contrary to F(O)A 1991;

(j) any offence involving the use, carrying or possession of an offensive weapon or firearm committed:
  (i)   during a period relevant to a regulated football match while the accused was at, or was entering or leaving the ground (or trying to do so), or
  (ii) if the court makes a declaration of relevance, while the accused was on a journey to or from a regulated football match;

(k) any offence involving the use, carrying or possession of an offensive weapon or firearm which does not fall within (j), which was committed during a period relevant to a regulated football match and as respects which the court declares that the offence related to that match or to that match and any other football offence during that period;

(l) ticket touting in relation to a regulated football match (Criminal Justice and Public Order Act 1994, s 166).

An attempt, conspiracy, incitement or aiding, abetting, counselling or procuring the commission of any such offence is included within these provisions. A person may be regarded as having been on a journey to or from a football match whether or not he attended or intended to attend the match. A journey includes breaks (including overnight breaks).

If, upon conviction for such an offence, a court is satisfied that there are reasonable grounds to believe that making a banning order would help to prevent violence or disorder at, or in connection with, any regulated football match, it *must* make such an order in respect of the offender. If it is not so satisfied, it must state its reasons in open court. A banning order is in addition to a sentence or order of conditional discharge.

Banning orders made on complaint

Under FSA 1989, s 14B, the chief officer of police of an area in which a person resides, or appears to reside, may make a complaint to a magistrates' court that the respondent has at some time contributed to violence or disorder in the United Kingdom or elsewhere.

In this respect, the terms 'violence' and 'disorder' carry their usual meanings, embracing violence against persons and property; threats of violence and endangering life; stirring up racial hatred; threatening, abusive and insulting behaviour; or displaying any such material, whether or not committed in connection with football.

If the court is satisfied as to the substance of the complaint and has reasonable grounds for believing that making a banning order would help to prevent violence or disorder at or in connection with any regulated football match it *must* make a banning order. In deciding these matters a court may take into account (among other things):

(a) any decision of a court or tribunal outside the United Kingdom;

(b) deportation or exclusion from a country outside the United Kingdom;

(c) removal or exclusion from football grounds in the United Kingdom or elsewhere; or

(d) conduct recorded by video or by any other means.

However, a court may only take note of matters occurring within the ten years preceding the application. It must also consider the reasons given by a court when, in relation to a relevant offence, it did not make a banning order.

The Court of Appeal has held that the making of such a banning order under FSA 1989, s 14B is compatible with European Community law as it is justified on the grounds of public policy in order to prevent violence or disorder at foreign football matches. If operated correctly, the scheme satisfies the requirements of proportionality. So far as the standard of proof is concerned, the court described it as an exacting one which would be hard in practice to distinguish from the criminal standard of proof beyond reasonable doubt. The high standard is imposed because of the serious restraints on an individual's freedom which a banning order imposes.

No application may be made under FSA 1989, s 14B after the end of the 'initial period' which is a period of five years beginning on 28 August 2002.

Banning order under FSA 1989, s 22

FSA 1989, s 22 governs the making of a banning order as a result of a conviction for a 'corresponding offence' outside England and Wales. A 'corresponding offence' is an offence under the law of a country specified outside England and Wales in an Order in Council. At the time that this book went to press, orders have been made in respect of Italy, Scotland, Sweden, Norway, the Republic of Ireland, France, Belgium and the Netherlands.

The effect of a banning order

A 'banning order' means an order made by a court under FSA 1989, Part II which:

(a) in relation to regulated football matches in England and Wales, prohibits the person who is subject to the order from entering premises for the purpose of attending such matches; and

(b) in relation to regulated football matches outside England and Wales, requires that person to report at a police station in accordance with Part II.

An order will apply to the whole range of matches which are prescribed, whatever the venue and whatever the club. This is sensible. Clearly, a banning order would not be very effective if it barred a person only from the ground at which the offence was committed.

The effect of a banning order must be explained by the court.

A banning order must require the person subject to the order to report to a police station specified in the order, within five days beginning with the day upon which the order is made. Unless there are exceptional circumstances, it must contain a requirement as to the surrender of a passport of the person subject to the order, in accordance with the requirements of the Act, in connection with regulated football matches. Such exceptional circumstances, if found, must be stated in open court. If the person concerned is detained in custody, the requirements apply upon release.

The court may impose additional requirements upon a person subject to such an order and may subsequently vary an order so as to impose, replace or omit requirements on the application of the person subject to the order or the person who applied for the order or the prosecutor. In addition, the court has power to require a constable to photograph the person or cause him to be photographed.

Duration of banning order

Where a banning order is made following conviction and is in addition to a sentence of imprisonment (any form of detention) taking immediate effect, the maximum is ten years and the minimum is six years. In any other case following conviction the maximum is five years and the minimum three. Orders which are made under s 14B (following complaint) may be for a maximum of three years and a minimum of two.

Termination of an order

After two-thirds of the period of the ban has passed, the person subject to it may apply to the court by which the order was made to terminate it. The court, in considering whether or not to terminate the ban, must have regard to a person's character; conduct since the order was made; the nature of the offence or conduct concerned; and any other relevant circumstances.

Functions of the enforcing authority and local police forces

Reporting at a police station

When a banned person initially reports at a police station, the officer responsible for that station may make such requirements of that person as are determined by the enforcing authority to be necessary or expedient for giving effect to the banning order, so far as matters are related to regulated football matches outside England and Wales. The 'enforcing authority' is the Football Banning Orders Authority established by the Secretary of State.

If, in connection with any regulated football match outside England and Wales, that authority considers that a requirement to report is necessary or expedient to reduce the likelihood of violence or disorder at or in connection with the match, the authority must give the person subject to the order a notice in writing to report as instructed and, if the match is outside the United Kingdom, to surrender his passport as instructed.

In the case of a regulated football match there may be a demand to comply with additional requirements.

A requirement to report at a police station is restricted to the 'control period' in relation to a regulated football match outside England and Wales or an external tournament and a requirement to surrender a passport in such circumstances must also be so restricted. The control period in relation to such a regulated football match is the period commencing five days before the date of the match and ending when the match is concluded or cancelled. In relation to an external tournament it means any period described in an order made by the Secretary of State beginning five days before the first match outside England and Wales and ending when the last match outside England and Wales has been concluded or cancelled. However, qualifying matches do not count in determining the start of the tournament.

If the Secretary of State considers it necessary or expedient to do so in order to secure the effective enforcement of these provisions, he may make an order extending the 'control period' in relation to any regulated football match to a maximum of not more than ten days.

Failure to comply with a requirement

It is an offence contrary to FSA 1989, s 14J(1), for a person subject to a banning order to fail to comply with:

(a) any requirement imposed by the order; or
(b) any requirement imposed by FSA 1989, s 19(2B) or s 19(2C), that is:
  (i) any requirement to report at a police station specified in a notice at a time, or between the times, specified and, if the match is outside the United Kingdom and the order requires the surrender of a passport, to surrender it at a police station specified in the notice at the required time, or between the required times (s 19(2B)); or
  (ii) any requirement made in relation to a regulated football match by the enforcing authority (s 19(2C)).

Summary measures

FSA 1989, ss 21A and 21B underpin the procedure for the application by way of complaint for a banning order. They provide for a constable in uniform to exercise powers of detention and of reference to a court in specified circumstances. The powers under ss 21A and 21B may be exercised only in relation to a British citizen.

FSA 1989, s 21A provides a constable in uniform with the power to detain a person in his custody if, during any 'control period' in relation to a regulated football match outside England and Wales or an external tournament:

(a) he has reasonable grounds to suspect that the person has at any time caused or contributed to any violence or disorder in the United Kingdom or elsewhere; and
(b) he has reasonable grounds to believe that making a banning order in his case would help to prevent violence or disorder at, or in connection with, any regulated football matches.

Such a person may be detained until the constable has decided whether or not to issue a notice under FSA 1989, s 21B requiring him:

(a) to appear before a magistrates' court at a specified time;
(b) not to leave England and Wales before that time; and
(c) if the control period relates to a regulated football match outside the United Kingdom or to an external tournament which includes such matches, to surrender his passport to the constable,

and stating the grounds upon which his decision is based.

Such detention may not exceed four hours or, with the authority of an officer of at least the rank of inspector, six hours. A person so detained may not be further detained within the same control period unless new information becomes available.

The notice referred to above may be issued where the officer is authorised to do so by an officer of at least the rank of inspector. The time at which such a person must appear before a magistrates' court must be within twenty-four hours of receiving the notice or that person's detention, whichever is the earlier. Such a notice will be treated as an application for a banning order by way of complaint.

Where a person to whom such a notice has been given appears before a magistrates' court, the court may remand him. If he is remanded on bail, he may be required not to leave England and Wales before his appearance before the court and, if the control period relates to a regulated football match outside the United Kingdom or to an external tournament which includes such matches, he may be required to surrender his passport to a constable.

By s 21C(2), it is an offence to fail to comply with a notice under s 21B.

No power under FSA 1989, s 21A or 21B may be exercised after the end of the period of five years beginning on 28 August 2002.

TICKET TOUTS

The Criminal Justice and Public Order Act 1994, s 166 makes it an offence for any unauthorised person to sell, or offer or expose for sale, a ticket for a designated football match, in any public place or place to which the public has access or, in the case of a trade or business, in any other place.

The only persons who are 'authorised' are those authorised in writing by the home club or organisers of the match. The term 'ticket' includes anything which purports to be a ticket, so that false tickets are included. However, where a false ticket is involved a charge of obtaining property by deception would be more appropriate where knowledge of such falsity can be proved. A 'designated football match' means an association football match (whether in England and Wales or elsewhere) of a description, or a particular match, designated for the purposes of the Football Spectators Act 1989, Part I or which is a regulated match under FSA 1989, Part II.

Police powers

The provisions of PACE, s 32 (search of an arrested person and his vehicle) are extended to the case where the vehicle is reasonably suspected to have been used for any purpose connected with the offence.

LABOUR LAWS

The police are inevitably involved in the enforcement of the law concerning trade disputes. Consequently, it is essential that that law is clearly understood by police officers, who are very much in the public eye when dealing with such disputes. The primary piece of legislation dealing with trade disputes is the Trade Union and Labour Relations (Consolidation) Act 1992 (TULR(C)A 1992).

Acts of 'interference' with workers

TULR(C)A 1992, s 241 is not directly concerned with picketing. Indeed, it is not confined to the context of trade disputes. However, that is its normal application. It deals with acts which may or may not be committed away from the picket line but which nevertheless amount to attempts to prevent a worker from exercising his own freedom of choice.

An offence is committed by any person who, with a view to compelling any other person to abstain from doing or to do any act which that other person has a legal right to do or abstain from doing, wrongfully and without legal authority does one of the following things:

Uses violence to or intimidates such other person or his spouse, civil partner or children, or injures his property

It is essential to realise that only peaceful picketing can be lawful. No matter what a mob may represent itself to be, if that mob or any particular person uses violence or intimidates another person an offence is committed against TULR(C)A 1992, s 241. Acts committed against a person's spouse, civil partner children or property are also punishable. It is not a form of peaceful persuasion to threaten a worker, his family or his property with violence. Instances have occurred in which the cars of workers who refused to join a strike have been damaged. In addition to the offence of criminal damage, the present offence is also committed.

Persistently follows such other person about from place to place

The word 'persistently' is not meant to convey any form of permanence in this activity and it is sufficient if a person, or part of the mob outside a works, follows a man from the works and through the streets, shouting at him or making hostile gestures. The following of an employer in an attempt to compel him to reinstate an employee is also covered by this provision.

Hides any tools, clothes or other property owned or used by such other person or deprives him of or hinders him in the use thereof

An effective way of preventing a skilled workman from carrying out his duties would be to prevent him from working by separating him from specialist tools required to carry out his task. If all the miners' lamps for a particular colliery were hidden, this could effectively prevent individual miners, and perhaps the entire workforce, from working.

Watches or besets the house or other place where such other person resides, or works, or carries on business, or happens to be, or the approach to such a house or place

'Watching or besetting' merely describes certain forms of picketing. It must be remembered that all the various types of conduct covered by TULR(C)A 1992, s 241 are only criminal if they are done wrongfully. As a result, a person engaged in lawful picketing is not guilty under s 241 by virtue of the present provision. What constitutes 'lawful picketing' is described below. There would be little purpose in restricting the nature of picketing at a works to forms of peaceful picketing if pickets could operate outside the houses of individual workers to prevent them from working. This mode of the offence is designed among other things to prevent the removal of picket lines or single persuaders from the works to a dwelling house or its approaches.

Since, like any other offence under TULR(C)A 1992, s 241, watching or besetting must be done with a view to compelling someone to abstain from doing something which he has a legal right to do, or vice versa, as opposed to with a view to simply persuading him, there cannot be a conviction on the ground of watching or besetting in the absence of proof that someone was either prevented or was likely to be prevented, or intended to be prevented, from doing something etc. The reason is that, in the absence of such evidence, there is no evidence of the watching or besetting being done with a view to compelling someone not to do something etc.

This was held in a case concerning alleged watching and besetting of an abortion clinic, where the accused sought to persuade women not to enter solely by verbal means, with no threat or actual use of force. A divisional court held that, in the absence of evidence that anyone was prevented, or likely to be prevented, or intended to be prevented, from undergoing an abortion, the accused had not acted with a view to compelling women not to do so.

Follows such other person with two or more other persons in a disorderly manner in or through any street or road

Although we have already considered the following of persons by those wishing to compel them not to work, this offence differs in that there is no need to prove any form of persistence. The aggravation by being accompanied by two or more persons and the incidence of disorderly conduct are sufficient. This mode of committing the offence can only be committed in a street or road.

Peaceful picketing: Trade Union and Labour Relations (Consolidation) Act 1992

It is extremely important to understand the law concerning peaceful picketing because of the necessity for police officers to ensure that the activities of the pickets are directed towards pursuits which are permitted by law and do not amount to intimidation of other workers, whether they are workers belonging to the same trade union or not.

TULR(C)A 1992, s 220(1) states that it shall be lawful for a person in contemplation or furtherance of a trade dispute to attend:

(a) at or near his own place of work; or
(b) if he is an official of a trade union, at or near the place of work of a member of that union whom he is accompanying and whom he represents,

for the purpose only of peacefully obtaining or communicating information, or peacefully persuading any person to work or abstain from working. These words contain key requirements for lawful picketing. They are concerned with *the place* where a person attends in contemplation or furtherance of a trade dispute and with *the purpose* for which he attends.

The place

TULR(C)A 1992, s 220(1) provides that it is lawful for a person in contemplation or furtherance of a trade dispute to attend at or near *his own place of work*; it does not, of course, authorise access to private premises without the consent of their owner. Except in the case of a trade union official accompanying a member whom he represents at or near the latter's place of work, picketing at some place other than the picket's own place of work is not declared to be lawful. Thus, picketing by 'flying pickets' or by other people who do not work at the place in question (and may not even be members of the trade union engaged in the dispute) is not declared to be lawful by s 220(1), and renders such a picket guilty from the outset of an offence against TULR(C)A 1992, s 241 on the ground of 'watching or besetting', however peaceful the picket may be.

It follows that the meaning of 'his own place of work' for the purposes of TULR(C)A 1992, s 220(1) is of crucial importance. In this respect, s 220(2) and (3) make special provision. TULR(C)A 1992, s 220(2) deals with the case of a worker who does not work at any one particular place (for example, a service engineer or train driver) or whose place of work is so located that it is impracticable for him to attend there to picket. It provides that the place of work of such a person is *any premises* of his employer *from* which he works or *from* which his work is administered.

Whether or not picketing is *at or near* the picket's place of work depends upon a common sense approach. In one case the Court of Appeal held that pickets, who stood at the entrance to a trading estate, 1,200 yards away from their employer's premises on that estate and would have been trespassing if they had picketed on the estate, were attending (picketing) near their place of work.

There are occasions when the provisions of TULR(C)A 1992, s 220 described so far would act unfairly against a worker who, having been dismissed from his employment, would be excluded from the right to protest because he would no longer have a place of work at or near which he could attend. TULR(C)A 1992, s 220(3) protects such a worker, by stating that where:

(a) his last employment was terminated in connection with a trade dispute; or
(b) the termination of his employment was one of the circumstances giving rise to the dispute,

his former place of work shall be treated as if it was his place of work.

The purpose

Even if the requirement that the picket must be obtaining or communicating information, or peacefully picketing at or near his own place of work is satisfied, his conduct is *only declared to be lawful by TULR(C)A 1992, s 220(1) if his attendance is for the purpose only of peacefully persuading any person to work or abstain from working.* A person who attends for some other purpose, for example forcibly to prevent workers or deliveries entering premises, is not protected by s 220(1) and is liable for any criminal offence which he may commit; he may also, of course, be liable to pay damages under the civil law for any harm which he causes by molesting a worker or interfering with his right to work. Thus, pickets who link arms and form a physical barrier to prevent movement in and out of works are criminally liable, even though they work there, for an offence against TULR(C)A 1992, s 241 and for any other offence which they may commit, as are members of a picket which by weight of numbers seeks to prevent others exercising their right to work since it cannot be said that they are there *only* for fulfilling one of the specified purposes peacefully: intimidation is not peaceful persuasion.

The physical presence of lawful pickets on a highway must represent some form of obstruction and this is permitted to the extent that it is reasonably necessary for such pickets to carry out their task of speaking to their colleagues. However, this right is restricted to those who are lawful pickets in accordance with the provisions of TULR(C)A 1992, s 220. It is a question of fact as to whether or not the degree of obstruction has passed beyond that reasonably required. Mass picketing clearly goes beyond what is reasonably required and is therefore illegal. So is the total obstruction of an entrance, and so are other measures which have the same effect. Where pickets kept moving by walking around in a circle outside the main entrance to a factory and were required to stop doing so by a police officer, they were held to have obstructed him in his duty by their refusal, as they were carrying out an illegal act.

The police have a duty to limit the size of lawful pickets to a number which appears to be reasonable in the circumstances and a refusal by the organisers to comply with reasonable requests made by the police may amount to a wilful obstruction contrary to the Police Act 1996, s 89(2).

The role of the police

The police must not be concerned with the merits of any trade dispute. Their role is the preservation of the peace, and they must impartially enforce and uphold the law where such action becomes necessary. They have a general discretion in relation to their handling of disputes and of pickets to ensure that all remains peaceful and orderly. It is no part of a police officer's duty to assist with civil remedies; if an employer wishes to identify persons on picket lines or outside his works with a view to civil process, that is his responsibility and police officers should not attempt to identify such persons on his behalf. Additionally, the enforcement of any orders made in favour of employers is the responsibility of officers of the court and police participation must be restricted to ensuring the maintenance of the peace.

The Code of Conduct on picketing issued for the guidance of pickets (which recommends that the number of pickets at any entrance to a workplace should not exceed six) is not a part of the criminal law. The number of pickets in particular circumstances is a matter for police discretion bearing in mind their primary purpose of maintaining the peace.

CHAPTER 33

Terrorism generally

As a result of the recent increase in offences and controls imposed as a result of terrorism, the material which previously appeared within Chapter 21 (Aliens) and Chapter 31 (Public order offences other than those related to sporting events etc), has been brought together within this new chapter.

The chapter is concerned with the special measures to be taken in respect of suspected international terrorists and with the offences and powers under the Terrorism Acts 2000 and 2006 and related legislation.

SUSPECTED INTERNATIONAL TERRORISTS: SPECIAL MEASURES

The Prevention of Terrorism Act 2005 (PTA 2005) provides for the making, against individuals involved in terrorism-related activity, of orders imposing obligations on them for purposes connected with preventing or restricting their further involvement in such activity. These provisions apply to any person and are not restricted to members of 'foreign' terrorist organisations. These orders are 'control orders' which impose obligations upon a person for a purpose connected with protecting members of the public from a risk of terrorism. Such orders can be made:

(a) except in the case of an order imposing obligations that are incompatible with the individual's right to liberty under art 5 of the European Convention on Human Rights, by the Secretary of State; and

(b) in the case of an order imposing obligations that are or include derogating obligations, by the court on an application by the Secretary of State.

The 'obligations' which are referred to are quite extensive but relate mainly to prohibiting the possession of articles, to restricting activities, freedom of movement or business activities, to requiring agreement to being photographed or electronically monitored, and to requiring reporting to a specified person or the surrender of a passport.

The obligations imposed by a particular control order must be such as the Secretary of State or (as the case may be) the court considers necessary for purposes connected with preventing or restricting involvement by the individual concerned in terrorism-related activity. A 'terrorism-related activity' is defined by PTA 2005, s 1(9) as:

(a) the commission, preparation or instigation of acts of terrorism;
(b) conduct which facilitates the commission, preparation or instigation of such acts, or which is intended to do so;
(c) conduct which gives encouragement to the commission, preparation or instigation of such acts, or which is intended to do so;
(d) conduct which gives support or assistance to individuals who are known or believed to be involved in terrorism-related activity; and for the purposes of s 1(9) it is immaterial whether the acts of terrorism in question are specific acts of terrorism or acts of terrorism generally.

There are two types of control order.

Non-derogating control order

A non-derogating control order may be made against an individual by the Secretary of State if he:

(a) has reasonable ground for suspecting that the individual is or has been involved in terrorism-related activity; and
(b) considers that it is necessary, for purposes connected with protecting members of the public from a risk of terrorism, to make a control order imposing obligations on that individual.

Such an order has effect for a period of twelve months but may be renewed on more than one occasion.

The Secretary of State may make such an order only where the High Court has given consent to the making of the order, except in an urgent case. In such an urgent case, the order must be referred to the High Court for consideration.

Derogating control order

By the European Convention on Human Rights, art 15, the United Kingdom can derogate from an article of the Convention in time of emergency. Such a derogation is known as a 'designated derogation'.

On receipt of an application by the Secretary of State, the court must hold an immediate preliminary hearing to determine whether to make a control order imposing obligations which are, or include, derogating obligations (a derogating control order). If such an order is made, the court must give directions for the holding of a full hearing to decide whether to confirm the order. Such orders cease to have effect after a period of six months, but may be renewed for a similar period.

'Derogating obligation' means an obligation on an individual which:

(a) is incompatible with his right to liberty under art 5 of the Convention on Human Rights; but
(b) is of a description of obligations which, for the purposes of the designation of a designated derogation, is set out in the designation order.

Offences

(1) A person who, without reasonable excuse, contravenes an obligation imposed on him by a control order is guilty of an offence.

(2) A person is guilty of an offence if:
- (a) a control order by which he is bound at a time when he leaves the United Kingdom requires him, whenever he enters the United Kingdom, to report to a specified person that he is or has been the subject of such an order;
- (b) he re-enters the United Kingdom after the order has ceased to have effect;
- (c) the occasion on which he re-enters the United Kingdom is the first occasion on which he does so after leaving while the order was in force; and
- (d) on that occasion he fails, without reasonable excuse, to report to the specified person in the manner that was required by the order.

(3) A person is guilty of an offence if he intentionally obstructs the exercise by any person of the power to enter and search premises for a person upon whom notice of a control order in to be served.

Arrest and detention pending derogating control order

(1) A constable may arrest and detain an individual if:
- (a) the Secretary of State has made an application to the court for a derogating control order to be made against that individual; and
- (b) the constable considers that the individual's arrest and detention is necessary to ensure that he is available to be given notice of the order if it is made.

(2) A constable who has arrested an individual under the above provision must take him to the designated place that the constable considers most appropriate as soon as practicable after the arrest.

(3) An individual taken to a designated place may be detained there until the end of forty-eight hours from the time of his arrest.

(4) If the court considers that it is necessary to do so to ensure that the individual in question is available to be given notice of any derogating control order that is made against him, it may, during the forty-eight hours following his arrest, extend the period for which the individual may be detained by a period of no more than forty-eight hours.

(5) An individual may not be detained under the above provisions at any time after:
- (a) he has become bound by a derogating control order made against him on the Secretary of State's application; or
- (b) the court has dismissed the application.

(6) A person who has the powers of a constable in one part of the United Kingdom may exercise the above power of arrest in that part of the United Kingdom or in any other part of the United Kingdom.

(7) An individual detained under the above provisions:
- (a) shall be deemed to be in legal custody throughout the period of his detention; and
- (b) after having been taken to a designated place shall be deemed:
  - (i) in England and Wales, to be in police detention for the purposes of the Police and Criminal Evidence Act 1984 (PACE); and

(ii) in Northern Ireland, to be in police detention for the purposes of the Police and Criminal Evidence (Northern Ireland) Order 1989;

but paragraph (b) has effect subject to (8).

(8) The provisions of the Terrorism Act 2000 Sch 8 (see pp 936–938) relating to the identification of a detained person and his rights apply to an individual detained under the above provisions, except that identification steps may only be taken by a constable and there are some modifications relating to the postponement of the detained person informing someone or consulting a solicitor.

(9) The power to detain an individual under the above provisions includes power to detain him in a manner that is incompatible with his right to liberty under art 5 of the Convention on Human Rights if, and only if:

(a) there is a designated derogation in respect of the detention of individuals under the above provisions in connection with the making of applications for derogating control orders; and

(b) that derogation and the designated derogation relating to the power to make the orders applied for are designated in respect of the same public emergency.

(10) In the above provisions 'designated place' means any place which the Secretary of State has designated under Sch 8 to the Terrorism Act 2000 as a place at which persons may be detained under s 41 of that Act.

The above provisions of the PTA 2005 must be renewed annually by order made by the Secretary of State subject to the approval of each House of Parliament. Unless renewed (and it can confidently be expected that they will be) these provisions will expire on 10 March 2007 when the current continuation order expires.

TERRORISM

The Terrorism Act 2000 contains a number of offences, as well as other provisions relating to matters such as arrest, detention and questioning, to deal with terrorism at home and abroad.

Meaning of 'terrorism' in the Terrorism Act 2000

The Terrorism Act 2000 (TA 2000) frequently refers to 'terrorism'. For the purposes of that Act, 'terrorism' is defined by s 1 as meaning the use or threat of action (inside or outside the United Kingdom) which:

(a) (i) involves serious violence against a person wherever he is;
   (ii) involves serious damage to property wherever situated;
   (iii) endangers a person's life, other than that of the person committing the action;
   (iv) creates a serious risk to the health and safety of the public or a section of the public; or
   (v) is designed seriously to interfere with or seriously to disrupt an electronic system;
(b) the use or threat is designed to influence the United Kingdom government, or any other government, or an international governmental organisation, or to intimidate the public or a section of the public anywhere; and

(c) the use or threat is made for the purpose of advancing a political, religious or ideological cause.

The use or threat of action falling within (a), which includes the use of firearms or explosives, is terrorism whether or not (b) is satisfied.

Proscribed organisations

The Terrorism Act 2000 contains a number of offences which can be committed in relation to a 'proscribed organisation' listed in TA 2000, Sch 2:

(a) to belong or profess to belong to a proscribed organisation, subject to a defence on 'proof' (interpreted by the House of Lords as only imposing an evidential burden) by the accused that he joined the proscribed organisation before it was proscribed and he has not taken part in the activities of the organisation since it became proscribed (TA 2000, s 11);

(b) to invite support for a proscribed organisation, other than support with money or property (TA 2000, s 12(1));

(c) to arrange, manage or assist in arranging or managing a meeting of three or more (whether or not the public are admitted) which the accused knows is:
   (i)   to support a proscribed organisation;
   (ii) to further the activities of a proscribed organisation; or
   (iii) to be addressed by a person who belongs or professes to belong to a proscribed organisation (where the offence relates to a private meeting), subject to a defence if the accused adduces sufficient evidence that he had no reasonable cause to believe that such an address would support a proscribed organisation or further its activities, whereupon the prosecution must disprove this (TA 2000, s 12(2));

(d) to address a meeting where the purpose is to encourage support for a proscribed organisation or to further its activities (TA 2000, s 12(3)).

For the purposes of the Act, the proscribed organisations associated with terrorism in Northern Ireland are at present:

the Irish Republican Army; Cumann na mBan; Fianna na hEireann; the Red Hand Commando; Saor Eire; the Ulster Freedom Fighters; the Ulster Volunteer Force; the Irish National Liberation Army; the Irish People's Liberation Organisation; the Ulster Defence Association; the Loyalist Volunteer Force; the Continuity Army Council; the Orange Volunteers and the Red Hand Defenders.

Other proscribed organisations are:

Al-Qa'ida, Egyptian Islamic Jihad; Al-Gama'at al-Islamiya; Armed Islamic Group (Groupe Islamique Armée) (GIA); Salafist ' Group for Call and Combat (Groupe Salafiste pour la Prédication et le Combat) (GSPC); Babbar Khalsa; International Sikh Youth Federation; Harakat Mujahideen; Jaish e Mohammed; Lashkar e Tayyaba; Liberation Tigers of Tamil Eelam (LTTE); Hizballah External Security Organisation; Hamas-Izz al-Din al-Qassem Brigades; Palestinian Islamic Jihad—Shaqaqi; Abu Nidal Organisation; Islamic Army of Aden; Mujaheddin e Khalq; Kurdistan Workers' Party (Partiya Karkeren Kurdistan) (PKK); Revolutionary Peoples' Liberation Party—Front (Devrimci Halk Kurtulus Partisi-Cephesi) (DHKP-C); Basque Homeland and Liberty (Euskadi ta Askatasuna

(ETA)); 17 November Revolutionary Organisation (N17); Abu Sayyaf Group; Asbat Al-Ansar; Islamic Movement of Uzbekistan; Jemaah Islamiyah; Al Itti-had Al Islamia; Ansar Al Islam; Ansar Al Sunna; Groupe Islamique Combattant Marocain; Harakat-ul-Jihad-ul-Islami; Harakat-ul-Jihad-ul-Islami (Bangladesh); Harakat-ul-Mujahadeen/Alami; Hezb-e Islami Gulbuddin; Islamic Jihad Union; Jamaat ul-Furquan; Jundallah; Khuddam ul-Islam; Lashkar-e Jhangvi; Libyan Islamic Fighting Group; Sipah-e Sahaba Pakistan; Al-Ghurabaa; The Saved Sect; Baluchistan Liberation Army; Teyrebaz Azadiye Kurdistan.

The Secretary of State has the power to add to, remove or amend a name included in TA 2000, Sch 2. He may only add the name of an organisation if he believes that it is concerned in terrorism, and for this purpose an organisation is concerned in terrorism if it commits, or participates in, acts of terrorism, prepares for terrorism, promotes or encourages terrorism, or is otherwise concerned in terrorism.

As can be seen, the provisions of TA 2000, ss 11 and 12 create a wide range of offences dealing with membership or professed membership of proscribed organisations, with the promotion of them, and meetings in support of them.

Contributions towards acts of terrorism

TA 2000, s 15 provides that a person is guilty of an offence if he:

(a) invites any other person to provide money or other property, and intends that it should be used, or has reasonable cause to suspect that it may be used, for the purposes of terrorism; or
(b) receives money or other property, and intends that it should be used, or has reasonable cause to suspect that it may be used, for the purposes of terrorism; or
(c) provides money or other property, and knows or has reasonable cause to suspect that it will or may be used, for the purposes of terrorism.

Within TA 2000, s 15, a reference to the 'provision' of money or other property is a reference to its being given, lent or otherwise made available, whether or not for consideration. Because it is irrelevant that the financial assistance is given for consideration, a person who purchases some article, object or property, knowing or having reason to suspect that the money he hands over will be used for terrorism commits an offence under s 15 unless he proves that he had no reason to suspect that it would benefit such an organisation.

TA 2000, s 16 prohibits the use of money or property for the purposes of terrorism. It creates a further offence of possessing money or other property intending that it should be used, or having reasonable cause to suspect that it may be used, for the purposes of terrorism.

TA 2000, s 17 prohibits a person entering into, or being concerned in, an arrangement which may make money or other property available, knowing, or having reasonable cause to suspect, that it may be used for terrorism. TA 2000, s 18 prohibits money laundering of terrorist property by concealment, removal from jurisdiction, transfer to nominees, or in any other way. Section 18 provides a defence for anyone who can prove lack of knowledge or reason to suspect that the arrangement was concerned with terrorist property.

Police powers

Arrest

TA 2000, s 41 provides that a constable may arrest without warrant a person whom he reasonably suspects to be a terrorist. For the purposes of this power of arrest a 'terrorist' is a person:

(a) who has committed an offence under TA 2000, s 11 (membership of a proscribed organisation); s 12 (support for it); ss 15 to 18 (fundraising etc and money laundering); s 54 (weapons training); or ss 56 to 63 (collecting information, inciting terrorism overseas and terrorist banking and finance offences); or

(b) who is, or has been, concerned in the commission, preparation or instigation of acts of terrorism.

A person who has been so detained may be held for forty-eight hours. Continued detention beyond that period is subject to a warrant granted in accordance with the procedures prescribed by TA 2000, Sch 8. This provides for the detention of persons arrested under TA 2000, s 41 or under Sch 7 (special powers at ports and border controls for a period of up to forty-eight hours (subject to reviews)).

Reviews and extensions of detention

A Crown Prosecutor and, in any part of the United Kingdom, a superintendent (or above) may apply to a judicial authority (or in some cases a High Court judge) for a warrant of further detention. A judicial authority ie the Senior District Judge (Chief Magistrate), or his deputy, or a designated district judge (magistrates' courts) or senior judge may issue a warrant for a shorter period where the application is for a shorter period or it is satisfied that there are circumstances that would make it inappropriate for the specified period to be as long as seven days. This may be extended, on application. Schedule 8 was amended by the Terrorism Act 2006 (TA 2006), ss 23 to 25 to make further provisions for warrants of further detention where there are reasonable grounds for believing that the further detention of the person concerned is necessary to obtain relevant evidence and the investigation is being conducted diligently and expeditiously

Code H (Code of Practice for Detention of Terrorism Suspects) includes significant changes from the provisions in PACE Code C in consequence of changes to maximum detention times by TA 2006. The original maximum period of detention of seven days was extended to a maximum of fourteen days by the Criminal Justice Act 2003, s 306. It is also provided that a detained person must be released if the grounds upon which his continued detention was authorised no longer exist and there is no other reason why he should be held.

The extended period of detention will normally be seven days but may be for less where seven days is inappropriate. In the case of warrants of extended detention, where the application is to extend beyond fourteen days, the application must be made to a senior judge (judge of the High Court). If for less than fourteen days, it may be made to a judicial authority (designated district judge). Applications for extension must be limited to seven days on each occasion and warrants may not be extended beyond twenty-eight days.

In the first instance, a review of the detention of a person arrested should be carried out by a review officer during the first forty-eight hours of his detention since arrest. He may authorise continued detention but his role ceases after the grant of a warrant of further detention. The grounds upon which he may do so are:

(a) to obtain relevant evidence, whether by questioning him or otherwise;
(b) to preserve relevant evidence;
(c) while awaiting the result of an examination or analysis of relevant evidence;
(d) for the examination or analysis of anything with a view to obtaining relevant evidence;
(e) pending a decision to apply to the Secretary of State for a deportation notice to be served on the detainee, the making of any such application, or the consideration of any such application by the Secretary of State;
(f) pending a decision to charge the detainee with an offence.

Notice that such an application has been made must be given to the detainee.

Applications for warrants of further detention may be made orally or in writing depending upon the circumstances of the case and fairness to the detainee. Applications may be made by means of video conferencing facilities. A judicial authority may require the physical presence of the detainee. Persons detained under a warrant of further detention beyond fourteen days must be transferred to a prison as soon as practicable.

Search of premises

By TA 2000, s 42, a justice of the peace may issue a warrant on the application of a constable in relation to the search of specified premises if satisfied that there are reasonable grounds for suspecting that a person, whom the constable reasonably suspects to be a person who is or has been concerned in the commission, preparation or instigation of acts of terrorism, is to be found there. Such a warrant authorises entry and search for the purpose of the arrest of a person subject to arrest under the provisions of TA 2000, s 41. This power of search includes a power to search a container on the premises.

Search of persons

A constable is given power by TA 2000, s 43 to stop and search a person whom he reasonably suspects to be a terrorist to discover whether he has in his possession anything which may constitute evidence that he is a terrorist. This power to stop a person includes the power to stop a vehicle. A constable of the same sex may also search anyone arrested under s 41 for similar evidence. Anything found in the search may be seized and retained if the constable reasonably suspects that it is evidence that the person is a terrorist. The additional powers of seizure under the Criminal Justice and Police Act 2001, s 51 are available: see p 74.

General point in relation to police powers

TA 2000, s 114 authorises the use of reasonable force for the purposes of exercising these powers.

In cordoned area

TA 2000, ss 33 to 36 permit the designation of an area as a 'cordoned area' for the purposes of a terrorist investigation. These matters are dealt with in Chapter 3 (p 57).

Taking of fingerprints and samples

This is dealt with on p 938–9.

Treatment of persons detained under Terrorism Act 2000, s 41 (or Sch 7)

The following rules relate to those detained under TA 2000, s 41 or Sch 7 (special powers to question at ports and—relevant only to police in Northern Ireland—border controls).

Place of detention

TA 2000, Sch 8 requires the Secretary of State to designate places at which persons may be detained under s 41 or Sch 7. A reference in Sch 8 to a police station includes a place so designated. A person arrested by a constable under the provisions of the Act must be taken, as soon as practicable, to the police station which the constable considers to be the most appropriate.

Identification

An 'authorised person' (which term includes a constable) may take any steps which are reasonably necessary for photographing, measuring, or identifying, the detained person. However, these initial measures do not include the taking of fingerprints, non-intimate samples or intimate samples as defined by PACE, s 65.

Interviews

As required by PACE, Sch 8, the Secretary of State has issued a Code of Practice dealing with the audio recording of interviews by police officers of persons detained in a police station under TA 2000. The term 'police station' includes any place designated as a place where a person may be detained under TA 2000, s 41. The Secretary of State has also issued an order requiring that interviews of persons detained under TA 2000, Sch 7 (port and border controls) or s 41 (arrest without warrant of a person reasonably suspected of being a terrorist) are audio recorded in accordance with that code of practice. It also empowers the Secretary of State to make an order requiring the video recording of interviews in relation to interviews to which the schedule applies, or those which take place in a particular part of the United Kingdom.

   The failure by a constable to observe a provision of a code of practice does not of itself make him liable to criminal or civil proceedings, but a code will be admissible in evidence in criminal and civil proceedings and must be taken into account by a court or tribunal in any case in which it is considered, by that court or tribunal, to be relevant.

Rights

A person detained under TA 2000, s 41 (or Sch 7) is entitled, if he so requests, to have a named person informed, as soon as is reasonably practicable, that he is being detained there. Such a person must be a friend, a relative, or a person who is known to the detained person or who is likely to take an interest in his welfare. If the detained person is transferred to another police station, he is entitled to exercise that right at the second police station.

In addition, the detained person is entitled, if he so requests, to consult a solicitor as soon as is reasonably practicable, privately and at any time. A record must be made of such a request. A direction may be given by an assistant chief constable (commander), if he has reasonable grounds for believing that the exercise of the right by the detained person will have any of the consequences set out below, that the consultation with a solicitor may take place only in the sight and hearing of a qualified officer. A 'qualified officer' must be a uniformed officer of at least the rank of inspector who has no connection with the case. Such a direction will cease to exist when the reason for it ceases to exist.

An officer of at least the rank of superintendent may authorise a delay in informing the person named by the detained person or in permitting the detained person to consult a solicitor, but he must be permitted to exercise these rights within forty-eight hours. Such an officer may give an authorisation only if he has reasonable grounds for believing that informing the named person or solicitor of the detained person's detention at the time when the person wishes this to be done, will lead to:

(a) interference with or harm to evidence of an indictable offence;
(b) interference with or physical injury to any person;
(c) the alerting of persons who are suspected of having committed an indictable offence but who have not been arrested for it;
(d) the hindering of the recovery of property obtained as a result of an indictable offence or in respect of which a forfeiture order in respect of fund raising or money laundering could be made under the Act;
(e) interference with the gathering of information about the commission, preparation or instigation of acts of terrorism;
(f) the alerting of a person and thereby making it more difficult to prevent an act of terrorism; and
(g) the alerting of a person and thereby making it more difficult to secure a person's apprehension, prosecution or conviction in connection with the commission, preparation or instigation of an act of terrorism.

In addition, a similar authorisation may be given where a superintendent (or above) has reasonable grounds for believing that the offence concerned is one in which there exist powers of confiscation in respect of the proceeds of an offence, and that the detained person has benefited from the offence and that, by informing the named person, or exercising the right to see a solicitor, the recovery of the value of that benefit will be hindered.

Where any delay is authorised the detained person must be told of the reason for the delay as soon as reasonably practicable and the reason must be recorded.

Fingerprinting; non-intimate and intimate samples

This is dealt with by TA 2000, Sch 8.

Fingerprints may be taken from the detained person by a constable with the written consent of the detainee, or without such consent where he is detained at a police station and an officer of at least the rank of superintendent gives an authorisation, or where the detainee has been convicted of a recordable offence. The same provisions apply to non-intimate samples provided that he was convicted of that offence on or after 10 April 1995.

An officer of at least the rank of superintendent may also authorise the taking of fingerprints from a person detained at a police station if he is satisfied that that person's fingerprints will facilitate the ascertainment of his identity, and that person has refused to identify himself or the officer has reasonable grounds for suspecting that that person is not who he claims to be. References to ascertaining a person's identity include references to showing that he is not a particular person.

Where two or more non-intimate samples suitable for the same means of analysis have been taken from a person and these samples have proved insufficient, and the person concerned has been released from detention, an intimate sample may be taken within the usual conditions. Where appropriate, if written consent to the taking of an intimate sample is refused without good cause, in any proceedings for an offence, either during committal or at trial, the court may draw such inferences from the refusal as appear proper.

If samples of hair, other than pubic hair, are taken, they may be taken by cutting or plucking provided that no more are plucked than is reasonably necessary to provide a sufficient sample.

Fingerprints and samples taken under TA 2000 may be retained but must not be used by any person except for the purposes of a terrorist investigation or for purposes related to the prevention or detection of crime, the investigation of an offence or the conduct of a prosecution.

An intimate sample may also be taken by a constable from a detained person at a police station with the written consent and authority of an officer of at least the rank of superintendent. However, an intimate sample other than a sample of urine or a dental impression, may be taken only by a registered medical practitioner acting on the authority of a constable. A dental impression may be taken only by a registered dentist acting on the authority of a constable.

An authorisation for the non-consensual taking of fingerprints or of a non-intimate sample, or an authorisation for the consensual taking of an intimate sample, may only be given if a person is detained under TA 2000, s 41, where the officer reasonably suspects that the person has been involved in an offence specified under TA 2000, ss 11 (p 932), 12 (p 932), 15 to 18 (p 933), 54 (weapons training) or 56 to 63 (p 941) and the officer reasonably believes that the fingerprints or sample will tend to confirm or disprove his involvement, or in any other case, the officer is satisfied that taking the fingerprints or sample is necessary to assist in determining whether the person has been concerned in the preparation, commission or instigation of acts of terrorism.

Before fingerprints or samples are taken, the person must be informed that they may be used for the purpose of checking against other fingerprints or samples held on behalf of police forces and, where taken with consent or in consequence of having been convicted of a recordable offence, of the reason for the fingerprints or samples being taken. All such matters must be recorded.

Display of support for a proscribed organisation

It is an offence contrary to TA 2000, s 13 for a person in a public place to wear any item of clothing or to wear, carry or display any article in such a way or in such circumstances as to arouse reasonable apprehension that he is a member or supporter of a proscribed organisation as defined on p 932. The carrying of banners or the wearing of favours indicating support for a proscribed organisation amount to offences against s 13.

Disclosure of information

TA 2000, s 19 provides that a person commits an offence if he does not disclose to a constable, as soon as reasonably practicable, a belief or suspicion, and the information upon which it is based, where he:

(a) believes or suspects that another person has committed an offence under any of TA 2000, ss 15 to 18 (fund raising etc, or money laundering); and
(b) bases his belief or suspicion on information which came to his attention in the course of a trade, profession, business or employment.

However, this section does not apply if the information came to the person in the course of a business in the regulated sector. A business is in the regulated sector to the extent that it engages in accepting deposits by persons with permission under Part 4 of the Financial Services and Markets Act 2000 to accept deposits. TA 2000, Sch 3A lists the organisations concerned which are banks, building societies, savings banks, bureaux de change; long-term insurance by an authorised business, or dealing in, advising in relation to, or managing investments. TA 2000, s 21A, which is set out below, provides offences which can be committed in those circumstances.

It is a defence to a charge under TA 2000, s 19 to prove reasonable excuse for non-disclosure. In the case of an employee, where there is an established procedure concerning disclosure, it is a defence for him to prove that disclosure was made within that procedure. The section does not require disclosure by a professional legal adviser of legally privileged information or of a belief or suspicion based on such information.

TA 2000, s 21 makes provision for those who act in co-operation with the police. An offence is not committed against ss 15 to 18 if the person is acting with the express consent of a constable.

The Anti-terrorism, Crime and Security Act 2001 (ACSA 2001) added ss 21A and 21B to TA 2000. They are aimed at preventing money laundering by terrorist organisations. TA 2000, s 21A creates an offence of failure by a person to disclose certain information or other matter to a constable or a nominated officer as soon as is practicable after that information comes into his possession. The offence occurs where:

(a) he knows or suspects or has reasonable grounds for knowing or suspecting that another person has committed an offence under any of TA 2000, ss 15 to 18;
(b) that information or other matter on which his knowledge or suspicion is based or which gives reasonable grounds for such knowledge or suspicion, came to him in the course of a business in the regulated sector.

A person will be taken to have committed an offence against TA 2000, ss 15 to 18 for these purposes if:

(a) he has taken action or been in possession of a thing; and
(b) he would have committed the offence if he had been in the United Kingdom at the time when he took the action or was in possession of the thing.

There is a defence of reasonable excuse for non-disclosure by a professional legal adviser where the information came to him in privileged circumstances. Such privilege does not apply where a communication is given with a view to furthering a criminal purpose.

In addition, TA 2000, s 21A requires that a court must consider whether the alleged offender had followed any relevant treasury approved guidance issued by a supervisory authority and properly brought to the attention of affected persons.

A disclosure to a 'nominated officer' is one made to a person nominated by the employer to receive such disclosures and is made in the course of the alleged offender's employment in accordance with established procedures.

By TA 2000, s 21B, a disclosure will not be taken to have breached any restriction upon the disclosure of information (however imposed) if it is made in the course of a business in the regulated sector and is such that it causes the person disclosing the information to know or suspect, or gives him reasonable grounds for knowing or suspecting, that another person has committed an offence under TA 2000, ss 15 to 18, if the disclosure is made to a constable or nominated officer as soon as is practicable.

TA 2000, s 39(1) is concerned with an offence which is committed by a person who knows or has reasonable cause to suspect that a constable is conducting, or proposes to conduct, a terrorist investigation and who:

(a) discloses to another anything which is likely to prejudice the investigation; or
(b) interferes with material which is likely to be relevant to the investigation.

Where a person knows or has reasonable cause to believe that a disclosure has been or will be made under TA 2000, ss 19 to 21 or 38B (below) he can commit an offence under TA 2000, s 39(4). This makes it an offence for a person:

(a) to disclose to another anything which is likely to prejudice an investigation resulting from the disclosure under one of these sections; or
(b) to interfere with material which is likely to be relevant to an investigation resulting from the disclosure under that section.

It is a defence to a charge under TA 2000, s 39(1) or (4) for a person to adduce evidence that he did not know and had no reasonable cause to suspect that the disclosure was likely to affect a terrorist investigation (whereupon the prosecution must disprove this) or to prove that he had a reasonable excuse for the disclosure or interference.

ACSA 2001 added a s 38B to TA 2000. It applies where a person has information which he knows or believes might be of material assistance:

(a) in preventing the commission by another person of an act of terrorism; or
(b) in securing the apprehension, prosecution or conviction of another person, in the United Kingdom, for an offence involving the commission, preparation or instigation of an act of terrorism.

The person commits an offence if he does not disclose the information as soon as reasonably practicable to a constable.

This offence may be treated as having been committed in any place where the person to be charged is, or has at any time been, since he first knew or believed that the information might be of material assistance, and proceedings may be taken in such places.

Possession of articles for terrorist purposes

TA 2000, s 57 prohibits the possession of articles in circumstances giving rise to a reasonable suspicion that the article is in a person's possession for a purpose connected with the commission, preparation or instigation of acts of terrorism.

Where it is proved that at the time of the commission of such an alleged offence, the person and the article were both present in any premises, or the article was in the premises of which he was the occupier, or which he habitually used other than as a member of the public, the court may assume that the person possessed the article, unless he adduces sufficient evidence to raise the issue that he did not know of the presence on the premises or that he had no control over it, whereupon the prosecution must disprove this.

Unlawful collection, recording or possession of information

TA 2000, s 58 provides offences of a person collecting or recording any information of a kind likely to be useful to a person committing or preparing an act of terrorism, or possessing a document or record containing information of that kind. The term 'record' includes a photographic or electronic record. It is a defence for the accused to adduce sufficient evidence to raise the issue that he had a reasonable excuse for his action or possession, whereupon the prosecution must disprove this.

The provisions of TA 2000, s 58 are wide enough to embrace the failure of close relatives of terrorists to disclose information in their possession as soon as reasonably practicable. It is recommended that relatives of a terrorist, who are not themselves involved in terrorism, should not be investigated with a view to obtaining evidence of offences by them against this section, unless particular extreme circumstances make this desirable. An example of such circumstances would be where the withholding of information could lead to death, serious injury or the escape of a terrorist offender.

Forfeiture of terrorist cash

ACSA 2001, s 1 and Sch 1 provide for the forfeiture of cash which is intended to be used for the purposes of terrorism, or consists of resources of a proscribed organisation, or which is, or represents, property obtained through terrorism. Such cash may be forfeited in civil proceedings before a magistrates' court. It is not essential to show that it is connected with any offence. ACSA 2001, s 4 provides that the Treasury may make a 'freezing order' if two conditions are satisfied:

(a) the Treasury reasonably believes that action to the detriment of the United Kingdom economy has been, or is likely to be, taken by a person or persons, or that action threatening life or property of one or more United Kingdom nationals has been, or is likely to be, taken by a person or persons; and

(b) if a person is believed to have taken, or to be likely to take, the action, that person must be the government of a country outside the United Kingdom or a resident of such a country.

ACSA 2001, ss 17 to 20 deal with the disclosure of information concerning such matters by various persons and bodies.

Terrorism and airport security

The Civil Aviation Act 1982, s 39 creates the offence of trespassing on any land forming part of an aerodrome licensed in pursuance of the Air Navigation Order 2000. In addition, the Aviation Security Act 1982, ss 21C and 21D create offences of unauthorised presence in a restricted zone and unauthorised presence on an aircraft. Before the offences related to aerodromes can be committed, notices must be displayed warning members of the public of this liability. A constable, manager of an aerodrome or a person acting on his behalf may use reasonable force to remove a person who fails to comply with a request to leave a restricted zone, and a constable, the operator of an aircraft or a person acting on his behalf may use such force to remove a person who fails to comply with a request to leave an aircraft made by the operator or person acting on his behalf. The provisions concerning removal by force were added to the sections by ACSA 2001.

Terrorist offences involving the use of noxious substances or things to cause harm and intimidate

ACSA 2001, s 113(1) creates the offence committed by any person who takes any action which:

(a) involves the use of a noxious substance or other noxious thing;
(b) has or is likely to have an effect which:
    (i)   causes serious violence against a person anywhere in the world;
    (ii) causes serious damage to real or personal property anywhere in the world;
    (iii) endangers human life or creates a serious risk to the health or safety of the public or a section of the public; or
    (iv) induces in members of the public the fear that the action is likely to endanger their lives or create a serious risk to their health or safety; and
(c) is designed to influence the government or an international governmental organisation or to intimidate the public or a section of the public.

In relation to (b) any effect upon the person taking the action is to be disregarded. ACSA 2001, s 113(3) creates another offence which is committed by a person who:

(a) makes a threat that he or another will take any action which constitutes an offence under ACSA 2001, s 113(1); and
(b) intends thereby to induce in a person anywhere in the world the fear that the threat is likely to be carried out.

ACSA 2001, s 114(1) provides that a person is guilty of an offence if he:

(a) places any substance or other thing in any place; or
(b) sends any substance or other thing from one place to another (by post, rail or any other means whatsoever),

with the intention of inducing in a person *anywhere in the world* a belief that it is likely to be (or contain) a noxious substance or other noxious thing and thereby endanger human life or create a serious risk to human health. An example would be sending what appeared to be anthrax spoor to someone in the USA.

A person is guilty of an offence under ACSA 2001, s 114(2) if he communicates any information which he knows or believes to be false with the intention of inducing in a person *anywhere in the world* a belief that a noxious substance or other noxious thing is likely to be present (whether at the time the information is communicated or later) in any place and thereby endanger human life or create a serious risk to human health.

For the purposes of both ACSA 2001, ss 113 and 114 'substance' includes any biological agent and any other natural or artificial substance (whatever its form, origin or method of production). In the case of offences against s 113(3) or 114 it is not necessary for the person concerned to have any particular person in mind as the person in whom he intends to induce the belief in question.

ENCOURAGEMENT ETC OF TERRORISM

Article 5 of the Council of Europe Convention on the Prevention of Terrorism requires member states to provide an offence of 'public provocation to commit a terrorist offence'. Pursuant to this, TA 2006, s 1(2) provides that a person commits an offence if:

(a) he publishes a statement to which s 1 applies or causes another to publish such a statement; and
(b) at the time he publishes it or causes it to be published, he:
    (i) intends members of the public to be directly or indirectly encouraged or otherwise induced by the statement to commit, prepare or instigate acts of terrorism or Convention offences; or
    (ii) is reckless as to whether members of the public will be directly or indirectly encouraged or otherwise induced by the statement to commit, prepare of instigate such acts or offences.

Section 1 applies to a statement that is likely to be understood by some or all of the members of the public to whom it is published as a direct or indirect encouragement or other inducement to them to the commission, preparation or instigation of acts of terrorism or Convention offences.

In TA 2006, an 'act of terrorism' includes anything constituting an action taken for the purposes of terrorism, within the meaning of TA 2000 (see p 931) (including a reference to action taken for the benefit of a proscribed organisation); and 'article' includes anything for storing data. A 'Convention offence' means an offence listed in TA 2006, Sch 1 (eg specified explosives offences, biological, chemical or nuclear weapons offences, hijacking, hostage-taking, and offences relating to terrorist funds or directing terrorist organisations) or an equivalent offence under the law of a country or territory outside the United Kingdom.

For the purposes of s 1, the statements that are likely to be understood by members of the public as indirectly encouraging the commission of acts of terrorism or Convention offences include every statement which glorifies the commission or preparation (whether in the past, future or generally) of such acts or offences, and is a statement from which those members of the public could reasonably be expected to infer that what is being glorified is being glorified as conduct that should be emulated by them. 'Glorification' includes any form of praise or celebration. In deciding how a statement is likely to be understood, the contents of the statement as a whole and the circumstances and manner of the publication must be taken into account. It is irrelevant, for the above purposes, whether particular acts of terrorism or particular offences are referred to, and whether any person is actually encouraged or induced to commit, prepare or instigate any such act or offence.

Section 1 provides a defence where it is not proved that the alleged offender intend-ed the statement directly or indirectly to bring about the commission, preparation or instigation of acts of terrorism or Convention offences. In such a case he has a defence if he can prove that the statement neither expressed his view nor had his actual endorsement, and that it was clear that this was so.

Dissemination of terrorist publications

TA 2006, s 2 prohibits the sale or other dissemination of terrorist publications, including information on the Internet, if (1) the accused intends his conduct to encourage or induce people to engage in the commission, preparation or instigation of acts of terrorism (2) he intends to assist in the commission or preparation of such acts, or (3) he is reckless as to whether his conduct will have either effect.

By s 2(2), the offence can be committed by distributing or circulating a terrorist publication; giving selling or lending a terrorist publication; offering such for sale or loan; providing a service which enables a person to obtain, read, listen to, or look at; transmitting it by electronic means, or possessing it with a view to it being dealt with in one of these ways.

A publication is a terrorist publication if it contains matter (a) likely to be understood by some or all of the persons to whom it may become available as an encouragement or inducement to them to the commission, preparation or instigation of acts of terrorism, or (b) likely to be useful in the commission or preparation of such acts or offences and is likely to be understood (by some or all of such persons) as contained in the publication, or made available, for the purpose of being so useful.

Where the publication is a terrorist publication by virtue of (a) and it is not proved that the accused acted with the intention of encouraging or inducing the commission, preparation or instigation of acts of terrorism, it is a defence for the accused to show that the material which encourages terrorism did not express his views, nor had his actual endorsement, and that it was clear, in all of the circumstances, that this was so. The defence will not be available where there has been a failure to comply with a notice (see 'Internet activity' below).

TA 2006, s 28 gives a justice of the peace power to issue a warrant authorising a constable to enter and search premises and seize any article on those premises if it is likely to be subject of conduct falling within s 2(2) and it would be treated as a terrorist publication, where he is satisfied that there are reasonable grounds for suspecting that such an article is on premises. Reasonable force may be used in effecting entry.

Bulk material may be removed in such circumstances for later examination, as opposed to examination on the premises. Notice must be given by the constable responsible for the seizure to every person whom he believes to be the owner of any material so seized. In the event of there being no such person, notice must be given to the person believed to be the occupier of the premises.

Internet activity

TA 2006, s 3 applies for the purposes of ss 1 and 2 in relation to cases where a statement is published or caused to be published in the course of, or in connection with, the provision or use of a service provided electronically, or conduct falling within s 2(2) was in the course of, or in connection with, the provision or use of such a service. Section 3(2) provides that the cases where the publishing etc of any statement or article electronically will be regarded as having the endorsement of a person at any time include a case where:

(a) that person has been given a notice by a constable which declares that in the constable's opinion the statement, article or record concerned is unlawfully terrorism-related, requires him to secure that the statement etc (so far as so related) is not available to the public, warns him that a failure to comply with the notice within two working days will result in the statement etc being regarded as having his endorsement, and explains how he may become liable by virtue of the notice if the statement etc becomes available to the public after he has complied with the notice;

(b) that time falls more than two working days after the notice was given, and

(c) that person has failed without reasonable excuse to comply with the notice.

The procedures relating to the giving of such notices are set out in s 4.

PREPARATION OF TERRORIST ACTS AND TERRORIST TRAINING

Pre-existing law deals with conspiracy and attempts to commit terrorist acts. TA 2006, s 5 bites at an earlier stage by prohibiting anyone intentionally preparing to commit, or assist others to commit, one or more acts of terrorism.

It is not essential that it is proved that a specific act or acts of terrorism was intended; an intention to carry out such acts generally will suffice.

Training for terrorism

TA 2006, s 6 prohibits knowingly giving or receiving (intending to use those skills) training in the making or handling of noxious substances, or the use of terrorist methods or techniques (including design or adaptation of, methods or techniques for, the purposes of terrorism) in preparation for acts of terrorism or Convention offences.

For these purposes, a 'noxious substance' means a pathogen or toxin or any other substance which is hazardous or noxious or which may or become hazardous or noxious only in certain circumstances.

Attendance at a place used for terrorist training

TA 2006, s 8 prohibits attending any place in the United Kingdom or elsewhere at which terrorist training is taking place. It must be proved that the accused knew or believed that training for those purposes was taking place, or that he could not reasonably have failed to understand that this was so.

OFFENCES INVOLVING RADIOACTIVE DEVICES AND MATERIALS AND NUCLEAR FACILITIES AND SITES

TA 2006, s 9 creates offences related to the making or possession of radioactive devices or the possession of radioactive material, for use in the commission or preparation of an act of terrorism or for purposes of terrorism.

Section 10 prohibits the use of such items in the course of, or in connection with, the commission of an act of terrorism, or for the purposes of terrorism. It also creates an offence of using or damaging a nuclear facility in the course of, or in connection with, acts of terrorism, in such a manner that radioactive material is released, or that the risk that such material will be released is created or increased.

Section 11 provides that it is an offence, in the course of or in connection with, the commission of an act of terrorism or for the purposes of terrorism, to demand the supply of a radioactive device or radioactive material, or that a nuclear facility, or access to a nuclear facility, is made available, if such a demand is supported by a threat of action if the demand is not met. The threat must be a credible one.

GENERAL

The consent of the Director of Public Prosecutions is required for any proceedings in relation to all of the above offences under the Terrorism Acts 2000 and 2006.

CHAPTER 34

Sexual offences

SEXUAL OFFENCES: INTRODUCTION

The law in relation to sexual offences was thoroughly overhauled and modernised by the Sexual Offences Act 2003 (SOA 2003). The only part of the previous principal Act, the Sexual Offences Act 1956, which survives is a handful of sections concerned with brothels. We deal with those sections in the next chapter.

Although the offender is often referred to as 'he' in the offences in SOA 2003, it must not be forgotten that, with the exception of rape and the offence of intercourse with an animal, contrary to SOA 2003, s 69(1), all the offences under that Act can be committed by a female person, as well as by a male person.

Sexual

For the purposes of the various offences in SOA 2003, s 78 provides that, except in relation to sexual activity in a public lavatory, penetration, touching or any other activity is sexual if a reasonable person would consider that:

(a) whatever its circumstances or any person's purpose in relation to it, it is because of its nature sexual; or
(b) because of its nature it *may* be sexual and because of its circumstances or the purpose of any person in relation to it (or both) it *is* sexual.

The Court of Appeal has held that (b) contains two requirements. The first is whether a reasonable person would consider that, because of its nature, the actual act could be sexual. In relation to this requirement, the circumstances before or after the act took place, or any evidence as to the purpose of any person in relation to it, are irrelevant. If the answer to the question posed by this requirement is 'No', the act is not sexual. If the answer to the question is 'Yes', the second requirement comes into play, and requires the jury or magistrates to ask themselves whether, because of the circumstances of the activity or the purpose of *any* person in relation to it (not just the person who does the act, but—for example—someone who encourages the act to be done), or both, the activity *is* sexual.

Consent

'Consent' is defined for the purposes of the offences under SOA 2003 involving the absence of consent by SOA 2003, s 74 as follows: a person consents if he agrees by choice, and has the freedom and capacity to make that choice.

SOA 2003, ss 75 and 76 lay down some evidential and conclusive presumptions as to the absence of consent in respect of rape and similar non-consensual sexual offences described in this chapter. These presumptions are dealt with at the relevant points.

Under the above definition, a person who is asleep or otherwise unconscious at the time of the relevant act will not normally consent because he will not normally agree to what is done. If there appears to be an agreement, it may be vitiated as follows.

Incapacity to make a choice

A person may, for example, lack the capacity to make a choice about whether or not to agree because of mental disorder, because he is drugged or intoxicated or because he is semi-comatose. A person will lack capacity to consent if at the time he has no real understanding of what is involved, or (in other words) he has such limited knowledge or understanding as not to be in a position to decide whether or not to agree.

Lack of freedom to choose

A person may not have a freedom to make a choice whether or not to agree if violence is being used against him, or he is caused to fear that it is being used against another, at the time of the relevant conduct or immediately beforehand. The same is the case if he is caused to fear at the time of the relevant act or beforehand that violence would be used against him or another person. A person may also lack freedom of choice for other reasons, as where someone agrees because he is unlawfully detained or where there was the use, or threat, of violence to destroy property which was of special value, financially or emotionally, or threat of dismissal by an employer to an employee, or a threat to remove children. It would all depend on the nature of the threat and the other circumstances, and the perception of the complainant, and whether in the light of these factors the complainant was not in reality free to agree or disagree.

By mistake

Some mistakes may vitiate an apparent agreement. This will certainly be the effect of a mistaken belief as to the nature of the act or that the accused is someone known personally to the complainant. In neither case does the complainant agree to what is done. The same is true, it would seem, where there is a mistake as to the purpose of the act.

It remains to be seen whether the judges will recognise that a mistake as to any quality of an act, other than its purpose, or a mistaken belief of identity not involving a belief as to someone known personally can prevent 'agreement by choice' for the purposes of the law of sexual offences.

Penetration and parts of the body

By SOA 2003, s 79, 'penetration' is a continuing act from entry to withdrawal. It has long been established by the courts that the slightest degree of penetration is enough. Section 79 also provides that references to a part of the body include references to a part surgically constructed (in particular through gender reassignment surgery); that 'vagina' includes vulva (external female genital organs); and that 'touching' includes touching with any part of the body, or with anything else, or through anything, and in particular includes touching through penetration. An example of a touching by something other than a part of anyone's body would be holding a sex toy against a private part of the victim's body. Since the touching can be through anything, it would be irrelevant that B was fully dressed at the time, provided that there was some physical contact, however slight, with B's body through the clothing.

NON-CONSENSUAL SEXUAL OFFENCES

Rape

By SOA 2003, s 1(1), a person (A) commits an offence if:

(a) he intentionally penetrates the vagina, anus or mouth of another person (B) with his penis;
(b) B does not consent to the penetration; and
(c) A does not reasonably believe that B consents.

The absence of consent does not have to be demonstrated by offering resistance or by communicating it to the accused.

SOA 2003, s 1(2) provides that whether a belief in consent is reasonable is to be determined having regard to all the circumstances, including any steps A (the accused) has taken to ascertain whether B (the victim) consents. The words 'all the circumstances' must refer to those which might be relevant to the issue, including any characteristic of the accused, permanent or transient, which might affect his ability to perceive or understand whether or not the victim is consenting. Examples would be a learning disability, mental illness, deafness, blindness, extreme youth and sexual inexperience.

Proof of lack of consent and of the fault element relating to it is assisted by special provisions, which also apply to the offences of assault by penetration, sexual assault and causing a person to engage in sexual activity without consent. Both these provisions refer to the accused having done 'the relevant act'. For the purposes of rape, 'the relevant act' is that the accused intentionally penetrated, with his penis, the vagina, anus or mouth of another person ('the complainant').

The first provision (SOA 2003, s 75) is that if in proceedings for an offence to which this section applies it is proved:

(a) that the accused did the relevant act;
(b) that any of the circumstances specified below existed; and
(c) that the accused knew that those circumstances existed,

the complainant is to be taken not to have consented to the relevant act unless sufficient evidence is adduced to raise an issue as to whether he consented, and the accused is to be taken not to have reasonably believed that the complainant consented unless sufficient evidence is adduced to raise an issue as to whether he reasonably believed it.

The specified circumstances are that:

(a) any person was, at the time of the relevant act or immediately before it began, using violence against the complainant or causing the complainant to fear that immediate violence would be used against him;

(b) any person was, at the time of the relevant act or immediately before it began, causing the complainant to fear that violence was being used, or that immediate violence would be used, against another person;

(c) the complainant was, and the accused was not, unlawfully detained at the time of the relevant act;

(d) the complainant was asleep or otherwise unconscious at the time of the relevant act;

(e) because of the complainant's physical disability, the complainant would not have been able at the time of the relevant act to communicate to the accused whether the complainant consented;

(f) any person had administered to or caused to be taken by the complainant, without the complainant's consent, a substance which, having regard to when it was administered or taken, was capable of causing or enabling the complainant to be stupefied or overpowered at the time of the relevant act.

The second provision (SOA 2003, s 76) is that if in proceedings for an offence to which this section applies it is proved that the accused did the relevant act and that either of the circumstances specified below existed, it is to be conclusively presumed:

(a) that the complainant did not consent to the relevant act; and

(b) that the accused did not believe that the complainant consented to the relevant act.

The specified circumstances are that: the accused intentionally deceived the complainant as to the nature or purpose of the relevant act; and that the accused intentionally induced the complainant to consent to the relevant act by impersonating a person known personally to the complainant.

Rape of a child under thirteen

By SOA 2003, s 5(1), a person commits an offence if:

(a) he intentionally penetrates the vagina, anus or mouth of another person with his penis; and

(b) the other person is under thirteen.

Whether or not the other person consents to the penetration is irrelevant; a child under thirteen is legally incapable of giving a legally significant consent.

The offence is one of the offences in respect of which there are exceptions from criminal liability under SOA 2003, s 73, on the basis of aiding, abetting or counselling the commission of the offence if a person acts for the purpose of:

(a) protecting the child from sexually transmitted infection;
(b) protecting the physical safety of the child;
(c) preventing the child from becoming pregnant; or
(d) promoting the child's emotional well-being by the giving of advice,

and not for the purpose of obtaining sexual gratification or for the purpose of causing or encouraging the activity constituting the offence or the child's participation in it.

Assault by penetration

By SOA 2003, s 2(1), a person (A) commits an offence if:

(a) he intentionally penetrates the vagina or anus of another person (B) with a part of his body or anything else;
(b) the penetration is sexual;
(c) B does not consent to the penetration; and
(d) A does not reasonably believe that B consents.

SOA 2003, s 2(2) provides that whether a belief is reasonable must be determined having regard to all the circumstances, including whether the accused has taken treasonable steps to ascertain whether the complainant consents.

If it is proved that the accused intentionally penetrated, with a part of his body (eg a finger or tongue) or anything else (eg a dildo or bottle), the vagina or anus of B ('the complainant') in circumstances where the penetration was sexual, and that (as the accused knew) one of the specified circumstances referred to in SOA 2003, s 75 existed, the evidential presumptions about the absence of consent and of a reasonable belief in consent referred to in relation to rape also apply to the present offence.

If it is proved that the accused (A) intentionally penetrated, with a part of his body or anything else, the vagina or anus of another person (B, 'the complainant') in circumstances where the penetration was sexual, and that A intentionally deceived B as to the nature or purpose of that act, or that A intentionally induced B to consent to that act by impersonating someone known to B, it is to be conclusively presumed under SOA 2003, s 76 that B did not consent to that act and that A did not believe that the complainant consented to the relevant act.

Assault of a child under thirteen by penetration

By SOA 2003, s 6(1), a person commits an offence if:

(a) he intentionally penetrates the vagina or anus of another person with a part of his body or anything else;
(b) the penetration is sexual; and
(c) the other person is under thirteen.

The absence of consent by the other person is not an element of this offence. The exceptions under SOA 2003, s 73 from liability for aiding, abetting or counselling apply to this offence.

Sexual assault

By SOA 2003, s 3(1), a person (A) commits an offence if:

(a) he intentionally touches another person (B);
(b) the touching is sexual;
(c) B does not consent to the touching; and
(d) A does not reasonably believe that B consents.

SOA 2003, s 3(2) provides that whether a belief is reasonable must be determined with regard to all the circumstances, including any steps the accused has taken to ascertain whether the complainant consents.

In terms of the requirement of the absence of consent by the complainant and 'no reasonable belief' in consent on the accused's part, the prosecution is assisted by the evidential and conclusive presumptions referred to on pp 949–950, which also apply to the present offence. For the purposes of the present offence, the 'relevant act' is that the accused intentionally touched the complainant, where the touching was sexual.

Sexual assault of a child under thirteen

By SOA 2003, s 7(1), a person commits an offence if:

(a) he intentionally touches another person;
(b) the touching is sexual; and
(c) the other person is under thirteen.

The absence of the other person's consent is not an element of the offence. The exceptions under SOA 2003, s 73 from liability for aiding, abetting or counselling apply to this offence.

Causing a person to engage in sexual activity without consent

By SOA 2003, s 4(1), a person (A) commits an offence if:

(a) he intentionally causes another person (B) to engage in an activity;
(b) the activity is sexual;
(c) B does not consent to engaging in the activity; and
(d) A does not reasonably believe that B consents.

A more serious offence is committed if the activity caused involved:

(a) penetration of B's anus or vagina;
(b) penetration of B's mouth with a person's penis;
(c) penetration of a person's anus or vagina with a part of B's body or by B with anything else; or
(d) penetration of a person's mouth with B's penis.

SOA 2003, s 4(1) provides that whether a belief is reasonable must be determined with regard to all the circumstances, including any steps the accused has taken to ascertain whether the complainant consents. In terms of the requirements of the absence of consent by the complainant and of no reasonable belief in consent, the prosecution is assisted by the evidential and conclusive presumptions referred to on pp 949–950, which also apply to the present offence. For the purposes of the present offence, the 'relevant act' is that the accused intentionally caused the complainant to engage in an activity, where the activity was sexual.

Causing or inciting a child under thirteen to engage in sexual activity

By SOA 2003, s 8(1), a person commits an offence if:

(a) he intentionally causes or incites another person (B) to engage in an activity;
(b) the activity is sexual, and
(c) B is under thirteen.

A more serious offence is committed if the activity caused or incited involved:

(a) penetration of B's anus or vagina;
(b) penetration of B's mouth with a person's penis;
(c) penetration of a person's anus or vagina with a part of B's body or by B with anything else; or
(d) penetration of a person's mouth with B's penis.

The absence of B's consent is not an element of an offence under s 8.

Advice in non-consensual sex cases

(1) To be fully effective, anonymity for complainants must start from the moment when the allegation is made to the police.
(2) Tactful and sympathetic questioning of complainants is important. Experience and sympathy in the interviewing officer are more important than his or her sex.
(3) Medical examination in a clinical environment, such as a hospital or surgery, should reduce distress, produce an atmosphere of care and concern, and provide for immediate treatment where desirable. As, however, there may be difficulties in the way of having such examinations away from a police station, adequate and suitable facilities for medical examination in police stations are needed in case it is necessary for such examinations to take place there.
(4) If possible, and if time permits, the police should ensure that the complainant is referred to the appropriate services, whether medical or social; this is best done before the complainant leaves the police station.

This advice is included in the report of the Advisory Group on the Law of Rape (1976). It is extremely important and is obviously applicable not just to rape but to any other non-consensual sexual offence. The complainant has just undergone an extremely frightening experience and will require all the assurance which it is possible to give.

CHILD SEX OFFENCES

In these offences, it is irrelevant that the child may have consented.

Sexual activity with a child

By SOA 2003, s 9(1), a person aged eighteen or over (A) commits an offence if:

(a) he intentionally touches another person (B);
(b) the touching is sexual; and
(c) either:
    (i) B is under sixteen and A does not reasonably believe that B is sixteen or over; or
    (ii) B is under thirteen.

A more serious offence is committed if the touching involved:

(a) penetration of B's anus or vagina with a part of A's body or anything else;
(b) penetration of B's mouth with A's penis;
(c) penetration of A's anus or vagina with a part of B's body; or
(d) penetration of A's mouth with B's penis.

The exceptions from liability for aiding, abetting or counselling under SOA 2003, s 73, described on pp 950–951, apply to such an offence.

Causing or inciting a child to engage in sexual activity

By SOA 2003, s 10(1), a person aged eighteen or over (A) commits an offence if:

(a) he intentionally causes or incites another person (B) to engage in an activity;
(b) the activity is sexual; and
(c) either:
    (i) B is under sixteen and A does not reasonably believe that B is sixteen or over; or
    (ii) B is under thirteen.

A more serious offence is committed if the activity caused or incited involved:

(a) penetration of B's anus or vagina (with a part of the body or anything else);
(b) penetration of B's mouth with a person's penis;
(c) penetration of a person's anus or vagina with a part of B's body or by B with anything else; or
(d) penetration of a person's mouth with B's penis.

Engaging in sexual activity in the presence of a child

By SOA 2003, s 11(1), a person aged eighteen or over (A) commits an offence if:

(a) he intentionally engages in an activity;
(b) the activity is sexual;
(c) for the purpose of obtaining sexual gratification, he engages in it:

(i) when another person (B) is present or is in a place from which A can be observed; and

(ii) knowing or believing that B is aware, or intending that B should be aware, that he is engaging in it; and

(d) either:

(i) B is under sixteen and A does not reasonably believe that B is sixteen or over; or

(ii) B is under thirteen.

'Observed' in (c) and elsewhere in the Act means observation whether direct or by looking at an image produced by any means.

Causing a child to watch a sexual act

By SOA 2003, s 12(1), a person aged eighteen or over (A) commits an offence if:

(a) for the purpose of obtaining sexual gratification, he intentionally causes another person (B) to watch a third person engaging in an activity, or to look at an image of any person engaging in an activity;

(b) the activity is sexual; and

(c) either:

(i) B is under sixteen and A does not reasonably believe that B is sixteen or over, or

(ii) B is under thirteen.

'Image' in (a), and elsewhere in the Act, includes a moving or still image, however produced, and, where—as here—the context permits, a three-dimensional image. It does not include written material. References to an image of a person include references to an image of an imaginary person. In this offence, and other similar offences, of 'causing to watch' under the Act, the purpose of obtaining sexual gratification need not relate to immediate gratification (eg from seeing the victim watch the images). The Court of Appeal has held that the purpose may relate to deferred sexual gratification, as where the accused's purpose is to put the victim in the mood for future sexual abuse.

Child sex offences committed by children or young persons

By SOA 2003, s 13(1), a person under eighteen commits an offence if he does anything which would be an offence under SOA 2003, ss 9 to 12 if he were aged eighteen. It is, however, a less serious offence than those offences. The exceptions from liability for aiding, abetting or counselling under SOA 2003 (pp 950–951) apply to this offence.

Arranging or facilitating the commission of a child sex offence

By SOA 2003, s 14(1), a person commits an offence if:

(a) he intentionally arranges or facilitates something that he intends to do, intends another person to do, or believes that another person will do, in any part of the world; and

(b) doing it will involve the commission of an offence under SOA 2003, ss 9 to 13.

SOA 2003, s 14(2) and (3) provides exceptions for people who seek to protect a child from pregnancy or sexually transmitted disease or to protect a child's physical safety or to give it advice, where they do not intend that the child will commit an offence under SOA 2003, ss 9 to 13 but believe that it will. They provide that a person does not commit an offence under s 14 if:

(a) he arranges or facilitates something that he believes another person will do, but that he does not intend to do or intend another person to do; and
(b) any offence within ss 9 to 13 which the doing of that thing would involve would be an offence against a child for whose protection he acts.

In this context, a person acts for the protection of a child if he acts for the purpose of:

(a) protecting the child from sexually transmitted infection;
(b) protecting the physical safety of the child;
(c) preventing the child from becoming pregnant; or
(d) promoting the child's emotional well-being by the giving of advice,

and not for the purpose of obtaining sexual gratification or for the purpose of causing or encouraging the activity constituting an offence within ss 9 to 13 or the child's participation in it.

Examples of conduct falling within these exceptions would be giving an under-age boy a condom (if done for the purpose of protecting the boy against a sexually-transmitted infection, but not if done to protect the boy against the risk of his sixteen-year-old girlfriend becoming pregnant); giving an under-age girl a condom (if done for the purpose of protecting her against a sexually-transmitted infection or pregnancy); giving advice (eg by an 'agony aunt' or counsellor) to an under-age child or children about protected sex (if done for the purpose of protection against sexually-transmitted infection, or, where the advice is given to a girl, pregnancy, or to promote the child's emotional well-being).

Meeting a child following sexual grooming with a view to engaging in sexual activity with it

Paedophiles have not been slow to make use of the Internet to gain the trust and confidence of children in 'chatroom conversations' and thereby to befriend them. Typically, the paedophile pretends that he is a teenager sharing the same interests and then arranges a meeting with the child. Grooming, however, is not limited to the Internet.

SOA 2003, s 15(1) deals with grooming by providing that a person aged eighteen or over (A) commits an offence if:

(a) having met or communicated with another person (B) anywhere in the world on at least two earlier occasions, he:
   (i) intentionally meets B; or
   (ii) travels with the intention of meeting B in any part of the world;

(b) at the time, he intends to do anything to or in respect of B, during or after the meeting, and in any part of the world, which if done will involve the commission by A of any offence described in this chapter or under the corresponding law of Northern Ireland or of another country;
(c) B is under sixteen; and
(d) A does not reasonably believe that B is sixteen or over.

ABUSE OF POSITION OF TRUST

Abuse of position of trust: sexual activity with a child

Provided that he has any necessary mens rea, a person aged eighteen or over (A) commits an offence under SOA 2003, s 16(1) if:

(a) he intentionally touches another person (B);
(b) the touching is sexual;
(c) A is in a position of trust in relation to B; and
(d) B is under eighteen.

B's consent is, of course, irrelevant in offences involving abuse of a position of trust. The exceptions from liability for aiding, abetting or counselling this offence under SOA 2003, s 73 (pp 950–951) apply to this offence if B is under sixteen.

Abuse of position of trust: causing or inciting a child to engage in sexual activity

Provided that he has any necessary mens rea, a person aged eighteen or over (A) commits an offence under s 17(1) if:

(a) he intentionally causes or incites another person (B) to engage in an activity;
(b) the activity is sexual;
(c) A is in a position of trust in relation to B; and
(d) B is under eighteen.

Abuse of position of trust: sexual activity in the presence of a child

Provided that he has any necessary mens rea, a person aged eighteen or over (A) commits an offence under SOA 2003, s 18(1) if:

(a) he intentionally engages in an activity;
(b) the activity is sexual;
(c) for the purpose of obtaining sexual gratification, he engages in it:
  (i) when another person (B) is present or is in a place from which A can be observed; and
  (ii) knowing or believing that B is aware, or intending that B should be aware, that he is engaging in it,
(d) A is in a position of trust in relation to B, and
(e) B is under eighteen.

Abuse of position of trust: causing a child to watch a sexual act

Provided that he has any necessary mens rea, a person aged eighteen or over (A) commits an offence under SOA 2003, s 19(1) if:

(a) for the purpose of obtaining sexual gratification, he intentionally causes another person (B) to watch a third person engaging in an activity, or to look at an image of any person engaging in an activity;
(b) the activity is sexual;
(c) A is in a position of trust in relation to B; and
(d) B is under eighteen.

Position of trust

For the purposes of the above offences, a person (A) is, by SOA 2003, s 22, in a position of trust in relation to another person (B) if:

(a) any of paras (1) to (12) below apply; or
(b) any condition specified in an order made by the Secretary of State is met. No order has yet been made.

(1)   If A looks after persons under eighteen who are detained in an institution by virtue of a court order or under an enactment, and B is so detained in that institution.
(2)   If A looks after persons under eighteen who are resident in a home or other place for children in residential care, and B is in residential care there.
(3)   If A looks after persons under eighteen who are accommodated and cared for in a hospital, an independent clinic, a care home, residential care home or private hospital, a community home, voluntary home or children's home, or the like, and B is accommodated and cared for in that institution.
(4)   If A looks after persons under eighteen who are receiving education at an educational institution and B is receiving, and A is not receiving, education at that institution.
(5)   If A is appointed to be the guardian of B under the Children (Northern Ireland) Order 1995, art 159 or 160.
(6)   If A is engaged in the provision of a careers service or similar service and, in that capacity, looks after B on an individual basis.
(7)   If A regularly has unsupervised contact with B (whether face to face or by any other means) in the provision of accommodation for children in need thereof or in police protection or detention or on remand.
(8)   If A, as a person who is to report to the court on matters relating to the welfare of B, regularly has unsupervised contact with B (whether face to face or by any other means).
(9)   If A is a personal adviser appointed for B under the Children Act 1989 or its Northern Irish equivalent, and, in that capacity, looks after B on an individual basis.
(10)   If:
    (a) B is subject to a care order, a supervision order or an education supervision order; and

(b) in the exercise of functions conferred by virtue of the order on an authorised person or the authority designated by the order, A looks after B on an individual basis.

(11) If A is an officer of the Children and Family Court Advisory Support Service (CAFCASS) or has a similar function in Northern Ireland, and, in that capacity, regularly has unsupervised contact with B (whether face to face or by any other means).

(12) If:

(a) B is subject to requirements imposed by or under an enactment on his release from detention for a criminal offence, or is subject to requirements imposed by a court order made in criminal proceedings; and

(b) A looks after B on an individual basis in pursuance of the requirements.

For the purposes of paras (1), (2), (3) and (4), a person looks after persons under eighteen at an institution or the like if he is regularly involved in caring for, training, supervising or being in sole charge of such persons there, not necessarily the child abused.

Paragraphs (6), (9), (10) and (12) refer to a person looking after another on an individual basis. A person (A) looks after another (B) on such a basis if:

(a) A is regularly involved in caring for, training or supervising B; and

(b) in the course of his involvement, A regularly has unsupervised contact with B (whether face to face or by any other means).

Mens rea

In addition to requiring the accused intentionally to do the thing specified by each individual section, ss 16 to 19 make further provision as to the mens rea required in respect of the child's age and the existence of a position of trust.

In terms of the mens rea as to the age of the child (B), the accused (A) must not reasonably believe that B is eighteen or over. However, this provision does not apply if B is under thirteen at the material time; in such a case the offences are undoubtedly ones of strict liability as to age. Although the prosecution ultimately has the persuasive burden of proof of the fault element as to the age of B where B is aged thirteen to seventeen, the prosecution is assisted by the provision that where in proceedings for an offence under these provisions it is proved that the other person was under eighteen, the accused is to be taken not to have reasonably believed that that person was eighteen or over unless sufficient evidence is adduced to raise an issue as to whether he reasonably believed it.

Where A is in a position of trust in relation to B by virtue of circumstances within para (1), (2), (3) or (4) above, ie:

(a) B detained in an institution by virtue of a court order or under an enactment;

(b) B in residential care;

(c) B accommodated and cared for in a hospital, care home, community home or the like; or

(d) B receiving education at an educational institution,

and, in each case, A is not also in a position of trust by virtue of other circumstances, it must be proved that A knew or could reasonably be expected to know of the circumstances by virtue of which he is in a position of trust in relation to B. Proof of this is aided by the provision that, where it is proved that A was in a position of trust in relation to the other person by virtue of the four circumstances just referred to, and it is not proved that he was in such a position of trust by virtue of other circumstances, it is to be presumed that A knew or could reasonably have been expected to know of the circumstances by virtue of which he was in such a position of trust unless sufficient evidence is adduced to raise an issue as to whether he knew or could reasonably have been expected to know of those circumstances.

Where a position of trust arises wholly or partly by virtue of the other categories of circumstance referred to above, the Act does not require proof of any mens rea as to the position of trust where such a position of trust is involved.

Exceptions: marriage, civil partnership and existing sexual relationships

Conduct by a person (A) which would otherwise be one of the offences under SOA 2003, ss 16 to 19 against another person (B) is not such an offence if:

(a) B was sixteen or over, and the accused proves that A and B were lawfully married (or civil partners under the Civil Partnership Act 2004) at the time of the conduct; or
(b) the accused proves that immediately before the position of trust arose, a sexual relationship existed between A and B, but this exception does not apply if at that time sexual intercourse between A and B would have been unlawful, eg because B was under sixteen.

FAMILIAL SEXUAL OFFENCES

Offences involving a child family member

Sexual activity with a child family member

A person (A) commits an offence under SOA 2003, s 25(1) if:

(a) he intentionally touches another person (B);
(b) the touching is sexual;
(c) the relation of A to B is within the specified relationships;
(d) A knows or could reasonably be expected to know that his relation to B is of a description falling within those relationships; and
(e) (i) either B is under eighteen and A does not reasonably believe that B is eighteen or over; or
    (ii) B is under thirteen.

The Act has the effect of distinguishing between three types of offence. The most serious is committed where A is eighteen or over at the time of the offence and the touching involved:

(a) penetration of B's anus or vagina with a part of A's body or anything else;
(b) penetration of B's mouth with A's penis;

(c) penetration of A's anus or vagina with part of B's body (but not with anything else); or

(d) penetration of A's mouth by B's penis.

The next offence is where A is eighteen or over at the material time but the activity is not penetrative in one of these ways. The least serious offence is where A was not eighteen or over at the material time, whatever type of activity was involved.

Where it is proved that the relation of the accused to the other person was of a description falling within the specified relationships, it is to be taken that the accused knew or could reasonably have been expected to know that his relation to the other person was of that description unless sufficient evidence is adduced to raise an issue (ie to raise a prima facie case) as to whether he knew or could reasonably have been expected to know that it was.

In respect of the mens rea in (e)(i) (no reasonable belief (where B is not under thirteen) that B is eighteen), where it is proved that B was under eighteen, A is to be taken not to have reasonably believed that B was eighteen or over unless sufficient evidence is adduced to raise an issue as to whether he reasonably believed it.

The exceptions under SOA 2003, s 73 from liability for aiding and abetting apply to an offence under s 25.

Inciting a child family member to engage in sexual activity

A person (A) commits an offence under SOA 2003, s 26 if:

(a) he intentionally incites another person (B) to touch, or allow himself to be touched by, A;

(b) the touching is sexual;

(c) the relation of A to B is within the specified relationships;

(d) A knows or could reasonably be expected to know that his relation to B is of a description falling within those relationships; and

(e) either:

    (i) B is under eighteen and A does not reasonably believe that B is eighteen or over; or

    (ii) B is under thirteen.

There are three types of offence under s 26, distinguished in a similar way as in s 25.

The mens rea in respect of the fact that the relation of A to B is within the specified relationships is the same as that in the offences described in relation to s 25. Thus, where it is proved that the relation of A to B was of a description falling within the specified relationships, it is to be taken that A knew or could reasonably have been expected to know that his relation to B was of that description unless sufficient evidence is adduced to raise an issue as to whether he knew or could reasonably have been expected to know that it was.

Likewise, in respect of the mens rea in para (e)(i) (no reasonable belief (where B is not under thirteen) that B is eighteen or over), where it is proved that B was under eighteen, A is to be taken not to have reasonably believed that B was eighteen or over unless sufficient evidence is adduced to raise an issue as to whether he reasonably believed it.

Family relationships

For the purposes of SOA 2003, ss 25 and 26, the relation of the accused and the 'victim' must be within s 27. The relation of one person (A) to another (B) is within the specified relationships if it is within paras (a) to (c) below, including an adoptive relationship (as well as a biological one).

The relation of A and B is within the specified relationships if:

(a) one of them is the other's parent, grandparent, brother, sister, half-brother, half-sister, aunt or uncle, or A is or has been B's foster parent;

(b) A and B live or have lived in the same household, or A is or has been regularly involved in caring for, training, supervising or being in sole charge of B, and:

    (i)   one of them is or has been the other's step-parent;

    (ii) A and B are cousins;

    (iii) one of them is or has been the other's stepbrother or stepsister; or

    (iv) the parent or present or former foster parent of one of them is or has been the other's foster parent;

(c) A and B live in the same household, and A is regularly involved in caring for, training, supervising or being in sole charge of B, eg a nanny or au pair. It will be noted that (c) only applies while A is living in the same household.

A 'step-parent' includes someone who is neither married to, nor the civil partner of, a parent, if that person is a parent's 'partner'. In (b)(i) and (iii) under this heading references to a step-parent or step-brother/step-sister of a person are to be read as follows: the step-parent of a person (X) includes someone who is the civil partner of X's parent (but is not X's parent), and X's step-brother or step-sister includes someone who is the son/daughter of the civil partner of X's parent (but not the son/daughter of either of X's parents).

Exceptions: marriage, civil partnership and existing sexual relationships

By SOA 2003, ss 28 and 29, conduct by a person (A) which would otherwise be an offence under s 25 or s 26 against another person (B) is not an offence thereunder if:

(a) B is sixteen or over, and A and B *are lawfully married (or civil partners* under the Civil Partnership Act 2004 (CPA 2004)); or

(b)

    (i)   the relation of A to B is not within para (a) of the specified relationships above, either biologically or adoptively; and

    (ii) immediately before the relation of A to B first became such as to fall within the specified relationships, a sexual relationship existed between A and B (as where when A's mother marries B's father, A and B were already in a sexual relationship).

The defence in para (b) does not apply if at the time referred to in para (b)(ii) sexual intercourse between A and B would have been unlawful, for example because one of them was under sixteen.

It is for the accused to prove the relationship mentioned in para (a) or para (b).

Sex with an adult relative

A person aged sixteen or over (A) commits an offence under SOA 2003, s 64(1) if:

(a) he intentionally penetrates another person's vagina or anus with a part of his body or anything else, or penetrates another person's mouth with his penis;

(b) the penetration is sexual;

(c) the other person (B) is aged eighteen or over;

(d) A is related to B in a specified way; and

(e) A knows or could reasonably be expected to know that he is related to B in that way.

A person aged sixteen or over (A) commits an offence under SOA 2003, s 65(1) if:

(a) another person (B) penetrates A's vagina or anus with a part of B's body or anything else, or penetrates A's mouth with B's penis;

(b) A consents to the penetration;

(c) the penetration is sexual;

(d) B is aged eighteen or over;

(e) A is related to B in a specified way; and

(f) A knows or could reasonably be expected to know that he is related to B in that way.

The specified ways that A may be related to B are as a parent, grandparent, child, grandchild, brother, sister, half-brother, half-sister, uncle, aunt, nephew or niece.

In terms of the requirement that the prosecution must prove that the accused (A) knew or could reasonably be expected to know that he is related to B in a specified way, it is to be taken that the accused knew or could reasonably have been expected to know that he was related in that way unless sufficient evidence is adduced to raise an issue as to whether he knew or could reasonably have been expected to know that he was.

OFFENCES AGAINST PEOPLE WITH A MENTAL DISORDER

Meaning of mental disorder

For the purposes of these offences, 'mental disorder' means 'mental illness, arrested or incomplete development of mind, psychopathic disorder and any other disorder or disability of mind'. A person with a learning disability falls within this definition.

Sexual activity with a person with a mental disorder impeding choice

A person (A) commits an offence under SOA 2003, s 30(1) if:

(a) he intentionally touches another person (B);

(b) the touching is sexual;

(c) B is unable to refuse because of or for a reason related to a mental disorder; and

(d) A knows or could reasonably be expected to know that B has a mental disorder and that because of it or for a reason related to it B is likely to be unable to refuse.

A person commits a more serious offence if the touching involved:

(a) penetration of B's anus or vagina with a part of A's body or anything else;
(b) penetration of B's mouth with A's penis;
(c) penetration of A's anus or vagina with a part of B's body (but not with anything else); or
(d) penetration of A's mouth with B's penis.

B is unable to refuse if:

(a) he lacks the capacity to choose whether to agree to the touching (whether because he lacks sufficient understanding of the nature or reasonably foreseeable consequences of what is being done, or for any other reason); or
(b) he is unable to communicate such a choice to A.

The exceptions under SOA 2003, s 73 from liability for aiding, abetting or counselling apply to an offence under s 30 and to an offence under s 34 (p 965).

Causing or inciting a person with a mental disorder impeding choice to engage in sexual activity

A person (A) commits an offence under SOA 2003, s 31(1) if:

(a) he intentionally causes or incites another person (B) to engage in an activity;
(b) the activity is sexual;
(c) B is unable to refuse because of or for a reason related to a mental disorder; and
(d) A knows or could reasonably be expected to know that B has a mental disorder and that because of it or for a reason related to it B is likely to be unable to refuse.

A person commits a more serious offence if the activity caused or incited involved:

(a) penetration of B's anus or vagina;
(b) penetration of B's mouth with a person's penis;
(c) penetration of a person's anus or vagina with a part of B's body or by B with anything else; or
(d) penetration of a person's mouth with B's penis.

B is unable to refuse if:

(a) he lacks the capacity to choose whether to agree to engaging in the activity caused or incited (whether because he lacks sufficient understanding of the nature or reasonably foreseeable consequences of the activity, or for any other reason); or
(b) he is unable to communicate such a choice to A.

Engaging in sexual activity in the presence of a person with a mental disorder impeding choice

A person (A) commits an offence under SOA 2003, s 32(1) if:

(a) he intentionally engages in an activity;
(b) the activity is sexual;
(c) for the purpose of obtaining sexual gratification, he engages in it:

(i)   when another person (B) is present or is in a place from which A can be observed; and

(ii)   knowing or believing that B is aware, or intending that B should be aware, that he is engaging in it;

(d)   B is unable to refuse because of or for a reason related to a mental disorder; and

(e)   A knows or could reasonably be expected to know that B has a mental disorder and that because of it or for a reason related to it B is likely to be unable to refuse.

B is unable to refuse if:

(a)   he lacks the capacity to choose whether to agree to being present (whether because he lacks sufficient understanding of the nature of the activity, or for any other reason); or

(b)   he is unable to communicate such a choice to A.

Causing a person with a mental disorder impeding choice to watch a sexual act

A person (A) commits an offence under SOA 2003, s 33(1) if:

(a)   for the purpose of obtaining sexual gratification, he intentionally causes another person (B) to watch a third person engaging in an activity, or to look at an image of any person engaging in an activity;

(b)   the activity is sexual;

(c)   B is unable to refuse because of or for a reason related to a mental disorder; and

(d)   A knows or could reasonably be expected to know that B has a mental disorder and that because of it or for a reason related to it B is likely to be unable to refuse.

B is unable to refuse if:

(a)   he lacks the capacity to choose whether to agree to watching or looking (whether because he lacks sufficient understanding of the nature of the activity, or for any other reason); or

(b)   he is unable to communicate such a choice to A.

Inducement, threat or deception to procure sexual activity with a person with a mental disorder

A person (A) commits an offence under SOA 2003, s 34(1) if:

(a)   with the agreement of another person (B) he intentionally touches that person;

(b)   the touching is sexual;

(c)   A obtains B's agreement by means of an inducement offered or given, a threat made or a deception practised by A for that purpose;

(d)   B has a mental disorder; and

(e)   A knows or could reasonably be expected to know that B has a mental disorder.

A person commits a more serious offence if the touching involved:

(a)   penetration of B's anus or vagina with a part of A's body or anything else;

(b)   penetration of B's mouth with A's penis;

(c) penetration of A's anus or vagina with a part of B's body; or

(d) penetration of A's mouth with B's penis.

It is not necessary in either of these offences or in the case of the related offences under SOA 2003, ss 35 to 37 that the victim's mental disorder made the victim unable to refuse. These offences are concerned with gaining the consent of a mentally vulnerable person by inducement (eg a reward), a threat (eg 'I won't tell on you if you agree . . .') or a deception (eg 'This is what everyone does').

Causing a person with a mental disorder to engage in, or agree to engage in, sexual activity by inducement, threat or deception

A person (A) commits an offence under SOA 2003, s 35(1) if:

(a) by means of an inducement offered or given, a threat made or a deception practised by him for this purpose, he intentionally causes another person (B) to engage in, or to agree to engage in, an activity;

(b) the activity is sexual;

(c) B has a mental disorder; and

(d) A knows or could reasonably be expected to know that B has a mental disorder.

A more serious offence is committed if the activity caused or agreed on is penetrative in the sense set out above.

Engaging in sexual activity in the presence, procured by inducement, threat or deception, of a person with a mental disorder

A person (A) commits an offence under SOA 2003, s 36(1) if:

(a) he intentionally engages in an activity;

(b) the activity is sexual;

(c) for the purpose of obtaining sexual gratification, he engages in it:

  (i) when another person (B) is present or is in a place from which A can be observed; and

  (ii) knowing or believing that B is aware, or intending that B should be aware, that he is engaging in it;

(d) B agrees to be present or in the place referred to in para (c)(i) because of an inducement offered or given, a threat made or a deception practised by A for the purpose of obtaining that agreement;

(e) B has a mental disorder; and

(f) A knows or could reasonably be expected to know that B has a mental disorder.

Causing a person with a mental disorder to watch a sexual act by inducement, threat or deception

A person (A) commits an offence under SOA 2003, s 37(1) if:

(a) for the purpose of obtaining sexual gratification, he intentionally causes another person (B) to watch a third person engaging in an activity, or to look at an image of any person engaging in an activity;
(b) the activity is sexual;
(c) B agrees to watch or look because of an inducement offered or given, a threat made or a deception practised by A for the purpose of obtaining that agreement;
(d) B has a mental disorder; and
(e) A knows or could reasonably be expected to know that B has a mental disorder.

Sexual activity by a care worker with a person with a mental disorder

A person (A) commits an offence under SOA 2003, s 38(1) if:

(a) he intentionally touches another person (B);
(b) the touching is sexual;
(c) B has a mental disorder;
(d) A knows or could reasonably be expected to know that B has a mental disorder; and
(e) A is involved in B's care in a way that falls within the provisions described on p 969.

A more serious offence is committed if the touching involved:

(a) penetration of B's anus or vagina with a part of A's body or anything else;
(b) penetration of B's mouth with A's penis;
(c) penetration of A's anus or vagina with a part of B's body; or
(d) penetration of Λ's mouth with B's penis.

If it is proved that the other person had a mental disorder, it is to be taken that the accused knew or could reasonably have been expected to know that that person had a mental disorder unless sufficient evidence is adduced to raise an issue as to whether he knew or could reasonably have been expected to know it.

The exceptions under SOA 2003, s 73 (pp 950–951) from liability for aiding, abetting or counselling apply to an offence under s 38.

Offences under s 38, and the other 'care worker offences' referred to below, are designed to protect those mentally disordered people who have the capacity to refuse consent from exploitation by a care worker of his or her relationship with the mentally disordered person.

Care worker causing or inciting a person with mental disorder to engage in sexual activity

A person (A) commits an offence under SOA 2003, s 39(1) if:

(a) he intentionally causes or incites another person (B) to engage in an activity;
(b) the activity is sexual;
(c) B has a mental disorder;
(d) A knows or could reasonably be expected to know that B has a mental disorder; and
(e) A is involved in B's care in a way that falls within the provisions described on p 969.

A more serious offence is committed if the sexual activity is penetrative in one of the ways described in relation to s 38. If it is proved that B had a mental disorder, it is to be taken as proved that the accused knew or could reasonably have been expected to know that B had a mental disorder unless sufficient evidence is adduced to raise an issue as to whether he knew or could reasonably be expected to know it.

Sexual activity by care worker in presence of person with mental disorder

A person (A) commits an offence under SOA 2003, s 40(1) if:

(a) he intentionally engages in an activity;
(b) the activity is sexual;
(c) for the purpose of obtaining sexual gratification, he engages in it:
  (i) when another person (B) is present or is in a place from which A can be observed; and
  (ii) knowing or believing that B is aware, or intending that B should be aware, that he is engaging in it;
(d) B has a mental disorder;
(e) A knows or could reasonably be expected to know that B has a mental disorder; and
(f) A is involved in B's care in a way that falls within the provisions described on p 969.

If it is proved that the other person had a mental disorder, it is to be taken that the accused knew or could reasonably have been expected to know that that person had a mental disorder unless sufficient evidence is adduced to raise an issue as to whether he knew or could reasonably be expected to know it.

Care worker causing person with mental disorder to watch a sexual act

A person (A) commits an offence under SOA 2003, s 41(1) if:

(a) for the purpose of obtaining sexual gratification, he intentionally causes another person (B) to watch a third person engaging in an activity, or to look at an image of any person engaging in an activity;
(b) the activity is sexual;
(c) B has a mental disorder;
(d) A knows or could reasonably be expected to know that B has a mental disorder; and
(e) A is involved in B's care in a way that falls within the provisions described on p 969.

If it is proved that the other person had a mental disorder, it is to be taken that the accused knew or could reasonably have been expected to know that that person had a mental disorder unless sufficient evidence is adduced to raise an issue as to whether he knew or could reasonably have been expected to know it.

Definition of care worker

For the purposes of the offences described in SOA 2003, ss 38 to 41, a person (A) is involved in the care of another (B) ('care worker' for short) if para (a), (b) or (c) below applies, that is:

(a) if:
    (i) B is accommodated and cared for in a care home, community home, voluntary home or children's home; and
    (ii) A has functions to perform in the home in the course of employment which have brought him or are likely to bring him into regular face-to-face contact with B;

(b) if B is a patient for whom services are provided:
    (i) by a National Health Service body or an independent medical agency; or
    (ii) in an independent clinic or an independent hospital, and A has functions to perform for the body or agency or in the clinic or hospital in the course of employment which have brought him or are likely to bring him into regular face to face contact with B;

(c) if:
    (i) A is, whether or not in the course of employment, a provider of care, assistance or services to B in connection with B's mental disorder, and
    (ii) as such, has had or is likely to have regular face to face contact with B.

Exceptions: marriage, civil partnership and existing relationships

By SOA 2003, ss 43 and 44, conduct by a person (A) which would otherwise be an offence under ss 38 to 41 against another person (B) is not such an offence if respectively:

(a) B was sixteen or over at the time of the conduct and the accused proves A and B were lawfully married (or civil partners under CPA 2004) at that time; or
(b) the accused proves that immediately before A became involved in B's care in a way described above, a sexual relationship existed between A and B. This exception does not apply if at that time—ie the 'immediately before' time—sexual intercourse between A and B would have been unlawful (eg because B was under sixteen).

PREPARATORY OFFENCES

Administering a substance with intent

A person commits an offence under SOA 2003, s 61(1) if he intentionally administers a substance to, or causes a substance to be taken by, another person (B):

(a) knowing that B does not consent; and
(b) with the intention of stupefying or overpowering B, so as to enable any person to engage in a sexual activity that involves B.

This offence is aimed at the activity which has become known as 'date rape' which is frequently carried out following the 'spiking' of a drink with a stupefying drug.

However, it would also include circumstances in which a person's drink was spiked with strong alcohol if that person believed that he or she was drinking a non-alcoholic drink. It would not, of course, cover circumstances in which a person was merely encouraged to drink alcoholic drinks where that person was aware that he or she was drinking alcohol.

The nature of the act is not restricted provided that it will have the specified effect. The victim could be given an injection which causes stupefaction or enables the person to be overpowered and the same effect could be caused by chloroform. The person need not carry out the act so that *he* may thereby be enabled to engage in sexual activity, it will be sufficient if he does so to enable some other person to so engage in that activity. The nature of the sexual activity envisaged by the section would include sexual intercourse, masturbation, oral sex and any other associated activity. It does not matter whether sexual activity actually takes place, it is sufficient that the perpetrator administered the substance, knowing that there was no consent and with the appropriate intention.

Committing an offence with intent to commit a sexual offence

A person commits an offence under SOA 2003, s 62(1) if he commits any offence with the intention of committing a relevant sexual offence. A 'relevant sexual offence' is any offence under SOA 2003, Part 1 (ss 1 to 79), dealt with on pp 949–972, including an offence of aiding, abetting, counselling or procuring such an offence. A person who commits such an offence by kidnapping or false imprisonment is guilty of a more serious offence.

Trespass with intent to commit a sexual offence

A person commits an offence under SOA 2993, s 63(1) if:

(a) he is a trespasser on any premises;
(b) he intends to commit a relevant sexual offence (as defined in the last paragraph) on the premises; and
(c) he knows that, or is reckless as to whether, he is a trespasser.

MISCELLANEOUS SEXUAL OFFENCES

Exposure

A person commits an offence under SOA 2003, s 66(1) if:

(a) he intentionally exposes his genitals; and
(b) he intends that someone will see them and be caused alarm or distress.

Although the common law offence of indecent exposure is now unlikely to be charged, it still exists. However, the 'public' element of such an offence requires that the act should be witnessed by more than one person. Where an unidentified woman carried out an act of oral sex on a man in a place where the act was likely to be seen by more than one person, the only evidence was that the act had later been seen on a video recording made by a security camera. A divisional court said that the witnessing of the commission of such a lewd act by one person was not enough for the common law offence to be committed. There had been no evidence of anyone other than the manageress of the security system seeing the video, nor evidence that the act was seen at the time it was committed.

Voyeurism: observing

A person commits an offence under SOA 2003, s 67(1) if:

(a) for the purpose of obtaining sexual gratification, he observes another person doing a private act; and
(b) he knows that the other person does not consent to being observed for his sexual gratification.

For the purposes of s 67, a person is doing a private act if the person is in a place which, in the circumstances, would reasonably be expected to provide privacy, and:

(a) the person's genitals, buttocks or breasts are exposed or covered only with underwear;
(b) the person is using a lavatory; or
(c) the person is doing a sexual act not of a kind ordinarily done in public.

A person commits an offence under SOA 2003, s 67(4) if he installs equipment, or constructs or adapts a structure or part of a structure, with the intention of enabling himself or another person to commit the above offence. 'Structure' includes a tent, vehicle or vessel or other temporary or movable structure.

Voyeurism: operating equipment

A person commits an offence under SOA 2003, s 67(2) if:

(a) he operates equipment with the intention of enabling another person to observe, for the purpose of obtaining sexual gratification, a third person (B) doing a private act (as defined above); and
(b) he knows that B does not consent to his operating equipment with that intention.

'Observation' means any observation, whether direct or by looking at a moving or still image (eg by installing a web cam).

Voyeurism: recording

A person commits an offence under SOA 2003, s 67(3), if:

(a) he records another person (B) doing a private act (as defined above);
(b) he does so with the intention that he or a third person will, for the purpose of obtaining sexual gratification, look at a moving or still image of B doing the act; and
(c) he knows that B does not consent to his recording the act with that intention.

Intercourse with an animal

A person commits an offence under SOA 2003, s 69(1) if:

(a) he intentionally performs an act of penetration with his penis;
(b) what is penetrated is the vagina or anus of a living animal; and
(c) he knows that, or is reckless as to whether, that is what is penetrated.

In relation to an animal, references to the vagina or anus include references to any similar part.

A person (A) commits an offence under SOA 2003, 69(2) if:

(a) A intentionally causes, or allows, A's vagina or anus to be penetrated;
(b) the penetration is by the penis of a living animal; and
(c) A knows that, or is reckless as to whether, that is what A is being penetrated by.

Sexual penetration of a corpse

A person commits an offence under SOA 2003, s 70(1) if:

(a) he intentionally performs an act of penetration with a part of his body or anything else;
(b) what is penetrated is a part of the body of a dead person;
(c) he knows that, or is reckless as to whether, that is what is penetrated;
(d) the penetration is sexual.

The wording of this offence shows that this offence is not committed if the person penetrated dies during the act of penetration.

Sexual activity in a public lavatory

A person commits an offence under SOA 2003, s 71(1) if:

(a) he is in a lavatory to which the public or a section of the public has, or is permitted to have access, whether on payment or otherwise;
(b) he intentionally engages in an activity; and
(c) the activity is sexual.

The definition of 'sexual' provided by SOA 2003, s 78, referred to on p 947, does not apply to this offence. Instead, for the purposes of s 71, an activity is sexual if a reasonable person would, in all the circumstances but regardless of any person's purpose, consider it to be sexual.

EVIDENCE

Corroboration

A trial judge is not required to give a corroboration direction to a jury in respect of the evidence of a complainant of any sexual offence. However, in some cases, such as failure to make an early complaint, or a history of the complainant making false allegations, the judge would be justified in warning the jury against relying on the complainant's unsupported evidence.

Restrictions on evidence or questions about complainant's sexual history

The Youth Justice and Criminal Evidence Act 1999 (YJCEA 1999), s 41 imposes such restrictions where a person is charged with any sexual offence under SOA 2003, Part 1 (ss 1 to 79), ie all the offences discussed so far in this chapter, as well as those under the 2003 Act relating to child prostitution, prostitution and sex trafficking referred to in the next chapter, or aiding, abetting, counselling or procuring the commission of such an offence or an incitement, conspiracy or attempt to commit such an offence.

YJCEA 1999, s 41 requires that where someone is charged with a sexual offence then, except with the leave of the court, no evidence may be adduced, and no questions may be asked in cross-examination, by or on behalf of any accused about the 'sexual behaviour' of the complainant. 'Sexual behaviour' means any sexual behaviour or other sexual experience, whether or not involving any accused or other persons.

If the defence wishes to introduce evidence or ask questions about such matters, it must apply to the court. The court will decide the application in private and in the absence of the complainant, after the prosecution has had the chance to oppose the application. The court can only grant leave when two conditions are satisfied. The first is that a refusal of leave might have the result of rendering unsafe a conclusion of the jury or (as the case may be) of the court on any relevant issue in the case. The second condition is that:

(a) the evidence in question relates to a relevant issue in the case and either:
 (i) that issue is not an issue of consent (for example, as the Court of Appeal has held, if the defence is that the accused *believed* the victim was consenting, evidence of recent consensual activity between them is admissible in relation to the issue of the accused's *belief*, but not as to whether the victim had consented); or
 (ii) it is an issue of consent and the complainant's sexual behaviour to which the evidence or question relates is alleged to have occurred at or about the same time as the event which is the subject matter of the charge against the accused (for example, that the complainant had consented to intercourse with the accused a couple of hours earlier, but not the fact that the complainant was a prostitute); or
 (iii) it is an issue of consent and the complainant's sexual behaviour to which the evidence or question relates is so similar either to any sexual behaviour of the complainant which (according to the defence's version) took place as part of the event which is the subject matter of the charge, or to any other sexual behaviour of the complainant which (according to the defence's version) took place at or about the same time as that event, that the similarity cannot reasonably be explained as a coincidence; or
(b) the evidence or question relates to any evidence adduced by the prosecution about any sexual behaviour of the complainant, and would go no further than necessary to enable the evidence adduced by the prosecution to be rebutted or explained by the accused.

To be admitted under the above provisions, the evidence must relate to a specific instance, or instances, of sexual behaviour. If the court considers that the purpose (or main purpose) of the evidence which the defence seeks to have admitted is to undermine or diminish the complainant's credibility, it will not allow the evidence to be given.

The House of Lords has held that (a)(iii) above must be construed, like any other statutory provision impinging on a Convention right, so as to give effect to that right so far as is possible. It held, therefore, that under (a)(iii) the test of admissibility was whether the evidence, and questioning relating to it, was so relevant to the issue of consent that to exclude it would endanger the fairness of the trial, contrary to the accused's right to a fair trial under art 6 of the European Convention on Human Rights. If that test was satisfied, the sexual behaviour evidence should not be excluded.

ANONYMITY OF COMPLAINANTS

The Sexual Offences (Amendment) Act 1992 provides for the anonymity of complainants (male or female) in the case of any offence under the provisions of Part 1 of the Sexual Offences Act 2003 except s 64 (sexual offence of penetration with an adult relative), s 65 (sex with adult relative where consent to penetration), s 69 (intercourse with an animal) or s 71 (sexual activity in a public lavatory). The same restrictions apply to similar offences against legislation which existed before SOA 2003.

Where an allegation is made that one of these offences has been committed against a person, no matter relating to that person may, during that person's lifetime, be included in any publication if it is likely to lead members of the public to identify that person as the person against whom the offence was committed. These matters include particularly (if their inclusion in any publication is likely to have such a result):

(a) the person's name;
(b) the person's address;
(c) the identity of any school or other educational establishment attended by the person;
(d) the identity of any place of work; and
(e) any still or moving picture of the person.

For the above purpose, and for the purpose of the next paragraph but one, 'publication' is widely defined. It includes, for example, a television or radio programme, a film, a written communication or a speech, addressed to the public at large or a section of the public.

This prohibition ceases to apply once a person has been accused of an offence. In such a case, the law thereafter is as set out in the next paragraph.

Where a person has been *accused* of one of the above offences, no matter whatsoever which is likely to lead to the identification of the complainant may be included in any publication during the complainant's lifetime. Provision is made for the requirements of the Sexual Offences (Amendment) Act 1992 to be set aside on application being made to the trial judge where it is considered necessary to induce persons to come forward as witnesses and that the applicant's defence will be substantially prejudiced if the direction is not given. The judge also has a 'public interest' discretion to set aside these provisions.

If any matter is published in breach of the above rules, an offence is committed:

(a) in the case of a newspaper or periodical, by any proprietor, editor or publisher of it;

(b) in the case of any other publication, by its publisher; or

(c) in the case of a programme, by any body corporate engaged in providing the service and by anyone involved in the programme corresponding to an editor of a newspaper.

NOTIFICATION REQUIREMENTS

SOA 2003, Part 2 requires a person subject to the notification requirements under the Act to notify the police of his date of birth, his national insurance number and his name and address (and any other name and any other address which he uses). Notification must be made within three days of the relevant date and must be made by attending at any prescribed police station in his local police area, and giving an oral notification to any police officer, or to any person authorised for the purpose by the officer in charge of the station. The relevant date is the date of conviction, finding or caution (including a reprimand or warning) but the three-day period does not include any time when the offender is in custody or in prison, detained in hospital or outside the United Kingdom. On giving notification, the person may be required by the police officer or authorised person to have his fingerprints and a photograph taken.

After such an original notification, a person subject to the procedure must give notice, within a period of three days of the change, of a new (ie unnotified) name, of a change of home address, of a new (ie unnotified) place of residence in the United Kingdom where he has resided for a qualifying period of seven days, or periods amounting to seven days in a twelve-month period, or of his release from custody, imprisonment or detention in hospital. (Although notification is permitted before use of the new name or the change of address, if the change subsequently takes place more than two days before the date notified that notification is invalid.) Moreover, if the event to which an advance notification relates has not occurred within three days of the date notified, the offender must within six days of the notified date notify the police that it did not occur within that period.

A person subject to the procedure must notify the police of his intention to leave the United Kingdom, and of his return, in accordance with the Sexual Offences Act 2003 (Travel Notification Requirements) Regulations 2004.

A person subject to the procedure must also annually re-notify the police of the information required to be given on initial notification. Where that person is in custody, prison, detained in hospital or outside the United Kingdom at the relevant time, the re-notification period is three days from release, or return to the United Kingdom.

The persons affected by the notification requirements under SOA 2003, Part 2 are those convicted of an offence listed in Sch 3 to that Act; those found not guilty of such an offence by reason of insanity; those found to be under a disability (ie unfit to plead) and to have done the act charged in respect of the offence; or cautioned (or reprimanded or warned in the case of a child) in respect of such an offence. Persons previously convicted of offences which made them subject to the Sex Offenders Act 1997, Part 1 remain subject to the notification requirements then imposed, until the completion of the period for which notification was required.

Schedule 3 offences

SOA 2003, Sch 3 includes the offences under previous legislation of rape; intercourse with a girl under thirteen; intercourse with a girl between thirteen and sixteen and abuse of a position of trust if in either case the offender was twenty years of age or more; gross indecency with a child; inciting a girl under sixteen to incest; taking, distributing etc indecent photographs of children (where the child was under sixteen); possessing indecent photographs of children (where the child was under sixteen); or importing indecent photographs of children (where the child was under sixteen); or causing the prostitution of, intercourse with, or indecent assault on a girl under sixteen. Where the victim is under eighteen, the offences of incest by a man; buggery if the offender was aged twenty or more; and assault with intent to commit buggery are also included. Indecent assault on a man or woman are included where the victim is under eighteen or where the offender was sentenced to at least thirty months' imprisonment or admitted to a hospital under a restriction order.

The schedule also includes offences under the 2003 Act of rape, assault by penetration, most sexual assaults, child sex offences, sexual grooming, offences involving an abuse of trust in relation to children, familial child sexual offences, offences against persons with a mental disorder including offences by care workers, paying for the sexual services of a child, administering substances with intent, trespassing with intent to commit a sexual offence, sex with an adult relative, exposure, voyeurism, intercourse with an animal, and sexual penetration with a corpse. In brief, this list includes every offence under SOA 2003, Part 1 (ss 1 to 79) besides those relating to prostitution or child pornography, to trafficking or to sexual activity in a public lavatory. These listed offences are described on pp 949–972 and 986 'paying for the sexual services of a child'. Reference should be made to the schedule as the offences often only give rise to the notification requirements in particular circumstances or in the case of particular penalties.

Attempts, conspiracy to commit, incitement and aiding and abetting such offences are also covered by these provisions.

Duration of notification requirement

Offenders who are sentenced to life imprisonment, or to thirty months' imprisonment or more, or who are admitted to hospital under a restriction order, are indefinitely subject to the notification requirement; offenders sentenced to more than six months but less than thirty months are subject for a period of ten years; offenders sentenced to less than six months or admitted to a hospital without a restriction order are subject for a period of seven years; and persons of any other description, for a period of five years. However, where the offender is under eighteen, the periods of ten, seven and five years are halved. Persons who are cautioned are subject to the requirements for two years (one year in the case of a reprimand or warning to an under-eighteen-year-old). Those who are conditionally discharged are subject to the requirements during the period of conditional discharge.

In the case of a young offender the court may direct a person with parental responsibility for the offender to comply with the notification requirements until the offender reaches the age of eighteen or until an earlier date specified in the order.

Offence of failure to comply with notification requirements

It is an offence for a person to fail without reasonable excuse to comply with these requirements. It is also an offence to notify to the police, in purported compliance with these requirements, any information which the person concerned knows to be false.

The offence of failure to notify is a continuing one so that proceedings may be taken at any time after such a failure. It may be dealt with at any place where the offender resides or where he is found.

PREVENTATIVE ORDERS

Notification orders

SOA 2003, s 97 provides that a chief officer of police may apply to a magistrates' court for a civil order (a notification order) in respect of a defendant who resides in his police area, or whom he believes is in, or is intending to come to, his police area, where it appears to him that the following conditions are satisfied with respect to the defendant:

(a) under the law in force in a country outside the United Kingdom:
  (i) he has been convicted of a relevant offence (whether or not he has been punished for it);
  (ii) a court exercising jurisdiction under that law has made in respect of a relevant offence a finding equivalent to a finding that he is not guilty by reason of insanity;
  (iii) such a court has made in respect of a relevant offence a finding equivalent to a finding that he is under a disability and did the act charged against him in respect of that offence; or
  (iv) he has been cautioned in respect of the relevant offence;
(b) condition (a) above is met because of a conviction, finding or caution which occurred on or after 1 September 1997 (or although a person was convicted before that date he was dealt with after it) or because, although there was a conviction before that date, the person concerned was detained in the foreign country, or subject to supervision or a community sentence;
(c) the period specified for the purposes of Part 2 in respect of the relevant offence has not expired.

If it is proved that these conditions exist the court must make a notification order. A 'relevant offence' means an act which constituted an offence under the law in force in the country concerned and would have constituted an offence listed in SOA 2003, Sch 3 if it had been done in any part of the United Kingdom.

The effect of a notification order is to subject the defendant to the notification requirements under SOA 2003, Part 2 for a period corresponding to that which would apply if he had been convicted in the United Kingdom. The notification period runs from the date of the foreign conviction etc. The initial notification must be made within three days of the service of the order.

Provision is made for an 'interim notification order' pending determination of an application for a notification order. Where a relevant offence has been committed abroad it may take some time to obtain the necessary documentation to put before the court. A person subject to an interim order is subject to the notification requirements while the order is in force and must make that notification within three days of service of the order.

Sexual offences prevention orders

Sexual offences prevention orders replace restraining orders and sex offender orders which existed under previous legislation. Such an order prohibits the person concerned from doing any act specified in the order. The order will remain in force for a period specified in the order (not less than five years). If, without reasonable excuse, a person does an act prohibited by a sexual offences prevention order, he is guilty of an offence. A person subject to the order is subject to the notification requirements of SOA 2003, Part 2 for the duration of the order.

By SOA 2003, s 104 a 'sexual offences prevention order' may be made when a court deals with a person convicted in respect of the offences listed in SOA 2003, Sch 3 or Sch 5, or where that court makes a finding in relation to a person charged with such an offence who is mentally incapacitated, if it is necessary to protect the public or any particular member of it from serious sexual harm from that person. Sch 3 offences were described above. Sch 5 offences include offences relating to child abuse through prostitution or pornography, to trafficking for sex, as well as murder and other offences of serious violence.

Sexual offences prevention orders may also be made under s 104 in civil proceedings in magistrates' courts on application by the chief officer of police for the police area. If, on a police application, it is proved that the defendant is a qualifying offender, the magistrates' court may make an order in respect of the defendant if satisfied that his behaviour since the 'appropriate date' makes it *necessary to make such an order, for the purpose of protecting the public or any particular members (or member) of the public from serious sexual harm from him* (ie protecting the public in the United Kingdom or any particular members of the public from serious physical or psychological harm caused by him committing a Sch 3 offence or offences).

A person is a qualifying offender if, whether before or after 1 May 2004, he has:

(a) been convicted of a Sch 3 or 5 offence;
(b) been found not guilty of such an offence by reason of insanity, or to be under a disability and to have done the act charged against him in respect of such an offence; or
(c) in England and Wales or Northern Ireland, been cautioned in respect of such an offence.

A person is also a qualifying offender if, under the law of a country outside the United Kingdom and before or after 1 May 2004:

(a) he has been convicted of a relevant offence;
(b) a foreign court has made, in respect of a relevant offence, a finding equivalent to a finding of not guilty by reason of insanity, or a finding that he is under a disability and did the act charged against him in respect of such an offence; or
(c) he has been cautioned in respect of a relevant offence.

A 'relevant' offence means an act which constituted an offence under the law of the country concerned, *and would have constituted a Sch 3 or 5 offence if it had been done in any part of the United Kingdom.*

The 'appropriate date', in relation to a qualifying offender, means the date (or first date) on which he was convicted, found or cautioned as mentioned above.

A sexual offences prevention order may be varied or discharged but it may not be discharged without the consent of both parties before the end of a period of five years.

Interim orders may also be obtained in appropriate circumstances in civil proceedings in a magistrates' court pending determination of an application.

Breach of an order or an interim order without reasonable excuse is an offence.

Foreign travel orders

SOA 2003, s 114 makes provision for the foreign travel order, a civil order which enables a court to prohibit for a period not exceeding six months persons who are 'qualifying offenders' (generally persons convicted of sexual offences against children under sixteen either in this country or abroad) from travelling abroad, where it is considered necessary to do so to protect children from serious sexual harm outside the United Kingdom. The order may be made by a magistrates' court on the application of a chief officer of police and it may refer to a named country or countries, or it may prohibit travel to any other country other than a named one, or to anywhere in the world. A person becomes a 'qualifying offender' if he is convicted of a relevant sexual offence or a corresponding foreign offence (or there is a 'finding' or 'caution' in this respect). It does not matter when such a person was dealt with for the relevant offence. It is an offence to breach without reasonable excuse any prohibition contained in such an order. An order may be varied or discharged. Breach of an order without reasonable excuse is an offence.

Risk of sexual harm orders

SOA 2003, s 123 makes provision for another type of civil order, the risk of sexual harm order, which enables a court to prohibit a defendant aged eighteen or over from doing anything described in the order for a fixed period (not less than two years) specified in the order or until further order. Such an order may only be made where:

(1) the defendant has on at least two occasions done an act of the following types:
  (a) engaging in sexual activity involving a child under sixteen or in the presence of such a child;
  (b) causing or inciting such a child to watch a person engaging in sexual activity or to look at a moving or still image that is sexual;
  (c) giving such a child anything that relates to sexual activity or contains a reference to such an activity (eg giving a child a condom, sending it a sex toy, a pornographic book or a video about sexual technique); or
  (d) communicating with such a child, where any part of the communication is sexual; and
(2) as a result, there is reasonable cause to believe that it is necessary for such an order to be made for the protection of children (or any child) under sixteen from harm from the defendant.

The order may be made by a magistrates' court on the application of a chief officer of police.

A risk of sexual harm order may be varied or discharged but it may not be discharged without the consent of both parties before the end of a period of two years.

Interim orders may also be obtained in appropriate circumstances in civil proceedings in a magistrates' court.

Breach of an order or interim order without reasonable excuse is an offence.

CHAPTER 35

Offences relating to prostitution, obscenity and indecent photographs

PROSTITUTION

Prostitute

Various statutes deal with prostitutes and prostitution. Except in the case of the Sexual Offences Act 2003 (SOA 2003), they do not define these terms. In the context of the other statutes reference must therefore be made to case law for the definition of 'prostitute' and 'prostitution' for the purposes of those statutes. Under that case law it has been established that a *prostitute* is a woman (or a man) who offers her (or his) body commonly for sexual intercourse or acts of a sexual nature, in return for payment, and it has been held by the Court of Appeal that it is immaterial that the woman (or man) is dishonest and intends simply to pocket advance payment and not to provide sexual services. The term 'sexual intercourse' requires no further explanation. The reference to other acts of a sexual nature extends the definition of 'prostitute'. Masseuses, for example, who carry out acts of masturbation on request are engaging in such acts. So are women who engage in sado-masochistic sessions for the sexual pleasure of their partner. Since sexual intercourse is not required, even a virgin can be a prostitute.

Some provisions refer to a '*common*' prostitute. Proof that a person is a common prostitute requires proof that in return for payment he or she is prepared to offer generally to engage in sexual intercourse or acts of lewdness. All these points must be proved. If a person offers intercourse for payment regularly to one person, the offerer is not a common prostitute as services are restricted to one person. If the offer is made to a number of persons because of the promiscuous nature of the offerer and no payment is required for the services, that person is not a common prostitute as no payment is received in return.

For the purposes of SOA 2003, 'prostitute' is defined as a person who, on at least one occasion and whether or not compelled to do so, offers or provides sexual services to another person in return for payment or a promise of payment to a particular person or a third person; 'prostitution' in SOA 2003 is interpreted accordingly. 'Payment' for the purposes of the 2003 Act means any financial advantage, including the discharge of an obligation to pay or the provision of goods or services (including sexual services) gratuitously or at a discount. Thus, any form of financial arrangement will be classified as payment. The settlement of a debt by the provision of sexual services, or the supply of drugs, or their provision at a discounted price will be sufficient. There is no doubt that a similar approach will be followed in relation to other statutes.

It is not an offence in itself to be a prostitute, but there are a number of offences which can only be committed by, or in respect of, prostitutes.

Loitering or soliciting by a common prostitute

The Street Offences Act 1959 (StOA 1959), s 1 creates the offence committed by a common prostitute (whether male or female) who loiters or solicits in a street or public place for the purposes of prostitution. To establish an intention to offer the body for prostitution there must be evidence of the accused's recent behaviour in a street or public place. Evidence of such recent behaviour should include evidence that on at least two previous occasions the person was seen accosting another person in the streets and was seen to leave with them. It must be remembered that it is possible for a perfectly respectable person to approach a number of others when asking for directions. However, if seen to walk off with others on a number of occasions it is much more likely that there has been soliciting. Loitering by a common prostitute does not need to be for the purpose of making approaches to others; it is sufficient that there is loitering for the purpose of being approached by others. Many streets are noted as the haunts of prostitutes and people go there to look for them. The prostitutes are loitering for such a purpose. In the same way a prostitute may loiter in a slowly moving vehicle but it must be shown that the purpose was to solicit others, or to be solicited by them. Soliciting need not be by words and can be carried out by all of the accepted forms of non-verbal communication. Movements of the body, arms, hands as well as facial expressions and gestures can be equally compelling forms of solicitation. A deaf and dumb prostitute solicited by making grunting noises accompanied by a gesture with a folded right arm, being bent and straightened. The meaning was never in doubt! Tapping on window panes, leaning out of windows with signals to indicate price, signalling the position of the entry door with the fingers are all forms of solicitation. The test to be applied should be, 'Is it clear to the reasonable man that he is being offered sex for money?'

Street or public place

'Street' for the purpose of StOA 1959 includes any bridge, road, lane, footway, subway, square, court, alley or passage, whether a thoroughfare or not, which is for the time being open to the public. In addition, the doorways and entrances to premises abutting on a street and the ground adjoining and open to a street are treated as forming part of the street.

The definition is quite wide; in effect, it prohibits loitering or soliciting by prostitutes in places which are upon private property if they are open to a street, and the courts have interpreted the legislation in this way. For example, prostitutes who solicited from balconies or from behind windows have been convicted of this offence. The words of Lord Parker describe the essence of this offence perfectly. He said:

I approach the matter by considering what is the mischief aimed at by this Act. Everybody knows that this was an Act intended to clean up the streets, to enable people to walk along the streets without being molested or solicited by common prostitutes. Viewed this way, it can matter little whether the prostitute is soliciting while in the street or is standing in a doorway or balcony, or at a window, or whether the window is shut or open or half open; in each case solicitation is projected to and addressed to somebody walking in the street.

The term 'public place' is not defined but generally the courts have accepted that a public place is one where the public go, no matter whether they have a right to go or not. The question of ownership of the property does not therefore arise and attention should be directed towards usage. A garden which is used for a garden party to which the public are invited is a public place while that party is in progress. Immediately the party ceases, the garden reverts to its status of a private place. Although the point has not been tested, it is unlikely that such places as public houses, restaurants, dance halls or similar places will be public places for the purpose of the Act. It is more likely that 'public place' will be interpreted in the light of the fact that it is used in the alternative to 'street' in deciding to what it applies.

Cautions

A Home Office Circular states that, before proceedings are taken against a prostitute aged eighteen or over for an offence under StOA 1959, s 1, at least two official cautions should have been given and particulars of such cautions should have been entered in an official cautions register maintained at the police station. If the person wishes to dispute that such actions amounted to an act in respect of which a caution should be given, application may be made to a court within fourteen days for an order directing that the caution be expunged.

The purpose of the provisions on cautioning was to prevent offences rather than to punish and the procedure to be followed by the police is directed towards giving the person every opportunity to reform. The procedure is as follows:

(1) On the first occasion that a person is suspected of this offence, obtain the assistance of a colleague as a witness (joint observation).
(2) Tell that person what you have seen and give a caution. Obtain name, date of birth, address and description to aid later observations. Check name and address, if possible from documents. There is no power to use or threaten force to detain a person for these purposes; consequently, the use or threat of force in such circumstances is unlawful.
(3) Ask if that person is willing to be put in touch with a welfare, social or probation service for help, or to attend at a police station to see a police officer, at that person's convenience.
(4) If seen on a second occasion, the same procedure should be followed.
(5) All cautions must be officially recorded.
(6) If seen loitering or soliciting after having been officially cautioned twice, that person may be dealt with for the offence. An officer must satisfy himself that two cautions have been so recorded and that they are sufficiently recent (some forces insist that they must be within the preceding twelve months) before proceeding.
(7) A complaint from such a person to the effect that the caution is without cause requires investigation in the same way as any other complaint. If the complaint

is justified the caution may be expunged without the need to refer the matter to a court.

(8) When a prosecution for an offence under StOA 1959, s 1 is in progress in court it is not necessary to mention cautions. However, the conduct which occasioned those cautions will probably have to be given to prove that the person is a common prostitute.

Child prostitutes

Although those under eighteen who engage in prostitution are subject to the above offences penalising the activities of a prostitute, a Home Office Circular issued in 2000 states that they are almost invariably victims and should be treated as such. Criminal justice action should only be taken against them (as opposed to those who abuse them or seek to exploit them) if all the relevant local agencies are satisfied that the child is involved in prostitution of his or her own free will, and attempts to divert the child out of prostitution have failed.

Solicitation by those using motor vehicles

The Sexual Offences Act 1985, s 1 deals with 'kerb crawling' and makes it an offence for a person persistently to solicit another person, or different persons, for the purpose of prostitution, from a motor vehicle while that motor vehicle is in a street or public place, or for a person persistently to solicit a another person, or different persons, for the purpose of prostitution, in a street or public place while in the immediate vicinity of a motor vehicle which the person soliciting has just got out of or off. 'Persistently' in StOA 1985 requires a degree of repetition by more than one invitation to one person or invitations to different people. As in the case of soliciting by a prostitute, soliciting can be by words or acts; the person must indicate to another by words or acts that services as a prostitute are required. Consequently, although merely driving round a red light district does not constitute soliciting, even if it is done persistently, an offence is committed by a person who persistently addresses requests to another person or persons, for the purposes of prostitution, from a slow-moving or stationary vehicle, if the vehicle is in a street or public place. If the person parks the vehicle, and leaves it, persistently to solicit for the purpose of prostitution, in the immediate vicinity of the vehicle, an offence is committed. This will be so even if the vehicle is parked in a private car park, provided that the solicitation takes place in a street or public place, in 'the immediate vicinity' of the motor vehicle. That which may be described as 'the immediate vicinity' is likely to form the subject of much legal argument. The critical question must be concerned with whether or not the use of the vehicle was one of a series of acts leading *directly* to the solicitation.

In cases where there is a doubt concerning the proximity of the vehicle in this respect, it will be advisable to consider an offence which is contained in SOA 1985, s 2. Section 2 creates the offence of a person persistently soliciting another or others, in a street or public place for the purpose of prostitution. The use of a motor vehicle is not an essential ingredient of this offence.

SOA 1985, s 1 also creates offences which are alternatives to those requiring evidence of 'persistent soliciting'. In either of the circumstances described above in relation to s 1 offences, if the evidence falls short of 'persistent soliciting', an alternative offence under s 1 may be committed if there is soliciting in such a manner or in such circumstances as to be likely to cause annoyance to the person or persons solicited, or nuisance to other persons in the neighbourhood. The likelihood of nuisance to other persons can be proved even though there is no evidence that other members of the public were present. Justices are entitled to take into account their local knowledge of the area in which the offence allegedly occurred when considering whether behaviour was likely to have caused a nuisance to other members of the public.

Placing of advertisements relating to prostitution

The Criminal Justice and Police Act 2001 (CJPA 2001), s 46 creates an offence of placing on, or in the immediate vicinity of, a public telephone, an advertisement relating to prostitution, with intent that the advertisement should come to the attention of any other person. An advertisement is covered by s 46 if it is for the services of a prostitute, whether male or female, or indicates that premises are premises in which such services are offered. Any advertisement which a reasonable person would consider to be an advertisement relating to prostitution is presumed to be so, unless shown not to be.

For the purposes of this section 'public telephone' means any telephone which is located in a public place for use by the public (or a section of the public) together with any structure in which it is housed. A 'public place' means any place to which the public have, or are permitted to have, access, whether on payment or otherwise, other than (a) any place to which children under the age of sixteen years are not permitted to have access, whether by law or otherwise, and (b) any premises which are wholly or mainly used for residential purposes.

CJPA 2001, s 47 permits the Secretary of State to extend these provisions to other public structures by order.

Exploitation of prostitution

SOA 2003, s 52 provides that it is an offence for a person intentionally to cause or incite another person to become a prostitute in any part of the world if he does so for or in the expectation of gain for himself or for a third person. Section 53 prohibits the intentional control by a person of any of the activities of another person relating to that person's prostitution in any part of the world for or in the expectation of gain for himself or a third person.

For the purposes of these offences the term 'gain' means:

(a) any financial advantage, including the discharge of an obligation to pay or the provision of goods or services (including sexual services) gratuitously or at a discount; or
(b) the goodwill of any person which is or appears likely, in time, to bring financial advantage.

The definition of 'gain' makes it clear that there in no requirement that money changes hands between the prostitute and the offender. It may be that the offender requires no more than an occasional 'freebee', or that the prostitute makes herself available at his club as an added attraction to customers. At the present time there is a lively trade in facilitating the illegal entry of women with the intention that they will become involved in prostitution and there are many people involved in taking percentages from their activities. All engaged in this 'trade' are involved in inciting or causing these women to become involved in prostitution for gain or in controlling their activities. The offence is also committed by those who are involved in the export of women from this country for the purposes of prostitution abroad.

These sections are not specifically aimed at protecting persons aged eighteen or over, but SOA 2003, ss 47 to 50 (below) specifically protect those under eighteen.

Trafficking for sexual exploitation

SOA 2003, ss 57 to 59 deal with this. Section 57 explicitly deals with those involved in 'trafficking' a person into the United Kingdom for the purpose of sexual activities. It is an offence for a person intentionally to arrange or facilitate the arrival of another person (B) in the United Kingdom, either intending to do anything to or in respect of B after B's arrival (but in any part of the world) which will amount to a relevant offence, or believing that another person will do something to or in relation to B, which if done will amount to a relevant offence. A 'relevant offence' is:

(a) an offence under Part 1 (ss 1 to 79) of SOA 2003;
(b) an offence under s 1(1)(a) of the Protection of Children Act 1978 (PCA 1978) (below).

Section 58 makes similar provision to deal with trafficking within the United Kingdom (travel within the United Kingdom); and s 59 with trafficking out of the United Kingdom. The sections apply to anything done outside the United Kingdom by any type of British citizen or a British protected person (including acts by a body corporate).

Involvement of children in prostitution and pornography

Paying for the sexual services of a child

SOA 2003, s 47 makes it an offence for a person intentionally to obtain for himself the sexual services of a person under eighteen where, in advance, such services have been paid for or where payment has been promised. The payment or promise may be made to the person under eighteen or to someone else. It may be that someone else has arranged for the person under eighteen to be available and has received the payment or been promised it. Where the victim is under thirteen the offence will be committed regardless of any belief which the accused may have concerning age. However, where the victim is thirteen or over the accused is only guilty if he did not reasonably believe that the victim was eighteen or over; it will be for the prosecution to prove that such a belief did not exist.

Causing or inciting child prostitution or pornography

SOA 2003, s 48 makes it an offence for a person intentionally to cause or incite a person under eighteen to become a prostitute or to be involved in pornography in any part of the world. Where the victim is under thirteen, it is irrelevant what belief the accused (however reasonably) may have had as to the victim's age. If the victim was thirteen or over, the prosecution must prove that the accused did not reasonably believe that the victim was under eighteen. This offence will be committed by those who recruit young persons into prostitution or pornography. It would be sufficient if a man caused his seventeen-year-old girlfriend to offer her services to others, either as a prostitute or as an actor in a pornographic film, so that they could afford a holiday. The section provides that the acts concerned can be intended to take place anywhere in the world; the offence lies in 'recruitment' for such purposes. There is no requirement to prove that this was done for gain.

Controlling a child prostitute or a child in pornography

SOA 2003, s 49 makes it an offence if a person intentionally controls any of the activities of another person relating to the prostitution of that person or involvement in pornography in any part of the world, and either the other person is under eighteen and the accused does not reasonably believe that the victim is eighteen or over or the victim is under thirteen.

Arranging or facilitating child prostitution or pornography

SOA 2003, s 50 makes it an offence for a person intentionally to arrange or facilitate the prostitution or involvement in pornography in any part of the world of another person, and either that person is under eighteen and the accused does not reasonably believe that the victim is eighteen or over, or the victim is under thirteen.

This offence is intended to punish those who are involved in child prostitution and pornography in other ways. It will cover those who 'convey' young persons to places or premises where such activities are intended to take place and those who merely make the administrative arrangements for such activities.

A person is involved in pornography for the purposes of ss 48, 49 and 50 if an indecent image of that person is recorded.

OFFENCES RELATING TO BROTHELS

Keeping a brothel

By the Sexual Offences Act 1956 (SOA 1956), s 33 it is an offence for a person to keep a brothel, or to manage it, or to act or assist in its management. Perhaps the first question to which we should address ourselves is 'What is a brothel?' Premises are a brothel if they are used by persons for illicit heterosexual or homosexual intercourse or other indecent behaviour. It is not necessary to show that some of the people resorting to the premises are prostitutes or that they received payment for their services, but there must be at least three people who use the premises in this way. It does not matter that one of them is the occupier, and it does not matter that only two people at a time ever use the premises for sexual activities.

Keeping a brothel for prostitution

By SOA 1956, s 33A, inserted by SOA 2003, it is an offence for a person to keep, or to manage, or act or assist in the management of, a brothel to which people resort for practices involving prostitution (whether or not also for other practices).

If separate and self-contained flats are separately let, each to one prostitute, it is likely that the building in its entirety will not be classed as a brothel as there is only one prostitute in each of the flats. However, if single rooms are let to prostitutes in one building, it may be sufficient if the rooms are sufficiently close to constitute what might be described as a nest of prostitutes.

In considering the charges to be preferred when it is established that a building is a brothel used for prostitution, we must look at the offence created by SOA 1956, s 33A. The keeper of the premises, who is most likely to be the residential landlord, a manager, who looks after the maintenance and day-to-day needs of the building and its tenants, the 'madame' of the trade and those who act or assist in the management of the brothel are all guilty of offences. 'Assisting in the management of a brothel' covers any conduct which contributes to the management of the brothel. Assistance in the management of a brothel does not require proof that the person actively exercised some control over the brothel or carried out some specific act of management. A person who takes advertisements to a post office and pays for them assists in the management of the brothel. So does a person who discusses with a potential customer the nature of the sexual activities on offer, or who negotiates the price. On the other hand, it has been held that a cleaner at a brothel does not assist in its management.

Related offences

SOA 1956, ss 34 and 35 go further and add offences to cover other possibilities in relation to responsibility for the brothel. First, a lessor or landlord of premises (or his agent) who has knowledge of their intended or actual use as a brothel is guilty of an offence (s 34). In addition, the tenant or occupier, or person in charge, of premises who knowingly permits the whole or part of them to be so used is also guilty of an offence (s 35). It will frequently be found that the same person might fit more than one description. For example, the occupier may frequently be the man whom you would consider to be the keeper of the brothel and it is of advantage to consider all possibilities.

OBSCENE PUBLICATIONS, INDECENT PHOTOGRAPHS OR PSEUDO-PHOTOGRAPHS, AND INDECENT DISPLAYS

Obscene publications

These are governed in general by the Obscene Publications Act 1959 (OPA 1959).

Under OPA 1959, s 2 an offence is committed by a person who:

(a) publishes an obscene article, whether for gain or not; or
(b) has an obscene article for publication for gain, whether for himself or another.

You may therefore sit at home and write as many obscene articles as you wish without committing an offence against the Act. If you circulate copies of these articles to other people, then you publish them and it does not matter that you have not received money or other reward for them. Having written the articles without any intention to publish, you may subsequently commit an offence if, having them in your possession, you decide that you will publish them for gain.

What is an 'obscene article'?

An 'article' for present purposes means any article containing or embodying matter to be read or looked at or both, any sound record, and any film or other record of a picture or pictures (such as a photograph, video cassette or computer disk). 'Article' for the purposes of the Act also includes any matter included in a television or sound broadcast or in a cable programme service; obscene publication via a broadcast or cable service is a rather specialised type of obscene publication, and we shall not deal with it further in the book.

An article is deemed to be obscene if its effect, or (where the article comprises two or more distinct items) the effect of any of its items is, taken as a whole, such as to tend to deprave and corrupt a significant proportion of persons who are likely, having regard to all the circumstances, to read, see or hear the matter contained in it.

Though a novel may be considered as a whole, a magazine must be considered item by item and, if any one of the items is obscene, this suffices. 'Deprave and corrupt' are strong words; to lead morally astray is not necessarily to deprave and corrupt. Obscenity is not confined to that which has a tendency to corrupt sexual morals; a book depicting the career of a drug addict has been held to be obscene because of its likely effect. On occasions, articles may be directed at persons who may already be considered to have become depraved and corrupted but this may still amount to an offence if the object is to maintain that state of depravity and corruption and to prevent escape from it. Whether an article is obscene because it is likely to deprave and corrupt is essentially a matter for the jury. A juror is as able as anyone to decide the effect upon people, whilst keeping in mind the current standards of ordinary, decent people.

In deciding whether to initiate action in these cases, police officers should take cognisance of current trends in society in coming to a decision regarding the effect of such articles; the reader, viewer or listener must also be considered. If the article tends to deprave and corrupt a significant proportion of those who receive it, it is obscene for the purposes of the Act. It would probably be insufficient if it was likely to affect only a few who were not representative of the 'ordinary man'.

Publication etc

To 'publish' means to distribute, circulate, sell, let on hire, give or lend, or to offer it for sale or hire. 'Publishing' also includes 'making available', as where X gives Y a key to a library containing obscene articles. Additionally, in the case of a record, a film etc 'publish' includes showing, playing, or projecting it. A person who enables another to access electronically stored obscene matter on a computer 'shows' the other that matter, and therefore 'publishes' it. Where the matter is data stored electronically, a person publishes it if he transmits that data.

We are, therefore, considering every method of passing the article from one person to another. If we return to our consideration of the obscene article written at home, to distribute the manuscript to only one person will amount to publication, whether for gain or not. However, at this stage, it will be difficult to prove that this one person was likely to be depraved and corrupted, particularly if he is a person with an interest in such obscene articles. As it is circulated to more people, the easier it will become to prove that the article was likely to deprave and corrupt them. We must also consider those who publish in the more generally accepted sense and offer on the market such articles for sale. Today, the article is quite likely to be a video recording, or even an audio tape. Those who distribute, sell etc commit offences but so do those who show, play or project obscene articles. The owner of a photographic studio who develops photographs which are obscene publishes them when he sells them or passes them back for gain to their owner; publication to a third party is not required. In deciding upon appropriate charges, once it is clear that an article is obscene for the purposes of the Act one must consider the role of every person who has in any way transmitted the material to someone else. If a person has actually published, the question of gain does not arise; if he merely possesses it for the purpose of publication he must intend to publish for gain, although not necessarily his own.

Defences

It is a defence for a person to prove he had not examined the article and had no reasonable cause to suspect that it was such that his publication of it, or possession, as the case may be, would make him liable under OPA 1959. He must prove both points. If he has examined it, it is no defence to allege that he had not realised its nature.

OPA 1959 provides a defence of 'public good'. If it is proved that publication was justified as being for the public good on the grounds that it is in the interests of science, literature, art or learning, or of other objects of general concern, a person must not be convicted of the above offences. Expert evidence may be given to establish or negative such a defence. This defence is only relevant once the jury has established obscenity, and is therefore of little operational significance to police officers.

Police powers

If an information on oath is laid before a justice that there are reasonable grounds for suspecting that obscene articles are kept on any premises, stall or vehicle in the justice's area for publication for gain, he may issue a warrant authorising a constable to search for and seize any articles which he has reason to believe to be obscene and to be kept for publication for gain. The additional powers of seizure provided by CJPA 2001, s 50 apply where a search warrant under OPA 1959 is executed. If the justice considers that any articles seized are obscene he may issue a summons to the occupier of the premises etc to appear before a magistrates' court and show cause why the articles should not be forfeited. If the court is satisfied that the articles seized are obscene and kept for publication for gain, it must order their forfeiture.

A search warrant including the words 'any other material of a sexually explicit nature' is invalid, since what is sexually explicit is not necessarily obscene.

Indecent photographs or pseudo-photographs of children

Photographs or pseudo-photographs

References in the above offences to an indecent photograph include an indecent film, a copy of an indecent photograph or film, and an indecent photograph comprised in a film. References to photographs also include the negative as well as the positive version.

To deal with the introduction of digital cameras, references to a 'photograph' include not only the negative as well as the positive version, but also include data stored on a computer disc or by other electronic means which is capable of conversion into a photograph. It is also possible to create 'fake' photographs (pseudo-photographs) by digital manipulation of photographs which have been electronically stored either by a digital camera or by scanning a conventional photograph. This digital manipulation is achieved by using widely available 'paint' and image-processing software to rearrange, colour and otherwise transform the objects in a scene. The same software can combine fragments of different images into one new image. Such indecent 'fake' photographs of children are already in circulation. It is for this reason that 'pseudo-photographs' have been included within the PCA 1978.

A 'pseudo-photograph' is an image, whether made by computer graphics or otherwise howsoever, which appears to be a photograph. The term includes:

(a) a copy of an indecent pseudo-photograph; and
(b) data stored on a computer disc or by other electronic means which is capable of conversion into a pseudo-photograph.

On the other hand, an exhibit obviously consisting of parts of two different photographs taped together cannot be said to 'appear to be a photograph' and is therefore not a pseudo-photograph, although if it was itself photocopied, it could.

Indecent

The term 'indecent' means offending against recognised standards of propriety. A photograph or pseudo-photograph can be indecent even though it is not obscene. The child's age (or in the case of a pseudo-photograph apparent age) is a relevant factor as to whether or not the photograph or pseudo-photograph is indecent, but the circumstances in which it was taken or made, or the motivation of the photographer (or the maker of a pseudo-photograph), is not. Something abstracted from a decent set of images is capable of being indecent if the abstracted matter satisfies the test of indecency. This was held by the Court of Appeal in a case where a man copied a television programme of a medical examination of the genitals of a naked boy and subsequently removed the commentary and slowed down the filming of the manipulation of the penis, the Court of Appeal held that the jury were entitled to look at the images independently of the original decent television programme in order to decide whether they were indecent.

Child

A photograph or pseudo-photograph must be of a child. In the case of a photograph, a child is someone under the age of eighteen. It is a matter for a court or jury to decide whether an unknown person depicted in an indecent photograph was under the age of eighteen. There is no need for expert evidence concerning age, the court or jury is as well placed as an expert to assess any argument concerning the age of the person depicted. Expert evidence would therefore be inadmissible. Since a pseudo-photograph will not be an image of a real person with a real age, it is provided that, if the impression conveyed by the pseudo-photograph is that the person shown is a child under the age of eighteen, the pseudo-photograph is to be treated for all purposes as showing such a child, and so is a pseudo-photograph where the predominant impression conveyed is that the person shown is a child under eighteen notwithstanding that some of the physical characteristics shown are those of an adult.

Taking, making, showing etc

The PCA 1978 is concerned with indecent photographs and pseudo-photographs of children. PCA 1978, s 1(1) provides that, subject to ss 1A and 1B (added by SOA 2003), it is an offence for a person:

(a) to take or permit to be taken, or to make any indecent photograph or pseudo-photograph of a child;
(b) to distribute or show such indecent photographs or pseudo-photographs;
(c) to have in his possession such indecent photographs or pseudo-photographs with a view to their being distributed or shown by himself or others; or
(d) to publish or cause to be published any advertisement likely to be understood as conveying that the advertiser distributes or shows such indecent photographs or pseudo-photographs or intends to do so.

A person who deliberately downloads an indecent image of a child from a web page on to a computer screen 'makes' a photograph or pseudo-photograph knowing that the image was, or was likely to be, an indecent photograph or pseudo-photograph of a child, commits an offence. It is irrelevant whether or not his motive is sexual gratification.

Even if the images originated outside the United Kingdom, the downloading or printing creates new material which has been *made* inside the United Kingdom.

'Showing' includes 'making available', as where a person gives another a key to a cupboard containing indecent photographs. The same would be so where a person makes available a password which enables someone to download a 'photograph' stored on a computer to his own computer. For an offence of 'possession with intent to show' to be committed under (c) above a person must be in possession with a view to showing the indecent photographs to a third party, it is not sufficient that he intends to show a cine film to himself.

A person possesses an indecent photograph etc with a view to it being distributed or shown by him to others only if one reason (not necessarily the primary reason) for possessing it is that it would be distributed or shown to others; thus a person who allows files containing indecent photographs etc to remain in his shared electronic folder, where they can be accessed and downloaded into the shared folders of other members of a file-sharing system, possesses those files with a view to their being shown or distributed only if one of his reasons, but not necessarily the primary reason, for doing so was to enable others to use them or download them.

PCA 1978, s 1(4) provides a defence to the charges *of distributing or showing or possession with a view to distribution or showing* if the accused proves either that:

(a) he had a legitimate reason for distributing or showing the photographs or pseudo-photographs or (as the case may be) having them in his possession; or
(b) he had not seen the photographs or pseudo-photographs and did not know, nor had any reason to suspect, them to be indecent.

In respect of an offence of proceedings for *taking* or *making*, PCA 1978, s 1A provides a defence of consent by the child or reasonable belief in consent. It states that, where in such proceedings, the accused proves that the photograph was of the child *aged sixteen or over*, and that at the time of the offence charged the child and he were married or civil partners of each other, or lived together as partners in an enduring family relationship, and sufficient evidence is adduced to raise an issue as to whether the child consented to the photograph being taken or made, or as to whether the accused reasonably believed that the child so consented, the accused is not guilty of the offence unless it is proved that the child did not so consent and that the accused did not reasonably believe that the child so consented.

In respect of proceedings for *distributing* or *showing* an indecent photograph of a child, PCA 1978, s 1A provides an additional defence for the case where the accused only distributes or shows the photograph to the child. It provides that where, in such proceedings, the accused proves that the photograph was of the child *aged sixteen or over*, and that at the time of the offence charged (ie the distributing or showing), or at the time when he obtained the photograph, the child and he were married or civil partners of each other, or lived together as partners in an enduring family relationship, the accused is not guilty of the offence unless it is proved that the showing or distributing was to someone other than the child.

In respect of proceedings for *possessing an indecent photograph of a child with a view to its being distributed or shown*, s 1A provides that it is a defence if the child consents to the accused's possession of the photograph (or that the accused reasonably believed in such consent) and the accused intended to distribute or show the photograph only to the child. It states that, where in such proceedings, the accused proves the photograph was of the child *aged sixteen or over*, and that at the time of the offence (ie the possession) charged, or at the time when he obtained the photograph, the child and he were married or civil partners of each other, or lived together as partners in an enduring family relationship, and sufficient evidence is adduced to raise an issue both:

(a) as to whether the child consented to the photograph being in the accused's possession, or as to whether the accused reasonably believed that the child so consented; and
(b) as to whether the accused had the photograph in his possession with a view to its being distributed or shown to anyone other than the child,

the accused is not guilty of the offence unless it is proved either that the child did not so consent and that the accused did not reasonably believe that the child so consented, or that the accused had the photograph in his possession with a view to its being distributed or shown to a person other than the child.

The above exceptions under s 1A apply whether the photograph showed the child alone or with the accused, but not if it showed any other person.

In addition, s 1B provides that in respect of a charge of *making* an indecent photograph or pseudo-photograph, for example downloading of an image from the Internet, or copying a photograph from a computer hard drive, a person will not commit an offence if it was done for the purpose of the prevention, detection or investigation of crime, or for the purpose of criminal proceedings. A similar defence also applies to a member of the Security Service or GCHQ who is able to prove that it was necessary to make the photograph or pseudo-photograph for the exercise of any functions of that Service or GCHQ.

Simple possession

The Criminal Justice Act 1988 (CJA 1988), s 160 makes it an offence for a person to have any indecent photograph or pseudo-photograph of a child in his possession.

For the purposes of an offence under the PCA 1978 or under CJA 1988, s 160, 'possession' means custody or control. It follows, for example, that an assistant in a sex shop containing indecent photographs of children is, like his employer, in possession of them. Where the image concerned is a computer file, the defendant is in possession of it at the relevant time if it is within his control—if, for example, he can produce it on his screen, make a hard copy of it or send it to someone else. Thus, images which have been emptied from the computer's recycle bin may be considered to be within the control of a defendant who is skilled in the use of computers and owns the software necessary to retrieve the images; whereas the images may not be considered to be within the control of a defendant who does not possess the requisite skill, and does not own the necessary software.

The offence is not committed unless the accused knew that he had, or once had, the photograph or pseudo-photograph in his possession.

By CJA 1988, s 160(2), a person charged under s 160 has a defence if he proves:

(a) that he had a legitimate reason for having the photograph or pseudo-photograph in his possession; the question of what constitutes a legitimate reason is a question of fact in each case; or

(b) that he had not himself seen the photograph or pseudo-photograph and did not know, nor had any reason to suspect, it to be indecent; or

(c) that the photograph or pseudo-photograph was sent to him without any prior request made by him or on his behalf and that he did not keep it for an unreasonable time.

The Court of Appeal has held that it is implicit in (b) that an accused who had not seen the photographs etc but had cause to suspect that they were indecent has a defence if he proves that he had no reason to suspect that they were indecent photographs of a child.

By CJA 1988, s 160A, if an accused proves that the photograph was of the child *aged sixteen or over*, and that at the time of the offence charged, or at the time when he obtained the photograph, the child and he were married or civil partners of each other, or lived together as partners in an enduring family relationship, and sufficient evidence is adduced to raise an issue as to whether the child consented to the photograph being in the accused's possession, or as to whether the accused reasonably believed that the child so consented, the accused is not guilty of the offence unless it is proved either that the child did not so consent or that the accused did not reasonably believe that the child so consented. The exception applies whether the photograph showed the child alone or with the accused, but not if it showed any other person.

Consent to prosecution

Proceedings for the above offences may only be instituted by or with the consent of the Director of Public Prosecutions.

Police powers

Under PCA 1978, s 4, a justice may issue a warrant to authorise entry, search for and seize indecent photographs or pseudo-photographs of a child on information laid on oath by a constable or by or on behalf of the Director of Public Prosecutions. The additional powers of seizure provided by CJPA 2001, s 50 apply where a search warrant under PCA 1978, s 4 is executed.

Harmful publications—children and young persons

The Children and Young Persons (Harmful Publications) Act 1955 (CYP(HP)A 1955) deals with books, magazines or similar works which are likely to fall into the hands of children or young persons. If such a publication consists wholly or mainly of stories *told in pictures* (with or without the addition of written matter), and those stories portray the commission of crimes, acts of violence or cruelty, or incidents of a repulsive or horrible nature, in such a way that the work as a whole would tend to corrupt a child or young person into whose hands it might fall, that publication is covered by the provisions of CYP(HP)A 1955. The terms 'child' and 'young person' are as defined by the Children and Young Persons Act 1933. A 'child' is someone under fourteen years of age, and a 'young person' someone under eighteen.

Clearly, the offence is concerned with 'horror comics' and the like. Those who print, publish, sell, let on hire or have in their possession for the purpose of selling or letting on hire such items commit offences. There is a defence to a selling or hiring charge: that the person concerned had not examined the contents of the publication and had no reason to suspect that CYP(HP)A 1955 would apply to it.

Police powers

The power of a justice to issue a search warrant is peculiar in relation to the CYP(HP)A 1955. One reason is that the consent of the Attorney-General is necessary before there may be a prosecution. Another reason is that a justice can only issue a search warrant at the time of, or after, the receipt of an information alleging an offence which leads him to authorise the issue of a summons or a warrant to arrest. In effect, therefore, proceedings for the present type of offence must have commenced in respect of a person allegedly involved in it. The additional powers of seizure provided by CJPA 2001, s 50 apply where a search warrant under CYP(HP)A 1955 is executed.

The CYP(HP)A 1955, and others similar to it, tend to cause difficulties for police officers considering charges to be preferred against those involved. Examination candidates share this concern. The correct approach is to examine the evidence at hand (or the information given) and from this to establish everyone who had been involved in the process from the outset. We must consider the responsibility of the printer, publisher, wholesaler, retailer or hirer: in other words, all those who handle the material.

Sending indecent etc matter through post

The Postal Services Act 2000, s 85 provides an offence which is concerned with sending a postal packet which encloses any indecent or obscene matter, or which has on the packet indecent or obscene words, marks or designs.

Indecent displays etc

The Indecent Displays (Control) Act 1981 (ID(C)A 1981) repealed all previous legislation dealing with indecent displays, advertisements etc. The offence prescribed by ID(C)A 1981 is quite simply one of publicly displaying indecent matter. Any person who does this, or who causes or permits it to be done by another, is guilty of an offence. The normal tests of indecency should be applied and matter is publicly displayed if it is displayed in a public place, or in a manner which makes it visible from a public place. The term 'public place' for the purposes of this Act means any place to which the public have access (whether on payment or otherwise) while that matter is displayed. It does not extend to places to which the public are permitted to have access only on payment which is for, or includes payment for, that display. Nor does it apply to a shop, or any part of a shop, to which public access can only be gained by passing beyond an adequate warning notice. However, both of these exemptions will only apply if persons under eighteen years of age are not allowed to enter such exempted premises whilst any such display is actually taking place.

The adequate warning notice described in ID(C)A 1981 should read as set out below and this notice should be looked for in premises where it is known that such displays are held:

WARNING
Persons passing beyond this notice will find material on display which they may consider indecent. No admittance to persons under 18 years of age.

'Matter', for the purposes of this Act, includes anything capable of being displayed, but does not include the actual human body or a part of it. Thus ID(C)A 1981 is not concerned with strippers. This is a useful Act to police officers as it can be applied to everything from the display of obscene graffiti scrawled on a wall to indecent film shows etc which are open to the public. The essential elements of the offence are indecency coupled with display to the general public.

Official TV programmes, art galleries, museums, Crown buildings, local authority buildings, theatres and arenas controlled by other legislation are totally outside the provisions of this Act.

Police powers

Under ID(C)A 1981, s 2, a constable may seize articles which he has reasonable grounds for believing to be indecent, or to contain indecent matter, or to have been used in the commission of an offence.

In addition, a justice may grant a search warrant, on information on oath, authorising entry within fourteen days and seizure of material suspected to have been used in an offence under ID(C)A 1981. The additional powers of seizure provided by CJPA 2001, s 50 apply where a search warrant under ID(C)A 1981 is executed.

CHAPTER 36

Drugs

Modern society could not operate as it does without drugs, and the ever-increasing prescription of drugs, the continuing search for new forms of drugs and the proportionate increase in the likelihood of drug dependence have created a need for strict forms of control. Arguments continue concerning which drugs are addictive and which are not, as do arguments for and against the permitted use of certain drugs such as cannabis which, though perhaps not addictive in themselves, create a feeling of well-being.

CLASSIFICATION OF DRUGS

The Misuse of Drugs Act 1971 (MDA 1971) provides a number of offences intended to control the misuse of drugs. Drugs which are subject to the Act are designated as 'controlled drugs'. A 'controlled drug' is any substance or product for the time being specified in Parts I, II or III of MDA 1971, Sch 2. Part 1 of Sch 2 lists 'Class A drugs'; Part II, 'Class B drugs'; and Part III, 'Class C drugs'. Drugs can be added to the lists contained in Sch 2 by Order in Council, or moved from one class to another. One of the points of the classification of controlled drugs is that it affects the punishment of some of the offences under the 1971 Act. As a result of a House of Lords' decision, what may appear to be one offence (eg unlawful supply) is in law divisible into distinct offences depending on the maximum penalty for the drug in question.

Class A drugs can be divided into two groups; first, narcotic drugs, such as cocaine, morphine, opium, pethidine, and heroin; and, second, hallucinogenic drugs, such as mescaline, LSD and MDMA (ecstasy), however the MDMA is produced, or fungus of any kind which contains psilocin or an ester of psilocin. Narcotic drugs are particularly dangerous because of their addictive qualities and hallucinogenic ones because of the violent conduct which the hallucinated taker may engage in. Class B drugs include amphetamines (which are stimulant drugs), such as mandrax. Class C drugs include cannabis, cannabis resin, benzyphetamine, chlorphentermine, mephentermine, phendimetrazine, pipradrol and temazapan.

Although there are a substantial number of substances listed as Class C drugs, they include only those which might generally be described as 'mild'. There are more than a hundred drugs listed in Class C and a similar number are listed in Class A. There are fewer Class B drugs; currently about twenty. Only an analysis of the substance will prove its nature, but (besides cannabis) the forms of drug in popular usage on the street are almost invariably Classes A and B or cannabis.

Because of its particular significance and the ease with which the plant can be grown, the expressions 'cannabis' and 'cannabis resin' are defined by the MDA 1971. 'Cannabis' (except in the expression 'cannabis resin') means any part of the genus Cannabis or any part of any such plant (by whatever name designated) except that it does not include cannabis resin, or any of the following products, after separation from the rest of the plant, namely:

(a) mature stalk of any such plant;
(b) fibre produced from mature stalk of any such plant; and
(c) seed of any such plant.

'Cannabis resin' means the separated resin, whether crude or purified, obtained from any plant of the genus Cannabis.

As indicated above a 'controlled drug' is a specified substance or *product*. In addition 'controlled drug' includes any 'preparation or other product' containing a specified substance or product. Some growing things, such as certain types of mushrooms, contain a specified substance. In their natural state such things are not a specified substance or product, but if they are picked and subjected to some process to enable them to be used as a drug, they become a 'preparation' containing a specified substance and become a controlled drug. If they are picked, packed and frozen they become a 'product' containing a specified substance and become a controlled drug.

The problem of enforcement which confronts police officers always appears to be a matter of identification of a substance. For example, reasonable suspicion that a person is in possession of a controlled drug will arise from circumstances other than the appearance or known character of the substance possessed. If, for example, persons are found on premises apparently under the influence of drugs, and tablets or other substances are found in their possession, it is not unreasonable to suspect that they are in possession of controlled drugs.

UNLAWFUL IMPORT AND EXPORT

The most effective way in which to limit drug trafficking in any country is to restrict the importation of drugs. MDA 1971, s 3 prohibits the importation or exportation of a controlled drug, otherwise than as authorised by regulations made under the Act or by a licence issued by the Secretary of State. Breach of this prohibition is not an offence under the Misuse of Drugs Act but it is an offence under the Customs and Excise Management Act 1979 (CEMA 1979), ss 50 and 68. Fraudulent evasion of such a prohibition is also punishable under CEMA 1979, s 170.

UNLAWFUL PRODUCTION

MDA 1971, s 4(2) states that it is an offence for any person unlawfully to produce a controlled drug or to be concerned in the production of a controlled drug. An offence under s 4(2) is subject to the defence provided by MDA 1971, s 28 (p 1007).

Unlawful

The production of any controlled drug other than as authorised by regulations is an unlawful production. The regulations authorise production by drug companies, by research establishments for experimental purposes and by chemists in the course of their business.

Produce

The term 'produce' means to produce a controlled drug by manufacture, cultivation or any other means, and 'production' has a corresponding meaning. A substance will pass through a number of processes in its production and a person charged must be clearly shown to have taken some identifiable part in the process of production before he can be convicted of this offence. It has been held that the conversion of cocaine hydrochloride into freebase cocaine, in which form it would vaporise and be capable of being inhaled, by dissolving cocaine hydrochloride in water and either baking powder or household ammonia, amounts to production of a Class A drug 'by other means' since the drug, in these two forms, is chemically different. It does not matter that the cocaine hydrochloride was already a Class A drug before the process began. By way of further example, where cannabis plants have been harvested and the plants are then stripped to take out those parts which could be used for smoking, it has been held that this amounts to production of a Class C drug (cannabis) as a controlled drug is produced by some 'other method' than cultivation or manufacture. However, the offence is to produce a controlled drug and it is therefore essential that a controlled drug is actually produced before the offence can be committed. If the process to produce a substance has not been completed, there can be a conviction for attempting to commit the offence of production. Where a person tries to produce a controlled drug but, because of insufficient knowledge, produces a substance which is not in fact a controlled drug, he may nevertheless be convicted of an attempt to produce a controlled drug.

Concerned in the production

The inclusion of these words is for the purpose of widening the net of criminal liability in relation to the production of controlled drugs. The effect of these words is that criminal liability is not limited to those who actually participated in the production of a controlled drug, since those who arrange for the delivery of ingredients to the place of manufacture of such a drug, knowing the purpose for which they are required, are concerned in its production, as is a person who knowingly allows his premises to be used. Not all types of activities covered by 'being concerned in' can properly be described as aiding, abetting, counselling or procuring the actual production of the drug. Consequently, the phrase 'being concerned' widens the ambit of the law beyond that which it would otherwise have.

UNLAWFUL SUPPLY

The unlawful supply of controlled drugs is another activity which is included in the general description of 'drug trafficking'. If a controlled drug is unlawfully imported or produced it must then have a distribution network. MDA 1971, s 4(3) states:

It is an offence for a person unlawfully to supply a controlled drug to another or to be concerned in the supplying of such a drug to another, or to offer to supply a controlled drug to another, or to be concerned in the making to another of an offer to supply such a drug.

The defence provided by MDA 1971, s 28 applies to an offence under s 4(3).

Unlawful

The circumstances in which a controlled drug may be supplied lawfully are set out in regulations made under the Act. They are not difficult to imagine: doctors may issue drugs direct from their own dispensaries; chemists may supply them upon prescription; nurses may supply patients in hospital; laboratory analysts, inspectors and quality controllers may also handle drugs and pass them from one to another. The inclusion of the term 'unlawfully' ensures that all circumstances in which controlled drugs are supplied to a person outside such exceptions amount to offences under the Act.

To supply to another

The term 'supply' means more than the mere transfer of physical control from one person to another: it means to furnish to another the drug in order to enable the other to use it for his own purposes. At one extreme there is the person who supplies the drug addict. He is the one who is usually described as a 'pusher', forming a rung in the distribution ladder between those who illegally import or produce drugs and those who use them. The person who distributes drugs at a party is supplying the drugs to another and is guilty of an offence under MDA 1971, s 4(3). So is someone who returns a drug to a person who already owns it so that he can use it, or who hands a 'reefer' to someone so that he can take a puff. On the other hand, a person who hands a drug to another for safe-keeping does not supply it to him. Nor does a person who injects another with heroin if that drug is already in the other's control.

Although a person who makes a joint purchase of drugs for consumption by himself and another, paying with their joint funds, supplies the other when he hands over the latter's share of the drugs, the Court of Appeal has stated that a charge of supplying the latter is undesirable.

Where police officers occupy a house used by suppliers, they may not be permitted to give evidence of things said by persons who call at the house to obtain supplies of drugs, as such evidence is hearsay. However, evidence given by police officers of incidents within eight days of observation upon premises, during which a great number of people were seen visiting the address, together with evidence of relevant convictions of eight of those persons for offences of possession or supply of heroin, is admissible as it is relevant to the nature of the transactions and the purpose for which the accuseds were letting the visitors into the house.

Before an offence of supplying can be committed the substance supplied must be a controlled drug. It is not sufficient that the supplier believed that the substance was a drug, when in fact it was not, although he could be convicted of an attempt to supply in such a case or, depending on the circumstances, of an offer to supply.

To be concerned in the supply

For the purpose of this offence, the wide meaning given to the term 'concerned' when discussed in its application to offences of production should be applied.

To offer to supply

It is the making of an offer which is the important factor in relation to this offence; the extension of the offence to those who may be concerned in the making of such an offer gives considerable width to its application. Whereas one must supply an actual controlled drug before committing the offence of supplying, this is not necessary in relation to the making of an offer and this will be appreciated if it is borne in mind that the offence lies in the making of the offer. Therefore, if an offer is made to supply a controlled drug, an offence is committed even though the substance is not in fact a controlled drug, and even though the accused knows this. Likewise, the offence of offering to supply a controlled drug is even committed if the offeror does not intend to supply anything. Many persons may be involved in the making of the offer. Those who approach people and seek to induce them to purchase drugs or merely receive them are offering to supply; those who send them out into the streets to canvass sale or distribution are concerned in the offer which is subsequently made.

SUPPLY OR OFFER TO SUPPLY ARTICLE

MDA 1971, s 9A creates offences of supplying or offering to supply an article which may be used or adapted to be used (whether by itself or in combination with another article) in the administration by a person of a controlled drug, or which may be used to prepare a controlled drug for administration, believing it would be so used in circumstances which would be unlawful.

However, it is not an offence under the section to supply a hypodermic syringe.

UNLAWFUL POSSESSION

The offences of unlawful possession of controlled drugs are those with which police officers are most commonly involved. MDA 1971, s 5(2) states that it is an offence for a person unlawfully to have a controlled drug in his possession.

Although magic mushrooms, ie fungus (of any kind) which contains psilocin or an ester of psilocin, are Class A drugs, prohibition of possession of controlled drugs does not have effect in relation to magic mushrooms where they:

(a) are growing uncultivated;

(b) are picked by a person already in lawful possession of them for delivery as soon as reasonably practicable into the custody of a person legally entitled to take custody of them and they remain in that person's possession for and in accordance with that purpose;

(c) are picked for either of the purposes specified in (d) below and are held for and in accordance with the purpose specified in (d)(ii) below, either by the picker or by another person; or

(d) are picked for the purpose specified in (d)(ii) below and are held for and in accordance with the purpose specified in (d)(i) below either by the picker or by another person.

For the purposes of (c) and (d) above, the purposes specified are:

(i) the purpose of delivering the magic mushrooms as soon as reasonably practicable into the custody of a person lawfully entitled to take custody of them; and

(ii) the purpose of destroying the magic mushrooms as soon as reasonably practicable.

Unlawful

The Misuse of Drugs Regulations 2001 specify when possession of a controlled drug is lawful. They provide that such possession is lawful if it is under the authority of a licence issued by the Secretary of State or under a doctor's, first level nurse's, nurse independent prescriber's, pharmacist's or registered midwife's prescription. In addition, a constable who comes into possession of controlled drugs in the course of his duties is in lawful possession of them, and so are carriers, postal workers, despatchers, workers in forensic laboratories who examine drugs on behalf of the police, medical personnel, ship's masters etc, in circumstances properly connected with their duties.

Possession

Physical custody of the drug is not necessary for possession but physical control over it is. It follows that a person who has bought a controlled drug is not in possession of it if it is still hidden in the seller's car or stored at the seller's home. On the other hand, a person who leaves a drug in his car or at home while he is away remains in possession of the drug since he retains physical control over it.

Possession can be joint: for example, if two people share a car which they know contains cannabis, they are both in possession of it if each shares with the other the right to control what is done with it. Moreover, MDA 1971, s 37(3) states that for the purposes of the Act the things which a person has in his possession shall be taken to include anything subject to his control which is in the custody of another. Therefore there may be a number of persons in possession of a particular controlled drug.

If a man imports cannabis and hands it to his business manager to store pending distribution, both are in possession as the drug is subject to their control. If the business manager then passes it on to the warehouseman to keep until either he or the importer send for the drug, all three are in possession of it for the purpose of the MDA 1971.

Possession cannot begin until the person with control is aware that the thing is under his control; if a drug is slipped into a person's pocket, unknown to him, he is not in possession of it. (As an exception, a person is in possession of a drug delivered to his home, even if he is unaware that it has arrived, provided it is delivered in response to a request by him.)

Knowledge of a thing's quality is not required. It follows that a mere mistake by the accused as to the quality of the thing under his control is not enough to prevent him being in possession. For example, if the accused knows that he is in control of some tablets which he believes to be aspirin (or, even sweets) but which are, in fact, heroin, he is in possession of the heroin tablets. Likewise, a divisional court has held that if the accused picks up a cigarette containing cannabis and puts it in his pocket, believing that it only contains tobacco, he is in possession of the cannabis.

In the case of drugs in a parcel, packet or other container in a person's physical control, he is in possession of those drugs if he knows that he is in control of that container and that it contains something, even though he thinks that the thing is something different in kind from a drug and even though he has no right to open the container to check its contents.

Possession, once begun, continues as long as the thing is in the person's control, even though he has forgotten about it or mistakenly believes it has been destroyed or disposed of.

Although it is not necessary to prove that a minimum or usable quantity of a controlled drug was unlawfully in the possession of the person charged he must have been in possession of a quantity of it which was visible, tangible and measurable. Persons who are found under the influence of a drug are not then in possession of it for the purposes of this offence, even though traces of it are found in a blood or urine sample. This is because, once consumed, the thing changes its character and can no longer be considered a controlled drug. However, evidence of the presence of a drug in a blood or urine sample can be given to support an allegation of possession of the drug in its true state at some earlier time, ie before it was taken into the body.

Defence

A person is not criminally liable for the unlawful possession of a controlled drug in the circumstances outlined by MDA 1971, s 5(4).

MDA 1971, s 5(4) provides that where, in any proceedings for an offence of unlawful possession contrary to MDA 1971, s 5(2), it is proved that the accused had a controlled drug in his possession it is a defence for him to prove that:

(a) knowing or suspecting it to be a controlled drug, he took possession of it for the purpose of preventing another from committing or continuing to commit an offence in connection with that drug and that as soon as possible after taking possession he took all such steps as were reasonably open to him to destroy the drug or to deliver it into the custody of a person lawfully entitled to take custody of it; or

(b) knowing or suspecting it to be a controlled drug, he took possession of it for the purpose of delivering it into the custody of a person lawfully entitled to the custody of it and that as soon as possible after taking possession of it he took all such steps as were reasonably open to him to deliver it into the custody of such a person.

The circumstances outlined at (a) would therefore cover the situation in which a mother found her child in possession of controlled drugs and took them from the child. Provided that she destroyed the drugs or handed them over to lawful custody as soon as possible, or took reasonable steps to do so, she would commit no offence. The Court of Appeal has held that concealing a controlled drug in the ground is not sufficient even though that drug may be destroyed in the course of time by the forces of nature. There must be an act of destruction. The situation outlined at (b) would cover the circumstances where a person found a bottle of amphetamine tablets in a park and took possession of the bottle to prevent the drugs from falling into the wrong hands. Once again, if steps were taken as soon as possible to hand over the drugs to lawful custody, the finder's possession would not be unlawful.

Despite the fact that MDA 1971, s 5(4) requires an accused to 'prove' a defence under it, it would seem likely from a House of Lords decision in 2001 that all an accused has to do is to adduce sufficient evidence to raise the defence, whereupon it will be for the prosecution to prove beyond reasonable doubt that the defence is not made out.

POSSESSION WITH INTENT TO SUPPLY

Offences concerned with supplying controlled drugs to another, or offering to supply such drugs, have already been discussed, but it is essential when considering drug offences to consider every stage of the movement of a controlled drug from person to person. MDA 1971, s 5(3) deals with offences of having a controlled drug in one's possession, whether lawfully or not, with intent to supply it unlawfully to another. Such an offence is one which is committed by a 'pusher' prior to his offer to supply the drug, or his actual supply of it. It fills a gap in the process of traffic in drugs. In the beginning, drugs are illegally imported or produced. They will then be possessed by any number of persons if they are stored within an organisation with knowledge on the part of a number of persons who have control over them. All will possess the drugs with intent to supply. Those who go out to peddle the drugs, the 'pushers', possess them with intent to supply them to others. Immediately they supply, or offer to supply, they commit a different offence. The persons who are supplied represent the end of the chain. They possess the drugs unlawfully for their own use.

An offence of possession with intent to supply may be committed by persons who are lawfully in possession in the first instance. For example, it can be committed by a doctor who is in possession of drugs lawfully, but has an intention to supply them unlawfully (eg merely for profit, as opposed to bona fide treatment). However, the offence is usually committed by drug pushers and the like.

A person can be convicted under MDA 1971, s 5(3) if it is proved that he was in possession of a controlled drug (whether or not it was the controlled drug specified in the charge) and that he intended to supply that substance unlawfully to another. It need not be proved that he knew the identity of the substance.

In terms of proving that possession was with intent unlawfully to supply, evidence of drug-related paraphernalia, evidence of an extravagant lifestyle and evidence of the possession of large amounts of cash *which are prima facie explicable only if derived from drug dealing* are relevant—but not conclusive—to the issue of *intent to supply* but not normally to the issue of possession. A case where such evidence might be relevant to possession, as well as to intent to supply, is where there is evidence of frequent brief visits by different young men, who then leave carrying small packages, and when the premises (whose occupant is long-term unemployed) are searched large sums of money and some drugs are found. Such evidence may be admitted as evidence that the occupant knew of the drugs and was in control of them (ie in possession) as well as of an intent to supply them. Whilst evidence in the form of documents relating to transactions and cash in the accused's possession is relevant, the relevance of the cash in the accused's possession must be related to evidence of ongoing (and not merely previous) drug transactions in order for it to be admissible. If there is a possibility that such money was in the accused's possession for a reason other than drug dealing, evidence of its possession together with drugs would not be probative of an intent to supply them. For example, where £150 was found in an ornamental kettle it was held that this was not admissible because it proved nothing in relation to a charge of possessing cannabis with intent to supply. On the other hand, where a sum of £ 16,000 and a gold necklace were found concealed beneath a cooker, it was held that the finding of a large sum of money was capable of being admissible in relation to the issue of intent to supply before the jury.

When MDA 1971, s 5(4A) to (4C), added by the Drugs Act 2005, is in force, if it is proved in any proceedings for an offence under s 5(3) that the accused had an amount of a controlled drug in his possession which is not less than an amount prescribed by regulations, the court or jury must assume that he had the drug in his possession with the intent to supply it as mentioned in s 5(3). However, this will not apply if evidence is adduced which is sufficient to raise an issue that the accused may not have had the drug in his possession with that intent.

CULTIVATION OF CANNABIS

The cultivation of cannabis is an offence. MDA 1971, s 6(2) states that it is an offence unlawfully to cultivate any plant of the genus Cannabis. The only lawful cultivation of cannabis is that authorised by a licence issued by the Secretary of State. The defence under MDA 1971, s 28 applies to an offence under s 6(2).

Cannabis plants grow quite easily in the British Isles and there are many persons now living in Great Britain who have the necessary knowledge to ensure successful cultivation of them. The word 'cultivate' indicates some form of attention to the plant during the process of its growth. A person who puts seeds in the ground cultivates, as does he who hoes, waters, prunes or generally cares for a plant during the process of its growth. It is doubtful if a person could be held to have cultivated plants merely because he failed to remove those which were growing wild but this would depend upon the circumstances. If they were deliberately preserved, by caring for the ground in which they were growing, this would amount to the type of care which could be described as cultivation. If any form of cultivation can be proved, then it merely remains for the prosecution to show that the plant was of the genus Cannabis.

MEDICAL NECESSITY

The defence of duress of circumstances is not available to an accused in relation to offences of cultivation, production or possession with intent to supply cannabis or resin, where his purpose is to alleviate pain arising from a pre-existing illness. Nor is it available to a person charged with possessing cannabis who claims that its use is for the purpose of alleviating pain and that such possession was a 'human right'.

SMOKING OF OPIUM

MDA 1971, s 9 prohibits a person from:

(a) smoking or otherwise using prepared opium; or
(b) frequenting a place used for the purpose of opium smoking; or
(c) having in his possession:
  (i) any pipes or other utensils made or adapted for use in connection with the smoking of opium, being pipes or utensils which have been used by him or with his knowledge and permission in that connection or which he intends to use or permit others to use in that connection; or
  (ii) any utensils which have been used by him or with his knowledge or permission in connection with the preparation of opium for smoking.

Offences under MDA 1971, s 9 are not common. The defence under MDA 1971, s 28 applies to an offence under s 9.

'Prepared opium' is opium prepared for smoking and includes dross and any other residue remaining after opium has been smoked.

Most of MDA 1971, s 9 is self-explanatory but further explanation must be given to the offence of frequenting.

The term 'frequenting' means to go there often. The more often a person visits a place at which opium is being smoked, the greater the presumption that he is attending that place for that purpose, in the absence of any other reasonable explanation. There is no requirement that a person who frequents a place used for opium smoking must have been shown to have been involved in opium smoking. Significant factors will be the duration and frequency of visits; the nature of the place (if it is a cafe the possibility of frequent visits being innocent increases); things which actually occurred whilst the accused was there; and his own behaviour when at or near that place. The offence is concerned with events which occur at a 'place'. That place does not need to be a building. Proof that the place is used as an opium den will be necessary.

STATUTORY DEFENCE

MDA 1971, s 28 provides a defence in relation to charges contrary to MDA 1971, s 4(2) (unlawful production), s 4(3) (unlawful supply), s 5(2) (unlawful possession), s 5(3) (possession with intent to supply), s 6(2) (unlawful cultivation of cannabis) and s 9 (smoking opium, frequenting places used for opium smoking, or possession of utensils used for opium smoking). For convenience, the defence will be explained in relation to the offence of unlawful possession but what is said will be equally applicable (with the appropriate changes of words) to the other offences just mentioned.

Assuming that the prosecution has proved that the accused was in unlawful possession of a controlled drug, he can be convicted of that offence, even though it is not proved that he knew he was in possession of a controlled drug. However, MDA 1971, s 28 provides the accused with a defence in the circumstances outlined below. Although s 28 says that the accused has to prove a defence under the section, the House of Lords held in 2001 that s 28 should be read as simply imposing an evidential burden on the accused so as to make it compatible with the presumption of innocence under art 6(2) of the European Convention on Human Rights. The result is that the accused does not have to prove a defence under s 28, despite the wording of the section. Instead, provided that sufficient evidence is adduced to raise a defence under s 28, the defence will succeed unless the prosecution proves beyond reasonable doubt that the terms of the defence are not satisfied.

The basic definition of the defence is contained in MDA 1971, s 28(2), which states that it is a defence for the accused to 'prove' that *he neither knew of, nor suspected, nor had reason to suspect* the existence of some fact alleged by the prosecution which it is necessary for the prosecution to prove if he is to be convicted of the offence charged. (This does not affect the need for the prosecution to prove the element of knowledge required to establish 'possession'.)

This provision is subject to a qualification, provided by MDA 1971, s 28(3), where the accused alleges, and 'proves', that he did not know, suspect or have reason to suspect that the thing in question was the controlled drug alleged, and proved, by the prosecution to have been involved. In this case, such 'proof' by the accused is not enough to give him a defence. In order to be acquitted he must also 'prove' one of two things:

(a)   that he neither believed nor suspected, nor had reason to suspect, that the thing in question was a controlled drug at all; or
(b)   that he believed that the thing in question was a controlled drug which he was, in fact, legally entitled to possess (or supply or produce etc as the case may be).

Paragraph (a) can be illustrated as follows: if A gives B for safekeeping a bottle of tablets which he alleges are aspirin tablets but which are in fact heroin, B will be in possession of the tablets because he is, to his knowledge, in control of the bottle (container) and knows that it contains something but he will have a defence to a charge of unlawful possession if he adduces sufficient evidence that he did not believe, suspect or have reason to suspect that the tablets were a controlled drug, and the prosecution does not disprove this. Had B been told or had reason to suspect that the bottle contained amphetamines whereas it in fact contained heroin, this would not be a defence as both are controlled drugs.

The following example demonstrates the operation of (b): if an addict is prescribed heroin and is given cocaine by mistake, he is technically in unlawful possession of the cocaine (since it has not been prescribed). If he adduces sufficient evidence that he neither knew, suspected or had reason to suspect that the thing was cocaine, and that he believed he was in possession of heroin, he will have a defence unless the prosecution disproves one or both parts of the defence.

CONTROLLED DRUGS ON PREMISES

MDA 1971, s 8 is concerned with a person who, being the occupier or concerned in the management of any premises, knowingly permits or suffers any of the following activities to take place on those premises:

(a) unlawfully producing or attempting to produce a controlled drug;
(b) unlawfully supplying or attempting to supply a controlled drug to another, or offering to supply a controlled drug unlawfully to another;
(c) preparing opium for smoking; or
(d) smoking cannabis, cannabis resin or prepared opium.

There must be proof that the conduct in (a), (b), (c) or (d) actually occurred; merely giving tacit approval in advance is insufficient.

The occupier

To be 'the occupier' a person does not have to be a tenant or have an estate in the premises. A person is the occupier of premises if he is entitled to exclusive possession of them, in the sense that he has the requisite degree of control over them to exclude from them those who might otherwise carry on one of the forbidden activities there. Thus, a student who had a room in a college hostel was held to be the occupier of it because his contractual licence gave him such exclusivity of possession, whether or not he was entitled to exclude the college authorities. If there is drug-taking in a dwelling house, and it is knowingly permitted by the householder (ie 'the occupier'), he commits an offence under MDA 1971, s 8. However, he would not commit that offence if, in his absence and unknown to him, his teenage son knowingly permits drug-taking on the premises. Nor would the son be guilty of an offence under s 8 on the basis of being 'the occupier' of the premises since he does not have that status. Nevertheless, depending on the circumstances, the son might be guilty of an offence under s 8 on the basis of 'being concerned in the management of the premises', to which phrase we now turn.

Concerned in management

To be 'concerned in the management of premises' a person need not necessarily have any legal interest in them, since the term includes anyone who is concerned in exercising control over the premises or in running or organising them on a day-to-day basis. It is possible that such a person will have some control over who shall be permitted to enter the premises and who shall not, but this is not a prerequisite for a person to be concerned in their management. If drug-taking was generally permitted on the premises of a gaming club, it is possible that only the general manager would have the right to permit entry but other officials of the club might control activities in different rooms. If drug use is generally and knowingly permitted, then all who are concerned in any way in the management of the premises (ie the general manager and other officials) would be guilty of this offence.

Persons who occupy premises as trespassers (and are therefore not 'occupiers' for the purpose of the offence) may nevertheless be concerned in the management of those premises. For example, if drug-taking activities are organised upon premises by squatters, all concerned in that organisation are guilty of the present offence.

Premises

The Act does not define the term 'premises'. The term should be given its normal, everyday meaning, and in this sense 'premises' includes any form of building and the grounds in which a building stands and also land without any building on it. Therefore, the organiser of an open air pop festival who knowingly permitted one of the activities described above would (as a person concerned in the management of the premises) be guilty of the present offence, as would the occupier of the site if he knowingly permitted one of these activities.

Knowingly permits or suffers

'Permit' and 'suffer' are synonymous. In law, a person only permits or suffers something to occur if, physically and legally, he could prevent it but does not do so. The Court of Appeal has held that 'permit' (and presumably 'suffer') require proof of unwillingness to prevent the prohibited activity, which can be inferred from failure to take reasonable steps readily available to prevent it. The fact that an accused believed that he had taken reasonable steps to prevent the prohibited activity is irrelevant.

The inclusion of the word 'knowingly' does not mean that actual knowledge that the premises were being used in the particular prohibited way must be proved since 'knowingly' also embraces wilful blindness, ie suspecting what is going on but deliberately refraining from making inquiries.

The smoking of cannabis results in a smell which is quite easily identifiable and if, at a party for instance, the occupier of the premises suspects that those assembled there are quite generally smoking cannabis but deliberately looks the other way, it is no defence for him to allege that he was not certain that cannabis was being smoked.

On a charge of permitting the premises to be used for producing or supplying a controlled drug, it is not necessary for the prosecution to prove more than that the accused 'knew' of the production or supply of a controlled drug; it need not be proved that he knew that it was the particular type of controlled drug supplied. It remains to be seen whether, on a charge of permitting the smoking of cannabis, an accused could be convicted even if he thought that cannabis resin or opium was being smoked, and so on.

Conclusion

The involvement of those in control of premises adds a further dimension to consideration of the offences which might be committed in particular circumstances. In addition to considering the passage of the controlled drug from person to person, it is necessary to consider the possible liability of the occupier or any person concerned in the management of any premises which may be involved.

POWERS

Search, seize and detain

MDA 1971, s 23(2) provides that, if a constable has reasonable grounds to suspect that any person is in possession of a controlled drug in contravention of the Act or regulations, the constable may:

(a) search that person, and detain him for the purpose of searching him;
(b) search any vehicle or vessel in which the constable suspects that the drug may be found, and for that purpose require the person in control to stop it;
(c) seize and detain, for the purpose of proceedings under MDA 1971, anything found in the course of the search which appears to the constable to be evidence of an offence under MDA 1971.

It must be emphasised that the exercise of these powers to search, seize and detain depends upon there being reasonable grounds to suspect possession of a controlled drug in contravention of the Act or regulations. It is impossible to set out a list of rules which might be applied in determining whether there is a reasonable suspicion that a person is in possession of a controlled drug. There is no general right to search persons who are found by night in areas which drug users are known to frequent. However, such circumstances, accompanied by observation of the passing of substances which have the appearance of being drugs from one person to another, could give rise to such suspicions in the minds of police officers. Reasonable suspicion may exist as a result of information received from another party; this will depend upon the reliability of the person providing the information and upon the likelihood of that information being true in all the circumstances.

The power to search a person must extend to searching things in his immediate possession, for example a suitcase or a holdall. If this was not so the power to search persons would be totally ineffective.

Search warrant

MDA 1971, s 23(3) also authorises a justice to grant a search warrant if satisfied by information on oath that there is a reasonable ground for suspecting that controlled drugs are, in contravention of the Act or any regulations, in the possession of a person on any premises, or that a document directly or indirectly relating to drug dealing is in the possession of persons on any premises. The warrant will name the particular premises, and it is only those premises (and persons in them) which may be searched on its authority. If necessary, force may be used to enter the premises.

If there is reasonable ground for suspecting that an offence has been committed in relation to any controlled drugs found on the premises or in the possession of anyone there, or that a document so found directly or indirectly relates to drug dealings, the drugs or document may be seized and detained.

A divisional court has held that, where a search warrant has been issued under both MDA 1971 and the Police and Criminal Evidence Act 1984 (PACE), the warrant refers to both persons and premises. MDA, s 23 provides the power to detain persons for the purpose of a search and PACE, s 117 provides the power to use reasonable force for the purpose of executing the warrant, including moving persons to one room while another was searched.

Additional powers of seizure

The additional powers of seizure provided by the Criminal Justice and Police Act 2001 (CJPA 2001), ss 50 and 51 apply where a search is made under the power in MDA 1971, s 23(2) or where a search warrant under s 23(3) is executed.

Closure of premises where drugs used unlawfully

The Anti-social Behaviour Act 2003, Part 1 (ss 1 to 11) provides that where a police officer not below the rank of superintendent has reasonable grounds for believing that, within the previous three months, premises have been used in connection with the unlawful use, production or supply of a *Class A controlled drug* and that the use of the premises is associated with the occurrence of disorder or serious nuisance to members of the public, the officer may, if satisfied that the local authority has been consulted, and that reasonable steps have been taken to identify any person who lives on the premises or who has control or responsibility for or an interest in the premises, issue a closure notice. The closure notice must give appropriate details and state when and where an application for a magistrates' closure order will be considered. When such a notice is served (by fixing notices to the building and serving copies upon relevant persons) it closes the premises to all members of the public except the owner or those who habitually reside there, until such time as a magistrates' court decides whether to issue a closure order. The court must hear the application within forty-eight hours. It may make a closure order only if satisfied that the premises in question have been used in connection with the unlawful use, production or supply of a Class A drug, that the use of the premises is associated with the occurrence of disorder or serious nuisance to members of the public, and that the making of a closure order is necessary to prevent the occurrence of such disorder or serious nuisance for the period of the order. If an order is made it prohibits entry to the premises by anyone for the period of the order.

The appropriate standard of proof in relation to such a closure order is the civil standard of proof, that is the balance of probabilities.

The maximum period for a closure order is three months, with a possibility of extension to a maximum of six months. The court may adjourn the proceedings for up to fourteen days to permit representations and may order that the existing notice continues in force during this period.

It is an offence contrary to s 4 for a person to remain on or enter premises subject to a closure notice without reasonable excuse, or to obstruct a constable serving a closure notice or enforcing an order, or to remain on or enter premises subject to a closure order without reasonable excuse.

Obstruction of a constable

It is an offence intentionally to obstruct a person in the execution of his powers to search under MDA 1971, s 23; or to conceal documents, drugs etc from such a person;

or to fail without reasonable excuse to produce such documents or books where the production is demanded by a person in the exercise of his powers under s 23.

Evidence—disclosure of site of observation posts

Where the police use hidden observation posts in an area where drug dealing is prevalent, the police officers concerned can refuse to answer questions about the location of those observation posts. There is no essential difference between informers and the providers of observation posts as both provide indispensable assistance in the detection of crime.

Entrapment

In order to prove that certain persons are supplying drugs, in situations in which it has proved difficult, if not impossible, to obtain evidence in any other way, undercover police operations have been mounted in an effort to secure the supply of drugs to an undercover officer. The issue of 'entrapment' in these circumstances has been considered by the House of Lords. It said that criminal proceedings might be stayed or evidence might be excluded under PACE, s 78, where there was evidence of entrapment. Usually, the proceedings would be stayed. The House said that the issue was whether the crime was 'state created' in that a person had been lured into doing something which he would not otherwise have done. However, where police conduct amounted to no more than might have been expected from any other person in those circumstances it should not be regarded as inciting or instigating crime. Proportionality must be considered. In the end it was a matter of whether police conduct was so seriously improper as to bring the administration of justice into disrepute.

TRAVEL RESTRICTIONS ON DRUG TRAFFICKING OFFENDERS

CJPA 2001, s 33 empowers a court to make a 'travel restriction order' where a person has been convicted of a drug trafficking offence and he is sentenced to four years' or more imprisonment. Such an order prohibits the offender from leaving the United Kingdom at any time after his release from prison until such date as is set out in the order (not less than two years). An order may contain a direction that his passport must be surrendered and it is an offence to fail to comply with a direction to do so. It is an offence to leave the United Kingdom while subject to a travel restriction. A person subject to such an order may apply for a suspension (which can only be granted in exceptional circumstances based on compassionate grounds). It is an offence not to be in the United Kingdom at a time when such a suspension ends.

The person affected by the travel restriction order may apply for its revocation at any time after the 'minimum period'. The 'minimum period' is two years, where the restriction was for a period of four years or less; four years for a restriction between four years and ten years; and five years in any other case.

For the purposes of CJPA 2001, s 33 a 'drug trafficking offence' means any of the following offences (including one committed by aiding, abetting, counselling and procuring of such offences):

(a) production and supply of controlled drugs: MDA 1971, s 4(2) or (3);
(b) assisting in or inducing commission outside United Kingdom of an offence punishable under a corresponding law: MDA 1971, s 20;
(c) any offence designated by order of the Secretary of State;
(d) improper importation, exportation or fraudulent evasion contrary to Customs and Excise Management Act 1979 in connection with any prohibition or restriction on importation or exportation of a controlled drug;
(e) conspiracy to commit any of the above offences: Criminal Law Act 1977, s 1;
(f) attempting to commit any of the above offences: Criminal Attempts Act 1981, s 1;
(g) inciting another person to commit any such offence: MDA 1971, s 19 or common law offence of incitement.

GLUE-SNIFFING

It is an offence, contrary to the Intoxicating Substances (Supply) Act 1985, for a person to supply, or offer to supply, a substance other than a controlled drug:

(a) to a person under eighteen whom he knows, or has reasonable cause to believe, to be under that age; or
(b) to a person who is acting on behalf of someone under eighteen, and whom he knows, or has reasonable cause to believe, to be so acting,

if he knows or has reasonable cause to believe that the substance is, or its fumes are, likely to be inhaled by the person under eighteen for the purpose of causing intoxication. Cigarette lighter fuel is such a substance.

It is a defence for a person who supplies or offers to supply such a substance to show that at the material time he was under eighteen and was not acting in the course or furtherance of a business.

CHAPTER 37

Theft and related offences, robbery and blackmail

THEFT

The Theft Act 1968 (TA 1968), s 1(1) provides:

A person is guilty of theft if he dishonestly appropriates property belonging to another with the intention of permanently depriving the other of it; and 'thief' and 'steal' shall be construed accordingly.

By TA 1968, s 30, the leave of the Director of Public Prosecutions is required for the institution of proceedings for the theft by one spouse or civil partner of the other's property, unless, by virtue of any judicial decree or order, the spouses were not obliged to cohabit at the material time or an order is in force providing for the separation of the civil partners, as the case may be.

Theft is a 'penalty offence' for the purposes of the Criminal Justice and Police Act 2001, Part 1 and may be dealt with by a police officer under a fixed penalty procedure: see p 874. This may be an appropriate course of action in minor cases, such as low-level shoplifting.

When one considers theft, it is usual to imagine the thief stealing so that he will benefit in some material way but this is not essential. TA 1968, s 1(2) states that it is immaterial whether the appropriation is made with a view to gain, or is made for the thief's own benefit. Thus, a postman who flushes postal packets down the lavatory to avoid delivering them, or who takes them to give to his son, is as guilty of theft as if he had taken them for his own benefit. The terms of the definition of theft in s 1(1) are defined, in whole or part, by TA 1968, ss 2 to 6.

For the purposes of exposition, it is best to start by noting that to be guilty of theft the accused must be proved:

(a) to have appropriated property belonging to another (the actus reus); and
(b) to have done so dishonestly and with the intention of permanently depriving the other of it (the mens rea).

Appropriation

TA 1968, s 3(1) describes appropriation in the following way:

Any assumption by a person of the rights of an owner amounts to an appropriation, and this includes, where he has come by the property (innocently or not) without stealing it, any later assumption of a right to it by keeping or dealing with it as owner.

The essence of this definition is an 'assumption of the rights of an owner'. An owner of property has many rights in relation to it, including the rights to use it, to destroy it, to give it away, to sell it, and so on. The House of Lords has held that, despite the use of the words 'the rights' at the beginning of TA 1968, s 3(1), s 3, as a whole, indicates that an appropriation does not require an assumption of all the rights of an owner and that it is enough that there has been an assumption of any of the rights of the owner. This conclusion does violence to the clear words of the section but it must now be regarded as representing the correct interpretation of the words in question. We shall see later on that it is possible to steal from a person who is not the owner but to whom the property 'belongs' for the purposes of theft and that an owner can steal his own property. Presumably, 'the owner' in the House of Lords' formulation must be read as 'the person to whom the property belongs' where the alleged theft is not from the owner.

The House of Lords has ruled that an act amounting to an assumption of a right of the owner done with the authority or consent of the owner can amount to an appropriation of goods for the purposes of TA 1968. In the case in question, the accused had been employed as an assistant manager at a shop trading in electrical goods. An acquaintance asked him to supply goods from the shop and accept payment by two stolen building society cheques. The accused agreed, prepared a list of goods and sought authority from his manager to release the goods. The manager agreed provided that the accused confirmed with the bank that the cheques were good. He alleged that he had done so. After the goods were released the cheques were returned endorsed, 'Orders not to pay—stolen cheque'. On these facts, the House of Lords held that the accused had properly been convicted of theft. In this case, the authority or consent was obtained by a deception, but the House of Lords has held that the result would be the same where the authority or consent was not so obtained.

The House of Lords also stated in the above case that it was irrelevant that what had happened might also have constituted an offence of obtaining property by deception. It also endorsed a previous decision of the House which affirmed that, where a taxi driver had dishonestly taken £6 from an Italian visitor's wallet, in addition to the £1 already proffered for a 10s and 6d (52.5 pence) journey, an appropriation could occur in such circumstances even though the owner had permitted or consented to the property being taken.

A pickpocket who takes someone's wallet clearly appropriates it. An appropriation can occur even though the assumption is only momentary. It has been held, for example, that there was an appropriation where a man wrested a bag from a woman's grasp, even though he then dropped it on the ground and did not make off with it. It remains to be decided whether the mere taking hold of a wallet, handbag or other article by a pickpocket or the like in order to take it constitutes an appropriation; if it is not it is certainly an attempt and could lead to a conviction for attempted theft.

A shopper who removes goods from a shelf in a supermarket and conceals them in his shopping bag thereby appropriates them (because this amounts to an assumption of one of the rights of the owner of the goods), and so does someone who simply puts goods in a supermarket basket without concealing them. In both cases, however, the person concerned would not be guilty of theft if he intended to pay at the checkout because he would not appropriate the goods dishonestly.

A fairly common practice among the dishonest is to switch the price labels on articles in a shop or supermarket, so that a lesser price than the true price is paid at the cash desk. This amounts to an assumption of the rights of the owner, and therefore to an appropriation.

There can be an appropriation by a person even though he never possesses the property concerned, as where, pretending to be the owner, he points to another's car and offers to sell it (because the right to sell is one of the rights of the owner and he has assumed that right). On the other hand, the Court of Appeal has held, a person who has never had possession or control of property but who deceives his victim into transferring it to a third party does not thereby appropriate it.

There may also be an appropriation through an innocent agent. If a person in authority signs a false invoice, intending that innocent people take further steps which result in money being debited and thus appropriated from a bank account, he is guilty of theft.

Appropriation by those already in possession

As already implied, a person can appropriate property even though he is already in possession or control of it. This is made clear by the latter part of TA 1968, s 3(1), which provides that 'appropriation' 'includes, where the accused has come by the property (innocently or not) without stealing it, any later assumption of a right to it by keeping or dealing with it as owner'. It follows that a shop assistant who knowingly sells goods at less than the marked price thereby appropriates them because she has assumed the owner's right to fix the price. Likewise, a watch repairer, who sells a watch left with him for repair, thereby appropriates it because he assumes the owner's right to sell. Another example would be where a person hires a car and later decides to sell it. When he sells, or—even—offers to sell, it to another, he thereby appropriates the car because he assumes the right of the owner to sell it.

An important aspect of the latter part of TA 1968, s 3(1) is that it can lead to the conviction of a person who originally came by the property dishonestly without stealing it. Suppose that X helps himself to Y's umbrella in order to go out during a shower but intending to return it. X does not steal the umbrella at that stage because, although he has appropriated it, he did not then intend permanently to deprive Y. However, if X subsequently decides to keep the umbrella or to sell it, and does so, he is then guilty of theft because his later assumption of a right to it by keeping or dealing with it as owner constitutes an appropriation which is accompanied by an intent permanently to deprive Y.

Where property is obtained by deception

Where a man obtains property by deception, he will, at the time of writing, be guilty of obtaining property by deception (see below) as soon as he obtains the money; and when the Fraud Act 2006, s 1 is in force he will be guilty instead of the offence of fraud as soon as he makes his false representation. However, the House of Lords has held that a person who obtains property by deception thereby appropriates it. A charge of obtaining the property by deception will be more appropriate than theft where both offences have been committed.

An express exception

TA 1968, s 3(2) excludes a particular type of case, which falls within the definition in s 3(1), from being an appropriation. It provides that 'where property or a right or interest in property is or purports to be *transferred for value* to a person *acting in good faith*, no later assumption by him of rights which he believed himself to be acquiring shall, by reason of any defect in the transferor's title, amount to theft of the property'. The effect of the subsection is that, if A steals goods from B and sells them to C who neither knows nor suspects that they are stolen, a refusal by C to restore the goods (or his actual disposal of them) after his discovery of the theft by A is not theft by him from B.

Property

'Property' is defined by TA 1968, s 4(1) as including money and all other property, real or personal, including things in action and other intangible property.

'Real property' means land and things forming part of the land, such as plants and buildings. Although land and things forming part of the land are 'property' for the purposes of theft; there are special provisions restricting the theft of them, which are dealt with later.

'Personal property', in its tangible sense, means movable things which can be owned, such as cars, cheque books and television sets.

A 'thing in action' is intangible property. It is a right to sue, and its inclusion in the definition of 'property' means that someone who dishonestly assumes rights (or a right) of ownership over a thing in action, such as a debt, copyright or trade mark, with the intention of permanently depriving the person entitled to it, is guilty of theft. Thus, if A dishonestly assigns to B a debt owed to A and his partner, C, in order to defeat C's rights, A is guilty of the theft of a thing in action belonging to C. Where a bank account is in credit the bank owes a debt to its customer for the amount of that credit. Consequently, if X dishonestly draws cheques on Y's account and uses the proceeds for his own purposes, he can be convicted of the theft of property belonging to Y because he will have appropriated a thing in action (the debt) owned by Y when he presents the cheque.

'Other intangible property' covers such things as gas stored in pipes, which is undoubtedly capable of being stolen, and patents.

Despite the wide terms of TA 1968, s 4(1), there are some things which do not, or may not, come within the definition and hence cannot be stolen. A live human body is not property because it can never be owned. The same is true in relation to a human corpse. However, where a body (or part of a body) has undergone a process or other application of human skill (such as embalming or dissecting) for exhibition or teaching purposes it becomes property for the purposes of s 4. In addition, there have been convictions in magistrates' courts for the theft of the products of the human body, such as hair and urine specimens.

It has been held that confidential information, such as a trade secret or the contents of an examination paper, is not property for the purposes of theft, so that the mere abstraction of the information is not theft, and it has also been held that electricity is not property for such purposes and cannot be stolen. There is, however, a separate offence of abstracting electricity, which we deal with later in this chapter.

Land and things forming part of the land

TA 1968, s 4(2) provides that:

A person cannot steal land, or things forming part of land and severed from it by him or by his directions, except in the following cases, that is to say:

(a) when he is a trustee or personal representative, or is authorised by power of attorney, or as liquidator of a company, or otherwise, to sell or dispose of land belonging to another, and he appropriates the land or anything forming part of it by dealing with it in breach of the confidence reposed in him; or

(b) when he is not in possession of the land and appropriates anything forming part of the land by severing it or causing it to be severed, or after it has been severed; or

(c) when, being in possession of the land under a tenancy, he appropriates the whole or any part of any fixture or structure let to be used with the land.

TA 1968, s 4(3) goes on to provide:

A person who picks mushrooms growing wild on any land, or who picks flowers, fruit or foliage from a plant growing wild on any land, does not (although not in possession of the land) steal what he picks, unless he does it for reward or for sale or other commercial purposes.

For the purposes of the subsection 'mushroom' includes any fungus and 'plant' includes any shrub or tree.

These complex provisions can be explained as follows:

(A) Land as a whole cannot be stolen except where the appropriator is of a defined class and acts in a defined way. The class of appropriators comprises a trustee or personal representative, or a person authorised by power of attorney, or as a liquidator of a company, or otherwise, to sell or dispose of land belonging to another. The defined mode of appropriation is dealing with the land in breach of the confidence reposed in him. The essence of the offence lies in the dishonest breach of a confidence placed in a person who enjoys a position of trust in relation to the land. As with theft offences generally, this disposition of property does not have to be to the benefit of the trustee etc who causes that disposition. The result of the rule that land as a whole cannot be stolen except by a trustee etc is that a person cannot steal land as a whole by moving a boundary fence or by occupying it as a squatter, although there could not be stronger examples of assumption of ownership rights. However, it is generally considered that these types of conduct, the former of which is not common today, are better dealt with by civil process.

(B) Things forming part of the land, such as soil, houses, bricks in a wall and fixtures, can only be stolen in the following cases:

  (1) As for land as a whole, by the defined persons in the defined way.

  (2) Where a person not in possession of the land appropriates the thing by severing it or causing it to be severed. If a trespasser digs up peat, turves or gravel, removes tiles or bricks from a building, digs up flowers or other growing things, picks flowers from a cultivated plant, cuts hay, or cuts down trees or saws off their branches, or causes such severance to be done, he may be convicted of theft (although in many cases it may be more appropriate to charge him with, and convict him of, criminal damage).

The present provision does not apply to the picking of *wild* mushrooms or fungi nor to picking *from wild* plants and the like. Such conduct is dealt with by TA 1968, s 4(3), as follows. First, the picking of wild mushrooms or other fungi by a person not in possession of the land cannot amount to theft (although clearly there has been a severance) unless it is done for reward or for sale or other commercial purpose. Second, where a person not in possession of the land picks flowers, fruit or foliage from a plant, shrub or tree growing wild, this cannot amount to theft (although, again, there has been a severance) unless the picking is done for reward or for sale or other commercial purpose.

The practice of wild mushroom gathering is therefore declared to be incapable of amounting to theft if it is done by a person who picks the mushrooms for his own use. It would be different if the mushroom picker arrived with a van and collected mushrooms on a large scale so that they might be sold in the local market. The same considerations apply to flowers, fruit or foliage. The person who picks buttercups or gathers elderberries, blackberries or wild apples, cannot be convicted of stealing them if this is not done for a commercial purpose. At Christmas time, many people pick a few sprigs of holly growing wild in the country. This cannot amount to theft, but it could if done for a commercial purpose (eg to sell it in the market). The term 'pick from' does not include uprooting, which is a clear case of severance covered by TA 1968, s 4(2)(b) and unaffected by TA 1968, s 4(3). In the same way, sawing the top off a Christmas tree is not 'picking from' it and the case is covered by s 4(2)(b) and not s 4(3).

As Christmas approaches, police officers become increasingly involved in the protection of growing things which are a traditional part of Christmas decorations. Vehicles carrying Christmas trees should be accompanied by delivery notes issued by the Forestry Commission or the landowner in question. If they are not, there is reason to suspect that the trees have been stolen.

Before leaving this area, it should be noted that a person who gathers or plucks any part of a 'protected' wild plant without uprooting thereby commits an offence under the Wildlife and Countryside Act 1981, s 13. These matters are discussed in Chapter 22, above.

(3) Generally, a person in possession of land under a tenancy cannot steal things forming part of the land. Thus, he cannot be convicted of theft if he digs up a plant on the land, or uproots a plant, or picks blackberries from wild plants on the land in order to sell them. The only exception relates to the whole or part of any structure or fixture let to be used with the land; such is stealable by the tenant. The obvious example of a 'structure' is a building but the term also includes a wall or bridge. A 'fixture' is an article, such as a washbasin or fireplace, which is attached to the land or to a building so as to make a permanent improvement to the land or building; by law it becomes part of the land.

The result of all this is that a tenant may be convicted of theft if he demolishes the garage on the land of which he is a tenant, or if he removes a fireplace there in order to sell it.

For the purposes of the above, a person is in possession under a tenancy regardless of whether the tenancy is a lease for 999 years or a weekly tenancy, and also if he is in possession merely under an agreement for such a tenancy. In addition, he must be treated as being in possession under a tenancy if he remains as a statutory tenant after the end of his tenancy.

Of course, once a thing has been severed from the land it ceases to be part of the land and may thereafter be the subject of theft in the same way as any other piece of personal property, which it has become. In other words, the special provisions of TA 1968, s 4(2) and (3) no longer apply to it.

Wild creatures

TA 1968, s 4(4) states that wild creatures, whether tamed or untamed, are to be regarded as property, but that a person cannot steal a wild creature, not tamed or ordinarily kept in captivity, or the carcass of any such creature, unless either it has been reduced into possession by or on behalf of another person and possession of it has not since been lost or abandoned or another person is in course of reducing it into possession.

This appears to be complex at first but it is more easily understood if it is borne in mind that, while they are alive, wild creatures which are neither tamed nor ordinarily kept in captivity are not owned by anyone, but on being killed or taken they become the property of the owner of the land on which they are killed or taken, or, if he has granted the sporting rights to someone else, the grantee of those rights.

A wild rabbit or pheasant, not tamed nor ordinarily kept in captivity, is not owned by anyone. A captured lion (undoubtedly a wild creature) which is kept in a zoo is in a different position. It is owned by the owner of the zoo. A peregrine falcon flying free is not owned by anyone, but if it has been caught and is kept in captivity, being trained for the purpose of falconry, it now has an owner. Homing pigeons are wild birds but have for years been bred in captivity. They are owned and even when released to fly freely they remain in the possession of the owner if they are trained to return to him. The position is different with bees which can hardly be said to be tamed or ordinarily kept in captivity. Bees kept in a hive are owned and possessed by the person keeping the hive but remain so only while they are in his sight and can be followed by him. If they swarm on land to which he has no access, they are no longer in his ownership or possession. These common law rules are based upon common sense; if bees escape and swarm in a person's house, that person may have cause to destroy them and would risk prosecution if they were still owned or possessed by someone else.

The Theft Act 1968 recognises these points, by declaring that wild creatures, tamed or untamed, are property and can therefore be stolen, except that untamed wild creatures which are not ordinarily kept in captivity (or their carcasses) can only be stolen in the circumstances outlined at the end of TA 1968, s 4(4).

These are:

(a) where the wild creature has been reduced into possession by or on behalf of another (in which case it remains stealable so long as possession is not subsequently lost or abandoned); or

(b) where another person is in the course of reducing the wild creature into possession.

Thus, it is not theft to poach game on another's land unless, for instance, the game is taken from a trap set by another, even another poacher (because another is in the course of reducing into possession), or from a sack into which another has put the product of his own shooting (because there has been a reduction into possession by another).

The term 'reduced into possession by or on behalf of another' in TA 1968, s 4(4) covers the shooting and taking of game by a gamekeeper on his master's behalf. If he shoots and takes the game, it is reduced into his master's possession and therefore the gamekeeper himself can be convicted of theft if he subsequently appropriates it.

If wild creatures are taken and kept alive in some place of confinement, for example in net traps set by poachers, they are temporarily reduced into possession, but if they are released to resume their free state, or escape, that possession ceases. Thus, for example, although it may be theft to shoot and take these creatures whilst in the net it would not be so to shoot them as they ran away after being released by someone else, because possession of them would have been 'lost or abandoned'.

Although TA 1968, s 4(4) means that poachers are not normally thieves, there are other offences, mentioned in Chapter 23, which they commit.

Belonging to another

The offence of theft requires that the property appropriated should belong to another when appropriated.

The basic rule

TA 1968, s 5(1) states that property shall be regarded as belonging to any person having possession or control of it, or having in it any proprietary right or interest (not being an equitable interest arising only from an agreement to transfer or grant an interest).

The question of whether the property appropriated belonged to some other person causes no problems in the vast majority of cases. If a wallet is taken from X's pocket it quite clearly belongs to X, since he will almost certainly be its owner (and complete ownership is the clearest example of a proprietary right) and, anyway, it will be in his possession. If goods are taken from a shop they clearly belong to the proprietor of the shop for the same reasons. When there are joint owners of property, one of them will steal from the other if he dishonestly assumes one of the rights of the owner, because the property will also belong to the other co-owner under TA 1968, s 5(1).

A man who takes his radio to a repairer still owns it and therefore it still belongs to him. The repairer now has possession of the radio and if it is then handed to one of his assistants to effect the repair, that assistant has control of it. The radio can now be stolen from either the owner, the repairer or his assistant, and it can be stolen by one of these from the other. For example, if the assistant takes the radio to the pub at lunchtime and sells it, he thereby appropriates property *belonging to another* (to the owner and to the repairer, since the radio is technically still in the repairer's possession). Likewise, if the owner sneaks into the repairer's shop and takes away the radio without paying for the repair he appropriates property belonging to another. A person (A) who lets to another (B) a television set or a motor car thereby parts with possession of it to that other but retains ownership of it. It follows that if B appropriates the thing (eg by unauthorisedly selling it to C) he will have appropriated property *belonging to another*, and so will A if he appropriates it during the hire period (eg by removing it back to his own premises contrary to the hiring agreement).

A person who loses property nevertheless still retains ownership of it, and he also retains possession until the property comes into the possession of another. Thus, 'lost property' is still capable of being stolen. This must be contrasted with the situation where the property has been abandoned. When a person throws away his old bicycle, not caring what happens to it (ie he abandons it), he loses ownership and possession of it. Since the property has no owner or possessor, it cannot thereafter be stolen. It would be different if the owner placed his cycle behind a hedge because the tyre had punctured and travelled the remainder of his journey by bus. In these circumstances the property is not abandoned because the owner cares about what may happen to the bicycle, and it therefore still belongs to him.

Property subject to a trust

Where property is subject to a trust, it is regarded as belonging to the beneficiaries (who have a proprietary interest in it) as well as to the trustees, with the result that trustees who appropriate trust property can be convicted of stealing it from the beneficiaries. There are two exceptions to this.

First, the beneficial interest of a beneficiary under one type of trust, a constructive trust, may not always be a sufficient proprietary interest under TA 1968, s 5(1). Consequently, there cannot always be a theft of the trust property, as against him.

Second, charitable trusts and certain other types of trust do not, in law, have beneficiaries, with the result that under TA 1968, s 5(1) the trust property belongs only to the trustees. To prevent trust property being unprotected in such a case against appropriations by the trustees, TA 1968, s 5(2) provides that, where property is subject to a trust, the persons to whom it belongs shall be regarded as including any person having a right to enforce the trust, and that an intention to defeat the trust shall be regarded accordingly as an intention to deprive of the property any person having that right. In the case of a charitable trust, the Attorney-General, although not a beneficiary, has the right to enforce the trust, so that appropriation of a charitable trust fund by the trustees is capable of amounting to theft since the fund belongs to the Attorney-General under s 5(2).

Property received under an obligation to retain and deal with it in a particular way

TA 1968, s 5(3) provides that, where a person receives property from or on account of another and is under an *obligation* (ie a legal obligation) to the other to *retain* and *deal* with that property, or *its* proceeds, *in a particular way*, the property or proceeds shall be regarded (as against him) as belonging to the other. Section 5(3) makes it clear that where a person has received property in accordance with its terms, that property or its proceeds (ie things into which it has been converted) is regarded (as against the recipient) as belonging to another for the purposes of theft, even though ownership, possession and control of the property may have been transferred to the recipient.

The essence of TA 1968, s 5(3) is that property (usually money) or its proceeds is regarded (as against the accused) as belonging to another from or on whose account the accused has received the property if the accused is under a *legal obligation* to that person *to retain and deal* with the property or its proceeds *in a particular way*. Section 5(3) is clearly satisfied where D receives money from P which he is legally obliged to P to use in a particular way (eg to pay it into a Christmas Club which D runs), or where D is legally obliged to P to use in a particular way the proceeds of money received from P (eg to use the money to buy some goods for P). In the latter case, both the money and the goods (its proceeds) will belong to another under s 5(3). Section 5(3) is also satisfied if a shop assistant receives money from a customer for some of his employer's goods, since he has received the money on account of another (the employer) and is under a legal obligation to deal with it in a particular way (to put it in the till). If D or the shop assistant dishonestly appropriates the property in question with intent permanently to deprive, theft is committed. On the other hand, s 5(3) is not satisfied where an employee receives money from a customer for goods which (contrary to his employer's instructions) he is selling on his own account since the money is not received from or on account of another person to whom the employee is legally obliged to retain and deal with it in a particular way.

Property got by another's mistake

TA 1968, s 5(4) states that:

where a person gets property by another's mistake, and is under an obligation to make restoration (in whole or in part) of the property or its proceeds or of the value thereof, then to the extent of that obligation the property or proceeds shall be regarded (as against him) as belonging to the person entitled to restoration, and an intention not to make restoration shall be regarded accordingly as an intention to deprive that person of the property or proceeds.

The important point about this provision is that it only applies where the recipient of property transferred under a mistake is thereby under an immediate legal obligation to restore it (or its proceeds or value). For practical purposes, this provision is only of importance where the recipient was ignorant of the mistake when he got the property and he has acquired ownership, possession and control of the property to the exclusion of anyone else. If he was aware of the mistake when he got the property he could be convicted of theft on the basis that his appropriation at that time was accompanied by mens rea. On the other hand, if the recipient only discovers the mistake later, but decides not to return the property his appropriation with mens rea will be of property which is then in his ownership, possession and control. Section 5(4) provides that if the recipient is under a legal obligation to restore the property, its proceeds or value, the property is regarded (as against him) as belonging to the person entitled to restoration. The best example of a case of a legal obligation to make restoration, where a person has received ownership, possession and control of property under a mistake, is where there is a transfer of money under a mistake which leads the transferor to believe that the transferee is legally entitled to the money. Thus, if A, by a mistake as to the number of hours of overtime worked, overpays his employee, B, and B, realising the mistake, appropriates the excess amount, B has appropriated money which by s 5(4) belongs to another. The same would be true if the excess payment was made by a cheque (since B would be obliged to make restoration of it to A); if B appropriates the cheque he will appropriate property belonging to another under s 5(4). Likewise, if B cashes the cheque and appropriates the cash received, he will appropriate property belonging to another under s 5(4) because the cash will be the proceeds of the cheque and B would be obliged to make restoration of it to A. On the other hand, if A is induced to give C some money as a gift by a self-induced mistaken belief that C is collecting for charity, C cannot be convicted of theft if he appropriates it later on discovering A's mistake because, the requirements of s 5(4) not having been fulfilled, the money will not belong to another (ie other than C) when C appropriates it.

Property of a corporation sole

TA 1968, s 5 contains one other provision, s 5(5), which can be disposed of briefly. Section 5(5) provides that the property of a 'corporation sole', such as a bishop or the Treasury Solicitor, shall be regarded as belonging to the corporation notwithstanding a vacancy in the corporation. Thus, the property of a bishopric 'belongs to another', and is therefore capable of being stolen, even though the bishop has just died and not yet been replaced by a successor.

Dishonesty

The appropriation of property belonging to another must be committed dishonestly.

The question of dishonesty is one of fact for the jury in the Crown Court and not of law for the judge, subject to the provisions of TA 1968, s 2(1) which expressly and as a matter of law exclude appropriations carried out with certain states of mind from being dishonest. Section 2(1) provides:

A person's appropriation of property belonging to another is *not* to be regarded as dishonest:

(a) if he appropriates the property in the belief that he has in law the right to deprive the other of it, on behalf of himself or a third person; or

(b) if he appropriates the property in the belief that he would have had the other's consent if the other knew of the appropriation and the circumstances of it; or

(c) (except where the property came to him as a trustee or personal representative) if he appropriates the property in the belief that the person to whom the property belongs cannot be discovered by taking reasonable steps.

These provisions are concerned with the accused's belief. It is legally irrelevant that a belief in this context is unreasonable, although, of course, magistrates or a jury are less inclined to accept an alleged belief as truly held if it is an unreasonable one.

Belief in legal right to deprive

By TA 1968, s 2(1)(a), the element of dishonesty is excluded if a person appropriating property belonging to another genuinely believed that he had a right in law to deprive the other of it, whether on behalf of himself or a third person. If his belief is genuine, it is immaterial that there is no legal reason for him to have such a belief or that it is unreasonable, for we are considering what motivated him to do the act, not how other people look upon it. A husband who genuinely believes that he has a legal right to sell his wife's car on the grounds that he considered that her property became his on marriage does not act dishonestly. If a person is owed money and in order to recover that money from his debtor he threatens him with a knife, this will not be theft if he truly believes that he has a legal right to deprive the other of property, even though he recognises that he should not use a knife.

TA 1968, s 2(1)(a) is limited to cases where the accused believes that 'he has in law the right to deprive'. Where a person acts under a belief in a moral right to deprive, the question of his dishonesty depends on certain tests which are described below.

Belief that the 'owner' would have consented if he had known

The exemption provided by TA 1968, s 2(1)(b) is a sensible one as it is quite possible for friends and neighbours to have the type of relationship which permits free usage of their respective personal possessions. The essence of this exemption is a belief that the person to whom the property belongs would have consented if he had known of the appropriation and its circumstances. A person may believe that his friend would consent to him taking a bottle of wine from his cellar for his own use, but he is less likely to believe the friend would consent if he takes it to sell it because he needs money. The circumstances surrounding the taking are different.

Belief that the 'owner' cannot be discovered by taking reasonable steps

The provisions of TA 1968, s 2(1)(c) are primarily, although not exclusively, concerned with those who find property belonging to another. As with the other provisions in s 2(1), they exempt the accused from dishonesty if he appropriated another's property under a genuine belief (whether reasonable or not) in a particular state of affairs, in this case that the person to whom the property belongs cannot be discovered by taking reasonable steps. The question is not whether the 'owner' could not be found by taking reasonable steps, but whether the accused believed this, but, of course, whether or not the owner could have been so found is of evidential importance in terms of the credibility of an alleged belief that he could not be so found.

If a person finds a £5 note in the street and appropriates it, it will be almost impossible to disprove a claim by him that he believed the owner could not be found by taking reasonable steps (since it would be very rare for the serial number of the note to have been recorded by the person who lost it). It will be different if the note is contained in a purse bearing the owner's name and address (or containing other material identifying the owner): in that case it will be much easier to disprove a claimed belief that the owner could not be found by taking reasonable steps.

The exemption is not restricted to things which are found. Suppose that A's friend, on emigrating, left property under A's care until he should return to this country. If, after many years, during which A has not heard from his friend, A sells the property, honestly believing that he will not return and that he could not be traced by taking reasonable steps, A will not be guilty of theft.

TA 1968, s 2(1)(c) expressly does not apply to a person who received the property as a trustee of property or a personal representative. This is sensible in view of the special obligations of such a person.

Dishonesty in a general sense

The negative definition of dishonesty in TA 1968, s 2(1) is only a partial definition; consequently, an accused's appropriation may not have been made dishonestly even though the case falls outside s 2(1). Whether or not an accused who appropriated property with some alleged state of mind other than one of the three referred to in s 2(1) did so dishonestly is a question of fact for the jury. This means that, unlike the situation in which a belief of the type referred to in s 2(1) is pleaded (where the judge must tell the jury that in law an appropriation with such a belief is not dishonest), it is not for the judge to tell the jury whether or not an appropriation with the alleged state of mind is dishonest but for the jury to decide this according to the following two-stage test.

In deciding this, the jury must first see whether, given his state of mind, the accused's actions were dishonest according to the ordinary standards of reasonable and honest people. If his actions were not dishonest according to those standards, the matter ends there and the prosecution fails. However, if his actions were dishonest by those standards, the jury must go on to decide whether the accused must have realised that what he was doing would be considered dishonest according to the standards of reasonable and honest people. If he did not realise this, his appropriation will not have been dishonest; if he did it will have been.

Where a theft charge is tried in a magistrates' court the above tests are, of course, applicable and are applied by the justices.

What has been said about dishonesty so far can be brought together as follows. X is charged with the theft of £10 taken from the till of the shop in which he is employed. If, at his trial, X pleads that his employer owed him £10 and he (X) believed that he was legally entitled to deprive the employer of the £10 taken in order to recoup his debt, the trial judge (assuming a Crown Court trial) must tell the jury that—as a matter of law (s 2(1))—X's alleged belief prevents his appropriation being dishonest and that they must acquit X unless the alleged belief is disproved. The same would be the case if X pleaded that he believed the employer would have consented to the taking if he had known of it and its circumstances.

Suppose, on the other hand, that X admits that he knew he had no legal right to the £10 and that he knew the employer would not have consented to his taking it, but claims instead that he took the money to tide him over to pay day, intending to put in £10 from his pay packet, and claims that what he did was a common practice in the shop. Here, X is not pleading one of the beliefs in s 2(1) and the trial judge must tell the jury that, if they do not find that X's claim that he intended to repay has been disproved by the prosecution, they must decide whether or not—given that intention—his appropriation was dishonest and must do so by applying the two-fold test referred to above.

For the sake of completeness, it should be mentioned that TA 1968, s 2(2) says what has already been implied, by providing that an appropriation *may* be dishonest notwithstanding that the person concerned intends to pay for what he took. If a collector fails to purchase a valuable antique at an auction, his appropriation would almost certainly be found to be dishonest if he took the antique from the home of the successful bidder and left money in payment, even if that money represented a reasonable purchase price. It has been judicially held that an appropriation can be dishonest even though the original owner of goods or money is not the poorer because of the accused's conduct.

Intention permanently to deprive

The appropriation of property belonging to another must be accompanied by an intention permanently to deprive the other of that property. Unless it can be shown that this intention existed at the time of appropriation there can be no theft. The Act does punish the removal of articles from places open to the public, for example paintings from art galleries, without an intention permanently to deprive, and it likewise punishes the taking, without such an intent, of motor vehicles and other conveyances without the consent of the owner, but these two types of conduct are punishable as separate offences and not as theft.

The presence of an intent permanently to deprive will usually be proved by evidence of what the accused did with the property appropriated. If a person takes Y's £5 note and spends it on drink this clearly indicates an intent permanently to deprive Y of the note as he has passed the note into circulation. It is no use the accused alleging that he intended to pay it back. Although this may prevent him being found to have been dishonest, and lead to an acquittal on that ground, he will nevertheless have intended permanently to deprive Y of the thing (the actual £5 note) which he has appropriated. If a car is appropriated and a false registration book is produced, the engine and chassis numbers are altered, and the colour of the car is changed, this is clear evidence of an intent permanently to deprive.

Where the victim of an appropriation only has a limited interest in the property, a person can intend permanently to deprive even though he intends only a purely temporary borrowing. For example, if a housewife hires a carpet cleaner from S for a period of one week to clean all of her carpets, and this is 'unlawfully' borrowed by an associate who is aware of the circumstances and who intends to retain it throughout that period and then to return it to S, the associate intends wholly to deprive the housewife of her special interest in the property, and that intended deprivation is therefore permanent in the circumstances.

In certain limited cases a person can be convicted of theft even though he did not mean permanently to deprive, and even though he positively intended to return the property at some future date (or did actually return it). A conviction in such a case is possible if the case falls within TA 1968, s 6, which extends the meaning of 'intention of permanently depriving'.

TA 1968, s 6(1) provides:

A person appropriating property belonging to another without meaning the other permanently to lose the thing itself is nevertheless to be regarded as having the intention of permanently depriving the other of it if his *intention is to treat the thing as his own to dispose of regardless of the other's rights;* and a borrowing or lending of it may amount to so treating it if, but only if, the borrowing or lending is for a period and in circumstances making it equivalent to an outright taking or disposal.

Treating as one's own to dispose of regardless of other's rights

For TA 1968, s 6(1) to operate to 'deem' a person to have intended permanent deprivation it must be shown that there was an intention to treat the thing as his own to dispose of regardless of the other's rights. If a thief takes a valuable painting belonging to B, intending to return it to B only if B pays a ransom for it, he clearly intends to treat the thing as his own to dispose of regardless of the other's rights, because he intends that the other should only get it back by paying for it. A similar solution applies to the practice, where such an opportunity exists, whereby boys take empty bottles from the rear of premises and immediately return them to the owner at the front of the premises to receive the deposit charge on the bottle.

TA 1968, s 6(1) also catches the rogue who purports to sell property belonging to another in circumstances where it is unlikely that the property will be removed, as where an employee purports to sell a grand piano belonging to his employer which he knows his employer is going to dispose of in a few minutes' time. The reason is that the rogue intends to treat the property 'sold' as his own to dispose of regardless of the rights of the other and it is irrelevant that such a disposal is unlikely to occur.

Another type of case falling within TA 1968, s 6(1) is where the accused abandons the property and is indifferent as to whether it is recovered by the person to whom it belongs. If, by the circumstances of the abandonment and/or the nature of the property, it is (to the accused's knowledge) extremely unlikely that the property will be recovered, he can be said to intend to dispose of it regardless of the rights of the other.

If A's car is taken and driven a distance of 200 miles by B and abandoned, the justices or jury are most unlikely to find that there was an intention to treat it as B's own to dispose of regardless of A's rights, as a car is easily identifiable and will certainly be returned to A. Had the property stolen been an overcoat which had been abandoned in a township some distance away this would indicate an intention to treat it as his own etc as B could not have believed that it was likely that the coat would be returned; consequently, he would have intended to treat it as his own to dispose of regardless of the other's right.

Borrowing or lending

TA 1968, s 6(1) provides that a borrowing or lending may amount to treating property as one's own to dispose of regardless of the other's rights, if the borrowing or lending is for a period and in circumstances which make it equivalent to an outright taking or disposal. The Court of Appeal has ruled that this provision is only satisfied by a borrower if his intention is to return the thing only when 'all its goodness or virtue has gone'. This covers the following types of cases:

E takes F's monthly season ticket, intending to return it at the end of the month. E's borrowing is clearly for a period and in circumstances making it equivalent to an outright taking since, when it is returned, the season ticket will be a virtually worthless piece of paper.

G takes H's rare plant and its pot, intending to return it and its pot once it has died. G's borrowing of the plant is for a period and in circumstances making it equivalent to an outright taking.

Because their borrowing is equivalent to an outright taking, or disposal, E and G's intention so to act is regarded by TA 1968, s 6(1) as an intent to treat as their own to dispose of regardless of the rights of F and H and, hence, as an intent permanently to deprive.

On the other hand, a cinema projectionist who borrows a film in order to make pirate copies would not intend to treat the film as his own to dispose of regardless of the owner's rights because on its return the film would not have lost all of its goodness or virtue.

An example of a case where a lending would satisfy the present provision would be where J, who has control of his employer, K's, non-refillable can of paint spray, lends it to L, telling L that he can keep it and use it for as long as he likes. J realises that the can may never be returned or may be returned empty. J intends to treat the can as his own to dispose of because, as he knows, the lending is for a period and in circumstances making it equivalent to an outright disposal.

Parting with property subject to a condition

TA 1968, s 6(2) provides a further explanation of 'treating as one's own to dispose of regardless of the other's rights'. It states that, without prejudice to the generality of s 6(1), where a person having possession or control (lawfully or not) of property belonging to another, parts with the property under a condition as to its return which he may not be able to perform, this (if done for purposes of his own and without the other's authority) amounts to treating the property as his own to dispose of regardless of the other's rights. The subsection applies to a person who lawfully holds property for another as well as to one who holds it unlawfully, perhaps a thief. If, without the owner's authority, such a person pawns the article under a condition as to its return which he may not be able to perform, he is deemed to intend to treat the property as his own to dispose of regardless of the other's rights. 'A condition as to return which he may not be able to perform' will have to be examined in the circumstances. If the property is pawned with seven days to redeem, and the pawner's pay cheque will arrive within two days and will provide him with more than sufficient money to redeem the property, it can hardly be said that he may not be able to fulfil the condition for the return of the property. On the other hand, if property is pawned for a large sum of money which the pawner has no prospect of receiving within the time allowed, then this is strong evidence that the pawner may not be able to fulfil the condition.

ABSTRACTING ELECTRICITY

As we have already said, it has been held that electricity is not property and therefore cannot be stolen. However, a special offence is provided by TA 1968, s 13, which states:

A person who dishonestly uses without due authority, or dishonestly causes to be wasted or diverted, any electricity shall be guilty of an offence.

For police purposes, the offence will usually be encountered when a person, who has had his electricity supply disconnected, reconnects it and thus uses electricity without authority; or when evidence is found that a consumer has by-passed his meter, since his authority to use electricity supplied by the Board is conditional upon that electricity having passed through the meter before use. No doubt the primary purpose of TA 1968, s 13 was to deal with these matters but the effect of the section is more widespread. If a trespasser enters into property and switches on the lights he undoubtedly uses electricity, and if this use in the circumstances is considered to be dishonest, he will commit this offence. Squatters who occupy premises and dishonestly use lighting, electric fires, refrigerators or appliances, dishonestly use electricity and are guilty of this offence. If, at the same time they use the gas supply, they steal the gas as gas is property for the purposes of theft (and consequently they can also be convicted of burglary).

The section covers wasting or diverting in addition to using. It seems that the person who by-passes his meter could be charged with either dishonest usage or dishonest diversion, as he does not have authority to use in that way and he has certainly caused electricity to be diverted. However, it is possible for one man dishonestly to divert electricity for dishonest usage by another.

There is no restriction within the section to mains electricity. A person who dishonestly uses the power stored in a battery could be guilty of this offence. The section could not be applied to the person who took a motor vehicle without consent, as a modern car recharges its battery as its power is used.

It is important not to forget that the element of dishonesty must be proved. The provisions of TA 1968, s 2(1) are limited to theft, and therefore do not apply to an offence under s 13, but the rest of our explanation of dishonesty for the purposes of theft applies equally to an offence under s 13.

DISHONESTLY OBTAINING ELECTRONIC COMMUNICATION SERVICE, AND POSSESSION OR SUPPLY OF APPARATUS FOR DOING SO

The Communications Act 2003 (CA 2003), s 125 provides that it is an offence dishonestly to obtain an electronic service with the intention of avoiding payment of a charge in respect of that service. However, the section exempts from its provisions the dishonest obtaining of a broadcasting or cable programme service provided from a place in the United Kingdom.

CA 2003, s 126 provides that it is also an offence to possess or have under one's control anything that may be used for obtaining an electronic communications service, or in connection with obtaining such a service, with certain specified intentions. The specified intentions are an intent: to use the thing to obtain such a service dishonestly; to use it for a purpose connected with the dishonest obtaining of such a service; dishonestly to allow it to be so used; or to allow it to be so used for a connected purpose. Once again, the section exempts dishonestly obtaining a broadcasting or cable programme service provided from a place in the United Kingdom. Section 126 also prohibits the supply, or offer to supply, of anything which may be used to commit the above offence where the supplier knows or believes that the person supplied etc has one of the above intentions.

REMOVAL OF ARTICLES FROM PLACES OPEN TO THE PUBLIC

As we have seen, an essential element of theft is an intention permanently to deprive the owner of his property. This being so, it is unlikely that a charge of theft would succeed against an art lover who takes a valuable painting from a public gallery, intending to enjoy its presence in his home for a year and thereafter to return it to the gallery. On a charge of theft, the only way of proving an intent permanently to deprive the gallery of its picture would be to have recourse to TA 1968, s 6 and to show that the 'borrowing' was for a period and in circumstances making it equivalent to an outright taking or disposal. Proof of this is unlikely, since in the particular circumstances the painting will not have deteriorated in such a way that it could be alleged that it has lost all its goodness or virtue on return and that the taking had therefore amounted to an outright taking. It is for this reason that TA 1968, s 11 creates a specific offence to cover cases such as this, whilst taking care not to extend the parameters of the offence beyond them. The section provides:

Where the public have access to a building in order to view the building or part of it, or a collection or part of a collection housed in it, any person who without lawful authority removes from the building or its grounds the whole or part of any article displayed or kept for display to the public in the building, or that part of it, or in its grounds, shall be guilty of an offence.

There are two key elements to this offence. First the removal of an article must be either from a building to which the public have access in order to view the building or part of it, or a collection or part of a collection housed in it, or from the grounds of such a building. We are therefore concerned with removals of articles from stately homes, national galleries, historic buildings etc, provided they are open to the public in the above sense, or from their grounds. A person who removes the portrait of an Edwardian mayor from the entrance of the town hall does not commit the present offence because, although the public have access to the town hall (or, at least, to the part in question), it is only for the purpose of paying council tax, making inquiries or seeing their councillors; they do not have access in order to view the building, or any collection in it, or any part of the building or collection. If a man removes a painting from a collection in a stately home, access to which is limited to members of the Women's Institute, he does not commit the present offence because the public do not have access to the building in question but only a particular section of the public.

Where an article is removed from a building to which the public have access in order to view a collection or part of a collection housed in it, the offence is not committed if the collection has been made or exhibited for the purposes of effecting sales or other commercial dealings. Thus, removals of paintings from commercial art galleries (which are really shops) are not caught by TA 1968, s 11. Subject to this, it does not matter that the collection in question is one got together for a temporary purpose. The annual art exhibition in the village hall is therefore caught by s 11.

Generally, an offence under TA 1968, s 11 can be committed whether or not the building is open to the public at the time of the removal. There is one exception: if the thing removed is there otherwise than as forming part of, or being on loan for exhibition with, a collection intended for permanent exhibition to the public, it must be removed on a day when the public has access. Thus, if a painting is removed from the collection at the National Gallery it is irrelevant that the Gallery is then closed over the Christmas period, whereas it is not an offence to remove a painting from the annual art exhibition in the village hall on a day when the hall is closed. In this way, TA 1968 recognises a distinction between permanent exhibitions (for example, in museums and galleries) as opposed to temporary or occasional exhibitions (for example, in stately homes). This is understandable as museums and galleries exist to contain treasures which require constant protection from visitors who might 'borrow' them, whereas on days when a stately home or the like is not open to the general public the building resumes its description of a dwelling house and is no different from any other dwelling house.

The second key element in the offence is that it only applies where the thing removed is the whole or part of any article displayed or kept for display to the public in the building, or part of it, to which the public have access or in its grounds. The purpose of this is to separate those things which are there for display and those which are not. If a visitor takes an old vase which forms a part of the display, he commits this offence. If he takes the attendant's coat on the way out he does not, as the coat is not a part of the display.

There must be a removal from the building or its grounds. A visitor who moves the vase from one room to another does not commit the offence, but one who takes it out of the building does. The grounds are protected because many stately homes will have articles in the grounds for display to the public. The value of the article is irrelevant to liability, as opposed to punishment. TA 1968, s 11 makes it clear that no offence is committed where the person removing an article covered by it has lawful authority for doing so.

There is no need to prove dishonesty in respect of the act of removal but the section does exempt those who believe that they have lawful authority, or that they would have been given authority by the person entitled to give it if he knew of the removal and its circumstances. Therefore, a furniture remover who was removing articles on behalf of their owner would not commit an offence if he took one of the exhibited articles, believing that he had lawful authority to remove it. Likewise, a restorer of oil paintings who carried out work for the owner from time to time would not commit an offence if in the owner's absence he took a painting for its five-yearly restoration, believing that, had the owner been present, he would have consented.

TAKING CONVEYANCES

TA 1968, s 12(1) created specific offences in relation to conveyances, a term which includes almost all 'motor vehicles', which are taken, not for the purposes of permanently depriving the owner of his property, but for the purposes of joyriding. Section 12(1) provides:

A person shall be guilty of an offence if, without having the consent of the owner or other lawful authority, he takes any conveyance for his own or another's use, or, knowing that any conveyance has been taken without such authority, drives it or allows himself to be carried in or on it.

There are two offences under TA 1968, s 12(1), that of taking a conveyance without authority and that of driving or allowing oneself to be carried in or on a conveyance which one knows has been so taken. The term 'conveyance' is defined to include any conveyance constructed or adapted for the carriage of a person or persons whether by land, water or air, but it does not include a conveyance constructed or adapted for use only under the control of a person not carried in or on it, and 'drive' is construed accordingly. The term 'conveyance' is therefore wide in meaning and covers almost all motor vehicles, as well as aeroplanes, hovercraft, ships, rowing boats and inflatable dinghies, but it does not cover pedestrian-controlled vehicles, such as some milk floats, electric trolleys which are drawn by hand, and similar conveyances. Nor does it cover pedal cycles. Pedal cycles are covered by a separate offence described on p 1036.

Taking without authority

Taking

The mere unauthorised assumption of possession or control is not enough to constitute a 'taking' of a conveyance; *there must be some movement, however small, of it*. The result is that a person who gets into the driving seat of a car and drives it a few feet takes a conveyance, as does a person who climbs into a rowing boat or dinghy and casts it off from the bank. On the other hand people who unlawfully occupy a conveyance, either to shelter or to make love in it, do not take it. Of course, someone who gets into another's car and tries to start it is attempting to take a conveyance, but as the taking would amount to a summary offence, there can be no charge of attempting to take it. In such a case there may be a conviction for the offence of interfering with vehicles, discussed on p 1107.

Unauthorised use of a conveyance by a person already in lawful possession or control of a conveyance may amount to a 'taking'. A lorry driver who uses his employer's lorry for his own purposes 'out of hours', or who appropriates it to his own use during the working day in a manner which is inconsistent with the rights of the employer and shows that he has assumed control for his own purposes, thereby 'takes' it. Thus, for example, a lorry driver who makes a serious deviation from his proper route for some private purpose can be convicted of the present offence. A similar principle applies to a person who has borrowed a conveyance if he uses it for a purpose other than that for which he has been given permission or after the time he is permitted to have the conveyance. By so using the conveyance, he takes it.

For the accused's or another's use

TA 1968, s 12(1) also requires that the taking be for the accused's own or another's use, and this means that either the conveyance must be used as a conveyance or it must be taken for later use as a conveyance. It follows that a person who cuts the mooring rope of a boat and allows it to drift away empty does not commit this offence, whereas he would if he was aboard or if he towed it away for later use as a boat.

Without consent or other authority

The taking must be without the consent of the owner or other lawful authority. An apparent consent to a taking obtained by intimidation (as where A stops a car, grabs the driver by his lapels and successfully demands the loan of the car) is not a true consent, so that the taking will be without consent. On the other hand, a consent which has been obtained by fraud is nevertheless valid and prevents the offence being committed, however fundamental (eg as to the identity of the deceiver) the mistake which is induced.

In relation to a conveyance subject to a hiring or hire-purchase agreement, 'owner' means the person in possession of it under that agreement. It follows that, during the currency of the agreement, such a person cannot commit the present offence in relation to that conveyance since he can hardly be said to take it without the consent of the owner.

The addition of the words 'or other lawful authority' is to excuse acts of removal which amount to taking, such as the removal by an authorised officer of a vehicle which is causing a serious obstruction. Finance companies on occasion reclaim vehicles which are on hire purchase from them when the terms of the agreement have been broken by the hirer, and they will usually have lawful authority to do so under the terms of the agreement.

Not only is the consent of the owner or other lawful authority a defence, but so also is a mistaken belief in the existence of such lawful authority or a mistaken belief that the owner would, if asked, have consented.

Drives or allows self to be driven

In relation to the taking of motor vehicles in particular, but not exclusively, it is frequently the case that, after a vehicle has been taken by one person, it is used to convey a number of persons, each of whom may take a turn at driving. The second offence in TA 1968, s 12(1) deals with this situation, by providing that an offence is committed by anyone who, *knowing* that a conveyance has been taken without the consent of the owner or other lawful authority, drives it or allows himself to be carried in or on it. In circumstances where a vehicle, known to have been 'taken' contrary to s 12(1), is seen to be moving (for it is essential that there is movement in order that a person can be said to be 'carried'), and all the occupants are seen to step out of the vehicle but all deny driving it, the issue of who was driving is unimportant because all have allowed themselves to be 'carried' in the vehicle (since that expression covers a person who was driving). If there is no evidence from the owner of the conveyance that it was taken without his consent, a memorandum of conviction for the offence of taking the conveyance without authority raises a strong prima facie case that it was taken without the owner's consent.

Where a person takes a vehicle without consent and later picks up friends and takes them for a drive, his friends commit no offence unless they know that the vehicle has been so taken. The same would apply to a person who was given a lift but, should the driver disclose that the vehicle has been unlawfully taken in the course of the journey, the passenger is guilty if he continues to allow himself to be carried.

Limitation upon proceedings for offence against TA 1968, s 12(1)

TA 1968, s 12(4A), (4B) and (4C) provide that proceedings for an offence under s 12(1) must not be commenced after the end of the period of three years beginning with the day on which the offence was committed but, subject to that, may be commenced at any time within six months beginning with the 'relevant day'. The 'relevant day', where the prosecution is conducted by a public prosecutor, is the day on which sufficient evidence to justify proceedings came to the knowledge of any person responsible for deciding whether to commence any proceedings. Where a prosecution by someone other than a public prosecutor follows the discontinuance of a public prosecution, it is the day on which such evidence came to the knowledge of the person who has decided to commence proceedings or, if later, the discontinuance of other proceedings. In any other case, it is the day on which sufficient knowledge to justify the proceeding came to the knowledge of the person who has decided to prosecute.

For the purpose of proceedings conducted by a public prosecutor within six months of such evidence coming to his knowledge, a certificate as to the date on which sufficient evidence to justify proceedings came to his knowledge will be conclusive evidence of that fact.

Aggravated vehicle-taking

Section 12A of the Theft Act 1968 provides offences of aggravated vehicle-taking. An offence under s 12A is committed where a person has committed an offence under

TA 1968, s 12(1) (the basic offence) in any way in relation to a mechanically propelled vehicle and it is proved that, at any time after the vehicle was unlawfully taken (whether by himself or another) and before it was recovered, the vehicle was driven, or injury or damage was caused, in one or more of the following circumstances that:

(a) the vehicle was driven in a dangerous manner on a road or other public place; the same test of such driving applies as in the offence of dangerous driving (see pp 568–571);

(b) owing to the driving of the vehicle, an accident occurred by which injury was caused to any person;

(c) owing to the driving of the vehicle, an accident occurred by which damage was caused to any property other than the vehicle; or

(d) damage was caused to the vehicle.

The prosecution does not have to prove that the dangerous driving, injury or damage was caused by the accused's driving or by the accused at all. Nor, under (b) or (c), need it be proved that there was any fault in the driving of the vehicle. 'Accident' in (c), however, includes a situation where a person has deliberately caused injury. Once it is proved that the driving, injury or damage was caused during the period between the taking of the vehicle contrary to TA 1968, s 12(1) and its recovery, the accused is fixed with liability for an offence contrary to s 12A, unless he has one of the defences referred to in the next paragraph. A vehicle is 'recovered' when it is returned to its owner or other lawful possession or custody.

The importance of the fact that the aggravating circumstances can occur at any time up to the recovery of the vehicle is shown by a case where a man, who was in the course of taking a vehicle, was 'locked in' the vehicle by an anti-theft device and he then damaged the vehicle in an attempt to escape before the police arrived. An aggravated vehicle-taking offence was committed as damage was caused to the vehicle before it was recovered. It is a defence for an accused to prove that such driving, accident or damage occurred before he committed the basic offence, or that he was neither in, nor on, nor in the immediate vicinity of the vehicle when such driving, accident or damage occurred.

Anyone who commits an offence (the basic offence) against TA 1968, s 12(1) is guilty of aggravated vehicle-taking if the motor vehicle is subsequently involved in one of the sets of circumstances set out at (a) to (d) above. As we have seen, s 12(1) embraces those who drive and those who allow themselves to be carried as well as those who take. Thus, the difficult problem of proving who was actually driving at the time, or who actually took the vehicle in the first instance, is avoided as all offend against s 12(1).

Since the maximum penalty is greater where death is caused, TA 1968, s 12A creates two offences: one where death is caused, and the other for other situations. It has been held that there is nothing to prevent charges of both aggravated vehicle-taking (involving an allegation that the vehicle was driven dangerously) and one of dangerous driving being preferred.

Pedal cycles

Pedal cycles are not conveyances for the purposes of TA 1968, s 12(1) but are separately dealt with by TA 1968, s 12(5). That subsection provides that a person commits an offence if, without having the consent of the owner or other lawful authority, he takes a pedal cycle for his own or another's use, or rides a pedal cycle knowing it to have been taken without such authority. What was said above about the various elements of the offence under s 12(1) is equally applicable to the present offence.

ROBBERY

The offence of robbery is often described colloquially as 'mugging'.
TA 1968, s 8(1) provides:

A person is guilty of robbery if he steals, and immediately before or at the time of doing so, and in order to do so, he uses force on any person, or puts or seeks to put any person in fear of being then and there subjected to force.

No theft; no robbery

Robbery is an aggravated form of theft, the theft being aggravated by the use of force or threat of force. This is the most essential point in understanding the offence. If there is no theft there is no robbery. Where a person uses or threatens force in order to steal but has not achieved the appropriation of any property, and is therefore not guilty of robbery, he can be convicted of assault with intent to rob. There can be no conviction for robbery if it is found that the person who used or threatened force in order to appropriate the property believed that he had a legal right to it, even though he did not believe he was entitled to use force to do so, because the essential ingredient for theft, 'dishonesty', is missing. Similarly, a person who, wishing to cross a river, forcibly dispossesses a man of his boat does not commit robbery if he does not 'intend permanently to deprive' the owner of his property, as that essential ingredient of theft is missing. Of course, in both cases there can be a conviction for some offence of assault (other than assault with intent to rob) and in the latter for taking a conveyance contrary to TA 1968, s 12.

Use or threat of force immediately before or at time of theft

To constitute robbery, the force must be used or threatened 'immediately before or at the time of' the theft. There can be no robbery if force is only used or threatened after 'the time' of the theft. A person who pushes an old lady to the ground and steals her handbag commits robbery, so does he who approaches her and threatens to punch her in the face unless she hands over her handbag. The first used force in a way which might be considered to be either immediately before or at the time of the theft and the other threatens force immediately before the theft. However, a person, who approaches a lady and steals her handbag without force but, being discovered by her in possession of the bag shortly afterwards, assaults her, cannot be convicted of robbery. This is because the time of the theft will have elapsed when the force is used. Such a man could, of course, be convicted of theft and assault. The 'time' of the theft is not limited to the split second of time during which the initial appropriation with mens rea occurs, since an act of appropriation may be a continuing one, in which case the 'time' of the theft lasts as long as the theft can be said still to be in progress in common sense terms. Thus, there can be a robbery where a person takes property in a shop and, when approached by the owner, uses violence. The act of 'appropriation' would still be continuing at that time.

Whether or not force has been used or threatened immediately before or at the time of stealing is not a difficult question to answer in the vast majority of cases, such as street robberies or house robberies where the accused enters a house, ties up the occupants and then steals property there. However, in a few other cases difficulties can arise. For example, is force used immediately before stealing where A enters the home of a bank manager, ties him up, takes his keys to the bank and drives five miles to the bank where he steals?

Where force is used, it must be used 'on' a person, but it has been held that the force need not be used directly against the person. Consequently, it is enough to use force to obtain possession of property in the physical possession of another. For example, the use of force to snatch a handbag from a woman's grasp is robbery.

In the case of a threat of force, a threat of future force is insufficient; the threat must be 'then and there' to subject another to force. A threat of violence to property will not suffice, nor will the actual use of force against it.

Use or threat of force in order to steal

The force used or threatened must be used in order to steal. If a man during an argument with another, threatens to give him a beating and the man threatened gives money to him not to do so, this cannot be robbery as the threat of force was not made with the intention of stealing. Likewise, a man who knocks a woman to the ground to rape her, but who then changes his mind and instead takes the handbag which she has dropped, is not guilty of robbery or of assault with intent to rob, although he may, of course, be convicted of theft and attempted rape.

Although the force must be used or threatened on a person, it is not essential that the theft is carried out in his presence, provided that it is used or threatened for the purpose of stealing. It is robbery, for example, where a security guard is tied up so that property may be removed from some other part of the warehouse in which he is on duty.

The theft need not be from the person against whom the force is used or threatened. Thus, if A threatens a married couple that he will stab the wife unless the husband hands over his wallet, A can be convicted of robbery.

BLACKMAIL

The offence of blackmail is dealt with by s 21 of the Theft Act 1968 (TA 1968) which provides that:

A person is guilty of blackmail if, with a view to gain for himself or another or with intent to cause loss to another, he makes any unwarranted demand with menaces; and for this purpose a demand with menaces is unwarranted unless the person making it does so in the belief:
(a) that he has reasonable grounds for making the demand; and
(b) that the use of the menaces is a proper means of reinforcing the demand.

The essence of the offence is a demand, so that a person may be guilty of blackmail if the other ingredients of the offence are present, and not merely of an attempt, if he obtains nothing as a result of his demand.

Demand with menaces

For a person to be guilty of blackmail he must have made an unwarranted demand with menaces (with the appropriate mens rea).

The nature of the act or omission demanded is immaterial. An oral demand is made when the words are said; if it is made by letter, it is made when that letter is posted. It is essential that a demand is made. If a person discovers a couple in the act of adultery and demands money for his silence he has made a demand, but not if he merely walks away and the couple follow him and offer to give him money with a plea that he maintains their secret. A demand need not, however, be express, since (taken together with the menaces) it may be implied by a request or suggestion or other conduct.

'Menaces' are not limited to threats of violence, since they include 'threats of action detrimental to or unpleasant to the person addressed'. It is immaterial whether the menaces do or do not relate to action to be taken by the person making the demand. The man who says, 'Pay me £5,000 or my daughter will tell the world that you seduced her', is as guilty of blackmail as the man who reinforces his demand with threats of action by himself.

The judge will not normally need to give the jury a definition of menaces, since it is an ordinary English word. However, in two types of case he will have to tell the jury one or other of the following. First, that if, on the facts known to the accused, his threats might have affected the mind of a person of ordinary stability, they would amount to menaces, even though they did not affect the person to whom they were addressed. Second, that if, although they would not have affected the mind of an ordinary person of normal stability, the threats affected the addressee's mind, they would amount to menaces if the accused was aware of the likely effect of his actions on the victim, eg because he knew of an unusual susceptibility on the victim's part.

With a view to gain or intent to cause loss

The accused must, of course, intend to make a demand with menaces. In addition, he must act either with a view to gain for himself or another, or with an intent to cause loss to another. The terms 'gain' and 'loss' are defined by TA 1968, s 34 as extending only to gain or loss in money or other property, whether temporary or permanent. TA 1968, s 34 also provides that:

(a) 'gain' includes a gain by keeping what one has, as well as a gain by getting what one has not; and

(b) 'loss' includes not getting what one might get, as well as a loss by parting with what one has.

The definition of these terms limits blackmail offences to cases with which one would expect a Theft Act to deal, namely, those concerned with intended or foreseen economic advantage or prejudice. If menaces are used with a view to sexual gratification, then (as one would expect) they are dealt with by the Sexual Offences Act 2003.

A person acts 'with a view to something' if he has it in his contemplation as something which might realistically occur; he need not intend or want it to occur.

Unwarranted

As already mentioned, the demand with menaces must be unwarranted; for this purpose s 21 provides that a demand with menaces *is unwarranted unless* the person making it does so in the *belief* that he has reasonable grounds for making the demand *and* that the use of the menaces is a proper means of reinforcing the demand. If a man has sex with a girl after promising payment of £500 and then refuses to pay, a demand by her for the money supported by a threat to inform the man's wife will not be blackmail by the girl if she *believes* that she has reasonable grounds for making such a demand *and* that her threat is a proper means of reinforcing the demand.

An accused does not have to prove these beliefs, but this does not mean that the prosecution must negative the existence of a belief for which there is no evidence since it need only negative the existence of one of the specified beliefs if there is evidence before the court in support of both types of belief; otherwise the jury is obliged to find that the demand with menaces was unwarranted.

Blackmail and robbery

Although it does not require any property to have been appropriated, the offence of blackmail is close in many respects to the more serious offence of robbery by putting in fear and, in many incidents where property has been taken by putting someone in fear, it is advantageous to consider both possibilities. In some cases which look like robbery at first glance, blackmail may be a much more appropriate charge. If a person offers violence to a child in a pram unless the mother parts with her money, it can be argued that this is robbery but the issue is not clear. For robbery to be committed the accused must put or seek to put someone in fear of immediate force to *him* or *herself* in order that the accused can steal. It need not be the person from whom the property is stolen who is put in fear, but in the case of the child in the pram it would be necessary to show that the accused put or sought to put the child in fear as it was against the child (and not the mother) that force was threatened. It would not be sufficient that the mother surrendered her money because she was in fear for her child. In such cases it is better to prefer a charge of blackmail in that an unwarranted demand was made of the mother with menaces directed towards the child. If the child was older and was clearly capable of recognising what was happening, there would be little difficulty in proving that the accused had put or sought to put it in fear of immediate force and it would therefore be much easier to prove the offence of robbery.

CHAPTER 38

Criminal damage

The Criminal Damage Act 1971 (CDA 1971) deals with most offences which are concerned with damage to property but other legislation still exists which is to some extent parallel with certain aspects of the law contained in CDA 1971. The Malicious Damage Act 1861 still deals with offences of obstructing railways, or interfering with railway signals, with intent to obstruct or damage a train, and of concealing or removing navigation marks or buoys. Damage related offences are retained under the Explosive Substances Act 1883; for example, causing an explosion likely to endanger life or cause serious injury to property. When considering the possible offences committed in particular circumstances it is advisable to examine possibilities under these Acts and, if an intention to injure persons can be shown, the provisions of the Offences Against the Person Act 1861 must also be considered (see Chapter 28).

CRIMINAL DAMAGE

CDA 1971, s 1(1) provides what is known as the simple offence of criminal damage:

A person who without lawful excuse destroys or damages any property belonging to another intending to destroy or damage any such property, or being reckless as to whether any such property would be destroyed or damaged, shall be guilty of an offence.

If the destruction or damage is by fire, there is a separate offence under s 1(1) and (3), required to be charged as arson, which carries a higher maximum punishment. As a result there are technically two offences of criminal damage otherwise than by fire contrary to s 1(1) and criminal damage committed by fire, contrary to CDA 1971, s 1(1) and (3).

By the Theft Act 1968 (TA 1968), s 30 the leave of the Director of Public Prosecutions is required for the institution of proceedings for criminal damage by one spouse (or civil partner) to the other's property, unless, by virtue of any judicial decree or order, the spouses were not obliged to cohabit at the material time (or an order is in force, providing for the separation of the civil partners).

Criminal damage contrary to CDA 1971, s 1(1) is a 'penalty offence' for the purposes of the Criminal Justice and Police Act 2001, Part 1 and may be dealt with under a fixed penalty procedure: see p 874. This may be an appropriate course of action in minor cases.

The terms of the definition of the simple offence in CDA 1971, s 1(1) involve more complexity than one might expect. What we have to say about them hereafter is equally applicable to the other offences under the Act, unless the contrary is indicated.

Destroy or damage

Property may be damaged if it suffers physical harm which involves permanent or temporary impairment of the property's use or value. If a motor car is scratched when a coin is scraped along its side it is damaged thereby, because its value is impaired; likewise a wall is damaged if slogans are painted on it, as is beer if water is poured into it. If part of a machine is removed, without which it cannot work, the machine may be damaged, even though neither it nor the part suffers actual physical injury, because its use is impaired. Consequently, a car may be damaged if the rotor arm is removed from its engine.

If the impairment of use or value is minimal it is likely to be found that there is no 'damage' for the purposes of CDA 1971. On the other hand, the fact that what is done is rectifiable does not prevent the property being damaged but the amount and cost of rectification are relevant factors in determining whether there has been damage; if they are minimal it may be found that the property has not been damaged. If a man trespasses in a field which is used for the grazing of cattle it will be difficult to prove that he thereby committed damage to the grass. It would be different if he walked through a field of corn, bending and severing the stalks with his feet. In each case the circumstances must be considered, together with the nature of the article alleged to have been damaged, what has happened to it and the above factors.

By the Computer Misuse Act 1990, s 3(6) any alteration, erasure or addition to a program or data held in a computer, which is made by the operation of any function of a computer, is not regarded as damaging any computer or computer storage medium (such as a hard or removable disc) unless the effect on that computer or medium impairs its physical condition.

The destruction of property involves something which goes beyond damage, such as the demolition of a machine, the pulling down of a wall or other structure, or the killing of an animal.

If arson is charged, it must also be proved that the destruction or damage was caused by fire.

Property

CDA 1971, s 10 defines property as being property of a tangible nature, whether real or personal, including money and:

(a) including wild creatures which have been tamed or are ordinarily kept in captivity, and any other wild creatures or their carcasses *if*, but only if, they have been reduced into possession which has not been lost or abandoned or are in the course of being reduced into possession; but

(b) *not* including mushrooms growing wild on any land or flowers, fruit or foliage of a plant growing wild on any land.

The term 'mushroom' includes any fungus and 'plant' includes shrubs and trees.

It can be seen that 'property' is defined by CDA 1971, s 10 in a similar way to the definition of that term in TA 1968 for the purposes of theft. One difference is that land itself, which generally cannot be stolen under the Theft Act definition, is not subjected to any limits on when it can be the subject of criminal damage. A man who moves his fence to capture a little of his neighbour's lawn cannot be convicted of theft of that piece of lawn, but he would be guilty of criminal damage if he damaged it. Another difference is that intangible things, such as copyright, cannot be the subject of criminal damage although they may be stolen.

It must be emphasised that wild mushrooms and wild flowers etc can never be the subject of *criminal* damage. However, as we saw in the last chapter, they can be the subject of theft in certain circumstances, and this is relevant because some cases of damage to such things also involve a theft. In addition, the provisions of the Wildlife and Countryside Act 1981 dealt with in Chapter 22 now offer protection to some wild creatures and plants in circumstances which would include forms of damage. Therefore damage to the flowers, fruit or foliage of wild plants, although not an offence of criminal damage, is likely to be an offence contrary to the provisions of the Wildlife and Countryside Act.

Belonging to another

The simple offence of criminal damage can only be committed against property belonging to another. If a person wishes to destroy a garden shed or motor car which belongs only to him he is at liberty to do so provided that he does not endanger any other person; if he did he could commit an offence under CDA 1971, s 1(2) (see p 1047). The class of persons to whom property is treated as belonging by CDA 1971, s 10(2) to (4) is by no means limited to the owners of property, but includes a range of other people with a connection with it.

CDA 1971, s 10(2) provides that property is to be treated for the purposes of the Act as belonging to any person:

(a) having the custody or control of it;
(b) having in it any proprietary right or interest (not being an equitable interest arising only from an agreement to transfer or grant an interest); or
(c) having a charge on it.

If a lawn-mower is hired to X he thereby obtains the custody or control of it. If anyone else, including the owner, intentionally or recklessly destroys or damages the lawn-mower without lawful excuse while it is in X's custody or control, that person can be convicted of criminal damage against X.

Co-owners of property each have a proprietary right or interest in the property and if one damages the property he may be convicted of criminal damage since the property 'belongs to another'. The adjective 'proprietary' is included to exclude those with what may be described as a second generation interest, such as insurance companies which, although they have an interest in the property, do not have a proprietary interest.

Finally, persons having a charge on property have a proprietary interest in it. The best example of a charge is where a house owner buys his house by mortgaging it by way of charge to a building society. As a result of the present provision, the house will belong to the building society, as well as to the house owner, and if the house owner intentionally or recklessly damages it without lawful excuse he can be convicted of criminal damage, since the house will 'belong to another'.

CDA 1971, s 10(3) and (4) provides that, as in the case of theft, where property is subject to a trust, the person to whom it belongs shall include any person having the right to enforce the trust; and that property belonging to a corporation sole (such as the Treasury Solicitor or a bishop) in his official capacity is to be treated as belonging to the corporation notwithstanding a vacancy in the corporation.

Mens rea

The mens rea required for an offence under CDA 1971, s 1(1) consists of either intention or recklessness as to the destruction of or damage to property belonging to another. To do an act deliberately, for example, deliberately throwing a stone, is not enough; the accused must have intended his conduct to result in property belonging to another being destroyed or damaged, or been reckless as to the risk of such destruction or damage resulting from his conduct.

Clearly, if W throws a stone at X's passing car and dents it, as he intended, he has the necessary mens rea, since he intended to damage property belonging to another. Moreover, because of the doctrine of transferred malice, W will still have the necessary intent if the stone misses X's car but damages Y's front door. This is not very important in practice because, even if the doctrine of transferred malice did not exist and apply to W's intention, he will have acted recklessly (in the sense explained below) as to the risk of damage to another's property if he was aware of that risk and unreasonably took it.

A person acts recklessly within the meaning of CDA 1971, s 1 as to whether or not any property would be destroyed or damaged with respect to:

(a) a circumstance when he is aware of a risk, that it exists, or will exist;
(b) a result when he is aware of a risk that it will occur, and it is in the circumstances known to him, unreasonable to take the risk.

For many years the courts had followed a previous interpretation of the meaning of s 1 given by the House of Lords to the effect that, in considering 'recklessness' under CDA 1971, a person was reckless if he carried out an act which created an obvious risk that property would be damaged and when he carried out that act he either had not given any thought to the possibility of there being any such risk or, having recognised that there was such a risk, nonetheless went on to do the act. This made no allowance for a defendant's youth or lack of mental capacity. When reconsidering this decision in a case involving two boys aged eleven and twelve who set fire to bundles of newspaper which they placed under a wheelie-bin at the rear of a shop, the fire spreading to another bin and then to a shop and adjoining commercial buildings, the House said that to make no allowance for a defendant's youth or lack of mental capacity was offensive to a jury's sense of justice and to the principle that a person should not be found guilty of a serious criminal offence unless he acted with appropriate mens rea. The boys, who had been charged with arson of the commercial buildings, claimed that they had not appreciated that there was any risk of the fire spreading to the commercial buildings. Applying the House's new definition of 'recklessness', the boys would have been unlikely to satisfy a court or jury that they were not reckless in relation to the damage to the wheelie-bins, but might have expected to be successful in persuading the court or jury that they had not been reckless in respect of the damage to the commercial buildings.

Recklessness in the present context can be illustrated as follows. Suppose that A fires a highly powered air rifle from his bedroom window at wild birds sitting on the eaves of houses opposite and that A misses the birds but breaks a window in B's house. A cannot be said to have intended to damage another's property; he did not fire with the purpose that someone else's property might be damaged. Nevertheless, A's act of firing the rifle creates an obvious risk that property belonging to another will be destroyed or damaged and he will be reckless as to that risk if, when he fires, he is aware of the risk and in the circumstances known to him, it is unreasonable to take that risk.

Another example would be where a tramp, who has decided to 'doss down' in a barn used for the storage of hay, lights a fire to warm himself and the fire spreads to the hay and burns down the barn. Clearly, the tramp's act of lighting the fire creates a risk that property will be destroyed or damaged and he will have acted recklessly if he is aware of the risk and it is, in the circumstances known to him, unreasonable to take that risk.

Without lawful excuse

In order to commit an offence under CDA 1971, s 1(1), the accused must destroy or damage another's property 'without lawful excuse'. For the purposes of s 1(1), s 5(2) provides that a person is to be treated as having a lawful excuse if he acted with one of two types of belief.

Belief in consent

CDA 1971, s 5(2)(a) provides that a person has a lawful excuse if, at the time of the act or acts alleged to constitute the offence, he believed that the person or persons whom he believed to be entitled to consent to the destruction of or damage to the property had so consented, or would have so consented if he or they had known of the destruction or damage and its circumstances.

If a business firm was altering its premises and, in the course of doing so, was clearing some old buildings from a yard at the rear, an employee who demolished a valuable building on the site would have a lawful excuse for doing so if he believed that he had been given permission by the foreman when given the general direction, 'Clear that yard at the back'. The test is whether his belief was honest, although the more reasonable the belief was the more likely it is that the justices or jury will find that it was honestly held. If no such direction had been given, but the worker honestly believed that he would have been given permission by the foreman had he asked, this would still amount to lawful excuse.

If an employee overheard his employer say that he would be delighted if the factory burned down so that he would receive money from the insurers, and the employee considered that this was in the nature of an instruction to him, this could amount to a lawful excuse if he honestly believed that his employer had consented to the damage.

Defence of property

CDA 1971, s 5(2)(b) provides that a person is to be treated as having a lawful excuse if he destroyed or damaged the property in question in order to protect his own property or that of some other person, or a right or interest (such as a right of way) in property which was or which he believed to be vested in himself or another, *and* at the time of the act he believed that the property, right or interest was in immediate need of protection, and at that time he believed that the means of protection adopted or proposed to be adopted were reasonable having regard to all the circumstances. It is immaterial whether the specified belief was reasonable or not, provided it was honestly held. It is also immaterial whether or not the threatened harm which the accused sought to prevent was unlawful or lawful.

In relation to CDA 1971, s 5(2)(b), the property intended to be protected, unlike that damaged, need not always be tangible; it can also consist of a right or privilege in or over land, whether created by grant, licence or otherwise. Just as a person is entitled in appropriate circumstances to shoot a dog attacking his sheep, so is he entitled to demolish a wall barring a right of way which he has (or believes he has).

The effect of s 5(2)(b) is that a person is treated as having a lawful excuse if:

(a) he can be said to have acted to protect property, whether his own or another's. This test is an objective one, but is answered on the basis of the facts as the defendant believed them to be, whether or not his belief was reasonable;

(b) at the time he acted, he believed that property was in immediate need of protection, and he believed that the means adopted were or would be reasonable, having regard to all the circumstances. This test is a subjective one; it is immaterial whether the beliefs referred to were reasonable, provided that they were held.

Not surprisingly, a person is not 'property' within the meaning of CDA 1971, s 5(2)(b). Consequently, for example, breaking down a door to recover a child who is being unlawfully detained does not fall within the defence of 'lawful excuse' under s 5(2).

An honest belief in a moral entitlement is not a lawful excuse, nor is an honest belief that the destruction or damage was reasonable in pursuit of some political objective.

The present provision clearly entitles the owner of livestock to kill dogs worrying his sheep if he honestly believes that such immediate action is necessary for their protection.

Lawful excuse in a general sense

Quite apart from the statutory instances of lawful excuse provided by CDA 1971, s 5, the ordinary, commonsense instances of lawful excuse still apply. A police officer, in executing a warrant to search premises, may, if denied entry, break a lock, thereby committing damage. He would certainly not have believed that the owner would have consented, nor have believed that this was necessary in the protection of property, but nevertheless he would have a lawful excuse for his actions because the various statutory powers under which search warrants may be granted authorise entry by force, if necessary. Other examples of lawful excuses besides those provided by CDA 1971, s 5 are self-defence and the defence of another.

On the other hand, a belief that in damaging property one is carrying out God's laws or instructions does not amount to a lawful excuse.

Attempt

When no actual destruction results from a deliberate act carried out with the *intention* of destroying or damaging property, a person may be charged with an attempt to commit criminal damage, however low the value of the property intended to be destroyed or of the intended damage. The moment of 'attempt' arrives as soon as something is actually done which is more than merely preparatory to the commission of the offence. Thus, the throwing of a brick at a window, which does not in fact break as it is intended it should, amounts to an attempt to commit criminal damage.

It must be remembered that, since a person is only guilty of an attempt if he intended to commit the crime, the attempted commission of which is charged, a person who was merely reckless as to the risk of destruction or damage resulting from his conduct cannot be guilty of an attempt to commit criminal damage.

RACIALLY- OR RELIGIOUSLY-AGGRAVATED CRIMINAL DAMAGE

A person commits an offence under the Crime and Disorder Act 1998, s 30 if he commits an offence under CDA 1971, s 1(1) which is racially or religiously aggravated.

An offence of criminal damage is racially or religiously aggravated if:

(a) at the time of committing it, or immediately before or after doing so, the offender demonstrates towards the person to whom the property belongs or is treated as belonging for the purposes of CDA 1971 hostility based on that person's membership (or presumed membership) of a racial or religious group; or

(b) the offence is motivated (wholly or partly) by hostility towards members of a racial or religious group based on their membership of that group.

For this purpose, in (a) 'membership of a racial or religious group' includes association with members of that group, and 'presumed' means presumed by the offender. A 'racial group' means a group of persons defined by reference to race, colour, nationality (including citizenship) or ethnic or national origins. A 'religious group' is a group of persons defined by reference to religious belief or lack of religious belief.

Although (a) requires proof of what the accused did at the time of committing the offence, (b) can be established by evidence relating to what the accused may have said or done on other occasions (since such evidence may be relevant to the accused's motivation at the time of the offence).

DESTROYING OR DAMAGING PROPERTY WITH INTENT TO ENDANGER LIFE OR RECKLESSNESS AS TO LIFE BEING ENDANGERED

CDA 1971, s 1(2) declares that it is an offence for a person without lawful excuse to destroy or damage any property, whether belonging to himself or another:

(a) intending to destroy or damage any property or being reckless as to whether any property would be destroyed or damaged; *and*
(b) intending the destruction or damage to endanger the life of another or being reckless as to whether the life of another would be thereby endangered.

By CDA 1971, s 1(3), an offence committed under s 1(2) by destroying or damaging property by fire is charged as arson and is charged as contrary to s 1(2) and (3).

Offences under s 1(2), or s 1(2) and (3) are generally described as aggravated criminal damage.

There are four separate offences under these provisions:

(a) criminal damage with intent to endanger life;
(b) criminal damage reckless as to whether life would be endangered;
(c) arson with intent to endanger life; and
(d) arson reckless as to whether life would be endangered.

As a result, the jury's verdict of guilty of one of the above offences provides a more specific basis of the facts on which their verdict has been based and thereby assists the judge in sentencing; arson is viewed as a particularly serious form of criminal damage and the two types of mens rea involved in the present offences involve very different degrees of mens rea. It is, of course, open to the prosecution to charge more than one count, alleging different offences in the above list, for example one alleging an offence committed with intent to endanger life and another an offence committed recklessly as to such endangerment. This course has been recommended by the Court of Appeal.

An offence under CDA 1971, s 1(2) can be committed in respect of property which 'belongs' only to the accused, and the reason for this can be easily appreciated. The essence of the offence is the endangering of life and life can as easily be endangered in the accused's own dwelling house as in other property. If a man sets fire to his house which 'belongs' only to him with his wife asleep inside it, it is to be expected that he may be charged with damage with intent to endanger life or recklessness as to life being endangered.

Except for the fact that the property need not belong to another, the provisions of CDA 1971, s 1(2) are an extension of the provisions of s 1(1). It is essential to prove the other elements of the offence of criminal damage first, including that the person charged either intended to destroy or damage the property or was reckless in that respect. If the jury are satisfied on these points they may go on to consider whether the accused additionally intended that the destruction or damage would endanger someone's life, or there was a recklessness as to whether human life would be endangered.

'Recklessness' is used in the same sense as in CDA 1971, s 1(1) and this is not only in relation to the risk of property being destroyed or damaged but also in relation to the 'risk' that another's life may be thereby endangered. Thus, as far as recklessness is concerned, the question is whether he was aware that a risk existed or would exist and it was, in the circumstances known to him, unreasonable to take that risk.

The accused must have intended to endanger life, or been reckless as to whether life would be endangered, *by the destruction or damaging* of property which he intentionally or recklessly caused; it is not enough that he merely intended to endanger life, or was reckless as to whether life would be endangered, by the act which caused the destruction or damage. Consequently, a person who fires a gun from outside a house at a person standing behind a window in it cannot be convicted under CDA 1971, s 1(2), even though he intended to endanger that person's life, if he did not intend the damaging of the window to endanger life (and was not reckless as to that damage doing so).

In the event of a charge under CDA 1971, s 1(2) being framed so as to charge the accused only with *intending* by the destruction or damage to endanger another's life, evidence of voluntary intoxication can be relevant as evidence that he lacked that intention.

This offence is an interesting one as it is close to the offence of attempted murder in so many respects. The difference lies in the distinction between an intention to kill and an intention to endanger life or recklessness as to whether life is endangered. If terrorists explode a bomb in a building intending to kill a political opponent they commit an offence of attempted murder, as well as the present offence. If it is exploded in a building occupied by supporters of a rival political group it is certainly likely to endanger life but there may not have been an intention to kill. Warnings of intended detonations given by such organisations go some way towards eliminating either of these intentions but, depending upon the circumstances, they may not always eliminate the element of recklessness.

Although the words 'lawful excuse' appear in this offence the excuses provided by CDA 1971, s 5(2) do not apply to this offence. 'Lawful excuse' for an offence of this nature will be restricted to those excuses which exist under the general law, such as self-defence and defence of another.

THREATS TO DESTROY OR DAMAGE PROPERTY

Threats to destroy or damage property are dealt with under CDA 1971, s 2:

A person who without lawful excuse makes to another a threat, intending that that other would fear it would be carried out:
(a) to destroy or damage any property belonging to that other or a third person; or
(b) to destroy or damage his own property in a way which he knows is likely to endanger the life of that other or a third person,
shall be guilty of an offence.

The threat must be to do something which would be an offence against CDA 1971, s 1. It must be carried out with the intention of inducing a fear in the mind of the recipient that it would be carried out. It does not matter how the threat is received; a letter, a telephone call, a verbal threat or any other means of conveying a message from one to another will suffice. It does not matter that the person who offers the threat does not intend to carry it out, provided that he intends to create the fear that he would do so in the mind of the recipient. Nor does it matter that the recipient is not actually put in fear by the threat.

The threat must be to destroy or damage the property of some other person, or to destroy or damage his (the maker of the threat's) own property in a way which will endanger life. It is interesting to consider this offence in relation to bomb hoaxes (see p 785). Someone who communicates the threat of an explosion to another person, intending that the recipient will fear that the threat will be carried out, commits this offence if the threat is concerned with destruction or damage to property etc. There is often confusion with the bomb hoax offences created by the Criminal Law

Act 1977, s 51. Although that section is largely concerned with persons who place or despatch false articles (which may be harmless) to induce fear of explosion, it also deals with the offence of communicating false information to induce such a fear. That offence is distinguished from the one under CDA 1971, s 2 by its limitations to false information whereas the offence under s 2 can be committed whether or not the threat involves false information.

The provisions of CDA 1971, s 5 relating to 'lawful excuse' apply to threats to destroy or damage another's property but do not apply to threats to destroy or damage the threatener's own property in a way likely to endanger the life of some person.

POSSESSING WITH INTENT

The possession of things to be used for the purpose of causing damage is dealt with by CDA 1971, s 3:

A person who has anything in his custody or under his control intending without lawful excuse to use or cause or permit another to use it—
(a) to destroy or damage any property belonging to some other person; or
(b) to destroy or damage his own or the user's property in a way which he knows is likely to
    endanger the life of some other person,
shall be guilty of an offence.

As can be seen, the possession of the 'thing' must be for the purpose of doing something (or causing or permitting something to be done) which would be an offence under CDA 1971, s 1. There must be a clear intention to use the thing in such a way or to cause or permit another to do so; and it is not sufficient to prove that the accused realised that it 'might' be so used. Provided that such an intention does exist it is immaterial that there is no immediate intention to use it but only a conditional one. A terrorist group which possesses explosives in a warehouse, intending to use them to destroy or damage property if, and when, the opportunity arises, can therefore be convicted of the present offence.

'Possession' is covered in the section not by the use of the actual word 'possession', but by the use of 'in his custody or under his control'. These precise terms cover the same situations as possession but their use avoids the technicalities of the concept of 'possession'. The explosives contained in a warehouse may be in the custody of the keeper of that warehouse but they may also be under the control of the leaders of the terrorist group, who can order their removal and use at any time.

The offence as described is sufficient to include instances of possession of a terrorist arsenal, the possession of pickaxe handles by protection racketeers, or even the possession of paint or sprays by those who intend to endorse graffiti on the walls of buildings.

Where the offence involves an intent falling within (a), ie to destroy or damage another's property, 'without lawful excuse' is subject to CDA 1971, s 5 (with minor modifications), but where the intent falls within (b), ie to destroy or damage property in a way known to be likely to endanger life, it is not.

POWERS

CDA 1971, s 6(1) allows a justice, following information given on oath, to grant a search warrant if there is reasonable cause to believe that a person has in his custody or under his control or on his premises anything which there is reasonable cause to believe *has been* used, or is *intended for use*, without lawful excuse to destroy or damage property belonging to another or to destroy or damage property in a way likely to endanger the life of another.

If such a search warrant is granted, a constable may enter (if need be by force) any premises and search for the thing in question. He may seize anything which he believes to have been used or to be intended to be used as aforesaid.

SALE OF AEROSOL PAINT TO CHILDREN

Although this is not an offence against CDA 1971 it is most conveniently dealt with here. The Anti-social Behaviour Act 2003, s 54 makes it an offence for a person to sell an aerosol paint container to a person under the age of sixteen.

It is a defence for a person to show that he took all reasonable steps to determine the purchaser's age and that he reasonably believed that the purchaser was not under sixteen. Where the sale was effected by another person it is a defence to prove that the defendant took all reasonable steps to avoid the commission of the offence.

CHAPTER 39

Burglary

The Theft Act 1968 (TA 1968), s 9(1) defines burglary as follows:

A person is guilty of burglary if—
(a) he enters any building or part of a building as a trespasser and with intent to commit any such offence as is mentioned in subsection (2) below; or
(b) having entered any building or part of a building as a trespasser he steals or attempts to steal anything in the building or that part of it or inflicts or attempts to inflict upon any person therein any grievous bodily harm.

It has been held that TA 1968, s 9(1) creates two types of offences, the first being set out by s 9(1)(a) and the second by s 9(1)(b). Because in each type of offence there is a higher maximum penalty if the building entered as a trespasser is a dwelling, each of the two types of offence has in it two offences one relating to dwellings and the other to other buildings. The definitions of the offences under s 9(1)(a) and (b) include many common terms which require explanation. We will give this as we describe the offence under s 9(1)(a) but what is said will be equally applicable to the offence under s 9(1)(b).

BURGLARY CONTRARY TO TA 1968, s 9(1)(A): ENTRY WITH INTENT

The effect of TA 1968, s 9(1)(a) is that a person is guilty of burglary if he enters any building, which term includes an inhabited vehicle or vessel, or part of a building as a trespasser and with intent to commit one of the offences listed in s 9(2), namely to steal anything in the building or part of a building in question, or to inflict on any person therein grievous bodily harm or to do unlawful damage to the building or anything therein. Prior to the Sexual Offences Act 2003 (SOA 2003), the offence under TA 1968, s 9(1)(a) also covered entry into a building (or part) with intent to rape any person therein, but this variant of the offence was repealed by SOA 2003. Section 63 of that Act now includes an offence of trespass on premises with the intent to commit any sexual offence included in Part 1 of SOA 2003. The following is an explanation of the various terms which are involved.

Enters

The Court of Appeal has adopted the test of an 'effective entry'. This test excludes minimal intrusions, as where the accused's fingers are inserted through a gap between a window and its frame in order to open the window. However, where a man was found stuck in a downstairs window of a house with his head and right arm inside the window but trapped by the window itself, which rested on his neck, the Court of Appeal held that there had been an entry. The issue of whether he was able, from that position, to steal anything was irrelevant.

Under the old law, an entry could be effected merely by the insertion of an instrument without the intrusion of any part of the body *provided it was inserted to commit a relevant further offence*, but not if it was inserted merely to facilitate access by a person's body. Assuming that this remains the law, a person who, whilst remaining outside a building at all times in a physical sense, inserts his walking stick in an endeavour to remove goods from the building enters the building for the purposes of burglary. So does a person who pokes the barrel of his rifle through the open window of a building in order to shoot at (and therefore seriously harm) someone inside. On the other hand, a person who inserts a jemmy behind a window which has been left ajar, or who pokes the barrel of his rifle through a letter box in order to intimidate the occupant into opening the front door, does not enter the building because the insertion of the instrument was merely to facilitate access by his body, not to commit an offence inside. It is almost certain that the rule which applied under the old law concerning entry by means of an innocent agent still applies. Under this rule a person who uses a child under the age of criminal responsibility to enter a building and steal is regarded as himself entering the building. The same considerations would apply to the use of a trained animal. Dogs are trained to perform a variety of tasks and to sniff out and locate particular articles. It would be possible to train a dog to bring to its master certain valuable articles of property normally found in houses. Entry by a dog in such circumstances would be entry by its handler.

These special rules should not be allowed to obscure the fact that in most circumstances the issue of entry will be quite clear.

As a trespasser

A person enters a building or part of a building as a trespasser if it is in the possession of another and he enters without a right by law or permission to do so; the entry need not involve any force at all.

Rights of entry are granted by statute to certain people, such as the police and public health inspectors, for certain purposes. For instance, a public health inspector entering the premises to check whether there has been a breach of the public health law is not a trespasser, because he has a statutory power to enter for this purpose, but he does enter as a trespasser if he enters premises for the purpose of stealing something inside.

Permission to enter for a particular purpose or purposes may be given by the occupier or by someone lawfully in the building (provided the purpose of entry is not contrary to the interests of the occupier). If a mature girl invites her lover into her parents' house for the purpose of lovemaking, his entry to the building is not as a trespasser, since she is lawfully entitled to be in the building and the purpose of her lover's entry is not contrary to her parents' interests. However, if she invited him on to the premises in order to steal property belonging to her parents, his entry would be as a trespasser as it would be contrary to the parents' interests and therefore the girl could not give a valid permission. These examples represent the extremes of non-trespassory entries and trespassory entries where some form of permission is given.

Permission to enter may be implied, instead of express. For instance, in the case of a shop there is an implied permission for members of the public to enter the public parts of the shop for the purposes of inspecting goods on display or making purchases, and a person who enters for such a purpose is not a trespasser.

This brings us to the next point. A permission to enter will be given for a particular purpose or purposes. A person who enters for a purpose other than one for which he has permission enters as a trespasser. For example, the Court of Appeal has held that a man, who had permission to enter his father's house, entered it as a trespasser when he entered to steal his father's television set because he entered in excess of his permission. Likewise, a person, who enters a shop for the purpose of stealing from the open shelves, enters the building as a trespasser and is technically guilty of burglary, although the practice is only to charge theft.

A permission to enter may not necessarily extend to every part of the building. Thus a person may lawfully enter a building such as a hotel or shop, but trespass in the manager's office or the stockroom; equally, he may be a lawful guest at a meal in a private house but enter a bedroom as a trespasser. In both of these cases the entry as a trespasser will be into a 'part of a building'. On the other hand, if a person enters a building (or part of a building) with a right by law or permission to do so and then stops on after the expiry of his entitlement (as where X, who has entered a shop for a lawful purpose, decides to hide and stay on after the shop closes, and does so, in order to steal) he cannot be convicted of burglary because, although he becomes a trespasser by staying after hours, he has not entered the building (or part) as a trespasser. If, however, he then moves into another part of the building to carry out the theft, he will then commit burglary because he will have entered that part as a trespasser with the requisite intent.

Where a person is given permission to enter a building under a mistake as to his identity, which will normally have been procured by his fraud, the apparent permission is of no effect and he will enter as a trespasser. It is very difficult to prove a mistake of identity, since it must be proved that the mistaken party believed positively that the person in front of him was some other particular person. This is not very important because a person who is given permission under a mistake concerning him is very likely to enter the building as a trespasser, even though the mistake is not as to his identity. For example, if A disguises himself as a meter reader and thereby is permitted to enter X's house, it will only be possible to prove a mistake of identity if X positively thought A was another person, B. Nevertheless, if, as is likely, A disguised himself so as to be able to enter the house for some purpose other than to read the meter, he will enter as a trespasser, as explained previously.

As a final point, it should be noted that the 'owner' of a building may trespass in part of it if that part is in the exclusive possession of someone else. For example, if a householder rents out the rooms in his attic to a student, on terms whereby the student obtains exclusive possession of them, the householder will enter them as a trespasser if he enters without the student's permission.

Building or part of a building

The term 'building' should be given its everyday meaning of a structure of some size with walls and a roof and of a permanent or semi-permanent nature. Although most such structures will be of block, brick or stone construction, this is not essential, and a wooden structure is a building if it satisfies the above test. Dwelling houses, warehouses, shops, office premises and the like are all buildings; so are outhouses and greenhouses (provided they are at least semi-permanent) and substantial portable structures with most of the attributes normally found in buildings, provided that there is an element of permanence in their site. On the other hand, tents, partially-built but unroofed houses, and open-sided barns, are not.

The term 'part of a building' refers to a particular area of a building and has no connection with unfinished buildings. In hotels there are a number of rooms. Guests at the hotel are permitted to use the room which has been allocated to them and those other parts of the hotel which are for general use, such as the bar and dining room, and therefore they do not enter those parts as trespassers. However, they do not have permission to enter the rooms of other guests and to do so is to enter a part of a building as a trespasser. As said on the previous page, a person who conceals himself on shop premises during business hours, emerges when the shop has been vacated and walks into another part of the shop, enters that part of the building as a trespasser because his permission to be on the premises expired with the closing of the shop.

A 'part of a building' does not necessarily mean a separate room; it also includes a physically marked out area in a room, such as the area behind a counter in a shop, from which the accused is plainly excluded, whether expressly or impliedly.

As already indicated, TA 1968, s 9 states that references to a building also apply to an inhabited vehicle or vessel, and this is so whether or not the person having a habitation in it is there at the time. Clearly, a caravan or houseboat which is someone's permanent home is an 'inhabited vehicle or vessel', even though he is not there at the time but, say, abroad on a holiday; so is a caravan or boat which is used as a holiday home, whether mobile or static, in the summer during those weeks or weekends in which it is being so used, but not at other times in the summer and not at all in the rest of the year when it is closed up.

Mens rea

The mens rea required by an offence of burglary contrary to TA 1968, s 9(1)(a) is that, when entering the building or part of a building, the accused must satisfy two requirements.

First, he must know he is entering the building, or part, as a trespasser, or at least be reckless as to whether he is so entering. In most circumstances the issue will be straightforward and it will be a relatively simple task to prove that the accused knew that he had entered as a trespasser; if, for example, a glass patio door is smashed to pieces then it is reasonable to assume that the person who entered through the gap realised that he had no permission to enter.

Second, he must enter with intent to commit one of the offences listed in TA 1968, s 9(2):

(a) to 'steal' anything in the building or, as the case may be, the part trespassed in;

(b) to inflict grievous bodily harm on any person in the building or, as the case may be, the part trespassed in; or

(c) to do unlawful damage to the building or anything therein (whether or not the accused has trespassed in the part in which the damage is intended to occur).

It is, of course, irrelevant that it is impossible for the accused to carry out his intent. The following is worthy of note in relation to this provision:

Intent to steal

On entering the building, or part, as a trespasser, the accused must have intended dishonestly to appropriate therein property (such as money or valuables) belonging to another with intent permanently to deprive the other of it. In this context, the reader is reminded that obtaining goods by deception can amount to theft, and that it is irrelevant that what has occurred might also constitute an offence of fraud.

Intent to inflict grievous bodily harm

On entering the building, or part, as a trespasser, the accused must have intended to inflict really serious harm on a person therein. Where A enters B's house with intent to break B's arm, having discovered that B is having an affair with his (A's) wife, he clearly commits this offence.

Intent to do unlawful damage

On entering the building, or part, as a trespasser, the accused must have intended to destroy or damage the building or other property (in the building) belonging to another without lawful excuse (ie to commit an offence contrary to the Criminal Damage Act 1971, s 1(1)). A man who enters the flat of his ex-lover as a trespasser with the intention of breaking up pieces of her furniture, as a punishment for rejecting him, commits burglary. If he enters as a trespasser but only intending to plead with her to take him back, he does not commit burglary if he then loses his temper in consequence of her insistence that the affair is over, and breaks up furniture before leaving.

General point

In most instances, unless there is an admission by the accused, the only way in which one of the requisite intentions will be apparent is if there has been some act almost amounting to an attempt to commit the intended offence.

BURGLARY CONTRARY TO TA 1968, s 9(1)(B): HAVING ENTERED AS A TRESPASSER, STEALING OR INFLICTING GRIEVOUS BODILY HARM, OR ATTEMPTING ONE OF THESE CRIMES

TA 1968, s 9(1)(b) provides:

A person is guilty of burglary if having entered a building or part of a building as a trespasser he steals or attempts to steal anything in the building or that part of it or inflicts or attempts to inflict on any person therein any grievous bodily harm.

What was said above in relation to TA 1968, s 9(1)(a) applies equally to the corresponding terms in this definition.

TA 1968, s 9(1)(a) distinguished

An important distinction between the offence of burglary under TA 1968, s 9(1)(a) and that under TA 1968, s 9(1)(b) is that the latter requires the accused, having entered a building or part of a building as a trespasser, actually to have committed or attempted to commit in the building or part trespassed in:

(a) the offence of theft (contrary to TA 1968, s 1);
(b) the offence of unlawfully and maliciously inflicting grievous bodily harm (contrary to the Offences Against the Person Act 1861, s 20); or
(c) the offence of unlawfully and maliciously administering poison so as to inflict grievous bodily harm (contrary to the Offences Against the Person Act 1861, s 23).

Another important distinction is that, unlike the offence under TA 1968, s 9(1)(a), the offence under s 9(1)(b) does not require the accused to have intended to commit one of the above offences when he entered as a trespasser. Consequently if A enters a building as a trespasser, but without one of the intents specified in TA 1968, s 9(2) (so that he is not guilty under s 9(1)(a)), he can only be guilty of burglary (under s 9(1)(b)) if he then steals or inflicts grievous bodily harm or attempts to do either.

Mens rea

Apart, of course, from having the mens rea required for theft, or an offence involving the infliction of grievous bodily harm, or an attempt to commit such, as the case may be, the accused must know or be reckless that he has entered as a trespasser when he commits one of these offences. It is irrelevant whether or not he realised at the time of entry that he was entering as a trespasser. Thus, if a person enters a building, thinking that he has permission, and later realises that he has not and then steals something inside or inflicts grievous bodily harm on someone inside (eg the occupier who is trying to eject him) he is guilty of burglary of the present type.

Examples of TA 1968, s 9(1)(b) offence

The boundaries of burglary contrary to TA 1968, s 9(1)(b) can be illustrated by the following examples. Theft requires the dishonest appropriation of property belonging to another with intent permanently to deprive the other of it. A person who enters an empty house as a trespasser to sleep in it for the night does not commit burglary contrary to s 9(1)(b), nor does he if he switches on the electric fire (because electricity is not property and cannot be stolen). But if he turns on a gas fire, he commits burglary contrary to s 9(1)(b) because gas is property and can be stolen. Likewise, he would be guilty of burglary contrary to s 9(1)(b) if, being discovered there by a security guard, he then deliberately strikes the guard with a piece of wood lying nearby and inflicts grievous bodily harm, whether he intended to or not, since he will have committed the offence of unlawfully and maliciously inflicting grievous bodily harm, contrary to the Offences against the Person Act 1861, s 20.

Fortunately most offences are quite straightforward. There is an unlawful entry and a theft of property, and the buildings usually attacked are dwelling houses, shops, warehouses and offices. However, caravan sites are increasingly visited for the purpose of theft of television sets and it will be necessary in those circumstances to consider the circumstances of the occupation of the caravan in question. As we have seen, if it is not lived in as a full-time residence it is only protected throughout those periods when it is a residence.

Of course, there is some overlap between the two offences of burglary. Where a person enters a building (or part) as a trespasser with intent to steal or to inflict grievous bodily harm therein, and he commits the intended offence or attempts to do so, he can be charged with either offence. In practice, it is normally best to charge burglary contrary to TA 1968, s 9(1)(b) in such a case since it is easier to prove.

AGGRAVATED BURGLARY

The element of aggravation lies in the possession of weapons or explosives at the time of the commission of the offence of burglary. Aggravated burglary is particularly serious because of the aggressive nature of the offence, which could well lead to loss of life for those inside the building.

TA 1968, s 10(1) states that a person is guilty of aggravated burglary if he commits any burglary and at the time has with him any firearm or imitation firearm, any weapon of offence, or any explosive. It goes on to define these terms as follows:

(a) 'firearm' includes an airgun or air pistol and 'imitation firearm' means anything which has the appearance of being a firearm, whether capable of being discharged or not;

(b) 'weapon of offence' means any article made or adapted for use for causing injury to or incapacitating a person, or intended by the person having it with him for such use; and

(c) 'explosive' means any article manufactured for the purpose of producing a practical effect by explosion, or intended by the person having it with him for that purpose.

Firearm, imitation firearm, weapon of offence or explosive

TA 1968, s 10(1)(a), which states that a 'firearm' includes an airgun or an air pistol, does not describe the term 'firearm' itself. There is no doubt that this omission is deliberate so that courts may apply the term in a realistic sense and apply it to anything which can be fired and can kill or wound. It is clear that the definition of a firearm given in the Firearms Act 1968 was not included in TA 1968 because it includes component parts. There is very little of a threat of bodily injury posed by the possession of a magazine case for a rifle.

Things which have the appearance of being a 'firearm' but cannot be fired are covered by the term 'imitation firearm'.

The definition of the term 'weapon of offence' covers not only articles which would be offensive weapons for the purposes of the Prevention of Crime Act 1953, such as coshes, knuckledusters, chains with sharpened links, caps with razor blades in the peak or even pickaxe handles, but also articles made, adapted or intended to be used for incapacitating a person. Articles made for incapacitation, that is, articles having no other real purpose, will include handcuffs, leg irons or a straitjacket: those adapted could include a scarf or a pair of tights knotted at intervals for use for strangulation, and those intended for such use might include drugs to induce sleep or handkerchiefs or pads for use with chloroform.

If the article in question is made or adapted for causing injury to, or incapacitating, a person it will be necessary to prove no more than that a burglary was committed by that person and that he was in possession of such a weapon of offence at the time. If it is alleged he was in possession of an article which he intended to use to cause injury or to incapacitate, such as a walking stick or a belt, it would be necessary to prove his intention so to use it. In the absence of an admission, this is only likely to occur where he threatens someone in the building in such a way that he indicates an intention to use that weapon. For the purposes of aggravated burglary, an article not made or adapted to injure or incapacitate can be a weapon of offence, even if the necessary intent is only formed an instant before it is used to injure or incapacitate (which makes an interesting contrast to the different rule which applies to the offence of having an offensive weapon in a public place, described on p 1109). Thus, a burglar who uses a screwdriver to enter a house and, when confronted by the occupant, then (and only then) decides to use it offensively in order to steal commits aggravated burglary when he steals, because he will then have with him a weapon of offence. Likewise, a burglar who, when confronted by an occupant in a building, picks up a poker (or some other article which is not offensive in itself) from the fireplace and seriously injures the occupier with it commits aggravated burglary.

As in the case of 'firearm', the definition of 'explosive' indicates Parliament's intention to limit the application of the term to offences where one might allege realistically that the possession of the particular explosive added aggravation to the offence of burglary. This is clear from the fact that the definition requires the article to be manufactured, or intended by the person having it with him, for the purpose of producing a 'practical effect by explosion' and makes no reference to those things which cause a 'pyrotechnic effect' described in the Explosive Substances Act 1883. The section is not aimed at the burglar who buys some sparklers, or other amusing fireworks for his children, immediately prior to committing the offence. It is aimed at the person who enters a building as a trespasser with explosives which are to be used to open a safe or some other secured part of the premises.

In most cases, an offender under the present section intends to use the article to injure or incapacitate someone in the course of a burglary. However, this is not essential; it suffices that he had it with him for such use on another occasion (as, for example, where the burglary is in an empty house and the offender intends to use a cosh to enable him to hijack a get-away car).

Has with him at time of burglary

In order for a burglar to 'have with him' a firearm etc, he must be armed with it; it is not enough that it is readily accessible to him. Thus, if the firearm etc is carried not by the burglar but by an accomplice waiting outside the building, aggravated burglary is not committed. This is a stricter approach than is taken to the phrase 'has with him' in other offences where the term appears. In addition, he must know that he has it with him: a burglar does not have with him a cosh which somebody has slipped into his swag bag, unknown to him, for example.

The person charged with aggravated burglary must be shown to have had with him a relevant article *at the time of committing* the offence of burglary. This is important.

Where the burglary is alleged to have been committed by committing or attempting theft or the infliction of grievous bodily harm after entry as a trespasser, then the possession must be proved at the time at which the theft etc was committed or attempted, because that is the time at which the offence of burglary will have been committed. Where the burglary is alleged to have been committed by an entry with intent to commit one of the offences specified for TA 1968, s 9(1)(a), the accused must be proved to have been in possession at the time of entry, because that is the time at which the offence of burglary will have been committed. Thus, if someone enters a building as a trespasser intending to steal and he has with him a cosh at the time of entry, he is guilty of aggravated burglary. The time of commission of the burglary is when he entered and a cosh is a weapon of offence per se. If he then only has with him a pocket knife, it would be very difficult on that evidence to secure a conviction for aggravated burglary *at that point of time*, because—since a pocket knife is not a weapon of offence per se—it would have to be proved that at that point of time he intended to use that knife as a weapon of offence. However, if, confronted by the householder, he pulls out the knife and threatens him, this would be very strong evidence that when he entered he intended to use the knife as a weapon of offence and a conviction for aggravated burglary would be far more likely. By way of further example, if someone enters a motor workshop without a weapon, merely intending to trespass there, he is not guilty of an offence of burglary at that stage; but if, when confronted by a security guard, he arms himself with a tyre lever stored in the workshop and uses it to strike the guard, causing him grievous bodily harm, he would be guilty not only of burglary at that stage but also of aggravated burglary. This is because he had the lever with him at the time of committing burglary and the lever was clearly intended by him for use for causing injury (and was therefore a weapon of offence).

CHAPTER 40

Offences of fraud and corruption

FRAUD: INTRODUCTION

In early times judges took an almost light-hearted attitude towards offences which deal with fraud. A judge said in 1704, 'Shall we indict one man for making a fool of another?'. However, attitudes have changed with the passage of time and the emergence of the professional cheat and we now have a number of offences dealing with fraudsters. The law relating to fraud was revised by the Fraud Act 2006 (FA 2006). The Act creates a general offence of fraud. It additionally creates new offences of obtaining services dishonestly and of possessing, making supplying articles for use in fraud, and of fraudulent trading which is applicable to non-corporate traders. The FA 2006 will come into force on a day or days to be appointed.

The offences of deception previously contained in the Theft Act 1968 (TA 1968), s 15, 15A, 16 and 20(2) and the Theft Act 1978, ss 1 and 2 have been repealed by the Fraud Act 2006, as recommended in the Law Commission's Report on *Fraud*. The offence of 'conspiracy to defraud' has been retained on the basis of serious practical concerns about the ability to prosecute multiple offences in the larger and most serious cases of fraud.

THE OFFENCE OF 'FRAUD'

FA 2006, s 1 creates an offence of fraud which is committed by a person who is in breach of FA 2006, s 2, 3 or 4. Section 2 is concerned with fraud by false representation; s 3 with fraud by failing to disclose information; and s 4 with fraud by abuse of position.

Fraud by false representation

Under FA 2006, s 2 a person is in breach of s 1 if he:

(a) dishonestly makes a false representation; and
(b) intends by making the representation:
   (i) to make a gain for himself or another; or
   (ii) to cause loss to another or to expose another to a risk of loss.

False representation

For these purposes, a representation is 'false' if it is untrue or misleading and the person making it knows that it is, or might be, untrue or misleading. A 'representation' means any representation, express or implied, as to fact or law, including a representation as to the state of mind of the person making the false representation or any other person. A representation may be regarded as made if it (or anything implying it) is submitted in any form to any system or device designed to receive, convey or respond to communications (with or without human intervention). There is no limitation upon how a representation may be made.

Among the types of conduct covered by s 2 is 'phishing' (dispatch of e-mails to large numbers of people claiming that the e-mail is sent by a legitimate financial institution). Such an e-mail may prompt a person to provide details of a credit card or bank account and enable access by the despatcher. Section 2 also covers goods sold upon the basis that the goods purchased are 'designer goods' but the seller knows this to be untrue.

Representation express or implied

A representation may be express or implied by words or conduct. In most circumstances there will be an express representation. An example of an express representation by words would be where the accused has described bottles of coloured water as whisky and as a result has obtained property, ie money, from the persons deceived. If a man knows that collectors visit certain houses every week to collect pools coupons and money on behalf of pools promoters and shoulders the same type of bag and dresses in similar fashion, it may only be necessary for him to knock on doors in order to be handed the coupons and the money; in such a case the representation is implied by conduct. If on any occasion the man is asked if he is an authorised collector and he says that he is, he will have added a further express representation by words. A person who wears the trappings of a bookmaker at a race meeting and receives bets, intending not to honour successful wagers but to abscond with the money, makes an implied representation by conduct as to his present intentions.

A representation would be made by way of conduct where a credit card was dishonestly used to make a payment. The tendering of the card amounts to a claim that the person using it had the authority to do so. If the person using the card knows that he has no such authority, or may not have such authority, he commits this offence. The offence is committed whether or not the person accepting the card is deceived by the representation.

The use of cheques involves a representation. If a person steals a cheque book, signs the name of the account holder on a cheque and gives it to someone else, there are various factors to consider outside the possibilities of forgery. There is a representation by conduct, in that such a person represents himself to be the account holder and therefore entitled to draw upon that account. If in answer to a question as to his identity he states that he is the person entitled to draw, the case is even stronger because a representation by words is thereby made.

A person who offers his own cheque which subsequently 'bounces' makes a false representation by his conduct that the state of affairs existing at the date of delivery of the cheque is such that the cheque will be honoured in the ordinary course of events on presentation for payment on or after the date specified in the cheque and, if the cheque bounces, this implied representation, being untrue, constitutes a false representation. It may be noted that the representation in such a case is not that the drawer then has sufficient funds in his account to meet the cheque; after all he may have an overdraft facility. Of course, the fact that a person obtains something by means of a 'bouncing' cheque does not necessarily make him guilty of an offence of fraud, since he may lack the necessary mens rea discussed later.

Today, most cheques are supported by the use of a banker's card and cheques so supported are guaranteed by the banker, provided certain conditions on the back of the cheque card are complied with, whether or not there are funds to meet them. The reason is that if someone (the drawer) offers to pay by cheque supported by a cheque card, and that offer is accepted, and the conditions on the cheque card are complied with, a contract is brought into effect between the payee and the bank whereby the bank is legally obliged to honour the cheque, and it is irrelevant that the drawer's authority to use the cheque card has been withdrawn or that he is exceeding it, or that the drawer was a thief (and not the authorised signatory) and had forged a signature resembling the authorised signatory's. In such a case, there will not be a representation of the type mentioned in the last paragraph. It could therefore be argued that when a person presents a cheque supported by a cheque card, there can never be a false representation, since the implied representation that the circumstances are such that the cheque will be honoured is true. However, this is not so. A person who offers a cheque supported by a cheque card thereby represents to the person to whom the cheque is offered that in the circumstances he is actually authorised by the bank to use his card and thereby to oblige the bank to honour the cheque if it is accepted. Therefore, if he is not actually authorised to use the banker's card in those circumstances, either because his authority to use it has been withdrawn or because he is using it in excess of his authorisation or because he has stolen it, he is making a false representation as to that authority upon the person to whom that cheque is offered. A similar analysis applies to the use of credit cards.

The issue of selling goods which are defective is surrounded by a number of problems. A man may sell a motor car which has a defective engine but he may complete that sale without the condition of the engine being debated. The car is there to be examined and test driven by the customer if he wishes to do so. The vendor is not obliged by law (see below) to disclose the engine defect. He does not practise a false representation by failing to do so. However, if he knows that the engine is defective but nevertheless assures the customer that it is in perfect working order, and thereby induces the customer to buy it, there is a false representation by words as a result of which property (ie the purchase price) is obtained.

As to fact or law

Most representations are in relation to fact. For example, the representations referred to above concerning cheques and cheque cards or the condition of a motor car are concerned with facts. Other common examples surround the claims made to social security officers. The woman, who falsely claims that she has lost her purse containing her husband's weekly pay and asks for assistance, obtains money by a false representation. Even if she does not, it was her intention to do so. Married women who are separated from their husbands may claim benefit for themselves and their children on the basis of there being no income from the husband coming in to the household. If the husband returns and once again contributes to the household budget, there is a false representation by conduct each time money is drawn on the assumption that the woman is solely responsible for the family's upkeep. This amounts to a false representation in relation to a fact.

As to present intentions of the person using the representation or any other person

For the purpose of fraud by false representation, a representation by words or conduct may be as to the present intentions of the person making the false representation or any other person. If a man obtains the payment of money as a deposit for the fitting of double glazed windows to houses, which he has no intention of fitting, he obtains that money by means of a false representation as to his present intentions. The inclusion of the phrase 'or any other person' covers the situation in which one person (the accused) misrepresents the present intentions of another person. This would be so where a salesman was used to make false promises on the instructions of his employer, who had no intention of honouring such agreements at that time.

Disputes concerning payments for meals in restaurants frequently result in police officers being called. If a customer intended to pay when he ordered the meal, but discovers after he has eaten it that he has left his wallet at home, he cannot be said to have obtained the meal by means of a false representation. On the other hand, if he knew that he had no money when he entered the restaurant and had no intention of offering payment in any other way, he will have falsely represented by his conduct his present intentions by sitting down and ordering from the menu since this conduct implies an intention to pay the price. However, for practical purposes, in the absence of an admission, it is almost impossible to prove that he did not intend to pay at the time of ordering the meal and that factor is always the important one.

Mens rea

'Dishonesty' involves a two-way test; whether a defendant's behaviour would be regarded as dishonest by the ordinary standards of reasonable and honest people; and where this is so, whether the defendant was aware that his conduct would be regarded as dishonest by reasonable and honest people. The answer to both tests must be 'yes'.

Although the accused must intend to make a gain for himself or another, or to cause loss to another or to expose another to a risk of loss, that gain or loss need not ensue. The terms 'gain' and 'loss' are defined by s 5. They extend only to gain or loss in money or other property, and include any such gain or loss whether temporary or permanent. 'Property' means any property whether real or personal (including things in action and other intangible property): see p 1018 as to these terms. A 'gain' may be made by keeping something which one already has as well, by getting something which one does not have, and 'loss' includes not getting what one might get, as well as parting with something which one already possesses. Thus, these terms have the same meaning as they have where they appear in sections of the Theft Act 1968.

Fraud by failing to disclose information

FA 2006, s 3 provides that a person is in breach of s 1 if he:

(a) dishonestly fails to disclose to another person information which he is under a legal duty to disclose, and
(b) intends, by failing to disclose the information:
  (i) to make a gain for himself or another, or
  (ii) to cause loss to another or to expose another to a risk of loss.

A 'legal duty' may be one prescribed by statute; from the fact that the transaction is one of good faith (such as a contract of insurance); from the express or implied terms of a contract; from the custom of a trade or market; or from the existence of a relationship (such as that of a trustee, agent or principal). This duty exists not only if the failure gives cause for action for damages, but also where there is a right to set aside any change in a victim's legal position to which that person may consent as a result of non-disclosure. A person in a position of trust has a duty to disclose material information when entering into a contract with a beneficiary. Because he is under a legal duty to disclose a material fact, s 3 would also cover a person who failed to disclose a relevant medical condition to a company offering life insurance.

The mens rea required under s 3 is similar to that required under s 2.

Fraud by abuse of position

By FA 2006, s 4 a person is in breach of s 1 if he:

(a) occupies a position in which he is expected to safeguard, or not to act against, the financial interests of another person;
(b) dishonestly abuses that position; and
(c) intends, by means of the abuse of that position:
  (i) to make a gain for himself or another; or
  (ii) to cause loss to another or to expose another to the risk of loss.

A person may be regarded as having abused his position even though his conduct consisted of an omission rather than an act.

The offence is aimed at those who are in a position to safeguard another's financial interests and have authority to exercise discretion and act on that person's behalf. Such persons may have access to assets, premises or equipment and need no further co-operation from that person to commit fraud against him. If such a person dishonestly acts against his client's interests for gain, he commits an offence of fraud. The term 'abuse' is not defined by the Act and it may cover a wide range of conduct. The offence might be committed by 'omission' where a person fails to act to obtain a contract in order to allow a rival company to obtain it.

The mens rea required under s 4 is similar to that required under s 2.

OBTAINING SERVICES DISHONESTLY

A person commits an offence against FA 2006, s 11(1) if he obtains services for himself or another:

(a) by a dishonest act; and
(b) in breach of the provisions of s 11(2) below.

By s 11(2), a person obtains services in breach of s 11 if:

(a) they are made available on the basis that payment has been, is being, or will be, made for or in respect of them;
(b) he obtains them without any payment having been made for, or in respect of, them or without payment having been made in full; and
(c) when he obtains them he knows:
   (i)   that they are being made available on the basis described in (a); or
   (ii) that they might be,

but intends that payment will not be made, or will not be made in full.

The offence does not require a false representation. There must be an 'obtaining' of a service. An example would be where a service has been made available to a person via the Internet on the understanding that payment would be made for access. The dishonest use of false credit card details or personal information for the purpose of obtaining a service would similarly amount to an offence against the section. Trespassory entry into premises to view an event will be an offence against the section as the service provided is one for which a person is expected to pay. The dishonest interception of a television broadcast, the receipt of which is intended to be limited to those who pay, would amount to such an offence.

Dishonesty bears the same meaning as described above.

MAKING OFF WITHOUT PAYMENT

Although not without its problems, TA 1978, s 3 is particularly helpful to those charged with the enforcement of the law in situations in which immediate action is essential. The section provides that a person who, knowing that payment on the spot for any goods supplied or service done is required or expected from him, dishonestly makes off without having paid as required or expected and with intent to avoid payment of the amount due is guilty of an offence. The section covers those circumstances generally referred to as 'bilking', for example leaving a restaurant without paying for a meal or leaving a self-service petrol station without paying for petrol received. These provisions are useful in that they cover opportunist offences in which it will often be difficult to prove that any particular intention existed at the time that the goods were supplied or the service was done (so that a deception as to intention cannot be proved). The payment which is required must be one which is legally enforceable.

Because the accused must make off 'without having paid as required or expected', an offence is not committed if the creditor (or his agent) has agreed that payment would be postponed, even if that postponement has been procured by a dishonest deception.

Because there is no reference to deception in TA 1978, s 3, the only dishonesty which needs to be shown is that which existed at the time of 'making off'. Dishonesty is a question of fact for the jury or justices and is approached in the same way as in offences of deception. It has been held by the House of Lords that an intention to evade payment permanently is part of the mental element to be proved by the prosecution.

Police officers are frequently called to incidents involving 'making off'. It is common in respect of restaurants where late night revellers eat well and look for opportunities to escape from the restaurant without paying. Restaurants demand payment on the spot from casual customers and this is well known by all. Officers called to such incidents need only be concerned with whether or not the persons concerned made off without paying and with intent to avoid payment. If they ran through the door and into the street that intention is quite obvious. In circumstances in which they discovered that they did not have sufficient money to pay, but gave their correct names and addresses to the proprietor and insisted upon leaving, they will certainly have made off without paying but their conduct does not indicate that they did so dishonestly nor with an intention to avoid payment.

The other common incident involves the self-service petrol station. These stations make it quite clear that payment is demanded on the spot, by posting notices which declare that self-service is in operation and that payment should be made at the kiosk. A motorist who drives out of such a station without paying will experience considerable difficulty in persuading a jury that his actions were not dishonest and not done with intent to avoid payment (although, of course, the onus of proving the offence is on the prosecution). Once again, it would be different if he left his name and address, together with the registration number of his car, with the attendant in the kiosk.

The words 'make off without payment' involve a departure without paying from the place where payment would normally be made. For example, in the case of a taxi, payment may be made while sitting in it or standing at the window and it can therefore be an offence to make off from either place without paying.

The person who is alleged to have made off without payment must be a person who knew that payment on the spot would be demanded from him. If Hales invites three friends to accompany him for a meal and promises to pay the total bill, his three friends do not know that payment will be expected from them. In such circumstances, Hales is the only one to commit this offence if the party leaves without paying.

The section differentiates between transactions which are on the spot cash transactions and those which involve trade credit. If an employee of a garage proprietor goes to his employer's wholesaler, collects spare parts and leaves without signing the invoice, he does not commit an offence. The wholesaler will send an account to the employer; payment was not expected on the spot. However, if such an employee went to an auto discount store at which all transactions were cash transactions and was given goods and then saw the opportunity to leave without paying, he would be guilty of this offence if he left with the intention of avoiding payment.

The term 'knowing that payment on the spot is required or expected' relates to the knowledge an accused must have of when payment must be made. It includes payment at the time of collecting goods on which work has been done or in respect of which a service has been provided. Therefore, a man who collects a radio set which has been repaired and makes off without paying will be guilty of the offence if he knows that payment on the spot is demanded. However, the section does not apply if the payment required or expected is not legally due (eg because the person demanding it is seriously in breach of contract). Nor does the section apply to the supplying of goods or the doing of services which is contrary to the law nor where the service done is such that payment is not enforceable. Consequently, for example, the offence is not committed by the man who makes off without paying a prostitute for services rendered.

FALSE ACCOUNTING

The offences of false accounting contrary to TA 1968, s 17 are not restricted to clerks and other people who are employed in the traditional sense for the purpose of bookkeeping. The falsity need not necessarily be with a view to gain since it is sufficient that the falsity is accompanied by an intent to cause loss to another.

TA 1968, s 17(1) states that:

Where a person dishonestly, with a view to gain for himself or another or with intent to cause loss to another,
(a) destroys, defaces, conceals or falsifies any account or any record or document made or required for any accounting purpose, or
(b) in furnishing information for any purpose produces or makes use of any account, or any such record or document as aforesaid, which to his knowledge is or may be misleading, false or deceptive in a material particular,
he is guilty of an offence.

TA 1968, s 17(1) creates two quite separate and distinct offences which might be described as the falsification of accounts (s 17(1)(a)) and the use of false or deceptive accounts (s 17(1)(b)). Before examining these offences separately a number of points can be made which apply to both of them.

Mens rea

For the purposes of either type of offence, the accused's conduct must be carried out dishonestly and with a view to gain for himself or another or with intent to cause loss to another. 'Dishonesty' in this context is understood in the same way as in the offences of deception. 'With a view to gain . . . or with intent to cause loss . . .' bears the same meaning as in blackmail.

Account, record or document made or required for any accounting purpose

Another general point is that the acts specified by TA 1968, s 17(1)(a) and (b) must be done in relation to 'any account, record or document made or required for any accounting purpose'. These terms should be given their ordinary meaning. An accounts book, balance sheet or a payroll record is made for an accounting purpose. That is the reason for its existence; it has no other real purpose as it can be used for little other than the keeping of accounts. Documents may be required for an accounting purpose, even though they have other purposes as well as an accounting purpose. For example, a delivery note is for the purpose of allowing the recipient of goods to check that all of the goods ordered have been delivered, but a firm may use that delivery note as an accounting document to be retained in the storeroom to account for stock in excess of that recorded on inventories or stock sheets. Until the additional stock is recorded on an inventory or stock sheet, the delivery note will provide the only account for its presence should an audit take place. It will therefore be used for an accounting purpose at that time. As a further example, a housing benefit claim form which contained the only information used to calculate housing benefit has been held to be a document required for an accounting purpose, despite the fact that it is also used to determine entitlement to benefit.

The forbidden acts relate to accounts, records or documents made or required for an accounting purpose. The terms 'account' or 'record' are wide enough to cover an account or record produced by a mechanical device, such as a taxi meter or the turnstile at a soccer ground which records the number of persons admitted so that the entries may be related to the money collected. The falsification of such an account or record is therefore punishable if done dishonestly and with a view to gain or loss. We now turn to the separate requirements of the two offences.

Falsification of accounts (TA 1968, s 17(1)(a))

What is required here is the destruction, defacement, concealment or falsification of any account etc. If entry to a cinema is recorded by the issue of a ticket by a process which produces a duplicate copy on a roll, the destruction of any part of that record, if carried out with the necessary intent, would be an offence. If some of the duplicate copies were not handed over to the manager so that a false total figure could be shown to cover deficiencies, those copies would be 'concealed' for the purposes of this section. If, to cover deficiencies in the accounts, a corrosive liquid, or other damaging agent, was applied to the duplicate records, this would amount to a defacement. However, the most common offence is always likely to be the falsification of figures in an account, record or document. 'Falsification' covers the preparation of false accounts, as well as the falsification of existing ones.

TA 1968, s 17(2) states that a person who makes or concurs in making in an account or other document an entry which is or may be misleading, false or deceptive in a material particular, or who omits or concurs in omitting a material particular from an account or other document, is to be treated as falsifying the account or document. However, this is not an exclusive definition of falsification. In one case, it has been held that a turnstile operator, who allowed two people through the turnstile while only recording one of them, falsified the record. It may be that the falsification was within TA 1968, s 17(2) (by omitting a material particular) but if not there was a 'falsification' within the ordinary meaning of that term.

A person can falsify an accounting document by completely failing to fill in a blank form required for an accounting purpose, and even though the particular document so falsified cannot be identified. This surprising ruling was made by the Court of Appeal in a case where it upheld the conviction of an international telephone operator who had failed to log calls on the forms provided for this purpose. The court held that, as soon as a call was made, it was the operator's duty to fill in one of the forms in a pile in front of him and that thereby one of them became a document required for an accounting purpose and the fact that the particular form could not be identified (since the operator might not have chosen to use the first form) did not matter.

Use of false or deceptive account (TA 1968, s 17(1)(b))

Whereas TA 1968, s 17(1)(a) is concerned with those who falsify or destroy etc any account etc, s 17(1)(b) deals with those who, in furnishing information for any purpose, produce or make use of any account or any record or document made or required for any accounting purpose, *knowing* it is or may be misleading, false or deceptive in a material particular.

Of course, a person who has falsified an account contrary to TA 1968, s 17(1)(a) may go on to use it contrary to s 17(1)(b), in which case he will have committed both offences. However, an offence under s 17(1)(b) may also be committed by a person who has not falsified the document in question, for it is not uncommon for persons with a view to gain to use in a dishonest way documents which have been made out erroneously by someone else. If a person, who is entitled to receive payment for money which he has spent on petrol for use in his firm's car, receives a receipt which he knows has been wrongly made out for a higher amount, he commits an offence against s 17(1)(b) if, when making out his claim (furnishing information), he makes use of that receipt since, to his *knowledge*, it is or may be misleading, false or deceptive in a material particular. However, if that employee had not noticed that the receipt was incorrect his actions would not be dishonest, nor would he have the necessary knowledge.

LIABILITY OF COMPANY OFFICERS FOR OFFENCES OF DECEPTION OR OF FALSE ACCOUNTING

Special provision is made for cases where a offence is committed by a company or other corporate body under TA 1968, s 17 or under FA 2006 through the act and state of mind of one of its 'controlling officers' being attributed to it. That officer will, of course, be liable for the relevant offence under general principles. In addition, it is specially provided by TA 1968, s 18 and FA 2006, s 12 respectively that if the offence is committed with the consent or connivance of any director, manager, secretary or other similar officer of the body corporate, or any person purporting to act in any such capacity, he is also guilty of that offence.

COMPUTER MISUSE

The misuse of computer hardware or software may involve one or more of the offences described elsewhere in this book. For example, a person who falsifies the data in an account held on computer by inputting false information can be convicted of falsification of accounts, contrary to TA 1968, s 17 if he acts with a view to gain or intent to cause loss.

In addition, the misuse of computer hardware or software may involve one or more of three offences under the Computer Misuse Act 1990 (CMA 1990):

(a) unauthorised access to computer material;
(b) unauthorised access with intent to commit or facilitate commission of a further offence;
(c) unauthorised modification of computer material.

Unauthorised access to computer material

By CMA 1990, s 1(1), a person commits an offence if:

(a) he causes a computer to perform any function with intent to secure access to any program or data held in the computer;
(b) the access he intends to secure is unauthorised; and
(c) he knows at the time when he causes the computer to perform the function that that is the case.

The intended access need not relate to any particular program or data or any particular type of program or data, nor to a program or data held in any particular computer. It is immaterial whether the program or data is unauthorisedly accessed directly from the computer containing it or indirectly via another computer.

The scope of this offence is wide, since it covers all forms of computer hacking. The section is not concerned with authority to access types of data, but with authority to access the actual data involved. It is designed to prevent all forms of unauthorised access whether by insiders or outsiders. Indeed, actual access to any program or data held in a computer is not required, since it is enough that the accused simply causes a computer to perform a function with intent to secure access to a program or data held in it, that intended access being unauthorised to his knowledge.

Access to a program or data is secured by a person if, by causing a computer to perform any function, he:

(a) alters or erases the program or data;
(b) copies or moves it to any storage medium other than that in which it is held or to a different location in the storage medium in which it is held;
(c) uses it; or
(d) has it output from the computer in which it is held (whether by having it displayed or in any other manner).

Intent to secure access to a program or data is to be understood accordingly.

Despite its width the offence does not cover computer eavesdropping; mere surveillance of data displayed on a VDU screen is not enough since the accused must cause the computer to perform a function if he is to be guilty.

The requirement in s 1 that the access be unauthorised means that all computer hackers are caught, including those 'computer enthusiasts' who seek access merely because of the challenge of breaking through a security system designed to restrict access.

By CMA 1990, s 17(5), access of any kind by any person to a program or data held in a computer is unauthorised if:

(a) he is not himself entitled to control access of the kind in question to the program or data; and
(b) he does not have consent to access by him of the kind in question to the program or data from any person who is so entitled.

Because the definition refers to 'access of the kind' in question, a person who has authority to view data may nevertheless unauthorisedly access it if he accesses it to alter or copy it if he has no authority to access for such a purpose.

Unauthorised access with intent

By CMA 1990, s 2(1), a person commits an offence if he commits the unauthorised access offence under s 1 with intent:

(a) to commit an offence to which this section applies; or
(b) to facilitate the commission of such an offence (whether by himself or by any other person).

CMA 1990, s 2 applies to any offence where sentence is fixed by law (eg murder) or for which an offender of eighteen or over may be sentenced to imprisonment for five years (eg the various deception offences under the Theft Acts, theft, forgery and criminal damage).

It is immaterial whether the further offence is to be committed on the same occasion as the unauthorised access offence or on any future occasion, and it is also immaterial that the facts are such that the commission of the further offence is impossible.

Unauthorised modification of computer material

By CMA 1990, s 3(1), a person is guilty of an offence if:

(a) he does any act which causes an unauthorised modification of the contents of any computer; and
(b) at the time at which he does the act he has the requisite intent and the requisite knowledge.

A modification of the contents of a computer takes place if, by the operation of any function of the computer concerned or any other computer, any program or data held in the computer is altered or erased, or any program or data is added to its contents. Thus, the offence can be committed in a variety of ways, for example, by the addition or deletion of material contained in a computer or software held in a computer or by interfering with a computer or software by introducing a computer virus by means of an infected disc or some other means. Any act which contributes towards causing a modification is regarded as causing it.

A modification is unauthorised if the person whose act causes it is not entitled to determine whether it should be made and he does not have consent to the modification from anyone who is so entitled. Although the owner of a computer which is able to receive email is ordinarily to be taken to consent to the sending of emails to the computer, such implied consent is not without limits. For example, a divisional court has held, it does not extend to emails which are not sent for the purpose of communicating with the owner, but are sent as a 'mail bombing campaign' for the purpose of interrupting the proper operation and use of the system.

The 'requisite intent' is an intent to cause a modification of the content of a computer and by so doing to impair its operation, or to prevent or hinder access to any program or data held in it, or to impair the operation of any such program or the reliability of any such data. An example would be where someone, by misusing or by-passing a password, places in the files of a computer a bogus email pretending that the password holder was the author; such an addition would result in an unauthorised modification of the contents of the computer and would clearly be done with intent to cause a modification of the contents and by so doing to impair the reliability of the data on the computer. The intent need not be directed at any particular computer program or data, or a particular kind of program or data, or at any particular modification or particular kind of modification.

The 'requisite knowledge' is knowledge that any modification which the accused intends to cause is unauthorised.

It is immaterial whether an unauthorised modification or any intended effect of it is, or is intended to be, permanent or merely temporary.

Search warrants

A circuit judge may issue a search warrant under CMA 1990, s 14 if satisfied by information on oath that there are reasonable grounds for believing that an offence under CMA 1990, s 1 has been or is about to be committed on any premises and that there is on the premises evidence of that offence. The additional powers of seizure provided by the Criminal Justice and Police Act 2001, s 50 apply where a search warrant under CMA 1990 is executed.

CORRUPTION

Common law

Where a person, who is in a position of trustee to perform any public duty, accepts a bribe to act in a corrupt manner in the discharge of that duty, he commits an offence of corruption contrary to common law. An offer of a bribe, or an attempt to bribe such a person, is also a common law offence.

Statutory offences

Public Bodies Corrupt Practices Act 1889, s 1

A person commits an offence who, by himself, or in conjunction with another person, corruptly solicits or receives, or agrees to receive for himself or another, any gift, loan, fee, reward, or advantage whatsoever as an inducement to, or reward for, or otherwise on account of any member, officer or servant of a public body, doing or forbearing to do anything in respect of any matter or transaction whatsoever, actual or proposed, in which the public body is concerned. A 'public body' is a council of a county, city or town, municipal borough, board, commissioners and any other body with power to act under legislation relating to local government, public health, poor law, or otherwise to administer money raised by rates. The term does not include a government department or the Crown, but it does include any body which exists in a country or territory outside the United Kingdom and is equivalent to any such body.

In addition, every person who by himself, or in conjunction with another person, corruptly gives, promises or offers any gift, loan, fee, reward or advantage whatsoever to any person, whether for the benefit of that person or another, as an inducement or reward for, or otherwise on account of any member, officer or servant of any public body, doing or forbearing to do anything in respect of any matter or transaction whatsoever, actual or proposed, in which the public body is concerned, commits an offence.

In relation to these offences, the word 'corruptly' does not mean dishonestly. It is concerned with purposely doing an act which the law forbids as tending to corrupt. Where an accused claimed that he had offered a bribe merely to expose corruption, it was held that 'corruptly' meant with intention to corrupt and that his motive was irrelevant. It is no defence to claim that the person given or offered the bribe etc did not in fact act in the manner forbidden.

A prosecution for an offence under the 1889 Act, s 1 may not be instituted without the consent of the Attorney-General.

Prevention of Corruption Act 1906, s 1

The offences created by this Act are similar to those set out above but are committed by 'agents' of a 'principal'. An agent is any person employed by or acting for another. A person serving under the Crown or under any corporation, or any borough, district or county council, or any board of guardians, is an agent. The corrupt act must relate to the principal's affairs or business. It is immaterial that the principal's affairs or business (or the agent's functions) have no connection with the United Kingdom and are conducted in a country or territory outside the United Kingdom. The term 'principal' includes an employer.

Offences are committed when corruptly giving or agreeing to give, or offering any gift or consideration to an agent to do, or forbear from doing, any act in relation to his principal's affairs or business, or for showing or forbearing to show favour or disfavour to any person in relation to those affairs. It is similarly an offence for such an agent to corruptly accept or obtain, or agree to accept or attempt to obtain from any person such a gift or consideration for those purposes. Offences are also committed by persons who give to an agent any receipt, account, or other document in respect of which the principal is interested and which contains any statement which is false, or erroneous, or defective in a material particular, and to his knowledge is intended to mislead the principal. Similarly, an offence is committed by an agent who knowingly uses, with intent to deceive his principal, such receipt etc.

Dishonesty is not an essential element of an offence under the Prevention of Corruption Act 1906, s 1. 'Corruptly' means deliberately offering money or other favours with the intention that this should operate on the mind of the person to whom the offer was made so as to encourage him to enter into a corrupt bargain.

CHAPTER 41

Handling stolen goods and related offences

HANDLING STOLEN GOODS

If goods which had been stolen had no sales outlet then the incidence of theft would undoubtedly diminish significantly. Some thefts occur because the person who appropriates the property wishes to use it himself but others, especially where the appropriator engages in widespread offences of burglary, are committed in the knowledge that there is a ready market for certain types of articles: stereo equipment, television sets and DVD recorders are all marketable products and seem to be constantly falling from lorries. The law concerning the handling of stolen goods is concerned with punishing not only the ultimate receiver, in the sense that he is the buyer of the property, but all persons who handle that property dishonestly. In considering handling offences the approach to adopt is straightforward. Who knew that the property was stolen and in what way were they concerned in its handling? The Theft Act 1968 (TA 1968), s 22(1), states:

A person handles stolen goods if (otherwise than in the course of the stealing) knowing or believing them to be stolen goods he dishonestly receives the goods, or dishonestly undertakes or assists in their retention, removal, disposal or realisation by or for the benefit of another person, or if he arranges to do so.

In terms of the maximum punishment, the offence is a more serious offence than theft.

In order to establish the nature of the offence it is necessary to consider the meaning of the words 'stolen', 'goods' and 'handling'. It is best to commence with 'goods'.

Goods

The term is defined by TA 1968, s 34(2)(b), as follows:

'Goods' includes money and every other description of property except land, and includes things severed from the land by stealing.

This description is close to that given to 'property' for the purposes of theft. Although s 34(2)(b) does not specifically mention 'things in action', the words 'every other description of property except land' are wide enough to include them, and the Court of Appeal has held that things in action are goods for the purposes of handling. Nevertheless, the handling of 'things in action' is likely to have little significance in the practical aspects of law enforcement.

Stolen

For the offence to be committed, the goods handled must be 'stolen goods' at that point of time. TA 1968, s 24 sets out the meaning of the term 'stolen goods':

(a) goods which have been stolen, contrary to TA 1968, s 1;

(b) goods which have been obtained as a result of blackmail, contrary to TA 1968, s 21

(c) goods which have been obtained by fraud, contrary to the Fraud Act 2006 (FA 2006), s 1;

(d) goods which have been 'stolen' abroad contrary to the law of that land, provided that had the 'stealing' occurred in England or Wales an offence contrary to TA 1968, s 1 or 21 or FA 2006, s 1, would have been committed.

Hereafter, we use the term 'stolen goods' in this wide sense.

References to stolen goods also include money which is dishonestly withdrawn from an account to which a 'wrongful credit' has been made, but only to the extent that the money derives from the credit. We define 'wrongful credit' below (see p 1085).

If a child who is below the age of criminal responsibility appropriates property in circumstances which would amount to theft in a person over that age, a person who dishonestly handles that property is not guilty of this offence as the goods are not 'stolen goods'. However, that person can be convicted of theft, just as a dishonest finder may be convicted of it.

The fact that goods were stolen goods at the time of the handling can be proved by evidence of the conviction of the thief, as such evidence is admissible at the trial of a person charged with dishonest handling. The acquittal of an alleged thief does not prevent the goods being found to be stolen goods. Another way of proving the status of the property is by offering evidence of ownership, the owner identifying the property and describing the circumstances of its loss. It is not necessary to prove that goods were stolen by any particular person; merely that they were stolen by someone and were dishonestly handled by the accused.

When goods cease to be stolen

The issue of proof that the goods were stolen when they were handled raises the issue of when goods which have been stolen cease to be stolen goods. The obvious example of goods ceasing to be stolen is where they are recovered from the thief and returned to the true owner. However, TA 1968, s 24(3) is helpful in this respect. It provides that no goods shall be regarded as having continued to be stolen goods after they have been restored to the person from whom they were stolen or to other lawful possession or custody. Clearly, this goes further than repossession by the owner, since it includes cases in which goods have been restored to other lawful possession or custody. When a police officer in the course of his duties takes possession of stolen goods, they are thereby restored to 'other lawful possession or custody' and are no longer stolen; consequently, it is not an offence to 'handle' them thereafter. If an officer interviews a thief at his home, and the thief admits stealing a watch and hands it over to the officer, it is now in the officer's lawful custody and is no longer stolen goods. If the thief then tells the officer that a man (X) is to call at any moment to examine the watch, which he knows to be stolen, with a view to buying it, there can be no successful charge of dishonest handling against X if the officer returns the watch to the thief in order to allow X to receive it and X does receive it. However, had the thief merely reached the stage at which he had admitted to the officer that he had stolen the watch but had not handed it over, the watch would remain stolen and X could be convicted of handling if he arrived a few minutes later and received the watch.

The issue is in reality whether or not the stolen goods have been taken into possession on the owner's account so that they may be returned to him. Where a security guard marked cartons of stolen cigarettes so that they would more easily be identified in the hands of a handler, they were not restored to the owner as physical possession did not take place. They were not taken out of the possession of the thief. If a police officer sees property inside a parked car which he suspects might be stolen and immobilises the car to ensure that he will have an opportunity of questioning the driver, he does not take possession of the stolen goods unless he immobilises the car with the intention of taking charge of those goods so that they cannot be removed. If he has retained an open mind as to whether he should take possession, and merely immobilises the car to prevent the driver getting away without questioning, he does not reduce the goods into his possession or custody. It is the state of mind of the officer which is the deciding factor in each case.

TA 1968, s 24(3) also provides that goods cease to be stolen goods where the person from whom they were stolen and any other person claiming through him have ceased to have rights of restitution in respect of the theft. The right to restitution of property is a matter of civil law.

There are various ways in which the right to restitution may have been lost. An example is where X obtains goods from Y by deception. If Y, on discovering the deception, nevertheless affirms the transaction he thereby ceases to have any right to restitution of the goods, which therefore cease to be stolen goods at that point of time.

In the circumstances in which goods have ceased to be classed as stolen goods for the purposes of this section, the provisions of the Criminal Attempts Act 1981 should be considered. A person may be guilty of an attempt to commit an offence, even though that offence could not be committed. This would be so in relation to handling if the accused handled the goods believing them to be stolen, even though the goods had lost their status as stolen goods.

Goods representing those originally stolen

TA 1968, s 24(2) provides that references to stolen goods include, in addition to the goods originally stolen and parts of them (whether in their original state or not):

(a) any other goods which directly or indirectly represent or have at any time represented the stolen goods in the hands of the thief as being the proceeds of any disposal or realisation of the whole or part of the goods stolen or of goods so representing the stolen goods; and

(b) any other goods which directly or indirectly represent or have at any time represented the stolen goods in the hands of a handler of the stolen goods or any part of them as being the proceeds of any disposal or realisation of the whole or part of the stolen goods handled by him or of goods so representing them.

'The thief' means the person by whose conduct the goods were originally stolen. 'A handler' means any person who has committed the actus reus of handling with the appropriate mens rea. The Court of Appeal has held that goods are in the hands of the thief or of a handler if they are in his possession or under his control; physical custody is not required.

The 'proceeds rule' provided by TA 1968, s 24(2) is essentially as follows: goods which directly or indirectly represent or have represented the originally stolen goods *in the hands of the thief or a handler as the proceeds* of the disposal or realisation of those stolen goods, or goods so representing those stolen goods, are themselves deemed to be stolen goods. Consequently, once goods have been deemed to be stolen goods by this rule, an offence is committed if they are 'handled' thereafter with the appropriate mens rea.

The rule can be illustrated as follows. A steals a car. He sells it to B for £1,000 and receives that sum in cash. The car and the cash are now both stolen goods, the latter because it directly represents the original goods (the car) in the hands of the thief—as the proceeds of the car's disposal or realisation. Therefore, if A then gives the £1,000 (or part of it) to C, who receives it knowing it has represented the original stolen goods in A's hands and C buys a camera with the £1,000, the camera becomes stolen goods once it is in C's hands because it indirectly represents the original stolen goods in the hands of a handler as the proceeds of the disposal or realisation of goods representing the original stolen goods. Consequently if D receives the camera from C, knowing it has represented the stolen goods in C's hands, D can be convicted of handling stolen goods. However, if E receives the camera from D, unaware that it represents the original stolen goods, and then sells it for cash, the cash which he receives will not become stolen goods because, lacking mens rea, he is not a handler and therefore *that* cash does not *represent the original stolen goods in the hands of a handler* as the proceeds of their disposal or realisation.

Various forms of handling

TA 1968, s 22 defines 'handling' as receiving stolen goods, or undertaking or assisting in their retention, removal, disposal or realisation by or for the benefit of another person, or arranging to do one of these things. The offence of handling therefore covers the passage or handling of the goods through as many pairs of hands as may be involved, on their passage to the receiver, and also dealings with them thereafter. An examination of the definition of 'handling' shows that there are eighteen different ways of doing so.

Selecting the correct charge

Although there are eighteen different ways in which handling can be committed, it is unnecessary to make exclusive selections of a particular variant of the offence. The section constitutes a single offence of handling stolen goods, which can be committed by receiving or by any of the other ways specified. Consequently, an information (or, when in force, a written charge) or indictment, which simply alleges that there had been a handling of stolen goods, is not bad for duplicity.

Nevertheless, in order to be fair and clear to the accused, the better practice is to particularise the form of handling relied on, and, if there is any uncertainty about the form of handling in question, it is advisable to have more than one information (or more than one count in the indictment). But only two informations (or counts) should generally be used in such a case: one charging receiving, and the other charging the various forms of 'undertaking or assisting in' by or for the benefit of another (or such forms of these as are clearly the only ones relevant).

It is essential to remember in the first instance that s 22 excludes from its provisions those who handle in the course of the original stealing. This is a commonsense approach to offences of handling. We are not concerned with thieves who handle stolen goods in the course of their theft as they are punishable in respect of the theft, whatever form that theft may take.

The forms of handling can be explained as follows.

Receiving

To prove this type of handling it must be shown that the accused obtained possession or control of stolen goods from someone else; a finder of goods does not receive them. The presence of stolen goods on the premises of another does not necessarily mean that they are in the possession or control of the owner of the premises. If a thief calls at the home of a friend and his pockets contain a number of items of stolen property, that stolen property is in the possession of the thief, not the householder. To be a 'receiver' a person need not have contact with the goods in any physical sense, since a person can have control of goods without any physical contact with them. For example, if a thief who is wanted for serious offences enlists the aid of a friend to assist him to escape from the country and, in payment for that assistance, tells his friend that he has hidden a stolen car in a wood and transfers control of that property to him by handing over the car keys, then the friend receives the car when he receives the keys. In the same way, a person may receive property into his possession or control through an employee or agent acting on his orders, in which case the employee or agent is also a receiver.

Often, a receiver is acting solely for his own benefit, but it is unnecessary that a receiver should act to gain any profit or even advantage from his possession of stolen goods. If a person, knowing that goods have been stolen, dishonestly allows the thief to store them in his warehouse so that they may be concealed from the police, he is guilty of handling by receiving whether or not he is offered payment for such use of his warehouse.

Arranging to receive

This requires a concluded agreement between the accused and another (eg the thief) for the receiving of stolen goods by the accused. It is essential that the goods are stolen goods at the time the arrangement to receive is made. Thus, a person (A) does not commit handling where he commissions others to steal a certain type of property which he agrees to receive from them if they succeed in the theft, because at the time of his arrangement to receive there are no stolen goods to which it can relate. (A would, of course, be guilty with the others of a conspiracy to steal and of a conspiracy to handle stolen goods; if the theft was actually committed, A would also be guilty of theft as an accomplice on account of his counselling or procuring.) It would be different if the goods in question had already been stolen and the thieves had approached A and contracted to sell them to him; A would thereby be guilty of arranging to receive stolen goods, and it would be irrelevant whether or not they were subsequently delivered to him.

The other forms of handling set out below differ in a vital respect from receiving, or arranging to receive, in that they must be done 'by or for the benefit of' a person other than the alleged handler (or, the Court of Appeal has held, a co-accused on the same charge of handling).

Undertaking the retention, removal, disposal or realisation of stolen goods for the benefit of another

These four forms of handling cover the case where the accused, either alone or with another, retains, removes, disposes or realises the stolen goods for the benefit of another.

The four activities can be explained as follows: '*Retention*' means 'keeping possession of, not losing, continuing to have'. '*Removal*' refers to the movement of stolen goods from one place to another, for example transporting stolen goods to a hideout for the benefit of the thief or another. '*Disposal*' covers dumping, giving away or destroying stolen goods, for example melting down candlesticks for the thief. '*Realisation*' means the exchange of stolen goods for money or some other property. A person who sells stolen goods as agent for a third party (eg the thief) undertakes their realisation for the benefit of another. However, the House of Lords has held that a person who sells stolen goods on his own behalf does not undertake their realisation for the benefit of another because the buyer benefits from the purchase and not from the realisation (which benefits only the accused).

Of course, a person who undertakes one of these four activities will often be in possession or control of the stolen goods. If he knew or believed they were stolen when he acquired possession or control, he is guilty of handling anyway on the basis of receiving. However, if he lacked such a state of mind at that point of time but realised the goods were stolen when he undertook one of the four activities, he can be convicted of handling on that basis, provided that his 'undertaking' was *for the benefit of another*.

Assisting in the retention, removal, disposal or realisation of stolen goods by another

These four forms of handling are appropriate to cover cases where the accused provides assistance to another person, the thief or another handler, who is going to undertake the retention, removal, disposal, or realisation of stolen goods.

For there to be 'assistance', the accused must do something for the purpose of enabling the goods to be retained etc, whether or not he succeeds.

There is some overlap with cases of 'undertaking'. For example, a person who joins with another in removing stolen goods not only undertakes their removal for the benefit of another but also assists in their removal by another.

A person *assists in the retention* of stolen goods by another if he puts the thief in touch with a warehouse keeper, or provides tarpaulins to conceal stolen goods in the possession of the thief or a handler, or tells lies so as to make it more difficult for the police to find or identify stolen goods retained by the thief or a handler. On the other hand, a refusal to answer questions put by the police as to the whereabouts of stolen goods does not amount to handling, although it may well assist in their retention by another. A person, who innocently allows goods to be left on his premises but later discovers that they are stolen, assists in their retention by another if he nevertheless permits them to continue to remain on the premises. Merely to use stolen goods does not suffice, since it does not in itself amount to assistance in their retention.

Turning to the other activities, the following examples can be given.

A person *assists in the removal* of stolen goods by another if he lends a lorry for their removal. He *assists in their disposal* by another if he advises the thief as to how to get rid of the goods. He *assists in their realisation* by another if he puts a 'fence' in touch with the thief.

Arranging to undertake or assist

The effect of the section is further extended by the addition of the words 'or arranging to do so'. Any arrangement to undertake or assist in one of the activities described above can suffice; it is irrelevant that nothing is done pursuant to the arrangement. However, as we mentioned in relation to the offence of 'arranging to receive', it must be proved that the arrangements in respect of these other forms of handling relate to stolen goods; ie the goods in question must be stolen goods at the time of that arrangement. If, at the time that a would-be receiver is arranging to collect and take into his possession crates of stolen whisky, arrangements are made with others (who are aware that the whisky is stolen), for them to help him to load and unload the stolen goods, these other people are guilty of handling in that they arrange to assist in the removal of the goods by another.

By or for the benefit of another person

As we have indicated, in all cases of handling (other than those of receiving and arranging to receive), it must be shown that the acts which were carried out were carried out to assist in retention etc by another or undertaken to retain etc for the benefit of another, and that person should be named in the charge if his identity is known. If it is not, the charge should indicate that the acts were done, as appropriate 'by or for the benefit of' some person unknown and such a charge will have to be supported by strong evidence that that other person existed.

Mens rea

It must be proved that, when he handled the stolen goods, the accused (a) knew or believed that they were stolen, and (b) acted dishonestly.

Knowledge or belief

Wilful blindness, ie deliberately turning a blind eye to the question of whether or not goods are stolen, does not suffice for 'knowledge' or 'belief', but it has been held that, if wilful blindness as to the goods being stolen is proved, knowledge or belief *may* be inferred from it. This is surprising if the suspicion involved in wilful blindness is not enough for 'knowledge or belief'. Nevertheless, it is important since, in the absence of an admission by the handler, knowledge or belief (at the time of the handling) that the goods were stolen can be difficult to prove, particularly in the common case of sales at bargain prices in public houses, clubs and other places where people assemble, of goods which 'fell off a lorry' and which turn out to have been stolen. Unless the buyer was of below average intelligence or there were other special circumstances, wilful blindness on his part as to the fact that the goods were stolen *may* be capable of proof. If it is, the jury *may* (not must) infer knowledge or belief therefrom. This knowledge or belief that the goods were stolen must exist at the time that the person committed the act of handling in question, and the same is true of the element of dishonesty. Subsequent knowledge or belief is not enough.

It need not be proved that a handler was aware of the precise nature of the goods. If it can be proved that a person received boxes believing them to contain stolen whisky, it is immaterial that the boxes contained stolen wine; he believed that he was receiving stolen goods and therefore he can be convicted of handling.

Frequently, knowledge or belief is proved by reference to the surrounding circumstances. If stolen goods have been carefully concealed on private premises, this suggests not only that the occupier of the premises did not wish to be found in possession of them but also that he knew that the goods were stolen. Likewise, if stolen goods have been altered in form or have had identifying marks removed, this suggests not only that the person who made the alteration or removal did not wish to be found in possession of the goods in their original state but also that he knew that they were stolen. Knowledge or belief that goods were stolen is also very likely to be inferred where the accused denied that stolen goods, subsequently found on his premises, were on the premises or where he claimed that goods contained in containers were of a different description from the stolen goods subsequently found in them.

In general, where a person is found in possession of property which has been recently stolen, a judge may direct a jury that they may infer knowledge or belief if the accused fails to offer an explanation for his possession, or if they are satisfied beyond reasonable doubt that any explanation which is offered is false. This rule is merely an application of the ordinary rules of circumstantial evidence. In addition, TA 1968, s 27 which applies where the accused is being prosecuted at the trial in question only for handling stolen goods, recognises the difficulties which may exist for the police in proving knowledge in handling offences by allowing special evidence to be offered in certain circumstances. It provides that, if evidence has been given of an act of handling by the accused in relation to the goods in question, the following evidence may be given to assist proof of knowledge or belief that the property was stolen:

(a) evidence that the person charged has had in his possession, or has undertaken or assisted in the retention, removal, disposal or realisation of, stolen goods from any theft taking place not earlier than twelve months before the offence charged; and

(b) provided that seven days' notice in writing has been given to the person charged of the intention to prove the conviction, evidence that he has, within the five years preceding the date of the offence charged, been convicted of theft or of handling stolen goods.

It must be emphasised that these provisions only permit the evidence described in (a) and (b) to be given to prove knowledge or belief that the goods were stolen. They do not enable such evidence to be used for any other purpose, for example to prove dishonesty on the accused's part or an act of handling by him.

These provisions are extremely helpful in relation to proof of knowledge. By virtue of (a) the police are able to offer to the court evidence that other stolen goods, that is goods other than those in respect of which the charge lies, have been in the possession of the handler and that those goods were stolen within the preceding twelve months. The handler is therefore shown to have been in possession of other recently stolen property. The more that he can be shown to have possessed, the less likely it becomes that such goods might have been acquired accidentally.

The provisions set out at (b) are exceptional. However, the nature of the offence of handling is somewhat unique in that the issue of guilt or lack of guilt is seated in the issue of knowledge. It is less likely that a person who has been convicted of theft or handling will have come into innocent possession of stolen goods.

The provisions in (b) must be read with the Police and Criminal Evidence Act 1984 (PACE), s 73(2) which provides that where evidence of a previous conviction on indictment is admissible by means of a certificate of conviction the certificate must give 'the substance and effect of the indictment and conviction'. When (b) is read together with PACE, s 73(2), a certificate of previous conviction should:

(a) where the conviction for theft or handling was on indictment, state the substance and effect of the indictment and conviction, including the nature of the property concerned; and

(b) where the conviction for theft or handling was in summary proceedings, record the nature of the property concerned.

The whole of such a certificate is admissible. These points were made by the House of Lords in a case where a person was charged with an offence of handling (in relation to the bodyshell of an Escort RS Turbo) and a certificate showed a previous conviction for dishonestly receiving property (a Ford RS Turbo motor car). The House admitted the certificate. Clearly the fact that the goods were similar was highly relevant to the issue of knowledge. See further as to PACE, s 73, p 221.

The Court of Appeal has ruled that the provisions set out at (a) do not permit the introduction of details of previous convictions for an offence of handling and this is easily appreciated. The provisions at (a) are concerned with the possession (or retention etc) of goods, other than those in respect of which the charge lies, not with previous convictions.

Dishonestly

This word is provided to excuse legitimate acts of handling. Dishonesty is always a question of fact for the jury or justices, and the same approach is to be taken by them, as it is in relation to the offences of deception. It follows, for example, that if a person knowingly receives stolen goods, but does so in order to restore them to their owner, or to hand them over to the police, his handling is not likely to be found to be dishonest by the jury or justices.

ADVERTISING REWARDS FOR RETURN OF STOLEN OR LOST GOODS

TA 1968, s 23 punishes the public advertisement of a reward for the return of any lost or stolen goods which uses any words to the effect that no questions will be asked, or that the person producing the goods will be safe from apprehension or inquiry, or that any money paid for the purchase of the goods or advanced by way of loan on them will be repaid. The printer and publisher of such an advertisement are liable, as well as the advertiser.

SEARCH FOR STOLEN GOODS

The following provision is contained in TA 1968, s 26.

A justice may grant a warrant, upon information being received on oath that there is reasonable cause to believe that any person has in his custody or possession or on his premises any stolen goods, to search for and seize those goods. The additional powers of seizure provided by the Criminal Justice and Police Act 2001, s 50 apply where a search warrant under TA 1968, s 26 is executed.

DISHONESTLY RETAINING A WRONGFUL CREDIT

The offence of handling is not committed by someone into whose bank account a 'wrongful credit', as defined below, has been received because that credit itself is not stolen goods.

This gap is filled by TA 1968, s 24A. TA 1968, s 24A provides that a person is guilty of an offence if:

(a) a wrongful credit has been made to an account kept by him or in respect of which he has any right or interest;
(b) he knows or believes that the credit is wrongful; and
(c) he dishonestly fails to take such steps as are reasonable in the circumstances to secure that the credit is cancelled.

Actus reus

What is required is the failure to take such steps as are reasonable in the circumstances to secure the cancellation of a wrongful credit made to an account kept by the accused or in respect of which he has any right or interest. Nothing need be done by the accused. The mere omission to take reasonable steps suffices.

A 'credit' refers to a credit of an amount of money in an account. 'Money' includes currencies other than sterling. A credit to an account is wrongful to the extent that it derives from theft, blackmail, fraud (contrary to FA 2006, s 1) or stolen goods. An account is an account kept with:

(a) a bank;
(b) a person carrying on a business (i) in the course of which money received by way of deposit which is lent to others; or (ii) any other activity which is financed, wholly or to any material extent, out of the capital of, or the interest on, money received by way of a deposit;
(c) an issuer of electronic money (as defined for the purposes of the Financial Services and Markets Act 2000, Pt 2)

In determining whether a credit to an account is wrongful, it is immaterial whether the account is overdrawn before or after the credit is made.

Mens rea

The accused must know or believe that the credit is wrongful; he must know or believe the facts which make the credit 'wrongful' in law, although he need not know that they have this effect since ignorance of the criminal law is no defence.

Because failing to take steps is an omission which can continue over a period of time, it suffices that mens rea exists at some point during it; it need not exist from the outset. It follows that those who only become aware of a wrongful credit after it has been made can commit an offence under TA 1968, s 24A.

The accused must dishonestly fail to take such steps which are reasonable in the circumstances to secure that the wrongful credit is cancelled. The approach to this question is the same as in offences of deception and of handling.

Width of offence

TA 1968, s 24A covers a range of situations. Suppose that X commits an offence of fraud by causing a money transfer to be made to D's account, unknown to D. If D dishonestly fails to take reasonable steps to cancel the credit on discovering the truth, he commits an offence under s 24A because the credit is wrongful under TA 1968, s 24A(3).

Suppose that Y pays money which he has stolen (or obtained by blackmail or by selling stolen goods) into his bank account, and that Y then transfers the credit thereby created to D's bank account. If D dishonestly fails to take reasonable steps to cancel that credit he can be convicted of an offence under TA 1968, s 24A, because the credit will be wrongful under s 24A(4). It would be likewise if the credit had derived from the transfer to D's bank account of a credit wrongfully obtained by Y by means of an offence of fraud against the FA 2006.

CHAPTER 42

Forgery and counterfeiting

The law relating to forgery and counterfeiting is governed by the Forgery and Counterfeiting Act 1981 (FCA 1981). Part I of the Act is concerned with forgery and related offences, and Part II with counterfeiting and related offences. Most of the offences described in this chapter refer to the verb 'believe'; in relation to this word, see p 1082.

FORGERY

This offence is defined by FCA 1981, s 1 which states that a person is guilty of forgery if he makes a false instrument, with the intention that he or another shall use it to induce somebody to accept it as genuine, and by reason of so accepting it to do or not to do some act to his own or any other person's prejudice.

The actus reus of this offence is 'making a false instrument', and by FCA 1981, s 9(2) this includes altering an instrument so as to make it false in any respect.

False instrument

'Instrument'

For the purpose of forgery and other offences involving false instruments, FCA 1981, s 8 defines the word 'instrument' as:

(a) any document, whether of a formal or informal character (other than a currency note);

(b) any stamp issued or sold by a postal operator (or a metered postage mark);

(c) any Inland Revenue stamp denoting any duty or fee; and

(d) any disc, tape, sound track or other device on or in which information is *recorded or stored* by mechanical, electronic or other means. To be 'recorded' or 'stored' the information must be preserved for an appreciable time with the object of subsequent retrieval. Examples of items covered are microfilm records and information on computer tapes or discs and tachograph record sheets, but not electronic impulses in a computer or its 'user segment' (which stores information momentarily while the computer searches its memory, eg to check a password). The result is that computer hacking is not forgery although it is an offence under the Computer Misuse Act 1990, s 1 (unauthorised access to computer material).

It is important to note that, for present purposes, 'instruments' are limited to the things just listed. The only part of this list which calls for further definition is (a), which tells us that a document, whether formal or informal (other than a currency note), is an instrument. But what is a 'document'? The Court of Appeal has held that a thing is only a document if it conveys two messages: a message about the thing itself (eg that it is a cheque) and a message to be found in the words or other symbols that is to be accepted and acted on (eg the message in a cheque to the banker to pay a specified sum). Thus, cheques, wills, and building society pass books are examples of documents (and are therefore instruments) but paintings (even if falsely signed), false autographs and any writing on manufactured articles or their wrappings indicating the name of the manufacturer or country of origin, are not.

'False'

FCA 1981, s 9(1) defines the adjective *'false'* in relation to 'instrument'. It states that an instrument is false for the purposes of forgery and other offences involving forged instruments:

(a) if it purports to have been *made* in the form in which it is made by *a person who did not in fact make it* in that form; or

(b) if it purports to have been *made* in the form in which it is made *on the authority of a person who did not in fact authorise its making* in that form; or

(c) if it purports to have been *made in the terms* in which it is made *by a person who did not in fact make it in those terms*; or

(d) if it purports to have been *made in the terms* in which it is made *on the authority of a person who did not in fact authorise its making in those terms*; or

(e) if it purports to have been *altered* in any respect *by a person who did not in fact alter it* in that respect; or

(f) if it purports to have been *altered* in any respect *on the authority of a person who did not in fact authorise the alteration* in that respect; or

(g) if it purports to have been *made* or *altered* on a *date* on which, or at a *place* at which, or *otherwise in circumstances* in which, it was *not in fact made or altered*; or

(h) if it purports to have been *made* or *altered* by an *existing person* but he did *not in fact exist.*

This definition of the falsity of an instrument is quite complex and needs to be simplified to assist understanding. The key point is that it is not enough that the document tells a lie (ie contains a false statement); what is required is that it should tell a lie about itself (ie the document itself must pretend to be something which it is not). If a man writes an application for a job as a chemical engineer and falsely alleges that he is studying for a postgraduate degree in that field, that instrument is not a forgery although its contents are untrue. It was made by the applicant, it has not been altered in any way or falsely dated and it is made by an existing person.

Should the applicant make out a reference which is allegedly from his former tutor then that would be a false instrument, as it alleges that it was made by a person who did not make it or authorise its making. We must therefore consider an instrument to be false if it lies about itself in relation to the person who made the instrument, or authorised its making, or in respect of an unauthorised alteration, or if it purports to have been made or altered on a date, or in a place, or otherwise in circumstances, in which it was not in fact made or altered, or if it represents itself as having been made or altered by an existing person, who in fact did not exist.

If a person finds a cheque book and makes out a cheque for £100 and signs it in his own name, the cheque is not a false instrument because, even though a person is not the holder of the cheque book, it bears the signature of the person who made out the cheque. However, if he signs the name of the person who holds the account, the cheque is a false instrument as it lies about itself by alleging that it was signed by another who did not make the instrument or authorise its making. On the other hand, a person who opens an account in a false name in order to pay in a stolen cheque, does not make a false instrument when he completes a withdrawal form in that name. The name of the drawer is the same as the depositor's (although false) and the withdrawal form does not purport to be made by a person who did not make it. The term 'authorise its making' is important. Another person may draw up a document on behalf of another (and even sign it on his behalf) without creating a false instrument, providing that he was authorised to do so. A cheque, made out quite properly by the holder of the bank account for the sum of £100, becomes a false instrument when another person alters that cheque to show a sum of £1,000 by adding another zero to the figure shown on the face of the cheque and writing alongside it the initials of the account holder without that person's authority. It would be different if the person making the alteration was authorised to do so.

What we have just said about a false instrument in relation to documents is of course equally applicable to the other types of instrument. The Court of Appeal has held that a coach driver who operates his tachograph in such a way as to produce a record which shows that someone else was driving for a certain period of time, produces a false instrument if there was no other driver with him. In such a case, the instrument purported to have been made in circumstances in which it was not made. There was no other driver present.

Mens rea

The accused must make the false instrument with the intention that he or another person shall use it to induce somebody to accept it as genuine, and with the intention to induce that person by reason of so accepting it to do or not to do some act to his own or any other person's prejudice (besides the accused). Consequently, it is not enough simply to intend to induce a person to believe that an instrument is genuine. For example, making a false birth certificate solely to induce a belief that one comes from a noble family is not forgery. Nor is it enough to make a copy of a false instrument if the copy-maker intends to represent it as a copy. If the accused acts with the necessary double intent, it is irrelevant whether it is communicated to anyone, whether anyone is induced to accept the instrument as genuine or whether prejudice (within the meaning set out below) is caused. There is no need for either of the two intended consequences to be achieved. The accused need not intend to induce another human being, it suffices that he intends to induce a machine to respond to the instrument as if it were genuine.

It has been held by the Court of Appeal that a person, who makes a false instrument intending to fax it to X and thereby to induce X to accept it (ie the false instrument) as genuine and to act prejudicially, intends to use it (ie the false instrument) to induce another to accept it as genuine and to act prejudicially. This is a somewhat strained interpretation since the fax would seem to be a copy and not the false instrument which has been made. A charge of copying a false instrument contrary to FCA 1981, s 2 (below) would be more appropriate.

The act or omission intended to be induced must be to the prejudice of the person induced or of someone else. FCA 1981, s 10(1) provides that, for the purposes of forgery and related offences, an act or omission intended to be induced is only to a person's prejudice if it is one which, if it occurs:

(a) will result:
    (i)   in his temporary or permanent loss of property (including a loss by not getting what he might get as well as a loss by parting with what he has);
    (ii) in his being deprived of an opportunity to earn remuneration or greater remuneration; or
    (iii) in his being deprived of an opportunity to gain a financial advantage otherwise than by way of remuneration; or
(b) will result in somebody being given an opportunity:
    (i)   to earn remuneration or greater remuneration from him (the person induced); or
    (ii) to gain a financial advantage from him otherwise than by way of remuneration; or
(c) will be the result of his having accepted a false instrument as genuine (or—and this is only relevant to offences under FCA 1981, ss 2 and 4 below—a copy of a false instrument as a copy of a genuine one) in connection with his performance of a duty.

(Where the intended inducement is of a machine (eg a cash dispenser), the act or omission intended to be induced by the machine responding to the instrument is treated as an act or omission to a person's prejudice.) This rather complicated provision can be illustrated as follows. If A signs a cheque in B's name, intending to give it to C as payment for a car which C is to hire to A for a day, A has made a false instrument and he intends to use it to induce C to accept it as genuine, and by reason of so accepting it to do some act to his own prejudice, because C's handing over of the car will result in his temporary loss of it (see (a)(i), above). A is therefore guilty of forgery.

If A learns that his rival, C, is about to be promoted and, to prevent this, A writes to C's employer, F, a letter purportedly written by X, a clergyman, which alleges that C is dishonest, A is guilty of forgery because he has made a false instrument with intent to induce F to accept it as genuine, and by reason of so accepting it not to do an act to the prejudice of some other person (C), because F's non-promotion of C will result in C being deprived of an opportunity to earn greater remuneration (see (a)(ii), above).

If, instead, the letter referred to above had said that C was highly efficient, in an effort to secure the promotion for him, A would still be guilty of forgery because he has made a false instrument with intent to induce F to accept it as genuine, and by reason of so accepting it to do an act to his own prejudice, because it will result in C being given greater remuneration (see (b)(i), above).

If A learns that his trading rival, C, is tendering to supply goods to F and, to prevent this, A writes a letter to F which purports to have been written by someone who does not in fact exist and alleges that C produces shoddy goods, A is guilty of forgery. The reason is that he has made a false instrument and intends to use it to induce F to accept it as genuine, and by reason of so accepting it to do some act to the prejudice of some other person (C), because the award of the tender to someone else will result in C being deprived of an opportunity to gain a financial advantage (see (a)(iii), above).

If A makes a false airline ticket in order to get a free flight, A is guilty of forgery because he intends to use the ticket to induce an airline employee to accept it as genuine, and by reason of so accepting it to do some act to the prejudice of the airline by giving a financial advantage (ie the free flight) to A (see (b)(ii), above).

It is clear from (c), above, that the intended prejudice need not be financial in any sense at all, since (c) provides that it is enough that the act or omission intended to be induced will be to a person's prejudice if it will be the result of his having accepted a false instrument as genuine in connection with the performance of any duty, as where a false pass is made to induce a doorkeeper to admit an unauthorised person to premises. The duty referred to here means a legal duty, as opposed simply to a moral one.

In conclusion, it should be noted that by virtue of FCA 1981, s 10(2), it is not forgery where the maker of a false instrument intends to induce someone to do something which he is under an enforceable legal duty to do (or to induce someone not to do something he is not legally entitled to do). Thus, if A, who is owed money by C, sends a letter purporting to come from a firm of solicitors and threatening legal action if the debt is not paid, A is not guilty of forgery. The reason is that, even though A intends to induce C to accept the letter as genuine, and by reason of this to pay the money and thereby suffer loss, the act intended to be induced (paying the debt) is something C is legally obliged to do. In one case, man produced forged documents in support of an application for housing benefit at three separate addresses. He claimed that he lived at all three addresses and that because the council had a legal obligation to pay him benefit he had not intended to induce some act to the prejudice of another person. The Court of Appeal said that he was only entitled to benefit if it was claimed as prescribed by regulations. Payment was dependent upon production of genuine documents.

Provided that the requirements of FCA 1981, s 10(1) are satisfied, an honest and reasonable belief in a legal or moral claim to the gain which the accused intended to make as a result of falsifying the instrument is no defence (unless s 10(2) applies). A worker may genuinely believe that he is entitled to the salary increase which he seeks to gain by use of a false instrument, but such a belief can never amount to a defence to a charge under FCA 1981. Indeed, it is not a defence in itself that the accused might actually have been entitled to have property transferred to him if he had made a true claim (but not if he made a false instrument). This was decided by the Court of Appeal in a case where the beneficiaries of a trust might have been paid expenses by the trustees if they had made a properly substantiated claim. The Court of Appeal held that the beneficiaries would have had the necessary intentions if they used a false invoice to make a claim. It was not the trustees' duty to pay on false claims.

COPYING A FALSE INSTRUMENT

FCA 1981, s 2 is concerned with the separate offence of copying a false instrument. It provides that it is an offence for a person to make a copy of an instrument which is, and which he knows or believes to be, a false instrument, with the intention that he or another will use it to induce somebody to accept it as a copy of a genuine instrument, and with the intention to induce that person by reason of so accepting it to do some act to the prejudice of himself or some other person.

It is important to remember that FCA 1981, s 2 is concerned with what might be described as second generation forgeries. We are considering copies of false instruments from the outset. The essence of the offence lies in the intention to induce a belief that it is a copy of a genuine instrument, whilst in reality it is a copy of a false instrument. The section is meant to close loopholes which might otherwise exist. The essential points to prove are that the original instrument is a false instrument; that the person who made the copy knew or believed this to be so; and that the copy was made to induce someone to act etc. If someone wished to avoid paying his gas bill, he could allege that he had already paid and in support of this he might falsify a receipt for the money made out to appear as if it had been issued by British Gas. Clearly, if he did that he would be guilty of forgery as he would have made a false instrument with the requisite intents. FCA 1981, s 2 ensures that it is equally an offence then to photocopy that false receipt with intent to use that copy in an attempt to avoid payment. The section overcomes the arguments which have surrounded the nature of false instruments. The original false receipt clearly tells a lie about itself as it represents itself to be a true receipt. Arguments have been advanced in the past that a photocopy, or any other copy, does not tell a lie about itself as it merely represents itself to be a copy. These arguments are now academic since FCA 1981, s 2 declares the making of such copies to be a separate offence, punishable in the same way as forgery, if done with the necessary intent.

So far we have concentrated on criminal liability for *making* a false instrument with intent that it be used to induce etc (forgery), and for *making* a copy of a false instrument with the like intent (offence of copying a false instrument). What of the user of a false instrument (or copy of such an instrument)? It may be the forger who uses the false instrument (or copy), and if this is so he commits an additional offence. Alternatively, it may be another person who uses it. FCA 1981, ss 3 and 4 deal with offences of use.

USING A FALSE INSTRUMENT

FCA 1981, s 3 makes it an offence for a person to use an instrument which is false, and which he knows or believes to be false, with the intention of inducing somebody to accept it as genuine, and with the intention of inducing that person by reason of so accepting it to do or not to do some act to his own or any other person's prejudice. Section 4 provides a similarly worded offence of using a copy of a false instrument which is, and which he knows or believes to be, a false instrument, with the intention of inducing somebody to accept it as a copy of a genuine instrument, and by reason of so accepting it to do or not to do some act to his own or any other person's prejudice. Any use of a false instrument (or, as the case may be, a copy of a false instrument) with the necessary intent suffices. The verb 'use' is wide in meaning and covers, for example, a person who offers, delivers, tenders in payment or exchange, or exposes for sale, a false instrument (or a copy of one).

CUSTODY OR CONTROL OF MONEY ORDERS, SHARE CERTIFICATES, PASSPORTS ETC

FCA 1981, s 5 provides a number of offences under this heading, which are concerned with the following instruments:

(a)   money orders or postal orders;
(b)   United Kingdom postage stamps;
(c)   Inland Revenue stamps;
(d)   share certificates;
(e)   passports and documents which can be used instead of passports;
(f)   immigration documents;
(g)   cheques or other bills of exchange;
(h)   travellers' cheques;
(i)   bankers' drafts;
(j)   promissory notes;
(k)   credit cards;
(l)   debit cards; and
(m)   birth, adoption, marriage, civil partnership or death certificates or officially certified copies thereof.

Any such instrument is hereafter referred to as a 'specified instrument'.

By FCA 1981, s 5(1), it is an offence for a person to have in his custody or under his control a specified instrument which is, and which he knows or believes to be, false, with the intention that he or another shall use it to induce somebody to accept it as genuine, and by reason of so accepting it to do or not to do some act to his own or any other person's prejudice.

This 'possession' offence completes the cycle of offences which are likely to be committed if a false instrument is made for the purposes previously described. If someone makes out a false cheque with intent to induce someone to accept it as genuine, and by reason of so accepting it to do something to his prejudice, he commits forgery contrary to FCA 1981, s 1. If he walks through the streets to a bank, with the false cheque, in order to cash it, he commits the present offence under FCA 1981, s 5(1). If he then passes the cheque to a bank official in order to induce him to part with money, he commits the offence of 'using' contrary to FCA 1981, s 3. Of course, it may be that different people will commit different offences in the cycle, as where the person who makes the false instrument gets other people to engage in the use of such false instruments.

If the intent required for an offence under FCA 1981, s 5(1) cannot be proved, one can fall back on FCA 1981, s 5(2). This makes it an offence for a person merely to have in his custody or control, without lawful authority or excuse, a specified instrument which is, and which he knows or believes to be, false. 'Lawful authority or excuse' is likely to be limited to such matters as possession by a police officer after seizure of a specified instrument or possession by some other person who is in the course of handing over to the police such an instrument.

FCA 1981, s 5(3) and (4) are aimed at the tools of a forger's trade. Section 5(3) provides that it is an offence for a person to make or to have in his custody or under his control a machine or implement, or paper or any other material, which to his knowledge is or has been specially designed or adapted for the making of a specified instrument, with the intention that he or another shall make a specified instrument which is false and that he or another shall induce somebody to accept it as genuine, and by reason of so accepting it to do or not to do some act to his own or another's prejudice. In this way the Act strikes at a would-be forger even before he starts to make a false instrument. Whether or not the necessary intent for an offence under s 5(3) can be proved will often depend, in part, on the amount of forging equipment etc in the accused's custody or control.

If the intent required under FCA 1981, s 5(3) cannot be proved, one can fall back on s 5(4), which makes it an offence for a person to make or to have in his custody or control any such machine, implement, paper or material, without lawful authority or excuse.

We discuss the powers of the police in relation to all the above offences (ie FCA 1981, ss 1 to 5) at the end of this chapter.

COUNTERFEITING OFFENCES: GENERAL POINTS

Definition of counterfeit

By FCA 1981, s 28(1), a thing is a counterfeit of a currency note or of a protected coin:

(a) if it is not a currency note or a protected coin, but *resembles a currency note or protected coin* (whether on one side only or on both) *to such an extent that it is reasonably capable of passing for a currency note or protected coin of that description*; or

(b) if it is a currency note or protected coin which has been *so altered that it is reasonably capable of passing for a currency note or protected coin of some other description*.

For the avoidance of any doubt on the matter, FCA 1981, s 28(2) goes on to provide that a thing consisting of one side only of a currency note, with or without the addition of other material, is a counterfeit of such a note, and that a thing consisting of parts of two or more currency notes (or of parts of such note(s) and other material) is capable of being a counterfeit of a currency note. Thus, for example, a supposed currency note composed of parts of true currency notes and other materials is a counterfeit, as is a thing which consists of one side only of a currency note as a result of that note being 'split'.

For the purposes of FCA 1981, 'currency note' means:

(a) any note which has been lawfully issued in the United Kingdom, Channel Islands, Isle of Man or Irish Republic, and *is or has been* customarily used as money in the country of issue; and is payable on demand; or

(b) any note which has been lawfully issued in some other country, and *is* customarily used as money in that country.

Thus, a £20 note, a 20 euro note and a 100 dinar note are all 'currency notes'; so is an old style £5 note, which is no longer legal tender, but not a note which is no longer valid currency in the country where it was issued.

A 'protected coin' is defined as any coin which is customarily used as money in any country, ie any coin which *is still* valid tender at the time. It also includes a sovereign, half-sovereign, krugerrand (or a coin denominated as a fraction thereof), a Maria-Theresia thaler dated 1780 and any euro coin.

Passing or tendering

In the offences which we now proceed to discuss, references to 'passing or tendering' a note or coin are not confined to passing or tendering it as legal tender, so that (for example) passing or tendering a note or coin to a coin dealer or as a collector's item is a 'passing or tendering' for the purpose of these offences. A person 'passes' a note or coin to somebody when the latter actually accepts it from him; a person 'tenders' a note or coin when he offers to pass it to somebody. Thus, X tenders a coin to Y if he offers to give it to Y but Y refuses to accept it. On the other hand, simply to produce a bundle of counterfeit notes to impress a lady friend does not constitute a tender of them, since it does not involve any offer to pass them to her or anyone else.

COUNTERFEITING

FCA 1981, s 14(1) states that it is an offence for a person to make a counterfeit of a currency note or protected coin, intending that he or another shall pass or tender it as genuine. FCA 1981, s 14(2) makes it an offence for a person to make a counterfeit of a currency note or protected coin without lawful authority or excuse.

Both offences punish those who make a counterfeit currency note or protected coin; the difference between them is this. If the maker's intention is that he or another shall pass it into circulation, he commits an offence under FCA 1981, s 14(1). If he did not so intend, or that intent cannot be proved, he can be convicted of the lesser offence under FCA 1981, s 14(2) unless he had a lawful authority or excuse for making the thing.

It is difficult to imagine many instances in which the intention required by FCA 1981, s 14(1) will not have existed where a person has made counterfeits; in terms of proof all the circumstances of the discovery of the false notes or coins may be taken into account, together with any explanations offered by the accused. If a particular intention cannot be established, it is difficult to imagine how the counterfeiter could escape the provisions of FCA 1981, s 14(2) as there are few circumstances in which one could make counterfeits with lawful authority or excuse. Even the making of such counterfeits as a hobby would be unlikely to be accepted as a lawful excuse for their 'making'.

PASSING COUNTERFEIT CURRENCY

Passing or tendering counterfeit as genuine

By FCA 1981, s 15(1)(a) it is an offence for a person to pass or tender as genuine anything which is, and which he knows or believes to be, a counterfeit of a currency note or of a protected coin.

We have already explained what is meant by 'pass' and 'tender'. The counterfeit must be passed or tendered as genuine before this offence can be committed. A man who sells to another coins or notes which are false and declares them to be such does not pass or tender them as genuine since he does not hide the fact of their falsity.

Finally, the person who offers the counterfeits as genuine must know or believe them to be false. This protects a person who, without realising their falsity, passes or tenders counterfeits which he has received quite innocently in his change. However, he would commit the offence if, recognising that he had received a false coin or note, he decided to put it back into circulation rather than accept the loss.

Delivering counterfeit to another with intent that it shall be passed or tendered as genuine

FCA 1981, s 15(1)(b) makes it an offence for a person to deliver to another anything which is, and which he knows or believes to be, a counterfeit of a currency note or protected coin, intending that the person to whom it is delivered or another shall pass or tender it as genuine. Section 15(1)(b) deals, for example, with the person who knowingly takes counterfeits from the maker and delivers them to a second person, intending that the second person should pass or tender them as genuine. It is irrelevant whether or not the second person is an innocent recipient.

Delivering counterfeit without lawful authority or excuse

In circumstances in which it cannot be proved that the person who delivered the counterfeit intended that the recipient or another should pass or tender it as genuine, he may be convicted of the offence of delivery without lawful authority or excuse, which is dealt with by s 15(2).

FCA 1981, s 15(2) makes it an offence for a person to deliver to another, without lawful authority or excuse, anything which is, and which he knows or believes to be, a counterfeit of a currency note or protected coin.

CUSTODY OR CONTROL OF COUNTERFEIT CURRENCY AND COUNTERFEITING IMPLEMENTS

The offences of 'possession' of false instruments and of materials and implements for their making dealt with above have their counterparts in FCA 1981, ss 16 and 17 in relation to people who have counterfeit currency or counterfeiting materials or implements in their custody or under their control.

Custody or control of counterfeit currency

By FCA 1981, s 16(1), it is an offence for a person to have in his custody or control a counterfeit of a currency note or of a protected coin, knowing or believing it to be so and intending either to pass or tender it as genuine or to deliver it to another with the intention that he or another shall pass or tender it as genuine. FCA 1981, s 16(2) makes it an offence for a person to have such custody or control, with such knowledge or belief, without lawful authority or excuse. On a charge under s 16(2) the accused's intention is irrelevant. Whilst a settled intention to hand in counterfeit currency may amount to a lawful excuse, the fact that a person has not yet decided what to do with it cannot amount to such an excuse.

The offences of 'possession' in respect of currency may be committed even though the coin or note is not in a fit state to be passed or tendered or even though its making or counterfeiting has not been finished or perfected. Consequently, these offences may be committed, for example, in relation to the part-finished efforts of a counterfeiter.

Making, custody or control of counterfeiting materials and implements

The distinction between FCA 1981, s 16(1) and (2) in terms of the accused's intention is mirrored by the provisions of FCA 1981, s 17, which is concerned with the making, custody or control of counterfeiting materials or implements, such as special paper or inks, metal plates and printing or reprographic equipment.

FCA 1981, s 17(1) makes it an offence for a person to make, or to have in his custody or under his control, anything which he intends to use, or to permit any other person to use, for the purpose of making a counterfeit of a currency note or of a protected coin with the intention that it be passed or tendered as genuine. The words 'anything which he intends to use' include *anything used as a part of the process of counterfeiting*. This includes chromolins (printers' proofs used to check the quality of an aluminium plate produced from a film) of a currency note.

FCA 1981, s 17(2) provides that it is an offence for a person without lawful authority or excuse to make or to have in his custody or under his control any thing which, to his knowledge, is or has been specially designed or adapted for the making of a counterfeit of a currency note; no intent that the counterfeit should be put into circulation needs to be proved.

By FCA 1981, s 17(3), it is an offence for a person to make or have in his custody or under his control, any implement which, to his knowledge, is capable of imparting to anything a resemblance:

(a) to the whole or part of either side of a protected coin; or
(b) to the whole or part of the reverse of the image on either side of a protected coin.

A person charged with this offence has a defence if he proves that he had the written consent of the Treasury or some other lawful authority or excuse. It is important to note that this is the only offence in the Act where the accused has the burden of proving a lawful authority or excuse.

SUMMARY ON COUNTERFEITING

In conclusion, it is helpful to consider the complete operation and the participation of each person involved when attempting to establish counterfeiting and related offences. If we consider at the outset the discovery of a counterfeiter's den, this discovery will almost certainly involve the finding of materials and implements for counterfeiting. Quite apart from the liability of the person in 'possession' of these things, there may be evidence as to who made them. Thus, a number of offences under FCA 1981, s 17 may be revealed at this stage. Any counterfeit currency which is discovered will almost certainly have been made with the intention that someone should pass or tender it as genuine, or at least have been made without lawful authority or excuse. In either event, an offence contrary to FCA 1981, s 14 will have been committed.

Where counterfeit currency has been made, there will almost certainly be someone who has it in his custody or control, and if he knows or believes it is counterfeit, he will be guilty of an offence under FCA 1981, s 16 if he intends that it should be passed or tendered as genuine, or if he has no lawful authority or excuse for his 'possession'. The first possibility will always embrace the second and this could be commented upon in such circumstances. These offences are complete even if the currency is not in a fit state to be passed or tendered.

If counterfeit currency is discovered at a counterfeiter's den, it is probable that finished currency will already have left the premises. This raises the question of whether it was delivered by some person to another for circulation, or whether it was merely delivered without lawful authority or excuse. Either way, provided the deliverer knew or believed the thing to be counterfeit, an offence under FCA 1981, s 15(1)(b) or (2) will have been committed.

Finally the actual introduction of the counterfeit currency into circulation must be considered, and in this context it must be remembered that the lawful authority or excuse exemption does not apply since FCA 1981, s 15(1)(a) (which governs this offence) merely requires the passing or tendering as genuine something which the accused knows or believes to be counterfeit.

REPRODUCING BRITISH CURRENCY

This heading can be misleading as it suggests serious offences of counterfeiting. However, the offences covered by this heading are neither serious (since they are punishable only by way of a fine, even if tried on indictment) nor do they require any counterfeiting. The offences in question are governed by FCA 1981, ss 18 and 19 which deal respectively with the reproduction of British currency notes without written consent to do so from the relevant authority, and with the making, sale or distribution of imitation British coins in connection with a scheme intended to promote the sale of any product or service.

These sections are not concerned with counterfeiting in its strict sense (ie notes and coins reasonably capable of passing as currency notes or protected coins), but set out to prevent the use of reproductions in any form, even though the copy reproduced would not fool any reasonable person. If there was no legislation to prevent the production of good quality 'stage money', this could lead to abuse. Colour supplement magazines could print a reproduction of one side of a currency note as a voucher entitling the holder to a reduction on the price of an article in certain stores. This would no doubt be done innocently, but the reproduction might be used falsely by some other person. Many modern copiers can produce good quality copies of colour documents and there is no reason to suppose that machines could not be produced which could reproduce reasonable copies. FCA 1981, s 18, which deals with notes, goes to the extent of prohibiting copies which are not reproduced on the correct scale, in order to prevent 'blow-ups' being produced which may be of assistance to a counterfeiter.

When considering offences of reproduction, one must not ignore the possibility of offences contrary to the previous provisions. If the reproductive processes lead to the production of a copy which is reasonably capable of passing for a currency note, the more serious offences under FCA 1981, s 14 of counterfeiting with intent to pass or tender, or of counterfeiting without lawful authority or excuse, should be considered.

PROCEDURE AND POWERS

Search

FCA 1981, ss 7 and 24 authorise a justice who is satisfied upon information on oath that there is reasonable cause to believe that a person has in his *custody* or under his *control*:

(a) anything which has been used, or is intended to be used, for the making of a false instrument or copy of a false instrument, contrary to FCA 1981, s 1 or 2;
(b) any false instrument or copy which has been used, or is intended to be used, contrary to FCA 1981, s 3 or 4;
(c) anything which it is unlawful to possess without authority etc, under FCA 1981, s 5 (false money orders, stamps etc);
(d) counterfeit currency notes or protected coins, or reproductions; or
(e) anything which has been used, or is intended to be used, for the making of such counterfeit or reproductions,

to issue a warrant authorising a constable to enter premises, search for and seize such objects. The additional powers of seizure provided by the Criminal Justice and Police Act 2001, s 50 apply where a search warrant under FCA 1981 is executed.

A constable may, at any time after seizure, apply to a magistrates' court for an order for the disposal of objects seized.

CHAPTER 43
Preventive justice

There are various offences which are specifically aimed at nipping crime in the bud. Legislation deals with criminal attempts, conspiracies, interference with motor vehicles, the possession of offensive weapons and going equipped to steal. The crime of incitement is still governed by the common law, as are certain types of conspiracy.

ATTEMPT

The Criminal Attempts Act 1981 (CAA 1981) abolished the common law offences of attempt and of procuring materials with which to commit crime and replaced them by a statutory offence of attempt, which is defined by CAA 1981, s 1. Section 1(1) provides:

If, with intent to commit an offence to which this section applies, a person does an act which is more than merely preparatory to the commission of the offence, he is guilty of attempting to commit the offence.

The offences to which the section applies are described by CAA 1981, s 1(4) which provides that the section applies to any offence which, if completed, would be triable in England and Wales as an indictable offence, except:

(a) conspiracy (at common law or under the Criminal Law Act 1977 (CLA 1977), s 1 or any other enactment);
(b) aiding, abetting, counselling, procuring or suborning the commission of an offence; and
(c) offences under the Criminal Law Act 1967, s 4(1) (assisting offenders) or s 5(1) (accepting or agreeing to accept consideration for not disclosing information about an indictable offence).

It follows that all attempts to commit indictable offences, other than those specified above, are offences contrary to CAA 1981, s 1 but attempts to commit summary offences are not. However, it should be noted that a number of statutes providing summary offences also provide specific offences of attempt in relation to them.

Mens rea

The requirement of mens rea plays a particularly important role in the crime of attempt because whether or not a particular act amounts to an attempt may well hinge on the intent with which it is done. For example, to strike a match near a haystack may or may not be attempted arson of a haystack, depending on whether there is an intent to set fire to the haystack or to light a cigarette: the intent colours the act.

The mens rea specified by CAA 1981, s 1(1) is an 'intent to commit an offence to which this section [ie s 1] applies' and which the accused is alleged to have attempted. This apparently straightforward statement needs further explanation since 'an intent to commit the offence attempted' may involve a number of mental states.

The accused must, of course, intend to commit an act or to continue with a series of acts which, when successfully completed, will amount to or lead to an offence. In addition, if the crime attempted requires some consequence to result from his conduct, the accused must *intend* to cause that consequence. This is so even though some other type of mens rea (eg recklessness) is required or suffices for the full offence. This requirement of mens rea in attempt can be illustrated as follows:

(1) On a charge of attempted murder, it must be proved that the accused intended the unlawful death of another human being. By way of comparison, if the accused had actually killed someone he could be convicted of murder merely because he intended his act unlawfully to cause grievous bodily harm to another person.
(2) On a charge of attempted criminal damage, it must be proved that the accused intended the destruction or damaging of property belonging to another, even though if he had actually destroyed or damaged that property he could have been convicted of criminal damage if he was reckless as to the risk that his act might possibly have this effect.

Where the actus reus of the crime attempted includes some circumstance, such as the absence of the victim's consent in rape or the fact that the goods handled are stolen in handling stolen goods, the accused will have sufficient mens rea as to that circumstance if he knew or believed that it existed. Moreover, where some lesser mental state as to a circumstance suffices for the full offence, or no mental state as to it is required at all, recklessness as to it suffices on a charge of attempt. This rule can mean that the requirements on an attempt charge are greater than on a charge for the full offence. For example, on a charge of attempting to commit the offence of rape of a child under thirteen, which offence requires no mens rea as to age, it must be proved not only that the accused had decided to have intercourse with the girl concerned but also that he knew or was reckless as to the fact that she was under thirteen, even though if he had succeeded in having intercourse with her he could have been convicted of the full offence despite the absence of any realisation on his part that she might be under thirteen and despite the fact that this absence was reasonable on his part.

One last point must be made. The requirement that the accused must intend to commit the offence attempted means that he must have any other mental element, additional to mens rea as to the elements of the actus reus of the crime attempted, required for that crime. Thus, to be convicted of attempted theft an accused must not only have intended to appropriate property belonging to another but have acted dishonestly and with intent permanently to deprive the 'owner' of the property in question. Likewise, to be convicted of attempting to commit the offence of damaging or destroying property, intending thereby to endanger the life of another, or being reckless whether another's life would thereby be endangered, the accused must not only have intended to destroy or damage property, but have intended thereby to endanger the life of another or been reckless as to the risk of this occurring.

Actus reus

CAA 1981, s 1(1) requires 'an act that is more than merely preparatory to the commission of the offence', ie the full offence which the accused intends to commit. The Act offers no explanation of the rather vague phrase just quoted. Nevertheless, it is obvious that an act is more than merely preparatory to the commission of an offence in a 'last act' case, that is one where the accused has done the last act towards the commission of the full offence which, to his knowledge, it was necessary for him to do in order to commit that offence, even though something more remains to be done by another, innocent, person. Two examples of such a case are where X puts poison in another's drink, intending him to drink it and be killed in consequence, and where X posts a parcel bomb to another, intending him to be killed when he opens it; in both cases it is inconceivable that a jury would not find that X had done an act that was more than merely preparatory to the commission of murder.

The 'more than merely preparatory' formula is not limited to 'last act' cases, since it *can* be satisfied where a person still has to take some further step or steps himself before the full offence can be committed by him. In this context it must be emphasised that the question is not whether the accused has done an act which was more than preparatory but whether he has done an act which was more than *merely* preparatory. If it was the former which was the test it would be virtually impossible to get a conviction for attempt, except in a 'last act' case, because every act in furtherance of a criminal intent, other than a 'last act', can be described as preparatory. On the other hand, not every such act can be described as *merely* preparatory. This is because if a person can be said to have got as far as being engaged in the commission of an offence (ie 'on the job'), it will be a major understatement to say that his acts were still *merely* preparatory to the commission of the crime, even though (since some further act was required of him) his acts were still at a preparatory stage.

It is difficult to be more precise than this. Nevertheless, if the approach just advocated is adopted, the solution in most cases where the issue is whether the accused has gone far enough to be guilty of attempt will be fairly easy. Suppose, for example, that X buys matches, paraffin, wellingtons and overalls with the intention of burning down a barn. These acts are clearly all merely preparatory acts and cannot amount to an attempt to commit arson. Suppose that X places all these articles in a car, drives to the scene, takes the articles out of the car and approaches the barn. If X gets no further than this, it is still inconceivable that a jury would find that he has gone beyond the merely preparatory. However, if X gets as far as pouring paraffin over the door of the barn, the jury is likely to find that this act is more than merely preparatory to the arson of it, and that therefore he is guilty of its attempted arson, and it is even more likely so to find if he has gone further and actually struck a match.

Another example can be drawn by reference to the case of a terrorist gunman who lies in wait for his victim before shooting him. Clearly his acts are merely preparatory when he first acquires a rifle for his murderous purpose and when he carries it to the spot where he is to lie in wait. On the other hand, if he gets as far as raising the rifle to his shoulder in order to take aim, a jury is likely to find that he has done an act that is more than merely preparatory and is therefore guilty of attempted murder, and it is even more likely so to find if he has actually taken aim.

Examples of cases where a judge has held that there is or is not sufficient evidence of a more than merely preparatory act are as follows.

In one case, where a man had loaded a gun, disguised himself and had gone to a place where his intended victim could be found, these acts were considered to be merely preparatory. When he later pointed the gun at his intended victim with the intention of killing him and, when foiled, placed a cord around his neck, these acts provided sufficient evidence of attempted murder for consideration by the jury. In another, a man dragged a girl to a secluded spot and threatened her before putting his hand up her skirt in contact with her vaginal area. He then moved his hand to the top of her tights. It was held that there was sufficient evidence of attempted rape upon which a jury could make a decision. Where a mother whose children were in local authority care bought three single ferry tickets for the Republic of Ireland before falsely telling a teacher at the children's school that she had come to take the children to the dentist, it was considered that the acts up to the point of asking the teacher for the children were merely preparatory, but that the jury was entitled to find that asking for the children involved an attempt to abduct them.

However, where a man was seen to approach a post office, ride around the area on a motor cycle and to walk around that area before donning sunglasses and putting his hand into a pocket which appeared to contain something heavy, it was held that this was not sufficient evidence on which a jury could find a more than merely preparatory act in relation to committing robbery at the post office. The fact that the man was later found to be in possession of an imitation gun and a threatening note were matters affecting the issue of 'intent'. His actions were too far removed from an offence of robbery to be considered more than merely preparatory.

In another case, a man was seen in the boys' lavatory block in a school. He was in possession of a rucksack which contained a large kitchen knife, lengths of rope and a roll of masking tape. The Court of Appeal said that there was not much room for doubt about the man's intention and there was clear evidence of preparation, but there was no evidence that he had even put himself in a position to commit an offence and he had had no contact or communication with, nor had confronted, any pupil. There was therefore, no evidence of an act which was more than merely preparatory to an act of wrongful imprisonment. The Court of Appeal also considered the importance of the word 'merely' in circumstances in which men provided themselves with oxyacetylene equipment, drove to a barn, had concealed that equipment in a hedge, and had approached the barn door and were found examining the padlock to see how best to go about effecting an entry. The Court said that those acts could be considered to be more than *merely* preparatory. The facts were sufficient to allow a jury to find that there had been an attempt. Essentially, the question is one of degree.

Impossibility

CAA 1981, s 1(2) deals with matters which have long been the concern of courts; could one attempt to steal from a pocket if that pocket was empty, or could one attempt to steal from an empty shopping bag? It puts the issue beyond doubt by declaring that a person may be guilty of attempting to commit an offence to which s 1 applies, even though the facts are such that the commission of the offence is impossible. Therefore, the person who puts his hand into an empty pocket with intent to steal can be convicted of attempting to commit an offence. Likewise, a person who intends to kill another by shooting him in a bed, but who discovers after he has fired the shot that the assumed and intended victim was a pillow, can be convicted of attempted murder.

CAA 1981, s 1(3) purports to reinforce the rule in s 1(2), by declaring that where:

(a) apart from s 1(3) a person's intention would not be regarded as having amounted to an intent to commit an offence; but

(b) if the facts of the case had been as that person believed them to be, his intention would have been so regarded,

he is to be regarded as having an intent to commit that offence.

The application of s 1(3) is illustrated by a case where the House of Lords held that there was an attempt where the accused had been arrested carrying a package he had brought from India which he believed to contain either heroin or cannabis. Scientific analysis later proved that the package did not contain a controlled drug but snuff or some similar harmless vegetable matter. The House of Lords held that the accused had properly been convicted of attempting to commit the offence of knowingly being concerned in dealing with a drug the importation of which was prohibited. He had had an intent to commit the offence in question, and, with that intent, he had done an act which was more than merely preparatory to the commission of that intended offence (since he had to be judged on the facts as he believed them to be). Likewise, where X handles what he believes to be stolen goods, when they are not in fact stolen, he is nevertheless guilty of an attempt to handle stolen goods. Such cases are no doubt covered by s 1(2) but s 1(3) makes it clear that they amount to an attempt.

Other statutory offences of attempt

CAA 1981, s 3 applies the provisions of the Act to other existing statutory attempts to commit offences, by stating that the same provisions apply to those attempts; that is that a person will be guilty of such an attempt if, with intent to commit the relevant full offence, he does an act which is more than merely preparatory to the commission of that offence. The section therefore ensures a common standard of approach to all offences of attempted crime, even where the specific offence of attempt is created by a particular statute and even where that specific offence relates to a summary offence.

INCITEMENT

It is an offence at common law to incite another person to commit any offence, including a summary one, other than conspiracy. The essence of the crime lies in the incitement; it is therefore irrelevant that the person incited does not in fact carry out the act. Incitement requires an element of persuasion or encouragement or of threats or other pressure. One example is where A offers B a large sum of money if B kills C. A is thereby guilty of incitement to murder, even though his efforts at persuasion or encouragement are totally ineffective and B refuses to have anything to do with the scheme. The element of persuasion or encouragement or of threats or other pressure may be implied as well as express. The incitement in question must, of course, come to the notice of the person intended to act on it. However, if it does not (eg because it is contained in a letter which never arrives), the person making it may be guilty of an attempt to incite.

CONSPIRACY: INTRODUCTION

There are two offences of conspiracy:

(1) It is a *statutory* offence to agree with any other person or persons for the commission of an offence. Statutory conspiracy was introduced, and is governed, by CLA 1977.
(2) It is a *common law* offence to agree to defraud or, to the extent that the conduct agreed on would not amount to or involve an offence if carried out by a single person, to engage in conduct which tends to corrupt public morals or outrages public decency. Prior to CLA 1977, an agreement to commit an offence or an agreement to do certain other things was a common law conspiracy but that Act abolished common law conspiracy except to the extent just stated.

Both types of conspiracy require a concluded agreement between two or more people. It is not sufficient for one person to have spoken in the presence of another of his intention to commit a crime, for example; that other person must agree with him that the crime be committed. Immediately such an agreement has been reached, the offence of conspiracy is complete; no steps need be taken in furtherance of it, although it will usually be most unlikely that the conspiracy will be discovered or capable of proof if no further steps are taken. A party cannot escape liability for conspiracy by withdrawing from the agreement.

For reasons which are not very convincing, a husband and wife cannot be convicted of conspiracy if they are the *only* parties to the agreement in question.

We now turn to the separate requirements of the two offences of conspiracy.

STATUTORY CONSPIRACY

CLA 1977, s 1(1) defines the statutory offence of conspiracy as follows:

If a person agrees with any other person or persons that a course of conduct shall be pursued which, if the agreement is carried out in accordance with their intentions, either:
(a) will necessarily amount to or involve the commission of any offence or offences by one or more of the parties to the agreement, or
(b) would do so but for the existence of facts which render the commission of the offence or any of the offences impossible,
he is guilty of conspiracy to commit the offence or offences in question.

Thus, a person commits statutory conspiracy if he agrees with any other person or persons *that a course of conduct shall be pursued which, if the agreement is carried out in accordance with their intentions, will necessarily amount to or involve the commission of an offence or offences by one or more of the parties to the agreement.* Special provision is made by CLA 1977, s 1(1)(b) for the case where the criminal objective is impossible, and we shall deal with this shortly. First, however, we must make the following points about the words italicised.

The key issue is whether the course of conduct agreed on by the parties would necessarily amount to or involve the commission of an offence by one or more of them if it was carried out in accordance with their intentions. Thus, if A and B agree to have intercourse with a woman without her consent, there is a statutory conspiracy to rape because the course of conduct agreed on—penile penetration—would necessarily amount to the commission of rape if it was carried out in accordance with their intentions, namely to have penile penetration with a woman without her consent.

The offence which the agreed course of conduct would necessarily amount to or involve may be of any type, including (with one exception) a summary offence. By CLA 1977, s 1A, s 1(1) applies in certain cases to an agreement to pursue a course of conduct in a foreign country which would amount to an offence under the law of the country concerned.

The exceptional case referred to above is provided by the Trade Union and Labour Relations (Consolidation) Act 1992, s 242. It is that where, in pursuance of any agreement, the acts constituting the offence are to be done in contemplation or furtherance of a trade dispute, that offence is not an 'offence' for the purposes of conspiracy if it is triable only summarily and *not* punishable with imprisonment. This exemption is provided, not to exempt trade union leaders from the criminal law in relation to conspiracies, since conspiracies to commit crimes punishable by imprisonment are still punishable, but to remove the potential danger of conspiracy charges in relation to the many minor offences which might be committed by union members in the course of a dispute, for example, simple obstructions of highways.

There cannot be a statutory conspiracy unless there are at least two parties to an agreement who intend that the agreement be carried out and that the offence they are alleged to have conspired to commit be committed. They can only have the latter intention if they intend or know that the elements of that offence shall or will exist when the conduct constituting that offence is to occur. If these requirements are satisfied, it is no defence to allege ignorance that the course of conduct agreed on was a criminal offence. Surprisingly, because it does violence to the wording of CLA 1977, s 1(1), the House of Lords has held that an individual party to an agreement can be convicted of conspiracy, even though he did not intend that it be carried out and the offence intended by the other parties be committed; in practice this ruling has been ignored and the courts require an intention that the agreement be carried out and that the offence be committed to be proved against an individual accused.

Impossibility

CLA 1977, s 1(1)(b) deals with agreements which are impossible of fulfilment. It provides that an agreement on a course of conduct which, if the agreement is carried out in accordance with the parties' intentions, would necessarily amount to or involve the commission of an offence or any offences by one or more of the parties *but for the existence of facts which render the commission of the offence or any of the offences impossible* is a statutory conspiracy. This is a sensible provision; the essence of the offence is hatching a plot to commit a crime and this is not made less blameworthy because the actual commission of that crime is rendered impossible because of some fact.

As a result of CLA 1977, s 1(1)(b), it is clear, for example, that A and B can be convicted of conspiracy to murder even though their intended victim was already dead when they agreed to kill him.

COMMON LAW CONSPIRACY

As we have already explained, the only types of common law conspiracy which still exist are conspiracy to defraud and, to the extent that the conduct agreed on would not amount to or involve an offence if carried out by a single person, conspiracy to engage in conduct which tends to corrupt public morals or outrages public decency.

Conspiracy to defraud requires further explanation. There can be a conspiracy to defraud without any element of deception since it is sufficient to prove an agreement by dishonesty to deprive a person of something which is his (or to which he is or would be or might be entitled) or an agreement by dishonesty to injure some proprietary right of his. Where the intended victim of an agreement is a person performing public duties, as distinct from a private individual, there can also be a conspiracy to defraud if the agreement is dishonestly to cause such a person to act contrary to his duty (eg in granting a licence or giving information). The causing of economic loss or prejudice, or (as the case may be) the deceiving of a public official into acting contrary to his duty, need not be the purpose of the parties to the agreement, since it suffices if they have dishonestly agreed to bring about a state of affairs which they realised would or might have such a result.

Clearly, the definition of conspiracy to defraud is wide enough to cover cases where the object of the agreement would itself be an offence as well as those where the object would not be criminal. Agreements to steal, or to forge, or to obtain property by deception, and so on, may, of course, be prosecuted as statutory conspiracies to steal etc but, by virtue of the Criminal Justice Act 1987, s 12, they may be charged as common law conspiracies to defraud instead, since they satisfy the definition of conspiracy to defraud.

INTERFERENCE WITH VEHICLES

CAA 1981, s 9 provides that a person is guilty of the offence of vehicle interference if he interferes with a motor vehicle or trailer or with anything carried in or on a motor vehicle or trailer with the intention that an offence of:

(a) theft of the motor vehicle or trailer or part of it;
(b) theft of anything carried in or on the motor vehicle or trailer; or
(c) an offence under the Theft Act 1968 (TA 1968), s 12(1) (taking and driving away without consent),

shall be committed by himself or some other person.

CAA 1981, s 9 states that if an accused person can be proved to have intended that one of these offences should be committed, it is immaterial that it cannot be shown which offence it was.

The section uses the term 'interference' and this interference is linked to the intended theft of vehicles, trailers or their parts, the intended theft of things in or on the vehicles, or the intended taking of the vehicle. The essential point to prove will therefore be interference of a nature which clearly indicates an intention to do one of those things. If a group of rowdy youths rock a vehicle in order to set off its intruder alarm, they certainly interfere with the vehicle but lack the intention to do any of the prohibited acts. On the other hand, if they start to unscrew the aerial or a wing mirror with the intention of stealing it, they commit an offence under the section. The removal of tarpaulins from goods vehicles carrying loads indicates an interference with the intention to steal part of the load, and the use of duplicate keys, is a clear indication of intention either to steal the vehicle or to take it without consent.

If a man is seen to try to open the door of one motor vehicle this is certainly an interference with that vehicle if it does not belong to him and he has no permission to do so. However, it is unlikely to satisfy a court that he intends to steal or take the vehicle, or to steal anything contained in it, unless there are further circumstances which point to an intention to commit one of those offences. The intention of the person interfering with vehicles becomes more apparent as attention is paid by him to more than one vehicle, or he is seen to examine the interior of the vehicle through its windows to check its contents, or even to try a number of doors on the same vehicle. The further the interference extends, the more likely it becomes that there is an appropriate criminal intent.

OFFENSIVE WEAPONS IN PUBLIC PLACES

When one is considering cases of possession of weapons in public places it is helpful to identify possible offences which may have been committed by first considering the nature of the weapon involved. If it is a firearm, it must be borne in mind that a person commits an offence if he has with him in a public place a loaded shotgun, an air weapon (whether loaded or not), or any other firearm (whether loaded or not) together with ammunition for it. This offence is governed by the Firearms Act 1968 and we have dealt with it in more detail in Chapter 24, above. We now turn to the Prevention of Crime Act 1953 (PCA 1953), which deals with offensive weapons in public places in general.

PCA 1953, s 1 provides that any person who without lawful authority or reasonable excuse, the proof whereof lies on him, has with him in any public place any offensive weapon is guilty of an offence. The court may make an order as to the disposal of a weapon following conviction.

A person may 'have with him' an offensive weapon even though he is not carrying the article in question, but he must have a close physical link with it and it must have been readily accessible to him. Consequently, 'have with him' is a narrower concept than 'possession', since a person can be in possession of something which is many miles away, as where a thing is left in his parked car in Harrogate while he is in Nottingham. On the other hand, he would still have with him an offensive weapon which he has left in his car while he goes into a nearby public convenience. A person does not 'have with him' something of whose presence he is unaware, such as a cosh which has been slipped into his bag, but once he knows of its presence it is no excuse that, at the material time, he has forgotten about it, as where he puts a cosh in the glove compartment of his car but has forgotten about it, when he is stopped by a patrol car a month later. The accused need not know of the facts which render the article an offensive weapon within the meaning of the statute.

An offensive weapon is any article made or adapted for use for causing injury to the person, or intended by the person having it with him for such use by him. This definition includes two classes of offensive weapons.

Articles made or adapted for causing injury to the person

These weapons are described as offensive per se (ie in themselves). Examples of articles made for causing injury to the person are bayonets, coshes, knuckledusters, swords, flick knives and butterfly knives. Examples of articles adapted for causing injury to the person are a piece of chain whose links have been sharpened and a man's cap in whose peak a razor blade has been inserted with the cutting edge exposed. In the latter type of case, articles which were harmless in themselves are made offensive weapons by their deliberate adaptation for use for causing personal injury.

Articles intended to be used for causing injury to the person

This class covers articles which are inoffensive per se (ie in themselves), because they have not been made or adapted for causing personal injury, but which are rendered offensive by the accused's intention to use them for causing injury to the person. Such articles include belts, stiletto-heeled shoes (or any other shoe), walking sticks (or umbrellas) and dog leads, provided it can be shown that there was an *intention* to use the article for causing injury to the person. The difficulty of proving such an intention increases in proportion to the generally non-offensive character of the article in question.

It is not enough that a man, who is in innocent possession of an article, suddenly uses it for an offensive purpose. Where a carpenter took a hammer from his tool bag during a fight and used it, a divisional court held that he was not guilty of an offence under PCA 1953, s 1 as he did not have the hammer with him for causing injury to the person. Similarly, where a defendant used abusive language to police officers, picked up her dog and put it behind a wall before swinging the metal and leather strap at the officers, a divisional court held that there was insufficient evidence to support the submission that her intention to use the lead as an offensive weapon had been formed prior to the occasion of its actual use. To support a conviction under PCA 1953, the prosecution must show that for an appreciable time before the offensive use the accused had the intention to use it offensively. This is a stricter rule than applies to similar wording in the offence of aggravated burglary (p 1059).

Public place

The accused must have with him the offensive weapon in a public place. For the purposes of this offence, the term 'public place' includes any highway, and any other premises or place to which at the material time the public have or are permitted (ie invited or tolerated) to have access, whether on payment or otherwise. The issue is generally whether the public have access, or are permitted to have it if they wish. Public access is a matter of fact and if access is restricted to certain classes of persons, it must be restricted to some considerable degree before it will be accepted that the public are not admitted. A dance restricted to those under twenty-five years is a public dance as all classes of those under that age have a right of access. A soccer ground is a public place if paying spectators are admitted; it would be unlikely to be considered so if entry was restricted to elected members, but regard would have to be paid to the nature and restriction of membership. If it was generally available to the public without interview or election by the committee it would probably be different.

The fact that a person is found with an offensive weapon in a private place may lead to a conviction for the present offence. For example, if a visitor to a dwelling house produces an offensive weapon, this gives rise to a strong inference that he brought it with him through the streets and therefore had it with him in a public place.

Lawful authority or reasonable excuse

A person does not commit the offence if he has lawful authority or reasonable excuse for having with him the offensive weapon; the accused has the onus of proving such authority or excuse.

Those who may have offensive weapons with lawful authority include members of the armed services, or police forces, who may carry weapons which are offensive in themselves as part of their duty. On the other hand, it has been held that private security guards do not have lawful authority to carry truncheons or the like. Whether there is reasonable excuse depends on whether a reasonable person would think it excusable in the circumstances to carry the weapon in question, but as a matter of law limitations have been imposed by the courts on what a reasonable man might think in this context. Thus, it has been held that he would not think it reasonable for a person to have with him a weapon for self-defence unless there is an immediate and particular threat to him (as opposed to a constant one), nor would he think it reasonable for a person to have with him a weapon in order to commit suicide with it or for a security guard at a dance hall to carry a truncheon 'as a deterrent' and 'as part of his uniform'. The Court of Appeal has held that a claim by a person who has been proved to be in possession of a weapon which is offensive per se, that he did not know that the article in question was an offensive weapon, cannot amount to a reasonable excuse.

ANCILLARY OFFENCES

Having article with blade or point in a public place

The Criminal Justice Act 1988, s 139 provides an ancillary offence to that under PCA 1953 which is useful where a knife or the like cannot be proved to have been made, adapted or intended to cause injury to the person. The section makes it an offence for a person to have with him in a public place an article which is sharply pointed or with a blade, other than a folding pocket knife with a blade not exceeding three inches. 'Has with him' has the same meaning as under the Prevention of Crime Act 1953. A butter knife without a handle and with no cutting edge and no point has been held to be a bladed article within CJA 1988, s 139. A folding knife which is secured in an open position by a locking device and can only be released from the open position by the pressing of a release button is not a folding pocket knife within the meaning of CJA 1988, s 139. 'Public place' is defined in essentially the same terms as in the PCA 1953. An accused has a defence if he proves lawful authority or good reason for having the article with him in a public place, or that he had it with him there for use at work, for a religious reason or as part of any national costume. Whether a person was in possession of such a knife 'for use at work' is a matter for the court or jury as the statute uses ordinary, everyday language. The Court of Appeal has held that requiring the accused to prove one of these defences is not in conflict with art 6 of the European Convention on Human Rights. The Court of Appeal has also held that the defendant's forgetfulness that he has the article is not a good reason, but that forgetfulness combined with another reason may be a good reason.

Having article with blade or point (or offensive weapon) on school premises

The Criminal Justice Act 1988 (CJA 1988), s 139A makes it an offence for a person to have with him on school premises any article to which CJA 1988, s 139 applies. It creates a similar offence in relation to an offensive weapon to which the PCA 1953 applies. The term 'school premises' means land used for the purpose of a school excluding any land occupied solely as a dwelling by a person employed at the school. Similar defences exist; a person who proves that he had good reason or lawful authority for having the article or weapon with him on the premises has a defence. So has a person who proves that he had the article or weapon with him for the purposes set out above in relation to CJA 1988, s 139. In addition, he may show possession 'for educational purposes'.

CJA 1988, s 139B provides a constable with a power of entry, using reasonable force if necessary, into school premises and the power to search those premises and any person on those premises for articles to which CJA 1988, s 139 applies, or to which s 1 of the PCA 1953, applies, if he has reasonable grounds for believing that an offence under CJA 1988, s 139A is being, or has been, committed. He may seize any articles or weapons discovered in the course of such a search which he reasonably suspects to be such articles or weapons.

General

As we saw in relation to the offence under PCA 1953, s 1, a person still has something with him when he has forgotten that he has it with him. This rule applies to the present offences. In addition, it has been held by the divisional court that, as in the case of 'reasonable excuse' in the PCA 1953, forgetfulness is not a 'good reason'. In the case in question a man was still in possession of a knife six days after he had used it in connection with his work. He had forgotten that he still had it with him but it was held that that was not a good reason for having it with him at the relevant time. A person charged with an offence under CJA 1988, s 139 or s 139A does not discharge the burden of proving 'good reason' simply by providing an explanation which is not contradicted by prosecution evidence. For example, in the case just referred to, the accused had advanced the excuse that he had the knife in his possession for the purpose of food preparation later in the evening; it was held that the justices were entitled to form the opinion that the alleged 'good reason' was most improbable.

As in the case of 'reasonable excuse' in the PCA 1953, a person has good reason for having one of the above articles with him for self-defence against an immediate threat (as opposed to a constant one).

RESTRICTION OF OFFENSIVE WEAPONS

Manufacture, sale etc of flick knives and gravity knives

The Restriction of Offensive Weapons Act 1959 is concerned with the manufacture and distribution of flick knives and gravity knives. It is an offence for any person to manufacture, sell, hire, offer for sale or hire, or to expose or have in his possession for the purpose of sale or hire, or to lend or give to any person, either of these weapons.

A 'flick knife' is any knife which has a blade which opens automatically by hand pressure applied to a button, spring or other device in or attached to the handle of the knife. A 'gravity knife' is one which has a blade which is released from the handle or sheath thereof by the force of gravity or the application of centrifugal force and which, when released, is locked in place by means of a button, spring, lever, or other device. The flick knife is therefore one with an up-and-over blade and a gravity knife is one which allows the blade to be shaken from the handle. These are weapons which are 'made' for the purpose of causing injury, so that a person who has such a weapon with him in a public place for sale or the like is guilty of the more serious offence under the PCA 1953, dealt with on pp 1108–1110.

Manufacture, sale etc of specified weapons

CJA 1988, s 141 creates a further offence. A person who manufactures, sells or hires or offers for sale or hire, exposes or has in his possession for the purpose of sale or hire, or lends or gives to any other person, any weapon specified by order by the Secretary of State, commits an offence. The importation of such weapons is also prohibited. The Secretary of State has since made the Criminal Justice Act 1988 (Offensive Weapons) Order 1988 listing the knuckleduster, swordstick, handclaw, belt buckle knife, push dagger, hollow kubotan (small truncheon with spikes), footclaw, death star, butterfly knife, telescopic truncheon, blow-pipe, kusari gama (sickle and chain), kyoketsu shoge (hooked knife and chain) and maurik kusari or kusari (weights joined by chain). An order of 2002 added a disguised knife, ie any knife which has a concealed blade or concealed sharp point and is designed to appear to be an everyday object of a kind commonly carried on the person or in a handbag, briefcase or other hand luggage (such as a comb, brush, writing instrument, cigarette lighter, key, lipstick or telephone). A further order of 2004 added (a) a stealth knife, that is a knife or spike, which has a blade or a sharp point, made from a material that is not readily detectable by apparatus used for detecting metal, and which is not designed for domestic use or for use in the processing, preparation or consumption of food or as a toy, and (b) a straight, side-handled or friction-lock truncheon (sometimes known as a baton). It is a defence to a charge under CJA 1988, s 141 to prove that the conduct in question was only for the purpose of making the weapon available to a public museum or gallery.

A justice may issue a warrant authorising entry and search on the application of a constable if he is satisfied that there are reasonable grounds for believing that there are on those premises knives such as are mentioned in the Restriction of Offensive Weapons Act 1959, s 1(1) or weapons to which CJA 1988, s 141 applies and that an offence under either of these provisions has been or is being committed in relation to them and that one of the essential conditions for a search warrant exists.

Sale of knives etc to persons under sixteen

By CJA 1988, s 141A, it is an offence for any person to sell to a person under the age of sixteen years a knife, knife blade or razor blade, any axe, and any other article which has a blade or which is sharply pointed and which is made or adapted for use for causing injury to the person. The section does not apply to articles already controlled by the Restriction of Offensive Weapons Act 1959, CJA 1988, s 141, or described in an order made by the Secretary of State under CJA 1988, s 141A. The Secretary of State has made an order in respect of a folding pocket knife with a blade which does not exceed three inches and razor blades permanently enclosed in a cartridge or housing.

The section provides a defence for a person who proves that he took all reasonable precautions and exercised all due diligence to avoid commission of the offence.

Marketing of combat knives

The Knives Act 1997 (KA 1997), s 1 represents a further attempt to ban particular types of weapons. It provides that it is an offence to market a knife in a way which:

(a) indicates, or suggests, that it is suitable for combat; or
(b) is otherwise likely to stimulate or encourage violent behaviour involving the use of the knife as a weapon.

The term 'market' includes selling or hiring, offering or exposing for sale or hire, or possession for the purpose of sale or hire. A 'knife' is an instrument which has a blade or is sharply pointed; 'suitable for combat' means suitable for use as a weapon for inflicting injury on a person or causing a person to fear injury; and 'violent behaviour' means an unlawful act inflicting injury on a person or causing a person to fear injury.

KA 1997, s 1 provides that, for the purposes of the Act, an indication or suggestion that a knife is suitable for combat may, in particular, be given or made by a name or description:

(a) applied to the knife;
(b) on the knife or its packaging; or
(c) in any advertisement which, expressly or by implication, relates to the knife.

KA 1997, s 2 creates the offence of publishing any written, pictorial or other material in connection with the marketing of any knife, which:

(a) indicates, or suggests, that the knife is 'suitable for combat'; or
(b) is otherwise likely to stimulate or encourage 'violent behaviour' involving the use of the knife as a weapon.

It is difficult to see what this legislation hopes to achieve in relation to public safety as it does not seek to prohibit particular weapons, merely to outlaw certain descriptions being applied to them.

Because of the wide range of the provisions of KA 1997, it provides some defences. In relation to the offence under KA 1997, s 1, the marketing of a knife for use by the armed forces of any country, or as an antique or curio is exempted. Likewise, in relation to the offence of publishing material under KA 1997, s 2, it is a defence to prove three things that:

(a) the material was published in connection with marketing a knife for use by the armed forces of any country or as an antique or curio;
(b) it was reasonable for the knife to be marketed in that way; and
(c) there were no reasonable grounds for suspecting that a person into whose possession the knife might come in consequence of the way in which it was marketed would use it for an unlawful purpose.

It is also a defence to a charge under KA 1997, s 1 or s 2 for a person to prove that he did not know or suspect, and had no reasonable grounds for suspecting, that the way the knife was marketed (s 1), or the material (s 2), amounted to an indication or suggestion that the knife was 'suitable for combat', or was likely to stimulate or encourage 'violent behaviour' involving the use of the knife as a weapon. Lastly, it is a defence to either offence for the accused to prove that he took all reasonable precautions and exercised due diligence to avoid committing the offence.

It may be that most police officers will issue a warning rather than attempt the perilous path of proving an offence under this Act!

The KA 1997 provides for the issue of search warrants authorising entry, using reasonable force, and search and seizure in respect of knives and publications. Reasonable force may be used in exercising the powers under the warrant. The additional powers of seizure provided by the Criminal Justice and Police Act 2001, s 50 apply where a search warrant under KA 1997 in respect of publications is executed.

GOING EQUIPPED TO STEAL

TA 1968, s 25 is concerned with a person, who, when not at his place of abode, has with him any article for use in the course of or in connection with any burglary or theft.

The mischief aimed at is the carrying of implements which a person intends to use in the course of or in connection with any burglary, or theft. The section does not, therefore, only punish possession in streets or public places; it also catches such persons who are found in possession of implements while trespassing upon private property or whilst anywhere else other than at their place of abode. As soon as the accused leaves his place of abode he is guilty of this offence if he has with him articles for one of the specified purposes. It has been decided that, where a person lives in a motor vehicle, it is his place of abode whilst on the site where he intends to abide, but that as soon as the vehicle leaves the site he is no longer at his place of abode.

Although the offence is described in the marginal note to TA 1968, s 25 as 'going equipped for stealing etc', and is commonly so described, it is not limited to conduct which could be described as 'going equipped'. The term 'has with him' has the same meaning as in the Prevention of Crime Act 1953.

The article does not need to be specifically made or adapted for use for one of the specified purposes; any article will do provided that the accused intends to use it for such a purpose.

The specified purposes are that the accused must intend to use the article in the course of or in connection with any burglary or theft to be committed in the future; it is not necessary to prove that the articles are to be used in connection with any particular burglary etc. Possession to enable someone else to use the articles is sufficient for the purposes of this section. TA 1968, s 25(5) states that, for the purposes of the present offence, an offence under TA 1968, s 12 of taking a conveyance, shall be treated as theft.

If a person is found with an article made or adapted for use in committing burglary or theft, proof of the offence under TA 1968, s 25 is assisted by s 25(3), which states that where there is proof that he had with him such an article that shall be evidence that he had it with him for such use. Of course, this can be rebutted by evidence of a contrary intention. The result of s 25(3) is that, if someone is found trespassing in the grounds of a dwelling house with a bunch of skeleton keys in his pocket, this is evidence that he had those articles with him for use in committing burglary. On the other hand, if he was found merely with the keys to his office and house this would provide no such evidence.

ARTICLES FOR USE IN FRAUD

Possession of articles for use in fraud

By the Fraud Act 2006 (FA 2006), s 6, a person commits an offence if he has in his possession or under his control any article for use in the course of or in connection with any fraud.

A general intention to commit fraud is sufficient for this offence.

The term 'articles' in this and s 7 below includes any program or data held in electronic form. Computer programs can generate credit card numbers; computer templates can be used for producing blank bills; and computer files may contain credit card details of persons.

Making or supplying articles for use in frauds

A person commits an offence against FA 2006, s 7 (not in force at the time of writing) if he makes, adapts, supplies or offers to supply any article:

(a) knowing that it is designed or adapted for use in the course of or in connection with fraud, or

(b) intending it to be used to commit, or assist in the commission of, fraud.

Where payment is made based upon energy consumed by a customer and consumption is measured by a meter, a person who makes or supplies a device intended to interfere with the record made by the device will intend it to be used to commit fraud.

Index

maintenance 392–4
bicycles 436
brakes 407, 410–11
construction and use of vehicles 427,
    429–30
fuel tanks 429
glass in vehicles 429
goods vehicle operators' licence 517
licensing of motor vehicles 335
lights 553–4
motor vehicles 429–30
motorways 481
petrol tanks 429
public service vehicle operator's licences 490
roads 335
seat belts 414
speedometers 420
tyres 429–30
windscreen wipers and washers 425

making off without payment 1066–8
bilking 1066
deception 1066
dishonesty 1066–7
meals in restaurants 1066
petrol stations, self-service 1066
postponement of payment 1066–7
prostitution 1067
taxis 1066
trade credit 1066

malice
battery 805
criminal damage 1044
indecent or grossly offensive
      communications 887
malice aforethought 843, 844
malicious communications 887
manslaughter 844
murder 843
transferred 805, 1044
wounding or grievous bodily harm 814–16

mandatory orders 35

manslaughter 844–8
accomplices 14
actus reus 847, 848
cause of death, unlawful act as 848
constructive 848
dangerous acts 848
death by dangerous driving, causing 573
diminished responsibility 844, 845–6
driving offences 566
gross negligence, killing by 847
involuntary 847–8
malice aforethought 844
murder 839
provocation 844–5
recklessness 847–8
suicide pacts 844, 846–7
unlawful and dangerous act, killing by an 848
voluntary 843–7

manufacturer's plates 512–13, 515

manufacturers' research vehicles 342, 345

markets, pedlars and 795

**mascots, emblems or ornamental items fitted
    to cars** 434

masseuses 981

masters of ships, drink and drugs and 631–2

matches or cigarette lighters 914

**matrimonial home, rights associated
    with** 830–2

maximum detention periods 164–8
24 hour period 164
authorisation 164
calculation of period of detention 164–5
continued detention 164
voluntary attendance at a police station 164
warrants of further detention 164

**meals, consumption by children of alcohol
    with** 679

meals in detention 140

meals in restaurants, failure to pay for 1064,
    1067

mechanically propelled vehicles 318–19
broken down vehicles 318
driving offences 566–7, 568
goods vehicles 513
immobilisation 318
licensing of motor vehicles 334
meaning of 318
off-road driving 397
plates 513
scrap yards, in 318
stripped down cars in garages 318

medical treatment
assault 806
children 637, 638
custody officers 151
custody records 151
detained persons, treatment of 141–3, 165
diseases or conditions, suffering from 142
drivers in need after accident of 563–4
medication, use of 142
murder 842
police surgeons, advice of 142
refusal of, murder and 842
requests for examination 142
review of detention 165
self-administration of medication 142

medication, suspects on 142, 617

meetings *see* **public meetings**

members' clubs
car parks 590
definition 710
gaming 710–12
licensing, sale and supply of alcohol and 662, 663
public service vehicles 484

Notes